Reader in

Comparative Religion

READER IN COMPARATIVE RELIGION

An Anthropological Approach

SECOND EDITION

WILLIAM A. LESSA
UNIVERSITY OF CALIFORNIA, LOS ANGELES

EVON Z. VOGT
HARVARD UNIVERSITY

Harper & Row, Publishers

NEW YORK, EVANSTON, AND LONDON

LIBRARY OF CONGRESS CATALOG CARD NUMBER: 65-12678

TABLE OF CONTENTS

1. THE ORIGIN AND DEVELOPMENT OF RELIGION

2. THE FUNCTION OF RELIGION IN HUMAN SOCIETY

v

3. MYTH AND RITUAL

4. SYMBOLISM

5. MANA AND TABOO

6. TOTEMISM

7. MAGIC, WITCHCRAFT, AND DIVINATION

8. THE MAGICAL TREATMENT OF ILLNESS

9. DEATH, GHOSTS, AND ANCESTOR WORSHIP

10. SHAMANS AND PRIESTS

11. DYNAMICS IN RELIGION

12. NEW METHODS OF ANALYSIS

FOREWORD

Three things appear to distinguish man from all other living creatures: the systematic making of tools, the use of abstract language, and religion. Some observers think they have detected among certain birds, mammals, and even other organisms the analogues of ritual. But no one has seriously suggested the presence of myth or theology. For these, another of the three distinctively human phenomena —abstract language—is surely a precondition.

Until the emergence of Communist societies we know of no human groups without religion. Even the Communists, as has often been said, have their "secular religion." While they repudiate the supernatural, they give allegiance in feeling as well as in thought to a body of doctrine that purports to provide life with a fairly immediate meaning. Nor is communism without its ritual and ceremonial side.

The universality of religion (in the broadest sense) suggests that it corresponds to some deep and probably inescapable human needs. All of these are repeatedly discussed in this book. There is the need for a moral order. Human life is necessarily a moral life precisely because it is a social life, and in the case of the human animal the minimum requirements for predictability of social behavior that will ensure some stability and continuity are not taken care of automatically by biologically inherited instincts, as is the case with the bees and the ants. Hence there must be generally accepted standards of conduct, and these values are more compelling if they are invested with divine authority and continually symbolized in rites that appeal to the senses. But no religion is solely a system of ethics. All religions also represent a response to the wonder and the terror of the ineluctable processes of nature. They supply some answer to the profound uncertainties of experience, most especially to the homogeneity of death—even though some religions make a pure acknowledgment of death and erectly, carelessly, undauntedly admit nothingness.

The needs met by religion are not, however, by any means limited to those of constituting or bolstering a social order or of providing cognitive "explanations." Man is a symbolic as well as a tool-making creature. Cassirer understandably considers myth as an autonomous form of symbolism comparable to language, art, and science. In many and varied respects religion is an expressive activity: an outlet in drama, poetry, dance, and the plastic and graphic arts for the diverse temperaments of individuals, for particular subgroups, for the total community or society. My teacher, R. R. Marett, used to say "primitive religion is danced, not believed."

He did not intend, of course, that this aphorism should be taken literally. And one of the strong points of this book is that Professors Lessa and Vogt have resolutely emphasized the continuity of all religious phenomena. Yet there is one matter on which the equivocal word "primitive" gives us a useful reminder. In so-called "primitive" societies religion encompasses philosophy, theater, "science," ethics, diversion, and other behavior spheres which recent Western civilization has tended to segregate. The student must be aware of this fact, though the adjective "comparative" in the title of this book is altogether factual.

Indeed this reader is more genuinely comparative than any volume I know. Careful study of it should free any student from a narrow and culture-bound conception of religion. And it will become quite apparent that at least the symbolic forms of all religions derive from the particular nature and specific experience of the peoples that created these forms. As Xenophanes (560–475 B.C.) wrote:

Yes, and if oxen and horses or lions had hands, and could paint with their hands, and

produce works of art as men do, horses would
paint the forms of their gods like horses, and
oxen like oxen, and make their bodies in the image of their several kinds. . . . The Ethiopians
make their gods black and snub-nosed; the
Thracians say theirs have blue eyes and red hair.

All religious systems—in practice if not in
theory—have had to make some concessions
to the frailties of human nature.

Because religious beliefs and practices,
learned so early in contexts intimately associated with the most intense human experiences, are the targets of strong positive
and negative feelings on the part of both
participants and observers and because religion embraces such a wide and such a complex area of human life, the scientific study
of religion is peculiarly difficult. The most
honest and best course is the one which the
editors have followed with great sensitivity
and skill: achieve a decent balance between
data and interpretation; present opposing
points of view fairly and in historical depth;
be as wide-ranging and comprehensive as
space will allow. Nevertheless, thanks to the
introductions to each chapter and the paragraphs linking the selections, the editors

have succeeded in making judicious contributions to the establishment of regularities,
to general theory. At the same time, the rich
bibliographic aids make it easy for teacher
and student to check and control the inductive generalizations which Professors Lessa
and Vogt set forth on all the major topical
areas of religion.

This, surely, is no parochial book. There
are passages from the sacred texts of many
religions. These passages and the descriptive
accounts swing through the centuries and all
the continents. The authors represent many
nationalities and professions. We have bishops and anthropologists, literary critics and
sociologists, psychiatrists and clergymen, administrators and psychologists. And the full
gamut of the religious experience emerges in
the materials: rationality and passion; the
supplication of bliss and of dread; a lurking,
snake-like fear; the carrion gobbling of the
garbage of sensations; mistrust and lurking
insolence, insolence against a higher creation; the drift of spent souls; the striving for
a center to life; the wheeling upon a dark
void; the unquenched desire to worship.

CLYDE KLUCKHOHN

ACKNOWLEDGMENT

The second edition of this volume has been made possible by the reception given the first, and so we must reaffirm the help given us in the past before we can go on to express our new indebtedness.

When the editors first contemplated the compilation of a book of readings that would be useful to them and possibly to others in teaching comparative and primitive religion, they received much encouragement and many significant suggestions from their friends and associates, particularly the late Clyde Kluckhohn, Robert N. Bellah, Clifford Geertz, and Melford E. Spiro, whose advice was gratefully absorbed in molding the form and content of the *Reader*. The junior author, while at the Center for Advanced Study in the Behavioral Sciences during 1956–1957, received further reinforcement through stimulating discussions with E. E. Evans-Pritchard, Morris E. Opler, and John M. Roberts. When it came time to put words on paper, Robert B. Edgerton and Roger C. Owen skilfully assisted in preparing some of the introductions to the selections and generally served as intellectual sounding boards, while Barbara Metzger wrote most of the original notes for the monographs on non-Western religious systems.

The new edition has turned once more to some of its old supporters and at the same time has added new names to its roster of collaborating colleagues, these being John W. M. Whiting, Michael G. Smith, and Philip L. Newman. We are also indebted to Jack Stauder for comments on this second edition.

The student assistants at the University of California, Los Angeles, who helped prepare the new manuscript for presentation to the publisher should also be given the recognition that belongs to them. Building on the foundation laid by Carol Romer Jones, who almost single-handedly worked on the first edition, Claudia Stevens, Carol Swartout, and Judy Wiseman collaborated on the second, which, strange to say, made more demands on time, patience, and ingenuity than one would have imagined necessary.

Finally, we must make note of the willingness with which publishers, editors, and authors responded to our requests for permission to reprint materials. In all instances we sought the consent of the authors involved, even when their articles were not copyrighted, and they responded with alacrity and enthusiasm. Indeed, in several instances they offered to substitute, add, or revise selections. A number of them suggested that they were flattered to be included, although of course we look at this the other way around. There would have been no *Reader* without their contributions.

W.A.L.
E.Z.V.

GENERAL INTRODUCTION

I

Religion may be described as a system of beliefs and practices directed toward the "ultimate concern" of a society. "Ultimate concern," a concept used by Paul Tillich, has two aspects—meaning and power. It has meaning in the sense of ultimate meaning of the central values of a society, and it has power in the sense of ultimate, sacred, or supernatural power which stands behind those values.

Viewed in this way, religion is concerned with the explanation and expression of the ultimate values of a society; in other words, it has important *integrative* functions for groups and for individual personalities. At the same time religion is concerned with the threats to these central values, or to social or individual existence; it has important *defense* functions in providing ways of managing tensions and anxieties. Thus, religion both maintains the ultimate values of a society and manages tensions in the personalities of individual members of a society.

The religious beliefs and practices that provide this double-barreled function are of course almost infinitely varied from culture to culture, and are developed and tailored with symbols, myths and rituals that fit the varying cultural contexts. But the basic functions, and the concept of an "ultimate concern" with meaning and power, are probably found universally in human societies.

Although the problem of the nature of religion has for centuries absorbed the imagination and energies of scholars in different cultures, the detached comparative approach to the matter is a relatively recent experience in history. Indeed, the first sustained and systematic efforts to understand and interpret the phenomenon stem from the works of nineteenth- and early twentieth-century British scholars, especially Sir Edward B. Tylor, William Robertson Smith, Andrew Lang, Sir James Frazer, and R. R. Marett. Many of these men were merely amateur or quasiprofessional anthropologists, but they were endowed with inquiring minds and fine intellects.

These writers were for the most part influenced by the Darwinian concept of biological evolution and were interested in describing what they conceived to be the stages in cultural evolution. They turned to the study of "primitive" peoples living in the far corners of the world because they believed that these cultures represented what amounted to an earlier evolutionary stage in our own cultural development. They were motivated by a basic question: What are the origins of religion in mankind's development? By careful study of the accounts of missionaries and travelers among primitive peoples—they did no field work themselves —they attempted to reconstruct what the earlier stages of religion were like and to answer such questions as: How did man first create myths and develop ritual? Was animism the first form of religion, or was there a preanimistic religion? Did an age of magic precede an age of religion?

1

A special problem related to this question of "origins" involved the inquiry into whether or not the most primitive peoples, such as the Ona and Yahgan of Tierra del Fuego, the Eskimo, or the Ainu of Japan, worshiped a "primitive high god" or "Supreme Being." The implication was that perhaps mankind developed polytheistic religions only later in history, and did not return to monotheism until the development of the great religions in the Near East. Father Wilhelm Schmidt was one of the principal investigators of this problem, as the reader will discover from the selection "The Nature, Attributes and Worship of the Primitive High God." That this matter is still one of concern among religious scholars is testified to by the recent work of Pettazzoni, who disagrees sharply with Father Schmidt in his paper on "The Formation of Monotheism."

Another major trend of thought is found in the works of the so-called French sociological school, and particularly in the work of Émile Durkheim. Some of Durkheim's ideas were foreshadowed by Fustel de Coulanges' *The Ancient City,* and we have added some selections from this classic to provide background information. In the work of Durkheim the emphasis is upon treating religion as an integral part of a society, but interestingly enough the question of origins still persists. Witness, for example, how Durkheim selects the case of the Australian aborigines to work out his theory that the reality underlying religion is society itself; he is interested in the origin of religious emotion and therefore selects a primitive culture. The works of this school are of crucial importance in that they form a kind of historical bridge between the earlier interests in "origins" and the later interests in the "functions" of religion, whatever their origin. The French school has exerted considerable influence outside its own national boundaries, thanks mostly to the prestige and international experience of an Englishman, Radcliffe-Brown. An American, W. Lloyd Warner, has also been an ardent supporter of the Durkheimian approach. Of course both of these men have made departures on their own, especially away from preoccupation with origins, but when writing in terms of the role of religion they hew close to the original line.

A third major theoretical strand also com-

ing from sociology is found in the works of Max Weber, especially in his explorations of the relationships between religious and economic institutions and his clear recognition of the fundamental importance of the problem of "meaning." This latter problem has two aspects: one is the difficulty of answers to the question of why unpredictable, unfortunate events occur in human life. This interest continues and is dealt with very perceptively in a selection from Evans-Pritchard, who shows with incisive clarity how witchcraft explains unfortunate events in Azande life. The second aspect has to do with the relationship between major institutional forms in a society. That is, the economic system must have some meaning in terms of the religious system and vice versa. Although we have not included a selection from Weber, his influence is evident in the writings of Talcott Parsons, and the questions we raise are clearly dealt with in the selection entitled "Religious Perspectives in Sociology and Social Psychology."

A fourth major theoretical thread was injected into the comparative study of religion by Sigmund Freud, who has been a crucial influence in thinking about the nature of religion, especially the relationship of religious thought and emotions to unconscious motivation and the treatment of religion as a projective system. Again it is significant that the interest in origins is also found here; witness how Freud concerned himself with the origin of the incest taboo in *Totem and Taboo.* Other writers have carried on the tradition, especially Géza Róheim and Bruno Bettelheim.

Meanwhile, influenced in part by the French sociological school and by their own firsthand field researches with primitive peoples, two major figures emerged who were to have a lasting impact on the anthropological treatment of religion: Malinowski and Radcliffe-Brown. In their "functional" approach to religion the question of origins in the older classical sense has shifted to a different question: What is the function of religion, whatever its origin, in any society and in particular societies? In other words, what does religion *do* for people and for social groups? There are great similarities but also important differences in the theoretical approach of these two scholars; Homans attempts to resolve the differences.

In recent decades the study of religion by

anthropologists has been more sporadic, but there is evidence that interest and research in the field is quickening both in the United States and Europe, as well as in Australia. A number of works by the American anthropologists A. Irving Hallowell, Morris Opler, and the late Clyde Kluckhohn favor a synthesis of the functional and psychoanalytic approaches to religion. We have included papers by Kluckhohn and Opler but not by Hallowell, since most of the latter's important papers were recently reprinted in *Culture and Experience* (1955). Other American and some British anthropologists have been busy studying the religions that have emerged in the acculturation situation, such as the Ghost Dance, Peyote Cult, and Cargo Cults, and have produced a number of remarkable publications like the paper by Anthony Wallace on "Revitalization Movements" (1956), which is now available in the "Bobbs-Merrill Reprint Series in Anthropology" and also in essence in Wallace's *Culture and Personality* (1961); a number of less available papers on the subject are included in Chapter 11. Other American scholars have been applying anthropological concepts to the study of the religions of the high cultures of the Far East, India, and Southeast Asia, and to the analysis of certain aspects of ritual in our own culture. There has also been a recent revival of interest in evolution in the religious aspects of societies, as exemplified in Bellah's interesting paper on "Religious Evolution" (1964), which has been added to Chapter 1.

The recent British publications on religion have included both a variety of stimulating papers and a number of excellent monographs that combine empirical data with theoretical analysis. Among the recent papers of general interest are Jack Goody's "Ritual and Religion: The Definitional Problem" (1961), Edmund Leach's "Magical Hair" (1958), and Robin Horton's "A Definition of Religion" (1960). Among the recent monographs there is S. F. Nadel's *Nupe Religion* (1954), E. E. Evans-Pritchard's *Nuer Religion* (1956), Meyer Fortes' *Oedipus and Job in West African Religion* (1958), Jack Goody's *Death, Property, and the Ancestors* (1962), Audrey I. Richards' *Chisungu: A Girl's Initiation Ceremony Among the Bemba of Northern Rhodesia* (1956), Godfrey Lienhardt's *Divinity and Experience: The Religion of the Dinka*

(1961), Max Gluckman's (editor) *Essays on the Ritual of Social Relations* (1962), and Victor Turner's *Chihamba: The White Spirit* (1962). In Australia special mention should be made of the series of papers on myth and rite by W. E. H. Stanner, that have appeared recently in *Oceania* and have been published as a monograph, *On Aboriginal Religion* (1963).

In France the most important recent development has been the stimulating publications from the pen of Claude Lévi-Strauss on myth and various aspects of ritual. Two of his articles, "The Structural Study of Myth" (1955, revised 1963) and "The Bear and the Barber" (1963), have been added to this second edition of our *Reader*. But the student should read his other publications that contain materials on religion, especially *Structural Anthropology* (1963), *Totemism* (1963), and *La Pensée Sauvage* (1962).

Among the recent general trends in the study of religion by anthropologists we have noted two of special significance: the analysis of symbolism in religion (see Chapter 4) and the development of new methods for eliciting and analyzing data on myths and rituals (see Chapter 12). The rapid growth of interest in the meaning and function of religious symbols is notable and promising. Our new chapter on this subject reprints four new essays on symbolism by Clifford Geertz, Eric Wolf, Edmund Leach, and Childe Herald, respectively, and includes two selections from W. Lloyd Warner and Bruno Bettelheim as samples of the excellent work that is appearing in both books and journals.

Also in evidence has been a promising recent interest, both in Europe and in the United States in the development of new and more precise methods for the study of religious phenomena, and we have added a sample of papers in this new edition that reflect this lively trend. We predict there will be much more work along these lines in the future.

But it is apparent that progress in theoretical treatment and methodological sophistication still lags behind the study of other aspects of culture (e.g., social structure, kinship, language), and we hope that this volume will stimulate younger generations of students to inquire further into the nature and function of religion.

II

At this point it may be appropriate to explain to some readers our seeming brashness in appropriating to our own use the term "comparative religion," in view of the fact that it has had different connotations for older students of religion as well as for modern theologians. Actually, the editors are not giving a special meaning to the term. It reflects a whole point of view in anthropology, and accordingly there occurs in the anthropological literature a series of related expressions, such as "comparative law," "comparative art," "comparative folklore," and "comparative institutions." The philosophy behind these terms will shortly be explained, but for the moment it will be well to examine the older and more traditional meaning of comparative religion.

Earlier studies of religion purported to be comparative—and indeed they often were—but these early studies used comparison as a sort of apologetics for the dominant Judaic-Christian religions.[1] During the latter stages of the nineteenth century several factors were combining to emancipate the comparative study of religion from this earlier goal of providing data for the validation of the origins and authority of Judaism or Christianity. One such factor was the accreting store of knowledge about primitive religions that was being collected by travelers, soldiers, missionaries, and administrators. Another was the Darwinian theory of biological evolution, which led to studies of other forms of evolution—among them that of religion. Several scholarly disciplines began to contribute stimuli to objective comparative studies; sociology, anthropology, philology, mythology, folk psychology, and history all began to eschew apologetics for science.

The new comparative religion as represented by the anthropological approach makes no effort to evaluate, and it encompasses all the religions of the world, past and present, about which there is any informa-

[1] In recent years theologians and others working in this more traditional and restricted field have veered away from the term "comparative religion" and substituted "history of religions" and "phenomenology of religions"—terms growing out of the general body of knowledge originally known as *Allgemeine Religionswissenschaft* (see Joseph M. Kitagawa, "The Nature and Program of the History of Religions Field," *Divinity School News,* November, 1957, pp. 13–25).

tion. By going beyond the complex cults of the great contemporary civilizations it is possible to gain not only a wider range of variation but also a greater degree of detachment. For example, those who are close to Christianity cannot always divorce themselves from the cultural and emotional associations that they entertain toward it. And they are apt to have preconceived notions regarding religions, such as Judaism and Islam, which have had intimate historical relationships with it. It is much more possible to retain an objective point of view when treating of the belief of the Koryak, Betsimisaraka, Kankanay, Witoto, or Ewe. In addition, the religions of the simpler societies have the advantage of being divested of the complex trappings characteristic of the faiths of civilized groups. They are more internally consistent, possessed of fewer alternatives of dogma, less complicated by sophisticated metaphysics, and freer of hierarchical superstructure. In short, they permit one to get down to the core—the fundamentals—of religion and its place in human life.

But what is the comparative method? Unfortunately, since it has meant many things to different people, the answer is not simple. Essentially, it is a method that attempts to achieve generalization through comparison of similar kinds of phenomena. It seeks to extract common denominators from a mass of variants. But the methods for which comparison has been utilized and the goals toward which these methods have been directed have not always been the same. The most comprehensive and fruitful effort to bring order out of the chaotic state into which the meaning of the expression has fallen is one made by Oscar Lewis in an article entitled "Comparisons in Cultural Anthropology" (1955). We shall take the liberty of reviewing some of his analysis.

According to Professor Lewis, there are two broad types of comparative studies in anthropology. The first examines societies that are historically related. Their common culture provides controls against which variables may be tested. This type, which has been given little recognition as an aspect of the comparative method, may in involve either comparisons within a single culture or community, within a single culture area, or within a single nation. There are many advantages to comparative studies of this more limited kind. The data are more intensively studied, usually along comparable lines, so there is greater assurance of comparability. The culture is seen as a whole and not in fractions, so that all aspects of the culture appear in context. Moreover, a large number of variables can be studied functionally. The objectives are usually modest and the research designs closer to those made in truly experimental studies. It is here that we find the greater proportion of recent studies based on comparative field research. The greatest drawback to the limited approach is that it has narrow vistas.

The second broad type of comparative study compares historically unrelated societies, taking a broader and more ambitious approach, often of a holistic character. It may make comparisons within a continent, between continents or nations, or on a random or global scale. The purpose is to utilize similarities in form, structure, and process as a basis for deriving typologies or establishing causal relationships among various aspects of culture. It might be observed parenthetically that in this case we are dealing with headier wine. This kind of comparison looks for universals, worldwide typologies, or evolutionary sequences. Here is where the work of men such as Tylor, Freud, Durkheim, and Radcliffe-Brown fits in. The weakness of this overall approach is that it does not have many of the controls possible in the more limited studies described in the previous paragraph. Moreover, when statistics are used they often artificially quantify the culture elements and control only a few of the variables. Recently there have been more sophisticated comparative studies along these lines in the "cross-cultural" works of Murdock, Whiting, and others who have used the Human Relations Area Files as a basis for careful samples of the world's societies and have successfully arrived at generalizations with high validity, as for example in Murdock's *Social Structure* (1949). Whiting's helpful paper on "The Cross-Cultural Method" (1954) provides an excellent description of the general approach.

Evans-Pritchard ("Religion," 1956) has in effect advocated a combination of these two approaches if we are to retain the objectivity necessary to reach general and significant conclusions regarding the nature of primitive religions as a whole. He says that we must, for example, first investigate the religion of one Melanesian people, then compare the religion of that group with several other Melanesian societies that are nearest to it in their culture. After that would come a comparative study of all Melanesian groups, and only then could one say something about Melanesian religion in general. This laborious kind of research is the only hope for eventually achieving broader conclusions about religion. This newer stress on careful comparisons on a smaller scale has also been emphasized by others, especially Eggan, who writes, "My own preference is for the utilization of the comparative method on a smaller scale and with as much control over the frame of comparison as it is possible to secure" ("Social Anthropology and the Method of Controlled Comparison," 1954). Eggan's masterful discussion of controlled comparisons shows that he is aware that there is much work ahead, and that no one approach is sufficient—the anthropological concepts of structure and function can and should be combined with the ethnological concepts of process and history.

More than mere painstaking labor is needed for valid comparisons. We must be sure that a comparative analysis is based on comparable data. Franz Boas' old warning on this score is still valid and has been eloquently renewed by Clyde Kluckhohn in a paper entitled "Universal Categories of Culture" (1953). As one of his examples he makes specific mention of the field of religion, which he says is a recurring pattern but not a uniform phenomenon, as evidenced by the lack of a clear-cut distinction between magic and religion. These concepts, he says, have heuristic usefulness in given situations but are not sufficiently distinct to serve as units from which larger concepts can be built up. As we shall see in our selections on such concepts as monotheism, totemism, taboo, mana, witchcraft, and others, there are by no means standard definitions of terms to fit all cases.

As for the aims which anthropologists have in their comparisons, Lewis (*op. cit.*) says that there are several: to establish general laws or regularities; to document the range of variation in the phenomena studied; to document the distribution of traits or aspects of culture; to reconstruct culture history; to test hypotheses derived from non-Western societies. This is a broad range, and it should be noted that it covers all the approaches in cultural anthropology, whether functional, diffusionist, *kulturkreis,* or evolutionary. The difference lies both in the ways in which they are used and in the objectives toward which they are directed.

The present volume is not concerned with documenting distributions or reconstructing history. Rather, as a work of science, it is concerned with comparison only insofar as it helps to establish regularities in religious phenomena. Of course, this would presuppose the testing of hypotheses in different cultural contexts. Some of the articles in the pages that follow do not explicitly state their aims, but these can be interpreted with reasonable accuracy. Many of the articles seem to be essentially descriptive or historical, but our purpose has been to use them as contributions to general theory and not as particular and discrete facts.

We can conclude by warning that anthropology cannot claim comparison as its brain child. Aside from the impressionistic comparisons of the layman, there are the systematic and controlled ones of all scientific disciplines, which use correlation and covariation in their study of similarities and differences. If we may at this point venture an opinion, it would be to the effect that anthropology can at least take pride in the fact that of all the social sciences it has most expanded the possibilities of comparison by adding to the general pool the thousands of case histories made available by its study of tribal societies. Moreover, some of the claims for exclusiveness were undoubtedly derived from the very special use of comparison made by the classical evolutionists of the last century—a specious method that employed a circular type of reasoning, but which nonetheless commanded considerable support in its time.

III

The basic purpose of this book of readings is to provide the student with a guide to the literature concerning what anthropologists have found out about religion in the last 100 years. In a few cases we have included selections from the pens of sociologists, psychologists, historians, and others, and particularly from scholars in these related fields whose works have especially influenced anthropological thinking or who have dealt with data from primitive cultures.

The book grew out of a need felt by the two editors as they attempted to teach courses in comparative and primitive religion at the University of California at Los Angeles and at Harvard University and discovered that many of the best materials were published in obscure journals or were inaccessible to large numbers of our students.

There are a number of interesting introductory texts on primitive religion, including William J. Goode's *Religion Among the Primitives,* W. W. Howells' *The Heathens,* Robert H. Lowie's *Primitive Religion,* Edward Norbeck's *Religion in Primitive Society,* Paul Radin's *Primitive Religion,* and J. Milton Yinger's *Religion, Society and the Individual.* But after students have read one of these texts in the opening weeks of a school term, there is then little for them to do except turn to the long, specialized monographs, or some of the smaller monographs such as "Case Studies in Cultural Anthropology" edited by George and Louise Spindler. It is hoped that this collection of readings will fill the gap between the introductory texts and the monographs and will give the student a significant overview of the anthropological literature. The teaching procedure that we recommend is, first, an introductory text, second, this volume, and third, exposure of the students to one or more of the monographs. We have included a selected list of the longer, specialized monographs on religion that we have found useful.

IV

Throughout the present collection we have attempted to strike a balance between the general and theoretical and the descriptive and concrete. The more general, theoretical selections on the origins and functions of religion have been placed in Chapters 1 and 2, followed by Chapter 3 on myths and rituals and Chapter 4 on symbolism. Chapter 5 on mana and taboo and Chapter 6 on totemism deal with basic concepts. Next come chapters dealing with stress situations—Chapter 7 on magic, witchcraft, and divination, Chapter 8 on the magical treatment of illness, and Chapter 9 on death, ghosts, and ancestor worship. Chapter 10 deals with religious specialists, and is followed by a chapter on the dynamics of religion. The final chapter deals with new methods of analysis of myth and ritual.

The introductions to each chapter and the introductory paragraphs for each selection are designed to place the material in context and to provide bibliographic and teaching aids.

CHAPTER 1

THE ORIGIN AND DEVELOPMENT OF RELIGION

INTRODUCTION

The origins of religion can only be speculated upon; they can never be discovered.
Theories with enormous "documentation"
and nimble imagination may temporarily de-
lude the impressionable reader into believing
that answers have been found, but sober reflection will always show the futility of accepting any one of them as constituting more
than a scholarly guess. Should we on this
account turn away from such speculations?
Not at all. The better and more responsible
of these hypotheses have pointed the way to
rewarding lines of investigation. Not only
have they caused an immense amount of
field data to be collected and studied, but
they have been ultimately responsible for
analytic contributions of lasting value. Even
scholars who have consciously renounced
historical interests in religion owe a great
debt to others who have had such interests
and helped found a science of religion.

One might ask what gave these early students the courage to proceed with reconstructions in the face of our inability to recover the past from actual documentary evidence. What did they substitute for fact?
The answer is, schemes, analogies, and
assumptions, all overlaid with rich imagination. One method of approach was through
the so-called comparative method. "Evidences" from tribes all over the world were
taken out of context and arranged in a sequential scheme. But this was done only according to a preconceived plan and was

justified on the grounds that it arranged the
data in such a way that they conformed to
the scheme and therefore proved its validity.
Another method was through the use of so-
called survivals—"processes, customs, opinions, and so forth, which have been carried
on by force of habit into a new state of society different from that in which they had
their original home, and thus they remain
proofs and examples of an older condition of
culture out of which a newer had been
evolved" (Tylor). In brief, existing survivals throw light on the history of the past.
But in the absence of written records there is
no way of knowing that a custom is actually
a vestigial remnant of a formerly widespread
condition. Again, reliance was firmly placed
on the principle of the psychic unity of mankind—human nature is basically uniform,
therefore similar results have come independently from the same causes. The implication of such panhumanism is that processes
and reactions which we can study and understand today can be used to reconstruct
the past because man's mind always reacts
in the same way to similar external stimuli.
Although anthropologists admit the great
force of such psychic unity, they feel that the
evolutionists did not take sufficient cognizance of the even greater effects of diffusion
in producing cultural similarity. Thus specific religious phenomena with which we are
acquainted through firsthand experience
may not be used to project back into the

8

past, because religious traits may be borrowed instead of developed independently. Such borrowing can disturb any picture of uniform development. Some evolutionists, notably Herbert Spencer, were guided by the principle of progress—society keeps advancing from a less desirable state to a better and better one. The way in which this principle operates is to regard the civilization of western Europe as the acme of man's achievements and to assume that the situation in the childhood of mankind must for each human institution have been exactly the opposite, with intermediate stages grading off from the one to the other. Thus if monotheism prevails today in western Europe, the belief in many spirits must have been a very early condition, polytheism being a less enlightened stage than belief in one God. Since progress is a matter of opinion and merely begs the question as to what is a desirable kind of change, such a theoretical plan rests on a tenuous base; it cannot tell us what the situation was like in primeval times. Moreover, the principle of progress as used by Spencer demands that it be regarded as an irresistible trend, an assumption that finds many objections. To reconstruct the past the surest evidences must come from archaeology; valuable leads have indeed been suggested by the study of old cultural remains. The burials of Neanderthal man and Cro-Magnon man have strong implications for the theory that they indicate an ancient belief in the soul and the afterworld. But since archaeological interpretations must so often rely on analogies with contemporary primitives they are not always conclusive. There is justifiable reason for being cautious in using archaeological data to say that the art of the Upper Paleolithic is magico-religious in nature.

The articles selected for this chapter, except for the last, consist of both representative theories of origins and critiques of such theories. It will be noticed that for the most part they do not bear a recent date, a reflection of the fact that the problem of origins is not a pressing current issue. But one should not minimize the value of these ideas, for they command serious attention as exploratory efforts and have had far-reaching and often fruitful effects. The first article is by Tylor, and represents the earliest of the major anthropological hypotheses of origins; it views religion as being rooted in the idea of

the soul, and argues that out of this rational creation by primeval man came the subsequent belief that a plurality of spirits is associated with various spheres of nature, human activities, and so on. The article by Father Schmidt takes issue with this view and reverses the sequence of development, maintaining that in the beginning man had belief in but one Spirit and that the multiplicity of gods we see in some contemporary societies is a degeneration from the earliest condition. Pettazzoni's article is critical of Schmidt's position regarding the origin of monotheism, especially attacking the motion that contemporary primitives give evidence of the original archaic situation described by Schmidt. The next selection, by W. Robertson Smith, takes an independent tack and makes some suggestions regarding the origin of sacrifice. It was influential in shaping the ideas of many subsequent writers, among them Freud, whose views are here represented only indirectly through two articles by Kroeber, who is at variance with the psychoanalytic interpretation of the origin not only of sacrifice but of religion in general. Durkheim's provocative theory of the origin of religion comes next in sequence, and since it has had strong and lasting influences in contemporary thinking, it is followed by a lengthy critique by Alexander Goldenweiser.

One important historical theory is not represented in the selections and deserves special notice. It is the naturism explanation originally offered in 1856 by F. Max Müller and subsequently expanded by him and other students of Sanskrit. The discovery of the ancient Vedas of the Hindus influenced Müller's ideas. The impulse to religious thought and language, he maintained, arises in the first instance from sensuous experience—from the influence of external nature on man. Nature contains surprise, terror, marvels, miracles. This vast domain of the unknown and infinite, rather than the known and finite, is what provided the sensation from which religions are derived. Fire, for example, could create such an impression on the mind of man. So could the sun and rivers and the wind, to name but a few phenomena. Religions only came into being, however, when the forces of nature were transformed by man from abstract forces to personal agents, that is, spirits. This came about through a "disease of language." Language influences the way in which people classify newly learned things. Natural phenomena came to be compared to human acts, and expressions originally used for human acts came to be applied to natural objects. A thunderbolt was called Something that tears up the soil or spreads fire, the wind Something that sighs or whistles, a river Something that flows, and so on. After this had been done, spirits had to be invented to account for the acts attributed to them by their names, and so arose pantheons of gods. The myth-making process then took hold and carried matters still further by endowing each god with a biography. Thus religion is really a fabric of errors. The supernatural world was composed of beings created out of nothing. In this developmental scheme Müller did not ignore Tylor's later theory of the origin of the soul, but he felt that it was a secondary idea. His chief error was in explaining primitive personalism about nature as if it were some sort of cognitive mistake— a disease of language—as if the primitive first saw the world in coldly objective and scientific terms and then through cognitive error lost this view. But the primitive never had such a world view, which was itself the product of cultural development. Müller's other error was in supposing that he could take ancient historic records from India and attribute religious developments there to the whole world. Writing is, after all, a recent phenomenon and does not even approach the antiquity ascribed to religion.

The final article, by Bellah, is the only one representing neoevolutionism.

EDWARD B. TYLOR

Animism

More than any other anthropologist, Sir Edward B. Tylor stressed the importance of the soul both in defining religion and in understanding the evolutionary stages through which religious phenomena have passed. To him, the belief in spirit beings— animism—constitutes the minimum definition of religion.

The present passage from Tylor's extensive account of animism does not clearly reveal his evolutionary position, but it is apparent that he is concerned with origin and development. First he delves into the question of how men came to create the concept of the soul, and finds the answer in men's efforts to interpret dreams, hallucinations, and other aberrant psychic phenomena which puzzle them. Tylor adduces what he considers to be evidences from primitive peoples that the idea of the soul is not only universal but is also consistent with his dream theory. Along the way he accounts for the origin of human sacrifice by asserting that it is a way of freeing the soul from the body and putting it into the service of the dead. It is only a reasonable step that early man should next extend the idea of the soul to animals, and then to plants, for they too live and die, enjoy health and suffer disease. This accounts for animal sacrifice, which is designed to aid the dead in the afterlife; however, there does not exist a counterpart among plants, for they are not sacrificed for the purpose of enlisting their souls for the service of the dead. Continuing to reason by analogy, says Tylor, early man extended the theory of the soul to stones, weapons, food, ornaments, and other objects which we who are civilized would endow with neither a soul nor life.

The portions of Tylor's theory of animism which have not been included in the accompanying article are lengthy, constituting six chapters of his *Primitive Culture*. They deal with such matters as transmigration and the future life; the expanding of the original

Reprinted in abridged form from Edward B. Tylor, *Primitive Culture* (2 vols.; 2d ed.; London: John Murray, 1873), Chap. 11, by permission of the publishers.

theory of souls into a wider doctrine of spirits, that is, an animistic theory of nature; the development of the view that spirits are personal causes of phenomena of the world; the origin of guardian spirits and nature spirits; the origin of polytheism; and, finally, the development of the idea of monotheism as the completion of the polytheistic system and the outcome of the animistic philosophy. All these are fitted into an unsystematic unilinear scheme of development, in which certain inevitable stages are passed through.

The first aspect of Tylor's theory, which is contained in the article that follows, has been attacked with far less severity than the evolutionary aspect, and even today it continues to impress scholars with its plausibility. The usual criticism is that it is an intellectualistic explanation, and that a rational need to explain the physiological phenomena of such unusual psychic states as dreams not only does not concern the primitive but fails to produce the emotional quality necessary for religion. It is for this reason that some theorists have substituted the criterion of supernaturalism for that of animism as a minimum requirement for religion. Another criticism is that primitive man could not have developed the concept of the soul through dreams because it would have been too easy for him to be contradicted when trying to check with his tribal mates on his hallucinatory experiences. Nevertheless, Tylor's theory has its admirers. Lowie remarks that it not only has a "high degree of probability" but to his knowledge has no serious competitor among rival theories. Even Marett, who put forth the theory that animatism preceded animism, expressed appreciation of Tylor's hypothesis and asserted that he himself was "no irreconcilable foe who has a rival theory to put forward concerning the origin of religion."

Greater vulnerability attaches to the second aspect of Tylor's theory, for when he attempts to show that out of the concept of the soul there evolved the concept of animism, then polydaemonism, then polytheism, and finally monotheism, he falls into most of the fallacies of the evolutionists of his time. In treating primitive man as primeval he had to assume that over a period of hundreds of thousands of years some of the simpler peoples of the world had retained religious beliefs unchanged. One could argue that religion shows a remarkable tenacity and indeed undergoes less alteration than other aspects of culture; but in this case it is asking too much. And, one could argue, too, as did the irrepressible Andrew Lang, that among the simplest peoples of the world there frequently appears a high god; therefore, while the idea of the soul as outlined by Tylor might itself be valid, it need not be supposed that it evolved into the concept of the high god. Other deficiencies in Tylor's chronological scheme could be mentioned, but they are mostly reducible to the use he made of survivals and the faulty comparative method of contemporary evolutionists.

Notwithstanding these limitations, there can be no doubt that Tylor made a challenging attempt to describe the origin of the soul and the general history of religion, and it stimulated subsequent and more sophisticated efforts.

The first requisite in a systematic study of the religions of the lower races is to lay down a rudimentary definition of religion. By requiring in this definition the belief in a supreme deity or of a judgment after death, the adoration of idols or the practice of sacrifice, or other partially diffused doctrines or rites, no doubt many tribes may be excluded from the category of religious. But such narrow definition has the fault of identifying religion rather with particular developments than with the deeper motive which underlies them. It seems best to fall back at once on this essential source, and simply to claim, as a minimum definition of religion, the belief in Spiritual Beings. So far as I can judge from the immense mass of accessible evidence, we have to admit that the belief in spiritual beings appears among all low races with whom we have attained to thoroughly intimate acquaintance; whereas the assertion of absence of such belief must apply either to ancient tribes, or to more or less imperfectly described modern ones.

I purpose here, under the name of Animism, to investigate the deep-lying doctrine of Spiritual Beings, which embodies the very essence of Spiritualistic as opposed to Materialistic philosophy. Animism is not a new technical term, though now seldom used. From its special relation to the doctrine of the soul, it will be seen to have a peculiar appropriateness to the view here taken of the mode in which theological ideas have been developed among mankind. The word "Spiritualism," though it may be, and sometimes is, used in a general sense, has this obvious defect to us, that it has become the designation of a particular modern sect, who indeed hold extreme spiritualistic views, but cannot be taken as typical representatives of these views in the world at large. The sense of Spiritualism in its wider acceptation, the general belief in spiritual beings, is here given to Animism.

Animism characterizes tribes very low in the scale of humanity, and thence ascends, deeply modified in its transmission, but from first to last preserving an unbroken continuity, into the midst of high modern culture. Doctrines adverse to it, so largely held by individuals or schools, are usually due not to early lowness of civilization, but to later changes in the intellectual course, to divergence from, or rejection of, ancestral faiths; and such newer developments do not affect the present inquiry as to the fundamental religious condition of mankind. Animism is, in fact, the groundwork of the Philosophy of Religion, from that of savages up to that of civilized men. And although it may at first sight seem to afford but a bare and meager definition of a minimum of religion, it will be found practically sufficient; for where the root is, the branches will generally be produced. It is habitually found that the theory of Animism divides into two great dogmas, forming parts of one consistent doctrine; first concerning souls of individual creatures, capable of continued existence after the death or destruction of the body; second, concerning other spirits, upward to the rank

of powerful deities. Spiritual beings are held to affect or control the events of the material world, and man's life here and hereafter; and it being considered that they hold intercourse with men, and receive pleasure or displeasure from human actions, the belief in their existence leads naturally, and it might almost be said inevitably, sooner or later to active reverence and propitiation. Thus Animism, in its full development, includes the belief in souls and in a future state, in controlling deities and subordinate spirits, these doctrines practically resulting in some kind of active worship. One great element of religion, that moral element which among the higher nations forms its most vital part, is indeed little represented in the religion of the lower races. It is not that these races have no moral sense or no moral standard, for both are strongly marked among them, if not in formal precept, at least in that traditional consensus of society which we call public opinion, according to which certain actions are held to be good or bad, right or wrong. It is that the conjunction of ethics and Animistic philosophy, so intimate and powerful in the higher culture, seems scarcely yet to have begun in the lower. I propose here hardly to touch upon the purely moral aspects of religion, but rather to study the animism of the world so far as it constitutes, as unquestionably it does constitute, an ancient and world-wide philosophy, of which belief is the theory and worship is the practice. Endeavoring to shape the materials for an inquiry hitherto strangely undervalued and neglected, it will now be my task to bring as clearly as may be into view the fundamental animism of the lower races, and in some slight and broken outline to trace its course into higher regions of civilization. Here let me state once for all two principal conditions under which the present research is carried on. First, as to the religious doctrines and practices examined, these are treated as belonging to theological systems devised by human reason, without supernatural aid or revelation; in other words, as being developments of Natural Religion. Second, as to the connection between similar ideas and rites in the religions of the savage and the civilized world. While dwelling at some length on doctrines and ceremonies of the lower races, and sometimes particularizing for special reasons the related doctrines and ceremonies of the higher nations, it has not seemed my proper task to work out in detail the problems thus suggested among the philosophies and creeds of Christendom. Such applications, extending farthest from the direct scope of a work on primitive culture, are briefly stated in general terms, or touched in slight allusion, or taken for granted without remark. Educated readers possess the information required to work out their general bearing on theology, while more technical discussion is left to philosophers and theologians specially occupied with such arguments.

The first branch of the subject to be considered is the doctrine of human and other souls, an examination of which will occupy the rest of the present theory of its development. It seems as though thinking men, as yet at a low level of culture, were deeply impressed by two groups of biological problems. In the first place, what is it that makes the difference between a living body and a dead one; what causes waking, sleep, trance, disease, death? In the second place, what are those human shapes which appear in dreams and visions? Looking at these two groups of phenomena, the ancient savage philosophers probably made their first step by the obvious inference that every man has two things belonging to him, namely, a life and a phantom. These two are evidently in close connection with the body, the life as enabling it to feel and think and act, the phantom as being its image or second self; both, also, are perceived to be things separable from the body, the life as able to go away and leave it insensible or dead, the phantom as appearing to people at a distance from it. The second step would seem also easy for savages to make, seeing how extremely difficult civilized men have found it to unmake. It is merely to combine the life and the phantom. As both belong to the body, why should they not also belong to one another, and be manifestations of one and the same soul? Let them then be considered as united, and the result is that well-known conception which may be described as an apparitional soul, a ghost-soul. This, at any rate, corresponds with the actual conception of the personal soul or spirit among the lower races, which may be defined as follows: It is a thin unsubstantial human image, in its nature a sort of vapor, film, or shadow; the cause of life and thought in the individual it animates; independently possessing the personal consciousness and volition of its corporeal owner, past or present; capable of leaving the body far behind, to flash swiftly from place to place; mostly impalpable and invisible, yet also manifesting physical power, and especially appearing to men waking or asleep as a phantasm separate from the body of which it bears the likeness; continuing to exist and appear to men after the death of that body; able to enter into, possess, and act in the bodies of other men, of animals, and even of things. Though this definition is by no means of universal application, it has sufficient generality to be taken as a standard, modified by more or less divergence among any particular people. Far from these world-wide opinions being arbitrary or conventional products, it is seldom even justifiable to consider their uniformity among distant races as proving communication of any sort. They are doctrines answering in the most forcible way to the plain evidence of men's senses, as interpreted by a fairly consistent and rational primitive philosophy. So well, indeed, does primitive animism account for the facts of nature, that it has held its place into the higher levels of education. Though classic and medieval philosophy modified it much, and modern philosophy has handled it yet more unsparingly, it has so far retained the traces of its original character, that heirlooms of primitive ages may be claimed in the existing psychology of the civilized world. Out of the vast mass of evidence, collected among the most various and distant races of mankind, typical details may now be selected to display the earlier theory of the soul, the relations of the parts of this theory, and the manner in which these parts have been abandoned, modified, or kept up, along the course of culture.

To understand the popular conceptions of the human soul or spirit, it is instructive to notice the words which have been found suitable to express it. The ghost or phantasm seen by the dreamer or the visionary is an unsubstantial form, like a shadow, and thus the familiar term of the *shade* comes in to express the soul. Thus the Tasmanian word for the shadow is also that for the spirit; the Algonquin Indians describe a man's soul as *otahchuk,* "his shadow," the Quiché language uses *natub* for "shadow, soul"; the Arawac *ueja* means "shadow, soul, image"; the Abipones made the one word *loákal* serve for "shadow, soul, echo, image." The Zulus not only use the word *tunzi* for "shadow, spirit, ghost," but they consider that at death the shadow of a man will in some way depart from the corpse, to become an ancestral spirit. The Basutos not only call the spirit remaining after death the *seriti* or "shadow," but they think that if a man walks on the river bank a crocodile may seize his shadow in the water and draw him in; while in Old Calabar there is found the same indentification of the spirit with the *ukpon* or "shadow," for a man to lose which is fatal. There are thus found among the lower races not only the types of those familiar classic terms, the *skia* and *umbra,* but also what seems the fundamental thought of the stories of shadowless men still current in the folklore of Europe, and familiar to modern readers in Chamisso's tale of Peter Schlemihl. Thus the dead in Purgatory knew that Dante was alive when they saw that, unlike theirs, his fingers cast a shadow on the ground. Other attributes are taken into the notion of soul or spirit, with especial regard to its being the cause of life. Thus the Caribs, connecting the pulses with spiritual beings, and especially considering that in the heart dwells man's chief soul, destined to a future heavenly life, could reasonably use the one word *iouanni* for "soul, life, heart." The Tongans supposed the soul to exist throughout the whole extension of the body, but particularly in the heart. On one occasion, the natives were declaring to a European that a man buried months ago was nevertheless still alive. "And one, endeavoring to make me understand what he meant, took hold of my hand, and squeezing it, said, 'This will die, but the life that is within you will never die'; with his other hand pointing to my heart." So the Basutos say of a dead man that his heart is gone, and of one recovering from sickness that his heart is coming back. This corresponds to the familiar Old World view of the heart as the prime mover in life, thought, and passion. The connection of soul and blood, familiar to the Karens and Papuas, appears prominently in Jewish and Arabic philosophy.

The act of breathing, so characteristic of the high animals during life, and coinciding so closely with life in its departure, has been repeatedly and naturally identified with the life or soul itself. It is thus that West Australians used one word *waug* for "breath, spirit, soul"; that in the Netela language of California, *piuts* means "life, breath, soul"; that certain Greenlanders reckoned two souls to man, namely, his shadow and his breath; that the Malays say the soul of the dying man escapes through his nostrils, and in Java use the same word *nawa* for "breath, life, soul." The conception of the soul as breath may be followed up through Semitic and Aryan etymology, and thus into the main streams of the philosophy of the world. Hebrew shows *nephesh,* "breath" passing into all the meanings of "life, soul, mind, animal," while *ruach* and *neshamah* make the like transition from "breath" to "spirit"; and to these the Arabic *nefs* and *ruh* correspond. The same is the history of Sanskrit *atman* and *prana,* of Greek *psyche* and *pneuma,* of Latin *animus, anima, spiritus.* German *geist* and English *ghost,* too, may possibly have the same original sense of breath. And if any should think such expressions due to mere metaphor, they may judge the strength of the implied connection between breath and spirit by cases of most unequivocal significance. Among the Seminoles of Florida, when a woman died in childbirth, the infant was held over her face to receive her parting spirit, and thus acquire strength and knowledge for its future use. These Indians could have well understood why at the deathbed of an ancient Roman, the nearest kinsman leant over to inhale the last breath of the departing (*ex excipies hanc animan ore pio*). Their state of mind is kept up to this day among Tyrolese peasants, who can still fancy a good man's soul to issue from his mouth at death like a little white cloud.

Among rude races, the original conception of the human soul seems to have been that of ethereality, or vaporous materiality, which has held so large a place in human thought ever since. In fact, the later metaphysical notion of immateriality could scarcely have conveyed any meaning to a savage. It is moreover to be noticed that, as to the whole nature and action of apparitional souls, the lower philosophy escapes various difficulties which down to modern times have perplexed metaphysicians and theologians of the civilized world. Considering the thin ethereal body of the soul to be itself sufficient and suitable for visibility, movement, and speech, the primitive animists had no need of additional hypotheses to account for these manifestations, theological theories such as we may find detailed by Calmet, as that immaterial souls have their own vaporous bodies provided for them by supernatural means to enable them to appear as specters, or that they possess the power of condensing the circumambient air into phantomlike bodies to invest themselves in, or of forming from it vocal instruments. It appears to have been within systematic schools of civilized philosophy that the transcendental definitions of the immaterial soul were obtained, by abstraction from the primitive conception of the ethereal-material soul, so as to reduce it from a physical to a metaphysical entity.

Departing from the body at the time of death, the soul or spirit is considered set free to linger near the tomb, to wander on earth or flit in the air, or to travel to the proper region of spirits—the world beyond the grave. The principal conceptions of the lower psychology as to a Future Life will be considered in the following chapters, but for the present purpose of investigating the theory of souls in general, it will be well to enter here upon one department of the subject. Men do not stop short at the persuasion that death releases the soul to a free and active existence, but they quite logically proceed to assist nature, by slaying men in order to liberate their souls for ghostly uses. Thus there arises one of the most widespread, distinct, and intelligible rites of animistic religion— that of funeral human sacrifice for the service of the dead. When a man of rank dies and his soul departs to its own place, wherever and whatever that place may be, it is a rational inference of early philosophy that the souls of attendants, slaves, and wives, put to death at his funeral, will make the same journey and continue their service in the next life, and the argument is frequently stretched further, to include the souls of new victims sacrificed in order that they may enter upon the same ghostly servitude. It will appear from the ethnography of this rite that it is not strongly marked in the very lowest levels of culture, but that, arising in the higher savagery, it develops itself in the barbaric stage, and thenceforth continues or dwindles in survival.

Of the murderous practices to which this opinion leads, remarkably distinct accounts may be cited from among tribes of the Indian Archipelago. The following account is given of the funerals of great men among the savage Kayans of Borneo: "Slaves are killed in order that they may follow the de-

ceased and attend upon him. Before they are killed the relations who surround them enjoin them to take great care of their master when they join him, to watch and shampoo him when he is indisposed, to be always near him, and to obey all his behests. The female relatives of the deceased then take a spear and slightly wound the victims, after which the males spear them to death." Again, the opinion of the Idaan is "that all whom they kill in this world shall attend them as slaves after death. This notion of further interest in the destruction of the human species is a great impediment to an intercourse with them, as murder goes further than present advantage or resentment. From the same principle they will purchase a slave, guilty of any capital crime, at fourfold his value, that they may be his executioners." With the same idea is connected the ferocious custom of "head-hunting," so prevalent among the Dayaks before Rajah Brooke's time. They considered that the owner of every human head they could procure would serve them in the next world, where, indeed, a man's rank would be according to his number of heads in this. They would continue the mourning for a dead man till a head was brought in, to provide him with a slave to accompany him to the "habitation of souls"; a father who lost his child would go out and kill the first man he met, as a funeral ceremony; a young man might not marry till he had procured a head, and some tribes would bury with a dead man the first head he had taken, together with spears, cloth, rice, and betel. Waylaying and murdering men for their heads became, in fact, the Dayaks' national sport, and they remarked "the white men read books, we hunt heads instead." Of such rites in the Pacific islands, the most hideously purposeful accounts reach us from the Fiji group. Till lately, a main part of the ceremony of a great man's funeral was the strangling of wives, friends, and slaves, for the distinct purpose of attending him into the world of spirits. Ordinarily the first victim was the wife of the deceased, and more than one if he had several, and their corpses, oiled as for a feast, clothed with new fringed girdles, with heads dressed and ornamented, and vermilion and turmeric powder spread on their faces and bosoms, were laid by the side of the dead warrior. Associates and inferior attendants were likewise slain, and these bodies were spoken of as "grass for bedding the grave." When Ra Mbithi, the pride of Somosomo, was lost at sea, seventeen of his wives were killed; and after the news of the massacre of the Namena people, in 1839, eighty women were strangled to accompany the spirits of their murdered husbands.

In now passing from the consideration of the souls of men to that of the souls of the lower animals, we have first to inform ourselves as to the savage man's idea, which is very different from the civilized man's, of the nature of these lower animals. A remarkable group of observances customary among rude tribes will bring this distinction sharply into view. Savages talk quite seriously to beasts alive or dead as they would to men alive or dead, offer them homage, ask pardon when it is their painful duty to hunt and kill them. A North American Indian will reason with a horse as if rational. Some will spare the rattlesnake, fearing the vengeance of its spirit if slain; others will salute the creature reverently, bid it welcome as a friend from the land of spirits, sprinkle a pinch of tobacco on its head for an offering, catch it by the tail and dispatch it with extreme dexterity, and carry off its skin as a trophy. If an Indian is attacked and torn by a bear, it is that the beast fell upon him intentionally in anger, perhaps to revenge the hurt done to another bear. When a bear is killed, they will beg pardon of him, or even make him condone the offense by smoking the peace-pipe with his murderers, who put the pipe in his mouth and blow down it, begging his spirit not to take revenge. So in Africa, the Kafirs will hunt the elephant, begging him not to tread on them and kill them, and when he is dead they will assure him that they did not kill him on purpose, and they will bury his trunk, for the elephant is a mighty chief, and his trunk is his hand that he may hurt withal. The Congo people will even avenge such a murder by a pretended attack on the hunters who did the deed. Such customs are common among the lower Asiatic tribes. The Stiens of Kambodia ask pardon of the beast they have killed; the Ainos of Yesso kill the bear, offer obeisance and salutation to him, and cut up his carcase. The Koriaks, if they have slain a bear or wolf, will flay him, dress one of their people in the skin, and dance round him, chanting excuses that they did not do it, and especially laying the blame on a Russian. But if it is a fox, they take his skin, wrap his dead body in hay, and sneering tell him to go to his own people and say what famous hospitality he has had, and how they gave him a new coat instead of his old one. The Samoyeds excuse themselves to the slain bear, telling him it was the Russian who did it, and that a Russian knife will cut him up. The Goldi will set up the slain bear, call him "my lord" and do ironical homage to him, or taking him alive will fatten him in a cage, call him "son" and "brother," and kill and eat him as a sacrifice at a solemn festival. In Borneo, the Dayaks, when they have caught an alligator with a baited hook and rope, address him with respect and soothing till they have his legs fast, and then mocking call him "rajah" and "grandfather." Thus when the savage gets over his fears, he still keeps up in ironical merriment the reverence which had its origin in trembling sincerity. Even now the Norse hunter will say with horror of a bear that will attack man, that he can be "no Christian bear."

The sense of an absolute psychical distinction between man and beast, so prevalent in the civilized world, is hardly to be found among the lower races. Men to whom the cries of beasts and birds seem like human language, and their actions guided as it were by human thought, logically enough allow the existence of souls to beasts, birds, and reptiles, as to men. The lower psychology cannot but recognize in beasts the very characteristic which it attributes to the human soul, namely, the phenomena of life and death, will and judgment, and the phantom seen in vision or in dream. As for believers, savage or civilized, in the great doctrine of metempsychosis, these not only consider that an animal may have a soul, but that this soul may have inhabited a human being, and thus the creature may be in fact their own ancestor or once familiar friend. A line of facts, arranged as waymarks along the course of civilization, will serve to indicate the history of opinion from savagery onward, as to the souls of animals during life and after death. North American Indians held every animal to have its spirit, and these spirits their future life; the soul of the Canadian dog went to serve his master in the other world; among the Sioux, the prerogative of having four souls was not confined to man, but belonged also to the bear, the most human of animals. The Greenlanders considered that a sick human soul might be replaced by the sorcerer with a fresh healthy soul of a hare, reindeer, or a young child. Maori taletellers have heard of the road by which the spirits of dogs descend to Reinga, the Hades of the departed; the Hovas of Madagascar know that the ghosts of beasts and men, dwelling in a great mountain in the south called Ambondromble, come out occasionally to walk among the tombs or execution-places of criminals. The Kamchadals held that every creature, even the smallest fry, would live again in the underworld. The Kukis of Assam think that the ghost of every animal a Kuki kills in the chase or for the feast will belong to him in the next life, even as the enemy he slays in the field will then become his slave. The Karens apply the doctrine of the spirit or personal life-phantom, which is apt to wander from the body and thus suffer injury, equally to men and to animals. The Zulus say the cattle they kill come to life again, and become the property of the dwellers in the world beneath. The Siamese butcher, when in defiance of the very principles of his Buddhism he slaughters an ox, before he kills the creature has at least the grace to beseech its spirit to seek a happier abode. In connection with such transmigration, Pythagorean and Platonic philosophy gives to the lower animals undying souls, while other classic opinion may recognize in beasts only an inferior order of soul, only the "anima" but not the human "animus" besides. Thus Juvenal:

Principio indulsit communis conditor illis
Tantum animas; nobis animum quoque. . . .

Through the middle ages, controversy as to the psychology of brutes has lasted on into our own times, ranging between two extremes; on the one the theory of Descartes which reduced animals to mere machines, on the other what Mr. Alger defines as "the faith that animals have immaterial and deathless souls." Among modern speculations may be instanced that of Wesley, who thought that in the next life animals will be raised even above their bodily and mental state at the creation, "the horridness of their appearance will be exchanged for their primeval beauty," and it even may be that they will be made what men are now, creatures capable of religion. Adam Clarke's argument for the future life of animals rests on abstract justice: whereas they did not sin,

but yet are involved in the sufferings of sinful man, and cannot have in the present state the happiness designed for them, it is reasonable that they must have it in another. Although, however, the primitive belief in the souls of animals still survives to some extent in serious philosophy, it is obvious that the tendency of educated opinion on the question whether brutes have soul, as distinguished from life and mind, has for ages been in a negative and skeptical direction.

Animals being thus considered in the primitive psychology to have souls like human beings, it follows as the simplest matter of course that tribes who kill wives and slaves, to dispatch their souls on errands of duty with their departed lords, may also kill animals in order that their spirits may do such service as is proper to them. The Pawnee warrior's horse is slain on his grave to be ready for him to mount again, and the Comanche's best horses are buried with his favorite weapons and his pipe, all alike to be used in the distant happy hunting-grounds. In South America not only do such rites occur, but they reach a practically disastrous extreme. Patagonian tribes, says D'Orbigny, believe in another life, where they are to enjoy perfect happiness, therefore they bury with the deceased his arms and ornaments, and even kill on his tomb all the animals which belonged to him, that he may find them in the abode of bliss; and this opposes an insurmountable barrier to all civilization, by preventing them from accumulating property and fixing their habitations. Not only do Pope's now hackneyed lines express a real motive with which the Indian's dog is buried with him, but in the North American continent the spirit of the dog has another remarkable office to perform. Certain Eskimos, as Cranz relates, would lay a dog's head in a child's grave, that the soul of the dog, who ever finds his home, may guide the helpless infant to the land of souls. In accordance with this, Captain Scoresby in Jameson's Land found a dog's skull in a small grave, probably a child's. Again, in the distant region of the Aztecs, one of the principal ceremonies was to slaughter a techichi, or native dog; it was burnt or buried with the corpse, with a cotton thread fastened to its neck, and its office was to convey the deceased across the deep waters of Chiuhnahuapan, on the way to the Land of the Dead. The dead Buraet's favorite horse, led saddled to the grave, killed, and flung in, may serve for a Tartar example. In Tonquin, even wild animals have been customarily drowned at funeral ceremonies of princes, to be at the service of the departed in the next world. Among Semitic tribes, an instance of the custom may be found in the Arab sacrifice of a camel on the grave, for the dead man's spirit to ride upon. Among the nations of the Aryan race in Europe, the prevalence of such rites is deep, wide, and full of purpose. Thus warriors were provided in death with horses and housings, with hounds and falcons. Customs thus described in chronicle and legend are vouched for in our own time by the opening of old barbaric burial places. How clear a relic of savage meaning lies here may be judged from a Livonian account as late as the fourteenth century, which relates how men and women, slaves, sheep, and oxen, with other things, were burnt with the dead, who, it was believed, would reach some region of the living, and find there, with the multitude of cattle and slaves, a country of life and happiness. As usual, these rites may be traced onward in survival. The Mongols, who formerly slaughtered camels and horses at their owner's burial, have been induced to replace the actual sacrifice by a gift of the cattle to the Lamas. The Hindus offer a black cow to the Brahmans, in order to secure their passage across the Vaitarani, the river of death, and will often die grasping the cow's tail as if to swim across in herdsman's fashion, holding on to the cow. It is mentioned as a belief in Northern Europe that he who has given a cow to the poor will find a cow to take him over the bridge of the dead, and a custom of leading a cow in the funeral procession is said to have been kept up to modern times. All these rites probably belong together as connected with ancient funeral sacrifice, and the survival of the custom of sacrificing the warrior's horse at his tomb is yet more striking. Saint-Foix long ago put the French evidence very forcibly. Mentioning the horse led at the funeral of Charles VI, with the four valets-de-pied in black, and bareheaded, holding the corners of its caparison, he recalls the horses and servants killed and buried with pre-Christian kings.

Plants, partaking with animals the phenomena of life and death, health and sickness, not unnaturally have some kind of soul ascribed to them. In fact, the notion of a vegetable soul, common to plants and to the higher organisms possessing an animal soul in addition, was familiar to medieval philosophy, and is not yet forgotten by naturalists. But in the lower ranges of culture, at least within one wide district of the world, the souls of plants are much more fully identified with the souls of animals. The Society Islanders seem to have attributed "varua," i.e., surviving soul or spirit, not to men only but to animals and plants. The Dayaks of Borneo not only consider men and animals to have a spirit of living principle, whose departure from the body causes sickness and eventually death, but they also give to the rice its "samangat padi," or "spirit of the paddy," and they hold feasts to retain this soul securely, lest the crop should decay. The Karens say that plants as well as men and animals have their "la" ("kelah"), and the spirit of sickly rice is here also called back like a human spirit considered to have left the body. There is reason to think that the doctrine of the spirits of plants lay deep in the intellectual history of South-East Asia, but was in great measure superseded under Buddhist influence. The Buddhist books show that in the early days of their religion it was matter of controversy whether trees had souls, and therefore whether they might lawfully be injured. Orthodox Buddhism decided against the tree-souls, and consequently against the scruple to harm them, declaring trees to have no mind nor sentient principle, though admitting that certain dewas or spirits do reside in the body of trees, and speak from within them. Buddhists also relate that a heterodox sect kept up the early doctrine of the actual animate life of trees, in connection with which may be remembered Marco Polo's somewhat doubtful statement as to certain austere Indians objecting to green herbs for such a reason, and some other passages from later writers. Generally speaking, the subject of the spirits of plants is an obscure one, whether from the lower races not having definite opinions, or from our not finding it easy to trace them. The evidence from funeral sacrifices, so valuable as to most departments of early psychology, fails us here, from plants not being thought suitable to send for the service of the dead. Yet, as we shall see more fully elsewhere, there are two topics which bear closely on the matter. On the one hand, the doctrine of transmigration widely and clearly recognizes the idea of trees or smaller plants being animated by human souls; on the other the belief in tree-spirits and the practice of tree-worship involve notions more or less closely coinciding with that of tree-souls, as when the classic hamadryad dies with her tree, or when the Talein of South-East Asia, considering every tree to have a demon or spirit, offers prayers before he cuts one down.

Thus far the details of the lower animistic philosophy are not very unfamiliar to modern students. The primitive view of the souls of men and beasts as asserted or acted on in the lower and middle levels of culture, so far belongs to current civilized thought, that those who hold the doctrine to be false, and the practices based upon it futile, can nevertheless understand and sympathize with the lower nations to whom they are matters of the most sober and serious conviction. Nor is even the notion of a separable spirit or soul as the cause of life in plants too incongruous with ordinary ideas to be readily appreciable. But the theory of souls in the lower culture stretches beyond this limit, to take in a conception much stranger to modern thought. Certain high savage races distinctly hold, and a large proportion of other savage and barbarian races make a more or less close approach to, a theory of separable and surviving souls or spirits belonging to stocks and stones, weapons, boats, food, clothes, ornaments, and other objects which to us are not merely soulless but lifeless.

Yet, strange as such a notion may seem to us at first sight, if we place ourselves by an effort in the intellectual position of an uncultured tribe, and examine the theory of object souls from their point of view, we shall hardly pronounce it irrational. In discussing the origin of myth, some account has been already given of the primitive stage of thought in which personality and life are ascribed not to men and beasts only, but to things. It has been shown how what we call inanimate objects—rivers, stones, trees, weapons, and so forth—are treated as living intelligent beings, talked to, propitiated, punished for the harm they do. Hume, whose "Natural History of Religion" is perhaps more then any other work the source of modern opinions as to the development of religion, comments on the influence of this personifying stage of thought. "There is an universal tendency among mankind to conceive all beings like themselves, and to transfer to every object those qualities with which they are familiarly acquainted, and of which they are intimately conscious. . . . The *unknown causes,* which continually employ their thought, appearing always in the same aspect, are all apprehended to be of the same kind or species. Nor is it long before we ascribe to them thought and reason, and passion, and sometimes even the limbs and figures of men, in order to bring them nearer to a resemblance with ourselves." Auguste Comte has ventured to bring such a state of thought under terms of strict definition in his conception of the primary mental condition of mankind—a state of "pure fetishism, constantly characterized by the free and direct exercise of our primitive tendency to conceive all external bodies soever, natural or artificial, as animated by a life essentially analogous to our own, with mere differences of intensity." Our comprehension of the lower stages of mental culture depends much on the thoroughness with which we can appreciate this primitive, childlike conception, and in this our best guide may be the memory of our own childish days. He who recollects when there was still personality to him in posts and sticks, chairs and toys, may well understand how the infant philosophy of mankind could extend the notion of vitality to what modern science only recognizes as lifeless things; thus one main part of the lower animistic doctrine as to souls of objects is accounted for. The doctrine requires for its full conception of a soul not only life, but also a phantom or apparitional spirit; this development, however, follows without difficulty, for the evidence of dreams and visions applies to the spirits of objects in much the same manner as to human ghosts. Everyone who has seen visions while light-headed in fever, everyone who has ever dreamt a dream, has seen the phantoms of objects as well as of persons. How then can we charge the savage with farfetched absurdity for taking into his philosophy and religion an opinion which rests on the very evidence of his senses? The notion is implicitly recognized in his accounts of ghosts, which do not come naked, but clothed, and even armed; of course there must be spirits of garments and weapons, seeing that the spirits of men come bearing them. It will indeed place savage philosophy in no unfavorable light, if we compare this extreme animistic development of it with the popular opinion still surviving in civilized countries, as to ghosts and the nature of the human soul as connected with them. When the ghost of Hamlet's father appeared armed cap-a-pie,

Such was the very armour he had on,
When he the ambitious Norway combated.

And thus it is a habitual feature of the ghost stories of the civilized, as of the savage world, that the ghost comes dressed, and even dressed in well-known clothing worn in life. Hearing as well as sight testifies to the phantoms of objects: the clanking of ghostly chains and the rustling of ghostly dresses are described in the literature of apparitions. Now by the savage theory, according to which the ghost and his clothes are alike imaginary and subjective, the facts of apparitions are rationally met. But the modern vulgar who ignore or repudiate the notion of ghosts of things, while retaining the notion of ghosts of persons, have fallen into a hybrid state of opinion which has neither the logic of the savage nor of the civilized philosopher.

It remains to sum up in a few words the doctrine of souls, in the various phases it has assumed from first to last among mankind. In the attempt to trace its main course through the successive grades of man's intellectual history, the evidence seems to accord best with a theory of its development, somewhat to the following effect. At the lowest levels of culture of which we have clear knowledge, the notion of a ghost-soul animating man while in the body, is found deeply ingrained. There is no reason to think that this belief was learnt by savage tribes from contact with higher races, nor that it is a relic of higher culture from which the savage tribes have degenerated: for what is here treated as the primitive animistic doctrine is thoroughly at home among savages, who appear to hold it on the very evidence of their senses, interpreted on the biological principle which seems to them most reasonable. We may now and then hear the savage doctrines and practices concerning souls claimed as relic of a high religious culture pervading the primeval race of man. They are said to be traces of remote ancestral religion, kept up in scanty and perverted memory by tribes degraded from a nobler state. It is easy to see that such an explanation of

some few facts, sundered from their connection with the general array, may seem plausible to certain minds. But a large view of the subject can hardly leave such argument in possession. The animism of savages stands for and by itself; it explains its own origin. The animism of civilized men, while more appropriate to advanced knowledge, is in great measure only explicable as a developed product of the older and ruder system. It is the doctrines and rites of the lower races which are, according to their philosophy, results of point-blank natural evidence and acts of straightforward practical purpose. It is the doctrines and rites of the higher races which show survival of the old in the midst of the new, modification of the old to bring it into conformity with the new, abandonment of the old because it is no longer compatible with the new. Let us see at a glance in what general relation the doctrine of souls among savage tribes stands to the doctrine of souls among barbaric and cultured nations. Among races within the limits of savagery, the general doctrine of souls is found worked out with remarkable breadth and consistency. The souls of animals are recognized by a natural extension from the theory of human souls; the souls of trees and plants follow in some vague partial way; and the souls of inanimate objects expand the general category to its extremest boundary. Thenceforth, as we explore human thought onward from savage into barbarian and civilized life, we find a state of theory more conformed to positive science, but in itself less complete and consistent. Far on into civilization, men still act as though in some half-meant way they believed in souls or ghosts of objects, while nevertheless their knowledge of physical science is beyond so crude a philosophy. As to the doctrine of souls of plants, fragmentary evidence of the history of its breaking down in Asia has reached us. In our own day and country, the notion of souls of beasts is to be seen dying out. Animism, indeed, seems to be drawing in its outposts, and concentrating itself on its first and main position, the doctrine of the human soul. This doctrine has undergone extreme modification in the course of culture. It has outlived the almost total loss of one great argument attached to it—the objective reality of apparitional souls or ghosts seen in dreams and visions. The soul has given up its ethereal substance, and become an immaterial entity, "the shadow of a shade." Its theory is becoming separated from the investigations of biology and mental science, which now discuss the phenomena of life and thought, the sense and the intellect, the emotions and the will, on a groundwork of pure experience. There has arisen an intellectual product whose very existence is of the deepest significance, a "psychology" which has no longer anything to do with "soul." The soul's place in modern thought is in the metaphysics of religion, and its especial office there is that of furnishing an intellectual side to the religious doctrine of the future life. Such are the alterations which have differenced the fundamental animistic belief in its course through successive periods of the world's culture. Yet it is evidence that, notwithstanding all this profound change, the conception of the human soul is, as to its most essential nature, continuous from the philosophy of the savage thinker to that of the modern professor of theology. Its definition has remained from the first that of an animating, separable, surviving entity, the vehicle of individual personal existence. The theory of the soul is one principle part of a system of religious philosophy, which unites, in an unbroken line of mental connection, the savage fetish-worshiper and the civilized Christian. The divisions which have separated the great religions of the world into intolerant and hostile sects are for the most part superficial in comparison with the deepest of all religious schisms, that which divides Animism from Materialism.

WILHELM SCHMIDT

The Nature, Attributes and Worship of the Primitive High God

Father Schmidt has vigorously propounded a theory of the development of religion that is diametrically opposed to that of Tylor. To him, the original religion revolved around the worship of a high god. Out of this *Urmonotheismus* there later arose, through a process of degenerative speculative thought, such concepts as spirits and ghosts, animal and plant souls, multiple gods, and wide variety in worship.

Andrew Lang had already in 1898 (*The Making of Religion*) challenged Tylor's theory of animism along similar lines. A literary writer and critic who stood outside the main stream of the anthropological thought of the times, he refused to be cowed either by Tylor's great erudition or by the evolutionary climate which then prevailed. He saw no unilinear progression toward a high god. Instead, to him the evidence of some of the simplest of living tribes demonstrated that the high god or "All-Father" was already present among them in their pristine condition, without influence from the Western world. In the course of time the All-Father, who is omniscient, omnipotent, eternal, and the creator of all things, comes to be supplanted by the ancestral dead, who are not so sublime as to be removed from direct dealings with the living. The ascendancy of the ghosts of the deceased is also due to the deterioration of the All-Father, who gradually loses his sublimity and acquires human or contemptible traits which may even reduce him to the status of a trickster. Another criticism made by Lang of the animistic doctrine was that the high god of the primitives need not be a spirit; he may merely be a highly superior being without having the characteristics of a soul or shadowy double. The evidence of some primitive tribes seems to bear him

Reprinted from Wilhelm Schmidt, *The Origin and Growth of Religion: Facts and Theories* (New York: Lincoln MacVeagh, 1931), Chap. 16, by permission of the Dial Press, Methuen & Co., Ltd., and Aschendorffsche Verlagsbuchhandlung.

out, for such people often view supernaturals as "magnified non-natural men" without being spiritual. In short, not all supernatural beings are spirits.

Developing Lang's theory that religion first manifested itself in the belief in high gods, Schmidt relaxed from the highly diffusionist, antievolutionist position of the *Kulturkreislehre,* of which he was an outstanding exponent, and embraced the concept of "survivals" to trace the origins of religion. The presence of high gods among tribal peoples meant to him that they reflected the existence of an original monotheism in the *Urkultur.* The belief in a Supreme Deity came to be so corrupted, twisted, and confused by magic and animistic views, he said, that only here and there among the most archaic cultures of today can we discover evidences of the belief in a high god.

A large number of Catholic missionary priests working with native peoples have been trained by Schmidt and have devoted considerable research toward finding evidences of a high god among their flocks. Along with their mentor, these scholars, who otherwise have made large positive contributions toward ethnology, have been accused of being uncritical and ecclesiastically biased. Often they have confused monolatry—the worship of one god out of many—with monotheism. One might be willing to admit the plausibility of their logical premises, but there remains a serious challenge to the facts that they have adduced in favor of their theory. They see eternity, omniscience, omnipotence, omnipresence, creativeness, complete beneficence, and righteousness—characteristics of a true supreme being—where they do not actually exist. Radcliffe-Brown's material from the Andaman Islands shows, for example, that Biliku does not really deserve to be called a monotheistic deity because the natives threaten and trick him (or her), steal from him, exile him, and even kill him in revenge. The Bushmen of South Africa do not really have a high god, for there both the moon and the stars are worshiped, and they not only have multiple forms but lack the immortality, unalterable goodness, and other qualities demanded of the monotheistic hypothesis. In short, the facts are not what they are represented to be. They are scanty, unreliable, contradictory, and distorted. Aside from all this, there is always present the objection that "primitive" is not the same concept as "primeval." The culture of the Pygmies is not the *Urkultur.*

A unique objection to the high-god hypothesis has been made by Radin (*Primitive Religion,* 1937), who not only maintains that true monotheism is extremely rare among primitive peoples, but that in any case it is not really a manifestation of religion at all but the philosophic speculation of a small part of the community—the medicine man or shaman among hunting and gathering tribes, the priest among agricultural tribes. The supreme beings created by these thinkers are not meant to be worshiped, and in cases where they do become the object of a religious cult they are quickly transformed into the highest gods of a polytheistic pantheon and lose much of their original character. Radin insists that the concept of supreme beings is not necessary for even the most complicated of primitive societies and has remained the possession of a few priest-thinkers. Nowhere among primitives is monotheism the official faith of the whole community.

Lang and Schmidt performed a service for the science of religion by stemming the influence of the theory of animism and demonstrating the plausibility of nonanimistic hypotheses of religious origins. While their counterproposals are themselves vulnerable, these two writers did help to keep thought on the subject fluid and critical.

1. THE PRIMITIVE RELIGION OF A HIGH GOD: A TRUE MONOTHEISM

That the Supreme Being of the primitive culture is really the god of a monotheism, and that the religion which includes him is genuinely monotheistic—this is the position which is most attacked by a number of authors. To this attack we may reply that there is a sufficient number of tribes among whom the really monotheistic character of their Supreme Being is clear even to a cursory examination. This is true of the Supreme Being of most Pygmy tribes, so far as we know them; also of the Tierra del Fuegians, the primitive Bushmen, the Kurnai, Kulin, and Yuin of South-East Australia, the peoples of the Arctic culture, except the Koryaks, and well-nigh all the primitives of North America.

Among other races, the fact of their monotheistic belief has been obscured. This is partly due to crosses with later forms, partly to differentiation, partly to other causes, all of which can be discovered only by exact historical analysis.

A. FORMS RESULTING FROM DIFFERENTIATION

(i) It is particularly characteristic of the Arctic primitives to differentiate a divine protector of beasts, both wild and tame. Originally it was none other than the Supreme Being who was lord of the beasts they hunted, these being one of their most important sources of food. But the process by which this differentiation took place can no longer be made out in much detail. Owing to the remarkable breadth which the concept of the Supreme Being has among them (for he includes in his sphere the sky, air, water, and often the whole of nature) other differentiations, corresponding to different parts of the universe, have also taken place.

(ii) In nearly every separate area of the primitive culture the First Father plays an important part, especially in the initiation ceremonies; originally, he and the First Mother were the parents of the race. Owing to the later influence of the matrilineal cultures, he develops a lunar character, is brought into connection with the moon and not uncommonly obscures the Supreme Being or blends with him. Where contact has been established with the solar mythology of the totemistic and patrilineal culture, the young and powerful morning sun is repre-sented as the child of the Supreme Being, who later becomes identified with the ageing evening sun and is obscured by the morning sun.

(iii) Another pluralizing of superior beings is brought about by the problem of the origin of evil, with which even these men of primeval days wrestled. The Supreme Being is everywhere represented among them as absolutely good, having nothing to do with evil either in conduct or in the outer world. Evil therefore must have another vehicle or originator; and he, especially in the mythology of the North American primitives and of those of the Arctic, is opposed to the Supreme Being; his origin, however, remains darkly mysterious.

(iv) Yet another source of a multiplicity of superior beings is the family relationships of the Supreme Being, when he appears with a wife and children. But here we must make the following observations. In the first place, there is a number of the peoples of the primitive culture who give their Supreme Being neither wife nor children, and even think it shocking or absurd to inquire if he has them. Such peoples are to be found in each of the several primitive circles and generally are the most ancient races of those circles; this is sufficient to make it probable in a high degree that this is the more nearly original state of things. Among these peoples are the Negrillos of Africa, the Negritos of the Philippines, the Kurnai in South-East Australia, the Samoyeds, the primitive Eskimo, the Ainu—the last three belong to the Arctic culture—and practically all the North American primitives. But in the case of the Supreme Being having acquired a wife and children, we can prove that these are later accretions from solar or lunar myths, and to some extent also from older sources than these. This is true of the Bushman Supreme Being, those of the Southern Andamanese and the Semang, of the Kulin, Yuin, and Wiradyuri-Kamilaroi in South-East Australia, and, in the Arctic culture, of the Koryaks. Thus the high probability already mentioned, that the Supreme Being of the primitive culture had originally neither wife nor child, rises to certainty.

B. TRUE MONOTHEISM WITH A PLURALITY OF SUPERIOR BEINGS

If we wish to estimate at its real value the objection which has been raised against the existence of a true monotheism, we must also inquire in what relation to the Supreme Being the other superior beings stand, when we find any such. If they are more or less clearly stated to have been created by him, and consequently have acquired their attributes and powers from him; or, still more, if their occupations and positions are assigned to them by him; but most of all if the Supreme Being still oversees and regulates the exercise of these functions, then we must declare such a religion to be still completely monotheistic. Such superior beings do not deserve the title of gods. If we add the cases in which there are almost no superior beings of any importance at all, as among the Central African Negrillos, the Negritos of the Philippines, the South Australian Kurnai and others, we find that for the primitive epoch, even supposing that there were numerous superior beings, the Supreme Being was in nature and in activities so much above them that the existence of a monotheism, as such, must be recognized. This is true of the Wiradyuri-Kamilaroi of South-East Australia, the Ainu, and the Algonkin tribes.

2. THE HABITATION, FORM AND NAME OF THE PRIMITIVE SUPREME BEING

A. HABITATION OF THE SUPREME BEING

(i) The Supreme Being of the primitive culture is not nearly so indissolubly connected with the sky as he is in the later cultures, especially that of the pastoral nomads. Among most peoples it is said that he used formerly to live on earth with men, whom he taught all manner of good and instructed in their social and moral laws. That alone is enough to show the close connection between this being and mankind. Such is, as we know, the case with the Southern Andamanese Supreme Being, Puluga, with that of the Semang, Kari, and those of the South-East Australians, North Central Californians, the Indians of the North-West and of many Algonkin tribes. However, another story is often told among North American primitives, namely that he came down to this earth from the sky, while among practically all peoples of the primitive culture the important doctrine is propounded that he left the earth, generally because of some sin of mankind, and went up to heaven, where he

now lives. Among the West Central Algonkin, the Ainu, and the Samoyeds it is believed that he lives in a higher heaven, the fourth, seventh, eighth, or even twelfth. Frequently, for instance among the North Central Californians and in South-East Australia, it is specified that in his departure from earth he went eastward.

(ii) While the connection of the primitive Supreme Being with the sky is undoubtedly clear, it is equally manifest that he is an independent and separate personality; there can be no possible identification of him with the material sky itself. As to the immediate reason for this connection with the sky and the sources to which that connection is due, that is a question we cannot answer until our available material is better put together and more narrowly examined than hitherto; no good purpose would be served by more or less ingenious hypotheses.

(iii) Closely associated with the heavenly habitation of the Supreme Being is the fact that lightning is very often represented as his weapon, thunder or the roaring and whistling of storm as the expression of his anger. However, in the whole Arctic culture-area and among nearly all North American primitives, these functions are transferred to the thunderbird. In the latter region there are usually four thunderbirds, one for each cardinal point; in North America the Supreme Being is himself a thunder-god only among the Kato and, most ancient of all, the Yuki. Very close connections are to be found between thunder and lightning and the Supreme Beings of the very ancient Bushmen, the Yuin god Daramulun, the Wiradyuri-Kamilaroi deity Baiame (the last two are South-East Australian), the Andamanese Puluga and particularly Kari among the Semang Pygmies, who whenever it thunders and lightens make their sin-offering by thing their own blood towards the sky.

(iv) Less frequent and less clearly expressed is the connection which we find the primitive Supreme Being to have with rain, as the source of fruitfulness in the vegetable kingdom and incidentally in the animal also. This exists among the Pygmies of Central Africa, the Bushmen and the Yuin and Wiradyuri-Kamilaroi of South-East Australia. It is therefore doubtful if we may count this among the oldest attributes of the Supreme Being, especially if we are to suppose that the idea of such a being first took shape in the tropics. The connection between rain and the fertility of plants probably was not a subject of very close observation until the agrarian, matrilineal culture; that between rain and animal fertility, not till the nomadic, patrilineal culture.

B. THE FORM OF THE SUPREME BEING

The information we have concerning the form of the Supreme Being may be divided into two groups. In the first, we are assured that he cannot be perceived by the senses; the second amounts to this, that he has human form, but also something remarkable in addition; from which it is clear that the point emphasized is not his humanity but his personality, a personality transcending all experience.

(i) To the first class belong such statements as that of the Kamilaroi man who said that Baiame, their Supreme Being, could not be seen but only heard or felt; or that of those Tierra del Fuegians who declared that their deity was like the wind and could not be grasped. Here then the Supreme Being is credited with a sort of invisibility. The same statement is distinctly made by the Boni Negrillos of East Africa, the Kalinga Negritos of Luzon, the Batwa of Ruanda, and the Andamanese; while the Samoyeds declare that he, like the sky, has no shape.

(ii) The other class of testimonies assure us that the Supreme Being is "like a man"; often his reverend age, marked by a long beard, is emphasized, for instance, among the Pučikwar of the Andaman Islands. If the race in question is dark-skinned, the same is of course said to be the color of the deity, as among some of the Semang tribes. But even there, on the other hand, his white color is insisted upon; thus certain other Semang tribes say he is "like cotton"; or his name is Keto ("Light"), for example among the South-Eastern Semang, or Batek Nogn.

(iii) This leads us to a whole series of other races, among whom the Supreme Being is described as "shining white" or "like fire"; for example, among the North-Western Semang, the Southern Andamanese, the Wiyot and Patwin of North Central California, the Lenape, an Algonkin tribe, and the Winnebago, a Sioux tribe influenced by the Algonkins. Among the Maidu of North Central California we are assured that the whole form of the Supreme Being shines like the light of the sun, but that his face is always covered and no one has ever seen it, except the Evil Spirit, who did so once. The Kurnai and Wiradyuri teach that the Supreme Being is surrounded by an aureole of sunrays. Among the Samoyeds a shaman saw him blazing with so bright a light that he could not look at him.

Baiame, the god of the Wiradyuri and Euahlayi, has also an apocalyptic vastness and majesty. He and his consort sit in heaven on thrones of transparent rock-crystal, and the lower part of his body has become one with the crystal, and crystal pillars rise about him, shining with rainbow hues. Among the Samoyeds, the rainbow is the hem of the mantle worn by their Supreme Being, Num; the Gabon Pygmies say that it is a hunter's bow with which their deity chases away the storm clouds.

(iv) No image of the primitive Supreme Being is made anywhere, save in those places where (as among the Yuin) he has coalesced with the First Father, or, as among the Wiradyuri-Kamilaroi, with the child of the sun.

C. THE NAME OF THE SUPREME BEING

The names by which the Supreme Being is called are various and expressive. Almost everywhere they are uttered only with reverence, and that but seldom and not without necessity; in many cases periphrases are substituted, or else gestures, such as pointing to the sky, as with the Yuin god Daramulun or the Kulin Bundjil. The most widely distributed names fall into three groups, denoting respectively fatherhood, creative power, and residence in the sky.

(i) The name "father" is applied to the Supreme Being in every single area of the primitive culture when he is addressed or appealed to. It seems, therefore, that we may consider it primeval and proper to the oldest primitive culture. We find it in the form "father" simply, also in the individual form ("my father") and the collective ("our father"). So far, this name has not been discovered among the Central African Pygmies, but it exists among the Bushmen and the Mountain Dama. It is lacking also among the Andamanese and the Philippine Negritos, but is found, although not commonly, among the Semang. Among the Samoyeds we find the formula "my Num-father," i.e., sky-father. In North Central

California the name occurs among the Pomo and the Patwin; all three forms of it are widely distributed among the Algonkins. It is also widely current among the two oldest Tierra del Fuegian tribes, the Yamana and the Halakwulup, who use the form "my father." Among all the tribes of South-East Australia it is in common use, in the form "our father." There it is the oldest name of all, and even the women and children know it; the oldest of the tribes, the Kurnai, have no other name for him. There is no doubt possible that the name "father" is intended in this connection to denote not physiological paternity (save in cases where the figures of the Supreme Being and of the First Father have coalesced), but an attitude of the greatest reverence, of tender affection and steadfast trust on the part of man towards his god.

(ii) The name "creator" is not so widely distributed; for the power to create is, as we shall see later, not predicated of all primitive Supreme Beings, or at least not in so many words of all. When creation is relegated to a subordinate being, usually the First Father, as the task of a sort of demiurgus, this being is fairly often styled "creator," as amongst the Koryaks. The Supreme Being is not, it would appear, called creator anywhere among the Pygmies, nor in the Arctic culture, with the exception of the Ainu, where he also is known as "divine maker of the world"; nor among the greater part of the groups belonging to the southern primitive culture, Bushmen, Tierra del Fuegians, and most South-East Australians; among the last, however, we do find it in one place, for the Wiradyuri-Kamilaroi call Baiame "the creator." The name of creator is most widely distributed among the Supreme Beings of the North American Primitives, where it takes the forms of "maker," "creator," "creator of the earth" and "creator of the world"; among the Samoyeds he is known as "creator of life."

(iii) More widely distributed names are those derived from his place of abode, or at least his present dwelling. Only the Samoyeds actually call the Supreme Being simply "Sky" (*Num*), however, and they are already in a state of transition from the primitive culture to that of pastoral nomads. The commonest forms are "He that is above" or "that lives above" (North Central Californians, American North-West, Tierra

del Fuego, and, doubtfully, Negritos, Bushmen, Koryaks), or "He that is in the sky," *Mirirul* (Yuin).

(iv) We must not omit a certain number of other names, less widely distributed but often of a very characteristic kind. One that is fairly common is that which indicates his continuance from of old, or from eternity. Among the primitive tribes of the American North-West he is styled "the old one" or "the old one above." The Yamana of Tierra del Fuego call him Watauinewa, i.e., "the primeval." Among the Koryaks he is "the one above" or "the master above," while his Ainu name is "the divine sky-lord." In the Andaman Islands the name of the Supreme Being, Puluga, is connected with the word meaning storm, especially thunderstorm; the name of the Semang deity, Kari, means "thunder," which is also the appellation of the Supreme Being among the Kato and the Coast Yuki in North Central California. Among the Yoshua Indians of the American North-West he has a beautiful name, "the Giver." The Supreme Being of the primitive Eskimo is Sila, whose name reflects excellently the indefiniteness and vastness of the deity of the Arctic primitives, for it means, among other things, "sky," "weather," and "power." The Ainu Supreme Being has three names, all of them beautiful; they are "Upholder" (of the universe), "Cradle" (of the child) and "Inspirer and Protector." Among many Algonkin tribes the Supreme Being is called the Great Manitu, signifying great and supreme spirit, or, more exactly, personality; in like manner Gauab or Gawab, the corresponding name among the Bushmen, applied to their ancient Supreme Being, does not mean "spirit" in any animistic sense, but "(invisible) personality." Among the Yamana of Tierra del Fuego the Supreme Being has many names, "the Primeval," "the good Old One," "the Most High," "the Most Mighty," but also "the Slayer in the sky," because he remorselessly sends death. The commonest name is, however, "my Father." We also find among the North Central Californian Maidu the appellation "Slayer"; this signifies supreme and sole power over death (and life). The Koryaks too have a long string of names for their Supreme Being, besides that already mentioned; they call him Master, He who Is, Overseer, Power, He who is Outside, and Universe.

3. ATTRIBUTES OF THE SUPREME BEING

The names of the Supreme Being which we have made the acquaintance of are enough to disclose a number of his attributes. However, we have in addition much definite information on the subject.

A. ETERNITY

A sort of eternity is ascribed to all these Supreme Beings more or less clearly, whenever we have anything like detailed information. The form of the statements is that they existed before all other beings, have always been and always will be, or that they never die; examples are the Andamanese Puluga and the Semang Kari. In two or three instances the death of the Supreme Being is spoken of, as in the case of Daramulun among the Ngarigo; but here we may be sure that a crossing with the First Father has taken place, he being of course mortal. The Wiradyuri of South-East Australia actually apply expressly to their Supreme Being, Baiame, a word *Burrambian,* which comes from *burrambin,* "eternity."

B. OMNISCIENCE

Omniscience is often ascribed to the Supreme Being, mostly in the interests of morality; it is a function of his eminently ethical character. The Supreme Being uses this omniscience especially to supervise the commissions and omissions of mankind. Thus the youths of the South-East Australian tribes are taught his omniscience in emphatic terms, with the added information that he also can punish. Among the Batwa of Ruanda it is emphatically said, "There is nothing which Imana does not know about, he knows everything"; he perceives even secret sins of thought. Among the Wiradyuri-Kamilaroi the omniscience of Baiame extends even to the thoughts of the heart. Puluga, in the Andamans, sees everything in the daytime; but among the Semang Batek Nogn, Keto's eyes are the sun and moon and so also among the Samoyeds, who believe, moreover, that the stars are God's ears; he therefore can see by night as well as by day. For the Halakwulup, the stars are the eyes of God, with which he views the whole earth. The Kensiu Semang believe in a sort of omnipresence of their Kari, who is near even to the most distant things; a similar statement is made concerning Gawab, the Supreme Being of the Mountain Dama, "he is everywhere and knows everything." In the Wiradyuri-Kamilaroi deity Baiame we find a beginning of inactivity, for he must learn from an all-seeing spirit what happens on earth; this spirit, however, is of his own creation. So also among the West Central Algonkin we find such intermediaries, while among some tribes of Bushmen the birds tell the Supreme Being everything.

C. BENEFICENCE

A quite typical attribute of the primitive Supreme Being is that he is altogether good; all good that men enjoy, and only good, comes from him. Among the North Central Californians he wishes men to live in a sort of paradise, with the least possible effort and the greatest possible pleasure. There, and also among the Algonkin, he did not want sickness or death to exist among men; when they grew old they were to bathe or plunge in the water of life, and come forth young again. When death came in spite of all, the Supreme Being of the West Central Algonkin instituted the life-ceremony, in order to make life last as long as possible. The Andamanese Puluga is characterized by sympathy and readiness to help; so also is the Wiradyuri-Kamilaroi Baiame, who likewise is glad to forgive sins and remit the punishment of them, on penitence and reformation. Among the Wiyot-Maidu of North Central California, the Old One Above bids men pray trustfully to him in all their troubles, for he will help them. Among the Wintun, He who lives Above makes careful preparation for the men who are to come into the world. The Supreme Being of the Yamana likewise is helpful and kind to those who pray to him. His strict insistence on sending death does, it is true, earn for him and also for the Kari of the Semang Pygmies the accusation of being "hard and cruel"; but this petulant reproach is at once set right for both these deities by the admission that they punish none but the wicked.

D. MORALITY

As regards morality, the primitive Supreme Being is without exception unalterably righteous; his only connection with anything morally bad is to abhor and punish it. The true source of this deeply moral character of the Supreme Being is the fact that he is the first and highest, the giver of the moral law, and consequently its origin; a point on which we shall have to say later. For the very reason that all evil is kept far from the Supreme Being, those peoples which lay especially great emphasis on his moral character oppose to him another being who is the representative of evil, who meets all his endeavors for good with protests and hindrances. We cannot properly call this dualism, for the good Supreme Being is represented as far the stronger and more important; but the origin and continuance of the evil being is often shrouded in a dim twilight which our present knowledge does not allow us to brighten. This is the state of the case among Arctic primitives, the Samoyeds and the Ainu, and the most part of the primitive peoples of North America, for instance the North Central Californians, the tribes of the North-West and both the Western and Eastern Algonkin.

E. OMNIPOTENCE

An attribute which is especially characteristic of the primitive Supreme Being is his enormous power, which indeed is often said to be boundless. This we must throughout consider to be omnipotence. Several tribes of South-East Australia say of him that he can go everywhere and do everything. For the Semang Pygmies he is mightier than all other beings, and this is tacitly implied of all other primitive Supreme Beings; there is no other being who can even distantly approach him in power, to say nothing of excelling him. Among North American tribes this idea is frequently expressed in legends to the effect that the Supreme Being engages in trials of strength with other superior beings, generally the First Father, for instance, to move a mountain or alter the course of a stream, to split a rock, to walk on the water, and so forth. In these contests the Supreme Being always wins. Examples may be found among the Kato, the Yuki, the Atsugewi, the Thompson River Indians, perhaps the Arapaho also. Even the strongest medicine man acknowledges that he is powerless against a mortal disease which is sent by the Supreme Being.

F. CREATIVE POWER

(i) The Supreme Being shows his power at its highest in creation. No primitive Supreme Being is definitely said to lack this power, although there are some who are not said in so many words to possess it, or concerning whom the point is obscure and indefinite. But such cases are comparatively few. Among them are a number of Bushman tribes, and in the Arctic culture, the Koryaks and both divisions of the Samoyeds lack the idea of creation in any decided and clear form. In Tierra del Fuego the Yamana and perhaps the Selknam are in like case. On the other hand, the Supreme Being is recognized as creator more or less definitely among all Pygmy peoples concerning whom we have anything like full information; also among the Ainu, the South-East Australians, the oldest Tierra del Fuegian people (the Halakwulup) and most especially among the primitives of the American North-West, the North Central Californians, the Algonkin, both Eastern and Western, and the Algonkinized Winnebago. In this last group we find the idea of creation in its highest form, that of creation *ex nihilo,* expressed with the greatest definiteness and explicitness. Their myths are concerned above all with creation, and their great national ceremonies are representations and repetitions of the creative process.

(ii) The Supreme Being is explicitly recognized as creator of the earth and of the universe among the Asiatic Pygmies (Andamanese, Semang, and Negritos); also among the Bushmen, the Ainu, the Samoyeds, all the North American primitives, the Halakwulup, and the South-East Australians. The raising of the earth from the primeval deep, in a myth found among the Samoyeds, some North Central Californians and Algonkins, is accomplished by the Supreme Being in the authentic Arapaho creation story, and not by waterfowl. Almost the same peoples acknowledge the Supreme Being as the creator of men also, or of the primal pair, which is the oldest form of the creation of man; here we must add the Batwa Negrillos of Urundi and the Gabon Pygmies to the list. As to the fashion in which he made the first man or men, that is by no means always explained. In North Central California, where our information on the subject is most complete, three methods are described. In the first, man was made from birds' feathers; this probably is due to totemic influences. In the second, he was made from sticks, which became human overnight. In the third, his body was formed out of clay, and life was put into the bodies of clay overnight by the Supreme Being sweating amongst them. Amongst the Kulin of South-East Australia, the body is made of clay and the Supreme Being breathes life into it through the nose, mouth, and navel. Among the East Kenta Semang also, Kari makes two children out of clay for his wife Manoid; among the Kensiu Semang he makes them out of fruits, but nothing is said of a separate creation or immission of the soul. Among the Gabon Pygmies the Supreme Being makes the body of the first man of wet clay, and gives it life by his almighty word. Among the Ainu, God makes the skeleton out of a piece of wood and fills in the gaps with earth.

4. RELATION OF THE SUPREME BEING TO MORALITY

We have already shown that the Supreme Being of the primitive period is always ethically good in himself, and that this is ultimately due to the fact that he is the creator and source of morality. This alone is enough to show his fundamental relation to it.

A. THE SUPREME BEING AS GIVER OF THE MORAL CODE

Among the primitive peoples there is a group which does not clearly, emphatically, and intensely express the relation of the Supreme Being to morality. This is especially true of the Bushmen, Koryaks, and primitive Eskimo. Clearly, not many tribes come under this head. Among all Pygmy peoples of whom we have fairly full information, and also among the Samoyeds, Ainu, North Central Californians, Algonkin, Tierra del Fuegians, and South-East Australians, he is the author of the moral code. The extent of his activities in this respect is not the same among all peoples, but in general his commands extend to the conduct of the ceremonies instituted by him, prayer and sacrifice, obedience to elders, care for the life of man and avoidance of unjustifiable homicide, sexual morality (avoidance of adultery, fornication, unnatural vices, prenuptial unchastity), honesty and readiness to help those who need it (the sick, weak, old, and those with many children). They are especially impressed upon the young men at their initiation or other ceremonies, as celebrated by the Ituri Pygmies, in South-East Aus-tralia, North Central California, among the Algonkin and the Algonkinized Sioux, and in Tierra del Fuego. These ceremonies are the creation of the Supreme Being himself, to be a lasting source of instruction in morals, social feeling and piety. In general, the morality of the primitive peoples is by no means low; a clear proof that they really follow the ethical commands and prohibitions of their Supreme Being. This obedience, this submission of their own wills, is all the more remarkable when we consider that in social and political life their freedom is unbounded, they acknowledge the right of no man to command, save for the authority of parents over minor children, and in particular there is no one who could give orders, positive or negative, to the whole community of his fellow tribesmen.

That the Supreme Being is also the guardian of morality and uses for this purpose especially his prerogative of omniscience has already been explained above.

B. THE SUPREME BEING AS AUTHOR OF MORAL REWARDS AND PUNISHMENTS

(i) The Supreme Being, thus exercising oversight on the doings of men, is likewise able to reward morally good action and punish that which is morally bad. A whole series of peoples declare with one voice that the reward is given on earth, in the form principally of long life, and the punishment also, consisting of early death. Among the Wiradyuri this is naïvely followed out to its logical conclusion, in the axiom that all old men are good, for otherwise God would not have let them live so long. The Supreme Being sends death by means of diseases; Kari for example, the Semang deity, sends them on evil winds, or among other tribes, for instance the Kulin of South-East Australia, the evil spirits of sickness carry them. It accords well with the goodness which many primitive peoples ascribe to the Supreme Being that they do not believe that he ever executes a sentence of death himself, but employs one of the evil spirits whose *raison d'être* this is; so for example among the Andamanese and the Ainu. Or it may be tigers or other dangerous beasts, as among the Semang; these creatures are his apparitors and messengers. Elsewhere, however, as also among the Semang, his lightning strikes evildoers directly.

(ii) But a whole array of primitive

peoples, the great majority, I think, of those of whom we have fairly detailed knowledge, extend the Supreme Being's rewards and punishments to the other world. All primitive peoples without exception believe in another life. As to what it is like, they cannot all say; for instance, the Yamana declare that they do not know, and give that as the reason why they are so sad when any of their relatives die. Others hold that in the other world there is no distinction between the good and the bad; this seems for instance to be the case with the Semang, who hold that all sins have already been atoned for in this world. Similar ideas exist among the Batwa of Ruanda. But the great majority of them recognize such a distinction of good and bad in a future life. Their most definite opinions concern the future lot of the good; as to the fate of the wicked, they are often uncertain or vague.

(iii) The good usually go, in cases concerning which we have any information, to the sky, where the Supreme Being lives. In many instances they enjoy his own company; there they live a life free from death, sickness, and pain, full of all manner of happiness. This is the belief of the North-Western Maidu in North Central California. Often this afterlife is nothing but a more fortunate replica of the present life; there are cases, however, in which gross sensual pleasures are definitely excluded, as among the Wiradyuri, in whose heaven they do not even eat. In many cases it is expressly stated that there will be no more begetting, for instance among the South Andamanese, Semang, and Mountain Dama. This is explained by the fact that there is no more dying. The road thither is sometimes said to be the Milky Way, and where that divides, the good are separated from the bad; this is for example the belief of the North-East and Hill Maidu. Often again the rainbow is the bridge leading to the other world, as among the South Andamanese. Among the Wiradyuri-Kamilaroi, the Supreme Being has prepared a stairway on the top of a mountain to the east, and by this the spirits bring men's souls up to heaven. In other cases, as among the most of the Semang Pygmies at present, the dwelling place of souls is in the west, on Islands of the Blessed in the midst of the sea. Among the Kulin of South-East Australia the soul goes to the west and then

climbs up to heaven on the beams of the setting sun. Among the Ainu, the heaven of the good, like the rest of the other world, is under the earth.

(iv) In some cases there is a regular judgment to decide the fate of the good and bad, the souls having to appear before the Supreme Being. This is the belief perhaps of the South Adamanese, certainly of the Halakwulup of Tierra del Fuego, where the soul presents an account of its life. The Wiradyuri hold that Grogoragally, the sun's son, brings the dead every evening to the Supreme Being, Baiame; Baiame then pronounces sentence, Grogoragally often advocating effectively the cause of those who were not altogether bad. The Yuin believe that Mirirul waits for the souls by the great tree of heaven, and judges them. Among the Ainu, the fire-goddess presents an exact picture, drawn by herself, of the whole life of the person on trial to the Supreme Being.

(v) The lot of the wicked is often described expressly as one of painful punishment, by fire and heat, as among the Ajongo Negrillos and the Southern Wiradyuri; but it may also be by cold, or by wanderings without rest. In other cases it consists simply in exclusion from the happiness of the good, or in an empty shadow-life. Among the Kamilaroi, the bad are annihilated. The place of the wicked is sometimes in the sky, but separate from that of the good. More commonly, however, it is in or under the earth, as among the Batwa of Ruanda and Urundi and the Kalinga Negritos; or on the western extremity of the earth, as among the Semang.

5. WORSHIP OF THE SUPREME BEING

A. GENERAL REMARKS

(i) Preuss, Söderblom and others have given it as a characteristic of high gods that they are elevated far above men, have little or no vital connection with them and also enjoy but scanty worship, if any. This is true for many high gods of the primary and secondary cultures, but as regards the Supreme Beings of the primitive culture it is wrong from beginning to end. The lively intercourse between the Supreme Being and men goes back to those primeval times when he himself lived among them on earth, teaching and instructing them. Even after leaving earth, none of these Supreme Beings has retired into a leisured existence, showing neither activity nor interest in mankind, but still influences this world and its inhabitants by his omnipotence and goodness, his oversight of what men do and leave undone in the moral sphere, the holy festivals and initiations which he founded and at which he is still often present, and finally by the judgment which he passes on the life of a man at its close. There are also cases, for instance the Halakwulup, the Semang, the Koryaks, and the Ainu, in which the Supreme Being sends down each individual human soul into a human body, and so makes the course of each several human life take its start from his own hand. Not all these relationships to mankind are to be found in every one of the Supreme Beings to an equal extent and with the same intensity; nevertheless, the number of cases which show a considerable proportion of such attributes is large enough to prohibit us from treating idleness and remoteness from mankind as the characteristic marks of these beings, the high gods of the primitive culture, in particular.

(ii) But men also have from their side lively intercourse with these Supreme Beings, and acknowledge by means thereof the many ways in which they are dependent upon them and their vast importance for human weal or woe. This results from the fear they feel of their punishments, if from nothing else, for this moves them to avoid what they forbid and to keep their commandments. It is shown likewise in the reverence and feeling with which they relate the myths which treat of the power and lovingkindness of these Supreme Beings; in the respect with which they pronounce their names, avoiding unnecessary mention of them; and finally by the significance of these names themselves, especially the appellations "Father" and "Creator." All these things are in themselves manifestations of respect, acts of worship, which they bestow on no other beings.

But we find among primitive peoples other ways of approaching the Supreme Being, which amount to actual cult, and are of such a kind as to set up a personal relationship between themselves and him, a relation of "I" and "thou," and therefore a real and full, because living, religion. This is done by prayer, sacrifice, and formal ceremonies.

B. PRAYER

(i) To establish the existence, among these primitive peoples especially, of the use of prayer is not an easy task; and we may be sure that many observers have quite missed certain forms of it, with the result that they have declared the peoples in question to have no such usage. This applies to two sorts of prayer in particular, the unspoken petition which has no outward expression at all and that which is expressed purely by gestures; these, however, may be combined with words, in which case the name of the Supreme Being will be uttered. Such a purely inward prayer, often combined with a strong effort of concentration in the soul, is to be found for instance among the primitive Eskimo, certain Algonkin tribes, and the Semang, whose seers pray on behalf of the rest of them in this fashion, and among the Bushmen. A prayer expressed in gestures, hardly to be recognized as such by others without further instruction, is practiced by the Semang, the Yuin and Wiradyuri-Kamilaroi of South-East Australia, and probably also, in the same continent, by the Kurnai and the Kulin.

(ii) But there is yet another kind of prayer not easy to discover, without a good knowledge of the native language and without having lived among the people for some time—two qualifications which it is especially rare to find in those who investigate these remote, retiring, and shy races. This is the spontaneous, informal prayer, still in use particularly among such peoples, the majority of whom have not yet advanced as far as fixed formulae. We have definite and beautiful instances of this from the Negritos of the Philippine Islands, the Yamana and Halakwulup in Tierra del Fuego, the Batwa of Ruanda and the Bushmen. We find also, however, even at this stage, long and elaborate liturgies, as that celebrated by night among these same Negritos, and other ceremonious prayers of the Gabon Pygmies and of Algonkin tribes here and there.

(iii) The commonest type of prayer is of course the petitionary. However, we have evidence for prayers of thanksgiving also among the Gabon Pygmies, in North Central California, among several Algonkin tribes, among the Yamana and Halakwulup of Tierra del Fuego and the Wiradyuri-Kamilaroi of South-East Australia. Among the last-named people we likewise find a prayer for the (male) dead, made at their grave, asking that they may be received into *bullimah,* or heaven. The sin-offering of the Semang is accompanied by prayers for the forgiveness of their sins.

(iv) If we survey the distribution of prayer among the primitive peoples, we can show that there is but one people among whom we cannot certainly prove its existence. This is the Andamanese; and even among them we find certain mysterious ceremonies the fundamental meaning of which we cannot arrive at; these may possibly represent a sort of prayer, consisting of gestures, not words. The Kurnai and Kulin of South-East Australia are in a very similar position, only the probability that such prayers exist among them is somewhat greater. The practice of prayer alone is uncommon among the Arctic primitives, the Samoyeds and Koryaks, and such prayers as they have are generally but short; in this region sacrifice is more developed; this, however, is almost always accompanied by prayer. The Wiradyuri-Kamilaroi also do not pray much, and have public and ceremonial prayers on two occasions only, the burial of men (not women) and at the conclusion of the youth's imitations. They expressly state that, since the Supreme Being is so benevolent and just, so much prayer as they have seen among the whites is not necessary, and can do little good, as may be seen from the life of these same whites. In Tierra del Fuego likewise, the Halakwulup say that petitionary prayer is not needed, for there is no avoiding any punishment inflicted by the Supreme Being, and he sends blessings unasked; they do, however, thank him for these. In the same region, we can already establish the existence of a comparatively abundant employment of prayer among the Yamana, and the same is true of a number of Algonkin tribes, also of the Gabon Pygmies and the Batwa of Ruanda. Probably better equipped investigators will be able to discover it in other places as well.

C. SACRIFICE

(i) Sacrifice appears to be entirely lacking among the South-East Australian primitives, except perhaps for certain offerings of leaves in some tribes, but they have developed the initiation ritual for their young men instead. It is also lacking among the two oldest tribes of Tierra del Fuego, the Yamana and the Halakwulup. In North Central California, also, it is hard to prove its existence, unless the feather-sticks of the Maidu and some others deserve the name; a view not without difficulties, if only because of their ethnological age. It is found, however, among the Arctic peoples, the Asiatic and African Pygmies, the Bushmen, the Selknam of Tierra del Fuego, and the Veddas.

(ii) The dominant form of sacrifice, the only one indeed among the Pygmies and Bushmen, is the offering of first fruits, presented by hunters and plant-gatherers, and of some small portions of food, offered before the people themselves eat of it. Such an offering is found also among the peoples of the Arctic culture, the Algonkins, and the Selknam. In all these cases the thing offered is nutriment, means of sustaining life, for according to the belief of these tribes, all such means are the absolute property of the Supreme Being. He gave man life to begin with; now he has given them the means to support and continue it, on certain conditions, which are that they shall own and use them within proper bounds, sparingly and respectfully. In this connection it is especially noteworthy that a similar offering of skulls and long bones of game (bears and reindeer), unopened and still retaining their precious contents, the brains and marrow, is found in the Arctic culture, and that we meet with it again in the older (pre-Mousterian) palaeolithic culture, as may be seen from the finds in the Drachenhöhle in the Tamina valley in Switzerland and that of the Petershöhle near Velden, Mittelfranhen, in Bavaria. The offering of first fruits is nothing but the recognition of the Supreme Being's sovereignty over the means of life, and therefore over life and death themselves. Outwardly, this type of offering is simple and natural; in content, it is high. Since we find it so widely distributed in these oldest culture-areas (it is the only form known among the Pygmies), we may rule out, as false from beginning to end, that theory of the origin of sacrifice which derives it from the feeding of the dead; especially as such feeding is practically unknown in any tribe of the primitive culture.

(iii) One Pygmy tribe, the Semang of Malacca, has no offering of first fruits, but has on the other hand a sin-offering of a sort unparalleled in the whole world. When the thunder rolls—this is the voice of their Supreme Being, Kari—they take a bamboo knife, make a little cut with it at the knee, mix the blood that comes from the wound with water in a vessel and throw the mixture skywards, praying at the same time for pardon for their sins and also, if the storm lasts a long while, making a detailed confession of their sins.

D. FORMAL CEREMONIES

Particularly among those tribes of the primitive culture who have no sacrifices, and to some extent also among those who seldom pray, we find solemn ceremonies especially well developed. They may last weeks and months, are regarded as having been founded by the Supreme Being himself, and are celebrated at his behest.

(i) Of special importance are the formal initiations of the youths, which are held among the Tierra del Fuegian tribes, the South-East Australians and the Andamanese with extraordinary rejoicing and devotion and with the most conscientious exactitude. Among the oldest of these tribes, the Kurnai for instance, also the Kulin, the Andamanese and the Tierra del Fuegians, the youth of both sexes are initiated and the ceremony has nothing secret about it. The object is to prepare the young people and make them capable of founding families (which are more or less monogamous), an institution of which the Supreme Being is himself the author. At the same time they are to be filled with all their tribe's wisdom and virtue, social, moral, and religious. Among many of these peoples, in South-East Australia for instance, the ceremonial is accompanied by invocations of the name of the Supreme Being, with or without accompanying gestures.

(ii) In North Central California and among the Eastern and Western Algonkin these ritual festivities occur almost every year, and have taken the form of grateful, we may even say sacramental, commemorations; they last four, eight, nine or twelve days and enact the creation of the world and of men. Thus they seek to bring the help and grace of God upon the family, the tribe, and the world at large, indeed in a manner of speaking to create the world anew.

(iii) In the Arctic culture, prayer, sacrifice, and ceremonies belonging to certain important seasons of the year have developed into elaborate festivals, in which thanks are given for help received and fresh help besought. The nocturnal litany of the Philippine Negritos, the Pano ceremony of the Semang, the rainbow ritual of the Gabon Pygmies, the ceremonial prayers for rain among the Khung Bushmen and the arrowrite and other ceremonies of the Veddas should probably be included in the same category.

E. RECAPITULATION

If now we briefly review the data, we find that, while this or that form of worship may be wanting in a particular tribe, no tribe is known in which there is not some form in use. As we might expect, prayer has the widest distribution; but even here we may be sure that there is still much to discover, and that much will be discovered. The wide distribution of the offering of first fruits in this, the oldest culture, is of great importance as a matter of principle. The cult of the Supreme Being has already reached a very high level among several Pygmy races, also in the Arctic culture, among the Algonkin, and in North Central California, in the combination of prayer and sacrifice in a solemn, expressive ceremonial. But it is to be noted that these are the areas where the best and most thoroughly trained observers have been employed. Perhaps equally competent researches in South-East Australia, for instance, might have discovered yet more; and it may be that the Pygmy races of Africa still have many surprises in store for us.

RAFFAELE PETTAZZONI

The Formation of Monotheism

An alternative and simple explanation of the origin of monotheism comes from Raffaele Pettazzoni: the only truly monotheistic religions are Yahwism, Zoroastrianism, Christianity, and Islam, and each originated as a reformist protest against polytheism. Monotheism is neither the culmination of a gradual and inevitable ideological development of evolutionary character nor the result of an original revelation. It is the consequence of a radical religious upheaval brought on through the effort of some great personality to deny extant polytheistic beliefs.

Pettazzoni's objection to the Lang and Schmidt theories of primitive monotheism is twofold. In the first place, they apply the name of monotheism ambiguously, regarding the primitives' idea of supreme beings as true monotheism when it is no more than an approximation to the ideal monotheism. It is fruitless to try to explain the difference as the result of a secondary degeneration or obscuration of the ideal. In the second place, they mistakenly transfer the idea of God to the most archaic religious culture when it in fact properly belongs only to our Western civilization. Monotheism is a relatively late historical phenomenon.

In passing, Pettazzoni's review of the history of modern debates on religious origins serves to remind us that they began with the philosophers and not the anthropologists. On the other hand, it is curious that the philosophers were inspired not by rationalistic philosophy but by early anthropological reports.

Reprinted from Raffaele Pettazzoni, *Essays on the History of Religions,* trans. H. J. Rose (Leiden: E. J. Brill, 1954), Chap. 1, by permission of the author and the publishers.

The problem of monotheism made its appearance in European thought during the eighteenth century. Voltaire, in his *Dictionnaire philosophique,* published in 1764, wrote:

Another scholar, . . . one of the profoundest metaphysicians of our time, gives strong reasons to show that polytheism was the first religion of mankind and that men began by believing in a plurality of gods before their reason was sufficiently enlightened to recognize but one Supreme Being.

The metaphysician to whom Voltaire alludes was the Scottish philosopher David Hume. We read, in fact, in one of Hume's essays, which came out in 1757 under the title *The Natural History of Religion:*

If we consider the improvement of human society, from rude beginnings to a state of greater perfection, polytheism or idolatry was, and necessarily must have been, the first and most ancient religion of mankind.

Voltaire was of a different opinion; after the words we have just quoted, he adds:

I venture to believe, on the contrary, that men began by knowing a single God, and that later, human weakness adopted a number of deities.

He held, therefore, that monotheism was the oldest form of belief in God, and that polytheism did not appear until a later date. Voltaire, the unbeliever, the rationalist, the pitiless mocker, was thus in agreement for once, on an important point, with the doctrine of the Church, according to which belief in one God was revealed by God Himself to the first man, while polytheism in its manifold forms was nothing but a diabolical counterfeit, or an alteration allowed by God Himself, these alternatives corresponding to the two leading theological doctrines in this connection, that of plagiarism and that of condescension. I need not say that Voltaire did not believe in revelation. Like the rationalist that he was, he postulated none but a rational and natural religion, the work of human reason, without any intervention of a supernatural kind; the idea of a single God he supposed to be an essential datum of this religion, and that it was not till later, owing to a "weakness" of the human mind, that the existence of many gods began to be supposed. It remains true that for Voltaire monotheism was earlier than polytheism, just as it was in the most orthodox theology.

At nearly the same time Jean-Jacques Rousseau came forward in support of Hume's theory. This is what he wrote in *Émile* (1764):

Laban's grotesques [the allusion is to the *teraphim* mentioned in Genesis 31, 19, in connection with Jacob's departure from his father-in-law Laban], savage *manitous,* Negro *fétiches,* all the works of nature and man, were the first deities of mortals; polytheism was their first religion and idolatry their first cult. They could not recognize a single God until, as they generalized their ideas more and more, etc.

Whence did Hume and Rousseau get this new theory which was so decidedly opposed to the Church's traditional teaching? Assuredly not from rationalistic philosophy, seeing that Voltaire, one of its most authoritative representatives, would have none of it. It was not so much philosophy that was in question as ethnology. At the base of the new theory lie the discoveries and information, the manifold observations on the uncivilized peoples of Africa and America, and especially on their religious beliefs, in short, the ethnographical data such as were to be found in the works of travelers, missionaries, and so forth. Hume indeed expressly appeals to the religion of the savage tribes of America, Africa, and Asia. Rousseau for his part expresses himself still more precisely, indeed in technical terms, for he definitely names, alongside of Laban's "grotesques" (*marmousets*), *manitous* and *fétiches.* The word "manitou" belongs to the religious vocabulary of the Algonkin peoples of North America, while "fetish" (*feitiço*) is a term invented by the Portuguese in the fifteenth century to signify the idols made and adored by the African blacks. We can even, I think, point out the sources from which it is likely that Hume and Rousseau got their information. It is enough to mention, on the one hand, the work of Father Lafitau, published in 1724, with the title *Les moeurs des sauv-ages amériquains comparés aux moeurs des premiers temps,* and dealing with the Indians of New France, in which the missions of the Society of Jesus were established; and on the other, the work of President de Brosses, *Du culte des Dieux Fétiches, ou Parellèle de l'ancienne Religion de l'Égypte avec la Religion actuelle de la Nigritie,* which came out in 1760 after having been rejected by the Académie des Inscriptions et Belles Lettres, "because of the boldness of its author's ideas."

In the nineteenth century de Brosses' fetishism made its way into the system of Auguste Comte, the positivist philosopher. In his *Cours de philosophie positive,* Comte drew a picture of the development of the human mind through three great successive epochs, the religious, from the beginnings to the fourteenth century, the metaphysical, from the fourteenth to the eighteenth, and the positive, at the present day. The religious epoch again subdivides into three periods, fetishism, polytheism, and monotheism.

Comte's scheme with its three grades was later taken up by the English anthropologist Edward Burnett Tylor in his classical work, *Primitive Culture,* 1871. Tylor however, who supposed animism to be the oldest form of religion, put that and not fetishism at the first stage of religious evolution, while keeping polytheism for the second stage and monotheism for the third.

It was not until the end of the nineteenth century that, starting from new data which concerned especially the uncivilized tribes of Australia, Andrew Lang, a brilliant Scottish writer who was a good anthropologist, was led to point to the idea of a Supreme Being as playing a part of the very first importance among the religious beliefs of savage peoples and in their religious life. This "discovery" was set forth by Lang in his book, *The Making of Religion,* published in 1898 (third edition in 1909).

At the same time a radical change of direction was coming about in ethnological science. That science, which had hitherto been thought of as a branch of physical anthropology, was breaking away more and more from the realm of the natural sciences and reaching full autonomy as a historical discipline. Dropping the idea of a uniform religious evolution fulfilling itself everywhere and always by the same stages, researchers henceforth preferred to keep in mind the manifold diversity of the various religious phenomena, charting for each of them its own area of distribution. It goes without saying that the theory which looked upon monotheism as the last stage of a gradual evolution, constant and uniform everywhere, was thus shattered from top to bottom.

A new theory was soon sketched out. According to it, monotheism, far from being regarded as the latest form of human religion, was thought of as the most primitive. This is the theory of "primitive monotheism" (*Urmonotheismus*), whose most ardent advocate Father Wilhelm Schmidt has made himself. It amounts to a return, by way of science, to the old position of the doctrine of revelation. The parenthesis which Hume and Rousseau had opened in the eighteenth century was now to be closed, and monotheism brought back to the very fountainhead of religion.

If we follow the problem of monotheism in the different stages of its development, as I have outlined them, since the abandonment of the traditionalist doctrine in the eighteenth century, passing through the nineteenth-century evolutionism to the rehabilitation of "primitive monotheism" in the twentieth, we find that the question has always been discussed with reference to the religions of uncivilized peoples. From Hume to Lang, from President de Brosses and Auguste Comte with their fetishist Negroes to Father Schmidt's Pygmies, it is always the uncivilized who have furnished the material for the different and mutually contradictory hypotheses concerning monotheism. This is explicable only if we keep in mind that the problem of monotheism was regularly envisaged, not in itself, but especially with regard to the more general problem of the primeval form of religion. The different theories were not so much the resultant of research having for its object monotheism itself, as the indirect outcome of acceptance or rejection of evolutionism.

This being the explanation, indeed the historical justification of the manner in which the monotheistic problem has been stated for two centuries, it still does not follow that that is a legitimate attitude. From an objective point of view, what justifies this preference for the religions of the uncivilized in the monotheistic controversy? Are they really the best qualified to impose themselves upon the study of such a religious phenomenon as

monotheism, which for its part has so much greater importance in the history of religion generally? Why then should we not devote ourselves, with as good grounds, to the polytheistic religions of the various civilized nations of antiquity?

What I have just said is no merely theoretical hypothesis. Welcker, in his great work on the mythology and religion of ancient Greece (*Die griechische Götterlehre*, 3 vols., 1857–62) himself, after his own manner, traced back Greek polytheism to a precedent monotheism, for he considered the various Olympian gods as so many variations or hypostases of the skygod Zeus, regarded as the purest representative of the monotheistic idea. Like a good "theologian," Welcker here clove to the theory of Schelling, who supposed that the primary form of the idea of God was a relative, rudimentary monotheism, or "henotheism," as he called it. Here we may add, in passing, that the ideas of Schelling had an even more noteworthy influence on Max Müller, the famous master of "comparative mythology," who took up the theory of henotheism, developing it particularly with reference to the religions of the Indo-European peoples in general and those of ancient India in particular. Monotheism in Greek religion was discussed from a more positive point of view later, by scholars such as Eduard Zeller, the historian of philosophy, Eduard Meyer, the historian of antiquity, Erwin Rohde, the historian of religion, and others. This interesting controversy came out to no appreciable result, and for a sufficient reason; the *sine qua non* of every positive inquiry into Greek monotheism was the previous possession of a precise idea of what monotheism is, and no one had the right to ask this of a polytheistic religion like that of Greece.

Now the same is true of our dealings with primitive religions. What we find in them is the notion of a Supreme Being. Is it allowable to identify such an idea with monotheism? If we do, are we not running the risk of importing among the uncivilized an idea peculiar to the sphere of the great modern monotheistic faiths? The great monotheistic religions, those whose monotheism is past all doubt, which have declared themselves monotheistic from their very birth, and have always represented themselves as that and nothing else, are surely those to which we must have recourse first of all in any inquiry concerning monotheism and its formation.

In my opinion, there is but one methodologically allowable manner of attacking the problem of monotheism, and that is, once more to advance from the known to the unknown, taking as our starting point the great monotheistic religions of history, to extract from them a positive and concrete notion of what monotheism is.

The religions whose monotheistic character is above doubt are in the first place Yahwism, Christianity, and Islam. Apart from these three great religions, which have well-known genetic relationships with each other, there is one other religion which, despite its dualistic structure, is yet to be included among monotheistic faiths, and that is Zoroastrianism. These then are the religions to which any inquiry regarding monotheism ought to be addressed in order to extract a historically allowable idea of monotheism and the manner in which it takes shape.

Now if we contemplate the monotheistic religions which I have just named, we find that every one of them arises as a new religion out of a previously existing polytheistic environment. It is a feature common to the monotheistic faiths that the appearance of every one of them is closely associated with a religious reform and with the work of a reformer. The monotheistic idea is invariably the subject of a prophet's preaching, and he appears as the founder of a new religion. We can verify this for the monotheism of Israel, the monotheism of Moses and the prophets, as opposed to the polytheistic cults of the ancient East. That is also the position of Christian monotheism, the prolongation of that of Israel, in relation to the various religions of the pagan Greco-Roman world and also to those of barbarous Europe. The monotheism of Mahomet in its turn is sharply opposed to the traditional religion of the Arabs, who until his coming were polytheists. In the same way, Zarathustra's monotheism is opposed to the polytheism of the Iranian peoples' traditional religion.

As to the religion of Zarathustra in particular, it furnishes an interesting observation. In the language of the Avesta, the Zoroastrian Bible, the word *daeva* means a devil, an evil spirit who is the enemy of the good Zoroastrian religion. Now *daeva* is nothing but the Iranian equivalent of the Vedic *deva,* which means a god (Latin *deus*). The Avestan *daeva* in the sense of "devil" therefore represents an inversion of meaning, a complete reversal of the original significance of the word, the result of which is that *daeva* has lost its original sense of "god" and come to indicate the very opposite.

Now this little linguistic and stylistic fact is but the reflection of a great fact belonging to the domains of history and of religion. This little fact opens us the door to the very spirit of Zoroastrian religion as it arises from the dynamics of its foundation.

Zarathustra's religion is marked by a very decided dualism between two sharply opposed Principles. The Principle of Good is represented by Ahura Mazda, that of Evil by Ahriman. In the Gathas, which are the oldest texts in the Avesta, we still find traces of the supremacy of Ahura Mazda in relation to Ahriman, while in the later texts the two antagonistic Principles are placed on a footing of complete equality. It is between these two Principles that man must choose, and when he has chosen, he finds himself involved in the never-ending conflict between Good and Evil, a conflict which lasts throughout the ages of the world until at last Evil is annihilated.

But this radical dualism does not prevent us from recognizing the monotheistic character of the Zoroastrian religion. For Zarathustra, there is but one God, namely Ahura Mazda; his opponent Ahriman is not a god, but the very negation of God. Here we encounter the true spirit of the new religion. Zarathustra opposed to the polytheism of the traditional religion of the Iranian peoples the idea of a single God. This one God, Ahura Mazda, the "Lord who knows," was not created out of nothing by Zarathustra. In all probability, his predecessor was an ancient Iranian skygod, who, like Zeus among the Greeks, Jupiter among the Romans, was the chief god of a polytheism, such as Herodotus shows us existing among the Persians (Herodotus i. 131).

From this supreme god of the old polytheism, Zarathustra made his one God. As to the other deities, he did not deny their existence, but denied them as gods, while keeping them in the only shape which could be got into agreement with monotheistic teaching, that is to say, as devils.

Here we have in a way an anticipation of

what was to happen later in Christianity. Christianity again could not but deny the old gods of Greek and Roman polytheism, yet it did not deny that they existed, but made them into demons: *omnes dii gentium daemonia,* says St. Augustine, "all the gods of the Gentiles are demons."

That is the importance, religious and historical, of the alteration in meaning of the word *daeva.* Its transition from the sense of "god" to that of "devil" lies very close to the profound religious revolution which was the work of Zarathustra. Across the history of the word we catch a glimpse of the deadly struggle which raged between two rival faiths during an acute crisis. On the one side was the traditional religion of Iran, inseparably attached to its old gods and its archaic structure; on the other, the new faith preached by a Prophet who, in his indomitable energy, set persecutions and sufferings at naught. "Whither could I fly? in what country could I take refuge?" This is one of the few passages in the Gathas and the whole Avesta which allow us to envisage the real personality of Zarathustra in its living humanity, in the bitterness of its poignant passion, in its expression of black despair. There is a drama in the life of Zarathustra, and it played itself out to the very end.

But the drama of Zarathustra is likewise in a way the drama of Moses, of Mahomet, and of Jesus, or if you like of Paul. The negation of polytheism, which expresses itself indirectly in Zoroastrianism by inverting the meaning of the word *daeva,* is expressed more directly and explicitly in Yahwism, Christianity, and Islam. Yahweh says to his people, in the Old Testament, "I am the LORD thy God . . . thou shalt have none other gods before me" (Exod. 20, 2–3, cf. Deut. 5, 6–7; 32, 39; Isaiah 43, 11; 44, 6). In the Gospel of Mark (12, 32) we read, "He is one; and there is none other but he." "There is no God but one," says the first Epistle to the Corinthians (8, 4). As to Islam, it is enough to remember the formula "There is no god but Allah, and Mahomet is the apostle of Allah." The affirmation of monotheism always is expressed by the negation of polytheism, and this negation is never anything but the verbal symbol of a combat in which no quarter is given, the combat between a faith in its death agonies and a new religious consciousness affirming

itself. Of this combat every prophet of monotheism has been the interpreter and at the same time the victim.

This, then, is the outcome of the study of the monotheistic religions. We have arrived at an idea of what monotheism really is, an idea which is not theological nor speculative, but purely historical, following the principle according to which the true nature of a historical fact is brought out by its formation and its development (*verum ipsum factum*).

It remains only to draw conclusions. It is now evident that my own point of view is as far from the evolutionist theory as from that of "primitive monotheism." According to the evolutionist theory, monotheism is represented as the outcome of a gradual ideological development, which, starting from belief in a plurality of spirits, very numerous and very little differentiated, came out through a series of reductions to a unitary idea of Deity. That is a strictly intellectualist manner of looking at the formation of monotheism; I depart from that position in order to hold to a point of view less intellectualist and more properly religious.

On the other hand, from the historical point of view I cannot attach myself to the theory of "primitive monotheism." If we keep, as I do and as one must do, the name of monotheism for the negation of polytheism, as it appears in the great monotheistic religions of history, the result is that monotheism presupposes polytheism by the very fact of denying it. In so far as it is a negation of polytheism, monotheism cannot be the first form of religion, as the theory of "primitive monotheism" supposes. What we find among uncivilized peoples is not monotheism in its historically legitimate sense, but the idea of a Supreme Being, and the erroneous identification, the misleading assimilation, of this idea to true monotheism can give rise only to misunderstandings.

Monotheism therefore is later than polytheism. Only, it does not evolve from it, as the evolutionist theory supposed. Far from developing out of it by an evolutionary process, monotheism takes shape by means of a revolution. Every coming of a monotheistic religion is conditioned by a religious revolution. Far from arising out of speculative thought, the formation of monotheism springs from religious life, from a fullness of religious life, such as has but seldom come to pass in the course of human history, and only by an unusual coincidence of favorable circumstances.

That is why the monotheistic religions properly so called are so few. Ancient India underwent a great religious revolution through Buddhism, but Buddhism is not monotheistic. This amounts to saying that, although the presence of a great religious personality is a necessary condition for monotheism to appear, it still is not a sufficient condition. Ancient Greece did not know monotheism. Greece, which reached the summits of genius in poetry, art, and speculative thought, the Greece of Homer, of Aeschylus and of Pindar, of Socrates, Plato, and Aris-

totle, never achieved the religion of the Only God. From the masters of the Ionian School down to Stoicism, Greek philosophy perfected more and more the idea of one God, without ever reaching that of an only God. Apart from the more or less monotheistic intuitions, which anyway are isolated, of such men as Xenophanes or Antisthenes, Greece never ceased to be polytheistic till the day when she was converted to Christianity.

If the monotheistic idea is so deeply rooted in our modern consciousness and in our civilization, we do not owe this so much to the progress of philosophical thought as to the propagation of the Christian faith.

W. ROBERTSON SMITH

Sacrifice Among the Semites

The origin of sacrifice has been speculated upon by many writers. Tylor (*Primitive Culture*) regarded it as being essentially a gift to a supernatural being to minimize its hostility; in the course of time sacrificial gifts develop into homage, and homage into abnegation. Frazer (*The Golden Bough*) saw it as kind of magic in which the slaying of an animal or human being is a way of rejuvenating a god: by killing the god to save him from decay and thus facilitate his rebirth; by killing a victim to feed and strengthen the god; by killing the rivals of the god to facilitate his resurrection. Hubert and Mauss ("Essai sur le Sacrifice"), stimulated by Durkheim, were not so much interested in the origin of sacrifice as in its role; nevertheless, historical implications adhere to their theory, which maintains that the thing sacrificed acts as a buffer between things sacred (the supernatural world) and things profane (the sacrificer), eliminating the great danger of direct contact. Westermarck (*Origin and Development of Moral Ideas*, 1906–1908) saw sacrifice as originally and fundamentally an expiation, and from this come secondary meanings, such as the transference of sin and the rejuvenation of a dying god. Freud's effort to link the origin of sacrifice with a primeval act of parricide, in which the sons ate their hated father and then continued to re-enact the original deed through commemorative rites, will be discussed in the next paper.

There remains a major theory of sacrifice, that of the brilliant W. Robertson Smith, who found the original motive of sacrifice to be an effort at communion among the members of the group, on the one hand, and between them and their god, on the other. Communion was effected through the sacrificial meal. Secondary developments emerged from this primitive sacramental stage. The meal came in time to be no more than a religious banquet, and then simply a good meal of animal food over which appropriate words had to be uttered. A piacular aspect also developed from the communion ritual, for the primitive community which felt that it had angered its god could reestablish rapport with him

Extracted from W. Robertson Smith, *Lectures on the Religion of the Semites* (New York: D. Appleton & Co., 1889), pp. 251–271, by permission of Appleton-Century-Crofts.

through a common sacrificial meal. A purificatory aspect also stemmed from the original ritual; it came to be believed that the blood of the animal sacrificed washed away impurity. Even the gift aspect of sacrifice can be seen to be derived from the primitive mystic communion, for as the deity became more and more sacred and taboo, his worshipers gradually stopped eating the sacrificial victim, handing it over instead to priests for consumption, or simply burning it. This came about at a time when the modern idea of property was developing, and the owner of the animal felt he could transfer the ownership of the victim to the god, at the same time relinquishing his right to eat or sell its flesh. The resemblance between the Christian Eucharist and primitive communion sacrifices did not escape Smith, who noted that the Christian idea that the Saviour sacrificed himself for humanity so it might live was foreshadowed to some degree by the oldest mystical sacrifices. (This argument appears on page 393 of the 1889 edition but not in the second and posthumous edition of 1894.)

Smith was led to his theory of sacrifice through his study of animal sacrifice among the ancient Arabs. These people would wound a sacrificial camel and then fall upon it and eat it as fast as possible in order that, says Smith, they could partake of its life for themselves. In doing so, the worshipers established a common bond among themselves, for they had eaten of the same flesh. They also established a bond with their god because the blood of the victim had been spilled upon the altar. There is ample evidence that Smith was to some extent influenced by his close friend, J. F. McLennan, a Scottish lawyer who discovered the importance of matrilineal descent and thought that totemism was a universal stage in human society. The relationship, however, was not one-sided, for Smith contributed both Biblical materials and insights for strengthening McLennan's theories.

Smith's theory of sacrifice was first presented in the ninth edition of the *Encyclopaedia Britannica* in the article, "Sacrifice." Later he discussed it in lectures given in 1886 and in 1888. But in his *Lectures on the Religion of the Semites,* published in 1889, the theory was most clearly formulated. This book was his most creative and important effort, although it was only one in a projected series which he was unable to complete because of his poor health, and it attracted considerable attention. It was the author's view that ancient religions could only be understood in terms of their rituals, for they had no established creeds. It was further his view that the religious unit was not the individual but the community to which he belonged; religion is part of the social order. Another point upon which he based his work was that the tie of blood was what held together the members of the primitive religious community, a community that included not only people but gods. The religion of the Semites, he said, was traceable to such a state in human society. In all nature religions there is always some expression of belief in a physical kinship which unites the human and superhuman members of the same religious and social community.

While many great minds of the period were lavish in their praise of the details of Robertson Smith's book, they tended to reject his central theme. Even James G. Frazer, an ardent admirer who dedicated the monumental *Golden Bough* to his memory, felt that the thesis was too simple and that too much reason was imputed to the primitives who allegedly first behaved and thought in the ways Smith postulated. Frazer said that the theory did not pay enough attention to the propitiatory or fear aspect of sacrifice. Others have felt that it is wrong to say that all religions have passed through a totemistic stage, that is, one in which the totem is eaten so as to establish communion with the god it represents. Still others maintain that gift, rather than communion, was behind the earliest Hebrew sacrifices known to us. Yet many of Smith's ideas have lasting merit and have exerted tremendous influence (see John Sutherland Black and George Chrystal, *The Life of William Robertson Smith,* 1912: James G. Frazer, "William Robertson Smith" in *Sir Roger de Coverley and Other Literary Pieces,* 1920: "Sacrifice" in Hastings' *Encyclopaedia of Religion and Ethics,* 1921: "Comparative Religion" in *Encyclopaedia of the Social Sciences,* 1937).

A recent contribution to theories of sacrifice has been made by Evans-Pritchard in his *Nuer Religion* (1956), in which he takes a cue from Georges Gusdorf (*L'Expérience humaine du sacrifice,* 1948) and asserts that for the Nuer, at least, the piacular sacrifice is a gift designed "to get rid of some danger of misfortune, usually sickness" (p. 276). Communication with God is established only to keep him away or get rid of him—not to establish a fellowship with him. The ox which is sacrificed represents the man who gives it in sacrifice; a life is substituted for a life. Evans-Pritchard acknowledges that the Nuer have more than one kind of sacrifice and that no simple formula covers all types. Furthermore, he does not maintain that his interpretations of his own materials are of universal applicability.

Enough has been said as to the significance of the sacrificial feast as we find it among ancient nations no longer barbarous. But to understand the matter fully we must trace it back to its origin in a state of society much more primitive than that of the agricultural Semites or Greeks.

The sacrificial meal was an appropriate expression of the antique ideal of religious life, not merely because it was a social act and an act in which the god and his worshipers were conceived as partaking together, but because, as has already been said, the very act of eating and drinking with a man was a symbol and a confirmation of fellowship and mutual social obligations. The one thing directly expressed in the sacrificial meal is that the god and his worshipers are *commensals,* but every other point in their mutual relations is included in what this involves. Those who sit at meat together are united for all social effects, those who do not eat together are aliens to one another, without fellowship in religion and without reciprocal social duties. The extent to which this view prevailed among the ancient Semites, and still prevails among Arabs, may be brought out most clearly by reference to the law of hospitality.

Among the Arabs every stranger whom one meets in the desert is a natural enemy, and has no protection against violence except his own strong hand or the fear that his tribe will avenge him if his blood be spilt.

But if I have eaten the smallest morsel of food with a man, I have nothing further to fear from him; "there is salt between us," and he is bound not only to do me no harm, but to help and defend me as if I were his brother. So far was this principle carried by the old Arabs, that Zaid al-Khail, a famous warrior in the days of Mohammed, refused to slay a vagabond who carried off his camels, because the thief had surreptitiously drunk from his father's milk bowl before committing the theft. It does not indeed follow as a matter of course that because I have eaten once with a man I am permanently his friend, for the bond of union is conceived in a very realistic way, and strictly speaking lasts no longer than the food may be supposed to remain in my system. But the temporary bond is confirmed by repetition, and readily passes into a permanent tie confirmed by an oath. "There was a sworn alliance between the Lihyan and the Mostalic, they were wont to eat and drink together." This phrase of an Arab narrator supplies exactly what is wanted to define the significance of the sacrificial meal. The god and his worshipers are wont to eat and drink together, and by this token their fellowship is declared and sealed.

The ethical significance of the common meal can be most adequately illustrated from Arabian usage, but it was not confined to the Arabs. The Old Testament records many cases where a covenant was sealed by the parties eating and drinking together. In most of these indeed the meal is sacrificial, so that it is not at once clear that two men are bound to each other merely by partaking of the same dish, unless the deity is taken in as a third party to the covenant. The value of the Arabian evidence is that it supplies proof that the bond of food is valid of itself, that religion may be called in to confirm and strengthen it, but that the essence of the thing lies in the physical act of eating together. That this was also the case among the Hebrews and Canaanites may be safely concluded from analogy, and appears to receive direct confirmation from Josh. ix. 14, where the Israelites enter into alliance with the Gibeonites by taking of their victuals, without consulting Jehovah. A formal league confirmed by an oath follows, but by accepting the proffered food the Israelites are already committed to the alliance.

But we have not yet got to the root of the matter. What is the ultimate nature of the fellowship which is constituted or declared when men eat and drink together? In our complicated society fellowship has many types and many degrees; men may be united by bonds of duty and honor for certain purposes, and stand quite apart in all other things. Even in ancient times—for example, in the Old Testament—we find the sacrament of a common meal introduced to seal engagements of various kinds. But in every case the engagement is absolute and inviolable, it constitutes what in the language of ethics is called a "duty of perfect obligation." Now in the most primitive society there is only one kind of fellowship which is absolute and inviolable. To the primitive man all other men fall under two classes, those to whom his life is sacred and those to whom it is not sacred. The former are his fellows; the latter are strangers and potential foemen, with whom it is absurd to think of forming any inviolable tie unless they are first brought into the circle within which each man's life is sacred to all his comrades.

But that circle again corresponds to the circle of kinship, for the practical test of kinship is that the whole kin is answerable for the life of each of its members. By the rules of early society, if I slay my kinsman, whether voluntarily or involuntarily, the act is murder, and is punished by expulsion from the kin; if my kinsman is slain by an outsider I and every other member of my kin are bound to avenge his death by killing the manslayer or some member of his kin. It is obvious that under such a system there can be no inviolable fellowship except between men of the same blood. For the duty of blood revenge is paramount, and every other obligation is dissolved as soon as it comes into conflict with the claims of blood. I cannot bind myself absolutely to a man, even for a temporary purpose, unless during the time of our engagement he is put into a kinsman's place. And this is as much as to say that a stranger cannot become bound to me, unless at the same time he becomes bound to all my kinsmen in exactly the same way. Such is, in fact, the law of the desert; when any member of a clan receives an outsider through the bond of salt, the whole clan is bound by his act, and must, while the engagement lasts, receive the stranger as one of themselves.

The idea that kinship is not purely an affair of birth, but may be acquired, has fallen out of our circle of ideas; but so, for that matter, has the primitive conception of kindred itself. To us kinship has no absolute value, but is measured by degrees, and means much or little, or nothing at all, according to its degree and other circumstances. In ancient times, on the contrary, the fundamental obligations of kinship had nothing to do with degrees of relationship, but rested with absolute and identical force on every member of the clan. To know that a man's life was sacred to me, and that every blood-feud that touched him involved me also, it was not necessary for me to count cousinship with him by reckoning up to our common ancestor; it was enough that we belonged to the same clan and bore the same clan name. What was my clan was determined by customary law, which was not the same in all stages of society; in the earliest Semitic communities a man was of his mother's clan, in later times he belonged to the clan of his father. But the essential idea of kinship was independent of the particular form of law. A kin was a group of persons whose lives were so bound up together, in what must be called a physical unity, that they could be treated as parts of one common life. The members of one kindred looked on themselves as one living whole, a single animated mass of blood, flesh, and bones, of which no member could be touched without all the members suffering. This point of view is expressed in the Semitic tongues in many familiar forms of speech. In a case of homicide Arabian tribesmen do not say, "The blood of M. or N. has been spilt," naming the man; they say, "Our blood has been spilt." In Hebrew the phrase by which one claims kinship is "I am your bone and your flesh." Both in Hebrew and in Arabic "flesh" is synonymous with "clan" or kindred group. To us all this seems mere metaphor, from which no practical consequences can follow. But in early thought there is no sharp line between the metaphorical and the literal, between the way of expressing a thing and the way of conceiving it; phrases and symbols are treated as realities. Now, if kinship means participation in common mass of flesh, blood, and bones, it is natural that it should be regarded as dependent, not merely on the fact that a man was born of his mother's body, and so was from his birth a part of her flesh, but also on the not less significant fact that he was nourished by her milk. And so we find that among the Arabs there is a tie of milk, as well as of blood, which unites the foster-child to his foster-mother and her kin. Again, after the child is weaned, his flesh and blood continue to be nourished and renewed by the food which he shares with his commensals, so that commensality can be thought of (1) as confirming or even (2) as constituting kinship in a very real sense.

As regards their bearing on the doctrine of sacrifice it will conduce to clearness if we keep these two points distinct. Primarily the circle of common religion and of common social duties was identical with that of natural kinship, and the god himself was conceived as a being of the same stock with his worshipers. It was natural, therefore, that the kinsmen and their kindred god should seal and strengthen their fellowship by meeting together from time to time to nourish their common life by a common meal, to which those outside the kin were not admitted. A good example of this kind of clan sacrifice, in which a whole kinship periodically joins, is afforded by the Roman *sacra gentilicia*. As in primitive society no man can belong to more than one kindred, so among the Romans no one could share in the *sacra* of two gentes—to do so was to confound the ritual and contaminate the purity of the gens. The *sacra* consisted in common anniversary sacrifices, in which the clansmen honored the gods of the clan and after them the "de-

mons" of their ancestors, so that the whole kin living and dead were brought together in the service. That the earliest sacrificial feasts among the Semites were of the nature of *sacra gentilicia* is a matter of inference rather than of direct evidence, but is not on that account less certain. For that the Semites form no exception to the general rule that the circle of religion and of kinship were originally identical, has been shown. The only thing, therefore, for which additional proof is needed is that the sacrificial ritual of the Semites already existed in this primitive form of society. That this was so is morally certain on general grounds; for an institution like the sacrificial meal, which occurs with the same general features all over the world, as is found among the most primitive peoples, must, in the nature of things, date from the earliest stage of social organization. And the general argument is confirmed by the fact that after several clans had begun to frequent the same sanctuary and worship the same god, the worshipers still grouped themselves for sacrificial purposes on the principle of kinship. In the days of Saul and David all the tribes of Israel had long been united in the worship of Jehovah, yet the clans still maintained their annual gentile sacrifice, at which every member of the group was bound to be present. But evidence more decisive comes to us from Arabia, where, as we have seen, men would not eat together at all unless they were united by kinship or by a covenant that had the same effect as natural kinship. Under such a rule the sacrificial feast must have been confined to kinsmen, and the clan was the largest circle that could unite in a sacrificial act. And so, though the great sanctuaries of heathen Arabia were frequented at the pilgrimage feasts by men of different tribes, who met peaceably for a season under the protection of the truce of God, we find that their participation in the worship of the same holy place did not bind alien clans together in any religious unity; they worshiped side by side, but not together. It is only under Islam that the pilgrimage becomes a bond of religious fellowship, whereas in the times of heathenism it was the correct usage that the different tribes, before they broke up from the feast, should engage in a rivalry of self-exaltation and mutual abuse, which sent them home with all their old jealousies freshly inflamed.

That the sacrificial meal was originally a feast of kinsmen, is apt to suggest to modern minds the idea that its primitive type is to be sought in the household circle, and that public sacrifices, in which the whole clan united, are merely an extension of such an act of domestic worship as in ancient Rome accompanied every family meal. The Roman family never rose from supper till a portion of food had been laid on the burning hearth as an offering to the Lares, and the current opinion, which regards the gens as nothing more than an enlarged household, naturally regards the gentile sacrifice as an enlargement of this domestic rite. But the notion that the clan is only a larger household is not consistent with the results of modern research. Kinship is an older thing than family life, and in the most primitive societies known to us the family or household group was not a subdivision of the clan, but contained members of more than one kindred. As a rule the savage man may not marry a clanswoman, and the children are of the mother's kin, and therefore have no communion of blood religion with their father. In such a society there is hardly any family life, and there can be no sacred household meal. Before the family meal can acquire the religious significance that it possessed in Rome, one of two things must take place: either the primitive association of religion with kinship must be dissolved, or means must have been found to make the whole household of one blood, as was done in Rome by the rule that the wife upon her marriage was adopted into her husband's gens. The rudest nations have religious rules about food, based on the principle of kinship, viz., that a man may not eat the totem animal of his clan; and they generally have some rites of the nature of the sacrificial feast of kinsmen; but it is not the custom of savages to take their ordinary daily food in a social way, in regular domestic meals. Their habit is to eat irregularly and apart, and this habit is strengthened by the religious rules, which often forbid to one member of a household the food which is permitted to another.

We have no direct evidence as to the rules and habits of the Semites in the state of primitive savagery, though there is ample proof of an indirect kind that they originally reckoned kinship through the mother, and that men often, if not always, took their wives from strange kins. It is to be presumed that at this stage of society the Semite did not eat with his wife and children, and it is certain that if he did so the meal could not have had a religious character, as an acknowledgment and seal of kinship and adherence to a kindred god. But in fact the family meal never became a fixed institution among the Semites generally. In Egypt, down to the present day, many persons hardly ever eat with their wives and children, and among the Arabs, boys who are not of full age do not presume to eat in the presence of their parents, but take their meals separately or with the women of the house. No doubt the seclusion of women has retarded the development of family life in Mohammedan countries; but for most purposes this seclusion has never taken much hold on the desert, and yet in northern Arabia no woman will eat before men. I apprehend that these customs were originally formed at a time when a man and his wife and family were not usually of one kin, and when only kinsmen would eat together. But be this as it may, the fact remains that in Arabia the daily family meal has never been an established institution with such a religious significance as attaches to the Roman supper.

The sacrificial feast, therefore, cannot be traced back to the domestic meal, but must be considered as having been from the first a public feast of clansmen. That this is true not only for Arabia but for the Semites as a whole might be inferred on general grounds, inasmuch as all Semitic worship manifestly springs from a common origin, and the inference is confirmed by the observation that even among the agricultural Semites there is no trace of a sacrificial character being attached to ordinary household meals. The domestic hearth among the Semites was not an altar as it was at Rome.

Almost all varieties of human food were offered to the gods, and any kind of food suffices, according to the laws of Arabian hospitality, to establish that bond between two men which in the last resort rests on the principle that only kinsmen eat together. It may seem, therefore, that in the abstract any sort of meal publicly partaken of by a company of kinsmen may constitute a sacrificial feast. The distinction between the feast and an ordinary meal lies, it may seem, not in the material or the copiousness of the repast, but in its public character. When men eat alone they do not invite the god to share their food, but when the clan eats together as a kindred unity the kindred god must also be of the party.

Practically, however, there is no sacrificial feast according to Semitic usage except where a victim is slaughtered. The rule of the Levitical law, that a cereal oblation, when offered alone, belongs wholly to the god and gives no occasion for a feast of worshipers, agrees with the older history, in which we never find a sacrificial meal of which flesh does not form part. Among the Arabs the usage is the same; a religious banquet implies a victim. It appears, therefore, to look at the matter from its merely human side, that the slaughter of a victim must have been in early times the only thing that brought the clan together for a stated meal. Conversely, every slaughter was a clan sacrifice, that is, a domestic animal was not slain except to procure the material for a public meal of kinsmen. This last proposition seems startling, but it is confirmed by the direct evidence of Nilus as to the habits of the Arabs of the Sinaitic desert towards the close of the fourth Christian century. The ordinary sustenance of these Saracens was derived from pillage or from hunting, to which, no doubt, must be added, as a main element, the milk of their herds. When these supplies failed they fell back on the flesh of their camels, one of which was slain for each clan (συγγένεια) or for each group which habitually pitched their tents together (συσκηνία)—which according to known Arab usage would always be a fraction of a clan—and the flesh was hastily devoured by the kinsmen in doglike fashion, half raw and merely softened over the fire.

To grasp the force of this evidence we must remember that, beyond question, there was at this time among the Saracens private property in camels, and that therefore, so far as the law of property went, there could be no reason why a man should not kill a beast for the use of his own family. And though a whole camel might be too much for a single household to eat fresh, the Arabs knew and practiced the art of preserving flesh by cutting it into strips and drying them in the sun. Under these circumstances private slaughter could not have failed to be customary, unless it was absolutely forbidden by tribal usage. In short, it appears that while milk, game, and the fruits of pillage

were private food which might be eaten in any way, the camel was not allowed to be killed and eaten except in a public rite, at which all the kinsmen assisted.

This evidence is all the more remarkable because, among the Saracens of whom Nilus speaks, the slaughter of a camel in times of hunger does not seem to have been considered as a sacrifice to the gods. For a couple of pages later he speaks expressly of the sacrifices which these Arabs offered to the morning star, the sole deity that they acknowledged. These could be performed only when the star was visible, and the whole victim—flesh, skin, and bones—had to be devoured before the sun rose upon it and the day-star disappeared. As this form of sacrifice was necessarily confined to seasons when the planet Venus was a morning star, while the necessity for slaughtering a camel as food might arise at any season, it is to be inferred that in the latter case the victim was not recognized as having a sacrificial character. The Saracens, in fact, had outlived the stage in which no necessity can justify slaughter that is not sacrificial. The principle that the god claims his share in every slaughter has its origin in the religion of kinship, and dates from a time when the tribal god was himself a member of the tribal stock, and when therefore his participation in the sacrificial feast is only one aspect of the rule that no kinsman must be excluded from a share in the victim. But the Saracens of Nilus, like the Arabs generally in the last ages of heathenism, had ceased to do sacrifice to the tribal or clan gods with whose worship the feast of kinsmen was originally connected. The planet Venus, or Lucifer, was not a tribal deity, but, as we know from a variety of sources, was worshiped by all the northern Arabs, to whatever kin they belonged. It is not therefore surprising that in case of necessity we should meet with a slaughter in which the nontribal deity had no part; but it is noteworthy that, after the victim had lost its sacrificial character, it was still deemed necessary that the slaughter should be the affair of the whole kindred. That this was so, while among the Hebrews, on the other hand, the rule that all legitimate slaughter is sacrifice survived long after householders were permitted to make private sacrifices on their own account, is characteristic of the peculiar development of Arabia, where as Wellhausen has justly remarked, religious feeling was quite put in the shade by the feeling for the sanctity of kindred blood. Elsewhere among the Semites we see the old religion surviving the tribal system on which it was based, and accommodating itself to the new forms of national life; but in Arabia the rules and customs of the kin retained the sanctity which they originally derived from their connection with the religion of the kin, long after the kindred god had been forgotten or had sunk into quite a subordinate place. I take it, however, that the eating of camels' flesh continued to be regarded by the Arabs as in some sense a religious act, even when it was no longer associated with a formal act of sacrifice; for abstinence from the flesh of camels and wild asses was prescribed by Symeon Stylites to his Saracen converts, and traces of an idolatrous significance in feasts of camels' flesh appear in Mohammedan tradition.

The persistence among the Arabs of the scruple against private slaughter for a man's own personal use may, I think, be traced in a modified form in other parts of Arabia and long after the time of Nilus. Even in modern times, when a sheep or camel is slain in honor of a guest, the good old custom is that the host keeps open house for his neighbors, or at least distributes portions of the flesh as far as it will go. To do otherwise is still deemed churlish, though not illegal, and the old Arabic literature leaves the impression that in ancient times this feeling was still stronger than it is now, and that the whole encampment was considered when a beast was slain for food. But be this as it may, it is highly significant to find that, even in one branch of the Arabian race, the doctrine that hunger itself does not justify slaughter, except as the act of the clan, was so deeply rooted as to survive the doctrine that all slaughter is sacrifice. This fact is sufficient to remove the last doubt as to the proposition that all sacrifice was originally clan sacrifice, and at the same time it puts the slaughter of a victim in a new light, by classing it among the acts which, in primitive society, are illegal to an individual, and can only be justified when the whole clan shares the responsibility of the deed. So far as I know, there is only one class of actions recognized by early nations to which this description applies, viz., actions which involve an invasion of the sanctity of the

tribal blood. In fact, a life which no single tribesman is allowed to invade, and which can be sacrificed only by the consent and common action of the kin, stands on the same footing with the life of the fellow tribesman. Neither may be taken away by private violence, but only by the consent of the kindred and the kindred god. And the parallelism between the two cases is curiously marked in detail by what I may call a similarity between the ritual of sacrifice and of the execution of a tribesman. In both cases it is required that, as far as possible, every member of the kindred should be not only a consenting party but a partaker in the act, so that whatever responsibility it involves may be equally distributed over the whole clan. This is the meaning of the ancient Hebrew form of execution, where the culprit is stoned by the whole congregation.

The idea that the life of a brute animal may be protected by the same kind of religious scruple as the life of a fellow man is one which we have a difficulty in grasping, or which at any rate we are apt to regard as more proper to a late and sentimental age than to the rude life of primitive times. But this difficulty mainly comes from our taking up a false point of view. Early man had certainly no conception of the sacredness of animal life as such, but neither had he any conception of the sacredness of human life as such. The life of his clansman was sacred to him, not because he was a man, but because he was a kinsman; and, in like manner, the life of an animal of his totem kind is sacred to the savage, not because it is animate, but because he and it are sprung from the same stock and are cousins to one another.

It is clear that the scruple of Nilus' Saracens about killing the camel was of this restricted kind; for they had no objection to kill and eat game. But the camel they would not kill except under the same circumstances as make it lawful for many savages to kill their totem, i.e., under the pressure of hunger or in connection with exceptional religious rites. The parallelism between the Arabian custom and totemism is therefore complete except in one point. There is no direct evidence that the scruple against the private slaughter of a camel was due to feelings of kinship. But, as we have seen, there is this indirect evidence, that the consent and participation of the clan, which was required to make the slaughter of a camel legitimate, is the very thing that is needed to make the death of a kinsman legitimate.

The presumption thus created that the regard paid by the Saracens for the life of the camel turned on the same principle of kinship between men and certain kinds of animals which is the prime factor in totemism, would not be worth much if it rested only on an isolated statement about a particular branch of the Arab race. But it is to be observed that the same kind of restriction on the private slaughter of animals must have existed in ancient times among all the Semites. We have found reason to believe that among the early Semites generally no slaughter was legitimate except for sacrifice, and we have also found reason, apart from Nilus' evidence, for believing that all Semitic sacrifice was originally the act of the community. If these two propositions are true, it follows that all the Semites at one time protected the lives of animals proper for sacrifice, and forbade them to be slain except by the act of the clan, that is, except under such circumstances as would justify or excuse the death of a kinsman. Now, if it thus appears that the scruple against private slaughter of an animal proper for sacrifice was no mere individual peculiarity of Nilus' Saracens, but must at an early period have extended to all the Semites, it is obvious that the conjecture which connects the scruple with a feeling of kinship between the worshipers and the victim gains greatly in plausibility. For the origin of the scruple must now be sought in some widespread and very primitive habit of thought, and it is therefore apposite to point out that among primitive peoples there are no binding precepts of conduct except those that rest on the principle of kinship. This is the general rule which is found in operation wherever we have an opportunity of observing rude societies, and that it prevailed among the early Semites is not to be doubted. Indeed among the Arabs the rule held good without substantial modification down to the time of Mohammed. No life and no obligation was sacred unless it was brought within the charmed circle of the kindred blood.

Thus the *prima facie* presumption, that the scruple in question had to do with the notion that certain animals were akin to men, becomes very strong indeed, and can hardly be set aside unless those who reject it are prepared to show that the idea of kinship between men and beasts, as it is found in most primitive nations, was altogether foreign to Semitic thought, or at least had no substantial place in the ancient religious ideas of that race. But I do not propose to throw the burden of proof on the antagonist.

I have already had occasion in another connection to show by a variety of evidences that the earliest Semites, like primitive men of other races, drew no sharp line of distinction between the nature of gods, of men, and of beasts, and had no difficulty in admitting a real kinship between (*a*) gods and men, (*b*) gods and sacred animals, (*c*) families of men and families of beasts. As regards the third of these points, the direct evidence is fragmentary and sporadic; it is sufficient to prove that the idea of kinship between races of men and races of beasts was not foreign to the Semites, but it is not sufficient to prove that such a belief was widely prevalent, and had prominence enough to justify us in taking it as one of the fundamental principles on which Semitic ritual was founded. But it must be remembered that the three points are so connected that if any two of them are established, the third necessarily follows. Now, as regards (*a*), it is not disputed that the kinship of gods with their worshipers is a fundamental doctrine of Semitic religion; it appears so widely and in so many forms and applications, that we cannot look upon it otherwise than as one of the first and most universal principles of ancient faith. Again as regards (*b*), a belief in sacred animals, which are treated with the reverence due to divine beings, is an essential element in the most widespread and important Semitic cults. All the great deities of the northern Semites had their sacred animals, and were themselves worshiped in animal form, or in association with animal symbols, down to a late date; and that this association implied a veritable unity of kind between animals and gods is placed beyond doubt, on the one hand, by the fact that the sacred animals, e.g., the doves and fish of Atargatis, were reverenced with divine honors; and, on the other hand, by theogonic myths, such as that which makes the dove-goddess be born from an egg, and transformation myths, such as that of Bambyce, where it was believed that the fish-goddess and her son had actually been transformed into fish.

Now if it thus appears that kinship between the gods and their worshipers, on the one hand, and kinship between the gods and certain kinds of animals, on the other, are deep-seated principles of Semitic religion, manifesting themselves in all parts of the sacred institutions of the race, we must necessarily conclude that kinship between families of men and animal kinds was an idea equally deep-seated, and we shall expect to find that the sacred animals, wherever they occur, will be treated with the regard which men pay to their kinsfolk.

Indeed in a religion based on kinship, where the god and his worshipers are of one stock, the principle of sanctity and that of kinship are identical. The sanctity of a kinsman's life and the sanctity of the godhead are not two things, but one; for ultimately

the only thing that is sacred is the common tribal life, or the common blood which is identified with the life. Whatever being partakes in this life is holy, and its holiness may be described indifferently, either as participation in the divine life and nature, or as participation the kindred blood.

Thus the conjecture that sacrificial animals were originally treated as kinsmen is simply equivalent to the conjecture that sacrifices were drawn from animals of a holy kind, whose lives were ordinarily protected by religious scruples and sanctions; and in support of this position a great mass of evidence can be adduced, not merely for Semitic sacrifice, but for ancient sacrifice generally.

ALFRED L. KROEBER

Totem and Taboo: An Ethnologic Psychoanalysis

In lieu of an abridgment of Freud's *Totem and Taboo* a critique has been offered instead, because while Freud's theory of the origin of sacrifice is well known and his book is available in reprinted forms, not too much is known of the anthropological reservations which have been made regarding it. Kroeber was admirably qualified to comment on the work, not only because of his regnant position in historical anthropology but also because of his experience as a practicing psychoanalyst from 1920 to 1923.

Freud's theory may be sharply different from that of others, but it was not derived out of thin air or psychoanalysis alone. He drew upon ideas from Bachofen, Atkinson, and Robertson Smith, to mention but a few. His "evidences" came from myth, totemic practices, and psychoanalysis, none of them documentary sources of the kind that historians or even anthropologists use to reconstruct the past. As a work of history, which it purports to be, Freud's reconstruction of the primal horde and the events which led to the slaying of the father and the instituting of commemorative sacrificial rites is the work of a fertile imagination. Prehistory is usually a reconstruction of a very tentative sort and all we can do is judge its plausibility. In this case the plausibility is low indeed.

Totem and Taboo, then, really falls back on whatever support it can derive from psychoanalytic theory. It is based on the assumption that the Oedipus complex is innate and universal. It is normal for the child to wish to have a sexual relationship with the mother and unwittingly will the death of its rival, the father, and this is often achieved vicariously through fantasy. In the primal horde, sexual gratification with their mothers was never consummated after the father had been slain by his sons; in fact, the sons set up specific taboos against sexual relations with their mothers, thus denying themselves the rewards of victory over the old man. The ritual slaughtering of an animal was instituted in order to commemorate the original parricide, says Freud, and in

Reprinted from *American Anthropologist,* XXII (1920), pp. 48–55, by permission of the author and the American Anthropological Association.

support of his view he points out that in the child's unconscious he frequently identifies his father with some animal. After the primal father had been killed, his sons felt some remorse for their action because they had felt some degree of admiration for his strength and protection. This ambivalent attitude is seen in the sacrificial ritual, which expresses not only the death-wish but *rapprochement* as well. The symbolism of the totem feast, then, is that it not only reenacts the original act of parricide, but establishes communion and reconciliation with the father through the father-substitute. Freud went so far as to say that all culture originated from the first sacrificial ritual.

Neo-Freudians discount the hereditary implications of the events in the primal horde. They feel that the Oedipus complex arises anew each time out of a familial configuration. Some even doubt that it is universal. The British psychoanalyst, Money-Kyrle (*The Meaning of Sacrifice,* 1930), has modified Freud's position and attempted to make it more palatable by denying the implications of a racial mind and the inheritance of acquired memory; instead, he says, sacrifice should be viewed as the symbolic expression of an unconscious desire for parricide that each individual has acquired for himself. Malinowski, the ethnologist (*Sex and Repression in Savage Society,* 1927), long ago showed that the complex was modifiable in terms of social structure. More recently Lessa ("Oedipus-Type Tales in Oceania," 1956) has indicated that Oedipus stories not only reflect such modifications, but apparently are not universal, being present only in a contiguous band extending eastward from Europe to the southwest Pacific. As Kroeber and many others have insisted, Freud was brilliant in his insights into psychological motivation, but his attempt to explain sacrifice as the result of a historic incident does not bear up under scrutiny. In all fairness, it should be pointed out that at least some have interpreted the "historical" description in *Totem and Taboo* as a brilliant image not to be taken literally as a historical event.

The recent translation into English of Freud's interpretation of a number of ethnic phenomena[1] offers an occasion to review the startling series of essays which first appeared in *Imago* a number of years ago. There is the more reason for this because, little as this particular work of Freud has been noticed by anthropologists, the vogue of the psychoanalytic movement founded by him is now so strong that the book is certain to make an impression in many intelligent circles.

Freud's principal thesis emerges formally only toward the end of his book, but evidently has controlled his reasoning from the beginning, although perhaps unconsciously. This thesis is (p. 258) "that the beginnings of religion, ethics, society, and art meet in the Oedipus complex." He commences with

[1] Sigmund Freud, *Totem and Taboo: Resemblances Between the Psychic Life of Savages and Neurotics.* Authorized English Translation, with Introduction, by A. A. Brill (New York: Moffat Yard & Co., 1918).

the inference of Darwin, developed farther by Atkinson, that at a very early period man lived in small communities consisting of an adult male and a number of females and immature individuals, the males among the latter being driven off by the head of the group as they became old enough to evoke his jealousy. To this Freud adds the Robertson Smith theory that sacrifice at the altar is the essential element in every ancient cult, and that such sacrifice goes back to a killing and eating by the clan of its totem animal, which was regarded as of kin with the clan and its god, and whose killing at ordinary times was therefore strictly forbidden. The Oedipus complex directed upon these two hypotheses welds them into a mechanism with which it is possible to explain most of the essentials of human civilization, as follows. The expelled sons of the primal horde finally banded together and slew their father, ate him, and appropriated the females. In this they satisfied the same hate impulse that is a normal infantile trait and the basis of most neuroses, but which often leads to unconscious "displacement" of feelings, especially upon animals. At this point, however, the ambivalence of emotions proved decisive. The tender feelings which had always persisted by the side of the brothers' hate for their father, gained the upper hand as soon as this hate was satisfied, and took the form of remorse and sense of guilt. "What the father's presence had formerly prevented they themselves now prohibited in the psychic situation of 'subsequent obedience' which we know so well from psychoanalysis. They undid their deed by declaring that the killing of the father substitute, the totem, was not allowed, and renounced the fruits of their deed by denying themselves the liberated women. Thus they created the two fundamental taboos of totemism" (p. 236). These are "the oldest and most important taboos" of mankind: "namely not to kill the totem animal and to avoid sexual intercourse with totem companions of the other sex." (p. 53), alongside which many if not all other taboos are "secondary, displaced and distorted." The renunciation of the women or incest prohibition had also this practical foundation: that any attempt to divide the spoils, when each member of the band really wished to emulate the father and possess all the women, would have disrupted the organization which had made the brothers strong (p. 237). The totem sacrifice and feast reflected the killing and eating of the father, assuaged "the burning sense of guilt," and brought about "a kind of reconciliation" or agreement by which the father-totem granted all wishes of his sons in return for their pledge to honor his life (p. 238). "All later religions prove to be . . . reactions aiming at the same great event with which culture began and which ever since has not let mankind come to rest" (p. 239).

This mere extrication and presentation of the framework of the Freudian hypothesis on the origin of socio-religious civilization is probably sufficient to prevent its acceptance; but a formal examination is only just.

First, the Darwin-Atkinson supposition is of course only hypothetical. It is a mere guess that the earliest organization of man resembled that of the gorilla rather than that of trooping monkeys.

Second, Robertson Smith's allegation that blood sacrifice is central in ancient cult holds chiefly or only for the Mediterranoid cultures of a certain period—say the last two thousand years B.C.—and cultures then or subsequently influenced by them. It does not apply to regions outside the sphere of affection by these cultures.

Third, it is at best problematical whether blood sacrifice goes back to a totemic observance. It is not established that totemism is an original possession of Semitic culture.

Fourth, coming to the Freudian theory proper, it is only conjecture that the sons would kill, let alone devour, the father.

Fifth, the fact that a child sometimes displaces its father-hatred upon an animal—we are not told in what percentage of cases—is no proof that the sons did so.

Sixth, if they "displaced," would they retain enough of the original hate impulse to slay the father; and if so, would the slaying not resolve and evaporate the displacements? Psychoanalysts may affirm both questions; others will require more examination before they accept the affirmation.

Seventh, granting the sons' remorse and resolve no longer to kill the father-displacement-totem, it seems exceedingly dubious whether this resolve could be powerful and enduring enough to suppress permanently the gratification of the sexual impulses which was now possible. Again there may be psychoanalytic evidence sufficient to allay the doubt; but it will take a deal of evidence to convince "unanalytic" psychologists, ethnologists, and laymen.

Eighth, if the band of brothers allowed strangers—perhaps expelled by their jealous fathers—to have access to the women whom they had renounced, and matrilinear or matriarchal institutions thus came into existence, what would be left for the brothers (unless they were able to be content with lifelong celibacy or homosexuality), other than individual attachments to other clans; which would mean the disintegration of the very solidarity that they are pictured as so anxious to preserve, even by denying their physiological instincts?

Ninth, it is far from established that exogamy and totem abstinence are the two fundamental prohibitions of totemism. Freud refers (p. 180) to Goldenweiser's study of the subject, which is certainly both analytical and conducted from a psychological point of view even though not psychoanalytical; but he fails to either accept or refute this author's carefully substantiated finding that these two features cannot be designated as primary in the totemic complex.

Tenth, that these two totemic taboos are the oldest of all taboos is pure assertion. If all other taboos are derived from them by displacement or distortion, some presentation of the nature and operation and sequence of these displacements is in order. An astronomer who casually said that he believed Sirius to be the center of the stellar universe and then proceeded to weave this opinion into the fabric of a still broader hypothesis, would get little hearing from other astronomers.

A final criticism—that the persistence into modern society and religion of this first "great event with which culture began" is an unexplained process—will not be pressed here, because Freud has anticipated it with a *tu quoque* (pp. 259–61) : social psychologists assume a "continuity in the psychic life of succeeding generations" without in general concerning themselves much with the manner in which this continuity is established.

No doubt still other challenges of fact or interpretation will occur to every careful reader of the book. The above enumeration has been compiled only far enough to prove the essential method of the work; which is to evade the painful process of arriving at a large certainty by the positive determination of smaller certainties and their unwavering addition irrespective of whether each augments or diminishes the sum total of conclusion arrived at. For this method the author substitutes a plan for multiplying into one another, as it were, fractional certainties— that is, more or less remote possibilities— without recognition that the multiplicity of factors must successively decrease the probability of their product. It is the old expedient of pyramiding hypotheses; which, if theories had to be paid for like stocks or gaming cards, would be less frequently indulged in. Lest this criticism be construed as unnecessarily harsh upon a gallant and stimulating adventurer into ethnology, let it be added that it applies with equal stricture upon the majority of ethnologists from whom Freud has drawn an account of the renown or interest of their books: Reinach, Wundt, Spencer and Gillen, Lang, Robertson Smith, Durkheim and his school, Keane, Spencer, Avebury; and his special vade mecum Frazer.

There is another cricism that can be leveled against the plan of Freud's book: that of insidiousness, though evidently only as the result of the gradual growth of his thesis during its writing. The first chapter or essay, on the Savage's Dread of Incest, merely makes a case for the applicability of psychoanalysis to certain special social phenomena such as the mother-in-law taboo. In the second, the psychoanalytic doctrine of the ambivalence of emotions is very neatly and it seems justly brought to bear on the dual nature of taboo as at once holy and defiling. Concurrently a foundation is laid, though not revealed, for the push to the ultimate thesis. The third chapter on Animism, Magic, and the Omnipotence of Thought refrains from directly advancing the argument, but strengthens its future hold on the reader by emphasizing the parallelism between the thought systems of savages and neurotics. The last chapter is not, in the main, a discussion of the Infantile Recurrence of Totemism, as it is designated, but an analysis of current ethnological theories as to the origin of totemism in society and the presentation of the theory of the author. This hypothesis, toward which everything has been tending, does not however begin to be divulged until page 233; after which, except for tentative claims to a wide extensibility of the principle arrived at and some distinctly fair admissions of weakness, the book promptly closes without any re-examination or testing of its proposition. The explanation of taboo on pages 52–58 is an essential part of the theory developed on pages 233 *seq.,* without any indication being given that it is so. Then, when the parallelism of savage and neurotic thought has been driven home by material largely irrelevant to the final and quite specific thesis, this is suddenly sprung. Freud cannot be charged with more than a propagandist's zeal and perhaps haste of composition; but the consequence is that this book is keen without orderliness, intricately rather than closely reasoned, and endowed with an unsubstantiated convincingness. The critical reader will ascertain these qualities; but the book will fall into the hands of many who are lacking either in care or independence of judgment and who, under the influence of a great name and in the presence of a bewilderingly fertile imagination, will be carried into an illusory belief. Again there is palliation—but nothing more—in the fact that the literature of theoretical anthropology consists largely of bad precedent.

But, with all the essential failure of its finally avowed purpose, the book is an important and valuable contribution. However much cultural anthropology may come to lean more on the historical instead of the psychological method, it can never ultimately free itself, nor should it wish to, from the psychology that underlies it. To this psychology the psychoanalytic movement initiated by Freud has made an indubitably significant contribution, which every ethnologist must sooner or later take into consideration. For instance, the correspondences between taboo customs and "compulsion neuroses" as developed on pages 43–48 are unquestionable, as are also the parallelism between the two aspects of taboo and the ambivalence of emotions under an accepted prohibition (p. 112). Again the strange combination of mourning for the dead with the fear of them and taboos against them is certainly illumined if not explained by this theory of ambivalence (pp. 87–107).

It is even possible to extend Freud's point of view. Where the taboo on the name of the dead is in force we find not only the fear that utterance will recall the soul to the hurt of the living, but also actual shock at the utterance as a slight or manifestation of hostility to the dead. It is a fair question whether this shock may not be construed as a reaction from the unconscious hate carried toward the dead during their life, as if speaking of them were an admission of satisfaction at their going. The shock is certainly greatest where affection was deepest; persons who were indifferent were mentioned without emotional reluctance if circumstances permit, whereas enemies, that is individuals toward whom hate was avowed instead of repressed, may have the utterance of their names gloated over.

Of very broad interest is the problem raised by Freud's conjecture that the psychic impulses of primitive people possessed more ambivalence than our own except in the case of neurotics: that their mental life, like that of neurotics, is more sexualized and contains fewer social components than ours (pp. 111, 121, 148). Neurosis would therefore usually represent an atavistic constitution. Whatever its complete significance, there exists no doubt a remarkable similarity between the phenomena of magic, taboo, animism, and primitive religion in general, and neurotic manifestations. In both a creation that has only psychic validity is given greater or less preference over reality. As Freud says, the two are of course not the same, and the ultimate difference lies in the fact that neuroses are asocial creations due to a flight from dissatisfying reality (p. 123). This is certainly not to be denied on any ethnological grounds; yet the implication that savages are essentially more neurotic than civilized men may well be challenged, although it cannot be dismissed offhand.

The experience of firsthand observers will probably be unanimous that primitive communities, like peasant populations, contain very few individuals that can be put into a class with the numerous neurotics of our civilization. The reason seems to be that primitive societies have institutionalized such impulses as with us lead to neuroses. The individual of neurotic tendency finds an approved and therefore harmless outlet in taboo, magic, myth, and the like, whereas the non-neurotic, who at heart remains attached to reality, accepts these activities as forms which do not seriously disturb him. In accord with this interpretation is the fact that neurotics appear to become numerous and characteristic in populations among whom religion has become decadent and "enlightenment" active, as in the Hellenistic, Roman Imperial, and recent eras; whereas in the Middle Ages, when "superstition" and taboo were firmly established, there were social aberrations indeed, like the flagellants and children's crusade, but few neurotics. Much the same with homosexuality, which the North American and Siberian natives have socialized. Its acceptance as an institution may be a departure from normality, but has certainly saved countless individuals from the heavy strain which definite homosexualists undergo in our civilization. It would be unfitting to go into these matters further here: they are mentioned as an illustration of the importance of the problems which Freud raises. However precipitate his entry into anthropology and however flimsy some of his syntheses, he brings to bear keen insight, a fecund imagination, and above all a point of view which henceforth can never be ignored without stultification.

While the book thus is one that no ethnologist can afford to neglect, one remark may be extended to psychologists of the unconscious who propose to follow in Freud's footsteps: there really is a great deal of ethnology not at all represented by the authors whom Freud discusses. To students of this side of the science the line of work initiated by Tylor and developed and most notably represented among the living by Frazer, is not so much ethnology as an attempt to psychologize with ethnological data. The cause of Freud's leaning so heavily on Frazer is clear. The latter knows nothing of psychoanalysis and with all acumen his efforts are prevailingly a dilettantish playing; but in the last analysis they are psychology, and as history only a pleasing fabrication. If psychoanalysts wish to establish serious contacts with historical ethnology, they must first learn to know that such an ethnology exists. It is easy enough to say, as Freud does on page 179, that the nature of totemism and exogamy could be most readily grasped if we could get into closer touch with their origins, but that as we cannot we must depend on hypotheses. Such a remark rings a bit naïve to students who have long since made up their minds that ethnology, like every other branch of science, is work and not a game in which lucky guesses score; and who therefore hold that since we know nothing directly about the origin of totemism or other social phenomena but have information on these phenomena as they exist at present, our business is first to understand as thoroughly as possible the nature of these existing phenomena; in the hope that such understanding may gradually lead to a partial reconstruction of origins—without undue guessing.

ALFRED L. KROEBER

Totem and Taboo in Retrospect

Almost two decades after writing the foregoing critique, Kroeber, in an issue of the *American Journal of Sociology* that was devoted to Freud in appreciation rather than in criticism of his contributions, again criticizes Freud's historical fantasies. He was writing at a time when anthropology was reaching the apex of psychoanalytic interest. In 1948 (*Anthropology*) he maintained perhaps an even stronger position, saying "the psychoanalytic explanation of culture is intuitive, dogmatic, and wholly unhistorical." In even more recent years he reiterated his disillusionment with the possibility of using psychoanalysis for historical reconstruction and was especially caustic concerning Freud's failure to advance beyond outmoded materials and approaches: "Freud preferred to forage in Frazer rather than to read the intellectually sophisticated works of his own age-mate Boas" (*The Nature of Culture*, 1952).

Nearly twenty years ago I wrote an analysis of *Totem and Taboo*—that brain child of Freud which was to be the precursor of a long series of psychoanalytic books and articles explaining this or that aspect of culture, or the whole of it.[1] It seems an appropriate time to return to the subject.

[1] "Totem and Taboo: An Ethnologic Psychoanalysis," *American Anthropologist,* XXII (1920), 48–55.

I see no reason to waver over my critical analysis of Freud's book. There is no indication that the consensus of anthropologists during these twenty years has moved even an inch nearer acceptance of Freud's central thesis. But I found myself somewhat conscience-stricken when, perhaps a decade later, I listened to a student in Sapir's seminar in Chicago making his report on *Totem and Taboo,* who, like myself, first spread out its gossamer texture and then laboriously tore it to shreds. It is a procedure too suggestive of breaking a butterfly on the wheel. An iridescent fantasy deserves a more delicate touch even in the act of demonstration of its unreality.

Freud himself has said of my review that it characterized his book as a *Just So* story. It is a felicitous phrase, coming from himself. Many a tale by Kipling or Andersen contains a profound psychological truth. One does not need therefore to cite and try it in the stern court of evidential confrontation.

However, the fault is not wholly mine. Freud does speak of the "great event with which culture began." And therewith he enters history. Events are historical and beginnings are historical, and human culture is appreciable historically. It is difficult to say how far he realized his vacillation between historic truth and abstract truth expressed through intuitive imagination. A historic finding calls for some specification of place and time and order; instead of which, he offers a finding of unique cardinality, such as history feels it cannot deal with.

Freud is reported subsequently to have said that his "event" is to be construed as "typical." Herewith we begin to approach a basis of possible agreement. A typical event, historically speaking, is a recurrent one. This can hardly be admitted for the father-slaying, eating, and guilt sense. At any rate, there is no profit in discussing the recurrence of an event which we do not even know to have occurred once. But there is no need sticking fast on the word "event" because Freud used it. His argument is evidently ambiguous as between historical thinking and psychological thinking. If we omit the fatal concept of event, of an act as it happens in history, we have left over the concept of the psychologically potential. Psychological insight may legitimately hope to attain to the realization and definition of such a potentiality; and to this, Freud should have confined himself. We may accordingly properly disregard any seeming claim, or half-claim, to historic authenticity of the suggested actual happening, as being beside the real point, and consider whether Freud's theory contains any possibility of being a generic, time-less explanation of the psychology that underlies certain recurrent historic phenomena or institutions like totemism and taboo.

Here we obviously are on better ground. It becomes better yet if we discard certain gratuitous and really irrelevant assumptions, such as that the self-imposed taboo following the father-slaying is the original of all taboos, these deriving from it as secondary displacements or distortions. Stripped down in this way, Freud's thesis would reduce to the proposition that certain psychic processes tend always to be operative and to find expression in wide-spread human institutions. Among these processes would be the incest drive and incest repression, filial ambivalence, and the like; in short, if one like, the kernel of the Oedipus situation. After all, if ten modern anthropologists were asked to designate one universal human institution, nine would be likely to name the incest prohibition; some have expressly named it as the only universal one. Anything so constant as this, at least as regards its nucleus, in the notoriously fluctuating universe of culture, can hardly be the result of a "mere" historical accident devoid of psychological significance. If there is accordingly an underlying factor which keeps reproducing the phenomenon in an unstable world, this factor must be something in the human constitution—in other words, a psychic factor. Therewith the door is open not for an acceptance *in toto* of Freud's explanation but at any rate for its serious consideration as a scientific hypothesis. Moreover, it is an explanation certainly marked by deeper insight and supportable by more parallel evidence from personal psychology than the older views, such as that familiarity breeds sexual indifference, or recourse to a supposed "instinct" which is merely a verbal restatement of the observed behavior.

Totemism, which is a much rarer phenomenon than incest taboo, might then well be the joint product of the incest-drive-and-repression process and of some other less compelling factor. Nonsexual taboo, on the other hand, which rears itself in so many protean forms over the whole field of culture, might be due to a set of still different but analogous psychic factors. Anthropologists and sociologists have certainly long been groping for something underlying which would help them explain both the repetitions and the variations in culture, provided the explanation were evidential, extensible by further analysis, and neither too simplistic nor too one-sided. Put in some such form as this, Freud's hypothesis might long before this have proved fertile in the realm of cultural understanding instead of being mainly rejected or ignored as a brilliant fantasy.

What has stood in the way of such a fruitful restatement or transposition? There seem to be at least three factors: one due to Freud himself, another jointly to himself and his followers, the third mainly to the Freudians.

The first of these is Freud's already mentioned ambiguity which leads him to state a timeless psychological explanation as if it were also a historical one. This tendency is evident elsewhere in his thinking. It appears to be the counterpart of an extraordinarily explorative imagination, constantly impelled to penetrate into new intellectual terrain. One consequence is a curious analogy to what he himself has discovered in regard to the manifest and the latent in dreams. The manifest is there, but it is ambiguous; a deeper meaning lies below; from the point of view of this latent lower content, the manifest is accidental and inconsequential. Much like this, it seems to me, is the historical dress which Freud gives his psychological insight. He does not repudiate it; he does not stand by it as integral. It is really irrelevant; but his insight having manifested itself in the dress, he cannot divest himself of this "manifest" form. His view is overdetermined like a dream.

A second factor is the curious indifference which Freud has always shown as to whether his conclusions do or do not integrate with the totality of science. This led him at one time to accept the inheritance of acquired traits as if it did not clash with standard scientific attitude. Here again we have the complete explorer who forgets in his quest, or represses, knowledge of what he started from or left behind. In Freud himself one is inclined not to quarrel too hard with this tendency; without it, he might have opened fewer and shorter vistas. Of his disciples, however, who have so largely merely followed, more liaison might be expected. I recall Rank, while still a Freudian, after expounding his views to a critically sympathetic audience, being pressed to reconcile certain of them to the findings of science at large and, after an hour, conceding that psychoanalysts held that there might be more than one truth, each on its own level and independent of the other. And he made the admission without appearing to realize its import.

A third element in the situation is the all-or-none attitude of most avowed psychoanalysts. They insist on operating within a closed system. At any rate, if not wholly closed, it grows only from within; it is not open to influence from without. A classical example is Ernest Jones's resistance to Malinowski's finding that among the matrilineal Melanesians the effects directed toward the father in our civilization are largely displaced upon the mother's brother, the relation of father and children being rather one of simple and relatively univalent affection. Therewith Malinowski had really vindicated the mechanism of the Oedipus relation. He showed that the mechanism remained operative even in a changed family situation; a minor modification of it, in its direction, conforming to the change in given condition. Jones, however, could not see this, and resisted tooth and nail. Because Freud in the culture of Vienna had determined that ambivalence was directed toward the father, ambivalence had to remain directed to him universally, even where primary authority resided in an uncle.

The same tendency appears in Roheim, whose "Psycho-analysis of Primitive Cultural Types" contains a mass of psychological observations most valuable to cultural anthropologists, but so organized as to be unusable by them. None have used it, so far as I know. This is not due to lack of interest on the part of anthropologists in psychological behavior within cultures, for in recent years a whole series of them have begun avowedly to deal with such behavior. Nor is it due to any deficiency of quality in Roheim's data: these are rich, vivid, novel, and valuable. But the data are so presented as to possess organization only from the point of view of orthodox psychoanalytic theory. With reference to the culture in which they occur, or to the consecutive life histories of personalities, they are inchoate. The closing sentence of the monograph—following immediately on some illuminative material—is typical: "We see then, that the sexual practices of a people are indeed prototypical and that from their posture in coitus their whole psychic attitude may be inferred." Can a conclusion be imagined which would appear more arbitrarily dogmatic than this to any psychologist, psychiatrist, anthropologist, or sociologist?

The fundamental concepts which Freud

formulated—repression, regression and infantile persistences, dream symbolism and overdetermination, guilt sense, the effects toward members of the family—have gradually seeped into general science and become an integral and important part of it. If one assumes that our science forms some kind of larger unit because its basic orientation and method are uniform, these concepts constitute the permanent contribution of Freud and psychoanalysis to general science; and the contribution is large. Beyond, there is a further set of concepts which in the main have not found their way into science: the censor, the superego, the castration complex, the explanation of specific cultural phenomena. To these concepts the several relevant branches of science—sociology, anthropology, psychology, and medicine alike—remain impervious about as consistently as when the concepts were first developed. It may therefore be inferred that science is likely to remain negative to them. To the psychoanalysts, on the contrary, the two classes of concepts remain on the same level, of much the same value, and inseparably interwoven into one system. In this quality of nondifferentiation between what the scientific world accepts as reality and rejects as fantasy, between what is essential and what is incidental, the orthodox psychoanalytic movement reveals itself as partaking of the nature of a religion—a system of mysticism; even, it might be said, it shows certain of the qualities of a delusional system. It has appropriated to itself such of the data of science—the cumulative representative of reality—as were digestible to it and has ignored the larger remainder. It has sought little integration with the totality of science, and only on its own terms. By contrast, science, while also of course a system, has shown itself a relatively open one: it has accepted and already largely absorbed a considerable part of the concepts of psychoanalysis. It is indicative of the largeness of Freud's mind that, although the sole founder of the movement and the originator of most of its ideas, his very ambiguities in the more doubtful areas carry a stamp of tolerance. He may persist in certain interpretations; he does not insist on them; they remain more or less fruitful suggestions. Of this class is his theory of the primary determination of culture. As a construct, neither science nor history can use it; but it would seem that they can both accept and utilize some of the process concepts that are involved in the construct.

I trust that this reformulation may be construed not only as an *amende honorable* but as a tribute to one of the great minds of our day.

Note.—Since the above was written and submitted, Freud has published *Der Mann Moses und die monotheistische Religion.* The thesis of *Totem and Taboo* is reaffirmed: "Ich halte an diesen Aufbau noch heute fest" (p. 231). One concession in the direction of my argument is made: the father-killing was not a unique event but "hat sich in Wirklichkeit über Jahrtausende erstreckt" (p. 146). Of his stimulator, Robertson Smith, Freud says superbly: "Mit seinen Gegnern traf ich nie zusammen" (p. 232). We, on our part, if I may speak for ethnologists, though remaining unconverted, have met Freud, recognize the encounter as memorable, and herewith resalute him.

ÉMILE DURKHEIM

The Elementary Forms of the Religious Life

Few books on the science of religion stand out as powerfully as Émile Durkheim's *The Elementary Forms of the Religious Life,* published originally in 1912 in France under the title *Les formes élémentaires de la vie religieuse: Le système totémique en Australie.* The author had already foreshadowed his views on religion in his *Le Suicide* (1897) and an article in the *Année Sociologique* (1899), and had even published some of the first portions of his forthcoming book. What Durkheim had to say has

Reprinted in abridged form from Émile Durkheim, *The Elementary Forms of the Religious Life,* trans. Joseph Ward Swain (London: George Allen & Unwin, Ltd., 1915), by permission of the publishers.

had a deep impact on subsequent theoreticians, particularly Rad-cliffe-Brown, Evans-Pritchard, and Warner. Durkheim's realization that religion plays a vital part in social life was impressed upon him by the writings of Robertson Smith and those British anthropologists who had been concerned with the subject of religion. While Durkheim was in Paris in 1885 for the purpose of rounding out his training, Lucien Herr, the librarian of the École Normale, guided him toward Frazer's articles on totemism, and from then on he made it his concern to study primitive religion so that he could understand the role of religion in general.

Durkheim became convinced that in order to understand this role one must examine religion in its simplest and original form, totemism; therefore he used materials from Australia to make his analysis. Totemism, he maintained, embodies all the essential aspects of religion: the division of things into sacred and profane; the notion of the soul, spirits, mythical personalities, and divinity; a negative cult wtih ascetic practices; rites of oblation and communion; imitative rites; commemorative rites; and expiatory rites. The sacred attitude necessary for religion is to be seen in the totem, which derives its sacredness from the fact that it is essentially the symbol of society. The totem represents the clan, which to the aborigine is virtually society itself. Primitive man, especially as a consequence of the social environment that results when he meets in large ceremonial gatherings, realizes, however unconsciously, that as a member of society he can survive but that as a lone individual he cannot. He comes to view society as something sacred because he is utterly dependent on it as a source of strength and culture. But it is easier for him to visualize and direct his feeling of awe and respect toward a symbol than toward so complex a thing as a clan. The totem becomes the object of the sacred attitude. It is virtually God. Society, in effect, deifies itself. Durkheim equates Society with God. Not only are the members of society sacred, but so are all things which stand for society: the totemic plants and animals and the images of such totems. They become the object of a cult because they possess mana. As Lowie (*Primitive Religion,* 1948) has so aptly put it, "In this interpretation of totemism there is something like an anticipation of the Freudian interpretation of dreams. Things are not what they seem on the surface but have a hidden meaning."

His preoccupation with origins was merely incidental to Durkheim's main goal, which was to study the role of religion. In effect, Durkheim saw religion as a vast symbolic system which made social life possible by expressing and maintaining the sentiments or values of the society. He especially analyzed the role of ceremonial and ritualistic institutions, and concluded that they are disciplinary, integrating, vitalizing, and euphoric forces. His method was what only in later years came to be labeled "functional." It stemmed from such predecessors as Fustel de Coulanges (who was one of his professors at the École Normale and whose *La Cité antique* [1864] linked religion with political organization and other institutions in a complex of interdependent relations) and Robertson Smith, whose effort to reveal causal nexuses has already been considered.

Religious phenomena are naturally arranged in two fundamental categories: beliefs and rites. The first are states of opinion, and consist in representations; the second are determined modes of action. Between these two classes of facts there is all the difference which separates thought from action.

The rites can be defined and distinguished from other human practices, moral practices, for example, only by the special nature of their object. A moral rule prescribes certain manners of acting to us, just as a rite does, but which are addressed to a different class of objects. So it is the object of the rite which must be characterized, if we are to characterize the rite itself. Now it is in the beliefs that the special nature of this object is expressed. It is possible to define the rite only after we have defined the belief.

All known religious beliefs, whether simple or complex, present one common characteristic: they presuppose a classification of all the things, real and ideal, of which men think, into two classes or opposed groups, generally designated by two distinct terms which are translated well enough by the words *profane* and *sacred* (*profane, sacré*). This division of the world into two domains, the one containing all that is sacred, the other all that is profane, is the distinctive trait of religious thought; the beliefs, myths, dogmas, and legends are either representations or systems of representations which express the nature of sacred things, the virtues and powers which are attributed to them, or their relations with each other and with profane things. But by sacred things one must not understand simply those personal beings which are called gods or spirits; a rock, a tree, a spring, a pebble, a piece of wood, a house, in a word, anything can be sacred. A rite can have this character; in fact, the rite does not exist which does not have it to a certain degree. There are words, expressions, and formulae which can be pronounced only by the mouths of consecrated persons; there are gestures and movements which everybody cannot perform. If the Vedic sacrifice has had such an efficacy that, according to mythology, it was the creator of the gods, and not merely a means of winning their favor, it is because it possessed a virtue comparable to that of the most sacred beings. The circle of sacred objects cannot be determined, then, once for all. Its extent varies infinitely, according to the different religions. That is how Buddhism is a religion: in default of gods, it admits the existence of sacred things, namely, the four noble truths and the practices derived from them.

* * *

. . . The real characteristic of religious phenomena is that they always suppose a bipartite division of the whole universe, known and knowable, into two classes which embrace all that exists, but which radically exclude each other. Sacred things are those which the interdictions protect and isolate; profane things, those to which these interdictions are applied and which must remain at a distance from the first. Religious beliefs are the representations which express the nature of sacred things and the relations which they sustain, either with each other or with profane things. Finally, rites are the rules of conduct which prescribe how a man should comport himself in the presence of these sacred objects.

* * *

The really religious beliefs are always common to a determined group, which makes profession of adhering to them and of practicing the rites connected with them. They are not merely received individually by all the members of this group; they are something belonging to the group, and they make its unity. The individuals which compose it feel themselves united to each other by the simple fact that they have a common faith. A society whose members are united by the fact that they think in the same way in regard to the sacred world and its relations with the profane world, and by the fact that they translate these common ideas into common practices, is what is called a "Church." In all history, we do not find a single religion without a Church. Sometimes the Church is strictly national, sometimes it passes the frontiers; sometimes it embraces an entire people (Rome, Athens, the Hebrews), sometimes it embraces only a part of them (the Christian societies since the advent of Protestantism); sometimes it is directed by a corps of priests, sometimes it is almost completely devoid of any official directing body. But wherever we observe the religious life, we find that it has a definite group as its foundation. Even the so-called "private" cults, such as the domestic cult or the cult of a corporation, satisfy this condition; for they are always celebrated by a group, the family, or the corporation. Moreover, even these particular religions are ordinarily only special forms of a more general religion which embraces all; these restricted Churches are in reality only chapels of a vaster Church which, by reason of this very extent, merits this name still more.

It is quite another matter with magic. To

be sure, the belief in magic is always more or less general; it is very frequently diffused in large masses of the population, and there are even peoples where it has as many adherents as the real religion. But it does not result in binding together those who adhere to it, nor in uniting them into a group leading a common life. *There is no Church of magic.* Between the magician and the individuals who consult him, as between these individuals themselves, there are no lasting bonds which make them members of the same moral community, comparable to that formed by the believers in the same god or the observers of the same cult. The magician has a clientele and not a Church, and it is very possible that his clients have no other relations between each other, or even do not know each other; even the relations which they have with him are generally accidental and transient; they are just like those of a sick man with his physician. The official and public character with which he is sometimes invested changes nothing in this situation; the fact that he works openly does not unite him more regularly or more durably to those who have recourse to his services.

* * *

Thus we arrive at the following definition: *A religion is a unified system of beliefs and practices relative to sacred things, that is to say, things set apart and forbidden—beliefs and practices which unite into one single moral community called a Church, all those who adhere to them.* The second element which thus finds a place in our definition is no less essential than the first; for by showing that the idea of religion is inseparable from that of the Church, it makes it clear that religion should be an eminently collective thing.

* * *

LEADING CONCEPTIONS OF THE ELEMENTARY RELIGION

Even the crudest religions with which history and ethnology make us acquainted are already of a complexity which corresponds badly with the idea sometimes held of primitive mentality. One finds there not only a confused system of beliefs and rites, but also such a plurality of different principles, and such a richness of essential notions, that it seems impossible to see in them anything but

the late product of a rather long evolution. Hence it has been concluded that to discover the truly original form of religious life, it is necessary to descend by analysis beyond these observable religions, to resolve them into their common and fundamental elements, and then to seek among these latter some one from which the others were derived.

To the problem thus stated, two contrary solutions have been given.

There is no religious system, ancient or recent, where one does not meet, under different forms, two religions, as it were, side by side, which, though being united closely and mutually penetrating each other, do not cease, nevertheless, to be distinct. The one addresses itself to the phenomena of nature, either the great cosmic forces, such as winds, rivers, stars, or the sky, etc., or else the objects of various sorts which cover the surface of the earth, such as plants, animals, rocks, etc.; for this reason it has been given the name of *naturism*. The other has spiritual beings as its object, spirits, souls, geniuses, demons, divinities properly so-called, animated and conscious agents like man, but distinguished from him, nevertheless, by the nature of their powers and especially by the peculiar characteristic that they do not affect the senses in the same way: ordinarily they are not visible to human eyes. This religion of spirits is called *animism*. Now, to explain the universal coexistence of these two sorts of cults, two contradictory theories have been proposed. For some, animism is the primitive religion, of which naturism is only a secondary and derived form. For the others, on the contrary, it is the nature cult which was the point of departure for religious evolution; the cult of spirits is only a peculiar case of that.

These two theories are, up to the present, the only ones by which the attempt has been made to explain rationally the origins of religious thought.

* * *

Finally, the animistic theory implies a consequence which is perhaps its best refutation.

If it were true, it would be necessary to admit that religious beliefs are so many hallucinatory representations, without any objective foundation whatsoever. It is supposed that they are all derived from the idea of the soul because one sees only a magnified soul in the spirits and gods. But according to Tylor and his disciples, the idea of the soul is itself constructed entirely out of the vague and inconsistent images which occupy our attention during sleep: for the soul is the double, and the double is merely a man as he appears to himself while he sleeps. From this point of view, then, sacred beings are only the imaginary conceptions which men have produced during a sort of delirium which regularly overtakes them every day, though it is quite impossible to see what useful ends these conceptions serve, nor what they answer to in reality. If a man prays, if he makes sacrifices and offerings, if he submits to the multiple privations which the ritual prescribes, it is because a sort of constitutional eccentricity has made him take his dreams for perceptions, death for a prolonged sleep, and dead bodies for living and thinking beings. Thus not only is it true, as many have held, that the forms under which religious powers have been represented to the mind do not express them exactly, and that the symbols with the aid of which they have been thought of partially hide their real nature, but more than that, behind these images and figures there exists nothing but the nightmares of private minds. In fine, religion is nothing but a dream, systematized and lived, but without any foundation in reality. Thence it comes about that the theorists of animism, when looking for the origins of religious thought, content themselves with a small outlay of energy. When they think that they have explained how men have been induced to imagine beings of a strange, vaporous form, such as those they see in their dreams, they think the problem is resolved.

In reality, it is not even approached. It is inadmissible that systems of ideas like religions, which have held so considerable a place in history, and from which, in all times, men have come to receive the energy which they must have to live, should be made up of a tissue of illusions. Today we are beginning to realize that law, morals, and even scientific thought itself were born of religion, were for a long time confounded with it, and have remained penetrated with its spirit. How could a vain fantasy have been able to fashion the human consciousness so strongly and so durably? Surely it ought to be a principle of the science of religions that religion expresses nothing which does not exist in nature; for there are sciences only of natural phenomena.

* * *

The spirit of the naturistic school is quite different.

* * *

They talk about the marvel which men should feel as they discover the world. But really, that which characterizes the life of nature is a regularity which approaches monotony. Every morning the sun mounts in the horizon, every evening it sets; every month the moon goes through the same cycle; the river flows in an uninterrupted manner in its bed; the same seasons periodically bring back the same sensations. To be sure, here and there an unexpected event sometimes happens: the sun is eclipsed, the moon is hidden behind clouds, the river overflows. But these momentary variations could only give birth to equally momentary impressions, the remembrance of which is gone after a little while; they could not serve as a basis for these stable and permanent systems of ideas and practices which constitute religions. Normally, the course of nature is uniform, and uniformity could never produce strong emotions. Representing the savage as filled with admiration before these marvels transports much more recent sentiments to the beginnings of history. He is much too accustomed to it to be greatly surprised by it. It requires culture and reflection to shake off this yoke of habit and to discover how marvellous this regularity itself is. Besides, as we have already remarked, admiring an object is not enough to make it appear sacred to us, that is to say, to mark it with those characteristics which make all direct contact with it appear a sacrilege and a profanation. We misunderstand what the religious sentiment really is, if we confound it with every impression of admiration and surprise.

But, they say, even if it is not admiration, there is a certain impression which men cannot help feeling in the presence of nature. He cannot come in contact with it, without realizing that it is greater than he. It overwhelms him by its immensity. This sensation of an infinite space which surrounds him, of an infinite time which has preceded and will follow the present moment, and of forces infinitely superior to those of which he is master, cannot fail, as it seems, to awaken within him the idea that outside of him there exists an infinite power upon which he depends. And this idea enters as an essential element into our conception of the divine.

But let us bear in mind what the question is. We are trying to find out how men came to think that there are in reality two categories of things, radically heterogeneous and incomparable to each other. Now how could the spectacle of nature give rise to the idea of this duality? Nature is always and everywhere of the same sort. It matters little that it extends to infinity: beyond the extreme limit to which my eyes can reach, it is not different from what it is here. The space which I imagine beyond the horizon is still space, identical with that which I see. The time which flows without end is made up of moments identical with those which I have passed through. Extension, like duration, repeats itself indefinitely; if the portions which I touch have of themselves no sacred character, where did the others get theirs? The fact that I do not see them directly, is not enough to transform them. A world of profane things may well be unlimited; but it remains a profane world. Do they say that the physical forces with which we come in contact exceed our own? Sacred forces are not to be distinguished from profane ones simply by their great intensity, they are different; they have special qualities which the others do not have. Quite on the contrary, all the forces manifested in the universe are of the same nature, those that are within us just as those that are outside of us. And especially, there is no reason which could have allowed giving a sort of pre-eminent dignity to some in relation to others. Then if religion really was born because of the need of assigning causes to physical phenomena, the forces thus imagined would have been no more sacred than those conceived by the scientist today to account for the same facts. This is as much as to say that there would have been no sacred beings and therefore no religion.

* * *

TOTEMISM AS AN ELEMENTARY RELIGION

Since neither man nor nature have of themselves a sacred character, they must get it from another source. Aside from the human individual and the physical world, there should be some other reality, in relation to which this variety of delirium which all religion is in a sense, has a significance and an objective value. In other words, beyond those which we have called animistic and naturistic, there should be another sort of cult, more fundamental and more primitive, of which the first are only derived forms or particular aspects.

In fact, this cult does exist: it is the one to which ethnologists have given the name of *totemism*.

* * *

With one reservation which will be indicated below, we propose to limit our research to Australian societies. They are perfectly homogeneous, for though it is possible to distinguish varieties among them, they all belong to one common type. This homogeneity is even so great that the forms of social organization are not only the same, but that they are even designated by identical or equivalent names in multitude of tribes, sometimes very distant from each other. Also, Australian totemism is the variety for which our documents are the most complete. Finally, that which we propose to study in this work is the most primitive and simple religion which it is possible to find. It is therefore natural that to discover it, we address ourselves to societies as slightly evolved as possible, for it is evidently there that we have the greatest chance of finding it and studying it well. Now there are no societies which present this characteristic to a higher degree than the Australian ones. Not only is their civilization most rudimentary— the house and even the hut are still unknown—but also their organization is the most primitive and simple which is actually known; it is that which we have elsewhere called *organization on basis of clans*.

* * *

Among the beliefs upon which totemism rests, the most important are naturally those concerning the totem; it is with these that we must begin.

At the basis of nearly all the Australian tribes we find a group which holds a preponderating place in the collective life: this is the clan. Two essential traits characterize it.

In the first place, the individuals who compose it consider themselves united by a bond of kinship, but one which is of a very special nature. This relationship does not come from the fact that they have definite blood connections with one another; they are relatives from the mere fact that they have the same name. They are not fathers and mothers, sons or daughters, uncles or nephews of one another in the sense which we now give these words; yet they think of themselves as forming a single family, which is large or small according to the dimensions of the clan, merely because they are collectively designated by the same word. When we say that they regard themselves as a single family, we do so because they recognize duties toward each other which are identical with those which have always been incumbent upon kindred: such duties as aid, vengeance, mourning, the obligations not to marry among themselves, etc.

* * *

The species of things which serves to designate the clan collectively is called its *totem.* The totem of the clan is also that of each of its members.

Each clan has its totem, which belongs to it alone; two different clans of the same tribe cannot have the same. In fact, one is a member of a clan merely because he has a certain name. All who bear this name are members of it for that very reason; in whatever manner they may be spread over the tribal territory, they all have the same relations of kinship with one another. Consequently, two groups having the same totem can only be two sections of the same clan. Undoubtedly, it frequently happens that all of a clan does not reside in the same locality, but has representatives in several different places. However, this lack of a geographical basis does not cause its unity to be the less keenly felt.

* * *

In a very large proportion of the cases, the objects which serve as totems belong either to the animal or the vegetable kingdom, but especially to the former. Inanimate things are much more rarely employed. Out of more than 500 totemic names collected by Howitt among the tribes of southeastern Australia, there are scarcely forty which are not the names of plants or animals; these are the clouds, rain, hail, frost, the moon, the sun, the wind, the autumn, the summer, the winter, certain stars, thunder, fire, smoke, water, or the sea. It is noticeable how small a place is given to celestial bodies and, more generally, to the great cosmic phenomena, which were destined to so great a fortune in later religious development.

* * *

But the totem is not merely a name; it is an emblem, a veritable coat-of-arms whose analogies with the arms of heraldry have often been remarked. In speaking of the Australians, Grey says, "each family adopt an animal or vegetable as their crest and sign," and what Grey calls a family is incontestably a clan. Also Fison and Howitt say, "the Australian divisions show that the totem is, in the first place, the badge of a group."

* * *

These totemic decorations enable us to see that the totem is not merely a name and an emblem. It is in the course of the religious ceremonies that they are employed; they are a part of the liturgy; so while the totem is a collective label, it also has a religious character. In fact, it is in connection with it, that things are classified as sacred or profane. It is the very type of sacred thing.

The tribes of Central Australia, especially the Arunta, the Loritja, the Kaitish, the Unmatjera, and the Ilpirra, make constant use of certain instruments in their rites which are called the *churinga* by the Arunta according to Spencer and Gillen, or the *tjurunga,* according to Strehlow. They are pieces of wood or bits of polished stone, of a great variety of forms, but generally oval or oblong. Each totemic group has a more or less important collection of these. *Upon each of these is engraved a design representing the totem of this same group.* A certain number of the churinga have a hole at one end, through which goes a thread made of human hair or that of an opossum. Those which are made of wood and are pierced in this way serve for exactly the same purposes as those instruments of the cult to which English ethnographers have given the name of "bull-roarers." By means of the thread by which they are suspended, they are whirled rapidly in the air in such a way as to produce a sort of humming identical with that made by the toys of this name still used by our children; this deafening noise has a ritual significance and accompanies all ceremonies of any importance. These sorts of churinga are real bull-roarers. But there are others which are not made of wood and are not pierced; consequently they cannot be employed in this way. Nevertheless, they inspire the same religious sentiments.

In fact, every churinga, for whatever purpose it may be employed, is counted among the eminently sacred things; there are none which surpass it in religious dignity. This is indicated even by the word which is used to designate them. It is not only a substantive but also an adjective meaning sacred. Also, among the several names which each Arunta has, there is one so sacred that it must not be revealed to a stranger; it is pronounced but rarely, and then in a low voice and a sort of mysterious murmur.

* * *

Now in themselves, the churinga are objects of wood and stone like all others; they are distinguished from profane things of the same sort by only one particularity; this is that the totemic mark is drawn or engraved upon them. So it is this mark and this alone which gives them their sacred character.

* * *

But totemic images are not the only sacred things. There are real things which are also the object of rites, because of the relations which they have with the totem: before all others, are the beings of the totemic species and the members of the clan.

* * *

Every member of the clan is invested with a sacred character which is not materially inferior to that which we just observed in the animal. This personal sacredness is due to the fact that the man believes that while he is a man in the usual sense of the word, he is also an animal or plant of the totemic species.

In fact, he bears its name; this identity of name is therefore supposed to imply an identity of nature. The first is not merely considered as an outward sign of the second; it supposes it logically. This is because the name, for a primitive, is not merely a word or a combination of sounds; it is a part of the being, and even something essential to it. A member of the Kangaroo clan calls himself a kangaroo; he is therefore, in one sense, an animal of this species.

* * *

We have seen that totemism places the figured representations of the totem in the first rank of the things it considers sacred; next come the animals or vegetables whose name the clan bears, and finally the members of the clan. Since all these things are sacred in the same way, though to different degrees, their religious character can be due to none of the special attributes distinguishing them from each other. If a certain species of animal or vegetable is the object of a reverential fear, this is not because of its special properties, for the human members of the clan enjoy the same privilege, though to a slightly inferior degree, while the mere image of this same plant or animal inspires an even more pronounced respect. The similar sentiments inspired by these different sorts of things in the mind of the believer, which give them their sacred character, can evidently come only from some common principle partaken of alike by the totemic emblems, the men of the clan and the individuals of the species serving as totem. In reality, it is to this common principle that the cult is addressed. In other words, totemism is the religion, not of such and such animals or men or images, but of an anonymous and impersonal force, found in each of these beings but not to be confounded with any of them. No one possesses it entirely and all participate in it. It is so completely independent of the particular subjects in whom it incarnates itself, that it precedes them and survives them. Individuals die, generations pass and are replaced by others; but this force always remains actual, living, and the same. It animates the generations of today as it animated those of yesterday and as it will animate those of tomorrow.

* * *

Thus the totem is before all a symbol, a material expression of something else. But of what?

From the analysis to which we have been giving our attention, it is evident that it expresses and symbolizes two different sorts of things. In the first place, it is the outward and visible form of what we have called the totemic principle or god. But it is also the symbol of the determined society called the clan. It is its flag; it is the sign by which each clan distinguishes itself from the others, the visible mark of its personality, a mark borne by everything which is a part of the clan under any title whatsoever, men, beasts, or things. So if it is at once the symbol of the god and of the society, is that not because the god and the society are only one? How could the emblem of the group have been able to become the figure of this quasi-divinity, if the group and the divinity were two distinct realities? The god of the clan, the totemic principle, can therefore be nothing else than the clan itself, personified and represented to the imagination under the visible form of the animal or vegetable which serves as totem.

But how has this apotheosis been possible, and how did it happen to take place in this fashion?

In a general way, it is unquestionable that a society has all that is necessary to arouse the sensation of the divine in minds, merely by the power that it has over them; for to its members it is what a god is to his worshipers. In fact, a god is, first of all, a being whom men think of as superior to themselves, and upon whom they feel that they depend. Whether it be a conscious personality, such as Zeus or Jahveh, or merely abstract forces such as those in play in totemism, the worshiper, in the one case as in the other, believes himself held to certain manners of acting which are imposed upon him by the nature of the sacred principle with which he feels that he is in communion. Now society also gives us the sensation of a perpetual dependence. Since it has a nature which is peculiar to itself and different from our individual nature, it pursues ends which are likewise special to it; but, as it cannot attain them except through our intermediacy, it imperiously demands our aid. It requires that, forgetful of our own interests, we make ourselves its servitors, and it submits us to every sort of inconvenience, privation, and sacrifice, without which social life would be impossible. It is because of this that at every instant we are obliged to submit ourselves to rules of conduct and of thought which we have neither made nor desired, and which are sometimes even contrary to our most fundamental inclinations and instincts.

Since religious force is nothing other than the collective and anonymous force of the clan, and since this can be represented in the mind only in the form of the totem, the totemic emblem is like the visible body of the god. Therefore, it is from it that those kindly or dreadful actions seem to emanate, which the cult seeks to provoke and prevent; consequently, it is to it that the cult is addressed. This is the explanation of why it holds the first place in the series of sacred things.

But the clan, like every other sort of society, can live only in and through the individual consciousnesses that compose it. So if religious force, in so far as it is conceived as incorporated in the totemic emblem, appears to be outside of the individuals and to be endowed with a sort of trancendence over them, it, like the clan of which it is the symbol, can be realized only in and through them; in this sense, it is immanent in them and they necessarily represent it as such. They feel it present and active within them, for it is this which raises them to a superior life. This is why men have believed that they contain within them a principle comparable to the one residing in the totem, and consequently, why they have attributed a sacred character to themselves, but one less marked than that of the emblem. It is because the emblem is the pre-eminent source of the religious life; the man participates in it only indirectly, as he is well aware; he takes into account the fact that the force that transports him into the world of sacred things is not inherent in him, but comes to him from the outside.

But for still another reason, the animals or vegetables of the totemic species should have the same character, and even to a higher degree. If the totemic principal is nothing else than the clan, it is the clan thought of under the material form of the totemic emblem; now this form is also that of the concrete beings whose name the clan bears. Owing to this resemblance, they could not fail to evoke sentiments analogous to those aroused by the emblem itself. Since the latter is the object of a religious respect, they too should inspire respect of the same sort and appear to be sacred. Having external forms so nearly identical, it would be impossible for the native not to attribute to them forces of the same nature. It is therefore forbidden to kill or eat the totemic animal, since its flesh is believed to have the positive virtues resulting from the rites; it is because it resembles the emblem of the clan, that is to say, it is in its own image. And since the animal naturally resembles the emblem more than the man does, it is placed on a superior rank in the heirarchy of sacred things. Between these two beings there is undoubtedly a close relationship, for they both partake of the same essence: both incarnate something of the totemic principle. However, since the principle itself is conceived under an animal form, the animal seems to incarnate it more fully than the man. Therefore, if men consider it and treat it as a brother, it is at least as an elder brother.

But even if the totemic principle has its preferred seat in a determined species of animal or vegetable, it cannot remain localized there. A sacred character is to a high degree contagious; it therefore spreads out from the totemic being to everything that is closely or remotely connected with it. The religious sentiments inspired by the animal are communicated to the substances upon which it is nourished and which serve to make or remake its flesh and blood, to the things that resemble it, and to the different beings with which it has constant relations. Thus, little by little, subtotems are attached to the totems and from the cosmological systems expressed by the primitive classifications. At last, the whole world is divided up among the totemic principles of each tribe.

We are now able to explain the origin of the ambiguity of religious forces as they appear in history, and how they are physical as well as human, moral as well as material. They are moral powers because they are made up entirely of the impressions this moral being, the group, arouses in those other moral beings, its individual members; they do not translate the manner in which physical things affect our senses, but the way in which the collective consciousness acts upon individual consciousnesses. Their authority is only one form of the moral ascendancy of society over its members. But, on the other hand, since they are conceived of under material forms, they could not fail to be regarded as closely related to material things. Therefore they dominate the two worlds. Their residence is in men, but at the same time they are the vital principles of things. They animate minds and discipline them, but it is also they who make plants grow and animals reproduce. It is this double nature which has enabled religion to be like the womb from which come all the leading germs of human civilization. Since it has been made to embrace all of reality, the physical world as well as the moral one, the forces that move bodies as well as those that move minds have been conceived in a religious form. That is how the most diverse methods and practices, both those that make possible the continuation of the moral life (law, morals, beaux-arts) and those serving the material life (the natural, technical, and practical sciences), are either directly or indirectly derived from religion.

ALEXANDER GOLDENWEISER

Religion and Society: A Critique of Émile Durkheim's Theory of the Origin and Nature of Religion

Those who have damned Durkheim have also heaped lavish praise on him, and those who have eulogized him have not failed to see serious shortcomings in his reconstruction and interpretation of religion. Bitterness is mingled with deep admiration for the tremendous intellectual tour de force which he produced in his *Elementary Forms;* praise is tempered by the haunting feeling that whereas in many specific details he showed astonishing insight, his major thesis was wrong. Lowie (*Primitive Religion*), for example, before going into a denunciation of his theory of origins, makes it clear that his book "represents an estimable intellectual achievement" and is "the only comprehensive effort since Tylor's day to unify religious data from a wholly novel

Reprinted from *The Journal of Philosophy, Psychology, and Scientific Methods,* XIV (1917), 113–124, by permission of *The Journal of Philosophy.*

angle." Radcliffe-Brown ("The Sociological Theory of Totemism"), who is a lineal descendant of Durkheimian sociology and adheres closely to many of the ideas contained in the *Elementary Forms,* says that Durkheim's attempt to provide a sociological theory of totemism "fails in certain important respects." Most criticisms are directed against that aspect of the theory that deals with origins; the part that deals with symbolism and role is usually unchallenged. Perhaps the most scathing critique of the former has come from the pen of Alexander Goldenweiser, a man of great intellectual talents and extensive philosophic background. He perhaps tends in some instances to warp Durkheim's meanings, as in the case of the part played by the "crowd" in generating an emotional state conducive to a feeling of the sacred, but on the whole his arguments are sound. Goldenweiser is interested in the problem of the origins of religion, not its functions.

Few problems have occupied the minds of thinking men so persistently and intensely as the problem of the origin and nature of religion. The psychologist vies with the sociologist and anthropologist, the philosopher with the philologist and theologian, in their attempts to enhance our comprehension of that peculiar phenomenon, which in its distribution is at least coextensive with man, and possesses, as an emotional value, but few rivals in the entire gamut of psychic experiences. Of the many theories on record three deserve our attention here: naturalism, animism, animatism. According to the naturalistic theory, proclaimed by Max Müller, Kuhn, and others, nature itself is responsible for the religious sentiment. The powers of nature, so often mysterious, inexplicable, gruesome, strange, frightful, arouse in man an emotional response, which constitutes the core of religion. The animistic theory, represented most prominently by Tylor and Spencer, is of interest in two of its aspects. On the one hand, it contains the doctrine of spirits; on the other (in the case of Spencer), a theory of worship. While agreeing with Tylor in the essentials of the animistic doctrine, Spencer derives all forms of worship from the cult of ancestors. The animatistic theory, finally, finds its most enthusiastic representative in R. R. Marett. By the adherents of this doctrine, the most recent and popular of the three, animism is regarded as a mere incident in the development of religion; the fundamental religious concept becomes that of power, impersonal magic potency, *mana,* to which, on the subjective side, corresponds the religious thrill.

Of these theories, only the animatistic one makes any attempt to analyze the religious consciousness, to interpret its nature psychologically. In the vision of the animist and the naturalist, the savage is very much alone with his religion; the social milieu is left out altogether; the process, moreover, through which religion comes to be, is conceived of as somewhat in the nature of a conscious rationalistic act, of a problem, posited and solved. In animatism the emphasis is shifted to the emotional side; we also hear that religion is "congregational" and must be treated sociologically. The derivation of the concept of mana, however, remains a purely individual affair; other individuals are understood to be there, but, so far as the origin of mana is concerned, their part is that of a stage setting.

An attempt to furnish a sociopsychological interpretation of religion, an attempt much more elaborate and pretentious than any of the above, has recently been made by Émile Durkheim, the French sociologist, in his *La vie religieuse.* The author aims to present a psychological analysis of the religious consciousness as well as an example of the most primitive religious complex. As the subtitle of the work indicates, the scene is laid in Australia, a field eminently within the competence of the author, whose Australian researches have extended over a quarter of a century. Durkheim's argument is, in brief, as follows.

All attempts to account for religion by drawing upon the properties of nature are doomed to failure. The savage knows no natural, hence he can have no conception of the supernatural. Nature, moreover, is utterly devoid of those characteristics which, in themselves, could arouse religious emotions. We must note, in addition, that the most insignificant objects or creatures often figure as recipients of religious regard. Religious values then are not derived from nature, but are superadded upon it. The derivation of fundamental religious conceptions from dreams and similar experiences is also at fault. Religion, with its universal appeal, cannot, in the last analysis, be due to an illusion; at the root of it must lie some concrete reality of experience.

Before proceeding with any analysis of religion, we must realize that a definition of religion may not be restricted to its emotional content, but must be extended so as to include the conceptional side of religion, theology, and its activational side, ritual. There is no religion without a church. When analyzed from this point of view the fundamental fact in all religions seems to be a dichotomy of experience into sacred and profane. Acts, things, beings, which are holy, sacred, are juxtaposed to acts, things, beings, which are commonplace, trite, profane. The quest for the origin of religion thus resolves itself into a search for that reality which underlies the dichotomy of experience into sacred and profane.

To find the fundamental core of religion we must turn to a religious complex which can be shown to be primitive. Such a complex is represented by Australian totemism; for totemism is based on the clan organization, and the clan is the most primitive social unit. Australian totemism reveals all the traits which, in higher forms, reappear in the world's great religions: it has a social aspect, clan totemism, and an individual aspect, the belief in guardian spirits; it possesses a cosmogony; it involves prayer and sacrifice and a belief in the soul.

An analysis of the totemic complex reveals the fact that the experience of the Australian is conceived as sacred or profane according to its inclusion in or exclusion from the totemic cycle of ideas, emotions, and activities. The totem is the criterion of sacredness. Further examination, morever, shows that while the totemic emblems, the totems, the totemites, all participate in the sacred realm, the veneration of the clan-mates is not directed to any of these beings or things or symbols, as such, but to a sacred and mysterious substance, the "totemic principle," which pervades them all.

A comparison of the "totemic principle" with mana, impersonal magic power, believed in by the Indians of North America, the Melanesians, and other peoples, discloses the identity of the two concepts. The "totemic principle" is mana which, when dominated by a clan system, as in Australia, appears in what might be called a pluralistic or distributive form; when, on the other hand, the tribe acquires precedence over the clan, as in North America, the mana concept, freed from the restraining influence of the social units, appears in its familiar form of an undifferentiated, impersonal, all-pervasive power. What will explain the "totemic principle," then, will explain mana, the sacred, religion.

The life of the Australian fluctuates between two radically distinct cycles of experiences. On the one hand, he fulfills the round of his daily pursuits, indifferent, monotonous, drab; on the other hand, he participates, at certain regularly recurring periods, in the ceremonial activities of the tribe, the clan, in the sacred totemic rites. At such periods, the gray monotony of daily experience gives way to excitement, frenzy, the charm of taboo, the passionate whirl of sacred songs and dances. The individual is transformed. His thoughts, emotions, acts, altogether transcend their accustomed level. He feels himself acted upon, carried away, by a power which is of himself, yet also external to him. That power which exalts and constrains arouses the sense of the sacred. Thus religion is born. The rest is infection through association, contact, deliberate transfer. Religion, then, the sacred, mana, the "totemic principle," are but so many symbols of society itself, and the most primitive form of a society is the totemic clan.

Durkheim's argument embraces the following fundamental propositions: nature, as such, cannot inspire the religious emotion; religion cannot, in the last analysis, be based on an illusion, but must be rooted in a concrete reality, derived from experience; an adequate definition of religion must recognize in it a complex of conceptual, emotional, and activational elements; the fundamental fact in all religions is a dichotomy of experience into sacred and profane; the most primitive religious complex is totemism; the "totemic principle," the source of the sacredness of the totemic cycle, is identical with mana; mana is a symbol of society, the "totemic principle," of the clan. We may now take up these propositions, one by one, and subject them to a brief critical analysis.

Nature as such cannot inspire the religious emotion.

When dealing with the remote periods in the course of which the birth of religion may be supposed to have occurred, one must of necessity take recourse to inference and analogy. In questions, however, of such generality as man's susceptibility to the impressions derived from his contact with nature, argument by analogy may be accepted as a guide of sufficient reliability. Now, our familiarity with man, modern, ancient, and primitive, leaves no room for doubt that at all times and places man was strongly susceptible to the impressions produced on him by the phenomena of nature and that such impressions assumed in his consciousness the form of quasi-religious sentiments. Earthquakes and the eruptions of volcanoes; tempests, floods, and torrential rains; comets, and the aurora borealis; eclipses of the sun and the moon; falling stars; forest and prairie fires, and extreme variations in weather and climate; these and many other manifestations of the powers of nature always did, as they still do, impress themselves on the mind of man and arouse in him that thrill or recoil which constitutes the emotional nucleus of all religion. And what is true of these phenomena applies with a difference of degree only to those slighter shocks and thrills evoked in man by the contact with his superiors, physically or mentally, whether these be animals or men. May we not, moreover, discern "the psychologist's fallacy" in Durkheim's assertion that primitive man, knowing no natural order, could have no concept of the supernatural? To be sure, the cleavage between the two realms does not, in primitive minds, fall where we would have it; transformations of animals into men and vice versa are to the savage natural everyday occurrences, while a visit to a chemical laboratory or even a stroll along Broadway would, for him, be replete with supernatural experiences. The study of primitive custom, mythology, language, moreover, brings irrefutable evidence of the presence of the concepts "natural" and "supernatural" in the mind of the savage. To these we must refer Professor Durkheim for particulars.

Religion cannot be based on an illusion, but must be rooted in a concrete basic fact of experience.

This view of Durkheim's might well be discarded as of secondary importance, but for the significant use made of it in his work. What, may we ask, does the author call an "illusion"? Surely, in a study of religion, we need not be concerned with the objective reality behind the conceptual constructs of the religious consciousness! The religious experience itself *is* the reality which counts. Is it not so with the esthetic experience, or the ethical experience as well? There are, of course, certain objective facts or relations underlying these experiences, but the subjective aspect of them does not in any of these situations, whether religious or esthetic or ethical, represent, or mimic, or symbolize, the objective aspect: it is the reaction of consciousness, in the form of an emotional intellectual complex, which counts. At best, moreover, it is the notion of spirit which is based on what Durkheim calls an illusion, not the emotional thrill or recoil attending the supernatural experience; in the latter, however, our author does not believe, at least not as an ultimate fact.

Religion must be defined as a complex of conceptual, emotional, and activational elements. There is no religion without a Church.

If the above proposition is merely taken to signify that every religion, as an institution, embraces a theology, a faith, a ritual, little exception can be taken to the statement. Although, even in that interpretation, it is true only in a most general way, as a limiting concept, to which every religion, in its institutional aspect, tends to approximate. Otherwise, the three aspects are most unevenly represented in different religions. Thus Buddhism and Confucianism represent conceptual edifices with but little faith and practically no ritual, whereas the religion of the Todas stands for pure ritualism with faith and theology attenuated to scarcely appreciable forms. The error involved in Durkheim's mode of approach is, however, a more serious one. The author defines and analyzes institutional religion, as if the conceptual-emotional-activational complex were a homogeneous phenomenon, culturally, historically, and psychologically, and, therefore, could be studied *in toto,* so to say, and with the use of the same methodological tools. This is very far from being the fact. A religion, like every other institution, represents historically and psychologically a highly heterogeneous complex. In such a complex live emotional elements go hand in hand with "evaporated emotions," serving as a petrified fringe to the religious concept or act; subjective experiences are intermingled with purely objective features; dynamic creative ideas exist side by side with traditional rite and form. Now, different as are the psychic and social mechanisms involved in these different aspects of institutional religion, so also must be the methods by means of which they can be investigated. The dogmas are recorded in written or oral tradition, and to them the scholastic methods of the bookman may well be applied. The rites must be seen and studied on the spot or laboriously reconstructed from written or oral accounts or numerous witnesses. The subjective experiences, finally, are varied in the extreme, and at best only a representative set of them can be secured by intensive investigation, involving great intimacy with the individuals concerned. In the domain of primitive religion, for instance, which for years has occupied the attention of scholars and practical workers of varied interests, training, abilities, only the last few years have brought glimpses into the psyche of the primitive devotee; and what meager results have been achieved were altogether due to the application of a painstaking linguistic method.

So much for institutional religion. But within every culture religious experiences occur which are but weakly institutionalized, while some of these, although likewise provided with a traditional background, remain almost altogether unsupported by similar experiences of other individuals. This vast domain of religious fact is completely eliminated through Durkheim's formal method.

The cardinal fact in all religions is the dichotomy of experience into sacred and profane.

A partial critique of this proposition is contained in the remarks on the preceding one. On the one hand, all acts, beings, objects, experiences, involved in a religion, are sacred—for such is the nature of the religious. So far, the statement, while true, is tautological. On the other hand, if any religion is analyzed in its concrete cultural setting, one finds that the domain of the sacred does not represent a psychologically homo-geneous phenomemon. In Australia, for instance, the sacredness of the magical act and of the magician is not that of the totem; nor the sacredness of the menstrual taboos that of the unclean animals, not eaten because possessed by evil spirits. Similarly, in our own society, the sacredness of the national flag is not that of the law, nor the sacredness of the family name that of the college pin or banner, nor the sacredness of the Church to which one belongs that of one to which he does not belong. The sacred, then, is an aggregate as psychologically heterogeneous as is the profane. To characterize religion, therefore, by a dichotomy of experience into sacred and profane, is to create an artificial situation as well as to establish a presumption in favor of an interpretation of the sacred through some one general principle, a pitfall which Professor Durkheim has not succeeded in evading.

Totemism is the most primitive religious complex.

Durkheim's selection of Australian totemism as the most primitive form of religion and as a proper setting for the origin of the religious emotion is supported by two considerations. Totemism, argues the author, is based on the most primitive type of social unit, the clan, hence totemism itself must be primitive; moreover, totemism, while primitive, embraces all the characteristic traits of the higher religions; hence it is a genuine religion. Durkheim's argument bristles with fallacies. We may not have reached final solutions in our search for the origins of organized society, but that the clan is not a primitive institution we may safely maintain, at the hand of ethnological fact and theory. The most primitive tribes known lack a clan system, the local groups and the family serving as a basis of organization. On the other hand, it is a priori obvious that a clan system, or any other system, cannot be regarded as a primitive institution, but that the most primitive society must have been based on a *natural* grouping, a natural biological grouping into families, combined with a natural territorial grouping into local communities. But were we to grant, for argument's sake, that the clan is primitive, the admission would not make totemism primitive; for, on the one hand, totemism might be regarded as associated only with highly evolved clan-systems (of which fact, indeed, there is plentiful evidence); on the other, the primitiveness of a social organization is no guarantee of the primitiveness of a form of religion associated with it, just as we find complex social organization coupled with primitive material arts, as in Australia, or primitive social organization with advanced arts, as among the Eskimo. Durkheim's identification of totemism with most primitive religion, moreover, implies an unexpressed belief in the universality of totemism, a thoroughly exploded doctrine, for there is not a shred of evidence that tribes like the Eskimo, or the Thompson, or the Blackfoot, or the Shoshone, ever were totemic.

Again, Durkheim's interpretation of totemism as a genuine religion must be regarded as one of the fatal consequences of his definition of religion. Most of the aspects of totemism carefully passed in review by the author can be shown, or at least suspected, to be of nontotemic origin. So-called "individual totemism" may not be regarded as a derivative of clan totemism. The guardian-spirit belief is most widespread among the Indians of North America, and nowhere does it flourish with greater exuberance than among the tribes of the so-called Plateau Area, tribes that are not totemic nor, for all we know, ever were totemic. Again, it would seem, at first sight, that what Durkheim calls the totemic cosmogony is a true offspring of totemism. But when one considers how common an ethnological feature is the cosmological projection of social organization, he is inclined to believe that the totemic cosmogony may also have been sociological, but not totemic in origin, having later become saturated with totemic values. A similar point may be raised with reference to the belief in souls which, in Australia, has a totemic coloring. But if various traits of totemism can be shown to have been nontotemic in origin, having become totemic through subsequent association, such traits may no longer be regarded as organic ingredients of a totemic religion.

What has been said in this section establishes a presumption against Durkheim's ultimate interpretation of religion, in so far as any "origin" of the religious emotion derived from the conditions given by a totemic complex must needs fall short in point of universality and primitiveness.

The "totemic principle" is identical with mana.

The "totemic principle" appears in Durkheim's argument somewhat after the fashion of a *deus ex machina,* and it may well be doubted whether the introduction of this concept does not involve a marked rationalization of the Australian totemic situation. Possibly, however, the author's idea of the "totemic principle" does not really imply that character of abstractness which the text suggests. We may, therefore, accept the term as a conceptualized interpretation of the sacred totemic cycle of participation. But the author identifies the "totemic principle" with mana, of which it is a forerunner, the two concepts being identical in content, but different in form. Mana is free, the "totemic principle" limited to the clan; mana is monistic, the "totemic principle" pluralistic.

At this point decided exception must be taken to the author's position. A full vindication of the concept of mana—which, if space permitted, could be shown to represent one of the two cardinal concepts of all religion, the other being the concept of spirit—cannot be given here. Suffice it to say that rapidly accumulating ethnological evidence brings abundant proof of the existence of the concept of mana, or impersonal power, among primitive peoples. On the other hand, the greater claim to universality and primitiveness of mana rather than the "totemic principle," may be gathered from the reflection that whereas the "totemic principle" is indissolubly bound to a definite form of social organization, itself of a limited distribution, mana requires nothing but nature, acting, and man's mind, acted upon; whereas the "totemic principle" can be psychologically derived only from the highly specialized conditions given by a totemic complex, the psychological derivation of the concept of mana can be made from almost any conceivable religious situation. Mana, then, not the "totemic principle," can claim universality and primitiveness. Hence, even if a similarity of nature were conceded to the two concepts, a psychological derivation of mana would not improbably apply also to the "totemic principle"; but the reverse would not be true.

The "totemic principle" is a symbol of the clan; the reality underlying religion is society.

This proposition represents the fundamental and ultimate aspect of Durkheim's theory. The thought is bold and original. No one before Durkheim, nor the author himself in his other works, has gone so far in effacing the individual in favor of the social. If the author's solution were found to be sound, a most significant step would have been made toward a final comprehension of the two problems which through the ages have occupied the minds of legions of thinkers: the problem of the relation of the individual to society, and that of the nature and origin of religion.

Three sets of arguments may be advanced against Durkheim's position: an ethnological one, a sociological one, and a psychological one.

In the first place, then, Durkheim's theory is by the very nature of his argument restricted to a totemic and ceremonial situation; it will, therefore, not hold for those tribes and areas which lack totemism as well as ceremonialism *en masse*. To make the point more specific: how does the case stand, for instance, in North America? The tribes of the Pacific Northwest, of the Southwest, part of the Plains tribes, those of the Southeast, and the Iroquois combine highly complex social systems with elaborate ceremonialism *en masse*. Most of these tribes are totemic. A large number of tribes, on the other hand, lack both of these features. To these belong the Eskimo of the Arctic littoral, the tribes of the Plateau, of California, and many isolated groups throughout the North American area. Among these tribes we find neither complex social organization nor elaborate ceremonialism. Whence, then—if we follow Durkheim—their religions? Unless indeed they have borrowed all their religious conceptions, nay, the very emotions of the religious thrill, from tribes more fortunately situated! So far the ethnological argument.

In the second place, the conception of the social, of society, in Durkheim's theory is strangely narrow. Notwithstanding the tremendous importance ascribed to it, society for Durkheim is but a sublimated crowd, while the social setting is the crowd-psychological situation. Society as a cultural, historical complex, society as the carrier of tradition, as the legislator, judge, as the standard of action, as public opinion; society in all of these varied and significant manifestations, which surely are of prime concern to the individual, does not figure in Durkheim's theory. All the marvels of social control are achieved through the medium of the crowd-psychological situation. Durkheim's theory, then, is a crowd-psychological one; but is his crowd psychology sound? The author will have us believe that the religious thrill, the sense of the sacred, arises from the reaction of the individual consciousness to social pressure, or rather from the ratiocination of that reaction. The elements involved in the situation utilized in the author's theory are still to be found in society, hence his contention is subject to verification by our modern experience. Now, how does the individual react to social pressure which overwhelms him in a crowd-psychological situation, and what construction does he place on his reaction? The reaction is very much as Durkheim has described it: in the theater, at a political meeting, in a mob, at a revival, in church, in a panic, the action of the group on the individual is characteristic and decisive. But how does he rationalize his participation in the group action or experience? Not by *contrasting* his daily life with the special crowd situation, nor by representing himself as actuated upon by a superior and external power—quite on the contrary: the individual *identifies* himself with the group, with the crowd; he represents himself as sharing in the power which is of the crowd, of the group. *We* thought, *we* felt, *we* did, is for him descriptive also of his own part in the proceedings. Social settings of this variety are so constant, so common an experience in the life of man, primitive or modern, that the average, that is, not exceptionally reflective individual, never thinks of contrasting these experiences with others, or of regarding his crowd or group self as transcending the self of his daily routine. On the contrary, the crowd or group self *is* the self par excellence, as well as the self at its best. Again, the crowd or group setting obviously does not create the specific psychic state involved. The joyful ecstasy of a jubilant crowd remains a feeling of joy; a panic of fear; the hatred of a lynching mob is hatred; the adoration of a religious gathering is adoration. In all of these instances, and ennumerable others, the specific emotion experienced is not of crowd derivation. What is common in the above situations is the crowd psychology: through a summation of stimuli, and through imitation, the emotions become intensified; the higher mental processes, involving deliberation and concentration, become paralyzed; the instinctive and reflexive responses, on the contrary, which have through past ages become attuned to the particular emotion involved, arise into prominence. What results then is an intensified expression of a given emotion in terms of instinctive and reflexive reactions, reactions, that is, which belong to a relative low level in human development. But the specific emotion so expressed is not born of the crowd, and differs in different crowd-psychological situations. Thus, a series of corroborees does not make an *intichiuma,* nor do the secular dances of the North American Indians become identified with the religious dances. A crowd-psychological situation may intensify or even transform a religious thrill, but it cannot create one. Thus the sociological argument is also opposed to Durkheim's theory.

In the third place, finally, we must take issue with the author on a psychological ground. The psychological argument has in part been forestalled in another section. The author's theory runs counter to the verdict of experience, ancient and modern, in denying nature the power to impress, shock, and thrill man, thus engendering in his psyche the emotional nucleus of the religious sentiment. The author, moreover, fails to do justice to the contribution of the individual of religious experience. While the religious emotion, deeply rooted as it is in instinctive reactions reaching far back into human and possibly pre-human history, is to a marked degree amenable to the transformations conditioned by the crowd, the mob, and other more complex types of social setting; religious experience has, on the other hand, been enriched, elaborated, refined, by the spiritual contributions of individuals. These were either individuals of average potentialities for religious experience, but placed in unusual circumstances, or they belonged to that group of exceptional individuals who, at all times and places, have shown uncommon proclivities for the religious life. The first category is exemplified by the Indian youth who, at the dawn of maturity, retires to a shanty in the woods, fasts, purifies himself until he is so pure that "the spirits can see through him"; then the vision of his life comes to him in the shape of a spiritual ani-mal or object; he receives a supernatural revelation of certain powers which henceforth are his for life, and never, after this, may he kill or eat the earthly representatives of the animal which, in spirit form, thus came to visit him in his vision. To the second category of individuals belongs that limited group of men from which history has recruited her religious teachers and reformers, fanatics and miracle workers, revivalists, founders and destroyers of religions, prophets and saints. Now, it is emphatically characteristic of both of these categories of men (and women) that, temporarily or permanently, they shun the crowd, they flee from the world, they live in solitude, they are proof against religions settings except those of their own making; in their psychic constitution lie infinite potentialities of religious experience and ecstasy. Their god is within them. The lives of such as they constitute a glaring refutation of Durkheim's theory.

Our critique is drawing to a close. The arguments advanced seem to show that Durkheim's theory of religion does not bear out the expectations aroused by the wisdom, scholarship, and noted brilliancy of the author. Durkheim errs in denying the savage the ability to differentiate between the natural and the supernatural, and in denying nature the power to cause the religious thrill; he errs in accepting a mongrel definition of religion and in regarding the dichotomy of experience into sacred and profane as a psychologically univocal determination of all religion; he errs in identifying primitive religion with totemism and the "totemic principle" with mana; he errs, finally, in claiming for mana, and its emotional concomitant, the religious thrill, an exclusively crowd-psychological origin.

Thus Durkheim does not succeed in furnishing a satisfactory solution of either of the two problems which stand in the center of his interest: the relation of individual to social experience and the interpretation of the nature and origin of the religious sentiment. Sharp as is the author's wit and brilliant as is his argumentation, one closes the book with a melancholy assurance that Durkheim has left these two perennial problems where he found them.

ROBERT N. BELLAH

Religious Evolution

In recent years little intellectual effort has been devoted to the construction of an evolutionary interpretation of religion. This sophisticated new article by Bellah, much of which emerged from a seminar given together with Talcott Parsons and S. N. Eisenstadt, is not only almost unique, but courageous as well. Cautiously assuming that contemporary preliterates and their religions represent earlier phases, and utilizing historical materials, Bellah proposes a sequence of five ideal typical stages of development: primitive, archaic, historic, early modern, and modern. He examines each of these states in terms of their religious symbol systems, religious actions, religious organizations, and social implications. Basically, he is interested in demonstrating that religious symbol systems have evolved from compact to complex ones; that religious collectivities have become increasingly differentiated from other social structures; and that consciousness of the self as a religious subject develops increasingly after its emergence in the historic stage. He is careful, however, to indicate that his stages are not inevitable, that there is a wide variety of types within each stage, and that actual cases present important features which cannot be neatly characterized in terms of any one stage.

Anticipated here to some extent is the interpretation of symbolism contained in Chapter 4, especially in the article by Geertz. Thus, Bellah views religion as symbolizing one's identity as well as concerning itself with imaging the ultimate conditions of man's existence.

There are of course other ways of looking at the broad sweep of change in religion, as Bellah explicitly reminds us. More conventional efforts at describing religious trends in industrial societies have stressed the diminishing importance of belief in the supernatural in the face of scientific advances and the intensification of the moral aspects of religious systems. But in our judgment, Bellah moves well beyond this simple generalization and formulates some propositions about religious evolution that will provoke controversy but will also stimulate further thinking and research along productive lines.

Reprinted from *American Sociological Review*, XXIX (1964), 358–374, by permission of the American Sociological Association and the author.

Time in its aging course teaches all things.
—Aeschylus: *Prometheus Bound*

Though one can name precursors as far back as Herodotus, the systematically scientific study of religions begins only in the second half of the 19th century. According to Chantepie de la Saussaye, the two preconditions for this emergence were that religion had become by the time of Hegel the object of comprehensive philosophical speculation and that history by the time of Buckle had been enlarged to include the history of civilization and culture in general. In its early phases, partly under the influence of Darwinism, the science of religion was dominated by an evolutionary tendency already implicit in Hegelian philosophy and early 19th century historiography. The grandfathers of modern sociology, Comte and Spencer, contributed to the strongly evolutionary approach to the study of religion as, with many reservations, did Durkheim and Weber.

But by the third decade of the 20th century the evolutionary wave was in full retreat both in the general field of science of religion and in the sociology of religion in particular. Of course, this was only one aspect of the general retreat of evolutionary thought in social science, but nowhere did the retreat go further nor the intensity of the opposition to evolution go deeper than in the field of religion. An attempt to explain the vicissitudes of evolutionary conceptions in the field of religion would be an interesting study in the sociology of knowledge but beyond the scope of this brief paper. Here I can only say that I hope that the present attempt to apply the evolutionary idea to religion evidences a serious appreciation of both 19th century evolutionary theories and 20th century criticisms of them.

Evolution at any system level I define as a process of increasing differentiation and complexity of organization which endows the organism, social system or whatever the unit in question may be, with greater capacity to adapt to its environment so that it is in some sense more autonomous relative to its environment than were its less complex ancestors. I do not assume that evolution is inevitable, irreversible or must follow any single particular course. Nor do I assume that simpler forms cannot prosper and survive alongside more complex forms. What I mean by evolution, then, is nothing metaphysical but the simple empirical generalization that more complex forms develop from less complex forms and that the properties and possibilities of more complex forms differ from those of less complex forms.

A brief handy definition of religion is considerably more difficult than a definition of evolution. An attempt at an adequate definition would, as Clifford Geertz has recently demonstrated, take a paper in itself for adequate explanation. So, for limited purposes only, let me define religion as a set of symbolic forms and acts which relate man to the ultimate conditions of his existence. The purpose of this definition is to indicate exactly what I claim has evolved. It is not the ultimate conditions, nor, in traditional language, God that has evolved, nor is it man in the broadest sense of *homo religiosus*. I am inclined to agree with Eliade when he holds that primitive man is as fully religious as man at any stage of existence, though I am not ready to go along with him when he implies *more* fully.

Neither religious man nor the structure of man's ultimate religious situation evolves, then, but rather religion as symbol system. Erich Voegelin, who I suspect shares Eliade's basic philosophical position, speaks of a development from compact to differentiated symbolization. Everything already exists in some sense in the religious symbol system of the most primitive man; it would be hard to find anything later that is not "foreshadowed" there, as for example, the monotheistic God is foreshadowed in the high gods of some primitive peoples. Yet just as obviously the two cannot be equated. Not only in their idea of God but in many other ways the monotheistic religions of Judaism, Christianity and Islam involve a much more differentiated symbolization of, and produce a much more complex relation to, the ultimate conditions of human existence than do primitive religions. At least the existence of that kind of difference is the thesis I wish to develop. I hope it is clear that there are a number of other possible meanings of the term "religious evolution" with which I am not concerned. I hope it is also clear that a complex and differentiated religious symbolization is not therefore a better or a truer or a more beautiful one than a compact religious symbolization. I am not a relativist and I do think judgments of value can reasonably be made between religions, societies or personalities. But the axis of that judgment is not provided by social evolution and if progress is used in an essentially ethical sense, then I for one will not speak of religious progress.

Having defined the ground rules under which I am operating let me now step back from the subject of religious evolution and look first at a few of the massive facts of human religious history. The first of these facts is the emergence in the first millennium B.C. all across the Old World, at least in centers of high cuture, of the phenomenon of religious rejection of the world characterized by an extremely negative evaluation of man and society and the exaltation of another realm of reality as alone true and infinitely valuable. This theme emerges in Greece through a long development into Plato's classic formulation in the Phaedo that the body is the tomb or prison of the soul and that only by disentanglement from the body and all things worldly can the soul unify itself with the unimaginably different world of the divine. A very different formulation is found in Israel, but there too the world is profoundly devalued in the face of the transcendent God with whom alone is there any refuge or comfort. In India we find perhaps the most radical of all versions of world rejection, culminating in the great image of the Buddha, that the world is a burning house and man's urgent need is a way to escape from it. In China, Taoist ascetics urged the transvaluation of all the accepted values and withdrawal from human society, which they condemned as unnatural and perverse.

Nor was this a brief or passing phenomenon. For over 2000 years great pulses of world rejection spread over the civilized world. The *Qur'an* compares this present world to vegetation after rain, whose growth rejoices the unbeliever, but it quickly withers away and becomes as straw. Men prefer life in the present world but the life to come is infinitely superior—it alone is everlasting. Even in Japan, usually so innocently world accepting, Shōtoku Taishi declared that the world is a lie and only the Buddha is true, and in the Kamakura period the conviction that the world is hell led to orgies of religious suicide by seekers after Amida's paradise. And it is hardly necessary to quote Revelations or Augustine for comparable Christian sentiments. I do not deny that there are profound differences among these various rejections of the world; Max Weber has written a great essay on the different directions of world rejection and their consequences for human action. But for the moment I want to concentrate on the fact that they were all in some sense rejections and that world rejection is characteristic of a long and important period of religious history. I want to insist on this fact because I want to contrast it with an equally striking fact—namely the virtual absence of world rejection in primitive religions, in religion prior to the first millennium B.C., and in the modern world.

Primitive religions are on the whole oriented to a single cosmos—they know nothing of a wholly different world relative to which the actual world is utterly devoid of value. They are concerned with the maintenance of personal, social and cosmic harmony and with attaining specific goods— rain, harvest, children, health—as men have always been. But the overriding goal of salvation that dominates the world rejecting religions is almost absent in primitive religion,

and life after death tends to be a shadowy semi-existence in some vaguely designated place in the single world.

World rejection is no more characteristic of the modern world than it is of primitive religion. Not only in the United States but through much of Asia there is at the moment something of a religious revival, but nowhere is this associated with a great new outburst of world rejection. In Asia apologists, even for religions with a long tradition of world rejection, are much more interested in showing the compatibility of their religions with the developing modern world than in totally rejecting it. And it is hardly necessary to point out that the American religious revival stems from motives quite opposite to world rejection.

One could attempt to account for this sequence of presence and absence of world rejection as a dominant religious theme without ever raising the issue of religious evolution, but I think I can account for these and many other facts of the historical development of religion in terms of a scheme of religious evolution. An extended rationale for the scheme and its broad empirical application must await publication in book form. Here all I can attempt is a very condensed overview.

The scheme is based on several presuppositions, the most basic of which I have already referred to: namely, that religious symbolization of what Geertz calls "the general order of existence" tends to change over time, at least in some instances, in the direction of more differentiated, comprehensive, and in Weber's sense, more rationalized formulations. A second assumption is that conceptions of religious action, of the nature of the religious actor, of religious organization and of the place of religion in the society tend to change in ways systematically related to the changes in symbolization. A third assumption is that these several changes in the sphere of religion, which constitute what I mean by religious evolution, are related to a variety of other dimensions of change in other social spheres which define the general process of sociocultural evolution.

Now, for heuristic purposes at least, it is also useful to assume a series of stages which may be regarded as relatively stable crystallizations of roughly the same order of complexity along a number of different dimensions. I shall use five stages which, for want of better terminology, I shall call primitive, archaic, historic, early modern and modern. These stages are ideal types derived from a theoretical formulation of the most generally observable historical regularities; they are meant to have a temporal reference but only in a very general sense.

Of course the scheme itself is not intended as an adequate description of historical reality. Particular lines of religious development cannot simply be forced into the terms of the scheme. In reality there may be compromise formations involving elements from two stages which I have for theoretical reasons discriminated; earlier stages may, as I have already suggested, strikingly foreshadow later developments; and more developed may regress to less developed stages. And of course no stage is ever completely abandoned; all earlier stages continue to coexist with and often within later ones. So what I shall present is not intended as a procrustean bed into which the facts of history are to be forced but a theoretical construction against which historical facts may be illuminated. The logic is much the same as that involved in conceptualizing stages of the life cycle in personality development.

PRIMITIVE RELIGION

Before turning to the specific features of primitive religion let us go back to the definition of religion as a set of symbolic forms and acts relating man to the ultimate conditions of his existence. Lienhardt, in his book on Dinka religion, spells out this process of symbolization in a most interesting way:

I have suggested that the Powers may be understood as images corresponding to complex and various combinations of Dinka experience which are contingent upon their particular social and physical environment. For the Dinka they are the grounds of those experiences; in our analysis we have shown them to be grounded in them, for to a European the experiences are more readily understood than the Powers, and the existence of the latter cannot be posited as a condition of the former. Without these Powers or images or an alternative to them there would be for the Dinka no differentiation between experience of the self and of the world which acts upon it. Suffering, for example, could be merely "lived" or endured. With the imaging of the grounds of suffering in a particular Power, the Dinka can grasp its na-

ture intellectually in a way which satisfies them, and thus to some extent transcend and dominate it in this act of knowledge. With this knowledge, this separation of a subject and an object in experience, there arises for them also the possibility of creating a form of experience they desire, and of freeing themselves symbolically from what they must otherwise passively endure.

If we take this as a description of religious symbolization in general, and I think we can, then it is clear that in terms of the conception of evolution used here the existence of even the simplest religion is an evolutionary advance. Animals or pre-religious men could only "passively endure" suffering or other limitations imposed by the conditions of their existence, but religious man can to some extent "transcend and dominate" them through his capacity for symbolization and thus attain a degree of freedom relative to his environment that was not previously possible.

Now though Lienhardt points out that the Dinka religious images make possible a "differentiation between experience of the self and of the world which acts upon it" he also points out earlier that the Dinka lack anything closely resembling our conception of the " 'mind,' as mediating and, as it were, storing up the experiences of the self." In fact, aspects of what we would attribute to the self are "imaged" among the divine Powers. Again if Lienhardt is describing something rather general, and I think there is every reason to believe he is, then religious symbolization relating man to the ultimate conditions of his existence is also involved in relating him to himself and in symbolizing his own identity.

Granted then that religious symbolization is concerned with imaging the ultimate conditions of existence, whether external or internal, we should examine at each stage the kind of symbol system involved, the kind of religious action it stimulates, the kind of social organization in which this religious action occurs and the implications for social action in general that the religious action contains.

Marcel Mauss, criticizing the heterogeneous sources from which Lévy-Bruhl had constructed the notion of primitive thought, suggested that the word primitive be restricted to Australia, which was the only major culture area largely unaffected by the neolithic. That was in 1923. In 1935 Lévy-Bruhl, heeding Mauss's stricture, published a book called *La Mythologie Primitive* in which the data are drawn almost exclusively from Australia and immediately adjacent islands. While Lévy-Bruhl finds material similar to his Australian data in all parts of the world, nowhere else does he find it in as pure a form. The differences between the Australian material and that of other areas are so great that Lévy-Bruhl is tempted to disagree with Durkheim that Australian religion is an elementary form of religion and term it rather "pre-religion," a temptation which for reasons already indicated I would firmly reject. At any rate, W. E. H. Stanner, by far the most brilliant interpreter of Australian religion in recent years, goes far to confirm the main lines of Lévy-Bruhl's position, without committing himself on the more broadly controversial aspects of the assertions of either Mauss or Lévy-Bruhl (indeed without so much as mentioning them). My description of a primitive stage of religion is a theoretical abstraction, but it is heavily indebted to the work of Lévy-Bruhl and Stanner for its main features.

The *religious symbol system* at the primitive level is characterized by Lévy-Bruhl as *"le monde mythique,"* and Stanner directly translates the Australians' own word for it as "the Dreaming." The Dreaming is a time out of time, or in Stanner's words, "everywhen," inhabited by ancestral figures, some human, some animal. Though they are often of heroic proportions and have capacities beyond those of ordinary men as well as being the progenitors and creators of many particular things in the world, they are not gods, for they do not control the world and are not worshipped.

Two main features of this mythical world of primitive religion are important for the purposes of the present theoretical scheme. The first is the very high degree to which the mythical world is related to the detailed features of the actual world. Not only is every clan and local group defined in terms of the ancestral progenitors and the mythical events of settlement, but virtually every mountain, rock and tree is explained in terms of the actions of mythical beings. All human action is prefigured in the Dreaming, including crimes and folly, so that actual existence and the paradigmatic myths are related in the most intimate possible way. The

second main feature, not unrelated to the extreme particularity of the mythical material, is the fluidity of its organization. Lienhardt, though describing a religion of a somewhat different type, catches the essentially free-associational nature of primitive myth when he says, "We meet here the typical lack of precise definition of the Dinka when they speak of divinities. As Garang, which is the name of the first man, is sometimes associated with the first man and sometimes said to be quite different, so Deng may in some sense be associated with anyone called Deng, and the Dinka connect or do not connect usages of the same name in different contexts according to their individual lights and to what they consider appropriate at any given moment." The fluid structure of the myth is almost consciously indicated by the Australians in their use of the word Dreaming: this is not purely metaphorical, for as Ronald Berndt has shown in a careful study, men do actually have a propensity to dream during the periods of cult performance. Through the dreams they reshape the cult symbolism for private psychic ends and what is even more interesting, dreams may actually lead to a reinterpretation in myth which in turn causes a ritual innovation. Both the particularity and the fluidity, then, help account for the hovering closeness of the world of myth to the actual world. A sense of gap, that things are not all they might be, is there but it is hardly experienced as tragic and is indeed on the verge of being comic.

Primitive *religious action* is characterized not, as we have said, by worship, nor, as we shall see, by sacrifice, but by identification, "participation," acting-out. Just as the primitive symbol system is myth *par excellence,* so primitive religious action is ritual *par excellence.* In the ritual the participants become identified with the mythical beings they represent. The mythical beings are not addressed or propitiated or beseeched. The distance between man and mythical being, which was at best slight, disappears altogether in the moment of ritual when everywhen becomes now. There are no priests and no congregation, no mediating representative roles and no spectators. All present are involved in the ritual action itself and have become one with the myth.

The underlying structure of ritual, which in Australia always has themes related to initiation, is remarkably similar to that of sacrifice. The four basic movements of the ritual as analyzed by Stanner are offering, destruction, transformation, and return-communion. Through acting out the mistakes and sufferings of the paradigmatic mythical hero, the new initiates come to terms symbolically with, again in Stanner's words, the "immemorial misdirection" of human life. Their former innocence is destroyed and they are transformed into new identities now more able to "assent to life, as it is, without morbidity." In a sense the whole gamut of the spiritual life is already visible in the Australian ritual. Yet the symbolism is so compact that there is almost no element of choice, will or responsibility. The religious life is as given and as fixed as the routines of daily living.

At the primitive level *religious organization* as a separate social structure does not exist. Church and society are one. Religious roles tend to be fused with other roles, and differentiations along lines of age, sex and kin group are important. While women are not as excluded from the religious life as male ethnographers once believed, their ritual life is to some degree separate and focused on particularly feminine life crises. In most primitive societies age is an important criterion for leadership in the ceremonial life. Ceremonies are often handed down in particular moieties and clans, as is only natural when the myths are so largely concerned with ancestors. Specialized shamans or medicine men are found in some tribes but are not a necessary feature of primitive religion.

As for the *social implications* of primitive religion, Durkheim's analysis seems still to be largely acceptable. The ritual life does reinforce the solidarity of the society and serves to induct the young into the norms of tribal behavior. We should not forget the innovative aspects of primitive religion, that particular myths and ceremonies are in a process of constant revision and alteration, and that in the face of severe historic crisis rather remarkable reformulations of primitive material can be made. Yet on the whole the religious life is the strongest reinforcement of the basic tenet of Australian philosophy, namely that life, as Stanner puts it, is a "one possibility thing." The very fluidity and flexibility of primitive religion is a barrier to radical innovation. Primitive religion gives little leverage from which to change the world.

ARCHAIC RELIGION

For purposes of the present conceptual scheme, as I have indicated, I am using primitive religion in an unusually restricted sense. Much that is usually classified as primitive religion would fall in my second category, archaic religion, which includes the religious systems of much of Africa and Polynesia and some of the New World, as well as the earliest religious systems of the ancient Middle East, India and China. The characteristic feature of archaic religion is the emergence of true cult with the complex of gods, priests, worship, sacrifice and in some cases divine or priestly kingship. The myth and ritual complex characteristic of primitive religion continues within the structure of archaic religion, but it is systematized and elaborated in new ways.

In the archaic *religious symbol system* mythical beings are much more definitely characterized. Instead of being great paradigmatic figures with whom men in ritual identify but with whom they do not really interact, the mythical beings are more objectified, conceived as actively and sometimes willfully controlling the natural and human world, and as beings with whom men must deal in a definite and purposive way—in a word they have become gods. Relations among the gods are a matter of considerable speculation and systematization, so that definite principles of organization, especially hierarchies of control, are established. The basic world view is still, like the primitives', monistic. There is still only one world with gods dominating particular parts of it, especially important being the high gods of the heavenly regions whose vision, knowledge and power may be conceived as very extensive indeed. But though the world is one it is far more differentiated, especially in a hierarchical way, than was the monistic world view of the primitives: archaic religions tend to elaborate a vast cosmology in which all things divine and natural have a place. Much of the particularity and fluidity characteristic of primitive myth is still to be found in archaic religious thinking. But where priestly roles have become well established a relatively stable symbolic structure may be worked out and transmitted over an extended period of time. Especially where at least craft literacy has been attained, the mythical tradition may become the object of critical reflection and innovative speculation which can lead to new developments beyond the nature of archaic religion.

Archaic *religious action* takes the form of cult in which the distinction between men as subjects and gods as objects is much more definite than in primitive religion. Because the division is sharper the need for a communication system through which gods and men can interact is much more acute. Worship and especially sacrifice are precisely such communication systems, as Henri Hubert and Marcel Mauss so brilliantly established in their great essay on sacrifice. There is no space here for a technical analysis of the sacrificial process; suffice it to say that a double identification of priest and victim with both gods and men effects a transformation of motives comparable to that referred to in the discussion of primitive religious action. The main difference is that instead of a relatively passive identification in an all-encompassing ritual action, the sacrificial process, no matter how stereotyped, permits the human communicants a greater element of intentionality and entails more uncertainty relative to the divine response. Through this more differentiated form of religious action a new degree of freedom as well, perhaps, as an increased burden of anxiety enters the relations between man and the ultimate conditions of his existence.

Archaic *religious organization* is still by and large merged with other social structures, but the proliferation of functionally and hierarchically differentiated groups leads to a mulitiplication of cults, since every group in archaic society tends to have its cultic aspect. The emergence of a two-class system, itself related to the increasing density of population made possible by agriculture, has its religious aspect. The upper-status group, which tends to monopolize political and military power, usually claims a superior religious status as well. Noble families are proud of their divine descent and often have special priestly functions. The divine king who is the chief link between his people and the gods is only the extreme case of the general tendency of archaic societies. Specialized priesthoods attached to cult centers may differentiate out but are usually kept subordinate to the political elite, which

at this stage never completely divests itself of religious leadership. Occasionally priesthoods at cult centers located interstitially relative to political units—for example, Delphi in ancient Greece—may come to exercise a certain independence.

The most significant limitation on archaic religious organization is the failure to develop differentiated religious collectivities including adherents as well as priests. The cult centers provide facilities for sacrifice and worship to an essentially transient clientele which is not itself organized as a collectivity, even though the priesthood itself may be rather tightly organized. The appearance of mystery cults and related religious confraternities in the ancient world is usually related to a reorganization of the religious symbol and action systems which indicates a transition to the next main type of religious structure.

The *social implications* of archaic religion are to some extent similar to those of primitive religion. The individual and his society are seen as merged in a natural-divine cosmos. Traditional social structures and social practices are considered to be grounded in the divinely instituted cosmic order and there is little tension between religious demand and social conformity. Indeed, social conformity is at every point reinforced with religious sanction. Nevertheless the very notion of well characterized gods acting over against men with a certain freedom introduces an element of openness that is less apparent at the primitive level. The struggle between rival groups may be interpreted as the struggle between rival deities or as a deity's change of favor from one group to another. Through the problems posed by religious rationalization of political change new modes of religious thinking may open up. This is clearly an important aspect of the early history of Israel, and it occurred in many other cases as well. The Greek preoccupation with the relation of the gods to the events of the Trojan War gave rise to a continuous deepening of religious thought from Homer to Euripides. In ancient China the attempt of the Chou to rationalize their conquest of the Shang led to an entirely new conception of the relation between human merit and divine favor. The breakdown of internal order led to messianic expectations of the coming of a savior king in such distant areas as Egypt on the one hand and Chou-period China on the other. These are but a few of the ways in which the problems of maintaining archaic religious symbolization in increasingly complex societies drove toward solutions that began to place the archaic pattern itself in jeopardy.

HISTORIC RELIGION

The next stage in this theoretical scheme is called historic simply because the religions included are all relatively recent; they emerged in societies that were more or less literate and so have fallen chiefly under the discipline of history rather than that of archaeology or ethnography. The criterion that distinguishes the historic religions from the archaic is that the historic religions are all in some sense transcendental. The cosmological monism of the earlier stage is now more or less completely broken through and an entirely different realm of universal reality, having for religious man the highest value, is proclaimed. The discovery of an entirely different realm of religious reality seems to imply a derogation of the value of the given empirical cosmos: at any rate the world rejection discussed above is, in this stage for the first time, a general characteristic of the religious system.

The *symbol systems* of the historic religions differ greatly among themselves but share the element of transcendentalism which sets them off from the archaic religions; in this sense they are all dualistic. The strong emphasis on hierarchical ordering characteristic of archaic religions continues to be stessed in most of the historic religions. Not only is the supernatural realm "above" this world in terms of both value and control but both the supernatural and earthly worlds are themselves organized in terms of a religiously legitimated hierarchy. For the masses, at least, the new dualism is above all expressed in the difference between this world and the life after death. Religious concern, focused on this life in primitive and archaic religions, now tends to focus on life in the other realm, which may be either infinitely superior or, under certain circumstances, with the emergence of various conceptions of hell, infinitely worse. Under these circumstances the religious goal of salvation (or enlightenment, release and so forth) is for the first time the central religious preoccupation.

In one sense historic religions represent a great "demythologization" relative to archaic religions. The notion of the one God who has neither court nor relatives, who has no myth himself and who is the sole creator and ruler of the universe, the notion of self subsistent being, or of release from the cycle of birth and rebirth, are all enormous simplifications of the ramified cosmologies of archaic religions. Yet all the historic religions have, to use Voegelin's term, mortgages imposed on them by the historical circumstances of their origin. All of them contain, in suspension as it were, elements of archaic cosmology alongside their transcendental assertions. Nonetheless, relative to earlier forms the historic religions are all universalistic. From the point of view of these religions a man is no longer defined chiefly in terms of what tribe or clan he comes from or what particular god he serves but rather as a being capable of salvation. That is to say that it is for the first time possible to conceive of man as such.

Religious action in the historic religions is thus above all action necessary for salvation. Even where elements of ritual and sacrifice remain prominent they take on a new significance. In primitive ritual the individual is put in harmony with the natural divine cosmos. His mistakes are overcome through symbolization as part of the total pattern. Through sacrifice archaic man can make up for his failures to fulfill his obligations to men or gods. He can atone for particular acts of unfaithfulness. But historic religion convicts man of a basic flaw far more serious than those conceived of by earlier religions. According to Buddhism, man's very nature is greed and anger from which he must seek a total escape. For the Hebrew prophets, man's sin is not particular wicked deeds but his profound heedlessness of God, and only a turn to complete obedience will be acceptable to the Lord. For Muhammad the *kafir* is not, as we usually translate, the "unbeliever" but rather the ungrateful man who is careless of the divine compassion. For him, only Islam, willing submission to the will of God, can bring salvation.

The identity diffusion characteristic of both primitive and archaic religions is radically challenged by the historic religious symbolization, which leads for the first time to a clearly structured conception of the self. Devaluation of the empirical world and the empirical self highlights the conception of a responsible self, a core self or a true self, deeper than the flux of everyday experience, facing a reality over against itself, a reality which has a consistency belied by the fluctuations of mere sensory impressions. Primitive man can only accept the world in its manifold givenness. Archaic man can through sacrifice fulfill his religious obligations and attain peace with the gods. But the historic religions promise man for the first time that he can understand the fundamental structure of reality and through salvation participate actively in it. The opportunity is far greater than before but so is the risk of failure.

Perhaps partly because of the profound risks involved the ideal of the religious life in the historic religions tends to be one of separation from the world. Even when, as in the case of Judaism and Islam, the religion enjoins types of worldly participation that are considered unacceptable or at least doubtful in some other historic religions, the devout are still set apart from ordinary worldlings by the massive collections of rules and obligations to which they must adhere. The early Christian solution, which, unlike the Buddhist, did allow the full possibility of salvation to the layman, nevertheless in its notion of a special state of religious perfection idealized religious withdrawal from the world. In fact the standard for lay piety tended to be closeness of approximation to the life of the religious.

Historic religion is associated with the emergence of differentiated religious collectivities as the chief characteristic of its *religious organization*. The profound dualism with respect to the conception of reality is also expressed in the social realm. The single religio-political hierarchy of archaic society tends to split into two at least partially independent hierarchies, one political and one religious. Together with the notion of a transcendent realm beyond the natural cosmos comes a new religious elite that claims direct relation to the transmundane world. Even though notions of divine kingship linger on for a very long time in various compromise forms, it is no longer possible for a divine king to monopolize religious leadership. With the emergence of a religious elite alongside the political one the problem of legitimizing political power enters a new phase. Legitimation now rests

upon a delicate balance of forces between the political and religious leadership. But the differentiation between religious and political that exists most clearly at the level of leadership tends also to be pushed down into the masses so that the roles of believer and subject become distinct. Even where, as in the case of Islam, this distinction was not supported by religious norms, it was soon recognized as an actuality.

The emergence of the historic religions is part of a general shift from the two-class system of the archaic period to the four-class system characteristic of all the great historic civilizations up to modern times: a political-military elite, a cultural-religious elite, a rural lower-status group (peasantry) and an urban lower-status group (merchants and artisans). Closely associated with the new religious developments was the growth of literacy among the elite groups and in the upper segments of the urban lower class. Other social changes, such as the growth in the market resulting from the first widespread use of coinage, the development of bureaucracy and law as well as new levels of urbanization, are less directly associated with religion but are part of the same great transformation that got underway in the first millennium B.C. The distinction between religious and political elites applies to some extent to the two great lower strata. From the point of view of the historic religions the peasantry long remained relatively intractable and were often considered religiously second-class citizens, their predilection for cosmological symbolization rendering them always to some degree religiously suspect. The notion of the peasant as truly religious is a fairly modern idea. On the contrary it was the townsman who was much more likely to be numbered among the devout, and Max Weber has pointed out the great fecundity of the urban middle strata in religious innovations throughout the several great historical traditions. Such groups developed new symbolizations that sometimes threatened the structure of the historic religions in their early form, and in the one case where a new stage of religious symbolization was finally achieved they made important contributions.

The *social implications* of the historic religions are implicit in the remarks on religious organization. The differentiation of a religious elite brought a new level of tension and a new possibility of conflict and change onto the social scene. Whether the confrontation was between Israelite prophet and king, Islamic ulama and sultan, Christian pope and emperor or even between Confucian scholar-official and his ruler, it implied that political acts could be judged in terms of standards that the political authorities could not finally control. The degree to which these confrontations had serious social consequences of course depended on the degree to which the religious group was structurally independent and could exert real pressure. S. N. Eisenstadt has made a comprehensive survey of these differences; for our purposes it is enough to note that they were nowhere entirely absent. Religion, then, provided the ideology and social cohesion for many rebellions and reform movements in the historic civilizations, and consequently played a more dynamic and especially a more purposive role in social change than had previously been possible. On the other hand, we should not forget that in most of the historic civilizations for long periods of time religion performed the functions we have noted from the beginning: legitimation and reinforcement of the existing social order.

EARLY MODERN RELIGION

In all previous stages the ideal type was based on a variety of actual cases. Now for the first time it derives from a single case or at best a congeries of related cases, namely, the Protestant Reformation. The defining characteristic of early modern religion is the collapse of the hierarchical structuring of both this and the other world. The dualism of the historic religions remains as a feature of early modern religion but takes on a new significance in the context of more direct confrontation between the two worlds. Under the new circumstances salvation is not to be found in any kind of withdrawal from the world but in the midst of worldly activities. Of course elements of this existed in the historic religions from the beginning, but on the whole the historic religions as institutionalized had offered a mediated salvation. Either conformity to religious law, or participation in a sacramental system or performance of mystical exercises was necessary for salvation. All of these to some extent involved a turning away from the world. Further, in

the religious two-class systems characteristic of the institutionalized historic religions the upper-status groups, the Christian monks or Sufi shaykhs or Buddhist ascetics, could through their pure acts and personal charisma store up a fund of grace that could then be shared with the less worthy. In this way too salvation was mediated rather than immediate. What the Reformation did was in principle, with the usual reservations and mortgages to the past, break through the whole mediated system of salvation and declare salvation potentially available to any man no matter what his station or calling might be.

Since immediate salvation seems implicit in all the historic religions it is not surprising that similar reform movements exist in other traditions, notably Shinran Shonin's version of Pure Land Buddhism but also certain tendencies in Islam, Buddhism, Taoism and Confucianism. But the Protestant Reformation is the only attempt that was successfully institutionalized. In the case of Taoism and Confucianism the mortgage of archaic symbolization was so heavy that what seemed a new breakthrough easily became regressive. In the other cases, notably in the case of the Jōdo Shinshū, the radical implications were not sustained and a religion of mediated salvation soon reasserted itself. Religious movements of early modern type may be emerging in a number of the great traditions today, perhaps even in the Vatican Council, and there are also secular movements with features strongly analogous to what I call early modern religion. But all of these tendencies are too uncertain to rely on in constructing an ideal type.

Early modern *religious symbolism* concentrates on the direct relation between the individual and transcendent reality. A great deal of the cosmological baggage of medieval Christianity is dropped as superstitition. The fundamentally ritualist interpretation of the sacrament of the Eucharist as a re-enactment of the paradigmatic sacrifice is replaced with the anti-ritualist interpretation of the Eucharist as a commemoration of a once-and-for-all historical event. Even though in one sense the world is more devalued in early Protestantism than in medieval Christianity, since the reformers re-emphasized the radical separation between divine and human, still by proclaiming the world as the theater of God's glory and the place wherein to fulfill his command, the Reformation reinforced positive autonomous action in the world instead of a relatively passive acceptance of it.

Religious action was now conceived to be identical with the whole of life. Special ascetic and devotional practices were dropped as well as the monastic roles that specialized in them and instead the service of God became a total demand in every walk of life. The stress was on faith, an internal quality of the person, rather than on particular acts clearly marked "religious." In this respect the process of identity unification that I have designated as a central feature of the historic religions advanced still further. The complex requirements for the attainment of salvation in the historic religions, though ideally they encouraged identity unification, could themselves become a new form of identity diffusion, as Luther and Shinran were aware. Assertion of the capacity for faith as an already received gift made it possible to undercut that difficulty. It also made it necessary to accept the ambiguity of human ethical life and the fact that salvation comes in spite of sin, not in its absolute absence. With the acceptance of the world not as it is but as a valid arena in which to work out the divine command, and with the acceptance of the self as capable of faith in spite of sin, the Reformation made it possible to turn away from world rejection in a way not possible in the historic religions. All of this was possible, however, only within the structure of a rigid orthodoxy and a tight though voluntaristic religious group.

I have already noted that early modern religion abandoned hierarchy as an essential dimension of its religious symbol system. It did the same in its *religious organization*. Not only did it reject papal authority, but it also rejected the old form of the religious distinction between two levels of relative religious perfection. This was replaced with a new kind of religious two-class system: the division between elect and reprobates. The new form differed from the old one in that the elect were really a vanguard group in the fulfillment of the divine plan rather than a qualitative religious elite. The political implications of Protestantism had much to do with the overthrow of the old conception of hierarchy in the secular field as well. Where Calvinistic Protestantism was powerful,

hereditary aristocracy and kingship were either greatly weakened or abandoned. In fact the Reformation is part of the general process of social change in which the four-class system of peasant societies began to break up in Europe. Especially in the Anglo-Saxon world, Protestantism greatly contributed to its replacement by a more flexible multi-centered mode of social organization based more on contract and voluntary association. Both church and state lost some of the reified significance they had in medieval times and later on the continent. The roles of church member and citizen were but two among several. Both church and state had their delimited spheres of authority, but with the full institutionalization of the common law neither had a right to dominate each other or the whole of society. Nonetheless, the church acted for a long time as a sort of cultural and ethical holding company, and many developments in philosophy, literature and social welfare took their initiative from clerical or church groups.

The *social implications* of the Protestant Reformation are among the more debated subjects of contemporary social science. Lacking space to defend my assertions, let me simply say that I stand with Weber, Merton, *et al.,* in attributing very great significance to the Reformation, especially in its Calvinistic wing, in a whole series of developments from economics to science, from education to law. Whereas in most of the historic civilizations religion stands as virtually the only stable challenger to the dominance of the political elite, in the emerging early modern society religious impulses give rise to a variety of institutional structures, from the beginning or very soon becoming fully secular, which stand beside and to some extent compete with and limit the state. The direct religious response to political and moral problems does not disappear but the impact of religious orientations on society is also mediated by a variety of worldly institutions in which religious values have been expressed. Weber's critics, frequently assuming a pre-modern model of the relation between religion and society, have often failed to understand the subtle interconnections he was tracing. But the contrast with the historic stage, when pressures toward social change in the direction of value realization were sporadic and often utopian, is decisive.

In the early modern stage for the first time pressures to social change in the direction of greater realization of religious values are actually institutionalized as part of the structure of the society itself. The self-revising social order expressed in a voluntaristic and democratic society can be seen as just such an outcome. The earliest phase of this development, especially the several examples of Calvinist commonwealths, was voluntaristic only within the elect vanguard group and otherwise was often illiberal and even dictatorial. The transition toward a more completely democratic society was complex and subject to many blockages. Close analogies to the early modern situation occur in many of the contemporary developing countries, which are trying for the first time to construct social systems with a built-in tendency to change in the direction of greater value realization. The leadership of these countries varies widely between several kinds of vanguard revolutionary movements with distinctly illiberal proclivities to elites committed to the implementation of a later, more democratic, model of Western political society.

MODERN RELIGION

I am not sure whether in the long run what I call early modern religion will appear as a stage with the same degree of distinctness as the others I have distinguished or whether it will appear only as a transitional phase, but I am reasonably sure that, even though we must speak from the midst of it, the modern situation represents a stage of religious development in many ways profoundly different from that of historic religion. The central feature of the change is the collapse of the dualism that was so crucial to all the historic religions.

It is difficult to speak of a *modern religious symbol system*. It is indeed an open question whether there can be a religious symbol system analogous to any of the preceding ones in the modern situation, which is characterized by a deepening analysis of the very nature of symbolization itself. At the highest intellectual level I would trace the fundamental break with traditional historic symbolization to the work of Kant. By revealing the problematic nature of the traditional metaphysical basis of all the religions and by indicating that it is not so much a

question of two worlds as it is of as many worlds as there are modes of apprehending them, he placed the whole religious problem in a new light. However simple the immediate result of his grounding religion in the structure of ethical life rather than in a metaphysics claiming cognitive adequacy, it nonetheless pointed decisively in the direction that modern religion would go. The entire modern analysis of religion, including much of the most important recent theology, though rejecting Kant's narrowly rational ethics, has been forced to ground religion in the structure of the human situation itself. In this respect the present paper is a symptom of the modern religious situation as well as an analysis of it. In the world view that has emerged from the tremendous intellectual advances of the last two centuries there is simply no room for a hierarchic dualistic religious symbol system of the classical historic type. This is not to be interpreted as a return to primitive monism: it is not that a single world has replaced a double one but that an infinitely multiplex one has replaced the simple duplex structure. It is not that life has become again a "one possibility thing" but that it has become an infinite possibility thing. The analysis of modern man as secular, materialistic, dehumanized and in the deepest sense areligious seems to me fundamentally misguided, for such a judgment is based on standards that cannot adequately gauge the modern temper.

Though it is central to the problems of modern religion, space forbids a review of the development of the modern analysis of religion on its scholarly and scientific side. I shall confine myself to some brief comments on directions of development within Protestant theology. In many respects Schliermacher is the key figure in early 19th century theology who saw the deeper implications of the Kantian breakthrough. The development of "liberal theology" in the later 19th century, partly on the basis of Schliermacher's beginnings, tended to fall back into Kant's overly rational limitations. Against this, Barth's reassertion of the power of the traditional symbolism was bound to produce a vigorous response, but unfortunately, due to Barth's own profound ambiguity on the ultimate status of dogma, the consequences were in part simply a regressive reassertion of the adequacy of the early modern theological formulation. By the middle of the

20th century, however, the deeper implications of Schliermacher's attempt were being developed in various ways by such diverse figures as Tillich, Bultmann and Bonhoeffer. Tillich's assertion of "ecstatic naturalism," Bultmann's program of "demythologization" and Bonhoeffer's search for a "religionless Christianity," though they cannot be simply equated with each other are efforts to come to terms with the modern situation. Even on the Catholic side the situation is beginning to be recognized.

Interestingly enough, indications of the same general search for an entirely new mode of religious symbolization, though mostly confined to the Protestant West, also appear in that most developed of the non-Western countries, Japan. Uchimura Kanzō's non-church Christianity was a relatively early indication of a search for new directions and is being developed even further today. Even more interesting perhaps is the emergence of a similar development out of the Jōdo Shinshū tradition, at least in the person of Ienaga Saburo. This example indeed suggests that highly "modern" implications exist in more than one strand of Mahayana Buddhism and perhaps several of the other great traditions as well. Although in my opinion these implications were never developed sufficiently to dominate a historical epoch as they did in the West in the last two centuries, they may well prove decisive in the future of these religions.

So far what I have been saying applies mainly to intellectuals, but at least some evidence indicates that changes are also occurring at the level of mass religiosity. Behind the 96 per cent of Americans who claim to believe in God there are many instances of a massive reinterpretation that leaves Tillich, Bultmann and Bonhoeffer far behind. In fact, for many churchgoers the obligation of doctrinal orthodoxy sits lightly indeed, and the idea that all creedal statements must receive a personal reinterpretation is widely accepted. The dualistic world view certainly persists in the minds of many of the devout, but just as surely many others have developed elaborate and often pseudo-scientific rationalizations to bring their faith in its experienced validity into some kind of cognitive harmony with the 20th century world. The wave of popular response that some of the newer theology seems to be eliciting is another indication that not only the intellec-

tuals find themselves in a new religious situation.

To concentrate on the church in a discussion of the modern religious situation is already misleading, for it is precisely the characteristic of the new situation that the great problem of religion as I have defined it, the symbolization of man's relation to the ultimate conditions of his existence, is no longer the monopoly of any groups explicitly labeled religious. However much the development of Western Christianity may have led up to and in a sense created the modern religious siuation, it just as obviously is no longer in control of it. Not only has any obligation of doctrinal orthodoxy been abandoned by the leading edge of modern culture, but every fixed position has become open to question in the process of making sense out of man and his situation. This involves a profounder commitment to the process I have been calling religious symbolization than ever before. The historic religions discovered the self; the early modern religion found a doctrinal basis on which to accept the self in all its empirical ambiguity; modern religion is beginning to understand the laws of the self's own existence and so to help man take responsibility for his own fate.

This statement is not intended to imply a simple liberal optimism, for the modern analysis of man has also disclosed the depths of the limitations imposed by man's situation. Nevertheless, the fundamental symbolization of modern man and his situation is that of a dynamic multi-dimensional self capable, within limits, of continual self-transformation and capable, again within limits, of remaking the world including the very symbolic forms with which he deals with it, even the forms that state the unalterable conditions of his own existence. Such a statement should not be taken to mean that I expect, even less that I advocate, some ghastly religion of social science. Rather I expect traditional religious symbolism to be maintained and developed in new directions, but with growing awareness that it is symbolism and that man in the last analysis is responsible for the choice of his symbolism. Naturally, continuation of the symbolization characteristic of earlier stages without any reinterpretation is to be expected among many in the modern world, just as it has occurred in every previous period.

Religious action in the modern period is, I

think, clearly a continuation of tendencies already evident in the early modern stage. Now less than ever can man's search for meaning be confined to the church. But with the collapse of a clearly defined doctrinal orthodoxy and a religiously supported objective system of moral standards, religious action in the world becomes more demanding than ever. The search for adequate standards of action, which is at the same time a search for personal maturity and social relevance, is in itself the heart of the modern quest for salvation, if I may divest that word of its dualistic associations. How the specifically religious bodies are to adjust their time honored practices of worship and devotion to modern conditions is of growing concern in religious circles. Such diverse movements as the liturgical revival, pastoral psychology and renewed emphasis on social action are all efforts to meet the present need. Few of these trends have gotten much beyond the experimental but we can expect the experiments to continue.

In the modern situation as I have defined it, one might almost be tempted to see in Thomas Paine's "My mind is my church," or Thomas Jefferson's "I am a sect myself" the typical expression of *religious organization* in the near future. Nonetheless it seems unlikely that collective symbolization of the great inescapabilities of life will soon disappear. Of course the "free intellectual" will continue to exist as he has for millennia but such a solution can hardly be very general. Private voluntary religious association in the West achieved full legitimation for the first time in the early modern situation, but in the early stages especially, discipline and control within these groups was very intense. The tendency in more recent periods has been to continue the basic pattern but with a much more open and flexible pattern of membership. In accord with general trends I have already discussed, standards of doctrinal orthodoxy and attempts to enforce moral purity have largely been dropped. The assumption in most of the major Protestant denominations is that the church member can be considered responsible for himself. This trend seems likely to continue, with an increasingly fluid type of organization in which many special purpose sub-groups form and disband. Rather than interpreting these trends as significant of indifference and secularization, I see in them

the increasing acceptance of the notion that each individual must work out his own ultimate solutions and that the most the church can do is provide him a favorable environment for doing so, without imposing on him a prefabricated set of answers. And it will be increasingly realized that answers to religious questions can validly be sought in various spheres of "secular" art and thought.

Here I can only suggest what I take to be the main *social implication* of the modern religious situation. Early modern society, to a considerable degree under religious pressure, developed, as we have seen, the notion of a self-revising social system in the form of a democratic society. But at least in the early phase of that development social flexibility was balanced against doctrinal (Protestant orthodoxy) and characterological (Puritan personality) rigidities. In a sense those rigidities were necessary to allow the flexibility to emerge in the social system, but it is the chief characteristic of the more recent modern phase that culture and personality themselves have come to be viewed as endlessly revisable. This has been characterized as a collapse of meaning and a failure of moral standards. No doubt the possibilities for pathological distortion in the modern situation are enormous. It remains to be seen whether the freedom modern society implies at the cultural and personality as well as the social level can be stably institutionalized in large-scale societies. Yet the very situation that has been characterized as one of the collapse of meaning and the failure of moral standards can also, and I would argue more fruitfully, be viewed as one offering unprecedented opportunities for creative innovation in every sphere of human action.

CONCLUSION

The schematic presentation of the stages of religious evolution just concluded is based on the proposition that at each stage the freedom of personality and society has increased relative to the environing conditions. Freedom has increased because at each successive stage the relation of man to the conditions of his existence has been conceived as more complex, more open and more subject to change and development. The distinction between conditions that are really ultimate and those that are alterable becomes increasingly clear though never complete. Of course this scheme of religious evolution has implied at almost every point a general theory of social evolution, which has had to remain largely implicit.

Let me suggest in closing, as a modest effort at empirical testing, how the evolutionary scheme may help to explain the facts of alternating world acceptance and rejection which were noted near the beginning of the paper. I have argued that the world acceptance of the primitive and archaic levels is largely to be explained as the only possible response to a reality that invades the self to such an extent that the symbolizations of self and world are only very partially separate. The great wave of world rejection of the historic religions I have interpreted as a major advance in what Lienhardt calls "the differentiation between experience of the self and of the world which acts upon it." Only by withdrawing cathexis from the myriad objects of empirical reality could consciousness of a centered self in relation to an encompassing reality emerge. Early modern religion made it possible to maintain the centered self without denying the multifold empirical reality and so made world rejection

in the classical sense unnecessary. In the modern phase knowledge of the laws of the formation of the self, as well as much more about the structure of the world, has opened up almost unlimited new directions of exploration and development. World rejection marks the beginning of a clear objectification of the social order and sharp criticism of it. In the earlier world-accepting phases religious conceptions and social order were so fused that it was almost impossible to criticize the latter from the point of view of the former. In the later phases the possibility of remaking the world to conform to value demands has served in a very different way to mute the extremes of world rejection. The world acceptance of the last two stages is shown in this analysis to have a profoundly different significance from that of the first two.

Construction of a wide-ranging evolutionary scheme like the one presented in this paper is an extremely risky enterprise. Nevertheless such efforts are justifiable if, by throwing light on perplexing developmental problems they contribute to modern man's efforts at self interpretation.

CHAPTER 2

THE FUNCTION OF RELIGION IN HUMAN SOCIETY

INTRODUCTION

While the earlier scholars, especially the writers on comparative religion in the nineteenth century, were concerned with the basic question of how various forms of religion originated in human history, the emphasis shifted in the twentieth century to the basic question of what functions religion has in human society. This shift of interest is well expressed by Radcliffe-Brown when he contrasts his own position with that of Sir James Frazer. He writes that

Sir James accounted for the taboos of savage tribes as the application in practice of beliefs arrived at by erroneous processes of reasoning, and he seems to have thought of the effect of these beliefs in creating or maintaining a stable orderly society as being accidental. My own view is that the negative and positive rites of savages exist and persist because they are part of the mechanism by which an orderly society maintains itself in existence, serving as they do to establish certain fundamental social values. . . . I would suggest that what Sir James Frazer seems to regard as the accidental results of magical and religious beliefs really constitute their essential function and the ultimate reason for their existence [*Taboo*].

In other words, scholars began to be less concerned with the question of how religious beliefs and practices arose out of human experience, and more concerned with the study of what these beliefs and practices *do* for individuals and societies, whatever their origins. When the question was posed in this

fashion, there began to be less disposition to study historical origins and stages of development, and less tendency to become embroiled in theological arguments. Instead, the student of comparative religion could start with the fundamental hypothesis that given the biological and social nature of man on this planet, some kind of religious system is a cultural universal; no human society can get along without a religion any more than it can survive without an economic system. The actual cultural content found in the religions of different societies may vary enormously, but underlying this diversity there may be impressive similarities in basic functions, involving the culturally prescribed solutions of human social and psychological problems and the ways of expressing and reaffirming the central values of a society. Viewed in this light, religion appears to be an essential ingredient of society.

To start with this position and to pose these questions, then, is a call for cross-cultural research and theoretical thinking that will lead both to a clear specification of those aspects of the human situation that require religious patterns and to a precise delineation of the functions religion does perform. We want to know what social and psychological problems are solved by religious beliefs and practices and how. We want to know to what extent and how a religious system helps to express, codify, and reaffirm the central values of a society in such a way

as to maintain the social fabric of that society.

The following selections are from writers
who have established landmarks in the development of functional thinking about the
nature of religion and associated beliefs and
practices. The first, by Fustel de Coulanges,
represents the seminal stage in such thinking. The works of Malinowski and Radcliffe-
Brown are clearly classics in this development of functionalism, and their publications
have sparked a stimulating controversy
over the concept of function as well as a disagreement over the relationships of anxiety
to ritual. Malinowski's use of the concept of
function revolved around the question:
What human needs (individual and social)
are fulfilled by cultural patterns? Radcliffe-
Brown's use of the concept was based upon
his "organismic analogy"; that is, just as
an organ of the body has a function in preserving the successful maintenance of the
body as a whole, so does a social custom or
usage have a function in preserving the
maintenance of a society as a whole. This
conceptual difference led to the disagreements between Malinowski and Radcliffe-
Brown over the relationship of anxiety to
ritual—a disagreement which Homans later
attempted to resolve in his paper.

Drawing upon these theories of the functions of religion, as well as upon the earlier
work of Émile Durkheim, Max Weber,
Vilfredo Pareto, and others, the selections
from Talcott Parsons and Robert H. Lowie
represent more recent syntheses of our theoretical knowledge concerning the role and
functions of religion in human society. The
selection from the pen of Clyde Kluckhohn
on "Myths and Rituals: A General Theory"
could also have been added to these recent
theoretical syntheses on the functions of religion, but since this paper provides such a
clear and cogent introduction to our next
section on "Myth and Ritual," it has been
placed there.

NUMA-DENYS FUSTEL DE COULANGES

The Ancient City   It is always rewarding to search for the antecedents of ideas and
influences which in the course of time have come to be accepted
almost as if they had burst upon us full-blown from out of the
blue. The functionalist approach in social anthropology is an excellent example of the manner in which a younger generation
without knowledge of the past history of a theory may erroneously assume it to have originated at a particular time with a
particular scholar. Without attempting to trace the entire history
of the functional concept of society, it is worthwhile to call attention to the influence of a single man, Fustel de Coulanges, on
subsequent generations of anthropologists and sociologists. This
great historian had as his pupil at the École Normale Supérieure
in Paris the young Émile Durkheim, on whom he exerted an
immediate and strong influence; the latter in turn attracted
eventually a number of important scholars who either directly or
indirectly came to adopt his approach. In his great work, *La Cité
antique,* first published in 1864 and now available in a paperback
edition in English, it is at once obvious that the author's goal was
to single out and trace the dynamic role of religion in ancient
Greek and Roman life, and to demonstrate its interrelatedness
with the laws and institutions of the Greeks and Romans. He
maintained that changes in the history of these peoples were due
directly to changes in religious beliefs. While the causal sequence
which he traced in the development of the city from its beginnings in the family can be challenged, as can his assertion that

Excerpted from [Numa-Denys] Fustel de Coulanges, *The Ancient
City,* trans. Willard Small (3d ed.; Boston: Lee and Shepard, 1877),
by permission of Lothrop, Lee & Shepard.

religion is the source of mores and institutions, he succeeded in elucidating the extent to which religious beliefs and institutions saturated Graeco-Roman social and political organization, especially in the family, marriage, property, morals, law, political authority, social class, and citizenship. *La Cité antique* tells us much more about the historical development of the ancient religion from familial ancestor worship (with the sacred fire as its principal symbol) to the worship of gods whom he says were a deification of nature. But for our purposes the essential value of the book is not as a work of history but as a force in developing a point of view towards religion that gave expression to the emancipated spirit of nineteenth century thought.

INTRODUCTION

It is proposed here to show upon what principles and by what rules Greek and Roman society was governed. We unite in the same study both the Greeks and Romans, because these two peoples, who were two branches of a single race, and who spoke two idioms of a single language, had also the same institutions and the same principles of government, and passed through a series of similar revolutions.

The cause which produces them [the revolutions] must be powerful, and must be found in man himself. If the laws of human association are no longer the same as in antiquity, it is because there has been a change in man. There is, in fact, a part of our being which is modified from age to age; this is our intelligence. It is always in movement; almost always progressing; and on this account, our institutions and our laws are subject to change. Man has not, in our day, the thinking he had twenty-five centuries ago; and this is why he is no longer governed as he was governed then.

The history of Greece and Rome is a witness and an example of the intimate relation which always exists between men's ideas and their social state. Examine the institutions of the ancients without thinking of their religious notions, and you find them obscure, whimsical, and inexplicable. Why were there patricians and plebeians, patrons and clients, eupatrids and thetes; and whence came the native and ineffaceable differences which we find between these classes? What was the meaning of those Lacedæmonian institutions which appear to us so contrary to nature? How are we to explain those unjust caprices of ancient private law; at Corinth and at Thebes, the sale of land prohibited; at Athens and at Rome, an inequality in the suc-

cession between brother and sister? What did the jurists understand by *agnation,* and by *gens?* Why those revolutions in the laws, those political revolutions? What was that singular patriotism which sometimes effaced every natural sentiment? What did they understand by that liberty of which they were always talking? How did it happen that institutions so very different from anything of which we have an idea to-day, could become established and reign for so long a time? What is the superior principle which gave them authority over the minds of men?

But by the side of these institutions and laws place the religious ideas of those times, and the facts at once become clear, and their explanation is no longer doubtful. If, on going back to the first ages of this race,—that is to say, to the time when its institutions were founded,—we observe the idea which it had of human existence, of life, of death, of a second life, of the divine principle, we perceive a close relation between these opinions and the ancient rules of private law; between the rites which spring from these opinions and their political institutions.

A comparison of beliefs and laws shows that a primitive religion constituted the Greek and Roman family, established marriage and paternal authority, fixed the order of relationship, and consecrated the right of property, and the right of inheritance. This same religion, after having enlarged and extended the family, formed a still larger association, the city, and reigned in that as it had reigned in the family. From it came all the institutions, as well as all the private law, of the ancients. It was from this that the city received all its principles, its rules, its usages, and its magistracies. But, in the course of time, this ancient religion became modified or effaced, and private law and political institutions were modified with it. Then came a series of revolutions, and social changes regularly followed the development of knowledge.

THE CITY FORMED

The tribe, like the family and phratry, was established as an independent body, since it had a special worship from which the stranger was excluded. Once formed, no new family could be admitted to it. No more could two tribes be fused into one; their religion was opposed to this. But just as several phratries were united in a tribe, several tribes might associate together, on condition that the religion of each should be respected. The day on which this alliance took place the city existed.

It is of little account to seek the cause which determined several neighboring tribes to unite. Sometimes it was voluntary; sometimes it was imposed by the superior force of a tribe, or by the powerful will of a man. What is certain is, that the bond of the new association was still a religion. The tribes that united to form a city never failed to light a sacred fire, and to adopt a common religion.

Thus human society, in this race, did not enlarge like a circle, which increases on all sides, gaining little by little. There were, on the contrary, small groups, which, having been long established, were finally joined together in larger ones. Several families formed the phratry, several phratries the tribe, several tribes the city. Family, phratry, tribe, city, were, moreover, societies exactly similar to each other, which were formed one after the other by a series of federations.

We must remark, also, that when the different groups became thus associated, none of them lost its individuality, or its independence. Although several families were united in a phratry, each one of them remained constituted just as it had been when separate. Nothing was changed in it, neither worship nor priesthood, nor property nor internal justice. Curies afterwards became associated, but each retained its worship, its assemblies, its festivals, its chief. From the tribe men passed to the city; but the tribe was not dissolved on that account, and each of them continued to form a body, very much as if the city had not existed. In religion there subsisted a multitude of subordinate worships, above which was established

one common to all; in politics, numerous little governments continued to act, while above them a common government was founded.

The city was a confederation. Hence it was obliged, at least for several centuries, to respect the religious and civil independence of the tribes, curies, and families, and had not the right, at first, to interfere in the private affairs of each of these little bodies. It had nothing to do in the interior of a family; it was not the judge of what passed there; it left to the father the right and duty of judging his wife, his son, and his client. It is for this reason that private law, which had been fixed at the time when families were isolated, could subsist in the city, and was modified only at a very late period.

The mode of founding ancient cities is attested by usages which continued for a very long time.

If we examine the army of the city in primitive times, we find it distributed into tribes, curies, and families, "in such a way," says one of the ancients, "that the warrior has for a neighbor in the combat one with whom, in time of peace, he has offered the libation and sacrifice at the same altar." If we look at the people when assembled, in the early ages of Rome, we see them voting by curies and by *gentes*. If we look at the worship, we see at Rome six Vestals, two for each tribe. At Athens, the archon offers the sacrifice in the name of the entire city, but he has in the religious part of the ceremony as many assistants as there are tribes.

Thus the city was not an assemblage of individuals; it was a confederation of several groups, which were established before it, and which it permitted to remain. We see, in the Athenian orators, that every Athenian formed a portion of four distinct societies at the same time; he was a member of a family, of a phratry, of a tribe, and of a city. He did not enter at the same time and the same day into all these four, like a Frenchman, who at the moment of his birth belongs at once to a family, a commune, a department, and a country. The phratry and the tribe are not administrative divisions. A man enters at different times into these four societies, and ascends, so to speak, from one to the other. First, the child is admitted into the family by the religious ceremony, which takes place six days after his birth. Some years later he enters the phratry by a new ceremony, which we have already described. Finally, at the age of sixteen or eighteen, he is presented for admission into the city. On that day, in the presence of an altar, and before the smoking flesh of a victim, he pronounces an oath, by which he binds himself, among other things, always to respect the religion of the city. From that day he is initiated into the public worship, and becomes a citizen. If we observe this young Athenian rising, step by step, from worship to worship, we have a symbol of the degrees through which human association has passed. The course which this young man is constrained to follow, is that which society first followed.

We should not lose sight of the excessive difficulty which, in primitive times, opposed the foundation of regular societies. The social tie was not easy to establish between those human beings who were so diverse, so free, so inconstant. To bring them under the rules of a community, to institute commandments and insure obedience, to cause passion to give way to reason, and individual right to public right, there certainly was something necessary, stronger than material force, more respectable than interest, surer than a philosophical theory, more unchangeable than a convention; something that should dwell equally in all hearts, and should be all-powerful there.

This power was a belief. Nothing has more power over the soul. A belief is the work of our mind, but we are not on that account free to modify it at will. It is our own creation, but we do not know it. It is human, and we believe it a god. It is the effect of our power, and is stronger than we are. It is in us; it does not quit us: it speaks to us at every moment. If it tells us to obey, we obey; if it traces duties for us, we submit. Man may, indeed, subdue nature, but he is subdued by his own thoughts.

Now, an ancient belief commanded a man to honor his ancestor; the worship of the ancestor grouped a family around an altar. Thus arose the first religion, the first prayers, the first ideas of duty, and of morals. Thus, too, was the right of property established, and the order of succession fixed. Thus, in fine, arose all private law, and all the rules of domestic organization. Later the belief grew, and human society grew at the same time. When men begin to perceive that there are common divinities for them, they unite in larger groups. The same rules, invented and

established for the family, are applied successively to the phratry, the tribe, and the city.

Let us take in at a glance the road over which man has passed. In the beginning the family lived isolated, and man knew only the domestic gods—Θεοι πάτρωοι, *dii gentiles.* Above the family was formed the phratry with its god—Θεὸς φράτριος, *Juno curialis.* Then came the tribe, and the god of the tribe —Θεὸς φύλιος. Finally came the city, and men conceived a god whose providence embraced this entire city—Θεὸς πολιεύς, *penates publici;* a hierarchy of creeds, and a hierarchy of association. The religious idea was, among the ancients, the inspiring breath and organizer of society.

The traditions of the Hindus, of the Greeks, and of the Etruscans, relate that the gods revealed social laws to man. Under this legendary form there is a truth. Social laws were the work of the gods; but those gods, so powerful and beneficent, were nothing else than the beliefs of men.

Such was the origin of cities among the ancients. This study was necessary to give us a correct idea of the nature and institutions of the city. But here we must make a reservation. If the first cities were formed of a confederation of little societies previously established, this is not saying that all the cities known to us were formed in the same manner. The municipal organization once discovered, it was not necessary for each new city to pass over the same long and difficult route. It might often happen that they followed the inverse order. When a chief, quitting a city already organized, went to found another, he took with him commonly only a small number of his fellow-citizens. He associated with them a multitude of other men who came from different parts, and might even belong to different races. But this chief never failed to organize the new state after the model of the one he had just quitted. Consequently he divided his people into tribes and phratries. Each of these little associations had an altar, sacrifices, and festivals; each even invented an ancient hero, whom it honored with its worship, and from whom, with the lapse of time, it believed itself to have been descended.

THE CITIZEN AND THE STRANGER

The citizen was recognized by the fact that he had a part in the religion of the city, and it was from this participation that he derived all his civil and political rights. If he renounced the worship, he renounced the rights. We have already spoken of the public meals, which were the principal ceremony of the national worship. Now, at Sparta, one who did not join in these, even if it was not his fault, ceased at once to be counted among the citizens. At Athens, one who did not take part in the festivals of the national gods lost the rights of a citizen. At Rome, it was necessary to have been present at the sacred ceremony of the lustration, in order to enjoy political rights. The man who had not taken part in this—that is to say, who had not joined in the common prayer and the sacrifice—lost his citizenship until the next lustration.

If we wished to give an exact definition of a citizen, we should say that it was a man who had the religion of the city. The stranger, on the contrary, is one who has not access to the worship, one whom gods of the city do not protect, and who has not even the right to invoke them. For these national gods do not wish to receive prayers and offering except from citizens; they repulse the stranger; entrance into their temples is forbidden to him, and his presence during the sacrifice is a sacrilege. Evidence of this ancient sentiment of repulsion has remained in one of the principal rites of Roman worship. The pontiff, when he sacrifices in the open air, must have his head veiled: "For before the sacred fires in the religious act which is offered to the national gods, the face of a stranger must not appear to the pontiff; the auspices would be disturbed." A sacred object which fell for a moment into the hands of a stranger at once became profane. It could not recover its religious character except by an expiatory ceremony. If the enemy seized upon a city, and the citizens succeeded in recovering it, above all things it was important that the temples should be purified and all the fires extinguished and rekindled. The presence of the stranger had defiled them.

Thus religion established between the citizen and the stranger a profound and ineffaceable distinction. This same religion, so long as it held its sway over the minds of men, forbade the right of citizenship to be granted to a stranger. In the time of Herodotus, Sparta had accorded it to no one except a prophet; and even for this the formal command of the oracle was necessary. Athens granted it sometimes; but with what precautions! First, it was necessary that the united people should vote by secret ballot for the admission of the stranger. Even this was nothing as yet; nine days afterwards a second assembly had to confirm the previous vote, and in this second case six thousand votes were required in favor of the admission—a number which will appear enormous when we recollect that it was very rare for an Athenian assembly to comprise so many citizens. After this a vote of the senate was required to confirm the decision of this double assembly. Finally, any citizen could oppose a sort of veto, and attack the decree as contrary to the ancient laws. Certainly there was no other public act where the legislator was surrounded with so many difficulties and precautions as that which conferred upon a stranger the title of citizen. The formalities to go through were not near so great in declaring war, or in passing a new law. Why should these men oppose so many obstacles to a stranger who wished to become a citizen? Assuredly they did not fear that in the political assemblies his vote would turn the balance. Demosthenes gives us the true motive and the true thought of the Athenians: "It is because the purity of the sacrifices must be preserved." To exclude the stranger was to "watch over the sacred ceremonies." To admit a stranger among the citizens was "to give him a part in the religion and in the sacrifices." Now, for such an act the people did not consider themselves entirely free, and were seized with religious scruples; for they knew that the national gods were disposed to repulse the stranger, and that the sacrifices would perhaps be rendered useless by the presence of the new comer. The gift of the rights of a citizen to a stranger was a real violation of the fundamental principles of the national religion; and it is for this reason that, in the beginning, the city was so sparing of it. We must also note that the man admitted to citizenship with so much difficulty could be neither archon nor priest. The city, indeed, permitted him to take part in its worship, but as to presiding at it, that would have been too much.

No one could become a citizen at Athens if he was a citizen in another city; for it was a religious impossibility to be at the same time a member of two cities, as it also was to be a member of two families. One could not have two religions at the same time.

The participation in the worship carried with it the possession of rights. As the citizen might assist in the sacrifice which preceded the assembly, he could also vote at the assembly. As he could perform the sacrifices in the name of the city, he might be a prytane and an archon. Having the religion of the city, he might claim rights under its laws, and perform all the ceremonies of legal procedure.

The stranger, on the contrary, having no part in the religion, had none in the law. If he entered the sacred enclosure which the priests had traced for the assembly, he was punished with death. The laws of the city did not exist for him. If he had committed a crime, he was treated as a slave, and punished without process of law, the city owing him no legal protection. When men arrived at that stage that they felt the need of having laws for the stranger, it was necessary to establish an exceptional tribunal. At Rome, in order to judge the alien, the praetor had to become an alien himself—*praetor peregrinus*. At Athens the judge of foreigners was the polemarch—that is to say, the magistrate who was charged with the cares of war, and of all transactions with the enemy.

Neither at Rome nor at Athens could a foreigner be a proprietor. He could not marry; or, if he married, his marriage was not recognized, and his children were reputed illegitimate. He could not make a contract with a citizen; at any rate, the law did not recognize such a contract as valid. At first he could take no part in commerce. The Roman law forbade him to inherit from a citizen, and even forbade a citizen to inherit from him. They pushed this principle so far, that if a foreigner obtained the rights of a citizen without his son, born before this event, obtaining the same favor, the son became a foreigner in regard to his father, and could not inherit from him. The distinction between citizen and foreigner was stronger than the natural tie between father and son.

At first blush it would seem as if the aim had been to establish a system that should be vexatious towards foreigners; but there was nothing of this. Athens and Rome, on the contrary, gave him a good reception, both for commercial and political reasons. But neither their good will nor their interest could abolish the ancient laws which religion had established. This religion did not permit the stranger to become a proprietor, because he could not have any part in the religious soil of the city. It permitted neither the foreigner to inherit from the citizen, nor the citizen to inherit from the foreigner; because every transmission of property carried with it the transmission of a worship, and it was as impossible for the citizen to perform the foreigner's worship as for the foreigner to perform the citizen's.

Citizens could welcome the foreigner, watch over him, even esteem him if he was rich and honorable; but they could give him no part in their religion or their laws. The slave in certain respects was better treated than he was, because the slave, being a member of the family whose worship he shared, was connected with the city through his master; the gods protected him. The Roman religion taught, therefore, that the tomb of the slave was sacred, but that the foreigner's was not.

A foreigner, to be of any account in the eyes of the law, to be enabled to engage in trade, to make contracts, to enjoy his property securely, to have the benefit of the laws of the city to protect him, must become the client of a citizen. Rome and Athens required every foreigner to adopt a patron. By choosing a citizen as a patron the foreigner became connected with the city. Thenceforth he participated in some of the benefits of the civil law, and its protection was secured.

THE REVOLUTIONS

Certainly we could imagine nothing more solidly constituted than this family of ancient ages, which contained within itself its gods, its worship, its priest, and its magistrate. There could be nothing stronger than this city, which also had in itself its religion, its protecting gods, and its independent priesthood, which governed the soul as well as the body of man, and which, infinitely more powerful than the states of our day, united in itself the double authority that we now see shared between the state and the church. If any society was ever established to last, it was certainly that. Still, like everything human, it had its revolutions. We cannot state at what period these revolutions commenced. We can understand that, in reality, this epoch was not the same for the different cities of Greece and Italy. All that is certain is, that from the seventh century before our era, this social organization was almost everywhere discussed and attacked. From that time it was supported only with difficulty, and by a more or less skilful combination or resistance and concessions. It struggled thus for several centuries, in the midst of perpetual contests, and finally disappeared.

The causes of its destruction may be reduced to two. One was the change which took place in the course of time in ideas, resulting from the natural development of the human mind, and which, in effacing ancient beliefs, at the same time caused the social edifice to crumble, which these beliefs had built, and could alone sustain. The other was a class of men who found themselves placed outside this city organization, and who suffered from it. These men had an interest in destroying it, and made war upon it continually.

When, therefore, the beliefs, on which this social *régime* was founded, became weakened, and the interests of the majority of men were at war with it, the system fell. No city escaped this law of transformation; Sparta no more than Athens, Rome no more than Greece. We have seen that the men of Greece and those of Italy had originally the same beliefs, and that the same series of institutions was developed among both; and we shall now see that all these cities passed through similar revolutions.

We must try to understand why and how men became separated from this ancient organization, not to fall, but, on the contrary, to advance towards a social organization larger and better. For under the semblance of disorder, and sometimes of decay, each of their changes brought them nearer an object which they did not comprehend.

PATRICIANS AND CLIENTS

Thus far we have not spoken of the lower classes, because we have had no occasion to speak of them. For we have been attempting to describe the primitive organization of the city; and the lower classes counted absolutely for nothing in that organism. The city was constituted as if these classes had not existed. We were able therefore to defer the study of these till we had arrived at the period of the revolutions.

The ancient city, like all human society, had ranks, distinctions, and inequalities. We know the distinction originally made at Athens between the Eupatrids and the Thetes; at Sparta we find the class of Equals and that of the Inferiors; and in Eubœa, that of the Knights and that of the People. The history of Rome is full of the struggles between the Patricians and Plebeians, struggles that we find in all the Sabine, Latin, and Etruscan cities. We can even remark that the higher we ascend in the history of Greece and Italy, the more profound and the more strongly marked the distinction appears—a positive proof that the inequality did not grow up with time, but that it existed from the beginning, and that it was contemporary with the birth of cities.

It is worth while to inquire upon what principles this division of classes rested. We can thus the more easily see by virtue of what ideas or what needs the struggles commenced, what the inferior classes claimed, and on what principles the superior classes defended their empire.

We have seen above that the city grew out of the confederation of families and tribes. Now, before the day on which the city was founded, the family already contained within itself this distinction of classes. Indeed, the family was never dismembered; it was indivisible, like the primitive religion of the hearth. The oldest son alone, succeeding the father, took possession of the priesthood, the property, and the authority, and his brothers were to him what they had been to their father. From generation to generation, from first-born to first-born, there was never but one family chief. He presided at the sacrifice, repeated the prayer, pronounced judgment, and governed. To him alone originally belonged the title of *pater;* for this word, which signified power and not paternity, could be applied only to the chief of the family. His sons, his brothers, his servants, all called him by this title.

Here, then, in the inner constitution of the family is the first principle of inequality. The oldest is the privileged one for the worship, for the succession, and for command. After several centuries, there were naturally formed, in each of these great families, younger branches, that were, according to religion and by custom, inferior to the older branch, and who, living under its protection, submitted to its authority.

This family, then, had servants, who did

not leave it, who were hereditarily attached to it, and upon whom the *pater,* or *patron,* exercised the triple authority of master, magistrate, and priest. They were called by names that varied with the locality: the more common names were Clients and Thetes.

Here was another inferior class. The client was inferior not only to the supreme chief of the family, but to the younger branches also. Between him and them there was this difference, that a member of a younger branch, by ascending the series of his ancestors, always arrived at a *pater,* that is to say, a family chief, one of those divine ancestors, whom the family invoked in its prayers. As he was descended from a *pater,* they called him in Latin *patricius.* The son of a client, on the contrary, however high he might ascend in his genealogy, never arrived at anything but a client or a slave. There was no *pater* among his ancestors. Hence came for him a state of inferiority from which there was no escape.

The distinction between these two classes of men was manifest in what concerned material interests. The property of the family belonged entirely to the chief, who, however, shared the enjoyment of it with the younger branches, and even with the clients. But while the younger branch had at least an eventual right to this property, in case of the extinction of the elder branch, the client could never become a proprietor. The land that he cultivated he had only in trust; if he died, it returned to his patron; Roman law of the later ages preserved a vestige of this ancient rule in what was called *jus applicationis.* The client's money, even, did not belong to him; the patron was the true owner of it, and could take it for his own needs. It was by virtue of this ancient rule that the Roman law required the client to endow the daughter of the patron, to pay the patron's fine, and to furnish his ransom, or contribute to the expenses of his magistracy.

The distinction is still more manifest in religion. The descendant of the *pater* alone can perform the ceremonies of the family worship. The client takes a part in it; a sacrifice is offered for him; he does not offer it for himself. Between him and the domestic divinity there is always a mediator. He cannot even replace the absent family. If this family becomes extinct, the clients do not continue the worship; they are dispersed.

For the religion is not their patrimony; it is not of their blood, it does not come from their own ancestors. It is a borrowed religion; they have not the enjoyment or the ownership of it.

Let us keep in mind that according to the ideas of ancient generations, the right to have a god and to pray was hereditary. The sacred tradition, the rites, the sacramental words, the powerful formulas which determined the gods to act,—all this was transmitted only with the blood. It was therefore very natural that in each of these ancient families, the free person who was really descended from the first ancestor, was alone in possession of the sacerdotal character. The Patricians or Eupatrids had the privilege of being priests, and of having a religion that belonged to them alone.

Thus, even before men left the family state, there existed a distinction of classes; the old domestic religion had established ranks. Afterwards, when the city was formed, nothing was changed in the inner constitution of the family. We have already shown that originally the city was not an association of individuals, but a confederation of tribes, curies, and families, and that in this sort of alliance each of these bodies remained what it had been before. The chiefs of these little groups united with each other, but each remained master in the little society of which he was already chief. This explains why the Roman law so long left to the *pater* the absolute authority over his family, and the control of and the right of judging his clients. The distinction of classes, born in the family, was continued therefore in the city.

The city in its first age was no more than an alliance of the heads of families. There are numerous evidences of a time when they alone were citizens. This rule was kept up at Sparta, where the younger sons had no political rights. We may still see vestiges of it in an ancient law of Athens, which declared that to be a citizen one must have a domestic god. Aristotle remarks that anciently, in many cities, it was the rule that the son was not a citizen during the life of his father, and that, the father being dead, the oldest son alone enjoyed political rights. The law then counted in the city neither the younger branches of the family, nor, for still stronger reason, the clients. Aristotle also adds that the real citizens were at that time very few.

We must not picture to ourselves the city

of these ancient ages as an agglomeration of men living mingled together within the enclosure of the same walls. In the earliest times the city was hardly the place of habitation; it was the sanctuary where the gods of the community were; it was the fortress which defended them, and which their presence sanctified; it was the centre of the association, the residence of the king and the priests, the place where justice was administered; but the people did not live there. For several generations yet men continued to live outside the city, in isolated families, that divided the soil among them. Each of these families occupied its canton, where it had its domestic sanctuary, and where it formed, under the authority of its *pater,* an indivisible group. Then, on certain days, if the interests of the city or the obligations of the common worship called, the chiefs of these families repaired to the city and assembled around the king, either to deliberate or to assist at a sacrifice. If it was a question of war, each of these chiefs arrived, followed by his family and his servants (*sua manus*): they were grouped by phratries, or curies, and formed the army of the city, under the command of the king.

THE PLEBEIANS

We must now point out another element of the population, which was below the clients themselves, and which, originally low, insensibly acquired strength enough to break the ancient social organization. This class, which became more numerous at Rome than in any other city, was there called the *plebs.* We must understand the origin and character of this class to understand the part it played in the history of the city, and of the family, among the ancients. The plebeians were not the clients; the historians of antiquity do not confound these two classes.

What constituted the peculiar character of the plebs was, that they were foreign to the religious organization of the city, and even to that of the family. By this we recognize the plebeian, and distinguish him from the client. The client shared at least in the worship of his patron, and made a part of the family and of the gens. The plebeian, at first, had no worship, and knew nothing of the sacred family.

What we have already seen of the social and religious state of ancient times explains to us how this class took its rise. Religion was not propagated; born in a family, it remained, as it were, shut in there; each family was forced to create its creed, its gods, and its worship. But there must have been, in those times, so distant from us, a great number of families in which the mind had not the power to create gods, to arrange a doctrine, to institute a worship, to invent hymns, and the rhythm of the prayer. These families naturally found themselves in a state of inferiority compared with those who had a religion, and could not make a part of society with them; they entered neither into the curies nor into the city. In the course of time it even happened that families which had a religion lost it either by negligence, forgetting the rites, or by one of those crimes which prevented a man from approaching his hearth and continuing his worship. It must have happened, also, that clients, on account of crime or bad treatment, quitted the family and renounced its religion. The son, too, who was born of a marriage in which the rites had not been performed, was reputed a bastard, like one who had been born of adultery, and the family religion did not exist for him. All these men, excluded from the family and from the worship, fell into the class of men without a sacred fire—that is to say, became plebeians.

We find this class around almost all the ancient cities, but separated by a line of demarcation. Originally a Greek city was double; there was the city, properly so called—πόλις, which was built ordinarily on the summit of some hill; it had been built with the religious rites, and enclosed the sanctuary of the national gods. At the foot of the hill was found an agglomeration of houses, which were built without any religious ceremony, and without a sacred enclosure. These were the dwellings of the plebeians, who could not live in the sacred city.

At Rome the difference between the two classes was striking. The city of the patricians and their clients was the one that Romulus founded, according to the rites, on the Palatine. The dwellings of the plebs were in the asylum, a species of enclosure situated on the slope of the Capitoline Hill, where Romulus admitted people without hearth or home, whom he could not admit into his city. Later, when new plebeians came to Rome, as they were strangers to the religion of the city, they were established on the Aventine—that is to say, without the pomœrium, or religious city.

One word characterizes these plebeians— they were without a hearth; they did not possess, in the beginning, at least, any domestic altars. Their adversaries were always reproaching them with having no ancestors, which certainly meant that they had not the worship of ancestors, and had no family tomb where they could carry their funeral repast. They had no father—*pater;* that is to say, they ascended the series of their ascendants in vain; they never arrived at a religious family chief. They had no family— *gentem non habent;* that is to say, they had only the natural family; as to the one which religion formed and constituted, they had not that.

The sacred marriage did not exist for them; they knew not its rites. Having no hearth, the union that the hearth established was forbidden to them; therefore the patricians, who knew no other regular union than that which united husband and wife in presence of the domestic divinity, could say, in speaking of the plebeians, *"Connubia promiscua habent more ferarum."* There was no family for them, no paternal authority. They had the power over their children which strength gave them; but that sacred authority with which religion clothed the father, they had not.

For them there was no right of property; for all property was established and consecrated by a hearth, a tomb, and termini— that is to say, by all the elements of the domestic worship. If the plebeian possessed land, that land had no sacred character; it was profane, and had no boundaries. But could he hold land in the earliest times? We know that at Rome no one could exercise the right of property if he was not a citizen; and the plebeian, in the first ages of Rome, was not a citizen. According to the juris-consult, one could not be a proprietor except by quiritary right; but the plebeians were not counted at first among the Quirites. At the foundation of Rome the *ager Romanus* was divided up among the tribes, the curies, and the gentes. Now, the plebeians, who belonged to none of these groups, certainly did not share in the division. These plebeians, who had no religion, had not the qualification which enabled a man to make a portion

of the soil his own. We know that they long inhabited the Aventine, and built houses there; but it was only after three centuries, and many struggles, that they finally obtained the ownership of this territory.

For the plebeians there was no law, no justice, since the law was the decision of religion, and the procedure was a body of rites. The client had the benefit of the Roman franchise through his patron; but for the plebeian this right did not exist. An ancient historian says formally that the sixth king of Rome was the first to make laws for the plebs, whilst the patricians had had theirs for a long time. It appears even that these laws were afterwards withdrawn from the plebs, or that, not being founded upon religion, the patricians refused to pay any attention to them. For we see in the historian that, when tribunes were created, a special law was required to protect their lives and liberty, and that this law was worded thus: "Let no one undertake to strike or kill a tribune as he would one of the plebs." It seems, therefore, that any one had a right to strike or to kill a plebeian; or, at least, that this misdeed committed against a man who was beyond the pale of the law was not punished.

The plebeians had no political rights. They were not at first citizens, and no one among them could be a magistrate. For two centuries there was no other assembly at Rome than that of the curies; and the curies did not include the plebeians. The plebs did not even enter into the composition of the army so long as that was distributed by curies.

But what manifestly separated the plebeian from the patrician was, that the plebeian had no part in the religion of the city. It was impossible for him to fill the priestly office. We may even suppose that in the earliest ages prayer was forbidden him, and that the rites could not be revealed to him. It was as in India where "the Sudra should always be ignorant of the sacred formulas." He was a foreigner, and consequently his presence alone defiled the sacrifice. He was repulsed by the gods. Between him and the patrician there was all the distance that religion could place between two men. The plebs were a despised and abject class, beyond the pale of religion, law, society, and the family. The patrician could compare such an existence only with that of the

brutes—*more ferarum.* The touch of the plebeian was impure. The decemvirs, in their
first ten tables, had forgotten to interdict
marriage between the two orders; for these
first decemvirs were all patricians, and it
never entered the mind of one of them that
such a marriage was possible.

We see how many classes in the primitive
age of the cities were superposed one above
another. At the head was the aristocracy of
family chiefs, those whom the official language of Rome called *patres,* whom the clients called *reges,* whom the Odyssey names
βασιλεύς or ἄνακτες. Below were the younger
branches of the families; still lower were
the clients; and lowest were the plebs.

This distinction of classes came from religion. For at the time when the ancestors of
the Greeks, the Italians, and Hindus still
lived together in Central Asia, religion had
said, "The oldest shall offer prayer." From
this came the pre-eminence of the oldest in
everything; the oldest branch in every family
had been the sacerdotal and dominant
branch. Still religion made great account of
the younger branches, who were a species of
reserve, to replace the older branch some
day, if it should become extinct, and to save
the worship. It also made some account of
the client, and even of the slave, because
they assisted in the religious acts. But the
plebeian, who had no part in the worship, it
reckoned as absolutely of no account. The
ranks had been thus fixed.

But none of the social arrangements
which man studies out and establishes is unchangeable. This carried in itself the germ of
disease and death, which was too great an
inequality. Many men had an interest in destroying a social organization that had no
benefits for them.

**NEW PRINCIPLES OF GOVERNMENT: THE
PUBLIC INTEREST AND THE SUFFRAGE**

The revolution which overthrew the rule
of the sacerdotal class, and raised the lower
class to a level with the ancient chiefs of
gentes, marked a new period in the history
of cities. A sort of social reconstruction was
accomplished. It was not simply replacing
one class of men in power by another. Old
principles had been thrust aside, and new
rules adopted that were to govern human
societies. The new city, it is true, preserved
the exterior forms of the preceding period.

The republican system remained; almost
everywhere the magistrates preserved their
ancient names. Athens still had its archons,
and Rome its consuls. Nor was anything
changed in the ceremonies of the public religion; the repasts of the prytaneum, the sacrifices at the opening of the public assembly,
the auspices and the prayers,—all were preserved. It is quite common with man, when
he rejects old institutions, to wish to preserve their exterior forms.

In reality all was changed. Neither institutions, nor laws, nor beliefs, nor manners
were in this new period what they had been
in the preceding. The old system disappeared, carrying with it the rigorous rules
which it had established in all things; a new
order of things was established, and human
life changed its aspect.

During long ages religion had been the
sole principle of government. Another principle had to be found capable of replacing it,
and which, like it, might govern human institutions, and keep them as much as possible clear of fluctuations and conflicts. The
principle upon which the governments of
cities were founded thenceforth was public
interest.

We must observe this new dogma which
then made its appearance in the minds of
men and in history. Heretofore the superior
rule whence social order was derived was
not interest, but religion. The duty of performing the rites of worship had been the
social bond. From this religious necessity
were derived, for some the right to command, for others the obligation to obey.
From this had come the rules of justice and
of legal procedure, those of public deliberations and those of war. Cities did not ask if
the institutions which they adopted were
useful; these institutions were adopted because religion had wished it thus. Neither
interest nor convenience had contributed to
establish them. And if the sacerdotal class
had tried to defend them, it was not in the
name of the public interest; it was in the
name of religious tradition. But in the period
which we now enter, tradition no longer
holds empire, and religion no longer governs. The regulating principle from which all
institutions now derive their authority—the
only one which is above individual wills, and
which obliges them all to submit—is public
interest. What the Latins call *res publica,*
the Greeks τὸ κοινόν, replaces the old reli-

gion. This is what, from this time, establishes institutions and laws, and by this all the important acts of cities are judged. In the deliberations of senates, or of popular assemblies, when a law is discussed, or a form of government, or a question of private right, or a political institution, no one any longer asks what religion prescribes, but what the general interest demands.

A saying is attributed to Solon which well characterizes this new *régime*. Some one asked him if he had given his country the best constitution. "No," he replied, "but the one which is the best suited to it." Now it was something quite new to expect in forms of government, and in laws, only a relative merit. The ancient constitutions, founded upon the rules of a worship, were proclaimed infallible and immutable. They possessed the rigor and inflexibility of the religion. Solon indicated by this answer that, in future, political constitutions should conform to the wants, the manners, and the interests of the men of each age. There was no longer a question of absolute truth; the rules of government were for the future to be flexible and variable. It is said that Solon wished at the most that his laws might be observed for a hundred years.

The precepts of public interest are not so absolute, so clear, so manifest, as are those of religion. We may always discuss them; they are not perceived at once. The way that appeared the simplest and surest to know what the public interest demanded was to assemble the citizens, and consult them. This course was thought to be necessary, and was almost daily employed. In the preceding period the auspices had borne the chief weight of the deliberations; the opinion of the priest, of the king, of the sacred magistrate was all-powerful. Men voted little, and then rather as a formality than to express an opinion. After that time they voted on every question; the opinion of all was needed in order to know what was for the interest of all. The suffrage became the great means of government. It was the source of institutions and the rule of right; it decided what was useful and even what was just. It was above the magistrates and above the laws; it was sovereign in the city.

The nature of government was also changed. Its essential function was no longer the regular performance of religious ceremonies. It was especially constituted to maintain order and peace within and dignity and power without. What had before been of secondary importance was now of the first. Politics took precedence of religion, and the government of men became a human affair. It consequently happened either that new offices were created, or, at any rate, that old ones assumed a new character. We can see this by the example of Athens, and by that of Rome. At Athens, during the domination of the aristocracy, the archons had been especially priests. The care of deciding causes, of administering the law, and of making war was of minor importance, and might, without inconvenience, be joined to the priesthood. When the Athenians rejected the old religious form of government, they did not suppress the archonship, for they had an extreme repugnance to abolishing what was ancient. But by the side of the archons they elected other magistrates, who, by the nature of their duties, corresponded better with the wants of the age. These were the *strategi*. The word signifies chief of the army, but the authority of these officers was not purely military; they had the care of the relations with other cities, of the finances, and of whatever concerned the police of the city. We may say that the archons had in their hands the state religion and all that related to it, and that the strategi had the political power. The archons preserved the authority such as the ancient ages had conceived it; the strategi had what new wants had caused to be established. Finally a time came when the archons had only the semblance of power, and the strategi had all the reality. These new magistrates were no longer priests; they hardly performed the ceremonies that were indispensable in time of war. The government tended more and more to free itself from religion. The strategi might be chosen outside the Eupatrids. In the examination which they had to undergo before they were appointed (δοκιμασία), they were asked, as the archons were, if they had a domestic worship, and if they were of a pure family; it was sufficient if they had always performed their duties as citizens, and held real property in Attica. The archons were designated by lot,—that is to say, by the voice of the gods; it was otherwise with the strategi. As the government became more difficult and more complicated, as piety was no longer the principal quality, and as skill, prudence, courage, and the art of commanding became necessary, men no longer believed the choice by lot was sufficient to make a good magistrate. The city no longer desired to be bound by the pretended will of the gods, and claimed to have a free choice of its chiefs. That the archon, who was a priest, should be designated by the gods, was natural; but the strategus, who held in his hands the material interests of the city, was better elected by the citizens.

If we closely observe the institutions of Rome, we see that changes of the same kind were going on there. On the one hand, the tribunes of the people so augmented their importance that the direction of the republic—at least, whatever related to internal affairs—finally belonged to them. Now, these tribunes who had no priestly character bore a great resemblance to the strategi. On the other hand, the consulship itself could subsist only by changing its character. Whatever was sacerdotal in it was by degrees effaced. The respect of the Romans for the traditions and forms of the past required, it is true, that the consul should continue to perform the ceremonies instituted by their ancestors; but we can easily understand that, the day when plebeians became consuls, these ceremonies were no longer anything more than vain formalities. The consulship was less and less a priesthood, and more and more a command. This transformation was slow, insensible, unperceived, but it was not the less complete. The consulship was certainly not, in the time of the Scipios, what it had been in Publicola's day. The military tribuneship, which the senate instituted in 443, and about which the ancients give us very little information, was perhaps the transition between the consulship of the first period and that of the second.

We may also remark that there was a change in the manner of nominating the consuls. Indeed, in the first ages, the vote of the centuries in the election of the magistrates was, as we have seen, a mere formality. In reality, the consul of each year was *created* by the consul of the preceding year, who transmitted the auspices to him after having obtained the assent of the gods. The centuries voted on the two or three candidates presented by the consul in office; there was no debate. The people might detest a candidate; but they were none the less compelled to vote for him. In the period at which we have now arrived, the election is quite different, although the forms are still the same. There is still, as formerly, a religious ceremony and a vote; but the religious ceremony is the formality, and the vote is the reality. The candidate is still presented by the consul who presides; but the consul is obliged, if not by law, at least by custom, to accept all candidates, and to declare that the auspices are equally favorable to all. Thus the centuries name those whom they honor. The election no longer belongs to the gods; it is in the hands of the people. The gods and the auspices are no longer consulted, except on the condition that they will be impartial towards all the candidates. Men make the choice.

CHRISTIANITY CHANGES THE CONDITIONS OF GOVERNMENT

The victory of Christianity marks the end of ancient society. With the new religion this social transformation, which we saw begun six or seven centuries earlier, was completed.

With Christianity not only was the religious sentiment revived, but it assumed a higher and less material expression. Whilst previously men had made for themselves gods of the human soul, or of the great forces of nature, they now began to look upon God as really foreign by his essence, from human nature on the one hand, and from the world on the other. The divine Being was placed outside and above physical nature. Whilst previously every man had made a god for himself, and there were as many of them as there were families and cities, God now appeared as a unique, immense, universal being, alone animating the worlds, alone able to supply the need of adoration that is in man. Religion, instead of being, as formerly among the nations of Greece and Italy, little more than an assemblage of practices, a series of rites which men repeated without having any idea of them, a succession of formulas which often were no longer understood because the language had grown old, a tradition which had been transmitted from age to age, and which owed its sacred character to its antiquity alone,—was now a collection of doctrines, and a great object proposed to faith. It was no longer exterior; it took up its abode especially in the thoughts of men. It was no longer matter; it became spirit. Christianity changed the nature and the form of adoration. Man no longer offered God food and drink. Prayer was no longer a form of incantation; it was an act of faith and a humble petition. The soul sustained another relation with the divinity; the fear of the gods was replaced by the love of God.

Christianity introduced other new ideas. It was not the domestic religion of any family, the national religion of any city, or of any race. It belonged neither to a caste nor to a corporation. From its first appearance it called to itself the whole human race. Christ said to his disciples, "Go ye into all the world, and preach the gospel to every creature."

In all this there was something new. For, everywhere, in the first ages of humanity, the divinity had been imagined as attaching himself especially to one race. The Jews had believed in the God of the Jews; the Athenians in the Athenian Pallas; the Romans in Jupiter Capitolinus. The right to practise a worship had been a privilege.

For this God there were no longer strangers. The stranger no longer profaned the temple, no longer tainted the sacrifice by his presence. The temple was open to all who believed in God. The priesthood ceased to be hereditary, because religion was no longer a patrimony. The worship was no longer kept secret; the rites, the prayers, the dogmas were no longer concealed. On the contrary, there was thenceforth religious instruction, which was not only given, but which was offered, which was carried to those who were the farthest away, and which sought out the most indifferent. The spirit of propagandism replaced the law of exclusion.

From this great consequences flowed, as well for the relations between nations as for the government of states.

Thus, by the single fact that the family no longer had its domestic religion, its constitution and its laws were transformed; so, too, from the single fact that the state no longer had its official religion, the rules for the government of men were forever changed.

Our study must end at this limit, which separates ancient from modern politics. We have written the history of a belief. It was established, and human society was constituted. It was modified, and society underwent a series of revolutions. It disappeared, and society changed its character. Such was the law of ancient times.

BRONISLAW MALINOWSKI

The Role of Magic and Religion

Few writers in modern times have written as lucidly and with as much firsthand field experience on the subject of magic and religion as has Bronislaw Malinowski. His classic paper on the subject is "Magic, Science, and Religion," which was first published in James Needham (ed.), *Science, Religion and Reality,* in 1925. But since this famous paper was reprinted by the Free Press in a book by the same name in 1948, and then in 1954 became available in a Doubleday Anchor Book edition, we are presenting a briefer statement of most of the same theoretical ground drawn from his article, "Culture," which appeared in the *Encyclopaedia of the Social Sciences.* For a more detailed version of the argument, the reader may turn to the readily available Anchor Book entitled *Magic, Science, and Religion.*

To understand Malinowski's thesis that every society, even the most primitive, has perfectly sound empirical knowledge to carry out many of its practical activities; that "magic is to be expected and generally to be found whenever man comes to an unbridgeable gap, a hiatus in his knowledge or in his powers of practical control, and yet has to continue in his pursuit"; and that "religion

Excerpted from Bronislaw Malinowski, "Culture," *Encyclopaedia of the Social Sciences,* IV (1931), 621–646. Copyright 1931 by the Macmillan Company and used with permission.

is not born out of speculation or reflection, still less out of illusion or misapprehension, but rather out ot the real tragedies of human life, out of the conflict between human plans and realities," one has to understand some of the thinking that was current about primitive religion at the time he wrote. Tylor had made primitive man into a kind of rational philosopher who tried to find answers to such problems as the difference between the living and the dead, and had developed the belief in animistic spirits which he regarded as the basis for primitive religion; Frazer had been concerned with showing that magic was a kind of "false science" and that an age of magic preceded an age of religion; Lévy-Bruhl had been engaging in brilliant speculations concerning the prelogical and mystical character of primitive thought. Into this cluster of ideas Malinowski brought some new insights—insights that were based for the first time on extensive, firsthand field experience. He was able to invite his readers "to step outside the closed study of the theorist into the open air of the Anthropological field," in this case the Trobriand Islands.

In addition to clarifying the relationships among magic, science, and religion, Malinowski clearly showed that the myths of primitive peoples also have important functions in social life. Thus he writes in the following article that "the function of myth is to strengthen tradition and to endow it with a greater value and prestige by tracing it back to a higher, better, more supernatural and more effective reality of initial events." For a more detailed version of his thesis on myths, and his classification of the oral literature into myths, legends, and folk tales, the reader may turn to his book *Myth in Primitive Psychology* (1926), which is also reprinted in the Anchor Book edition of *Magic, Science, and Religion*.

In spite of the various theories about a specific non-empirical and prelogical character of primitive mentality there can be no doubt that as soon as man developed the mastery of environment by the use of implements, and as soon as language came into being, there must also have existed primitive knowledge of an essentially scientific character. No culture could survive if its arts and crafts, its weapons and economic pursuits were based on mystical, non-empirical conceptions and doctrines. When human culture is approached from the pragmatic, technological side, it is found that primitive man is capable of exact observation, of sound generalizations and of logical reasoning in all those matters which affect his normal activities and are at the basis of his production. Knowledge is then an absolute derived necessity of culture. It is more, however, than a means to an end, and it was not classed therefore with the instrumental imperatives. Its place in culture, its function, is slightly different from that of production, of law, or of education. Systems of knowledge serve to connect various types of behavior; they carry over the results of past experiences into future enterprise and they bring together elements of human experience and allow man to co-ordinate and integrate his activities. Knowledge is a mental attitude, a diathesis of the nervous system, which allows man to carry on the work which culture makes him do. Its function is to organize and integrate the indispensable activities of culture.

The material embodiment of knowledge consists in the body of arts and crafts, of technical processes and rules of craftsmanship. More specifically, in most primitive cultures and certainly in higher ones there are special implements of knowledge—diagrams, topographical models, measures, aids to orientation or to counting.

The connection between native thought and language opens important problems of function. Linguistic abstraction, categories of space, time and relationship, and logical means of expressing the concatenation of ideas are extremely important matters, and the study of how thought works through language in any culture is still a virgin field of cultural linguistics. How primitive language works, where it is embodied, how it is related to social organization, to primitive religion and magic, are important problems of functional anthropology.

By the very forethought and foresight which it gives, the integrative function of knowledge creates new needs, that is, imposes new imperatives. Knowledge gives man the possibility of planning ahead, of embracing vast spaces of time and distance; it allows a wide range to his hopes and desires. But however much knowledge and science help man in allowing him to obtain what he wants, they are unable completely to control chance, to eliminate accidents, to foresee the unexpected turn of natural events, or to make human handiwork reliable and adequate to all practical requirements. In this field, much more practical, definite, and circumscribed than that of religion, there develops a special type of ritual activities which anthropology labels collectively as magic.

The most hazardous of all human enterprises known to primitive man is sailing. In the preparation of his sailing craft and the laying out of his plans the savage turns to his science. The painstaking work as well as the intelligently organized labor in construction and in navigation bears witness to the savage's trust in science and submission to it. But adverse wind or no wind at all, rough weather, currents and reefs are always liable to upset his best plans and most careful preparations. He must admit that neither his knowledge nor his most painstaking efforts are a guaranty of success. Something unaccountable usually enters and baffles his anticipations. But although unaccountable it yet appears to have a deep meaning, to act or behave with a purpose. The sequence, the significant concatenation of events, seems to contain some inner logical consistency. Man feels that he can do something to wrestle with that mysterious element or force, to help and abet his luck. There are therefore always systems of superstition, of more or less developed ritual, associated with sailing, and in primitive communities the magic of sailing craft is highly developed. Those who are well acquainted with some good magic have, in virtue of that, courage and confidence. When the canoes are used for fishing, the accidents and the good or bad luck may refer not only to transport but also to the appearance of fish and to the conditions under which they are caught. In trading, whether overseas or with near neighbors, chance may favor or thwart the ends and desires of man. As a result both fishing and trading magic are very well developed.

Likewise in war, man, however primitive, knows that well-made weapons of attack and defense, strategy, the force of numbers, and the strength of the individuals ensure victory. Yet with all this the unforeseen and accidental help even the weaker to victory when the fray happens under the cover of night, when ambushes are possible, when the conditions of the encounter obviously favor one side at the expense of the other. Magic is used as something which over and above man's equipment and his force helps him to master accident and to ensnare luck. In love also a mysterious, unaccountable quality of success or else a predestination to failure seems to be accompanied by some force independent of ostensible attraction and of the best laid plans and arrangements. Magic enters to insure something which counts over and above the visible and accountable qualifications.

Primitive man depends on his economic pursuits for his welfare in a manner which makes him realize bad luck very painfully and directly. Among people who rely on their fields or gardens what might be called agricultural knowledge is invariably well developed. The natives know the properties of the soil, the need of a thorough clearing from bush and weed, fertilizing with ashes and appropriate planting. But however well chosen the site and well worked the gardens, mishaps occur. Drought or deluge coming at most inappropriate seasons destroys the crops altogether, or some blights, insects, or wild animals diminish them. Or some other year, when man is conscious that he deserves but a poor crop, everything runs so smoothly and prosperously that an unexpectedly good return rewards the undeserving gardener. The dreaded elements of rain and sunshine, pests and fertility seem to be controlled by a force which is beyond ordinary human experience and knowledge, and man repairs once more to magic.

In all these examples the same factors are involved. Experience and logic teach man that within definite limits knowledge is supreme; but beyond them nothing can be done by rationally founded practical exertions. Yet he rebels against inaction because although he realizes his impotence he is yet driven to action by intense desire and strong emotions. Nor is inaction at all possible. Once he has embarked on a distant voyage or finds himself in the middle of a fray or halfway through the cycle of garden growing, the native tries to make his frail canoe more seaworthy by charms or to drive away locusts and wild animals by ritual or to vanquish his enemies by dancing.

Magic changes its forms; it shifts its ground; but it exists everywhere. In modern societies magic is associated with the third cigarette lit by the same match, with spilled salt and the need of throwing it over the left shoulder, with broken mirrors, with passing under a ladder, with the new moon seen through glass or on the left hand, with the number thirteen or with Friday. These are minor superstitions which seem merely to vegetate among the intelligentsia of the western world. But these superstitions and much more developed systems also persist tenaciously and are given serious consideration among modern urban populations. Black magic is practiced in the slums of London by the classical method of destroying the picture of the enemy. At marriage ceremonies good luck for the married couple is obtained by the strictest observance of several magical methods such as the throwing of the slipper and the spilling of rice. Among the peasants of central and eastern Europe elaborate magic still flourishes and children are treated by witches and warlocks. People are thought to have the power to prevent cows from giving milk, to induce cattle to multiply unduly, to produce rain and sunshine and to make people love or hate each other. The saints of the Roman Catholic Church become in popular practice passive accomplices of magic. They are beaten, cajoled and carried about. They can give rain by being placed in the field, stop flows of lava by confronting them and stop the progress of a disease, of a blight or of a plague of insects. The crude practical use made of certain religious rituals or objects makes their function magical. For magic is distinguished from religion in that the latter creates values and attains ends directly, whereas magic consists of acts which have a practical utilitarian value and are effective only as a means to an end. Thus a strictly utilitarian subject matter or issue of an act and its direct, instrumental function make it magic, and most modern established reli-

gions harbor within their ritual and even their ethics a good deal which really belongs to magic. But modern magic survives not only in the forms of minor superstitions or within the body of religious systems. Wherever there is danger, uncertainty, great incidence of chance and accident, even in entirely modern forms of enterprise, magic crops up. The gambler at Monte Carlo, on the turf, or in a continental state lottery develops systems. Motoring and modern sailing demand mascots and develop superstitions. Around every sensational sea tragedy there has formed a myth showing some mysterious magical indications or giving magical reasons for the catastrophe. Aviation is developing its superstitions and magic. Many pilots refuse to take up a passenger who is wearing anything green, to start a journey on a Friday, or to light three cigarettes with a match when in the air, and their sensitiveness to superstition seems to increase with altitude. In all large cities of Europe and America magic can be purchased from palmists, clairvoyants, and other soothsayers who forecast the future, give practical advice as to lucky conduct, and retail ritual apparatus such as amulets, mascots, and talismans. The richest domain of magic, however, is, in civilization as in savagery, that of health. Here again the old venerable religions lend themselves readily to magic. Roman Catholicism opens its sacred shrines and places of worship to the ailing pilgrim, and faith healing flourishes also in other churches. The main function of Christian Science is the thinking away of illness and decay; its metaphysics are very strongly pragmatic and utilitarian and its ritual is essentially a means to the end of health and happiness. The unlimited range of universal remedies and blessings, osteopathy and chiropractic, dietetics and curing by sun, cold water, grape or lemon juice, raw food, starvation, alcohol or its prohibition—one and all shade invariably into magic. Intellectuals still submit to Coué and Freud, to Jaeger and Kneipp, to sun worship, either direct or through the mercury-vapor lamp—not to mention the bedside manner of the highly paid specialist. It is very difficult to discover where common sense ends and where magic begins.

The savage is not more rational than modern man nor is he more superstitious. He is more limited, less liable to free imaginings and to the confidence trick of new inventions. His magic is traditional and he has his stronghold of knowledge, his empirical and rational tradition of science. Since the superstitious or prelogical character of primitive man has been so much emphasized, it is necessary to draw clearly the dividing line between primitive science and magic. There are domains on which magic never encroaches. The making of fire, basketry, the actual production of stone implements, the making of strings or mats, cooking and all minor domestic activities although extremely important are never associated with magic. Some of them become the center of religous practices and of mythology, as, for example, fire or cooking or stone implements; but magic is never connected with their production. The reason is that ordinary skill guided by sound knowledge is sufficient to set man on the right path and to give him certainty of correct and complete control of these activities.

In some pursuits magic is used under certain conditions and is absent under others. In a maritime community depending on the products of the sea there is never magic connected with the collecting of shellfish or with fishing by poison, weirs, and fish traps, so long as these are completely reliable. On the other hand, any dangerous, hazardous, and uncertain type of fishing is surrounded by ritual. In hunting, the simple and reliable ways of trapping or killing are controlled by knowledge and skill alone; but let there be any danger or any uncertainty connected with an important supply of game and magic immediately appears. Coastal sailing as long as it is perfectly safe and easy commands no magic. Overseas expeditions are invariably bound up with ceremonies and ritual. Man resorts to magic only where chance and circumstances are not fully controlled by knowledge.

This is best seen in what might be called systems of magic. Magic may be but loosely and capriciously connected with its practical setting. One hunter may use certain formulae and rites, and another ignore them; or the same man may apply his conjurings on one occasion and not on another. But there are forms of enterprise in which magic must be used. In a big tribal adventure, such as war, or a hazardous sailing expedition or seasonal travel or an undertaking such as a big hunt or a perilous fishing expedition or

the normal round of gardening, which as a rule is vital to the whole community, magic is often obligatory. It runs in a fixed sequence concatenated with the practical events, and the two orders, magical and practical, depend on one another and form a system. Such systems of magic appear at first sight an inextricable mixture of efficient work and superstitious practices and so seem to provide an unanswerable argument in favor of the theories that magic and science are under primitive conditions so fused as not to be separable. Fuller analysis, however, shows that magic and practical work are entirely independent and never fuse.

But magic is never used to replace work. In gardening the digging or the clearing of the ground or the strength of the fences or quality of the supports is never scamped because stronger magic has been used over them. The native knows well that mechanical construction must be produced by human labor according to strict rules of craft. He knows that all the processes which have been in the soil can be controlled by human effort to a certain extent but not beyond, and it is only this beyond which he tries to influence by magic. For his experience and his reason tell him that in certain matters his efforts and his intelligence are of no avail whatever. On the other hand, magic has been known to help; so at least his tradition tells him.

In the magic of war and of love, of trading expeditions and of fishing, of sailing and of canoe making, the rules of experience and logic are likewise strictly adhered to as regards technique, and knowledge and technique receive due credit in all the good results which can be attributed to them. It is only the unaccountable results, which an outside observer would attribute to luck, to the knack of doing things successfully, to chance or to fortune, that the savage attempts to control by magic.

Magic therefore, far from being primitive science, is the outgrowth of clear recognition that science has its limits and that a human mind and human skill are at times impotent. For all its appearances of megalomania, for all that it seems to be the declaration of the "omnipotence of thought," as it has recently been defined by Freud, magic has greater affinity with an emotional outburst, with daydreaming, with strong, unrealizable desire.

To affirm with Frazer that magic is a pseudo-science would be to recognize that magic is not really primitive science. It would imply that magic has an affinity with science or at least that it is the raw material out of which science develops—implications which are untenable. The ritual of magic shows certain striking characteristics which have made it quite plausible for most writers from Grimm and Tylor to Freud and Lévy-Bruhl to affirm that magic takes the place of primitive science.

Magic unquestionably is dominated by the sympathetic principle: like produces like; the whole is affected if the sorcerer acts on a part of it; occult influences can be imparted by contagion. If one concentrates on the form of the ritual only, he can legitimately conclude with Frazer that the analogy between the magical and the scientific conceptions of the world is close and that the various cases of sympathetic magic are mistaken applications of one or the other of two great fundamental laws of thought, namely, the association of ideas by similarity and the association of ideas by contiguity in space or time.

But a study of the function of science and the function of magic casts a doubt on the sufficiency of these conclusions. Sympathy is not the basis of pragmatic science, even under the most primitive conditions. The savage knows scientifically that a small pointed stick of hard wood rubbed or drilled against a piece of soft, brittle wood, provided they are both dry, gives fire. He also knows that strong, energetic, increasingly swift motion has to be employed, that tinder must be produced in the action, the wind kept off, and the spark fanned immediately into a glow and this into a flame. There is no sympathy, no similarity, no taking the part instead of the legitimate whole, no contagion. The only association or connection is the empirical, correctly observed and correctly framed concatenation of natural events. The savage knows that a strong bow well handled releases a swift arrow, that a broad beam makes for stability and a light, well-shaped hull for swiftness in his canoe. There is here no association of ideas by similarity or contagion or *pars pro toto*. The native puts a yam or a banana sprout into an appropriate piece of ground. He waters or irrigates it unless it be well drenched by rain. He weeds the ground round it, and he knows quite well

that barring unexpected calamities the plant will grow. Again there is no principle akin to that of sympathy contained in this activity. He creates conditions which are perfectly scientific and rational and lets nature do its work. Therefore in so far as magic consists in the enactment of sympathy, in so far as it is governed by an association of ideas, it radically differs from science; and on analysis the similarity of form between magic and science is revealed as merely apparent, not real.

The sympathetic rite although a very prominent element in magic functions always in the context of other elements. Its main purpose always consists in the generation and transference of magical force and accordingly it is performed in the atmosphere of the supernatural. As Hubert and Mauss have shown, acts of magic are always set apart, regarded as different, conceived and carried out under distinct conditions. The time when magic is performed is often determined by tradition rather than by the sympathetic principle, and the place where it is performed is only partly determined by sympathy or contagion and more by supernatural and mythological associations. Many of the substances used in magic are largely sympathetic but they are often used primarily for the physiological and emotional reaction which they elicit in man. The dramatic emotional elements in ritual enactment incorporate, in magic, factors which go far beyond sympathy or any scientific or pseudo-scientific principle. Mythology and tradition are everywhere embedded, especially in the performance of the magical spell, which must be repeated with absolute faithfulness to the traditional original and during which mythological events are recounted in which the power of the prototype is invoked. The supernatural character of magic is also expressed in the abnormal character of the magician and by the temporary taboos which surround its execution.

In brief, there exists a sympathetic principle: the ritual of magic contains usually some reference to the results to be achieved; it foreshadows them, anticipates the desired events. The magician is haunted by imagery, by symbolism, by associations of the result to follow. But he is quite as definitely haunted by the emotional obsession of the situation which has forced him to resort to magic. These facts do not fit into the simple scheme of sympathy conceived as misapplication of crude observations and half-logical deductions. The various apparently disjointed elements of magical ritual—the dramatic features, the emotional side, the mythological allusions, and the anticipation of the end—make it impossible to consider magic a sober scientific practice based on an empirical theory. Nor can magic be guided by experience and at the same time be constantly harking back to myth.

The fixed time, the determined spot, the preliminary isolating conditions of magic, the taboos to be observed by the performer, as well as his physiological and sociological nature, place the magical act in an atmosphere of the supernatural. Within this context of the supernatural the rite consists, functionally speaking, in the production of a specific virtue or force and of the launching, directing, or impelling of this force to the desired object. The production of magical force takes place by spell, manual and bodily gesticulation, and the proper condition of the officiating magician. All these elements exhibit a tendency to a formal assimilation toward the desired end or toward the ordinary means of producing this end. This formal resemblance is probably best defined in the statement that the whole ritual is dominated by the emotions of hate, fear, anger, or erotic passion, or by the desire to obtain a definite practical end.

The magical force or virtue is not conceived as a natural force. Hence the theories propounded by Preuss, Marett, and Hubert and Mauss, which would make the Melanesian mana or the similar North American concepts the clue to the understanding of all magic, are not satisfactory. The mana concept embraces personal power, natural force, excellence and efficiency alongside the specific virtue of magic. It is a force regarded as absolutely *sui generis,* different either from natural forces or from the normal faculties of man.

The force of magic can be produced only and exclusively within traditionally prescribed rites. It can be received and learned only by due initiation into the craft and by the taking over of the rigidly defined system of conditions, acts, and observances. Even when magic is discovered or invented it is invariably conceived as true revelation from the supernatural. Magic is an intrinsic, specific quality of a situation and of an object or

phenomenon within the situation, consisting in the object being amenable to human control by means which are specifically and uniquely connected with the object and which can be handled only by appropriate people. Magic therefore is always conceived as something which does not reside in nature, that is, outside man, but in the relation between man and nature. Only those objects and forces in nature which are very important to man, on which he depends and which he cannot yet normally control elicit magic.

A functional explanation of magic may be stated in terms of individual psychology and of the cultural and social value of magic. Magic is to be expected and generally to be found whenever man comes to an unbridgeable gap, a hiatus in his knowledge or in his powers of practical control, and yet has to continue in his pursuit. Forsaken by his knowledge, baffled by the results of his experience, unable to apply any effective technical skill, he realizes his impotence. Yet his desire grips him only the more strongly. His fears and hopes, his general anxiety, produce a state of unstable equilibrium in his organism, by which he is driven to some sort of vicarious activity. In the natural human reaction to frustrated hate and impotent anger is found the *materia prima* of black magic. Unrequited love provokes spontaneous acts of prototype magic. Fear moves every human being to aimless but compulsory acts; in the presence of an ordeal one always has recourse to obsessive daydreaming.

The natural flow of ideas under the influence of emotions and desires thwarted in their full practical satisfaction leads one inevitably to the anticipation of the positive results. But the experience upon which this anticipatory or sympathetic attitude rests is not the ordinary experience of science. It is much more akin to daydreaming, to what the psychoanalysts call wish fulfillment. When the emotional state reaches the breaking point at which man loses control over himself, the words which he utters, the gestures to which he gives way, and the physiological processes within his organism which accompany all this allow the pent-up tension to flow over. Over all such outbursts of emotion, over such acts of prototype magic, there presides the obsessive image of the desired end. The substitute action in which the physiological crisis finds its expression has a subjective value: the desired end seems nearer satisfaction.

Standardized, traditional magic is nothing else but an institution which fixes, organizes and imposes upon the members of a society the positive solution in those inevitable conflicts which arise out of human impotence in dealing with all hazardous issues by mere knowledge and technical ability. The spontaneous, natural reaction of man to such situations supplies the raw material of magic. This raw material implies the sympathetic principle in that man has to dwell both on the desired end and on the best means of obtaining it. The expression of emotions in verbal utterances, in gestures, in an almost mystical belief that such words and gestures have a power, crops up naturally as a normal, physiological reaction. The elements which do not exist in the *materia prima* of magic but are to be found in the developed systems are the traditional, mythological elements. Human culture everywhere integrates a raw material of human interests and pursuits into standardized, traditional customs. In all human tradition a definite choice is made from within a variety of possibilities. In magic also the raw material supplies a number of possible ways of behavior. Tradition chooses from among them, fixes a special type and endues it with a hallmark of social value.

Tradition also reinforces the belief in magical efficacy by the context of special experience. Magic is so deeply believed in because its pragmatic truth is vouched for by its psychological or even physiological efficacy, since in its form and in its ideology and structure magic corresponds to the natural processes of the human organism. The conviction which is implied in these processes extends obviously to standardized magic. This conviction is useful because it raises the efficiency of the person who submits to it. Magic possesses therefore a functional truth or a pragmatic truth, since it arises always under conditions where the human organism is disintegrated. Magic corresponds to a real physiological need.

The seal of social approval given to the standardized reactions, selected traditionally out of the raw material of magic, gives it an additional backing. The general conviction that this and only this rite, spell or personal preparation enables the magician to control chance makes every individual believe in it

through the ordinary mechanism of molding or conditioning. The public enactment of certain ceremonies, on the one hand, and the secrecy and esoteric atmosphere in which others are shrouded add again to their credibility. The fact also that magic usually is associated with intelligence and strong personality raises its credit in the eyes of any community. Thus a conviction that man can control by a special, traditional, standardized handling the forces of nature and human beings is not merely subjectively true through its physiological foundations, not merely pragmatically true in that it contributes to the reintegration of the individual, but it carries an additional evidence due to its sociological function.

Magic serves not only as an integrative force to the individual but also as an organizing force to society. The fact that the magician by the nature of his secret and esoteric lore has also the control of the associated practical activities causes him usually to be a person of the greatest importance in the community. The discovery of this was one of the great contributions of Frazer to anthropology. Magic, however, is of social importance not only because it gives power and thus raises a man to a high position. It is a real organizing force. In Australia the constitution of the tribe, of the clan, of the local group, is based on a system of totemic ideas. The main ceremonial expression of this system consists in the rites of magical multiplication of plants and animals and in the ceremonies of initiation into manhood. Both of these rites underlie the tribal framework and they are both the expression of a magical order of ideas based on totemic mythology. The leaders who arrange the tribal meetings, who conduct them, who direct the initiation and are the protagonists in dramatic representations of myth and in the public magical ceremonies, play this part because of their traditional magical filiation. The totemic magic of these tribes is their main organizing system.

To a large extent this is also true of the Papuan tribes of New Guinea, of the Melanesians and of the people of the Indonesian archipelagoes, where magical rites and ideas definitely supply the organizing principle in practical activities. The secret societies of the Bismarck Archipelago and West Africa, the rain makers of the Sudan, the medicine men of the North American Indians—all combine magical power with political and economic influence. Sufficient details to assess the extent and the mechanism by which magic enters and controls secular and ordinary life are often lacking. But among the Masai or Nandi in East Africa the evidence reveals that the military organization of the tribe is associated with war magic and that the guidance in political affairs and general tribal concerns depends on rain magic. In New Guinea garden magic, overseas trading expeditions, fishing and hunting on a big scale show that the ceremonial significance of magic supplies the moral and legal framework by which all practical activities are held together.

Sorcery in its major forms is usually specialized and institutionalized; that is, either the sorcerer is a professional whose services can be bought or commanded or sorcery is vested in a secret society or special organization. In all cases sorcery is either in the same hands as political power, prestige and wealth or else it can be purchased or demanded by those who can afford to do so. Sorcery thus is invariably a conservative force used at times for intimidation but usually for the enforcement of customary law or of the wishes of those in power. It is always a safeguard for the vested interests, for the organized, established privileges. The sorcerer who has behind him the chief or a powerful secret society can make his art felt more poignantly than if he were working against them or on his own.

The individual and sociological function of magic is thus made more efficient by the very mechanisms through which it works. In this and in the subjective aspect of the calculus of probability, which makes success overshadow failure, while failure again can be explained by countermagic, it is clear that the belief is not so ill founded nor due to such extravagant superstitiousness of the primitive mind as might at first appear. A strong belief in magic finds its public expression in the running mythology of magical miracles which is always found in company with all important types of magic. The competitive boasting of one community against another, the fame of outstanding magical success, the conviction that extraordinary good luck has probably been due to magic, create an ever nascent tradition which always surrounds famous magicians or famous systems of magic with a halo of supernatural reputation. This running tradition usually culminates retrospectively in a primeval myth, which gives the charter and credentials to the whole magical system. Myth of magic is definitely a warrant of its truth, a pedigree of its filiation, a charter of its claims to validity.

This is true not only of magical mythology. Myth in general is not an idle speculation about the origins of things or institutions. Nor is it the outcome of the contemplation of nature and rhapsodical interpretation of its laws. The function of myth is neither explanatory nor symbolic. It is the statement of an extraordinary event, the occurrence of which once for all had established the social order of a tribe or some of its economic pursuits, its arts and crafts or its religious or magical beliefs and ceremonies. Myth is not simply a piece of attractive fiction which is kept alive by the literary interest in the story. It is a statement of primeval reality which lives in the institutions and pursuits of a community. It justifies by precedent the existing order and it supplies a retrospective pattern of moral values, of sociological discriminations and burdens and of magical belief. In this consists its main cultural function. For all its similarity of form myth is neither a mere tale or prototype of literature or of science nor a branch of art or history nor an explanatory pseudo-theory. It fulfills a function *sui generis* closely connected with the nature of tradition and belief, with the continuity of culture, with the relation between age and youth and with the human attitude toward the past. The function of myth is to strengthen tradition and to endow it with a greater value and prestige by tracing it back to a higher, better, more supernatural and more effective reality of initial events.

The place of religion must be considered in the scheme of culture as a complex satisfaction of highly derived needs. The various theories of religion ascribe it to either a religious "instinct" or a specific religious sense (McDougall, Hauer) or else explain it as a primitive theory of animism (Tylor) or pre-animism (Marett) or ascribe it to the emotions of fear (Wundt) or to aesthetic raptures and lapses of speech (Max Müller) or the self-revelation of society (Durkheim). These theories make religion something superimposed on the whole structure of human culture, satisfying some needs perhaps, but needs which are entirely autonomous and have nothing to do with the hard-worked reality of human existence. Religion, however, can be shown to be intrinsically although indirectly connected with man's fundamental, that is, biological, needs. Like magic it comes from the curse of forethought and imagination, which fall on man once he rises above brute animal nature. Here there enter even wider issues of personal and social integration than those arising out of the practical necessity of hazardous action and dangerous enterprise. A whole range of anxieties, forebodings and problems concerning human destinies and man's place in the universe opens up once man begins to act in common not only with his fellow citizens but also with the past and future generations. Religion is not born out of speculation or reflection, still less out of illusion or misapprehension, but rather out of the real tragedies of human life, out of the conflict between human plans and realities.

Culture entails deep changes in man's personality; among other things it makes man surrender some of his self-love and self-seeking. For human relations do not rest merely or even mainly on constraint coming from without. Men can only work with and for one another by the moral forces which grow out of personal attachments and loyalties. These are primarily formed in the processes of parenthood and kinship but become inevitably widened and enriched. The love of parents for children and of children for their parents, that between husband and wife and between brothers and sisters, serve as prototypes and also as a nucleus for the loyalties of clanship, of neighborly feeling, and of tribal citizenship. Co-operation and mutual assistance are based, in savage and civilized societies, on permanent sentiments.

The existence of strong personal attachments and the fact of death, which of all human events is the most upsetting and disorganizing to man's calculations, are perhaps the main sources of religious belief. The affirmation that death is not real, that man has a soul and that this is immortal, arises out of a deep need to deny personal destruction, a need which is not a psychological instinct but is determined by culture, by co-operation and by the growth of human sentiments. To the individual who faces death the belief in immortality and the ritual of extreme unction, or last comforts (which in one form or another is almost universal), confirm his hope that there is a hereafter, that it is perhaps not worse than the present

life and may be better. Thus the ritual before death confirms the emotional outlook which a dying man has come to need in his supreme conflict. After death the bereaved are thrown into a chaos of emotion, which might become dangerous to each of them individually and to the community as a whole were it not for the ritual of mortuary duties. The religious rites of wake and burial—all the assistance given to the departed soul—are acts expressing the dogma of continuity after death and of communion between dead and living. Any survivor who has gone through a number of mortuary ceremonials for others becomes prepared for his own death. The belief in immortality, which he has lived through ritually and practiced in the case of his mother or father, of his brothers and friends, makes him cherish more firmly the belief in his own future life. The belief in human immortality therefore, which is the foundation of ancestor worship, of domestic cults, of mortuary ritual and of animism, grows out of the constitution of human society.

Most of the other forms of religion when analyzed in their functional character correspond to deep although derived needs of the individual and of the community. Totemism, for example, when related to its wider setting affirms the existence of an intimate kinship between man and his surrounding world. The ritual side of totemism and nature worship consists to a large extent in rites of multiplication or of propitiation of animals or in rites of enhancing the fertility of vegetable nature which also establish links between man and his environment. Primitive religion is largely concerned with the sacralization of the crises of human life. Conception, birth, puberty, marriage, as well as the supreme crisis death, all give rise to sacramental acts. The fact of conception is surrounded by such beliefs as that in reincarnation, spirit entry and magical impregnation. At birth a wealth of animistic ideas concerning the formation of the human soul, the value of the individual to his community, the development of his moral powers, the possibility of forecasting his fate, become associated with and expressed in birth ritual. Initiation ceremonies, prevalent in puberty, have a developed mythological and dogmatic context. Guardian spirits, tutelary divinities, culture heroes, or a tribal All-Father are associated with initiation ceremonies. The contractual sacraments, such as marriage, entry into an age grade, or acceptance into a magical or religious fraternity, entail primarily ethical views but very often are also the expression of myths and dogmas.

Every important crisis of human life implies a strong emotional upheaval, mental conflict and possible disintegration. The hopes of a favorable issue have to struggle with anxieties and forebodings. Religious belief consists in the traditional standardization of the positive side in the mental conflict and therefore satisfies a definite individual need arising out of the psychological concomitants of social organization. On the other hand, religious belief and ritual, by making the critical acts and the social contracts of human life public, traditionally standardized, and subject to supernatural sanctions, strengthen the bonds of human cohesion.

Religion in its ethics sanctifies human life and conduct and becomes perhaps the most powerful force of social control. In its dogmatics it supplies man with strong cohesive forces. It grows out of every culture, because knowledge which gives foresight fails to overcome fate; because lifelong bonds of cooperation and mutual interest create sentiments, and sentiments rebel against death and dissolution. The cultural call for religion is highly derived and indirect but is finally rooted in the way in which the primary needs of man are satisfied in culture.

A. R. RADCLIFFE-BROWN

Taboo

Another anthropological scholar whose writings on the function of religion in primitive society have been of major significance is Radcliffe-Brown. His three most important works on this subject are portions of his book, *The Andaman Islanders* (1922), his Frazer Lecture, *Taboo* (which is herewith reprinted), and a later paper, "Religion and Society" (1945).

Radcliffe-Brown's central thesis, that religious and magical rituals exist and persist because they are part of the mechanism by which society maintains itself in existence by establishing certain fundamental social values, should be understood in the wider context of his contributions toward the concepts and methods needed to pursue a systematic comparative study of societies, and especially of his thinking about the concept of "function." His series of papers reprinted in *Structure and Function in Primitive Society* (1952) are particularly useful.

In this paper on taboo Radcliffe-Brown begins by discussing the nature of one of the classic ideas in the primitive religions of Polynesia, but goes on to expound his thoughts on ritual and ritual values and their relationship to the essential constitution of a society. He reaches the conclusion that "the primary basis of ritual is the attribution of ritual value to objects and occasions which are either themselves objects of important common interests linking together the persons of a community or are symbolically representative of such objects." He then argues that men are more likely to experience concern and anxiety when a customary ritual is not performed than they are to turn to ritual procedures when they feel anxious.

Reprinted from A. R. Radcliffe-Brown, *Taboo* ("The Frazer Lecture," 1939). Cambridge: At the University Press, 1939. Reprinted by permission of Professor E. E. Evans-Pritchard, literary executor of the late Professor Radcliffe-Brown.

The purpose of this lecture, which you have done me the honor of inviting me to deliver, is to commemorate the work of Sir James Frazer, as an example of lifelong, single-minded devotion to scientific investigation and as having contributed, in as large a measure as that of any man, to laying the foundations of the science of social anthropology. It therefore seems to me appropriate to select as the subject of my discourse one which Sir James was the first to investigate systematically half a century ago, when he wrote the article on "Taboo" for the ninth edition of the *Encyclopaedia Britannica,* and to the elucidation of which he has made many successive contributions in his writings since that time.

The English word "taboo" is derived from the Polynesian word "tabu" (with the accent on the first syllable). In the languages of Polynesia the word means simply "to forbid," "forbidden," and can be applied to any sort of prohibition. A rule of etiquette, an order issued by a chief, an injunction to children not to meddle with the possessions of their elders, may all be expressed by the use of the word "tabu."

The early voyagers in Polynesia adopted the word to refer to prohibitions of a special kind, which may be illustrated by an example. Certain things such as a newly born infant, a corpse or the person of a chief are said to be tabu. This means that one should, as far as possible, avoid touching them. A man who does touch one of these tabu objects immediately becomes tabu himself. This means two things. In the first place, a man who is tabu in this sense must observe a number of special restrictions on his behavior; for example, he may not use his hands to feed himself. He is regarded as being in a state of danger, and this is generally stated by saying that if he fails to observe the customary precautions he will be ill and perhaps die. In the second place he is also dangerous to other persons—he is tabu in the same sense as the thing he has touched. If he should come in contact with utensils in which, or the fire at which, food is cooked, the dangerous influence would be communicated to the food and so injure anyone who partook of it. A person who is tabu in this way, as by touching a corpse, can be restored to his normal condition by rites of purification or desacralization. He is then said to be *noa* again, this term being the contrary of tabu.

Sir James Frazer has told us that when he took up the study of taboo in 1886 the current view of anthropologists at the time was that the institution in question was confined to the brown and black races of the Pacific,

but that as a result of his investigations he came to the conclusion that the Polynesian body of practices and beliefs "is only one of a number of similar systems of superstition which among many, perhaps all the races of men have contributed in large measure, under many different names and with many variations of detail, to build up the complex fabric of society in all the various sides or elements of it which we describe as religious, social, political, moral, and economic."

The use of the word taboo in anthropology for customs all over the world which resemble in essentials the example given from Polynesia seems to me undesirable and inconvenient. There is the fact already mentioned that in the Polynesian language the word tabu has a much wider meaning, equivalent to our own word "forbidden." This has produced a good deal of confusion in the literature relating to Polynesia owing to the ambiguity resulting from two different uses of the same word. You will have noticed that I have used the word "taboo" (with the English spelling and pronunciation) in the meaning that it has for anthropologists, and "tabu" (with the Polynesian spelling and pronunciation) in special reference to Polynesia and in the Polynesian sense. But this is not entirely satisfactory.

I propose to refer to the customs we are considering as "ritual avoidances" or "ritual prohibitions" and to define them by reference to two fundamental concepts for which I have been in the habit of using the terms "ritual status" and "ritual value." I am not suggesting that these are the best terms to be found; they are merely the best that I have been able to find up to the present. In such a science as ours words are the instruments of analysis and we should always be prepared to discard inferior tools for superior when opportunity arises.

A ritual prohibition is a rule of behavior which is associated with a belief that an infraction will result in an undesirable change in the ritual status of the person who fails to keep to the rule. This change of ritual status is conceived in many different ways in different societies, but everywhere there is the idea that it involves the likelihood of some minor or major misfortune which will befall the person concerned.

We have already considered one example. The Polynesian who touches a corpse has, according to Polynesian belief, undergone what I am calling an undesirable change of ritual status. The misfortune of which he is considered to be in danger is illness, and he therefore takes precautions and goes through a ritual in order that he may escape the danger and be restored to his former ritual status.

Let us consider two examples of different kinds from contemporary England. There are some people who think that one should avoid spilling salt. The person who spills salt will have bad luck. But he can avoid this by throwing a pinch of the spilled salt over his shoulder. Putting this in my terminology, it can be said that spilling salt produces an undesirable change in the ritual status of the person who does so, and that he is restored to his normal or previous ritual status by the positive rite of throwing salt over his shoulder.

A member of the Roman Catholic Church, unless granted a dispensation, is required by his religion to abstain from eating meat on Fridays and during Lent. If he fails to observe the rule he sins, and must proceed, as in any other sin, to confess and obtain absolution. Different as this is in important ways from the rule about spilling salt, it can and must for scientific purposes be regarded as belonging to the same general class. Eating meat on Friday produces in the person who does so an undesirable change of ritual status which requires to be remedied by fixed appropriate means.

We may add to these examples two others from other societies. If you turn to the fifth chapter of Leviticus you will find that amongst the Hebrews if a "soul" touch the carcase of an unclean beast or of unclean cattle, or of unclean creeping things, even if he is unaware that he does so, then he is unclean and guilty and has sinned. When he becomes aware of his sin he must confess that he has sinned and must take a trespass offering—a female from the flock, a lamb, or a kid of the goats—which the priest shall sacrifice to make an atonement for the sin so that it shall be forgiven him. Here the change in ritual status through touching an unclean carcase is described by the terms "sin," "unclean," and "guilty."

In the Kikuyu tribe of East Africa the word *thahu* denotes the undesirable ritual status that results from failure to observe rules of ritual avoidance. It is believed that a person who is *thahu* will be ill and will probably die unless he removes the *thahu* by the appropriate ritual remedies, which in all serious cases require the services of a priest or medicine man. Actions which produce this condition are touching or carrying a corpse, stepping over a corpse, eating food from a cracked pot, coming in contact with a woman's menstrual discharge, and many others. Just as amongst the Hebrews a soul may unwittingly be guilty of sin by touching in ignorance the carcase of an unclean animal, so amongst the Kikuyu a man may become *thahu* without any voluntary act on his part. If an elder or a woman when coming out of the hut slips and falls down on the ground, he or she is *thahu* and lies there until some of the elders of the neighborhood come and sacrifice a sheep. If the side-pole of a bedstead breaks, the person lying on it is *thahu* and must be purified. If the droppings of a kite or crow fall on a person he is *thahu,* and if a hyena defecates in a village, or a jackal barks therein, the village and its inhabitants are *thahu.*

I have purposely chosen from our own society two examples of ritual avoidances which are of very different kinds. The rule against eating meat on Friday or in Lent is a rule of religion, as is the rule, where it is recognized, against playing golf or tennis on Sunday. The rule against spilling salt, I suppose it will be agreed, is nonreligious. Our language permits us to make this distinction very clearly, for infractions of the rules of religion are sins, while the nonreligious avoidances are concerned with good and bad luck. Since this distinction is so obvious to us it might be thought that we should find it in other societies. My own experience is that in some of the societies with which I am acquainted this distinction between sinful acts and acts that bring bad luck cannot be made. Several anthropologists, however, have attempted to classify rites into two classes, religious rites and magical rites.

For Émile Durkheim the essential distinction is that religious rites are obligatory within a religious society or church, while magical rites are optional. A person who fails in religious observances is guilty of wrongdoing, whereas one who does not observe the precautions of magic or those relating to luck is simply acting foolishly. This distinction is of considerable theoretical importance. It is difficult to apply in the study of the rites of simple societies.

Sir James Frazer defines religion as "a propitiation or conciliation of superhuman powers which are believed to control nature and man," and regards magic as the erroneous application of the notion of causality. If we apply this to ritual prohibitions we may regard as belonging to religion those rules the infraction of which produces a change of ritual status in the individual by offending the superhuman powers, whereas the infraction of a rule of magic would be regarded as resulting immediately in a change of ritual status, or in the misfortune that follows, by a process of hidden causation. Spilling salt, by Sir James Frazer's definition, is a question of magic, while eating meat on Friday is a question of religion.

An attempt to apply this distinction systematically meets with certain difficulties. Thus with regard to the Maori, Sir James Frazer states that "the ultimate sanction of the taboo, in other words, that which engaged the people to observe its commandments, was a firm persuasion that any breach of those commandments would surely and speedily be punished by an *atua* or ghost, who would afflict the sinner with a painful malady till he died." This would seem to make the Polynesian taboo a matter of religion, not of magic. But my own observation of the Polynesians suggests to me that in general the native conceives of the change in his ritual status as taking place as the immediate result of such an act as touching a corpse, and that it is only when he proceeds to rationalize the whole system of taboos that he thinks of the gods and spirits—the *atua*—as being concerned. Incidentally, it should not be assumed that the Polynesian word *atua* or *otua* always refers to a personal spiritual being.

Of the various ways of distinguishing magic and religion I will mention only one more. For Professor Malinowski a rite is magical when "it has a definite practical purpose which is known to all who practice it and can be easily elicited from any native informant," while a rite is religious if it is simply expressive and has no purpose, being not a means to an end but an end in itself. A difficulty in applying this criterion is due to uncertainty as to what is meant by "definite practical purpose." To avoid the bad luck which results from spilling salt is, I suppose, a practical purpose though not very definite. The desire to please God in all our actions and thus escape some period of Purgatory is perhaps definite enough, but Professor Malinowski may regard it as not practical. What shall we say of the desire of the Polynesian to avoid sickness and possible death which he gives as his reason for not touching chiefs, corpses, and newly born babies?

Seeing that there is this absence of agreement as to the definitions of magic and religion and the nature of the distinction between them, and seeing that in many instances whether we call a particular rite magical or religious depends on which of the various proposed definitions we accept, the only sound procedure, at any rate in the present state of anthropological knowledge, is to avoid as far as possible the use of the terms in question until there is some general agreement about them. Certainly the distinctions made by Durkheim and Frazer and Malinowski may be theoretically significant, even though they are difficult to apply universally. Certainly, also, there is need for a systematic classification of rites, but a satisfactory classification will be fairly complex and a simple dichotomy between magic and religion does not carry us very far toward it.

Another distinction which we make in our own society within the field of ritual avoidances is between the holy and the unclean. Certain things must be treated with respect because they are holy, others because they are unclean. But, as Robertson Smith and Sir James Frazer have shown, there are many societies in which this distinction is entirely unrecognized. The Polynesian, for example, does not think of a chief or a temple as holy and a corpse as unclean. He thinks of them all as things dangerous. An example from Hawai'i will illustrate this fundamental identity of holiness and uncleanness. There, in former times, if a commoner committed incest with his sister he became *kapu* (the Hawai'ian form of tabu). His presence was dangerous in the extreme for the whole community, and since he could not be purified he was put to death. But if a chief of high rank, who, by reason of his rank was, of course, sacred (*kapu*), married his sister he became still more so. An extreme sanctity or untouchability attached to a chief born of a brother and sister who were themselves the children of a brother and sister. The sanctity of such a chief and the uncleanness of the person put to death for incest have the same source and are the same thing. They are both denoted by saying that the person is *kapu*. In studying the simpler societies it is essential that we should carefully avoid thinking of their behavior and ideas in terms of our own ideas of holiness and uncleanness. Since most people find this difficult it is desirable to have terms which we can use that do not convey this connotation. Durkheim and others have used the word "sacred" as an inclusive term for the holy and the unclean together. This is easier to do in French than in English, and has some justification in the fact that the Latin *sacer* did apply to holy things such as the gods and also to accursed things such as persons guilty of certain crimes. But there is certainly a tendency in English to identify sacred with holy. I think that it will greatly aid clear thinking if we adopt some wide inclusive term which does not have any undesirable connotation. I venture to propose the term "ritual value."

Anything—a person, a material thing, a place, a word or name, an occasion or event, a day of the week or a period of the year—which is the object of a ritual avoidance or taboo can be said to have ritual value. Thus in Polynesia chiefs, corpses, and newly born babies have ritual value. For some people in England salt has ritual value. For Christians all Sundays and Good Friday have ritual value, and for Jews all Saturdays and the Day of Atonement. The ritual value is exhibited in the behavior adopted towards the object or occasion in question. Ritual values are exhibited not only in negative ritual but also in positive ritual, being possessed by the objects towards which positive rites are directed and also by objects, words, or places used in the rites. A large class of positive rites, those of consecration or sacralization, have for their purpose to endow objects with ritual value. It may be noted that in general anything that has value in positive ritual is also the object of some sort of ritual avoidance or at the very least of ritual respect.

The word "value," as I am using it, always refers to a relation between a subject and an object. The relation can be stated in two ways by saying either that the object has a value for the subject, or that the subject has an interest in the object. We can use the terms in this way to refer to any act of behavior towards an object. The relation is exhibited in and defined by the behavior. The words "interest" and "value" provide a convenient shorthand by which we can describe the reality, which consists of acts of behavior and the actual relations between subjects and objects which those acts of behavior reveal. If Jack loves Jill, then Jill has the value of a loved object for Jack, and Jack has a recognizable interest in Jill. When I am hungry I have an interest in food, and a good meal has an immediate value for me that it does not have at other times. My toothache has a value to me as something that I am interested in getting rid of as quickly as possible.

A social system can be conceived and studied as a system of values. A society consists of a number of individuals bound together in a network of social relations. A social relation exists between two or more persons when there is some harmonization of their individual interests, by some convergence of interest and by limitation or adjustment of divergent interests. An interest is always the interest of an individual. Two individuals may have similar interests. Similar interests do not in themselves constitute a social relation; two dogs may have a similar interest in the same bone and the result may be a dogfight. But a society cannot exist except on the basis of a certain measure of similarity in the interests of its members. Putting this in terms of value, the first necessary condition of the existence of a society is that the individual members shall agree in some measure in the values that they recognize.

Any particular society is characterized by a certain set of values—moral, aesthetic, economic, etc. In a simple society there is a fair amount of agreement amongst the members in their evaluations, though of course the agreement is never absolute. In a complex modern society we find much more disagreement if we consider the society as a whole, but we may find a closer measure of agreement amongst the members of a group or class within the society.

While some measure of agreement about values, some similarity of interests, is a prerequisite of a social system, social relations involve more than this. They require the existence of common interests and of social values. When two or more persons have a common interest in the same object and are aware of their community of interest a social relation is established. They form, whether for a moment or for a long period, an association, and the object may be said to have a social value. For a man and his wife the birth of a child, the child itself and its well-being and happiness or its death, are objects of a common interest which binds them together and they thus have, for the association formed by the two persons, social value. By this definition an object can only have a social value for an association of persons. In the simplest possible instance we have a triadic relation; Subject 1 and Subject 2 are both interested in the same way in the Object and each of the Subjects has an interest in the other, or at any rate in certain items of the behavior of the other, namely those directed toward the object. To avoid cumbersome circumlocutions it is convenient to speak of the object as having a social value for any one subject involved in such a relation, but it must be remembered that this is a loose way of speaking.

It is perhaps necessary for the avoidance of misunderstanding to add that a social system also requires that persons should be objects of interest to other persons. In relations of friendship or love each of two persons has a value for the other. In certain kinds of groups each member is an object of interest for all the others, and each member therefore has a social value for the groups as a whole. Further, since there are negative values as well as positive, persons may be united or associated by their antagonism to other persons. For the members of an anti-Comintern pact the Comintern has a specific social value.

Amongst the members of a society we find a certain measure of agreement as to the ritual value they attribute to objects of different kinds. We also find that most of these ritual values are social values as defined above. Thus for a local totemic clan in Australia the totem-centers, the natural species associated with them, i.e., the totems, and the myths and rites that relate thereto, have a specific social value for the clan; the common interest in them binds the individuals together into a firm and lasting association.

Ritual values exist in every known society, and show an immense diversity as we pass from one society to another. The problem of a natural science of society (and it is as such

that I regard social anthropology) is to discover the deeper, not immediately perceptible, uniformities beneath the superficial differences. This is, of course, a highly complex problem which will require the studies begun by Sir James Frazer and others to be continued by many investigators over many years. The ultimate aim should be, I think, to find some relatively adequate answer to the question, *What is the relation of ritual and ritual values to the essential constitution of human society?* I have chosen a particular approach to this study which I believe to be promising—to investigate in a few societies studied as thoroughly as possible the relations of ritual values to other values including moral and aesthetic values. In the present lecture, however, it is only one small part of this study in which I seek to interest you—the question of a relation between ritual values and social values.

One way of approaching the study of ritual is by the consideration of the purposes or reasons for the rites. If one examines the literature of anthropology one finds this approach very frequently adopted. It is by far the least profitable, though the one that appeals most to common sense. Sometimes the purpose of a rite is obvious, or a reason may be volunteered by those who practice it. Sometimes the anthropologist has to ask the reason, and in such circumstances it may happen that different reasons are given by different informants. What is fundamentally the same rite in two different societies may have different purposes or reasons in the one and in the other. The reasons given by the members of a community for any custom they observe are important data for the anthropologist. But it is to fall into grievous error to suppose that they give a valid explanation of the custom. What is entirely inexcusable is for the anthropologist, when he cannot get from the people themselves a reason for their behavior which seems to him satisfactory, to attribute to them some purpose or reason on the basis of his own preconceptions about human motives. I could adduce many instances of this from the literature of ethnography, but I prefer to illustrate what I mean by an anecdote.

A Queenslander met a Chinese who was taking a bowl of cooked rice to place on his brother's grave. The Australian in jocular tones asked if he supposed that his brother would come and eat the rice. The reply was

"No! We offer rice to people as an expression of friendship and affection. But since you speak as you do I suppose that you in this country place flowers on the graves of your dead in the belief that they will enjoy looking at them and smelling their sweet perfume."

So far as ritual avoidances are concerned the reasons for them may vary from a very vague idea that some sort of misfortune or ill-luck, not defined as to its kind, is likely to befall anyone who fails to observe the taboo, to a belief that nonobservance will produce some quite specific and undesirable result. Thus an Australian aborigine told me that if he spoke to any woman who stood in the relation of mother-in-law to him his hair would turn gray.

The very common tendency to look for the explanation of ritual actions in their purpose is the result of a false assimilation of them to what may be called technical acts. In any technical activity an adequate statement of the purpose of any particular act or series of acts constitutes by itself a sufficient explanation. But ritual acts differ from technical acts in having in all instances some expressive or symbolic element in them.

A second approach to the study of ritual is therefore by a consideration not of their purpose or reason, but of their meaning. I am here using the words "symbol" and "meaning" as coincident. Whatever has a meaning is a symbol and the meaning is whatever is expressed by the symbol.

But how are we to discover meanings? They do not lie on the surface. There is a sense in which people always know the meaning of their own symbols, but they do so intuitively and can rarely express their understanding in words. Shall we therefore be reduced to guessing at meanings as some anthropologists have guessed at reasons and purposes? I think not. For as long as we admit guesswork of any kind social anthropology cannot be a science. There are, I believe, methods of determining, with some fair degree of probability, the meanings of rites and other symbols.

There is still a third approach to the study of rites. We can consider the effects of the rite—not the effects that it is supposed to produce by the people who practice it but the effects that it does actually produce. A rite has immediate or direct effects on the persons who are in any way directly concerned

in it, which we may call, for lack of a better term, the psychological effects. But there are also secondary effects upon the social structure, i.e., the network of social relations binding individuals together in an ordered life. These we may call the "social effects." By considering the psychological effects of a rite we may succeed in defining its psychological function; by considering the social effects we may discover its social function. Clearly it is impossible to discover the social function of a rite without taking into account its usual or average psychological effects. But it is possible to discuss the psychological effects while more or less completely ignoring the more remote sociological effects, and this is often done in what is called "functional anthropology."

Let us suppose that we wish to investigate in Australian tribes the totemic rites of a kind widely distributed over a large part of the continent. The ostensible purpose of these rites, as stated by the natives themselves, is to renew or maintain some part of nature, such as a species of animal or plant, or rain, or hot or cold weather. With reference to this purpose we have to say that from our point of view the natives are mistaken, that the rites do not actually do what they are believed to do. The rainmaking ceremony does not, we think, actually bring rain. In so far as the rites are performed for a purpose they are futile, based on erroneous belief. I do not believe that there is any scientific value in attempts to conjecture processes of reasoning which might be supposed to have led to these errors.

The rites are easily perceived to be symbolic, and we may therefore investigate their meaning. To do this we have to examine a considerable number of them and we then discover that there is a certain body of ritual idiom extending from the west coast of the continent to the east coast with some local variations. Since each rite has a myth associated with it we have similarly to investigate the meanings of the myths. As a result we find that the meaning of any single rite becomes clear in the light of a cosmology, a body of ideas and beliefs about nature and human society, which, so far as its most general features are concerned, is current in all Australian tribes.

The immediate psychological effects of the rites can be to some extent observed by watching and talking to the performers. The ostensible purpose of the rite is certainly present in their minds, but so also is that complex set of cosmological beliefs by reference to which the rite has a meaning. Certainly a person performing the rite, even if, as sometimes happens, he performs it alone, derives therefrom a definite feeling of satisfaction, but it would be entirely false to imagine that this is simply because he believes that he has helped to provide a more abundant supply of food for himself and his fellow tribesmen. His satisfaction is in having performed a ritual duty, we might say a religious duty. Putting in my own words what I judge, from my own observations, to express what the native feels, I would say that in the performance of the rite he has made that small contribution, which it is both his privilege and his duty to do, to the maintenance of that order of the universe of which man and nature are interdependent parts. The satisfaction which he thus receives gives the rite a special value for him. In some instances with which I am acquainted of the last survivor of a totemic group who still continues to perform the totemic rites by himself, it is this satisfaction that constitutes apparently the sole motive for his action.

To discover the social function of the totemic rites we have to consider the whole body of cosmological ideas of which each rite is a partial expression. I believe that it is possible to show that the social structure of an Australian tribe is connected in a very special way with these cosmological ideas and that the maintenance of its continuity depends on keeping them alive, by their regular expression in myth and rite.

Thus any satisfactory study of the totemic rites of Australia must be based not simply on the consideration of their ostensible purpose and their psychological function, or on an analysis of the motives of the individuals who perform the rites, but on the discovery of their meaning and of their social function.

It may be that some rites have no social function. This may be the case with such taboos as that against spilling salt in our own society. Nevertheless, the method of investigating rites and ritual values that I have found most profitable during work extending over more than thirty years is to study rites as symbolic expressions and to seek to discover their social functions. This method is not new except in so far as it is applied to the comparative study of many societies of diverse types. It was applied by Chinese thinkers to their own ritual more than twenty centuries ago.

In China, in the fifth and sixth centuries B.C., Confucius and his followers insisted on the great importance of the proper performance of ritual, such as funeral and mourning rites and sacrifices. After Confucius there came the reformer Mo Ti who taught a combination of altruism—love for all men— and utilitarianism. He held that funeral and mourning rites were useless and interfered with useful activities and should therefore be abolished or reduced to a minimum. In the third and second centuries B.C. the Confucians, Hsün Tze and the compilers of the *Li Chi* (Book of Rites), replied to Mo Ti to the effect that though these rites might have no utilitarian purpose they none the less had a very important social function. Briefly the theory is that the rites are the orderly (the *Li Chi* says the beautified) expression of feelings appropriate to a social situation. They thus serve to regulate and refine human emotions. We may say that partaking in the performance of rites serves to cultivate in the individual sentiments on whose existence the social order itself depends.

Let us consider the meaning and social function of an extremely simple example of ritual. In the Andaman Islands when a woman is expecting a baby a name is given to it while it is still in the womb. From that time until some weeks after the baby is born nobody is allowed to use the personal name of either the father or the mother; they can be referred to by teknonymy, i.e., in terms of their relation to the child. During this period both the parents are required to abstain from eating certain foods which they may freely eat at other times.

I did not obtain from the Andamanese any statement of the purpose or reason for this avoidance of names. Assuming that the act is symbolic, what method, other than that of guessing, is there of arriving at the meaning? I suggest that we may start with a general working hypothesis that when, in a single society, the same symbol is used in different contexts or on different kinds of occasions there is some common element of meaning, and that by comparing together the various uses of the symbol we may be able to discover what the common element is. This is precisely the method that we adopt in studying an unrecorded spoken language in order to discover the meanings of words and morphemes.

In the Andamans the name of a dead person is avoided from the occurrence of the death to the conclusion of mourning; the name of a person mourning for a dead relative is not used; there is avoidance of the name of a youth or girl who is passing through the ceremonies that take place at adolescence; a bride or bridegroom is not spoken of or to by his or her own name for a short time after the marriage. For the Andamanese the personal name is a symbol of the social personality, i.e., of the position that an individual occupies in the social structure and the social life. The avoidance of a personal name is a symbolic recognition of the fact that at the time the person is not occupying a normal position in the social life. It may be added that a person whose name is thus temporarily out of use is regarded as having for the time an abnormal ritual status.

Turning now to the rule as to avoiding certain foods, if the Andaman Islanders are asked what would happen if the father or mother broke this taboo the usual answer is that he or she would be ill, though one or two of my informants thought it might perhaps also affect the child. This is simply one instance of a standard formula which applies to a number of ritual prohibitions. Thus a person in mourning for a relative may not eat pork and turtle, the most important flesh foods, and the reason given is that if they did they would be ill.

To discover the meaning of this avoidance of foods by the parents we can apply the same method as in reference to the avoidance of their names. There are similar rules for mourners, for women during menstruation, and for youths and girls during the period of adolescence. But for a full demonstration we have to consider the place of foods in Andamanese ritual as a whole, and for an examination of this I must refer to what I have already written on the subject.

I should like to draw your attention to another point in the method by which it is possible to test our hypotheses as to the meanings of rites. We take the different occasions on which two rites are associated together, for example the association of the avoidance of a person's name with the avoidance by that person of certain foods, which we find in the instance of mourners on the one hand and the expectant mother and father on the other. We must assume that for the Andamanese there is some important similarity between these two kinds of occasions—birth and death—by virtue of which they have similar ritual values. We cannot rest content with any interpretation of the taboos at childbirth unless there is a parallel interpretation of those relating to mourners. In the terms I am using here we can say that in the Andamans the relatives of a recently dead person, and the father and mother of a child that is about to be, or has recently been, born, are in an abnormal ritual status. This is recognized or indicated by the avoidance of their names. They are regarded as likely to suffer some misfortune, some bad luck, if you will, unless they observe certain prescribed ritual precautions of which the avoidance of certain foods is one. In the Andaman Islands the danger in such instances is thought of as the danger of illness. This is the case also with the Polynesian belief about the ritual status of anyone who has touched a corpse or a newly born baby. It is to be noted that for the Polynesians as well as for the Andamanese the occasion of a birth has a similar ritual value to that of a death.

The interpretation of the taboos at childbirth at which we arrive by studying it in relation to the whole system of ritual values of the Andamanese is too complex to be stated here in full. Clearly, however, they express, in accordance with Andamanese ritual idiom, a common concern in the event. The parents show their concern by avoiding certain foods; their friends show theirs by avoiding the parents' personal names. By virtue of these taboos the occasion acquires a certain social value, as that term has been defined above.

There is one theory that might seem to be applicable to our example. It is based on a hypothesis as to the psychological function of a class of rites. The theory is that in certain circumstances the individual human being is anxious about the outcome of some event or activity because it depends to some extent on conditions that he cannot control by any technical means. He therefore observes some rite which, since he believes that it will ensure good luck, serves to reassure him. Thus an aeronaut takes with him in a plane a mascot which he believes will protect him from accident and thus carries out his flight with confidence.

The theory has a respectable antiquity. It was perhaps implied in the *Primus in orbe deos fecit timor* of Petronius and Statius. It has taken various forms from Hume's explanation of religion to Malinowski's explanation of Trobriand magic. It can be made so plausible by a suitable selection of illustrations that it is necessary to examine it with particular care and treat it with reasonable skepticism. For there is always the danger that we may be taken in by the plausibility of a theory that ultimately proves to be unsound.

I think that for certain rites it would be easy to maintain with equal plausibility an exactly contrary theory, namely, that if it were not for the existence of the rite and the beliefs associated with it the individual would feel no anxiety, and that the psychological effect of the rite is to create in him a sense of insecurity or danger. It seems very unlikely than an Andaman Islander would think that it is dangerous to eat dugong or pork or turtle meat if it were not for the existence of a specific body of ritual the ostensible purpose of which is to protect him from those dangers. Many hundreds of similar instances could be mentioned from all over the world.

Thus, while one anthropological theory is that magic and religion give men confidence, comfort, and a sense of security, it could equally well be argued that they give men fears and anxieties from which they would otherwise be free—the fear of black magic or of spirits, fear of God, of the Devil, of Hell.

Actually in our fears or anxieties as well as in our hopes we are conditioned (as the phrase goes) by the community in which we live. And it is largely by the sharing of hopes and fears, by what I have called common concern in events or eventualities, that human beings are linked together in temporary or permanent associations.

To return to the Andamanese taboos at childbirth, there are difficulties in supposing that they are means by which parents reassure themselves against the accidents that may interfere with a successful delivery. If the prospective father fails to observe the food taboo it is he who will be sick, according to the general Andamanese opinion. Moreover, he must continue to observe the taboos after the child is safely delivered.

Further, how are we to provide a parallel explanation of the similar taboos observed by a person mourning for a dead relative?

The taboos associated with pregnancy and parturition are often explained in terms of the hypothesis I have mentioned. A father, naturally anxious at the outcome of an event over which he does not have a technical control and which is subject to hazard, reassures himself by observing some taboo or carrying out some magical action. He may avoid certain foods. He may avoid making nets or tying knots, or he may go round the house untying all knots and opening any locked or closed boxes or containers.

I wish to arouse in your minds, if it is not already there, a suspicion that both the general theory and this special application of it do not give the whole truth and indeed may not be true at all. Skepticism of plausible but unproved hypotheses is essential in every science. There is at least good ground for suspicion in the fact that the theory has so far been considered in reference to facts that seem to fit it, and no systematic attempt has been made, so far as I am aware, to look for facts that do not fit. That there are many such I am satisfied from my own studies.

The alternative hypothesis which I am presenting for consideration is as follows. In a given community it is appropriate that an expectant father should feel concern or at least should make an appearance of doing so. Some suitable symbolic expression of his concern is found in terms of the general ritual or symbolic idiom of the society, and it is felt generally that a man in that situation ought to carry out the symbolic or ritual actions or abstentions. For every rule that *ought* to be observed there must be some sort of sanction or reason. For acts that patently affect other persons the moral and legal sanctions provide a generally sufficient controlling force upon the individual. For ritual obligations conformity and rationalization are provided by the ritual sanctions. The simplest form of ritual sanction is an accepted belief that if rules of ritual are not observed some undefined misfortune is likely to occur. In many societies the expected danger is somewhat more definitely conceived as a danger of sickness or, in extreme cases, death. In the more specialized forms of ritual sanction the good results to be hoped for or the bad results to be feared are more specifically defined in reference to the occasion or meaning of the ritual.

The theory is not concerned with the historical origin of ritual, nor is it another attempt to explain ritual in terms of human psychology; it is a hypothesis as to the relation of ritual and ritual values to the essential constitution of human society, i.e., to those invariant general characters which belong to all human societies, past, present, and future. It rests on the recognition of the fact that while in animal societies social co-aptation depends on instinct, in human societies it depends upon the efficacy of symbols of many different kinds. The theory I am advancing must therefore, for a just estimation of its value, be considered in its place in a general theory of symbols and their social efficacy.

By this theory the Andamanese taboos relating to childbirth are the obligatory recognition in a standardized symbolic form of the significance and importance of the event to the parents and to the community at large. They thus serve to fix the social value of occasions of this kind. Similarly I have argued in another place that the Andamanese taboos relating to the animals and plants used for food are means of affixing a definite social value to food, based on its social importance. The social importance of food is not that it satisfies hunger, but that in such a community as an Andamanese camp or village an enormously large proportion of the activities are concerned with the getting and consuming of food, and that in these activities, with their daily instances of collaboration and mutual aid, there continuously occur those interrelations of interests which bind the individual men, women, and children into a society.

I believe that this theory can be generalized and with suitable modifications will be found to apply to a vast number of the taboos of different societies. My theory would go further for I would hold, as a reasonable working hypothesis, that we have here the primary basis of all ritual and therefore of religion and magic, however those may be distinguished. The primary basis of ritual, so the formulation would run, is the attribution of ritual value to objects and occasions which are either themselves objects of important common interests linking together the persons of a community or are symbolically representative of such objects. To illustrate what is meant by the last part of this statement two illustrations may be offered. In the Andamans ritual value is attributed to the cicada, not because it has any social importance itself but because it symbolically represents the seasons of the year which do have importance. In some tribes of Eastern Australia the god Baiame is the personification, i.e., the symbolical representative, of the moral law of the tribe, and the rainbow-serpent (the Australian equivalent of the Chinese dragon) is a symbol representing growth and fertility in nature. Baiame and the rainbow-serpent in their turn are represented by the figures of earth which are made on the sacred ceremonial ground of the initiation ceremonies and at which rites are performed. The reverence that the Australian shows to the image of Baiame or towards his name is the symbolic method of fixing the social value of the moral law, particularly the laws relating to marriage.

In conclusion let me return once more to the work of the anthropologist whom we are here to honor. Sir James Frazer, in his *Psyche's Task* and in his other works, set himself to show how, in his own words, taboos have contributed to build up the complex fabric of society. He thus initiated that functional study of ritual to which I have in this lecture and elsewhere attempted to make some contribution. But there has been a shift of emphasis. Sir James accounted for the taboos of savage tribes as the application in practice of beliefs arrived at by erroneous processes of reasoning, and he seems to have thought of the effects of these beliefs in creating or maintaining a stable orderly society as being accidental. My own view is that the negative and positive rites of savages exist and persist because they are part of the mechanism by which an orderly society maintains itself in existence, serving as they do to establish certain fundamental social values. The beliefs by which the rites themselves are justified and given some sort of consistency are the rationalizations of symbolic actions and of the sentiments associated with them. I would suggest that what Sir James Frazer seems to regard as the accidental results of magical and religious beliefs really constitute their essential function and the ultimate reason for their existence.

NOTE.—The theory of ritual outlined in this lecture was first worked out in 1908 in a thesis on the Andaman Islanders. It was written out again in a revised and extended form in 1913 and appeared in print in 1922. Unfortunately the exposition contained in *The Andaman Islanders* is evidently not clear, since some of my critics have failed to understand what the theory is. For example, it has been assumed that by "social value" I mean "utility."

The best treatment of the subject of value with which I am acquainted is Ralph Barton Perry's *General Theory of Value*, 1926. For the Chinese theory of ritual the most easily accessible account is in Chapter XIV of Fung Yu-lan's *History of Chinese Philosophy*, 1937. The third chapter, on the uses of symbolism, of Whitehead's *Symbolism: Its Meaning and Effect*, is an admirable brief introduction to the sociological theory of symbolism.

One very important point that could not be dealt with in the lecture is that indicated by Whitehead in the following sentence: "No account of the uses of symbolism is complete without the recognition that the symbolic elements in life have a tendency to run wild, like the vegetation in a tropical forest."

GEORGE C. HOMANS

Anxiety and Ritual: The Theories of Malinowski and Radcliffe-Brown

With the publication of Malinowski's various books and papers on the function of ritual in allaying anxiety and inspiring confidence in men faced with an unbridgeable gap in their empirical knowledge, and of Radcliffe-Brown's lecture, *Taboo*, which presents the thesis that anxiety is frequently experienced when a customary ritual is *not* performed, students of religion and magic were confronted by a theoretical dilemma of how to resolve these two essentially opposing theories.

In this brief but penetrating paper Homans suggests a resolution by introducing the concepts of "primary" and "secondary" anxieties and rituals and by clarifying the relationship between the individual and societal level of analysis. His use of the term "rationalization" for the native's justification of his ritual may be misleading to some readers. This is rationalization not from the native's point of view—he *believes* in his rituals and thinks they are efficacious—but from the outside observer's point of view.

Reprinted from *American Anthropologist*, XLIII (1941), 164–172, by permission of the author and the American Anthropological Association.

In his Frazer Lecture for the year 1939, recently published as a pamphlet under the title *Taboo*, Professor A. R. Radcliffe-Brown restates certain of his views on magic and religion.[1] At the same time, he makes certain criticisms of Professor Malinowski's theories on the subject. The appearance of *Taboo*, therefore, offers the anthropologist an occasion for examining the present status of the theory of ritual by means of a study of a controversy between what are perhaps its two most important experts. Incidentally, the reader will find illustrated a type of behavior common in disputes in the world of science.

Malinowski's theory of magic is well known and has been widely accepted.[2] He holds that any primitive people has a body of empirical knowledge, comparable to modern scientific knowledge, as to the behavior of nature and the means of controlling it to meet man's needs. This knowledge the primitives apply in a thoroughly practical manner to get the results they desire—a crop of tubers, a catch of fish, and so forth. But their techniques are seldom so powerful that the accomplishment of these results is a matter of certainty. When the tiller of the soil has done the best he can to see that his fields are properly planted and tended, a drought or a blight may overwhelm him. Under these circumstances the primitives feel a sentiment which we call "anxiety"[3] and they perform

[1] Elsewhere most prominently stated in *The Andaman Islanders* (new ed., 1933).

[2] See "Magic, Science, and Religion," in J. Needham (ed.), *Science, Religion and Reality; Coral Gardens and Their Magic;* and *Foundations of Faith and Morals* ("Riddell Memorial Lectures").

[3] The word "anxiety" is used here in its ordinary common-sense meaning. This use is not to be confused with the psychoanalytic one, though of course the two are related.

magical rites which they say will ensure good luck. These rites give them the confidence which allows them to attack their practical work with energy and determination.

Malinowski clinches his argument with an observation made in the course of his field work:

An interesting and crucial test is provided by fishing in the Trobriand Islands and its magic. While in the villages on the inner Lagoon fishing is done in an easy and absolutely reliable manner by the method of poisoning, yielding abundant results without danger and uncertainty, there are on the shores of the open sea dangerous modes of fishing and also certain types in which the yield varies greatly according to whether shoals of fish appear beforehand or not. It is most significant that in the Lagoon fishing, where man can rely completely upon his knowledge and skill, magic does not exist, while in the open-sea fishing, full of danger and uncertainty, there is extensive magical ritual to secure safety and good results.[4]

On this understanding of magic, Malinowski bases a distinction between magical and religious ritual. A magical rite, he says,

has a definite practical purpose which is known to all who practice it and can be easily elicited from any native informant.

This is not true of a religious rite.

While in the magical act the underlying idea and aim is always clear, straightforward, and definite, in the religious ceremony there is no purpose directed towards a subsequent event. It is only possible for the sociologist to establish the function, the sociological *raison d'être* of the act. The native can always state the end of the magical rite, but he will say of a religious ceremony that it is done because such is the usage, or he will narrate an explanatory myth.[5]

This argument is the first with which Professor Radcliffe-Brown takes issue, and his criticism seems to the writer justified. He points out that the difficulty in applying this distinction between magic and religion lies in uncertainty as to what is meant by "definite, practical purpose." What is, in fact, the definite, practical purpose of a magical rite? To an anthropologist from western civilization, a magical rite and a religious rite are equally devoid of definite, practical results, in the usual sense of the phrase. The distinction between them must be based on other

grounds. A scrutiny of the methods we actually use to determine the purpose of a magical rite reveals that what we take to be the purpose of the rite is the purpose as stated by a native informant. The native performs one rite and says that it has a definite, practical purpose. He performs another rite and says that it is performed as a matter of custom. If we call the first rite magic and the second religion, we are basing our distinction on a difference between the verbal statements a native makes about the rites. For some purposes the distinction may be a useful one, but one of the truisms of the social sciences is that we shall do well to look at the statements men make about what they do with extreme care before we take the statements at their face value. Or, to use Radcliffe-Brown's own words:

The reasons given by the members of a community for the customs they observe are important data for the anthropologist. But it is to fall into grievous error to suppose that they give a valid explanation of the custom.[6]

Without doubt there are many factors involved in the performance of magic, but the least number which must be taken into consideration are apparently the following. A sentiment which we call anxiety arises when men feel certain desires and do not possess the techniques which make them sure of satisfying the desires. This sentiment of anxiety then manifests itself in ritual behavior. We may recall to mind here Pareto's third class of residues—the need of expressing sentiments by external acts. The situation is familiar in American folklore: a man and his wife are held up in a taxi in New York traffic and in danger of missing their liner to Europe. There is nothing that either one of them can do that would be of any use, but the wife screams to her husband: "But do something, can't you?" Furthermore, the action taken under such circumstances, however useless it may be, does do something to relieve the anxiety. In the usual phrase, it "works it off."

A better statement, from the point of view of psychology, is the following:

From clinical, physiological, and psychological data, it has been shown that throwing into conflict powerful excitations toward and against motor reaction regularly results in disorganization of behavior, subjective distress, and per-

---

[4] *Science, Religion and Reality*, p. 32.
[5] *Ibid.*, p. 38.

[6] *Taboo*, p. 25.

sistent drive toward relief. This syndrome has been called variously "affect," "tension," "anxiety," and "neurosis.". . . The drive toward relief tends to set into operation implicit or explicit forms of behavior, the principal characteristic of which is their abbreviated or condensed or symbolic character and their relative indifference and impermeability (because of the necessity of attaining relief as quickly as possible) to the ordinary checks, delays, and inhibitions imposed by objective reality; thus they are objectively non-adaptive, but are subjectively adaptive to the extent that the relief aimed at is actually effected.[7]

In magic in a primitive society there is a further factor which must be taken into consideration. The primitives feel anxiety and perform ritual actions which have some effect in relieving the anxiety, but they also produce a statement. They say that magical action does in fact produce a "definite, practical result." This statement is to be taken simply as a rationalization, similar in character to other rationalizations. If the rationalization is to be used as a means of distinguishing magic from religion, it should at least be recognized for what it is.

The writer doubts whether the distinction between magic and religion, as formulated by Malinowski, is a useful one. In an effort to get away from the rationalizations, magic might be defined as the ritual which is closely associated with practical activities: hunting, fishing, husbandry. Then religion would be the ritual which is not associated with practical activities, in the sense that, for instance, the Mass of the Catholic Church is not so associated. But could a distinction be made in many societies between magic and religion as so defined? Anthropologists will be aware that in many primitive societies native informants say of the most fundamental and sacred rituals, i.e., those ordinarily called religious, that if they are not performed the food supply will fail. Are these rituals closely associated with practical activities? The food supply is certainly a practical concern. Once more we are involved in the native rationalizations. In a sense these rituals are both magical and religious.

Nevertheless, Malinowski's general theory of magic seems sound, and it may be well to cite one of his statements as a summary:

We have seen that all the instincts and emotions, all practical activities, lead man into impasses where gaps in his knowledge and the limitations of his early power of observation and reason betray him at a crucial moment. The human organism reacts to this in spontaneous outbursts, in which rudimentary modes of behavior and rudimentary beliefs in their efficiency are engendered. Magic fixes upon these beliefs and rudimentary rites and standardizes them into permanent traditional forms.[8]

One word of explanation is needed here. The present paper is concerned with ritual so far as it arises out of the sentiment we call anxiety. But there is no implication that other sentiments besides anxiety do not give rise to ritual behavior.

There are other and more important criticisms which Radcliffe-Brown makes of Malinowski's theory of ritual. He wisely bases them upon a consideration of an actual case, the ritual of birth in the Andaman Islands. In order to follow his discussion, his material should first be cited:

In the Andaman Islands when a woman is expecting a baby a name is given to it while it is still in the womb. From that time until some weeks after the baby is born nobody is allowed to use the personal name of either the father or the mother; they can be referred to only by teknonymy, i.e., in terms of their relation to the child. During this period both the parents are required to abstain from eating certain foods which they may freely eat at other times.[9]

To be sure, this is an example of negative ritual—avoidance of behavior which under other circumstances might be proper—rather than of positive ritual, but the same problems arise in either case.

Radcliffe-Brown admits that Malinowski's theory might seem to be applicable as an interpretation of this body of ritual. For a woman, childbirth is always a dangerous process, in which tragedy may suddenly appear for inexplicable reasons. It is dangerous today; it was supremely dangerous under primitive conditions. Under these circumstances, the woman may feel great anxiety, and the husband is naturally interested in the fate of his wife. But the husband and the wife perform certain rites and say that they are efficacious in warding off the dangers of childbirth. Therefore their fears are, to a certain extent, lulled.

Without explicitly rejecting Malinowski's

[7] R. R. Willoughby, "Magic and Cognate Phenomena: An Hypothesis," in C. Murchison (ed.), *Handbook of Social Psychology*, p. 471.

[8] *Science, Religion and Reality*, p. 82.
[9] *Taboo*, p. 33.

interpretation, Radcliffe-Brown offers an alternative. He writes:

> The alternative hypothesis which I am presenting for consideration is as follows. In a given community it is appropriate that an expectant father should feel concern or at least make an appearance of doing so. Some suitable symbolic expression of his concern is found in terms of the general ritual or symbolic idiom of the society, and it is felt generally that a man in that situation ought to carry out the symbolic or ritual actions or abstentions.[10]

Radcliffe-Brown presents this interpretation as an alternative to Malinowski's. The point to be made here is that the question is not one of either/or. The hypothesis is not an alternative but a supplement: both hypotheses must be taken into consideration.

In fact the problem which is raised is the ancient one of the individual and his society. Malinowski is looking at the individual, Radcliffe-Brown at society. Malinowski is saying that the individual tends to feel anxiety on certain occasions; Radcliffe-Brown is saying that society expects the individual to feel anxiety on certain occasions. But there is every reason to believe that both statements are true. They are not mutually exclusive. Indeed the writer has difficulty in believing that it should have ever come about that "in a given community it is appropriate that an expectant father should feel concern" if individual fathers had not in fact showed such concern. Of course, once the tradition had been established, variations in two directions would naturally be produced. There would be, on the one hand, fathers who felt no concern but thought that the expedient thing to do was to put on a show of concern, and on the other hand, fathers who felt concern but did not express it in the manner appropriate in the given society. But on the whole these persons would be few. The average citizen would feel concern at the birth of his child but also would express his concern in the traditional manner. The custom of the society would provide the appropriate channel of his sentiments. In short, a theory adequate to the facts would combine the hypotheses of Malinowski and Radcliffe-Brown.

A statement made by Malinowski in another connection is appropriately quoted here:

The tendency represented largely by the sociological school of Durkheim, and clearly expressed in Professor Radcliffe-Brown's approach to primitive law and other phenomena, the tendency to ignore completely the individual and to eliminate the biological element from the functional analysis of culture, must in my opinion be overcome. It is really the only point of theoretical dissension between Professor Radcliffe-Brown and myself, and the only respect in which the Durkheimian conception of primitive society has to be supplemented in order to be really serviceable in field work, in theoretical studies, and in the practical application of sociology.[11]

Radcliffe-Brown makes a second and more important objection in applying Malinowski's theory to the ritual of childbirth in the Andamans. While a woman is expecting a child, and for some weeks after the birth of the child, both parents are required to abstain from eating certain foods which they may properly eat under ordinary circumstances, these foods apparently being dugong, pork, and turtle meat. Furthermore,

> If the Andaman Islanders are asked what would happen if the father or mother broke this taboo, the usual answer is that he or she would be ill, though one or two of my informants thought it might perhaps also affect the child. This is simply one instance of a standard formula which applies to a number of ritual prohibitions.[12]

On the basis of this observation, Radcliffe-Brown goes on to make the following attack on Malinowski's anxiety theory:

> I think that for certain rites it would be easy to maintain with equal plausibility an exactly contrary theory, namely, that if it were not for the existence of the rite and the beliefs associated with it the individual would feel no anxiety, and that the psychological effect of the rite is to create in him a sense of insecurity or danger. It seems very unlikely that an Andaman Islander would think that it is dangerous to eat dugong or pork or turtle meat if it were not for the existence of a specific body of ritual the ostensible purpose of which is to protect him from those dangers. Many hundreds of similar instances could be mentioned from all over the world.[13]

This attack on Malinowski's theory appears at first glance to be devastating. But

---

[10] *Ibid.,* p. 41.

[11] I. Hogbin, *Law and Order in Polynesia,* xxxviii. The introduction is by Malinowski.

[12] *Taboo,* p. 35.

[13] *Ibid.,* p. 39.

let us examine it a little more closely. Put in simpler language, what Radcliffe-Brown is saying is that the Andaman mother and father do not apparently feel anxiety at the fact of approaching childbirth. They feel anxiety only when the ritual of childbirth is not properly performed. There is no doubt that similar observations could be made of backward peoples all over the world. It is true that their techniques do not allow them to control completely the natural forces on which their lives depend. Nevertheless when they have done their practical work as well as they know how and have performed the proper rituals, they display little overt anxiety. If anxiety is present, it remains latent. They are, as we say, fatalists. What Thomas and Znaniecki have observed of the Polish peasant seems to be true of most primitive peoples. They write:

The fact is that when the peasant has been working steadily, and has fulfilled the religious and magical ceremonies which tradition requires, he "leaves the rest to God," and waits for the ultimate results to come; the question of more or less skill and efficiency of work has very little importance.[14]

When the primitive or the peasant has done his practical work as well as he knows how, and has "fulfilled the religious and magical ceremonies which tradition requires," he displays little overt anxiety. But he does feel anxiety if the ceremonies have not been properly performed. In fact he generalizes beyond this point and feels that unless all the moralities of his society are observed, nature will not yield her fruits. Incest or murder in the camp will lead to a failure of the crops just as surely as will a breach of ritual. In the shape of famine, pestilence, or war, God will visit their sins upon the people. Accordingly when, in a village of medieval Europe, the peasants, led by the parish priest, went in procession about the boundaries of the village in the Rogation Days in order to bless the growing crops, they offered up prayers at the same time for the forgiveness of sins. This association of ideas is characteristic: nature and morality are mutually dependent.

As a matter of fact, the above observations are implicit in Malinowski's theory, and he was undoubtedly aware of them. He

points to the initial anxiety situation, but he also states that ritual dispels the anxiety, at least in part, and gives men confidence. He implies, then, that anxiety remains latent so long as ritual is properly performed. Radcliffe-Brown's criticism does not demolish Malinowski's theory but takes the necessary further step. Once again, it is not an alternative but a supplement. Using the ritual of childbirth in the Andamans as an example, he asks what happens, or rather what would happen, if the ritual is not performed. And he shows that this occasion is the one in which the natives feel anxiety. The anxiety has, so to speak, been displaced from the original situation. But even granted that it has been displaced, Malinowski's general theory is confirmed by the existence of a secondary ritual which has the function of dispelling the secondary anxiety which arises from a breach of ritual and tradition. We call this the ritual of purification, of expiation.

In his description of the Australian Murngin, W. L. Warner sums up admirably what the writer has been trying to say. He writes:

The Murngin in their logic of controlling nature assume that there is a direct connection between social units and different aspects of nature, and that the control of nature lies in the proper control and treatment of social organization. Properly to control the social organization, the rituals must also be held which rid society of its uncleanliness. The society is disciplined by threat of what will happen to nature, the provider, if the members of the group misbehave.[15]

In summary, it appears from the discussion of the theories of Malinowski and Radcliffe-Brown that at least seven elements must be taken into consideration in any study of the rituals we are are accustomed to call magic. Of course, there are other elements which are not considered here. The seven are the following:

1. *Primary anxiety.* Whenever a man desires the accomplishment of certain results and does not possess the techniques which will make him certain to secure these results, he feels a sentiment which we call anxiety.

2. *Primary ritual.* Under these circumstances, he tends to perform actions which have no practical result and which we call ritual. But he is not simply an individual.

[14] W. I. Thomas and F. Znaniecki, *The Polish Peasant in Europe and America*, I, 174.

[15] W. L. Warner, *A Black Civilization*, p. 410.

He is a member of a society with definite traditions, and among other things society determines the form of the ritual and expects him to perform the ritual on the appropriate occasions. There is, however, evidence from our own society that when ritual tradition is weak, men will invent ritual when they feel anxiety.

3. *Secondary anxiety.* When a man has followed the technical procedures at his command and performed the traditional rituals, his primary anxiety remains latent. We say that the rites give him confidence. Under these circumstances, he will feel anxiety only when the rites themselves are not properly performed. In fact this attitude becomes generalized, and anxiety is felt whenever any one of the traditions of society is not observed. This anxiety may be called secondary or displaced anxiety.

4. *Secondary ritual.* This is the ritual of purification and expiation which has the function of dispelling secondary anxiety. Its form and performance, like those of primary ritual, may or may not be socially determined.

5. *Rationalization.* This element includes the statements which are associated with ritual. They may be very simple: such statements as that the performance of a certain magic does ensure the catching of fish, or that if an Andaman mother and father do not observe the food taboos they will be sick. The statements may be very elaborate. Such are the statements which accompany the fundamental rituals of any society: the equivalents of the Mass of the Catholic Church.

6. *Symbolization.* Since the form of ritual action is not determined by the nature of a practical result to be accomplished, it can be determined by other factors. We say that it is symbolic, and each society has its own vocabulary of symbols. Some of the symbolism is relatively simple: for example, the symbolism of sympathies and antipathies. Some is complicated. In particular, certain of the rituals of a society, and those the most important, make symbolic reference to the fundamental myths of the society. The ceremonies of the Murngin make reference to the fundamental myths of that society just as surely as the Mass makes reference to Christ's sacrifice on Calvary.

7. *Function.* Ritual actions do not produce a practical result on the external world—that is one reason why we call them ritual. But to make this statement is not to say that ritual has no function. Its function is not related to the world external to the society but to the internal constitution of the society. It gives the members of the society confidence; it dispels their anxieties; it disciplines the social organization. But the functions of ritual have been discussed elsewhere, and in any case they raise questions which are beyond the scope of the present paper.

Finally, a study of the theories of Malinowski and Radcliffe-Brown illustrates a common feature of scientific controversies: two distinguished persons talking past one another rather than trying to find a common ground for discussion, presenting their theories as alternatives when in fact they are complements. Such a study suggests also that the theory necessary for an adequate description of any phenomenon is often more complicated than the theories of the phenomenon which exist at any given time.

TALCOTT PARSONS

Religious Perspectives in Sociology and Social Psychology

Among the works of recent American sociologists, those of Talcott Parsons have been of the most general significance in defining the role and function of religion in human society. Parsons' classic paper on this subject is "The Theoretical Development of the Sociology of Religion," in which he synthesizes the theories of Durkheim, Pareto, Weber, and Malinowski. Since this earlier paper is readily available in his *Essays in Sociological Theory*

Adapted from Talcott Parsons, "Sociology and Social Psychology," in Hoxie N. Fairchild (ed.), *Religious Perspectives in College Teaching* (New York: Ronald Press, 1952), pp. 286–305. Copyright 1952, The Ronald Press Company. Used with permission.

(1949), a briefer and less available essay has been selected for inclusion in this volume.

In addition to setting forth a definition of religion as a universal feature of human society, Parsons (following leads suggested by Malinowski) also provides a cogent discussion of the two main types of frustration in the human situation that provide focal points for the development of religious patterns. One of these types is due to the fact that men are "hit" by events which they cannot either foresee and prepare for or control, such as the occurrence of premature death. The second type is present where there is a strong emotional investment in the success of human endeavor, where energy and skill count for much, but where unknown or uncontrollable factors often intervene to upset the balance between effort and success, such as in the exposure of agriculture to uncontrollable weather.

These frustrations of established expectations pose "problems of meaning," in the sense that Max Weber wrote much about; that is, we can explain how an automobile accident caused a premature death, but we cannot explain why it had to happen to a particular person at a particular time; we can explain how it is that "the wicked flourish like a green bay tree," but not why it has to come out this way in societies. Hence the significance of religion in human life is that it is made up of those aspects of the life situation to which men cannot remain indifferent, which they cannot in the long run evade, but which they cannot control or adjust to through the ordinary techniques and attitudes of practical utilitarian life.

The present essay is written from the point of view of the social scientist, not that of the representative of any religious denomination.

Sociology we will define as the science interested in the institutional structure of social systems, and the motivational processes in human beings which are involved in the maintenance and change of institutions. Social psychology is an interstitial science between psychology and sociology, much like biochemistry in the natural sciences. It is concerned with the study of motivational processes of behavior and the structure of personalities, in the context of their relevance to social systems and their problems, notably their institutional structure.

A religion we will define as a set of beliefs, practices and institutions which men have evolved in various societies, so far as they can be understood, as responses to those aspects of their life and situation which are believed not in the empirical-instrumental sense to be rationally understandable and/or controllable, and to which they attach a significance which includes some kind of reference to the relevant actions and events to man's conception of the existence of a "supernatural" order which is conceived and felt to have a fundamental bearing on man's

position in the universe and the values which give meaning to his fate as an individual and his relations to his fellows.

Defined in this way, a religion or religious system will include at a minimum: (1) a more or less integrated set of beliefs concerning entities which are "supernatural," sacred, or, as Durkheim said, "set apart" from the ordinary objects and events of utilitarian or instrumental significance for human affairs and interests on his relation to which the meaning of man's life is fundamentally dependent; (2) a system of symbols, objects, acts, persons, empirical and non-empirical, which have the quality of sacredness and in relation to which men express the emotional states relevant to the religious sphere, in short, a system of expressive symbols; (3) a set of more or less definitely prescribed activities which are interpreted as important and often obligatory in the light of the beliefs involved, but which from the point of view of the instrumental interests of daily life are "useless" in that they do not "accomplish anything." These activities will usually be prescribed for different types of occasions, forbidden on others and may be differentiated for different statuses in the social group; (4) to some degree a sense that "we" who share common beliefs of this character, and participate in what is felt to be an integrated system of such activities, constitute a "collectivity"—a group which by virtue of that fact is bound together in what Durkheim called a "moral community"; finally, (5) a sense that man's relation to the supernatural world is in some way intimately connected with his moral values, with the nature of the goals he is called upon to live for and the rules of conduct he is expected to comply with. The sharing of these common moral values as well as more specifically "religious" beliefs and practices will be constitutive of the moral community spoken of above.

In addition to these five minimum features of what the sociologist would call a religion or religious system, certain others may be expected to appear in different types of religious systems. These are all aspects of the differentiation and corresponding modes of organization of the social relationship systems which religious beliefs and practices involve. The most important aspect of differentiation is the differentiation of the roles of individuals and of classes of them relative to those of others participating in the same religious system. There are in turn two main aspects of this differentiation. The first is the differentiation of types of individuals and groups relative to their relations to the sacred and supernatural sphere independent of functions on behalf of the religious collectivity, while the second is differentiation of roles with such specialized functions. In the first direction we find such types as the individual ascetic or monastic order. In the second falls the minister or priest who functions on behalf of his congregation. The prophet can be regarded in both contexts, as having established a *new* relation to the supernatural and as the leader of a *movement* to implement its implications in the life of society.

Closely related to the differentiation of roles is the development of the character of the religious collectivity itself. There are several important aspects of this but two may be singled out for mention here. One is the mode of integration—or lack of it—of the religious collectivity itself with the rest of the group structure of the society. Thus it may be an aspect of a single overall collective organization as in the case of the most nonliterate societies, or there may be a distinctive religious grouping as with the Christian church or denominational organization. The other aspect is that of the internal organization of the religious collectivity above all the ways and extent of the development of formal organization of explicit canons formally interpreted and enforced, and the like.

The analysis of the conditions determining the specific type of belief or symbol system, of activities or moral roles, of differentiation of roles, of modes of collectivity organization, constitutes one main aspect of the sociology of religion in a more detailed sense. The other main aspect concerns the ways in which differences of religious systems in these respects are interdependent with other aspects of the social systems of which they are a part. Unfortunately limitations of space preclude entering into the fascinating analysis of these problems here. The reader should, however, keep in mind that solid grounding of many of the empirical generalizations stated in later sections of this essay would require carrying through the relevant analysis on this level in full detail. It is only space limitation which makes this impossible.

MOTIVATION OF RELIGIOUS BELIEF AND BEHAVIOR

With the above sketch of some of the principal components of religious systems on the social level in mind we may now turn to some aspects of the "social psychology" of religion, of the characteristic of man as an "actor" in a situation, and of that situation, which helps us to understand his need for and relations to religious institutions. We will develop this theme in two sections; in the present one we will attempt to sketch some of the main sources of the motivation to religious belief and behavior, and in that following to indicate some of the complicated interrelations between religious and secular motivations on this level.

Man is distinguished from the other animals, from the point of view of the social scientist, above all by the fact that he is a creator and bearer of culture. He creates and lives by systems of symbols and of artifacts; he not only modifies his environment but his orientation to it is generalized in terms of systems of symbolic meaning; he communicates with his fellow men through language and other symbols; he perpetuates and develops his knowledge, and he expresses his feelings, not directly and crudely, but in elaborately symbolic form.

A "culture" is not and cannot be just a discrete collection of disconnected artifacts and symbols, but to a greater or lesser degree must constitute a *system*. It must, that is, have coherence as a set of orientations which tie together the many particular aspects of men's experience and needs. Above all it has three types of functions. In the cognitive aspects, as a system of beliefs, it attempts to answer man's questions about himself and the world he lives in, and we all know that we cannot consciously hold contradictory beliefs without strain. Second, it provides "forms" or expressive symbols for expressing and communicating his feelings, forms which conform to standards of "taste." Finally, and from the sociological point of view perhaps most important, it provides standards for evaluation above all the moral standards which regulate man's conduct, particularly in his relation with his fellows. It can be proved quite definitely that once the step from regulation by "instinct" to the plastic dependence on learned patterns of behavior has been taken by man as organism, a society of men cannot subsist without what sociologists call the institutionalization of a relatively consistent system of patterns of culture, above all of moral values.

The role of culture in human life implies that men must be concerned, in a sense somewhat different from the animals, with the *meaning* of their experience, that is, not merely with whether a given experience gratifies a wish or fills a need or contrariwise involves pain or deprivation, but also with the *fit* between the *expectations* of experience which have been defined for him in his culture, and the actuality which he himself experiences.

There is in every system of human action, in every society, a smooth, "normal" pattern of everyday functioning, of ways in which people go "about their business" without particular strain, where the means available to them are adequate to attain the goals they have been taught to strive for, and where the all-important other people fulfill their expectations. But if all human life were like that, religion would certainly not have the significance that it does. We would be much more likely to think of the "problems" of life as

mainly of a practical "utilitarian" kind, to be solved by good "horse sense."

There are certain fundamental respects in which this is an inadequate picture of the human life situation. In whatever kind of society *some* human expectations, in the fulfillment of which people have acquired a deep emotional investment, are doomed to frustration. These frustrations are of two main types. One of them consists in the fact that men are "hit" by events which they either cannot foresee and prepare for, or control, or both; to which, however, they must make major adjustments, sometimes practical but always emotional. The type case of this kind of frustration is the occurrence of premature death. Certainly the fact that though we all know we have to die almost no man knows when he will die is one of the cardinal facts of the human situation. But not only for the person facing death himself, if he has time to think about it, but quite clearly for the survivors, there is a major problem of adjustment, for the simple reason that the human individual as an object of emotional attachment is of such fundamental importance. Even the loss of a "beloved enemy" can, we know, be very upsetting. Though religious orientations to death, which are universal and fundamental to religion, contain many shadings of belief about the "life after death," the fundamental feature of this orientation is not "wishful thinking." As one historian of religion has put it, "No major religion has ever claimed to be able to 'beat death.' " The dead are dead, and cannot be brought back to life; but the living must still adjust themselves to that fact. From the point of view of the social scientist, what they believe and do in this situation has significance as a set of "mechanisms" which in some ways facilitate this adjustment. From the secular social point of view to hold funeral ceremonies does not "accomplish anything," the functions of such ceremonies are "latent," but they may none the less be highly important.

In general it is extremely conspicuous that ceremonialism not only concerns the directly bereaved, but directly symbolizes the belongingness of the deceased and of the bereaved in larger social groupings. On the one hand these larger groups which are not so directly affected give their "support" to the bereaved, but on the other they set a "tone" for the occasion which in general says, "the traditional values of the society must be upheld." Death must be only a temporary interruption, the important thing on one level is to "get over it" and to go on living. Though it is by no means obvious, there are many features of funeral ceremonies which are closely similar to those of psychotherapy.

There are other types of uncontrollable events besides death which have what in certain respects is a similar bearing on human interests, natural catastrophes being one of them. Furthermore it should be noted that not only frustration in the usual sense, but unexpected and therefore "unearned" good fortune may also have an upsetting effect and require processes of adjustment. Perhaps our own Thanksgiving fits in that category. The Pilgrim Fathers may well have felt that they were extremely "lucky," or as they said, favored by God, to have survived their first terrible year in the wilderness at all.

A second type of frustrating experience is connected with what has come to be called in a special sense "uncertainty." By this is meant the very common type of situation where there is a strong emotional investment in the success of certain human endeavors, where energy and skill undoubtedly count for much, but where unknown and/or uncontrollable factors may and often do intervene to upset any "reasonable" balance between action and success. The exposure of agriculture the world over, with few exceptions, to the vagaries of uncontrollable and unpredictable weather, is one of the most important examples. No matter how industrious and capable a farmer may be, his crops may be ruined by drought or flood. The field of health is another classic example, and there are a variety of others. The unpredictable character of human conduct in many fields, from love to war, is also prominent.

In all these situations rational techniques must of course loom large; no farmer ever grew good crops by magic alone. But these are the classic situations in which what anthropologists call "magic" flourishes. Whatever the distinction made, magic is always continuous with religion, it always involves some relation to the strains occasioned by uncertainty, and to human emotional adjustment to such situations. Magical beliefs and practices constitute, from the point of view of social psychology, mechanisms of adjust-

ment to these situations of strain. They give an opportunity to "act out" some of the psychological products of that strain, thus to "place the blame" for the frustration—most conspicuous in the cases of belief in witchcraft. They give people the sense of "doing something about it" in areas where their rational techniques are powerless or untrustworthy. Above all they act as a tonic to self-confidence; they are a protection against allowing the risk of failure to lead to a fatalistic discouragement, the attitude that since success cannot be assured, it is no use trying at all. At the same time, magic may act as a stereotyping agency in situations where empirical knowledge and technique are applicable, and thus block technological advance—this in spite of the fact which Malinowski makes so clear, that magic cannot take the place of rational technique. The Trobriand Islander does not believe that he can make up for failing to cultivate his garden properly by more or better magic; it is a supplement, not a substitute.

The frustrations of established expectations of which we have been speaking pose "problems of meaning" in a double sense. On the one hand, man, being a culture-bearing animal, does not merely "take it" when things go as he does not expect. He has to give these things a meaning, in the first instance emotionally, so that his adjustments to such experiences can become integrated in the *system* of experience, which means among other things that his reactions are coordinated and organized with those of his fellows; he can communicate his feelings and receive adequate responses to his expressions of them.

But beyond this, as we have noted at the beginning of this section, the culture in which a social group lives constitutes a more or less integrated system. As such it must have a certain level of consistency; it must "cover" the principal ranges of men's experience in such a way that all of them to some degree "make sense," together as a whole.

Besides the direct problem of emotional adjustment to the frustration of particular experiences, the "generalization" which is involved in the integration of a cultural system brings up two further particularly crucial "problem" areas. The culture links the experience and expectations of any particular individual or subgroup with those of

others in a society. There is not only the
question of why must this happen *to me,* or
to those close to me, but why must it happen
at all to anyone? Above all, since men universally seek gratification of their wishes
and needs there is the generalized problem
of suffering, of why men must endure
deprivation and pain and so unequally and
haphazardly, or, indeed, at all, and, since
all societies must live by moral standards,
there is equally the problem of "evil," of
why men violate the moral standards of
their society and why the "economy" of
rewards and punishments fails, as it *always*
does to some extent, to balance out. Good
fortune and suffering must always, to
cultural man, be endowed with meaning.
They cannot, except in limiting cases, be
accepted as something that "just happens."
Similarly it is impossible to live by moral
standards and yet be wholly indifferent
either to the extent of conformity with
them or to the fate of conformists and
violators respectively. It is necessarily dis-
concerting that to some degree "the good die
young while the wicked flourish as the green
bay tree."

The sociologist is in a position to state
that some significant degree of discrepancy
between expectations in both these resepcts
and the actual state of affairs in a society is
inevitable, though it varies greatly in degree
and in incidence. Both expectations of gratification and moral standards vary from society to society, but this fundamental fact
of discrepancy seems to be a constant,
grounded in the nature of human personality, society, and culture and their relations
to each other.

This complex of circumstances constitutes
from a certain sociological point of view the
primary focus of the differential significance
of religion in human life. It is made up of
aspects of the life situation to which men,
being what they are, cannot remain emotionally indifferent, and which at the same
time in the long run they cannot evade. But
adequate adjustment on either the emotional
or the cognitive level to these situations cannot be worked out through the "ordinary"
techniques and attitudes of practical utilitarian life. The content and incidence of the
problems vary, but their presence is a constant. Almost another way of putting the essential point is to say that tragedy is of the
essence of the human situation.

ROBERT H. LOWIE

Religion in Human Life

Without writing as a self-conscious functionalist, Professor
Lowie has nevertheless left us in the following posthumous article
a sort of apologia for the positive role of religion in human life.
He has done so with the mellow introspection of a disbeliever
unable to escape from the implications of his field research among
people who do believe and have found comfort in their faith. In
expressing his personal convictions he may in fact be speaking
for many scholars in his discipline who have looked almost envi-
ously upon societies where there is little room for religious
skepticism. Coming from an anthropologist of great integrity who
came to be respected during his lifetime for his work in the field
of religion, this credo constitutes a fitting finale to a man of obvious erudition and sincerity.

Reprinted from *American Anthropologist,* LXV (1963), 532–542,
by permission of the American Anthropological Association.

Since this article is concerned with the moot
matter of religion, I should perhaps begin by
making clear my own point of view and my
reasons for coming to the conclusions that I
have come to. My first awareness of religious strife came from my grandfather before I left Vienna at the age of ten; he had
been an agnostic from his medical student
days, and he laid the foundations for my
own later attitudes. From my parents I re-

ceived no religious training of any kind. By the time I was sixteen, I was already reading the *philosophes* and imitating their violent anti-clericalism and bitterness toward all religion. This period continued, largely under the stimulus of and acquaintance with Ernst Haeckel, until I was about 25. At this point I was already going into the field as an ethnologist. It did not take long to discover that to the primitive mind religion was of paramount importance. If I wanted to understand the Indians of that period I simply had to study its values for them. Moreover, my constant field trips brought me into contact with dedicated men of all faiths who were certainly deriving neither money nor renown by being missionaries to a group of Indians on a remote reservation. They lived as other members of the community did, in poverty, and they remained with their charges through pestilence and famine. One day it occurred to me that both the Indians and the hardy souls who were trying to convert them to Christianity had some inner strength that I lacked. Nor was I unique in this lack. I began to wonder how many scientists would undergo for their science the years of poverty that the priests and ministers willingly accepted for their religion.

Here clearly was a phenomenon of both primitive and civilized life that warranted study. So I began to collect information about native religions on the same objective basis upon which I assembled data on basketweaving, social organization, hunting, or any other aspect of primitive life. Moreover, through my reading I discovered that no group of people had ever been found who did not have a religion of some kind. Since religion is a universal manifestation, it must have some value. I found also that despite the immense variations in the outward observances, the inner glow and the function of religion in the group were identical from one form to another. The Catholic priest, the Mormon missionary, the Eskimo shaman, the African witch-doctor, and the Protestant clergyman were all alike in their sense of inner conviction, in their intense desire to help others, and in their dependence upon some force outside themselves that gave them courage. Fanatic, ignorant, or rigid they might be, but they were men of faith. I cannot say that I have become a religious man as the result of my study, but I have become an informed one; and I have seen too much to believe now in the dicta that I accepted in my youth. I no longer doubt that religion has a definite place in human life.

My position towards religion as a cultural phenomenon springs directly from my conception of anthropology as a *science*. Since it is a science it must take cognizance of values because these form an essential part of its subject matter; but it must treat these values objectively—that is, it must refrain from judgment. Thus, an anthropologist who is studying West African fetishism must stick to what he can see and hear for himself and what he can find out from informants as to the meaning of fetishism to them, but he must not judge it in terms of his own religious standards. Probably my own lack of religious training was an asset rather than a drawback, because I could not condemn any form of worship merely because if differed from mine. I could only view it as a human manifestation worthy of scientific investigation. This same point of view should certainly be extended to include the religions of one's own day. Yet I have known anthropologists who accorded a benevolent understanding to the Hopi but denied it to Catholics, Mormons, Buddhists, or Mohammedans. This dichotomy of viewpoint strikes me as ridiculous and completely unscientific. In short, I will study as many religions as I can, but I will judge none of them. I doubt if any other attitude is scientifically defensible.

To a modern intellectual, religion is probably the most unfamiliar subject in the world. He cannot, of course, remain wholly ignorant of its role in the past, but the sentiments of such men as St. Francis of Assisi, George Fox, or John Wesley are utterly remote and unintelligible. For many people the religious issue is intertwined with an adolescent revolt against parental authority or with a struggle for intellectual freedom. For others it has become a symbol of restriction, repression, and reaction. To still others it is either just plain mumbo-jumbo or a narcotic. The former attitude is well illustrated by Voltaire's statement that religion began when the first knave duped the first fool. Marxians have their special brand of the second attitude: that it is an opiate with which exploiting capitalists lull the masses in order to fleece them with impunity. Most if not all of these attitudes are based upon a profound ignorance of what religion is and does.

While it is true that religion has lost ground during the past century, it has never ceased to sway the lives and fortunes of millions. And even if open allegiance to a church has become more rare as the decades have flowed past, the moral strength of religion has continued to influence people. During World War II many people either found religion for the first time or else returned to their former church for comfort and strength to bear the fears and pressures brought about by war. It should never be forgotten that all religions thrive on adversity. It is probable that the common attitude of indifference and apathy is caused primarily by too much prosperity.

The indifference is not confined to one church or to one country, as may be seen from the following two examples. In Italy the vast majority of the population is Catholic. Some of the people are certainly devout, but these come predominantly from the peasant class. The others—excluding a handful of freethinkers—are passive in their Catholicism. They have their children baptized by the Church; they are married and buried by the Church; but they seem to go through life without religious feeling or spiritual experience.

The situation is much the same in Protestant Sweden, where the people are overwhelmingly Lutheran and the king is constitutionally bound to profess the evangelical creed. But when one glances through a brief survey of Swedish life, one finds a good deal about the iron and match industries, about timbering and handicrafts, and about sports, but strangely little concerning the officially dominant faith as a force in shaping human lives. In the newspapers the sporting page, though shorter than in American dailies, is easily three times as long as the half-page or less that has to do with church or religion.

It was not of course like this in medieval Europe. Art, scholarship, philosophy, education, and crafts of every sort were all permeated by the Church. And the earlier crusades bear witness to the dynamic power of the Christian faith among the people. This all-pervasive character of religion has almost vanished from contemporary life, but in the days of my field work I found it still alive among the Indians whom I visited. For instance, when the Choctaw played an inter-village game, the performance started on the previous evening with 12 repetitions of a ceremonial dance by the players. The tribal prophets continued their magic rites throughout the night, and during the game itself the conjurers were almost as conspicuous as the players. The most matter-of-fact features in the daily routine of any primitive people are likely to be linked with magical observances, prayers, chants, or sacrifices. In New Zealand a Maori recited sacred spells when he began to build a canoe, when he launched it, when he planted his crops, when he harvested them; even when he taught a youngster to weave, he muttered a charm to increase the learner's receptiveness. During their farming period the Apinayé of Northern Brazil sang daily songs in honor of the sun. The Eskimo firmly believed that success in sealing hinged upon the favor of a powerful sea goddess. And so forth ad infinitum all over the savage world.

The field worker's business is always and everywhere to understand the true inwardness of the beliefs and practices of the people he studies. He is not content to record that infants are suffocated, aged parents abandoned, or enemies eaten. Unless he can also recover the accompanying sentiments, he has failed in his task. It is one thing if a parent throttles his newborn child from sheer brutality, another if he kills it because the mother died in delivery and a nurse cannot be found, and still another if his tribe has a superstitious fear of twins. And the field worker who consistently sees human civilization as one indivisible whole cannot logically apply a sympathetic attitude to Australian infanticide, Eskimo abandonment of old people, or Tupinamba cannibalism, and a prejudiced attitude to Catholics, Baptists, or Methodists. The touchstone of his anthropological conscience is whether or not he treats the communicant of some other faith than his own with the consideration he professionally metes out to an Indian medicine man or an Eskimo shaman.

In my own field experience the Hopi of Arizona and the Crow of Montana both impressed upon me the integrating power of religion, but from two instructively antithetical angles. The Pueblos illustrate ceremonialism par excellence, with a profusion of outward observances and paraphernalia. What first of all amazes the observer among the Hopi is the incredible amount of time consumed by their religious activities. Apart from an infinitude of minor performances there is a fixed calendar of major festivals lasting nine days each. While there is a slight variation from year to year, the average amount of time devoted to religious ceremonial is one day in three. In the Hopi village of Walpi, for instance, the "year" starts with a nine-day initiation of youths into adult status. At the winter solstice there is a celebration in honor of the Kachina spirits, impersonated by mummers. In January the people play shinny as a magic fertility rite; moreover, several fraternities and sororities prepare the characteristic Pueblo offerings, such as feathered sticks to be smoked and prayed over before they are deposited in caves, springs, or other appropriate places. Follows the Bean festival, with secret planting of the vegetable, distribution of beans and of seed corn, burlesques, masqueradings, and a legion of other ritualistic rites. After a period of spirit-impersonating dances, March ushers in the drama of the Water Snakes, with suckling of serpent images as part of a fertility ceremonial. In April, there is the first corn planting "for the Kachina"; in May, the Skeleton God is represented and ritualistically slain; in June, prayer-sticks must be made for the sun; in July, the Kachina spirits have their farewell ceremony. In August comes either of two festivals in regular alternation, the famous Snake Dance or the Flute Dance. In September and the early part of the fall the several feminine organizations perform, and in November youths are once more initiated.

Not all members of the community participate in the series in equal measure. Large portions of the esoteric rituals, the prerogative of special organizations, are barred to nonmembers; and within a fraternity the functions of the priest differ from those of the rank and file. However, even the outsider is affected by the solemnity that invests the community during the whole of a festival. Further, in a sense, everyone's welfare is involved, for whatever may be the special objects of major ceremonials, they are all meant to bring rain. As my interpreter quaintly put it, "The Hopi have no streams to irrigate with, so they must perform their ceremonies." These expert farmers who make a go of corn-growing where many White agriculturists would despair nevertheless believe unshakably in the indispensableness of ritual for gaining their ends. By wheedling the spirits, by mimicking whatever is associated with showers, they expect to wring rain from the powers of the universe. Now they offer their feathered sticks, now they draw pictures of clouds dropping precipitation, now they whirl a board through the air to simulate thunder.

The heavy display of fixed ritual in Hopi supernaturalism does not readily yield up its meaning from the worshipper's point of view. Literally thousands of pages in print about Pueblo ceremonies have until fairly recently left the reader almost wholly in the dark on this crucial point of the subject. As late as 1942 appeared Sun Chief's autobiography, which tells at least how one believer felt about it all.

Among the Plains Indians there was also some emphasis upon ritual, but it was overshadowed by the importance of the subjective thrill in visions, auditions, or particularly vivid dreams. The contrast between the Crow and the Hopi corresponds roughly to that popularly conceived between an established church and lay evangelism. However, if there were a ritual of however simple a nature it was observed with the same punctilio. I shall not readily forget the ceremonial opening of Flat-head-woman's sacred bundle. First he divided live embers into two heaps, strewed incense on both, then alternately lowered each end of the bundle toward the nearer heap. With muttered words of prayer he opened the bundle, its cloth wrappings being carefully folded back on the sides without disturbance of their relative positions. When possibly ten coverings had been gradually unfolded, nothing was visible but a large bunch of feathers. Flat-head-woman next combined the two heaps of embers, strewed more incense on top, then carefully arranged the feathers and extracted from among them, as the sacrosanct core, an arrow. This bundle was holy only because it had been revealed to the original owner (within Flat-head-woman's lifetime) by the Seven Stars. The arrow-spirit subsequently visited the first visionary's brother, Hillside, in his sleep. Hillside passed the bundle on to Flat-head-woman, who had never had a vision of his own; but after receiving the sacred bundle he began to have visions, seeing stalks of grass flying like arrows. For years he continued to receive revelations from the arrow-spirit. On one occasion it forbade him to throw ashes out of his lodge or to strike the lodge when removing snow from the tent cover. At another time it ordered him to visit the site of the original arrow revelation, where he was to find an eagle's feather in the cleft of a rock; and he found it.

The Crow, then, no less than the Hopi, attach extreme significance to things that we should regard as trivial. Both tribes insist upon a stereotyped procedure without the slightest deviation from the rules, lest you come to harm. Yet there is an immense difference between the tribes, for all those subjective experiences which are submerged in Hopi ritualism form the very warp and woof of Crow religion. The Crow Indians and their neighbors continually amazed me by their ever-recurring, face-to-face communication with the superhuman. It is such direct intercourse with the divine that is most distinctive of religion at its peak. As a veritable tyro I met Red-shirt, the Shoshone medicineman, who told me about his own death and resurrection. He had died, he said, because he had eaten salmon contrary to his familiar's orders and thus forever lost that spirit's protection. Fortunately, the Sun appeared to him in a dream, telling him he would die but promising resuscitation. This happened about 1880, and Red-shirt pointed out to me the spot where his tribesmen had built a special mortuary shelter for him. And now comes an illuminating detail. After his soul had stepped out of his thigh and taken a few steps forward, something suddenly descended clear through it, and it began to go downwards—not upwards, according to the general Shoshone belief. Red-shirt mistrusted the other Shoshone shamans no less than the Christian missionaries: Did he not have the direct evidence of his senses that the soul descended after death instead of rising? They were only guessing, but he *knew*. This adventure, though the most impressive in Red-shirt's career, was by no means the only one. Traveling at night on one occasion, he saw an Indian approaching; the face was invisible, but he was wearing a striped vest. As the figure got close, however, the stripes turned out to be bare ribs. Red-shirt fled from the specter, whom he headed off from pursuit by pronouncing a spell of exorcism: "You are only a ghost, leave me alone!" Then the figure wheeled about and vanished into the ground.

This type of experience was reported to me wherever I went in the Northern Plains.

The Stoney Assiniboine attached great importance to dreams. A man to whom a certain animal appeared in a dream would not kill or eat the flesh of its fellows. Only very young Stoneys dreamed of spirits, who would instruct them for several years and then depart for good. Jim Crack may be cited as an example: his benefactor, a dwarfish human, had taught him how to pursue every kind of game, so that Jim grew up to be a great hunter, after which his guide was seen no more. In Montana a blind Assiniboine recounted to me a series of personal revelations. Once he had been taken in a dream to a tent with a sun design on the cover; an old woman seated inside ordered him to decorate his own tent in the same manner and promised him that he and his family would enjoy good health. He did, and they did! On another occasion he received the right to doctor the sick. This was to be done in a special kind of painted tipi, the model being exhibited for his guidance; in it the practitioner was to be bound hand and foot and an invisible spirit would announce whether or not a cure was possible, and if so, would untie the doctor. Still another time my informant was shown a procession of Fool Dancers and bidden, on pain of premature death, to conduct their ceremony at least once a year. In 1908 he was still obeying this injunction, although total blindness had forced him to rely on the aid of a proxy.

It would be an exaggeration to say that every phase of a Crow's life was tinctured with religion, but it is literally true that every situation of strain or stress fused with the native concept of individual revelation. Thus, the young man who has been jilted goes off at once to fast in loneliness, praying for supernatural succor. An elk spirit may come and teach him a tune on a flute, as a means of luring the maiden back. The young man plays his tune, ensnares the haughty girl, and turns her away in disgrace, thus regaining his self-respect. Similarly, a wretched orphan who has been mocked by a young man of family hastens to the mountains to be blessed by some being, through whose favor he gains glory and loot on a raid, and can then turn the tables upon his tormentor. A woman big with child fasts and in a vision sees a weed which she subsequently harvests and through which she ensures a painless delivery. A gambler who has lost all his property retrieves his fortune through a revelation; and by the same technique a sorrowing kinsman identifies the slayers of his beloved relative and kills them. These are all typical instances, amply documented in personal recollections of informants and in traditional lore, showing the intrusion of religion into the frustrations of everyday living.

Out of this general atmosphere blossomed the notion that all conspicuous success in life is due to visions and revelations. Contrariwise, failure is interpreted as equivalent to lack of superhuman favor. As one informant put it: "All who had visions were well-to-do; I was to be poor, and that is why I had no visions." Such a man could still, however, tap hidden resources by borrowing a talisman—or a replica of one—from a more fortunate relative or friend. By its means he often managed to get a start, and later he might begin to have revelations of his own.

The question now arises as to how the ethnographer should appraise this faith in the reality, the paramount value, of visions. A casual estimate might suggest that the visionaries are all mystics or fools, but after several years' acquaintance with them, I am certain that they are neither. Every young man automatically went out to seek a vision, and those who claimed success were precisely the leaders of the tribe. The question still remains whether or not these men were intentional or unintentional frauds. My interpreter, a baptized Christian who was keenly aware of the inherent improbability by modern criteria of visions, thought otherwise. As he said, "When you listen to the old men telling their stories, you've just *got* to believe them." And in this impression I concur. Whatever the narrator's experiences may have been, he himself conceived them as being as he represented them.

But it is not necessary to rely upon subjective impressions, since there are at least four bits of evidence to suggest that the speakers were sincere. First, why should they lie to a white man, when they perfectly well knew that the more flamboyant their story the less likely I would be to believe it? Therefore, a pretense of wonderful experiences would serve no useful purpose for them. Second, among their own people, the rise to kudos through a vision required a good deal more than the palming off of a convenient hoax. Normally, the aspirant for a vision would go to the mountains, refrain

for four days from food and water, and mutilate himself, to convince the deities of his sincerity. These offerings of flesh are not figments of myth, for I have seen the mutilated fingers and the deep scars on back and chest. Even with such austerities, there were many who never succeeded in getting a vision. I doubt that sheer mountebanks would lacerate or starve themselves. Third, even assuming that a man's desire for status drove him to self-mutilation and the fabrication of a dream or vision, he would be no better off than before, because it was only the *demonstrably successful* healer or war leader who achieved a following. Until the revelation was backed up with results, and unless it were, the would-be visionary was held up to endless ridicule. A deliberate imposter would, therefore, be far more likely to lose prestige than to gain it. And fourth, the man who received power through a revelation also received usually at least one and perhaps more life-long and onerous restrictions. One old man of my acquaintance had not ridden a horse since the day of his vision thirty years earlier, for the spirits had forbidden him to do so. He had trudged on foot. Although the ownership of horses had great prestige value, he had sold the one he owned at the time of his vision and had never owned another. He would gain military renown by killing an enemy but not by the much simpler method of stealing an enemy's horse. Another Indian had been forbidden to eat eggs and was a constant nuisance because he would not eat anything unless he personally supervised its preparation, lest the cook slip in an egg without his knowledge. And a third was forbidden to touch salmon, one of the Crows' few delicacies; on one occasion he ate a mixture of prepared fish without knowing there was salmon there and attributed the following eleven years of rheumatism to his unwitting breaking of his taboo. So a vision was not an unmixed blessing, and a man could hardly hope to derive benefit from a fake.

The role of religion in the life of either community or individual has already been at least implied. A living faith serves to integrate the individual's behavior in society, to give him confidence in meeting the crises which life inescapably brings, and to introduce into his existence a stable central core in the light of which he can assign values. These same purposes are served by the religion of those more sophisticated than my Indian informants, although they may not show the basis of their integration in so clear a fashion. Religion should also provide the basis for ethics. It should enter into everything an individual does, every judgment he makes, every point of view he develops. It is admittedly true that religion is not the only integrator; the impulse may come from immersion in art, music, education, or science in the case of those who have the necessary abilities for such absorption. For the average citizen, however, religion is still the most available source of integration. This fact not only justifies its existence but also explains its universal appeal.

Perhaps it might be well to take a momentary look at what has happened in modern times to societies that have deliberately set about exterminating religion, at least in so far as they could. The Nazis are a case in point. It did not take Hitler long to discover that the churches and the clergy were his implacable enemies. Priests and ministers insisted upon doing what they considered right, they criticized him openly, they tried to rally their congregations to oppose him, they helped enemies of the state to escape, they harbored the persecuted. Hitler could not put his policies of suppression, incarceration, and extermination into effect until he had eliminated the clergy, who would not do as they were told and would not keep their mouths shut. Moreover, they were upheld by a power that he did not understand but which he feared. During the ten years of his dominance the one effective resistance that he could not completely eliminate came from organized religion. One main purpose of his "youth" groups was to bring up a generation that lacked the Christian virtues of compassion or mercy. The Soviets are attempting the same combination of repression and education of children without religious scruples. One *modus operandi* that has been used in totalitarian countries for the suppression of religion has been to carry away from each village as hostage one small child; thereafter, if any member of that village were caught at a secret religious gathering, if any gave aid to a member of the clergy, if any were seen saying his prayers, the child was killed. It is hard to imagine that in a country of even lukewarm Christianity such a method could be used. There are many people who might like to see the extermina-

tion of all religion, but perhaps they might take a closer look at what happens when religious attitudes are destroyed: the accompanying ethical standards also disappear, and one is left with a society not only without religion but also without restraining virtues. It is extremely doubtful that a nation can keep its ethics after it loses its religion.

For the last century at least much has been made of the conflict between religion and science and of the eventual and desirable substitution of the latter for the former. Perhaps before taking sides in this controversy one should consider to what extent the two systems of thought actually do contradict and interfere with each other. As soon as one stops to think, it is clear that there are vast bodies of scientific facts and principles that have never been challenged by any religious group—the ontogeny of silkworms, the expansion of mercury by heat, the predictability of an eclipse, the distance of the moon from the earth, the chemical constitution of water, the antiquity of man, the distinction between tame and domesticated animals, the germ theory of disease, the laws of gravity, and so on. In fact, the points upon which there is conflict are extremely few when compared to the sum total of scientific knowledge.

Perhaps the basic difficulty in seeing the relation of religion and science is that the majority of people do not know in the least what science is, much less what it can and cannot do. The man-in-the-street commonly regards scientific facts as eternal truths—things that cannot change. Nothing could be more incorrect. To take a very simple example: in my chemistry class I was taught that an atom was an absolutely indivisible particle of matter, but now it seems that it is not; and the theory of light waves, as expounded to me in my college days, has long since been amended. And so on, in every field of science. The layman seems to think that because a scientific theory is derived from experiments it *must* be true; such a theory is true only until further experimentation shows wherein it must be altered. A theory is only a hypothesis that will have to do until a better one comes along. There is nothing fixed about it. Another misconception arises from the notion that science is independent of the social and economic pressures of the environment. Quite the reverse is true. Thus, the very problems that are attacked at a particular stage in history are selected by irrational considerations or outside economic pressures, rather than in the light of eternal fitness. This statement explains why classical Greece was so sterile in useful inventions. It was certainly not because of any dearth in acute thinkers or of any ineptitude for experimentation. The reason is to be sought rather in the predominant ideology, which exalted speculation over utilitarian application. Further, the social scheme allocated manual work to slaves, of which there was an ample supply. The tone-setting classes thus had no urge to minimize human effort by labor-saving devices. Those who were mechanically gifted accordingly lavished their ingenuity upon clever but useless toys, such as wooden pigeons that flew by compressed air.

Still another erroneous notion that one often hears expressed is the idea of the scientist as a person who dwells in an ivory tower, remote from the common pressures of mankind, and reaches his conclusions by the exercise of pure reason. This notion, made familiar by various forms of mass communication, is mostly poppycock, as may be shown by taking at random a few samples from the history of science. Ideally, of course, a scientist should be a man who is uniformly critical, willing to follow proof, and insistent upon the application of reason, but unfortunately he is a man like other men, with the same dependence upon tradition in his field, upon his own prejudices, upon his own social milieu. Thus we find Tycho de Brahe, one of the foremost observational astronomers in the history of the science, piquing himself above all upon the accuracy not of his observations but of his horoscopes. History shows us again and again the whole guild of scientists rejecting epoch-making discoveries and advances that did not fit in with their traditional ideas. The scientists of his day branded Harvey as a charlatan for announcing his discoveries about the circulation of the blood, they martyrized Semmelweiss for expounding the cause of child-bed fever, they ridiculed Boucher de Perthes when he declared that man had been a contemporary of extinct animals. These examples are taken from previous centuries, but the ability of a scientist to free himself from tradition and to embrace novel ideas has not increased greatly. Moreover, even a well-balanced, objective scientist is frequently mistaken in his conclusions, not because he does not reason but because he does not yet have all the facts he needs to reason with. Thus, a generation or two ago Lord Kelvin estimated the age of the earth at a figure absurdly low in the light of subsequent research.

To return to the original argument, there are of course points upon which science and religion collide, and the intensity of the clash naturally varies with the circumstances. Medical science is intransigent against religious cults that reject vaccination. Religious leaders may be equally determined to resist the principle of birth-control. Both sides have argued endlessly and to no great profit about Christian Science. Medical men have attacked it as being both useless and dangerous. Its defenders can point to much good that has been done for individuals. Probably both sides are right; they are simply talking about different people and different problems. If a man is a diabetic, he will not be cured by Christian Science, and the period during which he tries to effect a cure by such means may postpone medical treatment until it is too late to do much good. But if a man has a psychosomatic condition, he cannot be cured by a doctor's prescription because the sickness in his body is only a symptom of the sickness in his emotional life. There is a chance that Christian Science can cure him; there is no chance that a pill can. I am reminded of a cousin who was unemployed, depressed, and down to her last hundred dollars, of which she spent fifty for a "course" given by a complete charlatan who actually sent her nothing but form letters, all encouraging her to have faith in the future. Everyone, including myself, thought she was out of her mind, but we were all wrong because the man cured her. She returned to work and remained emotionally adjusted and useful throughout the remainder of her life. This sort of thing illustrates one point about human nature that is often not recognized: that what the average person wants is a workable solution, and he does not in the least care how many mistakes have been made in the computation.

There is thus no warrant for the notion that Science consists of a body of doctrine established once and for all time in the realm of Pure Reason. At any particular stage science is a sportsmanlike adventure in ferreting the truth out of a coy universe. And it is by no means the only method of approach. When we compare what is now known with what was known, say, four hundred years ago, there is every reason for good cheer. But even today research is not wholly a matter of a earnest striving, specialized training, innate capacity for observation and deduction; it is the result of all these and of human frailty working under the handicap of a despotic heritage of traditional prejudice. The result is admittedly our best possible instrument for controlling physical environment and for formulating ideas of the material world. But it does not at all follow that it is soul-satisfying, or that it can serve as a basis for moral action.

If we keep before us the attitude of the man in the street, we shall understand why he can never be satisfied with science as a substitute for religion. That eternal striving for the truth without attaining it, which Lessing lauded as the highest good, has no appeal whatever for the generality of mankind. What the normal human being wants is peace, security, and relaxation. And he can never find these things in that dynamic, ever-growing, ever-disturbing thing that we have found science to be. In ringing words Ernst Mach has defined its nature: "The scientist's highest philosophy consists precisely in bearing an incomplete world-view and preferring it to one that is apparently complete, but inadequate." This is precisely the scientist's philosophy, but most people are nonscientists, and it is of them that I am speaking. The contrast is well expressed by Goethe's oft-quoted quatrain:

Wer Wissenschaft und Kunst besitzt
Hat auch Religion;
Wer jene beiden nicht besitzt,
Der *habe* Religion.

Whatever one may think of the snobbish flavor of these lines, they adumbrate an essential psychological truth. If a man's being is *wholly* absorbed in intellectual and esthetic pursuits, his interests may assume for him the place of spiritual guidance; without immersion in such activity, man had better rely upon the traditional faith. What an average man wants above everything else is security. But does science supply this? The answer is "No." That complete world-view that science explicitly renounces is precisely what the layman craves. In this perilous universe he is forever beset with dangers beyond his control. He wants at all odds to survive, and here science leaves him in the lurch—not everywhere and always, but often enough to make him keenly sensible of its imperfections. If he is dying of an incurable disease, it cheers him little to be told that medical science has made great strides in the past decades and that a remedy will almost certainly be found a hundred years hence, and probably sooner. Instead of running eagerly toward the latest scientific discovery, the average man is likely to wish the discovery had never been made, because it has proved so upsetting to his security. Science has achieved remarkable results, both practical and theoretical, but it has not made man a superman; so long as the enormous chasm yawns between man's rational control of nature and his biologico-psychological drives, there will still be room for belief in a Providence that grants not mere comfort, but security—not mere probability, but certainty. Religion and science thus perform different functions in the life of man, and it is not necessary that either should interfere with the other.

CHAPTER 3

MYTH AND RITUAL

❧❧❧❧

INTRODUCTION

Leaving the more general theoretical questions of the origin, development, and function of religion, it is now convenient to discuss matters concerning specific but universal features of religious systems.

Whatever one's view of the origin or function of religion, there is general agreement that all religions contain beliefs and practices. There are, on the one hand, sacred beliefs or ideas that the members of the society hold as to the nature of the universe and man's place in it; the nature of supernatural power and how man should relate himself to it; the role of the supernaturals in influencing human events; what constitutes good and evil, and so on. These beliefs make up a kind of dogma, since they are vouched for by tradition rather than experience, and are usually expressed in myths. The latter are sacred stories handed down through the generations, either by word of mouth or through books. Such stories are usually of crucial importance in providing explanations of how human life came to be as it is, and in providing justifications for the efficacy of ceremonials and rituals. On the other hand, there are always prescribed ways of carrying on religious acts and procedures, ways of worshiping, praying, chanting, sacrificing, making offerings, and so on, that are called "rituals." (Ceremonials may be looked upon as simply dramatized rituals.) In brief, the beliefs are found in myths; the practices are

prescribed in rituals. One of the best of the earlier efforts to show this linkage was made by Radcliffe-Brown in his special study, *The Andaman Islanders* (1922). The nature of myths and rituals and their functions and interrelationships are discussed in the first selection, written by Clyde Kluckhohn.

Some feeling for the kind of mythopoeic world in which some primitive peoples move is provided in the selection by W. E. H. Stanner on the Dreaming of the Australians. He has elaborated on this interpretation in a series of six articles now assembled as a monograph after they had appeared separately in *Oceania*. It will be recalled that Bellah, in his article on religious evolution in Chapter 1, took the Dreaming as his chief model in the depiction of the first or "primitive" stage of religion, which he saw among other things as a time out of time involving both particularity and fluidity—a close relationship between the mythical world and the details of the actual world on the one hand, and a free-associational lack of precise definition on the other, both of these traits bringing the world of myth close to the actual world. The point stressed by Stanner is that the tales of the Dreaming are a poetic key to Reality, a way of stating the principle which animates things. And of course Australian ritual action fuses man with the mythical beings.

An actual myth from the Gilbert Islands

is offered next as an illustration of the type of sacred story which commonly provides a cosmogony for a primitive culture.

The directions taken by studies of myth are numerous and can unfortunately be given no representation in this chapter. However, a few of them may be alluded to. For instance, there is an interest in examining the degree to which myths are expressive of culture, an important example of this line of investigation being Melville Jacobs' *The Content and Style of an Oral Literature* (1959), which lends excitement to a worthy tradition. A far-ranging and lengthy article by J. L. Fischer, "The Sociopsychological Analysis of Folktales" (1963), encompasses folkloristic writings in general but makes valuable reference to myth and dream, myth and ritual, symbolism, psychological function, and sociological function. Finally, there is a notable collection of contributions to the problem of myth in *Myth: A Symposium* (1955).

Returning to the selections contained in this chapter, there is a vivid account by Edmund Wilson of a Zuni ritual of the type called a "rite of intensification" by Chapple and Coon in their provocative book, *Principles of Anthropology* (1942). Such rites, they maintain, are designed to restore equilibrium to a society after a "crisis" or disturbance in equilibrium brought on by something affecting the whole group more or less equally, as in the alternation of day and night, the changes in the seasons, and various kinds of natural calamities. The Zuni Shalako is performed at a time when the winter solstice approaches. Contrasted with such rites are those which function to restore equilibrium after a crisis involving a change in a single individual, and here Chapple and Coon are content to follow closely Arnold van Gennep's classic interpretation as expressed in his *Les Rites de Passage* (1909), a work now paid new homage and published in an English translation. It will be remembered that van Gennep viewed certain rites as facilitating the passage by an individual from one state to another in the course of his lifetime: birth, puberty, marriage, death, and the like. In this chapter there are no examples of rites of passage but they may be found elsewhere, as in Bettelheim's article on symbolic wounds, which discusses a certain Australian puberty ritual in some detail, and in Geertz's analysis of a Javanese mourning ritual.

Of course there are many rites, including those characterized as magical, not belonging to either of the above cateories. The turtle ritual described in the article by William A. Lessa is predominantly politico-economic with no apparent connection with disequilibrium. The sacrificial rites discussed in the selection by Raymond Firth, although potentially having a restorative effect in the face of crises, are still further removed from any emphasis on equilibrium, communal or individual. Firth's interest in sacrifice is novel and centers around the organization of resources. To be sure, the vision quest of the North American Indians discussed in the brief article by Lowie sometimes has the character of a puberty rite but this was by no means its only or chief role; in fact, we have preferred to use it mostly as an illustration of the gaining of a mystical experience through a ritualistic act.

The possible relationship of many of these rites to "obsessional neuroses" in a given society has long been a matter of speculation and research since the suggestions set forth by Freud in his well-known paper, "Obsessive Acts and Religious Practices," which has been added to this collection.

CLYDE KLUCKHOHN

Myths and Rituals: A General Theory

The question of the relationship of myths and rituals is one that has concerned students of comparative religion for over a century. Are rituals developed as enactments of myths? Or are myths developed to justify rituals? This latter point of view is vigorously held to by such scholars as Lord Raglan (*The Hero*, 1936) and Stanley Edgar Hyman ("The Ritual View of Myth and the Mythic," 1955) but opposed by Bascom ("The Myth-Ritual Theory," 1957) and others.

In this illuminating paper Kluckhohn discusses the theoretical issues involved, and then shows that there is no necessary primacy of myth over ritual, or vice versa. In some cases, myths were composed to justify rituals. But, in general, there is a tendency for the two to be intricately interrelated and to have important functional connections with the social and psychological life of a particular people. Kluckhohn then tests these generalities by a review of the Navaho Indian case in which he shows in detail the interconnections between myth and ritual and the functions of both in Navaho society.

The identification of a "type anxiety" (that of concern for health) and the function of the ceremonial system (which in Navaho society is almost entirely composed of curing ceremonies) in dealing with this anxiety at both the societal and individual level brings the discussion into sharp focus and shows clearly how myths and rituals can be systematically studied as cultural products.

Reprinted by permission of the publishers from Clyde Kluckhohn, "Myths and Rituals: A General Theory," *Harvard Theological Review*, XXXV (January, 1942), 45–79. Cambridge, Mass.: Harvard University Press, 1942. The author kindly undertook some minor reworking of the text and deleted most of the footnotes.

I

Nineteenth-century students strongly tended to study mythology apart from associated rituals (and indeed apart from the life of the people generally). Myths were held to be symbolic descriptions of phenomena of nature. One prominent school, in fact, tried to find an astral basis for all mythic tales. Others, among whom Andrew Lang was prominent, saw in the myth a kind of primitive scientific theory. Mythology answered the insistent human HOW? and WHY? How and why was the world made? How and why were living creatures brought into being? Why, if there was life, must there be death? To early psychoanalysts such as Abraham and Rank myths were "group fantasies," wish fulfillments for a society strictly analogous to the dream and daydream of individuals. Mythology for these psychoana-

lysts was also a symbolic structure par excellence, but the symbolism which required interpretation was primarily a sex symbolism which was postulated as universal and all-pervasive. Reik recognized a connection between rite and myth, and he, with Freud, verbally agreed to Robertson Smith's proposition that mythology was mainly a description of ritual. To the psychoanalysts, however, mythology was essentially (so far as what they did with it is concerned) societal phantasy material which reflected impulse repression. (Many psychoanalysts today consider myths simply "a form of collective daydreaming." I have heard a prominent psychoanalyst say "Creation myths are for culture what early memories (true or fictitious) are to the individual.") There was no attempt to discover the practical function of mythology in the daily behaviors of the members of a society nor to demonstrate specific interactions of mythology and ceremonials. The interest was in supposedly panhuman symbolic meanings, not in the relation of a given myth or part of a myth to particular cultural forms or specific social situations.

To some extent the answer to the whole question of the relationship between myth and ceremony depends, of course, upon how wide or how restricted a sense one gives to "mythology." In ordinary usage the Oedipus tale is a "myth," but only some Freudians believe that this is merely the description of a ritual! The famous stories of the Republic are certainly called "μῦθος," and while a few scholars believe that Plato in *some* cases had reference to the Orphic and/or Eleusinian mysteries there is certainly not a shred of evidence that all of Plato's immortal "myths" are "descriptions of rituals." To be sure, one may justifiably narrow the problem by saying that in a technical sense these are "legends," and by insisting that "myths" be rigorously distinguished from "legends," "fairy tales," and "folk tales." If, however, one agrees that "myth" has Durkheim's connotation of the "sacred" as opposed to the "profane" the line is still sometimes hard to draw in concrete cases. What of "creation myths"? In some cases (as at Zuni) these are indeed recited during ritual performances (with variations for various ceremonies). In other cases, even though they may be recited in a "ritual" attitude, they do not enter into any ceremonial. Nevertheless, they definitely retain the flavor of "the sacred." Moreover, there are (as again at Zuni) exoteric and esoteric forms of the same myth. Among the Navaho many of the older men who are not ceremonial practitioners know that part of a myth which tells of the exploits of the hero or heroes but not the portion which prescribes the ritual details of the chant. Granting that there are sometimes both secular and sacred versions of the same tale and that other difficulties obtrude themselves in particular cases, it still seems possible to use the connotation of the sacred as that which differentiates "myth" from the rest of folklore.

But defining "myth" strictly as "sacred tale" does not carry with it by implication a warrant for considering mythology purely as a description of correlative rituals. Generally speaking, we do seem to find rich ritualism and a rich mythology together. But there are cases (like the Toda) where an extensive ceremonialism does not appear to have its equally extensive mythological counterpart and instances (like classical Greece) where a ramified mythology appears to have existed more or less independent of a comparatively meager rite system. For example, in spite of the many myths relating to Ares the rituals connected with Ares seem to have been few in number and highly localized in time and space. The early Romans, on the other hand, seemed to get along very well without mythology. The poverty of the ritual which accompanies the extremely complex mythology of the Mohave is well known. Kroeber indeed says, "Public ceremonies or rituals as they occur among almost all native Americans cannot be said to be practiced by the Mohave." The Bushmen likewise had many myths and very little ritual. On the other hand, one can point to examples like the Central Eskimo, where every detail of the Sedna myth has its ritual analogue in confessional, other rites, or hunting taboos, or, for contrast, to the American Indian tribes (especially some Californian ones) where the creation myth is never enacted in ceremonial form. In different sectors of one culture, the Papago, all of these possibilities are represented. Some myths are never ceremonially enacted. Some ceremonies emphasize content foreign to the myth. Other ceremonies consisting only of songs have some vague place in the mythological world; between these and the myths "there is a certain tenuous connection which may be a rationalization made for the sake of unity."

The anthropology of the past generation has tended to recoil sharply from any sort of generalized interpretation. Obsessed with the complexity of the historical experience of all peoples, anthropologists have (perhaps overmuch) eschewed the inference of regularities of psychological reaction which would transcend the facts of diffusion and of contacts of groups. Emphasis has been laid upon the distribution of myths and upon the mythological patterning which prevailed in different cultures and culture areas. Study of these distributions has led to a generalization of another order which is the converse of the hypothesis of most nineteenth-century

classical scholars that a ritual was an enactment of a myth. In the words of Boas: "The
uniformity of many such rituals over large
areas and the diversity of mythological explanations show clearly that the ritual itself
is the stimulus for the origin of the myth.
. . . The ritual existed, and the tale originated from the desire to account for it."

While this suggestion of the primacy of
ritual over myth is probably a valid statistical induction and a proper statement of the
modal tendency of our evidence, it is, it
seems to me, as objectionably a simple unitary explanation (if pressed too far) as the
generally rejected nineteenth-century views.
Thus we find Hocart recently asking: "If
there are myths that give rise to ritual where
do these myths come from?" A number of
instances will shortly be presented in which
the evidence is unequivocal that myths did
give rise to ritual. May I only remark here
that—if we view the matter objectively—the
Christian Mass, as interpreted by Christians, is a clear illustration of a ritual based
upon a sacred story. Surely, in any case,
Hocart's question can be answered very
simply: from a dream or a waking fantasy
or a personal habit system of some individual in the society. The basic psychological mechanisms involved would seem not
dissimilar to those whereby individuals in
our own (and other) cultures construct private rituals or carry out private divination—
e.g., counting and guessing before the clock
strikes, trying to get to a given point (a
traffic light, for instance) before something
else happens. As DuBois has suggested, "the
explanation may be that personal rituals
have been taken over and socialized by the
group." These "personal rituals" could have
their genesis in idiosyncratic habit formations (similar to those of obsessional neurotics in our culture) or in dreams or
reveries. Mrs. Seligman has convincingly
suggested that spontaneous personal dissociation is a frequent mechanism for rite
innovations. The literature is replete with
instances of persons "dreaming" that supernaturals summoned them, conducted them on
travels or adventures, and finally admonished
them thereafter to carry out certain rites
(often symbolically repetitive of the adventures).

Moreover, there are a number of well-
documented actual cases where historical
persons, in the memory of other historical
persons, actually instituted new rituals. The
ritual innovations of the American Indian
Ghost Dance cult and other nativistic cults
of the New World provide striking illustration. In these cases the dreams or fantasies—told by the innovators before the
ceremonial was ever actualized in deeds—
became an important part of traditionally
accepted rite-myths. Lincoln has presented
plausible evidence that dreams are the
source of "new" rituals. Morgan, on the
basis of Navaho material, says:

. . . delusions and dreams . . . are so vivid
and carry such conviction that any attempt to
reason about them afterwards on the basis of
conscious sense impressions is unavailing. Such
experiences deeply condition the individual,
sometimes so deeply that if the experience is at
variance with a tribal or neighborhood belief,
the individual will retain his own variation.
There can be no doubt that this is a very significant means of modifying a culture.

Van Gennep asserts that persons went to
dream in the sanctuary at Epidaurus as a
source for new rites in the cult of Asclepius.
To obtain ceremony through dream is, of
course, itself a pattern, a proper traditional
way of obtaining a ceremony or power. I do
not know of any cases of a society where
dreaming is generally in disrepute, as at
Zuni, and where ceremony has yet demonstrably originated through dream. But
where dreaming is accepted as revelation it
must not be assumed that the content (or
even, entirely, the structure) of a new myth
and its derived ceremony will be altogether
determined by pre-existent cultural forms.
As Lowie has remarked, "That they themselves (dreams) in part reflect the regnant
folklore offers no ultimate explanation." Anthropologists must be wary of what Korzyb-
ski calls "self-reflexive systems"—here, specifically, the covert premise that "culture
alone determines culture."

The structure of new cultural forms
(whether myths or rituals) will undoubtedly
be conditioned by the pre-existent cultural
matrix. But the rise of new cultural forms
will almost always be determined by factors
external to that culture: pressure from other
societies, biological events such as epidemics,
or changes in the physical environment.
Barber has recently shown how the Ghost
Dance and the Peyote Cult represent alternative responses of various American Indian
tribes to the deprivation resultant upon the

encroachment of whites. The Ghost Dance was an adaptive response under the earlier external conditions, but under later conditions the Peyote Cult was the more adaptive response, and the Ghost Dance suffered what the stimulus-response psychologists would call "extinction through non-reward." At any rate, the Ghost Dance became extinct in some tribes; in others it has perhaps suffered only partial extinction.

There are always individuals in every society who have their private rituals; there are always individuals who dream and who have compensatory fantasies. In the normal course of things these are simply deviant behaviors which are ridiculed or ignored by most members of the society. Perhaps indeed one should not speak of them as "deviant"— they are "deviant" only as carried to extremes by a relatively small number of individuals, for everyone probably has some private rituals and compensatory fantasies. When, however, changed conditions happen to make a particular type of obsessive behavior or a special sort of fantasy generally congenial, the private ritual is then socialized by the group, the fantasy of the individual becomes the myth of his society. Indeed there is evidence that when pressures are peculiarly strong and peculiarly general, a considerable number of different individuals may almost simultaneously develop substantially identical fantasies which then become widely current.

Whether belief (myth) or behavior (ritual) changes first will depend, again, both upon cultural tradition and upon external circumstances. Taking a very broad view of the matter, it does seem that behavioral patterns more frequently alter first. In a rapidly changing culture such as our own many ideal patterns are as much as a generation behind the corresponding behavioral patterns. There is evidence that certain ideal patterns (for example, those defining the status of women) are slowly being altered to harmonize with, to act as rationalizations for, the behavioral actualities. On the other hand, the case of Nazi Germany is an excellent illustration of the ideal patterns ("the myth") being provided from above almost whole cloth and of the state, through various organizations, exerting all its force to make the behavioral patterns conform to the standards of conduct laid down in the Nazi mythology.

Some cultures and subcultures are relatively indifferent to belief, others to behavior. The dominant practice of the Christian Church, throughout long periods of its history, was to give an emphasis to belief which is most unusual as seen from a cross-cultural perspective. In general, the crucial test as to whether or not one was a Christian was the willingness to avow belief in certain dogmas. The term "believer" was almost synonymous with "Christian." It is very possibly because of this cultural screen that until this century most European scholars selected the myth as primary.

II

To a considerable degree, the whole question of the primacy of ceremonial or mythology is as meaningless as all questions of "the hen or the egg" form. What is really important, as Malinowski has so brilliantly shown, is the intricate interdependence of myth (which is one form of ideology) with ritual and many other forms of behavior. He examines myths not as curiosa taken out of their total context but as living, vitally important elements in the day-to-day lives of his Trobrianders, interwoven with every other abstracted type of activity. From this point of view one sees the fallacy of all unilateral explanations. One also sees the aspect of truth in all (or nearly all) of them. There are features which seem to be explanatory of natural phenomena. There are features which reveal the peculiar forms of wish fulfillments characteristic of the culture in question (including the expression of the culturally disallowed but unconsciously wanted). There *are* myths which are intimately related to rituals, which may be descriptive of them, but there are myths which stand apart. If these others are descriptive of rituals at all, they are, as Durkheim (followed by Radcliffe-Brown and others) suggested, descriptions of rituals of the social organization. That is, they are symbolic representations of the dominant configurations of the particular culture. Myths, then, may express not only the latent content of rituals but of other culturally organized behaviors. Malinowski is surely in error when he writes ". . . myth . . . is not symbolic. . . ." Durkheim and Mauss have pointed out how various nonliterate groups (notably the Zuni and certain tribes of southeastern Australia) embrace nature within the schema of their social organization through myths which classify natural phenomena precisely according to the principles that prevail in the social organization.

Boas, with his usual caution, is skeptical of all attempts to find a systematic interpretation of mythology. But, while we can agree with him when he writes ". . . mythological narratives and mythological concepts should not be equalized; for social, psychological, and historical conditions affect both in different ways," the need for scrupulous inquiry into historical and other determinants must not be perverted to justify a repudiation of all attempts to deal with the symbolic processes of the all-important covert culture. At all events, the factual record is perfectly straightforward in one respect: neither myth nor ritual can be postulated as "primary."

This is the important point in our discussion at this juncture, and it is unfortunate that Hooke and his associates in their otherwise very illuminating contributions to the study of the relations between myth and ritual in the Near East have emphasized only one aspect of the system of interdependences which Malinowski and Radcliffe-Brown have shown to exist. When Hooke points out that myths are constantly used to justify rituals this observation is quite congruent with the observed facts in many cultures. Indeed all of these data may be used toward a still wider induction: man, as a symbol-using animal, appears to feel the need not only to act but almost equally to give verbal or other symbolic "reasons" for his acts. Hooke rightly speaks of "the vital significance of the myth as something that works," but when he continues "and that dies apart from its ritual" he seems to imply that myths cannot exist apart from rituals and this, as has been shown, is contrary to documented cases. No, the central theorem has been expressed much more adequately by Radcliffe-Brown: "In the case of both ritual and myth the sentiments expressed are those that are essential to the existence of the society." This theorem can be regarded as having been well established in a general way, but we still lack detailed observations on change in myths as correlated with changes in ritual and changes in a culture generally. Navaho material gives certain hints that when a culture as a whole changes rapidly its myths are also substantially and quickly altered.

In sum, the facts do not permit any universal generalizations as to ritual being the "cause" of myth or vice versa. Their relationship is rather that of intricate mutual interdependence, differently structured in different cultures and probably at different times in the same culture. As Benedict has pointed out, there is great variation in the extent to which mythology conditions the religious complex—"the small role of myth in Africa and its much greater importance in religion in parts of North America." Both myth and ritual satisfy the needs of a society and the relative place of one or the other will depend upon the particular needs (conscious and unconscious) of the individuals in a particular society at a particular time. This principle covers the observed data, which show that rituals are borrowed without their myths, and myths without any accompanying ritual. A ritual may be reinforced by a myth (or vice versa) in the donor culture, but satisfy the carriers of the recipient culture simply as a form of activity (or be rationalized by a quite different myth which better meets their emotional needs).[1] In short, the only uniformity which can be posited is that there is a strong tendency for some sort of interrelationship between myth and ceremony and that this is dependent upon what appears, so far as present information goes, to be an invariant function

[1] There are many striking and highly specific parallels between Navaho and Hopi ceremonial practices. For example, the mechanical equipment used in connection with the Sun's House phase of the Navaho Shooting Way chants has so much in common with similar gadgets used in Hopi ceremonials that one can hardly fail to posit a connection. Dr. Parsons has documented the intimate resemblances between the Male Shooting Way chant and Hopi Flute and Snake-Antelope ceremonies ("A Pre-Spanish Record of Hopi Ceremonies," *American Anthropologist,* Vol. XLII [1940], 541–543, n. 4, p. 541). The best guess at present would be that the Hopi was the donor culture, but the direction of diffusion is immaterial here: the significant point is that the supporting myths in the cases concerned show little likeness. For instance, Dr. Parsons regards the Flute Ceremony as a dramatization of the Hopi emergence myth, but the comparable ritual acts in Navaho culture are linked to chantway legends of the usual Holy Way pattern and not to the emergence story. In contrast, the White Mountain Apache seem to have borrowed *both* Snake myth and ritual from the Hopi. See E. C. Parsons, *Pueblo Indian Religion* (Chicago, 1939), p. 1060, and G. Goodwin, *Myths and Tales of the White Mountain Apache* ("Memoirs of the American Folklore Society," Vol. XXXIII [New York, 1939], p. vii).

of both myth and ritual: the gratification (most often in the negative form of anxiety reduction) of a large proportion of the individuals in a society.

If Malinowski and Radcliffe-Brown (and their followers) turned the searchlight of their interpretations as illuminatingly upon specific human animals and their impulses as upon cultural and social abstractions, it might be possible to take their work as providing a fairly complete and adequate general theory of myth and ritual. With Malinowski's notion of myth as "an active force" which is intimately related to almost every other aspect of a culture we can only agree. When he writes: "Myth is a constant byproduct of living faith which is in need of miracles; of sociological status, which demands precedent; of moral rule which requires sanction," we can only applaud. To the French sociologists, to Radcliffe-Brown, and to Warner we are indebted for the clear formulation of the symbolic principle. Those realms of behavior and of experience which man finds beyond rational and technological control he feels are capable of manipulation through symbols. Both myth and ritual are symbolical procedures and are most closely tied together by this, as well as by other, facts. The myth is a system of word symbols, whereas ritual is a system of object and act symbols. Both are symbolic processes for dealing with the same type of situation in the same affective mode.

But the French sociologists, Radcliffe-Brown, and—to a lesser extent—Malinowski are so interested in formulating the relations between conceptual elements that they tend to lose sight of the concrete human organisms. The "functionalists" do usually start with a description of some particular ritualistic behaviors. Not only, however, do the historical origins of this particular behavioral complex fail to interest them. Equally, the motivations and rewards which persons feel are lost sight of in the preoccupation with the contributions which the rituals make to the social system. Thus a sense of the specific detail is lost and we are soon talking about myth in general and ritual in general. From the "functionalist" point of view specific details are about as arbitrary as the phonemes of a language are with respect to "the content" of what is communicated by speech. Hence, as Dollard says, "What one sees from the cultural angle is a drama of life much like a puppet show in which 'culture' is pulling the strings from behind the scenes." The realization that we are really dealing with "animals struggling in real dilemmas" is lacking.

From this angle, some recent psychoanalytic interpretations of myth and ritual seem preferable. We may regard as unconvincing Roheim's attempts to treat myths as historical documents which link human phylogenetic and ontogenetic development, as we may justly feel that many psychoanalytic discussions of the latent content of mythology are extravagant and undisciplined. Casey's summary of the psychoanalytic view of religion, ". . . ritual is a sublimated compulsion; dogma and myth are sublimated obsessions," may well strike us as an oversimplified, overneat generalization, but at least our attention is drawn to the connection between cultural forms and impulse-motivated organisms. And Kardiner's relatively sober and controlled treatment does "point at individuals, at bodies, and at a rich and turbulent biological life"—even though that life is admittedly conditioned by social heredity: social organization, culturally defined symbolic systems, and the like.

In a later section of this paper, we shall return to the problem of how myths and rituals reinforce the behavior of individuals. But first let us test the generalities which have been propounded thus far by concrete data from a single culture, the Navaho.

III

The Navaho certainly have sacred tales which, as yet at all events, are not used to justify associated rituals. A striking case, and one where the tale has a clear function as expressing a sentiment "essential to the existence of the society," is known from different parts of the Navaho country.[2] The

[2] E. L. Hewett (*The Chaco Canyon and Its Monuments,* Albuquerque, N.M., 1936 p. 139) records the dissemination of this tale among the Chaco Canyon Navaho. Drs. A. and D. Leighton and I have obtained independent evidence that the same story was told, and believed by many, among the Ramah Navaho (one-hundred-odd miles away) at the same time. Those who believed the tale carried out ceremonials but not new ceremonials. Rather the old ceremonials (especially Blessing Way rites) were carried out in unusual frequency. In 1936 in the Huerfano country a young woman reported that she had been visited by White Shell

tales differ in detail but all have these structural elements in common: one of "the Holy People" visits one or more Navahos to warn them of an impending catastrophe (a flood or the like) which will destroy the whites—but believing Navahos will be saved if they retire to the top of a mountain or some other sanctuary. It is surely not without meaning that these tales became current at about the time that the Navahos were first feeling intensive and sustained pressure (they were not just prisoners of war as in the Fort Sumner epoch) from the agents of our culture.[3] Father Berard Haile has recently

published evidence that Navaho ceremonials may originate in dreams or visions rather than being invariably *post hoc* justifications for existent ritual practices. A practitioner called "son of the late Black Goat" instituted a new ceremonial "which he had learned in a dream while sleeping in a cave." Various informants assured Father Berard that chantway legends originated in the "visions" of individuals.[4] We have, then, Navaho data for (*a*) the existence of myths without associated rituals, and (*b*) the origin of both legends and rituals in dreams or visions.

It is true that all ceremonial practice among the Navaho is, in cultural theory, justified by an accompanying myth. One may say with Dr. Parsons on the Pueblos: "Whatever the original relationship between myth and ceremony, once made, the myth supports the ceremony or ceremonial office and may suggest ritual increments." One must in the same breath, however, call attention to the fact that myth also supports accepted ways of secular behavior. As Dr. Hill has pointed out, "Women are required to sit with their legs under them and to one side, men with their legs crossed in front of them, because it is said that in the beginning Changing Woman and the Monster Slayer sat in these positions." Let this one example suffice for the many which could easily be given. The general point is that in both sacred and secular spheres myths give some fixity to the ideal patterns of cultures where this is not attained by the printed word. The existence of rituals has a similar effect. Although I cannot agree with Wissler that "the primary function" of rituals is "to perpetuate exact knowledge and to secure precision in their application," there can be no doubt that both myths and rituals are im-

---

Woman who had been given instructions for Blessing Ways to be held—but with special additional procedures. These rites were widely carried out in the northeastern portion of the Navaho area. (See the article by Will Evans in the Farmington, N.M., *Times Hustler,* under date line of February 21, 1937.) Also in 1936 a woman in the Farmington region claimed to have been visited by Banded Rock Boy (one of the Holy People) and a similar story spread over the reservation. A famous singer, Left-handed, refused to credit the tale and many Navahos attributed his death (which occurred soon thereafter) to his disabelief. See *Mesa Verde Notes,* VII (March, 1937), 16–19. F. Gilmor (*Windsinger* [New York, 1930]) has used a story of the same pattern, obtained from the Navaho of the Kayenta, Arizona, region as a central episode in a novel.

[3] Jane Harrison (*Themis* [Cambridge, Eng., 1912]) says: "It is this collective sanction and solemn purpose that differentiate the myth alike from the historical narrative and the mere *conte* or fairy-tale . . ." (p. 330), and many agreeing with her will doubtless assert that my argument here is invalid because these tales, though unquestionably having "solemn purpose," lack "collective sanction." Some would also contend that since living persons claim to have seen the supernatural beings these stories must be called "tales" or, at any rate, not "myths." I see these points and, since I wish to avoid a purely verbal quarrel, I would agree, so far as present data go, that Navaho myths (in the narrow sense) are uniformly associated with ritual behaviors. Actually, *the* myth which most Navaho call their most sacred (the emergence story) is associated with rites only in a manner which is, from certain points of view, tenuous. The emergence myth is not held to be the basis for any single ceremonial, nor is it used to justify any very considerable portion of ceremonial practice. The emergence myth (or some part of it) *is* often prefaced to the chantway legend proper. In any case, I must insist (granting always that the line between secular and sacred folk literature must not be drawn too sharply) that the stories dealt with above are not part of the "profane" folklore of the Navaho in the sense in which the coyote tales, for example, are. The origin legends of the various clans are certainly not secular literature, but I imagine that a purist would maintain that we must call these "legends" as lacking "solemn purpose" (in Harrison's sense). Nevertheless I repeat that "myths" in

the broad sense of "sacred tale" are among the Navaho found quite dissociated from ritual.

[4] The assertion that ceremonials sometimes have their genesis in dreams and the like does not imply that this, any more than that between myth and ritual, is a one-way relationship. One can by no means dispose of the matter simply by saying "dreams cause myths and myths cause ceremonies." William Morgan ("Navaho Dreams," *American Anthropologist,* XXXIV [1932], 390–406), who was also convinced that some Navaho myths derive from dreams (p. 395), has pointed out the other aspect of the interdependence: ". . . myths . . . influence dreams; and these dreams, in turn, help to maintain the efficacy of the ceremonies. . . . Repetitive dreams do much to strengthen the tradiional beliefs concerning dreams" (p. 400).

portant agencies in the transmission of a culture and that they act as brakes upon the speed of culture change.

Returning to the connections between myth and rite among the Navaho, one cannot do better than begin by quoting some sentences from Washington Matthews: "In some cases a Navajo rite has only one myth pertaining to it. In other cases it has many myths. The relation of the myth to the ceremony is variable. Sometimes it explains nearly everything in the ceremony and gives an account of all the important acts from beginning to end, in the order in which they occur; at other times it describes the work in a less systematic manner. . . . Some of the myths seem to tell only of the way in which rites, already established with other tribes, were introduced among the Navajos. . . . The rite-myth never explains all of the symbolism of the rite, although it may account for all the important acts. A primitive and underlying symbolism which probably existed previous to the establishment of the rite, remains unexplained by the myth, as though its existence were taken as a matter of course, and required no explanation."

To these observations one may add the fact that knowledge of the myth is in no way prerequisite to the carrying out of a chant. Knowledge does give the singer or curer prestige and ability to expect higher fees, and disparaging remarks are often heard to the effect "Oh, he doesn't know the story," or "He doesn't know the story very well yet." And yet treatment by a practitioner ignorant of the myth[5] is regarded as efficacious. Navahos are often a little cynical about the variation in the myths. If someone observes that one singer did not carry out a procedure exactly as did another (of perhaps greater repute) it will often be said "Well, he says *his* story is different." Different forms of a rite-myth tend to prevail in different areas of the Navaho country and in different localities. Here the significance of the "personality" of various singers may sometimes be de-

tected in the rise of variations. The transvestite "Left-handed" who died a few years ago enjoyed a tremendous reputation as a singer. There is some evidence that he restructuralized a number of myths as he told them to his apprentices in a way which tended to make the hermaphrodite *be?gočidi* a kind of supreme Navaho deity—a position which he perhaps never held in the general tradition up to that point. I have heard other Navaho singers say that sand paintings and other ceremonial acts and procedures were slightly revised to accord with this tenet. If this be true, we have here another clear of myth-before-ritual.

Instances of the reverse sort are also well documented. From a number of informants accounts have been independently obtained of the creation (less than a hundred years ago) of a new rite: Enemy Monster Blessing Way. All the information agreed that the ritual procedures had been devised by one man who collated parts of two previously existent ceremonials and added a few bits from his own fancy. And three informants independently volunteered the observation "He didn't have any story. But after a while he and his son and another fellow made one up." This is corroborated by the fact that none of Father Berard's numerous versions of the Blessing Way myth mention an Enemy Monster form.

Besides these notes on the relations between myth and rite I should like to record my impression of another function of myth— one which ranges from simple entertainment to "intellectual edification." Myth among the Navaho not only acts as a justification, a rationale for ritual behavior and as a moral reinforcement for other customary behaviors. It also plays a role not dissimilar to that of literature (especially sacred literature) in many literate cultures. Navahos have a keen expectation of the long recitals of myths (or portions of them) around the fire on winter nights.[6] Myths have all the charm of the

---

[5] How much a practitioner knows of both legend and ceremonial depends upon the demands he made upon his instructor during his apprenticeship. The instructor is not supposed to prompt his pupil. Many practitioners are satisfied with quite mechanical performances, and there is no doubt that much information (both legendary and ritualistic) is being lost at present owing to the fact that apprentices do not question their instructors more than superficially.

[6] Why may the myths be recited only in winter? In Navaho feeling today this prohibition is linked in a wider configuration of forbidden activities. There is also, as usual, an historical and distributional problem, for this same prohibition is apparently widely distributed in North America. For example, it is found among the Berens River Salteaux and among the Iroquois. But I wonder if in a certain "deeper" sense this prohibition is not founded upon the circumstance that only winter affords the leisure for telling myths, that telling them in

familiar. Their very familiarity increases their efficacy, for, in a certain broad and loose sense, the function of both myths and rituals is "the discharge of the emotion of individuals in socially accepted channels." And Hocart acutely observes: "Emotion is assisted by the repetition of words that have acquired a strong emotional coloring, and this coloring again is intensified by repetition." Myths are expective, repetitive dramatizations—their role is similar to that of books in cultures which have few books. They have the (to us) scarcely understandable meaningfulness which the tragedies had for the Greek populace. As Matthew Arnold said of these, "their significance appeared inexhaustible."

IV

The inadequacy of any simplistic statement of the relationship between myth and ritual has been established. It has likewise been maintained that the most adequate generalization will not be cast in terms of the primacy of one or the other of these cultural forms but rather in terms of the general tendency for the two to be interdependent. This generalization has been arrived at through induction from abstractions at the cultural level. That is, as we have sampled the evidence from various cultures we have found cases where myths have justified rituals and have appeared to be "after the fact" of ritual; we have also seen cases where new myths have given rise to new rituals. In other words, the primary conclusion which may be drawn from the data is that myths and rituals tend to be very intimately associated and to influence each other. What is the explanation of the observed connection?

The explanation is to be found in the circumstance that myth and ritual satisfy a group of identical or closely related needs of individuals. Thus far we have alluded only occasionally and often obliquely to myths and rituals as cultural forms defining individual behaviors which are adaptive or adjustive responses. We have seen how myths and rituals are adaptive from the point of view of the society in that they promote social solidarity, enhance the integration of the society by providing a formalized statement

of its ultimate value-attitudes, and afford a means for the transmission of much of the culture with little loss of content—thus protecting cultural continuity and stabilizing the society. But how are myth and ritual rewarding enough in the daily lives of individuals so that individuals are instigated to preserve them, so that myth and ritual continue to prevail at the expense of more rational responses?

A systematic examination of this question, mainly again in terms of Navaho material, will help us to understand the prevailing interdependence of myth and ritual which has been documented. This sketch of a general theory of myth and ritual as providing a cultural storehouse of adjustive responses for individuals is to be regarded as tentative from the writer's point of view. I do not claim that the theory is proven—even in the context of Navaho culture. I do suggest that it provides a series of working hypotheses which can be tested by specifically pointed field procedures.

We can profitably begin by recurring to the function of myth as fulfilling the expectancy of the familiar. Both myth and ritual here provide cultural solutions to problems which all human beings face. Burke has remarked, "Human beings build their cultures, nervously loquacious, upon the edge of an abyss." In the face of want and death and destruction all humans have a fundamental insecurity. To some extent, all culture is a gigantic effort to mask this, to give the future the simulacrum of safety by making activity repetitive, expective—"to make the future predictable by making it conform to the past." From one angle our own scientific mythology is clearly related to that motivation, as is the obsessive, the compulsive tendency which lurks in all organized thought.

When questioned as to why a particular ceremonial activity is carried out in a particular way, Navaho singers will most often say "because the *divin diné*—the Holy People—did it that way in the first place." The *ultima ratio* of nonliterates strongly tends to be "that is what our fathers said it was." An Eskimo said to Rasmussen: "We Eskimos do not concern ourselves with solving all riddles. We repeat the old stories in the way they were told to us and with the words we ourselves remember." The Eskimo saying "we keep the old rules in order that we may live untroubled" is well known. The

Navaho and Eskimo thus implicitly recognize a principle which has been expressed by Harvey Fergusson as follows:

. . . man dreads both spontaneity and change, . . . he is a worshiper of habit in all its forms. Conventions and institutions are merely organized and more or less sanctified habits. These are the real gods of human society, which transcend and outlive all other gods. All of them originate as group expedients which have some social value at some time, but they remain the objects of a passionate adoration long after they have outlived their usefulness. Men fight and die for them. They have their high priests, their martyrs, and their rituals. They are the working gods, whatever the ostensible ones may be [*Modern Man,* p. 29].

These principles apply as well to standardized overt acts as to standardized forms of words. Thus Pareto considered the prevalence of ritual in all human cultures as perhaps the outstanding empirical justification for his thesis of the importance of nonlogical action. Merton writes:

. . . activities originally conceived as instrumental are transmuted into ends in themselves. The original purposes are forgotten and ritualistic adherence to institutionally prescribed conduct becomes virtually obsessive. . . . Such ritualism may be associated with a mythology which rationalizes these actions so that they appear to retain their status as means, but the dominant pressure is in the direction of strict ritualistic conformity, irrespective of such rationalizations. In this sense ritual has proceeded farthest when such rationalizations are not even called forth ["Social Structure and Anomie," p. 673].

Goldstein, a neurologist, recognizes a neurological basis for the persistence of such habit systems: "The organism tends to function in the accustomed manner, as long as an at least moderately effective performance can be achieved in this way."

Nevertheless, certain objections to the position as thus far developed must be anticipated and met. It must be allowed at once that the proposition "man dreads both spontaneity and change" must be qualified. More precisely put, we may say "most men, most of the time, dread both spontaneity and change in most of their activities." This formulation allows for the observed fact that most of us *occasionally* get irked with the routines of our lives or that there are certain sectors of our behavior where we fairly consistently show spontaneity. But a careful examination of the totality of behavior of any individual who is not confined in an institution or who has not withdrawn almost completely from participation in the society will show that the larger proportion of the behavior of even the greatest iconoclasts is habitual. This must be so, for by very definition a socialized organism is an organism which behaves mainly in a predictable manner. Even in a culture like contemporary American culture, which has made an institutionalized value of change (both for the individual and for society), conformity is at the same time a great virtue. To some extent, this is phrased as conformity with the latest fashion, but Americans remain, by and large, even greater conformists than most Europeans.

Existence in an organized society would be unthinkable unless most people, most of the time, behaved in an expectable manner. Rituals constitute "tender spots" for all human beings, people can count upon the repetitive nature of the phenomena. For example, in Zuni society (where rituals are highly calendrical) a man whose wife has left him or whose crops have been ruined by a torrential downpour can yet look forward to the Shalako ceremonial as something which is fixed and immutable. Similarly, the personal sorrow of the devout Christian is in some measure mitigated by anticipation of the great feasts of Christmas and Easter. Perhaps the even turn of the week with its Sunday services and mid-week prayer meetings gave a dependable regularity which the Christian clung to even more in disaster and sorrow. For some individuals daily prayer and the confessional gave the needed sense of security. Myths, likewise, give men "something to hold to." The Christian can better face the seemingly capricious reverses of his plans when he hears the joyous words "lift up your hearts." Rituals and myths supply, then, fixed points in a world of bewildering change and disappointment.

If almost all behavior has something of the habitual about it, how is it that myths and rituals tend to represent the maximum of fixity? Because they deal with those sectors of experience which do not seem amenable to rational control and hence where human beings can least tolerate insecurity. That very insistence upon the minutiae of ritual performance, upon preserving the myth to the very letter, which is character-istic of religious behavior must be regarded as a "reaction formation" (in the Freudian sense) which compensates for the actual in-transigence of those events which religion tries to control.

To anticipate another objection: do these "sanctified habit systems" show such ex-traordinary persistence simply because they are repeated so often and so scrupulously? Do myths and rituals constitute repetitive behavior par excellence not merely as reac-tion formations but because the habits are practiced so insistently? Perhaps myths and rituals perdure in accord with Allport's "principle of functional autonomy"—as in-terpreted by some writers? No, perform-ances must be rewarded in the day-to-day lives of participating individuals. Sheer repe-tition in and of itself has never assured the persistence of any habit. If this were not so, no myths and rituals would ever have be-come extinct except when a whole society died out. It is necessary for us to recognize the somewhat special conditions of drive and of reward which apply to myths and rituals.

It is easy to understand why organisms eat. It is easy to understand why a defense-less man will run to escape a charging tiger. The physiological bases of the activities rep-resented by myths and rituals are less ob-vious. A recent statement by a stimulus-response psychologist gives us the clue: "The position here taken is that human be-ings (and also other living organisms to varying degrees) can be motivated either by organic pressures (needs) that are currently felt *or* by the mere anticipation of such pres-sures, and that those habits tend to be ac-quired and perpetuated (reinforced) which effect a reduction in either of these two types of motivation." That is, myths and rituals are reinforced because they reduce the an-ticipation of disaster. No living person has died—but he has seen others die. The ter-rible things which we have seen happen to others may not yet have plagued us, but our experience teaches us that these are at least potential threats to our own health or hap-piness.

If a Navaho gets a bad case of snow blindness and recovers after being sung over, his disposition to go to a singer in the event of a recurrence will be strongly reinforced. And, by the principle of generalization, he is likely to go even if the ailment is quite dif-

ferent. Likewise, the reinforcement will be reciprocal—the singer's confidence in his powers will also be reinforced. Finally there will be some reinforcement for specta-tors and for all who hear of the recovery. That the ritual treatment rather than more rational preventatives or cures tends to be followed on future occasions can be under-stood in terms of the principle of the gradient of reinforcement. Delayed rewards are less effective than immediate rewards. In terms of the conceptual picture of experience with which the surrogates of his culture have furnished him, the patient *expects* to be relieved. Therefore, the very onset of the chant produces some lessening of emotional tension—in technical terms, some reduction of anxiety. If the Navaho is treated by a white physician, the "cure" is more gradual and is dependent upon the purely physico-chemical effects of the treatment. If the native wears snow goggles or practices some other form of prevention recommended by a white, the connection between the behavior and the reward (no soreness of the eyes) is so diffuse and so separated in time that rein-forcement is relatively weak. Even in those cases where no improvement (other than "psychological") is effected, the realization or at any rate the final acceptance that no help was obtained comes so much later than the immediate sense of benefit that the ex-tinction effects are relatively slight.

Navaho myths and rituals provide a cul-tural storehouse of adjustive[7] responses for individuals. Nor are these limited to the more obvious functions of providing individ-uals with the possibility of enhancing per-sonal prestige through display of memory, histrionic ability, etc. Of the ten "mecha-nisms of defense" which Anna Freud sug-gests that the ego has available, their myths and rituals afford the Navaho with institu-

[7] It is not possible to say "adaptive" here because there are not infrequent occasions on which cere-monial treatment aggravates the condition or ac-tually brings about death (which would probably not have supervened under a more rational treat-ment or even if the patient had simply been al-lowed to rest). From the point of view of the so-ciety, however, the rituals are with little doubt adaptive. Careful samples in two areas and more impressionistic data from the Navaho country gen-erally indicate that the frequency of ceremonials has very materially increased concomitantly with the increase of white pressure in recent years. It is tempting to regard this as an adaptive response similar to that of the Ghost Dance and Peyote Cult on the part of other American Indian tribes.

tionalized means of employing at least four. Reaction formation has already been discussed. Myths supply abundant materials for introjection and likewise (in the form of witchcraft myths) suggest an easy and culturally acceptable method of projection of hostile impulses. Finally, rituals provide ways of sublimation of aggression and other socially disapproved tendencies, in part, simply through giving people something to *do*.

All of these "mechanisms of ego defense" will come into context only if we answer the question, "adjustive with respect to what?" The existence of motivation, of "anxiety," in Navaho individuals must be accounted for by a number of different factors. In the first place—as in every society—there are those components of "anxiety," those "threats" which may be understood in terms of the "reality principle" of psychoanalysis: life *is* hard—an unseasonable temperature, a vagary of the rainfall does bring hunger or actual starvation; people *are* organically ill. In the second place, there are various forms of "neurotic" anxiety. In our own society it is probably sexual, although this may be true only of those segments of our society who are able to purchase economic and physical security. In most Plains Indians sexual anxiety, so far as we can tell from the available documents, was insignificant. There the basic anxiety was for life itself and for a certain quality of that life (which I cannot attempt to characterize in a few words).

Among the Navaho the "type anxiety" is certainly that for health. Almost all Navaho ceremonials (essentially every ceremonial still carried out today) are curing ceremonials. And this apparently has a realistic basis. A prominent officer of the Indian Medical Service stated that it was his impression that morbidity among the Navaho is about three times that found in average white communities. In a period of four months' field work among the Navaho, Drs. A. and D. Leighton found in their running field notes a total of 707 Navaho references to "threats" which they classified under six headings. Of these, sixty per cent referred to bodily welfare, and are broken down by the Leightons as follows:

Disease is responsible for sixty-seven per cent, accidents for seventeen per cent, and the rest are attributed to wars and fights. Of the diseases described, eighty-one per cent were evidently organic, like smallpox, broken legs, colds, and sore throats; sixteen per cent left us in doubt as to whether they were organic or functional; and three per cent were apparently functional, with symptoms suggesting depression, hysteria, etc. Of all the diseases, forty per cent were incapacitating, forty-three per cent were not, and seventeen per cent were not sufficiently specified in our notes to judge. From these figures it can easily be seen that lack of health is a very important concern of these Navahos, and that almost half of the instances of disease that they mentioned interfered with life activities ["Some Types of Uneasiness," p. 203].

While I am inclined to believe that the character of this sample was somewhat influenced by the fact that the Leightons were white physicians—to whom organic illnesses, primarily, would be reported—there is no doubt that these data confirm the reality of the health "threat." In terms of clothing and shelter which are inadequate (from our point of view at least), of hygiene and diet which similarly fail to conform to our health standards, it is not altogether surprising that the Navaho need to be preoccupied with their health. It is unequivocally true in my experience that a greater proportion of my Navaho friends are found ill when I call upon them than of my white friends.

The Navaho and Pueblo Indians live in essentially the same physical environment. Pueblo rituals are concerned predominantly with rain and with fertility. This contrast to the Navaho preoccupation with disease cannot (in the absence of fuller supporting facts) be laid to a lesser frequency of illness among the Pueblos, for it seems well documented that the Pueblos, living in congested towns, have been far more ravaged by endemic diseases than the Navaho. The explanation is probably to be sought in terms of the differing historical experience of the two peoples and in terms of the contrasting economic and social organizations. If one is living in relative isolation and if one is largely dependent (as were the Navaho at no terribly distant date) upon one's ability to move about hunting and collecting, ill-health presents a danger much more crucial than to the Indian who lives in a town which has a reserve supply of corn and a more specialized social organization.

That Navaho myths and rituals are focused upon health and upon curing has, then, a firm basis in the reality of the external world. But there is also a great deal of uneasiness arising from interpersonal relationships, and this undoubtedly influences the way the Navaho react to their illnesses. Then, too, one type of anxiousness always tends to modify others. Indeed, in view of what the psychoanalysts have taught us about "accidents" and of what we are learning from psychosomatic medicine about the psychogenic origin of many "organic" diseases we cannot regard the sources of disease among the Navaho as a closed question. Some disorders (especially perhaps those associated with acute anxieties) may be examples of what Caner has called "superstitious self-protection."

Where people live under constant threat from the physical environment, where small groups are geographically isolated and "emotional inbreeding" within the extended family group is at a maximum, interpersonal tensions and hostilities are inevitably intense. The prevalence of ill-health which throws additional burdens on the well and strong is in itself an additional socially disruptive force.[8] But if the overt expression of aggressive impulses proceeds very far the whole system of "economic" co-operation breaks down and then sheer physical survival is more than precarious. Here myths and rituals constitute a series of highly adaptive responses from the point of view of the society. Recital of or reference to the myths reaffirms the solidarity of the Navaho sentiment system. In the words of a Navaho informant: "Knowing a good story will protect your home and children and property. A myth is just like a big stone foundation—it lasts a long time." Performance of rituals likewise heightens awareness of the common system of sentiments. The ceremonials also bring individuals together in a situation where quarreling is forbidden. Preparation for and carrying out of a chant demands intricately ramified co-operation, economic and otherwise, and doubtless thus reinforces the sense of mutual dependency.

Myths and rituals equally facilitate the adjustment of the individual to his society. Primarily, perhaps, they provide a means of sublimation of his antisocial tendencies. It is surely not without meaning that essentially all known chant myths take the family and some trouble within it as a point of departure. Let us look at Reichard's generalization of the chant myth:

A number of chant legends are now available and all show approximately *the same* construction. People are having a hard time to secure *subsistence or have some grievance. A boy of the family is forbidden* to go somewhere or to do some particular thing. He does not observe the warnings and does that which was forbidden, whereupon he embarks upon a series of adventures which keep him away from home so long that *his family despairs of his return. . . .* After the dramatic episodes, the hero returns to his home bringing with him the ritualistic lore which he teaches to *his brother.* He has been away so long and has become so accustomed to association with deity that *his own people seem impure* to him. He corrects that fault by teaching them the means of purification. . . . He has *his brother* conduct the ritual over *his sister* . . . he vanishes into the air [*Navaho Medicine Man,* p. 76].

While as a total explanation the following would be oversimple, it seems fair to say that the gist of this may be interpreted as follows: the chant myth supplies a catharsis for the traumata incident upon the socialization of the Navaho child. That brother and sister are the principal *dramatis personae* fits neatly with the central conflicts of the Navaho socialization process. This is a subject which I hope to treat in detail in a later paper.

Overt quarrels between family members are by no means infrequent, and, especially when drinking has been going on, physical blows are often exchanged. Abundant data indicate that Navahos have a sense of shame which is fairly persistent and that this is closely connected with the socially disapproved hostile impulses which they have experienced toward relatives. It is also clear that their mistrust of others (including those in their own extended family group) is in part based upon a fear of retaliation (and

[8] Dr. A. Leighton has pointed out to me that these disruptive tendencies are reinforced by one of the techniques for survival which those Navahos who have intimate and competitive relations with whites have developed. He writes: "A group threatened by a stronger group can swing to one of two poles. (a) They can coalesce and form a highly efficient, highly integrated unit that can act with swiftness, power, and precision, and in which all individuals stand or fall together. (b) They can disperse like a covey of quail so as never to present a united target to the foe. This is the Navaho method of dealing with whites. It is every man for himself, and though individuals may fall, enough escape to survive. You don't rush to help your tribesman when trouble comes, you stay out of it, you 'let it go.' Such an attitude, however, does lead to mutual mistrust."

this fear of retaliation is soundly based upon experience in actual life as well as, possibly, upon "unconscious guilt"). Certain passages in the myths indicate that the Navaho have a somewhat conscious realization that the ceremonials act as a cure, not only for physical illness, but also for antisocial tendencies. The following extract from the myth of the Mountain Top Way Chant will serve as an example: "The ceremony cured Dsiliyi Neyani of all his strange feelings and notions. The lodge of his people no longer smelled unpleasant to him."

Thus "the working gods" of the Navaho are their sanctified repetitive ways of behavior. If these are offended by violation of the culture's system of scruples, the ceremonials exist as institutionalized means of restoring the individual to full rapport with the universe: nature and his own society. Indeed "restore" is the best English translation of the Navaho word which the Navaho constantly use to express what the ceremonial does for the "patient." The associated myths reinforce the patient's belief that the ceremonial will both truly cure him of his illness and also "change" him so that he will be a better man in his relations with his family and his neighbors. An English-speaking Navaho who had just returned from jail where he had been put for beating his wife and molesting his stepdaughter said to me: "I am sure going to behave from now on. I am going to be changed—just like somebody who has been sung over."

Since a certain minimum of social efficiency is by derivation a biological necessity for the Navaho, not all of the hostility and uneasiness engendered by the rigors of the physical environment, geographical isolation, and the burdens imposed by illness is expressed or even gets into consciousness. There is a great deal of repression and this leads, on the one hand, to projection phenomena (especially in the form of fantasies that others are practicing witchcraft against one) and, on the other hand, the strong feelings of shame at the conscious level are matched by powerful feelings of guilt at the unconscious level. Because a person feels guilty by reason of his unconscious hostilities toward members of his family (and friends and neighbors generally), some individuals develop chronic anxieties. Such persons feel continually uncomfortable. They say they "feel sick all over" without specifying organic ailments other than very vaguely. They feel so "ill" that they must have ceremonials to cure them. The diagnostician and other practitioners, taking myths as their authority, will refer the cause of the illness to the patient's having seen animals struck by lightning, to a past failure to observe ritual requirements, or to some similar violation of a cultural scruple. But isn't this perhaps basically a substitution of symbols acceptable to consciousness, a displacement of guilt feelings?

It is my observation that Navahos other than those who exhibit chronic or acute anxieties tend characteristically to show a high level of anxiety. It would be a mistake, however, to attribute all of this anxiety to intrafamilial tensions, although it is my impression that this is the outstanding pressure. Secondary drives resultant upon culture change and upon white pressure are also of undoubted importance. And it is likewise true, as Mr. Homans has pointed out, that the existence of these ritual injunctions and prohibitions (and of the concomitant myths and other beliefs) gives rise to still another variety of anxiety. In other words, the conceptual picture of the world which Navaho culture sets forth makes for a high threshold of anxiety in that it defines all manner of situations as fraught with peril, and individuals are instigated to anticipate danger on every hand.

But the culture, of course, prescribes not only the supernatural dangers but also the supernatural means of meeting these dangers or of alleviating their effects. Myths and rituals jointly provide systematic protection against supernatural dangers, the threats of ill-health and of the physical environment, antisocial tensions, and the pressures of a more powerful society. In the absence of a codified law and of an authoritarian "chief" or other father substitute, it is only through the myth-ritual system that Navahos can make a socially supported, unified response to all of these disintegrating threats. The all-pervasive configurations of word symbols (myths) and of act symbols (rituals) preserve the cohesion of the society and sustain the individual, protecting him from intolerable conflict. As Hoagland has remarked:

Religion appears to me to be a culmination of this basic tendency of organisms to react in a configurational way to situations. We must resolve conflicts and disturbing puzzles by closing some sort of a configuration, and the religious urge appears to be a primitive tendency, possessing biological survival value, to unify our environment so that we can cope with it.

v

The Navaho are only one case. The specific adaptive and adjustive responses performed by myth and ritual will be differently phrased in different societies according to the historical experience of these societies (including the specific opportunities they have had for borrowing from other cultures), in accord with prevalent configurations of other aspects of the culture, and with reference to pressures exerted by other societies and by the physical and biological environment. But the general nature of the adaptive and adjustive responses performed by myth and ritual appears very much the same in all human groups. Hence, although the relative importance of myth and of ritual does vary greatly, the two tend universally to be associated.

For myth and ritual have a common psychological basis. Ritual is an obsessive repetitive activity—often a symbolic dramatization of the fundamental "needs" of the society, whether "economic," "biological," "social," or "sexual." Mythology is the rationalization of these same needs, whether they are all expressed in overt ceremonial or

not. Someone has said "every culture has a type conflict and a type solution." Ceremonials tend to portray a symbolic resolvement of the conflicts which external environment, historical experience, and selective distribution of personality types have caused to be characteristic in the society. Because different conflict situations characterize different societies, the "needs" which are typical in one society may be the "needs" of only deviant individuals in another society. And the institutionalized gratifications (of which rituals and myths are prominent examples) of culturally recognized needs vary greatly from society to society. "Culturally recognized needs" is, of course, an analytical abstraction. Concretely, "needs" arise and exist only in specific individuals. This we must never forget, but it is equally important that myths and rituals, though surviving as functioning aspects of a coherent culture only so long as they meet the "needs" of a number of concrete individuals, are, in one sense, "supra-individual." They are usually composite creations; they normally embody the accretions of many generations, the modifications (through borrowing from other cultures or by intra-cultural changes) which the varying needs of the group as a whole and of innovating individuals in the group have imposed. In short, both myths and rituals are cultural products, part of the social heredity of a society.

W. E. H. STANNER

The Dreaming

The Australian concept of the Dreaming, a kind of epoch in which the mythical ancestors of the aborigines lived but which is not thought of as a time that is past in the ordinary sense of the word, has long fascinated anthropologists and psychologists. The myths of the dream time are the basis for the elaborate ritual of the Australians, seen particularly in the increase and initiation ceremonies. The highly sacred churingas of the aborigines are symbols of the heroes of the eternal dream time, as it has been called, and serve to transfer life and power from them to men. The myths of this state or time are connected at least psychically with dream-life, sharing many of its characteristics, and this has led such psychoanalysts as Róheim to interpret the Dreaming as representing a phase of totemism preceding the contrition that

Reprinted from W. E. H. Stanner, "The Dreaming," in T. A. G. Hungerford (ed.), *Australian Signpost* (Melbourne: F. W. Cheshire, 1956), pp. 51–65, by permission of the author and F. W. Cheshire Pty., Ltd.

was felt following the bloody prehistoric parricide hypothesized by Freud. Róheim believes that the myths of the Dreaming depict the various phases of the ontogenetic and phylogenetic Oedipus complex. Other interpretations have of course been made, but there is agreement that the Dreaming is no ordinary kind of past, not even the usual mythical past of other peoples. It has a strange quality that few investigators have truly understood, and we owe a great debt of gratitude to Dr. Stanner for his exquisite clarification of its true nature. He gives us a feeling of the remarkable beauty to be found in this focal point of Australian culture, and leaves us wondering anew that it could ever be asserted that here we have an "Old Stone Age" people representing the crudest level of human achievement. Those who wish to pursue further the interpretations of the religion may consult not only the monograph *On Aboriginal Religion* (1963), referred to in the introduction to this chapter, but also the author's recent "Religion, Totemism, and Symbolism" (1965).

I

The blackfellow's outlook on the universe and man is shaped by a remarkable conception, which Spencer and Gillen immortalized as "the dream time" or *alcheringa* of the Arunta or Aranda tribe. Some anthropologists have called it "The Eternal Dream Time." I prefer to call it what the blacks call it in English—"The Dreaming," or just "Dreaming."

A central meaning of The Dreaming *is* that of a sacred, heroic time long long ago when man and nature came to be as they are; but neither "time" nor "history" as we understand them is involved in this meaning. I have never been able to discover any aboriginal word for *time* as an abstract concept. And the sense of "history" is wholly alien here. We shall not understand The Dreaming fully except as a complex of meanings. A blackfellow may call his totem, or the place from which his spirit came, his Dreaming. He may also explain the existence of a custom, or a law of life, as causally due to The Dreaming.

A concept so impalpable and subtle naturally suffers badly by translation into our dry and abstract language. The blacks sense this difficulty. I can recall one intelligent old man who said to me, with a cadence almost as though he had been speaking verse:

> *White man got no dreaming,*
> *Him go 'nother way.*
> *White man, him go different,*
> *Him got road belong himself.*

In their own dialects, they use terms like *alcheringa, mipuramibirina, boaradja*—often almost untranslatable, or meaning literally something like "men of old." It is as difficult to be sure of the objective effects of the idea on their lives as of its subjective implications for them.

Although, as I have said, The Dreaming conjures up the notion of a sacred, heroic time of the indefinitely remote past, such a time is also, in a sense, still part of the present. One cannot "fix" The Dreaming *in* time: it was, and is, everywhen. We should be very wrong to try to read into it the idea of a Golden Age, or a Garden of Eden, though it was an Age of Heroes, when the ancestors did marvelous things that men can no longer do. The blacks are not at all insensitive to Mary Webb's "wistfulness that is the past," but they do not, in aversion from present or future, look back on it with yearning and nostalgia. Yet it has for them an unchallengeably sacred authority.

Clearly, The Dreaming is many things in one. Among them, a kind of narrative of things that once happened; a kind of charter of things that still happen; and a kind of *logos* or principle of order transcending everything significant for aboriginal man. If I am correct in saying so, it is much more complex philosophically than we have so far realized. I greatly hope that artists and men of letters who (it seems increasingly) find inspiration in aboriginal Australia will use all their gifts of empathy, but avoid banal projection and subjectivism, if they seek to borrow the notion.

Why the blackfellow thinks of "dreaming" as the nearest equivalent in English is a puzzle. It may be because it is by *the act* of dreaming, as reality and symbol, that the aboriginal mind makes contact—thinks it

makes contact—with whatever mystery it is
that connects The Dreaming and the Here-
and-Now.

II

How shall one deal with so subtle a conception? One has two options: educe its subjective logic and rationale from the "elements" which the blackfellow stumblingly
offers in trying to give an explanation; or
relate, as best one may, to things familiar in
our own intellectual history, the objective
figure it traces on their social life. There are
dangers in both courses.

The first is a matter, so to speak, of learning to "think black," not imposing Western
categories of understanding, but seeking to
conceive of things as the blackfellow himself
does.

In our modern understanding, we tend to
see "mind" and "body," "body" and "spirit,"
"spirit" and "personality," "personality"
and "name" as in some sense separate, even
opposed, entities though we manage to connect them up in some fashion into the unity
or oneness of "person" or "individual." The
blackfellow does not seem to think this way.
The distinctiveness we give to "mind,"
"spirit," and "body," and our contrast of
"body" versus "spirit" are not there, and the
whole notion of "the person" is enlarged. To
a blackfellow, a man's name, spirit, and
shadow are "him" in a sense which to us
may seem passing strange. One should not
ask a blackfellow: "What is your name?"
To do so embarrasses and shames him. The
name is like an intimate part of the body,
with which another person does not take lib-
erties. The blacks do not mind talking about
a dead person in an oblique way but, for a
long time, they are extremely reluctant even
to breathe his name. In the same way, to
threaten a man's shadow is to threaten him.
Nor may one treat lightly the physical place
from which his spirit came. By extension, his
totem, which is also associated with that
place, and with his spirit, should not be
lightly treated.

In such a context one has not succeeded in
"thinking black" until one's mind can, without intellectual struggle, enfold into some
kind of oneness the notions of body, spirit,
ghost, shadow, name, spirit-site, and totem.
To say so may seem a contradiction, or suggest a paradox, for the blackfellow can and
does, on some occasions, conceptually isolate
the "elements" of the "unity" most distinctly. But his abstractions do not put him
at war with himself. The separable elements
I have mentioned are all present in the
metaphysical heart of the idea of "person,"
but the overruling mood is one of belief, not
of inquiry or dissent. So long as the belief in
The Dreaming lasts, there can be no "momentary flash of Athenian questioning" to
grow into a great movement of skeptical unbelief which destroys the given unities.

There are many other such "onenesses"
which I believe I could substantiate. A
blackfellow may "see" as "a unity" two persons, such as two siblings or a grandparent
and grandchild; or a living man and something inanimate, as when he tells you that,
say, the woolly-butt tree, his totem, is his
wife's brother. (This is not quite as strange
as it may seem. Even modern psychologists
tend to include part of "environment" in a
"definition" of "person" or "personality.")
There is also some kind of unity between
waking-life and dream-life: the means by
which, in aboriginal understanding, a man
fathers a child, is not by sexual intercourse,
but by the act of dreaming about a spirit-
child. His own spirit, during a dream,
"finds" a child and directs it to his wife, who
then conceives. Physical congress between a
man and a woman is contingent, not a necessary prerequisite. Through the medium of
dream-contact with a spirit an artist is inspired to produce a new song. It is by
dreaming that a man divines the intention of
someone to kill him by sorcery, or of relatives to visit him. And, as I have suggested,
it is by the act of dreaming, in some way
difficult for a European to grasp because of
the force of our analytic abstractions, that a
blackfellow conceives himself to make touch
with whatever it is that is continuous between The Dreaming and the Here-and-
Now.

The truth of it seems to be that man, society, and nature and past, present, and future are at one together within a unitary
system of such a kind that its ontology cannot illumine minds too much under the influence of humanism, rationalism, and science. One cannot easily, in the mobility of
modern life and thought, grasp the vast intuitions of stability and permanence, and of
life and man, at the heart of aboriginal ontology.

It is fatally easy for Europeans, encountering such things for the first time, to go on to suppose that "mysticism" of this kind rules *all* aboriginal thought. It is not so. "Logical" thought and "rational" conduct are about as widely present in aboriginal life as they are on the simpler levels of European life. Once one understands three things —the primary intuitions which the blackfellow has formed about the nature of the universe and man, those things in both which he thinks interesting and significant, and the conceptual system from within which he reasons about them—then the suppositions about prelogicality, illogicality, and nonrationality can be seen to be merely absurd. And if one wishes to see a really brilliant demonstration of deductive thought, one has only to see a blackfellow tracking a wounded kangaroo, and persuade him to say why he interprets given signs in a certain way.

The second means of dealing with the notion of The Dreaming is, as I said, to try to relate it to things familiar in our own intellectual history. From this viewpoint, it is a cosmogony, an account of the begetting of the universe, a story about creation. It is also a cosmology, an account or theory of how what was created became an orderly system. To be more precise, how the universe became a moral system.

If one analyzes the hundreds of tales about The Dreaming, one can see within them three elements. The first concerns the great *marvels*—how all the fire and water in the world were stolen and recaptured; how men made a mistake over sorcery and now have to die from it; how the hills, rivers, and water holes were made; how the sun, moon, and stars were set upon their courses; and many other dramas of this kind. The second element tells how certain things were *instituted* for the first time— how animals and men diverged from a joint stock that was neither one nor the other; how the black-nosed kangaroo got his black nose and the porcupine his quills; how such social divisions as tribes, clans, and language groups were set up; how spirit-children were first placed in the water holes, the winds, and the leaves of trees. A third element, if I am not mistaken, allows one to suppose that many of the main institutions of present-day life were *already ruling* in The Dreaming, e.g., marriage, exogamy, sister-exchange, and initiation, as well as many of the well-

known breaches of custom. The men of The Dreaming committed adultery, betrayed and killed each other, were greedy, stole, and committed the very wrongs committed by those now alive.

Now, if one disregards the imagery in which the verbal literature of The Dreaming is cast, one may perhaps come to three conclusions.

The tales are a kind of commentary, or statement, on what is thought to be permanent and ordained at the very basis of the world and life. They are a way of stating the principle which animates things. I would call them a poetic key to Reality. The aborigine does not ask himself the philosophical types of questions: What is "real"? How many "kinds" of "reality" are there? What are the "properties" of "reality"? How are the properties "interconnected"? This is the idiom of Western intellectual discourse and the fruit of a certain social history. His tales are, however, a kind of answer to such questions so far as they have been asked at all. They may not be a "definition," but they are a "key" to reality, a key to the singleness and the plurality of things set up once-for-all when, in The Dreaming, the universe became man's universe. The active philosophy of aboriginal life transforms this "key," which is expressed in the idiom of poetry, drama, and symbolism, into a principle that The Dreaming determines not only what life *is* but also *what it can be*. Life, so to speak, is a one-possibility thing, and what this is, is the "meaning" of The Dreaming.

The tales are also a collation of *what is validly known* about such ordained permanencies. The blacks cite The Dreaming as a charter of absolute validity in answer to all questions of *why* and *how*. In this sense, the tales can be regarded as being, perhaps not a definition, but a "key" of Truth.

They also state, by their constant recitation of what was done rightly and wrongly in The Dreaming, the ways in which good men should, and bad men will, act now. In this sense, they are a "key" or guide to the norms of conduct, and a prediction of how men will err.

One may thus say that, after a fashion—a cryptic, symbolic, and poetic fashion—the tales are "a philosophy" in the garb of a verbal literature. The European has a philosophic literature which expresses a largely deductive understanding of reality, truth, goodness, and beauty. The blackfellow has a mythology, a ritual, and an art which express an intuitive, visionary, and poetic understanding of the same ultimates. In following out The Dreaming, the blackfellow "lives" this philosophy. It is an implicit philosophy, but nevertheless a real one. Whereas we hold (and may live) a philosophy of abstract propositions, attained by someone standing professionally outside "Life" and treating it as an object of contemplation and inquiry. The blackfellow holds his philosophy in mythology, attained as the social product of an indefinitely ancient past, and proceeds to live it out "in" life, in part through a ritual and an expressive art, and in part through nonsacred social customs.

European minds are made uneasy by the facts that the stories are, quite plainly, preposterous; are often a mass of internal contradictions; are encrusted by superstitious fancies about magic, sorcery, hobgoblins, and superhuman heroes; and lack the kind of theme and structure—in other words, the "story" element—for which we look. Many of us cannot help feeling that such things can only be the products of absurdly ignorant credulity and a lower order of mentality. This is to fall victim to a facile fallacy. Our own intellectual history is not an absolute standard by which to judge others. The worst imperialisms are those of preconception.

Custom is the reality, beliefs but the shadows which custom makes on the wall. Since the tales, in any case, are not really "explanatory" in purpose or function, they naturally lack logic, system, and completeness. It is simply pointless to look for such things within them. But we are not entitled to suppose that, because the tales are fantastical, the social life producing them is itself fantastical. The shape of reality is always distorted in the shadows it throws. One finds much logic, system, and rationality in the blacks' actual scheme of life.

These tales are neither simply illustrative nor simply explanatory; they are fanciful and poetic in content because they are based on visionary and intuitive insights into mysteries; and, if we are ever to understand them, we must always take them in their complex context. If, then, they make more sense to the poet, the artist, and the philosopher than to the clinicians of human life, let

us reflect on the withering effect on sensibility of our pervasive rationalism, rather than depreciate the gifts which produced the aboriginal imaginings. And in no case should we expect the tales, *prima facie,* to be even interesting if studied out of context. Aboriginal mythology is quite unlike the Scandinavian, Indian, or Polynesian mythologies.

III

In my own understanding, The Dreaming is a proof that the blackfellow shares with us two abilities which have largely made human history what it is.

The first of these we might call "the metaphysical gift." I mean ability to transcend oneself, to make acts of imagination so that one can stand "outside" or "away from" oneself, and turn the universe, oneself, and one's fellows into objects of contemplation. The second ability is a "drive" to try to "make sense" out of human experience and to find some "principle" in the whole human situation. This "drive" is, in some way, built into the constitution of the human mind. No one who has real knowledge of aboriginal life can have any doubt that they possess, and use, both abilities very much as we do. They differ from us only in the directions in which they turn their gifts, the idiom in which they express them, and the principles of intellectual control.

The blacks have no gods, just or unjust, to adjudicate the world. Not even by straining can one see in such culture heroes as Baiame and Darumulum the true hint of a Yahveh, jealous, omniscient, and omnipotent. The ethical insights are dim and somewhat coarse in texture. One can find in them little trace, say, of the inverted pride, the self-scrutiny, and the consciousness of favor and destiny which characterized the early Jews. A glimpse, but no truly poignant sense, of moral dualism; no notion of grace or redemption; no whisper of inner peace and reconcilement; no problems of worldly life to be solved only by a consummation of history; no heaven of reward or hell of punishment. The blackfellow's afterlife is but a shadowy replica of worldly life, so none flee to inner sanctuary to escape the world. There are no prophets, saints, or *illuminati.* There is a concept of goodness, but it lacks true scruple. Men can become ritually unclean, but may be cleansed by a simple mechanism. There is a moral law but, as in the beginning, men are both good and bad, and no one is racked by the knowledge. I imagine there could never have been an aboriginal Ezekiel, any more than there could have been a Job. The two sets of insights cannot easily be compared, but it is plain that their underlying moods are wholly unlike, and their store of meaningfulness very uneven. In the one there seem an almost endless possibility of growth, and a mood of censoriousness and pessimism. In the other, a kind of standstill, and a mood which is neither tragic nor optimistic. The aborigines are not shamed or inspired by a religious thesis of what men might become by faith and grace. Their metaphysic assents, without brooding or challenge, to what men evidently have to be because the terms of life are cast. Yet they have a kind of religiosity cryptically displayed in their magical awareness of nature, in their complex totemism, ritual, and art, and perhaps too even in their intricately ordered life.

They are, of course, nomads—hunters and foragers who grow nothing, build nothing, and stay nowhere long. They make almost no physical mark on the environment. Even in areas which are still inhabited, it takes a knowledgeable eye to detect their recent presence. Within a matter of weeks, the roughly cleared campsites may be erased by sun, rain, and wind. After a year or two there may be nothing to suggest that the country was ever inhabited. Until one stumbles on a few old flint tools, a stone quarry, a shell midden, a rock painting, or something of the kind, one may think the land had never known the touch of man.

They neither dominate their environment nor seek to change it. "Children of nature" they are not, nor are they nature's "masters." One can only say they are "at one" with nature. The whole ecological principle of their life might be summed up in the Baconian aphorism—*natura non vincitur nisi parendo:* "Nature is not to be commanded except by obeying." Naturally, one finds metaphysical and social reflections of the fact.

They move about, carrying their scant possessions, in small bands of anything from ten to sixty persons. Each band belongs to a given locality. A number of bands—anything from three or four up to twelve or fifteen, depending on the fertility of the area—make up a "tribe." A tribe is usually a language or dialect group which thinks of itself as having a certain unity of common speech and shared customs. The tribes range in size from a few hundred to a few thousand souls.

One rarely sees a tribe as a formed entity. It comes together and lives as a unit only for a great occasion—a feast, a corroboree, a hunt, an initiation, or a formal duel. After a few days—at the most, weeks—it breaks up again into smaller bands or sections of bands: most commonly into a group of brothers, with their wives, children, and grandchildren and perhaps a few close relatives. These parties rove about their family locality or, by agreement, the territories of immediate neighbors. They do not wander aimlessly, but to a purpose, and in tune with the seasonal food supply. One can almost plot a year of their life in terms of movement towards the places where honey, yams, grass seeds, eggs, or some other food staple, is in bearing and ready for eating.

The uncomplex visible routine, and the simple segmentation, are very deceptive. It took well over half a century for Europeans to realize that behind the outward show was an inward structure of surprising complexity. It was a century before any real understanding of this structure developed.

In one tribe with which I am familiar, a very representative tribe, there are about 100 "invisible" divisions which have to be analyzed before one can claim even a serviceable understanding of the tribe's organization. The structure is much more complex than that of an Australian village of the same size. The complexity is in the most striking contrast with the comparative simplicity which rules in the two other departments of aboriginal life—the material culture, on the one hand, and the ideational or metaphysical culture on the other. We have, I think, to try to account for this contrast in some way.

Their creative "drive" to make sense and order out of things has, for some reason, concentrated on the social rather than on the metaphysical or the material side. Consequently, there has been an unusually rich development of what the anthropologist calls "social structure," the network of enduring relations recognized between people. This very intricate system is an intellectual and social achievement of a high order. It is not, like an instinctual response, a phenomenon of "nature"; it is not, like art or ritual, a complex type of behavior passionately added to "nature," in keeping with metaphysical insight but without rational and intelligible purposes which can be clearly stated; it has to be compared, I think, with such a secular achievement as, say, parliamentary government in a European society. It is truly positive knowledge.

One may see within it three things: given customs, "of which the memory of man runneth not to the contrary"; a vast body of cumulative knowledge about the effects of these customs on a society in given circumstances; and the use of the power of abstract reason to rationalize the resultant relations into a system.

But it is something much more: It has become *the source of the dominant mode of aboriginal thinking*. The blacks use it to give a bony structure to parts of the world outlook suggested by intuitive speculation. I mean by this that they have taken some of its fundamental principles and relations and have applied them to very much wider sets of phenomena. This tends to happen if any type of system of thought becomes truly dominant. It is, broadly, what Europeans did with "religion" and "science" as systems: extended their principles and categories to fields far beyond the contexts in which the systems grew.

Thus, the blacks have taken the male-female social principle and have extended it to the nonhuman world. In one tribe I have studied, all women, without exception, call particular birds or trees by the same kinship terms which they apply to actual relatives. In the same way, all men without exception use comparable terms for a different set of trees or birds. From this results what the anthropologist calls "sex totemism." The use of other principles results in other types of totemism. An understanding of this simple fact removes much of the social, if not the ritual, mystery of totemism. Again, the principle of relatedness itself, relatedness between known people by known descent through known marriages, is extended over the whole face of human society. The same terms of kinship which are used for close agnatic and affinal relatives are used for every other person an aborigine meets in the course of his life: strangers, friends, enemies, and known kin may all be called by the same terms as one uses for brother, father,

mother's sister, father's mother's brother, and so on. This is what an anthropologist means when he says "aboriginal society is a society of kinship."

It might even be argued that the blacks have done much the same thing with "time." Time as a continuum is a concept only hazily present in the aboriginal mind. What might be called *social* time is, in a sense, "bent" into cycles or circles. The most controlled understanding of it is by reckoning in terms of generation-classes, which are arranged into named and recurring cycles. As far as the blackfellow thinks about time at all, his interest lies in the cycles rather than in the continuum, and each cycle is in essence a principle for dealing with social interrelatedness.

IV

Out of all this may come for some an understanding of the blackfellow very different from that which has passed into the ignorance and vulgarity of popular opinion.

One may see that, like all men, he is a metaphysician in being able to transcend himself. With the metaphysic goes a mood and spirit, which I can only call a mood and spirit of "assent": neither despair nor resignation, optimism nor pessimism, quietism nor indifference. The mood, and the outlook beneath it, make him hopelessly out of place in a world in which the Renaissance has triumphed only to be perverted, and in which the products of secular humanism, rationalism, and science challenge their own hopes, indeed, their beginnings.

Much association with the blackfellow makes me feel I may not be far wrong in saying that, unlike us, he seems to see "life" as a one-possibility thing. This may be why he seems to have almost no sense of tragedy. If "tragedy is a looking at fate for a lesson in deportment on life's scaffold," the aborigine seems to me to have read the lesson and to have written it into the very conception of how men should live, or else to have stopped short of the insight that there are gods either just or unjust. Nor have I found in him much self-pity. These sentiments can develop only if life presents real alternatives, or if it denies an alternative that one feels should be there. A philosophy of assent fits only a life of unvarying constancy. I do not at all say that pain, sorrow, and sadness have no place in aboriginal life, for I have seen them all too widely. All I mean is that the blacks seem to have gone beyond, or not quite attained, the human *quarrel* with such things. Their rituals of sorrow, their fortitude in pain, and their undemonstrative sadness seem to imply a reconciliation with the terms of life such that "peace is the understanding of tragedy and at the same time its preservation," or else that they have not sensed life as baffled by either fate or wisdom.

Like all men, he is also a philosopher in being able to use his power of abstract reason. His genius, his métier, and—in some sense—his fate, is that because of endowment and circumstance this power has channeled itself mainly into one activity, "making sense" out of the social relations among men living together. His intricate social organization is an impressive essay on the economy of conflict, tension, and experiment in a life situation at the absolute pole of our own.

Like all men, too, he pays the price of his insights and solutions. We look to a continuous unfolding of life, and to a blissful attainment of the better things for which, we say, man has an infinite capacity. For some time, nothing has seemed of less consequence to us than the maintenance of continuity. The cost, in instability and inequity, is proving very heavy. Aboriginal life has endured feeling that continuity, not man, is the measure of all. The cost, in the world of power and change, is extinction. What defeats the blackfellow in the modern world, fundamentally, is his transcendentalism. So much of his life and thought are concerned with The Dreaming that it stultifies his ability to develop. This is not a new thing in human history. A good analogy is with the process in Chinese poetry by which, according to Arthur Waley, its talent for classical allusion became a vice which finally destroyed it altogether.

A "philosophy of life," that is, a system of mental attitudes towards the conduct of life, may or may not be consistent with an actual way of life. Whether it is or is not will depend on how big a gap there is, if any, between what life *is* and what men think life *ought to be*. If Ideal and Real drift too far away from one another (as they did at the end of the Middle Ages, and seem increasingly to do in this century) men face some difficult options. They have to change their way of life, or their philosophy, or both, or live unhappily somewhere in between. We are familiar enough with the "war of the philosophies" and the tensions of modern life which express them. Problems of this kind had no place, I would say, in traditional aboriginal life. It knew nothing, and could not, I think, have known anything of the Christian's straining for inner perfection; of "moral man and immoral society"; of the dilemma of liberty and authority; of intellectual uncertainty, class warfare, and discontent with one's lot in life—all of which, in some sense, are problems of the gap between Ideal and Real.

The aborigines may have been in Australia for as long as 10,000 years. No one at present can do more than guess whence or how they came, and there is little more than presumptive evidence on which to base a guess. The span of time, immense though it may have been, matters less than the fact that, so far as one can tell, they have been almost completely isolated. Since their arrival, no foreign stimulus has touched them, except on the fringes of the northern and northwestern coasts. To these two facts we must add two others. The physical environment has, evidently, not undergone any marked general change, although there has been a slow desiccation of parts of the center into desert, and some limited coastline changes. The fourth fact is that their tools and material crafts seem to have been very unprogressive.

If we put these four facts together—an immensely long span of time, spent in more or less complete isolation, in a fairly constant environment, with an unprogressive material culture, we may perhaps see why sameness, absence of change, fixed routine, regularity, call it what you will, is a main dimension of their thought and life. Let us sum up this aspect as leading to a metaphysical emphasis on abidingness. They place a very special value on things remaining unchangingly themselves, on keeping life to a routine which is known and trusted. Absence of change, which means certainty of expectation, seems to them a good thing in itself. One may say, their Ideal and Real come very close together. The value given to continuity is so high that they are not simply a people "without a history": they are a people who have been able, in some sense, to "defeat" history, to become ahistorical in mood, outlook, and life. This is why, among them, the philosophy of assent, the glove, fits the hand of actual custom almost to perfection, and the forms of social life, the art, the ritual, and much else take on a wonderful symmetry.

Their tools and crafts, meager—pitiably meager—though they are, have nonetheless been good enough to let them win the battle for survival, and to win it comfortably at that. With no pottery, no knowledge of metals, no wheel, no domestication of animals, no agriculture, they have still been able not only to live and people the entire continent, but even in a sense to prosper, to win a surplus of goods and develop leisure-time occupations. The evidences of the surplus of yield over animal need are to be seen in the spider web of trade routes criss-crossing the continent, on which a large volume of non-utilitarian articles circulated, themselves largely the products of leisure. The true leisure-time activities—social entertaining, great ceremonial gatherings, even much of the ritual and artistic life—impressed observers even from the beginning. The notion of aboriginal life as always preoccupied with the risk of starvation, as always a hair's breadth from disaster, is as great a caricature as Hobbes' notion of savage life as "poor, nasty, brutish, and short." The best corrective of any such notion is to spend a few nights in an aboriginal camp, and experience directly the unique joy in life which can be attained by a people of few wants, an other-worldly cast of mind, and a simple scheme of life which so shapes a day that it ends with communal singing and dancing in the firelight.

The more one sees of aboriginal life the stronger the impression that its mode, its ethos, and its principle are variations on a single theme—continuity, constancy, balance, symmetry, regularity, system, or some such quality as these words convey.

One of the most striking things is that there are no great conflicts over power, no great contests for place and office. This single fact explains much else, because it rules out so much that would be destructive of stability. The idea of a formal chief, or a leader with authority over the persons of others in a large number of fields of life— say, for example, as with a Polynesian or African chief—just does not seem to make sense to a blackfellow. Nor does even the modified Melanesian notion—that of a man becoming some sort of a leader because he accumulates a great deal of garden wealth and so gains prestige. There are leaders in the sense of men of unusual skill, initiative, and force, and they are given much respect; they may even attract something like a following; but one finds no trace of formal or institutionalized chieftainship. So there are no offices to stimulate ambition, intrigue, or the use of force; to be envied or fought over; or to be lost or won. Power—a real thing in every society—is diffused mainly through one sex, the man, but in such a way that it is not to be won, or lost, in concentrations, by craft, struggle, or coup. It is very much a male-dominated society. The older men dominate the younger, the men dominate the women. Not that the women are chattels— Dr. Phyllis Kaberry in her interesting book *Aboriginal Woman* disposed of that Just-So story very effectively—but there is a great deal of discrimination against them. The mythology justifies this by tales telling how men had to take power from women by force in The Dreaming. The psychology (perhaps the truth) of it is as obvious as it is amusing. If women were not kept under, they would take over!

At all events, the struggle for power occurred once-for-all. Power, authority, influence, age, status, knowledge, all run together and, in some sense, are the same kind of thing. The men of power, authority, and influence are old men—at least, mature men; the greater the secret knowledge and authority the higher the status; and the initiations are so arranged (by the old men) that the young men do not acquire full knowledge, and so attain status and authority, until they too are well advanced in years. One can thus see why the great term of respect is "old man"—*maluka*, as in *We of the Never-Never*. The system is self-protective and self-renewing. The real point of it all is that the checks and balances seem nearly perfect, and no one really seems to want the kind of satisfaction that might come from a position of domination. At the same time, there is a serpent in Eden. The narrow self-interest of men exploits The Dreaming.

Power over things? Every canon of good citizenship and common sense is against it, though there are, of course, clear property arrangements. But what could be more useless than a store of food that will not keep, or a heavy pile of spears that have to be carried everywhere? Especially, in a society in which the primary virtues are generosity and fair dealing. Nearly every social affair involving goods—food in the family, payments in marriage, intertribal exchange—is heavily influenced by equalitarian notions; a notion of reciprocity as a moral obligation; a notion of generously equivalent return; and a surprisingly clear notion of fair dealing, or making things "level" as the blackfellow calls it in English.

There is a tilt of the system towards the interests of the men, but given this tilt, everything else seems as if carefully calculated to keep it in place. The blacks do not fight over the land. There are no wars or invasions to seize territory. They do not enslave each other. There is no master-servant relation. There is no class division. There is no property or income inequality. The result is a homeostasis, far-reaching and stable.

I do not wish to create an impression of a social life without egotism, without vitality, without cross-purposes, without conflict. Indeed, there is plenty of all, as there is of malice, enmity, bad faith, and violence, running along the lines of sex-inequality and age-inequality. But this essential humanity exists, and runs its course, within a system whose first principle is the preservation of balance. And, arching over it all, is the *logos* of The Dreaming. How we shall state this when we fully understand it I do not know, but I should think we are more likely to ennoble it than not. Equilibrium ennobled is "abidingness." Piccarda's answer in the third canto of the *Paradiso* gives the implicit theme and logic of The Dreaming: *e la sua volontate è nostra pace*, "His will is our peace." But the gleam that lighted Judah did not reach the Australian wilderness, and the blacks follow The Deaming only because their fathers did.

ARTHUR GRIMBLE

A Gilbertese Creation Myth

Every known culture has sacred stories of some kind which express the basic beliefs the people hold as to the nature of the universe and man's place in the cosmos. These may be little elaborated and without much emphasis placed upon them, or they may be greatly elaborated and emphasized by the culture. In the latter category are the creation myths of the peoples of Polynesia and Micronesia, of which the following specimen from the Gilbert Islands is a good example. The circumstances under which these myths are told and who tells them are beautifully illustrated by Sir Arthur Grimble. As an aside, it is interesting to note that the tale contains the fishing-up-of-islands motif in an attenuated form. This motif is common in Oceania and forms part of the great Maui cycle of Polynesia. Indeed, Naareau and Maui are similar.

Reprinted from *The Listener*, XIV, No. 1155 (1951), 621–625, by permission of John Murray, Ltd. A slightly altered version appears in Arthur Grimble, *A Pattern of Islands* (London: John Murray, 1952).

Taakeuta was an elder of the Gilbertese clan called Karongoa-of-the-Kings. This meant that, when he sat in the *maneaba*, or speak-house, of his village telling the story of the creation, nobody dared contradict him. It was perilous to gainsay an elder of Karongoa in the *maneaba*, for his sitting-place was up against the Sun stone. The Sun stone was only one of the many simple monoliths of hewn coral that held up the roof-plates of the enormous thatch. But it was the central

monolith of the eastern side, and the secret rituals of the Karongoa elders had turned it into the Sun's own person before another piece of the cathedral-like building had been put into place. Cross-legged under its shadow, Taakeuta spoke as irrefutably as a High Priest or Oracle, and he loved it.

The urge to expound the history of his people used to seize him every month anew, round about the full moon. You would find him sitting in the *maneaba* at any time of day between forenoon and dusk, a mighty-boned, gaunt old man, with the torso of a time-worn Achilles and the head of a saint. He would be girt in his most beautiful waist-mat and surrounded by listeners as massive and venerable as himself. If you were lucky, he might tell you a story of your own choosing. But it depended on what you asked for. Karongoa-of-the-Kings had its own peculiar versions of the basic traditions, which were not for the ears of outsiders. The rule of secrecy applied very particularly to its creation-story. The Karongoa cosmogony was wrapped up in a myth of a Sun-god named Au, the Lord of Heaven, who had risen from the depths into the sky on the crest of a pandanus tree. The other clans were allowed to know nothing of Au except under the name and style of Auriaria, a simple clan-ancestor. And so, whatever rendering of the creation-story you heard from Taakeuta in public, you could be sure that it was not Karongoa's private version. The Creating Spirits of whom he spoke under the Sun stone were Naareau the Elder and Naareau the Younger. The two Naareaus were, in fact, the popular First Causes as opposed to Au, the priestly one.

If (as I think) Karongoa-of-the-Kings was once, in days and lands but darkly remembered, a caste of royal priests who dictated the articles of popular belief from a temple of the Sun, it must have been a very wise priestcraft. The heritage of doctrinal tolerance that it handed down through the ages to old Taakeuta and his rustic peers was, at all events, a very liberal one. The elders of Karongoa, as I knew them, insisted publicly upon nothing but the barest essentials of dogma about Naareau the Elder and Naareau the Younger. That allowed scope for a stimulating variety of orthodoxies. A man was free to think, if he liked, that Naareau the Elder was a being evolved from the void through a genealogical series of abstractions and things; or, if he preferred, he could begin with an absolute Naareau seated in the void from all eternity. Original matter could be a ball of stuff timelessly coexistent with the god in the void; or, alternatively, a mixture of elements directly created by him. Nareau the Younger could be the son of the Elder, born of his sweat or a tear of his right eye; or he, too, could be the descendant of a genealogical series beginning with a man

and a woman created by the Elder. And so on multitudinously.

Every elder of every clan, of course, claimed that his particular rendering of the creation story was the one and only truth. They argued together about their pet cosmogonies as earnestly (shall I say?) as the physicists of civilization about their cosmologies. But when they took their differences to Taakeuta sitting by his Sun stone, he never failed to send them away friends. He would listen to each side's story in total silence and whisper at the end (Karongoa-of-the-Kings always whispered its judgments): "Sirs, there was Naareau the Elder, there was Naareau the Younger. They did what they did. They were great; we are little; no man among us knows all their works. Enough! Let each clan turn away content with its own knowledge." Having said which, he would treat them to an account radically different from either of theirs, and, usually, quite unlike the last one I had heard from him. But I found in the course of time that he never mixed his versions. He handed out each one intact, as it had come to him down the generations. I pass on to you now, after thirty-four years, the first rendering he ever gave me.

Dusk was falling as he told the story. All his listeners except myself had straggled away to the evening meal. Odors of cooking twined with sea-smells and the scent of crinum lilies hung poised in the *maneaba*'s sanctuaried gloom. The rumor of a chanted song came drifting in from far away. Taakeuta began as he always began: "Sir, I remember the voices of my fathers. Listen to the words of Karongoa. . . .

"Naareau the Elder was the First of All. Not a man, not a beast, not a fish, not a thing was before him. He slept not, for there was no sleep; he ate not, for there was no hunger. He was in the void. There was only Naareau sitting in the void. Long he sat, and there was none but he.

"Then Naareau said in his heart, 'I will make a woman.' Behold! a woman grew out of the void: Nei Teakea. He said again, 'I will make a man.' Behold! a man grew out of his thought: Na Atibu, the Rock. And Na Atibu lay with Nei Teakea. Behold! their child was born: Naareau the Younger. And Naareau the Elder said to Naareau the Younger, 'All knowledge is whole in thee. I will make a thing for thee to work upon.' So he made that thing in the void. It was called the Darkness and the Cleaving Together; the sky, and the earth, and the sea were within it; but the sky and the earth clove together, and darkness was between them, for as yet there was no separation. And when his work was done, Naareau the Elder said, 'Enough! It is ready. I go, never to return.' So he went, never to return, and no man knows where he abides now.

"But Naareau the Younger walked on the overside of the sky that lay on the land. The sky was rock, and in some places it was rooted in the land, but in other places there were hollows between. A thought came into Naareau's heart. He said, 'I will enter beneath it.' He searched for a cleft wherein he might creep, but there was no cleft. He said again, 'How shall I enter? I will do it with a spell.' That was the First Spell. He kneeled on the sky and began to tap it with his fingers, saying—

Tap, tap, on heaven and its dwelling-places!
It is stone. What becomes of it? It answers!
It is rock. What becomes of it? It answers!
Open, Sir Stone! Open, Sir Rock!
It is open—o—o!

"At the third striking, the sky opened under his fingers. He said, 'It is ready,' and he looked down into the hollow place. It was black dark, and his ears heard the noise of breathing and snoring in the darkness. So he stood up and rubbed his fingertips together. Behold! the First Creature came out of them: the Moth that he called Tiku-tiku-toumouma. And he said to the Moth, 'Thou canst see in the darkness. Go before me and find what thou findest.'

"The Moth went in. When he came to the underside, he called to Naareau, 'O—o!' and Naareau answered, 'O—o!' The Moth said, 'I see people lying in this place.' Naareau answered, 'What are they like?' And the Moth said, 'They move not; they say no word; they are all asleep.' Naareau answered again, 'It is the company of Fools and Deaf Mutes. They are a breed of slaves. Tell me their names.' Then the Moth settled on the forehead of each one as he lay in the darkness, and called his name to Naareau: 'This man is Uka,' 'Here lies Kotei,' 'Behold, Karitoro,' 'Now Naabawe,' 'Koteka-teka now': a great multitude. And when they were all named, Naareau said, 'Enough. I will go in.' So he crawled through the cleft and walked on the underside of the sky; and the Moth was his torch in the darkness. He stood among the Fools and Deaf Mutes and shouted, 'Sirs, what are you doing?' None answered: only his voice came back out of the hollowness, 'Sirs, what are you doing?' He said in his heart, 'They are not yet in their right minds, but wait.'

"He went to a high place in their midst; he shouted at them, 'Move!' They moved. He said again, 'Move! They sat up. The sky was lifted a little. He said again, 'Move! Stand!' They stood. He said again, 'Higher!' But they answered, 'How shall we lift it higher?' He made a beam of wood, saying, 'Lift it on this.' They did so. He said again, 'Higher! Higher!' But they answered, 'We can no more, we can no more, for the sky has roots in the land.' So Naareau lifted up his voice and shouted, 'Where are the Eel and the Turtle, the Octopus and the Sting-ray?' The Fools and Deaf Mutes answered, 'Alas! they are hidden away from the work.' So he said, 'Rest,' and they rested: and he said to that one among them named Naabawe, 'Go, call Riiki, the conger eel.'

"When Naabawe came to Riiki, he was coiled asleep with his wife, the short-tailed eel. Naabawe called him; he answered not, but lifted his head and bit him. Naabawe went back to Naareau, crying, 'Alas! the conger eel bit me.' So Naareau made a stick with a slipnoose, saying, 'We shall take him with this, if there is a bait to lure him.' Then he called the Octopus from his hiding place; and the Octopus had ten long arms. He struck off two arms and hung them on the stick as bait. Therefore the Octopus has only eight long arms to this day. They took the lure to Riiki, and as they offered it Naareau sang:

Riiki of old, Riiki of old
Come hither, Riiki, thou mighty one;
Leave thy wife, the short-tailed eel,
For thou shalt uproot the sky, thou shalt press down the depths.
Heave thyself up, Riiki, mighty and long,
Kingpost of the roof, prop up the sky and have done.
Have done, for the judgment is judged!

"When Riiki heard the spell, he lifted up his head and the sleep went out of him. See him now! He puts forth his snout, he seizes the bait. Alas! they tighten the noose: he is fast caught. They haul him, they haul him; he is dragged away from his wife the short-tailed eel, and Naareau is roaring and dancing. Yet pity him not, for the sky is ready to be lifted; the day of sundering has come.

"Riiki said to Naareau, 'What shall I do?' Naareau answered, 'Lift up the sky on thy snout; press down the earth under thy tail.' But when Riiki began to lift, the sky and the land groaned, and he said, 'They do not wish to be sundered.' Then Naareau lifted up his voice and sang:

Hark, hark, how it groans, the Cleaving To-
gether of old!
Speed between, Stingray, slice it apart.
Hump thy back, Turtle, burst it apart.
Fling out thy arms, Octopus, tear it apart.
West, East, cut them away!
North, South, cut them away!
Lift, Riiki, lift, kingpost of the roof, prop of the
sky.
It roars, it rumbles! Not yet, not yet is the
Cleaving Together sundered.

"When the Stingray, and the Turtle and the Octopus heard the words of Naareau, they began to tear at the roots of the sky that clung to the land. The company of Fools and Deaf Mutes stood in the midst; they laughed, they shouted, 'It moves! See how it moves!' And all that while Naareau was singing, and Riiki was pushing. He pushed with his snout; he pushed down with his tail; the roots of the sky were torn from the earth; they snapped; the Cleaving Together was split asunder. Enough! Riiki straightened out his body. The sky stood high, the land sank, the company of Fools and Deaf Mutes was left swimming in the sea. But Naareau looked up at the sky and saw that there were no sides to it. He said, 'Only I , Naareau, can pull down the sides of the sky,' and he sang:

Behold, I am seen in the West: it is West!
There is never a ghost, nor a land, nor a man;
There is only the Breed of the First Mother
with the First Father, and the First Beget-
ting of Things;
There is only the First Naming of Names and
the First Lying Together in the Void;
There is only the Lying Together of Na Atibu
with Teakea,
And we are flung down in the waters of the
western sea.
It is West!

"So also he sang in the East, and the North, and the South. He ran, he leapt, he flew, he was seen and gone again like the lightnings in the sides of heaven; and where he stayed, there he pulled down the side of the sky, so that it was shaped like a bowl. When that was done, he looked at the company of Fools and Deaf Mutes, and saw that they were swimming in the sea. He said in his heart, 'There shall be the First Land.' He called to them, 'Reach down, reach down—o—o! Clutch with your hands. Haul up the bedrock. Heave!' They reached down, they hauled up the First Land from the bottom of the sea. The name of it was Aba-the-Great, and there was a mountain that smoked in its midst. It was born in the Darkness. And after Aba-the-Great came Aba-the-Little, and after Aba-the-Little was Samoa in the South; but lay them aside, for they were not born in the Darkness.

"And Naareau stood on Aba-the-Great in the West. He said to his father, 'Na Atibu, it is dark. What shall I do?' Na Atibu answered, 'Take my eyes, so that it may be light.' Then Naareau slew his father and laid his head on the slope of the mountain that smoked. He took his right eye and flung it East. Behold, the Sun! He took his left eye and flung it West. Behold, the Moon! He took the fragments of his body and flung them into the sky. Behold, the stars! He took Riiki, the great Eel, and flung him overhead. Behold, his belly shines there to this day, the Milky Way! And Naareau planted in Aba-the-Great the beam of wood that lifted the sky. Behold, the First Tree, the Ancestor-Sun! The spirits of air and earth grew from its branches; the spirits of the underworld grew from its roots; and from the whirlpool where its roots went down to the sea grew the Ancestress, Nei Nimanoa, the far-voyager, from whom we know the navigating stars.

"And when it was light, Naareau made Aba-the-Little in the West and Samoa in the South. He planted in Samoa a branch of the First Tree, and ancestors grew from it. They were the Kings of the Tree of Samoa, the Breed of Matang, the company of red-skinned folk, whose eyes were blue. And Naareau plucked the flowers of the Tree of Samoa. He flung them northwards, and where they fell, there grew Tarawa, Beru, Tabiteuea, and a multitude of islands between South and West, not to be numbered.

All the lands of the earth were made by Naareau the Younger. Who shall know the end of his knowledge or his works? There is nothing that was not made by him. So at last all things were done according to his thought: he said in his heart, 'Enough. It is finished. I go, never to return'; and he went, never to return."

EDMUND WILSON

The Zuni Shalako Ceremony

One of the most important Southwestern Indian ceremonials is the Zuni Shalako, which is the high point in the annual Zuni ceremonial calendar. Since the ceremony takes place in late November or early December in Zuni Pueblo, located in an isolated region of western New Mexico, relatively few Americans have seen this colorful and dramatic affair. When one of our foremost writers and literary critics, Edmund Wilson, visited Zuni and attended the Shalako in the autumn of 1947, we were provided with this absorbing and perceptive account, which first appeared as an article in *The New Yorker* and was later published in Mr. Wilson's book, *Red, Black, Blond and Olive* (1956).

The account is an accurate ethnographic description of the main features of the Shalako, but more important, it provides in its interpretations an understanding of the meaning and significance of a rite of intensification for an American Indian culture. As Wilson expresses it, "It seems as if the dancer by his pounding were really generating energy for the Zunis; by his discipline, strengthening their fortitude; by his endurance, guaranteeing their permanence." Watching the dance, the people receive strength and revitalization. The dance is the climactic event of the year and sets the moral standard. As Wilson observes, the whole social structure of the Zuni revolves around the ceremony, and by keeping the dances up throughout the night "they know that their honor and stamina, their favor with the gods, are unimpaired."

An interesting treatment of the Shalako by a French scholar, Jean Cazeneuve, *Les Dieux dansant à Cibola* (1957), is the first full-scale account of the ceremony.

Reprinted in abridged form from Edmund Wilson, *Red, Black, Blond and Olive* (New York: Oxford University Press, 1956), pp. 3–4, 9–12, 23–31, and 33–42, by permission of the author and the publishers.

Ever since reading, some years ago, a book called *Dancing Gods,* by Miss Erna Fergusson, which describes the ceremonials of the Pueblo Indians in New Mexico and Arizona, I had had an ambition to attend what seemed from her account the most spectacular of them: the Zuni festival called Shalako. But this takes place under what are, for an Easterner, rather inconvenient conditions: in midwinter, at a date which varies and which may be set only a few days in advance; and at a place, in northwestern New Mexico, which is off the tourist route and not very easily accessible. When I did finally get a chance to visit the Shalako festival, I discovered certain other difficulties.

The little pueblo of Zuni is one of the Indian communities that have survived, since the arrival of the whites, most successfully as a social organism. Its strength and cohesion it seems mainly to owe to the extraordinary tribal religion: a complicated system of priesthoods, fraternities, and clans which not only performs the usual functions of religions but also supplies it with a medical service, a judiciary machinery, and year-long entertainment. This cult includes the whole community, distributing and rotating offices, and organizing it so tightly that it is completely self-contained, in a way that perhaps no white community is, and equipped to resist the pressures that have disintegrated other Indian groups. The ceremonies are partly in the nature of the enactment of a national myth, and they present a sort of sacred drama whose cycle runs through the entire year. The legends show a good deal of imagination and the impersonations a good deal of art, and the cast is so enormous that a very considerable proportion of the little town of twenty-six hundred has, at one time or another, a chance to play some role. With this, the Zuni religion imposes an effective discipline, involving periods of continence and fasting, and insisting on truthfulness— "speaking with one tongue"—and on civility and gentleness in personal relations. The Zunis as a group are extremely self-controlled, industrious, and self-reliant.

*   *   *

Coming down into the village proper— among one-story adobe houses and the beehive-shaped outdoor ovens that are both the same purplish pink as the bare grassless earth they are made of—is a descent into a foreign country. The air is full of piñon smoke that has a smell as rich and fragrant as roast chestnuts. The dogs come out everywhere to bark at you—half-wild and rather horrid mongrels: some look like degenerate huskies, others as if they were crossed with coyotes. I saw one family of half-grown pups in which every one was different. I was reminded for a moment by the earth and the smell, the women weraring gay shawls and carrying baskets or jars on their heads, of the towns in southern Europe. But this is something remote from Europe, at once newer and older: a piece of prehistoric America that has absorbed some of the customs of the United States.

There are great preparations in evidence: everywhere men chopping wood and women baking loaves in the ovens; outside the houses hang sheepskins, fresh from the dozens of sheep that will be barbecued or stewed for the feasts. Against the monotonous background, the blankets are bright green or red. The people have an Eskimo Mongoloid look: stout, compact, and not very tall, with round black eyes that shine. Some of the men have frank friendly faces, but all look as if they had been cut out of some very hard substance, and they are in general reserved and solemn, talking little among themselves and not even glancing at visitors. The women have bulky swathed bodies on feet and legs made enormous by a kind of wound puttees, and their wrapped and wadded bodies go along on legs that seem spindling. There are many small primitive corrals, mere rows of rough stakes, with sheep, burros, cattle, and horses. Here and there is a domesticated wild turkey or an eagle in a wooden cage, both kept to furnish feathers for costumes. Beyond rises Corn Mountain, which belongs to the Zunis and to which they belong, now transformed by the setting sun: the upper part of the mesa is for a moment vividly reddened, and its markings and outlines become distinct, then suddenly it is all left in shadow. On the other side of the sky, the clouds are a dull brickish red that corresponds with the color of the mesa and harmonizes with that of the soil. The little Zuni River shines palely as twilight falls.

The town is no longer the anthill (the Zunis themselves called it the Middle Anthill of the World) that the travelers of the eighteen-eighties found and that the Taos pueblo still is—with the houses piled up in terraces and scaled by outside ladders. There is a nucleus of these old buildings left that encloses the little plaza, but the Zunis have prospered so much that they have built themselves capacious houses, which now cover a relatively large area. They seem to put them wherever they like, at various distances from and angles to one another, and there is scarcely in the whole pueblo anything that can be called a street. The typical Zuni house has only a single story and not more than three or four rooms. These rooms are hung with shawls and blankets, and one of the more pretentious houses is decorated with maps. I saw none that showed any signs of squalor—though the Zunis' ideas about bedding are not so nice as ours—and none that did not smell clean. In spite of the generally high standard of living, there are different degrees of wealth, and the families I visited were pretty well off. Yet, even with their chairs and beds, these houses, to a non-Indian, seem rather bare, because they are still the dwellings of people who have for millennia been used to sitting and sleeping on the ground and have not yet had the time to acquire the sense of furniture. The pieces are set around without system, often at great distances from one another, just as the conversations that take place when a white visitor calls are full of immense silences that are the product not of embarrassment but of the natural taciturnity of the Indian. There are two of three houses with a second floor, but this is merely "conspicuous waste," as the owners do not live in the upper part but use it, if at all, to store corn. Lately, the Zunis have shifted from round to square beams, because the women have found that the latter are easier to dust—a motivation of a kind which, as a visiting anthropologist says, could hardly be guessed in the ruins of the past by a student of archaeology.

Some of these houses have curious features that are the result of their having been built to receive the Shalako gods, or Shalakos. There are six of these gods, and tradition demands that each of them be received in a house especially built for the purpose. There have also in the past been two houses to entertain other groups of divinities. Now, the building of these eight houses and the banquets, on a medieval scale, with which the gods are welcomed have in some cases ruined for the whole of the year the families that have undertaken them. So the Zunis sometimes cheat on the expense and merely replaster old houses or build on a new room or two or entertain two Shalakos in one house. Even so, this means that every year there are several new houses, equipped for the requirements of the Shalako dance. They must have each a long room, which sometimes runs to sixty feet, and a ceiling at least twelve feet high to accommodate the enormous masks. Each must also have a row of windows that opens on the Shalako room from another large chamber next to it and from which certain special groups have the privilege of watching the performance, as if from theater boxes. These windows, which have regular sashes and panes, with little paper stickers on them to advertise the company that makes them, are one of the queerest examples of the mixture in Zuni of the old and the new. When the celebration is over, and a family comes to live in the house, the windows become a nuisance and are usually walled up.

* * *

I started for the first night of the Shalako festival (December 16 this year), with a small party of other visitors, at about four in the afternoon. All cars going down the hill were stopped by the police and searched for liquor. This, I was later told, failed almost completely in its purpose, since the Zunis by way of their grapevine would send the word back to Gallup for their bootleggers to come in around the hills.

We arrived at the pueblo just in time for the advent of the Council of the Gods, a group in which the Shalakos are not included. A fording place of mud and stones had been built across the Zuni River, and the gods, coming down from a stone formation known as the White Rocks, made their entrance over it into the town. The young Fire God comes first—a boy in his early teens, his nude body painted black and spotted with red, yellow, white and blue, wearing a black spotted mask, like a helmet that covers the whole of his head, and carrying a smoldering brand. We missed his arrival, however, and did not see him till later. The main procession, which was now approaching, produced an uncanny impression. First comes the high god of the festival, Sayatasha, the Rain God of the North; and behind him his deputy, Hututu, the Rain God of the South. Sayatasha, in his mask, has what looks from a distance like a blank black-and-white pierrot face, between a black-banged wig and a black-and-white striped ruff, and he is dressed in a white gown. He stalks pompously in a long slow stride, accompanied by a short sharp rattle, made by shaking a cluster of deer scapulae every time he puts down his foot. It is the rhythm of authority and dignity which is reserved for him alone and—like the music for Wotan in the *Ring*—accompanies him all through the ceremonies. As he comes closer, we make out his accoutrements. A long flat horn, in place of an ear, sticks out from the right side of his mask, like an upcurved turquoise pennon; it has a heavy black fringe on its underside and a white feather dangling at the end. This horn presages long life for the Zuni people; and the left eye, a long black streak prolonged through an outstanding wooden ear, also heavily fringed, invokes a special long life for the "people of one heart." The right eye, not extended beyond the face, is intended to threaten short life to those who practice witchcraft. Sayatasha has a bow and arrows, and "prayer plumes"— that is, sticks with feathers attached that are

supposed to give wings to the prayers. His
follower Hututu is much the same, except
that he has two ears and no horn, and that
his eyes are set in a single black stripe which
stretches across his mask, and from the tip
of one ear to that of the other. Each is followed by a Yamuhakto, or Wood Carrier,
who comes to pray for the trees, so that the
people may have firewood and beams for
their houses. The masks of the Yamuhakto
are turquoise and bell-glass-shaped, with expressionless holes for the eyes and mouth,
and each of these masks is surmounted with
an untrimmed black wig, a tuft of yellow
macaw feathers, and a kind of long green
wand, from which hang down toward the
shoulders long tassels of many-colored
yarns. The Yamuhakto are wearing white
buckskin skirts, and the naked upper parts of
their bodies are painted a kind of purple and
festooned with great garlands of beads.
They carry deer antlers and bunches of
feathers. All four of these principal divinities
are wearing enormous round collars—
shaped like life preservers and striped black-
on-white like peppermints—that extend far
beyond their faces and conceal the joint
made by the mask. The two whippers, the
Salimopiya, come last, carrying yucca
switches. Both have bell-glass-shaped masks,
noses like long pipes, eyeholes that are connected like spectacles, yellow topknots of
feathers that stick out behind like weather
vanes, and huge ruffs of black raven feathers. Both are nude except for a loincloth and
wear spruce wreaths on wrists and ankles;
but they are decorated in different ways:
one, the Warrior of the Zenith, has a mask
that is checkered in bright squares of color,
with much yellow and red, which represents
a spectrum of the midday sun, and red sun-
bursts where the ears would be. The other,
the Warrior of the Nadir, is wearing a black
mask with blue eyes and a blue snout.

All these figures proceed at a rhythm that
is set by Sayatasha's rattle, but involves at
least three different gaits. Hututu paces at a
shorter stride than Sayatasha, and the Salimopiyas move with a quicker, a running
step. All the time one hears a soft lively
whistling that resembles the calling of birds.
One cannot tell which of the figures is
making these sounds, because one cannot see
their faces; and, arising from no visible
human source, scanning no human chant, yet
filling the quiet air, the song seems the

genuine voice of deities that are part of
Nature. So they pass, while the people wait
in silence, across the little dwindled river,
where a dead dog lies on the bank and old
tin cans and paper boxes have been caught
here and there on the mud flats; they march
up between the rude corrals, in one of which
a big sow is grunting.

The Council now blesses the village, proceeding to six different points, where small
holes have been dug in the ground. The
people come out of the houses and sprinkle
the divinities with sacred meal, and the
Council, at every excavation, plants prayer
plumes and sprinkles meal and performs
some solemn maneuvers. Sayatasha and Hututu, each with his Yamuhakto, make two
units that parade back and forth, while the
Salimopiya mark time, never slackening
their running pace but turning around in one
spot. The climax of the ceremony comes
when Sayatasha and Hututu walk up to one
another and stop. Sayatasha cries, "Hu-u-u,"
and his vis-à-vis answers "Hu-tu-tu. Hu-
tu-tu." The livelier calls, one decides,
must be made by the Salimopiya, since they
seem to match the brisker tempo. It is evident that all these calls have been imitated
directly from bird-cries—one remembers the
expertness at this of Fenimore Cooper's
Indians—bird-cries, perhaps, heard at dusk
or at night and attributed to elemental beings.
Though owls, with the Indians, have a bad
reputation, being usually connected with
witchcraft, Hututu is obviously an owl. I
assumed at first that the voices were whistles
in the snouts of the Salimopiyas, but learned
that they were produced by the throat and
lips. I was told of a conversation in English
in which one Zuni had said to another, "Gee,
you make that noise good!" At one year's
Shalako, Miss Bunzel says, the Salimopiyas
were severely criticized for not being sufficiently handsome, for not showing sufficient
animation, and for not giving loud enough
calls. Yet the whistling is never shrill, it is
always under perfect control; and the confrontation of Sayatasha and Hututu is performed with an unearthly impressiveness. At
last, with much ceremonial, they enter the
house prepared for them—it has a cozy,
brand-new, suburban look. Though we
whites have been behaving with discretion,
the Indians are afraid we may go too close
and warn us to keep our distance.

In the meantime, the six Shalakos, the

guests of honor, have been sitting out in front of a cabin, in which the actors put on their costumes, in a field back of one of the trading posts. These creatures are gigantic birds, the messengers of the rain gods, which, erect, stand ten or twelve feet tall. They have cylindrical turquoise faces with protruding eyes that roll up and down, long wooden beaks that snap, and upcurving tapering turquoise horns on either side of their heads. They wear big ruffs of raven feathers, black-banged wigs and towering fan-shaped crests of black-and-white eagle tail-feathers. But their entrance into the village is arranged to take place just at the moment when twilight is falling, and one can now see them only dimly as, proceeding in single file and escorted by men in black blankets, they make their way to the river and, with a rhythmic jingle of bells fastened around their ankles, come slowly across the ford. The dark is blotting them out at the moment they arrive on the hither side; they squat in a row of six on the road by which the Council came. Now, with night, it grows very cold. The visitors hang around for a time—there is a group of young men and women, anthropological students from the University of New Mexico—afraid to ask the Zunis what is going to happen next or when it is going to happen. We lean on the egg-shaped ovens, and one of the girls gets a present of a loaf of white Zuni bread, made from sour dough, which she breaks up and offers around: it is still warm and tastes delicious. But the last orange-yellow light has faded out of the sky to our left, and still the birds do not move. The Zunis have gone indoors, and the whites drift away, too. Only the Indian Agent and I remain.

An hour and a half pass. We walk up and down to unfreeze our feet. The Shalakos utter from time to time a single reiterated bird-note, which sounds as if it came, not from close at hand, but from the other side of the river; and at intervals they clack their beaks—which we can hear with remarkable distinctness—not at random, but one at a time, like counting-off in the Army. At one point, while they are making this sound, the bell in one of the churches, with a strange irrelevance, begins to ring. The men, wrapped in black blankets, go back and forth silently with flashlights, which are never allowed to play on the birds. They are only revealed now and then for a second by the

swerve of an occasional Zuni car. An airplane passes above us, winking green and red. The Indians begin to emerge and line up along the road; we assume that the show is starting, but we still have a long time to wait. At last, with other blanket-swathed figures, a group of twelve men arrives, jingling bells on their ankles; surprisingly, they seem costumed like characters in a production of *Romeo and Juliet*. These are the Shalako impersonators. (The birds, during the interval of waiting, have apparently been worked by "managers," who accompany and supervise them.) For each bird there are two dancers, who will alternate through the night. These twelve dancers, appointed a year ago, have been in training for their work ever since. Their roles, which bring much prestige, are exacting and responsible ones. Besides learning the difficult dances and memorizing endless speeches, they have had to build the Shalako houses. Though they begin by impersonating the gods, these latter, the night of the festival, will actually enter into them, and the men, with their masks, become sacred objects. If anyone touches a Shalako, or if the Shalako stumbles or falls—as it seems one of them did last year—the dancer is supposed to be struck dead by the god. A mistake on the part of the impersonator means either that someone has seen his mask while it was still in the dressing room and has not been whipped for impiety or that he himself has been making love to somebody else's wife and is unworthy to play the role. When a disaster of this kind occurs, the crowd must at once go away: the Salimopiya drive them off with whips. The dancer, of course, does not actually die, but his family go into mourning and behave as if he had. And though the Shalako actor must pull the cords that control the beak and the eyes, he is never—on pain of instant death—allowed to look up toward the top of the mask to watch the mystery in operation. Nobody except the manager may understand the Shalako's mechanics. These, then, were the dancers whom we now heard returning from six different points of the pueblo. We counted the jingling groups till the sixth had disappeared in the shadow where the birds were sitting.

Then suddenly, at some signal, a chorus of voices was raised. The Shalakos were on their feet. They came up from the road to the river and filed past us with their escort and choir; and the effect of this was thrilling and lovely in a way that it would be hard to imagine. The great birds, not rigidly erect but bent forward with the dignity of their kingly crests and their beardlike feathery ruffs, as if they were intent on their errand and knew each its destination, did not, in the frosty night, the pale moonlight, and the window lamplight, appear in the least comic, as they had in the pictures that one had seen; they hardly seemed even grotesque. And the welcoming hymns that accompanied them, in a harmony one did not understand but with the voices intertangled and singing against one another, had a beauty one could not have expected—not wild but both solemn and joyful—not entirely unlike our own anthems. Each of the Shalako birds is brought to the house prepared for it, and when it has come, it kneels down in front of the door, while prayer meal is sprinkled before it. The warm yellow light from inside gives comfort and life in the winter dark. The chants of reception are sung, and the bird, curt and proud in acceptance, snaps its beak in response to the welcome. Then the Shalako goes into the house and takes its seat before a turquoise altar. The impersonator comes out from inside, while a blanket is held up to screen him, and he and his alternate make offerings of seeds. Then they take seats beside the host, who hands them a cigarette, which he and they pass back and forth as they smoke it. The host addresses as "Father!" that one of the impersonators who is supposed to speak for the Shalako, and the latter replies, "Son!" They exchange other terms of relationship; then the host asks it, "How have you prayed for us? If you will tell us that, we shall be very glad to know it."

"I have come," says the Shalako, "from the sacred lake, and I have come by all the springs." He enumerates all the springs that the Zunis in their wanderings passed, when they were looking for a site for their town. "I have come to see my people. For many years I have heard of my people living here at Itiwana (the Middle), and for long I have wanted to come. I want them to be happy, and I have been praying for them; and especially I want the women to be fortunate with their babies. I bring my people all kinds of seeds, all the different kinds of corn, and all the different kinds of fruit and wild

green things. I have been praying for my people to have long life; and whoever has an evil heart should stand up in the daylight. I have been praying that my people may have all different kinds of seeds and that their rooms may be full of corn of all colors and beans of all colors and pumpkins and water gourds, and that they may have plenty of fresh water, so that they may look well and be healthy because of the pumpkins and the beans and the corn. I want to see them healthy. . . . Yes, I have worked hard and prayed for all my people. I do not want any of the roots to rot. I do not want anyone to sicken and die, but I want everyone to stand firmly on his feet all year. This is how I have prayed for you."

* * *

The dances do not begin till midnight, for the ceremonies connected with the reception of the gods are affairs of tremendous length. The speech made by Sayatasha alone—which the actor has had to learn by heart—takes him six hours to deliver. I did not try to visit the house where this god was being entertained. The old lady from California who was suspected of sinister designs, had walked in and sat down in front, and immediately been asked to leave. The Agent himself with his wife had been moved on from there by an officious visiting Navaho. The whole atmosphere was quietly hostile. Elsewhere a discourteous visitor was invited "kindly" to remove his hat; and another, who was standing at the door, was ordered not to come in by a boy of about twelve, who fixed him with a hateful eye. When the visitor tried to explain that his intention had been merely to look on from there, the boy grimly told him, "Don't look!" I did not, therefore, go into the house, but simply peered through the misted windows—where some of the Indians had also gathered—casually walking away and then walking up again. One cannot in the least blame the Zunis for wanting to keep strangers out of these ceremonies, for they are services of the most solemn kind, comparable in dignity and devotion to any that I have ever seen.

Besides the six houses prepared for the reception and the dances of the Shalakos, there are supposed to be one for the Council of the Gods and one for another group, called the Koyemshi, or Old Dance Men; but just as two pairs of Shalakos had doubled up this year, so the Koyemshi and the Council have combined. As I gazed in through the panes at these latter, the Council were beyond my vision, but I got a good view of the Koyemshi. These are a group of ten clown-priests, familiarly known as the Mudheads, who play roles of the first importance, being threaded in and out of ceremonies which continue through the whole year. When the Zunis, according to their legend, were wandering in search of a home, they sent out a brother and sister on a prospecting expedition. But the boy raped the girl in her sleep, and she gave birth to a brood of nine idiots These are the Mudheads, who stand as a warning of the danger of incestuous unions. Largely naked and painted pink, they wear masks that are pink and bald and knobbed with enormous warts, and have imbecile round pop-eyes, gaping mouths like tadpoles or frogs, and fleshy topknots or catfish antennae. Each of these masks differs slightly from the others, and the roles of the Mudheads differ. One tries to repeat sacred rituals and always breaks down into gibberish; one is a coward, who hides under ladders and hangs back behind the rest; another is called the Bat and is supposed to be blind, so that he is always stumbling about and bumping into things; another believes himself invisible and hides his head like an ostrich; another can only laugh; another is glum, etc. When they are in character and wearing their masks, they pass in and out of the houses, performing all sorts of antics or—in infantile simpleton voices that seem to whimper and wheedle, to bubble and ooze from their masks—entertaining the spectators with ribald jokes that often probe into their private affairs. When the festival was announced by them eight days before, it was in such terms as these: "In eight days my people come. You must look around for nice girls and stay with them. . . . I come to tell you that in eight days everyone will be happy and have a good time. Men should trade wives." But they, too, are sacred beings, venerated as well as loved. During the year of their impersonation, the actors in the mythical dramas partly lose their own identities and become for the people of the pueblo the personages they represent. In the case of Sayatasha, the actor even loses his own name and is known by the name of the god. The affection and reverence felt for the mythical role

that a man is playing is said sometimes to contrast sharply with the opinion his neighbors have had of him.

It is strange now to see these ten men (the incestuous Father makes the tenth), their masks pushed up on the tops of their heads, here dedicating themselves with prayer, after days of retreat and fasting, to the impish and ridiculous parts it is their duty to resume at midnight. Some of them are rather old, and have arms of skin-and-bone and aquiline Dantesque profiles. The audience sits on one side of the room, with a space between it and the celebrants. The Koyemshi, by themselves in a row, sit against the opposite wall; the man of the house sits facing them, flanked with five men of his own clan, the Dogwood, and four men of the Frog clan, his wife's, each drawn up so close to his vis-à-vis that their knees are almost touching. Long cigarettes made of reeds have been lighted from burning coals and are being passed back and forth between the Mudhead and the man who is receiving him, each taking six whiffs and waving the cigarette in the direction of the six Zuni points of the compass—North, South, East, West, Up, and Down. The Father recites a long speech like that of Sayatasha, while the others answer, *"Athlu"* (Amen). Says the Father of the Koyemshi to his hosts, "I leave my children with you for five days. They will dance in your houses; they will then go to the home of the gods in the East. . . . Give us food that we may eat, and next year we will bring you all kinds of seeds." They have little packets of seeds concealed under their black neckclothes, and the knobs on their heads are filled with seeds.

The young people came and went, looking in for a time through the windows or lingering on the porch. This part of the evening's ceremonies did not interest them much. A boy who had been in the war greeted two other boys with a *"Come sta, signori?"* and they showed off with Italian conversation. A boy and a girl had a moment of necking as they sat on the rail of the porch. He enveloped her plump round figure, dressed in poinsettia red, with a wing of his black blanket-cloak, and for a moment they rubbed their cheeks. Then he carried her off as she softly laughed, still with his cloak about her.

The monotonous chanting of the ritual went on without pause for hours: an unvarying repetition of six beats that ended in a kind of short wail.

The first Shalako house I visited, when, later, the dancing began, made upon me a tremendous impression. The rooms where the dances are held are dazzling with electric light and blazing with decorations. The walls are completely covered with brilliant blankets and shawls, pale buckskins, and queer blue or green hangings, made by the Navahos, on which square-headed elongated figures represent the Navaho gods. At one end of the room is a turquoise altar, ornamented with eagle feathers. A group of fetishistic animals, carved from stone, is set out in a row before it. In the audience, most of the men, having discarded their modern clothes, are wrapped in their best black blankets, and the women wear over their heads their best green or red or flowered shawls, and sometimes a kind of black apron, made of silk with fancy designs.

Against this background and before this audience, a Shalako and his alternate are dancing, balancing one another in a bizarre moving composition that seems to fill and charge the whole room. The unmasked dancer here is putting on such an extraordinary performance that he distracts attention from the bird. His costume has a suggestion of the Renaissance that may have been derived from the Spaniards. He wears a tight-fitting white buckskin cap with a curtain that hangs down behind, like the headwear of Giotto's Dante, and a fillet of red ribbon with silver bells. His black shirt is trimmed at the shoulders and sleeves with ribbons of many colors; his black kilts are embroidered in blue and circled with embroidered sashes. His knees are painted red, and the lower part of his legs is yellow, and he has tassels of blue yarn tied below the knees. With his brown bare feet he treads up and down—at a rate, as one observer has calculated, of about four times as many steps a minute as a marathon runner takes—in a quick, sharp, unflagging rhythm. This rhythm is also marked with a pointed yucca wand held before him in the right hand at an unwavering phallic angle. His eyelids are dropped, his eyes seem closed; the firm line of his mouth is drawn down—as if, in dedicating himself to his role, he has achieved a solemn sublimation and is shut off from the rest of the world. His whole demeanor is perfectly disciplined as he slowly moves thus back and

forth from one end of the room to the other. And the Shalako, towering above him, actually seems lighter than he and dancing to an easier rhythm, as it turns in place or marks time or—astonishing in its swiftness and grace—swoops the length of the floor in a birdlike flight, never butting into the wall or ceiling and never so much as brushing the spectators, who sit close on either side.

These spectators rarely move, they are receptive, quiet, and calm; and the white visitor, too, becomes rapt. He, too, feels the thrill and the awe at the elemental power summoned. It seems as if the dancer by his pounding were really generating energy for the Zunis; by his discipline, strengthening their fortitude; by his endurance, guaranteeing their permanence. These people who sit here in silence, without ever applauding or commenting, are sustained and invigorated by watching this. It makes the high point of their year, at which the moral standard is set. If the Zunis can still perform the Shalako dances, keeping it up all night, with one or other of the performers always dancing and sometimes both dancing at once, they know that their honor and their stamina, their favor with the gods, are unimpaired. The whole complicated society of Zuni in some sense depends on this dance. Our ideas of energy and power have tended to become, in the modern world, identified with the natural forces—electricity, combustion, etc. —which we manipulate mechanically for our benefit, and it is startling to see human energy invoked and adored as a force that is at once conceived as a loan from the nonhuman natural forces and as a rival pitted against them; or rather, to put it in terms that are closer to the Zuni point of view, to see all the life of the animal world and the power of the natural elements made continuous with human vitality and endowed with semihuman form.

Here, too, one finds theater and worship before they have become dissociated, and the spectacle suggests comparisons in the fields of both religion and art. In the theatrical connection, it seems curious at first to be reminded of the Russian Ballet, but the reason soon becomes quite plain. It must have been true that Dyaghilev brought into the conventional ballet, with its formal routines and patterns, something that was genuinely primitive. He had really opened the way for an infusion of old Russia—by giving new life to the music of Rimsky and Borodin, who had already returned to folk material; through the Mongolian wildness of Nizhinsky; through the barbaric splendors of Bakst; through the atavistic stridencies and iterative beat of the Stravinsky of *Le Sacre du Printemps*. The kind of thing one sees in the Shalako dance must be something like the kind of thing that was revived by the Russian Ballet—not brought to the point of refinement to which Dyaghilev was able to carry it, but, in its color and variety and style, in the thoroughness of the training involved and the scrupulous care for detail, a great deal more accomplished and calculated than one could easily conceive without seeing it. In the other, the religious, connection, one comes quite to understand the student of comparative religions quoted by Erna Fergusson, who said that it was "no wonder missionaries have had no luck in converting these people to Christianity. It will never be done. The essential mental rhythm of the two races is too far apart. You could imagine reducing that Shalako figure two feet or even four; you could not possibly turn it into Christ on the Cross." The difficulty, one sees, would be to induce the flourishing Zunis—who have maintained their community for centuries, as sound and as tough as a nut, by a religion that is also a festive art—to interest themselves in a religion that has its origin in poverty and anguish. The Zunis, moreover, have no sense of sin; they do not feel that they need to be pardoned. What the Shalako bird brings is not pardon, but good cheer and fecundity. It is formidable; the children hide from it the day it comes into town, and if anybody falls asleep, it leans over and wakes him by snapping its beak. But the great bird loves the people, and the people love the bird. They build a house for it and spread it a feast, and it dances before them all night to show them its satisfaction.

In each of the other two Shalako houses, two Shalakos were dancing together, occasionally assisted by Mudheads. At one place, where I looked through a window, I saw people holding a blanket while the Shalako sat down in a corner; and the alternate changed places with the weary man who had just been performing his role. In the house of Sayatasha, the Council of the Gods, with their masks off, were performing stately evo-

lutions, accompanied by the adolescent Fire God, who—slim and handsome in his speckled nudity—danced with the dropped eyelids and resolute lips of the Shalako impersonator. But the great success of the evening was a Shalako who danced alone. It was marvelous what this dancer could do, as he balanced his huge bird-body. He would slowly pavane across the floor; he would pirouette and teeter; he would glide in one flight the whole length of the room as smoothly as a bird alighting. The masks are constructed like crinolines; there are hoops sewn inside a long cylinder that diminishes toward the top; and the whole thing hangs from a slender pole attached to the dancer's belt. So the movements are never stiff. The Shalakos, ungainly though they may seem at first when one watches them from afar by daylight, are created in the dance as live beings; and this one was animated from top to toe, vibrating as if with excitement—gleaming with its turquoise face, flashing its white embroidered skirt, while its foxskins flapped like wings at the shoulders. The dance conveyed both delicacy and ecstasy, and the music—produced by a small group of men who sat, as if in a huddle, facing one another, as they chanted, beat a drum and shook rattles—exercised a peculiar enchantment. There are many different songs for the dances, and they vary in mood and pace; but each consists of a single theme repeated over and over, with a rest after so many bars and occasional changes in tempo, which momentarily relieve the dancer. In this case, the recurrent lapses—during which the Shalako, poised for flight, marked time and snapped his beak at the end of his room-long runway—would be followed by brisk pickings-up, when the bird would skim across the floor; and this reprise always had about it an element of the miraculous, of the miracle of the inexhaustible energy, leaping up after every subsidence with the same self-assertive joy. Carried along by the rhythm yourself, alternately let down and lulled, then awakened and stimulated, in a sequence that never faltered, you were held by a kind of spell. The great blue-and-white creature irresistibly took on for you, too, an extra-human personality, became a thing you could not help watching, a principle of bounding and soaring life that you could not help venerating. A white woman who had once seen the dance told me that it had given her a shudder and thrill, in her chair at the end of the room, to feel the eaglelike bird swooping down on her. And I found that it was only with effort that I, too, could withstand its hypnotic effect. I had finally to take myself in hand in order to turn my attention and to direct myself out of the house. For something in me began to fight the Shalako, to reject and repulse its influence just at the moment when it was most compelling. One did not want to rejoin the Zunis in their primitive Nature cult; and it was hardly worth while for a Protestant to have stripped off the mummeries of Rome in order to fall a victim to an agile young man in a ten-foot mask.

Yet the effect of it lingered and haunted me even after I was back in my guest-house. Kept wakeful as I was with coffee, the monotonously repetitive music, the indefatigable glowing bird that had dominated the crowded room, drawn toward it all upward-turned eyes, suspended in a trance all wills, stayed with me and continued to trouble me. I was glad to find a letter in my room which recalled me to my own urban world and which annoyed me, when I read it, so much that I was distracted from the vision of the Shalako.

WILLIAM A. LESSA

The Decreasing Power of Myth on Ulithi

This example from Micronesia shows in conventional fashion the enmeshment of myth with ritual, as well as the relationship of both to the native political system, but then it goes further and traces the actual decline of this three-fold linkage in the face of the subversive influences resulting from involvement with the outside world. As the myth lost strength, its grip on the ritual was weakened. Of course, myth is not really a force in itself, for it derives its strength and authority from a more ultimate body of beliefs and values and is therefore simply expressive of these. When this authority became undermined on Ulithi Atoll through the deterioration of the pagan religion, the myth no longer could draw upon its former support in controlling the ritual. As the myth crumbled, the ritual lost its pagan meaning and assumed a largely secular character. It will probably persist for a while as an economic rite with some political overtones, and eventually disappear entirely. It is interesting that it persists at all, having been able to do so partly by reason of custom and partly because of its lingering political and sportive roles.

Reprinted from *Journal of American Folklore*, LXXV (1962), 153–159, by permission of the American Folklore Society and the author.

On Ulithi, a Micronesian atoll in the Carolinian archipelago, mythology has always exercised an obvious part in maintaining rituals and supporting traditional values. It has "explained" the locus of supernatural power and provided a basis for tapping such power. Moreover, it has justified the political order by giving it a sacred rationale expressed in dramatic actions associated with gods, tricksters, and ancestral ghosts. In the economic and technological spheres it has explained the origin of various taboos.

In recent years, through contact with the outside world, the efficacy of Ulithian mythology has become rapidly diminished and altered to the extent that many rituals are no longer performed at all, while others are carried on perfunctorily or secularly. Thus, an elaborate kind of fish-making magic, formerly performed annually at the demand of the king, has been completely abandoned, due in part to the fact that the sacred narrative that lent it the support of the past has become a tale known only to a few old people. Already having had the seeds of religious disbelief implanted in them during the German and Japanese administrations of the present century, the natives found it difficult to maintain traditional fish-magic practices that depended on a belief in a sea spirit who rewarded a woman for having pleased him by giving him her skirt. The myth authenticated the ritual and provided its course of action, but when the myth lost acceptance it seemed useless to carry on its lengthy and risky ceremonial reenactment to ensure abundant fish for the atoll. Another myth once gave support to an important kind of palm leaf divination, asserting that the art had been taught to mortals by a group of spirits arriving in a large canoe. These spirits, together with the god of oracles, are no longer given credence and their names are almost forgotten, with the result that, despite the central place it used to hold until recently in the lives of the natives, the magical ritual has disappeared. Limiting ourselves, as we have done, to myths that support rituals, it is possible to cite another instance, this time involving the ritualistic use of sting-ray figurines of the patron god of navigators. These images used to be regarded with considerable awe by men at sea, who felt that they protected them from storms and misdirection. Knowledge of the great myth depicting the birth and power of the god is now held by few people, and even they feel no urge to implement its implications. A final example concerns the mythological origin of certain ritual prohibitions pertaining to canoe-building and navigation, which originated with certain terrestrial gods whose parents had exiled themselves from the sky world. Until recently, these prohibitions had continued to be in effect, even among Christians, but now they have virtually disappeared. Some awe still surrounds the names of the deities, but no one fears their wrath should their taboos not be maintained.

I do not mean to imply that the dissolution of the old rituals and the social system they helped to support is a simple consequence of the weakening of myths. After all, nowhere are myths prime movers. Rather, in loosely symbolic form they express the prevailing systems, structures, ideals, sentiments, and beliefs of the society that harbors them. They move as the culture moves.

Yet it is possible to trace social change through myths. It is possible to view them as instruments of more fundamental forces operative in a changing culture. They are not mere mirrors that reflect events without participating in them; instead, even though they are creatures of social forces, they are capable of exerting active influence and being influenced in return.

On Ulithi the primary movers in altering the traditional order of things have been westernization in general and Christianization in particular. Acculturation has undermined myth only to the extent that change has already penetrated into the economic, political, cognitive, ideational, and other aspects of native life.

If myths, then, are both indicators and instruments of change, it should be possible to select one and trace its waning influence in the maintenance of the old order. Specifically, we can select a Ulithian myth dealing with a certain turtle ritual and study its relationship to the political and religious institutions that were involved in the ritual. The altered import of the story parallels that of social change on the atoll.

According to the myth, three brothers lived in different villages on the island of Yap. They had a sister named Melehau, who left them and went to Ulithi Atoll. There she lived on the island of Losiep. She did not like it there, so she built a fire to see which way the smoke went. It went to the island of Mangejang, and she followed it to that island and went to live there. She did not like Mangejang, either, so she built another fire. The smoke wafted to the island of Mogmog, and she went there to live. She liked the island and remained on it, giving birth to a child named Iongolap. She told him that he and she were the chiefs of Yap and that when he went there, he would find that all the temples belonged to them. She told him that he should pray to the spirits to bring an abundance of plant foods and fish to Ulithi. Iongolap told the people of Ulithi that whenever they went anywhere and saw turtles, they should take them to him and his mother on Mogmog. After that he went to Yap and prayed for Ulithi.

Admittedly, this story has a fragmentary and not entirely consistent character. It seems to have originated on nearby Yap. However, from published reports about the western Carolines, as well as my own researches, we know a good deal about Iongolap. He is traditionally involved in the tribute relationship between Yap and the many islands to the east that have been part of its empire. Thus, another myth told on Ulithi concerns Bagau, who lived on Yap but left in a fit of madness. She strewed sand on the sea, and Ulithi was created from the grains. She gave birth to Iongolap on Ulithi and then returned to Yap, but before doing so she instructed the people to take annual offerings of oil, sails, and mats to her son, Iongolap. This myth sanctions the religious offerings that have been required in the past by the people of Gagil district on Yap. Another myth has Iongolap already living on Yap with his sister, Filtei. Filtei left Yap in anger because the people were killing turtles and giving her only the flippers. She created Ulithi out of sand and lived on the island of Mogmog. Iongolap came to her one day and told her that all the turtles killed by the people of Ulithi henceforth belonged to her.

The significance of these myths is that they sanction the obligation that Ulithians feel towards Iongolap or his family. These obligations involve, among other things, the giving of turtles. A locale on Mogmog, called the Rolong, is sacred to Iongolap, and offerings may be brought to him there when they are not taken to Yap. The Rolong has a political significance as well as a religious one. On it there once stood the atoll-wide council house, where the king was formally invested. In the last century the building was razed by a typhoon and never rebuilt, but investitures continued to be held in the open on the site of the great house.

In order to understand the intimate association between the turtle ritual and the political system, some remarks concerning the latter are necessary. The king of the atoll is normally the old king's next brother or the eldest son of the former king's eldest sister. He comes from the Lamathakh lineage, which dominates one of the two districts into which the island of Mogmog is divided. The other district is under the control of a chief from another lineage called Lamrui, which controls the other half of the island. This chief holds second place in the atoll-wide hierarchy of chiefs. All others, including the district chiefs of other islands, are ranked below these two in a descending pattern of authority. The king is the recognized political head of the atoll. He has certain prerogatives, among which are the right to receive certain kinds of gifts. These are mostly in the form of food and are called *maler tamol.* They include breadfruit, mountain apples, coconuts, and fish. The rationale behind the presentation of these gifts to the king is based on the mythological association between Mogmog and Iongolap. The king acts as an intermediary for Iongolap, receiving gifts in his name. Among these gifts are turtles, all of which rightfully belong to Iongolap or his mother and therefore to the king, since he is his surrogate. Turtles are caught mostly in the native months of *ermas* and *thomor,* corresponding approximately to May and June. This is when they most commonly lay their eggs. But occasionally they are caught at other times of the year, and the ritual is followed even then, thus distinguishing it from other gift offerings made to the king, which are annual and not continuous. In short, all turtles are sent to Mogmog at any time, whereas breadfruit, mountain apples, coconuts, and even fish are presented only once a year as "first fruits."

A description of the turtle ritual will illustrate its political and religious nature, providing us at the same time with a base from which to analyze recent departures from the traditional procedures. When the people of Falalop, or any of the islands under its political jurisdiction, catch green turtles (*Chelonia mydas*), they first assemble them on the beach and later load them on their sailing outriggers and proceed to Mogmog, the place where the king resides. En route to the island the men in the canoes perform the *hamath,* an obscene dance associated with whales and menstrual rites, and used as a means of public criticism. The women on the beach do the same dance. On reaching Mogmog, the men take the huge turtles to the Rolong, the sacred area mentioned above. The king kills the turtles, but before doing so he offers a prayer to Iongolap, the *tuthup bwol,* or "ancestor of the turtles," beseeching him to refrain from harming him: "I will kill these turtles. I am sorry I will kill these turtles. Do not kill me for killing the turtles." He addresses a similar prayer to the reptiles. The second ranking chief of the atoll also addresses a quiet prayer to Iongolap, but not to the turtles. The king then kills the reptiles by clubbing their heads with a stick of hard wood from the *Pemphis acidula* tree. A man selected at random by the chief from his own lineage cuts a slit in the throat of each turtle and pulls out the intestines, a separate basket being used as a receptacle for each. The slits are plugged up with coconut fiber and the reptiles are towed to the beach, where dried coconut leaves are placed over them and set afire. This is done to roast them slightly and make the carving of the meat easier. The carapaces and plastrons cannot avoid being scorched, but these dorsal and ventral portions of the bony case have no value. The chelonians are then hauled back to the Rolong.

A man from the king's lineage removes the head of the first turtle and gives it to the king, who may keep it for himself or share it with any relatives or friends whom he chooses. Then two men from the Lamathakh (king's) lineage begin to carve out the meat on one side of the reptile while two men from the Lamrui do the same on the other half. They use sharp knives and begin by making a hole under each flipper. The meat and eggs are drawn out of the holes and deposited in four receptacles. Each pair of men tries to outdo the other in extracting the contents of the bony case, and what they accumulate belongs to their lineage, to be disposed of in a manner described further on. The four flippers are then divided according to a formal plan. The proximal portions are "given" to the people of certain islands outside the Ulithian group: Fais, Ngulu, the Woleai, and Yap. Apparently, those people who are from Fais but living on Ulithi actually receive a portion; but the portions of the flippers assigned to the other islands are retained by the king, to give to his friends or relatives, or to eat himself if there is not much. The distal portions of the flippers are given to a certain lineage (unascertained).

Falalop is not left without some reward for its part in catching and delivering the turtles. First a gift of meat and eggs is given to the men who came over in the "turtle canoes," or *wal wol*. This is equally divided according to individual. Second, there is a more formal gift given to the chiefs of the Lipipi and Hachlau lineages, which have highest rank, respectively, over each of the two villages on Falalop. They are given the blood of the turtle, which has been collected in coconut shells, and they are given the carapace with the meat and fat that clings to it. The carapace is useless but the flesh is prized and divided equally. In addition,

these chiefs receive some of the proximal flippers.

The reader may be wondering how a single turtle, however large, can supply so many people. In point of fact, if only one reptile is caught, the division is meager, but usually many are obtained at one time. This involves an interesting procedure. The second, fourth, sixth and other even-numbered chelonians are butchered and distributed according to the above rite, but the third, fifth, seventh, and other odd-numbered ones are the object of a competitive sport. The two leading chiefs of Mogmog select a pair of men from each of their districts to enter a free-for-all competition to extract the meat and eggs. They must be agile and strong. Whatever they come up with is given to their districts. However, the flippers remain behind, to be allocated strictly according to the ritual for the first two turtles.

By custom, Falalop is not alone in sending turtles to Mogmog; so do all other islands, regardless of where the turtle may have been caught. The mythological warrant for this has already been referred to in the story of Melehau, who here is the mother of Iongolap. This also fits in with the tale about Filtei, allegedly Iongolap's sister. But one senses, and is told, that Falalop has a special obligation in this respect, the explanation being given in an account which is purportedly historical—if one can make such a distinction.

Stated briefly, we begin with a war won by Losiep island against Mogmog. The people of the latter island decided to retaliate by giving the king's daughter to the chief of the former. The plot was devious. The girl was to be such a model wife that she would put her husband to shame by her superior virtues. When the chief of Losiep detected that he was losing face, he decided to outvie his enemies by deluging them with gifts—turtles. He decreed that all turtles caught by the people under his authority must be turned over to Mogmog. By way of explanation, it should be pointed out that Losiep became uninhabited early in the present century, and the people moved to Falalop, establishing the village of Wililekh, headed by the Hachlau lineage. Howsoever we may choose to accept both the mythical and allegedly historical accounts, the fact remains that turtles must indeed be brought to

Mogmog, and that Falalop has a special obligation to do so.

It has been necessary to provide a background for the essential purpose of this article, which is to connect myth with cultural
change. From here on my presentation will
be anecdotal.

On 14 June 1960, the very day I had arrived on my third field trip to Ulithi, I
learned that some turtles—fifteen, to be exact—had been assembled on the beach at
Falalop, where I was temporarily staying.
The next morning, never having seen a sea
turtle on land, I went to the beach to satisfy
my curiosity, only to discover that almost all
the reptiles had been loaded in canoes and
were about to be taken to Mogmog. My interest aroused, for at that time, despite two
previous visits to the atoll in 1947 and 1948
I knew nothing whatsoever regarding the
ritual, I decided to accompany the several
outriggers that were sailing with their still-
thrashing cargoes of turtles. On reaching
Mogmog I discovered that some turtles had
already arrived and were being scorched.
Soon some men with turtles began to arrive
from the island of Fassarai, too. In the midst
of the welcome being accorded me by old
friends, I did not witness the killing of the
turtles and had to make a sudden departure
when the large canoe in which I had arrived
returned to Falalop. But the man in charge
of the fire had briefly informed me that this
was the renewal of an old custom suspended
because of the extinction of a certain type of
official, and that moreover, only one person,
acting on that spot, could perform the butchering.

Bit by bit I ascertained that the reason I
had not seen any turtles on Ulithi during
nine months I had previously lived there was
that the ritual had been terminated for religious reasons. About the year 1940—the
date is uncertain—a man named Rolmei had
become king of the atoll. For some reason,
he was not installed according to the usual
rite, which involved the presentation of a
special type of loincloth and invocations both
to the great celestial god, Ialulwe, and the
great underworld deity, Solal. He was a
pagan, and at that time Christianity had not
made great inroads. But on account of the
lacuna, he felt unauthorized to partake in the
ritual killing of the turtles, so he stopped the
practice.

His successor, Wegelemar, even though

he had become a Christian at least nominally, likewise feared the displeasure of Iongolap. He, too, fretted over his failure to be
installed according to the old religious procedure. As a consequence the turtle ritual
remained completely suspended.

But when Wegelemar died in 1953, some
of the leading chiefs on Mogmog, all of
whom by now were believing Christians, decided to defy the threat of punishment by
Iongolap. They wanted to prevent the wast-
age of turtles. Already, on the island of Fassarai, the people had occasionally violated
custom during Wegelemar's time and secretly eaten turtles. Even though their customary tribute to Mogmog had been quasi-
voluntary, when Wegelemar learned of their
acts he imposed a strict taboo against leaving the island, even to fish, on all of those
involved in the delict. After some months of
this, the culprits sent the king a gift of loin-
cloths, mats, turmeric, and other valuables,
and the taboo was lifted.

In its current form, the turtle ritual has no
religious meaning but does preserve some of
its political significance. It continues to recognize that Falalop and other islands whose
people catch turtles must take them to
Mogmog for butchering and distribution at
the Rolong site. Much of the form of the
ritual remains, except for the dances, but alterations in the details reflect the weakened
authority of Mogmog. Lineages do not participate in the formal way in which they used
to, and much of the meat, fat, and eggs is
given to other islands as if it were their
right.

The ritual retains some of its emotional
characteristics but is on the way to becoming
only an economic rite. The people's taste for
the meat will eventually supersede political
considerations.

The altered nature of the ritual reflects
the altered pattern of political authority that
is emerging in Ulithi. Until the death of
Wegelemar in 1953, each new king had come
from the Fasilus lineage (or the predecessor
lineage, Lamathakh, that it supplanted).
Wegelemar's successor should have been
Harongocheum, an elderly man of the Fasilus lineage. But Harongocheum demurred,
probably because of his lack of drive and
unwillingness to assume responsibility, especially towards the American authorities
with whom occasionally he would have to
deal. The next man in line, Malefich, also

declined the position, so for the first time in remembered history the old men who had informally assembled to select a new head went outside the traditional kin group. Amusingly, when the principals involved in the deliberations were on their way to Falalop from Mogmog to communicate their decision to the Trust Territory Administration via the radio facilities of the Coast Guard station on the former island, Malefich had a change of heart and offered to accept the kingship. The already named king willingly withdrew. But Malefich exerts only political responsibilities. The ritualistic aspects of his office—such as remain—are carried out by the aforementioned Harongocheum, who is content with this nonpolitical role. Despite all these changes, the right to kill the turtles remains completely in the hands of this chief. This is borne out by the fact that about three weeks after the performance of the ritual that I had partially witnessed soon after my arrival, some people from the island of Asor came to Mogmog with a chelonian they had captured on the island of Pig. Old Harongo-

cheum was notified and immediately made the long journey to Mogmog from his home on Fassarai in order to fulfill his role. Later, on two separate occasions when a turtle was brought to Mogmog, the chief was unable to make the trip because of an injury that he had sustained in the meantime. One of the reptiles escaped after lying on its back for several days, and the other was mercifully released to return to the sea.

In summary, influences from Christianity have militated to remove the fear of punishment should the turtle ritual be performed contrary to traditional religious procedures —specifically, where the man who wields the club has not been invested as king according to pagan custom. The ritual has had and still retains some political significance, reflecting Mogmog's authority; but eventually this will disappear under the impact of foreign political administration and changing political ideologies. Myth alone has not and cannot maintain a system in operation unless it is in turn energized by more basic institutions and beliefs.

RAYMOND FIRTH

Offering and Sacrifice: Problems of Organization

Firth approaches the problem of sacrifice in a manner distinct from the historical and functional positions taken by Robertson Smith and the other writers discussed in the introduction to Smith's article in Chapter 1. He looks behind the rite, which he considers in the final analysis to be a personal act—a giving of the self or a part of the self—to discover the influence and importance that a people's ideas about control of economic resources have on their concepts of sacrifice. He addresses himself to the organization of the rite, particularly the mobilizing of material objects and human beings and the way in which the solution to such problems as the determination of the time, the selection of the animal, and the drain on resources influence the central ideology, the style, and the frequency of sacrifice itself. He does not argue, however, that concepts of sacrifice can be reduced to economic rationality and prudent calculation, for sacrifice is fundamentally a symbolic act of critical significance for a human personality and has important social components.

Reprinted from *Journal of the Royal Anthropological Institute,* XCIII (1963), 12–24, by permission of the Royal Anthropological Institute and the author.

Offering in some form appears to occur in nearly all religious systems. The custom of making religious offering is part of a vast series of actions involving conceptions of

transfer of good or service from one person to another person, or to a putative entity, without direct and immediate counter-transfer of any visible equivalent. An offering is a species of gift. This means: (*a*) that the thing given is *personal* to the giver, his own property, or something over which he has rights of alienation; (*b*) that the thing transferred must have some *value* for the person who hands it over; and, (*c*) that it is transferred with some degree of *voluntary initiative*—it is not given by compulsion nor does it occur as a technical part of a series of actions dictated by some generally planned end. What distinguishes an offering from a gift—though the two terms are often used synonymously—is that an offering implies an asymmetrical *status relationship,* an inferiority on the part of the person making the offering and superiority on the part of the recipient. A gift may also involve a status relationship if not between equals, but this relationship tends to be created by the act of giving and receiving, not acknowledged or partially resolved by such act. (A subject in a kingdom may make an offering to his Sovereign, but the Sovereign does not make an offering to the subject; he makes a gift.) The effect of gift and offering may be directly opposite in social terms. A gift may put the recipient in a state of social inferiority and may indeed emphasize that inferiority. An offering emphasizes that it is the giver who is inferior and that the recipient is in a state of social superiority. *De facto,* the manner of transfer, the words and actions employed, may determine which terminology is most appropriately used in classification.

The concept of offering may carry other qualities. Linked with the notion of status difference is that of *uncertainty*—decision as to the acceptability of the transfer of value may be thought to rest with the person designated as recipient, who may refuse it. So also with a gift, but this concept carries with it a more positive idea of handing-over as a *fait accompli.* Another quality often attached especially to an offering is the suggestion of an *emotional element.* A gift may be emotionally neutral; an offering carries with it the notion of some outgoing sentiment of respect.

This brief semantic discussion is only in a very general sense, since neither gift nor offering are precise terms. I do not want to overdrive their meaning, especially since in common usage they shade into each other. But for analytical purposes it is useful to draw attention to such elements which frequently, though not necessarily always, oc-

cur implicitly in the usage of these terms, since they enter into an understanding of much religious practice and belief.

A religious offering or oblation embodies these ideas more definitely. Status difference, volitional aspect of acceptance, emotional attitudes of offerer—all are recognizable, and often present to a marked degree. They are correlated with the special notion of the recipient being an extra-human, supernormal being.

The concept of sacrifice includes a further element. As Gusdorf has pointed out, gift is a first approximation to sacrifice. Sacrifice is a species of offering or oblation, but implies a relation between what is offered and the *availability of resources.* Offering indicates an allocation or transfer of resources, but implies nothing about the degree or quality of allocation in relation to the total resources at the command of the giver. "Sacrifice" implies that the degree or quality is significant—that the resources are limited, that there are alternative uses for them, and that there is some abstention from an alternative use in making the offering. The sacrifice is giving up something at a cost. This is indicated in dictionary equivalents—that sacrifice means "the loss entailed by devotion to some other interest," or "the destruction or surrender of something valued or desired for the sake of something having a higher or more pressing claim."

The notion that a sacrifice is involved in the diversion of some valued object from one end to another which is regarded as more pressing, raises the question of alternative response or equivalents to be expected according to the end served. When a gift is made from one person to another, later reciprocity in the form of counter-gift or counter-service is common. If there is no such reciprocity, presumably the giver regards himself as compensated by the satisfaction arising from the knowledge of the effects of the gift or by the moral virtue attaching to the act of giving itself. Such vicarious action is characteristic of most forms of sacrifice. When in the religious sphere offering or sacrifice is made, no direct counter-gift of a material kind is normally expected, although ensuing material benefits—in the form of fertility of crops or health of persons maintained or restored—are frequently regarded as its outcome. But even where no such material benefit is thought to arise, religious offering and sacrifice have other compensatory functions. These may be generalized as benefits arising from belief in the establishment of appropriate relations between the offerer or sacrificer and some spirit entity or extra-human power. Commonly, too, the performance of sacrifice in particular is regarded as inducing or marking a change in the spiritual constitution of the sacrificer, renewing or intensifying his moral qualities. But sometimes the concept of sacrifice involves the ideal of a dual loss, to the victim as well as to the sacrificer. The issue is then not always clear from the moral point of view, as when Agamemnon sacrificed Iphigenia to his political loyalties and ambitions.

In a religious sense sacrifice is one of the most critical acts. In its Western etymology it is akin to the notion of consecration, of removal from secular to sacred sphere. It has been called "a peculiarly religious term" and to many people it expresses more than almost any other concept the heart of a religious system.

In the religious field various meanings have been given to the term. But the most common is that sacrifice is a voluntary act whereby, through the slaughter of an animal, an offering of food or other substance is made to a spiritual being. Sacrifice then ordinarily implies immolation, a living victim, e.g., the *zebah*, animal-offering or "bloody oblation" of the Hebrews. At the same time most anthropologists would probably be prepared to agree with Robertson Smith and with Hubert & Mauss that the notion of sacrifice can properly include even a vegetal offering, provided that some portion of it is destroyed with intent in the act. The element, if not of destruction, at least of transformation or transmutation of what is sacrificed is basic to the concept. It is related to what Hubert & Mauss and others have referred to as the aspect of abnegation, the denial of something to the self, which does seem to be involved in every sacrificial action. In the doctrines of many religions a concept of legitimacy is also strong; a sacrifice is valid only when offered by an authorized officiant or minister.

The theme of sacrifice in religion has provided copious literature, from William Outram and John Davison through Robertson Smith and Alfred Loisy to H. C. Trumbull, E. O. James, and R. K. Yerkes, and it has received special attention in recent Africanist anthropology. There has been a spate of theories to account for the origins of sacrifice and to describe its functions. The gift theory, the homage theory, the abnegation theory, are all in Tylor's writings, with the idea of development of one from another. The communion theory and the piacular theory of Robertson Smith have stimulated many later writers. The rejuvenation theory and the cathartic theory of Sir James Frazer, the intermediary theory of Hubert & Mauss, the symbolic parricide theory of Freud and Money-Kyrle, help to round out the interpretations. As Evans-Pritchard has shown, elements of many of these may be discerned in the sacrificial system of any one community.

The treatment of sacrifice in recent general anthropological studies of religion has been very uneven, though Goode (1951) has some significant observations. Apparent lack of interest in sacrifice as a feature of primitive religions may be partly because the view has been taken, as by Hocart or Howells, that sacrifices are special forms of ritual and not of first significance in general religious development. Recent ethnographic accounts, however, as by Evans-Pritchard, Middleton, and G. Lienhardt, have brought out in a most penetrating way the religious meaning of sacrifice, its relation to concepts of divinity and of human personality, its symbolic force, and its sociological significance.

But considering that sacrifice normally involves the use of material resources, often important ones, how much reference is there in the older or in the more recent literature to the means of mobilizing these resources, to the social problems posed by the procurement of sacrifices and to the implications of the solutions for the ideology of sacrifice itself?

When is the decision to make a sacrifice made? Which animal shall be sacrificed? These are unorthodox but relevant questions.

In studies of sacrifice, preoccupation has been with the concrete ritual procedures and with the underlying beliefs; the organization of the sacrifice has been neglected. From Robertson Smith, Lord Almoner's Professor of Arabic in the University of Cambridge or from Royden Keith Yerkes, a professional theologian, this is natural enough. But it is surprising to find how this aspect of the subject has been largely passed over by social anthropologists. Recent studies of African peoples, embodying several hundred references to sacrifices, give a good deal of interesting data on who provides the sacrifice and who attends it, together with occasional information about types and numbers of beasts furnished. But when one asks, what do the sacrifices represent in terms of proportionate loss to the people who make them? there is no adequate answer obtainable. These frontal problems, the drain upon the owner's resources which the sacrifice represents, the calculations involved in deciding what particular animals are to be sacrificed and when, and the relation of the sacrificial activities to other economic activities, are hardly ever studied. This is the more notable because, in theory at least, the necessity for such calculations may have some bearing upon the central ideology of the sacrificial act.

Briefly put, the problem may be expressed in this way. When people are said to make sacrifices, does this mean simply that they kill animals ritually? What is the relation of what they sacrifice to what they possess? What loss do they suffer? How can they afford this loss? What social movements do they go through in order to be able to make sacrifices? In case of illness, for example, do they make sacrifices even when they cannot "afford" them? How do they manage in such event? If they can afford sacrifices, what is the relation of religious dictate to personal initiative? Has this anything to do with the frequency and style of the sacrifices they do make?

Of course even bare information about numbers of available stock allows us to make some inferences. Evans-Pritchard gives some data about the average number of livestock in a Nuer byre in the early 1930s and Middleton gives data about livestock and about the number of sacrifices performed during a period of about a year in a Lugbara compound. But though Lienhardt has given a most impressive account of the significance of cattle to the Dinka, he seems to have taken their economic importance for granted, and one can therefore not find any details of the number of livestock at the command of a family or larger social group and the relation of those sacrifices to the group resources. (The Dinka dislike numbering their herds, but did this debar the anthropologist from counting? See Lien-

hardt 1961, p. 22.) We are told that the Dinka prefer in theory to sacrifice strong beasts (as a reflection of their own prowess) but "must often make the best of what they think they can afford" (Lienhardt 1961, p. 293). But what *do* they think they can afford? And if they must compromise, how do they explain it to themselves?

If one wished to be challenging, one might put forward as a hypothesis that, in default of information to the contrary, the frequency, amount, and quality of sacrifices in a given community are determined primarily not by the type of social structure, nor by the specifically religious ideology, nor by the chance events demanding resolution, but by the availability of material resources of the domestic animal population. (I use the term "domestic" because, as Robertson Smith has shown by implication, the sacrifice of wild animals which can be regarded as the free gift of nature is rarely allowable or efficient. The sacrifice must be something of the operator's own or his community's. The offering must be detached from himself.)

That sacrifices are the result not of ritual actions but of economic actions has some plausibility if one considers the utilization of the meat for food. Among many peoples, e.g., Dinka, Nuer, and Lugbara, livestock (or at least cattle), it is stated, should not be killed primarily for meat, but kept for sacrifice. But if cattle are very plentiful, then there need be no real problem in securing meat. Provided that the occasion can be found for a sacrifice—and it is usually simple—enough cattle could be sacrificed to provide a frequent meat supply. On the other hand, where cattle are not plentiful, sacrifices simply cannot be very frequent. But the number of them in a stated period, and their spacing, may reflect the relation between cattle supply and meat demand as well as the intensity of ritual obligations. The relation between sacrifice and ritual slaughter is also at times close. Sacrifice is presumably a killing which is not in the immediate food interest of the slaughterer, but of some more general obligation. But if each beast that is killed must, according to the dictates of the religion, be slaughtered according to a set ritual form, the line between killing for meat according to rules laid down by God, announcing the killing to God, and offering the slain beast to God must be very tenuous. As a reverse proposition to the local statement one might put it that implicitly cattle are killed for meat and only explicitly or nominally offered for sacrifice.

But in the crude form that sacrifice is a reflex of economic resources the hypothesis cannot of course be sustained. We remember at once that in many religious systems there are specific obligations to perform a sacrifice, irrespective of the economic situation. There may be a requirement for a regular annual or other periodic sacrifice: the Pawnee "Morning Star" sacrifice; the "year-minding" of the Beduin for their deceased male kin and ancestors; the Ketsá and other rituals of the Kede to secure the welfare of the people on the Niger River; or the sacrifices of the Tallensi at sowing and harvest. There are also the irregular but recurrent human contingencies to deal with: the sacrifice at the installation of a new chief as among the Ashanti; to rectify a homicide, as among the Tallensi and Nuer; to cure illness or avert accident as among the Swazi and Nuer; or after it as with the Lugbara; to expiate incest as among the Ashanti and Dinka; or to expiate fighting at some very sacred rites, as among the Owele Ibo. There are also the sacrifices to avert disasters of nature, as when the Lovedu try to secure rain. In all such cases the regular religious need, to establish communication with the god or with the spirit world, or in whatever other terms the sacrifice be defined, would seem to be pressing and primary. "Afford it or not," the attitude might seem to be, "we must offer up our cow, our goat, our chicken." There may be also implicit reasons of sociological pressure. A sacrifice may be necessary to seal a man's assumption of office; a sacrifice may be needed as a symbol of the restoration of threatened social relations between kin. Here too sanctions for a sacrifice may be so strong that postponement of it is inconceivable.

Yet this merely pushes the problem a stage further back. If indeed there are some types of sacrifice which are obligatory and immediate, brooking no omission or delay, then how are they effected? Some organizational devices in the economic sphere must come into play in order that the ritual need may be satisfied. If the would-be sacrificer has the resources at hand, how has he managed this: has he ample for all his wants, or has he had to practise prudent husbandry by careful anticipation, or has he just had luck?

How will he fare afterwards if a further unanticipated sacrifice is necessary? How well can he sustain a "run on the sacrifice-bank" if a series of misfortunes demanding the attention of gods and ancestors should strike him and his family? If he has not the resources at hand, to what shifts is he put to mobilize them? Does he forego sacrifice and risk the anger of the unseen world? Does he resort to makeshift devices or substitutes, and if he does, what is their validity for him and his belief in the views of his ancestors and gods? In particular, what additional social relations are entailed thereby, and with whom? Does he contract credit obligations, mortgaging his future income against his present demand? Does the system ever break down? If something has to go, some sacrifice to be omitted, which one? Some indication of the nature of the problem is given by the case of the Lugbara father reported by Middleton who, when his son was sick, waited and did not sacrifice a goat, having it in mind presumably that his son was not *very* sick. Here may be a test of the relative importance of values. In modern conditions of social change and of conflict between traditional and Western values, competing demands may well make these organizational issues of high significance.

In the ethnographic record, relatively thin in this matter as it is, there are enough examples of the prudent handling of resources to show that sacrifice does seem to be a matter of some economic calculation as well as ritual obligation. Goode notes that the religious goal of establishing one's ancestral dead by worship and sacrifice causes a decrease in immediate consumption and may necessitate prior saving. What he terms the "economic burden on the distributive system of the collectivity" should not be ignored. It is fairly common in the literature to state that sacrifices are performed in proportion to the issue at stake. This involves the concept that the less important the issue the less valuable the object sacrificed. But it leaves untouched another side of the question— granted that the issue was of major importance, how then were resources handled, and in particular were they so organized as to reduce as far as possible the economic loss? Evans-Pritchard has reported that normally (in the early '30's) the Nuer killed stock only for ritual purposes, not for food. Yet according to him they got thereby (apart from the odd cattle which died) enough meat to satisfy their craving. But the balance would seem to have been not altogether easy, and care to have been exercised lest the stock be unduly depleted. The "proper" Nuer sacrifice was an ox. But on minor occasions or "more usually" (including piacular sacrifices to God, who did not require larger beasts) sheep or goats were sacrificed by the Nuer rather than oxen because they were of less value. Again, a barren cow was sacrificed rather than a fertile one, which was immolated only in mortuary rites. Then again a cucumber might be presented instead of an ox, a point which I discuss again later. Moreover, the Nuer held that some men, in their desire for meat, sacrificed "without due cause." Yet there is inconsistency here, since on their own showing there were always spirits and ghosts to whom sacrifice would be appropriate and such sacrifices were often said to be long overdue.

The implication from all this is that the occasions for sacrifice have a strong economic control. Evans-Pritchard does mention the relevance of the smallness of their herds and says that "doubtless their high value is an important consideration." But he implies that religious intention, tradition, and convention are the prime factors involved in sacrifice, and that the requirements of the spirit are relevant rather than the prudent calculations of men. Yet the significance of the latter is reinforced when one remembers that Evans-Pritchard estimated the average stock at the time he worked with the Nuer to be only about ten head of cattle and five goats and sheep to a byre, the related personnel being about eight people. Cows probably composed about two-thirds of the cattle, which were fairly evenly distributed. Therefore, allowing for natural increase, these figures would seem to imply that, if the livestock average was to be maintained, not much more than one or two sacrifices a month per byre could occur. This does not seem to have allowed a very heavy meat diet, though the system of meat distribution presumably meant that the people of the byre shared in the flesh from other animals sacrificed elsewhere.

The general conclusion that frequency and quality of sacrifice are affected by economic position is supported by further evidence. In the general summary list of factors which

Fortes gives as responsible for the selection of animals among the Tallensi, he mentions: importance of the shrine; importance of the occasion; and status of the suppliant or his group. He does not include reference to the *resources* of the person or group as being in any way significant. Yet he does note in a few cases a direct relation between the size of the sacrifice and the wealth of the person making it. He also gives examples of the postponement of sacrifice on apparently economic grounds. Likewise Nadel who, in general, does not deal with this aspect of the subject, notes that the Muslim Nupe sacrifice of a fattened ram at the 'Id festival takes place "in every household that can afford it." He also gives a little information about the relative infrequency of Nupe sacrifice to ancestors which suggest that these, at least, occur so rarely as to present a small economic problem. That sacrifices are related to command of resources by the Ibo is made very clear by Meek. He records the view that stumbling or being bitten by a snake is interpreted by Ibo as possibly due to a man's personal genius being annoyed at the sacrifice of a chicken when the man could easily have afforded a goat (which indicates some prudent calculation somewhere). He notes also the ingenious mechanism whereby a diviner, it is alleged, thinking that a patient will die, prescribes as a sacrifice to save him one that is far beyond the means of the kinsman who consults him. In addition, he gives examples of the sharing of the expense of a sacrifice, as by dividing equally the cost of the sacrificial animal among the segments of relevant kinsfolk or, for public sacrifices, deciding at a general meeting the manner of earning the necessary funds.

Incidentally, the fact noted by Hubert & Mauss and others that the species, sex, colour, and other markings of the sacrificial animal are often laid down by traditional rule, divination or other ritual procedures has an organizational implication that is usually overlooked, the problem of finding one which will conform to specification. That this is not a purely academic question is indicated by instances given by Kuper and by Krige, showing the delay and difficulties that can result from such a ritual specification. Only where livestock are particularly abundant, as appears to be the case among the Dinka, can such prescriptions not be particularly onerous. Such economic control can be applied directly in two obvious ways, by spacing out at wider intervals the sacrifices it is deemed necessary to make, or by selecting among the possible recipients of sacrifices only those gods and ancestors deemed to be of primary importance. Social anthropologists have stressed the importance of the operation of selective mechanisms in the record of genealogies. It could be that considerations of such an economic kind have played some part in the reduction of spirit entities in communities which offer animals as sacrifice, and thereby have affected the structural character of the genealogical record.

But apart from its possible effect on the frequency of sacrifices, economic controls may affect their quality. R. K. Yerkes, who was not directly concerned with this problem, nevertheless stressed that for the ancient religions of the Near East sacrifices were always as large as possible, and that the larger they were the more joyful the occasion, and contrasted this with the "unworthy modern view" that a sacrifice is a loss and a misfortune, and that the outgo should be minimal. Robertson Smith, too, seems to have frowned on the notion that a sacrifice might be a matter of prudent calculation. He rejected, probably with justice, the allegation that the sacrifice of very young animals at the annual piacular rites of the ancient Semites was getting rid of a sacred obligation at the very cheapest rate. But in another context he said that "the introduction of ideas of property into the relation between men and their gods seems to have been one of the most fatal aberrations in the development of ancient religions," which looks as if he had had some inkling of an economic problem and was antipathetic to it. An anthropologist might surmise that this property idea was not an aberration but was in fact basic in the relationship.

Some writers not concerned with the more abstract aspects of the theory of sacrifice have seen the situation empirically and more clearly. C. M. Doughty, living among the Beduin in the nineteenth century, pointed out that sacrifices were performed according to ability, and gave examples. A suckling camel calf was killed, he noted, despite protestations that it was a female and that a sheep or goat should be slain instead. In reply to these arguments the answer was very sensibly, "she refuses the teat and we have

determined to kill her." He noted again that Beduin did not use a cow camel as a sacrifice to the dead because the households were so indigent, and it was impossible to cut off this "womb of the stock." In its place the Beduin bought, for three or four sheep or goats, a decrepit old camel that had lost its front teeth and was past bearing, and released it from work for several months to fatten it up. Thus the Beduin got meat as well as the credit for the religious act.

But variation in the quality of the sacrifice and use of low-grade animals on occasion is not just a matter of economic organization. It involves an interpretation of the ideology of the sacrifice.

A procedure of collective sacrifice involves concepts both of economy and of religious ideology. The collectivity of a sacrifice is commonly regarded as a symbol of group unity—the members of a descent group or a neighbourhood, by sharing in the common ritual act, give overt expression to social bonds which are significant for them, and strengthen the value of the sacrifice for an individual particularly concerned. But a collective sacrifice often means not only a common presentation of a victim, but also a lightening of the economic burden upon each participant. Collective sacrifices may be of various types. In one the sacrifice specifically represents an offering not by an individual who is the foremost participant but by the lineage or other group he represents. In another type no descent group as such may be involved, but some members of the community may in free association pool their contributions. Such a sacrifice is that of a bull or cow offered by Kelantan Malays in celebration of the annual pilgrimage in Mecca. The animal is usually bought by subscription from several people, the price always being made up in seven shares. Over a period of years, by accumulation of shares so contributed, a person may acquire as it were a complete sacrificial animal for himself and so secure the appropriate merit. Such collective acts of immolation of an animal may not necessarily reduce the number of sacrifices performed in a community, but they spread both the cost and the benefits. They also usually allow people with few resources to take advantage of the relative wealth of others, so that the ideology of charity may be subjoined to that of sacrifice. Again, the emphasis upon the ritual unity of the sacrificing group may be a virtue which is closely allied to necessity.

Another way of meeting the problem of resources in sacrifice which raises important questions of meaning is the use of permissible substitutes or surrogates. Robertson Smith mentioned this subject briefly, though he did not examine it. He regarded such substitution, as that of a sheep for a stag in a certain Roman rite if a stag could not be procured, as an evasion. (He called it bluntly a fraud.) Only in passing did he admit that otherwise the ceremony might fall through. More sophisticated discussion of this whole question is given by modern social anthropologists. Evans-Pritchard's argument takes the form that ultimately the sacrifice of an ox by the Nuer is a surrogate for the sacrifice of a man, and that man and ox are symbolic equivalents. For the Nuer, oxen are the appropriate sacrifice *par excellence*. If there were enough oxen a man might always sacrifice an ox; but there are not enough. Hence, a Nuer will sacrifice a lesser number of livestock or even in some circumstances will bisect a wild cucumber in sacrificial manner. Such a wild cucumber is a symbolic equivalent to an ox. For the Nuer, a cucumber is equivalent to an ox in respect to God who they think accepts it in the place of an ox. Ideologically the position here is very interesting. When a cucumber is so used as a "sacrificial victim" the Nuer speak of it as *yang,* "cow" i.e., normally an ox. Sometimes they appear to regard it as only a temporary substitute, an anticipatory offering in terms of an ox to be sacrificed later on. At other times they appear to regard it as a final substitute. It is spoken of as an ox and, for ritual purposes, an ox it is. The conception of a wild cucumber as an acceptable substitute for an ox involves an attribution to the cucumber of a quality not proper to it in any material sense.

A significant point to an anthropologist, though whether the Nuer clearly perceive it is not brought out, is that a wild cucumber is a most *economical* way of meeting one's *ritual* obligations. In order that what seems to be an expenditure of minimal resources shall be ritually valid, the Nuer have had to enlarge their sacrificial ideology and attribute to the cucumber an arbitrary religious quality. It is not clear from the evidence just how much trouble a person has to take in order to secure a cucumber for sacrifice, but

the inference is that it is not too difficult to find one. It may be suspected that this readiness of the Nuer to compromise in the sacrificial field, and to clothe cucumbers with the attributes of oxen for ritual purposes, is to some degree a reflex of their economic position—in particular their scarcity of oxen—perhaps by reference to their neighbours the Dinka. That in a somewhat analogous situation such a solution does not find favour is seen by the views of the Lugbara, who were incredulous when told of the Nuer practice, and obviously were not prepared to cheat the spirits by such worthless surrogates. The complexity of Nuer thought on this surrogate is indicated by the statement that the Nuer say that a man must make invocation "in truth," and if the sacrifice is to be effective what is said must be true. How they square this with calling a cucumber an ox is not apparent. The Dinka, who also split sacred cucumbers, use them specifically as temporary substitutes for animal victims and as an earnest of intention to provide such a victim when possible.

An interesting variant of this principle of substitution is the Swazi practice of the *licabi.* This is a particularly fine beast which every family priest dedicates to his ancestors. If a sacrifice is to be made the *licabi* animal is driven into the byre with the other cattle and the real victim is shepherded near it to acquire something of its ritual qualities, "so that by proxy the best goes to the dead." But the *licabi* itself serves the role many times; it is not killed until it becomes too old to serve as the display animal. By this practice clearly the proxy which is actually slain can be an inferior animal, thus conserving family resources.

The ideology of symbolic equivalents of things which may be offered in sacrifice may therefore be directly correlated with the problem of allocation of scarce resources. In the last resort the greatest surrogate of all is the sacrifice of the mind and heart, the abnegation of individual judgement and desire in favour of devotion to more general moral ends. Such a substitution is in line with very general trends of ethical and religious interpretation, and the material sacrifices are often regarded as one early developmental phase in a long line of substitutions. One ancient Rabbi is said to have held that the Mosaic laws appertaining to animal sacrifices were primarily designed for the generation of the desert; that burnt offerings were but time-conditioned ways of doing honour to God; that at a later time the sacrifices of righteousness would have precedence over offerings upon the altar. This view is clearly compatible with our modern attitudes towards human personality, but one need not overlook entirely that removal of the notion of sacrifice from the material to the immaterial plane does away with an awkward problem of organization. Readers of Max Weber and of R. H. Tawney do not need to be reminded how an ethical view can emerge side by side with a convenient economic doctrine.

If the elasticity of a surrogate is not possible, then other alternatives may be found. One method is to borrow for a sacrifice. But as Wagner has shown for the Logoli and Evans-Pritchard for the Nuer, this may lead to social difficulties for the borrower. In other words, though obligation is translated from the ritual to the social sphere the economic problem is apt to remain.

Again, the material of a sacrifice can be treated in either of two main ways: by complete destruction or by reservation. In destruction, if solid it can be consumed by fire, by water, or by exposure; if liquid it can be poured away. In reservation, it can be offered to god or spirit and then withdrawn for the consumption of the worshippers. Empirically, this latter seems to be by far the most usual course. Interest in the meat or other ingredients, as much ethnographic evidence shows, may be at least as important an element in attendance at the occasion as interest in the religious aspect of the sacrifice itself. While the sharing of sacrificial food may be a significant ritual act, it is very frequently nothing more than ordinary commensality.

The legitimization of such an economic rebate has very important implications for the practice and the theory of sacrifice. On the one hand it allows the sacrifice to be performed with much greater frequency than would certainly be the case if the sacrificial material was always destroyed. On the other hand it necessitates special beliefs about the manner in which the gods or spirits take their fill. Either they must be satisfied with the killing and display of the sacrificed object, or they must be satisfied to consume its least valuable portions, or to absorb some immaterial aspect or equivalent of it. In other words, the practice of reservation of the sacrificial material for the human participants almost inevitably demands some theory of essences, representations or symbols. Such, for example, is the theory of the Tikopia, who regard all their offerings as having an immaterial, invisible counterpart. They describe the immaterial counterpart in some detail, linking it with analogous spirit counterparts in man, and give it various names according to circumstances. This whole set of notions is part of an integral system of ideas about the meaning of ritual behaviour. When food offerings are set out it is this counterpart, invisible to men, that is thought to be taken away by the gods and spirits, and presumably consumed by them. The Tikopia describe in terms of such spirit action the wilting of fresh vegetable plants such as taro, set up on a grave as an offering to the spirit of the dead. But they are relatively uninterested in the process by which this abstraction of immaterial counterpart is believed to be done. They describe it as being "after the manner of spirits" and leave the subject there.

The point I wish to make here is this. From our Western angle of approach, like Robertson Smith, we probably regard the notion that it is the essence and not the substance of a sacrifice that is consumed by the god or spirit as a more refined idea than the crass belief that the god or spirit actually eats the material bread or meat or drinks the material beer. It may be so. But it is not only more refined; it is also more economical. The point was made essentially by Tylor many years ago. "Through the history of sacrifice it has occurred to many nations that cost may be economised without impairing efficiency. The result is seen in ingenious devices to lighten the burden on the worshipper by substituting something less valuable than what he ought to offer, or pretends to."

I think that one is entitled to say then that even at the heart of primitive religious ideology in such a basically important phenomenon as sacrifice, notions of rationality and prudent calculation enter. In other words, the concepts of sacrifice held by any people must be understood in relation to their notions about control of resources. I want to stress that it is not my argument that concepts of sacrifice can simply be reduced to rational, economic terms. Sacrifice is essentially a symbolic act of grave significance to human personality, and normally has important social components. But my basic point of view here is that, to understand the operations of a religious system even in such a highly symbolic rite as sacrifice, we must consider the implications of organization in men, material and timing of procedures. Much of the effect of these organizational concomitants is seen only in the magnitude and the style of the rites, but their quality, their content and their ideology can also be affected.

I conclude as follows: sacrifice is ultimately a personal act, a giving of the self or a part of the self. The self is represented or symbolized by various types of material object. Such a material object must have social significance or value, or the implication will be that the self is trivial or worthless. Part of the theory of sacrifice then is the giving of a valued object involving some immediate personal loss. In this giving of a valued object there are elements of rational calculation, or organization, of matching material loss against command of material resources, as well as against immaterial or spiritual gain. This element of rational calculation may condition the value or the quality of the object offered. It may also condition the mode of offering, for example by withdrawal of material once offered with the explanation that its essence has been taken. But rational calculation may also condition the ideology of the sacrifice, which may be elaborated in explanation of the particular operation of the offering. Into this field of ideas comes

the notion of the surrogate, of a ram instead of a human being, of a cucumber instead of an ox. These are physical substitutes, but they are often offered instead of a man not only as a physical substitute but also as a moral substitute. This notion interpreted conventionally is that it is not the thing itself but the spirit of the gift that is important. It is the act of giving rather than the gift that matters, that is, the expenditure of time and energy is significant, and beyond this the expenditure of thought and of emotion. But sacrifice as a moral act is a conception at a different level from sacrifice as a material loss.

All this implies that the value of the thing offered is attributed to it only conventionally by virtue of its being selected for offering. This is distinct from the value of the thing in ordinary economic transactions. Granting this, nevertheless one function of such beliefs is that they may allow the retention of objects of economic value. One may serve God without losing touch with Mammon. In the last resort, then, sacrifice in primitive religions is the action of giving up something to which has been allotted an arbitrary or specially circumscribed attribution of value. Communal objects of the highest economic value are regarded as most appropriate for sacrifice. But the use of them represents an equation of decision, the result of the effects of a number of variables in respect of the value put on the self and on its various properties in a specific social milieu. Sacrifice is a critical act for a human personality, but it is an act performed in terms laid down by the evaluations of the society.

ROBERT H. LOWIE

The Vision Quest Among the North American Indians

The vision quest among the Indians and Eskimo of North America was a ritualistic means of acquiring supernatural power through personal contact with the supernatural. But there have been many misunderstandings regarding the quest. As Ruth Fulton Benedict has demonstrated in her authoritative monograph, "The Concept of the Guardian Spirit in North America" (1923), the vision experience was not at all always associated with ac-

Reprinted with permission of McGraw-Hill Book Co., Inc., from *Indians of the Plains*, pp. 157–161, by Robert H. Lowe, published for the American Museum of Natural History by McGraw-Hill Book Co., Inc. Copyright 1954 by the American Museum of Natural History.

quiring a guardian spirit. It was used in California by shamans wishing to effect a cure; among the Montagnais and Mistassini to promote success in a hunt; among the Plains Indians for mourning, war paths, revenge, curing disease, calling the bison, naming a child, acquiring a design, entering a secret society, and so on; power or commands were received directly rather than by acquiring a guardian spirit. Nor was the vision quest, as Hutton Webster supposed, synonymous with the puberty rite; it was not a rite of passage except in certain areas. True, the two often went together, but frequently the vision cycle led only to supernatural power and the puberty rite qualified only for membership in the tribe. The two concepts were remarkably distinct in California. Another mistake is to regard the vision quest as something sought by all young men of the tribe. Some Indians reserved the quest only for shamans seeking a tutelary spirit to be used to punish trespassers on family hunting grounds and to fight with rival shamans in supernatural contests. Often the attempt to induce a vision failed and the individual might resort to acquiring a share in someone else's vision through purchase. It should be remembered, too, that visions were not always sought; west of the Rockies they ordinarily came involuntarily. Benedict has reminded us that guardian spirits could be acquired by means other than a vision. She insists that the vision and not the guardian spirit was the unifying religious fact of North America.

The hallucinatory side of the vision quest is of interest because it supports the hypothesis that religious ritual often affords an opportunity for self-transcendence, either through consciousness-changing drugs, purgatives, self-torture, or fasting. It leads to what is usually referred to as the "religious thrill," which many theorists regard as the source of religion. But while the experience is an individual and solitary one, it is culturally patterned both in the methods for inducing the vision and in the contents which are revealed. It is a socially created ritual, and not one whose genesis is to be sought in the unique experience of the individual.

The account of the vision quest that follows comes from Lowie's considerable field experience with American Indians, especially the Crow. The reader wishing to go beyond the descriptive type of account should consult the article by Benedict mentioned earlier.

Most North American Indians attached great importance to visions, and in the Plains these took precedence in the religious life. However, the spirits did not always appear to their prospective protégé, but might merely become audible to him, issuing instructions and promising definite benefits. In Siberia and parts of western North American supernatural visitants were not sought; in fact, often the spirit compelled a native to accept his guardianship much against the future protégé's wishes. By way of contrast, Woodland and Plains Indians deliberately went out to a lonely spot in order to obtain a revelation. Some Crow individuals received favors unsought when in a predicament. Occasionally it even happened that a spirit came under ordinary circumstances from a pure desire to befriend the mortal. However, the normal procedure was to go into solitude, fast and thirst for four days, and supplicate the spirits to take pity on the sufferer. A Crow usually cut off a finger joint of his left hand or in some other way mortified his flesh by way of arousing supernatural pity.

Certain tribal differences are noteworthy with respect to the vision quest. In the Woodlands, Ojibwa and Winnebago parents regularly instructed boys, possibly not over seven years of age, to fast in order to obtain the blessing of a spirit, and on the Plains the Hidatsa elders likewise prompted their children to seek a revelation at an early age. But no such admonition was customary among the Crow. There a lad grew up, constantly hearing that all success in life was derived from visions; hence, being eager for horses and for social recognition, an adolescent would go out to fast, praying for rich booty, for a chance to strike a coup, or for some other benefit. A mature man or woman would seek a vision whenever a special cause arose—if his children were sick, if he had lost his property, if he longed to revenge the killing of a close relative, and so on. Again, the Arapaho seem to have sought a vision only as adults.

We naturally wonder what really happened on such quests. There is no doubt that the vast majority of informants firmly believed in the reality of the experiences they described. In order to explain this phenomenon psychologically, several factors have to be considered. First of all, the god seeker was usually under a strong emotional impulse—either yearning to shine before his fellows or desiring relief from want or disease or the grief over an unavenged kinsman. By seclusion in a lonely spot, by his fast, by self-mutilation, he naturally intensified his emotional state. What is more, the myths told by his people and the accounts of the supernatural experiences of contemporary tribesmen had left an imprint on his mind and helped to shape the sense impressions that came to him. His longings at the time blended with the visionary pattern of his tribe and with the sounds or sights actually experienced under highly abnormal conditions so as to inspire an interpretation of things seen and heard. Individual peculiarities likewise entered: an Indian of a predominantly auditory type might imagine a whole series of distinguishable sounds—the call of a bird, the rustling of leaves, the neighing of a horse, the speech of an alien tribe, and what not. If his was a decidedly visual type, he would see specific details, as when a would-be raider caught sight of a mount he was to steal—say, a bay horse with docked tail, heavy mane, and a zigzag line painted down its legs. A man who subsequently arranged his sensations for his own enlightenment or to give a clear statement to an audience was in the position of ourselves when trying to give a coherent account of a dream. Without trying to deceive or to invent, he would unconsciously bridge over obscure points, filling in the gaps, adapting his memories of the experience to one of the tribal vision patterns familiar to him from listening to earlier accounts.

A good example of such a pattern is the following. Several Crow informants independently tell how on their lonely vigil they saw a spirit or several spirits riding along, how the rocks and trees in the neighborhood turned into enemies who attacked the horsemen, but were unable to inflict any harm. The symbolical meaning of these apparitions is that the spirits are making the visionary invulnerable. This is, of course, a generally prized blessing, but several persons could not independently conceive the identical image of spiritual riders shot at by transformed bits of the landscape, especially when the very same motif appears also in traditional stories apart from the narration of the teller's personal experiences. Evidently the image, however it may have originated, became part of tribal folklore and was readily worked into the report of their revelations by persons who particularly craved invulnerability. Again, it was certainly a part of the tribal pattern that most Crow Indians obtained their spiritual blessing on the fourth night of their seclusion, four being the mystic number within the area.

The supernatural beings who befriend man vary enormously in character. Animals were very frequent visitants of Plains Indians; buffalo, elk, bears, eagles (sometimes conceived as birds producing thunder by flapping their wings), and sparrow hawks constantly figure in the narratives, but also quite lowly beasts such as dogs or rabbits. A Pawnee legend even describes the invocation of mosquitoes, and according to Cree tradition a mosquito gave one tribesman the gift of chieftaincy. Curious contradictions do not seem to have been recognized as such by the Indians. In a Crow story a rabbit pursued by a hawk promises to give supernatural power to an Indian if he will shield him from the bird of prey. Correspondingly, a Pawnee boy gets supernatural aid from mice who are unable to extricate themselves from a relatively simple difficulty. That is, though animals are possessed of supernatural powers, they may be dependent on mortals for specific services, for which they reward them. Celestial patrons are also frequent, stars figuring prominently among the Pawnee. Fanciful creatures of more or less human shape likewise appear in visions, e.g., a dwarf with a very powerful musculature. Sometimes the patron comes in human guise but in disappearing assumes his true shape or otherwise gives a clue to his identity.

The Crow interpreted the relationship between patron and protégé as that of a father and his child, and accounts of visions often explicitly quote the spirit as pronouncing the formula of adoption: "I will have you for my child." In any case the spirit normally taught the Crow a sacred song, instructed him just how he must dress in battle or if a man was to become a doctor what medicines or curing devices he must use, and frequently imposed certain taboos as to diet or behavior. Any infraction of the rules was liable to precipitate a loss of the guardian's protection or even a dire calamity. Often the visionary not only wore some token of his vision or painted it on, say, his shield cover, but also on the strength of successive visions assembled the ingredients to build up a "medicine bundle," i.e., a wrapper containing a set of sacred objects indicated by the spirit. A Pawnee bundle contained as a minimum one pipe, tobacco, paints, certain birds, and corn—all assembled in a container of buffalo hide that was hung from the wall of the lodge. The opening of a bundle and the treatment of its contents were accompanied by definite rites. As already stated, it is often difficult to tell whether the native consistently considered such objects sacred in their own right, in other words, made them fetishes wholly independent of any personal spirit, or whether they become sacred only as gifts of the spirit; very likely the attitude of a person varied at different times.

If because of visions, one individual worshiped above all a supernatural buffalo, another an eagle, and a third the morning star, the question arises how these several beings ranked in relation to one another. With the Comanche and the Crow this problem arose only when there was a clash of interests between tribesmen, each man falling back on the protection of his own guardian and the issue showing whose patron was the stronger. In the absence of a coherent system of the universe, the religious consciousness assigned priority to individual visitants. Thus, an Indian once told the author that a feather he cherished as memento of his vision of a bird was the greatest thing in the world. At the opposite extreme stood the Pawnee, who had brought their beliefs into a logical system, venerating a Supreme Being named Tirawa, a sky-dwelling creator who rules the universe, his commands being executed by lesser deities. Utterances by Dakota medicine men suggest a similar fondness for metaphysical speculation and integration. A question that remains unanswered is whether the average Pawnee or Dakota individual in his daily life was actually guided by priestly generalizations or whether in practice, without overtly rejecting them, he followed the Crow pattern.

Though all persons coveted a revelation, not all were able to obtain one. Those who did not succeed naturally did not wish to be thereby doomed to failure throughout life. The Crow and some other tribes resolved the dilemma by permitting a successful visionary to sell part of his power to less fortunate tribesmen, adopting them as his supernatural patron had adopted *him,* making for each of his disciples a replica of his sacred paraphernalia, teaching him the sacred songs, and warning against breach of any taboo associated with his medicine.

SIGMUND FREUD

Obsessive Acts and Religious Practices

The probable relationship between the private ritual developed by neurotic individuals to alleviate their anxieties and the religious observances of a society has long been a matter of speculation for students of religion. As Freud recognizes in this selection, he was not the first to be struck by this resemblance. But his thinking on the subject has been most influential, and therefore we include

Reprinted from Sigmund Freud, *Collected Papers,* trans. Joan Rivière (5 vols.; London: Hogarth Press and the Institute of Psycho-Analysis, 1948–1950), II, 25–50), 25–35, by permission of the publishers.

this famous paper which sets forth his theory succinctly with some illustrations of the phenomena.

The problem posed is a difficult one and still far from solution, in part because it is not always clear whether one is noting the resemblance between obsessive acts in neurotics and religious practices in order to develop a theory about the origins of certain rituals in a given society, or whether one is arguing the thesis that whatever the origins (which often cannot be discovered anyway), the rituals serve the function of relieving the major stresses and anxieties felt by the members of a given society. If we focus on the first problem, the best we can say is that it does seem likely that many of the rituals now practiced in a society had their historical origins in the obsessional rituals developed in the lives of one or more individuals and that somehow these became extended to other members of the society and eventually became public ceremonials. But since all known societies already had complicated ceremonial systems by the time they were first studied, it is virtually impossible to reconstruct the necessary data to study this problem. All we can do is to examine the lives of people like Wovoka, whose vision was the point of origin of the 1890 Ghost Dance that swept through the Plains.

The second phrasing of the problem is more likely to be soluble, especially if we use the approach suggested by Kluckhohn, to the effect that we may be able to discover one or more "type anxieties" that are felt by the members of a society and then study the ways in which the ritual system carried by the culture functions to relieve these anxieties.

I am certainly not the first to be struck by the resemblance between what are called "obsessive acts" in neurotics and those religious observances by means of which the faithful give expression to their piety. The name "ceremonial," which has been given to certain of these obsessive acts, is evidence of this. The resemblance, however, seems to me to be something more than superficial, so that an insight into the origin of neurotic ceremonial may embolden us to draw by analogy inferences about the psychological processes of religious life.

Persons who are addicted to obsessive acts or ceremonials belong to the same class as those who suffer from obsessive thoughts and ideas, obsessive impulses and the like, and form with them a definite clinical group, the customary term for which is "obsessional neurosis." But one should not attempt to deduce the character of the disease from its name, for, strictly speaking, there are other morbid psychological phenomena which have an equal claim to the "obsessional character," as it is called. In place of a definition we must for the present be content with a detailed description of these conditions, for it has not yet been possible to demonstrate the essential feature which probably lies at the root of the obsessional neurosis, though one

seems to find indications of it at every turn in clinical manifestations of the disorder.

The neurotic ceremonial consists of little prescriptions, performances, restrictions, and arrangements in certain activities of everyday life which have to be carried out always in the same or in a methodically varied way. These performances make the impression that they are mere "formalities"; they appear quite meaningless to us. Nor do they appear otherwise to the patient himself; yet he is quite incapable of renouncing them, for every neglect of the ceremonial is punished with the most intolerable anxiety, which forces him to perform it instantly. Just as trivial as the ceremonial performances themselves are the occasions which give rise to them, and the kind of actions which are thereby caricatured, hindered, and invariably also delayed, e.g., dressing and undressing, going to bed, and the satisfaction of bodily needs. The carrying out of a ceremonial may be described as the fulfillment of a series of unwritten rules; for example, in the bed ceremonial the chair must stand in a particular place by the bed, and the clothes must be folded and laid upon it in a particular order; the coverlet must be tucked in at the bottom, and the bedclothes evenly spread; the pillows must be arranged in such and such a manner, and the body must lie in a particular position—only when all is correct is it permissible to go to sleep. In slight cases the ceremonial appears to be only an exaggeration of an ordinary and justifiable orderliness, but the remarkable conscientiousness with which it is carried out, and the anxiety which follows its neglect, gives the ceremonial the character of a sacred rite. Any disturbance of it is tolerated with difficulty, and the presence of other persons during the performance of it is almost always out of the question.

Any activities whatsoever may become obsessive acts in a wide sense if they become elaborated by petty modifications or develop a rhythmic character by pauses and repetitions. A sharp distinction between "obsessive acts" and "ceremonials" is not to be expected; as a rule an obsessive act develops from a ceremonial. Besides these, prohibitions and hindrances (abulia) complete the picture of the disorder; the latter only carry further the work of the obsessive acts, for in the one case a certain activity is interdicted altogether, and in the other it is only possible when the patient follows the prescribed ceremonial.

It is remarkable that both compulsions and prohibitions (that one thing must be done and another may not be done) originally relate only to the solitary activities of the persons concerned; for a long time their social activities remain unaffected, so that for many years such patients can treat their affliction as a private matter and hide it from others. Moreover, far more persons suffer from these forms of the obsessional neurosis than ever come to the knowledge of physicians. For many patients, too, concealment is not a difficult matter, because it is quite possible for them to fulfill their social duties during part of the day, after having devoted several hours to their secret perfromances in Melusina-like seclusion.

It is easy to see wherein lies the resemblance between neurotic ceremonial and religious rites; it is in the fear of pangs of conscience after their omission, in the complete isolation of them from all other activities (the feeling that one must not be disturbed), and in the conscientiousness with which the details are carried out. But equally obvious are the differences, some of which are so startling that they make the comparison into a sacrilege: the greater individual variability of neurotic ceremonial in contrast with the stereotyped character of rites (prayer, orientation, etc.); its private nature as opposed to the public and communal character of religious observances; especially, however, the distinction that the little details of religious ceremonies are full of meaning and are understood symbolically, while those of neurotics seem silly and meaningless. In this respect an obsessional neurosis furnishes a tragicomic travesty of a private religion. But this, the sharpest distinction between neurotic and religious ceremonials, disappears as soon as one penetrates by means of psychoanalytic investigation to insight into obsessive actions. By this process the outward appearance of being foolish and meaningless, which is characteristic of obsessive acts, is completely demolished, and the fact of their having this appearance is explained. It is found that obsessive acts are throughout and in all their details full of meaning, that they serve important interests of the personality, and that they give expression both to persisting impressions of previous experiences and to thoughts about them which are strongly charged with affect. This they do in two ways, either by direct or by symbolic representation, so that they are to be interpreted either historically or symbolically.

I must here give a few examples to illustrate these remarks. Those who are familiar with the results of the psychoanalytic investigation of the psychoneuroses will not be surprised to learn that what is expressed in an obsessive act or ceremonial is derived from the most intimate, and for the most part from the sexual, experiences of the patient.

(*a*) A girl of my acquaintance was under the compulsion to rinse out the basin many times after washing. The significance of this ceremonial lay in the proverbial saying, "Don't throw away dirty water until you have clean." The action had the meaning of a warning to her sister, to whom she was much attached, not to separate from her unsatisfactory husband until she had established a relationship with a better man.

(*b*) A woman who was living apart from her husband was subject to a compulsion to leave the best of whatever she ate; for example, she would only take the outside of a piece of roast meat. This renunciation was explained by the date of its origin. It appeared the day after she had refused marital relations with her husband, that is to say, had given up the best.

(c) The same patient could only sit on one particular chair, and could leave it again only with difficulty. In connection with certain details of her married life the chair symbolized to her her husband, to whom she remained faithful. She found the explanation of her compulsion in the sentence, "It is so hard to part from anything (chair or husband) in which one has once settled oneself."

(d) For a long time she used to repeat a very curious and senseless obsessive act. She ran out of her room into the next, in the middle of which stood a table with a cloth upon it. This she pulled straight in a particular manner, rang for the housemaid, who had to approach the table, and then sent her off again on some indifferent errand. During her efforts to explain this compulsion it occurred to her that at one place on the tablecloth there was a stain and that she always arranged the cloth so that the housemaid was bound to see it. The whole scene proved to be a reproduction of an incident in her marriage. On the wedding night her husband had met with a not unusual mishap. He found himself impotent, and "many times in the course of the night came hurrying from his room to hers" in order to try again. In the morning he said he would be shamed in the eyes of the hotel chambermaid who made the bed, so he took a bottle of red ink and poured its contents over the sheet; but he did it so clumsily that the stain came in a place most unsuitable for his purpose. With her obsessive act, therefore, she was reproducing the bridal night. ("Bed and board" indeed comprise marriage.)

(e) She started a compulsion to note the number of each currency-note before parting with it, and this also was to be interpreted historically. At a time when she had still had an intention to leave her husband if she could find a more trustworthy man, she allowed herself to become the object of the attentions of a man she met at a watering place, but was in doubt whether he was altogether in earnest. One day, as she was short of small change, she asked him to change a 5-kronen piece for her. He did so, and put the large coin in his pocket, saying with a gallant air that he would never part with it since it had passed through her hands. At their later meetings she was frequently tempted to challenge him to show her the 5-kronen piece, as if to convince herself that she could believe in his attentions. But she refrained, for the good reason that one cannot distinguish coins of the same value. Her doubts therefore remained unsolved; they left her with a compulsion to note the number of each currency-note by which each one can be distinguished from others of the same value.

These few examples, selected from many I have met with, are intended merely to illustrate the statement that in obsessive acts everything has its meaning and interpretation. The same is true of ceremonials in the strict sense, only that the evidence for this would require a more detailed presentation. I quite realize, however, how far we seem to be getting from any connection between this interpretation of obsessive acts and the line of thought peculiar to religious practices.

It is one of the features of the disease that the person who is affected with a compulsion submits to it without understanding its meaning—or at any rate its chief meaning. It is only under the influence of psychoanalytic treatment that the meaning of the obsessive act, and therewith of the impelling motive underlying it, becomes conscious. We express this important fact by saying that the obsessive act serves to express *unconscious* motives and ideas. Here we seem to find a further departure from religious rites; but we must remember that as a rule the ordinary religious observer carries out a ceremonial without concerning himself with its significance, although priests and investigators may be familiar with its meaning, which is usually symbolic. In all believers, however, the *motives* impelling them to religious practices are unknown, or are replaced in consciousness by others which are advanced in their stead.

The analysis of obsessive acts has already given us some sort of insight into their causes and into the network of motives which bring them to effect. One may say that a sufferer from compulsions and prohibitions behaves as if he were dominated by a sense of guilt, of which, however, he is ignorant—an unconscious sense of guilt, as one must call it in spite of the apparent contradiction in terms. The sense of guilt has its origin in certain early psychological occurrences, but is constantly revived by temptations which are renewed at every present opportunity; it gives rise, moreover, to a state of anxious expectation, or anticipation of misfortune, which through the idea of punishment is linked with the inner perception of temptation. When the compulsion is first being formed, the patient is conscious that he must do this or that lest misfortune occur, and as a rule the nature of the expected misfortune is also recognized in consciousness. But the relation between the occasion which gives rise to this anxiety and the danger to which it refers is already hidden from him, though it it always capable of demonstration. Thus a ceremonial begins as an act of defense or security—as a *protective measure.*

The protestations of the pious that they know they are miserable sinners in their hearts correspond to the sense of guilt of the obsessional neurotic; while the pious observances (prayers, invocations, etc.) with which they begin every act of the day, and especially every unusual undertaking, seem to have the significance of defensive and protective measures.

Deeper insight into the mechanism of the obsessional neurosis is gained when the primary factor underlying it is taken into account: this is always the repression of an impulse (one component of the sexual instinct) which is inherent in the constitution of the person, and which for a while found expression in his childhood but succumbed later to suppression. In course of this repression a special type of conscientiousness directed towards opposing the aim of the impulse is developed; but this mental reaction is felt to be insecure and constantly threatened by the impulse which lurks in the unconscious. The influence of the repressed impulse is felt as a temptation, and anxiety is produced by the process of repression itself, which is dealt with by directing it towards the future in the form of anxious expectation. The process of repression which leads to the obsessional neurosis must be described as imperfectly carried through and as constantly threatening to break down. It may be compared, consequently, with an insoluble conflict; fresh mental efforts are continually required to counterbalance the constant forward pressure of the impulse. Thus the ceremonial and obsessive acts arise partly as a defense against temptation and partly as a protection against the misfortune expected.

Against the temptation the protective measures seem to become rapidly ineffective; then the prohibitions come into play, for these are intended to keep at a distance situations which give rise to temptation. We thus see that prohibitions replace obsessive acts just as a phobia serves to hold off an hysterical attack. From another point of view a ceremonial represents the sum of all the conditions under which something not yet absolutely forbidden becomes permissible, just as the marriage ceremony of the Church signifies a sanction of sexual enjoyment, which is otherwise sinful. It is in the nature, moreover, of the obsessional neurosis—as of all similar affections—that its manifestations (symptoms, including also the obsessive acts) fulfill the condition of a compromise between the opposing forces in the mind. Thus they always reproduce something of the identical pleasure they were designed to prevent; they serve the repressed impulse no less than the repressing element. Indeed, as the disease develops the performances which at first were concerned chiefly with defense approximate ever more and more nearly to those proscribed actions in which the impulse was able to find an outlet in childhood.

This state of things has some counterparts in the sphere of religious life, as follows: the structure of a religion seems also to be founded on the suppression or renunciation of certain instinctual trends; these trends are not, however, as in the neurosis, exclusively components of the sexual instinct, but are egoistic, antisocial instincts, though even these for the most part are not without a sexual element. The sense of guilt in consequence of continual temptation, and the anxious expectation in the guise of fear of divine punishment, have indeed been familiar to us in religion longer than in neurosis. Possibly on account of the sexual elements which are also involved, possibly on account of some characteristic of instincts in general, the suppression active in religion proves here also to be neither completely effective nor final. Unredeemed backslidings into sin are even more common among the pious than among neurotics, and these give rise to a new form of religious activity; namely, the acts of penance of which one finds counterparts in the obsessional neurosis.

We saw a curious feature of the obsessional neurosis, one that seems to render it unworthy and trivial, in the fact that these ceremonials are concerned with such petty performances of daily life, and are expressed in foolish regulations and restrictions in regard to them. One first understands this remarkable feature of the clinical picture when one finds that the mechanism of the psychical displacement, which I first discovered in the formation of dreams, dominates the mental processes in the obsessional neurosis. It is already clear from the few examples of obsessive acts given above that their symbolism and the details of their execution are effected as if by a displacement from the actual important thing on to an insignificant one which replaces it, e.g., from the husband to the chair. It is this tendency to displacement which progressively changes the clinical picture of the symptoms, and eventually succeeds in turning apparently trivial matters into those of great and urgent importance. It cannot be denied that in the religious sphere also there is a similar tendency to a displacement of psychical values, and indeed in the same direction, so that petty ceremonials gradually become the essence of religious practices, and replace the ideas underlying them. It is for this reason that religions are subject to retroactive reforms which aim at the re-establishment of the original relative values.

The element of compromise in those obsessive acts which we find as neurotic symptoms is the feature least easy to find reproduced in corresponding religious observances. Yet here, too, one is reminded of this trait in the neurosis when one recalls how commonly all those acts which religion forbids—expressions of the instincts it represses—are yet committed precisely in the name of, and ostensibly in the cause of, religion.

In view of these resemblances and analogies one might venture to regard the obsessional neurosis as a pathological counterpart to the formation of a religion, to describe this neurosis as a private religious system, and religion as a universal obsessional neurosis. The essential resemblance would lie in the fundamental renunciation of the satisfaction of inherent instincts, and the chief difference in the nature of these instincts, which in the neurosis are exclusively sexual, but in religion are of egoistic origin.

A progressive renunciation of inherent instincts, the satisfaction of which is capable of giving direct pleasure to ego, appears to be one of the foundations of human civilization. Some part of this repression is effected by means of the various religions, in that they require individuals to sacrifice the satisfaction of their instincts to the divinity. "Vengeance is mine, saith the Lord." In the development of the ancient religions one seems to find that many things which mankind had renounced as wicked were surrendered in favor of the god, and were still permitted in his name; so that a yielding up of evil and asocial impulses to the divinity was the means by which man freed himself from them. For this reason it is surely no accident that all human characteristics—along with the crimes they prompt—were freely attributed to the ancient gods, and no anomaly that it was nevertheless not permissible to justify one's own misdeeds by reference to divine example.

CHAPTER 4

SYMBOLISM

INTRODUCTION

Man is a cultural being, which in essence means that he is a symbol-using animal. Indeed, his capacity to symbolize has often been given as a criterion placing him apart from the beasts. Language may be the most important kind of symbolization but it is not the only one. It has been said that religion may be viewed as a vast symbolic system, as indeed it may, and it is to this possibility that the present chapter addresses itself.

Reduced to its barest essentials, a symbol may be defined as something which stands for or represents something else. The idea of conventionality is implicit in the symbol. It is a sign that has been combined with a meaning. Rites and myths are of course the most obvious of religious symbols, and are usually, but not always, as we saw in Chapter 3, combined with one another. One may think of a myth as a verbal system expressing an inner system of sacred beliefs and values. When combined with a collective ritual it symbolically and overtly expresses the feelings and beliefs portrayed in the myth. It has been said that whatever is important in social life becomes the object of symbolic expression and will receive ritual attention. The collective rite is thus any social behavior intended to express a certain meaning which the group concerned feels is important. The forms taken by ritual symbols are numerous, consisting, for example, of places, things, animals, meteorological phenomena,

persons, and human relations, but always they must have meaningful contexts.

One could argue that man has a need for symbolization because it makes thought infinitely more possible and efficient. Writing with the "hero" in mind, Warner has said, "Abstract principles, precepts, and moral judgments are more easily felt and understood, and more highly valued, when met in a human being endowed with a symbolic form that expresses them" (1959, p. 14). If this is so, then the need for the symbolization of man's fears, hopes, insecurities, beliefs, values, and goals is at once apparent. They are best comprehended in terms of religion, which objectifies them through the medium of gods, sacred objects, myths, and rituals. The human mind comprehends ideas better when they are expressed in visual and auditory symbols, and responds more quickly to such symbols as stimuli. Religious symbols are not truly rational for they do not refer to meanings that belong to the ordinary workaday world or to referential and scientific concepts. They are "evocative," which is to say, nonrational, expressive, and emotional, arousing memories of past experiences vital to the social group. Such symbols condense and evoke in an effective manner not possible without symbols. Another function of symbols, mentioned by Kluckhohn in the previous chapter (p. 149). is that by expressing those realms of behavior and experience which he finds beyond rational and technological control, man feels he can manipulate them through the symbols.

Much of the explicit analysis of religious symbolism stems from the great work by Ogden and Richards, *The Meaning of Meaning* (1923, etc.), which dealt with the influence of symbols of all kinds on human affairs. Malinowski was greatly influenced by this volume and wrote an important supplement for one of the later editions. Perhaps W. Lloyd Warner was the first to make close utilization of the book, as he acknowledges in his *A Black Civilization* (1937), wherein he devotes considerable attention to the symbolic logic of Murngin myth and ritual. Warner has continued in his interest in symbol, as evidenced in his work *The Living and the Dead: A Study of the Symbolic Life of Americans* (1959), which was later published in revised form as a paperback, *The Family of God* (1961). However, he has incorporated much of the thinking of Durkheim and Radcliffe-Brown in his analyses. The latter's work *The Andaman Islanders* (1922) is mainly an effort to demonstrate that myths and rituals are essentially symbolic expressions of the common social sentiments upon which a society depends for its existence. Of course there have been other influences on social anthropologists, among them that of Alfred North Whitehead (*Symbolism*, 1927).

The subject of symbolism in religion is so vast that we are unable to include selections that are representative of important collective representations. It would have been desirable, for instance, to have illustrated the symbols of the Roman Catholic faith and its Mass. For the interested reader there is a little book by Dietrich von Hildebrand, *In Defense of Purity* (1935), which lays particular stress on the theme that the virgin is the Bride of Christ, as is indeed the priest and the Church itself. The liturgy of the Church is the subject of a highly authoritative work by Joseph A. Jungmann, *The Mass of the Roman Rite* (1961). Of a different sort is the study by W. H. Rassers, "On the Javanese Kris," which unfolds the complicated religious and social meanings attached to the Indonesian serpentine dagger, especially as an expression of dualism. But we must call a halt at this point, before the list of possibilities themselves becomes too lengthy.

The selections in this chapter are far ranging and represent varied approaches, including what might be termed functional, psychoanalytic, structural, and nonprofessional. Scattered throughout this book are other selections which might easily have been included here, which need not be surprising if we are right in our contention that the whole subject of religion can be seen symbolically.

CLIFFORD GEERTZ

Religion as a Cultural System

Man, says Professor Geertz in this splendidly written interpretation of religion as a symbolic system, is confronted with the constant impingement upon him of certain chaotic forces that give him a sense of analytic, emotional, and moral impotence. The first involves *ignorance*—bafflement in the face of his limited analytic ability to explain anomalous events; the second involves *pain*—making suffering sufferable when he can no longer endure; and the third involves *injustice*—coping with a sense of ethical paradox when he reaches the limits of his moral insight. The affirmation of these forces, as well as the denial that they are character-

Reprinted in greatly abridged form from Michael Banton (ed.), *Anthropological Approaches to the Study of Religion* ("Association of Social Anthropologists Monographs," No. 3 [London: Tavistock Publications, 1965]), by permission of the Association of Social Anthropologists, the publisher, and the author. The complete monograph is published in the United States by Frederick A. Praeger (1966).

istic of the world in general, is made in terms of religious symbolism.

For Geertz, a symbol means any object, act, event, quality, or relation that serves as a vehicle for a conception, the conception being the symbol's meaning. Cultural patterns are of course symbolic systems, religious symbols being those that induce and define dispositions in man. Geertz's aim is to demonstrate that sacred symbols deal with bafflement, pain, and moral paradox by synthesizing a people's ethos and their world view. The ethos of the group is rendered intellectually more reasonable by religious belief and practice. If man's denial of chaos comes to be believed in it is because of the special perspective of religion, which goes outside the realities of daily life to wider realities that complete them in a context of faith. Ritual is a powerful means for providing the conviction that religious concepts are truthful and that religious directives are sound, and the latter effective because they induce moods and motivations. They help make the group's ethos intellectually reasonable.

This article, which must be read in its unabridged form for substantiation of many of the author's premises, is at once both an interpretation of the role of symbolism and an appreciation of the importance of religion in transcending the chaos that threatens man.

Any attempt to speak without speaking any particular language is not more hopeless than the attempt to have a religion that shall be no religion in particular. . . . Thus every living and healthy religion has a marked idiosyncrasy. its power consists in its special and surprising message and in the bias which that revelation gives to life. The vistas it opens and the mysteries it propounds are another world to live in; and another world to live in—whether we expect ever to pass wholly over into it or no— is what we mean by having a religion.

—Santayana: *Reason in Religion* (1906)

As we are to deal with meaning, let us begin with a paradigm: *viz.,* that sacred symbols function to synthesize a people's ethos—the tone, character and quality of their life, its moral and aesthetic style and mood—and their world-view—the picture they have of the way things in sheer actuality are, their most comprehensive ideas of order. In religious belief and practice a group's ethos is rendered intellectually reasonable by being shown to represent a way of life ideally adapted to the actual state of affairs the world-view describes, while the world-view is rendered emotionally convincing by being presented as an image of an actual state of affairs peculiarly well-arranged to accommodate such a way of life. This confrontation and mutual confirmation has two fundamental effects. On the one hand, it objectivises moral and aesthetic preferences by depicting them as the imposed conditions of life implicit in a world with a particular structure, as mere common sense given the unalterable shape of reality. On the other, it supports these received beliefs about the world's body by invoking deeply felt moral and aesthetic sentiments as experiential evidence for their truth. Religious symbols formulate a basic congruence between a particular style of life and a specific (if, most often, implicit) metaphysic, and in so doing sustain each with the borrowed authority of the other.

Phrasing aside, this much may perhaps be granted. The notion that religion tunes human actions to an envisaged cosmic order and projects images of cosmic order onto the plane of human experience is hardly novel. But it is hardly investigated either, so that we have very little idea of how, in empirical terms, this particular miracle is accomplished. We just know that it is done, annually, weekly, daily, for some people almost hourly; and we have an enormous ethnographic literature to demonstrate it. But the theoretical framework which would enable us to provide an analytic account of it, an account of the sort we can provide for lineage segmentation, political succession, labor exchange or the socialization of the child, does not exist.

Let us, therefore, reduce our paradigm to a definition, for although it is notorious that definitions establish nothing in themselves they do, if they are carefully enough con-

structed, provide a useful orientation, or reorientation, of thought, such that an extended unpacking of them can be an effective
way of developing and controlling a novel
line of inquiry. They have the useful virtue
of explicitness : they commit themselves in a
way discursive prose, which, in this field especially, is always liable to substitute rhetoric for argument, does not. Without ado,
then, a *religion* is :

(1) a system of symbols which acts to (2)
establish powerful, pervasive and long-last-
ing moods and motivations in men by (3)
formulating conceptions of a general order
of existence and (4) clothing these conceptions with such an aura of factuality that (5)
the moods and motivations seem uniquely
realistic.

1. . . . A SYSTEM OF SYMBOLS WHICH ACTS TO . . .

Such a tremendous weight is being put on
the term "symbol" here that our first move
must be to decide with some precision what
we are going to mean by it. This is no easy
task, for, rather like "culture," "symbol" has
been used to refer to a great variety of
things, often a number of them at the same
time. In some hands it is used for anything
which signifies something else to someone :
dark clouds are the symbolic precursors of
an oncoming rain. In others it is used only
for explicitly conventional signs of one sort
or another : a red flag is a symbol of danger,
a white of surrender. In others, it is confined
to something which expresses in an oblique
and figurative manner that which cannot be
stated in a direct and literal one, so that
there are symbols in poetry but not in science, and symbolic logic is misnamed. In yet
others, however, it is used for any object,
act, event, quality or relation which serves
as a vehicle for a conception—the conception
is the symbol's "meaning"—and that is the
approach I shall follow here. The number
"6," written, imagined, laid out as a row of
stones, or even punched into the program
tapes of a computer is a symbol. But so also
is the Cross, talked about, visualized, shaped
worriedly in air or fondly fingered at the
neck, the expanse of painted canvas called
"Guernica" or the bit of painted stone called
a churinga, the word "reality," or even the
morpheme "-ing." They are all symbols, or
at least symbolic elements, because they are

tangible formulations or notions, abstractions from experience fixed in perceptible
forms, concrete embodiments of ideas, attitudes, judgments, longings or beliefs. To
undertake the study of cultural activity—
activity in which symbolism forms the positive content—is thus not to abandon social
analysis for a Platonic cave of shadows, to
enter into a mentalistic world of introspec-
tive psychology or, worse, speculative philosophy and wander there forever in a haze
of "Cognitions," "Affections," "Conations"
and other elusive entities. Cultural acts, the
construction, apprehension and utilization of
symbolic forms, are social events like any
other ; they are as public as marriage and as
observable as agriculture.

They are not, however, exactly the same
thing ; or, more precisely, the symbolic dimension of social events is, like the psychological, itself theoretically abstractable
from those events as empirical totalities.
There is still, to paraphrase a remark of
Kenneth Burke's, a difference between building a house and drawing up a plan for building a house, and reading a poem about
having children by marriage is not quite the
same thing as having children by marriage.
Even though the building of the house may
proceed under the guidance of the plan or—
a less likely occurrence—the having of children may be motivated by a reading of the
poem, there is something to be said for not
confusing our traffic with symbols with our
traffic with objects or human beings, for
these latter are not in themselves symbols,
however often they may function as such.
No matter how deeply interfused the cultural, the social and the psychological may
be in the everyday life of houses, farms,
poems and marriages, it is useful to distinguish them in analysis, and, so doing, to isolate the generic traits of each against the
normalized background of the other two.

So far as culture patterns, i.e., systems or
complexes of symbols, are concerned, the
generic trait which is of first importance for
us here is that they are extrinsic sources of
information. By "extrinsic," I mean only
that—unlike genes, for example—they lie
outside the boundaries of the individual organism as such in that intersubjective world
of common understandings into which all
human individuals are born, pursue their
separate careers, and leave persisting behind
them after they die. By "sources of informa-

tion," I mean only that—like genes—they provide a blueprint or template in terms of which processes external to themselves can be given a definite form. As the order of bases in a strand of DNA forms a coded program, a set of instructions or a recipe, for the synthesization of the structurally complex proteins which shape organic functioning, so culture patterns provide such programs for the institution of the social and psychological processes which shape public behavior. Though the sort of information and the mode of its transmission are vastly different in the two cases, this comparison of gene and symbol is more than a strained analogy of the familiar "social heredity" sort. It is actually a substantial relationship, for it is precisely the fact that genetically programmed processes are so highly generalized in men, as compared with lower animals, that culturally programmed ones are so important, only because human behavior is so loosely determined by intrinsic sources of information that extrinsic sources are so vital. To build a dam a beaver needs only an appropriate site and the proper materials—his mode of procedure is shaped by his physiology. But man, whose genes are silent on the building trades, needs also a conception of what it is to build a dam, a conception he can get only from some symbolic source—a blueprint, a textbook or a string of speech by someone who already knows how dams are built, or, of course, from manipulating graphic or linguistic elements in such a way as to attain for himself a conception of what dams are and how they are built.

This point is sometimes put in the form of an argument that cultural patterns are "models," that they are sets of symbols whose relations to one another "model" relations among entities, processes or what-have-you in physical, organic, social or psychological systems by "paralleling," "imitating" or "simulating" them. The term "model" has, however, two senses—an "of" sense and a "for" sense—and though these are but aspects of the same basic concept they are very much worth distinguishing for analytic purposes. In the first, what is stressed is the manipulation of symbol structures so as to bring them, more or less closely, into parallel with the preestablished non-symbolic system, as when we grasp how dams work by developing a theory of hydraulics or construct-

ing a flow chart. The theory or chart models physical relationships in such a way—i.e., by expressing their structure in synoptic form—as to render them apprehensible: it is a model *of* "reality." In the second, what is stressed is the manipulation of the non-symbolic systems in terms of the relationships expressed in the symbolic, as when we construct a dam according to the specifications implied in an hydraulic theory or the conclusions drawn from a flow chart. Here, the theory is a model under whose guidance physical relationships are organized: it is a model *for* "reality." For psychological and social systems, and for cultural models that we would not ordinarily refer to as "theories," but rather as "doctrines," "melodies" or "rites," the case is in no way different. Unlike genes, and other non-symbolic information sources, which are only models *for,* not models *of,* culture patterns have an intrinsic double aspect: they give meaning, i.e., objective conceptual form, to social and psychological reality both by shaping themselves to it and by shaping it to themselves.

It is, in fact, this double aspect which sets true symbols off from other sorts of significative forms. Models *for* are found, as the gene example suggests, through the whole order of nature, for wherever there is a communication of pattern such programs are, in simple logic, required. Among animals, imprint learning is perhaps the most striking example, because what such learning involves is the automatic presentation of an appropriate sequence of behavior by a model animal in the presence of a learning animal which serves, equally automatically, to call out and stabilize a certain set of responses genetically built into the learning animal. The communicative dance of two bees, one of which has found nectar and the other of which seeks it, is another, somewhat different more complexly coded, example. Craik has even suggested that the thin trickle of water which first finds its way down from a mountain spring to the sea and smoothes a little channel for the greater volume of water which follows after it plays a sort of model *for* function. But models *of*—linguistic, graphic, mechanical, natural, etc., processes which function not to provide sources of information in terms of which other processes can be patterned, but to represent those patterned processes as such, to express their structure in an alternative medium—are much rarer and may perhaps be confined, among living animals, to man. The perception of the structural congruence between one set of processes, activities, relations, entities, etc., and another set for which it acts as a program, so that the program can be taken as a representation, or conception—a symbol—of the programmed, is the essence of human thought. The inter-transposability of models *for* and models *of* of which symbolic formulation makes possible is the distinctive characteristic of our mentality.

2. . . . TO ESTABLISH POWERFUL, PERVASIVE AND LONG-LASTING MOODS AND MOTIVATIONS IN MEN BY . . .

So far as religious symbols and symbol systems are concerned this inter-transposability is clear. The endurance, courage, independence, perseverance and passionate willfulness in which the vision quest practices the Plains Indian are the same flamboyant virtues by which he attempts to live: while achieving a sense of revelation he stabilizes a sense of direction. The consciousness of defaulted obligation, secreted guilt and, when a confession is obtained, public shame in which [a] Manus' seance rehearses him are the same sentiments that underlie the sort of duty ethic by which his property-conscious society is maintained: the gaining of an absolution involves the forging of a conscience. And the same self-discipline which rewards a Javanese mystic staring fixedly into the flame of a lamp with what he takes to be an intimation of divinity drills him in that rigorous control of emotional expression which is necessary to a man who would follow a quietistic style of life. Whether one sees the conception of a personal guardian spirit, a family tutelary or an immanent God as synoptic formulations of the character of reality or as templates for producing reality with such a character seems largely arbitrary, a matter of which aspect, the model *of* or model *for,* one wants for the moment to bring into focus. The concrete symbols involved—one or another mythological figure materializing in the wilderness, the skull of the deceased household head hanging censoriously in the rafters, or a disembodied "voice in the stillness" soundlessly chanting enigmatic classical poetry—point in either direction.

They both express the world's climate and shape it.

They shape it by inducing in the worshipper a certain distinctive set of dispositions which lend a chronic character to the flow of his activity and the quality of his experience. A disposition describes not an activity or an occurrence but a probability of an activity being performed or an occurrence occurring under certain circumstances: "When a cow is said to be a ruminant, or a man is said to be a cigarette smoker, it is not being said that the cow is ruminating now or that the man is smoking a cigarette now. To be a ruminant is to tend to ruminate from time to time, and to be a cigarette-smoker is to be in the habit of smoking cigarettes." Similarly, to be pious is not to be performing something we would call an act of piety, but to be liable to perform such acts. So, too, with the Plains Indian's bravura, the Manus' compunctiousness or the Javanese's quietism which, in their contexts, form the substance of piety. The virtue of this sort of view of what are usually called "mental traits" or, if the Cartesianism is unavowed, "psychological forces" (both unobjectionable enough terms in themselves) is that it gets them out of any dim and inaccessible realm of private sensation into that same well-lit world of observables in which reside the brittleness of glass, the inflammability of paper and, to return to the metaphor, the dampness of England.

So far as religious activities are concerned (and learning a myth by heart is as much a religious activity as detaching one's finger at the knuckle), two somewhat different sorts of dispositions are induced by them: moods and motivations.

The major difference between moods and motivations is that where the latter are, so to speak, vectorial qualities, the former are merely scalar. Motives have a directional cast, they describe a certain overall course, gravitate toward certain, usually temporary, consummations. But moods vary only as to intensity: they go nowhere. They spring from certain circumstances but they are responsive to no ends. Like fogs, they just settle and lift; like scents, suffuse and evaporate. When present they are totalistic: if one is sad everything and everybody seems dreary; if one is gay, everything and everybody seems splendid. Thus, though a man can be vain, brave, willful and independent at the same time, he can't very well be playful and listless, or exultant and melancholy at the same time. Further, where motives persist for more or less extended periods of time, moods merely recur with greater or lesser frequency, coming and going for what are often quite unfathomable reasons. But perhaps the most important difference, so far as we are concerned, between moods and motivations is that motivations are "made meaningful" with reference to the ends toward which they are conceived to conduce, while moods are "made meaningful" with reference to the conditions from which they are conceived to spring. We interpret motives in terms of their consummations, but we interpret moods in terms of their sources. We say that a person is industrious because he wishes to succeed, we say that a person is worried because he is conscious of the hanging threat of nuclear holocaust. And this is no less the case when the interpretations invoked are ultimate. Charity becomes Christian charity when it is enclosed in a conception of God's purposes; optimism is Christian optimism when it is grounded in a particular conception of God's nature. The assiduity of the Navaho finds its rationale in a belief that, as "reality" operates mechanically, it is coercible; their chronic fearfulness finds its rationale in a conviction that, however "reality" operates, it is both enormously powerful and terribly dangerous.

3. . . . BY FORMULATING CONCEPTIONS OF A GENERAL ORDER OF EXISTENCE AND . . .

That the symbols or symbol systems which induce and define dispositions we set off as religious and those which place those dispositions in a cosmic framework are the same symbols ought to occasion no surprise. For what else do we mean by saying that a particular mood of awe is religious and not secular except that it springs from entertaining a conception of all-pervading vitality like mana and not from a visit to the Grand Canyon? Or that a particular case of asceticism is an example of a religious motivation except that it is directed toward the achievement of an unconditioned end like nirvana and not a conditioned one like weight-reduction? If sacred symbols did not at one and the same time, induce dispositions in human beings and formulate, however obliquely, inarticulately or unsystematically, general

ideas of order, then the empirical differentia of religious activity or religious experience would not exist. A man can indeed be said to be "religious" about golf, but not merely if he pursues it with passion and plays it on Sundays: he must also see it as symbolic of some transcendent truths. And the pubescent boy gazing soulfully into the eyes of the pubescent girl in a William Steig cartoon and murmuring, "there is something about you, Ethel, which gives me a sort of religious feeling," is, like most adolescents, confused. What any particular religion affirms about the fundamental nature of reality may be obscure, shallow or, all too often, perverse, but it must, if it is not to consist of the mere collection of received practices and conventional sentiments we usually refer to as moralism, affirm something. If one were to essay a minimal definition of religion today it would perhaps not be Tylor's famous "belief in spiritual beings," to which Goody, wearied of theoretical subtleties, has lately urged us to return, but rather what Salvador de Madariaga has called "the relatively modest dogma that God is not mad."

Usually, of course, religions affirm very much more than this: we believe, as James remarked, all that we can and would believe everything if we only could. The thing we seem least able to tolerate is a threat to our powers of conception, a suggestion that our ability to create, grasp and use symbols may fail us, for were this to happen we would be more helpless, as I have already pointed out, than the beavers. The extreme generality, diffuseness and variability of man's innate (i.e., genetically programmed) response capacities means that without the assistance of cultural patterns he would be functionally incomplete, not merely a talented ape who had, like some under-privileged child, unfortunately been prevented from realizing his full potentialities, but a kind of formless monster with neither sense of direction nor power of self-control, a chaos of spasmodic impulses and vague emotions. Man depends upon symbols and symbol systems with a dependence so great as to be decisive for his creatural viability and, as a result, his sensitivity to even the remotest indication that they may prove unable to cope with one or another aspect of experience raises within him the gravest sort of anxiety.

There are at least three points where chaos—a tumult of events which lack not just interpretations but *interpretability*—threatens to break in upon man : at the limits of his analytic capacities, at the limits of his powers of endurance, and at the limits of his moral insight. Bafflement, suffering and a sense of intractable ethical paradox are all, if they become intense enough or are sustained long enough, radical challenges to the proposition that life is comprehensible and that we can, by taking thought, orient ourselves effectively within it—challenges with which any religion, however "primitive," which hopes to persist must attempt somehow to cope.

Of the three issues, it is the first which has been least investigated by modern social anthropologists (though Evans-Pritchard's classic discussion of why granaries fall on some Azande and not on others, is a notable exception). Even to consider people's religious beliefs as attempts to bring anomalous events or experiences—death, dreams, mental fugues, volcanic eruptions or marital infidelity—within the circle of the at least potentially inexplicable seems to smack of Tyloreanism or worse. But it does appear to be a fact that at least some men—in all probability, most men—are unable to leave unclarified problems of analysis merely unclarified, just to look at the stranger features of the world's landscape in dumb astonishment or bland apathy without trying to develop, however fantastic, inconsistent or simpleminded, some notions as to how such features might be reconciled with the more ordinary deliverances of experience. Any chronic failure of one's explanatory apparatus, the complex of received culture patterns (common sense, science, philosophical speculation, myth) one has for mapping the empirical world, to explain things which cry out for explanation, tends to lead to a deep disquiet—a tendency rather more widespread and a disquiet rather deeper than we have sometimes supposed since the pseudoscience view of religious belief was, quite rightfully, deposed. After all, even that high priest of heroic atheism, Lord Russell, once remarked that although the problem of the existence of God had never bothered him, the ambiguity of certain mathematical axioms had threatened to unhinge his mind. And Einstein's profound dissatisfaction with quantum mechanics was based on a—surely religious—inability to believe that, as he put it, God plays dice with the universe.

But this quest for lucidity and the rush of metaphysical anxiety that occurs when empirical phenomena threaten to remain intransigently opaque is found on much humbler intellectual levels. Certainly, I was struck in my own work, much more than I had at all expected to be by the degree to which my more animistically inclined informants behaved like true Tyloreans. They seemed to be constantly using their beliefs to "explain" phenomena : or, more accurately, to convince themselves that the phenomena were explainable within the accepted scheme of things, for they commonly had only a minimal attachment to the particular soul possession, emotional disequilibrium, taboo infringement or bewitchment hypothesis they advanced and were all too ready to abandon it for some other, in the same genre, which struck them as more plausible given the facts of the case. What they were *not* ready to do was abandon it for no other hypothesis at all ; to leave events to themselves.

The second experiential challenge in whose face the meaningfulness of a particular pattern of life threatens to dissolve into a chaos of thingless names and nameless things—the problem of suffering—has been rather more investigated, or at least described, mainly because of the great amount of attention given in works on tribal religion to what are perhaps its two main loci : illness and mourning. Yet for all the fascinated interest in the emotional aura which surrounds these extreme situations, there has been, with a few exceptions such as Lienhardt's recent discussion of Dinka divining, little conceptual advance over the sort of crude confidence type theory set forth by Malinowski : *viz.,* that religion helps one to endure "situations of emotional stress" by "open [ing] up escapes from such situations and such impasses as offer no empirical way out except by ritual and belief into the domain of the supernatural." The inadequacy of this "theology of optimism," as Nadel rather drily called it, is, of course, radical. Over its career religion has probably disturbed men as much as it has cheered them ; forced them into a head-on, unblinking confrontation of the fact that they are born to trouble as often as it has enabled them to avoid such a confrontation by projecting them into sort of infantile fairy-tale world where—Malinowski again—"hope cannot fail nor desire deceive." With the possible exception of Christian Science, there are few if any religious traditions, "great" or "little," in which the proposition that life hurts is not strenuously affirmed and in some it is virtually glorified.

As a religious problem, the problem of suffering is, paradoxically, not how to avoid suffering but how to suffer, how to make of physical pain, personal loss, worldly defeat or the helpless contemplation of others' agony something bearable, supportable— something, as we say, sufferable.

The problem of suffering passes easily into the problem of evil, for it suffering is severe enough it usually, though not always, seems morally undeserved as well, at least to the sufferer. But they are not, however, exactly the same thing—a fact I think Weber, too influenced by the biases of a monotheistic tradition in which, as the various aspects of human experience must be conceived to proceed from a single, voluntaristic source, man's pain reflects directly on God's goodness, did not fully recognize in his generalization of the dilemmas of Christian theodicy Eastward. For where the problem of suffering is concerned with threats to our ability to put our "undisciplined squads of emotion" into some sort of soldierly order, the problem of evil is concerned with threats to our ability to make sound moral judgments. What is involved in the problem of evil is not the adequacy of our symbolic resources to govern our affective life, but the adequacy of those resources to provide a workable set of ethical criteria, normative guides to govern our action. The vexation here is the gap between things as they are and as they ought to be if our conceptions of right and wrong make sense, the gap between what we deem various individuals deserve and what we see that they get—a phenomenon summed up in that profound quatrain:

The rain falls on the just
And on the unjust fella;
But mainly upon the just,
Because the unjust has the just's umbrella.

Or if this seems too flippant an expression of an issue that, in somewhat different form, animates the Book of Job and the Baghavad Gita, the following classical Javanese poem, known, sung, and repeatedly quoted in Java by virtually everyone over the age of six, puts the point—the discrepancy between moral prescriptions and material rewards,

the seeming inconsistency of "is" and "ought"—rather more elegantly:

We have lived to see a time without order
In which everyone is confused in his mind.
One cannot bear to join in the madness,
But if he does not do so
He will not share in the spoils,
And will starve as a result.
Yes, God; wrong is wrong:
Happy are those who forget,
Happier yet those who remember and have deep insight.

The problem of evil, or perhaps one should say the problem *about* evil, is in essence the same sort of problem of or about bafflement and the problem of or about suffering. The strange opacity of certain empirical events, the dumb senselessness of intense or inexorable pain, and the enigmatic unaccountability of gross iniquity all raise the uncomfortable suspicion that perhaps the world, and hence man's life in the world, has no genuine order at all—no empirical regularity, no emotional form, no moral coherence. And the religious response to this suspicion is in each case the same: the formulation, by means of symbols, of an image of such a genuine order of the world which will account for, and even celebrate, the perceived ambiguities, puzzles and paradoxes in human experience. The effort is not to deny the undeniable—that there are unexplained events, that life hurts or that rain falls upon the just—but to deny that there are inexplicable events, that life is unendurable and that justice is a mirage. The principles which constitute the moral order may indeed often elude men in the same way as fully satisfactory explanations of anomalous events or effective forms for the expression of feeling often elude them. What is important, to a religious man at least, is that this elusiveness be accounted for, that it be not the result of the fact that there are no such principles, explanations or forms, that life is a surd and the attempt to make moral, intellectual or emotional sense out of experience is bootless.

The Problem of Meaning in each of its intergrading aspects (how these aspects in fact intergrade in each particular case, what sort of interplay there is between the sense of analytic, emotional and moral impotence, seems to me one of the outstanding, and except for Weber untouched, problems for comparative research in this whole field) is a matter of affirming, or at least recognizing, the inescapability of ignorance, pain and injustice on the human plane while simultaneously denying that these irrationalities are characteristic of the world as a whole. And it is in terms of religious symbolism, a symbolism relating man's sphere of existence to a wider sphere within which it is conceived to rest, that both the affirmation and the denial are made.

4. . . . AND CLOTHING THOSE CONCEPTIONS WITH SUCH AN AURA OF FACTUALITY THAT . . .

There arises here, however, a profounder question: how is it that this denial comes to be believed? how is it that the religious man moves from a troubled perception of experienced disorder to a more or less settled conviction of fundamental order? just what does "belief" mean in a religious context? Of all the problems surrounding attempts to conduct anthropological analysis of religion this is the one that has perhaps been most troublesome and therefore the most often avoided, usually by relegating it to psychology, that raffish outcast discipline to which social anthropologists are forever consigning phenomena they are unable to deal with within the framework of a denatured Durkheimianism. But the problem will not go away, it is not "merely" psychological (nothing social is), and no anthropological theory of religion which fails to attack it is worthy of the name. We have been trying to stage Hamlet without the Prince quite long enough.

It seems to me that it is best to begin any approach to this issue with frank recognition that religious belief involves not a Baconian induction from everyday experience—for then we should all be agnostics—but rather a prior acceptance of authority which transforms that experience. The existence of bafflement, pain and moral paradox—of The Problem of Meaning—is one of the things that drive men toward belief in gods, devils, spirits, totemic principles or the spiritual efficacy of cannibalism (an enfolding sense of beauty or a dazzling perception of power are others), but it is not the basis upon which those beliefs rest, but rather their most important field of application.

In tribal religions authority lies in the persuasive power of traditional imagery; in mystical ones in the apodictic force of supersensible experience; in charismatic ones in the hypnotic attraction of an extraordinary personality. But the priority of the acceptance of an authoritative criterion in religious matters over the revelation which is conceived to flow from that acceptance is not less complete than in scriptural or hieratic ones. The basic axiom underlying what we may perhaps call "the religious perspective" is everywhere the same: he who would know must first believe.

But to speak of "the religious perspective" is, by implication, to speak of one perspective among others. A perspective is a mode of seeing, in that extended sense of "see" in which it means "discern," "apprehend," "understand" or "grasp." It is a particular way of looking at life, a particular manner of construing the world, as when we speak of an historical perspective, a scientific perspective, an aesthetic perspective, a common-sense perspective, or even the bizarre perspective embodied in dreams and in hallucinations. The question then comes down to, first, what is "the religious perspective" generically considered, as differentiated from other perspectives; and second, how do men come to adopt it.

If we place the religious perspective against the background of three of the other major perspectives in terms of which men construe the world—the common-sensical, the scientific and the aesthetic—its special character emerges more sharply. What distinguishes common-sense as a mode of "seeing" is, as Schutz (1962) has pointed out, a simple acceptance of the world, its objects and its processes as being just what they seem to be—what is sometimes called naive realism—and the pragmatic motive, the wish to act upon that world so as to bend it to one's practical purposes, to master it, or so far as that proves impossible, to adjust to it. The world of everyday life, itself, of course, a cultural product, for it is framed in terms of the symbolic conceptions of "stubborn fact" handed down from generation to generation, is the established scene and given object of our actions. Like Mt. Everest it is just there and the thing to do with it, if one feels the need to do anything with it at all, is to climb it. In the scientific perspective it is precisely this givenness which disappears (Schutz, 1962). Deliberate doubt and systematic inquiry, the suspension of the pragmatic motive in favor of disinterested observation, the attempt to analyze the world in terms of formal concepts whose relationship to the informal conceptions of common-sense become increasingly problematic—there are the hallmarks of the attempt to grasp the world scientifically. And as for the aesthetic perspective, which under the rubric of "the aesthetic attitude" has been perhaps most exquisitely examined, it involves a different sort of suspension of naive realism and practical interest, in that instead of questioning the credentials of everyday experience that experience is merely ignored in favor of an eager dwelling upon appearances, an engrossment in surfaces, an absorption in things, as we say, "in themselves": "The function of artistic illusion is not 'make-believe' . . . but the very opposite, disengagement from belief—the contemplation of sensory qualities without their usual meanings of 'here's that chair,' 'That's my telephone' . . . etc. The knowledge that what is before us has no practical significance in the world is what enables us to give attention to its appearance as such" (Langer, 1953, p. 49). And like the common-sensical and the scientific (or the historical, the philosophical and the autistic), this perspective, this "way of seeing" is not the product of some mysterious Cartesian chemistry, but is induced, mediated, and in fact created by means of symbols. It is the artist's skill which can produce those curious quasi-objects—poems, dramas, sculptures, symphonies—which, dissociating themselves from the solid world of common-sense, take on the special sort of eloquence only sheer appearances can achieve.

The religious perspective differs from the common-sensical in that, as already pointed out, it moves beyond the realities of everyday life to wider ones which correct and complete them, and its defining concern is not action upon those wider realities but acceptance of them, faith in them. It differs from the scientific perspective in that it questions the realities of everyday life not out of an institutionalized scepticism which dissolves the world's givenness into a swirl of probabilistic hypotheses, but in terms of what it takes to be wider, non-hypothetical truths. Rather than detachment, its watchword is commitment; rather than analysis, encounter. And it differs from art in that instead of effecting a disengagement from the whole question of factuality, deliberately manufacturing an air of semblance and illusion, it deepens the concern with fact and seeks to create an aura of utter actuality. It is this sense of the "really real" upon which the religious perspective rests and which the symbolic activities of religion as a cultural system are devoted to producing, intensifying, and, so far as possible, rendering inviolable by the discordant revelations of secular experience. It is, again, the imbuing of a certain specific complex of symbols—of the metaphysic they formulate and the style of life they recommend—with a persuasive authority which, from an analytic point of view is the essence of religious action.

Which brings us, at length, to ritual. For it is in ritual—i.e., consecrated behavior—that this conviction that religious conceptions are veridical and that religious directives are sound is somehow generated. It is in some sort of ceremonial form—even if that form be hardly more than the recitation of a myth, the consultation of an oracle, or the decoration of a grave—that the moods and motivations which sacred symbols induce in men and the general conceptions of the order of existence which they formulate for men meet and reinforce one another. In a ritual, the world as lived and the world as imagined, fused under the agency of a single set of symbolic forms, turn out to be the same world, producing thus that idiosyncratic transformation in one's sense of reality to which Santayana refers in my epigraph. Whatever role divine intervention may or may not play in the creation of faith—and it is not the business of the scientist to pronounce upon such matters one way or the other—it is, primarily at least, out of the context of concrete acts of religious observance that religious conviction emerges on the human plane.

However, though any religious ritual, no matter how apparently automatic or conventional (if it is truly automatic or merely conventional it is not religious), involves this symbolic fusion of ethos and world-view, it is mainly certain more elaborate and usually more public ones, ones in which a broad range of moods and motivations on the one hand and of metaphysical conceptions on the other are caught up, which shape the spiritual consciousness of a people. Employing a useful term introduced by Singer (1955) we may call these full-blown ceremonies "cultural performances" and note that they represent not only the point at which the dispositional and conceptual aspects of religious life converge for the believer, but also the point at which the interaction between them can be most readily examined by the detached observer.

Of course, all cultural performances are not religious performances, and the line between those that are, and artistic, or even political ones is often not so easy to draw in practice, for, like social forms, symbolic forms can serve multiple purposes. But the point is that, paraphrasing slightly, Indians —"and perhaps all peoples"—seem to think of their religion "as encapsulated in these discrete performances which they [can] exhibit to visitors and to themselves" (Singer, 1955). The mode of exhibition is however radically different for the two sorts of witnesses, a fact seemingly overlooked by those who would argue that "religion is a form of human art." Where for "visitors" religious performances can, in the nature of the case, only be presentations of a particular religious perspective, and thus aesthetically appreciated or scientifically dissected, for participants they are in addition enactments, materializations, realizations of it—not only models *of* what they believe, but also models *for* the believing of it. In these plastic dramas men attain their faith as they portray it.

5. . . . THAT THE MOODS AND MOTIVATIONS SEEM UNIQUELY REALISTIC.

But no one, not even a saint, lives in the world religious symbols formulate all of the time, and the majority of men live in it only at moments. The everyday world of common-sense objects and practical acts is, as Schutz says, the paramount reality in human experience—paramount in the sense that it is the world in which we are most solidly rooted, whose inherent actuality we can hardly question (however much we may question certain portions of it), and from whose pressures and requirements we can least escape. A man, even large groups of men, may be aesthetically insensitive, religiously unconcerned and unequipped to pursue formal scientific analysis, but he cannot be completely lacking in common-sense and survive. The dispositions which religious rituals induce thus have their most important impact—from a human point of view—

outside the boundaries of the ritual itself as they reflect back to color the individual's conception of the established world of bare fact. The peculiar tone that marks the Plains vision quest, the Manus confession or the Javanese mystical exercise pervades areas of the life of these peoples far beyond the immediately religious, impressing upon them a distinctive style in the sense both of a dominant mood and a characteristic movement. Religion is sociologically interesting not because, as vulgar positivism would have it, it describes the social order (which, insofar as it does, it does not only very obliquely but very incompletely), but because, like environment, political power, wealth, jural obligation, personal affection, and a sense of beauty, it shapes it.

The movement back and forth between the religious perspective and the common-sense perspective is actually one of the more obvious empirical occurrences on the social scene, though, again, one of the most neglected by social anthropologists, virtually all of whom have seen it happen countless times. Religious belief has usually been presented as an homogeneous characteristic of an individual, like his place of residence, his occupational role, his kinship position, and so on. But religious belief in the midst of ritual, where it engulfs the total person, transporting him, so far as he is concerned, into another mode of existence, and religious belief as the pale, remembered reflection of that experience in the midst of everyday life are not precisely the same thing, and the failure to realize this has led to some confusion, most especially in connection with the so-called "primitive mentality" problem. Much of the difficulty between Lévy-Bruhl and Malinowski on the nature of "native thought," for example, arises from a lack of full recognition of this distinction; for where the French philosopher was concerned with the view of reality savages adopted when taking a specifically religious perspective, the Polish-English ethnographer was concerned with that which they adopted when taking a strictly common-sense one. Both perhaps vaguely sensed that they were not talking about exactly the same thing, but where they went astray was in failing to give a specific accounting of the way in which these two forms of "thought"—or as I would rather say, these two modes of symbolic formulation—interacted, so that where Lévy-

Bruhl's savages tended to live, despite his postludial disclaimers, in a world composed entirely of mystical encounters, Malinowski's tended to live, despite his stress on the functional importance of religion, in a world composed entirely of practical actions. They became reductionists (an idealist is as much of a reductionist as a materialist) in spite of themselves because they failed to see man as moving more or less easily, and very frequently, between radically contrasting ways of looking at the world, ways which are not continuous with one another but separated by cultural gaps across which Kierkegaardian leaps must be made in both directions.

For an anthropologist, the importance of religion lies in its capacity to serve, for an individual or for a group, as a source of general, yet distinctive conceptions of the world, the self and the relations between them on the one hand—its model *of* aspect—and of rooted, no less distinctive "mental" dispositions—its model *for* aspect—on the other. From these cultural functions flow, in turn, its social and psychological ones.

Religious concepts spread beyond their specifically metaphysical contexts to provide a framework of general ideas in terms of which a wide range of experience—intellectual, emotional, moral—can be given meaningful form. The Christian sees the Nazi movement against the background of The Fall which, though it does not, in a casual sense, explain it, places it in a moral, a cognitive, even an affective sense. A Zande sees the collapse of a granary upon a friend or relative against the background of a concrete and rather special notion of witchcraft and thus avoids the philosophical dilemmas as well as the psychological stress of indeterminism. A Javanese finds in the borrowed and reworked concept of *rasa* ("sense-taste-feeling-meaning") a means by which to "see" choreographic, gustatory, emotional and political phenomena in a new light. A synopsis of cosmic order, a set of religious beliefs is also a gloss upon the mundane world of social relationships and psychological events. It renders them graspable.

But more than gloss, such beliefs are also a template. They do not merely interpret social and psychological processes in cosmic terms—in which case they would be philosophical, not religious—but they shape them. In the doctrine of original sin is embedded

also a recommended attitude toward life, a recurring mood and a persisting set of motivations. The Zande learns from witchcraft conceptions not just to understand apparent "accidents" as not accidents at all, but to react to these spurious accidents with hatred for the agent who caused them and to proceed against him with appropriate resolution. Rasa, in addition to being a concept of truth, beauty and goodness, is also a preferred mode of experiencing, a kind of affectless detachment, a variety of bland aloofness, an unshakeable calm. The moods and motivations a religious orientation produces cast a derivative, lunar light over the solid features of a peoples' secular life.

The tracing of the social and psychological role of religion is thus not so much a matter of finding correlations between specific ritual acts and specific secular social ties—though these correlations do, of course, exist and are very worth continued investigation, especially if we can contrive something novel to say about them. More, it is a matter of understanding how it is that men's notions, however implicit, of the "really real" and the dispositions these notions induce in them, colors their sense of the reasonable, the practical, the humane and the moral. How far it does so (for in many societies religion's effects seem quite circumscribed, in others completely pervasive); how deeply it does so (for some men, and groups of men, seem to wear their religion lightly so far as the secular world goes, while others seem to apply their faith to each occasion, no matter how trivial); and how effectively it does so (for the width of the gap between what religion recommends and what people actually do is most variable cross-culturally)—all these are crucial issues in the comparative sociology and psychology of religion. Even the degree to which religious systems themselves are developed seems to vary extremely widely, and not merely on a simple evolutionary basis. In one society, the level of elaboration of symbolic formulations of ultimate actuality may reach extraordinary degrees of complexity and systematic articulation; in another, no less developed socially, such formulations may remain primitive in the true sense, hardly more than congeries of fragmentary by-beliefs and isolated images, of sacred reflexes and spiritual pictographs. One need

only think of the Australians and the Bushmen, the Toradja and the Alorese, the Hopi
and the Apache, the Hindus and the Romans, or even the Italians and the Poles, to
see that degree of religious articulateness is
not a constant even as between societies of
similar complexity.

The anthropological study of religion is
therefore a two stage operation: first, an
analysis of the system of meanings embodied
in the symbols which make up the religion
proper, and, second, the relating of these
systems to social structural and psychological processes. My dissatisfaction with so
much of contemporary social anthropological
work in religion is not that it concerns itself
with the second stage, but that it neglects the
first, and in so doing takes for granted what
most needs to be elucidated. To discuss the
role of ancestor worship in regulating political succession, of sacrificial feasts in

defining kinship obligations, of spirit worship in scheduling agricultural practices, of
divination in reinforcing social control or of
initiation rites in propelling personality
maturation are in no sense unimportant endeavors, and I am not recommending they
be abandoned for the kind of jejune cabalism
into which symbolic analysis of exotic faiths
can so easily fall. But to attempt them with
but the most general, common-sense view of
what ancestor worship, animal sacrifice,
spirit worship, divination or initiation rites
are as religious patterns seems to me not
particularly promising. Only when we have
a theoretical analysis of symbolic action
comparable in sophistication to that we now
have for social and psychological action,
we be able to cope effectively with those
aspects of social and psychological life in
which religion (or art, or science, or ideology) plays a determinant role.

W. LLOYD WARNER

An American Sacred Ceremony

Warner's vivid description of Memorial Day ceremonies in an
American community shows how a rite functions to tune up the
central values and sentiments of a culture and unify a community
that is divided into opposing churches and associations with conflicting symbol systems.

Associated with the ceremony are American collective representations, like the myth of Lincoln, that have become sacred
symbols of the idealism in our culture and that reenforce our
Memorial Day ceremonies and provide a coherent set of beliefs
and practices that organize, direct, and constantly revive the collective ideals of the community and nation.

This article of Warner's hews closely to the thinking of Durkheim, by whom he was greatly influenced. It attempts to do for
modern American society what Warner did with Murngin ritualistic symbolism in his book *A Black Civilization* (1937).

Reprinted with slight abridgment from W. Lloyd Warner, *American
Life* (Chicago: The University of Chicago Press, 1953), pp. 1–26, by
permission of the author and The University of Chicago Press. Copyright 1953 by The University of Chicago.

MEMORIAL DAY AND SYMBOLIC BEHAVIOR

Every year in the springtime when the
flowers are in bloom and the trees and
shrubs are most beautiful, citizens of the
Union celebrate Memorial Day. Over most
of the United States it is a legal holiday.
Being both sacred and secular, it is a holy
day as well as a holiday and is accordingly
celebrated.

For some it is part of a long holiday of
pleasure, extended outings, and great athletic events; for others it is a sacred day
when the dead are mourned and sacred
ceremonies are held to express their sorrow;
but for most Americans, especially in the
smaller cities, it is both sacred and secular.
They feel the sacred importance of the day
when they, or members of their family, par-

ticipate in the ceremonies; but they also enjoy going for an automobile trip or seeing or reading about some important athletic event staged on Memorial Day. This chapter will be devoted to the analysis and interpretation of Memorial Day to learn its meanings as an American sacred ceremony, a rite that evolved in this country and is native to it.

Memorial Day originated in the North shortly after the end of the Civil War as a sacred day to show respect for the Union soldiers who were killed in the War between the States. Only since the last two wars has it become a day for all who died for their country. In the South only now are they beginning to use it to express southern respect and obligation to the nation's soldier dead.

Memorial Day is an important occasion in the American ceremonial calendar and as such is a unit of this larger ceremonial system of symbols. Close examination discloses that it, too, is a symbol system in its own right existing within the complexities of the larger one.

Symbols include such familiar things as written and spoken words, religious beliefs and practices, including creeds and ceremonies, the several arts, such familiar signs as the cross and the flag, and countless other objects and acts which stand for something more than that which they are. The red, white, and blue cloth and the crossed sticks in themselves and as objects mean very little, but the sacred meanings which they evoke are of such deep significance to some that millions of men have sacrificed their lives for the first as the Stars and Stripes and for the second as the Christian Cross.

The ceremonial calendar of American society, this yearly round of holidays and holy days, partly sacred and partly secular, but more sacred than secular, is a symbol system used by all Americans. Christmas and Thanksgiving, Memorial Day and the Fourth of July, are days in our ceremonial calendar which allow Americans to express common sentiments about themselves and share their feelings with others on set days pre-established by the society for this very purpose. This calendar functions to draw all people together to emphasize their similarities and common heritage; to minimize their differences; and to contribute to their thinking, feeling, and acting alike. All societies, simple or complex, possess some form of ceremonial calendar, if it be no more than the seasonal alternation of secular and cere-

monial periods, such as that used by the Australian aborigines in their yearly cycle.

The integration and smooth functioning of the social life of a modern community are very difficult because of its complexity. American communities are filled with churches, each claiming great authority and each with its separate sacred symbol system. Many of them are in conflict, and all of them in opposition to one another. Many associations, such as the Masons, the Odd Fellows, and the like, have sacred symbol systems which partly separate them from the whole community. The traditions of foreign-born groups contribute to the diversity of symbolic life. The evidence is clear for the conflict among these systems.

It is the thesis of this chapter that the Memorial Day ceremonies and subsidiary rites (such as those of Armistice Day) of today, yesterday, and tomorrow are rituals of a sacred symbol system which functions periodically to unify the whole community, with its conflicting symbols and its opposing, autonomous churches and associations. It is contended here that in the Memorial Day ceremonies the anxieties which man has about death are confronted with a system of sacred beliefs about death which gives the individuals involved and the collectivity of individuals a feeling of well-being. Further, the feeling of triumph over death by collective action in the Memorial Day parade is made possible by re-creating the feeling of well-being and the sense of group strength and individual strength in the group power, which is felt so intensely during the wars when the veterans' associations are created and when the feeling so necessary for the Memorial Day's symbol system is originally experienced.

Memorial Day is a cult of the dead which organizes and integrates the various faiths and national and class groups into a sacred unity. It is a cult of the dead organized around the community cemeteries. Its principal themes are those of the sacrifice of the soldier dead for the living and the obligation of the living to sacrifice their individual purposes for the good of the group, so that they, too, can perform their spiritual obligations.

MEMORIAL DAY CEREMONIES

We shall first examine the Memorial Day ceremony of an American town for evidence. The sacred symbolic behavior of Memorial

Day, in which scores of the town's organizations are involved, is ordinarily divided into four periods. During the year separate rituals are held by many of the associations for their dead, and many of these activities are connected with later Memorial Day events. In the second phase, preparations are made during the last three or four weeks for the ceremony itself, and some of the associations perform public rituals. The third phase consists of the scores of rituals held in all the cemeteries, churches, and halls of the associations. These rituals consist of speeches and highly ceremonialized behavior. They last for two days and are climaxed by the fourth and last phase, in which all the separate celebrants gather in the center of the business district on the afternoon of Memorial Day. The separate organizations, with their members in uniform or with fitting insignia, march through the town, visit the shrines and monuments of the hero dead, and, finally, enter the cemetery. Here dozens of ceremonies are held, most of them highly symbolic and formalized. Let us examine the actual ritual behavior in these several phases of the ceremony.

The two or three weeks before the Memorial Day ceremonies are usually filled with elaborate preparations by each participating group. Meetings are held, and patriotic pronouncements are sent to the local paper by the various organizations which announce what part each organization is to play in the ceremony. Some of the associations have Memorial Day processions, memorial services are conducted, the schools have patriotic programs, and the cemeteries are cleaned and repaired. Graves are decorated by families and associations and new gravestones purchased and erected. The merchants put up flags before their establishments, and residents place flags above their houses.

All these events are recorded in the local paper, and most of them are discussed by the town. The preparation of public opinion for an awareness of the importance of Memorial Day and the rehearsal of what is expected from each section of the community are done fully and in great detail. The latent sentiments of each individual, each family, each church, school, and association for its own dead are thereby stimulated and related to the sentiments for the dead of the nation.

One of the important events observed in the preparatory phase in the community studied occurred several days before Memorial Day, when the man who had been the war mayor wrote an open letter to the commander of the American Legion. It was published in the local paper. He had a city-wide reputation for patriotism. He was an honorary member of the American Legion. The letter read: "Dear Commander: The approaching Poppy Day (when Legion supporters sold poppies in the town) brings to my mind a visit to the war zone in France on Memorial Day, 1925, reaching Belleau Wood at about 11 o'clock. On this sacred spot we left floral tributes in memory of our town's boys—Jonathan Dexter and John Smith, who here had made the supreme sacrifice, that the principle that 'might makes right' should not prevail."

Three days later the paper in a front-page editorial told its readers: "Next Saturday is the annual Poppy Day of the American Legion. Everybody should wear a poppy on Poppy Day. Think back to those terrible days when the red poppy on Flanders Field symbolized the blood of our boys slaughtered for democracy." The editor here explicitly states the symbolism involved.

Through the early preparatory period of the ceremony, through all its phases and in every rite, the emphasis in all communities is always on sacrifice—the sacrifice of the lives of the soldiers of the city, willingly given for democracy and for their country. The theme is always that the gift of their lives was voluntary; that it was freely given and therefore above selfishness or thoughts of self-preservation; and, finally, that the "sacrifice on the altars of their country" was done for everyone. The red poppy became a separate symbol from McCrae's poem "In Flanders Fields." The poem expressed and symbolized the sentiments experienced by the soldiers and people of the country who went through the first war. The editor makes the poppy refer directly to the "blood of the boys slaughtered." In ritual language he then recites the names of some of the city's "sacrificed dead," and "the altars" (battles) where they were killed. "Remember Dexter and Smith killed at Belleau Wood," he says. "Remember O'Flaherty killed near Château-Thierry, Stulavitz killed in the Bois D'Ormont, Kelley killed at Côte de Châtillon, Jones near the Bois de Montrebeaux, Kilnikap in the St.-Mihiel offensive, and the other brave boys who died in camp or on stricken fields. Remember the living boys of the Legion on Saturday."

The names selected by the editor covered most of the ethnic and religious groups of the community. They included Polish, Russian, Irish, French-Canadian, and Yankee names. The use of such names in this context emphasized the fact that the voluntary sacrifice of a citizen's life was equalitarian. They covered the top, middle, and bottom of the several classes. The newspapers throughout the country each year print similar lists, and their editorials stress the equality of sacrifice by all classes and creeds.

The topic for the morning services of the churches on the Sunday before Memorial Day ordinarily is the meaning of Memorial Day to the town and to the people as Christians. All the churches participate. Because of space limitations, we shall quote from only a few sermons from one Memorial Day to show the main themes; but observations of Memorial Day behavior since the second World War show no difference in the principal themes expressed before and after the war started. Indeed, some of the words are almost interchangeable. The Rev. Hugh McKellar chose as his text, "Be thou faithful until death." He said:

"Memorial Day is a day of sentiment and when it loses that, it loses all its value. We are all conscious of the danger of losing that sentiment. What we need today is more sacrifice, for there can be no achievement without sacrifice. There are too many out today preaching selfishness. Sacrifice is necessary to a noble living. In the words of our Lord, 'Whosoever shall save his life shall lose it and whosoever shall lose his life in My name shall save it.' It is only those who sacrifice personal gain and will to power and personal ambition who ever accomplish anything for their nation. Those who expect to save the nation will not get wealth and power for themselves.

"Memorial Day is a religious day. It is a day when we get a vision of the unbreakable brotherhood and unity of spirit which exists and still exists, no matter what race or creed or color, in the country where all men have equal rights."

The minister of the Congregational Church spoke with the voice of the Unknown Soldier to emphasize his message of sacrifice:

"If the spirit of that Unknown Soldier should speak, what would be his message? What would be the message of a youth I knew myself who might be one of the unknown dead? I believe he would speak as follows: 'It is well to remember us today, who gave our lives that democracy might live, we know something of sacrifice.'"

The two ministers in different language expressed the same theme of the sacrifice of the individual for national and democratic principles. One introduces divine sanction for this sacrificial belief and thereby succeeds in emphasizing the theme that the loss of an individual's life rewards him with life eternal. The other uses one of our greatest and most sacred symbols of democracy and the only very powerful one that came out of the first World War—the Unknown Soldier. The American Unknown Soldier is Everyman; he is the perfect symbol of equalitarianism.

There were many more Memorial Day sermons, most of which had this same theme. Many of them added the point that the Christian God had given his life for all. That afternoon during the same ceremony the cemeteries, memorial squares named for the town's dead, the lodge halls, and the churches had a large number of rituals. Among them was the "vacant chair." A row of chairs decorated with flags and wreaths, each with the name of a veteran who had died in the last year, was the center of this ceremony held in a church. Most of the institutions were represented in the ritual. We shall give only a small selection from the principal speech:

"Now we come to pay tribute to these men whose chairs are vacant, not because they were eminent men, as many soldiers were not, but the tribute we pay is to their attachment to the great cause. We are living in the most magnificent country on the face of the globe, a country planted and fertilized by a Great Power, a power not political or economic but religious and educational, especially in the North. In the South they had settlers who were there in pursuit of gold, in search of El Dorado, but the North was settled by people seeking religious principles and education."

In a large city park, before a tablet filled with the names of war dead, one of our field workers shortly after the vacant-chair rite heard a speaker in the memorial ritual eulogize the two great symbols of American unity—Washington and Lincoln. The orator said:

"No character except the Carpenter of Nazareth has ever been honored the way Washington and Lincoln have been in New England. Virtue, freedom from sin, and righteousness were qualities possessed by Washington and Lincoln, and in possessing these characteristics both were true Americans, and we would do well to emulate them. Let us first be true Americans. From these our friends beneath the sod we receive their message, 'Carry on.' Though your speaker will die, the fire and spark will carry on. Thou are not conqueror, death, and thy pale flag is not advancing."

In all the other services the same themes were used in the speeches, most of which were in ritualized, oratorical language, or were expressed in the ceremonials themselves. Washington, the father of his country, first in war and peace, had devoted his life not to himself but to his country. Lincoln had given his own life, sacrificed on the altar of his country. Most of the speeches implied or explicitly stated that divine guidance was involved and that these mundane affairs had supernatural implications. They stated that the revered dead had given the last ounce of devotion in following the ideals of Washington and Lincoln and the Unknown Soldier and declared that these same principles must guide us, the living. The beliefs and values of which they spoke referred to a world beyond the natural. Their references were to the supernatural. On Memorial Day morning the separate rituals, publicly performed, continued. The parade formed in the early afternoon in the business district. Hundreds of people, dressed in their best, gathered to watch the various uniformed groups march in the parade. Crowds collected along the entire route. The cemeteries, carefully prepared for the event, and the graves of kindred covered with flowers and flags and wreaths looked almost gay.

The parade marched through the town to the cemeteries. The various organizations spread throughout the several parts of the graveyards, and rites were performed. In the Greek quarter ceremonies were held; others were performed in the Polish and Russian sections; the Boy Scouts held a memorial rite for their departed; the Sons and Daughters of Union Veterans went through a rit-

ual, as did the other men's and women's organizations. All this was part of the parade in which everyone from all parts of the community could and did participate.

Near the end of the day all the men's and women's organizations assembled about the roped-off grave of General Fredericks. The Legion band played. A minister uttered a prayer. The ceremonial speaker said:

"We meet to honor those who fought, but in so doing we honor ourselves. From them we learn a lesson of sacrifice and devotion and of accountability to God and honor. We have an inspiration for the future today— our character is strengthened—this day speaks of a better and greater devotion to our country and to all that our flag represents."

After the several ceremonies in the Elm Hill Cemetery, the parade re-formed and started the march back to town, where it broke up. The firing squad of the American Legion fired three salutes, and a bugler sounded the "Last Post" at the cemetery entrance as they departed. This, they said, was a "general salute for all the dead in the cemetery."

Here we see people who are Protestant, Catholic, Jewish, and Greek Orthodox involved in a common ritual in a graveyard with their common dead. Their sense of separateness was present and expressed in the different ceremonies, but the parade and the unity gained by doing everything at one time emphasized the oneness of the total group. Each ritual also stressed the fact that the war was an experience where everyone sacrificed and some died, not as members of a separate group, but as citizens of a whole community.

LINCOLN—AN AMERICAN COLLECTIVE REPRESENTATION MADE BY AND FOR THE PEOPLE

Throughout the Memorial Day ceremony there were continual references to Lincoln and his Gettysburg Address. The symbol of Lincoln obviously was of deep significance in the various rituals and to the participants. He loomed over the memorial rituals like some great demigod over the rites of classical antiquity. What is the meaning of the myth of Lincoln to Americans? Why does his life and death as conceived in the myth of Lincoln play such a prominent part in Memorial Day?

Some of the answers are obvious. He was a great war president. He was the President of the United States and was assassinated during the Civil War. Memorial Day grew out of this war. A number of other facts about his life might be added; but for our present purposes the meaning of Lincoln the myth is more important to understand than the objective facts of his life-career.

Lincoln, product of the American prairies, sacred symbol of idealism in the United States, myth more real than the man himself, symbol and fact, was formed in the flow of events which composed the changing cultures of the Middle West. He is the symbolic culmination of America. To understand him is to know much of what America means.

In 1858, when Lincoln ran against Stephen Douglas for the United States Senate, he was Abraham Lincoln, the successful lawyer, the railroad attorney, who was noted throughout the state of Illinois as a man above common ability and of more than common importance. He was a former congressman. He was earning a substantial income. He had married a daughter of the superior classes from Kentucky. His friends were W. D. Green, the president of a railway, a man of wealth; David Davis, a representative of wealthy eastern investors in western property, who was on his way to becoming a millionaire; Jesse Fell, railway promoter; and other men of prominence and prestige in the state. Lincoln dressed like them; he had unlearned many of the habits acquired in childhood from his lowly placed parents and had learned most of the ways of those highly placed men who were now his friends. After the Lincoln-Douglas debates his place as a man of prestige and power was as high as anyone's in the whole state.

Yet in 1860, when he was nominated on the Republican ticket for the presidency of the United States, he suddenly became "Abe Lincoln, the rail splitter," "the rude man from the prairie and the river-bottoms." To this was soon added "Honest Abe," and finally, in death, "the martyred leader" who gave his life that "a nation dedicated to the proposition that all men are created equal" might long endure.

What can be the meaning of this strange transformation?

When Richard Oglesby arrived in the Republican convention in 1860, he cast about for a slogan that would bring his friend,

Lincoln, favorable recognition from the shrewd politicians of New York, Pennsylvania, and Ohio. He heard from Jim Hanks, who had known Lincoln as a boy, that Lincoln had once split fence rails. Dick Oglesby, knowing what appeals are most potent in getting the support of the politicians and in bringing out a favorable vote, dubbed Lincoln "the rail splitter." Fence rails were prominently displayed at the convention, to symbolize Lincoln's lowly beginnings. Politicians, remembering the great popular appeal of "Old Hickory," "Tippecanoe and Tyler too," and "The Log Cabin and Cider Jug" of former elections, realized that this slogan would be enormously effective in a national election. Lincoln, the rail splitter, was reborn in Chicago in 1860; and the Lincoln who had become the successful lawyer, intimate of wealthy men, husband of a well-born wife, and man of status was conveniently forgotten.

Three dominant symbolic themes compose the Lincoln image. The first—the theme of the common man—was fashioned in a form pre-established by the equalitarian ideals of a new democracy; to common men there could be no argument about what kind of man a rail splitter is.

"From log cabin to the White House" succinctly symbolizes the second theme of the trilogy which composes Lincoln, the most powerful of American collective representations. This phrase epitomizes the American success story, the rags-to-riches motif, and the ideals of the ambitious. As the equal of all men, Lincoln was the representative of the Common Man, as both their spokesman and their kind; and, as the man who had gone "from the log cabin to the White House," he became the superior man, the one who had not inherited but had earned that superior status and thereby proved to everyone that all men could do as he had. Lincoln thereby symbolized the two great collective but opposed ideals of American democracy.

When Lincoln was assassinated, a third powerful theme of our Christian society was added to the symbol being created by Americans to strengthen and adorn the keystone of their national symbol structure. Lincoln's life lay sacrificed on the altar of unity, climaxing a deadly war which proved by its successful termination that the country was one and that all men are created equal.

From the day of his death, thousands of sermons and speeches have demonstrated that Lincoln, like Christ, died that all men might live and be as one in the sight of God and man. Christ died that this might be true forever beyond the earth; Lincoln sacrificed his life that this might be true forever on this earth.

When Lincoln died, the imaginations of the people of the eastern seaboard cherished him as the man of the new West and translated him into their hopes for tomorrow, for to them the West was tomorrow. The defeated people of the South, during and after the reconstruction period, fitted him into their dark reveries of what might have been, had this man lived who loved all men. In their bright fantasies, the people of the West, young and believing only in the tomorrow they meant to create, knew Lincoln for what they wanted themselves to be. Lincoln, symbol of equalitarianism, of the social striving of men who live in a social hierarchy, the human leader sacrificed for all men, expresses all the basic values and beliefs of the Middle West and of the United States of America.

Lincoln, the superior man, above all men, yet equal to each, is a mystery beyond the logic of individual calculators. He belongs to the culture and to the social logics of the people for whom contradiction is unimportant and for whom the ultimate tests of truth are in the social structure in which, and for which, they live. Through the passing generations of our Christian culture the Man of the Prairies, formed in the mold of the God-man of Galilee and apotheosized into the man-god of the American people, each year less profane and more sacred, moves securely toward identification with deity and ultimate godhead. In him Americans realize themselves.

THE EFFECT OF WAR ON THE COMMUNITY

A problem of even greater difficulty confronts us on why war provides such an effective context for the creation of powerful national symbols, such as Lincoln, Washington, or Memorial Day. Durkheim gives us an important theoretical lead. He believed that the members of the group felt and became aware of their own group identity when they gathered periodically during times of plenty. For his test case, the Aus-

tralian aborigines, a hunting and gathering tribe, this was the season when food was plentiful. It was then when social interaction was most intense and the feelings most stimulated.

In modern society interaction, social solidarity, and intensity of feelings ordinarily are greatest in times of war. It would seem likely that such periods might well produce new sacred forms, built, of course, on the foundations of old beliefs. Let us examine the life of American communities in wartime as a possible matrix for such developments.

The most casual survey supplies ample evidence that the effects of war are most varied and diverse as they are reflected in the life of American towns. The immediate effect of war is very great on some towns and very minor on others. During its existence it strengthens the social structure of some and greatly weakens the social systems of others. In some communities it appears to introduce very little that is new, while in others the citizens are compelled by force of circumstances to incorporate whole new experiences into their lives and into the social systems which control them.

In some communities during the second World War there was no decided increase or decrease in the population, and war did not change the ordinary occupations of their people. Their citizens made but minor adjustments in their daily lives; no basic changes occurred in their institutions. For example, there were many small market towns servicing rural areas about them where the round of events substantially repeated what had occurred in all previous years from the time the towns grew to early maturity. A few of their boys were drafted, possibly the market crops were more remunerative, and it may be that the weekly paper had a few more war stories. Changes there were, but they were few and minor in their effect on the basic social system.

At the other extreme, most drastic and spectacular changes occurred in the second World War. Small towns that had formerly existed disappeared entirely, and their former localities were occupied by industrial cities born during the war and fathered by it. Sleepy rural villages were supplanted by huge industrial populations recruited from every corner of America. Towns of a few hundred people, traditionally quiet and well composed, suddenly expanded into brawling young cities with no past and no future. Market towns became industrial areas. The wives and mothers in these towns left their homes and joined the newcomers on the assembly line. The old people went into industry to take jobs they had to learn like the youngest boy working beside them. This and that boy and some of their friends left high school because they received tacit encouragement from their elders and the school authorities to go to work to help in the war effort. In some communities the whole system of control that had formerly prevailed ceased to function or was superseded by outside authority. The influx of population was so great that the schools could teach but a small portion of the children. The police force was inadequate. The usual recreational life disappeared, to be supplanted by the "taxi dance hall," "juke joint," "beer hall," and "gambling dive." Institutions such as the church and lodge almost ceased to function. In some towns one could drive through miles of trailer camps and small houses pressed against one another, all recently assembled, where the inhabitants lived in squalid anonymity with, but not of, the thousands around them. They were an aggregate of individuals concentrated in one area, but they were not a community.

We have described only the two extremes of the immediate influence of war on the community. Soon, however, those communities which had been little affected by the war felt some of its effects, and those which had been disorganized developed habits of life which conformed to the ordinary pattern of American town life. The two extremes soon approached the average.

But wars influence the average town quite differently. Changes take place, the institutional life is modified, new experiences are felt by the people, and the townsmen repeatedly modify their behavior to adapt to new circumstances brought them by new events. These modifications do not cause social breakdown. The contrary is true. The war activities strengthen the integration of many small communities. The people are more systematically organized into groups where everyone is involved and in which there is an intense awareness of oneness. The town's unity and feeling of autonomy are strengthened by competition in war activities with neighboring communities.

It is in time of war that the average American living in small cities and towns gets his deepest satisfactions as a member of his society. Despite the pessimistic events of 1917, the year when the United States entered the first World War, the people derived deep satisfaction from it, just as they did from the last war. It is a mistake to believe that the American people, particularly the small-towners, hate war to the extent that they derive no satisfaction from it. Verbally and superficially they disapprove of war, but at best this is only partly revealed in their deeper feelings. In simpler terms, their observed behavior reveals that most of them had more real satisfaction out of the second World War, just as they did in the previous one, than they had had in any other period of their lives. The various men's and women's organizations, instead of inventing things to do to keep busy, could choose among activities which they knew were vital and significant to them and to others.

The small-towner then had a sense of significance about himself, about those around him, and about the events which occurred, in a way that he had never felt before. The young man who quit high school during the depression to lounge on the street corner and who was known to be of no consequence to himself or to anyone else in the community became a seasoned veteran, fighting somewhere in the South Pacific—a man obviously with the qualities of a hero (it was believed), willing to give up his life for his country, since he was in its military forces. He and everyone else were playing, and they knew they were playing, a vital and significant role in the present crisis. Everyone was in it. There was a feeling of unconscious well-being, because everyone was doing something to help in the common desperate enterprise in a co-operative rather than in a private spirit. This feeling is often the unconscious equivalent of what people mean when they gather to celebrate and sing "Hail, hail, the gang's all here." It also has something of the deep significance that enters into people's lives only in moments of tragedy.

The strong belief that everyone must sacrifice to win a war greatly strengthens people's sense of their importance. Everyone gives up something for the common good— money, food, tires, scrap, automobiles, or blood for blood banks. All of it is contributed under the basic ideology of common sacrifice for the good of the country. These simple acts of giving by all individuals in the town, by all families, associations, schools, churches, and factories, are given strong additional emotional support by the common knowledge that some of the local young men are representing the town in the military forces of the country. It is known that some of them may be killed while serving their country. They are sacrificing their lives, it is believed, that their country may live. Therefore, all acts of individual giving to help win the war, no matter how small, are made socially significant and add to the strength of the social structure by being treated as sacrifices. The collective effect of these small renunciations, it is believed, is to lessen the number of those who must die on the altars of their country.

Another very strong integrative factor contributed by a war that strengthens the social structure of the small town and city is that petty internal antagonisms are drained out of the group onto the common enemy. The local antagonisms which customarily divide and separate people are largely suppressed. The feelings and psychic energies involved, normally expended in local feuds, are vented on the hated symbols of the enemy. Local groups which may have been excluded from participation in community affairs are given an honored place in the war effort, and the symbols of unity are stressed rather than the separating differences. The religious groups and the churches tend to emphasize the oneness of the common war effort rather than allow their differing theologies and competitive financing to keep them in opposing groups. The strongest pressure to compose their differences is placed against management and labor. (The small number of strikes is eloquent proof of the effectiveness of such pressure.) A common hate of a common enemy, when organized in community activities to express this basic emotion, provides the most powerful mechanism to energize the lives of the towns and to strengthen their feelings of unity. Those who believe that a war's hatreds can bring only evil to psychic life might well ponder the therapeutic and satisfying effects on the minds of people who turn their once private hatreds into social ones and join their townsmen and countrymen in the feeling of sharing this basic emotion in common symbols. Enemies as well as friends should be well chosen, for they must serve as objects for the expression of two emotions basic to man and his social system—hatred and love.

The American Legion and other patriotic organizations give form to the effort to capture the feelings of well-being when the society was most integrated and feelings of unity were most intense. The membership comes from every class, creed, and nationality, for the soldiers came from all of them.

Only a very few associations are sufficiently large and democratic in action to include in their membership men or women from all class levels, all religious faiths, and most, if not all, ethnic groups. Their number could be easily counted on the fingers of one hand. Most prominent among them are the patriotic associations, all of them structural developments from wars which involved the United States. The American Legion is a typical example of the patriotic type. Less than 6 per cent of several hundred associations which have been studied include members from all social classes. Of the remaining 94 per cent, approximately half have representatives from only three classes, or less than three, out of the six discussed in Chapter III. Although the associations which include members from all levels of the community are surprisingly few, those which stress in action as well as in words such other principles of democracy as the equality of races, nationalities, and religions are even fewer. Only 5 per cent of the associations are composed of members from the four principal religious faiths in America—Protestant, Catholic, Jewish, and Greek Orthodox—and most of their members come from the lower ranks of the society.

Lincoln and Washington and lesser ritual figures (and ceremonies such as Memorial Day) are the symbolic equivalent of such social institutions as the patriotic societies. They express the same values, satisfy the same social needs, and perform similar functions. All increase the social solidarity of a complex and heterogeneous society.

HOW SUCH CEREMONIES FUNCTION IN THE COMMUNITY

Memorial Day and similar ceremonies are one of the several forms of collective representations which Durkheim so brilliantly defined and interpreted in *The Elementary*

Forms of the Religious Life. He said: "Religious representations are collective representations which express collective realities." Religious collective representations are symbol systems which are composed of beliefs and rites which relate men to sacred beings. Beliefs are "states of opinion and consist in representations"; rites are "determined modes of action" which are expressions of, and refer to, religious belief. They are *visible* signs (symbols) of the invisible belief. The visible rite of baptism, for example, may express invisible beliefs about cleansing the newborn infant of sin and relating him to the Christian community.

Ceremonies, periodically held, serve to impress on men their social nature and make them aware of something beyond themselves which they feel and believe to be sacred. This intense feeling of belonging to something larger and more powerful than themselves and of having part of this within them as part of them is symbolized by the belief in sacred beings, which is given a visual symbol by use of designs which are the emblems of the sacred entities, e.g., the Cross of the Christian churches.

That which is beyond, yet part of, a person is no more than the awareness on the part of individuals and the collectivity of individuals of their participation in a social group. *The religious symbols, as well as the secular ones, must express the nature of the social structure of the group of which they are a part and which they represent.* The beliefs in the gods and the symbolic rites which celebrate their divinity are no more than men collectively worshiping their own images—their own, since they were made by themselves and fashioned from their experiences among themselves.

We said earlier that the Memorial Day rites of American towns are sacred collective representations and a modern cult of the dead. They are a cult because they consist of a system of sacred beliefs and dramatic rituals held by a group of people who, when they congregate, represent the whole community. They are sacred because they ritually relate the living to sacred things. They are a cult because the members have not been formally organized into an institutionalized church with a defined theology but depend on informal organization to bring into order their sacred activities. They are called a "cult" here, because this term most accurately places them in a class of social phenomena which can be clearly identified in the sacred behavior of non-European societies.

The cult system of sacred belief puts into the organized form of concepts those sentiments about death which are common to everyone in the community. These sentiments are composed of fears of death, which conflict with the social reassurances that our culture provides us to combat such anxieties. These assurances, usually acquired in childhood and thereby carrying some of the authority of the adults who provided them, are a composite of theology and folk belief. The deep anxieties to which we refer include anticipation of our deaths, of the deaths or possible deaths of loved ones, and, less powerfully, of the deaths or possible deaths of those we know and of men in general.

Each man's church provides him and those of his faith with a set of beliefs and a way of acting to face these problems; but his church and those of other men do not equip him with a common set of social beliefs and rituals which permit him to unite with all his fellows to confront this common and most feared of all his enemies. The Memorial Day rite and other subsidiary rituals connected with it form a cult which partially satisfies this need for common action on a common problem. It dramatically expresses the sentiments of unity of all the living among themselves, of all the living to all the dead, and of all the living and dead as a group to the gods. The gods—Catholic, Protestant, and Jewish—lose their sectarian definitions, limitations, and foreignness among themselves and become objects of worship for the whole group and the protectors of everyone.

The unifying and integrating symbols of this cult are the dead. The graves of the dead are the most powerful of the visible emblems which unify all the activities of the separate groups of the community. The cemetery and its graves become the objects of sacred rituals which permit opposing organizations, often in conflict, to subordinate their ordinary opposition and to co-operate in expressing jointly the larger unity of the total community through the use of common rites for their collective dead. The rites show extraordinary respect for all the dead, but they pay particular honor to those who were killed in battle "fighting for their country." The death of a soldier in battle is believed to

be a "voluntary sacrifice" by him on the altar of his country. To be understood, this
belief in the sacrifice of a man's life for his
country must be judged first with our general scientific knowledge of the nature of all
forms of sacrifice. It must then be subjected
to the principles which explain human sacrifice whenever and wherever found. More
particularly, this belief must be examined
with the realization that these sacrifices occur in a society whose deity was a man who
sacrificed his life for all men.

The principle of the gift is involved. In
simple terms, when something valuable is
given, an equally valuable thing must be returned. The speaker who quoted Scripture
in his Memorial Day speech, "Whosoever
shall save his life shall lose it and whosoever
shall lose his life in My name shall save it,"
almost explicitly stated the feelings and
principles involved. Finally, as we interpret
it, the belief in "the sacrifice of American
citizens killed in battle" is a social logic
which states in ultimate terms the subordinate relation of the citizen to his country and
its collective moral principles.

This discussion has shown that the Memorial Day ceremony consists of a series of
separate rituals performed by autonomous
groups which culminate in a procession of *all
of them as one group* to the consecrated area
set aside by the living for their dead. In such
a place the dead are classed as individuals,
for their graves are separate; as members of
separate social situations, for they are found
in family plots and formal ritual respect is
paid them by church and association; and as
a collectivity, since they are thought of as
"our dead" in most of the ceremonies. The
fences surrounding the cemetery place all the
dead together and separate all the living
from them.

The Memorial Day rite is a cult of the
dead, but not just of the dead as such, since
by symbolically elaborating sacrifice of human life for the country through, or identifying it with, the Christian church's sacred
sacrifice of their god, the deaths of such men
also become powerful sacred symbols which
organize, direct, and constantly revive the
collective ideals of the community and the
nation.

ERIC WOLF

The Virgin of Guadalupe: A Mexican National Symbol

There hardly exists a better example of a highly evocative national symbol than that of the Virgin of Guadalupe of Mexico.
Like her famous Polish counterpart, the Black Madonna of
Czenstochowa, she embodies abstract principles and precepts of
the nation to which she belongs. The complexity and heterogeneity of Mexico are reconciled in the Guadalupe in a special way
that no other symbol can rival. Political overtones are blended
with individual and societal aspirations, particularly for the Indian, for it was to an Indian that the Virgin revealed herself in
1531.

Reprinted from *Journal of American Folklore,* LXXI (1958), 34–
39, by permission of The American Folklore Society and the author.

Occasionally, we encounter a symbol which
seems to enshrine the major hopes and aspirations of an entire society. Such a master
symbol is represented by the Virgin of
Guadalupe, Mexico's patron saint. During
the Mexican War of Independence against
Spain, her image preceded the insurgents
into battle. Emiliano Zapata and his agrarian rebels fought under her emblem in the

Great Revolution of 1910. Today, her image
adorns house fronts and interiors, churches
and home altars, bull rings and gambling
dens, taxis and buses, restaurants and
houses of ill repute. She is celebrated in
popular song and verse. Her shrine at Tepeyac, immediately north of Mexico City, is
visited each year by hundreds of thousands
of pilgrims, ranging from the inhabitants of

far-off Indian villages to the members of socialist trade union locals. "Nothing to be
seen in Canada or Europe," says F. S. C.
Northrop, "equals it in the volume or the
vitality of its moving quality or in the depth
of its spirit of religious devotion."

In this paper, I should like to discuss this
Mexican master symbol, and the ideology
which surrounds it. In making use of the
term "master symbol," I do not wish to imply that belief in the symbol is common to all
Mexicans. We are not dealing here with an
element of a putative national character, defined as a common denominator of all Mexican nationals. It is no longer legitimate to
assume "that any member of the [national]
group will exhibit certain regularities of behavior which are common in high degree
among the other members of the society."
Nations, like other complex societies, must,
however, "possess cultural forms or mechanisms which groups involved in the same
overall web of relationships can use in their
formal and informal dealings with each
other." Such forms develop historically, hand
in hand with other processes which lead to
the formation of nations, and social groups
which are caught up in these processes must
become "acculturated" to their usage. Only
where such forms exist, can communication
and coördinated behavior be established
among the constituent groups of such a society. They provide the cultural idiom of behavior and ideal representations through
which different groups of the same society
can pursue and manipulate their different
fates within a coördinated framework. This
paper, then, deals with one such cultural
form, operating on the symbolic level. The
study of this symbol seems particularly rewarding, since it is not restricted to one set
of social ties, but refers to a very wide range
of social relationships.

The image of the Guadalupe and her
shrine at Tepeyac are surrounded by an
origin myth. According to this myth, the
Virgin Mary appeared to Juan Diego, a
Christianized Indian of commoner status,
and addressed him in Nahuatl. The encounter took place on the Hill of Tepeyac in the
year 1531, ten years after the Spanish Conquest of Tenochtitlan. The Virgin commanded Juan Diego to seek out the archbishop of Mexico and to inform him of her
desire to see a church built in her honor on
Tepeyac Hill. After Juan Diego was twice

unsuccessful in his efforts to carry out her
order, the Virgin wrought a miracle. She
bade Juan Diego pick roses in a sterile spot
where normally only desert plants could
grow, gathered the roses into the Indian's
cloak, and told him to present cloak and
roses to the incredulous archbishop. When
Juan Diego unfolded his cloak before the
bishop, the image of the Virgin was miraculously stamped upon it. The bishop acknowledged the miracle, and ordered a shrine built
where Mary had appeared to her humble
servant.

The shrine, rebuilt several times in centuries to follow, is today a basilica, the third
highest kind of church in Western Christendom. Above the central altar hangs Juan
Diego's cloak with the miraculous image. It
shows a young woman without child, her
head lowered demurely in her shawl. She
wears an open crown and flowing gown, and
stands upon a half moon symbolizing the
Immaculate Conception.

The shrine of Guadalupe was, however,
not the first religious structure built on
Tepeyac; nor was Guadalupe the first female supernatural associated with the hill.
In pre-Hispanic times, Tepeyac had housed
a temple to the earth and fertility goddess
Tonantzin, Our Lady Mother, who—like
the Guadalupe—was associated with the
moon. Temple, like basilica, was the center
of large scale pilgrimages. That the veneration accorded the Guadalupe drew inspiration from the earlier worship of Tonantzin is
attested by several Spanish friars. F. Bernardino de Sahagún, writing fifty years after
the Conquest, says: "Now that the Church
of Our Lady of Guadalupe has been built
there, they call her Tonantzin too. . . . The
term refers . . . to that ancient Tonantzin
and this state of affairs should be remedied,
because the proper name of the Mother of
God is not Tonantzin, but Dios and Nantzin.
It seems to be a satanic device to mask idolatry . . . and they come from far away to
visit that Tonantzin, as much as before; a
devotion which is also suspect because there
are many churches of Our Lady everywhere
and they do not go to them; and they come
from faraway lands to this Tonantzin as of
old." F. Martín de León wrote in a similar
vein: "On the hill where Our Lady of
Guadalupe is they adored the idol of a goddess they called Tonantzin, which means
Our Mother, and this is also the name they

give Our Lady and they always say they are going to Tonantzin or they are celebrating Tonantzin and many of them understand this in the old way and not in the modern way. . . ." The syncretism was still alive in the seventeenth century. F. Jacinto de la Serna, in discussing the pilgrimages to the Guadalupe at Tepeyac, noted: ". . . it is the purpose of the wicked to [worship] the goddess and not the Most Holy Virgin, or both together."

Increasingly popular during the sixteenth century, the Guadalupe cult gathered emotional impetus during the seventeenth. During this century appear the first known pictorial representations of the Guadalupe, apart from the miraculous original; the first poems are written in her honor; and the first sermons announce the transcendental implications of her supernatural appearance in Mexico and among Mexicans. Historians have long tended to neglect the seventeenth century which seemed "a kind of Dark Age in Mexico." Yet "this quiet time was of the utmost importance in the development of Mexican Society." During this century, the institution of the hacienda comes to dominate Mexican life. During this century, also, "New Spain is ceasing to be 'new' and to be 'Spain.' " These new experiences require a new cultural idiom, and in the Guadalupe cult, the component segments of Mexican colonial society encountered cultural forms in which they could express their parallel interests and longings.

The primary purpose of this paper is not, however, to trace the history of the Guadalupe symbol. It is concerned rather with its functional aspects, its roots and reference to the major social relationships of Mexican society.

The first set of relationships which I would like to single out for consideration are the ties of kinship, and the emotions generated in the play of relationships within families. I want to suggest that some of the meanings of the Virgin symbol in general, and of the Guadalupe symbol in particular, derive from these emotions. I say "some meanings" and I use the term "derive" rather than "originate," because the form and function of the family in any given society are themselves determined by other social factors: technology, economy, residence, political power. The family is but one relay in the circuit within which symbols are generated in complex societies. Also, I used the plural "families" rather than "family," because there are demonstrably more than one kind of family in Mexico. I shall simplify the available information on Mexican family life, and discuss the material in terms of two major types of families. The first kind of family is congruent with the closed and static life of the Indian village. It may be called the Indian family. In this kind of family, the husband is ideally dominant, but in reality labor and authority are shared equally among both marriage partners. Exploitation of one sex by the other is atypical; sexual feats do not add to a person's status in the eyes of others. Physical punishment and authoritarian treatment of children are rare. The second kind of family is congruent with the much more open, mobile, manipulative life in communities which are actively geared to the life of the nation, a life in which power relationships between individuals and groups are of great moment. This kind of family may be called the Mexican family. Here, the father's authority is unquestioned on both the real and the ideal plane. Double sex standards prevail, and male sexuality is charged with a desire to exercise domination. Children are ruled with a heavy hand; physical punishment is frequent.

The Indian family pattern is consistent with the behavior towards the Guadalupe noted by John Bushnell in the Matlazinca speaking community of San Juan Atzingo in the Valley of Toluca. There, the image of the Virgin is addressed in passionate terms as a source of warmth and love, and the *pulque* or century plant beer drunk on ceremonial occasions is identified with her milk. Bushnell postulates that here the Guadalupe is identified with the mother as a source of early satisfactions, never again experienced after separation from the mother and emergence into social adulthood. As such, the Guadalupe embodies a longing to return to the pristine state in which hunger and unsatisfactory social relations are minimized. The second family pattern is also consistent with a symbolic identification of Virgin and mother, yet this time within a context of adult male dominance and sexual assertion, discharged against submissive females and children. In this second context, the Guadalupe symbol is charged with the energy of rebellion against the father. Her image is the embodiment of hope in a victorious outcome of the struggle between generations.

This struggle leads to a further extension of the symbolism. Successful rebellion against power figures is equated with the promise of life; defeat with the promise of death. As John A. Mackay has suggested, there thus takes place a further symbolic identification of the Virgin with life; of defeat and death with the crucified Christ. In Mexican artistic tradition, as in Hispanic artistic tradition in general, Christ is never depicted as an adult man, but always either as a helpless child, or more often as a figure beaten, tortured, defeated and killed. In this symbolic equation we are touching upon some of the roots both of the passionate affirmation of faith in the Virgin, and of the fascination with death which characterizes Baroque Christianity in general, and Mexican Catholicism in particular. The Guadalupe stands for life, for hope, for health; Christ on the cross, for despair and for death.

Supernatural mother and natural mother are thus equated symbolically, as are earthly and otherworldly hopes and desires. These hopes center on the provision of food and emotional warmth in the first case, in the successful waging of the Oedipal struggle in the other.

Family relations are, however, only one element in the formation of the Guadalupe symbol. Their analysis does little to explain the Guadalupe as such. They merely illuminate the female and maternal attributes of the more widespread Virgin symbol. The Guadalupe is important to Mexicans not only because she is a supernatural mother, but also because she embodies their major political and religious aspirations.

To the Indian groups, the symbol is more than an embodiment of life and hope; it restores to them the hopes of salvation. We must not forget that the Spanish Conquest signified not only military defeat, but the defeat also of the old gods and the decline of the old ritual. The apparition of the Guadalupe to an Indian commoner thus represents on one level the return of Tonantzin. As Tannenbaum has well said, "The Church . . . gave the Indian an opportunity not merely to save his life, but also to save his faith in his own gods." On another level, the myth of the apparition served as a symbolic testimony that the Indians, as much as the Spaniard, was capable of being saved, capable of receiving Christianity. This must be understood against the background of the bitter theological and political argument which followed the Conquest and divided churchmen, officials, and conquerors into those who held that the Indian was incapable of conversion, thus inhuman, and therefore a fit subject of political and economic exploitation; and those who held that the Indian was human, capable of conversion and that this exploitation had to be tempered by the demands of the Catholic faith and of orderly civil processes of government. The myth of the Guadalupe thus validates the Indian's right to legal defense, orderly government, to citizenship; to supernatural salvation, but also to salvation from random oppression.

But if the Guadalupe guaranteed a rightful place to the Indians in the new social system of New Spain, the myth also held appeal to the large group of disinherited who arose in New Spain as illegitimate offspring of Spanish fathers and Indian mothers, or through impoverishment, acculturation or loss of status within the Indian or Spanish group. For such people, there was for a long time no proper place in the social order. Their very right to exist was questioned in their inability to command the full rights of citizenship and legal protection. Where Spaniard and Indian stood squarely within the law, they inhabited the interstices and margins of constituted society. These groups acquired influence and wealth in the seventeenth and eighteenth centuries, but were yet barred from social recognition and power by the prevailing economic, social and political order. To them, the Guadalupe myth came to represent not merely the guarantee of their assured place in heaven, but the guarantee of their place in society here and now. On the political plane, the wish for a return to a paradise of early satisfactions of food and warmth, a life without defeat, sickness or death, give rise to a political wish for a Mexican paradise, in which the illegitimate sons would possess the country, and the irresponsible Spanish overlords, who never acknowledged the social responsibilities of their paternity, would be driven from the land.

In the writings of seventeenth century ecclesiastics, the Guadalupe becomes the harbinger of this new order. In the book by

Miguel Sánchez, published in 1648, the Spanish Conquest of New Spain is justified solely on the grounds that it allowed the Virgin to become manifest in her chosen country, and to found in Mexico a new paradise. Just as Israel had been chosen to produce Christ, so Mexico had been chosen to produce Guadalupe. Sánchez equates her with the apocalyptic woman of the Revelation of John (12: 1), "arrayed with the sun, and the moon under her feet, and upon her head a crown of twelve stars" who is to realize the prophecy of Deuteronomy 8: 7–10 and lead the Mexicans into the Promised Land. Colonial Mexico thus becomes the desert of Sinai; Independent Mexico the land of milk and honey. F. Francisco de Florencia, writing in 1688, coined the slogan which made Mexico not merely another chosen nation, but the Chosen Nation: *non fecit taliter omni nationi,* words which still adorn the portals of the basilica, and shine forth in electric light bulbs at night. And on the eve of Mexican independence, Servando Teresa de Mier elaborates still further the Guadalupan myth by claiming that Mexico had been converted to Christianity long before the Spanish Conquest. The apostle Saint Thomas had brought the image of Guadalupe-Tonantzin to the New World as a symbol of his mission, just as Saint James had converted Spain with the image of the Virgin of the Pillar. The Spanish Conquest was therefore historically unnecessary, and should be erased from the annals of history. In this perspective, the Mexican War of Independence marks the final realization of the apocalyptic promise. The banner of the Guadalupe leads the insurgents; and their cause is referred to as "her law." In this ultimate extension of the symbol, the promise of life held out by the supernatural mother has become the promise of an independent Mexico, liberated from the irrational authority of the Spanish father-oppressors and restored to the Chosen Nation whose election had been manifest in the apparition of the Virgin on Tepeyac. The land of the supernatural mother is finally possessed by her rightful heirs. The symbolic circuit is closed. Mother; food, hope, health, life; supernatural salvation and salvation from oppression; Chosen People and national independence—all find expression in a single master symbol.

The Guadalupe symbol thus links together family, politics and religion; colonial past and independent present; Indian and Mexican. It reflects the salient social relationships of Mexican life, and embodies the emotions which they generate. It provides a cultural idiom through which the tenor and emotions of these relationships can be expressed. It is, ultimately, a way of talking about Mexico: a "collective representation" of Mexican society.

BRUNO BETTELHEIM

Symbolic Wounds

Puberty rites are rituals that initiate the individual into a new social position; they admirably fulfill Van Gennep's definition of rites of passage and may even be regarded as the most conspicuous examples of such ceremonies. And they usually show more clearly than other rites the three stages—separation, transition, and incorporation—which Van Gennep says are characteristic of all rites of passage. In the first stage the initiate is cut off from his boyhood ties; in the second he is brought into contact with things adult and sacred and is given instruction and knowledge pertaining to his adult role; in the third he is allowed to interact once again with the members of his community, often after having enacted a symbolic rebirth, such as crawling forward between the legs of a woman.

Reprinted from Bruno Bettelheim, *Symbolic Wounds, Puberty Rites and the Envious Male* (Glencoe, Ill.: The Free Press, 1954), pp. 11–19, 165–180, and 257–260, by permission of the author, The Free Press, and Thames and Hudson, Ltd.

In the following selection Bettelheim has addressed himself to the problem of interpreting the meaning of some of the more dramatic forms of the puberty rite as these are found among the Australian aborigines: circumcision and subincision. He discusses the various anthropological theories that have been advanced to account for puberty rites—theories which stress the social dimensions involved in the transition from youth to adulthood. He then rightly points out that these interpretations do not demonstrate why these rites should involve such matters as knocking out a tooth or circumcision or subincision. And this leads him to examine, and reject, the orthodox Freudian interpretation of circumcision in terms of castration and the Oedipal conflict. Instead, he provides us with the novel theory that subincision, and possibly also circumcision, have developed because men are envious of the female and her sexual organs and these ritual operations are symbolic attempts to acquire female organs and to gain power and control over the genitals of the female sex. And, unlike many previous psychoanalytic attempts to interpret such customs on the basis of little or insufficient data, Bettelheim makes an excellent case for his theory by careful use of anthropological field data. The theory needs testing on the basis of materials from other regions of the world, but meanwhile it stands as one of the most provocative theories that has been advanced in recent years.

Rudimentary forms of religious beliefs and rituals were probably the first inventions of the human mind once it ceased to be occupied solely with physical survival. The origin and primeval form of these first creations of man's imagination will be shrouded forever in that darkness that also hides the origin of man himself, the early development of his mind and the beginning of his social structures. The beliefs and rituals of present-day preliterate peoples represent only the most recent phases in a long, complex and, to us as well as to them, unknowable sequence. We cannot draw definitive conclusions as to their origin by studying the characteristics they exhibit today. Still, there is hardly a more fascinating topic for speculation; our curiosity leads us to wonder what were the forms of man's first religious thoughts and rituals and what were the emotional needs they were meant to satisfy.

Though conjectures on the beliefs and rituals of our own primitive ancestors must remain conjecture, we enter less mysterious territory when we begin to consider the lives and practices of modern preliterate people. This book represents an effort toward gaining better understanding of some aspects of present-day life through an analysis of certain ceremonies of preliterate people.

So closely interwoven in the lives of many tribes are religious rituals and those structures that make for social cohesion that it is often hard to know where the one ends and the other begins. This is particularly true of initiation rites, to the analysis of which this study is devoted. In many societies, especially among some of the most primitive, these rituals are extremely important as experiences that bind the group together; at the same time they are also the tribe's most elaborate religious ceremonies. Because of this dual importance, and perhaps also because of certain strange, even awe-inspiring features, they have attracted considerable attention from modern social scientists and psychologists. Though much has been written about them, basically only two sets of explanations as to their nature and meaning have been offered. One of these is anthropological, the other psychoanalytic. The first usually provides an interpretation of the rites as a total phenomenon; the second more commonly takes as its point of departure a certain specific feature, often the practice of circumcision, and explains the rites on its basis.

ANTHROPOLOGICAL INTERPRETATIONS

In the anthropological view, initiation is a *rite de passage* whose function is to introduce the young into adult society. Earlier anthropologists generally did not concern themselves with the reasons behind the application of particular means, and the role of central and formidable features such as circumcision and other mutilations therefore remained unclarified. Stressing the social aspects of the institution of initiation, these anthropologists tended to disregard the psychological motives that may account for it in general and the needs that man attempts to satisfy through some of its particular features. These needs, it seems to me, either are permanent or must recur with each generation, and, since the rites survive, they must be at least partly gratified (unless, of course, one concludes that the rites now satisfy needs different from those they served in the past).

Many anthropologists accept the view that the main purpose of many ritual details is to expedite the separation of the initiate from his old group, and, after a period of relative isolation, to introduce him more effectively into the new group; others think that the purpose of important features is to instruct the initiate in tribal lore. Speiser, for example, although looking for a psychological explanation, sees in initiation ceremonies merely efforts to speed the youngster on his road to adulthood by transmitting to him the "vital energy" of previous generations. He does not demonstrate *why* this should be accomplished by knocking out a tooth or by circumcision or subincision. Aware that this explanation does not account for subincision satisfactorily, he considers it to be little more than a supplement of circumcision. Without raising or answering the questions of why supplementation is needed and why this strange method was selected, he tacitly admits that such questions are justified by remarking that as yet he is unable to offer any more satisfactory psychological explanation.

According to Miller, initiation ceremonies "are intended to cut off the youth from his negligible past as if he had died and then to resurrect him into an entirely new existence as an adult." He sees in initiation "a systematic ceremonial induction of adolescent youths into the full participation in social life. . . . Such practices represent efforts to rivet the youth securely to the regnant social order and are devices for the development of social cohesion." This is undoubtedly true; but it does not clarify, for example, the function of mutilations regularly inflicted.

More recently functional anthropologists have paid greater attention to the social and psychological meaning of the rites. They describe the details and analyze the social aspects, but by and large they do not explain why the varied types of initiation experiences were developed in the first place and why one device is preferred to another. Malinowski, for example, has written at some length about the function initiation has for the society. The following statement illustrates his viewpoint:

They present right through the vast range of their occurrence certain striking similarities. Thus the novices have to undergo a more or less protracted period of seclusion and preparation. Then comes initiation proper, in which the youth, passing through a series of ordeals, is finally submitted to an act of bodily mutilation: at the mildest, a slight incision or the knocking out of a tooth; or, more severe, circumcision; or, really cruel and dangerous, an operation such as the subincision practiced in some Australian tribes. The ordeal is usually associated with the idea of the death and rebirth of the initiated one, which is sometimes enacted in a mimetic performance. But besides the ordeal, less conspicuous and dramatic, but in reality more important, is the second main aspect of initiation: the systematic instruction of the youth in sacred myth and tradition, the gradual unveiling of tribal mysteries and the exhibition of sacred objects.

The decision as to what elements of the rituals are "in reality more important" is the author's; it seems to me to lead to an overemphasis on an assumed end and an underemphasis on the means of attaining it. It is by no means certain whether that which the Western observer regards as means may not be in reality the end, while what he accepts as the end may be mainly a more or less fortuitous consequence or elaboration of the means.

Many anthropological reports on the rites of individual tribes, particularly more recent publications of functional anthropologists, seem to come much closer to what might be a correct explanation. Mead, for example, expresses the notion that in initiation men try to take over the functions of women. Ashley Montagu, Bateson, the Berndts, and others have recognized the important role played by female functions, especially menstruation and childbearing, in the emotional and ritual lives of primitives. If these interpretations were all collated and applied to the rituals of puberty, a different view of the ceremonies might emerge.

PSYCHOANALYTIC INTERPRETATIONS

Certain psychoanalytic ideas on initiation and circumcision, though never accepted by most anthropologists, have spread far beyond the circle of psychoanalysts and have influenced the thinking of many nonprofessional persons. Psychoanalytic investigators, in contrast to anthropologists, have given their attention almost entirely to interpreting ceremonial details. While any discussion of initiation rites must rely heavily on anthropological field observations, the psychoanalytic theories at present seem to offer a more workable frame of reference for explaining the nature, origin, function—in short, the meaning—of some of the seemingly fundamental features in which I am most interested.

Psychoanalytic theories on circumcision and related customs among preliterate peoples have been widely discussed, repeatedly quoted and, in recent times and by nonanthropologists, more often accepted than refused. If I find them in need of revision in several important respects, this implies, of course, no criticism of psychoanalysis as a frame of reference or method of investigation. On the contrary, my own efforts at understanding these rituals are based on both. Current psychoanalytic theory about initiation rites takes as its point of departure castration anxiety and the Oedipal conflict. The conclusion was forced upon me that, as we have learned to go farther back into childhood, beyond the age of the Oedipal situation, in psychoanalytic theory and practice, so also an adequate explanation of initiation ceremonies will have to consider the consequences of much earlier emotional experiences, including the infant's close attachment to his mother. Males' positive feelings and ambivalences toward female figures, and ambivalence of boys and girls, originating in pregenital fixations, about accepting the societally prescribed adult sex role, seem to me to offer a more adequate basis for understanding initiation rites than the theory that the events comprising these ceremonies result from the fathers' jealousy of their sons and that the purpose is to create sexual (castration) anxiety and to make the incest taboo secure.

As my study progressed, indeed, I became ever more keenly aware of the significance of a very different psychoanalytic premise for an understanding of the deeper meanings and functions of initiation rites : the premise that one sex feels envy in regard to the sexual organs and functions of the other.

Freud thought that all human beings are born with bisexual tendencies, and he spoke of "the great enigma of the biological fact of the duality of the sexes," a problem which, he felt, cannot be solved by psychoanalysis, though psychoanalysis is able to show in the mental lives of human beings many reactions to what he called "this great antithesis" of the sexes.

Once I began to view these rituals less on the basis of the concept of castration anxiety and more on that of the antithesis resulting from the duality of the sexes, it became ever clearer that the rites might originate in this antithesis, might even represent efforts to find a solution to the problems of sexual anxiety and envy that are its consequence.

But another contrast also demands attention in the study of puberty rites. Calling them age-grading ceremonies does not do justice to the particular age separation they mark. The antithesis between sexual immaturity and sexual maturity therefore must be considered also. Initiation rites, with certain very minor exceptions, are characterized by the fact that they occur at or around puberty; they are often called "puberty rites." Psychoanalysts were captivated particularly by circumcision, one of the most striking rituals, and, devoting their attention primarily to that rite, established a direct connection between it and infant circumcision. If psychoanalytic investigation had started, instead, with the fact that initiation occurs at puberty, more note might have been taken of Freud's remark that it is not until puberty that the sharp distinction between male and female character is established. Thus the rites seem to emphasize the end of a span of life in which this distinction has not been fully and securely established, and to herald a new life period which should be free of ambivalence about the adult sex role. This point of view concurs with the almost uniform contention of anthropologists that the definite separation of childhood from adulthood is a main purpose of the rites.

Once I had begun to consider these points,

a complex but comprehensible pattern, into which many customs reported by anthropologists seemed to fit, emerged. Other practices, of course, do not adjust easily to such an over-all pattern. This must be expected, if for no other reason because of the long history of the rites, during which they were made to serve a variety of other functions; these depend on the type of society and on the specific additional purposes. Still, certain basic features that on the surface seem to have nothing in common, such as subincision in Australia and the stopping up of the rectum in Africa, can be explained on the basis of these premises.

The possibility that the pattern might have implications far beyond the lives of the tribes studied also appeared. Envy of the genital apparatus and functions of the other sex is shown so generally that it begins to seem characteristic of all human beings. It plays an important role in civilized society. We do not generally ritualize this envy, either in circumcision or in re-enactment of childbirth by men. Nevertheless, direct or indirect derivatives of practices by which it is ritualized in many preliterate societies are part of our cultural heritage, and they are re-enforced in their psychological meaning and consequences by our present envy. Circumcision, as part of Judaic and thus of Christian tradition, is still common practice, though frequently camouflaged as a hygienic or prophylactic manipulation. Because circumcision has psychological consequences in both circumcised and noncircumcised persons, and because, I believe, it is originally derived from and feeds on and into sexual envy and anxiety, it is important to understand its significance.

AUSTRALIAN RITES

Anthropological literature on initiation is so abundant that it is very hard to make a selection of ceremonies for discussion. The problem is made even more difficult by the fact that many authors (most of them not strictly anthropologists but writers using anthropological data) who studied this subject after Freud formulated his theories on it were so profoundly influenced by him that they sometimes attached to observed facts meanings that were derived more from Freud than from empirical evidence. To circumvent this bias, and in justice to Freud, I

have relied mainly on the literature he used. My hypotheses must be substantiated or at least not contradicted by Freud's sources; otherwise, because of the great variety of rites, the conclusion would have to be that Freud's interpretations are valid for the tribes he discussed, while other hypotheses may be valid for others.

Freud's anthropological speculations, particularly those on initiation, were based on the writings of Spencer and Gillen and of Frazer, and since Frazer when discussing Australian aborigines relied heavily on the first authors, their reports will be used here primarily. Australian initiation seems to offer a good starting point because, as Freud remarked, the Australian aborigines, like the Australian fauna, preserved into our own time much that was archaic and no longer to be found elsewhere. The Arunta particularly, since they remained comparatively uninfluenced by contact with superior civilizations, are still considered to provide the most fertile ground for investigations aimed at gaining understanding of the spontaneous development or the acceptance and modification of the rites by preliterate people. In 1896, when they were first studied by Spencer and Gillen, the Arunta were indeed almost untouched by Europeans. Their isolated position in the heart of the continent had kept them from much contact even with other tribes, and had enabled them to preserve their culture in an unchanged form.

I shall quote only excerpts from Spencer and Gillen's accounts of initiation ceremonies, since a report on the Arunta rites alone covers several hundred pages. Also, the authors emphasize repeatedly that while certain features of certain rites are common to many tribes, almost every detail varies from tribe to tribe. Thus some quotations may apply only to one tribe, others to many or all. Each excerpt refers only to particular features of very long and detailed ceremonies lasting many months, and no claim is made to cover all or even most aspects.

MYTHS ON THE ORIGIN OF CIRCUMCISION

According to mythical accounts, circumcision of men was first performed by women. It should be realized, however, that the emotional impact of myths is different in preliterate society from our own. The events related take place in a past that seems very dim and remote, while at the same time it is all-embracing, since it shapes the activities of the present. In their emotional effects, events described in myths have an immediacy in the people's present lives that we may compare with the experiences of a young and unsophisticated child. To him, figures from fairy tales (witches, ferocious or protecting animals), if not the tales themselves, often are more real or more powerful in influencing his emotional life than many persons in the objective world. If the myths state that women originally circumcised men, then, in a way, they still do so, although the execution may now be vested in men. It is possible to conjecture that if people firmly believe that in mythical times women circumcised boys, and if the operation is now performed by men, they may experience it presently as circumcision by *both* women and men. Thus not only the circumcised boy but the circumcisor also may feel that he is taking part in an originally female function.

The Wawilak myth, the most important saga centering around *rites de passage* among several tribes, states simply and directly: "Circumcision started when those two women [the Wawilak sisters] tried to cut their boys" in mythical times.

In a myth current among the Adnjamatana tribe of South Australia, the originator of circumcision is described as neither male nor female human being but a semihuman bird, *Jurijurilja,* one of the totemic ancestors. This bird once threw a boomerang which, on returning, circumcised him and entered the vulvas of his wives, cutting them internally so that they bled. This caused their monthly menstrual period. Here, it seems, menstruation is viewed as a consequence of circumcision. This story not only establishes a direct and close connection between circumcision and menstruation; indirectly it also suggests that, since procreation in women cannot take place before they being to menstruate, circumcision is possibly viewed as an analogous necessary precondition for procreation.

Another legend, that of the Unthippa women, one of the most important myths of the Arunta, tells us that "When [these women] . . . found . . . people . . . about to perform the rite of circumcision upon some . . . boys . . . [the women] took the boys on their shoulders and carried them along with them, leaving them at various

spots en route, after performing circumcision on them." Then the women wandered on until they reached a place where, because of exhaustion from dancing, their sexual organs dropped out, forming deposits of red ochre. Similar stories are told also about other mythical women, and "the deposits of red ochre which are found in various parts [of the country] are associated with women's blood. . . . Tradition says that . . . women . . . caused blood to flow from the vulva in large quantities, and so formed the deposit of red ochre. . . . They did the same thing in other places."

The myth not only asserts that the Unthippa women invented circumcision (a belief that is acted out in present-day circumcision rites; see below) but also indicates that they bled from or lost their sex organs *after* they had circumcised the boys. If this sequence of events has any meaning, it suggests that bleeding from or loss or mutilation of the female sex organ as acted out in the introcision of girls is a consequence of (punishment for?) the circumcision of boys.

Red ochre, created from the female sex organs or vaginal blood according to the aborigines' belief, is of great importance in the rituals. Whenever the sacred bull-roarers are examined, for example, some of it is rubbed on them. In the thinking of these people, red ochre is not simply symbolic but actually is the mythical women's sex organs or genital blood; thus in its extensive ceremonial use red ochre must be considered to be menstrual blood or else very closely related to it.

According to Murngin tradition the great initiation rites were first performed by the mythical Wawilak sisters; it was only when the male ancestors dreamed of them that the rites passed into the hands of men. The people of the New Hebrides explicitly assert that women invented circumcision. They say that one day a man went into the jungle with his sister. She climbed a breadfruit tree to cut down the ripe fruit with a bamboo. When she had finished she threw down the bamboo, which accidentally cut the man's foreskin. After the man recovered, he had intercourse with a woman, who found it so good that she told another woman; soon this man was in great demand, to the fury of other men; "but their women sneer at them and say they need to be like that one. So they pay him to tell the secret. He tells, and they have in such wise cut their children ever after."

According to other myths women introduced or changed the tool with which circumcision is performed. In one region of Australia the mythical account states that women introduced the stone knife, where previously a fire stick had been used. These women threw a sharp piece of flint to the men, who then started to use it in circumcision of boys. Still another myth relates that a woman gave the ancestors the stone knife for circumcision; it also states that initiation of men was originally derived from that of women.

The important role women play in circumcision even in modern times is emphasized by the fact that the occasion of this rite is the only one at which they are permitted to decorate themselves as warriors and to carry men's weapons. After the novice has sat down among the men, "the women, who had been awaiting his arrival, at once began to dance, carrying shields in their hands. The reason assigned for this is that in the [mythical] times certain women called *Unthippa* carried along with them . . . young boys who were just being initiated. . . . They also carried shields: and therefore it is that, at the present day, the initiation ceremony must commence with an imitation of the Unthippa dance. . . . (Roth describes the women as decorated after the manner of warriors about to engage in a fight during the early part of the proceedings.) Except in connection with this ceremony women may never carry shields, which are exclusively the property of the men."

The women try to carry off the boys to be circumcised but are prevented by the men, the implication being that they wish to do it now as the mythical women did in the past:

. . . At a later time . . . in the ceremony . . . just before the performance of the actual ceremony [of circumcision] one of the women . . . placing her head between [the novice's] legs suddenly lifts him up on her shoulders and runs off with him, as . . . the *Unthippa* women did, but, unlike what happened in the past, the boy is again seized by the men and brought back.

After describing this ceremony, the authors remark that, whatever these Unthippa women may have been, the myth concerning them may be regarded as evidence that, in the past, women played an even more important part in such ceremonies than they do in modern times. They still attempt to take over the ceremonial ground just before circumcision is to take place, but nowadays are chased off by the men.

There are other indications that women formerly played a more important role in initiation. The tradition according to which the bull-roarers originally belonged to women may illustrate this. The swinging of these objects is a very important part of many aboriginal religious ceremonies, and there are many different bull-roarers, each representing some ancestral figure or totemistic subject. According to McConnell, in initiation four kinds of bull-roarers are used. Two, swung by young initiates at the end of the first ceremony, represent a young girl just entering the age of puberty; two others represent a girl fully mature and are swung by the initiates at the close of the ceremony. This seems to permit the interpretation that the changes initiation produces in the boys are parallel to those occurring in girls between onset of puberty and full sexual maturity.

According to the myth, these bull-roarers were originally swung by two young girls, who said, "It belongs to us women, really we have found it! But no matter! We leave it for the men! It is they who will always use it." Similarly in the Wikmunkan myth the women say, "This is a bull-roarer, we have found it! We women! It is we who have found it."

The Buka tell the story of the origin of the bull-roarer as follows:

A woman once went to cut firewood in the bush. . . . She picked up a piece of wood and knocked it on a log. It split in two. One piece flew up into the air and made a noise like this (the teller imitates it). The woman jumped up in a fright: "What is that?" Then she thought: "It is something very good. It belongs to me, I found it." . . . Then she went to her village [and all the women came together and] said "True, true, you have found a good thing. It belongs to us, you found it."

Then all the men came [and wanted to know what all the noise was about. The women told them, and] then all the men went back to their own side of the huts and talked. "Ah, we had better get this piece of wood, it can cry out." So the men went and took it away from the women, and they killed . . . them all, except some very tiny girls, hardly more than babies;

they were allowed to live because they did not know about the bull-roarer properly.

These myths seem to be parallel to those that maintain that circumcision was originally performed by women, and they might be viewed as mutually supporting since they are relatively independent of one another. The second suggests that the powers needed to initiate men into adult society originally belonged to women. Thus, again, it seems that male initiation depends or depended on women. The importance of women or of female sex organs and development in male initiation is further emphasized by the custom of subincision.

RITUAL SUBINCISION

Anatomically, and probably also psychologically, subincision, not circumcision, is the most far-reaching of all initiation ceremonies. Since it is practiced in only a few areas of the world it is relatively little discussed in the literature, although it involves very radical surgery on the male genital and probably also alters the sensations during coitus. It is described as follows:

The operation consists essentially in slitting open the whole or part of the penile urethra along the ventral or undersurface of the penis. The initial cut is generally about an inch long, but this may subsequently be enlarged so that the incision extends from the glans to the root of the scrotum, in this way the whole of the under part of the penile urethra is laid open. The latter form of the operation is universal among the Central tribes. As one proceeds outwards the intensity of the operation becomes reduced, until we meet with forms which strongly resemble the condition of hypospadias, that is, forms in which a small slit is made in the urethra towards either the glans or the scrotum, or both.

Subincision (*ariltha*) among the Arunta may take place five or six weeks after circumcision, depending on the time needed for recovery from the initial operation. In other tribes, the elapsed time may be much longer. From this ceremony women are excluded, and it proceeds, in part, as follows:

. . . As soon as ever [the novice] was in position another man sat astride of his body, grasped the penis and put the urethra on the stretch. The operator then approached and quickly, with a stone knife, laid open the urethra from below. . . . When all was over the

[newly initiated] were led to one side while they squatted over shields into which the blood was allowed to drain . . . and from which it is emptied into the center of a fire which is made for the purpose. . . . As a result of the operation . . . micturition is always . . . performed in a squatting position. . . .

It very often happens that, as soon as the operation has been performed on a novice, one or more of the younger men present, who have been operated on before, stand up and voluntarily undergo a second operation, considering that the incision has not been carried far enough. Standing out on the clear space . . . with legs wide apart and hands behind his back, the man shouts out . . . "Mura [wife's mother] mine, come and cut my subincision down to the root." . . . Most men . . . undergo the second operation and some come forward a third time, though a man is often as old as thirty or thirty-five before he submits to this second operation.

There are no accounts from these tribes of men requesting circumcision or circumcising themselves. Thus while the minor operation of circumcision is nearly always performed by others, the more radical subincision, like ritual castration in the service of the great maternal deities, is occasionally self-inflicted or, more often, inflicted on the subject at his request. We might therefore infer that subincision is more self-motivated than circumcision.

While the Arunta say that circumcision originated with the Unthippa women, no similar direct connection between subincision and mythical females is reported. Nevertheless, a connection between women and subincision is suggested by the subincised men's behavior on the morning following the operation:

At daylight on the morning of the next day the men provide themselves with fire sticks and, surrounding the young man, conduct him to the women. . . . When the party is within a short distance of the women . . . the young man steps out from the center of the group and throws his boomerang high up in the direction of the spot at which his mother was supposed to have lived in mythical times. This throwing of the boomerang in the direction of the mythical mother's camp . . . occurs [also] during the performance of . . . ceremonies . . . which accompany the knocking out of teeth.

Such attack against the mythical mother may represent either a desire for revenge or an effort on the young man's part to protect himself, by offensive action, against a danger. It might also be construed as symbolically putting women in their place, once the ritual mutilation has occurred. Whatever the reason, the fact remains that immediately after subincision (or the knocking out of teeth which in some tribes is substituted for circumcision or subincision) a symbolic attack is carried out against the symbolic mother. This time the men do not use relatively innocuous pieces of bark, as they do to frighten away the women who try to take over the circumcision ground earlier in the ceremonies. Now the most potent weapon of the tribe is used. And while the whole group of men threw bark at the women, this time only the victim throws the boomerang; it seems to be less a purely ceremonial act and more seriously meant as a symbol of personal revenge or attack.

Spencer and Gillen were puzzled by this custom, though they tried to rationalize it within the then prevalent frame of reference, according to which the purpose of initiation was to gain entrance into manhood and to break the ties between child and mother. Nevertheless, they remained dissatisfied by their own explanations and ended by stating that the significance of throwing the boomerang at the camp of the mythical mother is difficult to see. Such behavior would indeed be incomprehensible if aggression were directed against the real mother. It was not she, but the ancient, no longer existent mother who, either directly or through men's desire to be like women, caused subincision. Whether this suggests that maternal figures inflicted or demanded the operation as a precondition of marriage in prehistoric times; or whether the ancient mother image is that which every man carries within himself, the image received in childhood; or whether this figure is the man's own childish image of the mother, projected into ancient times—these possibilities are irrelevant here. It still may be inferred from the total behavior of the men that subincision is felt to be "caused" by an archaic mother.

Even if men at one time had been forced to submit to such an operation, however, they would hardly continue it and voluntarily request or inflict on themselves reopening of the wound if they were not motivated to do so by inner forces. No tribal lore is taught by it. It is no *rite de passage,* since it does not change the person's status.

It is a voluntarily chosen mutilation, not a mutilation of the son by the father. If, however, one begins with the fact that the subincision wound is called "vulva," then the operation itself and the repeated opening of and bleeding from the wound become understandable. Then it appears that the purpose of the ritual might be to reproduce symbolically the female sex organ, while the reopening of the wound may symbolize the periodic phenomenon of menstruation. Statements made by the people themselves confirm such an interpretation. The Murngin say: "The blood that runs from an incision and with which the dancers paint themselves and their emblems is something more than a man's blood—it is the menses of the old Wawilak women. . . . 'that blood we put all over those men is all the same as the blood that came from the old woman's vagina. It isn't the blood of those men any more because it has been sung over and made strong. The hole in the man's arm isn't that hole any more. It is all the same as the vagina of that old woman that had the blood coming out of it.' "

Other statements reveal similar attitudes. According to Roheim: "The ritual of subincision . . . consists in the older men (the initiators) running backwards and showing their subincision hole. The blood spurts forth from the subincision hole and the youngsters see the great mystery of initiation. It is quite clear what is meant when they call the subincision hole a 'vagina' or a 'penis womb.' . . . They are offering an artificial vagina as compensation for the real one . . ." and "the blood squirting from the penis is called woman, or milk." In another Central Australian tribe, the Urrabuna, subincision is known as *verrupu,* and the vagina is also occasionally designated by that term although its proper name is *pintha.*

Not only the Murngin but also the Wogeo and Kwoma of New Guinea use parallel names for menstrual bleeding and bleeding from the subincision opening. In New Guinea the penis is periodically incised, the operation usually being referred to as "men's menstruation." All avoidances imposed on women during the menstrual period also apply to men while they bleed from the incision wound.

These and other similar data suggested to Bryk that "through subincision the young man is supposed to be changed into a woman. . . . The initiation ceremonies change boys into women, or, rather, man-women."

Roheim stresses the significance of the use of the term "milk" in the sacred songs to describe the blood derived from the penis. Comparing food taboos, he remarks on the similarity between those applying to men bleeding from subincision and those for menstruating women. In further support of his contention that the men are playing the part of menstruating women, he quotes an Arunta, who stated that if a woman sees a man's blood flowing from the veins she must either be killed or a large group of men must have intercourse with her. Roheim feels that by this they reassert their manhood, which is in danger if their ("menstrual") blood is seen by a woman. Another parallel may be found in the stories according to which the women of the mythical period used their menstrual blood to smear their ceremonial poles, just as men now use blood drawn from the subincision wound for the same purpose.

It may well be that the magical qualities generally ascribed to menstruation and menstrual blood account for its supposed use for the ceremonial poles in mythical times. However, among these Australians, at any time a potent magic is to be invoked, blood is used. The magical quality ascribed particularly to menstrual blood forms the basis of the theory of subincision put forth by Ashley Montagu:

The element common to all forms of subincision is the inevitable effusion of blood. . . . Briefly, the suggestion here is that male subincision or incision corresponds, or is intended to correspond, to female menstruation. Indeed, I may at once state the hypothesis which I am about to offer as an explanation of the probable origin of subincision in Australia; it is that subincision in the male was originally instituted in order to cause the male to resemble the female with respect to the occasional effusion of blood which is naturally characteristic of the female, and possibly also with respect to producing some feminization in the appearance of the male organ.

While he recognizes that the purpose of subincision is to make men resemble women physiologically and anatomically, that subincision is "analogous" to menstruation, he thinks that it is only "for the purpose of permitting the bad humors of the body, and such as are likely to be produced during the performance of certain tasks with which a great deal of power is associated, to be liberated and voided. The analogy he suggests is, to my way of thinking, not broad enough.

Appearance of menstrual bleeding indicates the ability to bear children; the temporary stoppage of menstruation during pregnancy suggests a further relation between menstruation and the creation of new life. On the basis of such interrelation menstrual blood, or any blood drawn from the genitals, may appear as a substance that has powerful influence over life. The Arunta believe that it will restore endangered life, as in cases of sickness. While menstrual blood is supposed to restore power to the man, blood from the subincised penis is believed to have a similar effect on woman. When menstrual blood is not available and a man is seriously ill, blood is drawn from the labia minora and one of the women takes a witchetty grub, dips it into the blood and gives it to the man to eat. Afterward his body is rubbed over with the blood. When an aboriginal woman is very sick, one of the sons of her younger sisters draws blood from the subincision wound; she drinks part of it and he rubs the remainder over her body, adding a coating of red ochre and grease. In all cases of illness, the first remedy is to rub red ochre over the body.

FEMALE INITIATION RITES

Female initiation rites devised or imposed by women, such as extension of the clitoris and labia, in addition to providing a chance for socially approved masturbation, may be also the result of women's desire to possess a penislike organ. Dressing like men, wearing men's ornaments and weapons, etc., may help to satisfy related desires in respect to man's social functions.

Some examples may illustrate the procedures that give women a greater degree of clitoridean or "phallic" sexuality than nature grants them, as well as a penislike genital organ. The point to be emphasized is that women practice this without any encouragement from or interference by men; hence its motivation must lie in the desires of women. In Dahomey

Girls who are from nine to eleven years old—that is, whose breasts are beginning to develop—are assembled by compounds in groups —and engage in the practice . . . of massaging and enlarging the lips of the vagina. They gather in the evenings at sundown behind the house of the woman in whose care they have been placed. . . . With a shaped piece of wood, this woman manipulates the lips of the vagina of each girl, pulling at them, stretching them, and lightly puncturing the vaginal tissues in several places. This she does eight to nine times for each of her charges during the first year of instruction, and during the next year the girls do this for each other. . . . For two years at the very least this is continued, and in addition there is the other massaging of these "lips" to cause thickening and muscular development for "thin-lipped" women are considered lacking in comeliness.

According to another account

The Maxi people use a horn [for enlarging and developing the lips of the vagina], though in Abomey both a special wooden instrument and the root of the indigo plant are employed, and, in addition, ants . . . the purpose of the introduction of this vegetable irritant or the stinging ants is to stimulate the process of massage, by inducing irritation which encourages tugging and handling. The [female] teacher besides supervising this process, . . . also gives the girls instructions bearing on sexual life.

Among the Baganda and the Suaheli the girl before she reaches puberty is encouraged to enlarge her labia through frequent pulling and stroking and by use of some special herbs or leaves.

Such practices bring about changes of the genitals that can be connected neither with the teaching of tribal lore nor with wishes to bind the tribe together; they have no relation to *rites de passage,* nor to securing the incest taboo or inhibiting sexuality. They obviously increase the desire and opportunity for masturbation and, according to the teaching connected with them, enhance sex enjoyment for both men and women. It is an age-grading experience which prepares girls for their future sex role and seems well in line with the desires of girls of this age. It is not imposed by elders against the wishes of the young and serves hardly any other purpose than to provide sexual stimulation and to help the girls toward sexual maturity. Compared with such progressive experiences, those other female initiation rituals that seem to be mainly copies of male rites, even when apparently based on a desire for social equality with men, are lacking in conviction.

The writer on female initiation finds relatively little material on which to work. Partly because most investigators have been men, and partly because of the greater prominence of male rites, there is little in the literature on female initiation. But, on one point, female rites offer better evidence than male. In the myths explaining boys' rituals it is said that manipulation of the male genital was once executed by women. But in present practice the actual interference is nearly always performed by men. Manipulation of the female sex organs, on the other hand, is performed by both men and women. Thus in girls' rites we may find a clue as to what types of manipulation are imposed by the other sex (and possibly also why) and which are self-chosen or suggested and imposed by persons of the same sex on each other.

Comparing manipulation of the female sex apparatus by men and by women, it can be seen that, by and large, manipulation by men is destructive, showing an aggressive enmity that is most readily explained by fear or envy. Manipulation of female sex organs by women, on the other hand, more often than not results in greater sex enjoyment and in an extension of, if not an addition to, the sex apparatus which causes the existing organs to become more like those of men. That the labia, as Herskovits points out, by artificial manipulation become more muscular, harder, and less flexible is another change in the direction of the erect penis.

These practices suggest that human beings' envy of the genital apparatus of the other sex leads to the desire to acquire similar organs and to gain power and control over the genitals of the other sex. The former desire is represented in men by subincision and possibly also by circumcision; in women, it is shown in manipulation to enlarge the clitoris and labia. The wish for mastery—which might originate partly in an effort to deny and overcome fear—is no longer expressed directly by women, but it can be inferred from myths and from the fact that the foreskin is often given to women; the parallel desire of men still finds overt expression.

EDMUND R. LEACH

Two Essays Concerning the Symbolic Representation of Time

It is a truism that time, especially in its calendrical aspects, has been endowed by men everywhere with sacred meaning. A look at a Roman Catholic calendar gives testimony to the persistence of the ancient connection that has been made between sacred rituals and the yearly round, based in large measure on the ever-recurring change of seasons, in animal and plant life, and in celestial phenomena, these serving as a simple kind of measurement. The article "Pesach" in Chapter 11 furnishes an excellent example from the Jewish world. Social and religious life are regulated by and come to center around "natural" calendars, the moon being overwhelmingly important in the simpler societies, and traces of the lunar month can be found even today in almost all calendrical systems.

In his analysis of the symbolization of time, Leach has restated some of the standard notions of time and given them novel interpretations. His first essay, "Cronus and Chronos," opens with the suggestion that we tend to think of time both in terms of repetition and of irreversibility, especially the latter, and that much of religion is concerned with trying to deny the reality of death by equating the second of these two concepts with the first. Some primitives, however, do not experience time in either of these two ways but perceive it as a sequence of oscillations between opposite poles. The rest of the essay is devoted toward demonstrating that this third concept involves a third entity, to wit, the thing that does the oscillating, and that an animistic concept of this sort is bound up with a belief in reincarnation, justified by a mythology, an example of which is provided from classical Greece.

In his second article, "Time and False Noses," Leach's indebtedness to the Durkheimian school of sociology is again apparent, as it was in the first, where the influence of Lévi-Strauss was specifically acknowledged. Leach gives his solution to the question of why men throughout the world mark their calendars by festivals, at which time they indulge either in formality, masquerade, or role reversal. He sees these three involved, respectively, with three phases of sacred time: *separation,* with its rites of sacralization; a marginal state of *suspended animation,* when ordinary time stops; and *aggregation,* with its rites of desacralization. He attempts to structure the three practices of formality, masquerade, and role reversal in terms of opposites, placing the first and third in opposition to the second.

Reprinted from E. R. Leach, *Rethinking Anthropology* (London: The Athlone Press, University of London, 1961), pp. 124–136, by permission of the author and The Athlone Press.

INTRODUCTORY NOTE

These two short essays originally appeared in the Toronto University publication *Explorations.* The amendments which have been made to the text of "Cronus and Chronos" are largely due to the very helpful suggestions of Mr. M. I. Finley of Jesus College, Cambridge.

I. CRONUS AND CHRONOS

My starting point in this essay is simply *time* as a word in the English language. It is a word which we use in a wide variety of contexts and it has a considerable number of synonyms, yet is oddly difficult to translate. In an English-French dictionary *time* has one of the longest entries in the book; time is *temps,* and *fois,* and *heure,* and *age,* and *siècle,* and *saison* and lots more besides, and none of these are simple equivalents; *temps* perhaps is closest to English *time,* but *beau temps* is not a "lovely time"!

Outside of Europe this sort of ambiguity is even more marked. For example, the language of the Kachin people of North Burma seems to contain no single word which corresponds at all closely to English *time;* instead there are numerous partial equivalents. For example, in the following expressions the Kachin equivalent of the word *time* would differ in every case:

The *time* by the clock is	*ahkying*
A long *time*	*na*
A short *time*	*tawng*
The present *time*	*ten*
Spring *time*	*ta*
The *time* has come	*hkra*
In the *time* of Queen Victoria	*lakhtak, aprat*
At any *time* of life	*asak*

and that certainly does not exhaust the list. I do not think a Kachin would regard these words as in any way synonyms for one another.

This sort of thing suggests an interesting problem which is quite distinct from the purely philosophical issue as to what is the *nature* of Time. This is: How do we come to have such a verbal category as *time* at all? How does it link up with our everyday experiences?

Of course in our own case, equipped as we are with clocks and radios and astronomical observatories, time is a given factor in our social situation; it is an essential part of our lives which we take for granted. But suppose we had no clocks and no scientific astronomy, how then should we think about time? What obvious attributes would time then seem to possess?

Perhaps it is impossible to answer such a very hypothetical question, and yet, clocks apart, it seems to me that our modern English notion of time embraces at least two different kinds of experience which are logically distinct and even contradictory.

Firstly, there is the notion of repetition. Whenever we think about measuring time we concern ourselves with some kind of metronome; it may be the ticking of a clock or a pulse beat or the recurrence of days or moons or annual seasons, but always there is something which repeats.

Secondly, there is the notion of non-repetition. We are aware that all living things are born, grow old and die, and that this is an irreversible process.

I am inclined to think that all other aspects of time, duration for example or historical sequence, are fairly simple derivatives from these two basic experiences:

(*a*) that certain phenomena of nature repeat themselves
(*b*) that life change is irreversible.

Now our modern sophisticated view tends to throw the emphasis on the second of these aspects of time. "Time," says Whitehead, "is sheer succession of epochal durations": it goes on and on. All the same we need to recognize that this irreversibility of time is psychologically very unpleasant. Indeed, throughout the world, religious dogmas are largely concerned with denying the final "truth" of this common sense experience.

Religions of course vary greatly in the manner by which they purport to repudiate the "reality" of death; one of the commonest devices is simply to assert that death and birth are the same thing—that birth follows death, just as death follows birth. This seems to amount to denying the second aspect of time by equating it with the first.

I would go further. It seems to me that if it were not for religion we should not attempt to embrace the two aspects of time under one category at all. Repetitive and non-repetitive events are not, after all, logically the same. We treat them both as aspects of "one thing," *time,* not because it is rational to do so, but because of religious prejudice. The idea of Time, like the idea of God, is one of those categories which we find necessary because we are social animals rather than because of anything empirical in our objective experience of the world.

Or put it this way. In our conventional way of thinking, every interval of time is marked by repetition; it has a beginning and an end which are "the same thing"—the tick of a clock, sunrise, the new moon, New Year's day . . . but every interval of time is only a section of some larger interval of time which likewise begins and ends in repetition . . . so, if we think in this way, we must end by supposing that "Time itself" (whatever that is) must repeat itself. Empirically this seems to be the case. People *do* tend to think of time as something which ultimately repeats itself; this applies equally to Australian aborigines, Ancient Greeks, and modern mathematical astronomers. My view is that we think this way not because there is no other possible way of thinking, but because we have a psychological (and hence religious) repugnance to contemplating either the idea of death or the idea of the end of the universe.

I believe this argument may serve to throw some light upon the representation of time in primitive ritual and mythology. We ourselves, in thinking about time, are far too closely tied to the formulations of the astronomers; if we do not refer to time as if it were a coordinate straight line stretching from an infinite past to an infinite future, we describe it as a circle or cycle. These are purely geometrical metaphors, yet there is nothing intrinsically geometrical about time as we actually experience it. Only mathematicians are ordinarily inclined to think of repetition as an aspect of motion in a circle. In a primitive, unsophisticated community the metaphors of repetition are likely to be of a much more homely nature: vomiting, for example, or the oscillations of a weaver's shuttle, or the sequence of agricultural activities, or even the ritual exchanges of a series of interlinked marriages. When we describe such sequences as "cyclic" we innocently introduce a geometrical notation which may well be entirely absent in the thinking of the people concerned.

Indeed in some primitive societies it would seem that the time process is not experienced as a "succession of epochal durations" at all; there is no sense of going on and on in the same direction, or round and round the same wheel. On the contrary, time is experienced as something discontinuous, a repetition of repeated reversal, a sequence of oscillations between polar opposites: night and day, winter and summer, drought and flood, age and youth, life and death. In such a scheme the past has no "depth" to it, all past is equally past; it is simply the opposite of now.

It is religion, not common sense, that persuades men to include such various oppositions under a single category such as *time*. Night and day, life and death are logically similar pairs only in the sense that they are both pairs of contraries. It is religion that identifies them, tricking us into thinking of death as the night time of life and so persuading us that non-repetitive events are really repetitive.

The notion that the time process is an oscillation between opposites—between day and night or between life and death—implies the existence of a third entity—the "thing" that oscillates, the "I" that is at one moment in the daylight and another in the dark, the "soul" that is at one moment in the living body and at another in the tomb. In this version of animistic thinking the body and the grave are simply alternative temporary residences for the life-essence, the soul. Plato, in the *Phaedo,* actually uses this metaphor explicitly: he refers to the human body as the *tomb* of the soul (psyche). In death the soul goes from this world to the underworld; in birth it comes back from the underworld to this world.

This is of course a very common idea both in primitive and less primitive religious thinking. The point that I want to stress is that this type of animism involves a particular conception of the nature of time and, because of this, the mythology which justifies a belief in reincarnation is also, from another angle, a mythological representation of "time" itself. In the rest of this essay I shall attempt to illustrate this argument by reference to familiar material from classical Greece.

At first sight it may appear that I am arguing in a circle. I started by asking what sort of concrete real experience lies at the back of our abstract notion of time. All I seem to have done so far is to switch from the oscillations of abstract time to the oscillations of a still more abstract concept, soul. Surely that is worse than ever. For us, perhaps, yes. We can "see" time on a clock; we cannot see people's souls; for us, souls are more abstract than time. But for the Greeks, who had no clocks, time was a total abstraction, whereas the soul was thought of as a material substance consisting of the marrow of the spine and the head, and forming a sort of concentrated essence of male semen. At death, when the body was placed in the tomb this marrow coagulated into a live snake. In Greek ancestor cults the marked emphasis on snake worship was not a residue of totemism: it was simply that the hero-ancestor in his chthonic form was thought to be an actual snake. So for the Greeks, of the pre-Socratic period anyway, the oscillation of the soul between life and death was quite materially conceived—the soul was either material bone-marrow (in the living body) or it was a material snake (in the tomb).

If then, as I have suggested, the Greeks conceived the oscillations of time by analogy with the oscillations of the soul, they were using a concrete metaphor. Basically it is the metaphor of sexual coitus, of the ebb and flow of the sexual essence between sky and earth (with the rain as semen), between this world and the underworld (with marrow-fat and vegetable seeds as semen), between man and woman. In short, it is the sexual act itself which provides the primary image of time. In the act of copulation the male imparts a bit of his life-soul to the female; in giving birth she yields it forth again. Coitus is here seen as a kind of dying for the male; giving birth as a kind of dying for the female. Odd though this symbolism may appear, it is entirely in accord with the findings of psycho-analysts who have approached the matter from quite a different point of view.

All this I suggest throws light upon one of the most puzzling characters in classical Greek mythology, that of Cronus, father of Zeus. [Aristotle] (*de Mundo* Ch. 7) declared that Cronus (Kronos) was a symbolical representation of Chronos, Eternal Time—and it is apparently this association which has provided our venerable Father Time with his scythe. Etymologically, however, there is no close connection between *kronos* and *chronos,* and it seems unlikely that [Aristotle] should have made a bad pun the basis for a major issue of theology, though this seems to be the explanation generally put forward. Whatever may have been the history of the Cronus cult—and of that we know nothing—the fact that at one period Cronus was regarded as a symbol for Time must surely imply that there was something about the mythological character of Cronus which seemed appropriate to that of a personified Time. Yet it is difficult for us to understand this. To us Cronus appears an entirely disreputable character with no obvious temporal affinities.

Let me summarize briefly the stories which relate to him:

1. Cronus, King of the Titans, was the son of Uranus (sky) and Ge (earth). As the children of Uranus were born, Uranus pushed them back again into the body of Ge. Ge to escape this prolonged pregnancy armed Cronus with a sickle with which he castrated his father. The blood from the bleeding phallus fell into the sea and from the foam was born Aphrodite (universal fecundity).

2. Cronus begat children by his sister Rhea. As they were born he swallowed them. When the youngest, Zeus, was born, Rhea deceived Cronus by giving him a (phallic) stone wrapped in a cloth instead of the new-born infant. Cronus swallowed the stone instead of the child. Zeus thus grew up. When Zeus was adult, Cronus vomited up his swallowed children, namely: Hades, Poseidon, Hestia, Hera, Demeter, and also the stone phallus, which last became a cult object at Delphi. Zeus now rebelled against King Cronus and overthrew him; according to one version he castrated him. Placed in restraint, Cronus became nevertheless the beneficient ruler of the Elysian Fields, home of the blessed dead.

3. There had been men when King Cronus ruled but no women; Pandora, the first woman, was created on Zeus' instructions. The age of Cronus was a golden age of bliss and plenty, when the fields yielded harvests without being tilled. Since there were no women, there was no strife! Our present age, the age of Zeus, will one day come to an end, and the reign of Cronus will then be resumed. In that moment men will cease to grow older: they will grow younger. Time will repeat itself in reverse: men will be born from their graves. Women will once more cease to be necessary, and strife will disappear from the world.

4. About the rituals of Cronus we know little. In Athens the most important was the festival known as Kronia. This occurred at harvest time in the first month of the year and seems to have been a sort of New Year celebration. It resembled in some ways the Roman saturnalia (Greek Cronus and Roman Saturn were later considered identical). Its chief feature seems to have been a ritual reversal of roles—masters waiting on slaves and so on.

What is there in all this that makes Cronus an appropriate symbol for Time? The third story certainly contains a theme about time, but how does it relate to the first two stories? Clearly the time that is involved is not time as we ordinarily tend to think of it—an endless continuum from past to future. Cronus's time is an oscillation, a time that flows back and forth, that is born and swallowed and vomited up, an oscillation from father to mother, mother to father and back again.

Some aspects of the story fit well enough with the views of Frazer and Jane Harrison about Corn Spirits and Year Spirits (*eniautos daimon*). Cronus, as the divine reaper, cuts the "seed" from the "stalk" so that Mother Earth yields up her harvest. Moreover, since harvest is logically the end of a sequence of time, it is understandable enough that, given the notion of time as oscillation, the change over from year's end to year's beginning should be symbolized by a reversal of social roles—at the end point of any kind of oscillation everything goes into reverse. Even so the interpretation in terms of vegetation magic and nature symbolism does not get us very far. Frazer and Jane Harrison count their Corn Spirits and Year Spirits by the dozen and even if Cronus does belong to the general family this does not explain why Cronus rather than any of the others should have been specifically identified as a symbol of Time personified.

My own explanation is of a more structural kind. Fränkel has shown that early Greek ideas about time underwent considerable development. In Homer *chronos* refers to periods of empty time and is distinguished from periods of activity which are thought of as days (*ephemeros*). By the time of Pindar this verbal distinction had disappeared, but a tendency to think of time as an "alternation between contraries" active and inactive, good and bad, persisted. It is explicit in Archilochus (seventh century B.C.). In the classical period this idea underwent further development so that in the language of philosophy, time was an oscillation of vitality between two contrasted poles. The argument in Plato's *Phaedo* makes this particularly clear. Given this premise, it follows logically that the "beginning of time" occurred at that instant when, out of an initial unity, was created not only polar opposition but also the sexual vitality that oscillates between one and the other—not only God and the Virgin but the Holy Spirit as well.

Most commentators on the Cronus myth have noted simply that Cronus separates Sky from Earth, but in the ideology I have been discussing the creation of time involves more than that. Not only must male be distinguished from female but one must postulate a third element, mobile and vital, which oscillates between the two. It seems clear that the Greeks thought of this third element in explicit concrete form as male semen. Rain is the semen of Zeus; fire the semen of Hephaestos; the offerings to the dead (*panspermia*) were baskets of seeds mixed up with phallic emblems; Hermes the messenger of the gods, who takes the soul to Hades and brings back souls from the dead, is himself simply a phallus and a head and nothing more.

This last symbolic element is one which is found to recur in many mythological systems. The logic of it seems clear. In crude pictorial representation, it is the presence or absence of a phallus which distinguishes male from female, so, if time is represented as a sequence of role reversals, castration stories linked up with the notion of a phallus trickster who switches from side to side of the dichotomy "make sense." If Kerenyi and Jung are to be believed there are psychological explanations for the fact that the "messenger of the gods" should be part clown, part fraud, part isolated phallus, but here I am concerned only with a question of symbolic logic. If time be thought of as alternation, then myths about sex reversals are representations of time.

Given this set of metaphors Cronus's myth *does* make him "the creator of time." He separates sky from earth but he separates off at the same time the male vital principle which, falling to the sea reverses itself and becomes the female principle of fecundity. The shocking part of the first story, which at first seems an unnecessary gloss, contains, as one might have expected, the really crucial theme. So also in the second story the swallowing and vomiting activities of Cronus serve to create three separate categories—Zeus, the polar opposites of Zeus, and a material phallus. It is no accident that Zeus's twice born siblings are the five deities named, for each is the "contrary" of Zeus in one of his recognized major aspects: the three females are the three aspects of womanhood, Hestia the maiden, Hera the wife, Demeter the mother; they are the opposites of Zeus in his roles as divine youth (*kouros*), divine husband, divine father and divine son (Dionysus). Hades, lord of the underworld and the dead, is the opposite of Zeus, lord of the bright day and the living; Poseidon, earth shaker, god of the sea (salt water), is the opposite of Zeus, sky shaker (thunderer), god of rain and dew.

The theme of the child which is swallowed (in whole or part) by its father and thereby given second birth, crops up in other parts of Greek mythology—e.g. in the case of Athena and of Dionysus. What is peculiar to the Cronus story is that it serves to establish a mythological image of interrelated contraries, a theme which recurs repeatedly in mature Greek philosophy. The following comes from Cary's translation of the *Phaedo:*

"We have then," said Socrates, "sufficiently determined this—that all things are thus produced, contraries from contraries?"

"Certainly."

"What next? Is there also something of this kind in them, for instance, between all two contraries a mutual twofold production, from one to the other, and from the other back again . . . ?"

For men who thought in these terms, "the beginning" would be the creation of contraries, that is to say the creation of male and female not as brother and sister but as husband and wife. My thesis then is that the philosophy of the *Phaedo* is already implicit in the gory details of the myth of Cronus. The myth is a creation myth, not a story of the beginning of the world, but a story of the beginning of time, of the beginning of becoming.

Although the climate may seem unfamiliar, this theme is not without relevance for certain topics of anthropological discussion. There is for instance Radcliffe-Brown's doctrine concerning the identification of alternating generations, whereby grandfather and grandson tend to exhibit "solidarity" in opposition to the intervening father. Or there is the stress which Lévi-Strauss has placed upon marriage as a symbol of alliance between otherwise opposed groups. Such arguments when reduced to their most abstract algebraic form may be represented by a diagram such as this:

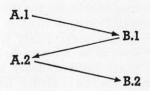

In Radcliffe-Brown's argument the As and the Bs, that are opposed yet linked, are the alternating generations of a lineage; in Lévi-Strauss's, the As and the Bs are the males of contending kin groups allied by the interchange of women.

My thesis has been that the Greeks tended to conceptualize the time process as a zig-zag of this same type. They associated Cronus with the idea of time because, in a structural sense, his myth represents a separation of A from B and a creation of the initial arrow $A \rightarrow B$, the beginning of life which is also the beginning of death. It is also nicely relevant that Heraclitus should have defined "a generation" as a period of thirty years, this being calculated "as the interval between the procreation of a son by his father and the procreation of a son's son by the son," the interval, that is $A.1 \rightarrow B.1 \rightarrow A.2$.

I don't want to suggest that all primitive peoples necessarily think about time in this way, but certainly some do. The Kachins whom I mentioned earlier have a word *majan,* which, literally, ought to mean "woman affair." They use it in three main contexts to mean (*a*) warfare, (*b*) a love-song, and (*c*) the weft threads of a loom. This seems to us an odd concatenation yet I fancy the Greeks would have understood it very well. Penelope sits at her loom, the shuttle goes back and forth, back and forth, love and war, love and war; and what does she weave? You can guess without looking up your *Odyssey*—a *shroud* of course, the time of Everyman. 'Tis love that makes the world go round; but women are the root of all evil. (The Greek Ares god of war was paramour of Aphrodite goddess of love.)

II. TIME AND FALSE NOSES

Briefly my puzzle is this. All over the world men mark out their calendars by means of festivals. We ourselves start each week with a Sunday and each year with a fancy dress party. Comparable divisions in other calendars are marked by comparable behaviours. The varieties of behaviour involved are rather limited yet curiously contradictory. People dress up in uniform, or in funny clothes; they eat special food, or they fast; they behave in a solemn restrained manner, or they indulge in license.

Rites de passage, which mark the individual's social development—rituals of birth, puberty, marriage, death—are often similar. Here too we find special dress (smart uniform or farcical make-believe), special food (feast or fast), special behaviour (sobriety or license). Now why?

Why should we demarcate time in this way? Why should it seem appropriate to wear top hats at funerals, and false noses on birthdays and New Year's Eve?

Frazer explained such behaviours by treating them as survivals of primitive magic. Frazer may be right, but he is inadequate. It is not good enough to explain a world-wide phenomenon in terms of particular, localized, archaic beliefs.

The oddest thing about time is surely that we have such a concept at all. We experience time, but not with our senses. We don't see it, or touch it, or smell it, or taste it, or hear it. How then? In three ways:

Firstly we recognize repetition. Drops of water falling from the roof; they are not all the same drop, but different. Yet to recognize them as being different we must first distinguish, and hence define, time-intervals. Time-intervals, durations, always begin and end with "the same thing," a pulse beat, a clock strike, New Year's Day.

Secondly we recognize aging, entropy. All living things are born, grow old and die. Aging is the irreversible fate of us all. But aging and interval are surely two quite different kinds of experience? I think we lump these two experiences together and describe them both by one name, time, because we would like to believe that in some mystical way birth and death are really the same thing.

Our third experience of time concerns the rate at which time passes. This is tricky. There is good evidence that the biological individual ages at a pace that is ever slowing down in relation to the sequence of stellar time. The feeling that most of us have that the first ten years of childhood "lasted much longer" than the hectic decade 40–50 is no illusion. Biological processes, such as wound healing, operate much faster (in terms of stellar time) during childhood than in old age. But since our sensations are geared to our biological processes rather than to the stars, time's chariot appears to proceed at ever increasing speed. This irregular flow of biological time is not merely a phenomenon of personal intuition; it is observable in the organic world all around us. Plant growth is much faster at the beginning than at the end of the life cycle; the ripening of the grain and the sprouting of the sown grain proceed at quite different rates of development.

Such facts show us that the regularity of time is not an intrinsic part of nature; it is a man made notion which we have projected into our environment for our own particular purposes. Most primitive peoples can have no feeling that the stars in their courses provide a fixed chronometer by which to measure all the affairs of life. On the contrary it is the year's round itself, the annual sequence of economic activities, which provides the measure of time. In such a system, since biological time is erratic, the stars may appear distinctly temperamental. The logic of astrology is not one of extreme fatalism, but rather that you can never be quite sure what the stars are going to get up to next.

But if there is nothing in the principle of the thing, or in the nature of our experience, to suggest that time must necessarily flow past at constant speed, we are not required to think of time as a constant flow at all. Why shouldn't time slow down and stop occasionally, or even go into reverse?

I agree that in a strictly scientific sense it is silly to pretend that death and birth are the same thing, yet without question many religious dogmas purport to maintain precisely that. Moreover, the make-believe that birth follows death is not confined to beliefs about the hereafter, it comes out also in the pattern of religious ritual itself. It appears not only in *rites de passage* (where the symbolism is often quite obvious) but also in a high proportion of sacrificial rites of a sacramental character. The generalizations first propounded by Hubert and Mauss and Van Gennep have an extraordinarily widespread validity; the rite as a whole falls into sections, a symbolic death, a period of ritual seclusion, a symbolic rebirth.

Now *rites de passage,* which are concerned with demarcating the stages in the human life cycle, must clearly be linked with some kind of representation or conceptualization of time. But the only picture of time that could make this death-birth identification logically plausible is a pendulum type concept. All sorts of pictorial metaphors have been produced for representing time. They range from Heraclitus's river to Pythagoras's harmonic spheres. You can think of time as going on and on, or you can think of it as going round and round. All I am saying is that in fact quite a lot of people think of it as going back and forth.

With a pendulum view of time, the sequence of things is discontinuous; time is a succession of alternations and full stops. Intervals are distinguished, not as the sequential markings on a tape measure, but as repeated opposites, tick-tock tick-tock. And surely our most elementary experiences of time flow are precisely of this kind: day-night day-night; hot-cold hot-cold; wet-dry wet-dry? Despite the word *pendulum,* this kind of metaphor is not sophisticated; the essence of the matter is not the pendulum but the alternation. I would maintain that the notion that time is a "discontinuity of repeated contrasts" is probably the most elementary and primitive of all ways of regarding time.

All this is orthodox Durkheimian sociology. For people who do not possess calendars of the Nautical Almanac type, the year's progress is marked by a succession of festivals. Each festival represents, for the true Durkheimian, a temporary shift from the Normal-Profane order of existence into the Abnormal-Sacred order and back again. The total flow of time then has a pattern which might be represented by such a diagram as this (Fig. 1):

or from sacred to profane. Viewed in this Durkheimian way, the total sequence embraces four distinct phases or "states of the moral person."

Phase A. The rite of sacralization, or separation. The moral person is transferred from the Secular-Profane world to the Sacred world; he "dies."

Phase B. The marginal state. The moral person is in a sacred condition, a kind of suspended animation. Ordinary social time has stopped.

Phase C. The rite of desacralization, or aggregation. The moral person is brought back from the Sacred to the Profane world; he is "reborn," secular time starts anew.

Phase D. This is the phase of normal secular life, the interval between successive festivals.

So much for Durkheim, but where do the funny hats come in? Well, let me draw your attention to three features in the foregoing theoretical argument.

Firstly let me emphasize that, among the various functions which the holding of festivals may fulfil, one very important function is the ordering of time. The interval between two successive festivals of the same type is a "period," usually a named period, e.g. "week," "year." Without the festivals, such periods would not exist, and all order would go out of social life. We talk of measuring time, as if time were a concrete thing waiting

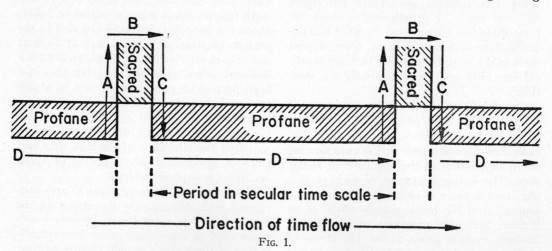

FIG. 1.

Such a flow of time is man made. It is ordered in this way by the Societies (the "moral persons" to use Durkheimian terminology) which participate in the festal rites. The rites themselves, especially sacrificial rites, are techniques for changing the status of the moral person from profane to sacred,

to be measured; but in fact we *create time* by creating intervals in social life. Until we have done this there is no time to be measured.

Secondly, don't forget that, just as secular periods begin and end in festivals, so also the festivals themselves have their ends and their beginnings. If we are to appreciate how neatly festivity serves to order time, we must consider the system as a whole, not just individual festivals. Notice for example how the 40 days between Carnival (Shrove Tuesday) and Easter is balanced off by the 40 days between Easter and Ascension, or how New Year's Eve falls precisely midway between Christmas Eve and Twelfth Night. Historians may tell you that such balanced intervals as these are pure accidents, but is history really so ingenious?

And thirdly there is the matter of false noses, or to be more academic, role reversal. If we accept the Durkheimian analysis of the structure of ritual which I have outlined above, then it follows that the rituals of Phase A and the rituals of Phase C ought, in some sense, to be the reverse of one another. Similarly, according to the diagram, Phase B ought somehow to be the logical opposite to Phase D. But Phase D, remember, is merely ordinary secular life. In that case a logically appropriate ritual behaviour for Phase B would be to play normal life back to front.

Now if we look at the general types of behaviour that we actually encounter on ritual occasions we may readily distinguish three seemingly contradictory species. On the one hand there are behaviours in which formality is increased; men adopt formal uniform, differences of status are precisely demarcated by dress and etiquette, moral rules are rigorously and ostentatiously obeyed. An English Sunday, the church ceremony at an English wedding, the Coronation Procession, University Degree taking ceremonials are examples of the sort of thing I mean.

In direct contrast we find celebrations of the Fancy Dress Party type, masquerades, revels. Here the individual, instead of emphasizing his social personality and his official status, seeks to disguise it. The world

goes in a mask, the formal rules of orthodox life are forgotten.

And finally, in a few relatively rare instances, we find an extreme form of revelry in which the participants play-act at being precisely the opposite to what they really are; men act as women, women as men, Kings as beggars, servants as masters, acolytes as Bishops. In such situations of true orgy, normal social life is played in reverse, with all manner of sins such as incest, adultery, transvestitism, sacrilege, and *lèse-majesté* treated as the natural order of the day.

Let us call these three types of ritual behaviour (1) formality, (2) masquerade, (3) role reversal. Although they are conceptually distinct as species of behaviour, they are in practice closely associated. A rite which starts with formality (e.g. a wedding) is likely to end in masquerade; a rite which starts with masquerade (e.g. New Year's Eve; Carnival) is likely to end in formality. In these puritanical days explicit role reversal is not common in our own society but it is common enough in the ethnographic literature and in accounts of Mediaeval Europe. You will find such behaviours associated with funerals, or with *rites de passage* (symbolic funerals) or with the year's end (e.g., in Europe: Saturnalia and the Feast of Fools).

My thesis is then that *formality* and *masquerade,* taken together, form a pair of contrasted opposites and correspond, in terms of my diagram, to the contrast between Phase A and Phase C. *Role reversal* on the other hand corresponds to Phase B. It is symbolic of a complete transfer from the secular to the sacred; normal time has stopped, sacred time is played in reverse, death is converted into birth. This Good King Wenceslas symbolism is something which has a world wide distribution because it makes logical sense independently of any particular folklorish traditions or any particular magical beliefs.

CHILDE HERALD

Freud and Football

"Childe Herald" is the pseudonym used by Thomas Hornsby Ferril, who regrets that the Freudians have never attempted to analyze the ritual of America's autumnal madness. He has attempted to correct this lapse by gratuitously supplying a symbolic exegesis of football. Interspersed with psychoanalytic symbols are some drawn from the naturistic school of mythology, but he does not say if this is fortuitous or an intentional effort to draw a parallel in methodology.

Reprinted from *The Rocky Mountain Herald,* September 10, 1955, by permission of the publisher and the author.

As I look back over the intellectual caprices of the past quarter century, I am amazed that neither the Marxists nor the Freudians ever took out after football. There's not a single book on the subject. It is now too late. In olympian cerebration, Marx and Freud are obsolete; the atom has taken over, and football, for the moment, seems reasonably safe from encroachment, although we may still see a few flurries; cobalt tracers, perhaps, for the study of the parabolas of flat passes, but it won't amount to much because the atom is cut out for graver duties.

If the Marxists had been more alert, they could have made something out of football as brutal capitalistic exploitation of the working class. They might have noted a few strikes for higher pay and a court decision entitling a college football player to workman's compensation benefits following injury.

But it was the Freudians who made the colossal blunder. You could argue that they overlooked football on the grounds that it was just too big to be noticed on those Saturday afternoons when the college library was free for their invasion of fiction, drama, poetry, painting, sculpture, music and economics.

Yet why, when the whole town was roaring over their heads, did they pay no attention to the emotional frenzy? Frankly, I think they must have, but the Freudians were notoriously selfish fellows; they wanted everything whole-hog; they were always extremely jealous of anthropologists, and, as you look back on their dilemma as far as football was concerned, their dog-in-the-manger attitude was perhaps justified,

for no self-respecting Freudian could ever have done a full-dress job on football without cutting some detested anthropologist in on the gravy.

But had the Freudians been less self-centered and had they welcomed a bit of anthropological assistance, just think of the monumental treatises by which the scientific literature of the period might have been enriched, great books wedding the wisdom of "Gesammelte Schriften" with the profundity of "The Golden Bough."

Let me set down, in nostalgic summary, some of the findings that might have been made, had the Freudians not been sulking in their tents.

Obviously, football is a syndrome of religious rites symbolizing the struggle to preserve the egg of life through the rigors of impending winter. The rites begin at the autumn equinox and culminate on the first day of the New Year with great festivals identified with bowls of plenty; the festivals are associated with flowers such as roses, fruits such as oranges, farm crops such as cotton, and even sun-worship and appeasement of great reptiles such as alligators.

In these rites the egg of life is symbolized by what is called "the oval," an inflated bladder covered with hog skin. The convention of "the oval" is repeated in the architectural oval-shaped design of the vast outdoor churches in which the services are held every sabbath in every town and city, also every Sunday in the greater centers of population where an advanced priesthood performs. These enormous roofless churches dominate every college campus; no other edifice compares in size with them, and they bear witness to the high spiritual development of the culture that produced them.

Literally millions of worshipers attend the sabbath services in these enormous open-air churches. Subconsciously, these hordes of worshipers are seeking an outlet from sex-frustration in anticipation of violent masochism and sadism about to be enacted by a highly trained priesthood of young men. Football obviously arises out of the Oedipus complex. Love of mother dominates the entire ritual. The churches, without exception, are dedicated to Alma Mater, Dear Mother. (Notre Dame and football are synonymous.)

The rites are performed on a rectangular area of green grass orientated to the four directions. The grass, symbolizing summer, is striped with ominous white lines representing the knifing snows of winter. The white stripes are repeated in the ceremonial costumes of the four whistling monitors who control the services through a time period divided into four quarters, symbolizing the four seasons.

The ceremony begins with colorful processions of musicians and semi-nude virgins who move in and out of ritualized patterns. This excites the thousands of worshipers to rise from their seats, shout frenzied poetry in unison and chant ecstatic anthems through which runs the Oedipus theme of willingness to die for love of Mother.

The actual rites, performed by 22 young priests of perfect physique, might appear to the uninitiated as a chaotic conflict concerned only with hurting the oval by kicking it, then endeavoring to rescue and protect the egg.

However, the procedure is highly stylized. On each side there are eleven young men wearing colorful and protective costumes. the group in so-called "possession" of the oval first arrange themselves in an egg-shaped "huddle," as it is called, for a moment of prayerful meditation and whispering of secret numbers to each other.

Then they rearrange themselves with relation to the position of the egg. In a typical "formation" there are seven priests "on the line," seven being a mystical number associated not, as Jung purists might contend, with the "seven last words" but actually, with sublimation of the "seven deadly sins" into "the seven cardinal principles of education."

The central priest crouches over the egg, protecting it with his hands while over his back quarters hovers the "quarterback." The transposition of "back quarters" to "quarterback" is easily explained by the Adler school. To the layman the curious posture assumed by the "quarter-back," as he hovers over the central priest, immediately suggests the Cretan origins of Mycenaean animal art, but this popular view is untenable. Actually, of course, the "quarter-back" symbolizes the libido, combining two instincts, namely (a) Eros, which strives for even closer union and (b) the instinct for destruction of anything which lies in the path of Eros. Moreover, the "pleasure-pain" excitement of the hysterical worshipers focuses entirely on the actions of the libido-quarter-back. Behind him are three priests representing the male triad.

At a given signal, the egg is passed by sleight-of-hand to one of the members of the triad who endeavors to move it by bodily force across the white lines of winter. This procedure, up and down the enclosure, continues through the four quarters of the ritual.

At the end of the second quarter, implying the summer solstice, the processions of musicians and semi-nude virgins are resumed. After forming themselves into pictograms, representing alphabetical and animal fetishes, the virgins perform a most curious rite requiring far more dexterity than the earlier phallic Maypole rituals from which it seems to be derived. Each of the virgins carries a wand of shining metal which she spins on her fingertips, tosses playfully into the air and with which she interweaves her body in most intricate gyrations.

The virgins perform another important function throughout the entire service. This concerns the mystical rite of "conversion" following success of one of the young priests in carrying the oval across the last white line of winter. As the moment of "conversion" approaches, the virgins kneel at the edge of the grass, bury their faces in the earth, then raise their arms to heaven in supplication, praying that "the uprights will be split." "Conversion" is indeed a dedicated ceremony.

Freud and Breuer in 1895 ("Studien über Hysteria") described "conversion" as hysterical symptoms originating through the energy of a mental process being withheld from conscious influence, and this precisely accounts for the behavior of the virgins in the football services.

The foregoing, I confess, scarcely scratches the surface. Space does not permit interpretation of football as related to dreams, or discussion of the great subconscious reservoirs of thwarted American energy that weekly seek expression through vicarious enjoyment of ritualized violence and infliction of pain. To relate football to the Oedipus complex alone would require, as it well deserves, years of patient research by scholarly men such as we find in the Ford Foundation.

I only regret that these studies were not undertaken a quarter century ago, when the Freudians were in full flower. It's just another instance, so characteristic of our culture, of too little and too late.

CHAPTER 5

MANA AND TABOO

☙☙☙☙

INTRODUCTION

Mana and taboo are conventionally grouped under one rubric because where mana exists there is bound to be taboo. The reverse, of course, does not always hold true, for much taboo stems from contexts not associated with mana.

Mana is not easy to define. It refers to sheer power—occult force independent of either persons or spirits. However, its usual *modus operandi* is through anything that lives or moves, and for this reason Marett referred to the belief in it as "animatism," thereby stressing the idea of animation. Yet inanimate objects, too, may possess such a force, especially if they are unusual in appearance. A certain degree of instability characterizes it, for it may move from persons to persons, things to persons, persons to things, or things to things, often without rhyme or reason. Of course, mana is neither good nor bad in itself, just as atomic power is neither one nor the other and may be manipulated in whichever direction its possessor chooses. But it is dangerous, and that is why restrictions are necessary to protect those who come in contact with it. One is reminded of the antiradiation measures that must be taken by those working with nuclear power. And just as decontamination is possible after atomic exposure, so is it possible to resort to purificatory rites after breaking a taboo. In both cases, the measures may fail.

As for the role of the belief in mana, it is multifold. It explains success, excellence, and potency when these qualities are not otherwise understandable to human beings in ordinary terms. True, alternate explanations are possible, as when the will of deities is advanced as a cause of conditions or events; but dynamism, as the belief in mana is sometimes called, is especially satisfying in puzzling conditions not aptly covered by such alternatives. A garden which has always produced poor yields of squash suddenly begins to give forth large crops after its owner has casually placed a queer-shaped rock in its midst, possibly only for him to sit on when tired. Ignorant of some of the vagaries of nature which probably could be explained simply enough in modern agronomic terms, an aborigine might attribute the change to the presence of the rock, which obviously must possess special potency. A championship football team may for no accountable reason lose a routine match against a mediocre opponent. What happened? Perhaps its mana left it, for how else can one explain why a well-drilled, well-conditioned, and alert group of young men should be overcome by another group habituated to losing? Some anthropologists would say that "luck" is our equivalent of mana, but while similar in some respects, explaining otherwise inexplicable success and good fortune, the analogy should not be overdrawn. Luck is a narrower and less comprehensive concept than mana.

Dynamism serves, too, to explain inequalities in human beings. One man is a better swimmer than his neighbor, or a richer canoe maker, because he is endowed with more of the impersonal power in question. It has been pointed out that the inequalities of men justify class distinctions because members of some social groups are born with more mana than others, for a hereditary quality often adheres to this power. Of course, such a role is not a general one, but in Polynesia it was of great use in maintaining the status quo, especially because of the taboo system that accompanied it.

Another role of the mana concept is not peculiar to it alone but is worth remembering, and that is that it defines and locates a special type of supernatural power, and in so doing also provides a way of handling and making use of it. Salomon Reinach expressed the pragmatic aspect of this power when he wrote, "If taboo is the principle of morality and decency, mana is that of the applied sciences" (*Orpheus: A History of Religions,* 1930).

While we are here concerned with the role of the concept of mana rather than its implications for theories of religious origins and development, mention should be made of the fact that its great simplicity has persuaded some theorists to view it as having come earlier in time than did the belief in spirits, being more generalized and undifferentiated. Marett (*The Threshold of Religion,* 1909) and Preuss are the chief exponents of this idea.

Turning to taboo, which we have already stated is not necessarily linked with mana, we encounter another term that is hard to define. Taboo is a prohibition not embodied in a legal code. But the question then arises as to whether a taboo is always linked to the sacred or even the supernatural. The answer depends on whose taboos are being looked at, those of urbanites or those of folklike peoples. In our idiom, it is taboo to discuss excretory functions in mixed company or to wear one tan and one black shoe at the same time. It is this meaning of the term that a sociologist had in mind when he wrote that taboos are "mores expressed in negative form." Supernaturalism is not involved here, and, according to Redfield, if the sacred is present it is only in the looser sense that the prohibition cannot be critically examined or rationally discussed.

Among primitives the sacred is more strongly present in taboo and is usually supplemented by the supernatural, but not always. Anthropologists tend to use the word in this sense, accepting the Polynesian point of view that the authority behind such interdicts rests in some kind of supernatural power. The fact that a chief may be the one to impose a taboo and apply a negative sanction when it is violated does not undermine this meaning of the term, for the chief would be considered either to have divine power or to be a surrogate for it. When Reinach (*Orpheus*) says that the distinctive mark of the taboo is that the prohibition is quite arbitrary, he is merely confirming its sacred nature and is applying the term to folk peoples. Drawing on Biblical examples, he supports his position by pointing out that when Adam was warned by the Lord not to eat the fruit of a certain tree under pain of death, he was given no reason for the interdict. The unreasoned and unreasonable nature of taboo, he says, is also seen in the prohibition against pronouncing the name of the Eternal, as well as in the way in which the well-meaning Uzzah was struck dead by the Lord after he had sprung forth to steady the Ark of the Covenant when the oxen that were pulling it stumbled on the road. Much as we see merit in Reinach's position, it cannot always be maintained, for even among primitives there are ample instances of taboos that are wholly reasonable, as when a chief of a coral atoll places a taboo on taro so that it may be used as a reserve after a typhoon has created a shortage of food. But if the quality of unreasonableness cannot always be ascertained in the taboos of folk peoples, that of sacredness can. In this instance the chief renders the taro sacred. This double meaning of taboo—prohibited and sacred—is of course well exemplified in Polynesia and elsewhere. In such places the authority behind the taboo is sacred. On Ulithi Atoll, where taro was indeed declared taboo about 1946 for the reason assigned, punishment to a violator would have come not from the chief or the people but from some undefined, vague supernatural source. We can close this discussion, then, by saying that the conventional, unlegal prohibitions of urban societies are mostly secular, while those of folk societies are essentially sacred.

Is taboo really, as Frazer suggested, a

kind of negative sympathetic magic, a homeopathic taboo? He said that taboo is based on the premise that "harmful consequences are averted when certain acts are *not* performed." If you do not spin or twist a rope, your unborn child will not have its guts entangled. If you do not break a marrow bone in a hut, your horse in the field will not break his leg. Ingenious as this suggestion may be, it does not stand up under scrutiny. Magic cannot be defined in terms of abstinence. Besides, many taboos are not in the least connected with it. To refrain from touching a Polynesian chief's head, from eating a Micronesian chief's special species of fish, or from having sexual intercourse after a wife's confinement involve no reverse sympathetic principle of magic. Moreover, magic, properly defined, involves ritual, and it is hard to see that doing nothing at all constitutes ritualistic activity.

Perhaps the chief role of taboo is as a quasilegal mechanism of social control. One might loosely say that taboo is to law as the sacred realm is to the secular. It helps maintain the social structure in a cohesive relationship by providing a standard of proper behavior to which the members of the society by and large subscribe. In individual or exceptional cases a set of taboos may seem unduly harsh and restrictive or partial to a dominanat class or select group, but looked at from the broad point of view it is no more so than a set of laws. For it should be borne in mind that as a whole taboos apply as much to those in high places as to those in lowlier ones. Taboos may even be more severe for a chief than a commoner, as witnessed by the case of Polynesian chiefs who were so immobilized by the taboo system that they dared not eat, drink, walk, sit, touch, talk, or mate without keeping an apprehensive eye on the possible consequences these might have not only for themselves but their subjects. The analogy with law ought not to be pressed too far, for taboo lacks the main ingredients of law—code and process backed by the force of the state—and remains comparatively amorphous, yet like law it gives a society reassurance that dangers have been delineated and a guide for avoiding them has been thought out for its benefit.

Taboo has many other roles. For example, as with magic and witchcraft, it serves to assign a cause to such matters as poor crops and barren ewes, bellyaches and boils, thwarted loves and lost battles. By defining and pigeonholing the matter in such terms, unpleasantnesses are rendered more tolerable. Paranoiac tendencies find little outlet in this respect, for whereas magic and witchcraft are sources of evil found outside the individual, the consequences of taboo breaking are usually due to something that he is responsible for and cannot attribute to others.

Radcliffe-Brown's work *Taboo,* which was included in the section on the function of religion rather than here, where taboo is treated mostly in terms of definition and description, is of course a major writing on the subject in question, demonstrating as it does that social sentiments and values are maintained through taboo. A whole volume by Hutton Webster called *Taboo: A Sociological Study* (1942) is a highly documented work in the Frazerian tradition and is of value mostly for systemizing the facets of taboo.

R. H. CODRINGTON

Mana

Bishop Codrington went to Melanesia as a missionary in 1863 and remained there until 1887, but most of his research was done while he was on Norfolk Island. This island, located between New Caledonia and New Zealand, was a retreat for native teachers and missionaries from Melanesia itself, and Codrington spent a good deal of time interviewing them. His discovery that the people of Melanesia had an abstract concept for all forms of su-

Reprinted from R. H. Codrington, "Religion," *The Melanesians: Studies in Their Anthropology and Folklore,* Chap. 7 (Oxford: Clarendon Press, 1891), pp. 118–120, by permission of the publishers.

pernatural power was destined to have surprising repercussions throughout the learned world. The power, called "mana," was described by Codrington as being not physical but supernatural, not fixed in anything but capable of being conveyed in almost anything. He pointed out that spirits could have it and impart it, and that men too might harbor it, but even stones, sticks, and other inanimate objects might possess it.

Once it had been discovered that the concept of an impersonal, nonanthropomorphized power existed in Melanesia it was not long before the idea was also found, under the same name, in Polynesia, as well as in the New World, where the Sioux called it *wakanda,* the Crow *maxpe,* the Iroquois *orenda,* and the Algonquins *manitou.* However, among the American Indians the power concept is not unadulterated, for sometimes it comes close to referring to a spirit being. Hints of a manalike power come also from Negro Africa, where the Ekoi refer to it as *njomm* and the Nkundu of the Belgian Congo as *elima.* The Moslems of North Africa have a concept like mana to which they apply the term *baraka* or "holiness." Actually, the idea of such dynamic potency is a very widespread phenomenon, even if it is not always clearcut. Thus while the Japanese term *kami* is a word for deity, in ancient usage it referred to anything outside the ordinary that possessed superior virtues or was awe-inspiring. Hutton Webster (*Magic,* 1948) has assembled a list of scores of places where a manalike concept is present. In addition to numerous tribes throughout Africa and America, he finds accounts in the literature for Australia, Torres Straits, New Guinea, many islands of Indonesia, Formosa, the Malay Peninsula, Annam, Indo-China, Burma, the Andaman Islands, India, and Madagascar. His list and documentation are very impressive. He even includes the ancient Egyptian *hike,* Hebrew *el,* Indian *brahma,* Greek *dynamis,* Latin *numen,* and so on. Not all of the beliefs he offers in evidence conform closely to Codrington's definition, and one could argue that several of them should be discarded as not comparable. For instance, the Indian notion of *brahma* is never applied to living individuals; it refers only to a cosmogonic concept which cannot be observed in events or human activities.

The very fact that conceptions resembling mana are almost ubiquitous helps to militate against regarding it as a distinctive and unusual belief. If a common denominator for all the similar beliefs throughout the world could be found, it would be so compromising as to render the notion almost valueless. Even for Polynesia it is impossible to find a word in English into which the idea could be translated. Handy (*Polynesian Religion,* 1927) mentions *power, might, influence, authority, prestige, glory, majesty, effectual,* and *effective* as words that have been used to translate "mana." The hazards of a restrictive definition are seen in the fact that Codrington himself did not always use the term consistently. His definition, then, must not be viewed as having called attention to a unique idea of special theoretical import. In showing that the pursuit of mana forms the basis of Melanesian religion and outrivals other aspects of religion, he performed a valuable service, for this is perhaps true of no other religious system—not even the Polynesian. But the term is not for export; it is best confined to those islands of the Pacific where the word is part of the vocabulary of the people. Similar manifestations elsewhere ought to be treated in their local contexts and resemblances should not be forced.

The Melanesian mind is entirely possessed by the belief in a supernatural power or influence, called almost universally "mana."

This is what works to effect everything which is beyond the ordinary power of men, outside the common processes of nature; it is present in the atmosphere of life, attaches itself to persons and to things, and is manifested by results which can only be ascribed to its operation. When one has got it he can use it and direct it, but its force may break forth at some new point; the presence of it is ascertained by proof. A man comes by chance upon a stone which takes his fancy; its shape is singular, it is like something, it is certainly not a common stone, there must be mana in it. So he argues with himself, and he puts it to the proof; he lays it at the root of a tree to the fruit of which it has a certain resemblance, or he buries it in the ground when he plants his garden; an abundant crop on the tree or in the garden shows that he is right, the stone is mana, has that power in it. Having that power it is a vehicle to convey mana to other stones. In the same way certain forms of words, generally in the form of a song, have power for certain purposes; a charm of words is called a mana. But this power, though itself impersonal, is always connected with some person who directs it; all spirits have it, ghosts generally, some men. If a stone is found to have a supernatural power, it is because a spirit has associated itself with it; a dead man's bone has with it mana, because the ghost is with the bone; a man may have so close a connection with a spirit or ghost that he has mana in himself also, and can so direct it as to effect what he desires; a charm is powerful because the name of a spirit or ghost expressed in the form of words brings into it the power which the ghost or spirit exercises through it. Thus all conspicuous success is a proof that a man has mana; his influence depends on the impression made on the people's mind that he has it; he becomes a chief by virtue of it. Hence a man's power, though political or social in its character, is his mana; the word is naturally used in accordance with the native conception of the character of all power and influence as supernatural. If a man has been successful in fighting, it has not been his natural strength of arm, quickness of eye, or readiness of resource that has won success; he has certainly got the mana of a spirit or of some deceased warrior to empower him, conveyed in an amulet of a stone round his neck, or a tuft of leaves in his belt, in a tooth hung upon a finger of his bow hand, or in the form of words with which he brings supernatural assistance to his side. If a man's pigs multiply and his gardens are productive, it is not because he is industrious and looks after his property, but because of the stones full of mana for pigs and yams that he possesses. Of course a yam naturally grows when planted, that is well known, but it will not be very large unless mana comes into play; a canoe will not be swift unless mana be brought to bear upon it, a net will not catch many fish, nor an arrow inflict a mortal wound.

E. S. CRAIGHILL HANDY

Mana in Polynesia

Even though it was not the most important aspect of the religion of Polynesia, the concept of mana was more highly refined there than in Melanesia, as the following article shows. Of course, in such places as Tahiti, Hawaii, and New Zealand the priesthood was elaborated to an unusual degree and there was much time and inclination to develop theological constructs. In addition, there existed an aristocratic hierarchy in which royalty was held to be divine and descended from the gods. One of the responsibilities of the priesthood, which included among its numbers some of the highest-born members of the tribe, was to give support to the godhood of the nobility by developing mythology, ritual, and religious concepts in favorable directions. The concept of mana, along with much else in Polynesian religion, has so impressed itself upon Handy that he assigns it to an ultimate origin in India.

Reprinted with slight abridgments from E. S. Craighill Handy, *Polynesian Religion* ("Bernice P. Bishop Museum Bulletins," No. 34 [Honolulu, 1927]), pp. 26–34, by permission of the author and the Bernice P. Bishop Museum.

He states that it "was really part and parcel with a systematic theory of dualism in nature which attributed divinity, power, the male principle, light, and life to the superior, heavenly realm; and commonness, impotence, the female principle, darkness, and death to lower nature, or the earth" (*Polynesian Religion,* p. 313). Both the claim for a Hindu origin of the concept of mana and its association with a dualistic system of thought have been seriously disputed by most anthropologists, but the very fact that Handy and others have taken such a point of view is eloquent testimony to the highly philosophic quality of Polynesian religion.

The most conclusive evidence of the existence in the native mind of the idea of the psychic dynamism of nature lies in the mana concept itself. The word "mana" referred to the manifestation of this aspect of nature when its dynamism was centered in or focused through specific gods, spirits, individuals, rites, or objects. Mana was exhibited in persons, in power, strength, prestige, reputation, skill, dynamic personality, intelligence; in things, in efficacy, in "luck"; that is, in accomplishment. These qualities were not mana; they were the evidences of mana, which was itself but the focusing and transmission of the potency of nature. It is my belief that mana was thought to come into individuals or objects only through the medium of gods or spirits. But no definite statement to this effect should be made without more extensive examination and analysis of instances than I am now prepared to make.

The primal mana was not merely power or energy, but procreative power, derived from an ultimate source and diffused, transmitted, and manifested throughout the universe. This was the original mana which was believed to be continuously passed down through the gods, the *mana atua* of which the Maori teacher in the New Zealand college of lore spoke as follows, deprecating its loss as a result of the influence of Christianity:

This [loss of the ancient knowledge] is in consequence of the decadence in power, authority and prestige of the conduct of the various rituals, of the (abrogation of) the *tapu,* of the (unbelief in) the gods, until at the present time, there is none of the ancient *mana,* or power, left . . . hence also it is that I impress on you the (former) aspect of these things, that you may be clear as to the descent of the *mana-atua* (the god-like powers) even from Io (the Supreme God), and from the Whatu-kuras, Mariekuras, and the Apas of each separate heaven. . . .

Another priest taught that the *mana-ariki* or chiefly power, the *mana-tapu* or sacred power (signifying apparently that which pertained to ritual), the *mana-ora* or life-giving power, and lastly the *mana-atuatanga* signifying the power pertaining to the gods, were "all held within the hands of Io," the Supreme Being.

The fact that the gods did not possess it of themselves but were the mediums or agents of this all-pervasive, divine force is indicated by these remarks of a learned Maori:

Mana is all round the world, and Tawhiri-matea [god of tempests], Ruaimoku [god of earthquakes], Maui [culture hero], and others are in the center of the circle and get hold of this *mana* and direct the elements and make the weather.

This teacher also says, "No one can rub out mana"; he then contrasts with it the borrowed mana of human beings, saying, "Personal mana can be overcome and annihilated, but the mana of the gods cannot."

Transmitted through the superior psychic mediums, the divine procreative energy was expressed in man in all qualities and attributes which rendered visible proof of this divine energy in MANIFEST ACCOMPLISHMENT; in objects, rites, and processes it was exhibited in PROVEN EFFICACY. No person or thing possessed intrinsic mana; but beings and objects of all kinds were capable, to a greater or less degree, of being mediums and reservoirs for the divine psychic potency.

The Polynesian ideas concerning the behavior of and laws governing mana are analogous in so many ways to the known nature of electricity that the simplest and clearest method of illustrating the native concept of the all-pervasive psychic force is by describing it in terms of this all-pervasive physical energy. The superior, divine aspect of nature, the "realm of light," was the reservoir of positive potential; while the inferior, common, earthly aspect, which sprang from and harbored darkness, was the impotent, the uncharged, the negative pole. In creation myths evolution is described as proceeding by the charging (impregnation) of the negative by the positive. In the world, all the children of the primal generations of the Cosmos, gods and spirits, men, animate and inanimate objects were transmitters and storage reservoirs. The energy was transmitted from one medium to another, or from a medium positively charged to one that was negative, through contact. When flow from superior positive to inferior negative occurred under improper circumstances, as when a common person came in contact with a high-born chief, there were two resultant effects: the superior was to some extent drained of potential energy; and the inferior, unsuited as a transmitter or container, was subject to various injurious effects as a result of the overload or surcharge. Hence the necessity for insulation of the transmitter and reservoir (the sacred chief or priest, for example) for his own protection and that of the higher mediums with which he was in contact (the gods), and for the protection of others, by means of tapu designed to prevent direct contact, or indirect contact through the medium of food, clothing, or other conductors; and hence also were various rites designed to relieve the commoner of a surcharge of mana, and to restore it to its rightful owner. Every person as a transmitter was the center of a field of psychic magnetic influence. The magnetic power and the extension of the field were proportionate to sacredness of the individual. Anything that came within that field became magnetized, and was thenceforth, unless demagnetized by one of the rites employed for this purpose, in intimate psychic rapport with the individual whose mana had affected it.

Mana may be compared not only to kinetic but also to static electricity. It could be generated by means of ritual prepared for the purpose by those having occult knowledge, just as electricity is generated through mechanical processes; and the conceptions of what actually took place are probably identical. Mana generated by means of dynamic ritual was evidently not believed to be created, but rather, like electricity, to be generated by induction, the all-pervasive and latent energy of nature being accumulated, to be stored or directly transmitted.

The divine chief was a transmitter: linked by an unbroken chain of first-borns to the primal gods, his was mana directly transmitted and made subject to conduction wherever the potential was needed—in agriculture, industry, war. On the other hand the mana of the priest or man of learning, which might be almost though not quite as great as that of the chief, was largely diffused mana, acquired as a result of consecrational ceremonies, and his continual association with sacred beings, objects, and rites. It may be said that while the chief transmitted mana, the priest was charged and magnetized with it. Like the chief, the gods or spirits whom the priest served were transmitters, as were also all objects animate or inanimate which had intimate generic relationship with superior power. And like the priest, all persons and objects that were charged with mana by means of dynamic rites and at the same time put in rapport or connected with the source of potential, or that were magnetized as a result of being placed in a magnetic field, may be said to have been charged, or magnetized. Any person or thing might, of course, become a transmitter by being connected with a terminal that was in contact with the ultimate source of potential, such as a chief, a spirit, or a god. Actually no being or object associated with Polynesian worship was believed to be purely a transmitter, or purely a reservoir or magnetic pole: the sacred chief's mana was in the main transmitted, but it was augmented by means of many consecrational rites, and by instruction; and no priest could through any amount of ritual consecration and teaching become a great priest unless he personally had inherited a capacity to transmit mana. Powerful priests were, in fact, almost always men of high birth in Polynesia.

Lest the description of the theory of mana in terms of electricity, which has been pursued only for the sake of illustration and not because I believe mana to have anything to do with electricity, or vice versa, become tedious, this method may now be abandoned in favor of specific illustration. The power—psychic and physical, religious and civil, productive and destructive—that the sacred chief in Polynesia was believed to embody was his first by reason of his direct descent from the higher beings and consequent close rapport with them through his illustrious ancestors; second, because of many rites that were performed to empower him and bring him into closer rapport with the higher beings; and last, as a result of knowledge acquired through education of the nature of the greater powers, of means of approaching, coming into rapport with, and influencing them—in a word, of superior psychic knowledge in general comparable to the superior worldly knowledge that was inevitably his through fortune of circumstances. Tregear writes that the mana of the Maori chiefs was a "part of their god-inheritance," which under unfortunate circumstances could be lost, but which was capable also of being greatly strengthened:

. . . it was not exactly success in battle, or acquisition of power and lands, or repute for wisdom, but the possession of these was a sign of the indwelling of *mana.* Its outward form might be what we vaguely call good luck, genius, reputation, etc., but it might also be recognizable in high courage, lofty social position, personal influence, etc. . . .

Interpreting mana from a rationalistic basis, Gudgeon considered it to be

. . . the result of hereditary characteristics transmitted through famous ancestors, and strengthened in every instance by the belief— shared by all true Maoris—that a man of this type must be under the special care of the gods.

The mana of the individual was believed to be concentrated in the head which, according to Polynesian philosophy, was associated with the superior, divine aspect of nature. This is evidenced by the figurative use in New Zealand of the phrase *kauwae runga* (upper jaw, or superior maxilla) to denote the heavens, the abiding place of the *ira atua* (superior godlike life). The same figure of speech was used in the Society Islands. This belief had to do with the widespread practice of secreting the skulls of deceased relatives.

A prophet or diviner who was the oracular medium of a spirit or god had little or no accretion of personal mana because of his inspirational talent—his mana was but that of the spirit or god be served. On the other hand a ritualistic priest (*tohunga*) was a personal embodiment of acquired mana, who exhibited his power in the efficacy of his ritual, and in his knowledge of occult influences and power to interpret omens.

In the case of a man of learning such a teacher of sacred lore, accuracy of memory, extensive knowledge, and keenness of mind were the evidences of his mana. In the Marquesas Islands any person who was an adept at any occupaton was a *tuhuna,* a master. Every *tuhuna* possessed mana for the particular activity in which he was skilled. But there were rare individuals whose learning and ability extended to all the departments of man's activity; knowledge, ritual, arts, and crafts. Such an adept, whose mana was so great that he was second to none in the tribe in sacredness, was honored with the title of *tuhuna nui,* great master or adept. The ability, talent, or capacity possessed by *tuhuna* appears to have been regarded as in part due to natural endowment, but more particularly to education, consecration, and experience. A Marquesan youth who could not memorize the ancient lore was spoken of as being "without mana"; but anyone who had great ability, showed sufficient persistence in learning from his teacher, and submitted to the required consecratory rites could become a master bard and ceremonial priest (*tuhuna oono*). Such a scholar grew in power and prestige as he demonstrated the superiority of his knowledge and wit in contests that were from time to time held between the wise men of different tribes; but if in such a contest with other *tuhuna* he proved incapable of meeting his opponents' sallies, or to be ignorant or in error, he was considered in some way to have lost the mana he once possessed. With his defeat his prestige and power were dissipated, he was no longer recognized as a master, and it was sometimes even believed that his defeat would cause his death. The mental darkness or blindness that would lead to such a downfall might, according to native ideas, result from the man's having come under a spell of witchcraft of an opponent or enemy, or from psychic defilement or broken tapu.

Another type of mana was that evidenced in physical prowess. Tregear writes that in New Zealand "the child of a slave could could by great daring, influence, and good fortune rise to be a dreaded chief or noted councilor." In the Marquesas it was through personal prowess that a tribesman became a war chief (*toa*). The warrior was thought to embody the mana of all those whom he had killed, his own mana increasing in proportion to his prowess. In the mind of the native, the prowess was the result, however, not the cause, of his mana. The mana of the warrior's spear was likewise increased with each death it inflicted. As a sign of his assumption of his defeated enemy's power, the victor in a hand-to-hand combat assumed his slain foe's name; with a view to absorbing directly his mana, he ate some of his flesh; and to bind the presence of the empowering influence in battle, to ensure his intimate rapport with the captured mana, he wore as a part of his war dress some physical relic of his vanquished foe—a bone, a dried hand, sometimes a whole skull.

Mana of the same type was exhibited by men in the more peaceful pursuits of industrial life. That of a canoe builder and his implements evidenced itself in his work and in the good fortune that accompanied the use of the products of his craftsmanship; that of the husbandman and his tools, in his crops; and that of the fisherman and his nets and hooks, in his catch. In this sense the mana of a man was regarded as power only partially inherent in or pertaining to the man himself. Much, perhaps most, of the mana of the warrior, craftsman, husbandman, and fisherman, came to him through his gods, through his rites and spells, and through the instruments he used. Again, mana manifested through instruments or rites was only partially inherent in these themselves, their efficacy when utilized being dependent upon the mana of the person using them. A great spear needed the hand of a great warrior, though it would give a common fighter more than his accustomed power. An adz, although it might embody mana in itself, could manifest its full efficacy only in the hands of an adept of great mana. A rite would demonstrate its highest mana only when performed by a priest endowed with that same mysterious quality. In the performance of rites not only the sacred instruments but the localities in which they were performed influenced the results; and in spells, the names or esoteric words that were recited, and the mode of utterance also had much to do with their efficacy. The mana directly applied or manifested in any circumstance may be said to have represented the sum total of psychic power brought to bear through the various mediums of rapport associated at the time—gods, men, rites, instruments, and localities.

The attribution of mana to spears and other implements and instruments has already been mentioned. Gudgeon describes "two weapons that were almost dangerous

to man by reason of the peculiar *mana* attached to them." One of these, a double-bladed club, served to give the tribe by which it was owned omens in wartime: if, as it lay on a mat it was observed by all to turn over, it was taken as a happy sign that the enterprise in hand would have a favorable outcome. "It was, however, in single combats that this weapon shone with its greatest luster, for then it never failed." The other object, characterized as being "almost dangerous to man" was an adz, said to be the very implement that was used by the gods in cutting the props that were made to hold up the Sky Father after he and the Earth Mother had been thrust apart.

In all the sections of Polynesia the bones of enemies were used for making fishhooks which were thought to have mana by reason of their rapport with the spirit of the deceased foe. Slightly different was the conception with regard to the stones commonly referred to as "fish gods" in the Marquesas Islands, Hawaii, and Tahiti. These possessed mana capable of aiding in fishing, not merely because they were in rapport with, but because they were supposed to be the actual shrines of gods or spirits which controlled particular kinds of fish.

Tregear has written that

Lands and localities were supposed to possess mana of their own, as well as men, weapons, etc. This influence when it pertained to land was on account of the spirits of famous men remaining on guard over them. If a man descended from, or related to one of these ancestors was in danger, he would feel much more security if he could reach such enchanted or sacred round, feeling that in some miraculous way he would obtain succor. Efforts would be made when a fight was impending to force the battle over into such a locality so as to obtain the "tribal luck" (mana) of the place.

The generation of mana by dynamic ritual may be illustrated by the custom of creating or empowering necromancer's familiars in Hawaii. The spirit selected was itself but the soul of a deceased infant. Such a spirit may have been chosen because of its supposed feeling of resentment against the world that had not welcomed it, and perhaps also because, being a child's soul, it was thought to be more easily subject to influence. According to J. S. Emerson, the spirit so chosen was supposedly raised to the power of a malicious demon by a process called *hoo-*

manamana, meaning literally to cause to have mana, a process which entailed continuous nourishing with offerings and the recitation of prayers or charms by the necromancer.

Now this word *hoomanamana* was applied not only to these rites of the necromancer, but also in a general sense to worship. In view of this, and of the remarks of the Maori teacher explaining the decadence of mana in modern times as being due to negligence of ritual, and lastly, in the light of the general intent of the worship of the higher powers through rapport, it may fairly be assumed that one main purpose of the prayer, sacrifice, and other elements of the Polynesian rites was to increase the mana of the gods worshiped, that, while they sought on the one hand to approach and draw on the strength embodied in their gods, these people were confident at the same time that their efforts in worship were capable of, indeed requisite for, empowering the very gods on whom they believed themselves to be dependent.

The empowering of a familiar demon with mana indicates that the divine psychic force might be diverted to, or coerced for, destructive ends; that the native mind accepted the possibility of worship of the evil beings, and of their being empowered by induction of the all-pervasive energy of nature in exactly the same manner as were the helpful, patron gods. Mana, indicating psychic power, may therefore signify destructive power as well as salutary. It was so applied when it was said of a sorcerer, "His is great mana for causing sickness and death." It was of this evil mana, diverted and at work against man's life and well-being, that a Maori sage spoke these words: "That which destroys man is the mana of the female organ."

WILLIAM ELLIS

The Tabu

It is refreshing and rewarding to read an account of taboo written by one who was on the spot when the taboo system in Hawaii had been overthrown but was still fresh in the minds of most people. Bishop Ellis gives us a flavor of things that could only have been sampled at that time. To be sure, the first missionary ship, the "Thaddeus," arrived in 1820, five months after the taboo system had been abrogated by Liholiho (King Kamehameha II), but he was on the scene so shortly after that momentous event that his account suffers little. One feels the marked and oppressive degree to which the system pervaded Hawaiian society and readily understands why the people, as they had already done in Tahiti, simply turned upon it. Opposition came only from some of the priesthood and nobility; the king took the lead in the daring deed. On a memorable day in 1819 he publicly broke the taboo which prohibited women from eating with men. Kroeber believes that it was all done because of "cultural fatigue"—weariness with an old system that had become a burden not only to the ordinary man but to royalty as well. Even the high priest of the islands took part in the dramatic revolt and carried it beyond its original scope. No doubt the forty-odd years of contact with Westerners after Captain Cook's discovery of the archipelago in 1778, as well as the knowledge that Pomare II had already led Tahiti into the camp of Christianity, played some part in Liholiho's bold move; but the evidence seems to indicate that the plotters were merely encouraged into taking a step that was almost inevitable.

To understand taboo in Hawaii as elsewhere in Polynesia, one

Reprinted from William Ellis, *Polynesian Researches, during a Residence of Nearly Eight Years in the Society and Sandwich Islands* (4 vols.; 2d ed., enlarged and improved; London: Fisher, Son, & Jackson, 1839–1842), IV, 385–391.

should bear in mind that the word refers not only to a prohibition but also to the sacred. It is interesting that Ellis so used the latter word many years ago, for this dual meaning is one which some writers today do not grasp. Things sacred are of course inevitably the object of taboo, even in modern society. The relation of all this to mana is obvious enough, because as a supernatural force mana partakes of the sacred. Just as the Latin *sacer* means something not only prohibited but dangerous, so does the Polynesian *tabu*. Contact with things sacred is dangerous; taboos must be established to prevent catastrophe. True, we do not think of taboo in connection with Melanesian mana. Undoubtedly some taboos, however mild and unorganized, were always connected with mana even there; but it remained for the Polynesians with their conquest states and elaborate hierarchy to translate the dangers of mana into a complex system designed to enhance and preserve the status of the aristocracy.

The tabu formed an important and essential part of their cruel system of idolatry, and was one of the strongest means of its support.

In most of the Polynesian dialects, the usual meaning of the word tabu is, *sacred*. It does not, however, imply any moral quality, but expresses a connection with the gods, or a separation from ordinary purposes, and exclusive appropriation to persons or things considered sacred; sometimes it means devoted as by a vow. Those chiefs who trace their genealogy to the gods are called *arii tabu,* chiefs sacred, from their supposed connection with the gods; and a temple is called a *wahi tabu,* place sacred, because devoted exclusively to the abode and worship of the gods. It is a distinct word from *rahui,* to prohibit, as the ohelo berries at Kirauea were said to be prohibited, being *tabu na Pele,* sacred for Pele, and is opposed to the word *noa,* which means general or common. Hence the system which prohibited females from eating with the men, and from eating, except on special occasions, any fruits or animals ever offered in sacrifice to the gods, while it allowed the men to partake of them, was called the *Ai tabu,* eating sacred; but the present state of things is called the *Ai noa,* eating generally, or having food in common.

This appears to be the legitimate meaning of the word tabu, though the natives, when talking with foreigners, use it more extensively, applying it to everything prohibited or improper. This, however, is only to accommodate the latter, as they use *kau-kau* (a word of Chinese origin) instead of the native word for eat, and *pikanniny,* for small, supposing they are thereby better understood.

The tabu separating whatever it was applied to from common use, and devoting it to the above purposes, was one of the most remarkable institutions among the South Sea Islanders; and though it prevailed, with slight variations, in the different groups of the Pacific, it has not been met with in any other part of the world. Although employed for civil as well as sacred purposes, the tabu was entirely a religious ceremony, and could be imposed only by the priests. A religious motive was always assigned for laying it on, though it was often done at the instance of the civil authorities; and persons called *kiaimoku,* island keepers, a kind of police officer, were always appointed by the king to see that the tabu was strictly observed.

The antiquity of the tabu was equal to the other branches of that superstition of which it formed so component a part, and its application was both general and particular, occasional and permanent. The idols, temples, persons, and names of the king, and members of the reigning family; the persons of the priests; canoes belonging to the gods; houses, clothes, and mats of the king and priests; and the heads of men who were the devotees of any particular idol—were always tabu, or sacred. The flesh of hogs, fowls, turtle, and several other kinds of fish, coconuts, and almost everything offered in sacrifice, were tabu to the use of the gods and the men; hence the women were, except in cases of particular indulgence, restricted from using them. Particular places, as those frequented by the king for bathing, were also rendered permanently tabu.

Sometimes an island or a district was tabued, when no canoe or person was allowed to approach it. Particular fruits, animals, and the fish of certain places, were occasionally tabu for several months from both men and women.

The seasons generally kept tabu were on the approach of some great religious ceremony, immediately before going to war, and during the sickness of chiefs. Their duration was various, and much longer in ancient than modern times. Tradition states that in the days of Umi there was a tabu kept thirty years, during which the men were not allowed to trim their beards, etc. Subsequently, there was one kept five years. Before the reign of Tamehameha, forty days was the usual period; during it, ten or five days, and sometimes only one day. In this respect, the tabus, or seasons of restriction, in Hawaii appear to have exceeded those of the South Sea Islands: the longest season of prohibition in Huahine known to the natives was the *rahui* of Mohono, which lasted ten or twelve years. It was during this period that the hogs became so numerous and large that they destroyed all the *feis,* or mountain plantains, excepting those growing on the summits of the highest mountains.

The tabu seasons were either common or strict. During a common tabu, the men were only required to abstain from their usual avocations, and attend at the *heiau* when the prayers were offered every morning and evening. But, during the season of strict tabu, every fire and light on the island or district must be extinguished; no canoe must be launched on the water, no person must bathe; and, except those whose attendance was required at the temple, no individual must be seen out of doors; no dog must bark, no pig must grunt, no cock must crow—or the tabu would be broken, and fail to accomplish the object designed. On these occasions, they tied up the mouths of the dogs and pigs, and put the fowls under a calabash, or fastened a piece of cloth over their eyes. All the common people prostrated themselves, with their faces touching the ground, before the sacred chiefs, when they walked out, particularly during tabu; and neither the king nor the priests were allowed to touch anything—even their food was put into their mouths by another person.

The tabu was imposed either by proclamation, when the crier or herald of the priests

went round, generally in the evening, requiring every light to be extinguished, the path by the sea to be left for the king, the paths inland to be left for the gods, etc. The people, however, were generally prepared, having had previous warning; though this was not always the case. Sometimes it was laid on by fixing certain marks called *unu unu,* the purport of which was well understood, on the places or things tabued. When the fish of a certain part are tabued, a small pole is fixed in the rocks on the coast, in the center of the place, to which is tied a bunch of bamboo leaves, or a piece of white cloth. A coconut leaf is tied to the stem of a tree, when the fruit is tabued. The hogs which were tabu, having been devoted to the gods, had a piece of cinet woven through a perforation in one of their ears.

The prohibitions and requisitions of the tabu were strictly enforced, and every breach of them punished with death, unless the delinquents had some very powerful friends who were either priests or chiefs. They were generally offered in sacrifice, strangled, or dispatched with a club or a stone within the precincts of the *heiau,* or they were burnt, as stated by Miomioi.

An institution so universal in its influence, and so inflexible in its demands, contributed very materially to the bondage and oppression of the natives in general. The king, sacred chiefs, and priests appear to have been the only persons to whom its application was easy; the great mass of the people were at no period of their existence exempt from its influence, and no circumstance in life could excuse their obedience to its demands. The females, in particular, felt all its humiliating and degrading force. From its birth, the child, if a female, was not allowed to be fed with a particle of food that had been kept in the father's dish, or cooked at his fire; and the little boy, after being weaned, was fed with his father's food, and, as soon as he was able, sat down to meals with his father, while his mother was not only obliged to take hers in an outhouse, but was interdicted from tasting the kind of which he ate. It is not surprising that the abolition of the tabu, effecting for them an emancipation so complete and an amelioration so important, should be a subject of constant gratulation; and that every circumstance tending in the smallest degree to revive the former tabu should be viewed with the most distressing apprehensions. The only tabu they now have is the Sabbath, which they call the *La tabu* (day sacred), and to its extension and perpetuity those who understand it seem to have no objection. Philanthropy will rejoice, that their fears respecting the former are not likely to be realized; for, should Christianity not be embraced by some, and only nominally professed by others, so sensible are the great body of the people of the miseries endured under the tabu system, that it is very improbable it will ever be reestablished among them. On the other hand, there is every reason to hope that pure Christianity, which imposes none but moral restrictions, and requires no appropriations but such as it will conduce to their own happiness to make, will eventually pervade every portion of the community; and that, while it teaches them to render a reasonable homage and obedience to the only living and true God, and prepares them for the enjoyment of his presence in a future state, it will elevate the degraded classes, especially the females, to the rank and influence for which they are designed, and render their domestic society as rational and happy as under the tabu it was abject and wretched.

HARRY TSCHOPIK, JR.

Taboo as a Possible Factor Involved in the Obsolescence of Navaho Pottery and Basketry

In the final article of this section, Tschopik offers an interpretation of the relation of taboo to the obsolescence of Navaho pottery and basketry. As these crafts became related to sacred ritual, they became correspondingly shrouded with taboos. This process illustrates factors basic to the concept of taboo. First, taboos are shown to proliferate in dangerous situations which cannot always be brought to a successful conclusion. Second, taboos operate to explain the failures which so often accompany difficult tasks.

The development of taboos in association with sacred ritual demonstrates a more general phenomenon, that of taboos being present in "culturally important" aspects of life. Sacred ritual is only one example of a culturally important aspect of life. Taboos do not surround unimportant things—things that are not dangerous, inexplicable, or difficult to control.

Finally, this article shows that the elaboration of taboos may eventuate in fear and tedium. It is thus, as exemplified by the 1819 Hawaiian abolition of their annoyingly restrictive taboos, that a taboo system may contribute to its own destruction.

Reprinted from *American Anthropologist*, XL (1938), 257–262, by permission of the American Anthropological Association.

The data presented in this paper are strictly applicable only to the Navaho in the vicinity of Ramah, New Mexico, and may not apply to the Indians on the Navaho reservation in all details. The purpose of the paper is an attempt to suggest in what manner taboo and related phenomena may have contributed to the decline of the very interesting Navaho crafts of basketry and pottery.

A brief description of the essential characteristics of these crafts may be in order. The baskets were made in the coiled technique, using sumac for the rods of the foundation and for the sewing material and *Yucca bac-*cata for the bundle. The shallow tray is the form which is still manufactured today. The designs are almost invariably broken at one point by a gap—which is oriented to the east when the basket is used ceremonially—and the last coil ends at precisely the point where the break in the design occurs. The rim is finished in the herringbone technique often referred to as "false braid." The pottery is a crude, unpainted, and unslipped ware, characterized by conical-bottomed vessels which are coated with piñon gum. A coarse painted ware was formerly made.

In studying the degeneration of these

crafts among the Navaho, three phases, roughly, may be inferred.

During the first phase—just after the termination of the captivity at Fort Sumner in the middle of the last century—basketry and pottery were a functioning part of Navaho everyday life. They were employed as utilitarian articles, serving as receptacles for food and water. Being the only containers and vessels, they served all purposes.

In the second phase the pots, pans, and buckets introduced by white traders largely replaced pots and baskets as utilitarian articles of Navaho material culture. Baskets continued to be used in weddings and in ceremonials. They continued to be manufactured, but to a lesser extent than formerly. The pots persisted for use in the Enemy Way or "Squaw Dance," as it is popularly called, and in other ceremonials. The painted ware dropped out.

In the third phase—which represents present-day conditions—baskets continue to be employed in the "sings," but their use in weddings has become largely obsolete. A few continued to be manufactured but many more, apparently, are purchased from the traders who in turn secure them from the Ute or Paiute. In the Ramah area, at least, pottery as a functioning craft has quite recently disappeared, while the pottery drums used in the Squaw Dance are heirloom pieces.

Pottery, therefore, has become a thing of the past, while basketry is well on the wane. Paradoxically enough, however, there are several reasons why these crafts should continue to be engaged in, at any rate, to a limited extent. In the first place, there is a need for baskets in the sings and for pottery drums in the Squaw Dance; and this need, though a ceremonial one, is a real need. Navaho ritual requires that a basket be used in every sing. From it the ritual bath must be taken. In some sings the basket is used as a drum and in others as a receptacle for medicine paraphernalia. In its manufacture, it must be begun to the east and finished to the east. The design should be broken to the east, and the whole basket must be in good condition in order that it may hold water during the ritual bath. As to the specifications regarding pottery, every Squaw Dance requires a Navaho-made drum, while pottery bowls are required for rites in other ceremonials. The drums are prepared under

ritual conditions, and after they have once been so employed, the vessels may never again be used for cooking purposes. In respect to the cup in which the medicine is administered and the pot from which the patient eats, the opinion of singers differs. Some maintain that they need only to be made of clay; others assert that they must be of Navaho manufacture. It seems possible that basketry survives, while pottery is lost, because of the differences in the rigidity of these ritual specifications; but perhaps in the case of the latter the specifications have been relaxed and rationalized to meet existing conditions.

The other reasons why basketry should continue to exist as a craft are more commonplace but none the less real. Baskets, as well as pots, are fragile objects and must be replaced from time to time. The baskets made by Navaho women are sold for use in sings at extremely good prices. On the other hand, the Paiute and Ute baskets, which are made according to Navaho ritual requirements and are practically indistinguishable from Navaho products, command high prices at the hands of the traders.

In an attempt to discover exactly why these crafts are so nearly extinct, we must observe the conditions under which they are pursued, or rather were pursued until recent times. In so doing there is one thing that is immediately outstanding, namely, the multiplicity of taboos which accompany and surround every phase of basketry and pottery manufacture.

First, let us consider pottery. A potter setting out to make pottery goes some distance from her hogan to do her work. No one may watch; especially is this true of children. Should anyone watch, the pot would split. Should anyone touch it, it would crack to pieces. While working on pottery one may not molest snakes nor frogs; one may harm neither dogs nor puppies. No one may step over the materials and clays used in pottery making. One may not break the metate on which the clay is ground nor may one break stones or bones. No one may touch the pottery with bloody hands. One may not jump across deep ditches but must go around them. When working on pottery during a rain, one must avoid getting under rock shelters or trees. One must stay out of caves. One may not swear. While working on the pottery, one may not hit another person, because he might be killed at this time.

In respect to basketry the array of taboos is even more varied and complex. Those applying to pottery also apply to basketry with the following additions. A woman must always work on the concave surface of a basket; if she turned it over, she would lose her mind. She must never allow a child to place the sumac on his head, else it would stunt his growth. If she works on the basket in a high wind, the materials will split. Should the basket or materials be burned, she would lose her mind. If a man works on a basket, he will become impotent. While a woman is working on a basket, she may not sleep with her husband. While menstruating, she may not work on the basket at all and must purify herself afterward before she may resume her work. If she is out during a rain, she must walk slowly and may never run. Should she be riding, she must get off her horse until the rain is over. If she neglected to put the doorway in the basketry design, she would lose her mind or else go blind. When the sumac is cut in preparation for making a basket, it must be tied with a yucca leaf, but never with string or anything else. After the design has been started she may eat only a little meat and bread, but no salt. In coiling the basket, the butt end of one rod must be placed next to the top end of the previous rod; the reverse of this situation may never occur, or the basket cannot be used in a sing. The scraps of the basketry material must be placed in a tree, or under a rock in the shade. When making basketry dyes, the mixture must be stirred with a stick of sumac, but this is not done when preparing the very same dyes for wool or cloth. The aforementioned taboos are representative, but by no means exhaust the list.

This complexity of taboo represents a very definite attitude and state of mind toward the crafts under consideration. The question is: was this the attitude and state of mind toward basketry and pottery when they were common, everyday articles? Old informants stated that in the "old days" there was no difference in appearance between food baskets and medicine baskets, pottery drums and cooking pots. But there are indications that the behavior toward these "sacred" and "profane" baskets—if we may so term them—was quite distinct.

While blood, for example, could come in contact with a food basket, it could never touch a medicine basket. Medicine baskets have been found archaeologically in Navaho graves. This is clearly based on the Navaho emphasis of the distinction between the living and the dead, between killing and curing. It is indeed probable that when pots and baskets were commonplace objects in Navaho culture there were no special emotional attitudes toward them, such as are manifested by taboos. But under special circumstances—that is to say, conditions wherein baskets and pots are no longer commonplace things, and are, furthermore, bound intimately to ritual—special attitudes toward them and ways of dealing with them have arisen.

It should be clear from the foregoing that the function of pottery and basketry has changed. It is no longer utilitarian; it has become wholly ceremonial. It is a well-known fact that objects of former utility survive in ritual—nor is this the only case of it that we find among the Navaho. Arrow points and fire drills are usually encountered in medicine bundles. As the pots and baskets were associated more and more closely with ceremony and ritual, this association manifested itself to an increasingly greater degree in the attitudes and behaviors displayed toward them, and this in turn served to identify them more and more closely with the ceremonial aspects of Navaho life.

It is difficult to get at the factors which have resulted in bringing about these special attitudes. The more obvious ones are the facts that baskets are used in a ceremonial association exclusively; that the sumac itself is used in the manufacture of ritual objects both in sings and at home; that the drum is both prepared and employed ceremonially. Although we may never wholly realize by what processes these bonds of association have come into being, the facts clearly indicate that they exist. Before a woman may start her first basket, she must have a certain sing. And again, after it is finished, she must have another sing. Old baskets are neither thrown away nor burned after they have become worn out; instead they must be disposed of in special ways. Myths relating to the origin of baskets are intimately bound up with the origins of certain sings. Basketry dyes must be made under conditions not applying to wool dyes. Finally, pots and baskets are no longer placed in graves, though other personal effects may be. The statement of an informant clearly indicates why this is so: "Pottery and baskets—they are medicine people. Medicine men always use them on sick persons to cure them; so I call them medicine people because they go with medicine."

In what ways, then, have these special attitudes contributed to the decline of the crafts under consideration? In the first place, these attitudes have served to reenforce the natural conservatism which governs any art tradition or native craft. Whether or not materials, designs, and colors in baskets have actually been specified verbally by singers is doubtful. The point, however, is that the women are afraid to experiment; hence individual expression has been largely stamped out. This also applies to a more limited extent to the pottery drum, which is no longer manufactured. Some women admitted that they had discontinued the pursuit of these crafts because the observation of the multiplicity of taboos was both tedious and uncomfortable. One informant states: "There are so many things that I can't do when I make baskets, that I don't know what I can do and what I cannot do any more." Furthermore, several women have not wished to learn basketry because

they consider the sumac dangerous, believing it a potential source of sickness. The very association of pottery and basketry with the sings makes them a convenient target for the diagnosticians seeking the cause of disease. There are several cases, indeed, where women were explicitly told by the singers that they should cease to make either pots or baskets, as the case may be. They were told that if they continued to make them, they would become sick. It is indeed not improbable that this one fact alone may have contributed extensively to the dying out of these crafts.

To sum up the foregoing: (1) Baskets and pots formerly had both utilitarian and ceremonial uses. (2) The extensive introduction of objects of our culture by traders practically extinguished the utilitarian need. (3) When these articles became wholly ceremonial in use, they became surrounded by so many ritual restrictions that they have recently become obsolete, or at least obsolescent.

In concluding, it may be stated that here we appear to be dealing with a peculiar phenomenon; namely, that crafts, surviving today solely in ritual context, have declined to the point of extinction principally, it would seem, because they do survive solely in a ritual context.

CHAPTER 6

TOTEMISM

⚒⚒⚒⚒

INTRODUCTION

Many human social groups recognize some type of relationship between themselves and some object in nature, either animate or inanimate. This phenomenon, commonly called "totemism," is difficult to characterize for all the cultural groups that manifest it, except in the diffuse way suggested in the definition given. At various times in the history of thought on the subject, writers have suggested universal features of the totemic "complex": totemism is the most primitive form of religion; it is always associated with marriage regulations; members of totemic groups have reverential attitudes toward the totem object; all clans are totemic; members of totemic groups are forbidden to eat the totem object; all totemic beliefs, wherever they are found, stem from a single geographico-cultural source; all totemic beliefs arise out of a panhuman psychological process; and many others. As ethnographic information has accumulated it has been shown that the only aspect of totemism shared by all cultures that contain the concept is the idea of association with the object in nature. The historical and psychological generalizations remain both unproven and highly suspect.

In primitive societies totemistic beliefs range in intensity and complexity from the clan symbols of the Iroquois, which are of little social significance and comparable to heraldic crests, to the immensely complex social and religious significance of the totemic beliefs found among many Australian aborigines. The content of various totemic systems is so varied, in fact, that Radcliffe-Brown ("The Sociological Theory of Totemism") was led to point out that the term does not refer to a single class of phenomena but rather to a large number of diverse institutions which have only very little in common. This view, common in contemporary anthropology, was not current around the turn of the century, when much speculation and theorizing was done regarding the origin and common characteristics of totemistic beliefs. A great deal of intellectual effort and printer's ink was expended before it became apparent that totemism, as a well-defined, clearly delimited system of beliefs and practices found among many cultural groups, simply did not exist. Instead, the concept basic to totemism exists in different groups, but surrounded by very different sets of beliefs and practices, having quite different roles in specific cultures, very likely having different psychological bases, and most certainly having different points of origin in the geographical sense. This is not to say that there are not cultures wherein totemism plays similar or identical roles. As Boas has said, "I do believe in the existence of analogous psychical processes among all races wherever analogous social conditions prevail; but I do not believe that ethnic phenomena are simply expressions of these psychological laws." There are many societies organized around totemic unilinear descent groups where marriage restrictions, some dietary customs, religious beliefs, and origin stories all reflect totemic beliefs. But in addition there are many societies which, harboring the totemic concept, have none of these supposed correlates.

It has also been pointed out by Lowie (*Primitive Society,* 1920) that totemism does not represent a single, unified field of inquiry, but rather that totemic beliefs are aspects of a series of specific but unrelated problems: the association of animal names with clans among Indian groups in the eastern United States is a problem in historical diffusion; Kariera totemic cults are best studied through social organization and religion, and so on.

Though it might be said that the preoccupation of many early anthropologists with the universality and origin of totemism was intellectual waste, this would be grossly unfair. Much of what we do know regarding the nature of primitive religion has arisen from the ashes of incinerated totemic theory. The articles in Chapter 1 by Durkheim, Kroeber, and Goldenweiser bear eloquent testimony to the intellectual explorations which such speculations have induced.

Current interest in totemism has been revived by a stimulating book by Lévi-Strauss, *Le Totémisme aujourd'hui* (1962; English translation, 1963), in which the author acknowledges agreement with Radcliffe-Brown's "second theory" of totemism, as opposed to the latter's "first theory," which was oriented toward utilitarianism and functionalism. This newer position sees that the rationale behind the selection of particular natural species as totems lies in the homology they make possible between them and the human groups they represent. There are two parallel sets of analogies, one natural and the other cultural, as may be seen in the equation: eagle: raven :: Eagle moiety: Raven moiety. But why, says Radcliffe-Brown, are particular species selected? It is because they express friendship and conflict, solidarity and opposition. "In other words," says Radcliffe-Brown, "the world of animal life is represented in terms of social relations similar to those of human society." This represents a great change of heart by the British anthropologist, who had earlier (1929) thought that animal and plant species were selected because they were already sacred on account of their importance for the well-being of the society as food. (Durkheim had said they were selected because they were easy to signify and that they became sacred *after* being selected.) Lévi-Strauss proceeds to adopt the "second theory," as he terms it, because he sees nature as providing a model for differentiation. His ideas are further expressed in his *La Pensée sauvage* (1962) and "The Bear and the Barber," the latter being the concluding selection of this chapter.

ALEXANDER GOLDENWEISER

Totemism

Inspired by Franz Boas' discontent with the concept of totemism as a real unit with a single psychological and historical origin, Goldenweiser published in 1910 an outstanding clarification of the concept in his article "Totemism: An Analytical Study," in which he laid bare its great diversity in form and content. He insisted that totemism had had diverse origins. However, he placed much stress on its emotional value, and in so doing agreed that it had a psychological unity, although not a common psychological source. In time, through a process of convergent evolution, a series of phenomena that had been different came to show overall resemblance.

Reprinted in abridged form from Alexander Goldenweiser, "Totemism: An Essay on Religion and Society," in V. F. Calverton (ed.), *The Making of Man: An Outline of Anthropology* (New York: Modern Library, 1931), pp. 363–392, by permission of the American Folklore Society and Random House, Inc.

Because Goldenweiser's original article is too cumbersome to reproduce here even in abridged form, we have chosen a later article, which is a reworking of the first one. In it there still appears the insistence that totemism is highly diverse and that many of the assumed criteria vanish in the face of worldwide comparison. Goldenweiser reviews some of the theories maintained by such men as McLennan, Freud, Durkheim, Wundt, and Schmidt, each of whom had untenable notions regarding both the nature and the origin of totemism.

After 1910, Goldenweiser began to alter his opinion about the specificity of totemism. He conceded that it had such a restricted character after all, being marked by an association of the totemic content with a clan system. That is, totemism and clans are part and parcel of a single complex. His change of heart, although only partial, has been lamented by his critics as being inconsistent with the facts. We must agree with their point of view, for clans are not always totemic and totemism is not always associated with clans.

DEFINITION AND GEOGRAPHICAL DISTRIBUTION OF TOTEMISM

In the cultures of many primitive tribes, features of religion and social organization are combined in a peculiar way. Anthropologists call such tribes *totemic,* while designating as a *totemic complex* the sum-total of features, whether religious, ritualistic, social, or artistic, which make up *totemism.*

Totemism is one of the most widespread institutions of primitive society. It is found in North America in several wide-flung areas; as our knowledge of South America increases, totemism there seems to be almost equally common; it is encountered in Africa throughout the enormous area south of the Sahara and north of the desert of Kalahari; in India we again discover it in numerous tribes, here in a crude, or perhaps, moribund form; in Australia totemism is practically universal, and it is found, in function or at least in traces, in several of the island clusters of Melanesia.

An institution so general in primitive society, and in it alone, is evidently tied to it by bonds far from casual. An understanding of totemism seems imperative if primitive life and thought are to be understood.

In his presidential address before Section H, Anthropology, of the British Association for the Advancement of Science, A. C. Haddon referred to totemism in the following terms: "Totemism, as Dr. Frazer and I understand it in its fully developed condition, implies the division of a people into several totem kins (or, as they are usually termed, totem clans), each of which has one or sometimes more than one totem. The totem is usually a species of animal, sometimes a species of plant, occasionally a natural object or phenomenon, very rarely a manufactured object. Totemism also involves the rules of exogamy, forbidding marriage between the kins. It is essentially connected with the matriarchal state of culture (mother-right), though it passes over into the partiarchal stage (father-right). The totems are regarded as kinsfolk and protectors of the kinsmen, who respect them and abstain from killing and eating them. There is thus a recognition of mutual rights and obligations between the members of the kin and their totem. The totem is the crest or symbol of the kin."

THEORIES OF TOTEMISM

In the *Fortnightly Review* for 1869–70, John Ferguson McLennan published two articles on "The Worship of Animals and Plants"; the first he called "Totems and Totemism," the second, "Totem-Gods among the Ancients." Ever since, and especially after the appearance of J. G. (now Sir John [*sic*]) Frazer's initial study, *Totemism* (1887), this subject has persistently evoked theories not from anthropologists alone but from sociologists, psychologists, psychoanalysts, and others. Some of these may now be passed in brief review.

In speculating about totemism some authors were primarily concerned with its origin while others attempted to place totemism against the background of primitive mentality or to indicate its place in the evolution of religion. Totemism was conceived as a "system of naming" by Major Powell, a theory partially maintained also by Pikler and Somlo and by Herbert Spencer. In the form given to it by the latter author the theory became known as the "misrepresentation of nicknames" theory. Spencer assumed that animal names were once given to individuals, that these names were subsequently confused with the animals themselves, owing to the vagueness of primitive languages, and that ultimately such animals came to be worshiped as ancestors. Andrew Lang in his *Secret of the Totem* (1905) partially subscribed to the naming theory with two important modifications. He held that, for one reason or another, the animal names were first applied to social groups, not to individuals, that later the origin of these names was forgotten, and speculative guesses were made by the primitives as to the provenience of the names. Thus the stage was set for a totemic origin. "No more than these three things"—argued Lang—"a group animal name of unknown origin; belief in a transcendental connection between all bearers, human and bestial, of the same name; and belief in the blood superstitions—were needed to give rise to all the totemic creeds or practices, including exogamy."

Frazer, who launched totemism upon its busy career and years later contributed to the subject his massive four-volume work, *Totemism and Exogamy* (1910), entertained at different times three different theories of totemic origin. The first became known as the "outward soul" or "bush soul" theory, the second as the "co-operative magic" theory, and the third as the "conceptional" theory. Initially, Frazer held that totemism developed out of the practice of tucking away human souls in animals, for preservation or safety. This enhanced the religious status of the animals. As it was not known, moreover, in which particular animal of a species the "bush soul" had its abode, the custom in time led to the veneration of the entire species. Frazer's second hypothesis was suggested by the *intichiuma* ceremonies described by Spencer and Gillen (1899) in their work on the Central Australians. These ceremonies, which have since been described and discussed so much, consist in somewhat dramatic rituals in which the natives dance and sing their magical rites for the multiplication of the totem animals. Each gens has the exclusive right to

perform the *intichiuma* for its own totem animal. From the resulting enhancement of the species the gens itself does not, to be sure, derive any benefit, for the totem is taboo to its members, but the other gentes do benefit. "In short," writes Frazer, "totemism among the Central Australian tribes appears, if we may judge from the *intichiuma* ceremonies, to be an organized system of magic intended to procure for savage man a plentiful supply of all the natural objects whereof he stands in need." Then, waxing enthusiastic, the author adds: "The thought naturally presents itself to us: 'Have we not in these ceremonies the key to the original meaning and purpose of totemism among the Central Australian tribes, perhaps even of totemism in general?'" Further pondering of the Australian material, meanwhile amplified by Spencer and Gillen's second study (1904), then led to the formulation of the third and final theory, the "conceptional" one (1905). It appeared that these natives ascribed conception, the physiology of which was obscure to them, to the impregnation of women by spirits or spirit carriers which they encountered, or thought they did, at the sacred totem spots (*oknanikilla*) haunted by the spirits. "If we use what in particular may have suggested the theory of conception which appears to be the taproot of totemism," says Frazer, "it seems probable that, as I have already indicated, a preponderant influence is to be ascribed to the sick fancies of pregnant women, and that so far, totemism may be described as a creation of the feminine rather than of the masculine mind." With this contribution to the psychology of the sexes, Frazer's speculations about totemism come to an end.

Pater Schmidt, the then editor of the *Anthropos,* saw the origin of totemism, at least in Australia and certain parts of the South Seas region, in primitive trade. He observed first that in Mabuiag the two totems used in the magical fertilization ceremonies are also the principal, or perhaps only, articles employed in intertribal trade. Reflection over this fact led to a theory which deduced totemism "seemingly so mysterious" from a "relatively prosaic and simple source." Here it is! Who does not know the familiar fact, writes the author in substance, that our peasants often abstain from using in their own households the food products they cultivate, but export them mostly to the neighboring town? What we find here in rudimentary form may develop everywhere under analogous conditions. Such conditions we find wherever the production and consumption of food articles are locally distinct, calling for supplementary intertribal exchange of food products. Local products intended for trade are tabooed to the inhabitants of the district. The food interdict, an economic custom in origin, becomes in time a moral law, and after a while the original motive of the interdict is forgotten (it is to be noted how Schmidt, and before him Lang, exploits the speculative possibilities of such an hypothesized amnesia). "There followed a time of doubt and uncertainty," quoth the author, "conditions pregnant with metaphysical associations." In recognition of its importance in the life of the tribe, the animal or plant becomes the mythical source of the life of the tribe, its ancestor. And what could be more natural than that the group should assume or be called by the name of the animal or plant so plentiful in its district!

After advancing a further argument in favor of the priority of plant-magic over animal-magic, Schmidt concludes that garden culture was the cradle of the magical multiplication rites: "I believe that these things develop quite naturally out of plant-cultivation followed by trade; starting from this base, the subsequent developments in the sphere of mythology explain equally naturally all the details of the fertilization rites and of the peculiar totemism of the Northern Australians." This theory, extravagant though it might seem, does not stand alone, for it was anticipated by A. C. Haddon, who in 1902 advanced a very similar theory, even though less elaborately argued.

There were other theories. Hill-Tout, basing his conclusions mainly on data from the Salish tribes of British Columbia, held that totemism grew out of the worship of individual guardian spirits. Ankermann, who worked largely with African material, saw the basis of totemism in a sort of compensation for the drabness of primitive life, accompanied by an urge to play with the man-animal relationship, to dramatize it. Graebner, faithful to his diffusionistic principles, identified totemism with localization and paternal descent, forming a culture area; and so on and on. For the sake of brevity I shall not consider these theories, turning instead to the more ambitious contributions of Émile Durkheim, Wilhelm Wundt, and Sigmund Freud.

No adequate analysis of Durkheim's theory contained in his *Elementary Forms of the Religious Life: The Totemic System in Australia,* 1915 (French original, 1912), can be given here; a brief summary attempted elsewhere will have to suffice. Religion is a complex of beliefs and activities referring to sacred things, and the characteristic fact in all religions is the division of beings, things, and activities into sacred and profane. If Australian totemism is a genuine religion, it must be the most primitive type of religion, for the social organization of the Australians is the most primitive known to us, being based on the clan.

The totemic symbol or emblem is the expression of the social solidarity of the clanmates. The symbol as well as the name of the clan are derived from the animal or plant which happens to be most common in the locality where the clan congregates. Totemic rituals arise spontaneously, as a direct expression of certain wishes regarding the food supply, and, whether imitative or representative, these rituals arouse pleasurable sensations in the participants by raising their social consciousness. These feelings of satisfaction are projected into the realm of physical nature, giving rise to the belief in the efficacy of the ritual.

The usual experiences accompanying the periodic ceremonial gatherings, when contrasted with the routine happenings of daily life, awaken in the mind of the totemite a sense of the sacred. Not being aware of the source of their exaltation, the individuals of the clan identify the sacred with the totemic symbols by which they find themselves surrounded on these ritualistic occasions. The true content of their beliefs, however, consists of a vague undifferentiated sense of an impersonal totemic principle, prototype of mana; but, unlike mana, the totemic principle, instead of becoming generalized, remains associated with the specific characteristics of the clans.

The totem represented in the symbol partakes of its nature and sacred character. The totemites, having become identified with the totem the name of which they bear, are, as such, also sacred. The entire physical universe is classified in accordance with the phratries and clans, and the beings and objects thus classified with a certain totem share its sacred character.

Thus totemism must be regarded as a religion not of the clan but of the tribe, each clan being sympathetically aware of the beliefs and practices of the other clans which, moreover, strictly correspond to its own.

Individual totemism is a derivative of clan totemism, and sex totemism partakes of the nature of both.

The individual soul is an incarnation of the spiritual essence of a totemic ancestor. The souls of these mythical totemic personages live on as spirits, the more prominent among them developing into tribal gods.

Thus totemism is revealed as a genuine religion. It comprises a division of beings, things, and activities into sacred and profane; it engenders the belief in souls, spirits, and gods; it has its cosmology; and its elaborate rituals embrace a form of sacrifice and ascetic practices. At the root of this religion lies the belief in a totemic principle, a belief which expresses the reaction of an individual psyche to its experience of the social control exercised by the clan. Indeed, the totemic principle *is* the clan. Society is God.

To Wundt totemism appears of interest from two angles. He places the origin of the institution in the period when the belief in a breath or shadow soul became differentiated from the earlier belief in a body soul. The first totem animals, therefore, were the soul-animals—hawk, crow, and lizard in Australia; eagle, falcon, and snake in America—in which human souls were deposited. As a culture historian, on the other hand, Wundt conceives of totemism as providing the sociopsychological and ideological background of nothing less than a "totemic era," one of the four or five great culture eras into which the history of mankind can be divided. With the totemic era Wundt identifies clan organization, exogamy, chieftainship, animal and plant culture, nature myths, zoömorphic and phytomorphic cults and a number of other cultural features.

And, finally, Freud's theory expounded in his book, *Totem and Taboo*. The theory runs, in brief, as follows: In very early times, before there was any definite social organization or religion, man lived in so-called "Cyclopean" families in which all the sex rights were monopolized by the dominant old man, while the younger men, his sons, had to submit to the restrictions imposed by him or be killed or expelled from the group. The great dominant male, the father, was revered by the others for his power and wisdom, but he was also hated on account of his monopolistic prerogatives. One day a great tragedy was enacted in such a primitive community. The brothers banded together—encouraged perhaps, adds Freud, by the invention of a new weapon—and dared to do openly together what each one had long secretly desired. They murdered the father. Then they consumed his body in the assurance of thus acquiring his prowess.

The patricidal act having been committed, the sons, tortured by remorse, reverted to a positive attitude toward the father. Obsessed by a belated desire to be obedient to him—"nachträglicher Gehorsam"—they decided to continue the taboo the oppressive character of which had led to the murder, and to abstain from sex contact with the women of the group. The consciousness of common guilt became the root of the new social bond. Thus arose the clan, protected and reinforced by the taboo on killing a clanmate, in order that the fate of the father might not befall any of the brothers. The totem of the clan is therefore but a transfigured image of the father, and the totemic sacrifice, an occasion for both joy and sorrow, but a dramatization of the remote tragedy in which the jubilant brothers murdered their despot father, then, conscience-stricken, reimposed upon themselves the oppressive taboo in the name of which the murder had been committed.

Freud goes still further. In the central setting of Greek tragedies he discovers another cultural symbolization of the gruesome event of earliest antiquity. The hero's part is to suffer, for he is but the dramatized memory of the murdered father, whereas the responsive chorus stands for the patricidal brothers. In this new setting, however, their part in the original tragedy is disguised under the cloak of a positive attitude toward the hero, a psychological subterfuge with which, in the domain of the individual psyche, psychoanalysis has made us familiar.

Thus four great institutions of mankind are ultimately reducible to one basic and pregnant event, a common psychosociological source. Common guilt lay at the root of the new social system, the clan, primitive Society. The consciousness of guilt expressed itself in a regard for the totem-father, the earliest Religion. In expiation of the crime came the self-imposed rule of exogamy, primal sex taboo, and the earliest embodiment of Morality. In the domain of Art, finally, Greek tragedy re-enacted the ancient deed in an expiatory disguise.

Details apart, a review of these theories leaves one with the impression that when we say "totemism" we have said all there is to be said about the history of human civilization. Give the speculator a thread and he will enmesh the world!

No systematic analysis of totemic theories can be undertaken here. But a few remarks will be in order for the sake of orientation.

The totemic origin theories which seek the first origin of totemism in some one of its features—name, descent, zoölatry, trade, taboo, magic co-operation, ideas of conception—all suffer from dogmatic one-sidedness. With reference to a particular place one or another of these theories may prove correct, but no ground is forthcoming why almost any of the others might not apply at some other place. It must be granted, however, that the theories stressing the totemic clan name come nearer to the essence of the problem than do the others. Even though this feature is not universal in totemic complexes, it is exceedingly common and must have provided in many, if not most, instances the link between the mystical and the social elements in totemism. Through the name, the locus and limits of each particular totemic connection—a particular clan with a particular totem—must have been established in numerous cases.

The theories stressing the role of totemism in religious evolution are in the wrong in so far as they overemphasize the religious aspect of totemism and assume its universality. This stricture applies particularly to F. B. Jevons' *Introduction to the History of Religion,* as has been pointed out by L. Marillier in his brilliant essay, "La place du totémisme dans l'évolution religieuse." In Durkheim's sense, totemism certainly qualifies as a religion, a tribal not a clan religion, for it belongs to the domain of the sacred, not the profane, in primitive life. But it must never be forgotten that the intensity of the religious *attitude* toward the totem is scarcely ever pronounced; also, that totemism, in *no* instance, constitutes the whole or even the center of the religious aspect of a tribal culture. Animism, ancestor or nature worship,

fetishism, idolatry, or even animal or plant worship, may each and all be present in a totemic tribe, side by side with totemism. Again, any of these features may become assimilated with a totemic complex in a particular place, so as to form an integral part of it, or they may not.

There is even something contradictory in the notion of a true religious regard and worship in connection with totemism. Primitives, it is true, have not as yet developed those extreme forms of religious partisanship and pugnacity so characteristic of later historic periods, but it may well be doubted whether totemic complexes could have sailed along as smoothly as they have if each family were divided against itself in point of its deepest religious attitudes. Equivalence of faith and practice in totemic clans and relative mildness of the specifically religious attitude seem equally important here.

Writers like Wundt, finally, and Lawrence Gomme in his *Folklore as a Historical Science,* who speak of a "totemic era" and the like, err in two important respects. On the one hand, they once more assume the universality of totemism of which, to say the least, there is no evidence. On the other, they identify with totemism, genetically or as historic coexistences, a variety of cultural features and tendencies which have nothing whatsoever to do with totemism, either psychologically or culturally or historically, even though they will occur in totemic tribes and cultures.

TOTEMISM AS A CONVERGENT HISTORIC-PSYCHOLOGICAL COMPLEX

By contrast with the older theorists of totemism who were, as a rule, concerned with the similarity and unity of totemic phenomena, my own preoccupation in *Totemism: An Analytical Study* (1910) was with the diversity of totemic complexes and the psychological and historical heterogeneity of the features entering into these complexes.

There is considerable variability in content in totemic complexes. The particular features entering a totemic complex are not always the same, nor is the part they play in the ideology or practice of the totemites.

It is equally apparent that the individual features figuring in totemic complexes are not inherently and necessarily totemic. This applies to *all* the features. We know of totemic exogamy, but it also occurs in clans, gentes, or phratries that are not totemic, as well as in families, local groups, and elsewhere. Similarly with taboos. Killing and eating taboos may or may not refer to totemic animals, in one or another group, but they also occur with reference to creatures other than totems. Killing and eating taboos, moreover, constitute only one aspect of the phenomenon of taboo which is world-wide. As cultural traits, taboo and totemism merely overlap. The same applies to the other features.

What we mean, therefore, when we say that totemism is historically and pyschologically complex is this. The features entering a totemic complex are not inherently totemic but become such in the particular context. As between complex and complex, the particular features composing one, vary. Also, the emphasis, the cultural or totemic status of a feature, varies as one passes from complex to complex.

This does not mean that all totemic features are equally rare, or common, in their occurrence. Far from it. An examination of a sufficient number of totemic complexes will show that exogamy, in one form or another, is almost always present. Also that a relation between humans and the rest of nature, especially animals and plants, is involved here. It may take the form of a "mystic affinity," or a belief in descent, or a taboo on the totem, or a mere eponymous function of the latter without any associated beliefs or practices with reference to it. It must be remembered, however, that the very assumption of an animal or other such name by a group or its acceptance of one given it by others, implies a certain ideological, if not emotional, relationship between humans and the rest of nature. This is a phenomenon not unknown in modern days but incomparably more common, and therefore more characteristic, in primitive society. As a background we discover a *Denkart,* a certain way of looking at things which makes such developments as totemism possible.

In addition to exogamy and a certain relationship between man and nature, the latter usually taking a mystical form, there is still another aspect of totemic complexes which, in this case, is *universal.* In every totemic community the tribal group is divided into a set of social units which are equivalent. The totemic functions of these social units, while different specifically, are also equivalent or homologous, as between unit and unit. It seems obvious that any attempt to find a general formula for totemism must rest on these three features.

TOTEMIC COMPLEXES AND RELIGIOUS SOCIETIES

Totemic communities, as complexes of historically and psychologically heterogeneous features, display certain striking similarities to another form of socioreligious association fairly common in primitive groups, namely, religious societies. A religious society is a group of individuals who have a common name (often derived from an animal, bird, or thing), share a set of religious and mythological beliefs, and perform together certain ceremonies. Where the societies occur, there is always more than one society in the tribe, while often a large part of the tribesmen may be grouped in societies either permanently or, as among the Kwakiutl, periodically. While male societies are more common, female societies also occur, but the membership of a society is almost invariably restricted to either one or the other sex. The geographical distribution of religious societies suggests some relation to totemism. In a large number of totemic areas religious societies also occur; for example, in several large areas in North America, in at least one area in South America, in West Africa, and Northern Melanesia.

On the basis of his Melanesian studies W. H. R. Rivers came to the conclusion that in Mota (one of the Banks Islands), the religious societies developed out of a pre-existing totemism which was, as it were, sucked up into these societies. Hutton Webster went further, representing secret societies in all areas as totemism in decay. In this version the societies appear as a normal stage of evolution from totemism to other forms of socioreligious organization.

In this sweeping form the theory must certainly be rejected, but it may nevertheless contain a germ of truth. In individual instances—in Mota, for example, or, perhaps, in the American Southwest—religious societies may actually have developed in this way. Also, the two institutions, resting against a similar sociopsychological and ideological background, must certainly be regarded as compatible, even though not genetically linked, except incidentally. The case of the Southern Kwakiutl is instructive here, among whom societies or totemic clans alternate: in the summer (the *profane* season) the clans constitute the social organization; whereas in the winter (the season of the *secrets*) these are replaced or, more accurately, overshadowed by a system of religious societies. One would not expect such periodic fluctuation between a system of clans, and, say, one of castes.

Of even greater interest than the geographical and the possible genetic relations of totemism and societies, are the similarities and contrasts between the two institutions from a theoretical standpoint. In both cases the tribe comprises a set of homologous social units; these unites exercise functions—ceremonial, religious, artistic—similar in kind but differing specifically in each clan or society. These functions, finally, cluster about or grow out of certain mystical attitudes toward creatures or objects in nature, the latter feature, however, being more nearly characteristic of totemism than it is of societies. In both cases, moreover, the institution—a totemic complex or a cluster of societies—must be regarded as an alloy of historically and psychologically disparate traits.

The similarity, from a theoretical angle, thus seems to be so close as almost to approach identity. But the contrasts are equally significant. While a society, like a clan, is a social unit, it is one solely by dint of the common functions of its members. Take away the functions and nothing remains but an aggregate of wholly disparate individuals. Not so in the clan. Here also the functions give the true cultural orientation of the social unit, but should the functions lapse, the unit remains; for a clan consists of related individuals (*de facto* or *de jure*)—it is a group of status, whereas a society is a purely functional group. While this contrast is, perhaps, most important, other differences are not lacking. The religious aspect is almost invariably more pronounced in a society than in a clan. Societies, as we saw, are largely unisexual, but not clans: a totemic complex with its supporting skeleton of clans necessarily comprises *all* the individuals of the tribe, whereas a tribal cluster of societies at best includes some of the women and never more than a majority of the men. This, of course, flows from the fact that a clan is a hereditary unit, part of the tribal

social system, whereas a society is merely a part of *a* social system within the tribe, even though some societies may tend to become hereditary or comprise hereditary officials.

While the two institutions—totemism and religious societies—present, from a theoretical standpoint, a set of similar problems, it seems imperative to keep them apart conceptually as well as for purposes of investigation.

TOTEMIC ANALOGUES IN MODERN SOCIETY

Evidence is not lacking that mystical and social features, once components of totemism, persist in modern society, if in less integrated form.

Of all things in nature, animals, both wild and tame, stand closest to us, and we find it difficult not to think of them in anthropomorphic terms. Similarities of physical and psychic traits in man and animal are stressed in verbal usage. We speak of the eagle eye, the leonine heart, the bull's neck, dogged perseverance. The fox and beaver, bear and rabbit, cat and cow, hog and ass, ape and shark, all figure in our scene in human disguise. The layman and the amateur naturalist as well find it difficult not to ascribe to animals qualities of intellect, affection, understanding, sensitiveness, vastly in excess of what sober judgment would allow.

While our attitude here is not strictly mystical, it leans dangerously in that direction.

Similarly with social tendencies. In modern as in primitive society, equivalent social units are known to adopt as classifiers names, badges, pins, flags, tattoo marks, colors. One thinks of high-school and college classes, baseball and football teams, political parties, the degrees of Elks and Masons, and the regiments of our armies.

The names and things thus used as classifiers rest against a background charged with potential emotion. In the case of regimental banners the emotional heat can on occasion become intense. Even the animal or bird mascots cultivated by military units become, under appropriate conditions, such as war, immersed in a complex of attitudes and rites so exotic as to suggest an exaggerated analogy with totemism.

In one form or another the mystic and

social tendencies of totemic days linger on in modern society. But we miss them on its highways. Here and there, under specially favorable conditions, these tendencies may flare up in a sort of totemic glow, presently to go out again, for lack of fuel. In primitive society the same tendencies, quickened and integrated by their association with sib systems, reach great heights of complexity and elaboration.

A. P. ELKIN

Australian Totemism

Several books and hundreds of articles have been written on the social organization of the Australian aborigines. Among these groups totemism pervades all aspects of the very complex kinship and territorial groups, and as then known provided a basis for most early theories regarding the nature of totemism. The intensity and complexity of totemic systems found here is unparalleled in any other culture area. Failure to recognize this fact led many theories astray.

In this discussion Elkin makes a very important distinction—that between social totemism and cult totemism, that is, totems associated with kinship and territorial groups as such, and totems involved in ritual and the sacred aspects of life. Social totemism serves to regulate marriage, to establish relationships between individuals, and to circumscribe social groups; cult totemism, to explain group origins, to maintain tribal customs, and ritually to attempt to increase the food supply.

For the sake of analysis, is there a least common denominator between the two? Is the totemic belief found in both the key to understanding interaction patterns, social integration, and ecological adjustment? Or is totemism in each case an entirely different phenomenon hiding behind similar masks? If the totems are symbolic representations created through psychological processes found in the individual members of the group, is it not possible that, instead of arising from identical processes, they have sprung from quite different ones?

Whatever the answer, quite unknowable at this time, totemistic beliefs in parts of Australia are associated with religion, economics, and social organization, and in each case the nature of the associated beliefs and practices is different and, in part at least, independent of the other. Totemism may be best studied, then, through an understanding of the rest of culture and not as a separate entity, even within a single culture where totemism is found associated with many aspects of the total cultural system.

Reprinted in abridged form from A. P. Elkin, *The Australian Aborigines: How to Understand Them* (3d ed.; Sydney: Angus & Robertson, 1954), pp. 132–155, by permission of the author and the publishers.

Probably Australian totemism has been more discussed in anthropological writings than any other feature of the culture, but the general reader has little, if any, understanding of it.

Totemism is a view of nature and life, of the universe and man, which colors and influences the Aborgines' social groupings and mythologies, inspires their rituals, and links them to the past. It unites them with nature's activities and species in a bond of mutual life-giving, and imparts confidence amidst the vicissitudes of life. The Aborigine is, from our point of view, a parasite on nature; he neither tills, fertilizes nor sows, but only reaps. His life, therefore, depends on nature's maintaining her normal course, but experience has proven that nature of herself is not always consistent. Droughts, floods, and diseases come and go. If man is to live, he must prevent or shorten the period of such disastrous occurrences. In other words, he must rouse himself into action and not be parasitic. Our reaction to this need has been to cultivate and irrigate the land—a reaction common to many primitive and prehistoric peoples, although in their case they have felt that cultivation needed supplementing; they have, therefore, tried to bring into operation unseen life-giving powers of a magical or religious nature or both. By the performance of rites and the adoption of circumspect behavior, they have assured themselves that their efforts would be rewarded—that rain and fine weather would come, each in its due season, and that crops would be abundant.

The Aborgine, on his part, brings nature into his social and ritual life, adopts an attitude of respect towards it, frequently performs ceremonies designed for its welfare and his own, and looks for its assistance not only as the source of food and water, but also as a protection from danger and a guide to the future. In other words, nature is thought of in an animistic, and indeed, personal way. This, however, is not a generalized view of nature as a whole, though such an aspect is not altogether absent. Just as normally, any one of us thinks not of mankind as a whole, but rather of this man, or of this or that group, so it is with the Aborigines' view of nature. They depend upon it, share a common life, and enter into mutual relations, with it. But this is not a relationship between black mankind or all the tribe and nature as a whole or in the abstract. It is a relationship between an individual or group of men on the one hand and a natural species or several species, that is, a part or parts, of nature on the other. In other words, there is a segmentary aspect to this relationship and bond which exists between man and nature, and it is this very feature which distinguishes totemism from a generalized nature-religion.

This feature is expressed in the usual definition of totemism as a relationship between an individual or group of individuals on the one hand and a natural object or species on the other—a relationship which is denoted by the bearing of the name of the latter, the totem, by the individual or group. Some such definition is useful provided we realize that it states rather than answers a question: namely, what is the nature of the relationship which exists between the totem and the human group associated with it? Does the totem do anything for the totemites, such as assisting or guarding them? Do they contribute anything to its welfare, such as performing ritual for its increase, guarding it from destruction or, at least, from disrespectful use? Do they themselves refrain from injuring, destroying, or eating it, and if so why? Is this because the relationship is a social and "physiological" one, such as exists between members of a blood-clan, or because it is religious and ceremonial? Does the totem merely exist to give a name to a group, and so provide a symbol of the common relationship of its members one to another, and incidentally serve as a method of classifying and denoting members of the tribe? And does the totem perform its functions of assisting, warning, and acting as a name in waking life only, in the dream life only, or in both? Then there is a second series of questions which concerns the human group rather than its totem. Thus, what is its constitution? Is it a local group, a patrilineal or matrilineal clan, a moiety, or some other subdivision of the tribe? Is membership of it determined by descent through the father or mother, or in some other way? Is it a social group only or a cult or religious group? And finally, there is the important question, what is the bearing and influence of totemism on the general economic, administrative, and social life of the tribe?

Such a list of questions must be borne in mind whenever we are confronted with any totemic phenomenon. At least it makes us realize first, that the subject is a very complex one, the understanding of which demands that we enter deeply into all aspects of native life; and second, that totemism does not stand just for one phenomenon of Aboriginal life. It is now regarded as a term used to cover a number of diverse phenomena of social, religious, and magical significance. Therefore it is necessary in every case of totemism to study the nature and function of the natural and human groups, and of the relationship which binds them together.

To do this we classify totemic phenomena from two points of view, namely, form and function. By form I mean the manner in which the totems are distributed amongst the members of a tribe and the way in which the totemic groups are constituted; such forms, for example, are moiety totemism, clan totemism, and sex totemism. By function, I mean the part played by the particular form of totemism in the life of the tribe; thus, it may help to regulate marriage, to preserve moral and social sanctions, or to provide a psychological adjustment to the conditions of life. In addition, each form of totemism has some meaning or significance for the individual totemite, and this must not be overlooked when studying its general social function; he regards the totem as his assistant, guardian, mate, or the symbol of his social or cult group, and he frequently regulates his thoughts and his behavior in accordance with his convictions in this regard.

FORMS OF TOTEMISM

The various forms of totemism are:

(i) *Individual totemism,* in which the totemic relationship is between one person on the one side and a species of nature on the other.

(ii) *Sex totemism,* which divides the whole tribe into two groups on the basis of sex and the possession by each of its own totem.

(iii) *Moiety totemism,* which also divides the tribe into two groups, but in this case on a principle of relationship and descent; this may be either patrilineal or matrilineal.

(iv) *Section and subsection totemism.* In this each of the four or eight groups of kin into which the tribe is respectively divided is associated with its own totem or totems. The descent of these groups and totems is indirectly matrilineal.

(v) *Clan totemism.* In its normal form a totemic clan consists of a group of kin directly related by patrilineal or matrilineal descent, the members of which share in common one or more totems. Sometimes, too, the local patrilineal patrilocal group (territorial clan) is also a totemic clan.

(v) *Local totemism.* In this, membership of the totemic group and the possession of its totem or totems depends on the principle of locality and not on that of descent. Membership of the territorial clan just mentioned is primarily a matter of the spiritual tie to the locality and not one of descent. Moreover, in some cases at least, the totems belong to the group because, like the totemites, they belong to the country. Mythology generally shows how the totems came to be associated with the locality.

(vii) *Multiple totemism.* In this form of totemism, a number of natural objects or species, as well as men and women, are grouped under the name of one or more principal totems. This can be a feature of moiety, section, clan, or local totemism. It is really a method of classifying natural phenomena.

To sum up: The forms of totemism are individual, sex, moiety, section and subsection, clan, local, and multiple. This variety of forms gives some idea of the complexity of totemism—a complexity which is increased by the coexistence in very many tribes, of several forms; it is quite common to find three or four in the one tribe; that is, each person has three or four totems or, rather, belongs to as many totemic groups. But this is only the beginning of the complexity, for as we shall see, on the one hand, one form may have more than one function and on the other hand, several forms perform a similar function. It is, therefore, necessary to study totemic phenomena from the point of view of the function which they perform in social and religious life.

THE FUNCTIONS OF TOTEMISM

Passing then from a study of the forms and organization of totemic phenomena to a study of their function and meaning, we may classify such phenomena under the following headings: social, cult, conceptional, dream, classificatory, and assistant.

Social totemism. Possibly the most important point to be made clear is the distinction between social and cult totemism. Had earlier investigators realized this distinction, less confusion would have resulted. The former is concerned with human relationships and marriage, whereas the latter has little if any concern with these matters; it has to do with mythology, ritual and the sacred side of tribal life.

Further, social totemism is nearly always, perhaps always, matrilineal in descent, while cult totemism is local and patrilineal. The former is very frequently expressed in matrilineal clans. The members of such a clan belong to it because their mothers do or did, and ultimately they have all been incarnated through the womb of a common ancestress. Now, it is this common flesh-and-blood relationship which is expressed by the term for social totem, namely, "flesh" or "meat." To ask a native what is his "flesh," is to receive the name of his matrilineal social totem, say, kangaroo or emu. It is his flesh, or rather the symbol of the common flesh shared by the members of the clan, who, therefore, speak of themselves as relations. As a result, they will not injure, kill, or eat their social totem, their flesh, nor will they marry any person who has the same social totem, never mind how distant is his genealogical relationship or how far away is his country, for he is one flesh. Such a marriage would break the fundamental incest laws which forbid marriage with mother or sister, because all who belong to one social clan are mothers and children or brothers and sisters.

This relationship is also very frequently shown in another way, namely, by an action on the part of the totemic partner; the animal or plant in actual life or in a vision or dream acts as a mate or friend of the persons whose totem it is; it warns them of danger, gives them courage or strength and imparts to them information regarding absent clansfolk. The very presence of the totem does this, or rather it sets the person meditating, and the condition in which, or the place where, he happens to be, has a lot to do with the interpretation put upon the action or presence of the social totem.

Matrilineal moiety totemism has in part a similar significance; all its members are relations, and the moiety totem (eagle hawk, crow, black cockatoo, white cockatoo, etc.) symbolizes the sharing of a common life based on descent through the mothers, though in a more extended sense than in the case of the social clan. In some cases, the members of a matrilineal moiety speak of themselves as one flesh, and will not eat the moiety totem unless driven to do so by hunger; in such a case, they express their sorrow for having eaten their friend or flesh. Such moieties are usually exogamous provided that *clan* exogamy and the kinship rules are observed, for the primary function of moieties, as previously stated, is not to regulate marriage.

Section (and subsection) totemism is either wholly or chiefly social in function. The sections group relations in certain ways for social purposes, separating generation lines and cross-cousins. Moreover, the members of any one group are, for certain purposes, regarded as relations, or all of one kind; this is even more true of subsections. But so close to nature do the Aborigines live and so all-pervading is the totemic attitude to life, that these groupings, comparatively recent as they must be, are mostly (and possibly were generally) thought of in a totemic manner; that is, the members of any one section are not only related to one another, but also to one or more natural species, their totems. Subsections are frequently referred to as "skins" in northwestern Australia; this corresponds to the use of the term "flesh" for the totem of the social clan; indeed, in one part of eastern Australia, "skin" is used instead of "flesh" for the latter. Moreover, the section and subsection totemic groups are indirectly matrilineal in descent, and in most of the tribes with sections in eastern Australia an individual adopts a ritual attitude towards his own totem, or even all the totems of his section. He neither kills nor eats it, and indeed, expresses sorrow when he sees it killed. The section totem, too, in some tribes, acts as the totemite's mate or guardian. Thus the section and subsection forms of totemism are similar in function and meaning to the totemism of the social clans. Like the latter also, the sections and subsections are ideally exogamous; often, however, this is not so in practice, though marriage between members of the same totemic group would not occur, for there are usually several totems in each section or subsection.

Sex totemism is also a variety of social totemism. It stands for the solidarity of each sex, a solidarity which is expressed in ritual quarrels and marriage preliminaries and is symbolized by the bearing by each sex of a bird or plant totem. But this is not just a matter of having a name or emblem, for the men and their totem on the one hand, and the women and their totem on the other hand, are said to share a common life. Some tribes believed that the men and women were each descended from their totems, and in this way all the men of the tribe were brothers and all the women were sisters, while the totem (bat and night owl, bat and woodpecker, emu-wren and superb warbler) was the mate or brother (or sister) of its totemic group, and indeed might itself be a transformed man or woman.

Thus sex totemism is social in nature because it functions as a social grouping and also because it symbolizes and expresses social and kinship relationships in much the same way as does social clan totemism.

Cult totemism. Over the greater part of Australia, perhaps formerly over all of it, there has existed a variety of totemism which may best be described as a secret religious or cult organization. In each tribe there are a number of cult societies or cult groups or lodges, each of which consists of a number of fully initiated male members whose affiliations were designated by right of birth. Each group exists to take care of and hand on a prescribed portion of the sacred totemic mythology and ritual of the tribe and often, also, to be the custodian of sacred totemic sites and to perform ceremonies for the increase of the species which is its totem. The portion of mythology and ritual and the sacred sites entrusted to such a cult group is defined by mythological history. It is fundamentally the mythology which records the travels and actions of the tribal heroes in its subdivision of the tribal territory. The country of each local group is crossed by the paths or tracks of these heroes along which there are a number of special sites where the hero performed some action which is recorded in myth; it may have been only an ordinary everyday act, or it may have been the institution or performance of a rite. A site with its heap of stones, standing stone, waterhole, or some other natural feature may mark the spot where he rested or went out of sight temporarily. Another may mark the final stopping place where his body was transformed into stone and his spirit was freed to watch everything which should happen afterwards or, possibly, it may be the "home" where his spirit awaits reincarnation. In some cases too, such a hero is believed to have left the preexistent children in the spirit-centers, in the same way as by his rites and actions and the virtue inherent in him, he caused certain places to be the life-centers or spirit-centers of natural species.

This conception of the mythological path is especially important in most of South Australia and the Northern Territory, and as we penetrate farther into the secret life of other regions, I doubt not that we shall find it exercising a constant influence in the cult-life. The special emphasis on the "paths" in South and Central Australia and adjacent areas of Western Australia is probably a reflection of geographical and economic facts,

namely, the dry nature of the country and scarcity of readily accessible water in the past, as in the present. Permanent rock holes and shallow soaks are few and often far between, with the result that, except immediately after rain, the natives are not free to roam far to the right or left of the shortest routes between the sources of water. Under such conditions it is not surprising that the natives are often vague concerning the boundaries of the countries of local groups, just as they sometimes are with regard to tribal boundaries. A kind of no-man's-land exists in which no one is particularly interested. It has no permanent economic value and is mythological in significance.

The existence of these paths explains one fact which sometimes puzzles students of Aboriginal cult-life. They notice that though the natives say they know quite well the direction and the exact location of a certain sacred site, they very seldom approach it by the shortest route; indeed, they frequently set out as though going somewhere else altogether, or they seem unable to find their way to the place. The explanation is that the sacred place must only be approached by the same path as that taken by the hero connected with it; this may lead for some time away from it, and some informants may have to search around until they find signs of the track before they can move with certainty.

These paths are intergroup and intertribal in character, that is to say, they pass through the countries and territories of local clans and of tribes and in doing so serve to bind these groups and tribes together. Certainly, all those whose countries, irrespective of tribe, are situated along the path of one hero or a group of heroes have a secret bond of friendship and a mutual claim to hospitality and protection. This enables members of a cult-group which is responsible for the myths and rites associated with the hero of the path to travel safely along that hero's path even when it leads into other tribal territories, provided their purpose is peaceful and associated at least indirectly with the cult. A notable instance of this is the expedition for red ochre from northeastern South Australia down to the deposits at Parachilna, a distance of three or four hundred miles; but all the way, the travelers could follow the path of the mythological emu and dogs whose blood ultimately caused the red ochre deposit.

The intergroup aspect of the path has another important effect, namely, it makes the various local groups and tribes mutually dependent for their cult-life. To obtain the whole story of many of the great myths and to see all the rites connected with it, we must pass from group to group and tribe to tribe —in other words, from lodge to lodge. Each one is the custodian of a particular chapter of the myth and of the particular rites and sites associated with that chapter. But as continuity with the past, a full knowledge of social and ritual sanctions, and a complete assurance for the present and future can only be maintained and gained by a knowledge of the myth as a whole and the performance of all the rites, it is essential that each "lodge" should do its part. Thus the groups and tribes are linked together by the cult-life.

This is particularly clear to us if we think of the rites which have to be performed for the increase of natural species—such as yams, fish, marsupials, rain, and other things on which life itself depends—and for the care of the sites associated with the life or spirits of these species. Each local cult-group is responsible for one, sometimes for a few, of these rites and sites, but as it requires for its sustenance the regular increase of other species, the rites and sites for which it does not possess, it is dependent on the ceremonial knowledge, sites, and activities of other local cult-groups for its own life. As this is mutual, we see that the cult-life is a vast system of ritual co-operation binding together local groups and also tribes.

The interdependence of groups is also brought about in another way, namely, by the fact that very often the paths of two or more heroes or bands of heroes pass through the country of the one territorial clan; these paths sometimes cross one another in space, though not necessarily in time, and the points of intersection are frequently known. This fact has two consequences: in the first place, members of a local group have an interest in the paths and myths of all the heroes who passed through their country, though they themselves are usually concerned primarily with only one, namely, the hero of special importance in their country; in the second place, according to the places in which their spirits were found, or in

which they were conceived or born, different members of the one local group may be attached to different mythological paths and heroes, and consequently their primary affiliations are to different "lodges," even though they may all assist each other in their respective cult duties. This sometimes explains why members of one local group have different totems, and at the same time each man has several or all the totems. It is a matter of the historical associations of the locality of his father's clan.

The question, however, might well be asked: "What has all this business of cult societies and 'lodges' to do with totemism?" The answer is simply that cult totemism is based on a belief in the mutual interdependence of man and nature, the need one has of the other, and the urge to bring the latter into the historical and ceremonial life of the former. The heroes whose paths we have been discussing are often referred to in totemic guise, that is, as animals or birds, though often too as human beings. Sometimes they are men and women bearing totemic names, possibly endowed with the power of assuming some of the characteristics and attributes of their totems when the occasion demands it, and sometimes they are animals or birds who always remain such, though they talk and think as human beings.

The cult lodges are responsible for two kinds of ceremonies. The first are solely historical and instructive in nature and function. They re-enact the doings of the hero or heroes concerned, and in so doing act out the myth. The actors, representing animals, birds, or human beings, "dress up," adorning themselves with the paint and design peculiar to the rite, and wearing or carrying symbols which express some fact about or incident in the life of the hero. Songs are chanted during the preparations for the rites, as well as during their performance. These are the poetical versions of the myths. At the conclusion of each act, which usually lasts only a couple of minutes or so, the old men explain it and the decorations and symbols to any newly initiated men present or to any whose memories need refreshing. In this way tribal history is handed down, and the patterns of life which the myths enshrine are instilled into the minds of the younger men present, for men must do today what the great heroes did in the dream-time.

The importance of the rites lies in two

important functions which they perform. In the first place, they preserve and inculcate the historical traditions and social sanctions (or authority) of the tribe and thereby strengthen the social sentiments; in the second place, they enable the members of the assembled group or groups to express and feel their unity and common life—a life which in the ritual wells up from the past and becomes available for the future.

Such means of maintaining the social sanctions and ideals and of strengthening the common life is essential for the Aborigines if not for all mankind. If the cohesion of the Aboriginal community is to be maintained, the cult-life must not be destroyed. The ceremonies might, however, be modified, or, indeed, replaced by others capable of performing the same essential functions.

There is no need to discuss here the second type of cult ceremony. Concerned with the increase of natural species, and like the ceremonies of the first type, it has an historical basis, being associated with the travels and deeds of the totemic heroes; moreover, the increase ceremony is usually performed at sites sanctified by those heroes, whose bodies were possibly transformed there, or where they themselves performed increase rituals. It is sufficient to state that the effect of these rites is once again to enable the groups concerned to realize their unity and common life. By the correct performance in the proper centers assurance is gained that nature will proceed on her wonted way and man will be able to get food and so live. The converse of the picture is that if the natives do not perform, or are prevented by us from performing, these increase rites, they cannot, and do not, have that assurance. Their life is based on a ritual co-operation with nature, and if they fail to do their part there is no certainty that nature will be able to perform hers; indeed, it is almost certain that she will not be able to do so.

It should be emphasized that the cult totem has nothing whatever to do with marriage, and if it appears to be implicated it is only because the totems are distributed amongst the local exogamous groups of the tribe.

A taboo on the cult totem is quite widely observed. In some tribes it is never eaten by the totemites except ritually once a year at the first gathering of the species; in other tribes, it cannot be eaten until after a period of abstinence, and [it must be] a ritual eating. In some cases, there seems to be no taboo at all. But in general there is a tendency or rule to regard the cult totem as too sacred a symbol to be used in a profane way; indeed, in symbolizing membership of a cult society it is often also the symbol of a patrilineal and spiritual relationship to a mythological ancestor; in this regard, the cult totem resembles the social totem, only the latter symbolizes a matrilineal physiological relationship.

We must also notice that cult totems and social totems frequently coexist in one tribe. The tribes of northeastern South Australia are the most striking examples of this: a man has his patrilineal local cult totem and a share in his mother's brother's cult totem; he also belongs to his mother's social totem (his flesh), and one may add, to her moiety; in addition, he has a sex totem. But these tribes are not alone in this regard. We know that many tribes of the Northern Territory and Eastern Kimberley have subsection social totems as well as cult totems, while some of them also have distinct social clan totems.

The women have cult totems just as their brothers and fathers have, but they are little more than a name to them, for they are not admitted to membership of the cult societies.

Conception totemism. From our point of view, conception can only be realized by the mother, nor would the Aborigines deny this, and in Central Australia they use this fact in determining cult totems. But the father may also play a part in conception—a spiritual role and not the physiological part that we know to be a fact. As already seen, in very many parts of Australia, the father finds in a vision of the day or night, the pre-existent child which ascertains from him who its mother is to be, and then enters her womb. The mother may dream of the spirit-child later. But the father knows ahead that a spirit is to be incarnated through his wife. In some parts, the spirit-child is "found" or dreamed of in association with some natural species; this is usually one of the totems of the father's own country or section or subsection—the vision being "controlled." In any case, this natural species becomes the child's conception totem—the tie between his spirit and the natural world; and although normally, it is also a cult totem or a section totem, there are instances which suggest that it is distinct.

Dream totemism. By dream totemism is meant the belief that a person is represented in dreams (especially the dreams of others) by a natural species or object, so that even the dream life has an intimate relationship with nature. In most of the great cult-totemic regions of Australia, the cult totem also acts as the dream totem; indeed, it is called the "dreaming," but not so much in reference to this function as to its significance as a link with the "eternal dream-time."

Classificatory totemism. Classificatory totemism is perhaps the most interesting variety of totemism; in form it is multiple totemism, and the latter may be a feature of moiety, clan, section, or local totemism. Broadly speaking, this means that each moiety, clan, section, or local group totem includes not only men and women but also certain natural species and objects. In the case of clan and local (cult) totems, these are often referred to as subsidiary totems, and in any case, a person looks upon the various species and objects grouped with or under his totem, as in some sense his own totems, and if he takes up any sort of ritual attitude to the primary totem, he acts towards the rest in much the same way. In other words, there is felt to be some kind of relationship between man and all natural species and objects: all things in heaven and earth—including man—are classified into moieties, clans, cult-groups, or sections. Totemism is then a method of classifying natural phenomena, and it does so by bringing them into man's social and cult-groups on the basis of the Aborigine's conviction that the life of nature and man is one. To us it may seem strange to be told that lightning is crow and so are thunder, rain, clouds, hail, and winter, that the moon and stars are black cockatoo, that fish, eels, and seals are *karato* (a nonpoisonous snake). But the major totems represent social clans, and by grouping in these all the other natural phenomena which come into his life in any way, he has a workable method of classification and one which does not add any further complications to ritual and social behavior.

We cannot always see the principle by which the classification was made, but no doubt there are, or were, associations in the Aboriginal mind and culture which would have no significance for us. Such animistic and social classification of natural phenomena, however, does at least show that Aboriginal man is at home in nature, and also that he makes nature at home within his own social organization.

Assistant totemism. In most parts of Australia the medicine man stands in a special relation to one natural species, usually an animal or reptile which acts as his assistant, going forth either to work his will for good or ill on the patient or victim or to gather information from a distance. This variety of totemism, which is individual in form, is most strongly developed in eastern Australia, but the possession of similar "familiars" is also a characteristic of the medicine men of northwestern Australia. Such totems and "familiars" are both within and without the individual. They are like a second self or spirit, and yet they are also externalized in the species, and may be exhibited in a tamed member of it. The lace lizard and certain snakes are the commonest varieties of assistant totems.

This totem is usually given by medicine men and generally only to persons who are destined, or desire, to be magical practitioners. A dying medicine man may leave his totem to someone else—in so doing, he bequeaths part of himself. In southeastern Australia, at least, assistant totemism is akin to social totemism; the totemite does not eat his totem; indeed, an injury to the latter will entail injury to him; and, for its part, the totem assists and guards the individual. It should also be noticed that the social totem and the dream totem are often believed to guard and warn the totemite and even to help him recover from illness. But the element of positive assistance in the performance of one's work or calling is not present; this seems to be limited to the profession of medicine men and the workers of magic, and so requires a subdivision for itself, namely, assistant totemism.

RALPH LINTON

Totemism and the A.E.F.

In this article Linton documents the development of totemic-like beliefs in the United States Army during World War I. The custom of naming army divisions which he cites has its counterpart in civilian life as well. Youth clubs, athletic teams, and many other social groups in modern societies commonly affiliate themselves with some object in nature. Names are chosen which in some way typify the spirit and goal of the group. Many such groups, as pointed out by Linton, have all but one prerequisite for full-blown totemic "complexes." It is important to note that, while the processes involved in the development of such modern totem beliefs may be identical to those which have occurred in some primitive societies, the basic similarity between the two is at the level of form—they "look" alike. Whether the sociopsychological processes involved in each case are the same, despite the apparent similarity of the end products, is open to question.

Reprinted from *American Anthropologist*, XXVI (1924), 296–300, by permission of the American Anthropological Association.

Many modern anthropologists discount the supposed differences in the mental processes of civilized and uncivilized peoples and hold that the psychological factors which have controlled the growth of the so-called "primitive" cultures are still at work in modern society. It is difficult to obtain evidence on this point, and a record of the development in the American army of a series of beliefs and practices which show a considerable resemblance to the totemic complexes existing among some primitive peoples may, therefore, be of interest. The growth of one of these pseudo-totemic complexes can be fully traced in the case of the 42nd or Rainbow Division. The name was arbitrarily chosen by the higher officials and is said to have been selected because the organization was made up of units from many states whose regimental colors were of every hue in the rainbow. Little importance was attached to the name while the division was in America and it was rarely used by enlisted men. After the organization arrived in France, its use became increasingly common, and the growth of a feeling of divisional solidarity finally resulted in its regular employment as a personal appellation. Outsiders usually addressed division members as "Rainbow," and to the question "What are you?" nine out of ten enlisted men would reply "I'm a Rainbow." The personal use of the name became general before any attitude toward the actual rainbow was developed. A feeling of connection between the organization and its namesake was first noted in February, 1918, five to six months after the assignment of the name. At this time it was first suggested and then believed that the appearance of a rainbow was a good omen for the division. Three months later it had become an article of faith in the organization that there was always a rainbow in the sky when the division went into action. A rainbow over the enemy's lines was considered especially auspicious, and after a victory men would often insist that they had seen one in this position even when the weather conditions or direction of advance made it impossible. This belief was held by most of the officers and enlisted men, and anyone who expressed doubts was considered a heretic and overwhelmed with arguments.

The personal use of the divisional name and the attitude toward the rainbow had both become thoroughly established before it began to be used as an emblem. In the author's regiment this phase first appeared in May, when the organization came in contact with the 77th Division, which had its namesake, the Goddess of Liberty, painted on its carts and other divisional property. The idea was taken up at once, and many of the men decorated the carts and limbers in their charge with rainbows without waiting for official permission. As no two of the painted rainbows were alike, the effect was grotesque and the practice was soon forbidden. Nevertheless it continued, more or less surreptitiously, until after the armistice, when it was finally permitted with a standardized rainbow.

The use of rainbows as personal insignia appeared still later, in August or September. The history of the development of shoulder insignia in the American army is well known and need not be given here. The idea apparently originated with the Canadian forces, but the A.E.F. received it indirectly through one of the later American organizations which had adopted it before their arrival in France. The use of such insignia became general in the rear areas before it reached the divisions at the front. The first shoulder insignia seen by the author's regiment were worn by a salvage corps and by one of the newer divisions. This division was rumored to have been routed in its first battle, and it was believed that its members were forced to wear the insignia as punishment. The idea thus reached the 42nd Division under unfavorable auspices, but it was immediately taken up and passed through nearly the same phases as the use of painted insignia on divisional property. The wearing of shoulder insignia was at first forbidden by some of the regimental commanders, but even while it was proscribed many of the men carried insignia with them and pinned them on whenever they were out of reach of their officers. They were worn by practically all members of the division when in the rear areas, and their use by outsiders, or even by the men sent to the division as replacements, was resented and punished. In the case of replacements, the stricture was relaxed as they became recognized members of the group.

All the other army organizations which were in existence long enough to develop a feeling of group solidarity seem to have built up similar complexes centering about their group names. The nature of some of these names precluded the development of the ideas of the namesake's guardianship or omen giving, but in such cases the beliefs which were associated with the rainbow by the 42nd Division were usually developed in connection with something other than the group namesake. In some organizations the behavior of an animal mascot, or even of an

abnormal person, was considered ominous. In one instance a subnormal hysteric acquired a reputation as a soothsayer and was relieved of regular duty by the other enlisted men on condition that he foretell the outcome of an expected attack. The successive stages in the development of these complexes were not always the same as in the case of the 42nd Division. Many of the later organizations seem to have taken over such complexes with little change except the substitution of their namesake for that of the group from which they borrowed.

By the end of the war, the A.E.F. had become organized into a series of well defined, and often mutually jealous, groups each of which had its individual complex of ideas and observances. These complexes all conformed to the same general pattern but differed in content. The individual complexes bound the members of each group together and enabled them to present a united front against other groups. In the same way the uniformity of pattern gave a basis for mutual understanding and tolerance and united all the groups against persons or organizations outside the system.

The conditions in the American army after these group complexes had become fully developed may be summarized as follows:

(1) A division of the personnel into a number of groups conscious of their individuality;

(2) the possession by each of these groups of a distinctive name derived from some animal, object, or natural phenomenon;

(3) the use of this name as a personal appellation in conversation with outsiders;

(4) the use of representations of the group namesake for the decoration of group property and for personal adornment, with a taboo against its use by members of other groups;

(5) a reverential attitude toward the group namesake and its representations;

(6) in many cases, an unformulated belief that the group namesake was also a group guardian capable of giving omens.

Almost any investigator who found such a condition existing among an uncivilized people would class these associated beliefs and practices as a totemic complex. It shows a poverty of content when contrasted with the highly developed totemism of the Australians or Melanesians, but is fully as rich as the totemic complexes of some of the North American Indian tribes. The main points in which it differs from true totemism are the absence of marriage regulations, of beliefs in descent from, or of blood relationship with, the totem, and of special rites or observances to propitiate the totem. Each of these features is lacking in one or another of the primitive complexes which are usually classed as totemic, and one of the most important, marriage regulation, is clearly a function of the clan or gentile system of organization and occurs in primitive groups for which totemism cannot be proved.

It seems probable that both the A.E.F. complexes and primitive totemism are results of the same social and supernaturalistic tendencies. The differences in the working out of these tendencies can readily be accounted for by the differences in the framework to which they have attached themselves and in the cultural patterns which have shaped their expression. In the army, the military unit offered a crystallization point for these tendencies, and this precluded the development of marriage regulations or of a belief in the common [descent] of the group. The American culture pattern stimulated the development of the eponymous and decorative features, but offered no formulae for the rationalization of the relation felt to exist between the group and its namesake, or for the development of observances for the namesake's propitiation. In primitive groups, on the other hand, the same tendencies usually crystallized about a clan or gentile system, and the marriage-regulation features of this system became incorporated into the complex. Membership in the clan or gens was based on common descent, and in a group which drew no clear line between mankind and the rest of nature, the idea of blood relationship provided a convenient formula for the explanation of the group-namesake relation. Animistic or polytheistic concepts, and the existence of observances for the propitiation of a number of supernatural beings,

afforded a pattern for the development of religious attitudes and special observances in connection with the namesake.

Even if we are willing to admit the essential unity of the tendencies which produced the army complexes on one hand and the totemic complexes on the other, it does not follow that the observed development of the army complexes will throw much light on the history of primitive totemism. Even in the army no universal rule of evolution was evident, for although the starting-points were always the group and name, the other features appeared in different order in the various units. The ease and rapidity with which the army complexes were developed suggests that the tendencies underlying them were deep-seated and only awaited a chance for expression. The importance of diffusion in the growth of these complexes is suggestive, and the army conditions may afford a clue to the true significance of some totemic phenomena. The often quoted example of the Australian who declared he was a kangaroo is a case in point. The author repeatedly heard soldiers declare that they were sunsets, wildcats, etc., and it would have required a good deal of questioning to obtain any coherent explanation of the relation which they felt existed between themselves and their namesakes. Such a cross-examination would have been impossible with the limited vocabulary of a trade jargon and very difficult with an ordinary interpreter. Although the army attitudes and practices were definite enough, their background was emotional rather than rational and the average soldier never attempted to formulate the ideas underlying them. Explanations elicited by questioning would be made up on the spur of the moment and would represent only his individual opinion. It seems probable that in primitive groups also a whole series of attitudes and practices could be developed without the individual feeling any need for their rationalization until he was confronted by some anthropological investigator.

CLAUDE LÉVI-STRAUSS

The Bear and the Barber

While Lévi-Strauss ostensibly addresses himself in this article to similarities between totemic groups and castes, he is really using them to express a methodological approach wherein he tries to reduce the variables of society to certain basic means for the solution of human problems. As in his provocative book on kinship and marriage, *Les Structures Elémentaires de la Parenté* (1949), which has exerted a profound influence on current social anthropology, his goal is to demonstrate that symmetry and exchange pervade human relations. He feels in the present instance that he has found a common language to express the structural relationship between totemic groups and castes, these two systems being ways that societies have evolved for allowing their members to express affiliation with the group into which they were born. But if exchange is to be possible between groups, social diversification must be established. In societies where there is no division of labor or specialization, as among the Australians, the only possible objective model that can be used by groups to define themselves is a natural rather than cultural one, namely, the diversity of natural species. This makes it possible for exogamous groups to exchange women between themselves even though women are biologically similar. In complex societies, nature is not taken as the model for diversification; instead, cultural products and services are used, these being true social species. But women cannot be exchanged outside their castes because they are not acknowledged to be similar from one occupational group to another. Australian totemic groups and Indian castes both specialize in "controlling" something necessary to the well-being of the whole group. Both are "exopractical" in that one produces women for marriage and the other produces goods and services. Both are "endopractical" in that each is kept closely self-contained—the Australian tribes through their preferred type of matrimonial exchange, the Indian castes by virtue of their rule of endogamy.

These ideas are admittedly involved and controversial, with insufficient testing on a wide scale, but at the same time they open the way to new insights regarding the nature of totemism.

Reprinted from *The Journal of the Royal Anthropological Institute,* XCIII (1963), 1–11, by permission of the author and the Royal Anthropological Institute of Great Britain and Ireland.

Human societies have evolved a number of means for allowing their members to express affiliation with the group into which they were born. Among these we shall single out two strongly contrasted ones. In one case, a given individual will make such a statement as "I am a bear," in the other case he will make such a statement as "I am a barber." One case exemplifies the so-called "totemic" groups, the other the caste system. My purpose is to examine the nature of the structural relationship—if there be one—between the two.

The words "bear" and "barber" were not chosen at random. Barbers cut and shave other people's hair, while—at least among the Chippewa Indians—people born in the Bear clan were reputed to have long, thick hair and never to grow bald. This doubly inverted relation—presence or absence of a given trait on the one hand, in respect to self or other on the other hand—plus perhaps an opposition between nature and culture (since the kind of hair one grows is a natural trait, while to remove it is a cultural custom), this threefold relation then is endowed, as I shall try to show, with an inner meaning since it symbolizes so to speak the structure of the scheme I am about to develop.

As a preliminary, I should like to caution the reader with regard to my use of the word "totemism."

Although I shall use it freely in the course of my talk, I fully endorse the general trend that has prevailed for a good many years among anthropologists to consider that there is no real institution which corresponds to the term "totemism" and that totemistic theories proceed from an arbitrary carving out of the objective facts. Nevertheless, it would be too easy simply to discard all past and present speculations concerning what is generally referred to as "totemism." If so many scholars whom we all admire have been, as it were, fascinated by the idea of "totemism," it is probably because, at a deeper level than the one they have been mistakenly considering, phenomena arbitrarily put together to make up a pseudo-institution are endowed with some inner meaning which makes them worthy of interest. This I believe was first discovered by Radcliffe-Brown, whose position in respect to "totemism" started by being a purely negative one in his early paper, "The Sociological Theory of Totemism" (1929), but who twenty-two years later in his Huxley Memorial Lecture entitled "The Comparative Method in Social Anthropology," without reverting in the least to a conception of "totemism" as an actual institution, succeeded nevertheless in unravelling the importance of the use of animal and plant names to characterize the relationship between the segments of human society. But this process led Radcliffe-Brown to modify considerably his earlier conception of this relationship.

In 1929, he believed that primitive people attached an intrinsic importance to animals for the reason that, as food, they were supposed to arouse man's spontaneous interest; whereas, in 1951 it was his theory that both animals and plants were to be regarded as mere figures of speech—symbols as it were. Thus, while in 1929, Radcliffe-Brown believed that interest was conferred upon animals and plants because they were "eatable," in 1951 he saw clearly that the real reason for this interest lay in the fact that they are, if I may use the word, "thinkable." It is interesting to note that each one of these two successive theories is in one way

more abstract and in another way more concrete than the other. The first theory is more abstract since all animals which can be consumed are merged into a vague category characterized by the one single aspect that has been abstracted: that of constituting merely animal food. From this point of view, animals that can be eaten are all regarded as similar, while men who partake of this common food are also held to be similar. Thus the link between the distinction of biological species and the segments of society is not perceived, though this first theory is also more concrete, since it only envisages the point of view of practical utility and physiological need. In its turn the second theory is more abstract, since it relies far less on the animals themselves than on the discovery that these animals or plants, or rather their properties, can be put to use as symbols to express contrasts and oppositions. Nevertheless, it is more concrete, because we are now asked in each special case to look for a definite reason which can account for the selection of a given animal and not of any other. So the choice made by one culture among the whole gamut of animals and plants which are empirically present becomes a means to express differences between men.

If Radcliffe-Brown's second theory is valid, as I believe it to be, we must admit that behind what was erroneously called "totemism" lie three very precise ideas. First, the idea of a culturally discrete set, that is, a segmentary society; second, the idea of a naturally discrete set, that is, the awareness of the empirical discontinuity of the biological species and third, the idea that there is some kind of homology between the above two systems of differences. Therefore totemic ideas appear to provide a code enabling man to express isomorphic properties between nature and culture. Obviously, there exists here some kind of similarity with linguistics, since language is also a code which, through oppositions between differences, permits us to convey meanings and since in the case of language as well as in that of "totemism," the complete series of empirical media provided in one case by vocal articulation, and in the other by the entire wealth of the biological world, cannot be called upon, but rather (and this is true in both cases) only a few elements which each language or each culture selects in order that they can be organized in strongly and unequivocally contrasting pairs. Such being the answer, we may be in a position to solve the problem raised by Boas in his paper "Mythology and Folk-tales of the North American Indians," where he says, "the essential problem regarding the ultimate origin of mythologies remains—why human tales are preferably attached to animals, celestial bodies and other personified phenomena of nature." The answer lies, so it seems, not, as the functionalist school assumes, in the utilitarian properties of biological species as mankind conceives them, but rather in their logical properties, that is, their ability to serve as symbols expressing contrasts and oppositions. This was demonstrated for a limited area by Dr. Freeman in his recent paper "Iban Augury," in which he shows how the Ibans by selecting a few species of birds out of a very large set provided by their forest environment, and by selecting for each species a very small number of significant properties, have been able to use these differential elements by opposing them and also combining them so as to convey different messages.

Having cleared up these general problems, I shall now enter into my subject proper. When going over the work of early investigators in Australia, I was struck by the fact that approximately between 1830 and 1850, these authors, although they knew that Australian sections and sub-sections were probably connected with the laws of intermarriage, nevertheless believed them to differ in rank; and to describe them, they frequently used the word "caste." This, I think, should not be neglected. In the first place, because there may have been something more "caste-like" in these divisions than what was subsequently found among interior, mostly desert, people and because it seems obvious that even from a superficial point of view there is something similar between Australian tribes and caste societies; each segment performs a special task which benefits the community as a whole and which is complementary to functions that devolve upon other segments. This appears clearly among the Australian tribes described by Spencer & Gillen in which moieties or clans are bound together by a rule of reciprocity. The Kaitish and the Unmatjera, who are northern neighbours of the Aranda, know of rules that require an individual who gathers wild seeds in a territory belonging to a totemic group named

after those seeds, to obtain permission from its head before consuming them; according to these rules, each totemic group is obliged to provide others with plants or animals whose "production" it allegedly controls. Thus the totemic food prohibition appears to be in such a case merely a negative way of expressing a positive obligation towards the others. This is clearly shown in a few well documented examples presented by Spencer & Gillen. The lone hunter belonging to the Emu clan cannot touch the bird, but in company he can and must kill it so as to present it as food to hunters belonging to other clans, and conversely the hunter belonging to the Water clan is permitted to drink alone, but when in company he can drink only if the water is presented to him by members of the opposite moiety. Among the Warramunga too each totemic group is held responsible for the natural species consumed by other groups. The Warramunga and the Walpari have secondary prohibitions against consuming the maternal totem but these are lifted when food is obtained from the opposite moiety. Generally speaking, and for each totem, there is a threefold distinction between those groups who never consume it because it is their own totem, those that may consume it when obtained from the opposite moiety (in case it should be the maternal totem), and those that can consume it in all circumstances, because it is not their totem. The same is true for the sacred wells which women may never approach, while uninitiated men, though they may approach them, may not drink from them, while still other groups of uninitiated men may both approach the wells and drink of the water, providing it is offered them by men belonging to the group that is allowed to drink freely.

Notwithstanding these similarities between totemic groups and castes, it is clear that the line which I have followed so far is too general to be convincing. It is well known that castes and totemic groups are widely different and opposed institutional systems, that one is linked with the highest cultures and the other with the lowest cultures with which anthropologists are acquainted. In a traditional way, totemism is linked to exogamy in its strictest forms, while in a game of free association, ninety-nine out of a hundred anthropologists would probably associate the word "caste" with the word "endogamy."

Thus the distinctive character of the extreme cases is clear, but would these appear as extreme if we could dispose of intermediary forms? In earlier writings I have tried to show that exchange in human society is a universal means of ensuring the interlocking of its constitutive parts and that this exchange can operate at different levels among which the more important are food, goods and services, and women. Two cases should be distinguished, however. Sometimes the three forms (or two of them) are called upon, so to speak, to cumulate their effects and to complement each other, either positively or negatively. In the second case, one form only is retained because it supplements the others. A good positive example of the first case is provided by those Australian groups where exchange of women and food prohibitions (which, as we have seen, can be equally well expressed as an obligatory exchange of foods), reinforce each other, and we find a negative example of the same phenomenon in some parts of Melanesia and in peasant Europe of the past, where endogamy or exogamy unwillingly practised seems to be connected with what we may call "endo-agriculture," that is, an extreme unwillingness to exchange seeds. Turning now to the second case, we may perhaps be permitted to consider the type of structure to be found in the so-called Crow-Omaha kinship systems as being in diametrical opposition to the Aranda systems in so far as, in the former, everything not forbidden is allowed, while in the latter the exact opposite is true: everything not allowed is forbidden. Now if this be granted, it is rather remarkable that in an African group such as the Nandi of Kenya, whose kinship system has been classified rightly or wrongly by Radcliffe-Brown as Omaha, there should be an extraordinary development of clan prohibitions bearing upon food and costume, and accompanied by individual marriage prohibitions based, not on clan affiliation, but on peculiar events pertaining to the individual history of each prospective groom and bride, which means that, in such a case, the structural arrangement of the alliance network—if any—would result from statistical fluctuations, exactly as happens with rules of marriage of the Crow-Omaha type. Let us consider a final example: that of the Baganda such as described by Roscoe. We are told that the Baganda had about forty clans, each possessing two totems, the first one being subject to food prohibition "so as to make it available to others in greater quantity," which is a modest counterpart of the Australian belief that, by refraining from consuming its totem, each clan acquires the power to multiply it. As in Australia too, each clan was linked to a territory which, in the case of the Baganda, was usually a sacred hill. In addition, each clan had a great many privileges, obligations, and prohibitions as, for instance, eligibility to kingship and other dignities, providing kingly wives, making and caring for regalia, providing other clans with certain kinds of food, and also special occupations. The Mushroom clan, for instance, was said to be sole maker of bark cloth and all the blacksmiths were supposed to come from the clan of the Tailless Cow. In such cases, we may well ask ourselves whether we are dealing with totemic clans, occupational castes, or with an intermediary form pertaining to both these types. Let us tackle this problem through application of our axiomatic principle.

We have seen that the so-called totemic concept amounts to a belief in an homology *not* between social groups and natural species, but between differences existing, on the one hand within the social system, and on the other within the natural system. Two systems of differences are conceived as isomorphic, although one is situated in nature, and the other in culture.

Let us now suppose that in addition to an homology of relationships, we have an homology of terms, and going one step further, that the homology of relationships shifts and becomes an homology between terms. The result will no longer be that Clan 1 can be held to differ from Clan 2 as for instance, Eagle differs from Bear, but that Clan 1 is in itself like Eagle and Clan 2 in itself like Bear. The system of differences will continue to exist, but, first, it will be conceived in reference to nature instead of to culture, and second, exogamy will inevitably break down because it implies that while women are sociologically conceived of as being different, they are naturally (though unconsciously) conceived of as similar, or else they could not be exchanged.

It so happens that this theoretical transformation may be exemplified by concrete examples. In volume 5 of the Haddon-Rivers Expedition to Torres Straits (p. 184) we find that at Mabuiag, for instance, "A definite physical and psychological resemblance was postulated for the human and animal members of the clan. There can be little doubt that this sentiment reacted on the clansmen and constrained them to live up to the traditional character of their respective clans." Thus the Cassowary, Crocodile, Snake, and Shark clans were reputed to love fighting, while the Shovel-nosed Skate, Ray and Sucker-Fish clans were said to be peaceable. Intermediate between the fierce and the gentle clans was the Dog clan, which was thought to be sometimes pugnacious and sometimes pacific, just like real dogs. The men of the Crocodile clan were said to be very strong and ruthless, while the men of the Cassowary clan were reputed for their long legs and their ability to run fast, like real cassowaries. Similar observations have been made in North America among Eastern Indians such as the Delaware, the Menomini, and the Chippewa. Among the latter, people of the Fish clan were reputed to be long lived, frequently to grow bald or to have thin hair, and all bald people were assumed to come from this clan. People of the Bear clan had long, thick, coarse hair that never turned white; they were said to be bellicose and quick to anger. People of the Crane clan had loud, ringing voices. Orators were always supposed to come from this clan.

From a theoretical point of view, we may now appraise the implications of these two opposite conceptions. In the first hypothesis, society on the one hand, nature on the other, will each retain its systematic integrity. Social segments will be referred to social segments; each natural species will be referred to other natural species. In the second hypothesis, instead of two "horizontal" systems situated at different levels, we shall have a plurality of "vertical" systems, considerably impoverished in fact, since instead of *two systems* each consisting of *numerous elements* we shall have *numerous systems* each consisting of *two elements,* heterogeneous (one natural, one cultural) instead of homogeneous (entirely natural or entirely cultural). Should this interpretation prove to be true, it should be possible, first to translate or re-code a "totemic" system into a caste system and conversely, and also to give

concrete examples of societies which have actually done so. This is what I intend to exemplify now.

Tribes of the Muskogi linguistic group in the South-Eastern United States such as, for instance, the Chickasaw and the Creek, did have clans and moieties the first of which were perhaps exogamous and the second endogamous. In any case moieties were noted for overt manifestations of exclusivism that bordered on hostility. Ritual was jealously guarded by each moiety and members of another moiety who had witnessed a ceremony, even inadvertently, were put to death (an attitude recalling that held by the Aranda in relation to their cult groups). What is even more important, moieties were said to differ by their respective ways of life and their disposition of mind; one was said to be warlike and to prefer open country, the other one to be peaceable and to live in the woods. They may also have been hierarchized, as is suggested by some of the names under which they were known, one moiety being called "their-hickory-choppings," meaning that they had susbstantial lodges, while the other moiety was called "their worn-out place," meaning that it consisted of inferior people living mostly under trees and in the woods. These differences were both more complex and more marked between clans, lineages, and hamlets. When informants were called upon to describe these secondary units, they used as a kind of leit-motiv, practically always the same words. "These people had ways of their own . . . they were very peculiar . . . different from all others . . . they had their own customs." These peculiarities were said to belong to different types: environment, economic activities, costume, food preferences, talents and tastes.

For instance, people of the Raccoon clan fed mostly on fish and wild fruits. Those of the Panther clan lived in mountains, avoided water, which they greatly feared, and fed on game. People of the Wild-Cat clan slept in the daytime, hunted by night since they were gifted with an especially keen sight, and were not interested in women. Those of the Bird clan woke up before daylight: "they were like real birds in that they would not bother anybody . . . the people of this clan have different sorts of minds, just as there are different species of birds . . . they had many wives . . . they did not work at all, but had an easy time going through life and went anywhere they wanted to . . . they had many offspring, as birds have."

People of the Red-Fox clan lived only in the woods, made a living by stealing from other people . . . doing whatever they liked. The "Wandering Iska" or "No-Home Iska" were a shiftless people "who did not want to own anything . . . they did not do anything for themselves . . . they were healthy looking, strong, for they did not do anything to run themselves down . . . they moved very slowly . . . they thought they were going to live forever . . . they did not care how they dressed or appeared . . . sometimes they wore dirty dresses . . . they were beggars and lazy."

The same kind of differences are emphasized between hamlets, for instance the Bending-Post-Oak-House Group lived in the wood, they were not very energetic, they loved to dance. They were prone to anxiety, had no foresight, were early risers, and made many mistakes, while people of the High-Corncrib House Group were not much esteemed by others but thought a great deal of themselves: "They were industrious, raised large crops, did not hunt much, bartered corn for venison. They were very wise, people of one mind, truthful, and they knew a great deal about the weather."

All these statements, which I have borrowed from Swanton, cannot be taken literally. They refer to a period when the traditional culture had already broken down and were obtained from old informants. They clearly belong to folk ethnology since, theoretically, it would be impossible for a human society to mimic nature to such an extent without running the risk of breaking down into several distinct groups hostile to one another. However, the testimony collected by Swanton is so rich, so concordant even when it comes from different tribes, that it must contain if not the literal truth at least the expression of a conceptual model which must have existed in the minds of the natives.

Allowing for these restrictive considerations, these statements have a threefold importance. In the first place, they describe what appears to have been a kind of caste system. In the second place, castes and their mutual relationships are being coded, so to speak, according to a natural model, after the diversity of natural species, as happens with totemic groups; and in the third place,

from an historical point of view, these Muskogi tribes constituted a kind of link between the "true" totemic societies of the Plains and the only "true" caste-societies which are known to have existed in North America, such as the Natchez. Thus, I have established so far that in two parts of the world traditionally conceived as "totemistic," Australia's so-called "totemic" groups can be interpreted as occupational groups, while in America, social segments which can actually function as castes, were conceived after a "totemic" model.

Let us now shift to India, also a classical land, though of castes rather than totemic groups. Here, instead of castes being conceived after a natural model, vestiges of totemic groups tend to be conceived after a cultural model. But before exemplifying this point let me remind the reader that I am using the word "totemic" in such a way as to be able to leave entirely aside the question of whether or not there are actual vestiges of totemism in India. From my present point of view, the problem is irrelevant since, when I make loose usage of the term totemism, I never refer to a past or present institution but to a classificatory device whereby discrete elements of the external world are associated with the discrete elements of the social world. Bearing this in mind, we may be struck by the fact that whereas so-called "totemic" names in Bengal are mostly of animal or vegetable origin, further south an increasing proportion of names borrowed from manufactured objects is to be found. For instance the Devanga who are a caste of weavers in Madras, use very few plant names for their clans and almost no animal names, but rather names such as buttermilk, cattle-pen, money, dam, houses, collyrium, knife, scissors, boat, clay lamp, female cloth, clothes, ropes for hanging pots, old plough, monastery, cart, funeral pyre, tile, etc., and the Kuruba of Mysore who have sixty-seven exogamous clans, with few plant and animal names, designate them by names such as, among others, drum, booth, cart, cup, woollen thread, bangle, gold, pick-axe, hut, gold ring, bell-metal, coloured border of a cloth, stick, blanket, measure, metal toe-ring, moustache, loom, bamboo tube, lace, ring, etc.

These manufactured objects are not only used as clan names, but they also receive attention, and serve to express obligations and prohibitions as in totemic systems. It is true that the use of manufactured objects as totemic names is well known elsewhere in the world, particularly in Northern Australia and in some parts of Africa, very good examples having been recently (1961) presented for the Dinka by Dr. Lienhardt in his book *Divinity and Experience*. However, this never happens to such an extent as in India. Thus it seems that while in America castes confusedly conceived have been contaminated by totemic classifications, in India, where products or symbols of occupational activities are clearly differentiated as such and can be put to use in order to express differences between social groups, vestiges or remnants of totemic groups have come to make use of a symbolism that is technological and occupational in origin.

This appears less surprising when one attempts to express Australian institutions (the first ones which we have envisaged) differently, and in a more direct way, in the language of the caste system. What we have done thus far was to compare Australian totemic groups one to another from the standpoint of their specialization in control of a given animal or vegetable species, while occupational castes "control" the technical activities necessary to the well-being of the whole group.

There are nevertheless two differences. In the first place, a potter caste makes pots, a laundryman caste does actual laundry work, and barbers do shave. The performances of Australian totemic groups, however, are unreal, imaginary, and even though the participants believe in their reality, we shall see later that this characteristic makes a great deal of difference. In the second place, the connexion between the sorcerer and the natural species that he claims to control is not of the same type as the link between the craftsman and his product. Only in mythical times did the animals or plants actually originate from the ancestor's body. Nowadays, kangaroos produce kangaroos and man can only help them to do so.

But the similarity is much stronger if we adopt a different point of view. An Australian section or sub-section actually produces its women for the benefit of the other sections, much as an occupational caste produces goods and services which the other castes cannot produce and must seek from this caste alone. Thus, it would be inaccurate to define totemic groups and caste systems as being simply one exogamous and another endogamous. These are not real properties existing as such, but superficial and indirect consequences of a similarity which should be recognized at a deeper level. In the first place, both castes and totemic groups are "exo-practical": castes in relation to goods and services, totemic groups in relation to marriage. In the second place, both remain to some extent "endo-practical": castes by virtue of the rule of endogamy and Australian groups as regards their preferred type of matrimonial exchange, which being mostly of the "restricted" type, keeps each tribe closely self-contained and, as it were, wrapped up in itself. It would seem that allowing for the above restrictive considerations, we have now reached a satisfactory formulation, in a common language, of the relationship between totemic groups and castes. Thus we might say that in the first case—totemic groups—women, that is, biological individuals or natural products, are begotten naturally by other biological individuals, while in the second case—castes—manufactured objects or services rendered through the medium of manufactured objects are fabricated culturally through technical agents. The principle of differentiation stems in the one case from nature and in the other from culture.

However, this kind of parallelism would be purely formal and without any concrete basis, for occupational castes are truly different from one another as regards culture, and also complementary. The same cannot be said, as regards nature, of exogamic groups which specialize, so to speak, in the production of women belonging to different "species." Occupational activities are true social species; they are objectively distinct. Women, on the other hand, even when they are born in different sections or sub-sections, belong nevertheless to one and the same natural species.

Social logic appears at this point to be caught in a dialectical trap. The assumed parallelism between natural products (actually, women) and social products is wholly imaginary. This explains why exogamous groups are so often inclined to define themselves as totemic groups, for over and above exogamy they need an objective model to express their social diversity. In societies where division of labour and occupational specialization do not exist, the only possible objective model has to be sought in the natural diversity of biological species; for there are only two objectively given models of concrete diversity: one on the level of nature, made up by the taxonomic system of natural species, the other on the level of culture, made up by the social system of trades and occupations.

The rules of exogamy establish an ambiguous system which lies somewhere in between: as regards nature, women are all alike, and only as regards culture may they be claimed to be different.

If the first point of view prevails, that is, when men borrow from nature their conceptual model of diversification, they must unconsciously abide also by a natural model of womankind. Exogamous groups make the overt claim that women are culturally different and, consequently, may be exchanged. But actually, they can only be exchanged because, at a deeper level, they are known to be similar. This provides an explanation to what I have said earlier and permits, so to speak, to deduce exogamy from more general principles.

Conversely, when the overt conceptual model is cultural, as in the caste system, women are acknowledged to be similar only within the limits of their respective social groups and this being projected on to the natural plane, their exchange between groups consequently becomes impossible.

In other words, both the caste system and the so-called totemic systems postulate isomorphism between natural and cultural differences. The validation of this postulate involves in each case a symmetrical and inverted relationship. Castes are defined after a cultural model and must define their matrimonial exchange after a natural model. Totemic groups pattern matrimonial exchange after a cultural model, and they themselves must be defined after a natural model. Women, homogeneous as regards nature, are claimed to be heterogeneous as regards culture, and conversely, natural species, although heterogeneous as regards nature, are claimed to be homogeneous as regards culture, since from the standpoint of culture, they share common properties in so far as man is believed to possess the power to control and to multiply them.

In totemic systems, men exchange culturally the women who procreate them naturally, and they claim to procreate culturally the animal and vegetable species which they exchange naturally: in the form of foodstuffs which are interchangeable, since any biological individual is able to dispense with one and to subsist on the others. A true parallelism can therefore be said to exist between the two formulas, and it is possible to code one into the terms of the other. Indeed, this parallelism is more complex than we believed it to be at the beginning. It can be expressed in the following tortuous way: castes naturalize fallaciously a true culture while totemic groups culturalize truly a false nature. "False" in two respects: first, from a natural point of view, women belong to one and the same natural species; and second, as a natural species, men do not have the power to increase and control other natural species.

However, this symmetry can never be rigorous; soon enough it reaches its limits. During their procreative period, women are naturally equivalent; anatomical structure and physiological function are, grossly speaking, identical in all female individuals. On the other hands, foods are not so easily replaceable. Speaking of the Karuba of Mysore, Thurston quotes the Arisana gotram which bears the name of turmeric. But since it is not easy to go without turmeric it has adopted as its food-prohibition *korra* seeds which can be more easily dispensed with. And in his book already referred to, Dr. Lienhardt states something similar about clans whose divinity is the giraffe. This is an all-important food, and instead of prohibiting it, these clans content themselves with avoiding to shed its blood. The same limitation exists with occupational castes. They too have to remain to some extent endo-functional, in order to render themselves the services they give to others. Otherwise who is going to shave the barber?

By way of conclusion I should like to emphasize four points. First, totemism which has been formalized in what may be called the "language of primitiveness" can equally well be formalized in the "language of castes" which were thought to be the very opposite of primitiveness.

Secondly, in its social undertakings, mankind keeps manoeuvering within narrow limits. Social types are not isolated creations, wholly independent of each other, and each one an original entity, but rather the result of an endless play of combination and re-combination, for ever seeking to solve the same problems by manipulating the same fundamental elements. This game always consists in a give-and-take, and what is given or taken must always belong either to the realm of nature (natural products) or to the realm of culture (goods and services), the exchange of women being the only for-mula that makes it possible to overcome this duality. Thus exchange of women not only ensures a horizontal mediation between groups of men, it also ensures a mediation, which we might call vertical, between nature and culture.

Thirdly, as we have seen, the tremendous differences existing between totemic groups and caste systems, in spite of their logical inverted similarity, may be ascribed to the fact that castes are right and totemic sys-tems are wrong, when they believe that they provide real services to their fellow groups. This should convince us that the "truth-value" is an unavoidable dimension of struc-tural method. No common analysis of reli-gion can be given by a believer and a non-believer, and from this point of view, the type of approach known as "religious phe-nomenology" should be dismissed.

Lastly, by analysing a specific example, I have attempted to validate a methodological approach which I have been trying to follow in France and which Dr. Leach is following in England. According to this approach so-cieties are not made up of the flotsam and jetsam of history, but of variables; thus widely different institutions can be reduced to transformations of the same basic figure, and the whole of human history may be looked upon merely as a set of attempts to organize differently the same means, but al-ways to answer the same questions.

CHAPTER 7

MAGIC, WITCHCRAFT, AND DIVINATION

🙖🙖🙖🙖

INTRODUCTION

The three concepts of magic, witchcraft, and divination are more than heuristic labels; they are real in that they represent actual classes of actions and beliefs intimately related to the human problem of control in known cultures. All men strive to control their social and physical environments and to determine, or at least to have prior knowledge of, their own lives. Through manipulation, explanation, and prediction the operations of magic, witchcraft, and divination work toward this vital human end.

Magic consists of a variety of ritual methods whereby events can be automatically influenced by supernatural means. While magic and religion have many mutual resemblances—both are supernatural, beyond the realm of experience, and dominated by symbolism and ritual—they are basically quite different. Religion is supplicative; by ritual it conciliates personal powers in order to request their favors. Magic is manipulative; it acts ritually upon impersonal powers in order automatically to make use of them. Magic is a formula or set of formulas. It is not a force as is mana. Magic is analogous to science in its use, but its premises—its theoretical bases—are supernatural and antithetical to science.

While magic is overwhelmingly private and individual in nature, there are many instances of magic being conducted publicly as an attempt to benefit a whole society. Private magic may be either malevolent (black) of well-intentioned (white); it may be designed to destroy a rival or to cure an ailing child. Public magic is always directed toward the welfare of the group which performs it, but it may be calculated to bring evil to other groups or tribes. The term "sorcerer" refers to a practitioner of black magic, while "medicine man" usually refers to a man who performs primarily white magic and cures through natural means, dealing only secondarily in black magic. The "law of sympathy," so basic to magic, will be thoroughly discussed by Sir James Frazer in the first article of this section.

The magical formula usually consists of a spoken and acted ritual, often called a "spell," and of material objects, often called "medicine." A "fetish" is an object or a bundle of objects, such as the famous Plains Indian medicine bundle, which has magical properties. While a fetish is sometimes thought to contain a spirit, it is used magically and is not, as is frequently claimed, worshiped. Neither should the term be used in the psychiatric sense of an inanimate object compulsively used in attaining sexual gratification.

When magic fails, as it often must, there are several explanations that serve to perpetuate belief in the particular formula: the ritual is said to have been incorrectly performed; the magician may have violated a taboo and thus have lost his power to perform the ritual, or there may have been strong counter-magic. When people want to believe, they will believe.

Although magic often has an emotional origin, the performance of magic is routine, and while the ritual may appear to be dramatic, it is almost always nonemotional. This is especially so if, as often happens, a client takes his complaint to a magical specialist who has no emotional involvement with the problem.

Magic gives the individual confidence in the face of fear and provides an outlet for hostility. Magic explains misfortune and failure and reveals the cause of illness. Magic assigns a human cause to terrifying events, and in so doing converts these events into a human rather than an extrahuman context. Socially, magic may act to drain off tensions which might otherwise result in physical combat and death. Unfortunately, magic creates problems as well. People die from fear of sorcery or fall ill from putatively magical attacks, and whole societies may live in constant fear of black magic. Whether magic is functionally more useful than it is harmful no one can positively say. However, magic is believed to have existed as early as the Upper Paleolithic in Europe, and it is known and practiced by all societies; this is strong positive evidence for its functional utility.

Witchcraft is the exercise of evil through an immanent power. Witchcraft, unlike sorcery, is derived from within, and cannot be learned. A witch's power to do evil may lie dormant and not be used or it may be increased by practice, but it is nearly always inherited. Whereas magic may be either malevolent or beneficent, witchcraft is invariably evil. A witch frequently has an animal form such as a cat, a werewolf, or a bat. Witches can project evil over great distances without moving, or they may transport themselves at great speeds in order to do some needed mischief. The evil eye and evil tongue are variants of witchcraft; some people can cause terrible harm simply by looking or speaking, often without evil intent. Witchcraft, like magic and divination, is undoubtedly worldwide, and its antiquity is great.

Witchcraft is far more than a grisly aberration of the human spirit; despite its macabre elements, it has positive functional value. All societies have the problem of providing an outlet for aggressions engendered by the conflicts, antagonisms, and frustrations of social living. Witches exist as convenient scapegoats for such aggressions. All societies also spawn individuals who in some degree do not find satisfactions within their culture, and a person of this sort may find an acceptable self-identity by considering himself to be a witch. Witchcraft may serve to regulate sex antagonisms (in some cultures, such as the Nupe of West Africa, witches are always women) or to provide a means of demanding cultural conformity by furnishing a criminal act or state of which deviants may be accused. Like magic, witchcraft may also explain unhappiness, disease, and bad luck. Similarly, witchcraft has its dysfunctional aspects. Witches do real harm, cause real fears, and promote dangerous conflicts. As with magic, it is difficult to construct a balance sheet which can indicate the relative value of these practices within any sociocultural system.

Divination, the art or practice of foreseeing future events or discovering hidden knowledge through supernatural means, is a cultural universal. From the Kaingang of South America, who seek answers in the volume of their belching, to the Hollywood movie star who daily consults a horoscope, divination assumes infinite forms and intensities. There are two general types of divination, inspirational and noninspirational. In the former, answers are revealed through a change in the psychology or emotional state of the individual. Shamanism, crystal gazing, and shell hearing are some inspirational forms of divination. Noninspirational divination may be either fortuitous, such as finding meanings in black cats, hairpins, sneezing, and countless other omens, or deliberate, by means of astrology, scapulimancy, chiromancy, ordeals, and the like.

All men, as we know them, eagerly seek to know the unknowable and to control the uncontrollable. Divination allows man to control chance and to know the future. Divination permits the man who is immobilized by a difficult decision to make a choice, and to make it with confidence. Or have you never flipped a coin? Man is an animal doubly cursed; he knows that there is a future, and he fears that he cannot control it. That divination lessens these curses is attested to by the flourishing vigor of many forms of divinatory art in modern Western European

culture, despite all the efforts of religion and
science to brand such practices as sinful or
ignorant.

Magic, witchcraft, and divination all aid

man in some respects and trouble him in
others. The articles that follow will do much
to clarify the nature and function of these
phenomena.

JAMES G. FRAZER

Sympathetic Magic

Although Sir James G. Frazer was not an outstanding theorist,
he was adept at compiling and classifying fact, had some feeling
for problem, and stimulated a whole generation of ethnologists to
take an interest in the theoretical questions involved in the subject of magic. His classic work, *The Golden Bough,* is one of the
best known of all ethnological publications. Many a layman who
has never heard of or read other anthropological books has at
least perused this one, usually in its abridged, one-volume form.

The portion of this vast work that is reprinted here presents
Frazer's well-known distinction between "imitative" and "contagious" magic. This classification, while it assuredly does not
encompass the whole range of magical phenomena, does cover the
greatest portion. Frazer shows that the common factor in these
two kinds of magic is the sympathetic principle: like to like, or
similar things are somehow capable of influencing each other. As
long as Frazer restricted himself to classificatory interests of this
sort, he remained unchallenged. But when he turned to either
historical or analytic problems, he enjoyed less immunity. For
example, his argument that magic is older than religion because it
is psychologically simpler than the concept of spirit agents and
because it is more uniform than religious cults does not stand up
against criticism. As Marett and Goldenweiser have demonstrated, Frazer's separation of magic from religion has some
merit, but it goes too far, because it overlooks the vast areas in
which the alleged differences actually overlap and because it
tends to obscure the common supernatural basis for each. Frazer's
view that magic is comparable to science because both involve
mental operations that are alike breaks down because, as Malinowski has insisted, the magical practitioner himself makes a distinction between things that lie in the empirical realm and those
that lie in the supernatural.

The following article contains a great many illustrative examples of the nature of magic. The functions of magic are not
explicitly considered, but many of them may be recognized in
Frazer's descriptions of diverse magical practices. It is cautioned
that the author's closing dictum that magic has been ". . . the
mother of freedom and truth," can be true only in a most allegor-
ical sense.

Reprinted in abridged form from James George Frazer, *The Golden
Bough: A Study in Magic and Religion* (12 vols.; 3d ed., rev. and
enl.; London: Macmillan & Co., Ltd., 1911–1915), I, 52–219, by permission of Trinity College, Cambridge, Macmillan & Co., Ltd., and
St Martin's Press, Inc.

1. THE PRINCIPLES OF MAGIC

If we analyze the principles of thought on
which magic is based, they will probably be
found to resolve themselves into two: first,

that like produces like, or that an effect resembles its cause; and, second, that things
which have once been in contact with each
other continue to act on each other at a dis-

tance after the physical contact has been severed. The former principle may be called the "Law of Similarity," the latter the "Law of Contact or Contagion." From the first of these principles, namely the Law of Similarity, the magician infers that he can produce any effect he desires merely by imitating it: from the second he infers that whatever he does to a material object will affect equally the person with whom the object was once in contact, whether it formed part of his body or not. Charms based on the Law of Similarity may be called "Homeopathic or Imitative Magic." Charms based on the Law of Contact or Contagion may be called "Contagious Magic." To denote the first of these branches of magic the term Homeopathic is perhaps preferable, for the alternative term Imitative or Mimetic suggests, if it does not imply, a conscious agent who imitates, thereby limiting the scope of magic too narrowly. For the same principles which the magician applies in the practice of his art are implicitly believed by him to regulate the operations of inanimate nature; in other words, he tacitly assumes that the Laws of Similarity and Contact are of universal application and are not limited to human actions. In short, magic is a spurious system of natural law as well as a fallacious guide of conduct; it is a false science as well as an abortive art. Regarded as a system of natural law, that is, as a statement of the rules which determine the sequence of events throughout the world, it may be called "Theoretical Magic": regarded as a set of precepts which human beings observe in order to compass their ends, it may be called "Practical Magic." At the same time it is to be borne in mind that the primitive magician knows magic only on its practical side; he never analyzes the mental processes on which his practice is based, never reflects on the abstract principles involved in his actions. With him, as with the vast majority of men, logic is implicit, not explicit; he reasons, just as he digests his food, in complete ignorance of the intellectual and physiological processes which are essential to the one operation and to the other. In short, to him magic is always an art, never a science; the very idea of science is lacking in his undeveloped mind. It is for the philosophic student to trace the train of thought which underlies the magician's practice; to draw out the few simple threads of which the tangled skein is composed; to disengage the abstract principles from their concrete applications; in short, to discern the spurious science behind the bastard art.

If my analysis of the magician's logic is correct, its two great principles turn out to be merely two different misapplications of the association of ideas. Homeopathic magic is founded on the association of ideas by similarity: contagious magic is founded on the association of ideas by contiguity. Homeopathic magic commits the mistake of assuming that things which resemble each other are the same: contagious magic commits the mistake of assuming that things which have once been in contact with each other are always in contact. But in practice the two branches are often combined; or, to be more exact, while homeopathic or imitative magic may be practiced by itself, contagious magic will generally be found to involve an application of the homeopathic or imitative principle. Thus generally stated the two things may be a little difficult to grasp, but they will readily become intelligible when they are illustrated by particular examples. Both trains of thought are in fact extremely simple and elementary. It could hardly be otherwise, since they are familiar in the concrete, though certainly not in the abstract, to the crude intelligence not only of the savage, but of ignorant and dull-witted people everywhere. Both branches of magic, the homeopathic and the contagious, may conveniently be comprehended under the general name of "Sympathetic Magic," since both assume that things act on each other at a distance through a secret sympathy, the impulse being transmitted from one to the other by means of what we may conceive as a kind of invisible ether, not unlike that which is postulated by modern science for a precisely similar purpose, namely, to explain how things can physically affect each other through a space which appears to be empty.

It may be convenient to tabulate as follows the branches of magic according to the laws of thought which underlie them:

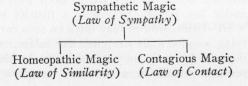

Sympathetic Magic
(*Law of Sympathy*)

Homeopathic Magic   Contagious Magic
(*Law of Similarity*)   (*Law of Contact*)

I will now illustrate these two great branches of sympathetic magic by examples, beginning with homeopathic magic.

2. HOMEOPATHIC OR IMITATIVE MAGIC

Perhaps the most familiar application of the principle that like produces like is the attempt which has been made by many peoples in many ages to injure or destroy an enemy by injuring or destroying an image of him, in the belief that just as the image suffers, so does the man, and that when it perishes he must die. A few instances out of many may be given to prove at once the wide diffusion of the practice over the world and its remarkable persistence through the ages. For thousands of years ago it was known to the sorcerers of ancient India, Babylon, and Egypt, as well as of Greece and Rome, and at this day it is still resorted to by cunning and malignant savages in Australia, Africa, and Scotland. Thus the North American Indians, we are told, believe that by drawing the figure of a person in sand, ashes, or clay, or by considering any object as his body, and then pricking it with a sharp stick or doing it any other injury, they inflict a corresponding injury on the person represented. So when a Cora Indian of Mexico wishes to kill a man, he makes a figure of him out of burnt clay, strips of cloth, and so forth, and then, muttering incantations, runs thorns through the head or stomach of the figure to make his victim suffer correspondingly.

If homeopathic or imitative magic, working by means of images, has commonly been practiced for the spiteful purpose of putting obnoxious people out of the world, it has also, though far more rarely, been employed with the benevolent intention of helping others into it. In other words, it has been used to facilitate childbirth and to procure offspring for barren women. Thus among the Eskimos of Bering Strait a barren woman desirous of having a son will consult a shaman, who commonly makes, or causes her husband to make, a small doll-like image over which he performs certain secret rites, and the woman is directed to sleep with it under her pillow. In Anno, a district of West Africa, women may often be seen carrying wooden dolls strapped, like babies, on their backs as a cure for sterility. In the seventh month of a woman's pregnancy common people in Java observe a ceremony which is plainly designed to facilitate the real birth by mimicking it. Husband and wife repair to a well or to the bank of a neighboring river. The upper part of the woman's body is bare, but young banana leaves are fastened under her arms, a small opening, or rather fold, being left in the leaves in front. Through this opening or fold in the leaves on his wife's body the husband lets fall from above a weaver's shuttle. An old woman receives the shuttle as it falls, takes it up in her arms and dandles it as if it were a baby, saying, "Oh, what a dear little child! Oh, what a beautiful little child!" Then the husband lets an egg slip through the fold, and when it lies on the ground as an emblem of the afterbirth, he takes his sword and cuts through the banana leaf at the place of the fold, obviously as if he were severing the navel-string.

The same principle of make-believe, so dear to children, has led other peoples to employ a simulation of birth as a form of adoption, and even as a mode of restoring a supposed dead person to life. If you pretend to give birth to a boy, or even to a great bearded man who has not a drop of your blood in his veins, then, in the eyes of primitive law and philosophy, that boy or man is really your son to all intents and purposes. Thus Diodorus tells us that when Zeus persuaded his jealous wife Hera to adopt Hercules, the goddess got into bed, and clasping the burly hero to her bosom, pushed him through her robes and let him fall to the ground in imitation of a real birth; and the historian adds that in his own day the same mode of adopting children was practiced by the barbarians. At the present time it is said to be still in use in Bulgaria and among the Bosnian Turks. A woman will take a boy whom she intends to adopt and push or pull him through her clothes; ever afterwards he is regarded as her very son, and inherits the whole property of his adoptive parents. In ancient Greece any man who had been supposed erroneously to be dead, and for whom in his absence funeral rites had been performed, was treated as dead to society till he had gone through the form of being born again. He was passed through a woman's lap, then washed, dressed in swaddling clothes, and put out to nurse. Not until this ceremony had been punctually performed might he mix freely with living folk.

Another beneficent use of homeopathic magic is to heal or prevent sickness. In ancient Greece, when a man died of dropsy, his children were made to sit with their feet in water until the body was burned. This was supposed to prevent the disease from attacking them. In Germany yellow turnips, gold coins, gold rings, saffron, and other yellow things are still esteemed remedies for jaundice, just as a stick of red sealing wax carried on the person cures the red eruption popularly known as St. Anthony's fire, or the bloodstone with its red spots allays bleeding. Another cure prescribed in Germany for St. Anthony's fire is to rub the patient with ashes from a house that has been burned down; for it is easy to see that as the fire died out in that house, so St. Anthony's fire will die out in that man.

One of the great merits of homeopathic magic is that it enables the cure to be performed on the person of the doctor instead of on that of his victim, who is thus relieved of all trouble and inconvenience, while he sees his medical man writhe in anguish before him. For example, the peasants of Perche, in France, labor under the impression that a prolonged fit of vomiting is brought about by the patient's stomach becoming unhooked, as they call it, and so falling down. Accordingly, a practitioner is called in to restore the organ to its proper place. After hearing the symptoms he at once throws himself into the most horrible contortions, for the purpose of unhooking his own stomach. Having succeeded in the effort, he next hooks it up again in another series of contortions and grimaces, while the patient experiences a corresponding relief. Fee five cents. In like manner a Dyak medicine man, who has been fetched in a case of illness, will lie down and pretend to be dead. He is accordingly treated like a corpse, is bound up in mats, taken out of the house, and deposited on the ground. After about an hour the other medicine men loose the pretended dead man and bring him to life; and as he recovers, the sick person is supposed to recover too.

Further, homeopathic and in general sympathetic magic plays a great part in the measures taken by the rude hunter or fishermen to secure an abundant supply of food. On the principle that like produces like, many things are done by him and his friends in deliberate imitation of the result which he seeks to attain; and, on the other hand, many things are scrupulously avoided because they bear some more or less fanciful resemblance to others which would really be disastrous.

Nowhere is the theory of sympathetic magic more systematically carried into practice for the maintenance of the food supply than in the barren region of Central Australia. Here the tribes are divided into a number of totem clans, each of which is charged with the duty of propagating and multiplying their totem for the good of the community by means of magical ceremonies and incantations. The great majority of the totems are edible animals and plants, and the general result supposed to be accomplished by these ceremonies or *intichiuma,* as the Arunta call them, is that of supplying the tribe with food and other necessaries. Often the rites consist of an imitation of the effect which the people desire to produce; in other words, their magic is of the homeopathic or imitative sort. Thus among the Arunta the men of the witchetty-grub totem perform a series of elaborate ceremonies for multiplying the grub which the other members of the tribe use as food. One of the ceremonies is a pantomime representing the fully developed insect in the act of emerging from the chrysalis.

The Indians of British Columbia live largely upon the fish which abound in their seas and rivers. If the fish do not come in due season, and the Indians are hungry, a Nootka wizard will make an image of a swimming fish and put it into the water in the direction from which the fish usually appear. This ceremony, accompanied by a prayer to the fish to come, will cause them to arrive at once. The islanders of Torres Straits use models of dugong and turtles to charm dugong and turtle to their destruction. The Toradjas of Central Celebes believe that things of the same sort attract each other by means of their indwelling spirits or vital ether. Hence they hang up the jawbones of deer and wild pigs in their houses, in order that the spirits which animate these bones may draw the living creatures of the same kind into the path of the hunter. In the island of Nias, when a wild pig has fallen into the pit prepared for it, the animal is taken out and its back is rubbed with nine fallen leaves, in the belief that this will make nine more wild pigs fall into the pit, just as the nine leaves fell from the tree.

The western tribes of British New Guinea employ a charm to aid the hunter in spearing dugong or turtle. A small beetle, which haunts coconut trees, is placed in the hole of the spear haft into which the spearhead fits. This is supposed to make the spearhead stick fast in the dugong or turtle, just as the beetle sticks fast to a man's skin when it bites him. When a Cambodian hunter has set his nets and taken nothing, he strips himself naked, goes some way off, then strolls up to the net as if he did not see it, lets himself be caught in it, and cries, "Hillo! what's this? I'm afraid I'm caught." After that the net is sure to catch game. A Malay who has baited a trap for crocodiles, and is awaiting results, is careful in eating his curry always to begin by swallowing three lumps of rice successively; for this helps the bait to slide more easily down the crocodile's throat. He is equally scrupulous not to take any bones out of his curry; for, if he did, it seems clear that the sharp-pointed stick on which the bait is skewered would similarly work itself loose, and the crocodile would get off with the bait. Hence in these circumstances it is prudent for the hunter, before he begins his meal, to get somebody else to take the bones out of his curry, otherwise he may at any moment have to choose between swallowing a bone and losing the crocodile.

This last rule is an instance of the things which the hunter abstains from doing lest, on the principle that like produces like, they should spoil his luck. For it is to be observed that the system of sympathetic magic is not merely composed of positive precepts; it comprises a very large number of negative precepts, that is, prohibitions. It tells you not merely what to do, but also what to leave undone. The positive precepts are charms: the negative precepts are taboos. In fact the whole doctrine of taboos, or at all events a large part of it, would seem to be only a special application of sympathetic magic, with its two great laws of similarity and contact. Though these laws are certainly not formulated in so many words nor even conceived in the abstract by the savage, they are nevertheless implicitly believed by him to regulate the course of nature quite independently of human will. He thinks that if he acts in a certain way, certain consequences will inevitably follow in virtue of one or the other of these laws; and if the consequences of a particular act appear to him likely to prove disagreeable or dangerous, he is naturally careful not to act in that way lest he should incur them. In other words, he abstains from doing that which, in accordance with his mistaken notions of cause and effect, he falsely believes would injure him; in short, he subjects himself to a taboo. Thus taboo is so far a negative application of practical magic. Positive magic or sorcery says, "Do this in order that so and so may happen." Negative magic or taboo says, "Do not do this, lest so and so should happen." The aim of positive magic or sorcery is to produce a desired event; the aim of negative magic or taboo is to avoid an undesirable one. But both consequences, the desirable and the undesirable, are supposed to be brought about in accordance with the laws of similarity and contact. And just as the desired consequence is not really effected by the observance of a magical ceremony, so the dreaded consequence does not really result from the violation of a taboo. If the supposed evil necessarily followed a breach of taboo, the taboo would not be a taboo but a precept of morality or common sense. It is not a taboo to say, "Do not put your hand in the Fire"; it is a rule of common sense, because the forbidden action entails a real, not an imaginary, evil. In short, those negative precepts which we call taboo are just as vain and futile as those positive precepts which we call sorcery. The two things are merely opposite sides or poles of one great disastrous fallacy, a mistaken conception of the association of ideas. Of that fallacy, sorcery is the positive and taboo the negative pole. If we give the general name of magic to the whole erroneous system, both theoretical and practical, then taboo may be defined as the negative side of practical magic. To put this in tabular form:

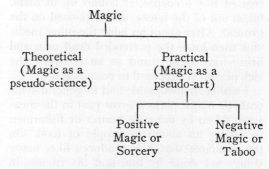

I have made these remarks on taboo and its relations to magic because I am about to give some instances of taboos observed by hunters, fishermen, and others, and I wished to show that they fall under the head of Sympathetic Magic, being only particular applications of that general theory. Among the Eskimos of Baffin Land boys are forbidden to play cat's cradle, because if they did so their fingers might in later life become entangled in the harpoon-line. Here the taboo is obviously an application of the law of similarity, which is the basis of homeopathic magic; as the child's fingers are entangled by the string in playing cat's cradle, so they will be entangled by the harpoon-line when he is a man and hunts whales. Again, among the Huzuls of the Carpathian Mountains, the wife of a hunter may not spin while her husband is eating, or the game will turn and wind like the spindle, and the hunter will be unable to hit it. Here again the taboo is clearly derived from the law of similarity. So, too, in most parts of ancient Italy women were forbidden by law to spin on the highroads as they walked, or even to carry their spindles openly, because any such action was believed to injure the crops. Probably the notion was that the twirling of the spindle would twirl the cornstalks and prevent them from growing straight. So, too, among the Ainos of Saghalien a pregnant woman may not spin nor twist ropes for two months before her delivery, because they think that if she did so the child's guts might be entangled like the thread. For a like reason in Bilaspore, a district of India, when the chief men of a village meet in council no one present should twirl a spindle; for they think that if such a thing were to happen, the discussion, like the spindle, would move in a circle and never be wound up. In the East Indian Islands of Saparoea, Haroekoe, and Noessalaut, any one who comes to the house of a hunter must walk straight in; he may not loiter at the door, for were he to do so, the game would in like manner stop in front of the hunter's snares and then turn back, instead of being caught in the trap. For a similar reason it is a rule with the Toradjas of Central Celebes that no one may stand or loiter on the ladder of a house where there is a pregnant woman, for such delay would retard the birth of the child; and in various parts of Sumatra the woman herself in these circumstances is forbidden to stand at the door or on the top rung of the house-ladder under pain of suffering hard labor for her

imprudence in neglecting so elementary a precaution.

Among the taboos observed by savages none perhaps are more numerous or important than the prohibitions to eat certain foods, and of such prohibitions many are demonstrably derived from the law of similarity and are accordingly examples of negative magic. Just as the savage eats many animals or plants in order to acquire certain desirable qualities with which he believes them to be endowed, so he avoids eating many other animals and plants lest he should acquire certain undesirable qualities with which he believes them to be infected. In eating the former he practices positive magic; in abstaining from the latter he practices negative magic.

The reader may have observed that in some of the foregoing examples of taboos the magical influence is supposed to operate at considerable distances; thus among the Blackfeet Indians the wives and children of an eagle hunter are forbidden to use an awl during his absence, lest the eagles should scratch the distant husband and father; and again no male animal may be killed in the house of a Malagasy soldier while he is away at the wars, lest the killing of the animal should entail the killing of the man. This belief in the sympathic influence exerted on each other by persons or things at a distance is of the essence of magic. Whatever doubts science may entertain as to the possibility of action at a distance, magic has none; faith in telepathy is one of its first principles. A modern advocate of the influence of mind upon mind at a distance would have no difficulty in convincing a savage; the savage believed in it long ago, and what is more, he acted on his belief with a logical consistency such as his civilized brother in the faith has not yet, so far as I am aware, exhibited in his conduct. For the savage is convinced not only that magical ceremonies affect persons and things afar off, but that the simplest acts of daily life may do so too. Hence on important occasions the behavior of friends and relations at a distance is often regulated by a more or less elaborate code of rules, the neglect of which by the one set of persons would, it is supposed, entail misfortune or even death on the absent ones. In particular when a party of men are out hunting or fighting, their kinsfolk at home are often expected to do certain things or to abstain from doing certain others, for the sake of ensuring the safety and success of the distant hunters or warriors. I will now give some instances of this magical telepathy both in its positive and in its negative aspect.

In Laos when an elephant hunter is starting for the chase, he warns his wife not to cut her hair or oil her body in his absence; for if she cut her hair the elephant would burst the toils, if she oiled herself it would slip through them. When a Dyak village has turned out to hunt wild pigs in the jungle, the people who stay at home may not touch oil or water with their hands during the absence of their friends; for if they did so, the hunters would all be "butterfingered" and the prey would slip through their hands. While a Gilyak hunter is pursuing the game in the forest, his children at home are forbidden to make drawings on wood or on sand; for they fear that if the children did so, the paths in the forest would become as perplexed as the lines in the drawings, so that the hunter might lose his way and never return. A Russian political prisoner once taught some Gilyak children to read and write; but their parents forbade them to write when any of their fathers was away from home; for it seemed to them that writing was a peculiarly complicated form of drawing, and they stood aghast at the idea of the danger to which such a drawing would expose the hunters out in the wild woods.

Many of the indigenous tribes of Sarawak are firmly persuaded that were the wives to commit adultery while their husbands are searching for camphor in the jungle, the camphor obtained by the men would evaporate. Husbands can discover, by certain knots in the tree, when their wives are unfaithful; and it is said that in former days many women were killed by jealous husbands on no better evidence than that of these knots. Futher, the wives dare not touch a comb while their husbands are away collecting the camphor; for if they did so, the interstices between the fibers of the tree, instead of being filled with the precious crystals, would be empty like the spaces between the teeth of a comb. In the Kei Islands, to the southwest of New Guinea, as soon as a vessel that is about to sail for a distant port has been launched, the part of the beach on which it lay is covered as speedily as possible with palm branches, and becomes sacred. No

one may thenceforth cross that spot till the ship comes home. To cross it sooner would cause the vessel to perish. Moreover, all the time that the voyage lasts three or four young girls, specially chosen for the duty, are supposed to remain in sympathetic connection with the mariners and to contribute by their behavior to the safety of and success of the voyage.

Where beliefs like these prevail as to the sympathetic connection between friends at a distance, we need not wonder that above everything else, war, with its stern yet stirring appeal to some of the deepest and tenderest of human emotions, should quicken in the anxious relations left behind a desire to turn the sympathetic bond to the utmost account for the benefit of the dear ones who may at any moment be fighting and dying far away. Hence, to secure an end so natural and laudable, friends at home are apt to resort to devices which will strike us as pathetic or ludicrous, according as we consider their object or the means adopted to effect it. Thus in some districts of Borneo, when a Dyak is out headhunting, his wife or, if he is unmarried, his sister must wear a sword day and night in order that he may always be thinking of his weapons; and she may not sleep during the day nor go to bed before two in the morning, lest her husband or brother should thereby be surprised in his sleep by an enemy. Among the Sea Dyaks of Banting in Sarawak the women strictly observe an elaborate code of rules while the men are away fighting. Some of the rules are negative and some are positive, but all alike are based on the principles of magical homeopathy and telepathy. Amongst them are the following. The women must wake very early in the morning and open the windows as soon as it is light; otherwise their absent husbands will oversleep themselves. The women may not oil their hair, or the men will slip. The women may neither sleep nor doze by day, or the men will be drowsy on the march. The women must cook and scatter popcorn on the veranda every morning; so will the men be agile in their movements The rooms must be kept very tidy, all boxes being placed near the walls; for if any one were to stumble over them, the absent husbands would fall and be at the mercy of the foe. At every meal a little rice must be left in the pot and put aside; so will the men far away always have something to eat and need never go hungry. On no account may the women sit at the loom till their legs grow cramped, otherwise their husbands will likewise be stiff in their joints and unable to rise up quickly or to run away from the foe. So in order to keep their husbands' joints supple the women often vary their labors at the loom by walking up and down the veranda. Further, they may not cover up their faces, or the men would not be able to find their way through the tall grass or jungle. Again, the women may not sew with a needle, or the men will tread on the sharp spikes set by the enemy in the path. Should a wife prove unfaithful while her husband is away, he will lose his life in the enemy's country.

Among the Thompson Indians of British Columbia, when the men were on the warpath, the women performed dances at frequent intervals. These dances were believed to ensure the success of the expedition. The dancers flourished their knives, threw long, sharp-pointed sticks forward, or drew sticks with hooked ends repeatedly backward and forward. Throwing the sticks forward was symbolic of piercing or warding off the enemy, and drawing them back was symbolic of drawing their own men from danger. The hook at the end of the stick was particularly well adapted to serve the purpose of a lifesaving apparatus. The women always pointed their weapons towards the enemy's country. They painted their faces red and sang as they danced, and they prayed to the weapons to preserve their husbands and help them to kill many foes. Some had eagledown stuck on the points of their sticks. When the dance was over, these weapons were hidden. If a woman whose husband was at the war thought she saw hair or a piece of a scalp on the weapon when she took it out, she knew that her husband had killed an enemy. But if she saw a stain of blood on it, she knew he was wounded or dead. When the men of the Yuki tribe of Indians in California were away fighting, the women at home did not sleep; they danced continually in a circle, chanting and waving leafy wands. For they said that if they danced all the time, their husbands would not grow tired. When a band of Carib Indians of the Orinoco had gone on the warpath, their friends left in the village used to calculate as nearly as they could the exact moment when the absent warriors would be advancing to attack the enemy. Then they took two lads, laid them down on a bench, and inflicted a most severe scouring on their bare backs. This the youths submitted to without a murmur, supported in their sufferings by the firm conviction, in which they had been bred from childhood, that on the constancy and fortitude with which they bore the cruel ordeal depended the valor and success of their comrades in the battle.

Among the many beneficent uses to which a mistaken ingenuity has applied the principle of homeopathic or imitative magic, is that of causing trees and plants to bear fruit in due season. In Thüringen the man who sows flax carries the seed in a long bag which reaches from shoulders to his knees, and he walks with long strides, so that the bag sways to and fro on his back. It is believed that this will cause the flax to wave in the wind. In the interior of Sumatra rice is sown by women who, in sowing, let their hair hang loose down their back, in order that the rice may grow luxuriantly and have long stalks. Similarly, in ancient Mexico a festival was held in honor of the goddess of maize, or "the long-haired mother," as she was called. It began at the time "when the plant had attained its full growth, and fibers shooting forth from the top of the green ear indicated that the grain was fully formed. During this festival the women wore their long hair unbound, shaking and tossing it in the dances which were the chief features in the ceremonial, in order that the tassel of the maize might grow in like profusion, that the grain might be correspondingly large and flat, and that the people might have abundance."

The notion that a person can influence a plant homeopathically by his act or condition comes out clearly in a remark made by a Malay woman. Being asked why she stripped the upper part of her body naked in reaping the rice, she explained that she did it to make the rice-husks thinner, as she was tired of pounding thick-husked rice. Clearly, she thought that the less clothing she wore the less husk there would be on the rice. The magic virtue of a pregnant woman to communicate fertility is known to Bavarian and Austrian peasants, who think that if you give the first fruit of a tree to a woman with child to eat, the trees will bring forth abundantly next year. On the other hand, the Baganda believe that a barren wife infects her husband's garden with her own sterility and prevents the trees from bearing fruit; hence a childless woman is generally divorced.

Thus on the theory of homeopathic magic a person can influence vegetation either for good or for evil according to the good or the bad character of his acts or states: for example, a fruitful woman makes plants fruitful, a barren woman makes them barren. Hence this belief in the noxious and infectious nature of certain personal qualities or accidents has given rise to a number of prohibitions or rules of avoidance: people abstain from doing certain things lest they should homeopathically infect the fruits of the earth with their own undesirable state or condition. All such customs of abstention or rules of avoidance are examples of negative magic or taboo.

In the foregoing cases a person is supposed to influence vegetation homeopathically. He infects trees or plants with qualities or accidents, good or bad, resembling and derived from his own. But on the principle of homeopathic magic the influence is mutual: the plant can infect the man just as much as the man can infect the plant. In magic, as I believe in physics, action and reaction are equal and opposite. The Cherokee Indians are adept in practical botany of the homeopathic sort. Thus wiry roots of the catgut plant or devil's shoestring (*Tephrosia*) are so tough that they can almost stop a plowshare in the furrow. Hence Cherokee women wash their hands with a decoction of the roots to make the hair strong, and Cherokee ballplayers wash themselves with it to toughen their muscles. It is a Galelareese belief that if you eat a fruit which has fallen to the ground, you will yourself contract a disposition to stumble and fall; and that if you partake of something which has been forgotten (such as a sweet potato left in the pot or a banana in the fire), you will become forgetful. The Galelareese are also of the opinion that if a woman were to consume two bananas growing from a single head she would give birth to twins. The Guarani Indians of South America thought that woman would become a mother of twins if she ate a double grain of millet. Near Charlotte Waters, in Central Australia, there is a tree which sprang up to mark the spot where a blind man died. It is called the Blind Tree by the natives, who think that if it were cut

down all the people of the neighborhood would become blind. A man who wishes to deprive his enemy of sight need only go to the tree by himself and rub it, muttering his wish and exhorting the magic virtue to go forth and do its baleful work. In this last example the infectious quality, though it emanates directly from a tree, is derived originally from a man—namely, the blind man—who was buried at the place where the tree grew. Similarly, the Central Australians believe that a certain group of stones at Undiara are the petrified boils of an old man who long ago plucked them from his body and left them there; hence any man who wishes to infect his enemy with boils will go to these stones and throw miniature spears at them, taking care that the points of the spears strike the stones. Then the spears are picked up, and thrown one by one in the direction of the person whom it is intended to injure. The spears carry with them the magic virtue from the stones, and the result is an eruption of painful boils on the body of the victim. Sometimes a whole group of people can be afflicted in this way by a skillful magician.

These examples introduce us to a fruitful branch of homeopathic magic, namely to that department of it which works by means of the dead; for just as the dead can neither see nor hear nor speak, so you may on homeopathic principles render people blind, deaf, and dumb by the use of dead men's bones or anything else that is tainted by the infection of death. Thus among the Galelareese, when a young man goes a-wooing at night, he takes a little earth from a grave and strews it on the roof of his sweetheart's house just above the place where her parents sleep. This, he fancies, will prevent them from waking while he converses with his beloved, since the earth from the grave will make them sleep as sound as the dead. Burglars in all ages and many lands have been patrons of this species of magic, which is very useful to them in the exercise of their profession. Thus a South Slavonian housebreaker sometimes begins operations by throwing a dead man's bone over the house, saying, with pungent sarcasm, "As this bone may waken, so may these people waken"; after that not a soul in the house can keep his or her eyes open. Similarly, in Java the burglar takes earth from a grave and sprinkles it round the house which he intends to rob; this throws the inmates into a deep sleep. In Europe similar properties were ascribed to the Hand of Glory, which was the dried and pickled hand of a man who had been hanged. If a candle made of the fat of a malefactor who had also died on the gallows was lighted and placed in the Hand of Glory as in a candlestick, it rendered motionless all persons to whom it was presented; they could not stir a finger any more than if they were dead. An ancient Greek robber or burglar thought he could silence and put to flight the fiercest watchdogs by carrying with him a brand plucked from a funeral pyre. Again, Servian and Bulgarian women who chafe at the restraints of domestic life will take the copper coins from the eyes of a corpse, wash them in wine or water, and give the liquid to their husbands to drink. After swallowing it, the husband will be as blind to his wife's peccadilloes as the dead man was on whose eyes the coins were laid.

Again, animals are often conceived to possess qualities or properties which might be useful to man, and homeopathic or imitative magic seeks to communicate these properties to human beings in various ways. Thus some Bechuanas wear a ferret as a charm, because, being very tenacious of life, it will make them difficult to kill. Others wear a certain insect, mutilated, but living, for a similar purpose. Yet other Bechuana warriors wear the hair of a hornless ox among their own hair, and the skin of a frog on their mantle, because a frog is slippery, and the ox, having no horns, is hard to catch; so the man who is provided with these charms believes that he will be as hard to hold as the ox and the frog. One of the ancient books of India prescribes that when a sacrifice is offered for victory, the earth out of which the altar is to be made should be taken from a place where a boar has been wallowing, since the strength of the boar will be in that earth. When you are playing the one-stringed lute, and your fingers are stiff, the thing to do is to catch some long-legged field spiders and roast them, and then rub your fingers with the ashes; that will make your fingers as lithe and nimble as the spiders' legs—at least so think the Galelareese. Among the western tribes of British New Guinea, a man who has killed a snake will burn it and smear his legs with the ashes when he goes into the forest; for no snake

will bite him for some days afterwards. If a South Slavonian has a mind to pilfer and steal at market, he has nothing to do but to burn a blind cat, and then throw a pinch of its ashes over the person with whom he is higgling; after that he can take what he likes from the booth, and the owner will not be a bit the wiser, having become as blind as the deceased cat with whose ashes he has been sprinkled. The thief may even ask boldly "Did I pay for it?" and the deluded huckster will reply, "Why certainly."

On the principle of homeopathic magic, inanimate things, as well as plants and animals, may diffuse blessing or bane around them, according to their own intrinsic nature and the skill of the wizard to tap or dam, as the case may be, the stream of weal or woe. In Samarkand women give a baby sugar candy to suck and put glue in the palm of its hand, in order that when the child grows up his words may be sweet and precious things may stick to his hands as if they were glued. The Greeks thought that a garment made from a fleece of a sheep that had been torn by a wolf would hurt the wearer, setting up an itch or irritation in his skin. They were also of opinion that if a stone which had been bitten by a dog were dropped in wine, it would make all who drank of that wine to fall out among themselves. Among the Arabs of Moab a childless woman often borrows the robe of a woman who has had many children, hoping with the robe to acquire the fruitfulness of its owner. The Caffres of Sofala, in East Africa, had a great dread of being struck with anything hollow, such as a reed or a straw, and greatly preferred being thrashed with a good thick cudgel or an iron bar, even though it hurt very much. For they thought that if a man were beaten with anything hollow, his inside would waste away till he died.

In Madagascar a mode of counteracting the levity of fortune is to bury a stone at the foot of the heavy house-post. The common custom of swearing upon a stone may be based partly on a belief that the strength and stability of the stone lend confirmation to an oath. Thus the old Danish historian Saxo Grammaticus tells us that "the ancients, when they were to choose a king, were wont to stand on stones planted in the ground, and to proclaim their votes, in order to foreshadow from the steadfastness of the stones that the deed would be lasting." But while a general magical efficacy may be supposed to reside in all stones by reason of their common properties of weight and solidity, special magical virtues are attributed to particular stones, or kinds of stone, in accordance with their individual or specific qualities of shape and color. The Indians of Peru employed certain stones for the increase of maize, others for the increase of potatoes, and others again for the increase of cattle. The stones used to make maize grow were fashioned in the likeness of cobs of maize, and the stones destined to multiply cattle had the shape of sheep. The ancients set great store on the magical qualities of precious stones; indeed it has been maintained, with great show of reason, that such stones were used as amulets long before they were worn as mere ornaments. Thus the Greeks gave the name of tree-agate to a stone which exhibits treelike markings, and they thought that if two of these gems were tied to the horns or neck of oxen at the plow, the crop would be sure to be plentiful. Again, they recognized a milkstone which produced an abundant supply of milk in women if only they drank it dissolved in honey-mead. Milkstones are used for the same purpose by Greek women in Crete and Melos at the present day; in Albania nursing mothers wear the stones in order to ensure an abundant flow of milk. Again, the Greeks believed in a stone which cured snake bites, and hence was named the snakestone; to test its efficacy you had only to grind the stone to powder and sprinkle the powder on the wound. The wine-colored amethyst received its name, which means "not drunken," because it was supposed to keep the wearer of it sober; and two brothers who desired to live at unity were advised to carry magnets about with them, which, by drawing the twain together, would clearly prevent them from falling out.

Dwellers by the sea cannot fail to be impressed by the sight of its ceaseless ebb and flow, and are apt, on the principles of that rude philosophy of sympathy and resemblance which here engages our attention, to trace a subtle relation, a secret harmony, between its tides and the life of man, of animals, and of plants. In the flowing tide they see not merely a symbol but a cause of exuberance, of prosperity, and of life, while in the ebbing tide they discern a real agent as well as a melancholy emblem of failure, of weakness, and of death. The Breton peasant fancies that clover sown when the tide is coming in will grow well, but that if the plant be sown at low water or when the tide is going out, it will never reach maturity, and that the cows which feed on it will burst. His wife believes that the best butter is made when the tide has just turned and is beginning to flow, that milk which foams in the churn will go on foaming till the hour of high water is past, and that water drawn from the well or milk extracted from the cow while the tide is rising will boil up in the pot or saucepan and overflow into the fire. According to some of the ancients, the skins of seals, even after they had been parted from their bodies, remained in secret sympathy with the sea, and were observed to ruffle when the tide was on the ebb. Another ancient belief, attributed to Aristotle, was that no creature can die except at ebb tide. In Portugal, all along the coast of Wales, and on some parts of the coast of Brittany, a belief is said to prevail that people are born when the tide comes in, and die when it goes out. Dickens attests the existence of the same superstition in England. "People can't die, along the coast," said Mr. Peggotty, "except when the tide's pretty nigh out. They can't be born, unless it's pretty nigh in—not properly born till flood."

Another application of the maxim that like produces like is seen in the Chinese belief that the fortunes of a town are deeply affected by its shape, and that they must vary according to the character of the thing which that shape most nearly resembles. Thus it is related that long ago the town of Tsuen-cheu-fu, the outlines of which are like those of a carp, frequently fell a prey to the depredations of the neighboring city of Yung-chun, which is shaped like a fishing net, until the inhabitants of the former town conceived the plan of erecting two tall pagodas in their midst. These pagodas, which still tower above the city of Tsuen-cheu-fu, have ever since exercised the happiest influence over its destiny by intercepting the imaginary net before it could descend and entangle in its meshes the imaginary carp.

Sometimes homeopathic or imitative magic is called in to annul an evil omen by accomplishing it in mimicry. The effect is to circumvent destiny by substituting a mock calamity for a real one. In Madagascar this mode of cheating the fates is reduced to a regular system. Here every mans' fortune is determined by the day or hour of his birth, and if that happens to be an unlucky one his fate is sealed, unless the mischief can be extracted, as the phrase goes, by means of a substitute. The ways of extracting the mischief are various. For example, if a man is born on the first day of the second month (February), his house will be burnt down when he comes of age. To take time by the forelock and avoid this catastrophe, the friends of the infant will set up a shed in a field or in a cattle fold and burn it. If the ceremony is to be really effective, the child and his mother should be placed in the shed and only plucked, like brands, from the burning hut before it is too late. Once more, if fortune has frowned on a man at his birth and penury has marked him for her own, he can easily erase the mark in question by purchasing a couple of cheap pearls, price three halfpence, and burying them. For who but the rich of this world can thus afford to fling pearls away?

3. CONTAGIOUS MAGIC

Thus far we have been considering chiefly that branch of sympathetic magic which may be called homeopathic or imitative. Its leading principle, as we have seen, is that like produces like, or, in other words, that an effect resembles its cause. The other great branch of sympathetic magic, which I have called Contagious Magic, proceeds upon the notion that things which have once been conjoined must remain ever afterwards, even when quite dissevered from each other, in such a sympathetic relation that whatever is done to the one must similarly affect the other. Thus the logical basis of Contagious Magic, like that of Homeopathic Magic, is a mistaken association of ideas; its physical basis, if we may speak of such a thing, like the physical basis of Homeopathic Magic, is a material medium of some sort which, like the ether of modern physics, is assumed to unite distant objects and to convey impressions from one to the other. The most familiar example of Contagious Magic is the magical sympathy which is supposed to exist between a man and any severed portion of his person, as his hair or nails; so that whoever gets possession of human hair or nails may work his will, at any distance, upon the

person from whom they were cut. This superstition is world-wide; instances of it in regard to hair and nails will be noticed later on in this work. I will now illustrate the principles of Contagious Magic by examples, beginning with its application to various parts of the human body.

The Basutos are careful to conceal their extracted teeth, lest these should fall into the hands of certain mythical beings called *baloi,* who haunt graves, and who could harm the owner of the tooth by working magic on it. In Sussex some fifty years ago a maidservant remonstrated strongly against the throwing away of children's cast teeth, affirming that should they be found and gnawed by any animal, the child's new tooth would be, for all the world, like the teeth of the animal that had bitten the old one. In proof of this she named old Master Simmons, who had a very large pig's tooth in his upper jaw, a personal defect that he always averred was caused by his mother, who threw away one of his cast teeth by accident into the hog's trough. A similar belief has led to practices intended, on the principles of homeopathic magic, to replace old teeth by new and better ones. Thus in many parts of the world it is customary to put extracted teeth in some place where they will be found by a mouse or a rat, in the hope that, through the sympathy which continues to subsist between them and their former owner, his other teeth may acquire the same firmness and excellence as the teeth of these rodents.

Other parts which are commonly believed to remain in a sympathetic union with the body, after the physical connection has been severed, are the navel-string and the afterbirth, including the placenta. So intimate, indeed, is the union conceived to be, that the fortunes of the individual for good or evil throughout life are often supposed to be bound up with one or other of these portions of his person, so that if his navel-string or afterbirth is preserved and properly treated, he will be prosperous; whereas if it be injured or lost, he will suffer accordingly. Certain tribes of Western Australia believe that a man swims well or ill, according as his mother at his birth threw the navel-string into water or not. In Ponape, one of the Caroline Islands, the navel-string is placed in a shell and then disposed of in such a way as shall best adapt the child for the career which the parents have chosen for him. Thus if they wish to make him a good climber, they will hang the navel-string on a tree. Among the Cherokees the navel-string of a girl is buried under a corn mortar, in order that the girl may grow up to be a good baker; but the navel-string of a boy is hung up on a tree in the woods, in order that he may be a hunter.

Even in Europe many people still believe that a person's destiny is more or less bound up with that of his navel-string or afterbirth. Thus in Rhenish Bavaria the navel-string is kept for a while wrapt up in a piece of old linen, and then cut or pricked to pieces according as the child is a boy or a girl, in order that he or she may grow up to be a skillful workman or a good seamstress. In Berlin the midwife commonly delivers the dried navel-string to the father with a strict injunction to preserve it carefully, for as long as it is kept the child will live and thrive and be free from sickness. In Beauce and Perche the people are careful to throw the navel-string neither into water nor into fire, believing that if that were done the child would be drowned or burned.

A curious application of the doctrine of contagious magic is the relation commonly believed to exist between a wounded man and the agent of the wound, so that whatever is subsequently done by or to the agent must correspondingly affect the patient either for good or evil. Thus Pliny tells us that if you have wounded a man and are sorry for it, you have only to spit on the hand that gave the wound, and the pain of the sufferer will be instantly alleviated. In Melanesia, if a man's friends get possession of the arrow which wounded him, they keep it in a damp place or in cool leaves, for then the inflammation will be trifling and will soon subside. Meantime the enemy who shot the arrow is hard at work to aggravate the wound by all the means in his power. For this purpose he and his friends drink hot and burning juices and chew irritating leaves, for this will clearly inflame and irritate the wound. Further, they keep the bow near the fire to make the wound which it has inflicted hot; and for the same reason they put the arrowhead, if it has been recovered, into the fire. Moreover, they are careful to keep the bowstring taut and to twang it occasionally, for this will cause the wounded man to suffer from tension of the nerves and spasms of tetanus. Similarly when a Kwakiutl Indian of British Columbia had bitten a piece out of an enemy's arm he used to drink hot water afterwards for the purpose of thereby inflaming the wound in his foe's body. If a horse wounds its foot by treading on a nail, a Suffolk groom will invariably preserve the nail, clean it, and grease it every day, to prevent the foot from festering. A few years ago a veterinary surgeon was sent for to attend a horse which had ripped its side open on the hinge of a farm gatepost. On arriving at the farm he found that nothing had been done to the wounded horse, but that a man was busy trying to pry the hinge out of the gatepost in order that it might be greased and put away, which, in the opinion of the Cambridge wiseacres, would conduce to the recovery of the animal. Similarly, Essex rustics opine that, if a man has been stabbed with a knife, it is essential to his recovery that the knife should be greased and laid across the bed on which the sufferer is lying. So in Bavaria you are directed to anoint a linen rag with grease and tie it on the edge of the axe that cut you, taking care to keep the sharp edge upwards. As the grease on the axe dries, your wound heals.

The sympathetic connection supposed to exist between a man and the weapon which has wounded him is probably founded on the notion that the blood on the weapon continues to feel with the blood in his body. For a like reason the Papuans of Tumleo, an island off German New Guinea, are careful to throw into the sea the bloody bandages with which their wounds have been dressed, for they fear that if these rags fell into the hands of an enemy he might injure them magically thereby. Once when a man with a wound in his mouth, which bled constantly, came to the missionaries to be treated, his faithful wife took great pains to collect all the blood and cast it into the sea. Strained and unnatural as this idea may seem to us, it is perhaps less so than the belief that magic sympathy is maintained between a person and his clothes, so that whatever is done to the clothes will be felt by the man himself even though he may be far away at the time. In Tanna, one of the New Hebrides, a man who had a grudge at another and desired his death would try to get possession of a cloth which had touched the sweat of his enemy's body. If he succeeded, he rubbed the cloth carefully over with the leaves and twigs of a certain tree, rolled and bound cloth, twigs, and leaves into a long sausage-shaped bundle, and burned it slowly in the fire. As the bundle was consumed, the victim fell ill, and when it was reduced to ashes, he died. In this last form of enchantment, however, the magical sympathy may be supposed to exist not so much between the man and the cloth as between the man and the sweat which issued from his body. But in other cases of the same sort it seems that the garment by itself is enough to give the sorcerer a hold upon his victim. In Prussia they say that if you cannot catch a thief, the next best thing you can do is to get hold of a garment which he may have shed in his flight; for if you beat it soundly, the thief will fall sick. This belief is firmly rooted in the popular mind. Some eighty or ninety years ago, in the neighborhood of Berend, a man was detected trying to steal honey, and fled, leaving his coat behind him. When he heard that the enraged owner of the honey was mauling his lost coat, he was so alarmed that he took to his bed and died.

Again magic may be wrought on a man sympathetically, not only through his clothes and severed parts of himself, but also through the impressions left by his body in sand or earth. In particular, it is a world-wide superstition that by injuring footprints you injure the feet that made them. Thus the natives of southeastern Australia think that they can lame a man by placing sharp pieces of quartz, glass, bone, or charcoal in his footprints. In North Africa the magic of the footprints is sometimes used for more amiable purposes. A woman who wishes to attach her husband or lover to herself will take earth from the print of his right foot, tie it up with some of his hairs in a packet, and wear the packet next her skin.

Similar practices prevail in various parts of Europe. Thus in Mecklenburg it is thought that if you drive a nail into a man's footprint he will fall lame; sometimes it is required that the nail should be taken from a coffin. A like mode of injuring an enemy is resorted to in some parts of France. It is said that there was an old woman who used to frequent Stow in Suffolk, and she was a witch. If, while she walked, anyone went after her and stuck a nail or a knife into her footprint in the dust, the dame could not stir a step till it was withdrawn. An old Danish mode of concluding a treaty was based on the same idea of the sympathetic connection between a man and his footprints; the covenanting parties sprinkled each other's footprints with their own blood, thus giving a pledge of fidelity. In ancient Greece superstitions of the same sort seem to have been current, for it was thought that if a horse stepped on the track of a wolf he was seized with numbness; and a maxim ascribed to Pythagoras forbade people to pierce a man's footprints with a nail or a knife.

The same superstition is turned to account by hunters in many parts of the world for the purpose of running down the game. Thus a German huntsman will stick a nail taken from a coffin into the fresh spoor of the quarry, believing that this will hinder the animal from escaping. The aborigines of Victoria put hot embers in the tracks of the animals they were pursuing. Hottentot hunters throw into the air a handful of sand taken from the footprints of the game, believing that this will bring the animal down. Thompson Indians used to lay charms on the tracks of wounded deer; after that they deemed it superfluous to pursue the animal any further that day, for being thus charmed it could not travel far and would soon die.

But though the footprint is the most obvious it is not the only impression made by the body through which magic may be wrought on a man. The aborigines of southeastern Australia believe that a man may be injured by burying sharp fragments of quartz, glass, and so forth in the mark made by his reclining body; the magical virtue of these sharp things enters his body and causes those acute pains which the ignorant European puts down as rheumatism. We can now understand why it was a maxim with the Pythagoreans that in rising from bed you should smooth away the impression left by your body on the bedclothes. The rule was simply an old precaution against magic, forming part of a whole code of superstitious maxims which antiquity fathered on Pythagoras, though doubtless they were familiar to the barbarous forefathers of the Greeks long before the time of that philosopher.

4. THE MAGICIAN'S PROGRESS

We have now concluded our examination of the general principles of sympathetic magic. The examples by which I have illustrated them have been drawn for the most part from what may be called private magic, that is, from magical rites and incantations practiced for the benefit or the injury of individuals. But in savage society there is commonly to be found in addition what we may call public magic, that is, sorcery practiced for the benefit of the whole community. Wherever ceremonies of this sort are observed for the common good, it is obvious that the magician ceases to be merely a private practitioner and becomes to some extent a public functionary. The development of such a class of functionaries is of great importance for the political as well as the religious evolution of society. For when the welfare of the tribe is supposed to depend on the performance of these magical rites, the magician rises into a position of much influence and repute, and may readily acquire the rank and authority of a chief or king. The profession accordingly draws into its ranks some of the ablest and most ambitious men of the tribe, because it holds out to them a prospect of honor, wealth, and power such as hardly any other career could offer. The acuter minds perceive how easy it is to dupe their weaker brother and to play on his superstition for their own advantage. Not that the sorcerer is always a knave and imposter; he is often sincerely convinced that he really possesses those wonderful powers which the credulity of his fellows ascribes to him. But the more sagacious he is, the more likely he is to see through the fallacies which impose on duller wits. Thus the ablest members of the profession must tend to be more or less conscious deceivers; and it is just these men who in virtue of their superior ability will generally come to the top and win for themselves positions of the highest dignity and the most commanding authority. The pitfalls which beset the path of the professional sorcerer are many, and as a rule only the man of coolest head and sharpest wit will be able to steer his way through them safely. For it must always be remembered that every single profession and claim put forward by the magician as such is false; not one of them can be maintained without deception, conscious or unconscious. Accordingly the sorcerer who sincerely believes in his own extravagant pretensions is in far greater peril and is much more likely to be cut short in his career than the deliberate impostor. The honest wizard always expects that his charms and incantations will produce their supposed effect; and when they fail, not only really, as they always do, but conspicuously and disastrously, as they often do, he is taken aback: he is not, like his knavish colleague, ready with a plausible excuse to account for the failure, and before he can find one he may be knocked on the head by his disappointed and angry employers.

The general result is that at this stage of social evolution the supreme power tends to fall into the hands of men of the keenest intelligence and the most unscrupulous character. If we could balance the harm they do by their knavery against the benefits they confer by their superior sagacity, it might well be found that the good greatly outweighed the evil. For more mischief has probably been wrought in the world by honest fools in high places than by intelligent rascals. Once your shrewd rogue has attained the height of his ambition, and has no longer any selfish end to further, he may, and often does, turn his talent, his experience, his resources, to the service of the public. Many men who have been least scrupulous in the acquisition of power have been most beneficent in the use of it, whether the power they aimed at and won was that of wealth, political authority, or what not. In the field of politics the wily intriguer, the ruthless victor, may end by being a wise and magnanimous ruler, blessed in his lifetime, lamented at his death, admired and applauded by posterity. Such men, to take two of the most conspicuous instances, were Julius Caesar and Augustus. But once a fool always a fool, and the greater the power in his hands the more disastrous is likely to be the use he makes of it. The heaviest calamity in English history, the breach with America, might never have occurred if George the Third had not been an honest dullard.

Thus, so far as the public profession of magic affected the constitution of savage society, it tended to place the control of affairs in the hands of the ablest man: it shifted the balance of power from the many to the one: it substituted a monarchy for a democracy, or rather for an oligarchy of old men; for in general the savage community is ruled not by the whole body of adult males, but by a council of elders. The change, by whatever causes produced, and whatever the character of the early rulers, was on the whole very beneficial. For the rise of monarchy appears to be an essential condition of the emergence of mankind from savagery. No human being is so hidebound by custom and tradition as your democratic savage; in no state of society consequently is progress so slow and difficult. The old notion that the savage is the freest of mankind is the reverse of the truth. He is a slave, not indeed to a visible master, but to the past, to the spirits of his dead forefathers, who haunt his steps from birth to death, and rule him with a rod of iron. What they did is the pattern of right, the unwritten law to which he yields a blind, unquestioning obedience. The least possible scope is thus afforded to superior talent to change old customs for the better. The ablest man is dragged down by the weakest and dullest, who necessarily sets the standard, since he cannot rise, while the other can fall. The surface of such a society presents a uniform dead level, so far as it is humanly possible to reduce the natural inequalities, the immeasurable real differences of inborn capacity and temper, to a false superficial appearance of equality. From this low and stagnant condition of affairs, which demagogues and dreamers in later times have lauded as the ideal state, the Golden Age, of humanity, everything that helps to raise society by opening a career to talent and proportioning the degrees of authority to men's natural abilities, deserves to be welcomed by all who have the real good of their fellows at heart. Once these elevating influences have begun to operate—and they cannot be forever suppressed—the progress of civilization becomes comparatively rapid. The rise of one man to supreme power enables him to carry through changes in a single lifetime which previously many generations might not have sufficed to effect; and if, as will often happen, he is a man of intellect and energy above the common, he will readily avail himself of the opportunity. Even the whims and caprices of a tyrant may be of service in breaking the chain of custom which lies so heavy on the savage. And as soon as the tribe ceases to be swayed by the timid and divided counsels of the elders, and yields to the direction of a single strong and resolute mind, it becomes formidable to its neighbors and enters on a career of aggrandizement, which at an early stage of history is often highly favorable to social, industrial, and intellectual progress. For extending its sway, partly by force of arms, partly by the voluntary submission of weaker tribes, the community soon acquires wealth and slaves, both of which, by relieving some classes from the perpetual struggle for a bare subsistence, afford them an opportunity of devoting themselves to that disinterested pursuit of knowledge which is the noblest and most powerful instrument to ameliorate the lot of man.

Intellectual progress, which reveals itself in the growth of art and science and the spread of more liberal views, cannot be dissociated from industrial or economic progress, and that in its turn receives an immense impulse from conquest and empire. It is no mere accident that the most vehement outbursts of activity of the human mind have followed close on the heels of victory, and that the great conquering races of the world have commonly done most to advance and spread civilization, thus healing in peace the wounds they inflicted in war. The Babylonians, the Greeks, the Romans, the Arabs are our witnesses in the past: we may yet live to see a similar outburst in Japan. Nor, to remount the stream of history to its sources, is it an accident that all the first great strides towards civilization have been made under despotic and theocratic governments, like those of Egypt, Babylon, and Peru, where the supreme ruler claimed and received the servile allegiance of his subjects in the double character of a king and a god. It is hardly too much to say that at this early epoch despotism is the best friend of humanity and, paradoxical as it may sound, of liberty. For after all there is more liberty in the best sense—liberty to think our own thoughts and to fashion our own destinies—under the most absolute despotism, the most grinding tyranny, than under the apparent freedom of savage life, where the indiviual's lot is cast from the cradle to the grave in the iron mold of hereditary custom.

So far, therefore, as the public profession of magic has been one of the roads by which the ablest men have passed to supreme power, it has contributed to emancipate mankind from the thralldom of tradition and to elevate them into a larger, freer life, with a broader outlook on the world. This is no small service rendered to humanity. And when we remember further that in another direction magic has paved the way for science, we are forced to admit that if the black art has done much evil, it has also been the source of much good; that if it is the child of error, it has yet been the mother of freedom and truth.

MISCHA TITIEV

A Fresh Approach to the Problem of Magic and Religion

There has recently been an intensified interest in defining religion, particularly as it relates to magic. The following article, by Mischa Titiev, is a modest effort to clear the atmosphere without departing from what is essentially a Frazerian position. It may be contrasted with two articles by Murray and Rosalie Wax, "The Magical World View" (1962) and "The Notion of Magic" (1963), which severely attack any effort to sustain the more traditional views of magic as expressed by not only Frazer himself but also Tylor, Durkheim, and others. The Waxes' articles provide a useful review of the controversy in its historical and intellectual aspects. Less polemic efforts at grappling with the definitional problems on a broad basis have been made by Horton (1960) and Goody (1961).

Titiev's proposal to distinguish between calendrical and critical rituals has a familiar ring, although his use of the distinction is novel. Chapple and Coon, in their *Principles of Anthropology*, had earlier made a distinction between rites of intensification and rites of passage, the first usually being cyclical and recurrent, the latter nonrecurrent, but their aim was to explore these rituals in terms of the restoration of disturbed equilibrium. What Titiev has done is to show that many of the traits adhering to calendrical rituals are those we usually regard as religious, whereas many of those associated with critical rites are customarily considered to be magical. Yet he does not press the use of these criteria beyond reason, recognizing, as do indeed even those who favor the Frazerian type of dichotomy, that there simply is no hard and fast rule.

Reprinted with omission of a figure from *Southwestern Journal of Anthropology*, XVI (1960), 292–298, by permission of the author and the *Southwestern Journal of Anthropology*.

About seventy years ago the great scholar of primitive religion, Sir James G. Frazer, found it advisable to divide all phenomena involving the supernatural into the two categories of magic and religion. Almost at once large numbers of social scientists found Frazer's dichotomy useful and began to emphasize the criteria which, in their opinion, separated the one category from the other. In the course of time it became customary to stress four factors, although others were sometimes invoked. The four attributes that came to be most often cited run somewhat as follows.

1. Magic *compels* the world of the supernatural to do its bidding. It fails to get results only if errors of procedure or text have been made, or if stronger countermagic has been brought to bear. Religion, on the other hand, say the supporters of Frazer's dichotomy, never guarantees results.

Its use is limited to *supplication,* and its practitioners never resort to manipulation or coercion.

2. Magic, according to Durkheim and his followers, has no "church." That is to say, magical rites may be public or private but, unlike those that are religious, they do not have to have a large body of celebrants; they do not need to be held in public before a congregation of worshippers; and they may have no social or communal aspects whatsoever.

3. Magical utterances have a tendency to degenerate into spells or formulas, some of which have little or no meaning even to those who say them. It is implied that religious pronouncements are usually meaningful in terms of a society's customary language.

4. Practitioners of magic, even in primitive societies, are often set apart in one

fashion or another from socially recognized priests. With occasional exceptions it is only acknowledged priests who go through a period of formal training and who then qualify to perform communal or publicly sanctioned religious exercises, leaving shamans and others to deal in magic.

Although most writers on the subject have continued to accept Frazer's distinction, somewhat apathetically, it must be confessed, others have held the criteria to be unsatisfactory because they cannot be precisely determined and because they so frequently overlap. Indeed, some contemporary anthropologists have found the customary divisions between magic and religion to be so vague and inderterminate that they have refused to recognize the traditional dichotomy and now prefer to treat both sets of practices as one. Indicative of this attitude is Dr. Hsu's statement, written only a few years ago, that "whichever criterion we employ, we are led to the conclusion that magic and religion, instead of being treated as mutually exclusive entities, must be grouped together as magico-religion or magico-religious phenomena. This is a position increasingly endorsed by anthropologists." Nevertheless, even if we grant that modern critics have many points in their favor, there are a number of anthropologists who still believe that a distinction needs to be made between what they feel are two essentially different kinds of human behavior, each of which makes an appeal to the supernatural world for help, guidance, or comfort.

As a fresh start toward a workable dichotomy, it may be well to distinguish two kinds of activities on a new basis, one that rests on a criterion that is precise, but has not been traditionally utilized by former analysts. In all primitive societies one set of practices involving the supernatural always takes place recurrently, and may, accordingly, be termed CALENDRICAL; while the other set, which is celebrated only intermittently, and then only when an emergency or crisis seems to have arisen, may be called CRITICAL.

Because of their very nature calendrical rituals can always be scheduled and announced long in advance of their occurrence. This gives the people of a community ample time to develop a shared sense of anticipation, and an opportunity to get ready for a big event. On the other hand, it must be realized that if a celebration is to be performed at a definite time or season in the future, it cannot possibly take into account the immediate desires for supernatural assistance or comfort of the whole society or of any of its parts. To cite one instance, the gigantic figure of Shalako appears in Zuni each December, regardless of the frame of mind of any particular inhabitants of the village.

One can find calendrical rites even in Christianity. Christmas is an excellent example. Throughout the Western world it is celebrated annually on the twenty-fifth day of December, regardless of the wants or needs, on that particular day, of individual Christians or of any congregation of Christians.

As a rule, calendrical performances are entrusted to officially-sanctioned priests, rather than to other persons who may deal with the supernatural; and since ceremonies based on a calendar cannot possibly be geared to anyone's immediate desires, they can be interpreted only as having value for an entire society. In this sense, especially, calendrical observances may be said always to have a "church", and to correspond, on the whole, more nearly to established concepts of religion than to those of magic.

Moreover, since they are always social or communal in character, calendrical rites invariably tend to disappear when a society loses its distinctiveness or radically alters its old ways of life. Thus, when the Hopi Indians of Oraibi began to show greater interest in White than in native culture, the pueblo's calendrical observances were among the first cultural items to suffer disintegration.

In a similar vein, long before the establishment of Israel, the Jews were of particular interest to social scientists partly because they managed to give the impression of being a single society, even though it was patently obvious that they were not, inasmuch as they were scattered among many, many nations. What, then, gave observers the impression that the Jews constituted *a society?* Above all else, it was the fact that regardless of their places of residence the Jewish people steadfastly continued to observe such traditional calendrical (social) ceremonies as Passover and Yom Kippur. It is noteworthy in this context that whenever Jews become assimilated into any originally alien society, they stop observing their ancient calendrical rituals.

Quite different in nearly every respect are those practices, also based on a belief in the supernatural, that we have termed critical. They are, let us recall, customarily designed to meet the pressing needs of a given moment. For this reason they can never be held only because a particular time has arrived, nor can they be announced, scheduled, or prepared for far in advance. In some cases critical ceremonies may be performed by priests, but in a large number of instances they are conducted by other personages.

Unlike calendrical observances which are *invariably* communal or broadly social, critical rituals may be designed to benefit either a whole society, a relatively small group, or even a single individual. It should be obvious that every now and then a critical rite may be held to counteract a public emergency, as when a prolonged drought affects all the farmers in a given community, or when an entire nation prays for peace. However, crises on this scale are comparatively rare. For the most part critical ceremonies are staged only when a private or personal emergency has arisen, as might be the case if something important has been stolen or mislaid, or if a child has fallen gravely ill, or in the event that an individual has entered on a new social position that disturbs his former dealings with the members of his society. In such cases critical rituals are designed to benefit only those who have asked, and sometimes paid, for them. A reëxamination of the rich material from Africa, as well as from other regions, pertaining to the services rendered by seers, diviners, fortune-tellers, medicine-men, and so forth, shows that their approach to the supernatural is far more often on behalf of persons who have a problem than it is for the sake of whole societies or communities. These instances show that critical observances do not inevitably need to have a "church." Since, at the same time, they do not necessarily have to be performed by socially sanctioned priests, they tend in a number of ways to correspond quite closely to traditional concepts of magic.

It should be noted further that whereas calendrical rites ordinarily disappear when a society diminishes in power or loses its identity, critical rites may persist long after an entire society has collapsed, and in a new social setting may form the basis for a large number of the carry-overs that students of religion generally call superstitions.

Since the distinction here made cannot be maintained without the existence of some form of a calendar, it is essential to show that even the most primitive and non-literate of people may have a simple way of keeping track of the year's progress. In the northern hemisphere, whose varied religions are far better known to anthropologists than are those of the people who live south of the equator, the easiest method involves no more than noting, from exactly the same spot each day, where the sun seems to rise. When this is done regularly the sun apparently travels from north to south between June 21 and December 21, and from south to north during the remaining six months. Whenever the eastern horizon happens to be irregular it appears as if the sun comes up now from a mountain peak, now from a bit of forest, now from an open stretch, and so on. In this way the coincidence of a sunrise with a particular landmark may serve as a seasonal checkpoint, and as an indication of the time when a given calendrical rite ought to be announced or performed. The terminal or turning points in the sun's annual course mark the solstices. In many communities of the northern hemisphere, even if the June solstice is unnoticed, it is customary to hold important calendrical rituals on or about December 21.

The main reason for this difference of attitude and behavior seems to stem from the fact that whenever it reaches either of its solstice points the sun at first makes so little daily progress in the opposite direction that it appears to rise in the same spot or, in a manner of speaking, to hesitate or to stand still for three or four days. When this "hesitation" takes place on June 21, there is little to fear, for vegetation is usually plentiful, crops are growing, and the weather is balmy. But it is quite another matter when the sun pauses at its southern terminal and appears reluctant to move northward, in the direction of spring and summer. Such a threatened stoppage would, indeed, be a calamity. It might result in perpetual winter, no fodder for animals, and no crops for man. That is why strenuous efforts are sometimes made to get the sun to turn from its southern to its northern path; and that is also why winter solstice observances so commonly take the form of new-fire rites, or else include a number of symbols expressive of man's desire for increased light and heat.

Never should it be thought that calendrical ceremonies, because they may disregard the needs of the moment, are only of secondary importance. Far from it! Analysis of their intent reveals that they are designed primarily to strengthen the bonds of cohesion that hold together all of a society's members or else to aid the individuals who form a social unit to adjust to one another and to their external environment.

Our dichotomy should not be interpreted as a device for classifying every conceivable aspect of primitive religion. For instance, it does not apply smoothly to all the manifestations of the famed rites of passage. It is true that three of Van Gennep's stages—birth, marriage, and death—are critical, because they are concerned primarily with individuals and cannot be precisely determined in advance; whereas the fourth—puberty or tribal initiation—is often calendrically observed. Yet, all of the rites of passage drastically change a person's social relationships, and, therefore, all of them may be classed, as they usually are, as critical.

For many anthropologists in the United Stages, especially, the old distinction between magic and religion has lost much of its pristine vitality and freshness. Unless we are prepared to lump all supernatural phenomena into a single category, we need a fresh basis for classification and analysis. That is what the proposed difference between calendrical and critical rites is meant to provide. The likelihood is strong that every social unit's system of supernatural practices contains both calendrical and critical elements. In partnership, these may be seen to function as vital parts of every primitive society's nonempirical method for trying to gain desired ends.

GEORGE GREY

The Two Sorcerers

This concise article, written in 1855 by Sir George Grey, is a legendary account of a lethal contest between two famed sorcerers. Kiki and Tamure, renowned New Zealand sorcerers, vie with one another in a fatal display of magical prowess. While magic and countermagic are everyday occurrences in most societies, actual vis-à-vis combat between sorcerers such as is here described is much less common; probably few men would be willing to risk reputation and life itself in one climactic battle. The author's style imparts an aura of supernaturalism, replete with spirits, demons, and genii, as well as magic. In actual practice, magic and other forms of supernaturalism often do commingle, revealing the fallacy in any rigid dichotomy between magic and religion.

Reprinted from George Grey, *Polynesian Mythology and Ancient Traditional History of the New Zealand Race* (London: John Murray, 1855), pp. 273–278.

Kiki was a celebrated sorcerer, and skilled in magical arts; he lived upon the river Waikato. The inhabitants of that river still have this proverb, "The offspring of Kiki wither shrubs." This proverb had its origin in the circumstance of Kiki being such a magician, that he could not go abroad in the sunshine; for if his shadow fell upon any place not protected from his magic, it at once became *tapu,* and all the plants there withered.

This Kiki was thoroughly skilled in the practice of sorcery. If any parties coming up the river called at his village in their canoes as they paddled by, he still remained quietly at home, and never troubled himself to come out, but just drew back the sliding door of his house, so that it might stand open, and the strangers stiffened and died; or even as canoes came paddling down from the upper parts of the river, he drew back the sliding wooden shutter to the window of his house, and the crews on board of them were sure to die.

At length, the fame of this sorcerer spread exceedingly, and resounded through every tribe, until Tamure, a chief who dwelt at Kawhia, heard with others, reports of the magical powers of Kiki, for his fame extended over the whole country. At length Tamure thought he would go and contend in the arts of sorcery with Kiki, that it might be seen which of them was most skilled in magic; and he arranged in his own mind a fortunate season for his visit.

When this time came, he selected two of his people as his companions, and he took his young daughter with him also; and they all crossed over the mountain range from Kawhia, and came down upon the river Waipa, which runs into the Waikato, and embarking there in a canoe, paddled down the river towards the village of Kiki; and they managed so well, that before they were seen by anybody, they had arrived at the landing-place. Tamure was not only skilled in magic, but he was also a very cautious man; so whilst they were still afloat upon the river, he repeated an incantation of the kind called "Mata-tawhito," to preserve him safe from all arts of sorcery; and he repeated other incantations, to ward off spells, to protect him from magic, to collect good genii round him, to keep off evil spirits, and to shield him from demons; when these preparations were all finished, they landed, and drew up their canoe on the beach, at the landing-place of Kiki.

As soon as they had landed, the old sorcerer called out to them that they were welcome to his village, and invited them to come up to it; so they went up to the village: and when they reached the square in the center, they seated themselves upon the ground; and some of Kiki's people kindled fire in an enchanted oven, and began to cook food in it for the strangers. Kiki sat in his house, and Tamure on the ground just outside the entrance to it, and he there availed himself of this opportunity to repeat incantations over the threshold of the house, so that Kiki might be enchanted as he stepped over it to come out. When the food in the enchanted oven was cooked, they pulled off the coverings, and spread it out upon clean mats. The old sorcerer now made his appearance out of his house, and he invited Tamure to come and eat food with him; but the food was all

enchanted, and his object in asking Tamure to eat with him was, that the enchanted food might kill him; therefore Tamure said that his young daughter was very hungry, and would eat of the food offered to them; he in the meantime kept on repeating incantations of the kind called Mata-tawhito, Whakangungu, and Parepare, protections against enchanted food, and as she ate she also continued to repeat them; even when she stretched out her hand to take a sweet potato, or any other food, she dropped the greater part of it at her feet, and hid it under her clothes, and then only ate a little bit. After she had done, the old sorcerer, Kiki, kept waiting for Tamure to begin to eat also of the enchanted food, that he might soon die. Kiki having gone into his house again, Tamure still sat on the ground outside the door, and as he had enchanted the threshold of the house, he now repeated incantations which might render the door enchanted also, so that Kiki might be certain not to escape when he passed out of it. By this time Tamure's daughter had quite finished her meal, but neither her father nor either of his people had partaken of the enchanted food.

Tamure now ordered his people to launch his canoe, and they paddled away, and a little time after they had left the village, Kiki became unwell; in the meanwhile, Tamure and his people were paddling homewards in all haste, and as they passed a village where there were a good many people on the river's bank, Tamure stopped, and said to them, "If you should see any canoe pulling after us, and the people in the canoe ask you, have you seen a canoe pass up the river, would you be good enough to say, 'Yes, a canoe has passed by here'? and then if they ask you, 'How far has it got?' would you be good enough to say, 'Oh, by this time it has got very far up the river'?" and having thus said to the people of that village, Tamure paddled away again in his canoe with all haste.

Some time after Tamure's party had left the village of Kiki, the old sorcerer became very ill indeed, and his people then knew that this had been brought about by the magical arts of Tamure, and they sprang into a canoe to follow after him, and pulled up the river as hard as they could; and when they reached the village where the people were on the river's bank, they called out and asked them, "How far has the canoe reached, which passed up the river?" and the villagers answered, "Oh, that canoe must have got very far up the river by this time." The people in the canoe that was pursuing Tamure, upon hearing this, returned again to their own village, and Kiki died from the incantations of Tamure.

Some of Kiki's descendants are still living—one of them, named Mokahi, recently died at Tau-ranga-a-Ruru, but Te Maioha is still living on the river Waipa. Yes, some of the descendants of Kiki, whose shadow withered trees, are still living. He was indeed a great sorcerer: he overcame every

other sorcerer until he met Tamure, but he was vanquished by him, and had to bend the knee before him.

Tamure has also some descendants living, amongst whom are Mahu and Kiake of the Ngati-Mariu tribe; these men are also skilled in magic: if a father skilled in magic died, he left his incantations to his children; so that if a man was skilled in sorcery, it was known that his children would have a good knowledge of the same arts, as they were certain to have derived it from their parent.

WALTER B. CANNON

"Voodoo" Death

The phenomenon of death caused by witchcraft and sorcery or due to taboo violation is common and widespread. Such deaths are frequent in aboriginal Australia, Polynesia, South America, and Africa. Similar phenomena are occasionally reported from almost every corner of the world.

Both early observers and modern investigators have accepted such deaths as being due to fear; that is, there is ample evidence that no poison or physical agent is necessary to bring about the demise of the victim. Where belief in sorcery, witchcraft, or supernatural sanctions is firmly held, fear alone can kill. While competent investigators had not doubted the actuality of "voodoo" death, it remained for Cannon to establish the physiological mechanisms by which fear, such as can be engendered by sorcery, can kill a human being. For this purpose, Cannon was able to draw upon his classic studies of the physiological changes due to hunger, rage, fear, and pain.

In this article the author demonstrates that through fear the body is stimulated to meet an emergency. Through the sympathetic nervous system, muscles are prepared for action by the production of large amounts of adrenalin and sugar and by the contraction of certain blood vessels. When the emergency is not met by action, or is prolonged, a state of shock may result. The blood pressure is reduced, the heart deteriorates, and blood plasma escapes into the tissues. Lack of food and water compound this deleterious physiological state. A continuation of this condition may lead to death within a very few days.

Although this article deals with witchcraft, fear, and death in primitive societies, its implications are far-reaching. The psychogenic ailments of modern "civilized" man defy understanding, but we know that fear through suggestion and autosuggestion afflicts the modern hypochondriac and ulcer patient much as it does the Australian who is bewitched or "sung."

Reprinted in abridged form from *American Anthropologist*, XLIV (1942), 169–181, by permission of the American Anthropological Association.

In records of anthropologists and others who have lived with primitive people in widely scattered parts of the world is the testimony

that when subjected to spells or sorcery or the use of "black magic" men may be brought to death. Among the natives of

South America and Africa, Australia, New Zealand, and the islands of the Pacific, as well as among the Negroes of nearby Haiti, "voodoo" death has been reported by apparently competent observers. The phenomenon is so extraordinary and so foreign to the experience of civilized people that it seems incredible; certainly if it is authentic it deserves careful consideration.

A question which naturally arises is whether those who have testified to the reality of voodoo death have exercised good critical judgment. Although the sorcerer or medicine man or chief may tacitly possess or may assume the ability to kill by bone-pointing or by another form of black magic, may he not preserve his reputation for supernatural power by the use of poison? Especially when death has been reported to have occurred after the taking of food may not the fatal result be due to action of poisonous substances not commonly known except to priests and wizards? Obviously, the possible use of poisons must be excluded before voodoo death can be accepted as an actual consequence of sorcery or witchcraft. Also it is essential to rule out instances of bold claims of supernatural power when in fact death resulted from natural causes; this precaution is particularly important because of the common belief among aborigines that illness is due to malevolence. I have endeavored to learn definitely whether poisoning and spurious claims can quite certainly be excluded from instances of death, attributed to magic power, by addressing inquiries to medically trained observers.

Dr. S. M. Lambert of the Western Pacific Service of the Rockefeller Foundation wrote to me concerning the experience of Dr. P. S. Clarke with Kanakas working on the sugar plantations of North Queensland. One day a Kanaka came to his hospital and told him he would die in a few days because a spell had been put upon him and nothing could be done to counteract it. The man had been known by Dr. Clarke for some time. He was given a very thorough examination, including an examination of the stool and the urine. All was found normal, but as he lay in bed he gradually grew weaker. Dr. Clarke called upon the foreman of the Kanakas to come to the hospital to give the man assurance, but on reaching the foot of the bed, the foreman leaned over, looked at the patient, and then turned to Dr. Clarke saying, "Yes,

doctor, close up him he die" (i.e., he is nearly dead). The next day, at 11 o'clock in the morning, he ceased to live. A postmortem examination revealed nothing that could in any way account for the fatal outcome.

Another observer with medical training, Dr. W. E. Roth, who served for three years as government surgeon among the primitive people of north central Queensland, has also given pertinent testimony. "So rooted sometimes is this belief on the part of the patient," Roth wrote, "that some enemy has 'pointed' the bone at him, that he will actually lie down to die, and succeed in the attempt, even at the expense of refusing food and succor within his reach: I have myself witnessed three or four such cases."

Dr. J. B. Cleland, Professor of Pathology at the University of Adelaide, has written to me that he has no doubt that from time to time the natives of the Australian bush do die as a result of a bone being pointed at them, and that such death may not be associated with any of the ordinary lethal injuries. In an article which included a section on death from malignant psychic influences, Dr. Cleland mentions a fine, robust tribesman in Central Australia who was injured in the fleshy part of the thigh by a spear that had been enchanted. The man slowly pined away and died, without any surgical complication which could be detected. Dr. Cleland cites a number of physicians who have referred to the fatal effects of bone-pointing and other terrifying acts. In his letter to me he wrote, "Poisoning is, I think, entirely ruled out in such cases among our Australian natives. There are very few poisonous plants available and I doubt whether it has ever entered the mind of the central Australian natives that such might be used on human beings."

Dr. Herbert Basedow, in his book, *The Australian Aboriginal,* has presented a vivid picture of the first horrifying effect of bone-pointing on the ignorant, superstitious, and credulous natives, and the later more calm acceptance of their mortal fate:

The man who discovers that he is being boned by any enemy is, indeed, a pitiable sight. He stands aghast, with his eyes staring at the treacherous pointer, and with his hands lifted as though to ward off the lethal medium, which he imagines is pouring into his body. His cheeks blanch and his eyes become glassy and the expression of his face becomes horribly distorted. . . . He attempts to shriek but usually the sound chokes in his throat, and all that one might see is froth at his mouth. His body begins to tremble and the muscles twist involuntarily. He sways backwards and falls to the ground, and after a short time appears to be in a swoon; but soon after he writhes as if in mortal agony, and, covering his face with his hands, begins to moan. After a while he becomes very composed and crawls to his wurley. From this time onwards he sickens and frets, refusing to eat and keeping aloof from the daily affairs of the tribe. Unless help is forthcoming in the shape of a countercharm administered by the hands of the Nangarri, or medicine man, his death is only a matter of a comparatively short time. If the coming of the medicine man is opportune he might be saved.

The Nangarri, when persuaded to exercise his powers, goes through an elaborate ceremony and finally steps toward the awe-stricken relatives, holding in his fingers a small article—a stick, a bone, a pebble, or a talon—which, he avows, he has taken from the "boned" man and which was the cause of the affliction. And now, since it is removed, the victim has nothing to fear. The effect, Dr. Basedow declares, is astounding. The victim, until that moment far on the road to death, raises his head and gazes in wonderment at the object held by the medicine man. He even lifts himself into a sitting position and calls for water to drink. The crisis is passed, and the recovery is speedy and complete. Without the Nangarri's intervention the boned fellow, according to Dr. Basedow, would certainly have fretted himself to death. The implicit faith which a native cherishes in the magical powers of his tribal magician is said to result in cures which exceed anything recorded by the faith-healing disciples of more cultured communities.

Perhaps the most complete account of the influence of the tribal taboo on the fate of a person subjected to its terrific potency has come from W. L. Warner, who worked among primitive aborigines in the Northern Territory of Australia. There are two definite movements of the social group, he declares, in the process by which black magic becomes effective on the victim of sorcery. In the first movement the community contracts; all people who stand in kinship relation with him withdraw their sustaining support. This means that all his fellows—everyone he knows—completely change their attitudes

toward him and place him in a new category. He is now viewed as one who is more nearly in the realm of the sacred and taboo than in the world of the ordinary where the community finds itself. The organization of his social life has collapsed, and, no longer a member of a group, he is alone and isolated. The doomed man is in a situation from which the only escape is by death. During the death-illness which ensues, the group acts with all the outreachings and complexities of its organization and with countless stimuli to suggest death positively to the victim, who is in a highly suggestible state. In addition to the social pressure upon him the victim himself, as a rule, not only makes no effort to live and to stay a part of his group but actually, through the multiple suggestions which he receives, co-operates in the withdrawal from it. He becomes what the attitude of his fellow tribesmen wills him to be. Thus he assists in committing a kind of suicide.

Before death takes place, the second movement of the community occurs, which is a return to the victim in order to subject him to the fateful ritual of mourning. The purpose of the community now, as a social unit with its ceremonial leader, who is a person of very near kin to the victim, is at last to cut him off entirely from the ordinary world and ultimately to place him in his proper position in the sacred totemic world of the dead. The victim, on his part, reciprocates this feeling. The effect of the double movement in the society, first away from the victim and then back, with all the compulsive force of one of its most powerful rituals, is obviously drastic.

The social environment as a support to morale is probably much more important and impressive among primitive people, because of their profound ignorance and insecurity in a haunted world, than among educated people living in civilized and well-protected communities. Dr. S. D. Porteus, physician and psychologist, has studied savage life extensively in the Pacific islands and in Africa; he writes:

Music and dance are primitive man's chief defenses against loneliness. By these he reminds himself that in his wilderness there are other minds seconding his own . . . in the dance he sees himself multiplied in his fellows, his action mirrored in theirs. There are in his life very few other occasions in which he can take part in concerted action and find partners. . . . The native aboriginal is above all fear-ridden. Devils haunt to seize the unwary; their malevolent magic shadows his waking moments, he believes that medicine men know how to make themselves invisible so that they may cut out his kidney fat, then sew him up and rub his tongue with a magic stone to induce forgetfulness, and thereafter he is a living corpse, devoted to death. . . . So desperate is this fear that if a man imagines that he has been subjected to the bone-pointing magic of the enemy he will straight away lie down and die.

Testimony similar to the foregoing, from Brazil, Africa, New Zealand, and Australia, was found in reports from the Hawaiian Islands, British Guiana, and Haiti. What attitude is justified in the presence of this accumulation of evidence? In a letter from Professor Lévy-Bruhl, the French ethnologist long interested in aboriginal tribes and their customs, he remarked that answers which he had received from inquiries could be summed up as follows. The ethnologists, basing their judgment on a large number of reports, quite independent of one another and gathered from groups in all parts of the world, admit that there are instances indicating that the belief that one has been subjected to sorcery, and in consequence is inevitably condemned to death, does actually result in death in the course of time. On the contrary, physiologists and physicians—men who have had no acquaintance with ethnological conditions—are inclined to consider the phenomenon as impossible and raise doubts regarding clear and definite testimony.

Before denying that voodoo death is within the realm of possibility, let us consider the general features of the specimen reports mentioned in foregoing paragraphs. First, there is the elemental fact that the phenomenon is characteristically noted among aborigines—among human beings so primitive, so superstitious, so ignorant that they are bewildered strangers in a hostile world. Instead of knowledge they have a fertile and unrestricted imagination which fills their environment with all manner of evil spirits capable of affecting their lives disastrously. As Dr. Porteus pointed out, only by engaging in communal activities are they able to develop sufficient *esprit de corps* to render themselves resistant to the mysterious and malicious influences which can vitiate their lives. Associated with these circumstances is the fixed assurance that because of certain conditions, such as being subject to bone-pointing or other magic, or failing to observe sacred tribal regulations, death is sure to supervene. This is a belief so firmly held by all members of the tribe that the individual not only has that conviction himself but is obsessed by the knowledge that all his fellows likewise hold it. Thereby he becomes a pariah, wholly deprived of the confidence and social support of the tribe. In his isolation the malicious spirits which he believes are all about him and capable of irresistibly and calamitously maltreating him, exert supremely their evil power. Amid this mysterious mark of grim and ominous fatality what has been called "the gravest known extremity of fear," that of an immediate threat of death, fills the terrified victim with powerless misery.

In his terror he refuses both food and drink, a fact which many observers have noted and which, as we shall see later, is highly significant for a possible understanding of the slow onset of weakness. The victim "pines away"; his strength runs out like water, to paraphrase words already quoted from one graphic account; and in the course of a day or two he succumbs.

The question which now arises is whether an ominous and persistent state of fear can end the life of a man. Fear, as is well known, is one of the most deeply rooted and dominant of the emotions. Often, only with difficulty can it be eradicated. Associated with it are profound physiological disturbances, widespread throughout the organism. There is evidence that some of these disturbances, if they are lasting, can work harmfully. In order to elucidate that evidence I must first indicate that great fear and great rage have similar effects in the body. Each of these powerful emotions is associated with ingrained instincts—the instinct to attack, if rage is present; the instinct to run away or escape, if fear is present. Throughout the long history of human beings and lower animals these two emotions and their related instincts have served effectively in the struggle for existence. When they are roused they bring into action an elemental division of the nervous system, the so-called "sympathetic" or sympathico-adrenal division, which exercises a control over internal organs, and also over the blood vessels. As a rule the sympathetic division acts to maintain a relatively constant state in the flowing blood and lymph, i.e., the "internal environment" of our living parts. It acts thus in strenuous muscular effort; for example, liberating sugar from the liver, accelerating the heart, contracting certain blood vessels, discharging adrenaline, and dilating the bronchioles. All these changes render the animal more efficient in physical struggle, for they supply essential conditions for continuous action of laboring muscles. Since they occur in association with the strong emotions, rage and fear, they can reasonably be interpreted as preparatory for the intense struggle which the instincts to attack or to escape may involve. If these powerful emotions prevail, and the bodily forces are fully mobilized for action, and if this state of extreme perturbation continues in uncontrolled possession of the organism for a considerable period, without the occurrence of action, dire results may ensue.

When, under brief ether anesthesia, the cerebral cortex of a cat is quickly destroyed so that the animal no longer has the benefit of the organs of intelligence, there is a remarkable display of the activities of lower, primary centers of behavior, those of emotional expression. This decorticate condition is similar to that produced in man when consciousness is abolished by the use of nitrous oxide; he is then decorticated by chemical means. Commonly the emotional expression of joy is released (nitrous oxide is usually known as "laughing gas"), but it may be that of sorrow (it might as well be called "weeping gas"). Similarly, ether anesthesia, if light, may release the expression of rage. In the sham rage of the decorticate cat there is a supreme exhibition of intense emotional activity. The hairs stand on end, sweat exudes from the toe pads, the heart rate may rise from about 150 beats per minute to twice that number, the blood pressure is greatly elevated, and the concentration of sugar in the blood soars to five times the normal. This excessive activity of the sympathico-adrenal system rarely lasts, however, more than three or four hours. By that time, without any loss of blood or any other events to explain the outcome, the decorticate remnant of the animal, in which this acme of emotional display has prevailed, ceases to exist.

What is the cause of the demise? It is clear that the rapidly fatal result is due to a persistent excessive activity of the sympathico-adrenal system. One of my associates, Philip Bard, noted that when the signs of emotional excitement failed to appear, the decorticate preparation might continue to survive for long periods; indeed, its existence might have to be ended by the experimenter. Further evidence was obtained by another of my associates, Norman E. Freeman, who produced sham rage in animals from which the sympathetic nerves had been removed. In these circumstances the behavior was similar in all respects to the behavior described above, excepting the manifestations dependent upon sympathetic innervation. The remarkable fact appeared that animals deprived of their sympathetic nerves and exhibiting sham rage, so far as was possible, continued to exist for many hours without any sign of breakdown. Here were experiments highly pertinent to the present inquiry.

What effect on the organism is produced by a lasting and intense action of the sympathico-adrenal system? In observations Bard found that a prominent and significant change which became manifest in animals displaying sham rage was a gradual fall of blood pressure towards the end of the display, from the high levels of the early stages to the low level seen in fatal wound shock. Freeman's research produced evidence that this fall of pressure was due to a reduction of the volume of circulating blood. This is the condition which during World War I was found to be the reason for the low blood pressure observed in badly wounded men— the blood volume is reduced until it becomes insufficient for the maintenance of an adequate circulation. Thereupon deterioration occurs in the heart, and also in the nerve centers which hold the blood vessels in moderate contraction. A vicious circle is then established; the low blood pressure damages the very organs which are necessary for the maintenance of an adequate circulation, and as they are damaged they are less and less able to keep the blood circulating to an effective degree. In sham rage, as in wound shock, death can be explained as due to a failure of essential organs to receive a sufficient supply of blood or, specifically, a sufficient supply of oxygen, to maintain their functions.

The gradual reduction of blood volume in

sham rage can be explained by the action of the sympathico-adrenal system in causing a persistent constriction of the small arterioles in certain parts of the body. If adrenaline, which constricts the blood vessels precisely as nerve impulses constrict them, is continuously injected at a rate which produces the vasoconstriction of strong emotional states, the blood volume is reduced to the degree seen in sham rage. Freeman, Freedman, and Miller performed that experiment. They employed in some instances no more adrenaline than is secreted in response to reflex stimulation of the adrenal gland, and they found not only marked reduction of the blood plasma but also a concentration of blood corpuscles as shown by the percentage increase of hemoglobin. It should be remembered, however, that in addition to this circulating vasoconstrictor agent there are in the normal functioning of the sympathico-adrenal system the constrictor effects on blood vessels of nerve impulses and the co-operation of another circulating chemical substance besides adrenaline, viz., sympathin. These three agents, working together in times of great emotional stress, might well produce the results which Freeman and his collaborators observed when they injected adrenaline alone. In the presence of the usual blood pressure, organs of primary importance, e.g., the heart and the brain, are not subjected to constriction of their vessels, and therefore they are continuously supplied with blood. But this advantage is secured at the deprivation of peripheral structures and especially the abdominal viscera. In these less essential parts, where constriction of the arterioles occurs, the capillaries are ill-supplied with oxygen. The very thin walls of the capillaries are sensitive to oxygen-want and when they do not receive an adequate supply they become more and more permeable to the fluid part of the blood. Thereupon the plasma escapes into the perivascular spaces. A similar condition occurs in the wound shock of human beings. The escape of the plasma from the blood vessels leaves the red corpuscles more concentrated. During World War I we found that the concentration of corpuscles in skin areas might be increased as much as fifty per cent.

A condition well known as likely to be harmful to the wounded was a prolonged lack of food or water. Freeman, Morison, and Sawyer found that loss of fluid from the body, resulting in a state of dehydration, excited the sympathico-adrenal system; thus again a vicious circle may be started, the low blood volume of the dehydrated condition being intensified by further loss through capillaries which have been made increasingly permeable.

The foregoing paragraphs have revealed how a persistent and profound emotional state may induce a disastrous fall of blood pressure, ending in death. Lack of food and drink would collaborate with the damaging emotional effects to induce the fatal outcome. These are the conditions which, as we have seen, are prevalent in persons who have been reported as dying as a consequence of sorcery. They go without food or water as they, in their isolation, wait in fear for their impending death. In these circumstances they might well die from a true state of shock, in the surgical sense—a shock induced by prolonged and tense emotion.

It is pertinent to mention here that Wallace, a surgeon of large experience in World War I, testified to having seen cases of shock in which neither trauma nor any of the known accentuating facts of shock could account for the disastrous condition. Sometimes the wounds were so trivial that they could not reasonably be regarded as the cause of the shock state; sometimes the visible injuries were negligible. He cites two illustrative instances. One was a man who was buried by the explosion of a shell in a cellar; the other was blown up by a buried shell over which he had lighted a fire. In both the circumstances were favorable for terrifying experience. In both all the classic symptoms of shock were present. The condition lasted more than 48 hours, and treatment was of no avail. A post-mortem examination did not reveal any gross injury. Another remarkable case which may be cited was studied by Freeman at the Massachusetts General Hospital. A woman of 43 years underwent a complete hysterectomy because of uterine bleeding. Although her emotional instability was recognized, she appeared to stand the operation well. Special precautions were taken, however, to avoid loss of blood, and in addition she was given fluid intravenously when the operation was completed. That night she was sweating, and refused to speak. The next morning her blood pressure had fallen to near the shock level, her heart rate was 150 beats per minute, her skin was cold and clammy, and the measured blood flow through the vessels of her hand was very slight. There was no bleeding to account for her desperate condition, which was diagnosed as shock brought on by fear. When one understands the utter strangeness, to an inexperienced layman, of a hospital and its elaborate surgical ritual, and the distressing invasion of the body with knives and metal retractors, the wonder is that not more patients exhibit signs of deep anxiety. In this instance a calm and reassuring attitude on the part of the surgeon resulted in a change of attitude in the patient, with recovery of a normal state. That the attitude of the patient is of significant importance for a favorable outcome of an operation is firmly believed by the well-known American surgeon, Dr. J. M. T. Finney, for many years Professor of Surgery at the Johns Hopkins Medical School. He has publicly testified, on the basis of serious experiences, that if any person came to him for a major operation, and expressed fear of the result, he invariably refused to operate. Some other surgeon must assume the risk!

Further evidence of the possibility of fatal outcome from profound emotional strain was reported by Mira in recounting his experiences as a psychiatrist in the Spanish war of 1936–1939. In patients who suffered from what he called "malignant anxiety" he observed signs of anguish and perplexity, accompanied by a permanently rapid pulse (more than 120 beats per minute), and a very rapid respiration (about three times the normal resting rate). These conditions indicated a perturbed state deeply involving the sympathico-adrenal complex. As predisposing conditions Mira mentioned "a previous lability of the sympathetic system" and "a severe mental shock experienced in conditions of physical exhaustion due to lack of food, fatigue, sleeplessness, etc." The lack of food appears to have attended lack of water, for the urine was concentrated and extremely acid. Towards the end the anguish still remained, but inactivity changed to restlessness. No focal symptoms were observed. In fatal cases death occurred in three or four days. Post-mortem examination revealed brain hemorrhages in some cases, but, excepting an increased pressure, the cerebrospinal fluid showed a normal state. The combination of lack of food and water, anxiety, very rapid pulse and respiration, associated with a shocking experience having persistent effects, would fit well with fatal conditions reported from primitive tribes.

The suggestion which I offer, therefore, is that voodoo death may be real, and that it may be explained as due to shocking emotional stress—to obvious or repressed terror. A satisfactory hypothesis is one which allows observations to be made which may determine whether or not it is correct. Fortunately, tests of a relatively simple type can be used to learn whether the suggestion as to the nature of voodoo death is justifiable. The pulse towards the end would be rapid and "thready." The skin would be cool and moist. A count of the red blood corpuscles, or even simpler, a determination by means of a hematocrit of the ratio of corpuscles to plasma in a small sample of blood from skin vessels would help to tell whether shock is present; for the "red count" would be high and the hematocrit also would reveal "hemoconcentration." The blood pressure would be low. The blood sugar would be increased, but the measure of it might be too difficult in the field. If in the future, however, any observer has opportunity to see an instance of voodoo death, it is to be hoped that he will conduct the simpler tests before the victim's last gasp.

E. E. EVANS-PRITCHARD

Witchcraft Explains Unfortunate Events

In few societies of the world does witchcraft assume a more focal interest than among the Azande, a large and complex group situated both north and south of the Sudan–Belgian Congo border. The Azande recognize witchcraft to be a psychic act, and they clearly differentiate it from sorcery, which concerns itself with spells and medicines. They believe that a person is a witch because of an inherited organ or substance called *mangu*. Mangu is oval, is located somewhere between the breastbone and the intestines, and is variously described as reddish, blackish, or hairy. A male can inherit mangu only from a male, a female only from a female. An autopsy may be performed to determine the presence or absence of mangu. Since an accusation of witchcraft may result in a stigma or a fine, or both, autopsies are sometimes carried out to clear a family name.

Witchcraft explains unfortunate events, but only if these events are unusual and inexplicable. An event which is clearly due to carelessness, sorcery, or a taboo violation would not be explained as being due to witchcraft. It is the uncommon event, the event which cannot be understood through normal causal interpretation, which is "obviously" due to witchcraft. The logic used in positing witchcraft as the cause of such strange events is impeccable. It is the basic premise, not the logic, which is at fault.

There are many plausible functions of Zande witchcraft. A man who is too successful, for example, one who finds three honeycombs in one day, is accused of witchcraft. Such accusations militate against any strong striving for success. The economic efficiency of the *kpolo* (extended family) is maintained by directing all conflicts outside the kpolo through accusations of witchcraft. A member of one's own extended family cannot be accused of witchcraft. The fact that the Azande have not engaged in feuds or raids may indicate the ability of accusations and angers against witches to absorb latent hostilities.

Most important however, is the usefulness of witchcraft in explaining why an event occurred. Science cannot tell us what happened, beyond mentioning the laws of probability. The Azande find both comfort and an opportunity to retaliate in their explanation of why an unfortunate and unusual event took place.

Reprinted in excerpted form from E. E. Evans-Pritchard, "The Notion of Witchcraft Explains Unfortunate Events," *Witchcraft, Oracles and Magic among the Azande* (Oxford: Clarendon Press, 1937), Part I, Chap. 4, by permission of the author and the publishers.

It is an inevitable conclusion from Zande descriptions of witchcraft that it is not an objective reality. The physiological condition which is said to be the seat of witchcraft, and which I believe to be nothing more than food passing through the small intestine, is an objective condition, but the qualities they attribute to it and the rest of their beliefs about it are mystical. Witches, as Azande conceive them, cannot exist.

The concept of witchcraft nevertheless provides them with a natural philosophy by which the relations between men and unfortunate events are explained and with a ready and stereotyped means of reacting to such events. Witchcraft beliefs also embrace a system of values which regulate human conduct.

Witchcraft is ubiquitous. It plays its part in every activity of Zande life; in agricultural, fishing, and hunting pursuits; in domestic life of homesteads as well as in communal life of district and court; it is an important theme of mental life in which it forms the background of a vast panorama of oracles and magic; its influence is plainly stamped on law and morals, etiquette and religion; it is prominent in technology and language; there is no niche or corner of Zande culture into which it does not twist itself. If blight seizes the groundnut crop it is witchcraft; if the bush is vainly scoured for game it is witchcraft; if women laboriously bail water out of a pool and are rewarded by but a few small fish it is witchcraft; if termites do not rise when their swarming is due and a cold useless night is spent in waiting for their flight it is witchcraft; if a wife is sulky and unresponsive to her husband it is witchcraft; if a prince is cold and distant with his subject it is witchcraft; if a magical rite fails to achieve its purpose it is witchcraft; if, in fact, any failure or misfortune falls upon any one at any time and in relation to any of the manifold activities of his life it may be due to witchcraft. Those acquainted either at firsthand or through reading with the life of an African people will realize that there is no end to possible misfortunes, in routine tasks and leisure hours alike, arising not only from miscalculation, incompetence, and laziness, but also from causes over which the African, with his meager scientific knowledge, has no control. The Zande attributes all these misfortunes to witchcraft unless there is strong evidence, and subsequent oracular confirmation, that sorcery or one of those evil agents which I mentioned in the preceding section has been at work, or unless they are clearly to be attributed to incompetence, breach of a taboo, or failure to observe a moral rule.

When a Zande speaks of witchcraft he does not speak of it as we speak of the weird witchcraft of our own history. Witchcraft is to him a commonplace happening and he seldom passes a day without mentioning it. Where we talk about the crops, hunting, and our neighbors' ailments the Zande introduces into these topics of conversation the subject of witchcraft. To say that witchcraft has blighted the groundnut crop, that witchcraft has scared away game, and that witchcraft has made so-and-so ill is equivalent to saying in terms of our own culture that the groundnut crop has failed owing to blight, that game is scarce this season, and that so-and-so has caught influenza. Witchcraft participates in all misfortunes and is the idiom in which Azande speak about them and in which they explain them. Witchcraft is a classification of misfortunes which while differing from each other in other respects have this single common character, their harmfulness to man.

Unless the reader appreciates that witchcraft is quite a normal factor in the life of Azande, one to which almost any and every happening may be referred, he will entirely misunderstand their behavior towards it. To us witchcraft is something which haunted and disgusted our credulous forefathers. But the Zande expects to come across witchcraft at any time of the day or night. He would be just as surprised if he were not brought into daily contact with it as we would be if confronted by its appearance. To him there is nothing miraculous about it. It is expected that a man's hunting will be injured by witches, and he has at his disposal means of dealing with them. When misfortunes occur he does not become awe-struck at the play of supernatural forces. He is not terrified at the presence of an occult enemy. He is, on the other hand, extremely annoyed. Some one, out of spite, has ruined his groundnuts or spoiled his hunting or given his wife a chill, and surely this is cause for anger! He has done no one harm, so what right has anyone to interfere in his affairs? It is an impertinence, an insult, a dirty, offensive trick! It is the aggressiveness and not the eeriness of these actions which Azande emphasize when speaking of them, and it is anger and not awe which we observe in their response to them.

Witchcraft is not less anticipated than adultery. It is so intertwined with everyday happenings that it is part of a Zande's ordinary world. There is nothing remarkable about a witch—you may be one yourself, and certainly many of your closest neighbors are witches. Nor is there anything awe-inspiring about witchcraft. We do not become psychologically transformed when we hear that someone is ill—we expect people to be ill—and it is the same with Azande. They expect people to be ill, i.e., to be bewitched, and it is not a matter for surprise or wonderment.

But is not Zande belief in witchcraft a belief in mystical causation of phenomena and events to the complete exclusion of all natural causes? The relations of mystical to common-sense thought are very complicated and raise problems that confront us on every page of this book. Here I wish to state the problem in a preliminary manner and in terms of actual situations.

I found it strange at first to live among Azande and listen to naïve explanations of misfortunes which, to our minds, have apparent causes, but after a while I learned the idiom of their thought and applied notions of witchcraft as spontaneously as themselves in situations where the concept was relevant. A boy knocked his foot against a small stump of wood in the center of a bush path, a frequent happening in Africa, and suffered pain and inconvenience in consequence. Owing to its position on his toe it was impossible to keep the cut free from dirt and it began to fester. He declared that witchcraft had made him knock his foot against the stump. I always argued with Azande and criticized their statements, and I did so on this occasion. I told the boy that he had knocked his foot against the stump of wood because he had been careless, and that witchcraft had not placed it in the path, for it had grown there naturally. He agreed that witchcraft had nothing to do with the stump of wood being in his path but added that he had kept his eyes open for stumps, as indeed every Zande does most carefully, and that if he had not been bewitched he would have seen the stump. As a conclusive argument for his view he remarked that all cuts do not take days to heal but, on the contrary, close quickly, for that is the nature of cuts. Why, then, had his sore festered and remained open if there were no witchcraft behind it? This, as I discovered before long, was to be regarded as the Zande explanation of sickness. Thus, to give a further example, I had been feeling unfit for several days, and I consulted Zande friends whether my consumption of bananas could have had anything to do with my indisposition and I was at once informed that bananas do not cause sickness, however many are eaten, unless one is bewitched. I have described at length Zande notions of disease in Part IV, so I shall record here a few examples of witchcraft being offered as an explanation for happenings other than illness.

Shortly after my arrival in Zandeland we were passing through a government settlement and noticed that a hut had been burnt to the ground on the previous night. Its owner was overcome with grief as it had contained the beer he was preparing for a mortuary feast. He told us that he had gone the previous night to examine his beer. He had lit a handful of straw and raised it above his head so that light would be cast on the pots, and in so doing he had ignited the thatch. He, and my companions also, were convinced that the disaster was caused by witchcraft.

One of my chief informants, Kisanga, was a skilled wood carver, one of the finest carvers in the whole kingdom of Gbudwe. Occasionally the bowls and stools which he carved split during the work, as one may well imagine in such a climate. Though the hardest woods be selected they sometimes split in process of carving or on completion of the utensil even if the craftsman is careful and well acquainted with the technical rules of his craft. When this happened to the bowls and stools of this particular craftsman he attributed the misfortune to witchcraft and used to harangue me about the spite and jealousy of his neighbors. When I used to reply that I thought he was mistaken and that people were well disposed towards him he used to hold the split bowl or stool towards me as concrete evidence of his assertions. If people were not bewitching his work, how would I account for that? Likewise a potter will attribute the cracking of his pots during firing to witchcraft. An experienced potter need have no fear that his pots will crack as a result of error. He selects the proper clay, kneads it thoroughly till he has extracted all grit and pebbles, and builds it up slowly and carefully. On the night before digging out his clay he abstains from sexual intercourse. So he should have nothing to fear. Yet pots sometimes break, even when they are the handiwork of expert potters, and this can only be accounted for by witchcraft. "It is broken—there is witchcraft," says the potter simply. Many similar situations in which witchcraft is cited as an agent are instanced throughout this and following chapters.

In speaking to Azande about witchcraft and in observing their reactions to situations of misfortune it was obvious that they did not attempt to account for the existence of phenomena, or even the action of phenomena, by mystical causation alone. What they explained by witchcraft were the particular conditions in a chain of causation which related an individual to natural happenings in such a way that he sustained injury. The boy who knocked his foot against a stump of wood did not account for the stump by reference to witchcraft, nor did he suggest that whenever anybody knocks his foot against a stump it is necessarily due to witchcraft, nor yet again did he account for the cut by saying that it was caused by witchcraft, for he knew quite well that it was caused by the stump of wood. What he attributed to witchcraft was that on this particular occasion, when exercising his usual care, he struck his foot against a stump of wood, whereas on a hundred other occasions he did not do so, and that on this particular occasion the cut, which he expected to result from the knock, festered whereas he had had dozens of cuts which had not festered. Surely these peculiar conditions demand an explanation. Again, if one eats a number of bananas this does not in itself cause sickness. Why should it do so? Plenty of people eat bananas but are are not sick in consequence, and I myself had often done so in the past. Therefore my indisposition could not possibly be attributed to bananas alone. If bananas alone had caused my sickness, then it was necessary to account for the fact that they had caused me sickness on this single occasion and not on dozens of previous occasions, and that they had made only me ill and not other people who were eating them. Again, every year hundreds of Azande go and inspect their beer by night and they always take with them a handful of straw in order to illuminate the hut in which it is fermenting. Why then should this particular man on this single occasion have ignited the thatch of his hut? I present the Zande's explicit line of reasoning—not my own. Again, my friend the wood carver had made scores of bowls and stools without mishap and he knew all there was to know about the selection of wood, use of tools, and conditions of carving. His bowls and stools did not split like the products of craftsmen who were unskilled in their work, so why on rare occasions should his bowls and stools split when they did not split usually and when he had exercised all his usual knowledge and care? He knew the answer well enough and so, in his opinion, did his envious, backbiting neighbors. In the same way, a potter wants to know why his pots should break on an occasion when he uses the same material and technique as on

other occasions; or rather he already knows, for the reason is known in advance, as it were. If the pots break it is due to witchcraft.

We must understand, therefore, that we shall give a false account of Zande philosophy if we say that they believe witchcraft to be the sole cause of phenomena. This proposition is not contained in Zande patterns of thought, which only assert that witchcraft brings a man into relation with events in such a way that he sustains injury.

My old friend Ongosi was many years ago injured by an elephant while out hunting, and his prince, Basongoda, consulted the oracles to discover who had bewitched him. We must distinguish here between the elephant and its prowess, on the one hand, and the fact that a particular elephant injured a particular man, on the other hand. The Supreme Being, not witchcraft, created elephants and gave them tusks and a trunk and huge legs so that they are able to pierce men and fling them sky high and reduce them to pulp by kneeling on them. But whenever men and elephants come across one another in the bush these dreadful things do not happen. They are rare events. Why, then, should this particular man on this one occasion in a life crowded with similar situations in which he and his friends emerged scatheless have been gored by this particular beast? Why he and not someone else? Why on this occasion and not on other occasions? Why by this elephant and not by other elephants? It is the particular and variable conditions of an event and not the general and universal conditions that witchcraft explains. Fire is hot, but it is not hot owing to witchcraft, for that is its nature. It is a universal quality of fire to burn, but it is not a universal quality of fire to burn *you*. This may never happen; or once in a lifetime, and then only if you have been bewitched.

In Zandeland sometimes an old granary collapses. There is nothing remarkable in this. Every Zande knows that termites eat the supports in course of time and that even the hardest woods decay after years of service. Now a granary is the summerhouse of a Zande homestead and people sit beneath it in the heat of the day and chat or play the African hole game or work at some craft. Consequently it may happen that there are people sitting beneath the granary when it collapses and they are injured, for it is a heavy structure made of beams and clay and may be stored with eleusine as well. Now why should these particular people have been sitting under this particular granary at the particular moment when it collapsed? That it should collapse is easily intelligible, but why should it have collapsed at the particular moment when these particular people were sitting beneath it? Through years it might have collapsed, so why should it fall just when certain people sought its kindly shelter? We say that the granary collapsed because its supports were eaten away by termites. That is the cause that explains the collapse of the granary. We also say that people were sitting under it at the time because it was in the heat of the day and they thought that it would be a comfortable place to talk and work. This is the cause of people being under the granary at the time it collapsed. To our minds the only relationship between these two independently caused facts is their coincidence in time and space. We have no explanation of why the two chains of causation intersected at a certain time and in a certain place, for there is no interdependence between them.

Zande philosophy can supply the missing link. The Zande knows that the supports were undermined by termites and that people were sitting beneath the granary in order to escape the heat and glare of the sun. But he knows besides why these two events occurred at a precisely similar moment in time and space. It was due to the action of witchcraft. If there had been no witchcraft people would have been sitting under the granary and it would not have fallen on them, or it would have collapsed but the people would not have been sheltering under it at the time. Witchcraft explains the coincidence of these two happenings.

GEORGE L. KITTREDGE

A Typical Case of Witchcraft in Old England

Witchcraft is not an exclusive property of primitive cultures. As anyone who knows about the witch trials of Old and New England will acknowledge, witchcraft has had an important place in the history of Western European civilization. The following article by Kittredge is not a study of the generic nature of functions of witchcraft; rather it is a specific study of Elizabethan witchcraft. To illustrate English witchcraft of this period, the author presents a detailed account of the charges against the Trevisard family in the years 1601 and 1602. Witchcraft is seen in cultural surroundings which the reader can understand and with which he can identify. This more than compensates for the fact that there is some information in this account that is tangential to a study of witchcraft. That the author is not an anthropologist is indicated by his misuse of the concept of culture and by rhetoric such as ". . . the abysmal pit of savagery."

The article insists that seventeenth-century English witches were accused of witchcraft because of their dangerous ill will— their power to injure goods, body, or life through supernatural means. It was through fear of this *maleficium* that Englishmen accused their neighbors of witchcraft. Any testimony as to an accused witch attending clandestine gatherings with devils, flying about on broomsticks, or brewing baneful potions were mere embellishment of the case; the cause for arrest was always the witch's power for evil.

Reprinted with abridgments from George Lyman Kittredge, *Witchcraft in Old and New England* (Cambridge, Mass.: Harvard University Press, 1929), pp. 3–22, by permission of the publishers. Copyright 1929, 1957 by the President and Fellows of Harvard College.

The accessible materials for a history of Elizabethan witchcraft are scattered and fragmentary. Much is lost, and much remains inedited. Yet we cannot hope to understand the prosecutions of the last sixty years of the seventeenth century, whether in

Old England or in New, until we arrive at a substantially accurate comprehension of what was thought and done at the close of the great queen's reign. It is not only the dogmas of the theologians, the tenets of the physicians, and the rules of the law that we need to know, but, above everything else, the beliefs and feelings of the populace—of the folk itself. For it is in this matter of witch-craft, if anywhere, that public opinion is supreme. The populace may, perhaps, be restrained by the more enlightened part of the community, but the so-called "governing classes" cannot prosecute with success if the populace does not approve. Witch-hunting never flourishes unless the common people are eager for it. It is to them that the officers of the law must look for testimony, and it is the jury of the vicinage that renders the verdict. Experience has taught, over and over again, how hard it is for the most skeptical judge to bring about an acquittal in a particular case when the neighborhood from which the jury comes is convinced of the reality of the crime in general.

In considering the tenacity of the popular belief on this subject, we should never forget that the essence of witchcraft is *maleficium.* The hatred and terror which a witch evokes is due to her will and her power to inflict bodily injury. Compacts with the devil, the suckling of imps, the violation of graves, the abominations of the Witches' Sabbath—these are mere incidentals, the paraphernalia of the art. They aggravate the offense, to be sure, and proof that a woman is implicated in such horrors may send her to the scaffold or the stake. But, in the last analysis, every witch is prosecuted, not because she amuses herself with riding a broomstick or because she has taken a fiend for a lover: she is hunted down like a wolf because she is an enemy to mankind. Her heart is full of malignity. For a harsh word, or the refusal of a bit of bread, she becomes your mortal foe. And her revenge is out of all proportion to the affront, for she is in league with spirits of evil who are almost infinite in strength. She sends blight upon your crops, the rot upon your sheep, the murrain on your cattle; your house takes fire; your ship is cast away. She visits you and your family with strange wasting diseases—with palsy, with consumption, with raging fever, with madness, with death. Witch trials are not prompted by theological hair-splitting, by

systems of devil lore, or by the text, "Thou shalt not suffer a witch to live." *These all come after the fact.* It is self-protection that incites the accuser. His cause is fear—and fear of bodily harm. The witch is a murderer, or may become a murderer on the slightest provocation. She cannot be spared, for there is no safety for life, body, or estate until she is sent out of the world.

Now the mere creed—the belief that witches exist and that they can work supernaturally to the injury and even to the destruction of their enemies—is the heritage of the human race. The Englishman of the sixteenth or seventeenth century did not excogitate or dream it for himself, or borrow it from the Continent, or learn it from his spiritual advisers whether before the Reformation or after. He inherited it in an unbroken line from his primeval ancestors. And along with it came another dogma, likewise of abysmal antiquity—the theory that all diseases are of supernatural origin. This dogma had, to be sure, been somewhat limited in scope as the shaman developed into the physician, but it was still extant and still vigorous. Every malady that baffled the doctors was ascribed to witchcraft, often by the doctors themselves; and all sudden or virulent or wasting maladies lay under suspicion. These things are truisms, but they are continually lost sight of by the investigators of English witchcraft. There is a constant assumption that such beliefs are abnormal, a persistent tendency to ignore the fact that it was rather a mark of exceptional enlightenment in popular diagnosis to look to natural causes than a mark of positive credulity or superstition to look to supernatural causes. In brief, the ordinary Elizabethan, in this essential particular—the doctrine of *maleficium* and its application to disease— had not yet emerged from barbarism. And it was the doctrine of *maleficium,* and nothing else, that made the witch creed terrible.

After a witch had been arrested, it is true, she often fell into the hands of the learned who asked her questions based on an elaborate system of demonology, and, when so interrogated, she often confessed strange things, which the industry of scholars may trace to foreign creeds or imported philosophies. Some of this erudite material, through the pulpit or otherwise, did certainly attach itself to the native and popular beliefs. And thus we may easily be led to fancy that judges, philosophers, divines—and even King James I—were to blame for the prevalence of English witchcraft in the seventeenth century. But such elaborations were merely incidental. They came into a particular case, if at all, only when the witch had once been cried out upon. Somebody falls sick, and the doctors cannot cure him; a child has hysterical fits and is grievously tormented. There are aged women in the village at whom we have long looked askance. They are foul-mouthed, perhaps, and prone to curse when we offend them; or they have laid claim to occult power, and have traded on the terror they inspire. They may even imagine themselves to hold intercourse with Satan, for they share the current superstitions and are not very strong in their wits. One of these beldames is mentioned as the bewitcher, perhaps because the patient's distempered fancy has seen a face and called a name. Then old rumors are revived: Smith's cattle died year before last, or Jones's little son. For there is ever at hand a huge mass of such latent evidence, all connected with the primitive doctrine of *maleficium,* and only waiting for a prosecution to bring it before the courts. When the trial begins, we may hear of compacts with Satan, of flights through the air, of sordid and hideous revels at the witches' Sabbath. But such things are mere confirmatory details. The essential point, the really efficient impulse, is always *maleficium*—injury to goods or body or life through supernatural means.

For England, the worst period of witch prosecution is, by common consent, the seventeenth century—the century of the Lancashire witches, of Matthew Hopkins and John Stearne, of Glanvil's *Saducismus Triumphatus.* The reign of James, we remember, covers exactly twenty-two years, from March, 1603, to March, 1625. In 1604 Parliament enacted a famous statute against witchcraft, usually called the statute of James I. The idea has been prevalent that the delusion was dying out at the close of Elizabeth's reign, and that the advent of the British Solomon gave it fresh vigor.

My purpose is to report an extremely interesting case of alleged witchcraft which occurred in Devonshire in 1601 and 1602, just before James came to the throne. This alone would make it significant enough. But it is still further noteworthy because it exhibits the phenomena in what we may call a pure

form. We have only the testimony of voluntary, and for the most part aggrieved, witnesses. There are no arguments, no confessions, no comments from the bench. There is nothing but the beliefs and experiences of the witnesses themselves, honestly detailed according to their lights. Hence the documents afford us a perfect picture of the witchcraft creed as held by the common people. And we find, as we should expect, that the sum and substance of it all was *maleficium*—injury to the property and the health of the victims, amounting even to ruin and death.

The documents consist of eleven "examinations," taken before a Devon justice of the peace, Sir Thomas Ridgeway, in 1601 and 1602. The manuscript was acquired by the Harvard College Library, in loose sheets, in 1905. The papers are the original records, each examination being written out by a clerk and signed by the magistrate. Most of them are in duplicate, both copies bearing Ridgeway's signature, and one is in triplicate. Sir Thomas Ridgeway was a man of first-rate intelligence, and is remembered as one of the Planters of Ulster. He was born about 1565. In 1600, shortly before the date of our examinations, he was appointed high sheriff of Devon and received the honor of knighthood. In 1616 he was raised to the Irish peerage by the title of Lord Ridgeway, and in 1623 he became Earl of Londonderry.

The scene of the trouble was Hardness, a village close to Dartmouth. Here lived Michael Trevisard, a fisherman, with his wife Alice and his son Peter. All were defamed for witchcraft, and suspicion against Michael and Alice was of long standing. The witnesses against them were persons of their own humble condition, belonging in Hardness or the vicinity. There is no trace of influence from the clergy or the gentry. It was the villagers themselves who appealed to the magistrate for protection. One witness speaks of a number of them as going to Tunstall, to the house of Sir Thomas Ridgeway, to make a complaint, and as meeting Alice Trevisard on the way back. Whether the accused persons were ever brought to trial we do not know, but it is clear that Ridgeway had these documents prepared for eventual use at the assizes.

The whole essential body of the witchcraft doctrine occurs, in a highly condensed form, in the examination of Alice Butler, of Hardness. This is in two parts, and may be quoted in full. The duplicate shows a number of variant readings, some of which I have inserted in brackets. I have modernized the spelling and regulated punctuation and capitals, and so elsewhere.

Devon Th' examination of Alice Butler of Hardness, in the County aforesaid, widow, taken before Sir Thomas Ridgway, Knight, the second of October, 1601.

1. This examinate saith that she, sitting at a door or bench in Hardness aforesaid about Christide last was twelvemonth with one Michael Trevysard of Hardness aforesaid, used these words: "I would my child were able to run as well as any of these children that run here in the street!" Then said Trevysard, "It shall never run!" "No? That's hard!" says this examinate again. "No, it shall never run," answered Trevysard, "till thou hast another," repeating the same words a dozen several times at the least with great vehemency. Whereupon this examinate, being much troubled in mind, especially upon a fear conceived by her before through the general bad report that went of him, departed from him. And the very same week the same child sickened, and consumed away, being well one day and ill another, for the space of seventeen weeks or thereabout, and then died.

2. This examinate further saith, that Peter Trevysard, son of the said Michael Trevisard, came to this examinate's house to borrow a hatchet, which Alice Beere, servant to this examinate, denied, to whom the said Michael answered [*var.* and he answered], "Shall I not have it? I will do thee a good turn ere twelve month be at an end." And shortly the said Alice Beere sickened, continuing one day well and another day ill, for the space of eleven weeks, and then died. In which case both the husband of this examinate and a [*var.* another] child of theirs fell sick, and so continued seventeen or eighteen weeks, and then died.

TH : RIDGWAY.

The regular fashion of commenting on such utterances as these is to cry out against the malicious folly of the accuser and to lament the hard lot of the accused. May I be permitted, for once, to abandon custom, and to express my sympathy with poor Alice Butler, who had lost her husband and two of her children by some strange wasting sickness, for which she had no name, and who could only revert to the primeval tenets of savage man in her attempt to explain so dreadful a visitation? Few utterances in any records are more artlessly pathetic.

To the student of English witchcraft the document is very valuable on account of the purity and simplicity of type which it exemplifies. *Maleficium* is the gist of the whole matter, and the process described is perfectly accordant to rule. We have the *damnum minatum* and the *malum secutum*. That is all. There are no complications whatever. There is not a trace of those foreign and learned elements that are often thought to constitute the bulk of the English witchcraft doctrine after the Reformation. There is no Black Man, no book to sign, no compact with Satan. There are no infernal revels, no fiendish lovers. In short, there is nothing that is nonessential. Alice Butler's evidence is precisely the kind of testimony that might have been offered against a witch in any land and in any stage of civilization, from the Stone Age to day before yesterday. It would be quite pertinent at the trial of a witch of Ashantee or Congo or the Australian bush. It exhibits the primitive and universal creed of the whole human race, preserved without the contamination of culture or education, and surviving every religious vicissitude, to the beginning of the seventeenth century, in one of the most enlightened countries in the world. Incidentally, it was quite enough to send Michael Trevisard to the scaffold if he came to trial and the jury believed Alice's story. Finally, nobody was to blame. The responsibility lay not upon the jurists or the theologians or the neighborhood: it was the burden of the human race as a whole.

An equally distressing case was that of Joan Baddaford. Alice Trevisard, it appears, had fallen out with John Baddaford, Joan's husband, and had "said unto him that he should go to Pursever Wood and gather up his wits." The precise meaning of this railing speech escapes me, but I fancy it was equivalent to calling John a scatterbrained fool. The phrase reminds one, though perhaps whimsically, of Pandar's contemptuous "Yea, hazelwood!" in Chaucer's Troilus. We may also adduce, tentatively, the common saying, "Your wits are gone woolgathering." It was manifestly possible, if the sequel should warrant, to interpret Alice's jeering words as a threat that John should lose his mind. The sequel did so warrant.

Within three weeks after [Joan alleged], the said John Baddaford made a voyage to Ro-

chelle, in the Hope of Dittsham, and returned
home again out of his wits, and so continued by
the space of two years, tearing and renting his
clothes, in such sort as four or five men were
hardly able to bind him and keep him in order.

On the occasion of the same quarrel, Joan
averred, Alice Trevisard had "further
threatened this examinate that within seven
years after she should not be worth a groat,
nor have a house to dwell in, nor a coat to
her back." And these threats came true, for
"whereas she had at that time the fee simple
of an house worth one hundreth pounds,
now is she worth nothing."

Let us bear in mind that the things to
which poor Joan Baddaford bore witness
must have been facts. Her insane husband
and her fallen fortunes were neither delusions nor superstitions. We cannot ridicule
or denounce; we can only pity. If Joan was a
bad logician—if she reasoned *post hoc ergo
propter hoc*—so do we, every day of our
lives. And as to threats, they are still ad-
missible as evidence against an accused
murderer.

The next section of Joan's examination
may seem trivial, but it was significant of
inveterate malice on the part of the alleged
witch, and thus was clearly pertinent. Some
three years before the date of this document,
Joan had asked a penny of Alice Trevisard
"for washing of clothes." Alice paid the
debt, but added that the penny should do
Joan "little good." Joan spent the coin for
drink, "and when the drink came, she had no
power to drink thereof, but the same night
fell sick, and continued so by the space of
seven weeks following." This is an excellent
instance of primeval magic. It is notoriously
dangerous to receive anything from a witch,
whether by way of gift or of payment. Joan's
inability to drink is a typical symptom. We
meet with it again in the Lancashire trials of
1612, as reported by Thomas Potts.

Joan Baddaford's experiences, or some of
them, convinced her that Alice Trevisard
was a witch. This, indeed, was the general
opinion in those parts. At all events, Joan,
with several of her neighbors, went to Sir
Thomas Ridgeway's house at Tunstall to lay
a complaint against her. On the way back,
Alice met them. A dispute ensued, as was
natural, and Alice said to Joan, "Thou or
thine may be burned before long be!" The
taunt, we may conjecture, was in answer to

some such remark as that Alice deserved to
be burnt for a witch. It is easy to imagine
the scene. The sharp-tongued Alice, a common railer and brawler, baited by a group of
villagers, all of whom believed that they had
suffered at her hands, was determined to
give as good as she got, regardless of the
risk that anything she said might be used
against her. The encounter was on a Mon-
day. From that day until the next Thursday
Joan Baddaford made no fire in her house,
whether from fear or from poverty we cannot tell. On Thursday, however, Joan began
to build a fire. She laid a few coals in her
chimney—brought from a neighbor's cot-
tage, no doubt—and turned aside to break
up some wood. Her child was sitting upon
the hearth. Suddenly she heard the child
scream, and saw that the band about his
neck was burning. Looking into his neck, she
found that the flesh was "burned to the
bone." Yet the child had not fallen into the
fire, but was "sitting on the hearth as before." Indeed, the fire was not kindled at all,
but the coals lay there just as she had put
them in. These facts Joan "presently shewed
to divers of the chief of Dartmouth, and
sought the best remedy she could, but found
neither salve nor anything else that did any
good, but within three weeks after the child
consumed and died." Here again is a grim
fact—superstition or no superstition—the
child perished miserably, and no one could
understand his disease.

The examination of William Tompson, of
Dartmouth, is uncommonly lively and pic-
turesque. William was a sailor. Some six
years before, he and a comrade (one William
Furseman, also of Dartmouth) had chanced
to meet Alice Trevisard upon the Force in
that town. It was about midnight. She was
dressed in a "long grayish cape down to her
foot," and wore a hood which covered almost all her face, "so that they took her for
some Seminary priest." They asked her
what she was doing in the street at that time
of night. Probably the sailors were not quite
sober. At any rate, they were uncivil, and if,
as William alleged, they mistook Alice for a
priest, we may be sure they were rough-
handed. An altercation followed—but we
will let Tompson tell his own story:

She fell out with them, and they were no
sooner gone from her than this examinate fell,
and was in great danger of breaking his neck.

Whereat the said Alice laughing, this examinate said to her, "Dost thou laugh at a shrewd turn [i.e., a bad accident]?" And then he struck her with a musket rod; whereupon she threatened this examinate, saying, "Thou shalt be better thou hadst never met with me!"

Vengeance was swift. Within three weeks after the *damnum minatum,* William Tompson went to sea. His ship caught fire—none knew how—and foundered. Out of twenty-five on board, only six were saved. As for William, he was picked up by a Portuguese vessel ("by a Portingalle") and carried to Spain, where he was imprisoned for a whole year. On his return Alice Trevisard said to Elizabeth Tompson, his wife, "Is he come home on life? He hath better luck than a good man! But it is no matter. He shall be there again within this twelve months." And the prophecy was fulfilled. In less than half a year William was captured once more, this time by the Spaniards, and he was kept in confinement for twenty-five months. "Elizabeth Tompson," adds the record, "being examined upon these last speeches of her husband's oath, affirmeth them to be true."

The next deposition in the manuscript is that of Christian Webbar. We will pass it over for a moment, to take up the examination of Christopher Honywell, since that, like William Tompson's, has to do with the sea. Christopher's deposition is unique. He was a lad of thirteen, and seems to have been playing about the harbor with another boy, Peter Trevisard, Michael and Alice's son, when the strange thing happened which tended to show that no member of the family was free from the taint of sorcery. The document is short and I shall append it entire. It would be quite charming in its naïve wonder if it were found in less sinister company.

Th' examination of Christopher Honywell aged thirteen years or thereabout, taken as aforesaid the 2 of October, 1601.

This examinate saith that about Whitsuntide last year he was with Peter Trevisard, son of the said Michael Trevisard, at a place at Hardness where the fishermen use to hang their nets; where the said young Trevisard did put off his father's boat, saying, "Go thy ways to New Quay, and go between the two lighters, and I will meet thee there." And farther this examinate saith that he ran with the young Trevisard to the New Quay presently after, and found the boat there between the two lighters,

the said quay being distant near two flightshoots from the place where the boat was so thrust off, as aforesaid, and not right against [i.e., opposite] the same place, but on one side, the said two lighters also being so near together that there was but room enough for the boat to go in.

TH: RIDGWAY.

The bearing of young Christopher's testimony should not be misconceived. It was merely confirmatory of the general proposition that the Trevisards possessed uncanny powers. To insist on its frivolity and hold up our hands in horror at the criminal folly of our forefathers in sending men and women to the gallows on such grounds is *parum ad rem.* No English witch was ever convicted on evidence like this, nor were such harmless feats of seamanship punishable at all under the law. There was plenty of serious evidence against the Trevisards, as we have seen. And with this caveat we may revert to the deposition of Christian Webbar, which is quite different from anything we have had before, and of very particular interest.

Christian was a widow in Hardness. She had let a tenement in the village to Michael Trevisard at a yearly rent of twenty-six shillings and eightpence. He had paid only six and eightpence, and Christian demanded the pound that was in arrears. "It shall be the worse for you!" was Alice Trevisard's response. Then followed a very curious piece of malignant sorcery. Alice cast water upon Christian's stairs. One Isabel Tozar saw it done, and warned Christian to

beware how she went up her stairs, which this examinate refrained accordingly for a space, in which mean space the said Alice Trevisard herself happened to pass through some part of the said stairs. And within one hour after, the said Alice, and this examinate also, fell grievously sick, and part of the hands, fingers, and toes of the said Alice rotted and consumed away, as yet appears by her.

The singularity of this piece of sorcery consists in the fact that the maleficent magic took effect on the witch herself when she heedlessly came under its influence. Alice fell into the pit which she had dug for another. Christian suffered too, on the principle of sympathy, but the virulence of the infection was felt chiefly by its contriver.

Joan Davye testified that her husband George had a quarrel with Michael Trevisard. Within a sennight thereafter Joan was sitting by the fire with a young child in her arms when the child leapt into the fire and was "very much scalded." When Trevisard heard of it, he said that he could help the child in twenty-four hours, if he wished, but that he would never do good to George Davye or any of his family. Davye seems to have been at sea at the time. At all events, the very week after, on "the same voyage" (so runs the testimony) "the said George Davye was hurt very grievously in shooting off a piece for pleasure." Joan also declared that one Henry Oldreeve had some differences with Trevisard, and that soon after Oldreeve lost twenty fat wethers in one week and "he himself languished and died."

William Cozen was another person who had fallen out with Trevisard. In this case the vengeance, though deferred, was nonetheless certain. Within a quarter of a year, William's daughter-in-law was sadly afflicted. Without a blow or any visible cause "her neck shrunk down between her two shoulders, and her chin touched her breast, and so remaineth still in a very strange manner." This accusation, like some others that we have already looked at, finds its parallel in the Lancashire case of 1612. Alison Device was the granddaughter of old Elizabeth Demdike, who had been a devotee of sorcery for fifty years and is described as "a general agent for the devil in those parts." Alison bore witness against both her mother and her grandmother; but she herself was implicated, confessed, and was hanged. Her offense was the laming of Abraham Law, a peddler. Abraham excited the compassion of the court by his miserable plight. Before his encounter with Alison Device, he

was a verie able sufficient stout man of Bodie, and a goodly man of Stature. But by this Devilish art of Witch-craft his head is drawne awrie, his Eyes and face deformed, his speech not well to bee understood; his Thighes and Legges starcke lame; his Armes lame especially the left side, his handes lame and turned out of their course, his Bodie able to indure no travell: and thus remaineth at this present time.

Alison was asked if she could cure the poor creature, and, though repentant, insisted that this was beyond her power. As in the case of Christian Webbar's infected stairs, the spells acted dynamically, when once they were set in motion, and passed quite beyond the witch's control. "The gods themselves cannot recall their gifts."

William Cozen's deposition closes with a bit of graphic horror which defies commentary in its simple impressiveness: "Further this examinate saith that Joan Cozen, wife of this examinate, being in her deathbed, requested this examinate that if Alice Trevisard, wife of the foresaid Michael Trevisard, did come to her grave, he should beat her away."

The evidence of Susan Tooker (or Turke) is very definite. It involves all three Trevisards, Michael and Alice and Peter their son. About four years ago, she declared, Alice Trevisard threatened her in plain terms: "I will not leave thee worth a gray groat!" Walter Tooker, Susan's husband, was just starting on a voyage. He lost both ship and goods, though the weather was fair. Further, it appears that young Peter Trevisard had been refused drink by Susan, whereupon he said "that it had been better to have delivered him drink." Next day Susan sickened, and she suffered for seven weeks. Finally, averred Susan, Mr. Martin, in the year of his mayoralty, set up a fold, or pound, at Hardness, to keep timber in. Michael Trevisard said: "Martin, hast thou made a fold? Wind and weather shall tear it up all!" And so it happened, nor could Mr. Martin keep his fold in place. "Since that time it hath been set up in the millpool, where no stormy weather can annoy it. Yet sithence it hath been plucked up very strangely, for it riseth up altogether, being timber of an exceeding great weight and bigness."

The trivial nature of some of the charges brought against alleged witches and wizards often excites the contemptuous mirth of the modern. But there is no sense or reason in such an attitude of mind. The importance of a piece of evidence should not be measured by the actual importance of the occurrence testified to, but by its significance with regard to the point at issue, that is, with regard to the question whether the defendant was or was not a practicer of "arts inhibited and out of warrant." Nobody scoffs at a prosecuting attorney nowadays for spending his energies over scraps of paper or thumbprints or scratched hands when a murder trial is in progress. It is just as absurd to jeer at our ancestors for troubling themselves about exploding ale barrels or butter that would not "come." The malice of a witch, according to the general hypothesis, may show itself in small things as well as in great. Jeering is poor business anywhere, but, if we must be contemptuous, let us concentrate our energies on the doctrine itself. No true philosopher will see anything ridiculous in the testimony of Joan Laishe, except the essential absurdity of the whole underlying thesis.

Joan, it seems, had once refused Alice Trevisard a halfpennyworth of ale, and Alice had retorted in the customary fashion. "That shall be a hard halfpennyworth!" and "I will not leave you worth a groat!" Two days after, one of Joan's ale casks "on the sudden leapt up of itself," and fell on the ground. The cask burst, and all the ale was lost.

Among the secondary causes of witch prosecution, the "healer," or white witch, regularly plays a conspicuous role. When consulted in sickness, she is quick to ascribe the ailment to evil arts, and is often ready enough to name the culprit. There need be no malice in this role of the white witch. She is simply in the same primitive stage of medical science which ascribes every malady to the personal enmity of a sorcerer. As to designating the guilty party, that is of course requisite. We must know who our enemy is if we are to resist or forestall his assault.

I have said that our Devon documents include all or most of the typical features of an English witchcraft case. Accordingly, the wise woman is not lacking. Her name was Blachford, Mother Blachford of Bridgetown. Alice Trevisard, it appears, called at John Denman's house in Kingswear, alleging that she had a letter for his wife. Mistress Denman was not at home. Alice showed a piece of paper to Denman's daughter, but the girl would not touch it, because she had heard that Alice was a witch. Soon after, one of Denman's children fell sick. Mother Blachford, to whom he resorted for medicine, told him that Alice Trevisard had bewitched the child. "When you go home," said Mother Blachford, "you shall find that Alice was at your house this morning with what she said was a letter." Denman inquired accordingly and learned what had happened in his absence. There is some vagueness at this point, which cross-questioning might have dissipated. It is obvious, however, that the paper was suspected to be a charm. At all events,

Denman declared that he never heard of the letter again. What became of the child is not stated. Probably it recovered, in spite of Alice's spell and Mother Blachford's remedy.

There is one more deposition in our manuscript—that of John Galsworthie of Hardness. It affords no novelties, but may be given in full to complete the record.

The examination of John Galsworthie of Hardness in the County aforesaid, husbandman, taken before Sir Thomas Ridgway, Knight, the eighth of April, 1602.

This examinate sayeth that about four years sithence, his wife demanded certain money of Alice Trevisard, the wife of Michael Trevisard of Hardness, which she owed her; whereunto the said Alice Trevisard answered, "I pray God that thou never prosper in body nor goods!" And never sithence did he, this examinate, or his wife, prosper in body or goods; for in very short time after that the said Alice Trevisard had spoken those words, he was taken lame in all his body and went by two crutches twelvemonth after. And further this examinate saith that his wife was never well in her body, sithence, but consumed away, and died at Christmas last past. And also this examinate sayeth that he had a sow great with pigs, which pigs rotted in the sow's belly within six weeks after his wife had demanded the money of the foresaid Trevisard, as aforesaid.

Th: Ridgway.

These documents are interesting enough as pictures of life and manners. But, as already suggested, their chief claim to our notice rests upon their date and upon the pure and unmixed form in which they exhibit the essential element in all witchcraft. The latter point needs no emphasis. The outcry against Michael Trevisard and his family was raised by the people itself—by the unadulterated, unsophisticated "folk," instigated only by its own primeval philosophy of *maleficium*. There were no social or political or theological complications. We have simply an upheaval from below, from the abysmal pit of savagery out of which the human race has had to struggle up. And such uncontaminated testimony, coming at this particular moment (in 1601 and 1602), is of very special consequence. If we are to comprehend the history of witchcraft in England, we must keep in mind, for this exact time, a clear idea of the intellectual condition of just that class to which Alice Butler and Joan

Baddaford and William Tompson and all the other complainants belonged. Queen Elizabeth died in 1603, and King James's witchcraft act was passed in 1604. There is a more or less general impression that this act was momentous, and that the accession of James gave an extraordinary impulse to

prosecution. If, as all will agree, our documents are typical of the state of popular feeling in 1601 and 1602, they offer an instant challenge to this idea. Anyhow, they make short work of the notion that English witchcraft was a theological importation from the Continent.

HENRY CALLAWAY

Divining by Familiar Spirits Among the Amazulu

Mediumship, or necromancy, is a common form of divination. The medium, or shaman, is possessed of extraordinary powers enabling him to discover hitherto unknown information by making contact with the spirit world. This unique power is often attributed to a familiar spirit or soul which either belongs to the medium or is somehow affiliated with him.

The following translated rendition of a first-person narrative by an Amazulu informant is a South African example of spirit divination. The South African medium, here called "doctor," dramatically utilizes some standard procedures of her art—ventriloquism, prior knowledge of the clients, the overhearing of the clients' unguarded conversation, and shrewd common sense—to enable her spirits to provide the clients with advice. In this example, a boy is suffering from a convulsive ailment. The spirits discover that an ancestral spirit is spitefully causing the boy's illness: the spirits decree that the location of the family's village must be moved; a goat must be sacrificed to the ancestor and the goat's bile poured over the boy; the boy must drink *Itongo* medicine. The treatment thus ranges from physical to social actions—from propitiation of wrathful ancestors to prescription of a medicinal potion.

Whatever the reason for the efficacy of the treatment, and the cure may have been wholly unrelated to the treatment, the boy did recover and the reputation of the medium must have risen correspondingly. Certainly not all spirit divination is as accurate as this case would indicate, but the inaccurate sessions are forgotten, while the accurate ones are remembered and extolled by persons sorely in need of answers to perplexing and worrisome questions.

Reprinted from Henry Callaway, *The Religious System of the Amazulu: Izinyanga Zokubula, or Divination, As Existing Among the Amazulu, in Their Own Words* ("Publications of the Folk-Lore Society," No. 15 [London, 1870]), pp. 361–374, by permission of the Folk-Lore Society. The account is given in the first person by an informant named Uguaise.

I once went to a person with a familiar spirit to inquire respecting a boy of ours who had convulsions. My father and brother and mothers and I wondered what was the nature of the disease, since it was a new thing. We saw at first sight that it was something about which we must inquire of the diviner. We set out and went to the person with a familiar spirit. We made obeisance, saying,

"Eh, friend; we come to you for good news." We waited. The doctor said, "Good day." We replied, saying, "Yes." She poured out some snuff, and took it; she then yawned and stretched, and also shuddered, and said, "They who divine are not yet here."

We remained a long time, and at length we too took some snuff; when we were no longer thinking of the reason of our coming, we heard that the spirits were come; they saluted us, saying, "Good day." We looked about the house to see where the voice came from.

The spirits said, "Why are you looking about, for we merely salute you?"

We said, "We look about because we cannot see where you are."

They said, "Here we are. You cannot see us. You will be helped by what we say only."

The voice was like that of a very little child; it cannot speak aloud, for it speaks above, among the wattles of the hut.

We replied to the salutation.

The spirits said, "You have come to inquire about something."

So we struck the ground.

They said, "That about which you have come is a great matter; the omen has appeared in a man."

We struck the ground, and asked, saying, "How big is the man in whom the omen has appeared?"

They replied, "It is a young person."

We struck the ground vehemently there, when we perceived that she had hit the mark.

They said, "I say the omen is a disease."

We smote the ground vehemently.

They said, "It is disease in the body of that young person." They said, "Let me see what that person is? It is a boy."

We assented strongly.

They said, "He does not yet herd. He is still small."

We smote violently on the ground.

They said, "But you wonder at what has occurred to him." They said, "Strike the ground, that I may see what that is which has occurred to the body of the little boy."

We struck the ground vehemently, and said, "We will hear from you, for you have seen that it is a little boy."

They said, "There he is; I see him; it is as though he had convulsions."

Upon that we smote the ground vehemently.

They said, "What kind of convulsions are they? Inquire of me."

We said, "We have nothing to ask about. For behold you know; you have already first told us. For it is proper that you should tell us to ask, if you were not going the right way; but as we perceive that you are going the right way, what have we to ask of you?"

They replied, "I tell you to ask, for perhaps I am going wrong."

We said, "No; you are not going wrong; you are going by the way which we ourselves see."

They said, "The disease began in the child when he began to walk. When he was very young, you did not see the disease—when he was a little infant; at length when he began to laugh, the disease had not yet appeared; at length he began to sit up, it not having yet appeared; at length he began to go on all fours, it not having yet appeared; at length he began to stand before he was affected by it; when he began to lift his foot from the ground to toddle, the disease came upon him. When you saw the disease, you saw it without expecting anything of the kind; he died in his mother's arms; his mother poured water on him when he was turning up his eyes; she uttered a great cry, you started, and ran into the house; when you entered he had again come to life. The mother said, 'You heard me cry; my child was dead. Do you not see he is wet? I poured water over him for some time, and therefore he has come to life again.'" The spirits continued, "I have now told you this; deny if what I say is not true."

We replied, "We can in no way dispute what you say; we have told you already that you were going by the right path."

The spirits said, "This disease resembles convulsions. You have come to me to know what is this disease which is like convulsions."

We said, "Just so, you say truly; we wish to hear from you, spirit; you will tell us the disease and its nature, that we may at length understand of what nature it is; for you have already told us the name of the disease; tell us also the medicines with which we shall treat it."

They replied, "I will tell you the disease. You are greatly alarmed because you say the child has convulsions; and a child with convulsions is not safe; he burns himself in the fire. I shall tell you what caused this disease. Just smite on the ground, boys, that I may understand if the child is the only son of his father."

We said, "Yes; he is his only son."

They said, "Smite the ground, that I may understand what relation you are to the child, since you come here to inquire."

We smote vehemently on the ground.

They said, "The boy is your brother. Smite the ground, that I may see if he is really your brother born of your own father, or not. Not so. He is not really the son of your father. Your fathers are brothers. He is your brother, because your fathers were brothers."

We smote the ground violently.

They said, "Smite, that I may understand which is the older of the two fathers. I say, boys, your own father is dead. Smite, that I may understand where he died. There he is; I see him; he died, boys, in the open country. He was stabbed with an assagai. By what tribe was he stabbed?"

We smote the ground vehemently.

They said, "He was stabbed by the Amazulu on this side the Utukela; that is where your father died, boys. The father of that child is your uncle, because he was your father's brother; he was the elder of the two."

They said, "Let me now tell you the disease which has attacked the boy. His disease is like convulsions; but it is not convulsions. And you are greatly alarmed because you think it is convulsions. But I shall tell you, for you will not again see him have a fit. I shall tell you what to do when you get home. Did you ever sacrifice for him? You have never sacrificed for him."

They said, "Let me just see where you live. You live among the Amathlongwa; that is the tribe where you live. Let me just see where you were born. You belong to the Amadunga. Just let me see, since you are here among the Amathlongwa, why you were separated from the Amadunga to come here. You quarreled with your own people, and so came here to the Amathlongwa. Smite the ground, that I may see if you have built your own village."

We smote the ground.

They said, "You have not yet built it. You live in the village of another; you have not yet built your own village on the hill. As for the boy, the disease attacked him in the village where you now are. Smite the ground, that I may see what relation the man with whom you live is to you."

We smote the ground.

They said, "He is your cousin on the mother's side. I see nothing wrong in the village of your cousin; he is good; I see no practicing of sorcery there; I see that the village is clear; you eat with your eyes shut, for you have nothing to complain of. What I shall tell you is this, it is the ancestral spirits that are doing this. It is not convulsions the child has. For my part I say he is affected by the ancestral spirits."

We wondered that we should continually hear the spirits which we could not see, speaking in the wattles, and telling us many things without our seeing them.

The spirits said, "I point out your ancestral spirits. When you reach home you shall take a goat. There it is, a he-goat; I see it."

We said, "How do you see it?"

They said, "Be silent, I will tell you, and satisfy you as to its color. It is white. That is it which has just come from the other side of the Ilovo from the Amanzimtoti. It is now a large he-goat. You shall sacrifice it, and pour its gall on the boy. You will go and pluck for him Itongo medicine. I see that Itongo; it says that your village is to be removed from its present place, and built on the hill. Does not the Itongo ask, 'Why has the village stayed so long in the midst of another?' It injures the lad, saying, 'Let the village remove from this place.' The he-goat you will sacrifice to your grandmother; it is she who refuses to allow the child to die, for your grandfather had been earnest to kill him, that he might die and be buried in accordance with his wish. I tell you this to satisfy you. I tell you that if the disease returns, you may come back to me and take your money. I tell you that this disease is caused by the ancestral spirit, because it wishes that your village should remove."

The spirits said, "Now I have divined for you; so give me my money."

We took out the money.

Then they said to her whose familiars they were, "Take it; there is the money."

They added, "I just take this money of yours. You will come and take it again if the disease returns. I say, it will never return again."

The woman with the familiar spirits sat in the midst of the house, at the time of full daylight, when we inquired of her; for the spirits cannot go alone when they are going to divine; their possessor goes with them. For if they wish to go they tell their possessor, saying to her, "Let us go to such a place," wherever they wish to go. The possessor of them cannot speak; she usually says little for she too inquires of the spirits, and says, "So-and-so, when you say so, do you tell the people who come to inquire of you, the truth?" In reply they say, they do tell the truth, and those who come to inquire will see it. She says, "Tell them the truth. They will come to me here if they come to take back their money; and if you tell them falsehoods, I shall give them back their money again. If you do not tell them the truth, I shall give it back to them." The spirits assent, saying, "You may give it back. For our parts we speak truly; we tell no lies."

So the possessor of the spirits took the money.

The spirits said to us, "Go in peace." We wondered when they bid us go in peace, without our seeing them. They told us to give their services to all our people at home. We said we would.

They said, "When you get home, do exactly what I have told you."

We replied, "Yes; we will do all you have told us to do."

So we went home. On our arrival we found the child better. As we were speaking with him, our father came into the house, and we said, "O father, we never had such confidence in a doctor. When we heard we said, 'The spirit has divined.' The spirits divined; they told us all things—our birth, and the order of our birth, and that he with whom we live is our cousin; they told us everything. They said the boy has nothing the matter with him that will kill him. They said we are alarmed, thinking he has convulsions; and we assented, saying, 'Yes, yes; we think he has convulsions.' The diviner denied, saying, 'No; he has not convulsions; he is possessed by a spirit. The spirit says that your village must be moved.' The spirits pointed out a white goat, and directed that it should be sacrificed for the child, and the village be moved; and they ordered us to pluck for him Itongo medicine, and sacrifice the goat. They said, if the disease returned, we were to go and take back our money."

Our father said, "O, they have divined, both as regards the disease and our relations with our cousin. We see they have divined. Why did not our ancestral spirits tell me in a dream that there was something which they wanted, instead of revealing themselves by coming to kill the child in this way? What prevented them from telling me in a dream what they complained about, instead of revealing themselves by coming to kill the child in this way, without saying anything to me first? These dead men are fools! Why

have they revealed themselves by killing the child in this way, without telling me? Go and fetch the goat, boys."

We went to fetch the goat from the house. We killed it, and poured the gall over the boy. Our cousin went to pluck the Itongo medicine; he squeezed the juice into a cup, and gave it to the boy to drink, and left the cup outside the kraal. The goat was eaten.

We worshiped the ancestral spirits, saying, "We shall see that the child is possessed by a spirit by his getting well, and not getting ill again; we shall say the spirit has lied if he is still ill. We shall see by his recovery; and shall then say, the spirits have told the truth. We do not understand why you have killed such a child as this. What prevents you from making old people ill? That is a good spirit which appears in dreams, and tells what it wants." Such were the words with which we addressed the spirits.

Our father said, "I shall now quit this place with my village in the morning, and put it in a place by itself. Why, when I thought I was living in peace, am I still obligated to be a wanderer? There is a site of an old village; I will examine it well. I shall now remove the village; may the new place be healthy and good, and this boy of mine be no longer ill. If he is still ill, I shall say he is not possessed with a spirit; and I will quarrel with the spirits, and say they have not divined properly." Our father said thus. He said, "I will look at the new site in the morning; let us go together, my cousin, and look at the new site, and inspect it well, for I say I am still a wanderer; for the ancestral spirits have killed me for staying here."

So he and his cousin went in the morning to inspect the site. They went to a place on the river Umathlongwa, and thoroughly inspected it and thought it good, and that it was a proper place for us to build on, for there was water near. They returned home.

In the morning we took our axes, and went to cut wattles and poles for the village. When we had finished cutting, the people of our village left that of our cousin and went to it, and then we completed it. The boy was not ill any more. It turned out in accordance with the word of the spirit; he was not ill again. At length he took out the calves at milking time, and herded the calves; at length he not only herded the calves and goats, but all the cattle—calves, goats, sheep, and cows. And at length he grew to be a man. His name is Umpini. He is now a diligent man. Next year he will milk the cows.

The name of the woman with the familiar spirits is Umkaukazi. It was not a man, but a woman. She saw us for the first time when

we saluted her on our arrival; for we too had been told by others that she was a great diviner. She lived on the Umtwalume by the sea, at a distance from us. It is a day and a half's journey from this.

E. E. EVANS-PRITCHARD

Consulting the Poison Oracle Among the Azande

The Zande practice of consulting a poison oracle is an outstanding example of the importance and elaboration that a form of divination may assume. With the Azande, the widespread African custom of divination by poisoning fowls reaches its apogee.

The Zande poison oracle is *benge,* a red paste which is related to strychnine. But benge is no mere poison—in fact, the Azande do not consider it to be a poison at all—it is a conscious supernatural substance. When fed to a chicken, benge does not kill the chicken because of its toxic qualities, but because of its willful decision to do so; therefore, before benge can make a decision as to killing or sparing a chicken, it must be apprised of all the relevant details. The Azande divine in many ways—their rubbing boards and termite sticks are frequently consulted—but for important queries and for legal decisions they consult benge.

Benge has a curious quality of killing about half the chickens it is applied to while sparing, for no apparent reason, the other half. Evans-Pritchard avers that neither the dosage of poison nor the health of the chicken seems related to the bird's survival. It is no wonder that benge is considered to be supernatural.

The Azande phrase their questions to benge in such a circumlocutory, ambiguous fashion that an unfavorable reply may be interpreted to be favorable, or some loophole may be found to justify asking benge a new series of questions leading to the desired answer.

The sociocultural involvements of the Zande poison oracle are considerable. As Evans-Pritchard indicates, control of the poison oracle is a paramount means by which old men assert their superordinacy over young men and over all women. The author also relates the institutional aspects of the poison oracle to marriage, status, and wealth. Furthermore, an unclean man—a man who has violated a taboo—cannot handle benge or even come near it. Politically, with the Zande kingship, the hegemony of the chiefs and subchiefs is buttressed by the belief that the chief's oracle is infallible; the Zande chief's oracle renders true legal decisions. In fact, the legal apparatus is based upon these oracular decisions.

The central importance of benge to the Azande is demonstrated by the class of questions put to it: a man may rhapsodically approach benge to discover the virtues of a potential wife, or he may venomously inquire as to the effect of his vengeance magic upon a witch, but he will not come to benge with trivial matters. The poison oracle provides important answers—answers about sickness, marriage, planting, adultery, and witchcraft. Through these answers, which are virtual assurances, much of the fear and uncertainty that attends the unknown and the future is removed.

Reprinted in excerpted form from E. E. Evans-Pritchard, "Consulting the Poison Oracle," *Witchcraft, Oracles and Magic among the Azande* (Oxford: Clarendon Press, 1937), Part III, Chap. 3, by permission of the author and the publishers.

The usual place for a consultation is on the edge of cultivations far removed from homesteads. Any place in the bush screened by high grasses and brushwood is suitable. Or they may choose the corner of a clearing at the edge of the bush where crops will later be sown, since this is not so damp as in the bush itself. The object in going so far is to ensure secrecy, to avoid pollution by people who have not observed the taboos, and to escape witchcraft, which is less likely to corrupt the oracle in the bush than in a homestead.

Oracle poison is useless unless a man possesses fowls upon which to test it, for the oracle speaks through fowls. In every Zande household there is a fowl house, and fowls are kept mainly with the object of subjecting them to oracular tests. As a rule they are only killed for food (and then only cocks or old hens) when an important visitor comes to the homestead, perhaps a prince's son or perhaps a father-in-law. Eggs are not eaten but are left to hens to hatch out. Generally a Zande, unless he is a wealthy man, will not possess more than half a dozen grown fowls at the most, and many people possess none at all or perhaps a single hen which someone has given to them.

Small chickens, only two or three days old, may be used for the poison oracle, but Azande prefer them older. However, one sees fowls of all sizes at oracle consultations, from tiny chickens to half-grown cockerels and pullets. When it is possible to tell the sex of fowls Azande use only cockerels, unless they have none and a consultation is necessary at once. The hens are spared for breeding purposes. Generally a man tells one of his younger sons to catch the fowls the night before a séance. Otherwise they catch them when the door of the fowl house is opened shortly after sunrise, but it is better to catch them and put them in a basket at night when they are roosting.

Old men say that fully grown birds ought not to be used in oracle consultations because they are too susceptible to the poison and have a habit of dying straight away before the poison has had time to consider the matter placed before it or even to hear a full statement of the problem. On the other hand, a chicken remains for a long time under the influence of the poison before it recovers or expires, so that the oracle has time to hear all the relevant details concerning the problem placed before it and to give a well-considered judgment.

Any male may take part in the proceedings. However, the oracle is costly, and the questions put to it concern adult occupations. Therefore boys are only present when they operate the oracle. Normally these are boys who are observing taboos of mourning for the death of a relative. Adults also consider that it would be very unwise to allow any boys other than these to come near their poison because boys cannot be relied upon to observe the taboos on meats and vegetables.

An unmarried man will seldom be present at a séance. If he has any problems his father or uncle can act on his behalf. Moreover, only a married householder is wealthy enough to possess fowls and to acquire poison and has the experience to conduct a séance properly. Senior men also say that youths are generally engaged in some illicit love affair and would probably pollute the poison if they came near it. It is particularly the province of married men with households of their own to consult the poison oracle and no occupation gives them greater pleasure. It is not merely that they are able to solve their personal problems; but also they are dealing with matters of public importance, witchcraft, sorcery, and adultery, in which their names will be associated as witnesses of the oracle's decisions. A middle-aged Zande is happy when he has some poison and a few fowls and the company of one or two trusted friends of his own age, and he can sit down to a long séance to discover all about the infidelities of his wives, his health and the health of his children, his marriage plans, his hunting and agricultural prospects, the advisability of changing his homestead, and so forth.

Poor men who do not possess poison or fowls but who are compelled for one reason or another to consult the oracle will persuade a kinsman, blood-brother, relative-in-law, or prince's deputy to consult it on their behalf. This is one of the main duties of social relationships.

Control over the poison oracle by the older men gives them great power over their juniors and it is one of the main sources of their prestige. It is possible for the older men to place the names of the youths before the poison oracle and on its declarations to bring accusations of adultery against them. Moreover, a man who is not able to afford poison is not a fully independent householder, since he is unable to initiate any important undertaking and is dependent on the good will of others to inform him about everything that concerns his health and welfare. In their dealings with youths older men are backed always by the authority of the oracle on any question that concerns their juniors, who have no means of directly consulting it themselves.

Women are debarred not only from operating the poison oracle but from having anything to do with it. They are not expected even to speak of it, and a man who mentions the oracle in the presence of women uses some circumlocutory expression. When a man is going to consult the poison oracle he says to his wife that he is going to look at his cultivations or makes a similar excuse. She understands well enough what he is going to do but says nothing.

The poison oracle is a male prerogative and is one of the principal mechanisms of male control and an expression of sex antagonism. For men say that women are capable of any deceit to defy a husband and please a lover, but men at least have the advantage that their oracle poison will reveal secret embraces. If it were not for the oracle it would be of little use to pay bridewealth, for the most jealous watch will not prevent a woman from committing adultery if she has a mind to do so. And what woman has not? The only thing which women fear is the poison oracle; for if they can escape the eyes of men they cannot escape the eyes of the oracle. Hence it is said that women hate the oracle, and that if a woman finds some of the poison in the bush she will destroy its power by urinating on it. I once asked a Zande why he so carefully collected the leaves used in operating the oracle and threw them some distance away from the bush, and he replied that it was to prevent women from finding them and polluting them, for if they pollute the leaves then the poison which has been removed to its hiding place will lose its power.

Occasionally very old women of good social position have been known to operate the poison oracle, or at least to consult it. A well-known character of the present day, the mother of Prince Ngere, consults the poison oracle, but such persons are rare exceptions and are always august persons.

When we consider to what extent social life is regulated by the poison oracle we shall at once appreciate how great an advantage men have over women in their ability to use it, and how being cut off from the main means of establishing contact with the mystical forces that so deeply affect human welfare degrades woman's position in Zande society. I have little hesitation in affirming that the customary exclusion of women from any dealings with the poison oracle is the most evident symptom of their inferior social position and means of maintaining it.

Great experience is necessary to conduct a séance in the correct manner and to know how to interpret the findings of the oracle. One must know how many doses of poison to administer, whether the oracle is working properly, in what order to take the questions, whether to put them in a positive or negative form, how long a fowl is to be held between the toes or in the hand while a question is being put to the oracle, when it ought to be jerked to stir up the poison, and when it is time to throw it on the ground for final inspection. One must know how to observe not only whether the fowl lives or dies, but also the exact manner in which the poison affects it, for while it is under the influence of the oracle its every movement is significant to the experienced eye. Also one must know the phraseology of address in order to put the questions clearly to the oracle without error or ambiguity, and this is no easy task when a single question may be asked in a harangue lasting as long as five or ten minutes.

Everyone knows what happens at a consultation of the poison oracle. Even women are aware of the procedure. But not every man is proficient in the art, though most adults can prepare and question the oracle if necessary. Those who as boys have often prepared the poison for their fathers and uncles, and who are members of families which frequent the court and constantly consult the oracle, are the most competent. When I have asked boys whether they can prepare the poison and administer it to fowls they have often replied that they are ignorant of the art. Some men are very expert at questioning the oracle, and those who wish to consult it like to be accompanied by such a man.

Any man who is invited by the owner of the oracle poison may attend the séance, but he will be expected to keep clear of the oracle if he has had relations with his wife or eaten any of the prohibited foods within the last few days. It is imperative that the man who actually prepares the poison shall have observed these taboos, and for this reason the owner of the poison, referred to in this account as the owner, generally asks a boy or man who is under taboos of mourning to operate the oracle, since there can be no doubt that he has kept the taboos, because they are the same for mourning as for oracles. Such a man is always employed when as in a case of sudden sickness, it is necessary to consult the oracle without warning so that there is no time for a man to prepare himself by observation of taboos. I shall refer to the man or boy who actually prepares the poison and administers it to fowls as the "operator." When I speak of the "questioner" I refer to the man who sits opposite to the oracle and addresses it and calls upon it for judgments. As he sits a few feet from the oracle he ought also to have observed all the taboos. It is possible for a man to be owner, operator, and questioner at the same time by conducting the consultation of the oracle by himself, but this rarely, if ever, occurs. Usually there is no difficulty in obtaining the services of an operator, since a man knows which of his neighbors are observing the taboos associated with death and vengeance. One of his companions who has not eaten tabooed food or had sexual relations with women for a day or two before the consultation acts as questioner. If a man is unclean he can address the oracle from a distance. It is better to take these precautions because contact of an unclean person with the oracle is certain to destroy its potency, and even the close proximity of an unclean person may have this result.

The owner does not pay the operator and questioner for their services. The questioner is almost invariably either the owner himself or one of his friends who also wishes to put questions to the oracle and has brought fowls with him for the purpose. It is usual to reward the operator, if he is an adult, by giving him a fowl during the séance so that he can place one of his own problems before the oracle. Since he is generally a man who wears a girdle of mourning and vengeance he will often ask the oracle when the vengeance magic is going to strike its victim.

To guard against pollution a man generally hides his poison in the thatched roof of a hut, on the inner side, if possible, in a hut which women do not use, but this is not essential, for a woman does not know that there is poison hidden in the roof and is unlikely to come into contact with it. The owner of the poison must have kept the taboos if he wishes to take it down from the roof himself, and if he is unclean he will bring the man or boy who is to operate the oracle into the hut and indicate to him at a distance where the poison is hidden in the thatch. So good a hiding place is the thatched roof of a hut for a small packet of poison that it is often difficult for its owner himself to find it. No one may smoke hemp in a hut which lodges oracle poison. However, there is always a danger of pollution and of witchcraft if the poison is kept in a homestead, and some men prefer to hide it in a hole in a tree in the bush, or even to build a small shelter and to lay it on the ground beneath. This shelter is far removed from human dwellings, and were a man to come across it in the bush he would not disturb it lest it cover some kind of lethal medicine. It is very improbable that witchcraft will discover oracle poison hidden in the bush. I have never seen oracle poison under a shelter in the bush, but I was told that it is frequently housed in this manner.

Oracle poison when not in use is kept wrapped in leaves, and at the end of a séance used poison is placed in a separate leaf-wrapping from unused poison. The poison may be used two or three times and sometimes fresh poison is added to it to make it more potent. When its action shows that it has lost its strength they throw it away.

Special care is taken to protect a prince's oracle poison from witchcraft and pollution because a prince's oracles reveal matters of tribal importance, judge criminal and civil cases, and determine whether vengeance has been exacted for death. A prince has two or three official operators who supervise his poison oracle. These men must be thoroughly reliable since the fate of their master and the purity of law are in their hands. If they break a taboo the whole legal system may become corrupted and the innocent be judged guilty and the guilty be judged innocent. Moreover, a prince is at frequent pains to discover witchcraft or sorcery among his wives and retainers which might do him an injury, so that his life is endangered if the oracle is not working properly.

An official consulter of a prince's oracles must also be a man of impeccable honesty, since he is given sole charge of many legal cases and tests of vengeance. He can ruin subjects of his master by fabricating oracular statements. Finally, the consulter of a prince's oracle must know how to maintain silence about his master's affairs. There is no offense more serious in the eyes of a Zande prince than "revealing the speech of the king's poison oracle." Hence the reason given for slaughtering a king's young servant at his graveside: "It is better they should die lest they reveal the speech of the king's poison oracle."

Each of these representatives of a prince supervises the oracle for about a month and then goes home to his wife and family and his place is taken by another. They need not prepare the poison themselves, though they may do so, but they supervise its preparation and bring from the prince the questions to which he desires answers, put them to the oracle, and inform the prince of its revelations. The actual preparation, in the old days, was generally performed by youths or boys who lived in a lonely hut in the bush at the back of the king's court where they had charge of the poison and the fowls. At the court of a great king like Gbudwe these boys were generally foreign captives, Moro, Munu, and so forth. At the courts of minor princes they were sons of his subjects who were acting as pages at court. Sometimes a small son of a king or prince would be in charge of these boys to see that they looked after the poison and fowls and kept the taboos. Today important princes in the old kingdom of Gbudwe maintain one or two oracle consulters, usually old men, and entrust to one of their own sons, or to a Zande boy whom they have proved worthy of trust, the task of preparing the poison. At the present time an important prince consults the oracles, either himself or through his representative, two or three times a week at least, but in the old days at the court of Gbudwe consultations were held daily.

All good oracle poison is the same, whoever owns, operates, and consults it. But its goodness depends on the care and virtue of owner, operator, and consulter. As the greatest precautions are taken with a prince's poison, it is considered more reliable than the poison of commoners. All *benge* is the same material, but people speak of "my *benge*" or of "so-and-so's *benge*," and they say that the poison of one prince is absolutely reliable while that of another prince is not so reliable. They make these judgments partly on the evidence of subsequent events which prove oracles right or wrong in their statements, and partly on the verdicts of the king's oracle, which is the final authority.

Control of the poison oracle in all legal cases gave the princes enormous power. No death or adultery could be legally avenged without a verdict from their oracles, so that the court was the sole medium of legal action and the king or his representative the sole source of law. Although the procedure was a mystical one it was carried out in the king's name and he was vested with judicial authority as completely as if a more commonsense system of justice had obtained.

Azande are very secretive about oracle séances and wish no one to be present when they are inquiring about private matters unless he is a trusted friend. They do not tell any one except trusted friends that they are going to consult the oracle, and they say nothing about the consultation on their return. It frequently happens when a man is about to set out from his homestead to the place of the oracle that he is visited by someone whom he does not wish to acquaint with his business. He does not tell the unwelcome visitor that he must hurry off to consult the oracle, but uses any pretext to get rid of him, and prefers to abandon the consultation rather than confess his intentions.

After this short introduction I will describe the manner in which poison is administered to fowls. The operator goes ahead of the rest of the party in order to prepare for the test. He takes with him a small gourdful of water. He clears a space by treading down the grasses. Afterwards he scrapes a hole in the earth into which he places a large leaf as a basin for the oracle poison. From *bingba* grass he fashions a small brush to administer the poison, and from leaves he makes a filter to pour the liquid poison into the beaks of the fowls; and from other leaves he makes a cup to transfer water from the gourd to the poison when it needs to be moistened. Finally, he tears off some branches of nearby shrubs and extracts their bast to be used as cord for attaching to the legs of fowls which have survived the test so that they can be eaily retrieved from the grass when the business of the day is finished. The operator does not moisten the poison till the rest of the party arrive.

There may be only one man or there may be several who have questions to put to the oracle. Each brings his fowls with him in an open-wove basket. As it has been agreed beforehand where the oracle consultation is to take place they know where to foregather. As each person arrives he hands over his basket of fowls to the operator who places it on the ground near him. A man who is used to acting as questioner sits opposite to it, a few feet away if he has observed the taboos, but several yards away if he has not observed them. Other men who have not kept the taboos remain at a greater distance.

When every one is seated they discuss in low tones whose fowl they will take first and how the question shall be framed. Meanwhile the operator pours some water from the gourd at his side into his leaf cup and from the cup on to the poison, which then effervesces. He mixes the poison and water with his finger tips into a paste of the right consistency and, when instructed by the questioner, takes one of the fowls and draws down its wings over its legs and pins them between and under his toes. He is seated with the fowl facing him. He takes his grass brush, twirls it round in the poison, and folds it in the leaf filter. He holds open the beak of the fowl and tips the end of the filter into it and squeezes the filter so that the liquid runs out of the paste into the throat of the fowl. He bobs the head of the fowl up and down to compel it to swallow the poison.

At this point the questioner, having previously been instructed by the owner of the fowl on the facts which he is to put before the oracle, commences to address the poison inside the fowl. He continues to address it for about a couple of minutes, when a second dose of poison is usually administered. If it is a very small chicken two doses will suffice, but a larger fowl will receive three doses, and I have known a fowl to receive a fourth dose, but never more than four. The questioner does not cease his address to the oracle, but puts his questions again and again in different forms, though always with the same refrain, "If such is the case, poison oracle kill the fowl," or "If such is the case, poison oracle spare the fowl." From time to time he interrupts his flow of oratory to give a technical order to the operator. He may

tell him to give the fowl another dose of poison or to jerk it between his toes by raising and lowering his foot (this stirs up the poison inside the fowl). When the last dose of poison has been administered and he has further addressed it, he tells the operator to raise the fowl. The operator takes it in his hand and, holding its legs between his fingers so that it faces him, gives it an occasional jerk backwards and forwards. The questioner redoubles his oratory as though the verdict depended upon his forensic efforts, and if the fowl is not already dead he then, after a further bout of oratory, tells the operator to put it on the ground. He continues to address the poison inside the fowl while they watch its movements on the ground.

The poison affects fowls in many ways. Occasionally it kills them immediately after the first dose, while they are still on the ground. This seldom happens, for normally a fowl is not seriously affected till it is removed from the ground and jerked backwards and forwards in the hand. Then, if it is going to die, it goes through spasmodic stretchings of the body and closing of the wings and vomits. After several such spasms it vomits and expires in a final seizure. Some fowls appear quite unaffected by the poison, and when, after being jerked backwards and forwards for a while, they are flung to the ground peck around unconcernedly. Those fowls which are unaffected by the poison generally excrete as soon as they are put to earth. Some fowls appear little affected by the poison till put to earth, when they suddenly collapse and die.

One generally knows what the verdict is going to be after the fowl has been held in the hand for a couple of minutes. If it appears certain to recover the operator ties bast to its leg and throws it to the ground. If it appears certain to die he does not trouble to tie bast to its leg, but lays it on the earth to die. Often when a fowl has died they draw its corpse in a semicircle round the poison to show it to the poison. They then cut off a wing to use as evidence and cover the body with grass. Those fowls which survive are taken home and let loose. A fowl is never used twice on the same day.

There is no stereotyped speech—no formula—in which the oracle must be addressed. As the content of each question differs from the others it is evident that this could not be the case. Moreover, the questioner addresses the oracle for more than five minutes, if it lives as long, in a flow of words. Nevertheless, there are traditional refrains, pieces of imagery, compliments to the oracle, ways of formulating a question, and so forth which occur in every consultation. After listening to a fair number of consultations I could easily have written out suitable addresses to the oracle on sickness, marriage, and other matters most frequently inquired into.

The main duty of the questioner is to see that the oracle fully understands the question put to it and is acquainted with all facts relevant to the problem it is asked to solve. They address it with all the care for detail that one observes in court cases before a prince. This means beginning a long way back and noting over a considerable period of time every detail which might elucidate the case, linking up facts into a consistent picture of events, and the marshalling of arguments, as Azande can so brilliantly do, into a logical and closely knit web of sequences and interrelations of facts and inference. Also the questioner is careful to mention to the oracle again and again the name of the man who is consulting it, and he points him out to the oracle with his outstretched arm. He mentions also the name of his father, perhaps the name of his clan, and the name of the place where he resides, and he gives similar details of other people mentioned in the address.

An address consists usually of alternate directions. The first sentences outline the question in terms demanding an affirmative answer and end with the command, "Poison oracle kill the fowl." The next sentences outline the question in terms demanding a negative answer and end with the command, "Poison oracle spare the fowl." The consulter then takes up the question again in terms asking an affirmative answer; and so on. If a bystander considers that a relevant point has been left out he interrupts the questioner, who then makes this point.

The questioner has a switch in his hand, and while questioning the oracle beats the ground, as he sits cross-legged, in front of it. He continues to beat the ground till the end of his address. Often he will gesticulate as he makes his points, in the same manner as a man making a case in court. He sometimes plucks grass and shows it to the poison and,

after explaining that there is something he does not wish it to consider, throws it behind him. Thus he tells the oracle that he does not wish it to consider the question of witchcraft but only of sorcery. Witchcraft is *wingi,* something irrelevant, and he casts it behind him. A single example of the kind of address made to the poison oracle is cited here. A man is consulting the oracle about the girl he wishes to marry:

"Poison oracle, that woman, since I intend to marry her, she is my wife? We will make a homestead together? We shall count the years together? Poison oracle listen, kill the fowl. It is not so, mine is the weariness of piercing boils—a man pierces a boil and can eat nothing—such is the affair of that woman. I must do without her and may not marry her, poison oracle listen and spare the fowl. It is not so, poison oracle, refuse to be deceived; you are marrying her to me, she is truly my wife. I will praise this verdict of yours, poison oracle, about that affair of my wife. Straight be your utterance like Zakiri, like Moragbondi. Poison oracle kill the fowl. It is not true, poison oracle, she is not my wife; although you are as fierce as Gbudwe if you see that that woman will not be my wife; poison oracle spare the fowl. Poison oracle do not make the fowl cry out on my account, make it cry out for that woman, the daughter of so-and-so. The poison oracle sees her that she is my wife; I will count the years together with her, ten years I will praise far off your verdict, poison oracle, and say that the poison oracle told me about that wife of mine and on account of its verdict we count our years together today—if I shall speak thus, poison oracle you slay the fowl. Ah! it is not true, poison oracle, for she may not be my wife; you are the poison oracle and though you may be as fierce as Gbudwe, poison oracle you spare the fowl since I may not marry her. Poison oracle spare the fowl."

The poison oracle considers the question and is sure that it is his wife. The poison oracle goes with a roar, as goes a Banginzo in a canoe, drags out the penis of the fowl like that of a powerful male beast, overwhelms the fowl, and kills it. The poison oracle ruffles its feathers. They have handed it over to the oracle, saying that it is the oracle which must settle the case, it will recover only if the oracle permits. The poison oracle cuts the fowl *zarrrrrr;* it sees that the affair of the woman is good and therefore kills it.

Such texts as the above are very difficult to translate as there is a special phraseology in speaking to the poison oracle and in describing its action on fowls. The imagery used is specially noteworthy. It is seldom that the oracle is addressed without analogies and circumlocutions. Thus in asking whether a man has committed adultery one frames the question in some such manner as follows:

"Poison oracle, poison oracle, you are in the throat of the fowl. That man his navel joined her navel; they pressed together; he knew her as woman and she knew him as man. She has drawn *badiabe* (a leaf used as a towel) and water to his side (for ablutions after intercourse); poison oracle hear it, kill the fowl."

While the fowl is undergoing its ordeal men are attentive to their behavior. A man must tighten and spread out his bark-cloth loin-covering lest he expose his genitals, as when he is sitting in the presence of a prince or parent-in-law. Men speak in a low voice as they do in the presence of superiors. Indeed, all conversation is avoided unless it directly concerns the procedure of consultation. If anyone desires to leave before the proceedings are finished he takes a leaf and spits on it and places it where he has been sitting. I have seen a man who rose for a few moments only to catch a fowl which had escaped from its basket place a blade of grass on the stone upon which he had been sitting. Spears must be laid on the ground and not planted upright in the presence of the poison oracle. Azande are very serious during a séance, for they are asking questions of vital importance to their lives and happiness.

Leaving out of consideration all peculiar circumstances and interpretations, the system of question and answer in oracle consultations is simple. There are two tests, the *bambata simi,* or first test, and the *gingo,* or second test. If a fowl dies in the first test then another fowl must survive the second test, and if a fowl survives the first test another fowl must die in the second test for the judgment to be accepted as valid. Generally the question is so framed that the oracle will have to kill a fowl in the first test and spare another fowl in the corroborative test to give an affirmative reply, and to spare a fowl in the first test and kill another fowl in the corroborative test to give a negative reply; but this is not invariably the case, and questions are sometimes framed in an opposite manner. The killing of a fowl does not give in itself a positive or negative answer. That depends upon the form of the question. I will illustrate the usual procedure by an example:

A

First Test. If X has committed adultery poison oracle kill the fowl. If X is innocent poison oracle spare the fowl. The fowl dies.

Second Test. The poison oracle has declared X guilty of adultery by slaying the fowl. If its declaration is true let it spare this second fowl. The fowl survives.

Result. A valid verdict. X is guilty.

B

First Test. If X has committed adultery poison oracle kill the fowl. If X is innocent poison oracle spare the fowl. The fowl lives.

Second Test. The poison oracle has declared X innocent of adultery by sparing the fowl. If its declaration is true let it slay the second fowl. The fowl dies.

Result. A valid verdict. X is innocent.

C

First Test. If X has committed adultery poison oracle kill the fowl. If X is innocent poison oracle spare the fowl. The fowl dies.

Second Test. The poison oracle has declared X guilty of adultery by slaying the fowl. If its declaration is true let it spare the second fowl. The fowl dies.

Result. The verdict is contradictory and therefore invalid.

D

First Test. If X has committed adultery poison oracle kill the fowl. If X is innocent poison oracle spare the fowl. The fowl survives.

Second Test. The poison oracle has declared X innocent of adultery by sparing the fowl. If its declaration is true let it slay the second fowl. The fowl survives.

Result. The verdict is contradictory and therefore invalid.

In the two tests one fowl must die and the other must live if the verdict is to be accepted as valid. If both live or both die the verdict is invalid and the oracle must be consulted on the matter a second time on another occasion. If the supply of oracle poison is sufficient the two tests may be made during the same séance, especially when the matter is important and urgent. Very often, however, a test is not completed at a single séance, for one of these reasons.

(1) The other part of the test may have been carried out previously or may be carried out at a future séance. Sometimes a

long interval elapses between two tests because the first one is considered sufficient justification for commencing an undertaking, but a second test has to be made before the undertaking is far advanced, e.g., a man is betrothed to a girl and begins to pay bride-spears to her father on the authority of a single test and leaves the corroborative test till months later. But the girl will not come to live with him permanently till both tests have been made. (2) One of the lesser oracles may have been consulted earlier so that a single verdict of the poison oracle is therefore regarded as an oracular confirmation. (3) Often Azande consider a single test sufficient, especially if the oracle gives its answer decisively by killing the fowl without hesitation. They are able to economize their oracle poison by this means. For example: a man who is well consults the oracle at the beginning of a new month and is assured that he will not fall sick during it. He is satisfied with this assurance and does not waste poison by asking the oracle to confirm what it has unequivocally stated. (4) Many confirmations of verdicts are contained in the oracle's answers to other questions, e.g., a man asks whether a witch will die if a certain kinsman observes taboos of vengeance magic. The oracle says "Yes." He then asks whether the kinsman will die during the period he is under taboos. If the oracle says "No" it confirms its previous verdict because the life of the kinsman is bound up with the accomplishment of vengeance. (5) Sometimes a single fowl is used to confirm different questions. If in answer to two different questions the oracle killed two fowls it may then be asked to spare a third fowl to confirm both its verdicts at the same time. (6) When a serious matter is not at stake Azande are sometimes content merely to know that the oracle is functioning correctly, and being assured of this, are prepared to accept its single statements and to dispense with repetitions of judgment. Thus five unconnected questions may be asked in a séance. The oracle spares fowls in answer to the first four questions and then kills a fowl in answer to the fifth question. This shows that the action of the particular bundle of poison is discriminating and therefore its first four verdicts may be assumed to be valid.

But two tests are essential in any question that concerns the relations between two persons, especially when they involve legal issues.

WILLIAM A. LESSA

Somatomancy: Precursor of the Science of Human Constitution

Humanistic writings abound in source materials for the social scientist, who unfortunately has shown a marked tendency to neglect them. An effort is made in this article to utilize humanistic data, especially as they relate to divination during the period of the Renaissance in Europe.

It was the renowned Jacob Burckhardt who, in his *Renaissance in Italy* (1878), stressed the emergence of the individual during the tumultuous change of this epoch. Others have expanded upon the implications of his thesis, a notable case being that of Erich Fromm, who is his *Escape from Freedom* (1941) suggests that the freedom that accompanies individualism may bring with it such uneasiness that in desperation people will seek security in the acceptance of dangerously authoritarian political systems.

The new individualism of the Renaissance suffered from concomitant loss of the traditional, dogmatic patterns of belief and action that had allayed some of the fears of medieval man. It is the contention of the present article that the insecurities of Renaissance individualism were commonly alleviated by body divi-

Reprinted from *Scientific Monthly*, LXXV (December, 1952), 355–365, by permission of the American Association for the Advancement of Science.

nation, particularly by the sort of body divination which allied itself with astrology. The inference is that the role of divination has been in all times and in all places the mitigation of anxiety about the unknown, and that where individuals have been shaken loose from their customary stability and security, divination will flourish.

From ancient times to the present, man has attempted to tear aside the veil that hides the unknown. In the days before there was any reliable body of science, his efforts to know himself and the world about him took forms which today seem both naïve and fantastic. In some instances, these bizarre pseudo sciences contained a germ of truth— a germ that was later to find new growth in a legitimate scientific field. Such an instance is offered by the pseudo sciences of somatomancy, a new term hereby proposed for all kinds of divination from the human body, whether involving phrenology, chiromancy, or various forms of astral physiognomy. Although these once flourishing arts have long since fallen into complete charlatanry and in some cases into oblivion, they were nevertheless among the forerunners of the modern science of human constitution, or "biotypology," as it is sometimes called.

Yet somatomancy has gone virtually unrecognized as a special and important effort on the part of man to pry loose the secrets of nature pertaining to his destiny and inner being. It deserves study along with its sister forms of divination, such as pyromancy, divination by flames; lithomancy, divination by stones; and hydromancy, divination by water. It must be made clear at the outset, however, that this discussion is not intended to demonstrate that human constitution is a form of divination. Biotypology is a branch of legitimate science; somatomancy is a form of supernaturalism. But, just as parallels can be drawn between magic and science (without, however, the mistaken equating of one with the other which Frazer ascribed to primitives), so can certain analogies be seen between somatomancy and biotypology.

An interesting thing about somatomancy is that it is absent among primitive peoples, being found only among higher cultures, in which it has a long history. This may seem curious upon first consideration, but there appear to be good reasons, implicit in the social and psychological factors involved in somatomancy, for this anomaly.

There are two main types of body divination. The first may be called *astral somatomancy;* it is more mystical, divinatory, and supernaturally oriented than the second type, termed *natural somatomancy.* The logic behind astral somatomancy establishes a linkage between body features and astrology. Astrologers believe, of course, that earth and sky are intimately related, and that the celestial governs the terrestrial. The pertinence of this doctrine to physiognomy (the art of discovering mental and moral characteristics from physical appearance) is that sidereal physiognomists maintain that every man is marked by signs which reveal his destiny, temperament, and character. This approach has many manifestations, a unique one of which is that man is merely the universe in miniature. All things contained in the universe, or macrocosm, are correspondingly represented in man, the microcosm. Saunders, the author of the first work in English (1653) on neomancy (divination from moles on the body), advanced an extensive argument to show that the position of markings on an individual has a bearing on the individual's relationship to the universe. Speaking of such markings, Saunders said, "It is a certain thing that every Humane Creature when it is born hath in some part of the body the mark of the Sign or Planet that governed at the hour and minute of their Conception and Nativity, which marks are in the parts of the body which are referred to those signs and Planets."

Astral physiognomy has many departments, depending upon the part of the body used in divination. Sometimes the whole body is correlated, part by part, with the stars (Fig. 1). Oftentimes it is the face that is scrutinized by the astral method (Fig. 2). But the most popular form of astral somatomancy is divination from the palm, or chiromancy. Here it is chiefly the lines and the seven "mounts" of the palm that are studied. The mounts are the small protuberances at the base of the fingers and thumb and along the outer edge of the palm (Fig. 3), and the characteristics of the individual

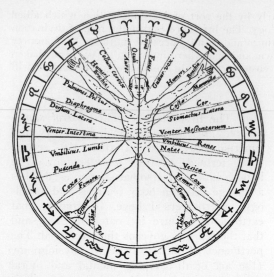

FIG. 1. Body astrophysiognomy. The relation of the body to the signs of the zodiac. (Fludd, *Microcosmi Historia* [1619].)

are discerned from the degree to which these mounts are developed. The method of assigning characteristics to the individual mounts offers a fascinating example of an anthropomorphic circle employed generally in astral somatomancy. Originally certain human characteristics were ascribed to various Greek and Roman gods. Later, these characteristics were transferred to the planets named for those gods. Later still, the characteristics found their way into general astrological doctrine and, finally, by adoption, back to man himself by being assigned

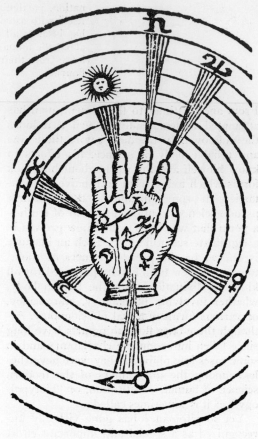

FIG. 3. Chiromancy. The relation of the palm to the planets. (Sicler, *La Chiromance Royale et Nouvelle* [1666].)

to specific parts of the human body, such as bumps on the palm (Fig. 4).

Thus, by this circuitous path, the mount of Jupiter at the base of the index finger indicates religion, ambition, love of honor, and felicity. Should this mount be very highly developed, it indicates an excess of the qualities represented—i.e., superstition, pride, and a tendency toward madness. If the mount is very weak or absent, the qualities suffer accordingly, becoming irreligion, shyness, sadness, and the lack of dignity. The other mounts are similarly read for their supposed significance.

Since the lines in the palm are not ordinarily linked with the stars, this part of chiromancy is not strictly astral. There are four principal lines—heart, life, head, and fortune. If they are deep and continuous, they indicate strength of the aspect with which they are involved; whereas if they are weak or broken, they are usually unfavorable.

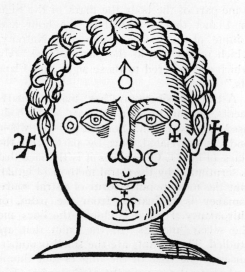

FIG. 2. Facial astrophysiognomy. The relation of the face to the planets. (Belot, *Oeuvres* [1654].)

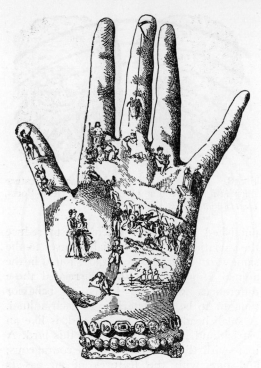

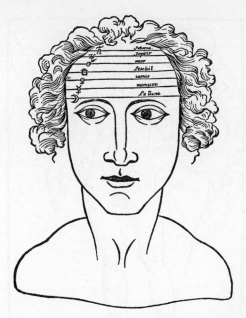

FIG. 6. Metoposcopy. The relation of the forehead to the planets. (Cardano, *Metoposcopia* [1658].)

FIG. 4. A pictorial representation of the mythological indications to be found in the hand. (Cerchiari, *Chiromanzie e Tatuaggio* [1903].)

In chiromancy, character divination of the individual is mixed with prophecy of his future prospects (Fig. 5), although some modern practitioners attempt to give the art a more "scientific" flavor by emphasizing the hand as a mirror of the traits of the individual rather than as a key to his fate.

In another form of astral somatomancy, metoposcopy, the lines of the forehead are studied in a manner analogous to the lines of the palm. Metoposcopy is of far greater recency than chiromancy, having been invented in the Renaissance, whereas chiromancy is at least 5,000 years old in China, where the reading of the feet, or pedomancy, was also practiced. The founder of metopos-

FIG. 5. Fate and the palm. An illustration from the earliest printed book on somatomancy. (Hartlieb, *Die Kunst Chiromantia* [1448].)

copy was Cardano, a famous and controversial Italian mathematician, philosopher, and physician. He mapped out the forehead into various regions, with each zone denoting a planet (Fig. 6). (As if in anticipation of modern basal metabolism technique, he decreed that the forehead must be examined in the morning before the subject had had breakfast.)

Mention has already been made of neomancy, or divination by moles. According to one convenient doctrine of this art, body moles are duplicated in the face according to their position on the body (Fig. 7), making it unnecessary for the neomancer to examine the body *in toto* and thus avoiding embarrassment to the client. We see here an example of the fact that, although body diviners frequently view the body in terms of its discrete parts, each part is not necessarily studied as if it were a self-contained system, but is correlated with other parts. Of this we shall say more later.

If space permitted it could be shown that practically every external part of the body has been studied by astral physiognomists, but perhaps it will be sufficient to name two more: ophthalmoscopy, which divines from the eyes, and onychomancy, which divines from the fingernails.

The second grand division of somatomancy, called "natural physiognomy,"

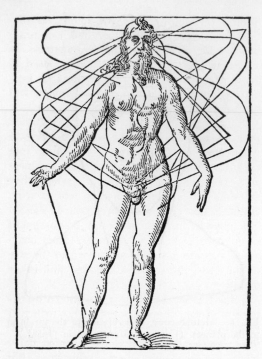

FIG. 7. Functional interrelationships. An early drawing showing the localities on the body that correspond to the localities of the face where moles are found. The figure is gynandromorphic. (Della Porta, *Della Fisonomia dell' Huomo* [1615].)

FIG. 8. Theriologic physiognomy. Early caricature illustrating the leonine type of man. (Della Porta, *De Humana Physiognomonia* [1601].)

makes no use of astrology. It is not particularly occult nor unduly mysterious. However, it is unquestionably divinatory, differing from astral somatomancy chiefly in its emphasis on uncovering the secrets of mental and moral character rather than in predicting the course of events affecting the individual. Natural physiognomy is of course of great antiquity, some evidences of it being found in the Bible.

The earliest workers in systematic natural physiognomy labored to show that within the human body there are signs indicative of a "sympathy" with other animals. Because the qualities of animals are easily understood (so the reasoning went), it is easy to assess the obscure inner nature of individual men by seeking the animal signs which mark them. The name "theriologic physiognomy" is given to divination employing such comparisons with animals. This was the favorite approach of the ancient Greeks, and it later received elaboration at the hands of Della Porta, the most honored of all natural physiognomists of the Renaissance (Figs. 8 and 9).

In Della Porta's chief work on the subject,

published in 1569, he attempted to reduce the variations in man's facial features to the same sort of differences as those found in the animal kingdom. He then correlated these differences with the kinds of behavior thought to be characteristic of each animal. A small-headed man, he believed, is like an ostrich and very often acts like this bird. A man with the face of a lion is courageous, and one with the features of an ass is stupid, and so on. It is interesting to note that here again we have anthropomorphism turned back upon itself, with the qualities traditionally bestowed by man upon animals reapplied to man himself in terms of animal features.

Another and altogether different kind of premise is sometimes employed in natural physiognomy. It is the concept which in recent years has been called the doctrine of the *homme moyen,* or "average man," and was much developed by the great Belgian mathematician and astronomer Quetelet. Without going into a description of the modern version of the premise, we can say that its basic tenet is the belief in an ideal: the mental-moral-aesthetic man who is what he is be-

FIG. 9. Theriologic physiognomy. Early caricature illustrating the asinine type of man. (Della Porta, *De Humana Physiognomonia* [1601].)

cause he manifests the least deviation from the average in the population. Individuals who depart from this ideal are, in proportion to their deviation, inferior in mentality, morality, and appearance.

A third type of logical approach may be termed the pseudo-inductive method. Mantegazza has spoken derisively of it in the following words: "A woman with a dimple in her chin has been found to be an angel, and hence it is concluded that all who have this dear dimple must be well-intentioned people." This method, which may also be called the single-case method, was used extensively in the more recent works on physiognomical endeavor. One of the disciples of Franz Joseph Gall, founder of phrenology, told how Gall had found the brain's "area of caution." He had chanced to stand behind two Viennese noted for their inability to make up their minds. Noting that both had heads which were rather narrow in a certain dimension, Gall at once decided that he had found the secret.

The fourth and final approach in natural physiognomy has no logical basis at all and may be termed the intuitive method. It is assumed by the physiognomist that because of a quasi-mystical power he is able automatically to divine the secrets of nature by scrutinizing the physiognomy of a man. This technique is employed by all the amateur character readers in the world, who can "size up a man the minute I see him." Perhaps this method, unformulated as it may be, is much older than the theriologic approach used by Aristotle, Zophirus, Hippocrates, and other men of the ancient world. But few physiognomists would admit that they relied upon it, even though in some ways it has less to condemn it than many of the more sophisticated approaches used in astral and natural physiognomy.

The varieties of natural physiognomy are rather like those of astral physiognomy, depending on what part of the body is studied. Generally, it refers to the face alone, and in modern usage the term "physiognomy" is synonymous with the face. Sometimes various parts of the body are examined, as in astral somatomancy; and at times the terminology is the same as in the astral version. Occasionally, to avoid astronomical connotations, the natural physiognomists use or coin special expressions, such as D'Arpentigny did when he spoke of "chirognomy," the natural physiognomy of the hands, as distinct from chiromancy, which had been practically taken over by astrophysiognomists. In a similar way "nevology" has been used to avoid the astrological implications of neomancy, although it, too, used moles and birthmarks for interpretation.

Natural ophthalmoscopy finds a champion in Fuchsius, who in 1615 issued a guide to what may be discovered by looking into eyes. Large pupils, he said, denote madness and incapacity. Small pupils, when they shine in the eye, betray a man who is wily, cunning, perverse, and libidinous. If the orbits move in an unequal circuit, it is a sign of a soul capable of horrible deeds. Other characteristics are assigned according to the size of the eyes, the color of the iris, and other details.

John Caspar Lavater, an eighteenth-century minister, demonstrated in his principal treatise an interest in warts. He suggested, for example, that women with brown hairy warts on the chin were industrious but "amorous to folly, or even to frenzy." He advised treating such warty specimens with "a mildly cold dignity of demeanor."

A special kind of natural physiognomy, phrenology, was founded, as mentioned above, by Gall, a Viennese medical philosopher, who gave his first lecture on the subject in 1796. He based his doctrine on the premise that every mental faculty is represented by a special cranial protuberance. Each bump, he declared, is an index of the development of the cerebral region underneath, where the seat of that particular faculty is located (Fig. 10). Most important of all was his belief that each part of the nervous system has special functions.

In order to discover which parts of the brain are linked with a special function, Gall examined the heads of persons who showed strong manifestations of certain qualities, and contrasted them with other persons in whom the quality was weak. For example, he contrasted the head of a mathematical wizard of the day with the head of one of his own followers who had difficulty with the simplest of arithmetical calculations. Once having determined the significance of each area of the skull, he expected to be able to analyze anyone simply by examining cranial bulges.

Gall's method of investigation was crudely empirical, though, as we have mentioned, he

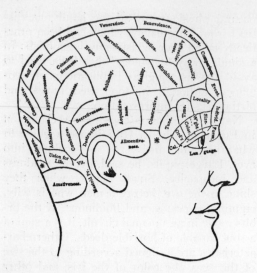

FIG. 10.   Phrenology. The location of the faculties.
(Fowler, *Practical Phrenology* [1851].)

resorted in some instances to the single-case
method. Although he may have made certain
erroneous assumptions, he was scientific in
spirit, and it is unfortunate that disciples
dragged his theory down to the level of charlatanry and into the realm of circus side
shows. Some, too, were unable to resist the
appeal of the stars and brought them into
their schemes (Fig. 11).

What are the claims of somatomancy?
This is a pertinent question, because in answering it we see many things which relate
to the interests of modern human constitution, even though, of course, somatomancy

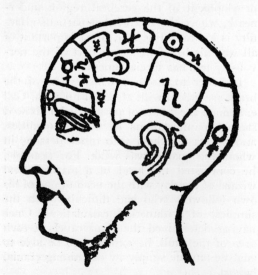

FIG. 11.   Phrenological astrophysiognomy. The relation of the head to the planets. (Saint-Germain,
The Study of Palmistry [1900].)

lies almost wholly in the sphere of the divinatory arts. The hidden knowledge that
physiognomists seek to reveal may lie in the
future, the present, or the past. It may concern itself with happenings, with character,
or with a condition of the mind or body. For
example, one type of information which
body divination claims to be able to supply
is the criminal propensity of men. The
phrenologist says that the potential murderer has a certain development of the organ
of destructiveness, located under the temporal lobe just above the ear. The palmist
says that the thief has, among other things,
an exaggerated development of the Mount of
Mercury. Efforts such as these adumbrate
the more specifically formulated ideas of the
nineteenth-century criminal anthropologists,
among whom were Lombroso, Ferri, Garo-
falo, and Benedikt. Sometimes body divination goes beyond the determination of criminal propensities and enters the field of "discovery divination," which is used to detect
and apprehend criminals or to decide guilt.

In medicine the part played by body divination has not been inconsequential. During
the first half of the fifteenth century, when
much medicine was astrological in character,
the great physicians of the time who supported this approach had an influence on a
whole host of lesser physicians, who, instead
of consulting the stars directly, looked for
celestial clues in the bodies of their patients.
A perusal of the illustrious names in astral
physiognomy during the Renaissance
shows that the majority were in fact practicing physicians and that body divination
was an accoutrement of their art. Nonastro-
logical somatomancy has been even more influential than the celestial sort in medical
practice, claiming greater antiquity and application as well as more respectability.

One other application of body divination
may be mentioned. In the business world,
hardheaded employers have utilized principles of somatomancy in the selection of
personnel. During the early part of the twentieth century an especially popular book by
Blackford and Newcomb, called *The Job,
the Man, the Boss,* gave advice for the hiring of men. This book set up certain "physical variables," as they were called, and
described the variations in character which
were supposed to accompany each. Even the
Greeks were guided by physiognomy in filling positions.

For a wider understanding of somatomancy, we must turn to its sociocultural base. As a part of the universal phenomena of supernaturalism, it is man's response to the fulfillment of a need—the need to gain security in a world rendered fearful and worrisome by uncertainty, chance, and inadequate understanding of a wide variety of natural phenomena. Body divination, then, exists for the same reasons that magic and religion do.

The Renaissance and its beginnings provide a case study to support this statement. The great flowering of divination in general accompanied the revival of learning which took place during this period, when the foundations of modern life were taking on their unique features. In the general ferment leading to a period different in many ways from the preceding Middle Ages, Roger Bacon and Albertus Magnus, among others, were accused of crimes having to do with divination. The significance of the coming of the Renaissance is implicit in Cassirer, who has said that if proof of the historical reality of the period were needed, it would be enough to point to two major works—Galileo's *Dialogues concerning Two New Sciences* and Machiavelli's *Prince*. These strangely diverse books had one element in common. They were original and novel, and since they could not have been conceived by medieval minds, were sharp indicators of the sociocultural changes sweeping over Western Europe.

The Middle Ages had provided intense confidence in the *status quo*, in the neat, consistent, and dogmatic view of the world which medieval thought had adapted from Aristotelian philosophy. Security was provided for the individual by feudal collectivism, by the permanent station in society which the feudal system sanctioned, and by a clear and preordained meaning of life. In this world the individual had not been free, but he had been secure, and he was relatively incapable of seeing himself as a separate entity.

Contrasted with this, the Renaissance saw the accomplishment of great changes. The heliocentric theory inspired by Galileo and Copernicus not only shattered the terracentric view of the universe, but also severely weakened scholastic dogma and theology. Medieval collectivism foundered in the capitalism and competition sanctioned by the rise of individualism and personal initiative. The feudal system and the ideal of a great Christian commonwealth became attenuated in the rise of nationalism and the modern state. Hence, with these changes, status became no longer so rigidly a matter of birth but was instead increasingly subject to individual action and the insecurities engendered by chance and uncertainty. Man could no longer search for an understanding of himself and his goals by referring to the traditional religious concepts. The new ruling force in the world of the Renaissance came to be not Divine Providence, but Fortune.

The dominant theme of the Renaissance, as far as we are concerned, is that man had "returned to himself." Man was forced to look to himself for the answers to questions which tradition and religious concepts no longer explained adequately, for although he ceased to be concerned with whence he had come, he became immensely concerned with whither he was going. Understanding of present position became essential, and in trying to establish a course of behavior, the element of chance intervened. The role of divination came to be that of attempting to control chance.

One more force related to the foregoing factors impelled the individual of the Renaissance to turn to divination. Torn loose from the moorings of the Middle Ages, he had achieved a new, but insecure and anxiety-loaded freedom; being one's own master proved to be thoroughly discomforting. The feeling of anxiety and insecurity that freedom is capable of inflicting has been discussed by Fromm.

We have examined a plausible theory to explain divination as resulting from man's need for comfort and reassurance, and to account for the greatly increased interest in divination which came about in Renaissance times. But we have not explained how the human body came to be used for divinatory purposes in the civilized world. The answer is not clear, but good guesses may be made. Physiognomy had been employed in the ancient civilized centers, probably as the result of an incipient spirit of "scientific" inquiry not incompatible with urban sophistication; but this form of divination had never attained first rank, as had nonsomatic varieties. Perhaps individualism as such did not really emerge until the Renaissance. At any rate, it seems reasonable for us to associate the use of the body for divinatory purposes with the new interest in man in himself as an individual; for somatomancy was in tune with the spirit of the times—with the search of man to understand himself. If clues to his own nature were to be found, what was more obvious than for the individual to look within himself for those clues, rather than in sand patterns, animal scapulae, pendulums, or natural phenomena—especially when new learning in medical and anatomical science fortified the particular orientation, and the two interstimulated each other?

Somatomancy merits the attention of historians, scientists, and theorists because it is clearly one of the forerunners of the modern field of human constitution, which studies the total biological make-up of the individual in terms of varieties or types. It shares with it certain common assumptions, methods, and motivations. The first and most obvious circumstance which attracts our notice is that for each of them the human body is the starting point. Each makes classifications according to morphological traits, sometimes stressing over-all appearance and at other times selecting special features. The books of the physiognomist Della Porta are studded with pictures illustrating types of breasts, nates, trunks, knees, legs, feet, and facial profiles (Fig. 12). So are the writings of

Fig. 12. An early attempt at classification. Three types of facial profiles. (Della Porta, *Della Fisonomia dell' Huomo* [1615].)

Taisnier, Lavater, Combe, and Delestre, to name but a few. Similarly, a perusal of books by constitutionalists is apt to reveal the use of drawings and photographs to illustrate classifications of various types of noses, palates, fingers, calves, hips, hair patterns, and the like. In describing various physiques as they see them, body diviners use such terms as "jupiterian," "solar," "leonine," "bovine," and "lymphatic," whereas constitutionalists employ such ex-

pressions as "microsplanchnic," "pyknic," "muscular," "cerebral," and "ectomorphic" (Fig. 13). Cassifications may vary considerably from one writer to another but are always indispensable, even where modern investigators ardently insist that they are not dealing with "types."

Regardless of the soundness of the typologies used and the methods employed for achieving them, the fact of the matter is that neither somantomanticists nor constitutionalists set up their classifications as mere exercises. Rather, they feel that through an inspection of the body they can achieve more ultimate objectives. We find, accordingly, that each is interested in matters of disease, temperament, crime, and the like. Lombroso's writings on criminal types were to some extent inspired by the phrenological climate of the times and illustrate the gradual transition that in many cases has been made from somatomancy to constitution.

These grander objectives depend for their logical justification on a principle that is all-important. In modern jargon we might call it "functional consistency." Constitutionalists have insisted over and over again that the human organism is an integral entity, and without this premise they cannot proceed. They say that the biotype may be studied from various aspects, and that regardless of the approach used the ultimate results will be the same. If this sounds familiar and like what such ethnologists as Malinowski, Benedict, and others have said in the field of culture study, it is because of a similarity in outlook. Yet it forms part of the corpus of somatomantic belief, too. Three hundred years ago in his treatise on moles Saunders wrote, "And so, when as in the body all parts and qualities are so fitly dispensed and composed that they consist together in a unified fit natural proportion, so likewise is it in the soul, all things being so moderated and fitly composed that all the affections, as it were in apt and set numbers and figures, conspire an harmonious accord."

The reason that physique is the most commonly used approach is obvious—it is the aspect most readily observed and classified, although it is vastly less amenable to classification than has generally been realized. Some authors are willing to go much further, seeing physique as a causal factor in the determination of other components of the biotype. Thus Seltzer declares,

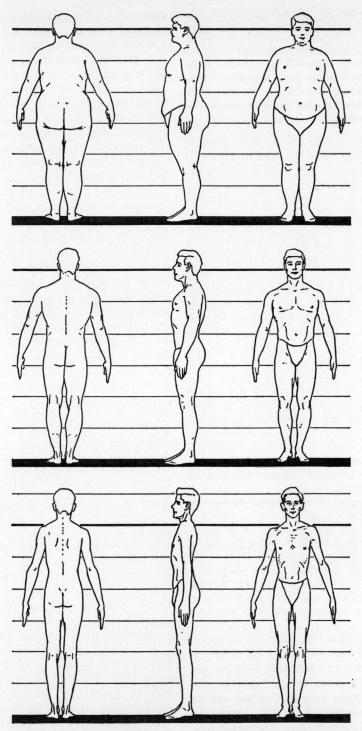

Fig. 13. A modern attempt at classification. Three extreme Sheldonian somatotypes: endomorphic, mesomorphic, and ectomorphic. (From an original of plate 1, C. W. Dupertuis, *Am. J. Phys. Anthrop.*, n.s. VIII, 385 [1950].)

Not only does it [physqiue] provide the basic framework through which the individual functions, but its importance is more far-reaching in that the individual's physique is, in the main, biologically inherited, genetically determined. Body build being thus "a product of influences emanating from the germ plasm," is therefore a constitutional determinant in the personality formation.

To illustrate one of the common meeting grounds of body divination and biotypology, we may examine their attitudes toward "ugliness." Each sees it as indicative of undesirable inner traits. Long ago the Greeks coined a word, *kalosagathos* ("beautiful" plus "good"), which expressed their conviction that beauty and goodness go hand in hand. A reverse application of this is found in the medieval dictum that if two men were brought to trial for a crime and there should be indecision as to who was guilty, then the uglier of the two was to be hanged. Similar ideas, expressed variously in terms of dysplasia, disharmony, body disproportions, and bad modeling, appear in the constitutional literature. Mention has already been made of Quetelet's doctrine of the medial man. Further along these lines is a statement by Draper, the great American pioneer in constitution:

In this connection one is reminded of the ancient German medical adage "Hässlichkeit stellt eine schlechte Prognose vor." Indeed if one notes the general appearance of hospital ward inmates the average standard of beauty in the ordinarily accepted sense is surprisingly low. It is as though ugliness, being an expression of bad modelling in respect of features and body proportions, expressed in the morphological panel a sort of genetic bungling. In such folk, inadequacies in other phases of the total personality may not unreasonably be expected.

Body disproportions have been the subject of a special study by Seltzer, who maintains that when they are present they indicate predisposition to a sensitive and complex personality, and when relatively absent are associated with vitality, directness, relative insensibility to fine influences, and good integration.

Under the somatomantic and constitutional approaches, the individual rather than the group is the focus of attention. Insofar as constitution is part of physical anthropology, such an emphasis is notable for its novelty, for physical anthropologists are traditionally concerned with "human populations, their physical evolution, gene distributions, anatomical peculiarities, and patterns of physical growth, maturation, and aging." This shift in emphasis corresponds to a similar shift in cultural anthropology, with its recent excursions into ethnopsychology. Interest in the group as such is not altogether absent, however, and in somatomantic writings of the sixteenth century and earlier we find attempts at racial, sexual, age, and familial patterns of morphology.

An unfortunate but all too real similarity between somatomancy and constitution is that both are almost authoritarian in their emphasis on biological factors. In medieval and Renaissance times an attempt was made to arbitrate the problem of human immutability versus human plasticity by invoking the concept of "free will" as a counterproposal to predeterminism, but foredestiny has nevertheless always remained implicit in most body divination. In analogous fashion, among constitutionalists there has long been a healthy division of opinion as to whether constitution partakes of environmental-cultural modification. Under the forceful leadership of W. H. Sheldon, the hereditary point of view has had new popularity by conceiving of the somatotype as immutable from birth. However, because of the barrage of censure leveled at him by critics (mostly outside the field), Sheldon has recently made a concession and coined the term "morphophenotype" to express the fixed genetic influence which persists in the organism, reserving the old term "somatotype" for the tentative representation of the morphogenotype. He declares that the morphophenotype changes with growth, aging, nutritional variations, and pathology, but that the somatotype delves beneath this and attempts to approximate the morphogenotype.

It is abundantly evident that both somatomancy and human constitution have pragmatic goals, for both wish to enable individuals to benefit by the information which their findings disclose. They want to "accentuate the positive and eliminate the negative" by having people make the best of their favorable traits and carefully avoid the consequences inherent in their malignant ones. They believe in situational adjustments. Viewed from this angle, physiognomists, palmists, metoposcopists, phrenologists, and the rest of their kind are essentially advisers. On the other hand, biotypologists have not yet reached the practitioner stage because their discipline is still undergoing exploration, but it is nevertheless the avowed intention of these men ultimately to cast their lot with applied science. Indeed, some have already conducted considerable experimental research for the armed forces of the United States in the determination of various aptitudes. In Boston, Sheldon had begun therapy with the juvenile delinquents he was studying at the Hayden Goodwill Inn, when he was forced to stop because of the war.

If space permitted it would be profitable to explore the possibility that both somatomancy and constitution are, in part, responses to man's need to establish security. We have already examined the role of the mantic arts in this respect. Much of the appeal of the science of biotypology rests similarly on the hope that it can interpret for the individual his characteristics, capacities, and weaknesses. It forecasts, to some extent, and it also interprets some of the present and the past. There can be no doubt that if constitutionalists accepted clients in the same way that somatomanticists do, even though their findings are still highly tentative, they would have a tremendous practice.

It would be grossly unfair to stop at this point and leave the reader with an exaggerated notion as to the likeness between what is essentially an art resting on supernaturalism and a discipline based on experimental research. As we noted in our earlier discussions, somatomancy is often intuitive and eschews the experimental method. No serious account is taken of obvious discrepancies, except to explain them away with implausible excuses—the intervention of chance, errors in computation, and so on. When Cardano made the mistake of predicting a long life for Edward VI of England, who promptly died the next year at the age of sixteen, he re-examined his calculations and discarded the method of Ptolemy, which he declared he should not have used.

In contrast to all this, the science of human constitution is overwhelmingly experimental. Hundreds and sometimes thousands of subjects are studied in order to discover even the simplest of correlations. Discrepancies are found, but ordinarily they are not glossed over; instead, they call for further research, further methods and techniques, and further revision of theory. Although interrelationships sometimes are observed

without being understood, no recourse is had to mysticism to resolve the dilemma.

Unhappily, however, subjectivity is not altogether wanting in constitutional studies. One of the more obvious examples, afforded by the work of Sheldon, may be cited. When his *Varieties of Human Physique* appeared in 1940, his method of somatotyping (i.e., assessing physique) was described by some critics as involving a personal equation. Even Hunt, who uses the technique, concedes that "the attempt to rate the morphogenotype of an individual is highly subjective, has few operational referents, and is impossible to validate." Howells has recently termed it "too much of an art and too little of a science." Of Sheldon's *Varieties of Juvenile Delinquency* a famous criminologist wrote that "his definition of delinquency effectively removes this study from the area of empirical research and fixes it firmly in the area of homiletics," and "his method of scoring delinquency is subjective and unreliable." W. C. Reckless says that some of his themes are "fanciful" and certain methods of rating "dubious." Washburn, noting with dismay that Sheldon has said phrenology is on the right track, concludes that his system has its roots in characterology, not science, and is "the new Phrenology in which the bumps of the buttocks take the place of the bumps of the skull." Many critics impugn not only Sheldon's intellectual integrity but also his motives. They see in his eugenical crusade a new and virulent form of racism. Because his writings contain a mission, they have led Sutherland to say that his constitutional psychology is offered to us as "the Messiah for a world rushing into societal chaos," and Garn to add, "the author assumes the mantle, and preaches more like Jeremiah than Hosea." Similar, though milder, accusations of subjectivity have been applied to other constitutionalists, such as Hooton and Kretschmer.

To sum up, it is clear that somatomancy and constitution, despite differences, manifest many analogies as well as downright resemblances. As has been shown, the origins of both not only spring from similar needs, but also are frequently embodied in the writings of the same investigators. Furthermore, the roots of science often are to be found among precursory magical and divinatory arts, and again are contained in the works of Renaissance giants or the culture of ancient endeavor.

EVON Z. VOGT

Water Witching:
An Interpretation
of a Ritual
Pattern in a
Rural American
Community

The next article of this chapter is concerned with divination in a contemporary American rural community. This community, Homestead, New Mexico, presents a rare opportunity for a systematic study of water witching. Water witching is a divinatory ritual; both ritual and divination are considered to be responses to emotional anxiety and cognitive frustration in a situation of uncertainty.

Because of irregularities in geological strata, ground water in the Homestead area varies considerably in depth. The area is geologically so complex that modern geologists are unable accurately to predict where a well should best be drilled. In this uncertainty, water witching has flourished.

It was possible to approach the origin and role of the Homestead water-witching pattern from several theoretical positions. These positions are, briefly: (1) water witching is technologically valid—it finds water; (2) water witching is a superstition accepted only by the uneducated; and (3) water witching has a positive sociopsychological value for its users. These theories are empirically examined by means of comparison between Homestead and a town in the center of the area from which the Homesteaders migrated, and by comparison between Homestead and nearby Mormon, Spanish-American, Navaho, and Zuni communities. Further, statistical data from Homestead and New South Wales are presented, as are experimental data from New Zealand.

This study indicates that the technological utility of water witching is no better than chance—somewhat worse, in fact—and that many well-educated people subscribe to it in some degree. The evidence substantiates the third theory, that water witching does reassure people in a situation of uncertainty; it tells an individual just where and how deep a well should be dug and it is in accord with the Homesteader's value of a rational mastery over nature.

The article tends to corroborate the thesis that water witching in particular and divination in general are responses to uncertainty—to that which man is unable to know and control through rational means.

Further information on water witching as magical divination is provided in the book by Vogt and Hyman, *Water Witching U.S.A.* (1959), which offers evidence that 25,000 water dowsers are currently practicing this ancient form of divination in America today and that the general conclusions of this article can be extended to the United States as a whole.

Reprinted from *Scientific Monthly*, LXXV (September, 1952), 175–186, by permission of the American Association for the Advancement of Science.

This paper will attempt an interpretation of the phenomenon of water witching as a folk-ritual pattern which has been extraordinarily persistent in rural American culture and which has not been replaced by the services of competent ground-water geologists in locating family-size wells in countless rural American communities. There is a vast literature on this water-divining pattern, but by and large the writings have centered on the problem of whether dowsing does or does not work as an empirical technique for locating underground supplies of water. The latest publication of note in this vein is the best seller by Kenneth Roberts, *Henry Gross and His Dowsing Rod,* which, as a spirited defense of the empirical validity of the dowsing technique, has renewed and publicized the age-old controversy. But, so far as this writer has been able to determine, there has been no systematic attempt to analyze the phenomenon as a folk-ritual pattern functionally equivalent to the magical practices found in the nonliterate cultures of the world.

Emanating from the writings of Pareto, Malinowski, and Weber, and continuing in the present generation of theorists—notably Parsons, Kluckhohn, and Homans—a general body of theory concerning the function of ritual in the situation of human action has emerged. Briefly stated, the essence of this theory is that when human beings are confronted with situations that are beyond empirical control and that are, therefore, anxiety-producing both in terms of emotional involvement and of a sense of cognitive frustration, they respond by developing and elaborating nonempirical ritual that has the function of relieving emotional anxiety and of making some sense of the situation on a cognitive level. Kroeber has recently questioned the universality of this relationship by pointing out that the Eskimos, who live in a far more uncertain and anxiety-producing environment than do Malinowski's Trobriand Islanders, have little ritual as compared to the Trobrianders, whereas given Malinowski's formulation one would expect more Eskimo ritual. Kroeber goes on to indicate that the arctic environment is so severe that had the Eskimos devoted much energy to the development of ritual patterns, they would long since have perished. This latter point is sound, but further analysis of Eskimo culture may reveal that, although there is little elaboration of ritual, the ritual patterns that do exist are still clustered around the greatest uncertainties of Eskimo life.

Others, notably Radcliffe-Brown, have raised the issue as to whether rituals do not create anxiety (when they are not performed or are not performed properly) rather than alleviate it. Homans has treated this problem in terms of "primary" and "secondary" rituals focused around "primary" and "secondary" types of anxiety. Primary anxiety describes the sentiment men feel when

they desire the accomplishment of certain results and do not possess the techniques that make these results certain; secondary anxiety describes the sentiment resulting when the traditional rites are not performed or are performed improperly. Kluckhohn has carried the analysis further by demonstrating that ritual patterns have both a "gain" and a "cost" from the point of view of the continued functioning of a society, and that problems are created as well as solved by the presence of ritual patterns in a given culture.

Finally, I should like to advance the theory that ritual patterns which initially emerge as responses to critical areas of uncertainty in the situation of action are elaborated and reinterpreted in terms of certain selective value-orientations in a given culture.[1]

We are brought, then, to a dynamic conception of ritual which includes the following considerations: Ritual patterns develop as a response to emotional anxiety and cognitive frustration in a situation of uncertainty; but ritual patterns come to have both "functional" and "dysfunctional" aspects (both a "gain" and a "cost") for the continuing existence of a society as the patterns are elaborated and developed in terms of the selective value-orientations of a given culture.

In this paper I shall analyze the relationship of the water-witching pattern to the critical area of uncertainty in the location of underground water supplies, explore the functional and dysfunctional aspects of this pattern for the continuing survival of the community, and try to show how the pattern has become an expression of the value stress on "rational" environment control in a rural American community.

FOLK RITUAL IN RURAL AMERICA

The continuing existence of a large body of folk ritual in rural American culture is a fact of common observation by anyone who has lived in such communities and by those who have done systematic research in rural areas. For example, in *Plainville, USA,* James West wrote that "many magical practices still exist for planting crops, castrating livestock, weaning, gardening, girdling

[1] This theoretical point is developed in the writer's book, *Modern Homesteaders: The Life of a Twentieth-century Frontier Community* (Cambridge: Harvard University Press, 1955).

trees." Taylor reported that he had gathered 467 different signs and superstitions that are known and to some extent believed in rural communities.

Although these magical practices are found in connection with many aspects of rural culture, including the preparation of food, the curing of illness, and the weaning of babies, they are apparently concentrated in the area of farming technology and have to do mainly with weather, crops, the care of animals, and the locating of water wells. Taylor asserted that over one fourth of his 467 signs and superstitions refer to climate and weather and that the majority refer to plants and animals in addition to weather and climate.

THE WATER-WITCHING PATTERN

The phenomenon by means of which one is supposed to find underground supplies of water by the use of a divining rod is variously known as dowsing, divining, witching, and rhabdomancy. The indicator employed in water divining is called a divining rod, witching stick, dowsing rod, dipping rod, striking stick, or wand; and the practitioner may be called a diviner, dowser, witch, or finder. In current usage the word "dowsing" is more common in the literature and is used by rural people along the Eastern seaboard; "water witching" is the more common term used by rural folk who utilize the technique in the South, Middle West, and Far West.[2]

It is certain that the water-witching pattern has a respectable antiquity in Western culture and it is highly probable that the basic ideas of the technique derive ultimately from ancient divining practices that are widespread among the nonliterate cultures of the world. The "rod" is mentioned many times in the Bible in connection with miraculous performances, especially in the books of Moses. The much-quoted reference to Moses' striking the rock with his rod, thus producing water for his followers in the wilderness (Numb. xx: 9–11), has been re-

garded by enthusiasts of water witching as a significant reference to the divining rod. Herodotus mentions the use of the divining rod by the Persians, Scythians, and Medes; and Marco Polo reports its use throughout the Orient.

But whatever significance one may attach to such references, authorities agree that the divining rod in its present form was in use in Germany by the first half of the sixteenth century. The first complete published description is contained in Agricola's *De re metallica,* published in 1556. Barrett considers that the birthplace of the modern divining rod was in the mining districts of Germany, probably in the Harz Mountains, where it was used to prospect for ore. During the reign of Queen Elizabeth (1558–1603), when German miners were imported to England to lend an impetus to the mining industry in Cornwall, they brought the *schlagruthe* ("striking rod") with them. As mining declined in Cornwall, the use of the rod was transferred to water finding. At about the same time there is mention of the use of the rod for locating water supplies in France.

Before the end of the seventeenth century the use of the divining rod had spread through Europe, everywhere arousing controversy. Its champions, among whom were some of the most learned men of the time, explained its operation on the principle of "sympathy" or "attraction and repulsion." Its adversaries, like Agricola, condemned its use as a superstitious and vain practice. Indeed, the practice even became a subject of ecclesiastical controversy when Martin Luther proclaimed in 1518 that the use of the rod violated the First Commandment, and the Jesuit Father Gaspard Schott later denounced it as an instrument controlled by the devil. From Europe the water-witching pattern spread to the New World and to such regions as Australia and New Zealand, and it is reported that as late as 1931 the government of British Columbia hired an "official" water diviner to locate wells.

Over the past four centuries the phenomenon has also been the subject of innumerable scientific (or allegedly scientific) investigations and controversies, beginning with Pierre Lebrun in 1692 and continuing off and on to the present controversy stimulated by Roberts' best-selling book. The key

[2] Roberts objects to the use of the term "water witch" on the ground that it perpetuates the idea of its association with witchcraft and prefers the term "dowsing." "Dowsing" comes from the Cornish word *douse* and the Middle English word *duschen,* both meaning "to strike" or "to fall." "Rhabdomancy" comes from two Greek words, *Rhabdos* ("rod") and *manteia* ("divination").

figures in these investigations and controversies have been such men as Sir William Barrett (professor of physics in the Royal College of Science for Ireland), Henri Mager (in France), J. W. Gregory (Glasgow University), O. E. Meinzer (U.S. Geological Survey), and more recently Solco W. Tromp (professor of geology at Fuad I University, Cairo).

The core of the water-witching pattern as it is now found in rural American culture may be characterized as follows:

Equipment. The most common item of equipment utilized is the witching stick, typically a Y-shaped green twig cut from a hazel, willow, or peach tree. The two forks vary from 14 to 18 inches in length, and the neck from 4 to 11 inches. The diameter of the stick may vary from one-eighth inch to almost an inch. Alternative types of wood used include maple, apple, dogwood, and beach twigs and, in the southwestern United States, twigs cut from piñon and juniper trees. There is even one case on record of a diviner who uses a leaf from the broad-leafed yucca plant. Less common, but widespread, are various metallic materials used for witching, including barbed wire from the nearest fence, a clock or watch spring, and especially constructed aluminum rods. Finally, some water witches use various kinds of pendulums such as small bottles of "chemicals" suspended on a string, or a key suspended by string from either a Bible or an arithmetic book.

Technique. The most common technique is to grasp the two branches of the forked twig, one in each hand, with the neck (or bottom of the Y) pointing skyward. Usually the twig is grasped with the palms of the hands up, but an alternative method is to hold the stick with the palms down. In either case, the forked twig is placed under tension in such a way that the slightest contraction of the muscles in the forearm or a slight twist of the wrists is sufficient to cause the twig to rotate toward the ground. The water witch walks over the ground in the area where a water supply is desired. When he walks over an underground supply of water, the witching stick is supposed to dip down, and a stake is then driven into the ground to mark the spot. Although most dowsers function only to locate a suitable spot to drill for a well or to dig for a spring, some also have techniques for determining the depth of the water supply. Perhaps the most common of these is to measure the distance from the place where the stick starts to dip to where it dips straight down over the water supply. Few, if any, other practitioners profess to have the sophisticated "powers" of Henry Gross that would enable them to ask questions and receive answers (by the way the rod nods) as to the quality and amount of the underground water, or to locate a water supply by "long-distance" dowsing, as Henry Gross did when he dowsed over a map of Bermuda while in New England and located water there.

Ideology. Like most ritual patterns, water witching carries with it an elaborate mythology, the core of which involves two aspects: the dowser's definition of the geological situation, summarized by the belief held by dowsers that underground water occurs in two forms: *sheet water,* which underlies a total area, and *water veins,* which may vary in magnitude from "the size of a pencil" to "underground rivers" and which run through the earth like the veins in the human body. The important thing is to locate and trace these veins, because either there may be no sheet water in a given area or it may be located at so deep a level that the only way to find suitable shallow water is "to hit a vein." The most elementary knowledge of groundwater geology is sufficient to prove that this dowsing concept bears little relation to known facts. The second aspect concerns the many and varied "explanations" and justifications advanced by dowsers for the efficacy of dowsing and the rationalization provided to account for failures. The "explanations" on record range from supernaturalistic interpretations (such as the notion that dowsers derive their mysterious power from Moses, "who was the first water witch") to supposedly scientific interpretations (such as the notion that the muscles of the water witch are affected by electromagnetic disturbances emanating from underground water supplies). Most of the ordinary and less articulate water witches in rural America provide explanations in terms of (1) a kind of magical principle by which the water in the green twig is attracted by the water in the ground, or (2) a theory—which they regard as "scientific"—that the dipping of the stick has something to do with "electricity" or "electrical currents" which run from the water through their bodies and into the stick, causing it to dip. Equally important are the rationalizations advanced to account for failures. These typically take the form of attributing the failure either to faulty equipment (e.g., "I couldn't find a straight stick that day") or to some aspect of the situation that negates the findings of the dowser (e.g., "I found I had a knife in my pocket which short-circuited the electric current," or "The vein dried up before they got around to drilling the well").

Institutionalization of role. There is considerable variation in the prestige the dowser has in a rural community, depending upon various factors. But it is clear that he occupies a special role. In the first place, the basic ability to do witching is usually believed to be a skill with which one is born and which he later discovers; it cannot be acquired by training or experience. In this respect it comprises a skill which is acquired by "divine stroke," as in the "shamanistic" tradition, rather than a body of knowledge transmitted by training in a "priestly" tradition. To be sure, it is necessary for a person to have observed (or to have heard about) the basic techniques, but it is impossible for one water witch to impart the skill to another. One is either born with it or one is not.[3] By virtue of this inborn ability, the dowser assumes a specialized role that is recognized by the total community—both by the proponents and by the adversaries of dowsing.

In the second place, the water witch is almost always paid for his services, in amounts ranging from $5 to $25 (in the Southwest) for locating each well site. In this respect his position becomes a part-time occupation and some dowsers derive a substantial income from their activities. It should be pointed out that some dowsers charge a set price and collect the money in businesslike fashion; others volunteer their services and take whatever contributions are offered them. But I have not yet known a water witch who was a charlatan or who performed the operation purely for the monetary gain involved. Usually they are sincere individuals who believe thoroughly in their ability to find water. Finally, it should be noted that dowsers are usually men, although women sometimes have the witching skill. Indeed, the water diviner reported to have been employed by the government of British Columbia in 1931 was a woman.

Having described the history and general pattern of dowsing, let us turn to a more intensive treatment of water witching in terms of the concrete data from a single community—Homestead, New Mexico[4]—where the relevant historical, geological, and social facts are well known.

[3] However, there are reputedly differences among dowsers as to the amount of skill they possess. Thus Roberts describes Henry Gross as being a highly skilled dowser. And once a dowser finds that he has the basic ability, it is possible for him to become more skilled with experience. It would be interesting to know the incidence of dowsing skill in the rural population, but no data are yet available. It is worth noting that in the community of Homestead (pop. 250) there is one dowser; and in the nearby Mormon community of Rimrock (pop. 300) there is only one. Neither community has ever been without at least one dowser. For short periods of time there have been two in each community, but never more than two at any given time.

[4] Homestead is a fictitious name, used to protect the anonymity of my informants.

WATER WITCHING IN HOMESTEAD

The community of Homestead was established by families from the South Plains area of western Texas and Oklahoma who settled on homesteads in the semiarid area of western New Mexico in the early 1930's. The economy focuses around the production of pinto beans on dry-land farms, supplemented by crops of corn, winter wheat, and beef cattle. Farms now average two sections in size and are scattered as far as twenty miles from the crossroads center of the community which contains the stores, school, post office, repair shops, and other service institutions. Farming technology has shifted through the years from horse-drawn implements to mechanized equipment.

The natural environment provides an unusually hazardous setting for dry-land farming. Until the homesteaders arrived, the land had been used only for grazing purposes, and the area is still regarded as submarginal farming land by authorities in the U.S. Department of Agriculture. The soil is excellent for beans, but the necessary 90-day growing season is often cut short by late spring frosts or early fall frosts at this elevation (7,000 feet). Heavy windstorms in the spring add the hazard of serious wind erosion. But the basic environmental problems are those of inadequate and fluctuating rainfall and the development of water resources for livestock and household use. Annual precipitation averages 12.5–15 inches, depending upon locality and elevation, but has varied over the past two decades from 6 to 19 inches.

The people who established this community defined themselves as pioneers, leaving the "civilized" centers of Texas and Oklahoma to seek new homes on the "frontier" west of the Continental Divide. As pioneers, they emphasize many of the values characteristic of newly settled American farming communities: a stress on self-reliance and independence of the individual, a drive to subdue and control the natural environment, an abiding faith in the progressive development of their community, and a perennial optimism about the future. With these values they confronted the semiarid environment of western New Mexico and set about the business of developing dry-land farms.

One of the first critical problems the homesteaders faced was the development of adequate water supplies. When they first arrived in 1930–31, they found it necessary to haul water in barrels by team and wagon from a lake three miles from the center of the community. When the lake went dry, they hauled water from a spring seven miles distant. If a farmer had livestock, it meant that he had to haul water at least every other day. A few tried drilling wells in the early years, but it was soon discovered that, although in some places water was struck at shallow depths (80–100 feet), in others dry holes were the only result after drilling over 500 feet. At a cost of $1–$3 a foot for drilling a well, few homesteaders were willing or able to take the risk.

It was in this situation that one farmer suddenly "discovered" in 1933 that he had the "power" to witch for water. As a young boy in Texas he had observed witching. One day he simply cut a forked stick from his wife's peach tree, tried out the technique as he remembered it, and it worked. He found two water veins on his farm, traced them to a point where they crossed each other, and had a successful well drilled at this spot at a depth of 230 feet. He rapidly achieved community-wide reputation as a water witch and successfully witched 18 wells in the next few years. Six wells were dowsed by a second water witch who lived in the community for a few years, making a total of 24 wells that were located in this manner. During the same period, however, the original water witch dowsed five locations where dry holes resulted after drilling; and he often missed calculating the depth by as much as 200–400 feet. For, in addition to using the common technique for locating the water vein by walking over the ground with a forked twig and putting a stake in the ground where the rod dipped, he developed a special technique for determining depth. He would hold a thin, straight stick (5 feet in length) over the water vein, and it would "involuntarily" nod up and down. The number of nods indicated the depth in feet to the water. During the same period 25 wells were successfully drilled without benefit of dowsing, and seven dry holes were drilled in locations that were not dowsed (Table 1).

As time went on, the water witch killed his wife's lone peach tree by cutting witching sticks from it. He then made an adjustment to the New Mexican environment by shifting to the use of forked twigs from piñon

TABLE 1

	Wells Divined	Wells Not Divined
Successful wells	24	25
Dry holes	5	7

trees. He explains his dowsing in terms of "electricity" and usually attributes errors to the presence of iron (like a knife in his pocket, or an old piece of farm machinery in the vicinity) or to the fact that he could not find a straight stick.

There is, of course, more than a casual relation between the early water supply problems of homesteaders and the geology of the Homestead area.[5] The community is bordered on the south by a high escarpment that exposes the upper formations underlying the area. These consist of Quaternary basalt flows which are exposed in portions of the eastern and northern parts, Tertiary sands and conglomerates which underlie the western part, and the Mesa Verde formation of Upper Cretaceous age which underlies the above formations at variable depths. The Mesa Verde formation is about 1,800 feet thick and consists of alternating gray to buff sandstones, gray clay shales, and coal.

During Tertiary time the shales and sandstones of the upper Mesa Verde formation were eroded, and subsequent deposition of the Tertiary sands and conglomerates filled the old channels. The existence of these buried channels and ridges, and recent erosion of the Tertiary formation, resulted in variations in the thickness of the Tertiary formation and the upper member of the Mesa Verde formation.

Ground water occurs in the Mesa Verde formation, which is the main aquifer, and in the Tertiary formation; small quantities may also be available in the recent alluvium in the valleys, especially in the north and northeast. Structural conditions are not well known, but there are indications of a number of faults and of one syncline, which also affect ground-water supplies.

Several shallow wells near the center of the community and a few wells to the west obtain water from the Tertiary formation. These wells range in depth from 225 to 260 feet, and the yield is usually small. The erosion of the Mesa Verde formation, and sub-

---

[5] I am indebted to Tom O. Meeks for the geological data.

sequent deposition of the Tertiary formation, have caused the base of the Tertiary sands to be an irregular surface. This accounts for the variable depth of wells and the variation in yields. Wells drilled into the old channels are likely to yield more water than others drilled on the buried ridges of the underlying Mesa Verde formation.

The majority of wells in the Homestead area, and all the wells a mile or more east of the center of the community, obtain water from the Mesa Verde formation. The yield of these wells is generally greater than those obtaining water from the Tertiary sands, but it is necessary to drill deeper. The depth varies from about 80 feet in the Tertiary sands in the western part of the area to 800 feet in the Mesa Verde formation in the eastern portion.

Thus it is readily seen that geological conditions have resulted in substantial variations in ground-water resources in different parts of the area. In some localities water is found in the Tertiary sands, usually at relatively shallow depths, but with variations running from 88 to over 300 feet. In other localities it is necessary to drill to a greater depth into the Mesa Verde formation. And the situation is further complicated by structural conditions that are not yet well known by geologists.

In the dowsing of his own well the local water witch was over the Tertiary formation, and water in small quantities was located at 230 feet. The wells which the dowser "successfully" located were either drilled into the Tertiary formation or the farmers were willing to drill to greater depths and thus reach the Mesa Verde formation. The dry holes were cases in which the wells were either (*a*) located where the Tertiary sands did not exist and the farmer was unwilling to go deep enough to strike the Mesa Verde formation (two cases), or (*b*) located over the Tertiary formation but in places where buried channels or the presence of the syncline in the underlying Mesa Verde formation made the depth to water greater than the wells were drilled (three cases). The same geological facts account for the dry holes that resulted from drilling in locations that were not dowsed. The frequent errors in estimating depth were undoubtedly due to these same geological conditions, especially since the dowser usually named a depth that approximated, or was less than, the depth of his own well.

In addition to the water-witching pattern there are two other types of institutionalized folk ritual in Homestead: (1) the use of natural phenomena, such as the winds, clouds, or moon to predict the weather (especially the occurrence of frost) and to judge the proper time for planting crops; and (2) the use of the signs of the zodiac to know when to perform certain farming or livestock operations,[6] such as when to castrate calves "so they won't bleed to death," when to wean calves "so they won't bawl around for several days,"[7] or when to hoe weeds "so they won't come up again." Farmers who believe in and practice these three types of folk ritual are known, respectively, as "witch men," "moon men," and "sign men."

Not all the homesteaders believe in and practice these rituals. Our data indicate that opinions range from those of farmers who are wholly oriented in terms of the rational-technological methods of modern agricultural science and scoff at "those silly superstitions," to those who believe firmly in and practice all three types of ritual—e.g., the water witch who is also full of knowledge about and belief in "signs," "planting by the moon," etc. The data further indicate that, of the three areas of ritual, the water-witching pattern is the most widespread and the most persistent in the face of formal education in the theories and methods of modern science. When the recorded instances of the practice of these rituals from our running field notes for the year's period were classified, it was found that 57 per cent of the instances were in the area of water witching, 29 per cent were in the area of the use of the almanac and the signs of the zodiac, and 14 per cent referred to the use of natural phenomena to predict and control events. It was further discovered that some of the most

[6] For the signs the homesteaders depend mainly upon *Dr. J. H. McLean's Almanac* (now in its 98th year of publication), which is distributed free through the local stores by the Dr. J. H. McLean Medicine Company of St. Louis.

[7] The same sign is used to judge the proper times to wean infants. Other researchers interested in the socialization process in Homestead were startled when the response to their question "When do you wean your babies?" was "I wean them when the sign is right." This would appear to be an aspect of the socialization process in rural America that has not yet been explored.

highly educated individuals in the community were having wells dowsed (for example, the principal of the school, who possesses an M.A. degree). Again, research revealed that opinion varied from utter skepticism on the part of some farmers who said that "the best witching stick is the end of the driller's bit" to complete faith in the ability of the dowser to locate water. The most frequent response was an attitude expressed by such statements as, "Well, I'm not sure I believe in it, but it don't cost any more," or "I'll always give it the benefit of the doubt."

Comparative data from a recent study in the Texas Panhandle, which was initiated to provide controls over certain variables in the Homestead study, are illuminating for the analysis of water witching. The Panhandle study was focused on the small community of Cotton Center (pop. 100), near the geographical center of the area that provided the families for the present population of Homestead. The kinship and intervisiting ties between the two communities are unusually close, despite the distances involved, and there is ample evidence that the cultures of the two communities are still quite similar.

Specific inquiries as to water witching and the geology and ground-water resources were made in Cotton Center. The community is located in Hale County, which is extremely flat, consisting of slightly undulating hills interspersed with many poorly drained depressions that fill with water during the rainy season. Annual rainfall averages 22 inches, or almost twice the precipitation found in Homestead. Most of the usable ground water is found in the Ogallala formation, a sandy deposit lying at or near the surface throughout the region. The ground-water table stands at a depth of about 125 feet below the surface, and good wells can be obtained at almost any point. Wells are located where water can be used to best agricultural advantage on the farms. Water witching is widely known, but it is almost never practiced. It can be classified as an unused skill in Cotton Center.

There is also evidence from this area of the Panhandle to indicate that the practice of water witching in Homestead is not due to selective migration—with the "superstitious people" moving west to New Mexico and leaving the families with a more rational-technological orientation behind. For, less

than 25 miles to the southeast of Cotton Center in Floyd and Crosby counties, the ground-water situation is more variable, there is more difficulty locating wells, and water witching is currently practiced. Indeed, there are men from Cotton Center who assist their relatives in dowsing for water in these other counties.

ALTERNATIVE THEORIES OF WATER WITCHING

There are three theories to account for the persistence of water witching in rural American culture. The first may be designated as the "technological theory," which accounts for the continuing practice of water witching on the basis of the empirical validity of the technique as a reliable method for locating wells. The second theory may be designated as the "survival theory," which assumes that water witching is a folk-ritual pattern but accounts for its continued practice by defining the pattern as a "survival" from a previous, less technically oriented phase of our cultural development. The third theory may be designated as the "functional theory," which also defines water witching as a ritual pattern but emphasizes the relationship between situations of technological uncertainty in the present scene and the pattern of water witching as a ritual means of coping with situations that are beyond empirical control.

THE TECHNOLOGICAL THEORY

As indicated earlier, the controversy about water witching has centered around the problem of whether it does or does not work as a reliable empirical method for locating underground supplies of water. This theory must be examined first, because if water witching is an empirically reliable technique, it can then be regarded as part of the rational farming technology in rural American culture, and no further explanation of its continuing use is necessary.

It would be patently impossible to summarize here all the arguments pro and con on the empirical validity of water witching; our task is merely to examine the most relevant evidence. At the outset we may rule out the various "supernaturalistic" claims—as, for example, the claim that dowsers have some kind of mysterious power transmitted through the generations from Moses which enables them to find water. We may also eliminate the simple explanation of many dowsers to the effect that the water in the ground attracts and pulls the water in the freshly cut witching stick. There would appear to be no naturalistic basis for believing that water located (in some cases) as much as several hundred feet under the surface could directly affect the water in a freshly cut stick. Furthermore, as Finklestein points out, the claims of the dowsers lead one to the inevitable conclusion that if there is an empirical basis for the technique, it must be independent of the type of witching device utilized; because the same claims are made for the effectiveness of all devices.

Although we may eliminate the possibility that some kind of external physical force acts directly upon the dowsing rod, there remains the possibility that some kind of external physical force is stimulating the dowser's muscles, which then contract and cause the rod to dip. In this case the rod is merely an indicator of muscular contractions and the type of witching rod used would make no difference.

This approach to the problem has recently been explored by Tromp, who presents experimental evidence indicating that some individuals are more sensitive than others to changes in the strength and polarity of electrical fields associated with both natural and artificial objects. And the problem then becomes one of assessing the possibility that underground supplies of water may affect variations in electromagnetic fields to the extent that these changes in electrical field strength are registered in the dowser's muscles, stimulating them to contract, and thereby indicating the presence of underground water. As matters now stand, even Tromp does not appear to claim that dowsers can identify the cause of a particular change in electrical field strength (such as might result from the presence of underground water), but only that it exists. And the judgment of competent geologists is that it is impossible that changes in electromagnetic fields caused by the *specific* presence of underground water can be registered in *specific* ways in the muscular contractions of dowsers.[8]

The question may also be raised as to whether the dowser is not merely a sound practical geologist who knows the groundwater situation from experience in a given area, and that he is responding to certain surface outcroppings or other indications of underground water when his witching stick dips. In other words, perhaps the witching stick is merely an indirect way of communicating sound geological knowledge.

It is true that many dowsers respond to certain cues in the environment while they are going through the dowsing process. For example, the dowser in Homestead utilizes anthills, and piñon trees with branches that hang down unusually far, as general guides to underground water. But our evidence indicates that these are merely cues for the dowser and have no specific connection with shallow underground water. Furthermore, the dowser makes no attempt to collect information about the location and depth of other wells in the vicinity or to utilize other types of empirical data in the location of new wells.

In other areas of the world, however, there is suggestive evidence that the dowsers occasionally do possess some sound geological knowledge and that their "successes" are due to these empirical observations that are then recorded by the witching stick. But in this case it is obviously the geological observations made by the dowser (and neither the attraction of the rod by underground water nor the stimulation of the muscles of the dowser by variations in electrical fields caused by the presence of underground water) which give the technique an empirical basis.

A second approach to the problem of the empirical validity of water witching is to examine the best evidence available as to the reliability of the dowsing technique. There have been two recent relevant systematic studies. In 1939 the New South Wales Water Conservation and Irrigation Com-

---

[8] Personal communication from Kirtley F. Mather, April 10, 1952, as follows: "Although he [Tromp] claims that the results of his own experiments and those of other qualified scientists indicate 'that divining phenomena are not due to charlatanry and suggestion but really exist,' he also states that 'many diviners make the mistake of claiming that they are able to indicate certain hidden objects, underground ore deposits, water, etc. They fail to realize that many external influences can create the same physiological reaction, similar to readings with modern geophysical instruments, which could be the same under different external conditions.' My conclusion is that Tromp presents no valid evidence that there is any scientific basis, other than psychological, for the procedures followed by dowsers in their efforts to locate underground water supplies."

mission issued a report containing full data on wells drilled in New South Wales from 1918 to 1939. The commission drills wells and issues licenses for wells drilled by private companies, so that full statistical data are available. Table 2 gives the totals from 1918 to 1939.

cating that chance or common sense is a little more reliable.

Finally, I have observed two cases in Homestead in which the well driller was already drilling in a water-bearing formation when the water witch appeared with his forked twig and announced (after dowsing

TABLE 2

	Wells Divined		Wells Not Divined	
	Number of Wells	Percentage	Number of Wells	Percentage
Bores in which supplies of serviceable water estimated at 100 gal./hr. or over were obtained	1234	70.4	1406	83.9
Bores in which supplies of serviceable water estimated at less than 100 gal./hr. were obtained	180	10.2	88	5.3
Bores in which supplies of unserviceable water were obtained	82	4.7	55	3.3
Bores—absolute failures, no water of any kind obtained	257	14.7	126	7.5
Total	1753	100.0	1675	100.0

In 1948 P. A. Ongley, of the medical school at the University of Otago, published the results of controlled experiments performed on 58 different New Zealand water dowsers. Not a single dowser showed any reliability in any of the experiments, which consisted of the following:

1. Asking the dowser to locate an underground stream and then return to it with his eyes closed.
2. Having the dowser locate an underground stream and then later identify which pegs were on the stream and which were not—the experimenter having placed one half of a number of pegs over the underground stream designated by the dowser and the other half of the pegs off the stream.
3. Asking two or more dowsers to check one another on the location of underground water.
4. Asking the dowser to say whether a hidden bottle was full of water or empty.
5. Asking two or more dowsers to determine the depth of the water below the surface of the ground.

To these observed facts, we may add the data on dowsing from Homestead which are reported in Table 1. Although the number of wells involved is small as compared to the series from New South Wales, it is plain that the same negative results are indicated. In both instances, it does not appear to make much difference whether a well is dowsed or not; if anything, there would appear to be fewer complete failures when wells are located by methods other than dowsing, indi-

around the immediate area of the well rig) that the driller had best move his drill since he would never hit water in the hole he was then drilling!

It is difficult to avoid the conclusion that water witching is not an empirically reliable method for locating underground supplies of water.[9] It is plain that the witching stick dips in response to muscular contractions of the dowser that are due to some type of unconscious mental or psychic processes and *not* in response to the physical presence of underground water supplies. But the question remains as to why water witching con-

[9] For an answer to the problem of how Henry Gross was able to locate wells in Bermuda by merely dowsing over a map, the reader is referred to Nichols' review of Kenneth Roberts' book on *Henry Gross and His Dowsing Rod.* Briefly, Nichols points out that limestone islands of the Bermuda type have little fresh water, because the limestone is so permeable that the rain water runs through it rapidly and mixes with the salt water. Most of these islands have a thin lens of fresh water floating on salt water, its thickness depending on the size of the island, the permeability of the rock, and the rainfall. The problem is not that there is no fresh water in Bermuda, but that there is not very much. What there is must be developed by a "skimming" process in which wells are dug to or just below sea level and the water is pumped at a rate just above that of the sea, thus preventing salt water from rising into the well. So Henry Gross did not locate "domes" of fresh water in Bermuda (where there was previously nothing but rain water trapped from the runoff of roofs); he merely located wells which reached to lenses of fresh water floating on the salt water.

tinues to be practiced if it is not an empirical method for locating water. To answer this question we must turn to the other two theories.

THE SURVIVAL THEORY

A second theory that is held implicitly, and sometimes stated explicitly, by many rural sociologists, government agricultural experts, and other observers of the rural scene is the view that water witching is one of many "superstitions" that survive among the unenlightened farmers who learned them from their fathers and grandfathers. It is firmly believed by these observers that the "superstitions" will be replaced by rational-technological methods for coping with the environment as soon as there is sufficient education in the methods of modern agricultural science. Indeed, the disposition of many of these writers is to behave as if the superstitions had already been replaced by scientific methods; and despite their prevalence in rural American culture, it is rare to find an explicit treatment of the problem in rural sociology textbooks. An exception is Sims, who writes that:

> The magical mind, rather than the scientific attitude, tends to prevail (in rural America). . . . This is an emotional and unreflective attitude which does not clearly perceive the steps between thoughts and actions. . . . Expressions of magical mindedness are seen in numerous superstitious beliefs and practices in regard to harvesting and planting.

Sims goes on to argue that science will eventually cause the disappearance of ritual from the rural scene, as he writes:

> The impress of science is already marked and the agencies carrying it to the farmers persistent. . . . With much prestige already established for this method, there is every reason to think that fairly rapid headway will be made in the immediate future. To the degree such progress is made, the magical mindedness will disappear.

There is certainly a grain of truth in this explanation of water witching. It *is* a "superstitious" practice from the point of view of the educated observer, and the pattern has obviously been transmitted to the current generation of farmers from earlier generations. But does it persist *merely* because farmers are lacking in education and are "magical minded"? Two observations on the basis of Homestead data may be made here. The first is that many of the most highly educated individuals in Homestead still resort to the practice when they have a well drilled. The second is the fact that although the educational level is approximately the same in the present population of Homestead as in the population of Cotton Center in the Texas Panhandle, water witching is not utilized to locate wells in Cotton Center (where the water table stands at a uniform depth), whereas the practice flourishes in Homestead (where the underground water supply is highly variable in depth). These facts strongly suggest that there is more to the phenomenon of dowsing than that it is a "superstitious survival" from an earlier phase of cultural development.

THE FUNCTIONAL THEORY

A few rural sociological writers have given some attention to this third theory in which such practices as water witching are viewed not merely as "superstitious survivals" but as ritual responses to situations of technological uncertainty in the contemporary scene. Carl Taylor, in his *Rural Sociology,* has made the following statement:

> The reliance of the old-time farmer upon the almanac was proverbial, and his belief in signs, although sometimes exaggerated, is by no means extinct. . . . The point we wish to make here is not that superstitions, signs, and charms have greater influence among rural than urban people (although this is probably the case), but that farming as an enterprise is influenced by the uncertainty of weather and seasons to such an extent that specious explanations of the causes and effects of this uncertainty have become widespread among rural people.

In the elaboration and application of this functional theory to the phenomenon of water witching, we must first specify the aspects of the Homestead situation that are technologically uncertain (and hence productive of emotional and cognitive frustration) from the point of view of modern science. It is clear that a competent groundwater geologist can provide a sound general description of the geology and the water resources of the region, and that this geological knowledge indicates that ground water is available in two of the formations that underlie all or part of the region. One or the other of these aquifers can always be reached if wells are drilled deep enough. But it is equally clear that even with the most careful geological mapping, there exists a high degree of uncertainty as to the depth and amount of ground water available in any *particular* location where one may choose to drill. This factor of indeterminacy arises from the fact that surface outcroppings do not provide complete knowledge of the buried channels and ridges that resulted from erosion of the Mesa Verde formation in Tertiary times, or of the structural conditions resulting from faults. Both these geological facts result in substantial variations in the depth and quantity of ground water.

We have, then, a situation in which family-size wells on the scattered farmsteads were needed to relieve farmers of the expensive and time-consuming task of hauling water from some distance, and a situation in which there existed a zone of indeterminacy in the exact location of adequate ground-water resources. The stage was set, so to speak, for the development of a method to cope with the situation. Two things happened. On the one hand, a local farmer "discovered" that he had the power to dowse wells and began to do so throughout the community; on the other, geologists from the Soil Conservation Service began to visit the community and to make certain recommendations on the location of wells. The two alternative methods were in competition. But the geologists came to the community infrequently[10] and could only provide answers to the question of location and the depth to water in a given well in *general* terms, whereas the water witch was always available and could specify an *exact* location and an *exact* number of feet of water. These reassuring answers encouraged many homesteaders to drill wells. When good wells were obtained at near the depth named by the water witch, his praises were sung throughout the community. When a dowsed well was a failure (because it was not deep enough), there were ready-made rationalizations to account for the failure. And the most frequent stories told about dowsing involve the cases in which a farmer tried drilling without dowsing and obtained a dry hole; then he hired the water witch to locate a well on his farm and obtained good water.

In brief, there would appear to be a functional connection between technological uncertainty in locating wells in this arid environment with a complicated geological structure and the flourishing of the water-witching pattern. This conclusion is fortified by the observed fact that the area of highest anxiety in the community—the location and development of adequate water resources—is also the area of the most persistent and most utilized ritual pattern—the water-witching technique (57 per cent of the observed instances of ritual practice)—and by the fact that water witching, which is an unused skill in the ancestral region of the Texas Panhandle, was activated and has flourished in Homestead.

Thus, although a relationship can be demonstrated between technological uncertainty and ritual in the case of water witching, the pattern has been elaborated and rationalized in terms of one of the central value-orientations of Homestead. For in their relationships with the natural environment the homesteaders strongly emphasize an orientation which may be described as "rational mastery over nature"; the environment is viewed as something to be controlled and exploited for man's material comfort. And for the adherents of water witching in the community, the pattern becomes an important expression of this value stress upon "rational" environmental control. It is part of the farming process—along with clearing the land with bulldozers, plowing, planting, and cultivating the fields with power machinery—to locate a well by witching before one employs a driller. Explanations of how dowsing works are predominantly sought in terms of "electricity" and other "scientific" concepts. Rationalization for errors is provided in terms of the presence of metal objects which "short-circuit" the process, or in terms of technologically faulty equipment.

There are clearly certain functional "gains" in the practice of water witching for the development and continuing survival of a community like Homestead. The *certain* answers provided by the dowser relieve the farmers' anxiety about ground-water resources and inspire confidence to go ahead with the hard work of developing farms. The pattern also provides a cognitive orientation to the problem of why water is found (at a certain depth) on one farm and not on an-

[10] Mr. Meeks has called my attention to the fact that the Soil Conservation Service maintains only two geologists in the Southwest who give advice on locating wells; hence their visits to any given community are necessarily infrequent.

other—in terms of the ideas about water veins that run irregularly under the ground.

But it is equally clear that the practice of dowsing involves certain functional "costs" in this situation. Energy and resources are invested in a technique which does not provide any better information as to the location of shallow underground water supplies than does the good judgment of individual farmers. It is also often the case that dowsed wells will be located at spots that are highly inconvenient and inefficient for the most economical operation of the farm. Some farmhouses in the community have been built in inaccessible places on the sides of hills "because that is where the water witch found the water." But the homesteaders who are adherents of dowsing believe that they are being "scientific" about locating underground water. These attitudes detract from the effort of obtaining more precise geological information which, even if it does not tell the farmer in terms of so many feet how far it is to water at a given location, is at least a more promising long-range approach to the development of water resources for the community.

SOME COMPARATIVE DATA

Homestead is located in a region inhabited by four other cultural groups: Mormon, Spanish-American, Zuni, and Navaho. The water-witching pattern is part of the cultural equipment of the Mormons and the Spanish-Americans, but it is generally absent among the Navahos and Zunis. The Mormon experience with water dowsing parallels that of Homestead. The Mormon community is located in a well-watered valley at the base of a mountain range. In this valley wells can be drilled at almost any location, and ample ground water obtained at 30–40 feet. Some of the Mormon settlers have dry-land farms and ranches in the area to the south and east in which the ground-water situation, with a high degree of variability in amount and depth, is comparable to that of Homestead. Although the Mormon community has a water witch, he has dowsed only five wells in the irrigated valley during the past forty years. On the other hand, he has been employed to witch more than fifty wells in the dry-land farming and ranching region where the ground-water situation is highly uncertain. Occasionally, the Mormon water witch is employed to dowse for the homesteaders, and the water witch from Homestead has been employed on at least three occasions to dowse for the Mormons.

Water witching is also used by the Spanish-Americans in the area. About fifty years ago there was a practicing Spanish-American dowser, but at present the Spanish-American population does not have its own dowser. Instead, water witches from Homestead or the Mormon community dowse wells.

So far as we can determine, the water-witching pattern is unknown to the Zunis and to most Navahos, and there is no evidence that aboriginal divining techniques—such as Navaho hand-trembling—have ever been used to locate springs or wells. The only exception in the Navaho community is found in the case of three older Navahos who in the 1930's observed the techniques of the Mormon water witch. When the Navahos tried the technique themselves, the witching stick "worked" for only one of the three. This Navaho still claims to be a water witch and reports that he has (on his own initiative) dowsed three wells, two of which produced water, and one of which was a dry hole. The powers of this one Navaho water witch are not generally recognized by others in the Navaho community, and, indeed, he is usually ridiculed when he talks about dowsing. It should be noted that this dowser is the only one of the local Navahos who has become an earnest convert to Mormonism; he is now an elder in the Mormon church.

The general absence of the pattern among the Zunis and Navahos is partly a matter of history, in that it was not a part of the cultural tradition of these groups as it was in the case of the homesteaders, Mormons, and Spanish-Americans. But it is also partly a matter of geographical situation and the use made of water resources by the Indians. Before the Indian Service began to drill wells for these two tribes, the Navahos depended upon springs, natural water holes, and lakes for water; the Zunis depended upon springs, natural lakes, and the Zuni River. Although both tribes now have wells on their reservations, the problem of locating and drilling the wells is completely in the hands of Indian Service technicians.

There is one interesting case of a highly acculturated Navaho who decided to have his own well drilled. At the suggestion of the Mormon trader, he employed the Mormon water witch and paid him $25 to locate a well. The dowser designated a location with his witching stick and told the Navaho that it would be 12 feet to water. A well driller was then employed, but the only result was a dry hole 400 feet deep which cost the Navaho $1200. The Mormon trader commented, "First time I've seen the water witch miss"; the water witch explained the situation by asserting that "the vein must have dried up," since it was several months after the dowsing took place that the well was drilled. The Navaho is thoroughly disillusioned about the powers of water-diviners.

Our conclusion is that water witching is a ritual pattern which fills the gap between sound rational-technological techniques for coping with the ground-water problem and the type of control which rural American farmers feel the need to achieve. The best geological knowledge of ground-water resources that is currently available still leaves an area of uncertainty in the task of predicting the exact depth to water at a *given* location in a region with a variable ground-water table. The water-witching pattern provides a reassuring mode of response in this uncertain situation.

Thus, although water witching is to be regarded by the scientific observer as a non-empirical means for achieving empirical ends —and is functionally equivalent to the magical practices of nonliterate societies—it is generally viewed as a rational-technological procedure by its adherents in rural communities. The technique can, therefore, best be described as a type of "folk science" or "pseudo science" in the rural American cultural tradition. As a body of pseudoscientific knowledge, the water-witching pattern in our rural farming culture is the same order of phenomena as the pseudoscientific practices that cluster around situations of uncertainty in other areas of our culture; as, for example, in modern medical practice where there appears to be a pattern of "fashion change" in the use of certain drugs, an irrational "bias" in favor of active surgical intervention in doubtful cases, and a general "optimistic bias" in favor of the soundness of ideas and efficacy of procedures which bolsters self-confidence in uncertain situations.

OMAR KHAYYAM MOORE

Divination—A New Perspective

The author proposes that divination, by supplying a chance mechanism, directs some human activities towards randomness and may thereby serve a useful role in avoiding regularity where such lack of deviation may be deleterious. In the article by Park following this one, the probability theory of divination is given some credence but with the caution that the act of divining is seldom purely random, that randomness is not always necessarily useful, and that divination in some societies thrives without the actual prevalence of "objective," i.e., nonsubjective, procedures. Park nevertheless sees the scapulimancy of the Naskapi as serving the useful function of establishing an effective consensus upon a particular project. It is well to bear in mind that not all divination is directed towards randomness, as Winston Churchill realized when during World War II he hired Louis de Wohl, an astrologer, to tell him what Hitler's five astrologers were most likely advising the Führer to do in making his military decisions. In any event, Moore's position is ingenious.

Reprinted from *American Anthropologist,* LIX (1957), 69–74, by permission of the author and the American Anthropological Association.

The purpose of this paper is to suggest a new interpretation of certain kinds of magical practices, especially divination. First, however, I should perhaps explain briefly the motivation for undertaking this analysis. The initial impetus came from experimental investigations of the problem-solving activities of groups. These experiments quite naturally involved the study and classification of ineffective problem-solving techniques, and it appeared that fresh insight into this whole matter might be gained through examining some "classic" cases of ineffective solutions to problems. Magic is, by definition and reputation, a notoriously ineffective method for attaining the specific ends its practitioners hope to achieve through its use. On the surface, at least, it would seem then that magical rituals are classic cases of poor solutions to problems, and for this reason should be of theoretical interest from the standpoint of research on human problem solving.

Most, if not all, scientific analyses of magic presuppose that these rituals as a matter of fact do not lead to the desired results. If the carrying out of a magical rite is followed by the hoped for state of affairs, then this is to be explained on other grounds. Scientific observers, of course, employ the criteria furnished by modern science to judge the probable efficacy of magical activities as methods for producing the ends-in-view of magicians. One of the puzzles most theories of magic seek to resolve is why human beings cling so tenaciously to magic if it does not work. Many contemporary explanations of this puzzle make use of the concept "positive latent function," that is, that even though magic fails to achieve its "manifest" ends, except by accident or coincidence, it serves its practitioners and/or their society in other critically important ways. The position developed here is compatible with the viewpoint that magical rituals may be sustained by numerous latent functions. However, it conceivably could serve as a prophylaxis against the overelaboration of these functions; in any case, it could serve as a supplementary explanation of the phenomena.

Put baldly, the thesis to be advanced here is that some practices which have been classified as magic may well be directly efficacious as techniques for attaining the ends envisaged by their practitioners. Perhaps the best way to render plausible this somewhat counter-intuitive proposition is to consider in some detail an actual magical rite as it has been described by a highly competent anthropologist.

The Montagnais-Naskapi, most northerly of eastern Indian tribes, live in the forests and barren ground of the interior plateau of the Labradorian Peninsula. Speck (1935) has conducted field studies of the Naskapi and in the account that follows, primary reliance is placed upon his reports. According to Speck, "The practices of divination embody the very innermost spirit of the religion of the Labrador bands. Theirs is almost wholly a religion of divination" (p. 127). It is of interest to learn exactly how divination is carried out and what ends the Naskapi expect to achieve through it.

Animal bones and various other objects are used in divination. The shoulder blade of the caribou is held by them to be especially "truthful." When it is to be employed for this purpose the meat is pared away, and the bone is boiled and wiped clean; it is hung up to dry, and finally a small piece of wood is split and attached to the bone to form a handle. In the divinatory ritual the shoulder blade, thus prepared, is held over hot coals for a short time. The heat causes cracks and burnt spots to form, and these are then "read." The Naskapi have a system for interpreting the cracks and spots, and in this way they find answers to important questions. One class of questions for which shoulder-blade augury provides answers is: What direction should hunters take in locating game? This is a critical matter, for the failure of a hunt may bring privation or even death.

When a shoulder blade is used to locate game, it is held in a predetermined position with reference to the local topography, i.e., it is directionally oriented. It may be regarded as "a blank chart of the hunting territory . . . " (Speck, p. 151). Speck states (p. 151) " . . . as the burnt spots and cracks appear these indicate the directions to be followed and sought." If there is a shortage of food, the shoulder-blade oracle may be consulted as often as every three or four days and, of course, the directions that the hunts take are determined thereby.

There are certain other relevant aspects of divination that must be mentioned before turning to an analysis of the ritual. Speck explains (p. 150) :

In divining with the burnt shoulder blade the procedure is first to dream. This, as we shall see, is induced by a sweat bath and by drumming or shaking a rattle. Then, when a dream of seeing or securing game comes to the hunter, the next thing to do is to find where to go and what circumstances will be encountered. And since the dream is vague, and especially since it is not localized, the hunter-dreamer cannot tell where his route is to lie or what landmarks he will find. So he employs the shoulder blade. As one informant put it, the divination rite cleared up the dream. "We generally use the caribou shoulder blade for caribou hunting divination, the shoulder blade or hip bone of beaver for beaver divination, fish-jaw augury for fishing, and so on." Drumming, singing, and dreaming, next divination by scapula, then, combine as the modus operandi of the life-supporting hunt.

It is well to pause at this point to take note of certain features of these rites.

The Naskapi do not control the exact patterning of cracks and spots in the shoulder blade and, furthermore, it would not be in accord with their beliefs about divination to attempt such control; rather, they are interested in observing whatever cracks and spots appear. This means that the final decision about where to hunt, for instance, does not represent a purely personal choice. Decisions are based on the outcome of a process extrinsic to their volition—and this outcome is dependent upon the interaction of a number of relatively uncontrolled variables such as bone structure, temperature of fire, length of time bone is exposed to heat, etc.

It may be clarifying to perform a "mental experiment" in order to analyze some of the possible consequences of basing a decision on the outcome of an impersonal and relatively uncontrolled process. Imagine that the Naskapi carried out their divinatory rites as described with this exception; they did not base their decisions on the occurrence of cracks and spots in the burnt blade. They dreamed, sang, drummed, burned a shoulder blade, but ignored the cracks and spots. Under these hypothetical circumstances, decisions still would have to be made about where to hunt to game.

One question which this "mental experiment" raises is: Would the Naskapi be likely to enjoy more success in hunting if they did not permit decisions to rest upon the occurrence of cracks and spots? Would it not be sounder practice for them simply to decide where, in their best judgment, game may be found and hunt there? Of course, when the Naskapi do have information about the location of game, they tend to act upon it. Ordinarily, it is when they are uncertain and food supplies get low that they turn to their oracle for guidance.

It can be seen that divination based on the reading of cracks and spots, serves to break (or weaken) the causal nexus between final decisions about where to hunt and individual and group preferences in this matter. Without the intervention of this impersonal mechanism it seems reasonable to suppose that the outcome of past hunts would play a more important role in determining present strategy; it seems likely their selections of hunting routes would be patterned in a way related to recent successes and failures. If it may be assumed that there is some interplay between the animals they seek and the hunts they undertake, such that the hunted and the hunters act and react to the other's actions and potential actions, then there may be a marked advantage in avoiding a fixed pattern in hunting. Unwitting regularities in behavior provide a basis for anticipatory responses. For instance, animals that are "overhunted" are likely to become sensitized to human beings and hence quick to take evasive action. Because the occurrence of cracks and spots in the shoulder blade and the distribution of game are in all likelihood independent events, i.e., the former is unrelated to the outcome of past hunts, it would seem that a certain amount of irregularity would be introduced into the Naskapi hunting pattern by this mechanism.

We can indicate the point of the foregoing discussion in the following way. In the first place, the Naskapi live a precarious life; their continued existence depends on the success of their day-to-day hunting. And it is prima facie unlikely that grossly defective approaches to hunting would have survival value. Like all people, they can be victimized by their own habits; in particular, habitual success in hunting certain areas may lead to depletion of the game supply—it may lead, that is, to a success-induced failure. Under these circumstances, a device which would break up habit patterns in a more or less random fashion might be of value. The question is: To what degree, if any, does shoulder-blade augury do this?

It should be remembered that it is difficult for human beings to avoid patterning their behavior in a regular way. Without the aid of a table of random numbers or some other randomizing instrument, it is very unlikely that a human being or group would be able to make random choices even if an attempt were made to do so. The essential soundness of the last statement is recognized in scientific practice. Whenever, in the course of a scientific investigation, it is essential to avoid bias in making selections, every effort is made to eliminate the factor of personal choice. As Yule and Kendall have succinctly stated, "Experience has, in fact, shown that the human being is an extremely poor instrument for the conduct of a random selection."

Of course, it is not maintained here that the burnt shoulder blade is an unbiased randomizing device. It is likely that the bones would crack and form spots in certain ways more often than others. Regularity stemming from this source may to some degree be lessened because the Naskapi change campsites, yet in the rituals they maintain the same spatial orientation of the bones (for, as previously mentioned, the bones are oriented map-like with reference to the topography). Hence, a crack or spot appearing in the same place in the bone on a new occasion of divination at another campsite, would send them on a different route. An impersonal device of the kind used by the Naskapi might be characterized as a crude "chance-like" instrument. It seems that the use of such a device would make it more difficult to anticipate their behavior than would otherwise be the case.

It is not possible on the basis of the available evidence to determine even approximately whether shoulder-blade divination as practiced by the Naskapi actually serves to increase their hunting success, although a plausible argument has been advanced indicating that this might be the case.

If the Naskapi were the only people who engaged in scapulimancy, the question of its efficacy would perhaps not be of general theoretical interest. However, scapulimancy was widely practiced in North America and has been reported from Asia, India, and Europe. There are other divinatory rituals that also involve the use of impersonal chance-like devices in arriving at decisions, for example, the ancient Chinese divination by cracks in burnt tortoise shells. One hundred and twenty-five different figures formed by these cracks were distinguished for oracular purposes. All manner of objects and events have been used in divination. Some arrangements are perhaps not obviously chance-like,

but prove to be so when analyzed, as for instance Azande divination. The basic divinatory equipment associated with the Azande "poison oracle" consists of poison, probably strychnine, and fowls. The Azande have little control over the potency of the poison they administer to the fowls since they do not make their own poison, and not all fowls have the same tolerance for this poison. The Azande ask questions of the poison oracle and base decisions on whether the fowls live or die. They have no way of knowing in advance what the outcome will be.

The heuristic analysis given here is potentially relevant to all situations in which human beings base their decisions on the outcome of chance mechanisms. It is obvious, however, that light would be shed on the actual workability of these procedures only in terms of a thorough-going investigation of the problems men face within the societal context in which these problems occur. Certainly the apparent irrelevance of such techniques is no guarantee of their inutility. On the contrary, if shoulder-blade augury, for example, has any worth as a viable part of the life-supporting hunt, then it is because it is in essence a very crude way of randomizing human behavior under conditions where avoiding fixed patterns of activity may be an advantage. The difficulty of providing an empirical test for this hypothesis points to the fact that it is an open question.

Years ago Tylor noted that "the art of divination and games of chance are so similar in principle that the very same instrument passes from one use to the other." Tylor's observation is acute. However, it would appear that the relationship in "principle" is not between divination and games of chance, but between divination and games of strategy. It is only very recently that the distinction between games of chance and games of strategy has been drawn clearly. We are indebted to von Neumann and Morgenstern for clarifying this. It is beyond the scope of this paper to discuss the theory of games of strategy, but it is worth pointing out that this theory makes evident how some classes of interactional problems can be solved optimally by means of a "mixed" or "statistical" strategy. In order to employ a statistical strategy it is necessary to have, adapt, or invent a suitable chance mechanism. Its being "suitable" is critical, for unless the chance device will generate appropriate odds for the problem at hand, then its potential advantage may be lost. It should go without saying that no one assumes that preliterate magicians are in any position to get the most out of their crude chance-like devices. Nevertheless, it is possible that through a long process of creative trial and error some societies have arrived at some approximate solutions for recurring problems.

SUMMARY

It is the object of this paper to suggest a new interpretation of some aspects of divina-tion. It should be emphasized that this inter-pretation is offered as a supplement to exist-ing theories of magic and not as a replace-ment. An examination of many magical practices suggests that the utility of some of these techniques needs to be reassessed. It seems safe to assume that human beings require a functional equivalent to a table of random numbers if they are to avoid unwit-ting regularities in their behavior which can be utilized by adversaries. Only an ex-tremely thorough study of the detailed struc-ture of problems will enable scientists to de-termine to what degree some very ancient devices are effective.

GEORGE K. PARK

Divination and Its Social Contexts

The title of this article succinctly expresses the point of view with which Park chooses to treat divination. Divinatory proce-dures, he says, must always be seen in relation to the social situa-tion, and with this as his theme he convincingly imparts to us an appreciation of the positive role they play in affecting the social processes by eliminating an important source of disorder in social relationships. Park stresses the legitimizing function of divina-tion. An African Yoruba who uses divination to select the site of a house does more than perform an isolated bit of personal magic; viewed in its social context, the procedure imparts a legitimizing sanction to a process of structural realignment that would be diffi-cult to sanction in any other way. Appreciation of the social con-text of divination is also of help in determining the appropriate-ness of divination *per se,* or the appropriateness of a truly random device. It is a paradox that divination has a derandomizing effect, for it establishes a consensus and thereby makes action more pre-dictable and regular. This can be seen among the Naskapi, who gain a collective decision on the direction of hunting through the use of scapulimancy, even though the procedure has subjective elements. In dealing with guilt divination or ordeals, which in-volve a series of cumulative trials, the author makes a clever comparison between such procedures and the decisions beginning at a lower court and leading upward to the highest court, with only the "guilty" passing on to a further trial. To illustrate the unevenness in the distribution of divination among the folk socie-ties (where, however, it is found more typically than in urban societies) he cites the contrast between the Azande, whose divina-tion is important in the detection of witches but is nevertheless formal and undramatic, and the Buye, who use divination to lead to a public vengeance-murder and cannibalism; each procedure is suited to each social situation.

To sum up, Park suggests that a sociological rather than a

Reprinted from *The Journal of the Royal Anthropological Institute,* XCIII (1963), 195–209, by permission of the author and the Royal Anthropological Institute of Great Britain and Ireland. Some slight editorial revisions suggested by the author have been included.

psychological interpretation of divination is more general and fruitful. To be appreciated, divination has to be viewed in its context of private sentiment and public opinion according to the particular structure of the society in question. For a given situation one must look into the context provided by the social structure, conventional thought, and the immediate circumstances.

In a good many societies studied by anthropologists divination holds, or has held, a fairly exalted place; yet the argument is not often put forward that the working of any particular social system has hinged in any critical way upon the performances of its diviners. In a general way, diviners are to be classed with the native herbalist and the shaman as private practitioners of an art to which natural science lends little support; and when it is once assumed that the "doctor" does not do what he manifestly claims to do—that a diviner does not, in fact, divine—reason would seem to suggest that on the whole he is likely to do as much harm as good. In particular would that reasoning seem to apply for the many societies in which the diviner is most conspicuously employed in the finding of witches, and where a normal consequence of his fallible accusations may be the destruction of innocent persons.

There will be occasion to examine a few such cases in later sections of this paper, where I shall argue that their crueller aspects tell us less about the nature of divination than about the general problem of order in human societies. But first I should like to present, in the light of some less dramatic facts, an argument for taking divination seriously as a characteristic social institution of which our understanding needs to be improved. From the study of divining, I think we may properly expect to gain some insight into the working of other, and perhaps more reputable, institutions also exhibiting the phenomenon which I shall describe as "procedural intervention." It will be a thesis of this paper that developed systems of divination should not be regarded as mere excrescences upon the body politic, doing none of its work; but that the diviner, with all his peculiar skills and his characteristic paraphernalia, does in a controlled way intervene in and affect the social process with rather definite and socially useful results. I do not suggest that the consequences of any given act of divination are more likely to be just than unjust: nor

shall I claim to have become convinced, by an examination of cases, that witch-doctors usually help to rid their societies of disagreeable deviants. But I shall argue that, quite apart from such considerations as these, divination has as its regular consequence the elimination of an important source of disorder in social relationships.

I

Divination is always, I think, associated with a situation which, from the point of view of the client or instigator, seems to call for decision upon some plan of action which is not easily taken. Even the urban addict to fortune-telling is probably no exception to that rule; though the point need not be laboured. Typically, divination is called for in cases of illness and death, and in other life-crises; in the corroboration of a marriage-choice and in individual or collective moves involving some change in social alignments or, perhaps, economic condition; and in situations of loss, calamity, or unresolved conflict, whether on a personal or a much larger scale. For each society in which divination is practised there is, to be sure, a proper list of its occasions; and such a list may say much about the sources of strain in that society—the Chinese diviner in Singapore does not receive the same pattern of cases as does the Zulu; nor has European contact failed to change (by enlargement) the scope of the institution among the Plateau Tonga. Divination is associated with the sense of danger, and often seems to relieve it. But those who have regarded the diviner only as a sort of primitive therapist, relieving his client of doubt and indecision, or explaining away such phenomena as convulsions, may surely be accused of understating the case. For it is generally true that where convention calls for divination, its omission might have genuinely difficult consequences for the person or group who acted without it. Divination normally provides more than the "psychological release that comes from the conviction that subsequent action is in tune with the wishes of supernatural forces"; the association of divination with situations of problematical action is best explained, after all, by the fact that it lends to a client's subsequent act a peculiar but effective type of legitimation.

What I propose is, put most simply, that a "sociological" interpretation of divination will be found more general, and more satisfactory, than the "psychological" analysis which is so much more readily suggested by the usual circumstances of actual observation in the field. The ethnographer to-day seldom observes divination in conjunction with what Durkheim called "collective representations"; far more often it is a mere matter of individual purpose—irrelevant, almost, to anything so grand as the collective welfare. A Yoruba employs Ifa divination, for example, in the selection of a house site. Stripped of its social context, and taken only from the immediate point of view of the actor, divination for such a purpose would seem to have doubtful value. On the one hand, as Bascom (1941, p. 45) observes, "the elimination of fruitless hesitation and indecision would seem to enable the individual to concentrate his entire energy, without distraction, upon the task at hand." But against this one must weigh a heavy material cost and all the added "distractions" which, among the Yoruba, that is likely to entail. Yet the choice of a house site by a Yoruba has, in fact, a special gravity readily apparent from the point of view of social-structural analysis, although perhaps unlikely to be intelligibly conceived by the actor himself. Where one builds must decide where a particular family is to be placed in social space. Thus the inclusive lineage splits whenever a member establishes a compound in a separate town; while within the town the assortment of households into small, tightly localized, lineage units (*omole*) is similarly dependent upon voluntary choice of residence. Overcrowding and quarrelling within the *omole* leads to the formation of a secedent group which co-operates over an extended period in establishing a new compound, and hence a new *omole*. A "first chamber" is established for the leader, who is helped and will gradually be followed by "any other men of the *omole* who may care to join him."

On the testimony of the ethnographer himself, then, the choice of a house site is scarcely to be regarded as a decision affecting the principal actor alone. The *omole* is defined by agnatic descent *and* by common residence in a given compound. In building a house one must either desert or remain with that nuclear kinship unit of which one has been a part; one must join or fail to join a particular party of secession; whatever choice one adopts must be comparatively permanent. I suggest that the custom of prescribing divination in such a context is eminently understandable on the ground of social function. For it is the peculiar property of the diviner's role that he is able, in the public conscience, to remove the agency and responsibility for a decision from the actor himself, casting it upon the heavens where it lies beyond cavil and beyond reproach. In the Yoruba case which has been cited, the diviner in effect provides a legitimating sanction upon a process of structural realignment which, depending as it does upon a voluntary act, would be difficult indeed to sanction in any remarkably different manner.

Nor is the Yoruba case exceptional, unless in the fact that one is able to reconstruct, from the ethnographer's material, the social context of a procedure which too often is presented simply as an isolated bit of magic, of no social consequence. In other societies where a similar insight is to be gained, divination appears to play a similar "structural" role, sanctioning by depersonalizing the various types of action which may normally be required in the process of sorting and resorting local living arrangements. Often the diviner plays a part in the cleavage of groups through conflict. By means of divination, a groundless and merely personal or private accusation may be given publicity as an apparent fact, shorn of the obvious bias of its original sponsor. Thus among the Yao a large measure of voluntarism is involved in the process by which, in a matrilineal and largely uxorilocal society, a headman comes to command a village or hamlet mainly composed, on the male side, of a congeries of individuals tied to him only by marriage. There are strains toward virilocal marriage which are countered by the stress laid upon matrifiliation, which increases, the more successful a woman may be in producing children. Again, succession within the matrilineage to the position of headman or chief is competitive and often transitory; it depends upon political ability and upon that peculiar social talent by which a leader is able to avoid serious accusation of such acts as sorcery, incest for the sake of maleficent power, or lack of diligence in protecting the interests of the lineage women who hold the balance of power in the village. Inevitably, the cycle of alignment, succession, and secession is moved by accusation and counter-accusation; and in virtually every new initiative the diviner plays a part. But Yao divination differs in form and degree of "objectivity" from the Ifa divination of the Yoruba; and this characteristic difference accords with the more nearly transitory and, apparently, more "emotional" character of Yao social relationships.

Ifa divination has been carefully described; and perhaps needs no special recounting here. The questions asked of the oracle are often kept secret, in the precise form asked, even from the diviner himself; the diviner repeats set verses, corresponding to the throw of a chance device; recognition of the applicability of a verse by the client is the chief means by which subjective selection is allowed to enter the procedure. Mitchell describes Yao divination as follows:

The type of divining is usually by gourd and object (*ndumba*). The diviner first of all establishes the reason for the visit, i.e. death, illness, theft, or whatever it is. He then consults his gourd and throws into his hand a variety of symbolic objects. He builds a story round these objects, and finally pronounces that he sees some person whom he vaguely defines. The consultor is then asked to mention who this could be. Though sorcery is supposed to be practised mainly in order to get human flesh for ghoulish feasts, it is not believed to act haphazard. In other words, a sorcerer is supposed to select his victims for revenge as well as for meat. The selective processes at work, therefore, when the consultor seeks to reconcile the diviner's findings with his own suspicions, are that he should select someone who is obviously evil, i.e. from his own point of view, one with whom he has been quarrelling, and he should appraise the possible motivation for sorcery. After he has made the selection the name is tested by the diviner and the consultor may later submit a chicken to the poison ordeal to test the diviner's findings (Mitchell 1956, p. 153 n.).

It is notable that the form of divination, as described here, allows a degree of flexibility and publicity to which an accused might reasonably object; nor in the cases which Mitchell presents is there any hint that determinations of this sort are normally unchallenged by the accused. On the contrary, an inconvenient divination is often doubted and belittled; and it may be tried again elsewhere. In the end, it is not so much the choice of the divining instrument but that of the public, reflecting the alignment of interpersonal loyalties, which decides whose divination will prevail, and how far.

II

It may be objected that in a system like that of the Yao, since divination is ultimately overridden by opinion, the diviner can play no functionally significant part. But public credence goes by degrees; it is not absolute. Moreover, divination is not simply a weapon to be taken in hand by any who wishes to increase his influence; the call upon the diviner requires a particular sort of occasion, and the diviner must look to his own rules and to his own need for professional independence. An important aspect of divination as institutionalized procedure is just this—that it provides "resistance" in its own right to any client's proposal.

An interesting but, I think, not all-important source of such "resistance" lies in the employment of chance or chance-like mechanisms in the rendering of decisions. In Moore's brief but suggestive analysis of scapulimancy among the Naskapi of Labrador (Moore 1957) the point was made that the chance elements in divination may sometimes have a very practical effect in dispersing hunting activities, and the like, so as to prevent over-use of a favourite resort. The emphasis was here upon the practical consequences of the use of a randomizing device in the selection of certain critical courses of action. One is led to conceive of the diviner as a sort of spinner of a wheel of fate, which is wiser than any human judge.

But there are objections to what may be called the "probability theory" of divination, even when full justice be done to it. One is that it puts an incongruous emphasis upon the actual "objectivity" of the divining process, an emphasis very hard to justify on ethnographic testimony. A related objection is the obvious one that the theorist must dig very hard amongst the descriptive materials to find only a few examples where a random device, by scattering choices, might have some use; while he is surrounded by implausible cases. (Is it useful or not to scatter accusations of witchcraft?) Finally, divination in many societies thrives in the face of the fact that it possesses no truly "objective" forms at all. Among the Dinka, chance devices are evidently mere imports with no firm standing and uncontrolled by the safeguard of known and respected rules; the diviner of repute is "one who is thought to have an important Power, a free-divinity, in his body" and who divines by uncontrolled possession (Lienhardt 1961, pp. 68 seq., 71). If we are to identify a generic function in divination, then, it must be one of more general applicability.

We have considered the point that the Yao override the decisions of their diviners in many cases, and yet that the practitioner thrives among them. The Azande, who refer major questions to a procedurally guarded poison oracle for which the probability of a given outcome in response to a given query is subject to mathematical calculation, certainly possess a more "objective" procedure; and they honour its objectivity frankly, by relegating other important oracles to lesser places. But complementary to their respect for the major oracles is their disinclination to take seriously others, which none the less persist in use. Such is the *makama,* which, though it is only used to indicate a witch, "is regarded lightly by every one and rather in the nature of a joke" (Evans-Pritchard 1937, p. 376). If we now ask why Yao divination persists in the face of obvious scepticism, the answer may perhaps be phrased analogously to the drama of *makama* divination among the Azande. The instrument is a cone of wood, inserted in a tight-fitting sheath which is held by the witch-doctor at a seance. No one supposes that the witch-doctor cannot, by the way he inserts the conical peg, decide whether or not the man he hands it to is likely to be able to pull it out. Yet when one who has taken the peg is unable to tug it away, the force of the demonstration upon the audience is clear enough. The *makama* has been told to stick tight if the man is a witch "and has come to spoil divination"; and behold, tug as he may, that man cannot dislodge the peg from the sheath held by the diviner. In this way (I think we may suppose) the witch-doctor who chooses to manipulate his audience may gain its

effective consent in barring a certain person from the seance. And so in a great variety of other and less artificial situations may an act of divination become the occasion for the emergence of consensus where before there was none. That all shall agree, the previous commitments of some must meet resistance in a moment of unanimity.

My point is that divinatory procedure, whether "objective" in quality or merely inter-subjective, constitutes a technique for establishing an effective consensus upon a rather particular project. If that project be conceived in its entirety by the client prior to his seeking the corroboration and quasi-religious sanction of the diviner, the requirement to divine yet proves an obstacle to him. By deflecting his plan, divination may tame it. But more often, I judge, a client's "project" is but vaguely formed; he has a grievance or cause for acute anxiety but no clear path before him. Then divination may act as a decision-making mechanism by taking the matter, as it were, out of the client's hands. Here a random device, for which intelligent alternative proposals must be framed, is most appropriate. Such was Moore's case among the Naskapi. A band must hunt together or its essential unity would be lost; yet in the context of Naskapi culture the band had no permanent structure. Scapulimancy was much used by the Naskapi in connexion with the broadest imaginable range of purposes, and seems to have permitted of fairly free interpretation. As an instrument for achieving a collective decision on the direction of hunting it was probably not particularly "random"; but it was suited by its apparent impartiality and its association with prescience to the task of rendering a decision with exceptional authority.

By contrast to the Naskapi, differently situated migratory groups may make no use at all of divination in determining routes, which may be determined by politically established rules of precedence or on economic grounds; for the little-structured organization of the Naskapi is not universal. The appropriateness or inappropriateness of divination *per se* is thus one question; and the appropriateness of a truly random device is another. Both questions require analysis of the context of social structure and conventional thought as well as of the immediate situation of divining. External or "objective" divination may be called for where the status of the diviner is relatively low; but "objective" divination which is also truly random may have very limited uses. Azande *makama* divination has its own proper context, as does, in great measure, each separate oracle used in that society. Divination by "objective" oracle characterizes the Azande social system as clearly as prophetic divination characterizes the Dinka. In both societies divination is rather clearly stratified, in the sense that there is greater attribution of reliability to pronouncements from one source than to those from another. On the other hand, the Yao know no such universal stratification. For better reliability one has no fairer alternative than to take the trouble of going farther away from home, where the atmosphere of contention may be less heavy. The consequence of such egalitarianism is one of a general tentativeness in all social arrangements predicated on moral allegations which were legitimated by divination; and that, indeed, would seem as essential to the operation of the Yao social system as is formal procedure to the Azande or depth of faith to the Dinka.

III

I have attempted to place divination among the important institutions of the primitive world by comparing its operation in several different social contexts, and suggesting that in each case divinatory procedure has the effect of stamping with a mark of special legitimacy a particular decision or a particular kind of response to crisis. Paradoxically, divination appears to have a de-randomizing function; establishing consensus, it renders action more predictable and regular. We have thus come to the point of regarding divination as a practice closely related to the problem of controlling and channelling public opinion and belief; and thus we come close to the more general subject of ritual and its sociological meaning.

Ritual occasions presuppose an underlying consensus; and by demonstrating that consensus in a dramatic fashion they strengthen it. The "field" of ritual in time and space is indefinitely extended to the borders of the social world known to its congregation. By contrast, the "field" of the diviner's seance is restricted, centering upon an immediate problem, and dissipating as distance and time rob the problem of reality. Yet divina-

tion and ritual interplay; nor is the scale of divination always so small as the situation of the "seance" suggests. Ritual is employed to solemnize attitudes toward the diviner and toward his paraphernalia amongst his public, and even to solemnize his own attitudes toward his professional role. Thus an Ovimbundu divining-basket is to be "put to bed" each night by a procedure suggesting the "ritual" of psycho-analytic literature. The basket is further set apart from ordinary things by containing the skull of a poisoned child, bits of the corpse of a famed diviner, and durable remains from animals who appeared in portentous circumstances. The conceived "power" of such a basket, it would seem, must be equal to the dramatic effect required of it in use.

The same theme of solemnization may be remarked in the close association of divination with sacrifice. The consultant diviner may invariably prescribe sacrifice, as among the Yoruba; in priestly divination omens are sought through solemn ritual. The context within which a class of priestly diviners might intervene in affairs of state has been suggested by Sidney Smith in an essay, "The Practice of Kingship in Early Semitic Kingdoms" (1958, p. 31):

The subjection of the individual actions of the king to a procedure—the framing of a question capable of only a positive or negative response, the examination of the liver or the flight of birds or the like, the decision as to how the many omens were to be interpreted to procure a majority of favourable or unfavourable results —shows that no king acted according to his own judgment alone, without the possibility of interference by others. They were themselves well instructed in the devices of divination. . . . But they cannot always have forced measures through, if the diviners were in opposition.

The suggestion of a check-and-balance system, stabilized by a qualitative division of role, is supported by what is known of the importance attributed to divination by the Assyrian kings themselves, and by records of the severe ritual constraints to which the king, at the hands of the priest, was subject. The point upon which I would insist, however, is that of the necessary relationship inhering between omen and public attitude in a society which so exalts the diviner. The warlord who disregards published omens cannot but prejudice victory and, in the case of reversal, invite disaster: such is the plot of many an ancient tale.

It is perhaps then a little less important to know how such a system actually worked than to understand how, of necessity, it must have been supposed to work. The stability of ritual and structure over centuries, which for ancient Mesopotamia is subject to careful documentation, bespeaks a rootedness in universally shared conventional understandings. The favour of the gods was regularly tested in public by the king himself; and the procedures were patently such as to lie convincingly beyond public suspicion—they possessed a genuine drama. If the effect of that drama was, directly, only to enhance the verity of myth, yet the resulting sacredness of myth and ritual—as being the whole basis for the legitimacy of the system of authority itself—was such as to provide a terrible safeguard of due procedure against the depredations of expedience. It is most unlikely, I suggest, that a critical military decision ever was thrown up to mere chance; or that chance ill-omens ever were allowed in fact to shake the legitimacy of a king's rule. Such possibilities are no more likely than that the Naskapi of Labrador ever went off in a completely wrong direction as the result of an odd crack in a scapula. The function of the ritual precautions, then, was precisely indicated by their manifest purpose of colloquy with the gods. No enterprise of state could proceed without the drama of suspense by which the eventual approval of the gods was made known, and the fact of the direction of such enterprise by beings higher yet than the king was demonstrated to all.

The verity and the power of the myth are thus of greater importance to us than the genuineness of the chance or inspirational devices employed, which need have only dramatic truth. If we would correctly understand Yoruba precautions against contamination of the "objectivity" of their oracles, or Zande down-grading of devices which they believe may sometimes be rigged, we should think of such precautions as protective of the essential credibility possessed by their more solemn procedures of divination—procedures which, having ceased to be convincing, cease to have value. For while in one social context the requisites of compelling drama may be music, dancing and shouting, and the appearance of sudden "possession" in an immoderately decorated

diviner, in a quite different context a drama of markedly different quality may be the only appropriate one. The canons of popular drama are not everywhere the same.

We began with the point that divination must "resist" in order to produce conviction; and we have been brought to the point of conceiving that resistance in dramatic terms. Where it is used, the genuine randomizing mechanism effects a set of baffles contravening direct movement toward a goal, and the drama is that of a maze; but it is functionally equivalent to the merely ritual or emotive dramatization found in other contexts. If the types of divination should be named, then, I would call them mechanical, ritual, and emotive; although the three types easily shade into one another in many systems of divinatory practice. Thus the drama of "possession" is not necessarily a frightening one; it may merely serve, like a mechanical device, to establish the apparent presence of otherwise invisible beings. Clairvoyance and mediumship or ventriloquism are in different contexts the functional equivalents of the induced convulsion of the body. Divining bones and similar collections of paired and named objects, even though they be cast out in public view or cast by the client himself, and even though they be interpreted by a wholly exoteric calculus, as Junod made it quite clear that they might be, only dramatically resist nice application to the case in hand—they do not refuse but parry, reverse, and redirect the questioning until it finally culminates in a meaningful resolution, a denouement which, ideally, suddenly reveals the hidden clue to the turns of the drama, like the verb in Virgilian verse. Among the Sotho by 1935 the element of chance, or fate, or direct communication by spirits was merely asserted in the formal act of casting the bones; the emphasis lay not there but in the skill with which the diviner was able to achieve insight into the problems of his client and to bring what was usually a protracted seance to an impressive conclusion. Thus the great work of the Sotho diviner was not in the cure or charm which he finally sold to the client, but in the artificial task of discovering what the client had come about—by skilful diagnosis he must establish his own extraordinary powers as a practitioner; and that would give to his cures their value.

So among the Buye it was the lesser diviners who employed the more random and emotionally less impressive devices; the *kilumbu* diviner, upon whose word a man might be seized for a witch and submitted to the poison ordeal, was in his body but in strange voice the medium of communication from a spirit world. The finding of a witch was through a culminative process. It began with an "objective" seance; and sorcery could only be divined when, after spirits and ancestors all alike had been tried and refused, it was necessary to hint at living persons. There followed an impressive seance with the *kilumbu* diviner, whose mechanical devices only supplemented and coloured his own charismatic aura. Beyond, there was a sort of "high oracle" of final recourse, or the poison ordeal. It is my suggestion that these various forms of trial should be conceived as ranging along a gradient of increasing unimpeachability; and that each item of procedure should be understood as essentially contributing toward that end—the dramatic establishment of an ostensibly irrevocable judgment.

IV

There is perhaps a certain lack of logic in a cumulative system of trials, each of which is ritually exalted to the pitch of infallibility, but any one of which may contradict the preceding. But there is no lack of drama here; nor does the same characteristic in the developed court system in the urban society prevent the lower courts from pronouncing final judgments. Instead, there is an enhancement of the sense that truth, eventually, must always be found out. A hierarchical system of guilt-divination parallels, in the logical frame of its organization, a system of courts. The drama and seriousness of procedure increases, as only the "guilty" pass on to a further trial; suspense holds, for each succeeding test offers a chance of exoneration; only no person or body present is invested with apparent responsibility for the critical judgment. At the bottom of the system is the lowly consultant diviner; at the top, perhaps, the ordeal, divination by invisible diviner—that *ne plus ultra,* as it has so often been pictured, of human irrationality.

But ordeals in many societies are interchangeable with other forms of guilt-divination. Bourgeois reports from Rwanda and Burundi techniques of guilt-determination ranging from accusation by a jumping grasshopper to a series of ordeals, some of which could manifestly operate only on a "psychological" basis, and others which as clearly are insensitive to the psychic state of the accused. Here the social context of the ordeal as a trial for sorcery is perhaps epitomized in the fact that torture must be used to extract confession where the signs indicated guilt but the accused denied; and by the further fact that the drama might even then turn: for a stout submission to torture could result in pardon by the highest authority.

The analytical problem, I suggest, which such facts present is essentially one of showing a constant relation between a divining procedure, insusceptible to any but a procedural criterion of validity, and the public conception of right. As the Yoruba, moving in social space, legitimates his move by submitting alternative plans to divination, so a movement of witch-killing, whatever its true determining conditions, must have legitimation. Moreover, as in the political theory of legitimacy, we must distinguish between formal and substantive manifestations: it is in the necessity of achieving more than formal grounds for public execution that the puzzle of the mortal ordeal may be understood. At the moment of action, I would argue, it is substantive legitimacy which is most essential; the act which is predicated upon the decision of divinatory proceedings must be the one which, as all concerned now concede, ultimate wisdom would find true. But there is the further fact that, in the long run, the emotional consensus created by the divining session will fade; so that the legitimacy of the action, in retrospect, will rest upon formal considerations. Both conditions, the formal and the substantive, must therefore be met; the latter to prevent immediate disorder, the former to preserve the chartering myth of constituted authority—its claim of embodying transcendent justice.

The immediate importance of substantive legitimation is well illustrated in the materials reported by Bourgeois, Weeks, and Colle. Where a confession is required before execution, it is evident that the formal indication of guilt is felt to have insufficient weight. We must imagine, I think, that in a segmentary society no accused is without his kin, disposed to support him if the matter is not handled well; and that it is their acquiescence above all which must be publicly demonstrated before an exacted death will become an act of the greater collectivity and quite distinct from action by a vengeance group. But public torture can, in certain contexts, bring about a revolution in group sentiment. One way of handling that emergency would be to reserve the possibility of a pardon; another, I think, is to be found where procedure relies more fully on the logic of the mortal ordeal.

A comparison of Buye and Kongo ordeals is instructive. The importance of the state of public sentiment, and an indication of the logic in the ordeal, emerge from the Kongo materials of Weeks. A duly accused witch is given bark poison and may exonerate himself by vomiting it in four successive trials. Normally, on succeeding in this way, he is fêted with great enthusiasm; no taint of the earlier indictment remains against him. Yet in some cases there is no immediate reversion of public sentiment. A person "very obnoxious to the people generally" (a person deserted even by his kin?) is subjected to a further procedure, a sort of intellectual torture or ordeal. Dazed from the effects of the poison, he must none the less show normally quick powers of discrimination, identifying the species of twig thrown to him, or the type of ant, butterfly, or bird pointed out; and a single miss legitimates execution on the spot. The poison ordeal is intended, as it were, not so much to determine guilt as to demonstrate it. Where opinion is divided, it may demonstrate either guilt or innocence. But where opinion is one, and the poison yet fail to demonstrate its truth, a more certain ordeal may be added, whose form is tinsel but whose decision will validate the popular mandate. The same bark poison which, in four administrations, should kill a witch is employed in a single dose in a lesser case; yet the value of the poison is here reversed. Innocence is demonstrated by retaining the poison unharmed; and vomiting demonstrates guilt, whose punishment is short of death. Yet there is a consistency of logic, when the ordeal is perceived as demonstration and not merely trial: if the poison is to demonstrate guilt in a capital offence, it cannot fail to kill; if poison is to demonstrate innocence in a less-than-capital offence, it must be retained without killing. Here is divination by "objective" sign.

The procedures of Buye law in connexion with the poison ordeal suggest a rather different social context, in which the poison in fact operates as legitimating divination, of the highest order, in what is not a public execution but a public vengeance-murder. If the accused failed quickly to vomit the poison upon the first trial, he was set upon by the waiting relatives of his supposed victim, who cut off head and limbs and threw them into "un grand brasier," probably then to be bought from the group by an anthropophage, whose secret society would obtain from such a body the sense of increased supernatural power. The ceremonial ordeal here recounted was administered, away from the village of the deceased, by a ritual specialist of official standing; but it might be duplicated on a less imposing, though equally mortal, scale in private vengeance trials administered wholly by the vengeance group itself. The interplay of formal procedure and direct, vengeful aggression indicates the immediate translation of formal legitimation into substantive right. Presumably, the divinatory system could be said to have reduced bloodshed as against a putative vengeance system requiring a death for a death. Since Colle remarks that the ceremonial ordeal would be imposed in a given case by the *kilumbu* diviner himself, we may suppose that he was not unaware of the relation inhering between the social situation of achieving formal legitimation and the certainty with which it may be expected to resolve the problem of substantive right. Divination without the diviner is peculiarly suited to such a context of controversy. As a public demonstration of guilt, or equally of innocence, the mortal ordeal could possess a dramatic quality unequalled by the other techniques we have examined. The mere publicity of the event as a mortal trial, with its apparent acceptance as such by a great crowd suffering it to proceed, appears to rule out the possibility that, in the public conception, the actual result might have been predetermined by the official mixer of what the modern reader must regard as a merely chemical poison. It was not so regarded by the Buye.

There are, I think, two major puzzles in connexion with the ordeal. One, however, is simply an artifact of the meeting between believer and sceptical observer; it evaporates when attention is shifted from the superficial plausibility of the beliefs which support divinatory practice to the problem of understanding how such beliefs in fact become established and reinforced in collective experience. The other puzzle is the technical one of understanding the peculiar properties of the ordeal which have made it a widespread phenomenon in various parts of the world at various times. I have suggested in this paper that the poison ordeal has in several societies functioned as the apical procedure in a system of guilt-determination; and it is in those terms that I have offered a functional analysis of the custom. The ordeal, like other forms of divination, has been presented as an instrument by which, in concrete situations calling for action, a particular construction may be put upon a problem, and a particular resolution socially established as the right one. In the context of guilt-divination, the consequence is legitimation of demands for punishment or restitution. The ordeal is characteristic of societies in which the right to demand punishment has not been successfully pre-empted by constituted authority, or where that authority requires the drama of human sacrifice to penetrate the public conscience.

v

Divination is typical of the folk, and not of the contemporary urban, form of the social life; its distribution is also uneven within the folk world. "Divination," wrote Lowie (1935, p. 255), "is rightly considered atypical for American Indians." His perspective was that of the Plains Indians, possessed of a social life in which loss, theft, illness, and death were met in a manner wholly different to that which has characterized most of the African societies considered in this paper. As the individualistic quest-religion of the Plains differed diametrically from a congregational religion centred in the regard for common ancestry, so was the relation of man to man amongst such groups as the Crow or Cheyenne distinct, whether in war, in hunting, in marriage, or in the ceremonial solemnification of those peculiar values which characterize a tribe's commitment to the life it has known. If one were to set oneself the task of discovering what particular cluster of human sentiments might most probably be found in constant association with a developed system of divination, the contrast between Plains Indian and Bantu African responses to physical helplessness, loss by death, characterological deviance, and mortal danger would offer a starting-point of obvious merit. Nor can such a task, I think, ultimately be avoided if we are to understand the ethnographic distribution of divination, and thence to establish a scientific comprehension of its nature.

It has been the tendency of this paper to suggest that divination is regularly associated, in a comprehensible manner, with certain types of social situation; and it is perhaps unnecessary to insist that, while some regard is due to the operational fictions of "pure structuralism" in anthropological analysis, equivalent social situations cannot occur in two widely different cultures. That is because actual human situations arise as much out of actor-perception and actor-definition as they do out of such events as death or cattle-theft. If divination is to be known as an important institution of the folk world, and not as a mere example of what unscientific thought can uncork, I have suggested that it must be appreciated in its context of private sentiment and public opinion as these are found in variously structured societies. Guilt-divination among the Buye culminated in a public vengeance-murder and cannibalism; among the Azande neither cannibalism or the mortal ordeal had any such firm place; rather, by historical times, the very sentiments which were celebrated in the Buye practice had been subjected among the Azande to firm and formalistic control:

It is apparent that when a witch is exposed by the oracles a situation fraught with danger is created, since the injured man and his kinsmen are angry at an affront to their dignity and an attack on their welfare by a neighbour. No one accepts lightly that another shall ruin his hunting or undermine his health out of spite and jealousy, and Azande would certainly assault witches who are proved to be injuring them if their resentment were not directed into customary channels backed by political authority (Evans-Pritchard 1937, p. 85).

The active role of witch is all but wholly imaginary amongst the Azande; yet persons identified as witches abound and are neither cut off from most normal social ties nor usually killed. The witch is identified by formal and "objective" systems of corroborative divination, which accept and reject proposals at random; and the act by which a witch recalls and cancels his psychic aggression is equally formal. Public opinion is little roused; substantive legitimacy is not a problem but follows from general acceptance of the correctness of those formal procedures of divination which are supposed to have been followed. When substantive legitimacy does, rarely, prove a matter of some concern, the case may be put to a test; although normally not until the accused dies a natural death, when public examination of entrails again puts to proof, by corroborative divination, the proposal that in life he was indeed a witch. A particular belief, moreover, would appear specifically to discourage the relatives of a deceased from insisting upon such a test—witchcraft is thought to be inherited, and the taint, in the case of a damaging finding, then falls upon the living. It would be only an already embattled group of kinsmen who would stand to gain from raising the issue; in general, the Azande are content with formal and undramatic procedure, so that public feeling fairly readily subsides, excuses, and forgets. While all may agree that the witches about them are many, there is no general agreement as to who they may be (Evans-Pritchard 1937, pp. 23 seq., *et passim*).

The social system of the Azande, I submit, is very different from that of the Buye; nor is there any obvious need that we should trace the reason for this general difference to a source, as it were, in one of its parts. The differences of political and social organization are manifestly important; but so are the differences of ecological setting; nor would an analysis betraying preference for "psychological" causes be barren of pertinent evidence. The concern of this paper is with systems of divination, and it seems evident to the author that these, also, have some explanatory value. It should be clear that Zande divination is suited to the character of Zande life, as Buye divination is suited to another; but divination, I have insisted, has a logic of its own and is not an inconsequential institution. We may as reasonably propose, then, that Zande ideas about witchcraft follow from Zande divinatory practices, as we may put the case the other way round. And in similar fashion we may insist that the drama of Buye divination was not merely a fierce sort of entertainment, but was an instrument by which the prevailing social appetites, fears, and ideas, as reported for the Buye at the beginning of this century, had been shaped. It is in this light, I think, that we may best perceive the affinity between ordeal and crucifixion, or between the poisoning and the burning of witches.

As a legitimating procedure, divination in the folk world has much in common with what we may call the "licensing and certifying complex" in the contemporary urban world, which is similarly concerned with such matters as birth, marriage, and death, and which functions in connexion with movement over social boundaries and the infringement of property rights, as well as with crime and dangerous or irksome insanity. Yet a world which is cleansed and ordered by a vast hierarchy of licensing bureaux has a quality lacking in the world which must resort to supernatural ratification of all its minor changes of status. In peasant China, as exemplified in West Town (Hsu 1948), there was no ritual intervention in marriage, of the sort which requires a solemn commitment to the choice by the two individuals or families concerned. There was, however, at a preliminary stage in the betrothal, a quiet procedure of submitting the "eight characters" of a son and prospective daughter-in-law to divination, which should expose an unsuitable match before the start of a long and eventful schedule of gift-giving and negotiation essential to the establishment of the match as a duly acknowledged contract. The social context was that of a seclusionist society, in which publicity had a peculiarly symbolic and putative quality, centring in notions of family dignity and honour, which required objective expression from time to time in the form of elaborately ceremonial feasts, processions, and gifts to the living and the dead. The submission of a marriage-choice to divination was felt to be genuine, even though a negative result was not necessarily final: if one diviner found the "characters" incompatible, the father of the boy might, on consideration, simply go to another. Divination then provided no more than a formalistic ratification of the choice; yet in its context it had function and meaning. The negotiation during betrothal was pre-eminently a test of the status of the boy's family; and as such it strained the family's economic resources to the utmost. Divination here preceded and legitimated the launching of a peculiar, ceremonial splurge by which the family must pair itself in the public eye with another and unrelated family, demonstrating its own means in the negotiated size of its gifts in money and kind, only a portion of which would probably be returned as dowry.

More usually, divination in West Town had an even more routine character—it was employed only to hold and check ceremonial proceedings at each point until the auspicious hour was met. Yet even in this form divination betrays, on analysis, its peculiar usefulness; for the longer, in West Town, one might stretch a ceremony, the greater was one's demonstrable importance. That proposition illuminates particularly, I think, the use of divination in burial. Predetermining and saving for the cost of an old man's death could become a major preoccupation for his family, which recognized an impending test of its public and heavenly standing. The extent of mourning, feasting, and economic outlay for a procession must be wisely decided. In the event itself, much depended upon the length of the dead man's stay, as a corpse, with his family; for this was a sign, not only of the family's regard for the man, but also of its regard for the house whose fortune he had guided in life. Thus it was, I suggest, that divination must determine "the hour when the coffin lid will be nailed on the coffin, the hour when the coffin will be removed from the house, and the day when the coffin will be lowered into the pit for burial." But the system of divination was not here one which left the matter to chance. Poor families divined only the hour, not the date; while an important burial amongst the well-to-do might be delayed for one or two months. The diviner who set the worth of a family by thus timing its funeral shared the universal exemption from reproach of a peculiar institution: he was the midwife of decision, knowing not its author.

I have attempted to sketch the meaning which divination might have had in the context of Chinese family institutions because it has usually been treated only as a minor part of an intellectual or criteriological system and because I have found it illustrative of the manner in which divinatory legitimation may parallel and supplement in its working the most formal ritual sanction. Legitimation is a process whereby a particular act, event, or establishment is declared to be an example of a class already defined in the presupposed norms of a society; and where formal legitimation only is concerned the movement is simply, as in a lower court of law, from "norm" to "case." But as in a higher court the movement has a tendency to reverse, and the "case" from providing precedent comes to modify the "norm," so I think we should regard divination as a two-edged instrument of social control. Earlier anthropologists were not sufficiently impressed, perhaps, with the airiness of "norms" in the preliterate society: Sumner's *mores* were forces in themselves, as real as Durkheim's mechanically-conceived Society or as the Church to earlier unsympathetic historians of mediaeval life. Yet Durkheim had the insight to perceive that Society is the creation of ceremony, and to stress the importance of emotional interaction in the ceremonial gathering; later anthropologists have come to see that the *mores* do not live on of themselves but must be recreated by ritual, ceremony, and the act of constituted authority in the experience of each individual; and history has perceived that the ordeals of witches and the torture of heretics may have been more than the mere application of secure "norms" to "cases"—that such cruel and dramatic phenomena reveal to us a crisis in the security of the norms themselves.

CHAPTER 8

THE MAGICAL TREATMENT OF ILLNESS

⚘⚘⚘⚘

INTRODUCTION

The question of whether primitive behavior is rational, or irrational and supernatural, has long been surrounded by confusion. Words such as "rational" and "supernatural" are relative words, and may be defined in relation to any cultural standard. Behavior which is clearly irrational or nonrational in our terms may be quite rational for the native who lives in a more supernatural world. Before the turn of the century Tylor proposed his theory of the rational nature of the primitive; he represented the primitive to be essentially a rational being hampered only by a lack of knowledge. Later the social philosopher Lévy-Bruhl insisted that primitive man is prelogical and dominated by supernaturalism. The truth probably lies somewhere between these antipodes; even by modern criteria primitive man is often rational in his mundane, easily controlled affairs, but in his treatment of disease he turns very largely to supernatural means.

This is not to say that all primitive societies have a like amount of supernaturalism in their treatment of disease; they certainly do not. The Aztecs were often empirics, although not scientists, and were so successful in treating disease that Cortez was said to have preferred an Aztec physician to his own sixteenth-century Spanish "medicine man." Furthermore, probably even the simplest society has some medical treatments which are rational. Bloodletting, cathartics, massages, sweat baths, trepanning (if not

trephining), and bonesetting are common in primitive societies. But even these manifestly rational treatments are likely to have mystical supernatural treatments associated with them—the Comanche could skillfully set a broken bone but would have considered the treatment incomplete if it were not accompanied by magical incantations and prayerful entreaties.

The primitive man in his supernatural world assigns a supernatural cause to disease. Disease may be caused by object intrusion and cured by a sucking shaman; if a spirit possesses you, it must be driven out; if your soul has left you, it must be found by divination and made to return by a medium; and if the disease is merely due to some malfunction of one's internal organs, a good shaking or beating may suffice.

Despite the bizarre aspects of many supernatural treatments, despite the fact that fantastic magical curing formulas may have been passed down for centuries, and despite the fact that many treatments have no apparent empirical derivation, primitive treatment often does cure. First of all, most illnesses cure themselves anyhow; most people recover in spite of the treatment they undergo. However, supernatural treatment may have real medical utility. The psychotherapeutic bedside manner of the primitive curer removes fear and creates faith. Again, some of the drugs magically administered to the patient may actually have value (see A. H. and D. C. Leighton, "Elements of Psychotherapy in Navaho Religion," *Psychiatry,* IV [1941], 515–524). The typical primitive supernatural treatment involves elements of shock or stress analogous to modern shock treatment—treatment which stimulates an internal reaction capable of returning the organism to health. Finally, the assignation of a cause, even a supernatural cause, for an illness allows both the patient and those concerned about him to take action against something—anything. The primitive is provided with a culturally acceptable cause of disease, such as sorcery or a taboo violation, and is given "normal" means of acting to combat the illness and its

cause. Compare this with the debilitating anxiety which accompanies inactivity and it will be evident why the primitive is told what to do and is kept busy doing it.

The prominence and affluence of the cancer quack is unfortunate testimony to the failure of even modern medicine to cure all disease by rational procedures; as the modern sufferer seeks any cure in his misery, so does the primitive accept any supernatural balm he can find in his agonizing fear of sickness and death.

Modern medicine is primarily rational with some magical elements while primitive medicine is primarily supernatural with some rational elements. This chapter is designed in greater part to illustrate the latter.

ERWIN H. ACKERKNECHT

Problems of Primitive Medicine

In the following article Ackerknecht, who has written extensively in the area of primitive medicine and medical history, presents a brief but comprehensive discussion of primitive medicine in contrast to modern scientific medicine. He stresses the supernatural character of primitive medicine. As he states it, "primitive medicine is essentially magic medicine."

For the most part the author's presentation of relevant data and his analyses of them are both sound and instructive. However, he does occasionally take positions which are unorthodox. The espousal of Lévy-Bruhl's theories and terminology is not justified on the basis of present knowledge; indeed, Lévy-Bruhl's theories of the prelogicality of primitive man are roundly denounced by the majority of contemporary anthropologists. Similarly, the primitive is not always the "poet" or "dreamer" we meet in his pages. Malinowski, Marett, and many others have convincingly demonstrated the fact that some areas of primitive society are primarily rational and empirical. The contrast between a modern scientist and a primitive is often misleading, for only a small number of persons in European societies live even partially scientific lives. It would seem untenable to argue that primitive man does not employ the same principles of deductive and inductive logic that modern man does. What leads the primitive to magical acts and beliefs is not his system of logic but his errors in correlating irrelevant causes with particular outcomes. The primitive who attributes his recovery from a fever to the performance of a supernatural curing ceremony has not committed a logical error, he has simply made a bad correlation. Scientists make the same sort of error every day, although they are much more likely to detect their error than is the primitive. If we view magical treatment not as a different and curious form of logic but as the result of inaccurate causal relations of variables, then we can begin to

Reprinted from *Bulletin of the History of Medicine,* XI (1942), 503–521, by permission of the author, the American Association of the History of Medicine, and the Johns Hopkins Institute of the History of Medicine.

seek reasons for the primitive man's magical treatment of illness.
Some additional warnings are necessary. The "instinct" theory
adduced as the reason for the discovery of useful drugs is possible, but is is not probable and certainly has not been proved.
The fourth cause of the success of primitive medicine is said to be
due to the fulfillment of a "deep metaphysical need." By this the
author apparently refers to a general human desire to be in harmony with his social and physical universe.

Ackerknecht's theories about the relation of the medicine man
to the priest rather than to the physician are well worth consideration, and his discussion of primitive psychotherapy is excellent.
Read critically, this article presents a number of controversial
and important problems. It should serve as a stimulating introduction to the study of the supernatural treatment of illness.

Lacking a better expression, we call "primitive medicine" the medicine of the so-called
"savage" or "uncivilized" people. We wish
by no means to indicate by this expression
that this medicine gives us a simple picture
of the first stages of medicine. Although the
medicine of these tribes is the main and almost the only source at our disposal for the
study of these first stages, conclusions have
to be drawn with extreme caution. These
tribes and their culture have their own history, sometimes as complex and as tortuous
as our own. From all that we know today,
evolution followed not one, but multiple
lines.

Although primitive medicine covers an
enormous field in time and space, it has been
studied to a surprisingly small degree by
both medical historians and anthropologists.
The approach taken especially by medical
historians was not always a very happy one.
Students either decided that certain primitives have no medicine at all, because their
medicine fits so badly into our patterns of
medicine, or they regarded it only as a mere
immature or degenerate variety of our medicine. But our medicine is not *the medicine*
nor our religion *the religion,* and there are
not one medicine but numerous and quite
different medicines in the different parts of
the world and in the past, present, and future. Measuring everything with our everyday standards, we will never understand
either the past or the future. Primitive medicine is not a queer collection of errors and
superstitions, but a number of living unities
in living cultural patterns, quite able to function through the centuries in spite of their
fundamental differences from our pattern.
This method of seeking in primitive medicine
only for what it has in common with ours
and of projecting into primitive medicine our

categories leads to somewhat strange results.
Demonology was put in the same class with
bacteriology. Primitive medicine was studied
by putting aside consciously every magic and
religious element and served even as a model
of logical and causal thinking. There developed a myth of primitive "empiricism." A
great handicap also was the clinging of medical historians to outmoded anthropological
theories (Tylor, Spencer) and the permanent confusion with folk medicine. Folk
medicine seems still to complicate the problem by its strange mixture of true primitive
traits with degenerate high cultural elements.

The strong difference made by Lévy-
Bruhl between irrational primitive mentality
and rational modern mentality may be discussed, although Lévy-Bruhl's real thought
is much more sensible than his critics imply.
This pragmatic approach to the question
proved to be more laborious, of course, but
also much more fertile than any other
method. But there can be no doubt that there
is such an opposition between modern medicine based essentially on rationalism in spite
of its magical elements and between primitive medicine based essentially on supernaturalism in spite of its rational elements. A
short study of the most salient features of
primitive medicine will show us that primitive medicine is essentially magic medicine.

PRIMITIVE MEDICINE IS MAGIC MEDICINE

The expression "magic" is used here in a
very broad sense, as is sometimes done by
anthropological authors. "Magico-religious"
would perhaps be more correct for the complex which concerns us. In the relatively
little-differentiated societies we are studying,
magic and religion like their representatives

have generally not yet differentiated from their common background. The attempt of Rivers to classify the medical rites in the religious with respect to their more personal, propitious and ideal character, and in the magic with respect to their more coercitive, impersonal, and utilitarian character has proved somewhat arbitrary and seems not to advance very much our understanding of the question.

Illness, like death or an accident, is generally not regarded by the primitive as a natural event. It is the consequence of supernatural actions or forces. Even a cold may be explained by such causes. Mystical object intrusion, loss of the soul or one of the souls, spirit intrusion, breach of the taboo, or witchcraft are the most common causes of illness. Very often not only one but several of them are accepted in one tribe. The witchcraft theory, which is distributed all over the world, leads especially in Africa to a kind of witch psychosis even more murderous than our own medieval outbreak. The object-intrusion theory is absent only in the Eskimo districts and on the Asiatic continent. The soul-loss conception has its greatest elaboration among the Eskimos in Siberia and on the North Pacific coast. Of course the soul-notion of the primitive is quite different from our soul-notion. Often it is something rather material, like the kidney fat of the Australians, and can be eaten by the captor. The widespread spirit intrusion, associated with exorcism and transference, seems most elaborated in the regions of higher culture (China, India, Egypt, Mexico). Again the spirit should not be regarded as the true spiritual being. It can be materialized in a snake, bird, etc. Taboo transgression unites in a strange blending of medical, juridical, and economic elements on a religious background.

The belief in such causes can of course only occur in a world quite different from ours, in a magical world where the natural is supernatural but the supernatural quite natural, where causality in our sense does not exist but things, animals, and plants are tied together by mystical participations and moved by occult forces. Primitive causality is not afraid of contradictions, and looks for the cause of a material effect in another supernatural dimension or vice versa, because it sees no limits between the two realms. That makes Mr. Evans-Pritchard say: "In-deed we may ask whether they have any notion that approximates to what we mean when we speak of physical causes." Here is much more than the usual *post hoc–propter hoc* fallacy. It is quite clear that this "logic" can never become more than the mother of pseudo sciences. The primitive is not merely surprised by the unusual, because in his world everything is possible; but he reacts with intense emotion. The emotion governs his thought and produces new images and delusions which he takes for realities. While our world had become the world of the *homo faber*, his is rather the world of the poet or the dreamer.

Nevertheless among the countless tribes which do not know natural causes for disease there are no doubt tribes which recognize natural causes for certain diseases. The overemphasis of this fact created an entirely false picture of primitive medicine. After a closer examination a number of these cases appear as magic. Some appear clearly as a result of European influence. And the rest seem still so well integrated in the magical system that the primitive does not resent any contradiction between these and supernatural causes, does not feel compelled to employ this new system of thought. Instead it seems to be their very frequency that takes these diseases out of the emotional, magical, religious sphere. The famous process of rationalization (Max Weber) is only its first beginning and magic has been submitted to ordeals like inquisition and puritanism before going to pieces.

To find out such unusual causes of disease unusual methods of diagnosis are needed and used. Every kind of divination, trance, astrology, and dreams are the current methods. Among the Cherokees the latter method even produces the disease names. Our experience stops at the frontiers of the natural. The most important part of the primitive's experience is on the other side of this frontier in his contact with the dead, the spirits, and the mystic ancestors. What for us is a mere hallucination is for him a privileged experience.

The primitive's treatment is deeply embedded in the whole magico-religious system, hence his extreme traditionalism, conservatism, and conformity. Everything new is resented as highly dangerous, and fear, the kernel of primitive man's faith, makes him cling so closely to rules and customs.

This traditionalism on the other hand makes him so surprisingly insensible to experience. Dreams again reveal very often the best ways of healing. Countermagic with its different manual and vocal rites and dances, soul hunts, exorcism, and purification are the most common irrational methods of healing. Of course they often contain measures which we now employ rationally as bloodletting, massage, baths, and drugs. But they are employed in a magical sense. Amulets serve as magical preventive methods. The primitive treatment centers around symbolical actions, for the symbol is of enormous importance in primitive thought. But while our symbol dematerializes, the primitive symbol remains concrete and material, and permits action by mystical participation upon invisible forces which it cannot attain otherwise.

The mechanism of these participations becomes quite obvious in the much decried couvade. The primitive father does not lie down as a result of laziness, but to protect his child. He takes the child's medicine, or the whole family confesses or keeps a diet when one member is ill. The borderlines of primitive man's individuality are located differently from ours. As his treatment is magical and miraculous, it has to be strong and short. He distrusts the long treatment of the white man. His magico-religious ideas make the primitive sometimes not only flee the ill person, but even kill him, as he kills twins and monsters. If we finally remember that time and space are qualitative in primitive man's thought, that his classifications separate what we unite and unite what we separate (men, plants, animals), that his medical thought is full of the conception of a mysterious power (*mana, orenda, mori, ngye,* etc.), we can only wonder about the identification of his "causality" and his "logic" with ours by some of the best students of this problem.

IS THE MEDICINE MAN THE ANCESTOR OF THE MODERN PHYSICIAN?

Since Spencer, it has become a kind of axiom that the medicine man is the forefather of the modern physician. This strange personality is very often the first and only professional man in primitive society. His magic tries to produce prosperity in every field for his tribe and to fight its foes by magic. Very often the medicine man is not only magician, priest, and sorcerer, but also chief and king, an almost superhuman being. His calling is generally inherited from the father or the maternal uncle. But being cured of a severe illness, being a twin, or becoming possessed may equally qualify him. A strange and widespread custom is his wearing of women's clothes. He undergoes a very severe initiation and is surrounded by strong taboos, which isolate him from society. His costume, food, dwelling, customs (he does not work and sleeps during the day, being awake at night), name, and language are different from the ordinary. He has his special drums and rattles, his magical stick and medicine bag. Sometimes he kills his own son to get more magical power. To fail is often very dangerous for him; the killing of the inefficient (or too successful) medicine man is reported all over the world. Different even in death, he goes to another heaven than that of his fellow tribesmen.

A careful analysis of both medicine man and modern physician reveals them rather as antagonists than as colleagues. All that they have in common is that both take care of diseases; everything else is different. The conservative medicine man plays his role as the most irrational man in an irrational pattern. The critical modern doctor gains social leadership by expressing the rational tendencies in society, rationalizing even the irrational as for instance the psychoanalyst, and invading in this way the oldest domain of the priest. The medicine man is rather the ancestor of the priest, the antagonist of the physician for centuries. If there is any ancestor or colleague of the modern physician in primitive society, it is the lay healer, usually a woman, the midwife. This female lay healer is not to be confused with the female "medicine man," the priestess. Though she is relatively nearer to empiricism, common sense, or rationalism, it should not be forgotten that she also is entirely penetrated by the magic faith.

We are fully aware that with the preceding short description of magic medicine, taking our examples from quite different cultures we sometimes oversimplified and built up one of those anthropological monsters which Ruth Benedict so wittily describes. There is not one kind of primitive medicine; there are many. In Liberia it is the mystical power of the drug that heals; among the Bantu the power of the medicine man;

among the Zuni the medical society. Among the Navahos the greatest part of the religious ceremonial is primarily concerned with disease; elsewhere it is entirely free from such purposes. Smallpox may be fled from in panic here and venerated there. Here the medicine man is rich; there he is extremely poor. Here he is priest, sorcerer, and magician in one person; there an extreme differentiation takes place.

Here medical practices are genuine; there they are imported and modified, and so on. The reason is quite obvious: "the significant sociological unit is not the institution but the cultural configuration." Medicine is nowhere independent and following only its own motivations. Its character and dynamism depend on the place it takes in every cultural pattern; they depend on the pattern itself. Therefore in order to reach a better understanding of the whole problem, we will describe in a following article the different medicines of some primitive tribes in relation to their different cultures.

THE STONE OF THE MEDICINE MAN

The question of whether the medicine man is a deceiver or believes in his own practices seems to us of the greatest importance. It is obvious that our whole attitude toward primitive medicine will depend on this question. Among people less acquainted with the subject, the former assumption prevails. It is highly interesting that among specialists only Sir J. G. Frazer defends this point of view. It is also expressed by A. B. Ellis Cator, Leonard, and Read, but by the latter two with many limitations. Still more limited are the accusations of Hrdlička and Evans-Pritchard. On the other hand, Maddox reaches some conclusions, based on the writings of Kingsley, Sieroszewski, Hoffman, Laflesche, Roth, and Nansen, about the proportion of quacks and frauds among primitive medicine men to those who are honest and sincere: "Investigation indicates the fact that the ratio of the false to the true among the uncivilized is practically the same as among the civilized." May we mention further positive testimonials in favor of the subjective honesty of the medicine man by Boas, Rivers, Lowie, Harley, von Martius, Hill-Tout, Jerome Dowd, Howitt, B. Gutmann, Driberg, Hofstra, J. W. Hauer, Wright, Hubert-Mauss, Sumner and Keller, Stone, and Marett. And it may be said that the majority of these men are not "armchair anthropologists" but fieldworkers.

There is no other practice that arouses as much suspicion about the treachery of the medicine man as his sucking out a stone (hidden before in his mouth) from the body of the patient. It seems to be just the same humbug as the stone of the medieval stone-cutter, at least as long as we see things from our own medical standpoint and not from the point of view of the primitive. But as im Thurn states: "This foreign substance, at least among the Indians of Guiana, is often if not always regarded not as simply a natural body but as the materialized form of a hostile spirit." The conclusion is rather obvious: "Given the true point of view which is not empirical but transcendental, the procedure is perfectly sincere and in its way rational. An invisible force is dealt with visibly by means that are meant and understood to be symbolic. An evil magician must have projected a crystal in the patient that is invisible. It becomes now necessary to provide a therapeutic in the form of a manual rite." Or as Lévy-Bruhl points out: "To destroy the misunderstanding it is sufficient to know that the extraction of the stone, insect, etc., in short, of the materialized disease, is by no means a sleight of hand. The doctor prefigures the intended expulsion of the evil influence. In the same way the Nagas, in order to get a rich harvest, come down the slope where they planted the rice with their bodies bent forward as if the weight of the future harvest lay already on their shoulders." Similar conclusions are reached by H. Meyer and F. E. Williams. The patients know about the substitution. We should not forget that in some Indian tribes, for instance among the Dakotas, the same characteristic stone is always used for the procedure, and consequently it is almost impossible for the patient and the public not to know the real fact. But this side of the question is not important for them. They still believe in the act because they believe in its symbolic effect. Besides, why should it be impossible for us to understand this mechanism, since the central rite of our religion, the eating of the savior's body and the drinking of his blood, is still based on a very similar symbolism?

**THE REASONS FOR THE SUCCESS OF
PRIMITIVE MEDICINE I**

Why primitive medicine and primitive
mentality took this strange course is still a
riddle. We know of no biological difference
between the savage and us which necessitated this course. But one thing seems to be
certain: in its strange ways primitive medicine nevertheless fulfills its role. In looking
for the reasons for its effectiveness we may
perhaps come nearer to an understanding of
the whole problem.

There is no doubt that primitive medicine
contains a sufficiently large number of objectively effective factors which we employ in a
rational way: massage, bloodletting, dry
cupping, baths, cauterization, surgery from
appropriate fracture treatment to trephining; even inoculation against smallpox or
snake bite are found among the uncivilized.
But we should never forget that this, as well
as isolating the sick or hiding the excrements
or keeping a diet, is not done in a rational
sense, but in an entirely magical sense accompanied by spells or prayers or manual
rites or dances! The same holds true for native drugs which we find even among the
most primitive tribes (Andamanese, Australians, Kubus, and Tasmanians). The
"spirit" of the herb fights against the disease
"spirit." It is amazing what an enormous
number of effective drugs is known to the
primitives. From twenty-five to fifty per cent
of their pharmacopoeia is often found to be
objectively active. Our knowledge of opium,
hashish, hemp, coca, cinchona, eucalyptus,
sarsaparilla, acacia, kousso, copaibo, guaiac,
jalap, podophyllin, quassia, and many others
is a heritage from the primitive.

There is little doubt that further inquiries
in the field of primitive plant lore, unfortunately wholly neglected by our too proud
"synthetic" chemists, would still give very
important results.

Even in the best textbooks of medical history the knowledge of these drugs by the
primitive is generally derived from "empiricism," "observation," the "process of trial
and error" (Castiglioni, Meyer-Steineg and
Sudhoff, Neuburger, Diepgen, and Pagel);
only Cumston speaks of the instinctive state
of medicine. But the strange fact is that such
primitive empiricism was never observed.
Besides, it is a rather grotesque picture to
imagine that the primitive should have taken
the thousands of herbs and plants and tried
one after the other until he had found out
the few dozen effective drugs. We may like it
or not; we may call it superstitition or even
stupidity like Preuss, Briffault, and Ch.
Richet; we may judge it a necessary way for
the development of human thought; in any
case the first human thought we know and
we observe is magical. Under the enormous
pressure of his terrifying surroundings man
starts to think; but he does not think rationally, in a "plain" and "natural" way with
"common sense" about his tools, for instance, which he continues to handle in a
rather instinctive way. He first creates supernatural causes and forces.

On the other hand, it is not very likely
that magical thought could find or invent the
effective drugs. As magical thought could
gather them only by chance, and as they are
otherwise too numerous to have been found
only in this way, we have to look elsewhere
for the sources of this drug knowledge. It is
the merit of Artelt to have formulated and
first proved the probable solution: "Neither
empiricism nor magic are the beginning of
the inner application of drugs by men, but
the animal function of instinct." Just as the
ill man and the ill animal still instinctively
choose their food, just as the ill animal eats
herbs and performs other reflex-like healing
measures (rubbing, scratching, licking, sucking, blowing, extracting foreign bodies) in
the same way man or pre-man chooses his
herbs. If what we call instinct were finer or
differently developed sense organs, "natural-
somnambulic perceptions of primitive sense
organs" as the school of Uexkull formulates
it, if there were specially endowed individuals leaving their knowledge to their heirs,
we do not yet know it. In any case magic
replaced to a certain degree "useful instinct-
actions by unuseful actions of thought"
(Preuss). It counteracted surgery by mystical fears, perhaps introduced cannibalism,
paralyzed growing empiricism by its traditionalism, entangled the materially effective
measures in an enormous body of materially
useless acts and beliefs. Then only empiricism slowly grew up. The birth of scientific
thought in the middle of the eighteenth century is just such a revolutionary act against
every magical-religious influence that it first
throws away everything with a magical past,
the effective (opium, quinine, iodine, mercury) as well as the ineffective.

THE REASONS FOR THE SUCCESS OF PRIMITIVE MEDICINE II

"Although remedies acting through the mind were probably the earliest to be employed by man, the knowledge that the remedies act in this way is one of the most important recent acquisitions of medicine." It is only since we have been applying psychotherapy consciously ourselves that we understand one of the main conditions of the medicine man's success. There are too many well-testified cases in primitive tribes where magic kills by suggestion for the fact to be doubted. Why should the power that kills not be able to heal? The medicine man is a soul doctor and his fellow primitive whom we know as an emotionalist needs him badly. He gives peace by confessing his patient. His rigid system (which ignores doubt) dispels fear, restores confidence, and inspires hope. And as Charcot said: the best inspirer of hope is the best physician. The primitive patient "comes into complete harmony with the infinite and as such, must of course be free of all ills and evils." In a certain sense the primitive psychotherapist uses more and stronger weapons than the modern psychotherapist. He works not only with the strength of his own personality. His rite is part of the common faith of the whole community which not seldom assists *in corpore* at his healing act or even participates in singing and dancing. The whole weight of the tribe's religion, myths, history, and community spirit enters into the treatment. Inside and outside the patient he can mobilize strong psychic energies no longer available in modern society.

He unchains hypobulical mechanisms, and thinking with his whole body (Janet) he makes his patient think with his whole body. Here lies even one of the strongest points of primitive medicine. In spite of all that has been said and written about the soul-body problem, our thought is still dualistic. We still know illnesses of the body and of the soul. We differentiate between objective physical treatment and psychotherapy; and in my description, unable to employ other categories than those of my time, I too did so; but the primitive does not. He is no dualist. He knows only one kind of disease and one kind of therapy. When Rivers called primitive medicine "even more rational than ours, because its modes of diagnosis and treatment followed more directly from their ideas concerning the causation of disease" the conclusion was grotesque, but the statement was correct. He might even have continued: and their ideas about disease are more closely connected with their general thinking and feeling. We differentiate between the magical and the rational in their thought and behavior, because we do it in our own. But they do not do the same. This unity of medical lore, this unity of the whole life and thought, makes primitive medicine very strong in a certain sense.

THE REASONS FOR THE SUCCESS OF PRIMITIVE MEDICINE III

Primitive medicine is but a part of the magical system. This system is a pure creation of society. No special natural perception or association, these qualities being common in all races and cultures, builds this strange system. Society creates these collective representations; society conserves them *and they conserve society*. The strength of the magician and his own belief in himself is the consequence of the belief of the community. Magic is not built on experience; sensual experience never furnished the proofs of a magical judgment. "The general character and the apriorism of the magical judgments seems to indicate their collective origin." Development of social organization, prior to technical development, is based on magical belief, and strange as it seems, magic forms an excellent cement for primitive society. It maintains public order without coercion. If the chief is not the magician or medicine man himself, there is the closest co-operation between them. Or in rather democratic forms of primitive government, he strengthens the influence of the old men's council which rules the tribe. "The social function of the sorcerer is therefore to preserve inviolate the power of the chief (who may or may not be a sorcerer himself), to suppress an anarchical or disorderly tendency, to give the community a sense of security in the face of known and unknown danger, to effect cures, to combat epidemics, to inflict injuries on the enemies of the clan, to counter the evil magic of the sorcerers of hostile tribes, to punish those who have offended the chief or the communal susceptibilities of the clan, and, in short, to hold the pulse of the tribe and sustain all those subtle influences that go to form the social cement that marks the difference between a community and a horde of men" (Pitt-Rivers). In a social formation where primitive mentality dominates, the medicine man is a vital organ. It is no wonder that he is generally a strong personality, the man who was strong enough to undergo the initiation, who is strong enough to live isolated from his very community-minded fellows. He thinks for his people. He knows them quite well and uses that knowledge when, in the ordeal, he detects the culprits. He has an aura of secular and eternal power. And that, no doubt, helps him a great deal in healing.

THE REASONS FOR THE SUCCESS OF PRIMITIVE MEDICINE IV

Besides its materially useful and psychotherapeutical characteristics, besides its social interrelations, magic medicine seems to have another essential element of success. Magic medicine satisfies, much more than our medicine, a basic craving in humanity, a certain metaphysical need. We are generally very suspicious of such general statements. We have seen too many errors and fallacies in this way; but we cannot on the other hand refuse to recognize a general rule when facts seem to impose it.

"Man has among his most powerful instincts a kind of need for the ideal, a kind of deep and irresistible appetite for dreams, for the unreal. This tendency manifests itself imperiously and exteriorized in the primitive, restrained and perfected in the civilized, but quite precise in all epochs of history" (Hesnard).

"Man is more proud of his metaphysical tendencies than of his scientific conquests; we have seen it already and we will see it without interruption when studying human history" (Le Dantec).

"Every individual has a representation of the reality where he lives and acts, corresponding to the structure of his group. Here the spirits are attached to other things than to the objective relations on which practical activity and industry are based" (Lévy-Bruhl).

"In the middle of the ruins of the old moral world stays still intact the triumphant column of religious need" (Michels).

If they state it as a matter of fact or if they state it with deep anger like the old supermaterialist Le Dantec, if they call it ideal, religious, or metaphysical—they could still find other more or less precise names like emotional, irrational, etc.—all of them, psychologists, biologists, sociologists, state the fact of this metaphysical need. Whether we like it or not, man has this irrational tendency, his behavior responds to this symbolical appeal to his unconscious. "Throughout man's history it has been the mechanistic theory that he has found phantastic, not the animistic one."

This need is still strong, because in its fulfillment man finds a satisfaction never reached elsewhere. "Compared with ignorance, at least conscious ignorance—knowledge undoubtedly means a possession of its object; but compared with the participation which prelogical mentality realizes, this possession is never anything but imperfect, incomplete, and as it were external. It is the very essense of participation that all duality is effaced. Now the need of participation assuredly remains something more imperious and more intense even among people like ourselves than the thirst of knowledge and the desire of conformity with the claims of reason."

Because magic gives this mystical unity which we feel so important, this deep satisfaction by metaphysical participation, it could be repressed, condemned to a hidden and almost unconscious existence (like ratio lives in primitive mentality) but it could not die, it still lives and acts. As the primitive esteems his medicine man more than his lay healer independently of their mutual effectiveness, during centuries civilized men placed the physician higher than the surgeon even though the usefulness of the latter may have been much greater than the usefulness of the former. It is not by chance that Lewis Carroll's "Alice in Wonderland," the spirit of which is so near to primitive mentality, became one of the most influential books in English literature. Since Sighele's discovery of the relationship between the mentality of sects and primitive mentality, we have been more attentive to these questions. In a small but very intelligent book, *Hidden Religions,* C. C. Bry describes the magical character in such movements as Esperanto, Sex-Reform, Christian Science, Anti-Alcoholism, Anti-Semitism, Occultism. We are witnesses of a strange hunger for idols in the masses (dictators, film stars, etc.). We observe the mystical transformations that scientific discoveries undergo in popular thought (vitamins, microbes, etc.). Some thirty years ago W. G. Sumner announced another outburst of magical thinking and feeling in our society. Unfortunately it seems that he was not mistaken.

To understand primitive medicine, we had

to go very far from our standsards and concepts. But these apparently very remote studies are by no means unrelated to our time. Besides presenting their problems to us, they lead us back to some of our own problems and thus appear as a legitimate branch of real social sciences.

JOHN GILLIN

Magical Fright

This article by Professor Gillin describes and analyzes a case of magical fright (*espanto*) in a Guatemalan community. The anxiety or fear of the patient is ostensibly caused by soul loss. An untreated case of magical fright is said to result in death in much the same manner that Victorian heroines took to their beds and languished.

The cure of magical fright is effected by a curing shaman through massage, imitative magic, shock, and suggestion, administered while he persuades evil spirits to return the stolen soul to the patient. Although the shaman can explain many of his techniques in a fashion that makes good sense to members of that culture, the treatment is clearly supernatural by our criteria.

It is interesting to note the relaxation which is reported to follow the patient's confession, as well as the juxtaposition of pagan and Christian elements in the curing ceremony.

We do not know the cause of the patient's illness; neither do we know what part, if any, of the shaman's treatment helped to bring about the cure. We do know that the patient, the audience, and the shaman himself attributed the cure to the shaman's efforts. We can easily understand the increased confidence a future patient would have in this shaman and his treatment.

Reprinted in abridged form from *Psychiatry,* XI (1948), 387–400, by permission of the author and the William Alanson White Psychiatric Foundation.

A seemingly widespread syndrome or group of ailments current among folk peoples in various parts of the Latin American area is the condition which one might call "magical fright." In Spanish it is known as *espanto* or *susto*. Both of these words mean "fright," but they are used in two different types of context. On the one hand, they are used to describe "ordinary" incidents which involve fear but which do not affect the "soul"—that is, they are not believed to have serious psychological consequences. For example, one may be "frightened" by the prospect of rain before the harvest is completed, by the power of one's opponent in a quarrel, by the announcement of an epidemic, and so on. In the second type of context, however, *espanto* and *susto* always refer to an illness or ab-

normal condition of body and personality. For this reason it seems best to render the latter concept in English by the qualifying expression "magical fright."

In general, magical fright is manifested in a person by symptoms of depression, withdrawal from normal social activity and responsibility, and signs of a temporary collapse of the ego organization. Although these are symptoms which are apparent to an objective observer, the condition is universally interpreted culturally in the contexts where it occurs as being caused by loss of the soul. The soul, in turn, is believed to have escaped from the body of its owner during a sudden fright involving startle. Hence the Spanish words used to label the illness. In cultures where this type of soul loss is recognized it is likewise believed that a person cannot live indefinitely without the presence of his soul. Therefore the "cure" of *susto* or *espanto* involves magical procedures carried out by curing shamans or *curanderos,* the main objective of which, as understood by patients and curers alike, is to effect the recapture and return of the soul to the patient.

In the course of ethnological field work I have had the opportunity to become acquainted with this condition, with patients suffering from it, and with professional curers who treat it in two widely separated Latin American communities, the Peruvian coastal town of Moche and the Eastern Guatemalan community of San Luis Jilotepeque.

In this article I propose merely to outline one typical case, to offer some suggestions of parallelism between the native treatment and scientific therapeutics, to sketch the cultural setting of this sort of ailment and its treatment, and to offer a few comparative ethnographic data.

In 1946 William Davidson and I observed all phases of the cure of several authentic cases in San Luis Jilotepeque (Guatemala) and persuaded six Indian *parcheros* or *curanderos* (shaman curers) to demonstrate and discuss their techniques in special sessions arranged for our benefit. We were also able to do the same with two female Ladino curers.

The patient in this case was a Pokomám Indian woman, aged 63, married to an Indian man two years her senior. The couple were born in San Luis and have lived there all their lives. The husband is a small farmer, and the wife makes pottery to sell. They are relatively poor and do not have distinguished status in the community, although they are respected. Of four children born to them only one survives, a man 36 years of age, married, and the father of three children. I shall use fictitious names in this account and shall call the patient Alicia.

The curer or *parchero* is an Indian who is also a native and lifelong resident of San Luis. He has a wide reputation, not only in San Luis but also in many other communities of the Oriente, as one of the most successful curers of *espanto* in the region. He works his own and rented land, but also makes a considerable income from curing. I shall call him Manuel.

The patient complained of not feeling well. She was in a depressed state of mind, neglected her household duties and her pottery making, and reduced her contacts with friends and relatives. Physical complaints included diarrhea, "pains in the stomach," loss of appetite, "pains in the back and legs," occasional fever. Verbalizations were wheedling and anxious. She alternated between moods of timorous anxiety and tensions, characterized by tremor of the hands and generally rapid and jerky movements, and moods of profound, though conscious, lethargy. Orientation was adequate for time and place, and normal reflexes were present. Before arranging her magical cure I administered to her for two weeks, with the advice of the local druggist and empirical physician, the standard remedial quinine treatment for malaria, without securing remission of her recurring fever symptoms. This was not surprising, however, because her feverish episodes did not present a clinical picture of malarial infection, although this complication cannot, of course, be ruled out. In general she gave the appearance seen in patients suffering from an anxiety attack with depressions. She herself expressed the opinion that her condition was due to "*espanto.*" Among her other anxieties was the fact that she lacked the funds to hire a competent *parchero.* A successful expert like Manuel charges two quetzales for his service, and the incidental expenses of the cure bring the total to about six quetzales. Alicia was preoccupied with the belief universal in her culture that an untreated *espanto* will eventually result in death. This, of course, added to her anxieties.

I undertook to pay for her treatment by Manuel, but, in order to avoid placing undue importance on my part in the cure, my payments were made piecemeal. In other words, I offered no guarantee at the start that any and all expenses would be paid by me. In this way the patient's anxiety concerning the financial aspects of the treatment was maintained throughout the preliminary stages.

A diagnostic session was the second step in the proceedings. This took place in the patient's house, a one-room thatched-roof dwelling with cane walls, on the outskirts of San Luis. Present at the session were the patient's husband, a male friend of the family (not a kinsman) who had acted as intermediary between the curer and the patient, Davidson, and myself. Alicia had been "cured" by Manuel before, so that she had confidence in him.

After a bit of conversation apparently intended to set the patient at ease, the curer proceeded to take her pulse. He placed the ball of his right thumb, not his fingers, on each pulse in turn for about 30 seconds, looking directly at the patient as he did so. When she attempted to drop her eyes from his gaze, he told her to continue looking him in the eyes. His demeanor throughout was one of calm and thoughtful confidence, not greatly different from that of a medical specialist in our own country when examining a patient. After he had felt the pulse he was silent for a few moments. The patient pleaded anxiously for him to tell what he had discovered. He announced calmly that the trouble was clearly *espanto*.

The second phase of the diagnostic session was what might be called "the confession" on the part of the patient. A certain amount of resistance was exhibited by the patient. A technique of the curer was to look her directly in the eyes and to announce in a calm, authoritative manner that she had been *"espantado* near the river when you saw your husband foolishly lose your money to a loose woman." (This was already known to the curer, as we discovered later.) He urged her to "tell the whole story." After several minutes of fidgeting, the patient "broke down" and loosed a flood of words telling of her life frustrations and anxieties. The *manifest,* or obvious, content of this material was to the effect that she had been the oldest of five siblings, was apparently dominated by her father who was an undistinguished Indian farmer, seemingly had developed a strong attachment to him, was forced to marry an amiable, ne'er-do-well drunkard whom she did not respect and who did not fully arouse her sexually, had from childhood a stronger than common desire for money or economic security, and had been constantly annoyed by the poverty-stricken condition of herself and her husband, a condition which she blamed upon her mate. During the recital of this story the curer, Manuel, nodded noncommittally, but permissively, keeping his eyes fixed on her face. Then he said that it was good that she should tell him of her life. "But," he said, "you have been *espantado* seven times before. What is it that 'frightened' you this

time?" She then told about a recent experience when she and her husband were passing near the spot where he had been deceived by the loose woman. Manuel had her specify the spot in precise detail. She had upbraided her husband, and he had seized a rock and struck her. This had precipitated the present *susto*. It seemed to us that the patient was noticeably more relaxed after her recital than previously.

The curer told the patient that he was confident that the present condition could be cured. Then he outlined to her the herbs, pharmacy preparations, food, and other items, which she must procure for the curing session per se. Also it was agreed between them that the curing session would take place the following Thursday.

It seems that in this session at least three well-known psychiatric mechanisms are exhibited. (1) The patient enjoys an emotional catharsis, even though somewhat superficial. (2) The patient "transfers" to the curer whom she respects and who by his procedures and air of knowledge inspires confidence. (3) The curer provides reassurance both verbally and by his prescriptions of medicines.

The following interval of four days was occupied by the patient in making preparations for the cure and its associated social activities. The responsibility for arrangements was laid upon the patient herself, both for securing the necessary drugs and foods and for obtaining the participation of the other people specified in the curing ritual. It is not necessary to describe these preparations in detail, but they are of the following types: the patient must secure and prepare food for a feast; she must secure and prepare or have prepared according to close specifications a considerable number of herbs, potions, incense, and other "medicines" used in the cure itself; she must persuade a woman friend or kinswoman to become her "servant" during the days of preparation and to be at her orders in the preparation and serving of the food on the night of the cure; she must invite to the feast at her house a number of friends and relatives who, in addition to enjoying the hospitality, will be at the service of the curer during the ceremony; she must persuade one of the six principal men of the Indian community to participate in the cure itself with the medicine man.

It will be perceived that these requirements which are laid upon the patient involve several apparently sound therapeutic procedures. (1) The patient's preoccupation with her complaints is broken and her attention is fixed upon goals outside herself. (2) She is given activity patterns to perform and social as well as somatically derived motivation. (3) A pattern is offered for the re-establishment of social contacts, and prestige motivation is rewarded by the fact that she is ostensibly placed in the "managerial" role. A "servant" is placed at her disposal, a luxury which is very uncommon in Indian homes. (4) Reassurance is given the patient by the co-operative attitude of friends and relatives who gather around to aid her in the preparations and to assist in the ceremony itself. (5) Sanction of the most powerful mundane authority in the local Indian social organization is furnished through the co-operation and acquiescence of the Principal. The group of the Principals is the repository, among the Indians at least, of the local version of the Christian religion in this community which has no resident priests. Only they among the Indians know the proper prayers and are believed to have direct spiritual access to the Christian saints. They are also the holders of political and social power among the Indians, although not recognized as such by the Ladino government. The participation of a Principal in any undertaking means that it is blessed with both wisdom and holiness.

The curing ceremony itself got under way Thursday afternoon. All of the invited guests and participants gathered at the patient's house about 4:00 P.M. The house altar, with a lithographed picture of the household saint, was decorated with fresh tissue paper and pine boughs. The entire inside of the one-room dwelling was adorned with pine boughs, and pine needles covered the earth floor. A group of women were working about the hearth and over grinding stones under the direction of the patient. The latter in her role of hostess was in considerable state of tension, evidenced by her snapping remarks and her air of great preoccupation. Nevertheless it was also apparent that she was enjoying her role as the center of interest. After all the others were present—including Miguel, the Principal— Manuel, the curer, made his entrance. He calmly shook the patient's hand and checked on the preparations. He made it clear that every phase of the succeeding events would be under his direction and that all those present were subject to his orders. No one objected to his assumption of the role, and it was followed throughout the night. A light refreshment was served by the woman "servant," and we chatted easily for about an hour and a half.

This phase seems to serve two purposes. (1) The organization of a social group about the patient and the manifestation of its interest in the patient's welfare are exhibited. (2) Such interpersonal tensions within the group or between its members and the patient which might develop from the strangeness and seriousness of the situation are relaxed.

After dusk a delegation left for the church in the center of town to pray to the saints, explaining to them the necessity for this cure, and to plead for their aid and benign interest. The delegation consisted of the curer carrying a large bundle of candles, the Principal carrying a native-made clay censer in which copal incense burned, and the patient's son carrying a large armful of pine boughs with which to decorate the altars of the various saints in the church. The curer and the Principal prayed together at the main altar and set up large candles before it and at the church door. Then the curer began a long series of prayers in Pokomám before each of the 14 images of saints in the church. All prayers were much the same. The curer knelt with two lighted candles in his right hand and swung the copal censer with the left hand while he explained in somewhat stylized fashion the loss of the soul of Alicia and invoked aid in its recovery. At the end of each prayer he placed two lighted candles before the saint and swung the censer in the sign of the cross, while the patient's son decorated that particular altar with pine boughs. When each of the saints had been properly appealed to, both the curer and the Principal knelt before the main altar and prayed long and loud to the Virgin and to Jesus Christ. Then two extra candles and another prayer were offered to San Marcos "because he is said to be the saint of the *brujos* [evil witches]." After this the group returned to the patient's house where the curer explained what had been done. The prayers had lasted about two hours.

The function of this part of the cure seems to be primarily to relieve the patient's anxiety concerning the Christian saints. From the phrasing of the prayers it is also evident that all participants in the "cure," including the medicine man himself, receive reassurance against the fear that the Christian deities may intervene unfavorably in what is essentially a pagan proceeding. For soul loss itself lies outside the realm of Christian affairs, and the recovery of a soul involves dealing with renegade saints and familiar spirits certainly not approved of by God Almighty.

After we returned to the house a large meal of native dishes was served. The scene was lighted with pine splinters. The patient did not eat but looked on, complaining about the efforts she had put forth, but clearly enjoying her misery. The guests and the curer complimented her on the food. Then the curer asked that the herbs and essences and other medicines which had been procured be brought out so that he could inspect them and give instruction to the women as to how they should be prepared.

During this phase also the curer was engaged in making a pair of small images, representing "Don Avelín Caballero Sombrerón" (the chief of the evil spirits) and "his wife." These images, made from a ball of beeswax which he carried in his pocket, were about three inches tall. The male figure had a wide-brimmed hat, and the female figure displayed a typical married woman's hairdress, arranged in a sort of crown or filet around the head. The female figure has a needle placed in her hands. The curer explained that if the appeal to Avelín for the return of the patient's soul was unsuccessful, he would implore the wife who would prod her husband with her "lance."

The patient was instructed to stand in her clothes before the house altar. The curer took two eggs in the shell from a gourd plate included in the collection of necessities for the cure. Holding one egg in his right hand he passed it over her forehead, then down her neck to the inside of her right forearm, stroking the inside of the right forearm 12 times from below elbow to wrist. With a second egg he repeated the process on the left side. Then he took two more eggs, one in each hand. After making the sign of a cross before her face, he moved both eggs, one on each side, up her arms to her head, down her back and legs all the way to her feet, up the inside of her legs to the crotch, and over her abdomen and breasts to her mouth. He placed the four eggs which he had used in a gourd plate and lighted a small candle on the house altar. This, explained Manuel, removes some of the sickness from the body into the eggs. The eggs are taken to "The Place" where the fright occurred and constitute evidence to be offered to the spirits of the harm which has befallen the patient as the result of soul loss.

The native theory here is that the organism is seriously weakened at the time the soul is frightened out of the body and that in this condition *aires* (evil winds) may enter the body. The physical symptoms of a person suffering soul loss are believed to be caused by the *"aires de espanto."* The eggs used in this fashion have the effect of drawing the *aires* into themselves and out of the patient's body. This in itself, however, is not a sufficient "cure," according to the local theory of etiology, for the soul has not yet been restored to its owner and consequently the patient is still in a "weakened" condition, peculiarly susceptible to invasion by other *aires*.

The curer and the Principal, together with two male helpers, now went to "The Place" where the precipitating fright of the present *espanto* occurred. They carried with them in a gourd the four eggs just used to draw the *aires* out of the patient, digging sticks, pine splinters for light, two candles, and a collection of gifts to be offered the evil spirits. These gifts included a cigar, a bunch of handmade cigarettes, an earthen pitcher of *chilate* (a maize gruel used as ceremonial drink among the Pokomám), four cacao seeds, some sweet biscuits, and a small bottle of drinking alcohol. We walked in single file through the darkness, following a dim path among the bushes upstream along the river. Finally we came to a spot about ten feet above the river which the curer announced was "The Place" where Alicia had lost her soul. A pine splinter was lighted. While the two men helpers started digging a hole in the ground, the curer and the Principal turned their backs and faced across the river to the west. All previous prayers had been in Pokomám, but now the curer spoke in Spanish and in familiar, man-to-man terms. He addressed five spirits, calling them by name and addressing them as *compadres* (a form of ceremonial kinship). The names of the five were "Avelín Caballero Sombrerón, Señor Don Justo Juez, Doña María Diego, Don Manuel Urrutia, and San Graviel [Gabriel]." After saluting the others he directed his remarks to Don Avelín. He explained in detail that he had brought them a feast to eat and alcohol to drink. He explained that here Alicia had lost her soul through a *susto*. He dwelt upon her symptoms and said that the eggs would bear him out. He said that he knew that his compadres knew where her soul was hidden and that they had it in their power to return it to her. As a favor to him, the curer, would they not help him to secure the lost soul? And so on. This discourse delivered into the darkness lasted about twenty minutes. During it the old Principal stood by the curer's side, saying nothing, but swinging the smoking censer in a regular rhythm. The two wax images of Avelín and his wife were set on a stone, the food and other offerings were laid out, drinks were poured for the spirits. Then everything was buried in a shallow hole, and we departed for the patient's house. Some earth and pebbles dug up by the helpers were placed in a gourd dish and carried back with us. "That the soul might follow," the earth and pebbles were rattled in their gourd container as we walked through the night.

This step in the cure was the crucial one from the native point of view. The theory is that the evil spirits, which the Indians call *tiéwu* in their own language and *diablos* (devils) when speaking Spanish, hid a disembodied soul somewhere in the mountains. Only a medicine man who has established friendly relations with these occult powers is able to persuade them to release the soul.

As we left the spot a roll of thunder rumbled through the mountains as the rainstorm which had been going on all evening moved off toward the west, and a flash of lightning illuminated the slope across the river. The curer remarked that this was a "good sign."

We were met at the door of the house by the patient. She showed an intense desire to know if the mission had been successful. The curer spoke noncommittal but comforting words.

The curer and the Principal set up two large candles on the house altar and prayed in Pokomám, explaining to the picture of the household patron saint why it had been nec-

essary to talk with the spirits and to make offerings to them.

A ground altar was laid out on the tamped earth outside the door of the house in the form of a square about a yard on each side. Each corner was marked by a stake to which a pine bough was tied upright. Each side faced one of the cardinal directions. Now the curer with the Principal beside him knelt on a goatskin and began a long series of prayers in Pokomám. First they knelt on the south side facing north, then on the north side facing west, then on the west side, and finally on the east side. The whole sequence of prayers was repeated in each position. Although the cardinal directions were not named or personified, this procedure seems to be a survival of earlier Mayan beliefs in the sacredness of the directions. The prayers were actually directed to Jesus Christ and a list of 44 saints, "if you happen to be now in the north [south, east, west]." The ground-altar phase lasted about ninety minutes and ended about 1:30 A.M.

The house was purified and sanctified. The Principal set up two candles at each inside corner of the house, while the curer, holding the copal censer swinging from his hand, prayed over each pair of candles in Pokomám. Then he knelt before the house altar once more explaining briefly to the patron saint what he had done. He perfumed the altar with copal smoke and went into the yard and did the same to the ground altar. He came back into the house and sat down to smoke a cigarette while he wiped the weariness from his eyes.

The son and daughter-in-law of the patient now began to grind the medicinal herbs and to mix the magic potions under directions of the curer. When the mixture was completed a gourd bowlful of greenish liquid was handed to the curer who muttered an invocation over it and placed it on the altar.

Under instructions from the curer all the guests sat down on the floor, leaving a small open space in front of the altar. The curer took off his jacket and shirt, tying the arms of the shirt around his neck so that it hung down his back. The patient, her mumbling complaints silenced for once, took off her clothes and tied a scanty piece of cloth around her loins, just sufficient to cover her genitals. The curer took a long drink of *aguardiente* (beverage alcohol). The patient cried and whimpered, standing naked before the company. She and the curer stood for a moment facing the altar while he prayed. It was now about 2:00 A.M.

The curer went out of the house and the patient followed. He walked about a hundred yards into the cornfield. The rest of the party was instructed to stand about in such a way as to form a crude square. The only light was a single burning pine splinter. The sky had cleared, and the night air was uncomfortably chilly. The patient stood naked in the center of the square, facing north. The curer offered her the bowl of magic potion. She took a quick gulp, making a face as she did so and whining with complaint.

The curer put his lips to the bowl and took a large mouthful, stepping back from the patient about three feet. For approximately sixty seconds everyone present stood rigid. Suddenly and without warning a blast of fine spray burst from the curer's mouth straight into the face of the patient. The shock of the alcoholic liquid in the cold air rocked her. He continued, systematically spraying her whole body—front and rear—with the medicine, ignoring her protests and her shivering. A stool was brought and the patient sat down trembling while the curer rinsed his mouth with a bowl of water. After she had sat for about ten minutes the curer gave her a bowl of the mixture and she drank it all, about a pint. Then everyone returned to the house.

A mat was laid on the damp earth floor in front of the altar, and the patient, still naked and shivering, stretched out on it. The curer took off his shirt entirely and with a gourd plate of six eggs in the shell in his hands he offered a short prayer before the altar. First he took two eggs in his right hand and massaged the patient's head, abdomen, and chest with them. Then, with a second pair of eggs he massaged her right arm, front of her body, trunk, head, and ears. A third pair of eggs were used to massage both legs. Then four eggs, two in each hand, were pressed against each side of her chest. She turned over, and the whole back side of her body was similarly massaged. This whole procedure was not superficial but a systematic and thorough rubbing of skin and muscle. Although the curer did not touch the genitals, he did not hesitate to massage the nipples. Gradually her shivering and complaints ceased. She was obviously enjoying the treatment and was relaxed. The curer removed one of his sandals and with it massaged all parts of her body.

The patient rose and put on her clothes and was led to the rustic platform bed where she lay down and was covered with blankets. She emitted a long humming sigh of relaxation. One of the assistants placed a broken pot full of coals under the bed, and the curer crawled through the smoke and placed under the bed the gourd of earth and pebbles brought from "The Place" of the fright. As he did so the copal suddenly burst into flame. "Ha," said the medicine man, "the soul is here."

As the smoke cleared away a large gourd bowl half full of water was brought to the curer. He broke the six eggs he had used in the massage one by one into the water. Slowly the whites coagulated in the water, forming swirling shapes. For a long time the curer gazed into the bowl by the vague light of the candles on the altar behind him. Then he nodded affirmatively, saying that he saw that all was confirmed in the eggs. He went through the entire history of the patient's eight *espantos* pointing out "proofs" in the eggs. Then as the whites sank slowly to the bottom of the bowl he said that this showed that all previous *sustos* had been cured and that the present symptoms would shortly disappear. He pronounced the cure finished. The patient roused herself briefly on the bed and shouted hoarsely, "That is right." Then she sank back into a deep snoring sleep.

The curer, the Principal, and guests left the patient's house about 5:00 A.M., leaving her in the care of her son, her daughter-in-law, and her husband.

The immediate aftermaths of the treatment were of two types—physical and psychological.

Next day about noon I was called to the patient's house by her son. She was in her bed with a temperature of 105°F. She was very "happy" and felt that her soul was restored. But her verbalizations showed some delirium. Her condition was not surprising in view of the violent chill she had received during the "shock treatment" of the night before when she was sprayed naked with liquid by the curer. Alicia had left her bed three times while sweating heavily. I gave her aspirin and had her husband rub her down with aromatic oil. Then I consulted with the curer, Manuel. He did not seem concerned. "Once the soul has returned," he said, "the body usually has to readjust itself. A short sickness often comes after a cure of this sort. Alicia will be restored in a few days." I asked him if his patients ever died after treatment. "Yes," he said calmly. "Not often, but occasionally. But it is better to die with the soul. They would die anyway. To die without one's soul is to condemn the spirit to eternal wandering upon this earth. A lost soul can never see *La Gloria*. He refused to visit the patient, saying his work was done. I am certain that there was nothing cowardly in his attitude. It was simply his view that in such cases events must take their course.

We had with us ample supplies of sulfadiazine. Since I am of course not a licensed medical man, I arranged that I should administer this medication officially under the supervision of the local pharmacist who held a Guatemalan license as pharmacist and empirical physician. In two days the fever had disappeared, and in a week Alicia was up and about her usual tasks.

The patient was under our observation for four weeks after the curing ceremony. She seemed to have developed a new personality, temporarily at least. The hypochondriacal complaints, nagging of her husband and relatives, withdrawal from her social contacts, and anxiety symptoms, all disappeared following the cure. One not entirely surprising result was a heavy emotional transference to myself. She believed that by arranging the cure I had saved her life. Thereafter she insisted on calling me her "papa" and in every way endeavored to develop a dependency relationship with me. Emotional instability was indicated during the four weeks following the ceremony only by an occasional tendency to break into tears when telling someone how "good" I had been to her by seeing that she was "cured."

In this and other cases seen, therefore, it is evident that the magical treatment is followed by a remission of presenting symptoms. I believe that evidence is clear, however, that this type of treatment resolves no fundamental or deep-lying conflicts of personality. This particular woman has suffered *espanto* eight times and the chances are that she will continue to have recurring episodes of this type. On the other hand we have a case of an Indian man of the same age, an

apparently well-integrated personality, who had one episode of *espanto* in his twenties of which he was "cured" in the manner just described and has never suffered a recurrence. One concludes that the permanence of the readjustment effected by this type of "cure" depends primarily upon the personality structure of the patient.

Three methods were used to assess the personalities of the patient and the curer: (1) life sketches, (2) Rorschach tests, and (3) opinions gathered directly and indirectly from other members of the community.

Alicia, the patient, seems to be rather a dull person on the intellectual side and a person whose life story has been full of frustrations and repressions. As she exhibits her personality at the present time one can characterize it as hypochondriacal and compulsive with numerous manifestations of insecurity and anxiety.

The curer, Manuel, from all points of view would probably be labeled as a schizophrenic in North American society. This diagnosis is unequivocally brought out, according to Dr. Billig, in his Rorschach protocol. Also, behavioristic material tends to support such a diagnosis. Manuel exhibits the typical masklike countenance, flat emotional reactions, high development of fantasy life which is unshared with others, and typical disregard of opinions and reactions of the members of his social group. However, in the society of San Luis, Manuel does not occupy a position corresponding to that of a schizophrenic patient in our own society. On the contrary, he fills a highly respected status as an important and much respected curer who has had considerable success. He carries on his farming with skill, and he manages his business affairs, such as renting and trading new plots of lands, with a certain shrewdness. His income is considerably more than that of an ordinary Indian because of the fees which he collects for curing sessions. Many people come to him for advice which he gives in a calm and rather dissociated manner. In short, whatever the final diagnosis of Manuel may be, there is a recognized and, from the local point of view, a useful place for him in the social structure of San Luis. As Dr. Billig says in his Rorschach report, "His society does not exert any pressure to bring his drive-dominated fantasy life under a more rigid control, and it does not regard thorough testing of reality as necessary. It enables Manuel not only to live in a dream world of his own but also enables him to find an accepted escape for others, as in the case of Alicia's difficulties, by the powerful convictions evolving from the symbolic strength of his own traumatic experiences."

It may be interesting to note that the five other Indian curers on whom we have life-history material and Rorschach protocols exhibit fairly uniform personality structure. All share, according to Billig's Rorschach results, basic "introversive tendencies," and in our society would be considered "schizoid." Nevertheless, although all the shaman

curers in the Indian sector of San Luis society exhibit similar status personalities, and occupy similar positions in the social structure of the community, they are, as regards other personality traits, rather distinct personalities whose types vary throughout a certain range.

In a tentative way, we may say that the Indian curers are all people whose basic personality is in some way "peculiar," but that they have found an application of their talents and a toleration of their peculiarities in the status of shaman curer as recognized among the Indians of San Luis.

KNUD RASMUSSEN

An Eskimo Shaman Purifies a Sick Person

Knud Rasmussen, in this account of the purification of an Eskimo woman, has succeeded in capturing the lyrical rhythm of this ceremony—a ceremony that is a good example of the emotional catharsis of confession.

Confession is quite rare among primitives, by whom it is often viewed as a virtually physical act of catharsis (see Pettazzoni, *La Confession des Péchés,* 1931), and although we have already witnessed an attenuated form of confession in Gillin's "Magical Fright," the Guatemalan practice of confession may be due to Spanish influence. Eskimo culture, however, assigns confession a central role in the treatment of disease. The interaction between the patient, audience, shaman, and the shaman's helping spirit is directed toward eliciting confessions from the patient herself. The shaman and the audience pose leading questions, call upon their own knowledge of the patient's covert acts, and make educated guesses about her possible transgressions. Each confession is thought to act so as to purge a part of the patient's illness.

Very clearly, the process of confession, expiation of guilt, and forgiveness has a salutary effect on the sick woman. But even should the illness continue, the confessional ceremony serves to reinforce the norms and values of Eskimo culture. By Rasmussen's sensitive rendition of this ceremony, the reader is given an inside, empathetic knowledge of the patient's struggle to regain her health while trying to avoid the shame of public confession.

Reprinted from Knud Rasmussen, *Report of the Fifth Thule Expedition, 1921–24,* Vol. VII, No. 1, *Intellectual Culture of the Iglulik Eskimos* (Copenhagen: Gyldendalske Boghandel, Nordisk Forlag, 1929), pp. 133–141, by permission of Rudolf Sand.

A woman named Nanoraq, the wife of Mákik, lay very ill, with pains all over her body. The patient, who was so ill that she could hardly stand upright, was placed on the bench. All the inhabitants of the village were summoned, and Angutingmarik [a

shaman] inquired of his spirits as to the cause of the disease. The shaman walked slowly up and down the floor for a long time, swinging his arms backwards and forwards with mittens on, talking in groans and sighs, in varying tones, sometimes breathing deeply as if under extreme pressure. He says: "It is you, you are Aksharquarnilik, I ask you, my helping spirit, whence comes the sickness from which this person is suffering? Is it due to something I have eaten in defiance of taboo, lately or long since? Or is it due to the one who is wont to lie beside me, to my wife? Or is it brought about by the sick woman herself? Is she herself the cause of the disease?"

The patient answers: "The sickness is due to my own fault. I have but ill fulfilled my duties. My thoughts have been bad and my actions evil."

The shaman interrupts her, and continues: "It looks like peat, and yet is not really peat. It is that which is behind the ear, something that looks like the cartilage of the ear? There is something that gleams white. It is the edge of a pipe, or what can it be?"

The listeners cry all at once: "She has smoked a pipe that she ought not to have smoked. But never mind. We will not take any notice of that. Let her be forgiven. tauva!"

The shaman: "That is not all. There are yet further offenses, which have brought about this disease. Is it due to me, or to the sick person herself?"

The patient answers: "It is due to myself alone. There was something the matter with my abdomen, with my inside."

The shaman: "I espy something dark beside the house. Is it perhaps a piece of a marrowbone, or just a bit of boiled meat, standing upright, or is it something that has been split with a chisel? That is the cause. She has split a meat bone which she ought not to have touched."

The audience: "Let her be released from her offense! tauva!"

The shaman: "She is not released from her evil. It is dangerous. It is matter for anxiety. Helping spirit, say what it is that plagues her. Is it due to me or to herself?"

Angutingmarik listens, in breathless silence, and then speaking as if he had with difficulty elicited the information from his helping spirit, he says: "She has eaten a piece of raw, frozen caribou steak at a time when that was taboo for her."

Listeners: "It is such a slight offense, and means so little, when her life is at stake. Let her be released from his burden, from this cause, from this source of illness, tauva!"

The shaman: "She is not yet released. I see a woman over in your direction, towards my audience, a woman who seems to be asking for something. A light shines out in front of her. It is as if she was asking for something with her eyes, and in front of her is something that looks like a hollow. What is it? What is it? Is it that, I wonder, which causes death? Can it indeed be something which will not be taken from her? Will she not be released from it? I still see before me a woman with entreating eyes, with sorrowful eyes, and she has with her a walrus tusk in which grooves have been cut."

Listeners: "Oh, is that all? It is a harpoon head that she has worked at, cutting grooves in it at a time when she ought not to touch anything made from parts of an animal. If that is all, let her be released. Let it be, tauva!"

Shaman: "Now this evil is removed, but in its place there appears something else; hair combings and sinew thread."

The patient: "Oh, I did comb my hair once when after giving birth to a child I ought not to have combed my hair; and I hid away the combings that none might see."

Listeners: "Let her be released from that. Oh, such a trifling thing; let her be released, tauva!"

Shaman: "We have not yet come to the end of her offenses, of the causes of her sickness. Here is a caribou breast come to light, a raw caribou breast."

Listeners: "Yes, we know! Last summer, at a time when she was not allowed to eat the breast of a caribou she ate some all the same. But let her be released from that offense. Let it be taken from her, tauva!"

Shaman: "She is not yet free. A seal comes forth, plain to be seen. It is wet. One can see how the skin has been scraped on the blubber side; it is all plain as could be."

The patient: "I did scrape the skin of a seal which my son Qasagâq had killed at a time when I ought not to have touched seal skins."

Shaman: "It is not yet removed. It has shifted a little way back. Something very like it, something of the same sort, is visible near by."

Listeners: "Oh that was last summer, when her husband cut out the tusk from a walrus skull, and that was shortly after he had been ill, when he was not yet allowed to touch any kind of game. Let her be released from that. Do let it be taken from her! tauva!"

Shaman: "There is more to come. There are yet cases of work, of occupations which were forbidden; something that happened in the spring, after we had moved over to this place."

The patient: "Oh, I gave my daughter a waistbelt made of skin that had been used for my husband's quiver."

Listeners: "Let this be taken away. Let her be released from it. tauva!"

Shaman: "It is not yet taken away. She is not released from it as yet. Perhaps it has something to do with the caribou. Perhaps she has prepared caribou skins at a time when she ought not to have touched them."

Listeners: "She has prepared caribou skins. She helped to stretch out the skins at a time when she was living in the same house with a woman who had her menses. Let her be released from that tauva!"

Shaman: "She is not freed from guilt even yet. It seems now as if the earth beneath our feet were beginning to move."

Patient: "I have picked moss at a time when I ought not to have touched earth at all, moss to melt lead with for my husband's rifle bullets."

Shaman: "There is more yet, more forbidden work that has been done. The patient has not only melted lead for her husband when it was taboo, but she did it while still wearing clothes of old caribou skin, she did it before she had yet put on the garments made from the new autumn skins."

Listeners: "Oh these are such little things. A woman must not be suffered to die for these. Do let her be released."

Shaman: "She is not released. It may perhaps prove impossible to release her from these burdens. What is it that I begin to see now? It must be blood, unless it is human filth. But it is outside the house, on the ground. It looks like blood. It is frozen, and covered with loose snow. Someone has tried to hide it."

Patient: "Yes, that was in the autumn. I had a miscarriage, and tried to conceal it, I tried to keep it secret to avoid the taboo."

Listeners: "This is certainly a great and serious offense. But let her be released nevertheless. Let her be released, tauva!"

Shaman: "We wish her to get well again. Let all these obstacles be removed. Let her get well! And yet I see, and yet I espy things done which were forbidden. What do I see? It looks as if it were a caribou antler. It looks like that part of the antler nearest the head."

Patient: "Oh that was a caribou head I once stole in order to eat it, though it was forbidden food for me at the time."

Listeners: "That was very wrong, but all the same, let her be released, let her be released from that. tauva!"

Shaman: "There is still something more I seem to see; something that as it were comes and disappears just as I am about to grasp it. What is it? Can it be the man Amarualik, I wonder? It looks like him. I think it must be he. His face is bright, but he is blushing also. He is as bright as a living being. It looks as if he wanted to show me something. And yet another person. Who is that? The patient must have no secrets. Let her tell us herself. Let her speak to us herself. Or can it be my cousin Qumangâpik? Yes, it is he. It is Qumangâpik. The size is right, and he has a big nose."

Patient: "Alas, yes, it is true. Those men have I lain with at a time when I ought not to have lain with any man, at a time when I was unclean."

Listeners: "It is a very serious offense for a woman to lie with men when she is unclean. But never mind all that. Let her be released, let her get well."

Shaman: "But there is more yet to come." And turning to his spirit, he says:

"Release her from it all. Release her, so that she may get well. There is still something hereabout, something I can faintly perceive, but cannot yet grasp entirely."

The patient: "Before the snow came, and before we were allowed to work on the skins of newly captured caribou, I cut up some caribou skin for soles and sewed them on to our boots."

Shaman: "That is there still! There is yet more. The sources of disease are doubtless all in the patient herself, or can it be that any are in me? Can it be my fault, or that of my helping spirits? Or can those here present as listeners be guilty in any way? Can they have any part in the disease? (This was a reference to Therkel Mathiassen and Jacob Olsen, who had been digging among the ruins. It is considered sacrilege to touch the houses of the dead.) What can be the cause of that which still torments her? Can it be forbidden work or forbidden food, something eatable, something eaten of that which was forbidden, and nothing said? Could it be a tongue?"

Patient: "Alas, yes, I ate a tongue when it was forbidden me to eat caribou tongue."

Listeners: "tauva, let her be released from this burden, from this offense."

Shaman: "She is not yet released. There is more yet about forbidden food."

Patient: "Can it be because I once stole some salmon and ate it at a time when salmon was forbidden me?"

Listeners: "Let her foolishness, let her misdeeds be taken from her. Let her get well."

Shaman: "She is not yet released. There is more yet; forbidden occupations, forbidden food, stealing. Can it be that she is trying to hide something from us? Is she trying to conceal something, I wonder?"

Listeners: "Even if she is trying to keep something concealed, let her be released from that, let her get well."

Shaman: "There are still offenses, evil thoughts, that rise up like a heavy mass, and she was only just beginning to get clean. The confessions were beginning to help her."

Listeners: "Let all evil thoughts disappear. Take away all evil thoughts."

Shaman: "Many confessions has the patient made, and yet it seems difficult! Can it be that she is beyond cure? But let her get well, quite well. Raise her up. But you cannot. You are not able to relieve her of her illness, though many of the causes have now been removed. It is terrible, it is dangerous, and you, my helping spirit, you whom I believe to be here with us, why do you not raise her up and relieve her of her pain, of her sickness? Raise her up, hold her up. Now once more something appears before my eyes, forbidden food and sinews of caribou."

Listeners: "Once more she has combed her hair although she was unclean. Let her be released from that; let it be taken away from her. Let her get well. tauva!"

Shaman: "Yet again I catch a glimpse of forbidden occupations carried on in secret. They appear before my eyes, I can just perceive them."

Listeners: "While she was lying on a caribou skin from an animal killed when shedding its coat in the spring, she had a miscarriage, and she kept it secret, and her husband, all unwitting, lay down on the same skin where that had taken place, and

so rendered himself unclean for his hunting!"

Shaman: "Even for so hardened a conscience there is release. But she is not yet freed. Before her I see green flowers of sorrel and the fruits of sorrel."

Listeners: "Before the spring was come, and the snow melted and the earth grew living, she once, wearing unclean garments, shovelled the snow away and ate of the earth, ate sorrel and berries, but let her be released from that, let her get well, tauva!"

Shaman: "She is not yet released. I see plants of seaweed, and something that looks like fuel. It stands in the way of her recovery. Explain what it can be."

Listeners: "She has burned seaweed and used blubber to light it with, although it is forbidden to use blubber for sea plants. But let her be released from that, let her get well, tauva!"

Shaman: "Ha, if the patient remains obstinate and will not confess her own misdeeds, then the sickness will gain the upper hand, and she will not get well. The sickness is yet in her body, and the offenses still plague her. Let her speak for herself, let her speak out. It is her own fault."

Patient: "I happened to touch a dead body without afterwards observing the taboo prescribed for those who touch dead bodies. But I kept it secret."

Shaman: "She is not yet released. The sickness is yet in her body. I see snow whereon something has been spilt, and I hear something being poured out. What is it, what is it?"

Patient: "We were out after salmon, and I happened to spill something from the cooking pot on the snow floor." (When salmon are being sought for, care must be taken never to spill anything from a cooking pot either in the snow, in a snow hut, or on the ground in a tent.)

Shaman: "There are more sins yet. There is more to come. She grows cleaner with every confession, but there is more to come. There is yet something which I have been gazing at for a long time, something I have long had in view. . . ."

Listeners: "We do not wish that anything shall be dangerous. We do not wish anything to plague her and weigh heavily upon her. She is better now, it is better now. Let her get well altogether."

Shaman: "Here you are, helping spirit,

dog Púngo. Tell me what you know. Explain yourself. Tell me, name to me, the thing she has taken. Was it the feet of an eider duck?"

Patient: "Oh, I ate the craw of a goose at a time when I was not allowed to eat such meat."

Listeners: "Never mind that. Let her be released from that, let her get well."

Shaman: "But she is not yet released. There is more yet. I can still see a hollow that has been visible to me all the time, ever since I began taking counsel of my helping spirit this evening. I see it, I perceive it. I see something which is half naked, something with wings, I do not understand what this can mean."

Patient: "Oh, perhaps a little sparrow, which my daughter brought into the tent at a time when I was unclean, when it was forbidden me to come into contact with the animals of nature."

Listeners: "Oh, let it pass. Let her be excused. Let her get well."

Shaman: "She is not yet released. Ah, I fear it may not succeed. She still droops, falling forward, she is ill even yet. I see a fur garment. It looks as if it belonged to some sick person. I suppose it cannot be anyone else who has used it, who has borrowed it?"

Listeners: "Oh, yes, it is true, she lent a fur coat to someone at a time when she was unclean."

Shaman: "I can still see a piece of sole leather chewed through and through, a piece of sole leather being softened."

Patient: "The spotted seal from the skin of which I removed the hair, and the meat of which I ate, though it was taboo."

Listeners: "Let it pass. Let her be released from that. Let her get well."

Shaman: "Return to life, I see you now returning in good health among the living, and you, being yourself a shaman, have your helping spirits in attendance. Name but one more instance of forbidden food, all the men you have lain with though you were unclean, all the food you have swallowed, old and new offenses, forbidden occupations exercised, or was it a lamp that you borrowed?"

Patient: "Alas yes, I did borrow the lamp of one dead. I have used a lamp that has belonged to a dead person."

Listeners: "Even though it be so, let it be removed. Let all evils be driven far away, that she may get well."

Here the shaman ended his exorcisms, which had taken place early in the morning, and were now to be repeated at noon and later, when evening had come. The patient was by that time so exhausted that she could hardly sit upright, and the listeners left the house believing that all the sins and offenses now confessed had taken the sting out of her illness, so that she would now soon be well again.

HORACE MINER

Body Ritual Among the Nacirema

One of the best examples of the extreme degree to which a culture may be dominated by ritualized, magical treatments of illness is that of the Nacirema, here described by Miner. The Nacirema focus considerable attention upon the body, which is thought to be utterly fulsome to the eye and naturally liable to infirmity. The result of this belief is an elaborate household shrine complex of charms, magic, potions, and holy ablutions which are intended to prevent physical debility. Should the household shrine prove inadequate, medical specialists such as "holy mouth men" and "listeners" may be consulted. Miner's discussion of the shock treatments which are accepted and regularly employed in the *latipso* ceremony confirms the native's surpassing faith in what, by modern standards, must be deemed supernatural, even abhorrent,

Reprinted from *American Anthropologist*, LVIII (1956), 503–507, by permission of the author and the American Anthropological Association.

techniques. The prevalence of a ritual torture theme in Nacirema therapy leads the author to suggest the possibility of sado-masochistic personality structure. Despite the sundry magical elements in the Nacirema approach to physical ills, it would be a mistake to assume that these people are "magic-ridden." It is principally in the area of sickness and death, where science and rationalism have yet to provide assurance, that the Nacirema turn to the supernatural; in their mundane affairs magic and ritual are less important.

The anthropologist has become so familiar with the diversity of ways in which different peoples behave in similar situations that he is not apt to be surprised by even the most exotic customs. In fact, if all of the logically possible combinations of behavior have not been found somewhere in the world, he is apt to suspect that they must be present in some yet undescribed tribe. This point has, in fact, been expressed with respect to clan organization by Murdock. In this light, the magical beliefs and practices of the Nacirema present such unusual aspects that it seems desirable to describe them as an example of the extremes to which human behavior can go.

Professor Linton first brought the ritual of the Nacirema to the attention of anthropologists twenty years ago, but the culture of this people is still very poorly understood. They are a North American group living in the territory between the Canadian Cree, the Yaqui and Tarahumare of Mexico, and the Carib and Arawak of the Antilles. Little is known of their orgin, although tradition states that they came from the east. According to Nacirema mythology, their nation was originated by a culture hero, Notgnih-saw, who is otherwise known for two great feats of strength—the throwing of a piece of wampum across the river Pa-To-Mac and the chopping down of a cherry tree in which the Spirit of Truth resided.

Nacirema culture is characterized by a highly developed market economy which has evolved in a rich natural habitat. While much of the people's time is devoted to economic pursuits, a large part of the fruits of these labors and a considerable portion of the day are spent in ritual activity. The focus of this activity is the human body, the appearance and health of which loom as a dominant concern in the ethos of the people. While such a concern is certainly not unusual, its ceremonial aspects and associated philosophy are unique.

The fundamental belief underlying the whole system appears to be that the human body is ugly and that its natural tendency is to debility and disease. Incarcerated in such a body, man's only hope is to avert these characteristics through the use of the powerful influences of ritual and ceremony. Every household has one or more shrines devoted to this purpose. The more powerful individuals in the society have several shrines in their houses and, in fact, the opulence of a house is often referred to in terms of the number of such ritual centers it possesses. Most houses are of wattle and daub construction, but the shrine rooms of the more wealthy are walled with stone. Poorer families imitate the rich by applying pottery plaques to their shrine walls.

While each family has at least one such shrine, the rituals associated with it are not family ceremonies but are private and secret. The rites are normally only discussed with children, and then only during the period when they are being initiated into these mysteries. I was able, however, to establish sufficient rapport with the natives to examine these shrines and to have the rituals described to me.

The focal point of the shrine is a box or chest which is built into the wall. In this chest are kept the many charms and magical potions without which no native believes he could live. These preparations are secured from a variety of specialized practitioners. The most powerful of these are the medicine men, whose assistance must be rewarded with substantial gifts. However, the medicine men do not provide the curative potions for their clients, but decide what the ingredients should be and then write them down in an ancient and secret language. This writing is understood only by the medicine men and by the herbalists who, for another gift, provide the required charm.

The charm is not disposed of after it has served its purpose, but is placed in the charm-box of the household shrine. As these magical materials are specific for certain ills, and the real or imagined maladies of the people are many, the charm-box is usually full to overflowing. The magical packets are so numerous that people forget what their purposes were and fear to use them again. While the natives are very vague on this point, we can only assume that the idea in retaining all the old magical materials is that their presence in the charm-box, before which the body rituals are conducted, will in some way protect the worshiper.

Beneath the charm-box is a small font. Each day every member of the family, in succession, enters the shrine room, bows his head before the charm-box, mingles different sorts of holy water in the font, and proceeds with a brief rite of ablution. The holy waters are secured from the Water Temple of the community, where the priests conduct elaborate ceremonies to make the liquid ritually pure.

In the hierarchy of magical practitioners, and below the medicine men in prestige, are specialists whose designation is best translated "holy-mouth-men." The Nacirema have an almost pathological horror of and fascination with the mouth, the condition of which is believed to have a supernatural influence on all social relationships. Were it not for the rituals of the mouth, they believe that their teeth would fall out, their gums bleed, their jaws shrink, their friends desert them, and their lovers reject them. They also believe that a strong relationship exists between oral and moral characteristics. For example, there is a ritual ablution of the mouth for children which is supposed to improve their moral fiber.

The daily body ritual performed by everyone includes a mouth-rite. Despite the fact that these people are so punctilious about care of the mouth, this rite involves a practice which strikes the uninitiated stranger as revolting. It was reported to me that the ritual consists of inserting a small bundle of hog hairs into the mouth, along with certain magical powders, and then moving the bundle in a highly formalized series of gestures.

In addition to the private mouth-rite, the people seek out a holy-mouth-man once or twice a year. These practitioners have an impressive set of paraphernalia, consisting of a variety of augers, awls, probes, and prods. The use of these objects in the exorcism of the evils of the mouth involves almost unbelievable ritual torture of the client. The holy-mouth-man opens the client's mouth and, using the above-mentioned tools, enlarges any holes which decay may have created in the teeth. Magical materials are put into these holes. If there are no naturally occurring holes in the teeth, large sections of one or more teeth are gouged out so that the supernatural substance can be applied. In the client's view, the purpose of these ministrations is to arrest decay and to draw friends. The extremely sacred and traditional character of the rite is evident in the fact that the natives return to the holy-mouth-men year after year, despite the fact that their teeth continue to decay.

It is hoped that, when a thorough study of the Nacirema is made, there will be careful inquiry into the personality structure of these people. One has but to watch the gleam in the eye of the holy-mouth-man, as he jabs an awl into an exposed nerve, to suspect that a certain amount of sadism is involved. If this can be established, a very interesting pattern emerges, for most of the population shows definite masochistic tendencies. It was to these that Professor Linton referred in discussing a distinctive part of the daily body ritual which is performed only by men. This part of the rite involves scraping and lacerating the surface of the face with a sharp instrument. Special women's rites are performed only four times during each lunar month, but what they lack in frequency is made up in barbarity. As part of this ceremony, women bake their heads in small ovens for about an hour. The theoretically interesting point is that what seems to be a preponderantly masochistic people have developed sadistic specialists.

The medicine men have an imposing temple, or *latipso,* in every community of any size. The more elaborate ceremonies required to treat very sick patients can only be performed at this temple. These ceremonies involve not only the thaumaturge but a permanent group of vestal maidens who move sedately about the temple chambers in distinctive costume and headdress.

The *latipso* ceremonies are so harsh that it is phenomenal that a fair proportion of the really sick natives who enter the temple ever recover. Small children whose indoctrination is still incomplete have been known to resist attempts to take them to the temple because "that is where you go to die." Despite this fact, sick adults are not only willing but eager to undergo the protracted ritual purification, if they can afford to do so. No matter how ill the supplicant or how grave the emergency, the guardians of many temples will not admit a client if he cannot give a rich gift to the custodian. Even after one has gained admission and survived the ceremonies, the guardians will not permit the neophyte to leave until he makes still another gift.

The supplicant entering the temple is first stripped of all his or her clothes. In everyday life the Nacirema avoids exposure of his body and its natural functions. Bathing and excretory acts are performed only in the secrecy of the household shrine, where they are ritualized as part of the body-rites. Psychological shock results from the fact that body secrecy is suddenly lost upon entry into the *latipso*. A man, whose own wife has never seen him in an excretory act, suddenly finds himself naked and assisted by a vestal maiden while he performs his natural functions into a sacred vessel. This sort of ceremonial treatment is necessitated by the fact that the excreta are used by a diviner to ascertain the course and nature of the client's sickness. Female clients, on the other hand, find their naked bodies are subjected to the scrutiny, manipulation, and prodding of the medicine men.

Few supplicants in the temple are well enough to do anything but lie on their hard beds. The daily ceremonies, like the rites of the holy-mouth-men, involve discomfort and torture. With ritual precision, the vestals awaken their miserable charges each dawn and roll them about on their beds of pain while performing ablutions, in the formal movements of which the maidens are highly trained. At other times they insert magic wands in the supplicant's mouth or force him to eat substances which are supposed to be healing. From time to time the medicine men come to their clients and jab magically treated needles into their flesh. The fact that these temple ceremonies may not cure, and may even kill the neophyte in no way decreases the people's faith in the medicine man.

There remains one other kind of practitioner, known as a "listener." This witch doctor has the power to exorcise the devils that lodge in the heads of people who have been bewitched. The Nacirema believe that parents bewitch their own children. Mothers are particularly suspected of putting a curse on children while teaching them the secret body rituals. The countermagic of the witch doctor is unusual in its lack of ritual. The patient simply tells the "listener" all his troubles and fears, beginning with the earliest difficulties he can remember. The memory displayed by the Nacirema in these exorcism sessions is truly remarkable. It is not uncommon for the patient to bemoan the rejection he felt upon being weaned as a babe, and a few individuals even see their troubles going back to the traumatic effects of their own birth.

In conclusion, mention must be made of certain practices which have their base in native aesthetics but which depend upon the pervasive aversion to the natural body and its functions. There are ritual fasts to make fat people thin and ceremonial feasts to make thin people fat. Still other rites are used to make women's breasts larger if they are small, and smaller if they are large. General dissatisfaction with breast shape is symbolized in the fact that the ideal form is virtually outside the range of human variation. A few women afflicted with almost inhuman hypermammary development are so idolized that they make a handsome living by simply going from village to village and permitting the natives to stare at them for a fee.

Reference has already been made to the fact that excretory functions are ritualized, routinized, and relegated to secrecy. Natural reproductive functions are similarly distorted. Intercourse is taboo as a topic and scheduled as an act. Efforts are made to avoid pregnancy by the use of magical materials or by limiting intercourse to certain phases of the moon. Conception is actually infrequent. When pregnant, women dress so as to hide their condition. Parturition takes place in secret, without friends or relatives to assist, and the majority of women do not nurse their infants.

Our review of the ritual life of the Nacirema has certainly shown them to be a magic-ridden people. It is hard to understand how they have managed to exist so long under the burdens which they have imposed upon themselves. But even such exotic customs as these take on real meaning when they are viewed with the insight provided by Malinowski when he wrote:

Looking from far and above, from our high places of safety in the developed civilization, it is easy to see all the crudity and irrelevance of magic. But without its power and guidance early man could not have mastered his practical difficulties as he has done, nor could man have advanced to the higher stages of civilization.

CHAPTER 9

DEATH, GHOSTS, AND ANCESTOR WORSHIP

INTRODUCTION

Universal problems faced by all human societies are created by what Malinowski has called "the supreme and final crisis of life"—death. These problems, many-faceted to be sure, may be considered on two levels: those that face the individual, and those that force adjustments on the society as a whole.

For all sane individuals eventual extinction of the organism, in the corporeal sense at least, forms an ever-present part of life expectancy; no normal human considers his own potential span to be eternal. Further, the death of a spouse or close relative disturbs an individual's social relations, often necessitating deliberate changes in family relations, economic activities, emotional exchange, and many other areas where the life pattern of the deceased formerly impinged on the lives of the survivors. Moving to a higher level of abstraction—the societal rather than the individual—the death of any member of the interacting group is likely to create points of stress which will pervade the entire social structure, particularly in small societies living in face-to-face relationships. Depending on the social importance of the deceased, the amount of disturbance felt within the system will vary. When the middle-aged but still vigorous male family head dies he leaves a vastly greater number of roles and functions unfulfilled than does, let us say, a female infant from a socially unimportant family. Yet the loss of any member from the group will have repercussions in a much wider circle than that composed of kin alone.

All cultures have techniques and methods which serve, if not to eliminate, at least to reduce problems arising out of the fact of human mortality. This they do both by reducing the individual's anxiety stemming from the contemplation of his own demise and by facilitating the orderly resumption of interpersonal relations following the death of a member of the group.

It could hardly be said that members of any culture anticipate with relish the prospect of passing from the delights of earthly existence, regardless of how few these may be; it is probably a fair generalization to say that most humans, given the option, would choose to remain among the living a while longer when the final moment of departure arrives. Myth and fiction sometimes permit an alternative but life itself never does. But though it is not possible to postulate eternal corporeal existence for members of a culture—the corpse is difficult to overlook—it is possible to extend culture-like conditions, bridging out from the known to the unknown, for the departed spirit to enjoy. Without attempting to suggest causality or primacy to either the spirit concept or that of life after death, it may be said that virtually all cultures provide both the concept of some nonmaterial aspect of life which will survive death and some beliefs regarding where and how this spirit would exist.

It might be suggested, though it is at present a better research hypothesis than a cultural law, that the individual's attitude toward death is strongly conditioned by the cultural belief regarding what becomes of that part of consciousness which survives the death crisis. Implicit belief in, and anticipation of, the survival of the cognitive being beyond the grave might do much to alleviate individual anxieties regarding termination of the material self—it merely continues to exist in another, and possibly more pleasant, form. The willingness of members of religious groups to die for causes justified by religious beliefs stands in evidence for this point. Attitudes of early Christians sacrificed for their faith, the willingness of Moslems to engage in "holy wars," and the apparent acceptance of their fates by many Aztec sacrificial victims, all attest to the overcoming of individual fears of death when promised recompense in an afterworld. This same point could be made for the Masai, the Plains Indian, and the Eskimo; death loses its sting when it is not conceived of as the complete end of the self. This cultural potential, the possibility of partially alleviating individual fears regarding death through the implicit belief in an afterlife, stands as another virtually universal feature of human existence. Referring to the belief in the survival of the human spirit after death, Frazer wrote with some petulance that "it seems probable that the great majority of our species will continue to acquiesce in a belief so flattering to human vanity and so comforting to human sorrow."

But what of the living, those who are not immediately contemplating an exit? Belief in an afterworld may assuage an individual's fears but, at the same time, it places him in more or less intimate contact with a host of nonmortal beings, either the departed members of his own group, as in the case with many simple cultures, or with the spirits of all departed human beings, as in the case with Christianity. Does the knowledge that the spirits of the dead were formerly relatives, countrymen, or fellow humans result in the enthusiastic participation of the living with the nonliving? Apparently not, except

in a few cases. As Frazer has so convincingly demonstrated in a three-volume study of the subject (*The Fear of the Dead in Primitive Religion* [1933–1936]), most cultures have developed attitudes of fear and dread regarding the spirits of the deceased. Sometimes these fears are mild and noninstitutionalized, as among the Hopi. At other times they are expressed through elaborate mechanisms which serve to pacify the ghosts or to mislead them by guile, as when the Bambwa sacrifice a goat near a shrine close to the ghost's alleged abode, or certain Australian tribes impose years of silence on widows so that the spirits of their jealous husbands will not be able to detect them. Anthropological literature is filled with fantastic examples of the efforts to which the living will go to ensure against the return of ghosts, even to the extent of supplying the dead with money for their expenses of the journey to the other world—a custom not only of the Khasis of Assam, the Burmese, the Lolos, and the Mosquito Indians, but the ancient Greeks as well, who inserted a coin in the mouth of the corpse so that the deceased could pay Charon for ferrying him across the river Styx.

Apparently basic to the institutionalized fear of ghosts is the belief that after death, though the spirit of the individual continues to exist in the afterworld, the basic "personality" structure of the spirit undergoes a striking change—it becomes malevolent. Regardless of what the person may have been like in life, his spirit is potentially dangerous to the living. As the following articles reveal, however, this conception of spirits of the dead is not always the case. In many groups, ghosts may be only partially evil or dangerous, and in still others, they may be conceived of as ever-present members of the social group who have increased powers to influence the lives of the living, either favorably or unfavorably. When the ghosts are thought to be most concerned with members of their own kin groups, and the members of the kin groups feel that the ghosts require propitiation in order to aid their living kinsmen, ancestor worship prevails. The spirits of the dead are revered, though that reverence is possibly never free from some feelings of fear and awe. Sometimes repressive and harsh, at other times benign and beneficial, the ghosts or ancestral spirits coexist with the living, influencing and even determining the fortunes of the tribal members.

The articles in this chapter are intended to indicate something of the range of attitudes and beliefs that exist regarding death and ghosts, to indicate the ways in which these attitudes and practices are interrelated with other aspects of culture, and to offer some analyses of the various phenomena.

MORRIS E. OPLER

An Interpretation of Ambivalence of Two American Indian Tribes

This article, prefaced by a Freudian proposition regarding ambivalence, contains excellent ethnographic documentation of attitudes and behaviors associated with death in Chiricahua and Mescalero Apache cultures. The ambivalent feeling that living members of the groups manifest toward the dead—mourning and grief expressed on the one hand, and dread and possibly hatred expressed on the other—is explained in purely cultural terms. Rejecting the Freudian position regarding "primordial parricides" and a consequent guilt feeling arising from this hypothetical event, Opler suggests that the apparent ambivalences may be explained through an analysis of interpersonal relations, the nature of power, and the ecological circumstances of the cultures. Fear of the dead is seen as a function of kinship and local group systems, of patterns of authority, of fear of sorcery and witchcraft, plus the basic need for interpersonal cooperation as a requisite for survival in the hostile environment.

As is true of most conclusions drawn from bodies of data partially inferred from individual psychological processes, other interpretations could be made than that presented here by Opler. Nonetheless, Opler's work stands as a well-documented, closely reasoned analysis of what is possibly a panhuman phenomenon— ambivalent feelings on the part of the living toward the deceased.

Opler has provided further data to substantiate his thesis in an article, "Further Comparative Anthropological Data Bearing on the Solution of a Psychological Problem," published in 1938.

Reprinted in abridged form from *Journal of Social Psycholgy*, VII, No. 1 (February, 1936), 82–115, by permission of the author and the Journal Press.

Sometime ago, in a review of *Totem and Taboo*, A. L. Kroeber referred to a number of Freud's suggestions as contributions "which every ethnologist must sooner or later take into consideration." Kroeber singled out Freud's discussion of ambivalence as particularly provocative and, in part, said of it: "Again the strange combination of mourning for the dead with the fear of them and taboos against them is certainly illumined if not explained by this theory of ambivalence."

Whether or not the ethnologist has taken this phase of Freud's writings into consideration, it remains true that few students of preliterate peoples have conducted inquiries designed to test or modify the psychoanalytic theory and conclusions upon the point.

At one time during my stay on the [Mescalero Apache] reservation, a very able and intelligent informant who wished to give me the fullest possible understanding of the culture undertook to explain native customs and beliefs for me. This Apache offered a number of native rationalizations pertaining to various rites and practices, and then bravely started to explain the peculiar belief that an Apache who possesses supernatural power and successfully practices the rite connected with it for any length of time, finally will be forced to sacrifice a close relative or permit himself to die. My informant floundered in a web of ambiguities for a few minutes and then had to confess that the whole matter was not clear to him. He could see, he said, why the power of some outsider, one who wished you ill perhaps, was to be feared; but why the power of a relative, one who could refuse you nothing in everyday life, should be a source of terror, he was unable to explain. This Apache was manifestly bewildered by the glaring inconsistency in the attitude toward kin upon which he had stumbled. On one hand he had been urged throughout his life to assist, and, in turn, to depend upon his relatives in all matters, to support them, whatever the consequences to himself, and even to avenge all wrongs inflicted upon them. Yet it was also within the traditional pattern to believe that these same people become, par excellence, a source of morbid fear for him. This contradiction or conflict in emotion and attitude towards the same person or group of people which this native sensed, we readily recognize as an expression of ambivalence.

The example cited is one of the most striking cases of contradictory attitude in respect to the same person which Apache culture affords and is the one which would, perhaps, be most noticeable to the native. But this instance by no means stands alone. The cultural forms are marked, at many points, by unmistakable evidence of such contrary emotions, and whole complexes are liberally tinged with such mixed feelings. A conspicuous affirmation of the last statement is the entire complex which has to do with death and the disposal of the dead. It will repay us to turn to this set of practices and beliefs.

One of the most impressive elements of Apache burial is the dispatch with which it must be conducted. Whenever possible burial takes place the same day on which death occurred. If this is impossible because the deceased has died in the evening, the burial always takes place the following day. The time during which the living and the dead are in contact is reduced to a minimum, a logical procedure in view of the dread sickness it is believed can be contracted from the dead, from the sight of the corpse, or from the possessions of the deceased.

As the last statement may suggest, no time is lost in disposing of the personal possessions of the dead. A certain number of his belongings are taken along by the burial party and interred with him; the rest are burned or broken into pieces at the spot where death took place. It is incumbent upon a dead Apache's relatives to dispose, in this way, of everything which had been used by him or had been in close personal contact with him. Even articles owned jointly with other members of the family, if they had been used to any extent by the deceased, had to be sacrificed. To retain any of these objects would bring back the ghost; the dead would return to claim his possessions. In any case the retention of some personal possession of a dead man would be sure to act as a reminder of him, and to think of the dead is one way of inviting the presence of the ghost and of subsequently succumbing to the serious "ghost" or "darkness sickness." In keeping with this fear of the return of the ghost to claim objects recognized by him, it is considered dangerous even to cherish presents given one by the deceased before his death.

Not only are the possessions of the dead relative destroyed or buried, but the very dwelling in which death took place is razed as well. The framework is usually burned, but even if it is not reduced to ashes, one may be sure that no Apache will enter a deserted house or use wood from it unless he is very certain that no death has occurred there. Nor does the destruction of the dwelling pave the way for a new, uncontaminated home on the old site. The family moves immediately to a new locality, one that will not be conducive to memories centering about the departed.

The effort to efface the memory of the dead relative goes much further. Those who assume the unwelcome task of dressing the corpse and burying it, burn, upon their return, all the clothes they wore while performing these duties. They also bathe their bodies in the smoke of a sage called "ghost medicine" which is thought unpleasant to ghosts and efficacious in keeping them at a distance. In fact, all members of the bereaved family are likely to "fumigate" themselves in this manner and to resort for some days to various devices which are considered useful in avoiding dreams of the dead or in warding off the visits of ghosts. Such practices consist in crossing the forehead or bed with ashes, or hanging some crossed pieces of "ghost medicine" above the head before retiring.

At the grave, just before their return, the members of the burial party take a final precautionary measure. They brush off their own bodies with green grass which they then lay at the grave in the form of a cross. The conception is that when this is done, any danger of falling victim to "ghost sickness" will be brushed away and left at the grave of the dead.

No more people than are strictly necessary to carry the possessions and prepare the grave participate in the burial. The site of the grave is not discussed thereafter; ordinarily no one would ask about the location of the grave, and no one would volunteer such information.

After the foregoing it is almost unnecessary to add that the grave is never revisited and that anyone found lingering around a grave site is suspect of witchcraft. As among so many other peoples, graves and the bones and possessions of the dead play a prominent role in ideas concerning sorcery.

To this point we have been primarily concerned with the measures taken to erase from the scene any material reminders of a dead relative and to avoid illness which may derive from actual contact with or sight of the corpse. But there are quite as many steps taken to obliterate less tangible reminders of the loss the family has suffered, and it may be instructive to turn to some of these now.

There is, first of all, a strong taboo against mentioning the name of the deceased. If it becomes necessary, for any reason, to mention his name, a phrase meaning "who used to be called" must be added.

As a result of this taboo it proved extremely difficult for me to obtain reliable genealogical material. It was considerably easier to persuade Apaches to discuss and reveal rites and ceremonies than it was to bring them to the point of talking freely of the kinship ties which had existed between them and those now dead.

The unwillingness to utter the name of the recent dead is a characteristic true of all members of these two tribes, whether they are relatives of the deceased or not. With the passage of time the taboo becomes less binding upon nonrelatives. Not so in respect to the relatives, however. For them there is no diminution of the strength of the taboo, and others, no matter what they may do elsewhere, must strictly refrain from any mention of the dead in the presence of these relatives. In fact, nothing is more insulting,

provocative, and certain to precipitate conflict than to call out the name of a dead man in the presence of his relative. A surprising number of feuds between families have had such an origin or include such an episode in their histories.

Just as the calling of a dead man's name within the hearing of his relative is accounted the gravest of insults and acts of hostility, so it is considered a graceful compliment to the family of the deceased and to the memory of the dead to take elaborate precautions that the name be not called. In cases of the death of prominent men who have been named after some object or animal, that animal or object is given an alternative name or another name. Thus when a Mescalero leader named Beso (from the Spanish *peso*) died, everyone was obliged to say *dinero* instead of *peso,* especially when within earshot of members of the dead man's family.

There is another practice which utilizes similar reasoning. If an Apache called two relatives by the same kinship term, and one of these relatives dies, for a long time afterward he will refrain from using this term to the survivor. To use the term formerly addressed to the one who has died will awaken memories of him and deepest grief, it is felt.

It is interesting to note that the very existence of death cannot be allowed terminological sanction. The verb that connotes the coming of death is used only in connection with animals. Of a person the most that can he said in everyday speech is, "He is gone."

The insistence that nothing be left as it was before a death, lest it act as a reminder of the bereavement, finds expression in all departments of native life. There is the practice, for example, of never leaving the bedding as it was when in use, when camp is to be broken. If death should occur and the individual should not return to that place, the sight of his bed as last used by him would only bring sorrow to his relatives.

These attitudes are reflected in the ceremonial complex, moreover. Ceremonies usually continue through four days or nights. If a death occurs in any nearby camp after the rite has begun, when the news is brought to the officiating shaman, he terminates his work at once. The ceremonial gifts which had to be given him before he could enter upon his duties he returns to the donors. Now all is as it was before, and after the passage from one to four days the whole ceremony is repeated from the beginning.

Despite the brevity and condensation of this description of Apache customs concerning death rites, it should be reasonably clear that there is a whole set of important practices designed to suppress and obliterate all mention and memory of the dead relative. In introducing this material I have termed it an indicator of ambivalent attitudes. In the Freudian sense this would suggest that the struggle to remove the possessions, the name, even the memory of the deceased from consciousness, is nothing else than an elaborate attempt to guard against the fear of the dead which results from the unconscious hate and resentment felt for this person during his life.

It may be asked why such an interpretation, so farfetched at first thought, need be accepted. The Apaches themselves say that there is no deep-seated mystery concerning the genesis of these acts and rites. They will tell you that an Apache loves his kin—a great deal more than the white man cares for his relatives, they may add significantly. To dwell on the memory of the dead would be to emphasize the loss and deepen the grief. Therefore they engage in the practices which arouse our curiosity.

The reasoning sounds honest and logical and might be acceptable if it were not for another congeries of attitudes and practices of an altogether different flavor which exists at the time of death, side by side with those we have already noted. These last are direct and vehement expressions of grief and evidences of mourning which are in no way subdued, curbed, or repressed. When an Apache learns of a close relative's death, he tears the clothes from his back. The women wail, the men cry openly and unashamed. Close relatives cut their hair, an act which alone will mark their bereavement for at least a year. For some time they wear only such clothing as is absolutely necessary for minimum warmth, and for a generous span of time they shun the dances and festivities. Often relatives mourn thus for a long time. An old woman, whose husband has been dead many years, still can be heard bewailing her loss occasionally.

Without laboring the point or extending the discussion, enough has been said, perhaps, to indicate that contradictory practices mark the Apache rites of death; there is the tendency to publicly signify grief and attest to the loss, and an elaborately socialized machinery for banishing that grief and the objects and words which might awake it.

But to state the Freudian conception, namely, that these two sets of practices result from ambivalent emotional attitudes toward the dead; that one set derives from the affection and regard which normal human relations sponsor, and the other from unconscious dislike and fear that are no less poignant and real; to state this, merely, is not to prove it.

Indeed, it could be most reasonably argued that it is gratuitous elaboration and special pleading to conjure up fear and unconscious hate as the stimulus for the practices which serve to eradicate mention and memory of the dead. It might be insisted with as much cogency that both sets of practices can be reasonably traced to one source, the affection and regard for the dead relative. It takes no great imaginative powers to suppose that genuine love for the dead relative could expend itself through more than one channel, and that the actualizations of these emotional flows could even appear contradictory. It is intelligible that under the impact of a deeply felt loss there would be the impulse to cry out and testify to grief, and no less the realization that the future must be faced alone, that the living must somehow carry on, that memories which weaken without aiding must be laid aside.

With these two interpretations possible from the data, the inquiry is reduced bluntly to this question: Is there any concrete and conclusive evidence in Apache culture of avowed fear of the dead, and especially of dead relatives, which might give body and validity to the hypothesis that the avoidance of the dead, of their graves, their names, their possessions, and their memories is attributable to fear rather than to regard?

Fortunately the study of Apache culture affords an unequivocal answer. Fear of the dead, and fear of the dead relatives particularly, does not have to be inferred. Instead its existence is asserted and emphasized by the natives. This fear is not merely an amorphous dread which seizes individuals in varying ways and must be relieved according to personal requirements. It has become formalized into a body of beliefs and concepts, and these have been woven into the fabric of the ceremonial life.

Now Apache ceremonial life, while it has other functions, is principally concerned with the healing of the sick. The gravest illnesses are contracted, it is believed, from contact with certain animals, such as bear, snake, and the like, or from being frightened or endangered by certain natural forces, such as lightning. Each of these sicknesses has its own characteristics and symptoms, and such diseases can be cured by shamans who have supernatural power from, and therefore considerable influence over, the animal or agency which has caused the illness. But there are also some people of malevolent disposition who have likewise had supernatural experiences with these potent animals or forces of nature and who have gained a ceremony and considerable power thereby. These are the witches, who manipulate their power for evil often, and are the ultimate source of much sickness and death. The witch who "knows" Bear may cause his enemy to suffer from "bear disease." His victim's sole hope is to command the services of another who "knows" Bear, who uses such power for beneficent purposes only, and whose power is stronger than that of the witch. It is likewise possible for a person to use his ceremony for the benefit of some, yet seek to harm others. He may be a shaman at one point of his career and a witch at another. He may be both at the same time.

With this hint of background we may proceed to the expression of the fear of the dead in Apache society. The fear, in obedience to the native pattern, is expressed in terms of sickness, and the sickness, eloquently enough for our argument, is expressed in terms of fear.

The particular illness attributable to persecution by the ghosts of the dead is known by three names, "ghost sickness," "owl sickness," and "darkness sickness." Ordinarily the Apache will not dare to use the words "ghost" or "owl" and will therefore give the last name only. The term "ghost sickness" is self-explanatory. The disease is also called "owl sickness" because the ghost is said to come back in the shape of an owl; owls are the ghosts of the departed. The blackest omen of which an Apache can think is the hoot of an owl around camp. The proximity of the bird, especially shortly after the death of a relative, evokes the greatest terror, and is often sufficient grounds for the requisite "ghost" or "owl ceremony." I could fill many more pages with native accounts of the dread and despair inspired by the appearance of the owl around camp or by its call. Ghosts are said to trouble people most often at night when it is dark, and most shamans who cure "ghost sickness" will not conduct their ceremony except at night. For these reasons, and also because a person afflicted with the malady is especially nervous and easily frightened at night, the name "darkness sickness" is the approved euphemism for the disease.

It is of special interest to note that the disease always strikes "from the head to the heart." All its symptoms are those of fright and include irregular beating of the heart, a choking sensation, and faintness at first seizure. As long as the illness lasts the patient suffers from excessive timidity, much trembling, weeping, and headache.

Although ghosts of nonrelatives may and do cause fear and sickness, it is far more common that the disease be the result of an encounter with the ghost of a deceased relative.

In the first place it is noteworthy that the most elaborate precautions are entered upon by the close relatives immediately after an Apache's death. Since these relatives have most contact with the corpse and the possessions of the dead, this is quite to be expected. Nevertheless, the end result and the general feeling are that the relative has more to fear from the ghost than anyone else.

Again, it is a matter of interest that most ghost ceremonies are held soon after a death in a family, and that the patient or patients are usually relatives of the deceased.

There is another impressive indication of the close nexus between relationship and fear of ghosts and owls. The hooting of the owl is accepted as speech in the Apache language which can be understood if one listens closely. The owl, according to my informants, has many unpleasant remarks to make to its uneasy hearers. It has been known to make the hair-raising statement, "I'm going to drink your blood." But more often the words of the owl have to do with its relationship to the one it is addressing. "I am your dead relative"—this is the most common sentence discerned by the tortured imagination of the Apache when the owl hoots nearby.

The owl is also prone to give ominous warnings concerning relatives. The bird is not infrequently heard reporting such melancholy news as, "All your people (relatives) are going to die." One woman, after the departure of a war party, heard this message repeated over and over by an owl, "I used to be one of your relatives." The next day the men returned without her son; he had been killed.

The owl, according to one Apache, "represents the spirit of a person" which "works by entering the body of an owl and exercises evil influence in this way." "That man is already dead and comes back. He turned to owl." "It's a ghost. It comes out of the grave, and it goes back." These are representative dicta of the natives concerning the owl.

From this equation of ghost with owl flows the belief that the ghost can appear as an owl and then transform itself at will into the semblance of the figure it bore in life. And it is possible for a shade of the dead to appear and, upon being accosted, to change into an owl and disappear.

Now to see or hear an owl is unlucky and harrowing enough, but to see the form of a ghost as you knew him in life, or, worse still, to be able to distinguish his features, is well-nigh fatal. It is the general consensus of opinion, backed by the authority of many cases, that the person who can discern the features of the ghost before him has not long to live.

Even though the evidence which has been offered is but a fraction of what could be presented, I hope that enough has been said to establish the connection between the taboos directed against the dead and fear of the dead. It should be abundantly clear, too, that the burden of both the taboos and the fear falls primarily and with unremitting force on the relatives of the deceased. But if the Apache must guard against the ill will of the dead, he must guard himself just as sedulously against the machinations of the living. Something has been said above of the duality of supernatural power as conceived of by the Apache, and of the possibility of wielding such power in the spirit of malice and revenge as well as for purposes good and holy. Granting the existence and duality of supernatural power, there is nothing obscure about the basis of fear of witches. A case will illustrate this. I was once talking to a man about charges of witchcraft which had been directed against X. The man with

whom I was talking then admitted to me, "Well, I'm a little afraid of X myself." He told me how he and X had opposed each other in a dispute which nearly ended in blows. Knowing X's reputation for possessing much supernatural power, and believing him to be thoroughly unscrupulous, he wondered whether X's resentment might not spill over into supernatural channels and work some immense disaster to him. In this case there was a cause for revenge and a subsequent outgrowth of fear. In all cases of ordinary witchcraft, some reason for the murderous supernatural attack is advanced, if it is only that the witch was jealous of the sick one's good looks or envious of his promising career. When a shaman sings over a patient and determines that his client is witched, he very often describes what led the witch to such extremes. "Do you remember when you attended that dance two years ago?" he might ask. "You gave something to drink to everyone there but one woman. You did not know it, but you forgot her and she was very angry. She determined to get even for this insult. She has waited till now so no suspicion will fall upon her." The conception is that always, if one can but put a finger on it, there is some injury or insult which will account for recourse to witchcraft.

But the Apache is not only beset by fear of the supernatural power of those who have reason to hate and harm him; he must also face the possibility that the supernatural power of those who are closest and dearest to him, the supernatural power of his own relatives, may be utilized to effect his very death. The reader will remember that we began our paper with this very paradox. At that time it seemed an insoluble contradiction which puzzled my willing Apache informant as much as it puzzled us. Now we are in a position to see the concept as one more mark of the underlying fear directed towards relatives. We have already dealt with the fear of the ghosts of the dead felt by living relatives. Now we have to consider the Apache's fear of the supernatural power of his living relatives.

The fear is based on the peculiar belief which already has been introduced. It is asserted that if one who has a ceremony from a certain power, heals and prospers by means of it for many years, the time will come when his power will remind him of the benefits bestowed, of the long life that has been permitted him, of the guidance and security that have been granted. Then the power will ask payment in return for all this help, and, coming to the point, will announce that the payment must be the sacrifice of a child or close relative of the shaman. To refuse is to sign one's own death warrant; if the relative does not die, the shaman must die in his stead. Thus there is the saying, "He sacrifices his relative to prolong his own life."

I was once working in his tent with an Apache well above middle age, when I happened to glance out of the doorway and saw his father, a very old man, approaching on horseback. I innocently said, "Here comes your father. Shall I call him over?" I was not a little disturbed to hear an emphatic, "No!" uttered in a hoarse, strained whisper. Instead, I was directed in that same tense tone of voice, to stand at the door and describe the old man's movements. "Where is he now? What's he doing? Is he going away?" These were the questions thrown at me, and I answered in some bewilderment. As it happened the old man was just passing through his son's field on the way to another camp. I reported his departure and turned to demand an explanation of such unusual conduct. My friend was perspiring freely and breathing heavily. He talked readily enough about the matter. "I don't mind admitting I'm afraid of the old man" he said. "He's got all kinds of power. They say he has done a lot of good with it. Well, maybe he has done good years ago. But I haven't seen any good that he's done in the last ten years. I don't like to have him monkeying around this camp."

It is decidedly easier to establish the existence of ambivalence in Apache society, and to advance material concerning the fear of the ghosts of dead relatives and the power of living ones, than it is to account for and explain all this. One explanation has already been offered us. It is Freud's suggestion "that ambivalence, originally foreign to our emotional life, was acquired by mankind from the father complex. . . ."

There are a number of objections to such a view. In characteristic Freudian manner it would derive ambivalence from the omnipotent Oedipus complex, that hypothetical source from which so much is made to flow. Freud would have us believe that Apache ambivalence exists, not because there is any-

thing in present Apache culture to warrant it, but because some of the younger men of a protohuman horde slew their father countless years ago. A "psyche of mass" which no psycholgists have been able to understand, explain, or substantiate is supposed to have carried on and preserved the memory of the parricide for the unconscious of our Apaches. Just how this parricide can account for the fear of dead female relatives and the fear of the power of living female relatives it is difficult to imagine, and how this hypothesis can illuminate the equally strong fear of relatives other than parents has yet to be demonstrated. Divorce from reality in the interests of a threadbare theory and insistence upon tying excellent clinical data to the coattails of the unconvincing Oedipus story have done not a little to delay the benefits which should result from Freud's contributions.

I have found it more convincing, realistic, and illuminating to interpret Apache ambivalence in terms of forces and elements which actually operate in the society and whose effects are open to observation and evaluation. It will be profitable, therefore, to outline one or two aspects of Apache culture which I feel have a direct bearing upon our problem.

The Mescalero and Chiricahua Apaches were hunting and food-gathering nomads ranging over the semiarid territory which now includes northwestern Texas, southern New Mexico, southeastern Arizona, and the adjoining section of northern Old Mexico. They lived on the wild game and plant life of the region and so were constantly on the move as the fruits ripened in one locality or game seemed more abundant in another. As one would expect from this simple economy and roving life, their artifacts were few and crude. The life was arduous, and productivity was achieved only as a result of earnest effort to which all individuals had to contribute. It was the obligation of the Apache to fit himself for any situation, and, if possible, to excel his fellows in all important pursuits. From his earliest years the Apache boy was taught to develop his strength and talents and to compete with others in tests of endurance and fortitude. Most of the games played by the children were designed to prepare them for the strenuous life of the future. At the time of puberty the boy was subjected to a prolonged ordeal of hardening and training. With this successfully passed there remained a series of four warpath expeditions which he had to attend, not as a warrior, but as an apprentice, and on these trips he was again under the severe scrutiny of the older men who looked for any signs of weakness or incompetence in the youth. Often a relative would arrange to have a distinguished hunter or warrior with much supernatural power perform a ceremony for the young man, so that he would become outstanding in those activities.

The girl, too, was urged quite as much to perfect herself in the women's tasks. In short, the Apache had infinite pride in his strength, his hunting ability, his warpath prowess, and in all the traits and aptitudes which marked him as an exceptional individual.

In the light of the meager technological advancement of the Apaches, this attitude is what might be expected. Each warrior had to know how to make his bow and arrows and to use them effectively. Everyone had to be trained and encouraged to take his place in the economy and to help win a livelihood from the barren country which constituted a large part of the Apache range. The point I wish to emphasize is the appreciation of himself as an individual of capacity and ability which every normal Apache was likely to develop. This personal independence was manifest throughout life and pervaded all types of activity.

But while it is true that each Apache had to be trained to cope with the dangers and trials which a nomadic life of hunting, raiding, and warfare imposed, it is certainly not true that he was an arrant individualist, owing obedience, co-operation, and discipline to no group. I should like, very briefly, to outline the composition of a strong unit to which the individual owed deepest loyalty, to touch upon the probable reasons for its strength, and to indicate the part it normally played in the affairs of each Apache.

It is apparent that the economy which the Apache practiced would not support a large population. From the time of earliest records to the present, the two tribes we are considering were few in numbers and there is no reason to think that their population was on the increase at the time of first white contact. Yet these two small tribes traversed and controlled a vast territory, necessary to

a hunting and gathering people in a locality where soil and climate combine to limit the food supply. It was imperative, moreover, that the people be well distributed over the range; too great a number trying to subsist in a limited area would have soon exhausted the available plant and animal life. Yet some concentration of population was required, if only for defense. As far back as my informants could remember, they had always had invaders to repel. For the Mescaleros, first it was the Tonkawas, then the Comanches, later the Mexicans and the Americans. Again, a good many of the tasks which had to be discharged required the assistance of a number of men or women. A raid to obtain valuable horses is a case in point. Enough men had to participate to secure and drive away the animals quickly, and the raid was most likely to succeed when lookouts could be posted before and behind the line of march. When the women were roasting the mescal in underground ovens and preparing this important food for winter use, enough of them had to assist to perform the necessary labor.

It occasions no surprise, then, to learn that the Apaches were distributed over their range in groups whose size and composition reflected the need for a small, close-knit body of people, sufficient for the execution of the necessary tasks dictated by the simple technology, possessing means of defense and the requisite mobility.

The group which offered these valuable characteristics and which became the central unit of Apache social organization was the extended domestic family. Residence after marriage among the Apaches was matrilocal, and so the extended domestic family ordinarily included an older married couple, their married and unmarried daughters, their sons-in-law, their married daughters' children, and their unmarried sons. The individual dwellings of the several families comprising this group were scattered a short distance from one another; altogether these camps composed a cluster of related families who shared the varied fortunes of battle, feast, work, and ceremony.

It was not uncommon for two or more extended domestic families which were united by marriage to camp near one another. This larger social division I have called the local group, for its members were generally known by a name descriptive of some mountain or natural landmark near which they roamed. This local group represented the greatest concentration of population realized by these Apaches except during brief periods of feast or ceremony. The Apache's life, therefore, was spent largely in company with his relatives by blood and affinity.

Apache social organization is characterized by other social divisions but they are of minor importance. There are the band and the tribe. Each is demarcated from the other by a definite range and slight differences of dialect and customs. While their existence was recognized by the native, he was considerably less interested in them than is the anthropologist. The Apache was sensible of the greater uniformity of speech and culture within what we call a tribe, but the Apache tribe was so remotely concerned with the problems and activities of the individual that neither of the two peoples under discussion possessed native tribal names. For all practical purposes, the allegiance and fundamental interest of the Apache were limited to the group of relatives represented by the extended domestic family, or at least by the local group.

It would be difficult to overestimate the unity of the extended domestic family. The women, the mother and daughters, were inseparable. They acted together in the accomplishment of all tasks, whether it were food gathering, food preparation, or the cooking. The mother's home was the center of all domestic activity. All game shot by the father, unmarried sons, or sons-in-law was brought to this domestic hub. Here the daughters aided their mother with the cooking, and then each married daughter carried some of the prepared food to her own dwelling and ate with her husband and children, since the son-in-law must never see his wife's mother.

There is powerful opposition to the disruption of this nucleus of relatives. The son-in-law, as has been mentioned, is bound to his wife's family by ties of avoidance, by special forms of speech and conduct, and these carry with them obligations of continuous economic assistance and absolute respect. He must live near his parents-in-law and work for them. He is always at their command. If the young man should wish to marry a second wife (for polygyny was practiced) it would have to be a younger sister or cousin

of his first wife, a member of the same relationship cluster. If his wife died, her relatives could force the widower to take a sister or female cousin of the deceased to wife. In case of domestic discord, the husband could not take easy offense and leave the camp of his parents-in-law without sufficient provocation. To do so would be to excite the enmity of a large and powerful group, and to be a marked man in its territory thereafter. So much for the structural safeguards which maintain the extended domestic family.

It will be appreciated that an organization of such strength and rigidity must exercise tremendous influence over the children which are reared in its charge. Something of the domination of this body of relatives over the affairs of the growing child has already been indicated when we were discussing that part played by relatives in the marriage choice. In all other matters of import the child is quite as dependent. If he needs a ceremony performed, it usually rests upon the bounty of his relatives to defray expenses. His instruction and training are supplied by relatives, or if outsiders are involved, the relatives pay for such services. Even as a mature person the individual can accomplish little without the aid of his relatives.

It may be wondered, perhaps, why so much space has been devoted to a discussion of Apache social groupings in a paper supposedly concerned with psychological problems. I think it is sufficient justification to point out that since the ambivalences we are attempting to comprehend are directed primarily against the members of the extended domestic family and the local group, it is plainly necessary (if we take the position that the ambivalences are stimulated by present, determinable factors) to study the common interests and also the probable causes of antagonism which these social units engender.

I am going to suggest the hypothesis that the ambivalences marked by the Apache practice of mourning for the dead and yet barring from sight or hearing anything that may arouse memories of the dead and consequent distress marked by fear, and the equally contradictory convention of avowing affection for kin and yet living in perpetual fear of their power—that these are the result of repressed and unconscious resentment and dislike of relatives which have their roots in the actual circumstances and events of Apache life.

The reader may smile at this. He may think, "Well, it is probably less fantastic to derive ambivalence from unconscious resentment against meddling relatives than it is to seek its meaning in fear of the vengeance of the sire of a primal horde, but, unfortunately, this hypothesis seems as impossible to prove as the other."

The situation may not be quite so desperate, however. After all, it should be possible to determine whether there are tangible causes of antagonism between relatives in Apache culture and whether these points of friction are substantial enough to cause noticeable disruption, and thus find a way into the field notes of the ethnologist. An affirmative answer of these two inquiries would afford much more conviction to my hypothesis. Therefore I am going to subject my hypothesis to four germane questions: (1) Is there any reason, inherent in Apache society, to expect conflict of desires between an Apache and his relative or body of relatives? (2) Do such conflicts occur openly enough and frequently enough to call themselves to the attention of an observer of the culture? (3) Can such open and public conflicts as do occur be definitely correlated with the existence or strength of ambivalence? (4) Agreeing that clashes between relatives may occur because of marked divergences in personalities and aims, how shall we account for the socialization of such oppositions, and their appearances as ambivalences, taboos, and customs to which all, including those who seemingly get along well with their kin, are subject?

In answer to the first question it may be said that while the strength and unity of the extended domestic family were prime necessities for the functioning of Apache culture at its technological level, and while innumerable benefits and kindnesses flowed to the individual Apache from such an arrangement, it also had its suppressive and irritating side. Merely to view the matter theoretically and apart from actual cases, it would seem inevitable that to train the youth to self-reliance and pride in personal achievement and yet leave him so completely under the control of a body of kin, would be to invite dissatisfaction and discord.

Let us now turn to our second inquiry and determine whether the undercurrent of revolt and dissatisfaction that seems theoretically possible really existed. I have abundant reason to believe that the absolutism of control over the individual by older kin or kin in a greater position of authority is compensated for by a definite tenseness in these relations which not infrequently flares up into acrimonious disputes.

The matter is not one into which it is easy to delve. The important material bearing on the point is not obtained through general questions which aim at understanding the formal outlines of the culture. Only considerable contact with the natives over a respectable length of time, and the establishment of close and friendly contacts can furnish the requisite data. An actual incident of field work will illustrate the point. During the early stages of my Mescalero research I hired an elderly informant and had no reason to complain of his services. As many others did after him, he gave me the ideal picture of Apache society. He emphasized, as will any reliable informant, the great respect and obedience which the Apache husband owes to his wife's relatives, and he enumerated the avoidances, polite forms, and usages which mark such observances. No one would have gathered from his sober and consistent discourse, that any Apache would dare slight these obligations or could live among his people if he had done so. About a year later I learned that this same informant, when a young man, had not only violated the proprieties to the extent of seeing his mother-in-law, but had come within an ace of scalping the poor lady. He had led an armed, one-man revolt against his wife's family, bottled them up together in a dwelling, and was only subdued by force in a successful attack from the rear.

Once the surface of things was scratched, it was not difficult to find comparable material which told a tale of resistance of individuals against domination by relatives of blood and affinity. Stories were obtained describing how girls fled from home rather than submit to marriage with repugnant men chosen by their relatives. A number of such unfortunates are said to have been killed by bears. I have the case of a young woman forced into a "shotgun" marriage by her father. She was so incensed that she refused to see her father any more, and she lived, in contrast to the usual Apache rule, with her husband's relatives.

One elderly informant, after I had absorbed considerable Apache decorum, rather shocked me by asserting that his mother-in-law was "no good." Upon investigation it turned out that the mother-in-law, after some family difficulties, had insulted him outrageously. Angered at something he had done, and in spite of the strict rule of avoidance, she faced him in the company of some others and freely aired her opinion of him. Another bitter antagonism between son-in-law and mother-in-law was masked behind avoidance and polite forms for some years. Then it culminated in a hand-to-hand scuffle in which the man emerged victorious but with consideral damage to his reputation. Still another mother-in-law, after scrupulous attention to all the forms for a long time, is reported to have assisted her daughter in driving her son-in-law out of camp under a barrage of rocks.

If we are satisfied that differences between Apache kin can arise and often terminate somewhat violently, we can pass to the next question and ask whether there is any discernible correlation between the expressions of ambivalence and conflicts such as we have been describing above. To answer briefly, I believe that evidence for such a correlation exists. It is certain that when conflict between relatives occurs, the fear of the power of the relative becomes stronger and avowed. The reader will remember the informant who was thrown into such a panic at the approach of his father. It will perhaps clarify the incident to remark that at the time of this scene, these two were opposing each other upon an issue which meant much to them. The father was about to instruct the son's bitterest political foe in his personal power.

We may say that when fear of the ghosts of relatives or fear of the power of living relatives is admitted and avowed, there is a definite correlation between this fear and tangible factors which led these people to oppose and dislike each other. We also note that exceptionally tranquil and satisfactory relations between individuals who are kin diminish the likelihood of the development of such fears, at least in overt form. If these be accepted as valid generalizations a long stride has been taken towards the validation of my hypothesis, for the connection between ambivalence and experience has been made in these instances.

But, while we have accounted for such manifestations of ambivalence in terms of conflict between the respect which the Apache is taught to tender all relatives and the antagonism and dislike which he cannot help feeling towards some of them, the general problem of ambivalence in Apache society is not yet entirely clarified.

After all, most Apache youths do not attempt to scalp their mothers-in-law, and most Apache mothers-in-law do not stone their sons-in-law. . . . While I have listed a number of the more spectacular deviations from Apache canons of good conduct, the truth of the matter is that the ordinary Apache obeyed the mores of his society and behaved himself so as to precipitate little scandal. And yet every Apache, though most were not involved in any open and discernible conflicts with relatives, practiced all the taboos of the death rite and believed in the possibility of their sacrifice by relatives— elements which we have said are indicative of fear and resentment felt towards kin.

I believe we will understand the matter better if we regard the cases of admitted and overt hostility towards relatives as symptoms of a far more general psychic disorder. These are the exceptional cases where friction has been so continuous and galling that the trouble could not subside and be dismissed.

While the occasional explosions furnish valuable clews to the nature of disagreements in the society, such incidents were not the general rule. Nevertheless, I have little doubt that most Apaches at some stage of their careers found the control of their affairs by relatives somewhat at variance with their own plans and desires. There is ample evidence to show that individual marriage choices were overruled and personal inclinations rejected any time they interfered with the best interests of the larger group. But, though the individual often felt circumscribed, limited, and curbed by the decisions of his relatives, he generally subordinated his personal inclinations to their rulings. To do otherwise, to invite an open rupture, would be to cut himself off from future economic and moral assistance. No man stood more isolated and alone than one who could not depend on his kin to furnish him a haven. It goes without saying that only extreme provocation would induce an Apache to break with his relatives. What resentment he felt when his wishes were thwarted, he swallowed. . . . He bowed to the inevitable and was guided by tradition and his own best interests. He suppressed the memory of the whole inicdent, banished it from consciousness, and followed whither the cultural forms led.

But the repression of conscious wishes does not make them less real for unconscious mental life. The longings, which had to be denied that the extended domestic family might flourish, lodged their protest in the unconscious. The resentment, which could not normally be expressed in everyday life if the solidarity and unity essential to the health of the society were to be maintained, emerged in the guise of a mysterious terror of the dead relatives and a puzzling dread of the power of living relatives. The disguise is ingenious. Everything is arranged to mask from consciousness the reality of the ill feeling against the relative. The ghost of the dead becomes an owl, and one can revile the owl, shoot at it, drive it away from camp with good conscience. The fact that it is your relative whom you treat in this manner is obscured by the feeling that you are thus harassing an evil bird. You fear the supernatural power of your relative, but again the grim truth is glossed over. For some unexplained reason his power forces him to act against you. In conscious thought the power is represented as malevolent and blameworthy, and the relative escapes the greater part of the censure. But these sops to the traditions and amenities which guide conscious thought are rather transparent, and, as we have seen, they yield readily to analysis when a total picture is presented.

In conclusion I would say that the material and interpretation offered are an attempt to explain aspects of Apache psychology, conscious and unconscious, from the circumstances under which actual people lived in a society that really existed. Such an approach stands in direct contrast to the general trend of "depth psychology" wherein it has been the fashion to derive psychological phenomena, and even social phenomena, from such remote events and concepts as "primal parricides" and "primordial images." If what has been written here proves suggestive and worthy of consideration, it is hoped that other and more penetrating studies of mental life from this angle will be accomplished, and that the important relationship between culture and psychology will be richly exploited.

MELFORD E. SPIRO

Ghosts, Ifaluk, and Teleological Functionalism

Attitudes toward the dead found among the inhabitants of the small atoll of Ifaluk are in many ways similar to those expressed among the Apaches. Here fear and hatred of the spirits of the dead are focused on only one type of ghost, the malevolent *alusengau* (it should be noted that Spiro deals primarily with the psychosocial effect of the belief in the malevolent spirits only), yet these beliefs approximate those found in Apache culture directed toward all spirits of the dead. Spiro raises the question, as the Ifaluks might themselves, "Would not the people be better off if there were no *alusengau?*" He concludes that the fear and personal anxieties that stem from the culturally created belief in malevolent ghosts, so apparently dysfunctional, are balanced in the culture on the manifest level by the contributions that the concept makes to the understanding of the causes of disease and pathological behavior, and on the latent level by the outlet that the concept provides for the culturally and environmentally engendered hostility and aggression which is unacceptable when expressed interpersonally.

Reprinted from *American Anthropologist*, LIV (1952), 497–503, by permission of the author and the American Anthropological Association.

Points of similarity between the conclusions presented by Opler and Spiro are striking when their different points of departure are considered. Opler makes an analysis on the manifest cultural level; Spiro utilizes a neo-Freudian framework. Hatred and fear of the dead are seen by both authors as stemming, in part, from the size and nature of the society, and from the necessity of maintaining extremely amicable in-group relations.

Parenthetically, it should be noted that Lessa (1961) and De Beauclair (1963) have recently established that sorcery exists on Ifaluk. Spiro (1961) feels this does not invalidate his general thesis.

Ifaluk, a small atoll in the Central Carolines (Micronesia), is inhabited by about 250 people, whose culture, with minor exceptions, reveals very few indications of acculturation. The subsistence economy consists of fishing and horticulture, the former being men's work and the latter, women's. Politically, the society is governed by five hereditary chiefs, who are far from "chiefly," however, in their external characteristics. Descent is matrilineal and residence is matrilocal. Though clans and lineages are important social groups, the extended family is the basic unit for both economic and socialization functions. This culture is particularly notable for its ethic of nonaggression and its emphasis on helpfulness, sharing, and cooperation.

Ifaluk religion asserts the existence of two kinds of supernatural beings, or *alus*: high gods and ghosts. The former, though important, do not play as significant a role in the daily lives of the people as the latter. Ghosts are of two varieties—benevolent and malevolent. Benevolent ghosts (*alusisalup*) are the immortal souls of the benevolent dead, while malevolent ghosts (*alusengau*) are the souls of the malevolent dead. One's character in the next world is thus not a reward or punishment for activity in this one, but rather a persistence in time and space of one's mortal character.

Malevolent ghosts delight in causing evil. They are ultimately responsible not only for all immoral behavior, but, more importantly, for illness which they cause by indiscriminately possessing any member of their lineage. Benevolent ghosts attempt to help the people, and with their assistance the shaman may exorcise the malevolent spirits. These malevolent ghosts are the most feared and hated objects in Ifaluk by persons of all ages and both sexes. This fear and hatred, found on both a conscious and unconscious level, is attested to by abundant evidence, derived from linguistics, overt behavior, conscious verbal attitudes, projective tests, and dreams. As a consequence, most Ifaluk ceremonial life is concerned with these *alusengau,* and much of their nonceremonial life is preoccupied with them.

We must now ask ourselves, what are the functions of the belief in the alus in Ifaluk? On a manifest level this belief is both functional and dysfunctional, providing both for the individual and for the group a consistent theory of disease. In the absence of scientific medicine, this function is not to be lightly dismissed. The two areas of life over which the Ifaluk have no technological control are illness and typhoons, and the belief in alus serves to restrict the area of uncertainty. For it affords not only an explanation for illness, but also techniques for its control, minimizing the anxieties arising from intellectual bewilderment in the face of crucial life crises, and the feeling of impotence to deal with them.

Furthermore, the belief serves to explain another problem—the existence of evil and defective people. Native psychological theory has it that man is born "good" and "normal." In the absence of the concept of the alus, the people would be hard put to explain such phenomena as aggression and abnormality, for it also serves to explain these inexplicable and potentially dangerous phenomena. All abnormalities—in which the Ifaluk include violations of the ethic of nonaggression, as well as what we would label mental subnormality, neurosis, and psychosis—are termed *malebush,* and are explained by possession by an alus. The manifest functions of this belief, however, seem to be outbalanced by its obvious dysfunctions. The alus cause worry, fear, and anxiety, as well as sickness and death; and by causing the death of individuals they can, potentially, destroy the entire society. From the point of view of the people, it would be better if there were no alus.

We are thus presented with a difficult question: Why does such a manifestly dysfunctional belief continue to survive? To answer this question we must turn to other aspects of Ifaluk culture. This culture, we have observed, is characterized by a strong sanction against aggression. No display of aggression is permitted in interpersonal relationships; and in fact, no aggression is displayed at all. The people could not remember one instance of antisocial behavior, aside from the malebush, nor were any examples of it observed in the course of this investigation. To this striking fact another, equally striking, may be added: namely, that the absence of overt aggression in interpersonal relationships is found in persons who may be characterized as having a substantial amount of aggressive drive. But aggressive drives, like other imperious drives, demand expression; if they are not permitted expression they are deflected from their original goal and are either inverted or displaced. Some Ifaluk aggression is inverted; but that all aggression should be turned inward is impossible, assuming even the lowest possible level of psychological functioning. For if this were the case, we would have to predict the probable disintegration of personality, if not the destruction of the organism. This has not happened in Ifaluk, because the Ifaluk have a socially acceptable channel for the expression of aggression—the alus.

The alus, as already observed, are feared and hated; and this hatred is expressed in conversation, dreams, and fantasies, as well as in overt behavior patterns of public exorcism, ritual, and ceremony, whose purpose is to drive off the alus and to destroy them. Thus, though the intrinsically hated qualities of the alus are sufficient to arouse aggressive responses, the belief in their existence allows the individual to displace his other aggressions onto the alus, since all the hatred and hostility which is denied expression in interpersonal relationships can be directed against these evil ghosts. As Dollard, following Lasswell, has put it, in any instance of direct aggression, "there is always some displaced aggression accompanying it, and adding additional forces to the rational attack. Justifiable aggressive responses seem to break the way for irrational and unjustifiable hostilities. . . . The image of the incredibly hostile and amoral out-grouper is built up out of our own real antagonism plus our displaced aggression against him."

Thus antisocial aggressive drives are canalized into culturally sanctioned, aggressive culture patterns. The possibility for this is important in any society: it is particularly important for the Ifaluk because of their ethic of nonaggression, as well as of the smallness of the land mass which they inhabit. Kluckhohn, for example, points out that belief in witchcraft provides an outlet for Navaho aggression and, as such, serves a crucial function for the Navaho, despite the fact that they have other channels for aggression as well. The Navaho show aggression in interpersonal relationships by quarreling, murder, and violent physical fighting. These avenues are closed to the Ifaluk; indeed, they are inconceivable to them. Furthermore, Kluckhohn points out, the Navaho can "withdraw" from unpleasant situations, either physically or emotionally, by drinking. The Ifaluk cannot "withdraw." As Burrows has put it: "The people of Ifaluk are so few (two-hundred fifty of them); their territory so restricted (about one-half square mile of land surrounding a square mile of lagoon); and their lives all forced so much of the time into the same channels by the routine of getting a livelihood, that it would be nearly impossible for any part of them to keep aloof from the rest. So there is next to no segregation. Each individual surely has some face-to-face contact with every other." Nor can they "withdraw" by drinking, since they have no liquor that is genuinely intoxicating.

Given this situation, therefore, as concerns both the physical and cultural reality, there is no way to deal with aggression except to displace it. Hence a latent psychobiological function of the alus is to provide an outlet for Ifaluk aggressions, preventing the turning of all aggression inward, and thus precluding the collapse of Ifaluk personality. That this problem is not unique to Ifaluk, but is found with equal intensity on other tiny atolls, is revealed in Beaglehole's discussion of Puka-Puka. Here, too, we find an ethic of nonaggression in a tiny Pacific atoll, whose culture is similar to that of Ifaluk.

And here, too, socially sanctioned channels exist for the expression of aggression, serving the same functions that the alus serve in Ifaluk. "Life is such," writes Beaglehole, "that no one may get away from his fellow villagers. Privacy and solitude as we know them are almost nonexistent. Day and night, month in and month out, the individual is continuously in contact with others. He cannot get away from them no matter what the provocation. Were it not for certain socially approved ways of expressing otherwise repressed emotions the society would disintegrate under the weight of its own neuroses."

But the Ifaluk must deal with their anxieties, as well as with their aggressions. The Ifaluk experience certain anxieties in childhood which establish a permanent anxiety "set" in the Ifaluk personality. This anxiety is particularly crippling, for it is "free-floating"; that is, its source is unknown or repressed, so that there is no way of coping with it. In this connection, belief in alus serves another vital latent function for the individual, since it converts a free-floating anxiety into a culturally sanctioned, real fear. That is, it provides the people with a putative source of their anxiety—the alus—at the same time that it provides them with techniques to deal with this fear by the use of time-proven techniques, in the form of ritual, incantations, and herbs, whereby the imputed source of the anxiety may be manipulated and controlled.

Thus we see that the belief in the alus has certain consequences for the psychological functioning of the Ifaluk, which, though they are unaware of them, are nonetheless vital and crucial for their functioning at an optimum level of psychological adjustment. For the Ifaluk individual, that is, the latent function of the cultural belief in alus is to protect him from psychological disorganization. Without this belief—or its *psychological equivalent*—the tensions arising within the individual as a result of his anxieties and repressed aggressions could well become unbearable.

But the belief in alus has important sociological functions, as well. If there were no alus and the people repressed their aggressions, the society, as well as individual personalities, would disintegrate. On this level, then, the consequences for the group follow from the consequences for the individual; if

all individuals collapse, it follows that the group collapses. But the probabilities of the repression of all aggression in any society are very small. In all likelihood, the strength of the Ifaluk ethic of nonaggression would be weaker than the strength of the aggressive drives, because of the strength of the tensions created by the latter, so that these drives would seek overt expression. But this is exactly what could not occur in Ifaluk without leading to the disintegration of the entire society. The Ifaluk ethic of nonaggression is a necessary condition for the optimal adaptation of a society inhabiting a minute atoll. The minimal aggression permitted in other societies inhabiting large land masses does not lead to disastrous consequences; but here even this minimum cannot be permitted because of the impossibility of isolation. The physical presence of others is a constantly obtruding factor, and the existence of even a modicum of aggression could set up a "chain reaction" which could well get out of control. This fact is recognized by some of the people. Thus our interpreter told of an individual who had offended others by his unseemly conduct, who had made no attempt to rebuke him. When asked for an explanation of their behavior, it was pointed out that any action on their part would have led to strife, and since "very small this place," other people would become involved, until "by'm-by no more people this place."

Even if the expression of aggression in interpersonal relationships would not lead to the physical destruction of Ifaluk society, it would result in the dissolution of the distinctive aspect of its culture—sharing, co-operation, and kindliness toward others. Sharing and co-operation have enabled the Ifaluk to exploit their natural environment to its fullest extent with the technology at their disposal, and to live at peace with one another, in mutual trust and respect. In short, it has given them both physical and psychological security. The breakdown of the Ifaluk ethic of nonaggression, even a minimum of aggressive behavior, would destroy the positive attitudes that make co-operation and sharing possible, which would seriously reduce economic efficiency and psychological security. The disappearance of co-operation, then, would result in a precariously low level of adaptive integration.

With their belief in the alus, however, it is possible for the people to turn their aggressions from their fellows and direct them against a common enemy. The common hatred that results not only enables the people to displace most of their aggressions from the in-group to the out-group, but also serves to strengthen the bonds of group solidarity. For all the people may suffer the same fate—attack by the alus. All must defend themselves against this, and all attempt to defend others from it. The resultant solidarity is both expressed and symbolized in the medicine ceremonies, both therapeutic and prophylactic, which are occasions for convening the entire group.

Thus we again see that the belief in alus has certain latent consequences of which the people are unaware, but which are vital to the functioning of this society and the preservation of its culture. The absence of this belief, or of some other institution with the same functions, would be disastrous for Ifaluk society as we know it today.

Having assessed the belief in malevolent ghosts in terms of the total social functioning of one society, it may be instructive to compare this belief with institutions in other societies, which have the same functional importance. Sorcery and witchcraft play the same functional role among the Ojibwa and Navaho, respectively, that ghosts play in Ifaluk. But we can now perceive the superiority of the belief in ghosts over witchcraft and sorcery for the achievement of their common latent end—the release of aggression. For though the latter beliefs serve to deflect some aggressive drives from other members of society onto the sorcerers or witches, they also serve to instigate other aggressive drives. Since witches and sorcerers are members of one's society, and since their identity is usually obscure, one

tends to become suspicious, wary in interpersonal relationships, and insecure with one's fellows. Thus though the belief in witches and sorcerers succeeds in deflecting aggressive drives and contributing to social solidarity, it also increases aggressive drives and decreases social solidarity. Belief in ghosts, however, serves the dual function of both decreasing in-group aggression and increasing group solidarity. It may not be irrelevant to observe in this connection that societies, such as Dobu, Kwoma, Ojibwa, and Navaho, which practice sorcery or witchcraft, are also characterized by individualism and insecurity, whereas Ifaluk is characterized by communalism and mutual trust.

We have observed that the belief in the alus is crucial to the psychobiological functioning of the individual and to the survival of Ifaluk society and its culture. This analysis thus enables us to understand how an apparently irrational belief continues to survive with such tenacity. As Merton points out: "Seemingly irrational social patterns" may be seen to "perform a function for the group, although this function may be quite remote from the avowed purpose of the behavior."

This interpretation of the Ifaluk malevolent ghosts is not meant to imply that no dysfunctions can be attributed to this belief. We have already indicated the important manifest dysfunctions. The latent dysfunctions are equally severe: the belief serves to drain energy from creative enterprise to that of defense against the alus; it serves to preclude investigations of alternative disease theories; it channels much economic activity into nonproductive channels; finally, though it resolves many anxieties, it creates a very serious one in its own right—the anxiety created by fear of the alus itself.

ELIZABETH COLSON

Ancestral Spirits and Social Structure Among the Plateau Tonga

Among the Tongas, individuals are considered to have several spirits which are released at the time of death. As among the Ifaluks, some such spirits are evil, others are beneficial. The Tongas make the added distinction that each individual contributes at least one of each, and that the number and kind of spirits he contains is determined, in part, by the social position he held during life. The ease with which Colson describes the social structure of the group by listing and analyzing the types of *mizimu,* points strongly to the intimate relationship that exists here, and in many other cultures, between social structure and religious beliefs.

To be noted especially here is the way in which the mizimu serve to validate the Tonga life pattern, tie together potentially divergent kin groups, and reinforce the major status changes encountered by the Tonga adult.

Reprinted in abridged form from *International Archives of Ethnography,* XLVII, Part 1 (1954), 21–68, by permission of the author and the publishers.

In this paper I am going to describe beliefs held by the Plateau Tonga about the activities of a particular type of spirits, the *mizimu,* and attempt to show how these reflect the ideal organization of Tonga social structure. The term *mizimu* (*muzimu* in the singular) is usually translated by anthropologists as "ancestral spirits," but I shall use the native term since this translation does not cover the various ways in which the Tonga use the term and I can find no adequate English equivalent.

I have already published a sketch of Tonga social organization. I need only say here in introduction that the Plateau Tonga are a Bantu-speaking people inhabiting Mazabuka District in the Southern Province of Northern Rhodesia. Their number today has been variously estimated as between 80,000 and 120,000 people. Until the British administration introduced a Native Authority system, they had no large-scale political organization of their own. The basis of their own system was twofold: an organization into a large number of small dispersed groups of matrilineal kinsmen, and an organization into local neighborhoods composed of a few villages with a common rain shrine and cult. Although the rain shrines no longer hold the allegiance of many Tonga, the local neighborhoods continue. To most Tonga they are

of greater importance than the chiefdoms or the Pleateau Tonga Native Authority, which have been imposed upon the old structure. The matrilineal groups are still important units, although their functions have been curtailed with the outlawing of self-help and the institution of courts. They have also been affected by the diminished importance of the cult of the mizimu which is an integral element in the organization of such groups.

In this paper I shall write as though all the Tonga still held to the old beliefs about the mizimu. This, of course, is not true. Missions have worked in the area since 1905. Many Tonga are Christians, of eight different sects. Others are skeptics who deny the old beliefs without accepting those introduced by the missionaries. Many claim that they have forgotten the mizimu, and that these no longer affect them in any way. There are whole villages where no one makes offerings to the mizimu or considers them in any way. On the other hand, there are many Tonga to whom the mizimu are a vital part of life. They would claim, along with the old man who heard a woman suggest that the mizimu had disappeared since people stopped believing in them: "No, the mizimu can never die. They will always be there affecting us."

THE NATURE OF THE MIZIMU

Mizimu and ghosts (*zelo*) are both thought to be the spirits of former living people, but the two are distinct. A few Tonga have told me that mizimu and ghosts are one and the same thing. Others have argued that the ghost exists only for the period between a death and the time when the kinsmen assemble for the final mourning rite and that this transforms the ghost into the muzimu. But most maintain that the two are completely different entities, and a study of their actions on different occasions is consistent with this interpretation and not with any identification of ghost and muzimu.

When a person dies, therefore, two spirits remain, one the muzimu and one the ghost. The ghost is always a newly created spirit, some saying that it originates in the dying breath. Not all people produce a new muzimu when they die, and I have never been able to get a clear statement as to how the muzimu originates. Indeed, various people have told me: "I have never been able to understand this myself, and I don't think anyone else does either." There is general agreement, however, that only those who have achieved a certain status during their lifetime give rise to a new muzimu after death, while others leave behind them only the already existing muzimu associated with them since their naming. Once created, moreover, the mizimu are not immortal like the ghosts, who are independent of the devotion of living people for their continued existence. When the living cease to remember the mizimu and no longer call upon them by name, they become nameless spirits wandering at large, who now work only for evil. "They have become like ghosts." Over these the living have no control, for in forgetting the names they have lost the means of summoning or propitiating the spirits.

Over ghosts the living have no direct control, unless they are sorcerers, and ghosts are presumed to be only evil. They may act against the living of their own volition, or they may be agents of sorcerers who have pressed them into service. A sudden dangerous or mortal illness is therefore usually attributed to ghosts. The muzimu is not actively evil in the same way. It may cause injury to the living, but this is not its primary purpose, nor is it free like the ghost to cause injury to anyone with whom it comes

in contact. The muzimu is dependent upon the living for its own continued existence, and it causes injury to keep its memory alive in the living so that they may provide the offerings on which it depends. If the living refuse to listen to its demands, then it is thought to enlist the aid of the ghosts to inflict more drastic punishment. Some Tonga say that the muzimu travels always with the ghost which originated with it on a person's death and which acts as its intermediary with other ghosts.

The mizimu are thought to be concerned that they should not be forgotten, and so they send sickness and other misfortune to the living as a reminder that beer and other offerings must be provided. They are anxious that the living should maintain the customs that they practiced when they were alive, and therefore they punish departures from custom. In return they offer to the living some protection against other spirits and against sorcery. They should also assist the living to obtain the good things of life—children, good harvests, herds of cattle, and an orderly existence. These in turn permit the living to procure grain for beer, to marry wives who will brew the beer for offerings, and to perpetuate the names of the mizimu through the children whom they beget and who, to some extent, are regarded as the living representatives of the mizimu. The living propitiate the spirits to ensure for themselves the good things which they desire; the spirits assist the living to these goods so that they in turn may continue to exist. Each is dependent upon the other, and there is partnership between the living and the mizimu in achieving their common ends.

But the mizimu are not concerned with all the living, and the living are not concerned with all the mizimu. The relationships between them are a projection of those which exist between living persons organized in the kinship system. Mizimu and living members of a kinship group are parts of a single whole, and the ties between them transcend the bounds of time and space. Or rather, since the Tonga kinship system is not given a local focus, nor does an ordered genealogical framework or any scheme of historical incidents create a time scale into which the living and the mizimu can be fitted—the system exists outside time and space in a perpetual present.

INDIVIDUALS AND THEIR MIZIMU

The Tonga maintain that the mizimu which are concerned with them, and therefore with which they are concerned, are the spirits of former members of the matrilineal kinship groups of their mothers and fathers, though they also say that the spirits of the matrilineal groups of their two grandfathers may occasionally intervene in their affairs. Nevertheless, it is the affiliation with the two parental groups which is primarily stressed in relation to the mizimu, as it is throughout social life. Some of these mizimu, however, are of more importance to an individual than are others. When a Tonga speaks of his mizimu, or refers to the mizimu of someone else, he may be using the term very broadly to include all those spirits which are concerned with him, or more narrowly to refer to particular mizimu who stand in a special relationship to him. His meaning is usually clear from the context. For analysis, however, it is necessary to distinguish the different uses of the term, and I shall therefore use the following classification in writing about the role of the mizimu in any one individual's life.

1. *Mizimu* as a general term includes all the spirits of former members of the lines of the father and mother, and may even be used still more generally for all the spirits of former members of any group with which a person feels a kinship relationship. If I write of the mizimu of a matrilineal group, however, it refers only to the spirits of former members of this group.
2. *Guardian Mizimu* are those associated with the names which each person receives soon after birth. They act as his special guardians throughout life, and from them he is thought to derive his personality.
3. *House Mizimu* are the particular spirits which an adult person installs as the guardians of his household.
4. *Inherited Mizimu* are those which are associated with a person because he has been given the name of someone recently deceased as part of the funeral rites.
5. *Own Muzimu.* This is the new muzimu which comes into existence only after a person's death. No living person has his own muzimu.

The guardian mizimu have a special significance in each person's life. They can be regarded as symbolic representations of the overwhelming importance of the paternal and maternal matrilineal groups in determining the original social status of any individual, and of their responsibility for his well-being throughout life. Names are identified with mizimu, and the giving of a name implies assumption of social responsibility for a child. A man who begets a child by an unmarried woman may obtain the right to name his child, which is then affiliated to his matrilineal group and comes under the power of its mizimu in the same fashion as any child born in wedlock. A man who begets an adulterine child by a married woman has no such right. The woman's husband is the legal father. He names the child, thus bestowing upon it a guardian muzimu, and it comes under the protection of the mizimu of his line quite as much as do children he has begotten. The names, which thus recognize the existence of the child and give it its initial place in society, are bestowed some months after birth. The first name is given by the father or his relatives, and it is a name belonging to a former member of this line. The second is given by the mother's relatives and is the name of a former member of her line. Each name is associated with a muzimu. The Tonga say that the mizimu themselves may decide which of their living kin shall receive their names, and thus become their special charges. When a woman is in labor, the midwives call the names of various mizimu, saying, "Nangoma, come forth! Mavwali, come forth! Nankambula, come forth! Cimuka, come forth!" The child should be born when they call the appropriate name, and they then know that it is this muzimu which has chosen to give its name to the child. They may have no such indication, and may later learn the appropriate name through divination. If the child becomes ill, the diviner may attribute the illness to the desire of a particular muzimu to give its name to the child. Even if the child's name has been decided at its birth, the name may still be changed since the guardian muzimu has failed in its duty by permitting the illness, or the relatives may decide that henceforth the child shall bear both names and both mizimu will be regarded as its guardians and as concerned with its fate. In addition, it will have a name and a guardian muzimu from the other parent's side. Occasionally the name is chosen by the relatives without any form of divination. However a name is chosen, it is not identified with the child until the time of the formal naming rite.

The guardian mizimu may thus be viewed as symbols of the identification of a person with his kinship groups. But when as an adult he establishes his own independent household, he acquires a new social position. His household is one of the units in the local community, and he takes his place within the community as its head. Within the household are joined not only the interests of his own paternal and maternal matrilineal kinship groups, but also of the matrilineal groups of his wife. The importance of his new position is ritually recognized, for he now for the first time becomes capable of making offerings to the mizimu. At the same time, the new household is also given a ritual recognition, by the installation of one or more of the husband's mizimu as special guardians of the house. Significantly enough, these are rarely the husband's guardian mizimu, which stress his identification with his paternal and maternal kinship groups. These remain as his individual guardians, but henceforth his house mizimu will hold a dominant position in all that concerns him as his interests are centered in the well-being of his household.

The fact that he has achieved a position of his own is further recognized, for when he dies he himself will become a muzimu. Those who die before they set up a household leave behind them only the guardian mizimu of their names. I argue that this is because their social personality is still derived from attachment to their matrilineal groups, and their death is of concern only to these two groups. The head of a household is of importance to others besides his own paternal and maternal kinsmen, and his importance to his kinsmen is now at least partially a reflection of the position which he occupies in the community. This is given recognition by attributing to him a muzimu of his own when he dies.

At the same time, the primary affiliation of each person to his matrilineal kinsmen is stressed, for the new muzimu which he has created bears the name of his guardian muzimu from his maternal line, and it has power to affect only those of his line and their offspring. His death breaks the tie which has been created between his own matrilineal group and that of his father by their common interest in him. His father's group have no concern with his own muzimu, and it cannot affect them. Part of the funeral rite emphasizes the finality of the break with the father's line in contrast to the continuity with the maternal line. This is embodied in every funeral, whether or not a new muzimu is thought to be involved. For, although not every person becomes a muzimu, each person once named is associated with his guardian mizimu. Formerly, when a child died before it was named, there was no mourning, for no mizimu were involved. Even today, the old women will tell the mother to hush her wailing, saying that this is only a ghost (*celo*) or only a person (*muntu*), and the mourning is usually curtailed. But if a person dies after being named, someone must be chosen to inherit the muzimu (*kwanga muzimu*). This is the deceased's guardian muzimu from his maternal line in the case of one who dies before establishing a household; it is his own muzimu otherwise. The father's group come to the mourning, and they are said to take away with them the name which they gave to their child and with it the associated guardian muzimu. The name from the maternal side is perpetuated in another member of the group. The person chosen is anointed with oil at the nape of the neck, given tobacco, and as beads are placed about his neck, he is told: "Your name is now such and such." This rite is thought to continue the attachment of the now inherited muzimu to the group to which it belongs. If it is a newly created muzimu, however, a further rite is performed some months after the death, when the people gather for the final mourning. In the interim, though the muzimu has been inherited, it is thought to be wandering disconsolately in the bush. At the final rite, an offering is poured in its name, and it is told to take its place among the other mizimu of the line with the assurance that the living will not forget it while it remembers them. Henceforth it may appear in many different roles—it may be installed as the guardian of a household, its name may be given to any number of children to whom it will be thought to act as guardian, or it may only be invoked occasionally by a diviner who attributes illness to its anger at being neglected. Its importance will reflect the importance which the person attained in life. Those of little importance to their kinsmen are usually soon forgotten.

THE MIZIMU AND THE MATRILINEAL GROUP

So far this analysis of the cult of the mizimu has been concerned with the way in which it reflects the identification of the individual with the kinsmen of his father and mother. In this section I shall analyze the way in which the cult reflects the relationships which exist between kinsmen within a matrilineal group. Each such group claims that it is a united body in relationship to the mizimu of its line, and indeed the members are likely to describe the common tie that binds them together as due to the fact that all of them are affected by the same mizimu.

The matrilineal group is the basic kinship unit of Tonga society. It is a group of kinsmen who claim a putative descent through females from a common ancestress, though they are not concerned to trace their descent and are frequently ignorant of their exact relationship to each other. The duties of members of the group involve the obligation of visiting each other when ill, of mourning the deaths of members of each other's families, of helping to provide bride-wealth for the males of the group, of assisting each other to pay fines and damages, of purifying the spouses of those who die, and of finding people to inherit the positions and mizimu of their dead. In case of need, they should assist each other with food and other gifts. In former days they formed a vengeance group to uphold each other's right against outsiders, and were held jointly responsible by outsiders for each other's actions. They also have certain joint rights. They should share in the bride-wealth given for the women of the group and they share the estates of their deceased members.

SUMMARY

In the foregoing paper it has been shown that various aspects of the Tonga social system are reflected in the set of beliefs they hold about the mizimu.

1. The affiliation of each individual with the two matrilineal groups of his father and his mother is reflected in the belief that a person receives at his naming a guardian muzimu from each line, which is important in determining character and actions. It is further reflected in the belief that all mizimu of either line may affect him.

2. The system of matrilineal inheritance, and the primary affiliation with the matrilineal group of the mother, is reflected in the belief that when a person dies his own muzimu is inherited by the matrilineal line, and has no power over members of the father's group.

3. The dogma that the matrilineal group is undifferentiated is reflected in the belief that any muzimu belonging to the line may affect any member of it.

4. The lack of instituted formal leadership within the group is reflected in the belief that every adult may approach the mizimu of his matrilineal line on his own behalf, and in the fact that no one person acts as priest for the rest of the group or for any division within it.

5. The local dispersion of the matrilineal group is reflected in the absence of local shrines for the propitiation of the mizimu, and in the belief that they are present wherever living members of the line live.

6. The importance of the household is reflected in the belief that only men and women who have formed their own households become mizimu in their own right when they die.

7. The dominant role of the husband as representative of the household is reflected in the domination of his mizimu over the mizimu of the wife in household ritual.

8. The necessity for integrating people into a local community composed of members of many matrilineal groups is reflected in the stress upon the importance of the paternal mizimu for whose propitiation an intermediary is necessary.

RUTH BUNZEL

The Nature
of Katcinas

One of the most common souvenirs bought by travelers in the American Southwest is the small, brightly painted wooden doll called the "katcina." Often erroneously called an Indian "god" or "fetish," the dolls, in fact, serve as visual aids in educating Pueblo Indian children in the intricacies of the Katcina Cult found among these Indians. The katcina spirits, in part thought to be tribal ancestral spirits and in part the spirits of departed tribal members, are of many forms and fill many roles: Pautiwa is the chief of katcina village; Chakwena Woman aids in rabbit hunts; the Koyemshi are clowns. Katcina spirits are participants in, rather than the objects of, Pueblo ceremonials. Enacted by men in the masks and body decorations appropriate to particular spirits or types of spirits, katcinas take part in fertility ceremonies, rain dances, and many of the ceremonies involved in the yearly round. They mingle in the streets with the people, discipline unruly children in their homes, chide deviants publicly, and, in front of all the people during ceremonials in the plazas, they often dramatize the values and beliefs basic to Pueblo Indian culture.

Recalling that katcinas are thought to be, in part, the spirits of the dead, Zuni attitudes toward these "ghosts" stand in contrast to those of the Apaches and the Ifaluks cited in the previous articles.

Extracted with editorial modifications from "Zuni Katcinas," *47th Annual Report of the Bureau of American Ethnology*, pp. 837–1086 (Washington, D.C.: 1932), by permission of the author and the Bureau of American Ethnology.

The Katcina Cult is one of the six major cults of Zuni, and might indeed be called the dominant Zuni cult. It includes many of the most beautiful and spectacular ceremonies, and the ceremonies which attract the most popular attention. Furthermore, it is the one cult which personally reaches all people, since all males belong to it and are required to participate in its ceremonies. Moreover, at the present time it is an ascendant cult. At a time when the societies are declining in membership, and the priesthoods experience difficulties in filling their ranks, when ceremonies lapse because no one competent to perform them survives, the Katcina Society is extending its activities. More katcina dances are held each year than in Mrs. Stevenson's time, and the dances last longer. It is true that some of the older dances are no longer performed, but on the other hand for each dance that lapses two new ones are introduced. It is the most vital, the most spectacular, and the most pervasive of Zuni cults; whatever foreign elements it may at one time or another have incorporated, its ideology and form are aboriginal and characteristic, and for the average Zuni it is the focal point of religious, social, and aesthetic experience.

The Katcina Cult is built upon the worship, principally through impersonation, of a group of supernaturals called in Zuni terminology *koko*. The koko live in a lake, *Hatin kaiakwi* (whispering spring), west of Zuni, near St. Johns, Arizona. In the bottom of this lake they have a village (*Koluwalawa*, katcina village) reached by ladders through the lake. Here they spend their time singing and dancing, and occasionally they come to Zuni to dance for their "daylight" fathers. They live on the spiritual essence of food sacrificed to them in the river, and clothe themselves with the feathers of prayer sticks. They turn into ducks when traveling back and forth to Zuni.

The first katcinas were the children of humans lost through contact with contamination, unwilling sacrifices to atone for sin. By origin and later association they are identified with the dead. Mortals on death join the katcinas at katcina village and become like them.

In addition to being identified with the dead the katcinas are especially associated with clouds and rain. When they come to dance they come in rain. They are equivalent to the Shiwana of Keresan pueblos.

In ancient times, the katcina used to come to Zuni to dance for their people in order that they might be gay. But always when they left someone "went with them," that is, died, and so they decided not to come any more. But they authorized masked dances and promised "to come and stand before them." So now when a katcina dance is held the katcinas come merely as rain, and no one dies. So the institution of masked dancing, originated according to legend to assuage the loneliness of parents for their lost children, has become a rain-making ceremony.

The power of katcina ceremonies resides in the masks which, whether ancient tribal property or individually owned modern masks, are believed to contain divine substance, by means of which the katcina whose representation is worn "makes himself into a person." Masks are treated with the utmost reverence. The awe which Zunis feel for all sacred and powerful objects is intensified in this case by the fact that masks are representations of the dead, and, indeed, the very substance of death. Therefore the use of masks is surrounded by special taboos. One must never try on a mask when not participating in a ceremony, else one will die. One must never use human hair or the hair of a live horse on a mask, else that person or horse will surely die. If one is incontinent during a katcina ceremony the mask will choke him or stick to his face during the dance.

The katcinas are very intimate and affectionate supernaturals. They like pretty clothes and feathers; they like to sing and dance, and to visit. Above all they like to come to Zuni to dance.

The folk tales about individual katcinas describe them at home in their kitchens, scrambling for their feathers at the solstices, quarreling amiably among themselves, meddling in one another's affairs. They have a village organization similar to that of Zuni. Pautiwa is "the boss," as Zunis say. His pekwin, who delivers his messages, is Kaklo. His principal administrative duties seem to be to keep his people quiet long enough to give a courteous welcome to visitors, to receive messages from Zuni, and to decide when to dance there and who shall go. Pautiwa "makes the New Year" at Zuni. His representative brings in the Ca'lako crook and crooks for other special ceremonies, such as the initiation and the dance of the Kanakwe, thus determining the calendar of katcina ceremonies for the year. Whenever the people at Zuni decide they want one of the regular katcina dances they send prayer sticks to katcina village (kiva chiefs plant prayer sticks four days before a dance) and Pautiwa decides whom to send.

Hamokatsik, the mother of the katcinas, looks after their clothing when they prepare for dances.

In addition to the official visits of the katcinas when invited with prayer sticks, they sometimes pay unexpected visits on missions of good will. They come to plant and harvest for deserted children, to affirm the supernatural power of the pious and despised. Pautiwa visits in disguise poor and despised maidens, and leaves wealth and blessing behind him. Katcinas in disguise bring proud girls to their senses by the amiable disciplinary methods so characteristically Zunian.

In reading these folk tales we cannot but be struck by their resemblance in feeling and tone to medieval tales of saints and angels—such tales as that of the amiable angel who turned off the wine tap left open by the monk who was so pious that he didn't even stop to turn off the tap when summoned for prayer. The particular situations in which katcinas prove helpful and their special techniques differ, of course, from those of saints and angels. Medieval saints do not ordinarily humble proud maids by contriving in spite of impossible tests to sleep with them and so instruct them in the delights of normal human association and the advantages of humility. But in spite of these differences the popular attitudes and feeling for the role of supernaturals in commonplace human affairs are curiously similar. Undoubtedly this modern folklore concerning katcinas has been strongly colored by Catholic influences.

But for all their generally amiable and benign character, there is a certain sinister undertone to all katcina ceremonies. It is said more often of the katcinas than of other supernaturals that they are "dangerous." The katcinas inflict the most direct and dramatic punishments for violation of their sanctity. If a priest fails in his duties, he does not get rain during his retreat, he may suffer from general bad luck, he may become sick and may even die if he does nothing to "save his life." But the katcina impersonator who fails in his trust may be choked to death by his mask during the ceremony. There is always a certain feeling of danger in wearing a mask. In putting on a mask the wearer always addresses it in prayer: "Do not cause me any serious trouble." A man wearing a mask or, in katcina dances without mask, one wearing katcina body paint, is untouchable. He is dangerous to others until his paint has been washed off. Zunis watching katcinas dance shrink from them as they pass through narrow passages, in order not to touch their bodies.

The first katcinas were children sacrificed to the water to atone for sin; afterwards when they came to dance, bringing their blessing of rain and fertility, "they took someone with them"; that is, they exacted a human life from the village. It was only when masks were substituted for the actual presence of the katcinas that this heavy toll was lightened.

There are hints in ritual that ideas of human sacrifice may lie but a little way beneath the surface in the concept of masked impersonation. The great ceremony of the Ca'lako opens with the appointment of a group of impersonators of the gods. For a year they are set apart. They do no work of their own. In the case of the Saiyataca party they even assume the names of the gods whom they are to impersonate. At the end of their term of office they have elaborate ceremonies in which they appear in mask; that is, in the regalia of death. After all-night ceremonies they depart for the home of the dead. "Everyone cries when they go," as a Zuni informant says. "It is very sad to see them go, because we always think that we shall never see them again." The final ceremony of the departure of the Ca'lako is especially suggestive of this interpretation. When out of sight of the village the Ca'lako

are pursued by young men. When caught they are thrown down and killed, and the mask is treated like the body of a fallen deer—"for good luck in hunting." On returning the impersonators are met outside the village by their aunts and taken at once to their houses to be bathed before they are safe for human contact.

Identification with the god, and the killing of the god, for fecundity, as found in ancient Mexico, seem to be ideas in keeping with Zuni concepts. But Zuni temperament would repudiate the bloody sacrifice. It may well be that the particular technique of impersonation, with its atmosphere of the sinister and dangerous, is the symbolic representation of the extirpated fact. Tales of the former existence of human sacrifice in the pueblos continually crop up.

Frazer, quoting Bourke, gives an account of the sacrifice of a youth at the fire festival (tribal initiation) of the Hopi. Mrs. Stevenson refers to the report of human sacrifice at Zia. There are cases of human sacrifices for fertility among the Pawnee and the Sioux. The prevalence of all forms of human sacrifice among the Aztecs is too well known to require comment. Among the Aztecs, however, are found two striking features: The dancing of priests in the flayed skin of the sacrificial victim, and the identification of the sacrificial victim with god, as for example, in the sacrifice of Tezcatlipoca. In the battle with the katcinas at Acoma the katcinas are ritualistically slain so that their blood may fertilize the earth. In the prayers of the scalp dance there are frequent allusions to blood as a fertilizing medium, so possibly the whole complex of human sacrifice is not so remote historically or conceptually as might at first appear.

The persistent rumors of an early prevalence of human sacrifice in the pueblos may be without foundation, but the reworking of a cult that once included human sacrifice is quite in accord with pueblo tendency to absorb ritual from all sides and mitigate all its more violent features.

BERTHOLD LAUFER

The Development of Ancestral Images in China

The complex mosaic that is Chinese ancestor worship has yet to be perfectly understood; at least, no two scholars have yet reached "perfect understandings" which are similar. Even less susceptible to definitive analysis is its historical development. However, the selection by Berthold Laufer accomplishes a great deal toward bringing ancestor worship and the development of ancestral tablets into historical focus.

Laufer suggests that the general failure to recognize ancestral tablets as a development from real anthropomorphic images representing ancestors is in large measure the result of the policy of suppression of knowledge by the authors of sacred books of confucianism because of their desire to emancipate Confucianism from the "idolatry" of Buddhism. The author maintains that the present (as of 1913) form of ancestor worship is at most eight- to nine-hundred years old and that earlier forms were quite different. Before the development of writing, another form of symbolic representation on ancestral tablets must have been in use. Since images in China long antedate Buddhism, there is at least suggestive evidence that images of ancestors preceded ancestral tablets.

Laufer also directs his analysis to Chinese social evolution, which is causally related—or so we must assume—to the evolution of ancestral tablets. Prior to 300 B.C. the large territorial clan group was the politically significant unit, the family being politically insignificant. These clans chose ancestors, or culture heroes who were putatively ancestors, to aid and protect the clan. The collapse of the feudal organization and the rise of Confucian doctrines in the third century B.C. led to family hegemony, and with it, filial piety. Thus Laufer reverses the common notion of social evolution in which the family temporally precedes the clan. Furthermore, as Laufer posits a developmental sequence in which clan ancestors became clan gods and are then reduced to mere family ancestors, he adds a new dimension to the theoretical viewpoints of Spencer and Tylor, who believed that gods arose from ancestral ghosts. There is recent ethnological evidence from Micronesia which indicates that ancestral spirits actually have become gods. However, this is only one case. No matter how tempting such instances may be, there are insufficient data to support either proposition as a generalization.

Finally, Laufer submits a theory of causal priority by designating a desire for protection as the fundamental stimulus to the creation of ancestral images and tablets. He considers the present Chinese emphasis on filial piety in ancestor worship to be a recent (twelfth century), Confucian-inspired elaboration of a basic and earlier conception of ancestors as protectors.

Reprinted in abridged form from *Journal of Religious Psychology*, VI (1913), 111–123, by permission of Clark University Press.

For reasons of state policy the authors of the sacred books of Confucianism have vehemently suppressed the greater part of ancient popular lore and beliefs, retaining only what seemed to them reasonable and in keeping with their standard of morality or relating myth and legend in forms mutilated or newly digested, as best suited their purpose. An attempt at reconstructing the ancient mythology of China, for this reason, is fraught with great obstacles. The gradual development into conventionality, formalism, and dogmatism has, moreover, obscured the clear conception of the ancient ideas and converted the oldest history into the dream of a golden age which is purely the outcome of fabulous speculation. One of the favorite dogmas of later official Confucianism is the sweeping statement that in times of antiquity there was no image of any shape nor idol worship of any kind, and it is no wonder that this axiom has crept as a gospel truth into all foreign books on the religion of the Chinese and still holds sway in the minds of students.

The tendency of this tenet is obvious: it was directed as a blow against Buddhism, whose idolatry is so odious to the literati, and should serve, positively, as a glorification of the purity and sublimity of the dearly cherished antiquity. But the existence of images representative of dieties in the earliest periods of Chinese culture can no longer be disclaimed, and a close study of this subject, thus far, has brought to light four large classes of images:

1. A group of images of geometric forms, usually carved from jade of required color, used in the worship of the cosmic deities, Heaven, Earth, and the Four Quarters.
2. A group of zoomorphic images in the shape of tigers, fishes, dragons, and numerous other monsters.
3. Human clay figures of shamanistic origin serving the purpose of healing disease and protecting the corpse in the grave, and representations of the shaman himself.
4. Statues of heroes and ancestors.

Under the title of "Ancestral Images" I take the liberty to present a few notes on the last subject. The principal idea by which I am guided is that the so-called "ancestral tablets," such as are still found and worshiped in every family of China, have developed from real anthropomorphic images representing the ancestor. The subject, simultaneously, has an interesting bearing on the question as to how ancestral worship arose, was formed, and grew. It will be most advantageous to follow up the problem in a retrospective manner.

What is called at present the ancestral tablet is merely a conventional mode of translating a much more significant Chinese term which means "the wooden lord or master (*mu chu*)." It consists of a rectangular slip of planed wood, rounded on the top and inserted in a pedestal, and inscribed in black ink on both sides according to a stereotyped formula: "Seat of the soul of such and such a one," giving the posthumous name of the deceased, followed by rank and title, if any, and by the date of his birth and death, with the addition of the name of the oldest son who has erected the tablet. Everybody on his death receives a special posthumous name, and the name of his lifetime is forever tabooed. During the first hundred days after burial, this tablet receives daily offerings of food and drink, and is, in every respect, treated as the representative of the dead man. In other words, it is apparently conceived as his animate image. At the lapse of that period, an auspicious day is chosen to convey the tablet into the ancestral temple, such as is owned only by families of high standing, or into a shrine kept in the house, as is done by the majority of people; the ancestral shrine is always arranged in close proximity to the one sheltering the domestic gods, so that the deified ancestors, in the estimation of the living ones, are placed on a par with the latter. From this moment the tablet has ceased to act as a live image and sinks to the function of a symbol. It is to the son a reminder of his departed father, an object on which, to speak with the Chinese, the bereaved one will fix his heart. The tablet, however, becomes animate periodically, i.e., on the occasion of a sacrifice to the ancestor, when his soul is supposed to descend into, and to be present in, the tablet, in order to take part in the offerings. To an ethnological mind, an observation here presents itself spontaneously, and this is, that the symbol of ancestor worship becomes effective through the medium of writing, that it is the function of writing which has resulted in the use of a conventional tablet, and, consequently, that, in times when writing was not yet in existence or not yet fully developed, the object of ancestor worship cannot have been a tablet, but must have been something of a different character. A survival of the older form is still preserved in the most important custom connected with the making of a tablet. This is the ceremony of punctuating the tablet, which in northern China has shriveled into a much abridged, conventionalized form. As already mentioned, the tablet is inscribed with the posthumous name of the dead followed by the words "seat of the soul of," *shên chu*. The last word, meaning "seat," is first written incompletely, the dot on the top being omitted. In the punctuation ceremony, this dot is added by a high official, for the alleged reason of rendering a particular honor to the dead. This practice becomes quite intelligible through another more complete series of rites still observed in the southern parts of China. There the tablet, wrapped up with red cloth, is carried in the funeral procession in an open palanquin preceding the bier. When the coffin is lowered into the grave, the eldest son kneels down at the end of the pit where the feet of the dead are, being surrounded by his brothers in the same posture. Then he turns his face toward the sun and receives from the hands of a relative or friend the tablet, which he holds with both his hands on his back, bending his head. A member of the family who is highest in rank, or an official who is on friendly terms with the family, now removes the red cover from the tablet and touches it six times with dots in vermilion, two pairs of dots in the middle denoting eyes and ears, one above and another below representing head and feet and interpreted from the thoughts of nature philosophy as symbolizing heaven and earth, man being considered the product of the union of the two. This explanation is recited in a verse by the officiating writer during the ceremony, and this verse, doubtless, is very old:

I am painting heaven, may heaven always be bright over his grave.
I am painting earth, may the site of the grave be of powerful effect.
I am painting the ears, may the ears well listen [i.e., to the prayers of the descendants].
I am painting the eyes, may his eyes penetrate through all [i.e., be open to the needs of the descendants].

In this punctuation rite, accordingly, a mystic and magic shorthand figure of a man is drawn, and it is this very act which renders the tablet alive and useful, capable of serving as the domicile of a soul. A most interesting parallel of this practice is offered by the process of the Taoist priests of enlivening the images destined for worship in their temples. When a new religious image has left the workshop of the artist, it is brought in solemn procession to a temple where an older image of the same deity exists. With offerings of incense, the participants invoke this deity to allow part of its inherent soul substance to migrate into the newly completed image. The notion that images are not merely representative but animated with a soul and living realities is most ancient in China and by no means due to Buddhism; on the contrary, the images of Buddhism have originally had quite another significance, and the Chinese people have merely transferred their own long-inherited ideas regarding images to those instituted by Buddhism. As soon as the new image is installed in its temple, the ceremony of consecration, called the "opening of the eyes," is performed by Taoist priests, who celebrate a mass (sometimes lasting for several days) and then, accompanied by prayers and music, daub with a dot the eyes, mouth, nose, ears, and even hands and feet of the image, by availing themselves of blood or vermilion, vermilion being a substitute for blood as in the case of the ancestral tablet. By this procedure, the organs of sense of the god are opened. This very act enables him to become conscious of his new senses, and to commune with the external world; now he is capable of listening to the prayers of his votaries, acting upon them, and enjoying their offerings. This usage apparently rests on the same psychical foundation as the one mentioned before in regard to the ancestral tablet, and the parallel becomes still more striking, as the Taoist images are also accompanied by wooden tablets inscribed with the name of the god, of the same form and scope as the ancestral tablets. It hence follows, and the fact is, that the ancestors are conceived as gods, and that the same designation *shên* (spirit, ghost, soul) is applied to both. The employment of blood in the consecrating of images goes back to times of great antiquity when the ancestral temple and all paraphernalia of a sacred character were sanctified with the blood of sacrificial animals. The single dot added in the north of China to the word *chu* denotes the eye of the ancestor. It is an echo of the ancient idea that the drawing of the eye is a magic rite rendering the image alive (even a sacred act to the great artist).

While a survival of the image character is thus manifest in the ancestral tablets, and their association with the established cult of the national gods becomes apparent, there are also real ancestral images still in existence of a decidedly realistic shape. In many parts of southern China a paper doll representing the dead is made for the occasion of the funeral ceremony; it is designated "the body for the soul" (*hun shên*) and often dressed in the costume of an official, the supposition being that this image should serve as a resting place for the roaming soul who may leave it at will to partake of the offerings. On the last day of the ceremony, the paper image is cremated with all the sacrificial paraphernalia, in order to be the body of the soul in the other world. Cremation, in funeral ceremonies, does not mean destruction but a transposition of an object from the visible into the spirit world. The soul-body impersonated by the paper image, accordingly, has the same function as the tablet, except that the role it plays on earth is limited in time and is then continued in the beyond. Universal, at the present time, is the custom of having a portrait of a deceased father and mother painted. These painted portraits are allowed to take the place of the tablets during the sacrifices, but altogether have more of a social and sentimental significance. The time when they came into vogue is not exactly known, but surely goes back into the first centuries of our era; it is clear that this practice could arise only at a period when the art of portrait painting was fully developed. In other words, the painted ancestral portrait is a thought-manifestation *sui generis,* which was not by any means evolved from a primitive conception of the ancestral image. It was merely an adaptation of pictorial art to the specific needs of ancestor worship. It is also doubtful whether the paper images alluded to can be considered in the light of a survival, and historical investigation seems to prompt us to the belief that they should rather be regarded as a comparatively recent innovation actuated by the more sensual needs of the masses. The present coexistence of ancestral tablets, images, and portraits must not lead us astray into a preposterous evolutionary construction of these three phenomena, rather, we must consult the data of history, in order to arrive at a proper understanding of the development.

In studying ancestor worship in its historical aspect, we are, first of all, confronted by the surprising fact that the present condition of affairs is only about 800–900 year old (dating from the time of the Sung dynasty), i.e., considering Chinese developments, quite a recent affair. In this modern period, every individual is entitled to render a cult to his ancestor, and obliged to have the ancestral tablet; ancestor worship is universal and individual, while in earlier times it was neither the one nor the other. Among a number of Chinese scholars the opinion prevails that in times of antiquity the officials and the literary class had not the privilege of a tablet; the former were honored by a sort of figure or puppet, made of a textile in silk supported in the interior by a wooden frame, and the literati were distinguished by a similar contrivance of plaited straw. This subject, like many others, is one of great controversy among the scholars of China, and no unanimity of opinion has been reached. The one important fact remains that the present regulations were set up only as late as in the twelfth century, and that prior to that date neither all classes of the population were covered by this practice nor were tablets in general vogue. The whole question is closely interwoven with that of the development of social organization in China, on which (it is sad but true) no sensible investigation as yet exists. In the beginning, the social unit was not the natural family but the territorial clan group, each comprising from five to several thousands of families. In the ancient law only these groups play a conspicuous role, while the family has no independent existence in the political organism. There were, correspondingly, at first only clan or tribal ancestors, whereas the family ancestor is a much later product. Briefly stated, the development was this, that the family gradually grew in importance within the boundaries of the clan. This movement was furthered by the debacle of the feudal organization of the Chou period in the third century B.C. and the progress of Confucian teachings which placed the family in the foreground. The strengthening of the family resulted in an extending and deepening of ancestor worship. The number of tribal ancestors was comparatively small, and the object and meaning of clan ancestor worship differed to a marked degree from the later family ancestor worship. Confucius inculcated the worship of ancestors as an action of filial piety, as a continuation of that respect and devotion which the good son owed to his parents during their life; while adopting and endorsing this ancient feature of the national religion, he impressed on it the seal of moral duty and obligation. This is certainly the final conclusion but not the beginning nor the real cause of ancestor worship. The chief agency instrumental in the formation of ancestor worship in ancient China seems to me to be the idea of protection. The ancestors supposed to reside in heaven had full charge of their descendants on earth and could avert from them disease, drought, or other calamities, bestow blessings upon them, and punish them for misdemeanor. The clan ancestor, as a rule, was a powerful hero of superior bodily and mental strength, who had impressed his fellow mates by an extraordinary deed or deserved well of them by a new invention, a new law or institution. In all likelihood, they were not in all cases blood ancestors at all, but culture heroes, chosen as ancestors by the clan or tribe and then designated as "spiritual ancestors." Often enough it happened that a clan adopted the ancestor of another more powerful clan as its own or affiliated itself with other clans under the guidance of the same ancestor god. The ancestor was the chief protector of the clan in all conditions of life and responsible for its welfare; events of importance were communicated to him before his shrine, and many state affairs were transacted in his temple; he was invoked for success in war and consulted by means of divination in difficult predicaments; vows were made to him to ensure the realization of a wish, for the fulfillment of which he was rewarded by a sacrifice. These ancestors were worshiped under images of stone or wood, and as we have now recognized the essential features in the development of ancestor worship, we are prepared to grasp the difference between ancestral image and ancestral tablet. The clan ancestor, whether real or alleged, whether real or mythical, was a personage of individual traits imbued with well-defined characteristics and equipped with certain attributes in popular imagination: he was capable of having a statue erected to him. No doubt also, and there are records to this effect, family ancestors were revered in the shape of a simulacrum in ancient times, but the rapidly increasing number of this class of ancestors necessarily led to a generalization of the entire ancestral subject and resulted in the mechanical tablet, generalized and conventionalized as the ancestor himself. The clan ancestors then disappeared entirely, and a host of colorless souls or spirits, one exactly like the other, remained, corresponding to the same instrument of expression.

The development of ancestral images may be finally summed up as follows: First, the great dead of past generations magnified in the eyes of subsequent men were worshiped as guardian spirits and adopted as ancestor gods by the clan groups; crude images were erected in their memory and honored with regular sacrifices to ensure their blessings for the community, or as a recompense for favors received. The notions were still blended in these tribal ancestor spirits, and remained for a long period latent also in the family ancestors, particularly in those of imperial, royal, and other noble houses. The clan images were therefore adapted to the individual ancestors, whose souls were believed to dwell in their images while simultaneously a living substitute for the ancestor during the sacrifices was a prerogative of aristocracy. The ancestral wooden tablet, on the whole, represents a secondary development, as it could spring up only at an advanced period of civilization when writing had reached a perfect state. The magic of writing takes the place of the visual elements of the likeness, and the form of the tablet is suggested by two factors—the wooden or bamboo slips, which were the ordinary writing material before the invention of rag paper in 105 A.D., and an assimilation to the external shape of the images, which were simple rectangular stone slabs or pillars with a rude face carved on the top. The tablet is throughout a counterpart of the image and inhabited by the soul or spirit of the ancestor. As the growth of ancestor worship advanced, the tablet became more and more formal and conventional; ancestor worship developed into a thoroughly democratic institution, and the effect was that ancestors sank in value and became at a discount. While in the beginning on a par with the rest of the gods, they could no longer withstand their keen competition, for gods multiplied in China at a tremendous rate of speed, and a clear and net distinction between gods and ancestors was the consequence. Images therefore fell into disuse for ancestors, and were reserved exclusively for the gods. This movement was fostered by the coming into power of Buddhism and Taoism, which set up a systematic code of elaborate iconography. The immense host of Buddhist and Taoist images has swallowed the ancient national gods and finally brought about the purely formal and ritualistic character of the ancestral tablets. In the consecration ceremony their relation to the primeval cult is still manifestly retained, and what they may have lost in artistic expression, at the expense of their greater rivals, is largely compensated by an increase in spirituality, by their magnificent simplicity, by their social power and ethical influence, and by their equalizing democratic tendency, which is surely one of the most imposing emanations of Chinese genius.

CHAPTER 10

SHAMANS AND PRIESTS

INTRODUCTION

In the comparative analysis of religious organization one of the most useful analytical distinctions has been the contrast between the "shaman" and the "priest." These two polar types of ceremonial practitioners are found in all parts of the world, and the difference between their religious roles provides a significant index of contrasts between different types of religious systems.

As defined in the first selection, by Robert H. Lowie, a "shaman" is a ceremonial practitioner whose powers come from direct contact with the supernatural, by divine stroke, rather than from inheritance or memorized ritual; a "priest" is a ceremonial practitioner who often inherits his position and who learns a body of codified and standardized ritual knowledge from older priests and later transmits it to successors. Shamanism is more usually found in the loosely structured food-gathering cultures, where the more common ceremonial is a curing rite performed for one or more patients within the context of an extended family group. The ceremonial takes place on a noncalendrical basis, usually when a person falls ill and needs the ritual. The priest, and especially the organization of priests into elaborate sets of priesthoods, is characteristically found in tightly structured and relatively elaborate food-producing—usually agricultural—societies, where the more common ceremonial is a public rite performed for the benefit of a whole village or community. The ceremony typically takes place on a calendrical basis at the proper time within the annual ceremonial calendar. Many societies, of course, have both shamans and priests, as, for example, in Navaho society where the hand-tremblers who diagnose illness are technically shamans, in the sense that they derive their power directly from a supernatural source, while the singers who perform the curing ceremonies are technically priests, in the sense that they have learned standardized ritual by apprenticing themselves to an older singer. But our evidence suggests that the presence of these singers has been a relatively recent development in Navaho history, a pattern which the Navahos borrowed from contact with the Southwestern Pueblos. Earlier in their history all Navaho ceremonial practitioners were probably of the shamanistic type. Among the neighboring Apache tribes the practitioners are still more shamanistic in type, as indicated in the Opler article in the preceding chapter.

Another way of looking at the difference between shamans and priests is in terms of communication between supernaturals and men. Shamans are essentially mediums, for they are the mouthpieces of spirit beings. Priests are intermediaries between people and the spirits to whom they wish to address themselves. This is what Evans-Pritchard has in mind when, writing about the priests and prophets (shamans) of the Nuer of the Sudan, he says: "Whereas in the priest man speaks to God, in the prophet . . . God speaks to man."

The outstanding area for the study of shamanism has been Siberia—in fact, the very word comes from the Tungus word "shaman"—and northern and western North America. The selections from Bogoras and Rasmussen provide excellent descriptive accounts of shamanistic performances among the Chukchee and Eskimo. But the phenomenon is by no means restricted to this area, as will be apparent in Lowie's article on the Indians of the Plains and in Nadel's "A Study of Shamanism in the Nuba Mountains," in which he describes comparable patterns of religious behavior in Africa.

The behavior of priests and the organization of priesthoods are touched upon in many selections in this *Reader,* especially in the pieces from Edmund Wilson and Ruth Bunzel; but their activities are most clearly characterized in the Sahagún description of Aztec sacrifice and the Thompson description of a Maya priest in action. It is obvious that in the simpler cultures shamans and priests tend to be interwoven with one another and with magicians, and that only when one goes up the scale in social complexity does the priest emerge as a more sharply defined specialist, operating full time within an organized cult.

ROBERT H. LOWIE

Shamans and Priests Among the Plains Indians

Shamanism is a salient feature of the religion of the Indians of both North and South America. North of Mexico, the individual wishing to become a shaman deliberately sets out to acquire a vision. South of that area, visions are not sought after, but if they come they are accepted, not resisted as they often are in northeastern Siberia. Lowie, in his account of the shaman of the Great Plains, does not make the common mistake of calling any medical practitioner by that term. He adheres closely to the original sense of the Tungus word "shaman," which refers to a person who has entered into direct communication with spirits. Therefore, while Lowie makes mention of the "tricks" and the doctoring of shamans, he does not lose sight of their source of power—the spirit world. Shamans and priests may coexist, as we see in the article that follows. Among the Plains Indians the latter hold a subordinate position. The difference between the two is not defined except in terms of the source of power. A priest may supplement his ritual by a vision, but basically his position depends on learning standardized ritual beliefs and practices by becoming an apprentice and enduring a long period of formal training with older priests. The Plains priest was markedly less developed as compared, for example, with those of the Hopi, Maya, Aztec, and Incas.

Reprinted with permission of McGraw-Hill Book Co., Inc., from *Indians of the Plains,* pp. 161–164, by Robert H. Lowie, published for The American Museum of Natural History by McGraw-Hill Book Co., Inc. Copyright 1954 by The American Museum of Natural History.

At the opposite pole from those unable to gain a personal vision were the Indians who, as demonstrated by their conspicuous success, had obtained exceptional power from the spirits. Such persons were said to be *maxpé* or *wakan* and in English may be called "medicine men" or, to borrow a convenient Siberian term, "shamans."

According to the Wahpeton Dakota, their medicine men lived a prenatal existence among the Thunders and enjoyed a knowledge, prior to birth, of all that would happen to them as mortals. Their social role began with maturity, when they received a sign from the Thunders to start performing shamanistic duties; any shaman disobeying the divine orders would suffer punishment or even be killed by the Thunders. The services rendered to tribesmen included curing the sick, discovering the whereabouts of the enemy, and helping to recover lost or stolen property. By way of proving his powers a shaman summoned people to large meetings, at which he performed tricks in order to establish himself as a wonder-worker.

The most elaborate organization for such miraculous performances appeared among the Pawnee. Their medicine men in some measure partook of the nature of priests since they were trained, a great master of legerdemain being surrounded by a number of disciples. However, all medicine men were supposed to obtain their powers from living creatures, so that the subjective experience of the vision remained a vital element. In the late summer or early fall all the accepted masters at sleight-of-hand gathered in one of two earth lodges reserved in the village for that purpose and with the aid of pupils erected their several booths. A turtle effigy was modeled at the cleared fireplace, a new fireplace put on its back, and a ceremonially felled tree was planted by the Skidi Pawnee in the forked tail of an image representing a mythical water monster encircling the fireplace. The clay statue of a woman, life size, was set up on the south side, a large male figure of rawhide was placed upon a pole above the lodge, and many small human figures, also of rawhide, were attached about the assembly place. The fire symbolized the sun; the clay female, the moon; the large male effigy, the morning star; and the many little images, the stars.

After a dedication ceremony there was an impressive procession through the village, each shaman wearing a costume in mimicry of his animal protector. Then the participants re-entered the lodge for a secret ritual, after which the door was opened for the spectacular show. Among other tricks there was the magical maturing of cornstalks before the onlookers' gaze; and the Bear shamans pretended to tear out a man's liver, to eat it, and then to make him rise unharmed.

Sleight of hand was a common technique for impressing the laity. The Iruska shamans of the Pawnee handled burning corn husks with their bare hands, took meat out of a kettle of boiling soup, and stood on red-hot rocks. These tricks were closely paralleled by the Dakota, who among other things shared a fire-walking feat with Arapaho, Gros Ventre, and Cheyenne performers. Another marvelous stunt, noted by Maximilian among the Mandan and Hidatsa, was to harbor some animal or plant inside one's body and have it emerge to the amazement of the spectators. The Prince actually saw a Hidatsa woman "dance a corncob out of herself," and another Indian professed to feel a buffalo calf kicking around inside his body. A Crow informant declared that when a certain song was sung a horse inside her would try to come out, protruding his tail from her mouth.

Sometimes Crow shamans offered a public competitive exhibition of their powers, one man or a group trying to overcome those pitted against them.

More important from the laity's point of view was the shaman's doctoring. The treatment of illness did not necessarily require supernatural power, for there were liniments, herbs, therapeutic potions, and other home remedies. However, in serious cases recourse was generally had to a practitioner who derived his techniques, even when rational, from a visionary experience. Because of the usually specific nature of the instruction given by the spirit, a doctor was likely to cure only particular ailments. Thus, he might treat only women in childbirth or men bitten by a snake.

Perhaps the commonest primitive theory of disease ascribes the cause to a foreign object in the patient's body; hence the physician tries to extract it, usually by suction, exhibiting to the patient and his kin the splinter, thorn, or what not that supposedly caused the disturbance. These notions occur also in our area. For example, in recent times a Crow named Bull-all-the-time cured several patients by sucking at the afflicted parts with a pipestem and pulling out, respectively, a bone, a black beetle, a morsel of meat; but he deprecated any competence in dealing with wounds or snake bites. The treatment by suction obviously implies sleight-of-hand.

Sickness would smite a shaman or his patient if rules laid down by his spiritual patron were disobeyed, whether willingly or not. Thus, it might be fatal for a sick man if a dog crossed his doctor's path. Anyone who ate food forbidden to him in a dream or vision was bound to suffer.

Though witchcraft was less pronounced than among the Pueblos, the Plains Indians did sometimes resort to effigy magic. In the 1890's some Comanche suspected an interpreter of treason, made an image of him, and pelted it with mud; in consequence, they assert, he had a hemorrhage and died. The same people used to kill a sorcerer after he had repeatedly worked harm against his fellows. This act was in line with Basin custom, but at least the central Plains tribes probably did not proceed in this way, rather counteracting the malevolent shaman's magic by the aid of another shaman.

Other medical techniques included massage, smoking, bleeding, cupping, and applying burning sage. Arapaho doctors fumigated a sick infant with the smoke from heated roots or cedar twigs or made it inhale the fumes from herbs laid on hot coals. Though the sweat lodge was prominent in ceremonialism, it was also used for medicinal purposes, at least by a number of tribes, such as the Arapaho and the Comanche.

Whereas a shaman by definition acquires his status through a personal communication by supernatural beings, the priest need not have this face-to-face relationship with the spirit world but must have competence in conducting ritual. In other words, he has

been trained for his activities. As stated, the medicine men of the Pawnee were shamans by virtue of their animal mentors; but they were likewise priests in so far as they had to undergo special instruction. One might even speak of their ordination, for being allowed to take a permanent place in the lodge each had to demonstrate his skill to the leaders, being ejected if he failed. However, the Pawnee had a number of other men who combined official standing with a knowledge of sacred songs in their sequence and of the meaning of ritual procedures. Accordingly, the tribe can properly be said to have had a priesthood. More particularly, the priests were associated with the sacred-bundle scheme that underlay Pawnee political organization. Each of the thirteen Skidi villages owned a bundle, which had to be opened at the first thunder in the spring, when the keeper made offerings and went through the traditional rites. Four of the bundles were pre-eminent, and a fifth, associated with the evening star, took absolute precedence; the priests of these bundles rather than the titular chiefs held supreme authority. Normally, the four priests in turn assumed responsibility for the welfare of the people for the period of a year and specifically for the success of the buffalo hunt. If this miscarried, the Evening Star priest was asked to supersede his officiating colleague. The priesthood was strictly hereditary, passing from its holder to the next of kin in the maternal line.

WALDEMAR BOGORAS

Shamanistic Performance in the Inner Room

The anthropological literature reveals few phenomena more interesting, and none more dramatic, than the shamanistic performance. In the following selection Bogoras calls upon his intimate knowledge of the nomadic, reindeer-herding Chukchee of Siberia to provide a description of the shaman in action. He reveals the consummate artistry of the shaman without becoming so enamored of the shaman's skill as to be unable to view his performance objectively. The Chukchee shaman employs superb verbal and manual skills—ventriloquism, singing, beating the omnipresent

Reprinted from Waldemar Bogoras, *The Chukchee*, Vol. VII of Franz Boas (ed.), *The Jesup North Pacific Expedition* ("Memoirs of the American Museum of Natural History," Vol. XI, Parts 2 and 3 [Leyden: E. J. Brill, 1904–1909]), pp. 433–441, by permission of the American Museum of Natural History.

drum, sleight of hand—to capture his audience in a semitrance state.

Although Bogoras discusses the procedural techniques of the shaman and at times tends to portray him as a ventriloquist and conjurer, it must be remembered that the Chukchee do not visit a shaman with a critical analysis of his technique in mind. They cannot suspect him of fraud or wither him with ruthless logic, for if he is a fraud then so are they, and if he is open to logical criticism then so are they, since they both share the same logical premises. It should be clear then that the Chukchee cannot afford the luxury of skepticism, for they need the shaman and his wonderful powers. When the shaman becomes hysterical in his spirit possession, the audience knows this as a sign that they will soon hear the voices of powerful spirits able to divine their vital problems. When the shaman transports himself to the spirit world to divine or cure, the audience does not look for tricks; they anxiously and respectfully await answers.

The typical shamanistic performance is carried out in the following manner. After the evening meal is finished and the kettles and trays are removed to the outer tent, all the people who wish to be present at the séance enter the inner room, which is carefully closed for the night. Among the Reindeer Chukchee, the inner room is especially small, and its narrow space causes much inconvenience to the audience, which is packed together in a tight and most uncomfortable manner. The Maritime Chukchee have more room, and may listen to the voices of the spirits with more ease and freedom. The shaman sits on the "master's place," near the back wall; and even in the most limited sleeping-room, some free space must be left around him. The drum is carefully looked over, its head tightened, and, if it is much shrunken, it is moistened with urine and hung up for a short time over the lamp to dry. The shaman sometimes occupies more than an hour in this process, before he is satisfied with the drum. To have more freedom in his movements, the shaman usually takes off his fur shirt, and remains quite naked down to the waist. He often removes also his shoes and stockings, which of course gives free play to his feet and toes.

In olden times, shamans used no stimulants; but at present they often smoke a pipeful of strong tobacco without admixture of wood, which certainly works like a strong narcotic. This habit is copied from the Tungus shamans, who make great use of unmixed tobacco as a powerful stimulant.

At last the light is put out and the shaman begins to operate. He beats the drum and sings his introductory tunes, at first in a low voice; then gradually his voice increases in volume, and soon it fills the small closed-up room with its violent clamor. The narrow walls resound in all directions.

Moreover, the shaman uses his drum for modifying his voice, now placing it directly before his mouth, now turning it at an oblique angle, and all the time beating it violently. After a few minutes, all this noise begins to work strangely on the listeners, who are crouching down, squeezed together in a most uncomfortable position. They begin to lose the power to locate the source of the sounds; and, almost without any effort of imagination, the song and the drum seem to shift from corner to corner, or even to move about without having any definite place at all.

The shaman's songs have no words. Their music is mostly simple, and consists of one short phrase repeated again and again. After repeating it many times, the shaman breaks off, and utters a series of long-drawn, hysterical sighs, which sound something like "Ah, ya, ka, ya, ka, ya, ka!" After that, he comes back to his songs. For this he draws his breath as deep as possible in order to have more air in his lungs, and to make the first note the longest.

Some of the tunes, however, are more varied, and are not devoid of a certain grace. Not a few are improvised by the shaman on the spot; others are repeated from séance to séance. Each shaman has several songs of his own, which are well known to the people; so that if anybody uses one of them, for instance at a ceremonial, the listeners recognize it immediately, and say that such and such a man is using the particular song of such and such a shaman.

There is no definite order for the succession of the songs, and the shaman changes them at will, sometimes even returning to the first one after a considerable interval has elapsed. This introductory singing lasts from a quarter of an hour to half an hour or more, after which the ke'let make their first appearance.

The shaman sings all alone, and the auditors take no part in the performance. From time to time, however, some one of the listeners will cry out, "Hɪk, hɪk!" or "Hɪč, hɪč!" (interjection of wonder) or "Qai'vo" ("of course") or "Emño'lɪk" ("certainly")—all of which are meant to express the full approbation by those present of the doings of the shaman. The Chukchee have a special word for these exclamations, "o'cɪtkək" ("to give answering calls"). Without an očɪtke'lɪn (participle), a Chukchee shaman considers himself unable to perform his calling in a proper way; therefore novices, while trying to learn the shamanistic practices, usually induce a brother or a sister to respond, thus encouraging the zeal of the performer. Some shamans also require those people who claim their advice or treatment to give them answering calls during the particular part of the performance which refers to their affairs. The storytellers of the Chukchee also usually claim the assistance of their listeners, who must call out the same exclamations.

Among the Asiatic Eskimo, the wife and other members of the family form a kind of chorus, which from time to time catches up the tune and sings with the shaman. Among the Russianized Yukaghir of the lower Kolyma the wife is also the assistant of her shaman husband, and during the performance she gives him encouraging answers, and he addresses her as his "supporting staff."

In most cases the ke'let begin by entering the body of the shaman. This is marked with some change in his manner of beating the drum, which becomes faster and more violent; but the chief mark is a series of new sounds, supposed to be peculiar to the ke'let. The shaman shakes his head violently, producing with his lips a peculiar chattering noise, not unlike a man who is shivering with cold. He shouts hysterically, and in a changed voice utters strange, prolonged shrieks, such as "O to, to, to, to," or "I pi, pi, pi, pi"—all of which are supposed to characterize the voice of the ke'let. He often imitates the cries of various animals and birds which are supposed to be his particular assistants. If the shaman is only a "single-bodied" one—that is, has no ventriloquistic power—the ke'let will proceed to sing and beat the drum by means of his body. The only difference will be in the timbre of the voice, which will sound harsh and unnatural, as becomes supernatural beings.

With other shamans the ke'let appear all at once as the "separate voices." They manifest themselves with sounds and shrieks of the same harsh and unnatural character, and these are located outside the body of the shaman. After that a varied exhibition begins, in which the performance of the shaman far transcends anything attainable by a person of ordinary powers.

The Chukchee ventriloquists display great skill, and could with credit to themselves carry on a contest with the best artists of the kind of civilized countries. The "separate voices" of their calling come from all sides of the room, changing their place to the complete illusion of their listeners. Some voices are at first faint, as if coming from afar; as they gradually approach, they increase in volume, and at last they rush into the room, pass through it and out, decreasing, and dying away in the remote distance. Other voices come from above, pass through the room and seem to underground, where they are heard as if from the depths of the earth. Tricks of this kind are played also with the voices of animals and birds, and even with the howling of the tempest, producing a most weird effect.

I heard a voice which professed to be an echo. It repeated faithfully all sounds and cries which we chose to produce in its presence, including phrases in English or Russian. The foreign words were, of course, slightly mispronounced, still the reproduction proved the "spirit" to be possessed of a fine ear, catching quickly the sounds of an unknown language. The only way in which the "spirit" could imitate the clapping of our hands (another test to which we put him) was by clacking his tongue, which caused much mirth even among the native listeners. I heard also the "spirits" of a grasshopper, horsefly, and mosquito, who imitated exceedingly well the sounds produced by the real insects.

In proof of his accuracy as to the location of the sounds, the shaman Qora'wge, previously spoken of, made one of his "spirits" shout, talk, and whisper directly into my ear, and the illusion was so perfect that involuntarily I put my hand to my ear to catch the "spirit." After that he made the "spirit" enter the ground under me and talk right in between my legs, etc. All the time that he is conversing with the "separate voices," the shaman beats his drum without interruption in order to prove that his force and attention are otherwise occupied.

I tried to make a phonographic record of the "separate voices" of the "spirits." For this purpose I induced the shaman Scratching-Woman to give a séance in my own house, overcoming his reluctance with a few extra presents. The performance, of course, had to be carried out in utter darkness: and I arranged my machine so as to be able to work it without any light. Scratching-Woman sat in the farthest corner of the spacious room, at a distance of twenty feet from me. When the light was put out, the "spirits," after some "bashful" hesitation, entered, in compliance with the demand of the shaman, and even began to talk into the funnel of the graphophone. The records show a very marked difference between the voice of the shaman himself, which sounds from afar, and the voices of the "spirits," who seemed to be talking directly into the funnel.

All the while, Scratching-Woman was beating the drum incessantly to show that he was in his usual place, and occupied with his usual function, that of beating the drum without interruption. He brought some of the entering "spirits" to my special notice. One was a fawn of a wild reindeer, found by him in the wilderness beside the carcass of its mother, which had been killed by a wolf. The fawn, when he found it, was trying to suck the carcass. The strange sight had evidently struck Scratching-Woman, and he took the fawn for one of his assisting ke'let. The "spirit" manifested his presence by characteristic short snorts, peculiar to the fawn when calling for its mother. Another "spirit" entered with a dismal howl. This was the wolf who killed the reindeer dam.

Scratching-Woman explained that when he desired to wreak his vengeance on some one of his foes, he transformed himself into this wolf, taking care beforehand to turn the other party into a reindeer. Then, of course, he was quite certain of victory. The idea that shamans, in case of need, not only may send their "spirits" to a destined place, but also may turn themselves into any of their "spirits," and carry out their intentions, appears in many tales.

For instance, in the tale of the Shaman with Warts (Kuku'lpin), this shaman, during a shamanistic contest asks his adversary, "Which ke'lE are you going to employ?" The other answers, "The small black hawk." —"And you?"—"The great diver." Then they turn into these birds, and the contest begins.

Those episodes of the tales in which men in distress have recourse to their animal amulets—either reviving them and bidding them fight their enemies, or transforming themselves into their living likenesses—are evidently quite analogous.

Still another of the ke'let introduced by Scratching-Woman was a raven who cawed lustily. The shaman used him when working with magic medicine, because the raven could devour all germs of sickness and disease. Still another was a little mouse, who could travel very fast underground, and was employed on errands requiring haste.

There followed the leather bucket, which forms a part of a "bonebreaking set," and is used as a receptacle for pounded bones. Once when Scratching-Woman was hunting wild reindeer, he succeeded in wounding a strong buck in the right foreleg, but still he could not overtake it. Then he called for the Skin Bucket, bade it overtake the buck and entrap its head. After that the reindeer was easily caught.

After having entered the room and produced a few sounds, by way of making his presence known, the "spirit" usually offers to "try his breath," that is, he beats the drum for a while, singing a tune in the special harsh voice peculiar to the "spirits." This, however, lasts only a short time, after which the "spirit" declares that his breath is ebbing away. Then he either begins to talk, or straightway takes his departure with characteristic quivering sounds somewhat similar to the buzzing of a fly. These sounds are called by the Chukchee "gibbering" (moomga'tɪrgɪn), and are always associated with the "spirits." The same name is applied to the chattering alluded to before.

Often the shaman declares to the "spirit" first entering, that the sound of his drum is bad, or even that the cover of it is broken, and this is corroborated by a few dull strokes. The "spirit" must then mend the drum by breathing upon it, which he does accordingly. This treatment is resorted to especially in cases of magic medicine. After the drum is mended, the shaman explains to the patient that it is a good sign. He says also, that, if the "spirit" were not able to mend the drum, it would forebode a bad turn in the disease.

I must again repeat that the animal "spirits" produce their own characteristic sounds. The walrus and the bear roar, the reindeer snorts, the wolf howls, the fox bays, the raven caws. The last three, however, are able to talk but use a particular timbre of voice, and intersperse among their words, from time to time, their peculiar cries.

In most cases the ventriloquistic performance soon takes on a dramatic character. A number of "spirits" appear in succession. They talk to the shaman and to one another, pick quarrels, abuse and denounce one another. It is superfluous to add that only one voice may talk at a time, so that even the most lively dialogue consists of a series of interpolations following each other in succession. The talk of the "spirits" is often carried on in strange, quite unintelligible words, such as "papire kuri muri," etc. To make it understood, the shaman has to call for an interpreter, who from that time on takes part in all conversations, and also explains to the auditors the words of the other "spirits." Thus the shaman is supposed to be unable to understand the language of the "separate spirits."

The same idea obtains among other neighboring tribes. The most curious case of all is that of the shamans of the Russians and the Russianized natives of the Kolyma and the Anadyr, who know no other language than the Russian. The "spirits," however, even when speaking through the mouth of the shaman, employ only the usual unintelligible gibberish mixed with some distorted and mispronounced phrases in the Koryak, Yakut, and Yukaghir languages. After a while the shaman calls for an interpreter, and at last, after some controversy, the spirits send for one who can speak Russian and who translates the orders of the "spirits."

The Chukchee shamans have no special language of their own, with the exception of a few words and expressions. Thus the drum is called "a'ᶜtwet" ("canoe"), which is an additional proof of the preponderance of maritime pursuits in the former life of the people. The idea of shamanistic ecstasy is expressed by the word "an·ña'arkɪn" ("he sinks"), which refers to the belief that the shaman, during the period of ecstasy, is able to visit other worlds, and especially that underground.

Among the northwestern branch of the Koryak, the "spirits" are said to use a special mode of pronunciation, similar to that used by the southeastern Koryak and the Chukchee. A few words are also said to be peculiar to them. Among the Asiatic Eskimo the "spirits" are said to have a special language. Many words of it were given to me by the shamans, and most of them are analogous to the "spirit" language known to various Eskimo tribes of America, both in Alaska and on the Atlantic side.

Tricks of various kinds break up the monotony of the performance, which may last for several hours. The "spirits" will scratch from the outside at the walls of the sleeping-room, running around it in all directions, so that the clattering of their feet is quite audible. In contrast to this, the motion of the ke'let inside of the room produces but slight noise. The rustling of their flight is similar to the buzzing of a mosquito, and the rattling of their tiny feet as they run over the surface of the drum is hardly perceptible.

Often, however, a mischievous "spirit" suddenly tugs at the skin spread in the center of the room with such force that things lying on it fly about in all directions. Therefore the housemates of the shaman usually take the precaution to remove kettles and dishes from the room. Sometimes an invisible hand seizes the whole sleeping-room by its top, and shakes it with wonderful strength, or even lifts it up high, letting in for a moment the twilight from the outer tent. This, of course, is possible only with the movable tent of the Reindeer people, where the sleeping-room is fastened none too firmly. Other invisible hands toss about lumps of snow, spill cold water and urine, and even throw blocks of wood, or stones, at the imminent risk of hurting some of the listeners.

All these things happened several times in my presence. The "spirits" would ask me, through the shamans, whether I really felt afraid; and, when I did not give a satisfactory answer, the "spirits" would try to increase my respect for them by such material manifestations. I must mention that the audience is strictly forbidden to make any attempts whatever to touch the "spirits." These latter highly resent any intrusion of this kind, and retaliate either on the shaman, whom they may kill on the spot, or on the trespassing listener, who runs the risk of having his head broken, or even a knife thrust through his ribs in the dark. I received warnings of this kind at almost every shamanistic performance. In some cases the shaman would lay a bare knife within his own reach as an additional warning against any infringement.

The size of the sleeping-room is so small that it is really wonderful how a shaman can keep up the illusion even under cover of the dark and with the protection of his resentful "spirits." Many times I sat so near the performer that I could almost touch him with my outstretched hand, and the warning against too great inquisitiveness on my part was of course quite necessary.

All these tricks strangely resemble the doings of modern spiritualists, and without doubt they cannot be carried out without the help of human assistants.

The second part of the shamanistic performance is of a magical character. To give a clearer idea of it, I will describe a few instances.

The shaman Tilu'wgi, of whom I shall speak again, after some preliminary intercourse with the "spirits," called a peculiar ke'lE of his, who said she was an old maid, living alone in her house, and she expressed apprehension lest we should laugh at her talk with the peculiar feminine pronunciation. After that, however, she proceeded to give the magic instructions and explanations.

She told one of those present, Enmu'wgi by name, who had recently been vanquished in a wrestling-match, that his defeat was caused by the use of malignant incantations by his adversary, and she advised him to take the matter into his own hands.

This female "spirit" reproached one of my fellow travelers, a great hunter, with ill-treating those "walking afoot," which is the usual periphrasis for the bears. When he tried to defend himself, the female "spirit" reminded him of a hunting expedition, in which he took part about two months before, which was directed against a bear sleeping in its den. From the old Chukchee point of view, this certainly was a rather dangerous pursuit. In the end the "spirit" said that the man in question, because of his offenses against those "walking afoot," was in danger of losing his powers of endurance in walking. To his question as to the means of warding off the danger, the female "spirit" said that he must procure for himself the skin of the nose of a newly killed bear, and perform a thanksgiving ceremonial over it. That, probably, would appease those "walking afoot."

Afterward she told another listener that she saw that in the last autumn he had killed a wild reindeer buck. Though this happened far away from his herd, he should have made a sacrifice to the buck, which he omitted to do; therefore the following winter he was visited by bad luck, in that the wolves attacked his herd, and killed nine fat bucks. To check the recurrence of such a misfortune, it is necessary to take a small crotch of willow cut on the place of the attack by wolves, and perform over it the required ceremonial.

Galmu'urgin, the soothsaying shaman already spoken of, who gave a prescription at the very beginning of the séance, predicted in my presence to the master of the tent that the next fall many reindeer would come to his house. "One buck will stop on the right side of the entrance, and pluck at the grass, attracted by a certain doe of dark-gray hair. This attraction must be strengthened with a special incantation. The reindeer buck, while standing there, must be killed with a bow, and the arrow to be used must have a flat rhomboid point. This will secure the successful killing of all the other wild reindeer."

After that the shaman recollected himself for a while, and addressed the brother of the master, who, with one companion, lived in a separate camp. This companion was married to one of his relatives. The shaman said that, before the fall, they would part company, nor would they look at each other with clear eyes; and, by the way, his prediction was fulfilled much earlier than the time designated.

To still another of the listeners he said that he feared lest the "bad beings" might conceive a desire to approach his house. By this he meant the "spirits of disease." In order to thwart their intentions, the man was told to go through some special preventive ceremonies during the celebration of the ceremonial of the antlers, which was then at hand. The ceremonies consisted in drawing several lines across the snow near the tent, and putting some small stones before the entrance. These were supposed to transform themselves into a large river, and high, inaccessible cliffs, on the route of the "bad beings."

In this way the usual shamanistic performance is carried on in the inner room, and with the light put out.

In other cases the shaman actually "sinks"; that is, after some most violent singing, and beating of the drum, he falls into a kind of trance, during which his body lies on the ground unconscious, while his soul visits "spirits" in their own world, and asks them for advice. Chukchee folklore is full of episodes referring to such shamanistic trances; but in real life they happen very rarely, especially in modern times, when shamans are so much less skillful than of old. Even the word "an·ña'arkɪn" ("to sink"), from the explanation of modern shamans, has reference simply to the immersion of the performer into the depths of shamanistic ecstasy without its literal fulfillment.

In folk stories the shamans sink into the other worlds chiefly for the purpose of finding one of the missing souls of a patient who claims their power for his treatment. In important cases, even at the present day, the shamans, when treating a well-to-do patient, will at least pretend to have sunk into the required unconsciousness. On one or two occasions I had an opportunity of witnessing such a state, but the whole performance was of a rather poor kind.

It began, as usual, in the dark; but when the shaman suddenly broke off beating the drum, the lamp was again lighted and the face of the shaman immediately covered with a piece of cloth. The mistress of the house, who was the wife of the shaman, took up the drum and began to beat it with light, slow strokes. This lasted the entire time that the shaman lay under the cloth, or about a quarter of an hour. Then he suddenly awoke, and, removing the cloth from his face, sat up in his place, took the drum from his wife, beat it for a while, and sang a few tunes as in the beginning. After that he began to give the patient magical advice regarding his illness, which, however, was nothing else than an elaborate incantation in dramatized form.

KNUD RASMUSSEN

A Shaman's Journey to the Sea Spirit

Shamans ordinarily deal with spirits by acting as their mouthpieces while in a state of possession; this article illustrates a less usual procedure in which the shaman's soul dissociates itself from his body and travels to the spirit world.

In this moving account, Knud Rasmussen, one of the great authorities on the Eskimo, describes one of the principal rituals of an Eskimo shaman—to make a journey to the bottom of the sea to propitiate the Spirit of the Sea (often called "Sedna" or "Sea Goddess" in other monographs on the Eskimo). The Eskimos believe that this goddess controls the sea mammals, whence come the most important food, fuel, and skins for clothing, and sends nearly all the worst misfortunes to the Eskimo people. These misfortunes are due to misdeeds and offenses committed by men and they gather in dirt and impurity over the body of the goddess. It is necessary for the shaman to go through a dangerous ordeal to reach the sea goddess at the bottom of the sea. He must then

Reprinted in abridged form from Knud Rasmussen, *Report of the Fifth Thule Expedition, 1921–24,* Vol. VII, No. 1, *Intellectual Culture of the Iglulik Eskimos* (Copenhagen: Gyldendalske Boghandel, Nordisk Forlag, 1929), pp. 123–129, by permission of Rudolf Sand.

stroke her hair and report the difficulties of his people. The goddess replies that breaches of taboos have caused her to send the misfortunes. Whereupon the shaman returns for the mass confession from all the people who have committed misdeeds. Presumably when all sins are confessed, the sea goddess releases the game, returns lost souls, cures illnesses, and generally makes the world right with the Eskimos again.

The girl who was thrown into the sea by her own father and had her finger joints so cruelly cut off as she clung in terror to the side of the boat has in a strange fashion made herself the stern goddess of fate among the Eskimos. From her comes all the most indispensable of human food, the flesh of sea beasts; from her comes the blubber that warms the cold snow huts and gives light in the lamps when the long arctic night broods over the land. From her come also the skins of the great seal which are likewise indispensable for clothes and boot soles, if the hunters are to be able to move over the frozen sea all seasons of the year. But while Takánakapsâluk gives mankind all these good things, created out of her own finger joints, it is she also who sends nearly all the misfortunes which are regarded by the dwellers on earth as the worst and direst. In her anger at men's failing to live as they should, she calls up storms that prevent the men from hunting, or she keeps the animals they seek hidden away in a pool she has at the bottom of the sea, or she will steal away the souls of human beings and send sickness among the people. It is not strange, therefore, that it is regarded as one of a shaman's greatest feats to visit her where she lives at the bottom of the sea, and so tame and conciliate her that human beings can live once more untroubled on earth.

When a shaman wishes to visit Takánakapsâluk, he sits on the inner part of the sleeping place behind a curtain, and must wear nothing but his kamiks and mittens. A shaman about to make this journey is said to be ᴎak·a·ʒɔq: one who drops down to the bottom of the sea. This remarkable expression is due perhaps in some degree to the fact that no one can rightly explain how the journey is made. Some assert that it is only his soul or his spirit which makes the journey; others declare that it is the shaman himself who actually, in the flesh, drops down into the underworld.

The journey may be undertaken at the instance of a single individual, who pays the shaman for his trouble, either because there is sickness in his household which appears incurable, or because he has been particularly unsuccessful in his hunting. But it may also be made on behalf of a whole village threatened by famine and death owing to scarcity of game. As soon as such occasion arises, all the adult members of the community assemble in the house from which the shaman is to start, and when he has taken up his position—if it is winter, and in a snow hut, on the bare snow; if in summer, on the bare ground—the men and women present must loosen all tight fastenings in their clothes, the lacings of their footgear, the waistbands of their breeches, and then sit down and remain still with closed eyes, all lamps being put out, or allowed to burn only with so faint a flame that it is practically dark inside the house.

The shaman sits for a while in silence, breathing deeply, and then, after some time has elapsed, he begins to call upon his helping spirits, repeating over and over again: "The way is made ready for me; the way opens before me!"

Whereat all present must answer in chorus: "Let it be so!"

And when the helping spirits have arrived, the earth opens under the shaman, but often only to close up again; he has to struggle for a long time with hidden forces, ere he can cry at last:

"Now the way is open."

And then all present must answer: "Let the way be open before him; let there be way for him."

And now one hears, at first under the sleeping place: "Halala—he—he—he, halala—he—he—he!" and afterwards under the passage, below the ground, the same cry: "Halele—he!" And the sound can be distinctly heard to recede farther and farther until it is lost altogether. Then all know that he is on his way to the ruler of the sea beasts.

Meanwhile, the members of the household pass the time by singing songs in chorus, and here it may happen that the clothes which the shaman has discarded come alive and fly about round the house, above the heads of the singers, who are sitting with closed eyes. And one may hear deep sighs and the breathing of persons long since dead; these are the souls of the shaman's namesakes, who have come to help. But as soon as one calls them by name, the sighs cease, and all is silent in the house until another dead person begins to sigh.

In the darkened house one hears only sighing and groaning from the dead who lived many generations earlier. This sighing and puffing sounds as if the spirits were down under water, in the sea, as marine animals, and in between all the noises one hears the blowing and splashing of creatures coming up to breathe. There is one song especially which must be constantly repeated; it is only to be sung by the oldest members of the tribe, and is as follows:

> We reach out our hands
> to help you up;
> We are without food,
> we are without game.
> From the hollow by the entrance
> you shall open,
> you shall bore your way up.
> We are without food,
> and we lay ourselves down
> holding out hands
> to help you up!

An ordinary shaman will, even though skillful, encounter many dangers in his flight down to the bottom of the sea; the most dreaded are three large rolling stones which he meets as soon as he has reached the sea floor. There is no way round; he has to pass between them, and take great care not to be crushed by these stones, which churn about, hardly leaving room for a human being to pass. Once he has passed beyond them, he comes to a broad, trodden path, the shaman's path; he follows a coastline resembling that which he knows from on earth, and entering a bay finds himself on a great plain, and here lies the house of Takánakapsâluk, built of stone, with a short passageway, just like the houses of the tunit. Outside the house one can hear the animals puffing and blowing, but he does not see them; in the passage leading to the house lies Takánakapsâluk's dog stretched across the passage taking up all the room; it lies there gnawing at a bone and snarling. It is

dangerous to all who fear it, and only the courageous shaman can pass by it, stepping straight over it as it lies; the dog then knows that the bold visitor is a great shaman, and does him no harm.

These difficulties and dangers attend the journey of an ordinary shaman. But for the very greatest, a way opens right from the house whence they invoke their helping spirits; a road down through the earth, if they are in a tent on shore, or down through the sea, if it is in a snow hut on the sea ice, and by this route the shaman is led down without encountering any obstacle. He almost glides as if falling through a tube so fitted to his body that he can check his progress by pressing against the sides, and need not actually fall down with a rush. This tube is kept open for him by all the souls of his namesakes, until he returns on his way back to earth.

Should a great shelter wall be built, outside the house of Takánakapsâluk, it means that she is very angry and implacable in her feelings towards mankind, but the shaman must fling himself upon the wall, kick it down and level it to the ground. There are some who declare that her house has no roof, and is open at the top, so that she can better watch, from her place by the lamp, the doings of mankind. All the different kinds of game: seal, bearded seal, walrus, and whale are collected in a great pool on the right of her lamp, and there they lie puffing and blowing. When the shaman enters the house, he at once sees Takánakapsâluk, who, as a sign of anger, is sitting with her back to the lamp and with her back to all the animals in the pool. Her hair hangs down loose all over one side of her face, a tangled, untidy mass hiding her eyes, so that she cannot see. It is the misdeeds and offenses committed by men which gather in dirt and impurity over her body. All the foul emanations from the sins of mankind nearly suffocate her. As the shaman moves towards her, Isarrataitsoq, her father, tries to grasp hold of him. He thinks it is a dead person come to expiate offenses before passing on to the Land of The Dead, but the shaman must then at once cry out: "I am flesh and blood" and then he will not be hurt. And he must grasp Takánakapsâluk by one shoulder and turn her face towards the lamp and towards the animals, and stroke her hair, the hair she has been unable to comb out herself, because she has no fingers; and he must smooth it and comb it, and as soon as she is calmer, he must say:

"Those up above can no longer help the seals up by grasping their foreflippers."

Then Takánakapsâluk answers in the spirit language: "The secret miscarriages of the women and breaches of taboo in eating boiled meat bar the way for the animals."

The shaman must now use all his efforts to appease her anger, and at last, when she is in a kindlier mood, she takes the animals one by one and drops them on the floor, and then it is as if a whirlpool arose in the passage, the water pours out from the pool and the animals disappear in the sea. This means rich hunting and abundance for mankind.

It is then time for the shaman to return to his fellows up above, who are waiting for him. They can hear him coming a long way off; the rush of his passage through the tube kept open for him by the spirits comes nearer and nearer, and with a mighty "Plu—a—he—he" he shoots up into his place behind the curtain: "Plu-plu," like some creature of the sea, shooting up from the deep to take breath under the pressure of mighty lungs.

Then there is silence for a moment. No one may break this silence until the shaman says: "I have something to say."

Then all present answer: "Let us hear, let us hear."

And the shaman goes on, in the solemn spirit language: "Words will arise."

And then all in the house must confess any breaches of taboo they have committed.

"It is my fault, perhaps," they cry, all at once, women and men together, in fear of famine and starvation, and all begin telling of the wrong things they have done. All the names of those in the house are mentioned, and all must confess, and thus much comes to light which no one had ever dreamed of; everyone learns his neighbors' secrets. But despite all the sin confessed, the shaman may go on talking as one who is unhappy at having made a mistake, and again and again break out into such expressions as this:

"I seek my grounds in things which have not happened; I speak as one who knows nothing."

There are still secrets barring the way for full solution of the trouble, and so the women in the house begin to go through all the names, one after another; nearly all women's names; for it was always their breaches of taboo which were most dangerous. Now and again when a name is mentioned, the shaman exclaims in relief:

"Taina, taina!"

It may happen that the woman in question is not present, and in such a case, she is sent for. Often it would be quite young girls or young wives, and when they came in crying and miserable, it was always a sign that they were good women, good penitent women. And as soon as they showed themselves, shamefaced and weeping, the shaman would break out again into his cries of self-reproach:

"I seek, and I strike where nothing is to be found! I seek, and I strike where nothing is to be found! If there is anything, you must say so!"

And the woman who has been led in, and whom the shaman has marked out as one who has broken her taboo, now confesses:

"I had a miscarriage, but I said nothing, because I was afraid, and because it took place in a house where there were many."

She thus admits that she has had a miscarriage, but did not venture to say so at the time because of the consequences involved, affecting her numerous housemates; for the rules provide that as soon as a woman has had a miscarriage in a house, all those living in the same house, men and women alike, must throw away all the house contains of qituptɔq: soft things, i.e., all the skins on the sleeping place, all the clothes, in a word all soft skins, thus including also ilupɛrɔq: the sealskin covering used to line the whole interior of a snow hut as used among the Iglulingmiut. This was so serious a matter for the household that women sometimes dared not report a miscarriage; moreover, in the case of quite young girls who had not yet given birth to any child, a miscarriage might accompany their menstruation without their knowing, and only when the shaman in such a case as this, pointed out the girl as the origin of the trouble and the cause of Takánakapsâluk's anger, would she call to mind that there had once been, in her menstruation skin (the piece of thick-haired caribou skin which women place in their underbreeches during menstruation) something that looked like "thick blood." She had not thought at the time that it was anything particular, and had therefore said nothing about it, but now that she is pointed out by the shaman, it recurs to her mind. Thus at last the cause of Takánakapsâluk's anger is explained, and all are filled with joy at having escaped disaster. They are now assured that there will be abundance of game on the following day. And in the end, there may be almost a feeling of thankfulness towards the delinquent. This then was what took place when shamans went down and propitiated the great Spirit of the Sea.

S. F. NADEL

A Study of Shamanism in the Nuba Mountains

In this interesting account Nadel describes the patterns of shamanism among the Nuba peoples of the southern Sudan. Although drumming, dancing, and other techniques used by Asiatic and American shamans are absent, the shaman is possessed by supernatural spirits and thereby functions both as a mouthpiece of the spirits and the officiant of the cult addressed to them.

It is significant to note that shamanism is not universal in these Nuba tribes. Only six of the eighteen tribes Nadel visited had the practice, where it was used for divination and guidance on what to do about troublesome situations—when and under what conditions to go to war, what has caused and what should be the cure for illnesses, and so forth. Note also that unlike many of the Asiatic and American shamans, the Nuba shamans do not undertake therapy for illnesses—this is done by healing experts, or medicine men proper—rather they merely discover what the proper treatment should be. Apparently in some cases the spirit can be inherited in family lines, but the prevailing pattern is nonhereditary spirit possession, as it is in Asia and America.

The Nuba have two general types of shamans—those who concern themselves with the irregular, contingent needs of individuals, such as illness or barrenness, and those who concern themselves with the needs of the community, such as annual rituals, the control of rain, or luck in war. The latter have much more prestige within the society; in fact, they exercise functions that are performed by "priests" in other societies. Nadel makes it clear that the Nuba also have priests, and he has an illuminating discussion of the relationship between the shamanistic and the nonshamanistic (priestly) aspects of the culture.

He also raises interesting theoretical questions in his discussion of the role of the shaman in culture change, pointing out how the unpredictable leadership of spirit-inspired individuals is an important force for change, since they can be social reformers with no fear of disbelief or resentment on the part of the people. He discusses the psychology of shamanism, and raises the question of whether the trances are genuine. He asks whether shamanism serves to absorb abnormal personalities and offers these deviants a legitimate social niche, and whether shamanistic performances provide an institutionalized catharsis that stabilizes hysteria and related psychoneuroses, thus reducing a psychopathic incidence which would otherwise be much larger in the society. He favors the hypothesis that shamanism exploits and at the same time canalizes existing neurotic leanings and relieves mental stresses. But he is frank in recognizing that he has not verified the hypothesis, for mental stresses may find different paths for their expression, such as witchcraft, evil magic, or hysteria and psy-

Reprinted from *Journal of the Royal Anthropological Institute*, LXXVI (1946), 25–37, by permission of the Royal Anthropological Institute of Great Britain and Ireland.

choses that are undisguised and unfettered. To verify the hypotheses it would have to be shown that psychoses and kindred disorders are increasing among nonshamanistic groups under stress, while in comparable shamanistic groups under comparable stress the increase of shamanism would go hand in hand with a relatively undisturbed mental stability. Nadel's thoughts about the psychology of shamanism are similar to the observations and impressions of observers of shamanistic behavior in other areas of the world. For example, Bogoras commented that many Chukchee shamans he knew were "half crazy." Margaret Lantis has described the condition of the Eskimo shaman in his novitiate, and to some extent in his later shamanistic performances, as resembling the progress of schizophrenia. It is clear that a relationship exists between psychiatric abnormalities and the practice of shamanism which provides defense mechanisms both for the shaman and his clientele, although further research is needed to determine the precise nature of this relationship.

THE CULT AND THE PEOPLE

The religious cult described in this paper is, I think, properly named *shamanism*. It corresponds in all essentials to the classical shamanism of Central Asia and North West America. Like the latter, it rests on the belief that spirits may possess human beings, and on the practice of establishing communication with the supernatural through human beings so possessed. The person possessed—the shaman—is more than merely a temporary and passive medium through which others place themselves *en rapport* with the spirit world. He is an incarnation of the spirit, and so a person lifted above all others. He is a passive medium when possessed; but through his ability to induce possession he is also a master of these supernatural powers. He is an instrument which others may use only in the sense in which priests are instruments for the communication with deities. The shaman, then, is both a mouthpiece of the spirits and an officiant of the cult addressed to them.

So far, I have used the phraseology believers might use. Psychologically, the spirit possession represents a "hysterical dissociation," a fit or trance which is often self-induced, through autosuggestion, and may materialize either spontaneously or in prearranged séances. The stimulants of drumming and dancing, familiar from Asiatic and American shamanism, are absent in the Nuba Mountains—at least in the ordinary spirit séance; they play a part only in the ceremonial which surrounds the consecration of the Nuba shaman.

The group of Negro tribes known by the collective name "Nuba" lives in the hills and mountains of Kordofan, in the Southern Sudan, wedged in between Arabs and Nilotes. The common name stands for no marked ethnic or cultural unity. The Nuba are divided into numerous autonomous tribes, perhaps 30 or more, of very unequal size and widely varying language and culture. Only a few groups here and there speak related and mutually intelligible dialects, or share a wide range of cultural features. In spite of the diversity, certain cultural traits are typical of all or nearly all Nuba groups. The common environment may account for much that is identical in their economy, which is that of sedentary farmers owning considerable stocks of cattle, sheep, and goats. But we also meet with such common features as the belief in a supreme deity; the conception of leprosy as a sanction for kinship offenses; double exogamy; and a clan organization entailing eating prohibitions between different clans. Other cultural traits appear irregularly dispersed: shamanism belongs to this category.

Of the 18 Nuba tribes which I visited six practice shamanism (ignoring offshoot tribes of recent diffusion). These are the people of Nyima, Dilling, Koalib, Tabak, Tima, and Miri. With the exception of the Miri, they all live in the north or northwest of the Nuba Mountains, and with the exception of the Tima, they all belong to the group of Nuba tribes which have a patrilineal kinship system. But the relevance of this distribution is uncertain, since a considerable number of tribes in the west and southwest are still ethnographically unknown. Apart from the method of reckoning descent, the six sha-

manistic groups have little in common : they
speak entirely different languages and differ
widely in size, social organization, and culture at large.

The present account deals with one of
these tribes—the Nyima. They are a large
group, with a population of about 37,000
which lives fairly closely packed on seven
neighboring hills, the different hill communities maintaining close though (in the past)
not always friendly contacts. Nyima social
organization is built upon small individual
families and nonlocalized clans. Their political system, in its traditional form, lacked
chieftainship; as we shall see, the shaman
represented the nearest approach to institutionalized political leadership.

THE SPIRIT FACULTIES

The Nyima call the shaman *kujur* and the
spirit which possesses him *kuni*.

The *kuni* spirits are to some extent conceived of as anthropomorphous beings. Sex
and offspring are ascribed to them, and their
kinship relationships are often traceable;
they are also said to have human interests,
emotions, and moods, as well as individual
names. But no more tangible physical characteristics are associated with these quasi-
human aspects : the spirits are invisible and
cannot be described—they are "like the air."
These beliefs are more definite only where
they are concerned with the varying gifts
and faculties of spirits. Some spirits are
more powerful than others, and the nature of
their powers equally varies. The human vessel shares in these spirit faculties and in turn
becomes a "specialist" in one or the other
sphere of life—in war or farming, in the
treatment of barrenness or disease, in helping lovers, or assisting people to recover lost
or stolen property. Certain of the spirit
faculties are firmly bound up with the institutional life of the group: age-grades, circumcision, a number of communal rites, all
require the intervention of spirits and so the
ministrations of particular shamans.

The inventory of spirit faculties is large
and, as we shall see, ever-changing. The aid
offered by the spirit vessels, however, falls
under the two headings "divination" and
"guidance." In trance, the shaman divines
auspicious times and conditions for various
tasks such as war, farmwork, or rituals; he
warns the people of impending events and

prescribes the procedure, ritual or otherwise,
to avoid or ensure particular happenings
(rain, a famine, the discovery and punishment of offenders). Always, the shaman's
orders express the likes and dislikes of the
spirits, and the conditions under which they
will help or hinder.

The healing powers of the shaman correspond to the same conceptions. Consulted
by the patient or his family, the shaman goes
into trance and discovers the cause and cure
of the disease. Typical causes are the anger
of ancestors, a sin committed by the patient,
the power of the evil eye, or the hostility
(perhaps employed by a human enemy) of
other spirits. Typical remedies are expiatory
sacrifices, gifts to the shaman's spirit, or redress of the wrong which provoked the hostility. In simple ailments the shaman may
merely announce their harmlessness and
predict their eventual disappearance. In no
case does the shaman perform anything in
the nature of a therapeutic manipulation :
this is the field of other healing experts,
medicine men proper, and the shaman sometimes instructs his clients to seek treatment
of this sort. Spirit possession is a means of
discovering the right treatment, and not a
part of it. The therapeutic effects that the
shaman's practices may have are entirely
psychological and rest on the suggestibility
of the subjects. Clearly, where psychoneu-
rotic disorders are at the root of the illness,
the shaman may indeed effect a cure. But
this does not mean that he wisely refrains
from treating ailments not responsive to
such treatment by suggestion. This criterion,
though not ignored, is only crudely applied.
The cure of all mental diseases falls to the
shaman, and no shaman would undertake
the treatment of a broken leg, an ulcer, or a
septic wound; but the main conception underlying this division of labor seems to be
that diseases of obscure origin which attack
the whole being of man concern the shaman
while diseases whose origin is empirically
understood and whose effect is localized are
outside his sphere.

Thus shamans do not hesitate to "treat"
sterility, leprosy, and what seems to be tu-
berculosis or infantile paralysis. Occasionally, they are reported to be completely successful; but where a check is possible the
reports prove to be inaccurate. I was told of
a certain famous epilepsy expert whose cures
were infallible; I found at least one patient

whom he had not cured. More often however, no such extravagant claims are made. The patient who fails to be cured by one shaman will try another; for as we have noted, shamans and spirits are not equally powerful. And if the patient fails everywhere (provided he lives long enough to try all the shamans), there is still the nature of the spirits to be reckoned with: for they are often unpredictable and capricious, or jealously interfere in each other's work.

THE IDEOLOGY OF INCARNATION

The existence of the spirits before or apart from their manifestation in human beings is ill-defined. There is general agreement that the spirit comes to the shaman "from outside" and, in the trance, gains hold of his body. But no one knows where the spirits dwell in between trances; nor is the nature of the spirit possession clearly visualized. It is described by the word *koyidi,* which is also employed when referring to the mounting of a horse or to the way in which slaves are tied by the neck to a forked wooden post. But the parallel is not precise; for the Nyima maintain that the spirit does not ride on the shaman's shoulders or neck, but "seizes his head from above," or "enters his head."

The origin of the spirits is again largely a matter of speculation. A few famous shamans offer detailed accounts and quote appropriate myths. But other old men and experts, though they accept the main facts, consider the legends themselves both apocryphal and irrelevant, and the large majority of Nyima know nothing about them.

According to these myths the first spirits to enter human beings were the souls of the tribal ancestors, men of the "culture hero" type, who founded the hill communities, brought circumcision to Nyima, and established rituals and sacrifices. Incarnated in the descendants of these first ancestors, the spirits taught the people, above all, to wage war against enemies and conquer other countries. These spirits of human origin were jealous of each other, bloodthirsty and evil, and their work ended in bloodshed and unhappiness. Taking pity upon humanity, God sent another kind of spirit down from the sky. These spirits were good and kind; they became the masters of helpful magic, the magic of fertility, of rain, of cultivation,

and of health. A third kind of spirit is vaguely referred to in a few disconnected legends; these were spirits which, in the mythical past, had lived in rocks, caves, or in the ground, waiting to be released and incarnated in man.

The spirit cult corresponds only in a very general sense to the picture painted in myths and legends. All three kinds of spirits appear in the shamanistic manifestations; but the third kind plays a very unimportant part, while the spirits "from the sky" are the most numerous. Moreover, many spirits believed to be at present incarnated are "just spirits" and not further identified. The distinction in kind between the spirits of war and peace is not maintained in practice; the simple juxtaposition of good and evil spirits does not resolve the complex relation between the spirit beliefs and moral values; nor is the identification of certain spirits with the souls of ancestors quite consistent with the Nyima conception of death, afterlife, and the nature of the soul. Moreover, the tenet that only mythical ancestors are capable of reincarnation admits of one notable exception. The hereditary rainmaker Agemna who led the Nyima in the rebellion of 1918 and was later executed by the Government, is now (since 1936) reincarnated in his surviving brother. Agemna was not a shaman; he had no spirit which he might have bequeathed to his descendants. It is he himself, his own soul, which has now found a human vessel. The heroic and unhappy memory of the rebellion evidently proved strong enough to rival the legendary past in the creation of a "culture hero" turned spirit.

Spirits may at any time step out of this nebulous existence to take possession of human beings. All *kuni* spirits are males, but they may seek incarnation both in men and women. At least, this is the theory; for the overwhelming majority of spirit incarnations occurs in men, and female incarnations are mistrusted, and actively discouraged. This is done quite simply by refusing to arrange the consecration rites for female shamans. These are the views and actions of a society controlled by men. Husbands complain that a wife turned shaman would neglect the house; fathers, that their daughters would find no husbands; and all men agree that it would be unbecoming for a woman to become rich in livestock, as shamans usually do. These practical reasons are combined with more mystic arguments. Thus it is said that spirits hate visiting human beings who (like women) have no house of their own, and so turn evil and vicious; or it is bluntly stated that "it is bad for women to dream" —dreams being one of the prerequisites for the shaman's vocation. The opposition to female shamans differs, however, in different clans, and the varying attitude appears linked with a significant aspect of the clan structure. The Nyima consider any offense against marital fidelity a grave sin, which would be visited with death on one of the culprits. In one group of clans, the man would be the victim, in another the girl. It is the former group of clans which opposes female spirit priestship most violently; while the other clans have accepted several women shamans. Thus in the clans, where the scales of sin are more heavily weighted against the male, female authority in the spiritual sphere is resented. Let me add that this moral balance fits well into the schematic and often dualistic conceptions which dominate Nyima culture.

The shaman may be any age between 17 and 50 when he first experiences the manifestation of spirits. These take the form of unusual and perhaps prophetic dreams or of striking events which, to the people, are clearly supernatural. Sooner or later he begins to exhibit the chief symptom of spirit possession, the hysterical attack and dissociation. Though the spirit manifests itself in this fashion only intermittently, its incarnation is conceived of as lasting, and normally ends only with the shaman's death. Afterwards, the spirit is free to return to the limbo in which it previously existed or, perhaps, to seek another incarnation. This may or may not be in the family or clan of its previous vessel, and if it is, not necessarily in the next generation; for there is no rigid rule, the decision lying with the spirit alone. A reincarnated spirit is identified by the familiar manner of its manifestation, which the old men would remember and recognize; where this is unfamiliar, the experts will diagnose a new, different spirit. The large majority of known spirits are reincarnations, mostly in the same family; some have been identified in individuals belonging to different families or clans; others have appeared as it were from nowhere or are at least of unknown antecedents. The same family may be visited by several spirits at the same time,

and the same person may even own up to three different spirits. The number of incarnated spirits is extremely large; no hamlet is without one, and the village on Salara Hill where I stayed boasted seven shamans in a population of about 1500. Of the ten shamans whose life histories I recorded eight possessed "hereditary" spirits, though four shamans had new spirits besides.

Every man in Nyima would wish to have a spirit and to enjoy the exalted position of a shaman. But it is not possible, nor is the attempt ever made, to force a spirit whose existence is known to choose a particular human vessel. The spirit incarnation is conceived of as being free, entirely spontaneous, capricious even. Cases are known of spirits which chose their vessels tentatively and abandoned them again. But when the spirit visits become regular and lead to impressive-manifestations, this is taken as a sign that the spirit desires to stay.

THE CONSECRATION OF THE SHAMAN

This bond is confirmed and strengthened by two consecration ceremonies which take place some years after the first manifestations, though the shaman might start "practicing" before that, if he finds clients ready to consult him. Hereditary or reincarnated spirits are very soon identified, but "new" spirits reveal their name and full powers only at the first consecration ceremony. Only after the second ceremony, however, does the shaman attain the full status of a spirit priest. Until then he is an ordinary mortal; if he died, his funeral would in no way differ from that of other people, while the funeral of a fully fledged spirit priest involves special ceremonies and observances. Before the second consecration rite, the shaman is known as *kuni da koyidi*—"one mounted by the spirit"; afterwards he is called *kujur* and addressed as "Grandfather of the Spirit." Full *kujurs* are much rarer than ordinary shamans; of the seven shamans in Salara only two were consecrated spirit priests at the time of my visit.

The first ceremony is usually performed 2 to 3 years after the first manifestation. The shaman himself, in trance, announces the date, which announcement concludes a period both sufficient to prove the genuineness of the spirit and adequate in a practical sense; for the ceremony is not expensive by

Nyima standards, and the shaman needs comparatively little time to collect the livestock required for it. It is called *tir*, meaning "head," and is said to "open the head for the spirit to enter." It is not compulsory, unless the spirit manifests itself in a frightening manner, when the ritual is needed to clear the shaman's mind of fear and confusion. The ceremony is businesslike and on a small scale; there is no beer, nor any dancing or singing, and only clansmen of the shaman are invited.

The second ceremony, which is both more important and expensive, also takes longer to prepare—mostly 8 to 12 years. It is called *difira tay*, "Entering the grass shed," after the grass hut erected by the shaman's family inside the compound, where the shaman must stay for 15 days, sitting and sleeping on a mat on the ground, being allowed to leave the hut only at night, to relieve nature. During this period the shaman as well as all men of his clan must refrain from sexual intercourse, lest death befall them or their children, or barrenness their wives. On the fifteenth day a big feast takes place, when numerous animals are killed, beer is offered to the huge number of guests of all clans, and there is singing, drumming, and dancing.

On this day the shaman is expected to be seized by the spirit, the seizure being the signal for the first sacrifice. This consists in the killing of a he-goat, which is thrown outside through the gate of the house to be later collected by people from other clans. The meaning of this act is to purify the shaman of such blood guilt as he may have loaded upon himself, wittingly or unwittingly; as the people put it—"the blood is thrown away." A series of sacrifices follows, all performed with elaborate ritual, the whole ceremony ending at nightfall. The symbolism of some of the ritual acts is uncertain, while others conspicuously dramatize the social structure. Thus the shaman's father, mother-brother [*sic*], wife, and mother each has an appointed task in one or the other sacrifice, as have also the members of the shaman's sub-clan, clan and age-grade.

On the next day the shaman assumes the many emblems of *kujur* status—four iron bangles worn round the left wrist. In subsequent years the *kujur* may acquire more iron bangles, up to 8–10; but these are mere signs of wealth, and not, like the first four, insignia of priestly status. A big white bead worn round the neck, brass bangles, spiral cuffs, rings on the fingers and through the ears, a ceremonial axe and throwing knife, are more paraphernalia of this kind, which may be assumed only after the final consecration ritual but whose connotation is not entirely sacred, and which testify to the *kujur's* wealth and prestige rather than to his achieved vocation.

LIFE HISTORIES OF SHAMANS

Let me now illustrate this account by typical life histories of Nyima shamans. The first case is that of the *kujur* Layin, a shaman of great fame. At the time of my visit he was between 60 and 70. His spirit was said to be powerful in several spheres—it could make grain grow and cure illness; its most outstanding gift was the cure and prevention of barrenness (coupled with the faculty of causing it). In consequence Layin's intervention was sought at every marriage in the neighborhood; as the fee was a cow per marriage, and this particular ministration offered a steady income, Layin became one of the wealthiest men in the community. Previously, there had been no spirit possession in Layin's family. When the spirit first seized him he was 25 or 30 and already married. First, he had a number of striking dreams; he paid no attention to them at the time, realizing their significance only in the light of subsequent events. In his first dream he saw a horse, red with a white belly. In his second dream he saw a leopard, a small animal which raised itself on its hind legs and grew miraculously; Layin was afraid the leopard would eat him, but it did not harm him, merely placing its paws on Layin's shoulders. Red-and-white horses or leopards frequently occur in the dreams of shamans-to-be. In his final dream, before the first trance, Layin was bitten by a snake; this, too, is a common shaman dream. Layin still occasionally has striking dreams, which now turn out to be prophetic. During my stay there was a short threat of drought, and Layin maintained that he had foretold it, having heard in his dream people crying out "there is no rain! the world has become dry!" The spirit also visits Layin at night without showing itself, in the form of vague, terrifying nightmares.

This is Layin's account of his first possession: in the middle of the day he was suddenly seized by a fit of trembling, and lost consciousness. He afterwards learned from the people who had come to watch and listen that he was shouting wildly at first, but then calmed down and made this speech: "This year I am looking after the grain. All who will plant this year will reap a rich harvest. The women who are present—let them sacrifice, and they will bear children." The listeners all agreed that there was a spirit manifesting itself and outlining its future interests. Presently the spirit became more specific, addressing itself to Layin himself. Layin's children had all died young; now the spirit ordered him to perform a certain ritual to remove the curse. Layin subsequently obeyed the spirit instructions, and his wife in due course had five healthy children. In Layin's case it took considerable time until the incarnation could be fully proved and accepted. Layin waited 12 years for the first, and another 3 years for the second consecration rite.

The shaman Harib, a man of about 50, was still only a *kuni* when I met him. His spirit had previously been incarnated in several of his ancestors, the last time in his grandfather; its nature and identity were therefore already known. This spirit was most versatile; its faculties embraced locust magic, the fertility of women, the cure of various diseases, and grain and rain magic. Unlike other shamans, Harib had no warning dreams, and started having prophetic dreams when already a shaman, but he was made aware of his vocation by an extraordinary event. He was asleep at night during a thunderstorm, when the lightning struck his hut and he lost consciousness; as he put it— "he was dead for two days." His stupor was followed by the familiar "possession," during which (in his words) he yelled, babbled, and trembled all over; enough to convince the people that his ancestral spirit had reappeared. Shortly afterwards there was a locust plague and the threat of famine. Once more the spirit seized Harib, and through him promised to stop the locusts if the people would sacrifice a ram, a lamb, and a cock. This they did, and the locusts disappeared— which established another of the spirit's faculties. Harib's period of probation was short. He underwent his first consecration one year after the first manifestation. Six years later (when I visited his village) he

was thinking of undergoing the final ritual in two years' time. Harib, incidentally, had two more spirits: but these appeared only occasionally, were unnamed, and played a subordinate part; they were likened to "servants" of the main spirit.

THE MALEVOLENCE OF SPIRITS

In cases such as these the spirit possession appears on the whole to work smoothly, and, from the shaman's point of view, entirely benevolently. The violence of the first possessions, the fear dreams or attacks which announce the spirit's coming, tend to give way to the controlled dissociations of the séance and to dreams which are unusual only in that they prove to be prophetic. This, however, is not always the case. As I have mentioned, certain spirits are conceived of as vicious, possessive, and jealous, even evil, and their vessel suffers under their hard mastery. This conventional mystical interpretation seems to bear on an empirical fact—that in the case of some individuals the hysterical fit does not lose its violence and spontaneity, and that their particular sensitivity goes hand in hand with lasting or repeated illness. I have met with shamans who were openly reluctant to undergo a trance, which, they claimed, weakened them and made them suffer. The presence of several spirits in the same human body, especially, often assumes such a threatening aspect.

The chief of Salara was thus unhappily possessed of three spirits. The first spirit of which he became possessed was gentle and friendly: it announced itself by the dream of a red horse with white legs; this the chief knew to be the manifestation of a hereditary spirit previously incarnated in his father. The second spirit was more puzzling and disturbing, and appeared to him in a dream during a severe illness. It took the shape of an enormous wooden telegraph pole of frightening appearance; he could not take his eyes off it until, terrified, he pulled his eyelids down with his hands. The pole then spoke to him and told him what to do to recover from his illness. The spirit also announced its name—which was *li,* a concept of vague meaning: *li* means, literally, the "whole world," but is also used to refer to all that is unaccountable, uncontrollable, and evil. This spirit called *li* was a new spirit, unknown to all the old men whom the chief consulted: but they voiced the opinion, most comforting to an ambitious chief, that if the spirit had indeed revealed itself as *li,* it must be "the greatest spirit of all." The chief's third spirit, also new and announcing itself in a dream, appeared in the curious shape of a small motorcar. The chief was driving it to a dark place, surrounded by high mountains, and filled with vast heaps of iron. The chief, this time trusting his own interpretation, suggested that this new spirit was an "English" spirit—"for why else should it take the shape of a motorcar such as the District Commissioner has?"

This chief was an ambitious man; and I have no doubt that his consuming ambition shaped his dreams or at least colored their interpretation. The fact that his spirits appeared in terrifying dreams and subjected his body to severe illness, was to him (as to the people) only another instance of the power of his spirits and their jealous struggle for his person. One dream may here be quoted: one night the chief saw himself in the dream and knew that he was *li,* the spirit called "the whole world." He had a whip in his hand and was lashing out furiously. Then he saw his hereditary spirit standing outside the door of his house, in the shape of his dead father. The dreamer, as *li,* threatened his father's spirit with the whip, shouting: "I do not want you any more; it is I who will now minister to the whole world." Whereupon the father-spirit grew smaller and smaller, until it turned into a fly sitting on the dreamer's hand. The interpretation of the dream was strikingly incongruous; it was thought to mean that "hereditary spirits never abandon you."

Prospective shamans often have dreams or undergo experiences in which their father (or father's spirit) appears in similar frightening and morally ambiguous contexts. Ordinary people, it is maintained, never have dreams or experiences of this kind. One shaman had what appeared to be cerebrospinal meningitis in his youth; it was divined to have been caused by his dead father's spirit, which had to be persuaded to leave and to return in a less hostile manner. Another future spirit priest had dreamt that he was digging a grave for his father, who was dead at the time but appeared alive in the dream; the dreamer was deeply disturbed but, on consulting a shaman, learned that the dream merely foreshadowed the reincarnation of his father's spirit.

These instances, to which I could add others, seem to me to be of greatest importance for the understanding of Nyima shamanism. I am not, however, thinking only of their psychological (or psychopathological) implications, much as the nature of the dreams would seem to invite such an approach. For such an approach would lead us only to the individuals who become shamans, and to the expression or solution of their particular conflicts. The importance of shamanism would in this case seem to rest only on the private experiences separating the visionary from the rest of the community. This is far from being the true picture. The dreams of the shaman are public property; his vocation is a public ideal; and it is by persons such as he and by visions such as he is apt to have that the community is guided. It is here that the full significance of dreams and other spirit manifestations is revealed. These individual experiences build up the world of the supernatural which all must accept. It is a malevolent world—or at least one that is not unequivocally benevolent. Not only does it subject its vessels to disturbing experiences, in the physical as well as moral sense, but it appears itself as "disturbed"—full of threats, unpredictable, and essentially amoral. And this, as we shall see, is the leitmotif of Nyima shamanism.

THE SOCIAL ROLE OF THE SHAMAN

To return for the moment to our descriptive task. When speaking of the two consecration ceremonies which shamans must undergo we touched upon the economic implications of the spirit cult, and this aspect requires fuller exploration. There is no need, however, to dwell on the heavy expenditure involved in the attainment of full *kujur* status. It is clear that only a successful shaman can meet it; and it is clear also that here beliefs and rational factors sustain each other. For a powerful spirit, whose gifts have been amply proved, will soon make its vessel wealthy and so capable of attaining full priesthood; while the shaman of a weak and unimportant spirit will neither, in general belief, deserve full priesthood nor, in practice, amass the necessary wealth. Let us note also that it is only the power of spirits that counts—not their morals: service of vicious spirits is as lucrative as of benevolent ones, and no one would dare to refuse recognition to the former.

Wealth alone, however, does not determine the social status of the shaman or the consecrated *kujur*. To begin with, his association with the spirit confers upon his person supernatural benefits and a supernatural protection which separate him sharply from all ordinary mortals. Thus, one day during the rainy season, *kujur* Harib had engaged a large working party on his land; on this day it did not rain, although it was pouring both the day before and the day after. The people saw in this the work of Harib's spirit (one of whose faculties was control of rain). During my stay in Salara the wife of another *kujur* was struck by lightning: the explanation offered was that she had been unfaithful to her husband and that the spirit had by this means avenged his servant's reputation. It is, in fact, generally believed, that all injuries done to a shaman are punished by lightning.

The exceptional position of the *kujur* is also reflected in the special rules surrounding his death. Ordinary people are buried in the daytime, up to three in one grave, no sacrifice is performed at the burial, and the grave bears no particular marks. *Kujurs* are buried at night, always in a new grave, a bull is sacrificed, and a circle of stones placed on the grave.

The shaman's position in the community is defined more closely by the nature of his spiritual faculties. These may be grouped in two main categories: one concerns the irregular, contingent needs of individuals, such as illness or barrenness, the desire to capture the favors of a woman, to recover stolen property, and the like; the other concerns the needs of the community as such and events and activities framed in the institutions of the group—age-grades, circumcision, annual rituals, the control of rain, and the luck of war.

Shamans qualified to deal only with the first kind of contingency do not rank very high, although they may acquire fame and wealth—as did the epilepsy expert mentioned before. But their influence is only that of experts in a special field. They share this field, moreover, with the medicine men and women who practice their profession without (or essentially without) the intervention of spirits. The shamans whose faculties also

bear on the life and institutions of the community occupy a much higher position, and sometimes the highest position this society can offer. They become the leaders of the community in the widest sense. Not only are they appealed to regularly, on behalf of the whole community, but their guidance is also sought on matters not implicit in their spiritual vocation.

This leadership contains certain elements which are not otherwise represented in the Nyima social system. This is characterized by a rigid segmentation into clans, sub-clans and linked clans, all irregularly scattered over villages and hill communities. Human life almost in its totality is dominated by the principle of descent. Now, shamanism introduces into the lineage framework a different order of alignment. The spirit priest is the center of a new, more fluid grouping, which extends as far as does his reputation. This extent is localized, and coincides with the zone of community life. Shamanism thus provides a spiritual focus for a community otherwise rigidly divided along lines of descent.

In the case of war *kujurs* this focus is secular as well. In the past the Nyima were a most bellicose tribe, at war with many of the neighboring groups and also divided among themselves, hill community fighting hill community. The war *kujurs* would advise on blood feuds between clans and ordain the wars to be fought against other tribes. Equally, the war *kujurs* might recommend peace and reconciliation, and negotiate on behalf of the communities or kinship groups. The people maintain that no war *kujur* would ever sanction or lead wars between the Nyima communities; yet if the *kujurs* thus stood for tribal peace they did so only passively and in a platonic fashion. In the narrower group, and in the sphere of "offense and defense," the war shaman was the nearest approach to chieftainship under traditional conditions.

Even so, the shaman leadership did not make for real unity. The leadership was irregular, fluid, and often conflicting. One shaman, entrusted with the supervision of some ceremonial, would unite the community in one way and on certain occasions; the war shaman would unite it in a different way and for different purposes. The leadership of each would last only while he was alive or unrivaled by the priest of a stronger spirit. Rival war shamans and other *kujurs* frequently divided the people. The Nyima rebellion of 1918 collapsed so easily because a *kujur,* prophesying the downfall of its leader, caused a large section of the community to desert the cause. Even today, two rival war *kujurs* live side by side on Salara Hill, though their rivalry now has little practical effect.

Modern chieftainship is still based on the hill community, the tribe being constituted as a federation of semi-autonomous groups. Only few among the modern chiefs are men who had been *kujurs,* of war or peace, before Government was established. The majority were appointed on more rational grounds, for service in the army or police, or for administrative efficiency. But the old conception of spirit-inspired leadership has survived: among eighteen chiefs and headmen nine were shamans at the time of my visit.

SHAMANISM AND CULTURE CHANGE

There is, then, no dearth of spirits. On the contrary, rival spirits claim supremacy in the same field, and the various social institutions which need spirit intervention are hardly ever without suitable shamans. If at any time the appropriate spirit remains without incarnation, a spirit relative of kindred and adequate faculties is nearly always discovered. It is reasonable to assume that the pervasive knowledge of the necessities of social life causes the shamans-to-be to produce subconsciously the required manifestations.

But these need not be, and are not expected to be, uniform. New spirits, as we have seen, are also appearing, and the shamans who are their mouthpieces may modify a traditional task or offer a new one to the community.

The unpredictable leadership of spirit-inspired individuals would thus seem to facilitate culture change in all its forms. The shaman is, at least potentially, a social reformer who need fear no inertia, disbelief, or resentment on the part of the people, and whom no ordinary mortal can gainsay. I found, in fact, several instances of shamans upholding, in the name of their spirits, not tradition, but departure from it. I also found that one conspicuous recent aspect of culture change in the Nuba Mountains, Arab assimilation, was most strongly pronounced (under otherwise equal conditions) in the communities which have shamanism. But let me leave the question of a nexus between visionary cults and susceptibility to change at this tentative suggestion, and point instead to another fluid feature of Nyima shamanism.

Through the spirit-inspired innovations the group is constantly adjusting and enriching its supernatural mastery over the universe. This enrichment of the magic armory is, I believe, another subconscious motive behind the varying spirit manifestations. Nor is it a motive peculiar to Nyima shamanism; for similar motives are also visible in many other, differently organized, forms of primitive religion.

THE PLACE OF SHAMANISM IN NYIMA RELIGION

We have so far considered Nyima shamanism as a belief and practice isolated from the wider religious framework. It must now be shown, if only briefly, that such a framework exists; that it is not filled completely with shamanistic conceptions and usages; and that these have, as it were, their appointed place and function.

To some extent shamanistic and non-shamanistic beliefs and usages exist side by side, without closer integration. The *kuni* spirits, for example, are not the only immaterial entities discoverable in man. Like all animate beings man possesses a life principle, called dam, which resides somewhere in the body, weakens with illness, and disappears at death. Man (unlike animals) further possesses two souls, called *swe;* one is located in the left shoulder (and accounts for all that is evil in his nature), the other in the right shoulder (representing the good in human nature). Certain individuals have an unusually powerful *swe.* If it is evil, they are gifted with the evil eye and a mild form of witchcraft (*koro*); if the powerful *swe* is good, its owner becomes a great man or a tribal leader. The mythical culture heroes were such men of powerful souls, and the tribal rain maker is endowed with an immensely strong and good *swe* (though in his case it has a special name—*musluz*). When I see people in my dreams, it is their *swe* I see, just as my own *swe* visits people and places when I dream of them. At death, the *swe* returns to God, and is later reincarnated in other humans, not necessarily of the same family or clan.

Continued individual existence beyond death is made possible by a final attribute of man: the shadows of the living—*lu*—turn into the spirits of the dead—*geshin,* and these once more appear in dreams, roam about with no fixed abode, and may cause illness and misfortune among their kinsfolk if these neglect their duties towards the deceased. It is this action of the *geshin* which the shaman divines. But he is not otherwise involved in the service of the spirits of the dead, and in ordinary kinship ceremonials the ancestors are approached without his intervention. Numerous rituals, moreover, of the crisis-of-life type (birth, puberty, marriage, funerals) stand completely apart from shamanistic practice.

This side-by-side existence of shamanistic and nonshamanistic beliefs is blurred by certain inconsistencies in the beliefs and by the tendency (perhaps at the root of the inconsistencies) to let shamanism encroach upon the neighboring field. Thus in certain contexts the concepts *swe, geshin* and *kuni* appear to be interchangeable. If a shaman dreams of his father or grandfather, it may not be their *geshin* he sees but their *kuni.* The *swe* of the dead although it returns to God to be presently reincarnated at random, is also effective in a way which suggests that it exists as a loose, free element in the universe, much like *kuni* spirits awaiting reincarnation. For in all kinship rituals the *swe* of ancestors is invoked (although it might have found another, alien body), and is addressed, not only as *swe* but often as *kuni.* Most people maintain that the *swe* is different from the *kuni,* and that, in addressing ancestral spirits as *kuni,* one merely addresses any shamanistic spirit that might have been incarnated in previous generations. But there is no dogmatic certainty on this point. Opinion is even more sharply divided concerning the reincarnation of the culture heroes; according to some, their immensely powerful *swe* has reappeared as *kuni;* according to others, the men themselves—the owners of the *swe*—became spirits.

The encroachment of shamanistic ideas is most conspicuous in Nyima priestship. And here we also meet with a final, sharply defined relationship between shamanistic and nonshamanistic beliefs—the relationship of two principles opposed yet complementary. The Nyima have three kinds of priests: the shaman, who is fully a servant of spirits; the *medo eran* or Hill Priest, whose office illustrates the encroachment of shamanistic concepts; and the *shirra* or Rain Maker, whose office is nonshamanistic but in vital respects appears as the counterpart, or opposite pole, of shamanism.

The Hill Priest is conceived of as the guardian of the hill on which the community lives—the Hill being understood in a mystical, sacred sense. He officiates in the most important communal rites, which are concerned with the land, the seasons, and circumcision, that is, with the continuity (physical and social) of life on the Hill. The Hill Priests' office is hereditary, being transmitted from father to son. But, since the mythical founders of the Hill community and its rituals have become spirits, their reincarnation equally enters into the qualifications for this priesthood. Thus a few Hill Priests are both hereditary priests and shamans of these mythical spirits; others are only the former, though they possess, as it were incidentally, *kuni* spirits of some other kind. The mythical spirits or some of their relatives have also appeared in individuals other than the Hill Priests. Finally, "new" spirits now incarnated in shamans, while not mythically associated with the hill rituals, yet claim knowledge and control of these rites. This confused situation is resolved, in practice, through the co-operation and scrupulous division of labor between all the individuals who are so variously entitled to share in the spiritual custody of the Hill.

The priestship of the *shirra,* on the other hand, is free from all interference by spirits or spirit incarnations. The office is strictly hereditary, passing from father to son. It is, moreover, a tribal office, and, in fact, the only office, secular or sacred, which embraces the tribe as a whole. In translating *shirra* into Arabic, the people use the word *Sultan*—an apt translation, since this office has conspicuous aspects of paramount political leadership. The *shirra* lives, with his family, in a small hamlet in the valley, which belongs to none of the seven hill communities of Nyima—a kind of primitive Washington, D.C. It fell to the *shirra* to guide the whole tribe in war (while the *kujur* led only his community) or to establish peace between the whole of Nyima and other tribes. Like the *kujurs,* the *shirra* stood aloof from all internal warfare, neither sanctioning nor forbidding it; but he would also attempt to reconcile warring hill communities. The war *kujurs* would submit to the *shirra*'s orders and acknowledge his supremacy with a share in the booty made in their "private" wars. Any attempt to challenge the leadership of the *shirra* was short-lived; for he had the most powerful sanction at his command—the threat to stop the rain. He would use it, too, in the sphere of law, to break a blood feud which had lasted too long, or to enforce the punishment of a criminal by a reluctant clan or local community.

All this was in the past; today the *shirra* is only a rain priest. Here again, he wields greater power than the rain shamans or indeed any spirit priest. While they minister only to the needs of their communities, the *shirra* secures rain, health, and fertility for the whole tribe. The shamans officiate in special rituals, annual or contingent; the *shirra*'s office in a sense embraces all the permanent religious tasks, for every annual ritual celebrated in Nyima contains some expression of deference to the *shirra* and involves some offering to him and to the powers he serves. Nor is the *shirra* merely a shaman on a tribal scale; his is a different office entirely; he holds it, not by the favor of the spirits, but by the right of descent and as a gift from *abradi,* the Supreme Deity.

In comparing *shirra* and shaman we grasp a fundamental aspect of Nyima religion. The *shirra,* servant of a remote deity, personifies the supernatural in a remote and all-embracing sense, as something existing for the widest group and bearing upon the widest perspective of human life. The shaman, on the other hand, can deal with the needs of individuals and communities, and with the needs of the moment. If the former offers guidance of a general and often predestined order, the latter offers aid *ad hoc,* in everyday perplexities. There are rival shamans and spirits, but only one *shirra.* Spirits are capricious and unpredictable; there are good and evil ones, and their servants accordingly lead the community into actions which are good or evil. The *shirra* is by definition good; he serves a benevolent power; he stands for a moral order of things and for all that is certain in the universe.

I do not think that I have exaggerated the contrast or read into it a meaning it does not

have for the people. The relation between *shirra* and shaman reveals a dichotomy which underlies the whole edifice of Nyima religion—as it underlies all religious systems. The people, confused and vague about many aspects of the spirit beliefs, are clear as to this crucial relationship. The *shirra*'s soul, they say, has direct access to God (*abradi*); "God hears the *shirra*'s speech." And God is clearly conceived as the giver of rain, health, fertility, food—of the many good things in this world. The spirits, too, exist by the will of God; but there is no direct link between the two. The spirits cannot influence God, nor does their action express His influence, although some spirits are thought to have come from the sky and God. The spirits are intermediaries between man and supernatural forces which do not reflect an unambiguously ordered and moral universe. The good spirits divine such sources of human grief as the anger of the dead, and so affirm the moral obligations of the living; they combat the power of evil *swe,* or the action of the vague evil force summarized in the concept of *li.* The evil spirits add to the uncertainty of the universe. Their manifestations, as we have seen, may belie the moral principles of filial and parental duty. It is these evil spirits that cause shamans to lead the community to bloodshed and to be prompted by jealousy and envy of each other. Nor are the human servants free to reject their evil masters or to seek out benevolent ones. The spirits are not only unpredictable but, ultimately, beyond the Law. They stand for moral indeterminacy and an uncertain universe.

Here we return to the leitmotif of Nyima shamanism. It expresses a philosophy of life—a philosophy of uncertainty. That it is frightening is shown by the desire of the people to read into it the reassuring knowledge that the spirits are good, act according to moral standards, and that only man is vile. The spirit mythology would seem to leave no doubt as to the evil nature of certain spirits; the people also state in general terms that a shaman is good or evil according to the spirit that possesses him. Yet in spite of these beliefs the Nyima tend to place the blame for any evil resulting from the actions of a shaman upon the human vessel rather than the spirit. This contradiction is most clearly pronounced in the spirit-inspired ordeals and sanctions of crimes.

Any person who alleges he has suffered injury at the hand of another (be the culprit known or unknown) can appeal to a spirit for redress and vengeance. The shaman, in trance, will announce the punishment—illness or death, and unless the culprit repents and makes good his crime, the spirit curse will come true. This curse is thought to be effective only against persons really guilty of the alleged offense. Yet the Nyima also believe that the deadly services of certain spirits can be engaged against innocent people, and for no other reason than spite or revenge. And again, there will be an attempt to whitewash the spirit. The Nyima have a proverb, "the *kuni* does not kill without reason," and some reason, trifling and far-fetched though it might seem, will be adduced: the spirit may have resented another person being wealthier than its servant; or the spirit may have wished to punish the successful suitor of a girl who had jilted a clansfellow of the shaman, thus supporting, in partisan fashion, the social group of its human vessel. But some time, in some case, the contradiction between the doctrine and its exegesis will remain unresolved. Thus we know that spirits jealously watch over their servants' property and honor. This responsibility, however, is restrained by moral scruples; it is held that a really great spirit would not, for example, punish a thief who steals from hunger, or adultery of or with a shaman's wife: for, in the words of my informants, such spirits are "the fathers of all the people." But the same informants attributed the death by lightning of a famous *kujur*'s wife to her adultery and the consequent punishment by the spirit.

Much, then, in the confusion of the spirit beliefs expresses the desire to gloss over their moral indeterminacy and to overcome this frightening "philosophy of uncertainty." Yet though frightening, it is inescapable. It has its place in the universal scheme of creation as the Nyima see it. The spirits, like everything else, are created by God. But in creating the spirits, He created something that is exempt from the physical and moral order for which He stands. Now, all religion offers, in whatever disguise, the certainty of a physical and moral order; and all religion must offer, too, a loophole for all that conspicuously eludes or contradicts that order. This "loophole" takes many forms—witchcraft, the temptations of the devil, or the

curse of sins visited on children and children's children. The Nyima have no witchcraft in the full sense of the word, and no conception of a sin that cannot be diagnosed and rendered harmless by spirit guidance. Here shamanism absorbs all that is unpredictable and morally indeterminate: it saves the conception of an ordered universe from self-contradiction.

It is this dichotomy that I spoke of before as one underlying all religious systems. Its nature varies widely. Among the Nyima, the universal order belongs to the background of their philosophy of life: it is expressed in the simple conception of a Supreme Deity, and materializes in the one *shirra*. The foreground is filled with the array of shamanistic ideas and practices. They alone do justice to everyday happenings and to the lifelong problems of man, in which an unchanging law can only dimly be discerned.

THE PSYCHOLOGY OF SHAMANISM

I have left until the last the most difficult aspect of shamanism—its psychological (or psychopathological) implications. Picture a shamanistic trance. It may materialize anywhere and at any time. If it occurs by request, at a séance arranged for the benefit of clients, it usually takes place in the shaman's hut, in the presence of his attendants or relatives, whose duty it is to translate his sometimes indistinct or incoherent utterances to the audience. The clients sit opposite the shaman, as far away as possible.

The séance begins in silence, the shaman sitting with his eyes closed, at first not moving. Usually he has smoked heavily all day, which undoubtedly assists in provoking the attack. The first signs of the oncoming trance are rapid breathing, probably leading to superoxygenation, and attempts to twist his arms and neck into a cramped and unnatural position. Suddenly the shaman will jump up, yelling, and walking stiffly and rapidly up and down. The stiffness of all movements is one of the most striking characteristics; so is the cramped posture of the head, which is craned backwards or upwards, or bent downwards, throughout the trance. Some shamans turn and twist their heads all the time. The shaman will seize anything that stands near—a spear or doorpost—and hold on to it with utmost strength. If the spirit seizes the shaman, not in an arranged séance, but spontaneously, for example at a feast or ceremony, everything is more intense; the shaman would contort his face, twist his body, and act with violent and uncontrolled motions. Sometimes shamans appear to experience olfactory hallucinations or to suffer from difficulties of vision. One shaman whom I observed was sniffing and complaining of tobacco smoke, though no one present was smoking at the time; others were shading their eyes as though they could not see well. All these features are familiar from hysterical or epileptic attacks; I have not, however, seen any actual epileptic or cataleptic fit. Towards the end of the trance the shaman becomes quiet, sits down and seems to collapse. Finally, he stirs from his trance, looks around, lifts his arms, and clenches his hands above his head, cracking his fingers—which is the sign that the spirit has departed.

At some time during the trance the shaman begins to talk, a forced falsetto being often the accepted spirit voice. In arranged séances the flow of language is fairly even and easy to follow. There are a great many repetitions and some long pauses, but few interruptions by yells or incomprehensible language. In spirit possessions which come upon the shaman spontaneously the position is different; the shaman shouts, bellows, and babbles, often endlessly repeating the same word, and even experienced men may be unable to understand his utterances.

On the whole, relatively little in trance speech or behavior is conventionalized. There are, of course, the varying set models indicating particular hereditary spirits. But they are not binding; the frequent "discovery" of new spirits shows this clearly. "Models" in a more general sense are offered in every spirit possession; for, as will have been gathered, they are in no way secret or private affairs. They can be watched by everyone, children included, and this is especially true of the spontaneous trances which may occur at public gatherings and feasts. Thus all can learn what trances look like (or should look like) and all are exposed, from early youth, to their stimulation.

Are all these trances genuine? The answer is—no. I witnessed six trances in Nyima; two were quite clearly put on, involuntary glimpses at the audience (or me), or too well-controlled movements and speech

betraying the conscious management. Three were undoubtedly genuine attacks: when they were over, the shama was covered with perspiration and completely exhausted; his pulse was shallow and irregular; he was seized by violent hiccups, or broke into uncontrollable sobbing. I watched these "spirit possessions" happening in a crowd in the middle of a feast, when the attack of one shaman was followed by that of a second and third, in the familiar manner in which hysterical fits stimulate each other. And I also observed one séance which, starting as make-believe, ended as genuine seizure and dissociation; consciously planned at first, the aids of deep breathing, cramped posture, and violent motion gradually became effective, and brought on the full trance.

The people are well aware that spirit possession can be simulated. Usually, they maintain, this deception can easily be detected. But their criteria are not ours; to them, the proof lies in the vindication of the prophecies and guidance offered by the shaman. Moreover, their skepticism is probably awake only during the early manifestations; once the shaman's vocation is accepted, subsequent manifestations are no longer critically judged. At a séance which I attended and which I at once recognized to be a fake, the audience remained fully satisfied: it was enacted by a famous *kujur* whose genuine trances in the past obviously overshadowed this and similar routine exhibitions.

Since, then, many, perhaps the majority, of the shamanistic performances are genuine cases of hysterical dissociation; and since the cult of shamanism always finds a sufficient number of congenial personalities to continue as an institution, the question arises how far we must assume the existence of a specific psychological predisposition in the groups where this form of mental instability plays so prominent and socially attractive a part. The predominantly hereditary nature of Nyima spirit-possession clearly adds weight to the question.

The problem, needless to say, is beset with difficulties. Not the least is a technical one: for its examination hinges on a psychological or psychiatrical comparison of shamanistic and nonshamanistic groups of otherwise kindred cultures, and adequate data are simply not available. In the present case I was fortunate in being able to draw on information which I obtained from the resident medical mission in Nyima. But even so, I can offer only a tentative answer, or perhaps merely a pointer to where the answer may be found.

These are the facts such as I have been able to ascertain. Insanity seems to be rare in Nyima, but epilepsy is widespread, amounting perhaps to 1 in 100. Of the ten shamans whose life histories I collected, six had epilepsy in their family, and of the eight hereditary shamans only two claimed that none of their relations had been an epileptic. The people themselves emphasized the high incidence of epilepsy in the Nyima Hills. And here it is important to stress that neither epilepsy nor insanity, nor yet other minor mental derangements, are in themselves regarded as symptoms of spirit possession. They are diseases, abnormal disorders, not supernatural qualifications. No shaman is, in everyday life, an "abnormal" individual, a neurotic or a paranoiac; if he were, he would be classed as a lunatic, not respected as a priest. Nor finally can shamanism be correlated with incipient or latent abnormality; I recorded no case of a shaman whose professional hysteria deteriorated into serious mental disorders.

Certain anthropologists hold the view that shamanism and similar cults are designed to absorb abnormal personalities and to offer to these "deviants" from the norm a legitimate social "niche." Stated in this form, the theory is inapplicable to the society here discussed. Shamanism still leaves in existence, and without a social niche, the deviant and abnormal personality, though the borderline between normal and abnormal differs from that valid in nonshamanistic groups. But it remains an open question whether shamanism does not in a different sense "absorb" mental derangement; the institutionalized catharsis which it offers may well have the therapeutic effect of stabilizing hysteria and related psychoneuroses, thus reducing a psychopathic incidence which would otherwise be much larger.

The comparative data show that another shamanistic group in the Nuba Mountains (the Dilling tribe) has a relatively high incidence of insanity (perhaps 1 in 300) and no or little epilepsy; while a third shamanistic group (the Koalib) seems to have a much lower incidence of both insanity and epilepsy, which I estimated as between 1 in 500 and 1 in 1,000 respectively. In nonshamanistic Nuba groups I found the incidence of serious mental derangements to be both lower and higher; emotional instability in a wider sense, as it is visible in the general behavior of individuals, is again both more and less marked in nonshamanistic groups as compared with the Nyima.

Shamanism, then, neither absorbs mental abnormality at large nor rests on uncommonly widespread psychopathic predispositions; it certainly cannot be explained merely as a cultural mechanism designed either to achieve the former or to exploit the latter. But it is possible that shamanism both exploits *and* canalizes neurotic predispositions, so that they remain relatively stable and confined within one sphere. And it is equally possible that shamanism operates, above all, as a suggestive "model" for behavior, provoking its congenial personality from "neutral" human material, that is, from a group with a normal incidence of hysteria and related disorders.

The answer to our question is thus inconclusive. But perhaps the ambiguous issue of psychological cause and cultural effect ought not to have been raised at all? Elusive though the problem is, it cannot be left aside entirely. For it confronts us today in conspicuous form. Without doubt, shamanism is on the increase; spirit manifestations have become more numerous; and the cult is also spreading under our eyes from traditionally shamanistic to nonshamanistic groups.

This process to some extent merely expresses the tendency inherent in shamanism, to enrich the spiritual armory of the group: this is being enriched, logically, in the face of rapid and radical extraneous change, of new perplexities and new conflicts which the group must overcome. Understood in this sense, the culture change must have the effect of enlarging the clientele of shamans and multiplying the occasions which require shaman intervention. But the same impact would also be responsible for an increase in shamanistic manifestations. For the enforced change must be psychologically unsettling; among the Nyima as among all primitive communities, it must create and foster emotional instability, neurotic and hysterical leanings, that is, the constitutional qualifications of shamanism. This twofold effect was strikingly visible among the Nyima soldiers, before and during the [Second World] War: repeatedly, on critical occasions, they would ask for leave to consult a shaman at home; and in camps and barracks shamanism was rife.

How far do these facts help us to reduce the ambiguity of the conclusions previously arrived at? The equation now discovered, greater nervous instability—spreading of shamanism, seems to weigh the scales in favor of the hypothesis that shamanism exploits and at the same time canalizes existing neurotic leanings and relieves mental stresses. The human material which demonstrates the increase in hysterical dissociation is no longer "neutral"; the congenital mentality is not, today, provoked merely by the model of shamanism. Yet the existence of the model

remains an irreducible fact which we must take for granted. Without it, the mental stresses might find different paths for their expression. These paths are familiar in many societies: they are manifest in the spread of belief in witchcraft and evil magic; and in hysteria and psychoses undisguised and unfettered. Thus the hypothesis I suggest is verifiable—though I cannot myself verify it. For if it is true, it must be possible to show that psychoses and kindred disorders are increasing among the nonshamanistic groups, while in the shamanistic groups the increase of shamanism would go hand in hand with a relatively undisturbed mental stability.

BERNARDINO DE SAHAGÚN

Aztec Sacrifice

Bernardino de Sahagún was probably the first "ethnologist" to interview and record the customs and way of life of the American Indians. He was a Franciscan friar who arrived in Tenochtitlan (Mexico City) in 1529, shortly after the Conquest, and after some years of experience as a missionary he began to devote himself to the compilation of data on Aztec culture. Sahagún's method was to systematically question small-town native Aztecs, who knew no Spanish, about their customs. The answers were provided by hieroglyphic paintings, which were later submitted to other natives who had been educated in Mexico City and who provided a written translation in the Nahuatl language spoken by the Aztecs. These data were cross-checked in other areas of Mexico, and then finally combined by Sahagún into a Nahuatl version of his *General History of the Things of New Spain.* Sahagún later added a Spanish translation of the Aztec texts, and the manuscript was sent off to Madrid, where it disappeared. In the nineteenth century it was finally recovered and in 1829–1830 editions were published for the first time, nearly three centuries after the data were collected.

Anderson and Dibble have recently undertaken the translation of the Aztec texts directly into English in their monumental *Florentine Codex: General History of the Things of New Spain* (13 volumes). The following selection from Book II, *The Ceremonies,* provides a classic description of Aztec sacrificial ritual as exemplified by the great feast of Tezcatlipoca.

The Aztecs believed in a great pantheon of gods and had an elaborate ceremonial calendar which scheduled and regulated the ceremonies performed for these gods. It was thought that men depended upon the gods for their continuing existence; the gods, in turn, depended upon offerings from men for continuing welfare. The most precious offerings, and hence the most effective in sus-

Reprinted from *The Florentine Codex,* Book II, *The Ceremonies,* trans. A. J. O. Anderson and C. H. Dibble ("Monographs of the School of American Research," No. 14, Part III [Santa Fe, N.M.: Museum of New Mexico, 1951]), pp. 64–68, by permission of the translators and the Museum of New Mexico.

taining the gods, were the human hearts offered up during the year. Tezcatlipoca was one of the principal gods in the pantheon and consequently enjoyed one of the most elaborate ceremonies, as described below.

It should also be noted that among the Aztecs, priests were the important religious practitioners; shamanistic manifestations were reduced to a minimum. Further information on the religion of the Aztecs may be found in George C. Vaillant, *Aztecs of Mexico* (1941), and Alfonso Caso, *El Pueblo del Sol* (1953).

Sixth [Twenty-fourth] Chapter, which relateth the feast and blood sacrifices made during all the days in the fifth month, which was called Toxcatl.

In [the month of] Toxcatl, the great feast of Tezcatlipoca was [held]. At that time he was formed and set up. Wherefore died his impersonator, who for one year had lived [as Tezcatlipoca].

And at that time once more was offered [to the people] his [new] impersonator, who would again live for one year.

For many impersonators [thus] lived, whom guardians kept and maintained. Perchance there were ten. These were select captives, chosen when captives were taken. Then was one chosen if he was good to look upon and fair of body. Then such were taken, and the guardians cared for them. But one whom they destined to be a slave, the captor slew.

For he who was chosen was of fair countenance, of good understanding and quick, of clean body—slender like a reed; long and thin like a stout cane; well-built; not of overfed body, not corpulent, and neither very small nor exceedingly tall.

For anyone who was formed [thus] defective, who was too tall, to him the women said: "Tall one; head-nodder; handful of stars!" He who was chosen impersonator was without defects.

[He was] like something smoothed, like a tomato, or like a pebble, as if hewn of wood. [He did] not [have] curly hair, [but] straight, long hair; [he had] no scabs, pustules, or boils on the forehead, nor skin growths on the forehead, nor [was he] large-headed, nor with the back of the head prominent; nor of a head shaped like a carrying-net, nor with the sutures of the crown yet soft; not broad-headed, nor with a square head; not bald, nor with a bulbous forehead; not of swollen eyelids, nor enlarged ones; not with swollen cheeks; not of disfigured eyes or cheeks, nor with swollen face; not with cleft chin; not with a gross face, nor a downcast one; not flat-nosed nor with wide nostrils, nor with an arched, Roman nose nor a bulbous nose, nor bent nor twisted nor crooked—but his nose should be well-placed, straight; not thick-lipped nor gross- nor big-lipped, nor with bowl-like ones, nor enlarged; neither one who stammered, nor [one who talked] as if his tongue were pierced for a ring; nor one with welts on his tongue; nor one who spoke a barbarous language, or spoke thickly, or lisped, or was dumb; nor buck-toothed, nor large-toothed or fang-toothed, nor of yellowed teeth, nor darkened, nor decayed—but his teeth were like seashells, well arrayed in order; his teeth were not shaped like bowls. Neither had he scarred eyes, nor poor vision, nor squinting eyes, nor scarified; not blinded, nor of small, seedlike eyes, nor angry-eyed, nor sunken, nor hollow, nor cuplike, nor stupid-looking, nor gouged, pierced, or wounded; nor had he a scarred neck, [like one which hath been] choked, nor one with lacerations, nor with double chin, nor with pocks on the neck. Not with protruding or long ears, nor with torpid neck, nor hunch-backed, nor stiff-necked, nor with neck elongated, much elongated, nor twisted, nor kinked; neither with unduly long hands, nor lacking one hand, nor wanting both hands, nor fat-fingered; not emaciated, nor fat, nor big-bellied, nor of prominent, hatchet-shaped navel, nor of wrinkled stomach, nor shrunken stomach; not cringing; not of hatchet-shaped buttocks; nor of flabby buttocks or thighs.

He who was thus, without flaw, who had no [bodily] defects, who had no blemishes, nor moles, who had no lacerations or wrinkles on his body, they then looked well that he be taught to blow the flute; that he might pipe and play his flute well; and that with it he hold his flowers and his smoking tube and blow and suck upon it, and smell [the flowers].

Thus he went bearing [his flute], his flowers, and his smoking tube together as he walked through the streets.

And while yet he lived and was cared for in the house of the guardian, before he appeared [before the people], care was taken that he might be prudent in his discourse, that he might talk graciously, converse well, and greet people agreeably on the road, if he met anyone.

For he was much honored when he appeared as the impersonator; because he was the likeness of Titlacauan; he was acknowledged as our lord, treated like a lord, one begged favors, with sighs; before him the common people bowed in reverence and kissed the earth.

And if they noted that his body became even a little fat, they made him drink brine, so that he became thin; the salt water thinned him, so that he became lean; he became hard; his flesh became firm.

And for one year he [thus] lived; at [the feast of] Toxcatl, he appeared [before the people.] And when the man died who had been the impersonator for one year, he who had led the way, he who had cast [the spear] for one year, who had given commands for one year, forthwith was one chosen to be set in his place, from all whom the temple guardians had saved and cared for at the time that [the captives] appeared [before them.]

Thereupon he began his office; he went about playing his flute. By day and by night he followed whatever way he wished.

His eight young men went following him. Four [of them] had fasted for a year; their hair was shorn like [the hair] of slaves, cut and clipped, not smooth like a gourd, nor cut [too] short, not [made like] growing whiskers on the head.

And four warriors, who instructed youths in the art of war, [were] similarly shorn. Their hairdress lay upright on their foreheads.

Then Moctezuma adorned [the impersonator] well and arrayed him in varied garb; he provided him [his appropriate indumentary]. He ornamented him, he adorned him in great pomp with all costly articles, which he caused to be placed upon him; for verily he took him to be his beloved god. His face was anointed with black; it was said: "He fasteth with blackened face." A thick layer of black was smeared on his cheeks. White feathers were placed upon his head—the soft down of eagles. They placed it on his hair, which fell to his loins.

And when he was attired, he went about with sweet-smelling flowers upon his head, a crown of flowers. And these same were hung over both shoulders, as far down as his armpits. This was called "the flowery garment."

And from both ears hung curved, gold, shell pendants. And they fitted [his ears] with ear plugs made of a mosaic of turquoise. And [he wore] a shell necklace. Moreover, his breast ornament was of white sea shells.

And then his lip plug was a slender snail shell lip plug. And hanging from his shoulders was what was like a cord bag called *icpatoxin*.

Then they placed golden bracelets on both upper arms, and on both wrists they put carved bracelets with precious stones, covering almost all the forearm. And he put on his net cape like a fish-net of wide mesh with a fringe of brown cotton thread. And his costly breech clout reached to the calves of his legs.

And then they placed his bells on both legs, all golden bells, called *oioalli*. These, as he ran, went jingling and ringing. Thus they resounded. And he had princely sandals with ocelot-skin ears. Thus was arrayed he who died after one year.

When [the feast] of Toxcatl was drawing near, when it was approaching him, when it was coming to him, first they married him to [four] women whom they sought out [for him]. He was married in [the month of] Uey toçoztli.

And he left off, scattered in various places, and abandoned the ornaments he had had, in which he had walked about fasting, painted black. His hair was shorn; he was given a tuft of hair tied upon his forehead, like that of a war captain. Thus they bound [his hair], knotting it [with brown cotton thread] called *tochiacatl;* and they tied to his long hair his forked heron-feather ornament with single quetzal feathers attached.

Only twenty days he lived, lying with and married to the women. Four women he lived with, who also were cared for, for one year, in the guardian's house.

The first one was named Xochiquetzal; the second, Xilonen; the third, Atlatonan; the fourth, Uixtociuatl.

And still on the eve of [the feast of] Toxcatl, still five days from it, on the fifth day
[before it], when in five days the feast day
of Toxcatl would come, then they began to
sing [and dance].

Now, during this time, Moctezuma came
not forth; those who had been [the impersonator's] companions provided the people
with food and favors.

On the first day they sang [and danced]
at a place called Tecanman. On the second
day, in the place where they kept the image
of Titlacauan, in the house of the keeper
who guarded it. On the third day, at Tepetzinco, in the midst of the lagoon. On the
fourth [day], at Tepepulco, which is also
near Tepetzinco.

After they had sung [and danced], then
he embarked in a canoe. The women went
traveling with him; they went consoling him
and keeping him merry. Then the canoe arrived; then it touched the shore; then it was
beached at a place called Acaquilpan or
Caualtepec.

For here he was abandoned, a little [dis-
tance] from Tlapitzauhcan. The women
then returned; and only they who had freely
become his pages accompanied him while he
yet lived.

So, it was said, when he arrived where he
was to die, [where] a small temple stood,
called Tlacochcalco, he ascended by himself,
of his free will, to the place where he was to
die. When he climbed the first step, as he
passed one [step], he there broke, shattered,
his flute, his whistle, etc.

And when he had mounted all the steps,
when he had reached the summit, then the
priests fell upon him; they threw him on his
back upon the sacrificial stone. Then [one]
cut open his breast, seized his heart, and
raised it as an offering to the sun.

For in this manner were all [these] captives offered up. But his body they did not
roll down; rather, they lowered it. Four men
carried it.

And his severed head they strung on the
skull-rack. Thus he ended in the adornment
in which he died. Thus he there ended his
life, there he terminated his life, when he
went to die there at Tlapitzauaian.

And this betokeneth our life on earth. For
he who rejoiceth, who possesseth riches, who
seeketh and coveteth our lord's sweetness,
his gentleness—riches and prosperity—thus
endeth in great misery. For it is said: "None
come to an end here upon earth with happiness, riches, and wealth."

J. ERIC S. THOMPSON

A Maya
Priest in
Action

This delightfully written selection from the pen of J. Eric
Thompson represents an interesting departure from the usual
ethnographic reconstruction. It is a fictitious sketch with the actions largely derived from actual information we possess on Maya
life but with some incidents drawn from Aztec or other Mexican
sources whose religious ideas were close to those of the Maya.
Thompson writes in the "Preamble" to his sketches, "In this
chapter I have brought together a series of miniatures of Maya
life, each in a fictional setting, in an effort to give quickening
color to the dead past. I submitted one of these sketches to a well-
known anthropologist, who was inexpressibly shocked at the
mingling of fiction with science; the deep impress of the typed
words on the sheet of paper showed how upset he was that science should be draped in such intangibles as thought processes
not susceptible to tabulation or graphing. If I shared his belief
that archaeology is a science, I might feel a trifle uneasy, but,

Reprinted from J. Eric S. Thompson, *The Rise and Fall of Maya
Civilization* ("The Civilization of the American Indian Series," Vol.
XXXIX [Norman, Okla.: University of Oklahoma Press, 1954]), pp.
189–197. Copyright 1954, University of Oklahoma Press. Used by
permission.

regarding archaeology as a backward projection of history, I see no reason why such reconstructions should not be used" (*The Rise and Fall of Maya Civilization*, p. 188). The editors agree with Thompson and feel that, taken for what it is, the sketch does indeed give quickening color to the dead past.

The Mayas lived in what is now Guatemala and the Mexican state of Yucatán; their culture was similar to that of the Aztecs on the high central plateau of Mexico.

Young Balam ached all over. His tongue was swollen; the lobes of his ears, his arms, and other parts of his body were tender from drawing blood from them continuously. Also he was hungry and worn from lack of sleep. For eighty days, from 13 Xul, all through the months Yaxkin, Mol, Ch'en, and over half of Yax, he had fasted, tended the temple, kept vigils, and made sacrifices of his own blood. In another three or four hours all this would be ended, for by then he and everyone else in the world would have been destroyed, or he would be sitting down to a feast, the anticipation of which kept coming to him when his thoughts should have been on more serious matters. Still, it was difficult not to look forward to turkey and venison stewed with sweet potatoes, when for so long one had eaten nothing but very skimpy tortillas, and drunk only weak corn gruel.

It was now about three hours before sunset of the day 4 Ahau 13 Yax. The fifteenth katun (twenty-year period) of Cycle 10 (9.15.0.0.0, 4 Ahau 13 Yax) would end at sunset. This was three-quarters of the way through Cycle 10 (we speak of this as Cycle 9, but to the Maya it was Cycle 10), and the day was the lucky 4 Ahau. That alone was of good augury, but Yax was the month of the planet of Venus, and that baleful god would be visible at sunset, blazing high in the evening sky. In another four months he would be lost in the sun's rays before reappearing as morning star. Everyone knew that the world would be destroyed at the end of a katun; the real question was whether this particular one was the appointed one; favorable and unfavorable factors seemed about equally balanced. Extra care in the performance of every bit of the ritual might save the day.

The first of the big ceremonies was about to start. Today, as on every day 4 Ahau, the fire-walking ceremony was to be held, and, in addition, persons were to be sacrificed to the god Venus, since he was the patron of this month in which the katun closed. Balam should get a ringside seat at these ceremonies since he was to be the front legs and head of the sky monster of the east.

From the building where they were living during this period of fasting and preparation, he and his fellow novitiates had seen fire set to the great pile of wood stacked in the court before the temple of the rain gods, and the heat from the blaze had been terrific. Now the attendants had just finished spreading the glowing embers with long poles of green wood to form a field of fire. Inside the temple, the four priests who were to walk the fire had completed their prayers and offerings of copal incense and *balche* (a mead drink). As Balam and his friends watched, they came out one behind the other, stooping as they emerged so that their high masks and headdresses would not catch against the lintel of the doorway. Slowly they descended the steep stairway.

At the head of the little procession came the high priest, dressed in red as the red rain god of the east, but with his headdress, enshrining the long-nosed mask of the rain god Chac, bedecked with a mass of quetzal plumage, green to represent the greenness of young corn and the new leaves on the trees, verdure which the rains would bring. Behind him in order followed the Chacs of the north, west, and south, all wearing similar headdresses, but dressed respectively in white, black, and yellow. Each carried in his right hand an axe with stone blade set in a wooden haft, the end of which curled up to form a snake's head. Each had in the left hand a zigzag stick symbolizing the lightning, and, slung from one shoulder, a calabash of water, from which the rain gods sprinkle the rain.

At the edge of the field of glowing embers, the little party halted, and sandals were removed. The high priest took a bowl of burning copal and a gourd of *balche* from an attendant, and turning to the east, offered both to the red Chac. Then picking up an aspergillum formed of the rattles of rattlesnakes, he started without hesitation to walk across the carpet of live coals, dipping the aspergillum in the bowl of *balche,* and sprinkling the embers with it as he advanced. Reaching the far side, he paused a moment and then started on the return journey. Safely back at the starting point and seemingly unharmed by the fire, he offered copal and *balche* once more to the east, and then drank the *balche* remaining in the gourd.

In turn the impersonators of the white, black, and yellow Chacs went through the same procedure. Balam watched the performance of the white Chac with particular attention. This priest was unpopular with the young men training for holy orders, and Balam found himself half wishing that he would slip and get badly burned. He put the idea away, for it was not seemly that such thoughts should occupy one's attention on such a solemn occasion, and such a misadventure would mean the failure of the ceremony, with the consequence that the dissatisfied gods would deny the people rain.

Balam could not wait to see the conclusion of the ceremony, for he had to make ready for his part in the ritual to mark the end of the katun. Inside the hut the four great frames of wood, covered with bark cloth and bedecked with plumage to represent the sky monsters, had been placed ready to mount. Balam moved to the red one, which he and his friend Tutz were to wear. He put his feet in the forelegs of the monster and thrust his head through the throat and into the open jaws, taking care not to scratch himself against the huge fangs. Tutz did the same for the rear part of the monster. Poles resting on the shoulders of the young men held rigid between them the creature's long body.

The master of ceremonial paraphernalia inspected the two youths and, satisfied, placed masks on both of them. That of Balam had slits for his eyes so that he could see where he was going; Tutz was not so lucky. His mask was put on front to back, for it must appear as emerging from the rear end of the monster, whereas Tutz faced faced front, and eyepieces would have been useless to him. They would only have given him a close-up of the monster's rear throat.

At a signal from the master of the paraphernalia, the four pairs of young men lined up in single file, Balam and Tutz with their red monster of the east heading the line. Their movements had been rehearsed sev-

eral times, and Balam knew exactly what to do when the order to start was given.

The four monsters emerged one after the other from the hut, and, crossing the court down a corridor kept clear of squatting onlookers, they passed slowly up the great stairway of the pyramid of the Temple of Venus. At every few paces the bearers made short barking noises to represent the alligator's call. Arriving at the platform before the temple on the summit, Balam and Tutz wheeled to the east, and the other monsters placed themselves on the north, west, and south sides of the open spaces. As they faced in, Balam had a splendid view of the proceedings; Tutz, of course, was unable to see anything, and soon began to find the weight of the frame on his shoulders and the heavy mask on his head irksome.

The high priest and his three assistants had doffed their costumes of rain gods and now were inside the Temple of Venus, praying to him to spare the world from destruction. Attendants led up the stairway five young men who were to be sacrificed on the stone block standing before the temple. The victims appeared resigned; they had been given quantities of *balche* to purify them, and, incidentally, to give them courage. Furthermore, they firmly believed that they would be united with the gods to whom they were about to take the messages of the people.

Balam gazed at them curiously. Three of them did not have Maya features and were probably Olmec or Zoque slaves purchased some time ago from merchants from the Gulf of Mexico. Balam knew the fourth, a young man who had grown up as a slave in his father's household, a rather stupid youth who had been the butt of many a practical joke. There had been no need to convince him that his sacrifice was for his own glory; his simple faith had required no strengthening, and he seemed to anticipate with a subdued zeal his coming honor. The occasion had given him a dignity he had never before enjoyed. Terror was in the dark eyes of the fifth victim, a sculptor who was to pay with his life for a mistake he had made in copying the work sheets for the glyphs on the stela about to be dedicated.

As the priests issued from the temple at the conclusion of their prayers, attendants brought forward one of the foreigners and placed him on the sacrificial stone. Two junior priests, called "Chacs," held his feet; two, his hands. Assistant priests held smoking copal censers and sprinkled *balche* as the high priest, with the long flint knife in his hand—"the hand of God," the Maya called it—advanced toward the victim, for in a ceremony of such importance only he could perform the sacrifice. Balam felt himself swept by a wave of emotion, in which impulses of elation, pity, and sadism were strangely mingled. The Olmec, his arms and legs curving down from the small of his back resting on the sacrificial stone, was between Balam and the sun, now low in the afternoon sky. His shadow on the stuccoed floor lay like the arc of a grotesque bow at Balam's feet.

The high priest, bending over the victim, struck a savage blow at the base of the left ribs. At the moment of impact the body gave a last convulsive jerk. The high priest wrenched out the heart and raised it above his head, facing toward the setting sun. His clothing was stained deep red and more blood had spattered his face. A second time the heart was raised to the west, the direction of the god Venus, who would soon be visible if the world were to be spared. A great shout arose from the congregation squatting in the court below as the priest walked to the edge of the platform, showing the heart to those assembled there.

The body was placed to one side as the second victim was brought forward and similarly dispatched, and then the third. The former slave of Balam's father was the fourth victim. Balam felt a certain shame that this simple, harmless youth should die. It was considered an honor to contribute a victim, but it would have been easier to bear had the man been sullen or had he shown bravado; this eager faith was upsetting. Balam averted his gaze, watching instead two flies that hovered around the gaping wound in the stomach of one dead man. He did not look to his front again until the shout of the crowd told him all was over.

The fifth man, who had revealed terror, struggled as he was brought forward, and had to be dragged to the block. Even after he had been thrown on it, and was tightly grasped in the requisite position, he continued to try to free himself. Balam frowned beneath his mask. Such conduct was unseemly, and by such ignominy the man was disregarding the welfare of the whole community, for such a spectacle must be offensive to the god Venus. The man had already jeopardized the well-being of all by his careless carving of an error on the stela. Now he was once again upsetting the rhythm of the ritual. His struggles soon ended, however, and his body was placed beside those already sacrificed. The whole ceremony had taken but a few minutes.

Balam and Tutz moved forward to take their place in the procession. At the head walked the high priest and his three assistants. Behind came five more priests wearing masks of the Venus god, each carrying a bowl in which reposed one of the hearts of the sacrificial victims. The four sky monsters swung in behind them and were, in turn, followed by other priests with smoking censers of copal; junior priests and attendants, carrying offerings to be dedicated to the new stela, brought up the rear.

The procession passed down the stairway of the pyramid, across the court of the Venus Temple, passed the end of the ball court, and so into the great ceremonial court. A halt was made in front of the newly erected stela, which stood on the east side of the court. Because of its width, the court was still lighted by the rays of the setting sun. The blues, reds, yellows, and greens of the freshly applied stucco glowed in the soft light. At the foot of the monument a large hole, reaching to level with the base of the butt, stood ready to receive the offerings, stout transversal poles against the butt holding the mass of carved stone in position.

Balam and Tutz had to mount several steps of the pyramid, against the base of which the stela was set, in order to occupy their position to the east of the ceremony and still be visible. Thus overlooking the stela, Balam again had a full view of the proceedings. He was relieved that Tutz and he had made the difficult trip down and up the steep steps without mishap; it had taken many rehearsals to co-ordinate their movements. As soon as all were in their assigned positions, the priests, junior priests, attendants, and all the spectators gathered in the great court and squatted on their haunches. From bags they drew sharp points of obsidian and bundles of sticks all cut to the same size. The drums set at each corner of the great court were thudding to a slow rhythm. Gradually the tempo increased until the beats cascaded in the same sequence with great rapidity. Balam's pulse quickened to the pounding measure; he wanted to shout and dance. It was almost unbearable to have to stand motionless. Now the trumpets and rattles and conch shells were sounding and antlers were beating on turtle carapaces.

The high priest raised his hand as a signal to the assembly, and then, lowering it, plunged an obsidian point in quick succession into his tongue, the lobes of his ears, and the fleshy parts of his arms and legs. Every man, for there were no women present, did the same save the eight novices inside the sky monsters. Then the sticks were passed through the gashes.

The high priests and his attendants advanced in turn to the pit in front of the stela, and cast in the blood-smeared sticks and pieces of bark cloth on which the blood had dripped; the ordinary people arranged their bloody sticks on the ground before them. The music had slowed and died. The lower part of the stela was now in shadow.

In turn, the five impersonators of the Venus god approached, holding the bowls with the hearts in them. The high priest took a heart from each in order. He smeared the first over the face of the god carved on the front of the stela and then dropped it in the center of the pit before the stela. The corners of the stela were rubbed in turn with the remaining four hearts, which were immediately dropped in the hole, one at each corner. As the high priest performed these acts, the assistants and junior priests squatted behind lines of braziers, from which rolls of smoke rose and, carried by the breath of evening wind, wreathed the stela. More attendants advanced carrying bundles of quetzal feathers, carved jades, finely worked flints, *balche,* food, and cacao beans. The high priest raised each offering in turn to the west and next to the stela, and then cast it into the pit.

When all the offerings had been deposited in the pit, attendants scooped earth into the cavity, and as soon as it had been tamped down, masons hurriedly laid a floor over it.

By then the sun was on the point of setting, and as it sank below the horizon, Balam could see the dim light of the god Venus growing brighter each minute; the world had been given respite from destruc-tion for another twenty years. The day 5 Imix had started. He raised a hand and quietly jerked the pole resting on his right shoulder, the signal he had agreed to give Tutz if Venus was visible.

At a sign from the high priest, the drums began to beat a triumphant fast measure. The flutes joined in. Priests lighted a fire, and into it the men threw their bloodstained sticks and offerings of copal. Young men from the college hastily lighted pine torches in the blaze and ran with them to all the pyramids in the ceremonial center. Soon the court was ablaze with fires burning before every temple and stela. Other fires illumined the ball court and the market place; on the outskirts lights began to twinkle in the houses of the theocrats.

The assembly was beginning to disperse. The four sky monsters wended their way back to the storeroom of the masks. When the cumbrous masks and serpent bodies had been doffed, Balam's empty stomach reminded him of the feast that was to follow. Everyone was in a happy mood. The eighty days of tension were over, the ceremonies in which they had participated had been crowned with success, and the day 5 Imix had started without any untoward occurrence. Balam had completely forgotten his father's slave, whose heart now was buried at the base of the stela.

Tutz, who was barely seventeen, started some horseplay, catching the end of his partner's loincloth and twisting it around his leg in an effort to trip him. The keeper of the paraphernalia chided him half jokingly, to which Tutz replied that he was hardhearted, "with a face like a tree trunk," as the Maya saying goes. All laughed, for the master of the paraphernalia was known to everyone as one of the kindliest of men.

When the two friends left the building, it was completely dark, and many of the fires had died down. They walked to the edge of the ceremonial center, entering the residential quarter of the nobility. Frogs were croaking their monotonous chorus; drooping leaves of cohune palms were silhouetted against a sky silvered by a moon ten days old. Passing one house, the boys' nostrils caught the odor of turkey stewing in chili sauce. They quickened their pace.

CHAPTER 11

DYNAMICS IN RELIGION

🐜🐜🐜🐜

INTRODUCTION

Like other aspects of culture, religious systems are in constant process of alteration, either in response to internal pressures within the social system, to environmental changes, or to the impact of acculturation. Anthropologists have especially recently stressed the problems of change, in part because they wished to correct the common misconception that primitive religion does not undergo modification, in part because changes in the religious sphere have given us some of our most important data and insights on the general processes of culture change. The following selections focus upon these dynamic aspects of religion.

First there are provided two selections that illustrate processes of growth and development of religious practices. The Frankforts show how variations in the Near East religions may be related to natural environmental differences; Schauss discribes how the Jewish Pesach, or Passover, changed in response to the changing circumstances of Jewish life over the centuries.

A series of papers on "nativistic movements" has been included to show how these movements develop in response to stresses set up by the impact of Western culture upon non-Western cultures. Ralph Linton's paper is a classic attempt to define the essence of the phenomena and to provide a workable typology of the movements. The Barber, Hill, and Slotkin selections deal

with problems connected with the Ghost Dance and the Peyote Cult, which are two of the most important movements of the nativistic type among North American Indians. Belshaw's contribution takes us to another part of the world and provides materials on similar cults that have developed in Melanesia. The Cargo cults are still active in New Guinea and are continuing to be studied by anthropologists at the present time.

The term "nativistic" has become increasingly inadequate as a discriminating label for the various kinds of cult movements alluded to above. Currently, much stress is being placed on the notion of millenarism, a phenomenon dealt with in terms of social change by Yonia Talmon in her "Pursuit of the Millennium." The article following hers, "A Note on Relative Deprivation Theory" by David Aberle, goes a long way towards providing a unifying theme.

The next selection, from the works of Herskovits on the Negro in the New World, adds another important dimension in the acculturation process—the syncretism that occurs between the old and the new cultural forms in culture-contact situations. This process is common in the religious systems of primitive peoples, who often eagerly accept alien beliefs and practices so long as they feel they can benefit by them. This contrasts sharply with the point of view of the great world religions, which tend to be intolerant of other systems and to resist syncretism, although it usually occurs surreptitiously.

The final selection, "Ritual and Social Change: A Javánese Example," by Clifford Geertz, could have been placed in the section dealing with death and ghosts but has been included here because its real stress is on change in religion, especially the changes generated by internal pressures due to incongruities between the social and cultural dimensions of a society.

H. AND H. A. FRANKFORT

Interrelationships Between Religion and Nature in the Ancient Near East

This masterful selection from the Frankforts characterizes in bold and sweeping strokes the similarities and differences in world view among the religions of ancient man in the Near East—Egyptians, Mesopotamians, and Hebrews—and then sketches in some detail the possible interrelationships between the natural environments and the differences in religious conceptions.

The Egyptians and Mesopotamians, living agricultural lives in small urban centers, agreed in the fundamental assumptions that the individual is part of society, that society is imbedded in nature, and that nature is but the manifestation of the divine. There were, however, far-reaching differences between them in world view. The Egyptians believed that the gods were powerful without being violent, that nature was an established order, that the divine Pharaoh occupying the throne ensured a harmonious integration between nature and society at all times—all features which possibly related to the regular natural rhythms along the Nile. But in Mesopotamia the assembly of gods assigned a mere mortal to rule men, and the divine favor might at any time be withdrawn from him. Man was more at the mercy of decisions he could neither influence nor gauge. Hence the king and his counselors watched for portents on earth and in the sky that might reveal changes in divine grace, so that catastrophe might be foreseen and possibly averted—features which appear to have been related to the more irregular natural setting in Mesopotamia. Nevertheless, both peoples comprehended the divine as immanent; the gods were in nature. And man and society were intimately connected with nature.

The Hebrew world view was very different. The dominant tenet was the absolute transcendence of God. Yahweh was not in nature, but was pure being, unqualified and ineffable. Not cosmic phenomena but history itself had here become pregnant with meaning; history became a revelation of the dynamic will of God. The human being was not merely the servant of the god as he was in Mesopotamia; nor was he placed, as in Egypt, at a preordained station in a static universe. Man, according to Hebrew thought, was the interpreter and the servant of God; he was even honored with the task of bringing about the realization of God's will. The Frankforts suggest that this world view arises from the fact that the Hebrews were tribal nomads, living not in boundless steppes but between the agricultural valleys and desert, between the most fertile of lands and the total negation of life. They suggest that nomadic freedom can be bought only at a price. For whoever rejects the complexities and mutual dependencies of agricultural society not only gains freedom but also loses the bond with the natural phenomenal world; in fact, he gains his freedom at the cost of significant form.

The Frankforts are careful to point out that they are not advancing an "unwarranted naturalism" and claiming that cultural phenomena can be derived from physiographical causes; they are merely suggesting that a relation between land and culture may exist. The hypothesis is an interesting one that needs further exploration in the Near East, as well as in other areas of the world, as research on the dynamics of religion is pursued in the future.

When we read in Psalm 19 that "the heavens declare the glory of God; and the firmament sheweth his handwork," we hear a voice which mocks the beliefs of Egyptians and Babylonians. The heavens, which were to the psalmist but a witness of God's greatness, were to the Mesopotamians the very majesty of godhead, the highest ruler, Anu. To the Egyptians the heavens signified the mystery of the divine mother through whom man was reborn. In Egypt and Mesopotamia the divine was comprehended as immanent: the gods were in nature. The Egyptians saw in the sun all that a man may know of the Creator; the Mesopotamians viewed the sun as the god Shamash, the guarantor of justice. But to the psalmist the sun was God's devoted servant who "is as a bridegroom coming out of his chamber, and rejoiceth as a strong man to run a race." The God of the psalmists and the prophets was not in nature. He transcended nature—and transcended, likewise, the realm of mythopoeic thought. It would seem that the Hebrews, no less than the Greeks, broke with the mode of speculation which had prevailed up to their time.

The mainspring of the acts, thoughts, and feelings of early man was the conviction that the divine was immanent in nature, and nature intimately connected with society. Dr. Wilson emphasized this fact by calling the Egyptians monophysites. Dr. Jacobsen indicated that his approach to Mesopotamian thought could not do full justice to it; but the myths and beliefs which he discussed reflect it at every turn. And in our first chapter we found that the assumption of an essential correlation between nature and man provided us with a basis for the understanding of mythopoeic thought. Its logic, its peculiar structure, was seen to derive from an unceasing awareness of a live relationship between man and the phenomenal world. In the significant moments of his life, early man was confronted not by an inanimate, impersonal nature—not by an "It"—but by a "Thou." We have seen that such a relationship involved not only man's intellect but the whole of his being—his feeling and his will, no less than his thought. Hence early man would have rejected the detachment of a purely intellectual attitude toward nature, had he been able to conceive it, as inadequate to his experience.

As long as the peoples of the ancient Near East preserved their cultural integrity—from the middle of the fourth to the middle of the first millennium B.C.—they remained conscious of their close bond with nature. And that awareness remained vivid notwithstanding the conditions of city life. The efflorescence of civilization in Egypt and Mesopotamia brought with it the need for a division of labor and a diversification of life possible only when people congregate in sufficient numbers for some to be freed from preoccupation with earning a livelihood. But the ancient cities were small by our standards, and their inhabitants were not cut off from the land. On the contrary, most of them derived their sustenance from the surrounding fields; all of them worshiped gods personifying natural powers; and all of them participated in rites which marked the turning-points in the farmer's year. In the great metropolis of Babylon the outstanding annual event was the New Year's Festival celebrating the renewal of the generative force of nature. In all Mesopotamian cities the business of everyday life was interrupted several times in the course of each month when the moon completed one of its phases or other natural events called for appropriate action on the part of the community. In Egypt, too, the husbandman's preoccupations found expression in festivals at Thebes, Memphis, and other Egyptian cities where celebrations marked the rise of the Nile, the end of the inundation, or the completion of the harvest. Thus urban life in no way diminished man's awareness of his essential involvement in nature.

When we accentuate the basic conception of ancient Near Eastern thought, as we have just done, we are necessarily obscuring its richness and diversity. Within the scope of mythopoeic thought a great variety of attitudes and outlooks are possible; and contrast as well as variety become apparent when we compare the speculative myths of Egypt and Mesopotamia. It is true that the same natural phenomena were often personified in these two countries and that the same images were often used to describe them. Yet the mood of the myths and the significance of the images are most unlike.

In both countries, for instance, the existing world was believed to have emerged from the waters of chaos. In Egypt this primeval ocean was male—the god Nūn. In other words, it was conceived as a fertilizing agent, and as such it was a permanent factor in the created universe recognized in the subsoil water and in the annual flood of the Nile. In Mesopotamia the fertilizing power in water was personified as the god Enki or Ea. But he was entirely unrelated to the primordial ocean. This ocean was a female, Ti'amat, the mother who brought forth gods and monsters in such profusion that her unbounded fruitfulness endangered the very existence of the universe. She was killed in combat by Marduk, who formed the world from her body. Thus water was significant to both Babylonians and Egyptians as the source and also as the sustainer of life. Yet these conceptions were very differently expressed by the two peoples.

A similar contrast appears in relation to earth. Mesopotamia worshiped a beneficial Great Mother whose fertility was seen in the produce of the earth and who gained additional religious importance by a variety of associations. The earth was viewed as the counterpart (and hence the spouse) of Heaven, Anu; or of the water, Enki; or even of Enlil, the kingly storm-god. In Egypt, on the other hand, the earth was a male—Geb or Ptah or Osiris: the ubiquitous mother-goddess was not connected with the soil. Her image was either cast in the primitive and ancient guise of the cow or projected on the sky which, as Nūt, gave birth to the sun and stars each day at dawn and dusk. Moreover, the dead entered her body to be reborn as immortals. The sustained Egyptian preoccupation with death and the hereafter, however, found no equivalent in Mesopotamia. On the contrary, death was understood there as an almost complete destruction of personality; and man's chief desires were for a worthy life and freedom from disease, with a good reputation and descendants to survive him; and the sky was not a goddess bending over her children but the most unapproachable of male gods.

The differences which we have enumerated do not merely represent a meaningless variety of images; they betray a thorough contrast between the Egyptian and Mesopotamian views as to the nature of the universe in which man lives. Throughout the Mesopotamian texts we hear overtones of anxiety which seem to express a haunting fear that the unaccountable and turbulent powers may at any time bring disaster to human society. But in Egypt the gods were powerful without being violent. Nature presented itself as an established order in which changes were either superficial and insignificant or an unfolding in time of what had been preordained from the beginning. Moreover, Egyptian kingship guaranteed stability to society. For, as Dr. Wilson explained, one of the gods occupied the throne. Pharaoh was divine, the son and image of the Creator. Thus Pharaoh ensured a harmonious integration of nature and society at all times. But in Mesopotamia the assembly of the gods assigned a mere mortal to rule men, and the divine favor might at any time be withdrawn from him. Man was at the mercy of decisions he could neither influence nor gauge. Hence the king and his counselors watched for portents on earth and in the sky which might reveal a changing constellation of divine grace, so that catastrophe might be foreseen and possibly averted. In Egypt neither astrology nor prophecy ever developed to any great extent.

The contrast between the temper of the two countries was concisely expressed in their creation myths. In Egypt creation was viewed as the brilliant act of an omnipotent Creator disposing of submissive elements. Of the lasting order which he created, society formed an unchanging part. In Mesopotamia the Creator had been chosen by a divine assembly helpless before the threat of the powers of chaos. Their champion, Marduk, had followed up his victory over these antagonists by the creation of the universe. This took place almost as an afterthought, and man was especially designed as a servant of the gods. There was no permanence in the human sphere. The gods assembled on every New Year's Day to "establish (such) destinies" for mankind as they pleased.

The differences between the Egyptian and Mesopotamian manners of viewing the world are very far-reaching. Yet the two peoples agreed in the fundamental assumptions that the individual is part of society, that society is imbedded in nature, and that nature is but the manifestation of the divine. This doctrine was, in fact, universally accepted by the peoples of the ancient world, with the single exception of the Hebrews.

The Hebrews arrived late upon the scene and settled in a country pervaded by influences from the two superior adjacent cultures. One would expect the newcomers to have assimilated alien modes of thought, since these were supported by such vast prestige. Untold immigrants from deserts and mountains had done so in the past; and many individual Hebrews did, in fact, conform to the ways of the Gentiles. But assimilation was not characteristic of Hebrew thought. On the contrary, it held out with a peculiar stubbornness and insolence against the wisdom of Israel's neighbors. It is possible to detect the reflection of Egyptian and Mesopotamian beliefs in many episodes of the Old Testament; but the overwhelming impression left by that document is one, not of derivation, but of originality.

The dominant tenet of Hebrew thought is the absolute transcendence of God. Yahweh is not in nature. Neither earth nor sun nor heaven is divine; even the most potent natural phenomena are but reflections of God's greatness. It is not even possible properly to name God:

And Moses said unto God, Behold, when I come unto the children of Israel and shall say unto them, The God of your fathers hath sent me unto you; and they shall say to me: What is his name: what shall I say unto them?
And God said unto Moses: I AM THAT I AM: and he said, Thus shalt thou say unto the children of Israel, I AM hath sent me unto you [Exod. 3:13–14].

The God of the Hebrews is pure being, unqualified, ineffable. He is *holy*. That means that he is *sui generis*. It does not mean that he is taboo or that he is power. It means that all values are ultimately attributes of God alone. Hence all concrete phenomena are devaluated. Dr. Irwin has pointed out that in Hebrew thought man and nature are not necessarily corrupt; but both are necessarily *valueless* before God. As Eliphaz said to Job (and we use the Chicago translation):

Can a mortal be righteous before God
Or a man be pure before his Maker?
Even in his servants he does not trust,
And his angels he charges with error.
How much less them that dwell in Houses of clay,
Whose foundation is in the dust . . . [Job 4:17–19a].

A similar meaning lies in the words of Deutero-Isaiah (64:6a): "We are all as an unclean thing, and all our righteousnesses are as filthy rags." Even man's righteousness, his highest virtue, is devaluated by the comparison with the absolute.

In the field of material culture such a conception of God leads to iconoclasm; and it needs an effort of the imagination to realize the shattering boldness of a contempt for imagery at the time, and in the particular historical setting, of the Hebrews. Everywhere religious fervor not only inspired verse and rite but also sought plastic and pictorial expression. The Hebrews, however, denied the relevancy of the "graven image"; the boundless could not be given form, the unqualified could but be offended by a representation, whatever the skill and the devotion that went into its making. Every finite reality shriveled to nothingness before the absolute value which was God.

The abysmal difference between the Hebrew and the normal Near Eastern viewpoints can best be illustrated by the manner in which an identical theme, the instability of the social order, is treated. We have a number of Egyptian texts which deal with the period of social upheaval which followed the great era of the pyramid builders. The disturbance of the established order was viewed with horror. Neferrohu said:

I show thee the land in lamentation and distress. The man with a weak arm (now) has (a strong) arm. . . . I show thee how the undermost is turned to uppermost. . . . The poor man will acquire riches.

The most famous of the sages, Ipuwer, is even more explicit. For instance, he condemns as a disastrous parody of order the fact that

gold and lapis lazuli are hung about the necks of slave girls. But noble ladies walk through land and mistresses of houses say: Would that we had something to eat. . . . Behold they that possessed beds now lie upon the ground. He that slept with dirt upon him now stuffeth for himself a cushion.

The upshot is unmitigated misery for all: "Nay but great and small say: I wish I were dead."

In the Old Testament we meet the same theme—the reversal of established social conditions. When Hannah, after years of barrenness, had prayed for a son, and Samuel was born, she praised God:

There is none holy as the Lord: for there is none beside thee: neither is there any rock like our God. . . . The bows of the mighty men are broken, and they that stumbled are girded with strength. They that were full have hired out themselves for bread; and they that were hungry ceased. . . . The Lord maketh poor and maketh rich: he bringeth low, and lifteth up. He raiseth up the poor out of the dust, and lifteth up the beggar from the dunghill, to set them among princes, and to make them inherit the throne of glory: for the pillars of the earth are the Lord's and he hath set the world upon them [I Sam. 2:2-8].

Notice that the last verses state explicitly that God created the existing social order; but, quite characteristically, this order did not derive any sacredness, any value, from its divine origin. The sacredness and value remain attributes of God alone, and the violent changes of fortune observed in social life are but signs of God's omnipotence. Nowhere else do we meet this fanatical devaluation of the phenomena of nature and the achievements of man: art, virtue, social order—in view of the unique significance of the divine. It has been rightly pointed out that the monotheism of the Hebrews is a correlate of their insistence on the unconditioned nature of God. Only a God who transcends every phenomenon, who is not conditioned by any mode of manifestation —only an unqualified God can be the one and only ground of all existence.

This conception of God represents so high a degree of abstraction that, in reaching it, the Hebrews seem to have left the realm of mythopoeic thought. The impression that they did so is strengthened when we observe that the Old Testament is remarkably poor in mythology of the type we have encountered in Egypt and Mesopotamia. But this impression requires correction. The processes of mythopoeic thought are decisive for many sections of the Old Testament. For instance, the magnificent verses from the Book of Proverbs quoted in chapter ix describe the Wisdom of God, personified and substantialized in the same manner in which the corresponding concept of ma'at is treated by the Egyptians. Even the great conception of an only and transcendent God was not entirely free from myth, for it was not the fruit of detached speculation but of a passionate and dynamic experience. Hebrew thought did not entirely overcome mythopoeic thought. It created, in fact, a new myth—the myth of the Will of God.

Although the great "Thou" which confronted the Hebrews transcended nature, it stood in a specific relationship to the people. For when they were freed from bondage and roamed in "a desert land . . . the waste howling wilderness . . . the Lord alone did lead (them) and there was no strange god with (them)" (Deut. 32:10-12). And God had said:

But thou, Israel, art my servant, Jacob whom I have chosen, the seed of Abraham my friend. Thou whom I have taken from the ends of the earth, and called thee from the chief men thereof, and said unto thee, Thou art my servant; I have chosen thee, and not cast thee away [Isa. 41:8-9].

Thus God's will was felt to be focused on one particular and concrete group of human beings; it was asserted to have manifested itself at one decisive moment in their history and ceaselessly and relentlessly to have urged, rewarded, or chastised the people of its choice. For in Sinai, God had said, "Ye shall be unto me a kingdom of priests and an holy nation" (Exod. 19:6).

It is a poignant myth, this Hebrew myth of a chosen people, of a divine promise made, of a terrifying moral burden imposed—a prelude to the later myth of the Kingdom of God, that more remote and more spiritual "promised land." For in the myth of the chosen people the ineffable majesty of God and the worthlessness of man are correlated in a dramatic situation that is to unfold in time and is moving toward a future where the distant yet related parallels of human and divine existence are to meet in infinity.

Not cosmic phenomena, but history itself, had here become pregnant with meaning; history had become a revelation of the dynamic will of God. The human being was not merely the servant of the god as he was in Mesopotamia; nor was he placed, as in Egypt, at a preordained station in a static universe which did not need to be—and, in fact, could not be—questioned. Man, according to Hebrew thought, was the interpreter and the servant of God; he was even honored with the task of bringing about the realization of God's will. Thus man was condemned to unending efforts which were doomed to fail because of his inadequacy. In the Old Testament we find man possessed of a new freedom and of a new burden of responsibility. We also find there a new and utter lack of *eudaimonia*, of harmony—whether with the world of reason or with the world of perception.

All this may help to explain the strange poignancy of single individuals in the Old Testament. Nowhere in the literature of Egypt or Babylonia do we meet the loneliness of the biblical figures, astonishingly real in their mixture of ugliness and beauty, pride and contrition, achievement and failure. There is the tragic figure of Saul, the problematical David; there are countless others. We find single men in terrible isolation facing a trascendent God: Abraham trudging to the place of sacrifice with his son, Jacob in his struggle, and Moses and the Prophets. In Egypt and Mesopotamia man was dominated, but also supported, by the great rhythm of nature. If in his dark moments he felt himself caught and held in the net of unfathomable decisions, his involvement in nature had, on the whole, a soothing character. He was gently carried along on the perennial cosmic tides of the seasons. The depth and intimacy of man's relationship with nature found expression in the ancient symbol of the mother-goddess. But Hebrew thought ignored this image entirely. It only recognized the stern Father, of whom it was said: "He led him (Jacob, the people) about, he instructed him, he kept him as the apple of his eye" (Deut. 32:10b).

The bond between Yahweh and his chosen people had been finally established during the Exodus. The Hebrews considered the forty years in the desert the decisive phase in their development. And we, too, may understand the originality and the coherence of their speculations if we relate them to their experience in the desert.

The reader will remember that preceding chapters took great care to describe the Egyptian and Mesopotamian landscapes. In doing so, the authors did not succumb to an unwarranted naturalism; they did not claim that cultural phenomena could be derived from physiographical causes. They merely suggested that a relation between land and culture may exist, a suggestion we can accept the more readily since we have seen that the surrounding world confronted early man as a "Thou." We may ask, then, what was the natural setting which determined the Hebrew's experience of the world around him. Now, the Hebrews, whatever their ancestry and historical antecedents, were tribal nomads. And since they were nomads in the Near East, they must have lived, not in boundless steppes, but between the desert and the sown, between the most fertile of lands and the total negation of life, which, in this remarkable corner of the earth, lie cheek by jowl. They must, therefore, have known through experience both the reward and the cost of existence in either.

The Hebrews craved to settle for good in the fertile plains. But characteristically they dreamed of lands overflowing with milk and honey, not lands of superabundant crops like those the Egyptians imagined for their hereafter. It seems that the desert as a metaphysical experience loomed very large for the Hebrews and colored all their valuations. It is, perhaps, the tension between two valuations—between a desire and a contempt for what is desired—that may explain some of the paradoxes of ancient Hebrew beliefs.

The organized states of the ancient Near East were agricultural; but the values of an agricultural community are the opposites of those of the nomadic tribe, especially of the extreme type of nomads of the desert. The settled peasant's reverence for impersonal authority, and the bondage, the constraint which the organized state imposes, mean an intolerable lack of personal freedom for the tribesman. The farmer's everlasting preoccupation with phenomena of growth and his total dependence on these phenomena appear to the nomad a form of slavery. Moreover, to him the desert is clean, but the scene of life, which is also the scene of decay, is sordid.

On the other hand, nomadic freedom can be bought only at a price; for whoever rejects the complexities and mutual dependencies of agricultural society not only gains freedom but also loses the bond with the phenomenal world; in fact, he gains his freedom at the cost of significant form. For, wherever we find reverence for the phenomena of life and growth, we find preoccupation with the immanence of the divine and with the *form* of its manifestation. But in the stark solitude of the desert, where nothing changes, nothing moves (except man at his own free will), where features in the landscape are only pointers, landmarks, without significance in themselves—there we may expect the image of God to transcend concrete phenomena altogether. Man confronting God will not contemplate him but will hear his voice and command, as Moses did, and the prophets, and Mohammed.

When we compared the lands of origin of Hebrews, Egyptians, and Mesopotamians, we were concerned, not with the relation between group psychology and habitat, but with profound differences in pristine religious experience. The peculiar experience which we have just described seems characteristic for all the most significant figures of the Old Testament. It is important to realize this, not because it enables us to understand them better as individuals, but because we then recognize what colored and integrated their thought. They propounded, not speculative theory, but revolutionary and dynamic teaching. The doctrine of a single, unconditioned, transcendent God rejected time-honored values, proclaimed new ones, and postulated a metaphysical significance for history and for man's actions. With infinite *moral* courage the Hebrews worshiped an absolute God and accepted as the correlate of their faith the sacrifice of a harmonious existence. In transcending the Near Eastern myths of immanent godhead, they created, as we have seen, the new myth of the will of God. It remained for the Greeks, with their peculiar *intellectual* courage, to discover a form of speculative thought in which myth was entirely overcome.

HAYYIM SCHAUSS

Pesach: Its Origins

From the general treatment of the growth and dynamics of different religious traditions in the ancient Near East provided by the Frankforts, we move to a smaller canvas and present a selection that deals with the dynamics of change in a particular ceremony in the Jewish religion.

Schauss shows how the Pesach, or Passover, changed from a spring festival of shepherds wandering the desert to an agricultural festival when the Jewish peasants settled in Palestine; how it was later reinterpreted and associated with the deliverance from Egypt; and how still later, under the oppression of the Romans, it became associated with the belief in a Messiah who would be a second Moses and would free the Jews from the bondage of Rome, just as their ancestors were released from Egyptian slavery. Incidentally, it also shows the universal linkage between seasonal and calendrical change and religion—a tie-up apparent in such Christian holidays as Christmas, New Year's, and Easter —all derived from solar seasons.

Reprinted from Hayyim Schauss, *The Jewish Festivals* (Cincinnati, Ohio: Union of American Hebrew Congregations, 1938), by permission of the Commission on Jewish Education.

INTRODUCTION

Pesach, usually called Passover, is first in the calendar of Jewish festivals. It is the greatest of Jewish festivals. For over two thousand years it has been more than a holiday; it has been *the* holiday, the festival of redemption.

In addition, Pesach is the oldest of Jewish

festivals. Jews observed it in the most ancient of times, in the days when they were still nomadic shepherds in the wilderness.

Pesach is the Jewish spring festival. It begins on the eve of the fourteenth day of the Jewish month Nisan. Originally it was a seven-day festival and is so observed today in Palestine and among Reform Jews, with only the first and seventh days as days of rest. Due, however, to the unsettled state of the Jewish calendar in olden times the festival was extended to last eight days amongst Jews not resident in Palestine. The full holiday, with cessation of work, is observed only the first two and the last two days of the festival. The four intervening days are semi-holidays.

A FESTIVAL OF THE SHEPHERDS

Pesach was not always the holiday that we know today. Generation after generation came and went, epoch upon epoch of Jewish life passed by, and each contributed its strivings and ideals, its hopes and emotions to the festival before it became the great holiday of deliverance and freedom.

Festivals change and develop in accordance with various modes of life and periods of history. Holidays usually start as nature festivals and are observed in that season of the year when nature itself changes, and the ceremonies attending the holiday grow out of these manifestations of nature. Later, however, when men reach a higher cultural level, they give a deeper spiritual meaning to the festival and the old ceremonies assume a new symbolic significance.

It is, therefore, true that a holiday is always older than the interpretation which is given to it. First comes the custom, the ceremony, the observance; no interpretation for them is needed or sought. The ceremony explains itself. Later, after a long time passes, need is found for an interpretation of the festival and its rites. So, Pesach was originally a nature festival, an observance of the coming of spring. Later, as time went on, it became a historic and national holiday, the festival of the deliverance from Egypt, and it thus assumed a newer and higher meaning.

Pesach as a spring festival is very old. Jews observed a spring festival long before the deliverance from Egypt. The beginnings of Pesach carry us back to those prehistoric days when Jews were still tribes of shepherds wandering in the desert. Wherever they found pasturage for their herds, they pitched their tents and grazed their flocks. In the month when the kids and lambs were born, the month that ushered in spring, they observed a festival at full moon (the fourteenth to the fifteenth day of the month). Every member of the family took part in the observance of this festival, which was featured by the sacrifice of a sheep or goat from the flock. The sacrifice occurred just before nightfall, after which the animal was roasted whole and all members of the family made a hasty meal in the middle of the night. It was forbidden to break any of the bones of the sacrificial animal or to leave uneaten any part of it by the time daybreak came. One of the chief ceremonies attendant upon the festival was the daubing of the tent-posts with the blood of the slain animal. It was clear to these primitive shepherds why certain ceremonies were commanded and other practices forbidden. They knew that observance was an antidote to plagues, misfortunes, and illnesses, and that it was an assurance of good luck and safety for the coming year. Similar beliefs, customs, and fetishes were prevalent amongst other peoples, too.

These primitive nomads knew why the sacrifice that was so hastily eaten and the festival with which it was connected were called *Pesach*. It was not till a long time later that the meaning of the word was lost and a new interpretation given to it. To this day we cannot be certain what the word meant originally; neither can we be certain of the details of the ceremonies and rites that accompanied the observance. We do know, however, that the celebration was held at night and that morning brought with it the end of the festival. We also know that the ceremony was not tied up with any sanctuary or priesthood; it was a family festival, conducted by the head of the family.

A time came when the Jews ceased to be nomads and settled in Palestine. But even then they did not forgo observing the spring festival of the shepherds which they had brought with them from the desert. It was observed, naturally, in the rural districts only, in those sections where there were still shepherds who made a living from their flocks. There were more shepherds in Judah, in the south, than in Israel, where the land was more fertile and the inhabitants gained their main livelihood from tilling the soil.

AN AGRICULTURAL FESTIVAL

The Jewish peasants of Palestine, those who lived by tilling the soil, had another form of spring festival, one related to the cutting of the grain, which they called "The Festival of Matsos" (Unleavened Bread). The grain harvest began in the spring with the cutting of the barley and ended with the reaping of the wheat, a season that lasted about seven weeks.

Before the start of the barley harvest, the Jews would get rid of all the *sour dough* (fermented dough used instead of yeast to leaven bread) and the old bread they possessed; everything, in fact, connected with *chomets,* the leaven of the last year's crop. We cannot know for certain, by now, what was the origin of the removing of all sour dough and the eating of unleavened bread. It was probably regarded as a safeguard against an unproductive year. In later years the Jews created a new interpretation for this old custom, just as they evolved a new meaning for the Pesach eve ceremonies.

The real importance of the holiday, however, centered in the ceremony of the *omer,* the first sheaf of newly cut barley that was offered to the priest on the first day of the harvest as a sacrifice, as a gift to God. For all people, in those days, had the belief that everything that man used belonged to the gods and they must, therefore, offer the best of everything, the very first, to these gods as a gift.

There was more than just this one seasonal, agricultural festival observed by the Jews in Palestine. In addition to the "Festival of Unleavened Bread," they also observed the "Feast of Harvest" (Shovuos) and the "Feast of Ingathering" (Sukkos). These three occasions were the greatest and most festive holidays of the year and were always observed in a sanctuary. In those days Jerusalem was not yet the only holy spot in Palestine; temples were situated in many parts of the country. In addition, there were holy sites known as "high places" in many small towns and villages. These were hills considered holy by the Canaanites. When the Jews settled in the land, they also used these hills as places of sacrifice and worship. The Canaanites served their gods, the *baalim,* in these "high places"; the Jews used the same spots to serve their God. The "high places" were open to the sky and on each one was a stone slab which was used as an altar for sacrifices; each one also contained a holy stone (*matsevoh*) and a holy tree (*asheroh*), objects which were taken over by the Jews. The services on these "high places" were performed by a priest, who was not only the most learned member of the community and its spiritual leader, but who also acted as the judge in settling all disputes of the region.

The village generally stood on the slope of the hill, within easy reach of the "high place" on top of the hill. At the coming of a festival, the entire village would make its way to the "high place" and there offer its sacrifices; they would then hold a huge feast of the meat of the sacrificial animals, singing holy songs and dancing religious dances. All were joyous and merry. In fact, holy services in the sanctuaries were called "eating before God" and "being merry before God."

Pesach and Shovuos were the seasons for the grain harvest, the time of the year when there was much work to do in the fields, and it was difficult for the Jewish peasant to leave his home and travel to a great sanctuary in a large center. He could do this only at Sukkos, the autumn festival, when he had finished his work and the produce of his field and orchard was stored away; therefore he observed the Feast of Unleavened Bread generally at his local "high place." It is not hard for us to picture the simple, joyous scene on that occasion; we can see festive Jewish peasants from hilly Ephraim or from the Valley of Jezreel, winding up the hill in a joyful procession, bearing the *omer,* the first sheaf of barley, to the "high place." The priest takes the sheaf and, chanting prayers and blessings, waves it over the altar, symbolically giving it to God.

We must thus bear in mind that Pesach and the Feast of Unleavened Bread were originally two distinct festivals, observed at the same time. Pesach was the older holiday, the one the Jews brought with them from the desert; the Feast of Unleavened Bread was newer, instituted only after the Jews had settled in Palestine and become farmers. Both were spring festivals, but the Feast of Unleavened Bread was observed by the entire community gathered in a holy place, while Pesach was celebrated in the home as a family festival.

A DAY OF DELIVERANCE

Holidays are closely bound up with the life of a people and with their spiritual culture. In the course of time when the life of the people changes, then the festivals of that people also change and assume a new character. The ceremonies and rites, to a great extent, remain but they take on new meaning. They are interpreted differently, given symbolic values, and in this way become something almost entirely new.

This has happened with all festivals, ceremonies, and customs, as it happened to Pesach. Jewish culture and Jewish life evolved and changed during the early centuries that the Jews spent in Palestine. Newer and higher conceptions and ideals arose and, in time, the Jews forgot the meaning and spirit of the old customs and ceremonies of Pesach and the Feast of Unleavened Bread. Above all, the idea of observing nature and the harvest festivals ceased to appeal to the Jews. They had a much greater desire to observe, in the spring of the year, a holiday with a historic background, a festival that would represent symbolically the social and spiritual strivings and ideals of the day. In answer to this desire they began to emphasize Pesach as the festival of the deliverance from Egypt.

This transition came very easily. The memory of the exodus from Egypt burned brightly in the minds of the Jews, and with it the memory that it was in the first spring month of the year that they had left the land of the Pharaohs. The reliving of that great event in the dawn of Jewish history became the chief motive for the celebration of the spring festival. Spring, the time of liberation for nature, and the idea of human freedom seemed to fit very well together; in this way Pesach became the festival of the freedom of the Jewish people, its deliverance from slavery, and its awakening to a new life.

All the customs and ceremonies which were bound up with Pesach and the Feast of Unleavened Bread were then reinterpreted and became associated with the deliverance from Egypt. *Pesach,* for instance, was declared to mean "passing by or over"; and the holiday was called by that name because God passed over the Jewish homes when he slew the first-born of Egypt. The quickly baked *matsos,* according to the new interpretation, were eaten because the Jews were in such a hurry to get out of Egypt that they had no time to leaven their bread and bake it properly. The bitter herbs eaten on Pesach eve were declared to be reminders of the bitterness of the Jewish lot in Egypt. Even the fruit salad of the Pesach night, the *charoses,* was in later times bound up with the deliverance; it was considered symbolic of the mortar mixed by the Jews when they were slaves in Egypt.

These new interpretations were intended for a new generation, to whom the old ceremonies lacked meaning. And one of the foremost problems in those days of change was that of enlightening the new generation, making clear to the young son the symbolic meanings which the old ceremonies had assumed, for the children were entirely strangers to the customs handed down from the old days. "And it shall be when thy son asketh thee in time to come, saying, 'What is this?' that thou shalt say unto him: 'By strength of hand the Lord brought us out from Egypt, from the house of bondage.'"

It was in this way that Pesach and the Feast of Unleavened Bread were joined together, and two distinct spring festivals become one historical holiday, a symbol of the striving of the people toward national freedom. But, since the festival was still bound up with the family, or, at most, the village community, it could not yet become a great national holiday. It was only later, when Pesach was observed by all Jews in one place, in one great sanctuary, that it gained national importance.

This happened in the last few decades before the destruction of the first Temple, in the time of Josiah, King of Judah. Israel, the great Jewish kingdom of the north, was no more. All that remained was Judah, the smaller kingdom of the south. In the reign of Josiah there was a strong progressive party, seeking to reconstruct Jewish national life and establish it on a new basis of justice and right. Sweeping reforms were instituted. One of the most outstanding was the elimination of all the "high places" because Jerusalem was declared the one sanctuary for all the Jews. Sacrifices were forbidden anywhere else and only Jerusalem was to be the goal of the pilgrimages made at holiday time. The festivals, therefore, lost their local character and became national observances that united all Jews in the one holy place, the Temple in Jerusalem.

Through this reform the Pesach ceremonial took on almost a new character. Since it was forbidden to make the Paschal sacrifice anywhere but in the Temple at Jerusalem, it was impossible to smear the blood of the sacrificial lamb upon the doorposts of the houses. In general, the observance lost its ancient weird character. The Book of Kings tells us truly that such a Pesach as was observed in the eighteenth year of the reign of Josiah, the year in which the reform was instituted, had not been celebrated since the Jews settled in Palestine.

We cannot be certain how long a time passed before the Jews accepted these reforms in practice and ceased to offer the Pesach sacrifice in their own homes. Nor can we be certain how long it took for Pesach and the Feast of Unleavened Bread to become as one festival. But we do know that the importance of the festival grew and that it became, in time, the greatest Jewish national holiday. Sukkos remained the most festive and most joyous of the holidays, but Pesach attained the greatest national importance.

THE GREATEST JEWISH HOLIDAY

The highest point in the evolution of Pesach came in the last century of the second Temple, when the Jews suffered from the heavy oppression of the Romans. It was during this period that the Messianic hope flamed up, and in the minds of the Jews the deliverance of the future became bound up with the first redemption in Jewish history: the deliverance from Egypt. Jews had long believed that in the deliverance to come, God would show the same sort of miracles that he had performed in redeeming the Jews from Egypt. This belief gained added strength in this period of Roman occupation and oppression. Jews began to believe that the Messiah

would be a second Moses and would free the Jews the selfsame eve, the eve of Pesach. So Pesach became the festival of the second as well as the first redemption; in every part of the world where Jews lived, especially in Palestine, Jewish hearts beat faster on the eve of Pesach, beat with the hope that this night the Jews would be freed from the bondage of Rome, just as their ancestors were released from Egyptian slavery.

The ritual of the Pesach eve had, by that time, developed to rich proportions and was entirely different from the spring festival of the Jewish shepherds of old. The great Greco-Roman civilization ruled almost the entire known world and influenced the Jews to observe their holiday in a richer, more luxurious fashion. They adopted the wine and the soft sofas and the other luxuries that in those days were part of a feast. Jews still partook of the meat of the sacrificial lamb, but not in haste, as the Samaritan sect does to this very day; they ate leisurely and reclined on the softest of cushions.

The Pesach ritual at that time was a compromise between the Pesach of the very old days that was observed in the home, and the Pesach that followed it, the holiday that was observed only in the Temple. Observance, therefore, was divided into two main parts, and was celebrated in two different places, the Temple and the home. In the afternoon of the day before Pesach, the sacrificial animal was slaughtered with elaborate ceremonies in the Temple; it was then taken home, roasted, and eaten in groups, with ceremonies that are almost identical with the Seder observed by Jews today. Outside of Jerusalem the offering of sacrifices was not allowed and Pesach eve was observed in the home, in the family circle, and in the synagogue. In some places, however, it was customary to eat roast lamb, though no sacrifice was offered.

RALPH LINTON

Nativistic Movements

The impact of European culture upon the small, primitive societies of the world during the past four centuries has frequently led to the appearance of what have come to be known as "nativistic movements," wherein the primitive societies have reacted, sometimes violently, against domination by the Europeans and engaged in organized attempts to revive or perpetuate certain aspects of their native cultures in the face of this pressure to change. Since the religious systems of the primitive societies typically embodied the central values of their cultures, these nativistic movements almost always involved some type of religious or magical procedures as their essential elements and hence have provided us with crucial data on dynamics in religion.

This general paper of Ralph Linton's is an attempt to define and classify the types of nativistic movements that have occurred in culture-contact situations and to identify the conditions under which these various types of movements arise. Linton makes it clear that nativism can appear in the dominant group as well as in the subordinate group in a culture-contact situation, although the more dramatic manifestations tend to occur in the subordinate society.

More recently Anthony Wallace has added important new theoretical dimensions to our understanding of nativistic movements in his paper "Revitalization Movements" (1956).

Reprinted from *American Anthropologist*, XLV (1943), 230–240, by permission of the American Anthropological Association.

At the time that the centennial meeting of the American Ethnological Society was planned, the writer was invited to contribute a paper on nativistic movements in North America. When he attempted to prepare this it soon became evident that there was a need for a systematic analysis of nativistic phenomena in general. Although the Social Science Research Council's Committee on Acculturation had made some progress in this direction much remained to be done. The present paper is an attempt to provide such a systematic analysis and is presented in the hope that its formulations may be modified and expanded by further research.

The first difficulty encountered in the study of nativistic movements was that of delimiting the field. The term "nativistic" has been loosely applied to a rather wide range of phenomena, resembling in this respect many other terms employed by the social sciences. For the writer to determine arbitrarily which of several established usages is to be considered correct and which incorrect is not only presumptuous but also one of the surest ways to promote misunderstanding of the theoretical contributions he hopes to make. The only satisfactory definition under such circumstances is one based upon the common denominators of the meanings which have come to be attached to the term through usage. With this as a guide, we may define a nativistic movement as "Any conscious, organized attempt on the part of a society's members to revive or perpetuate selected aspects of its culture."

Like all definitions, the above requires amplification to make its implications clear. Its crux lies in the phrase "conscious, organized effort." All societies seek to perpetuate their own cultures, but they usually do this unconsciously and as a part of the normal processes of individual training and socialization. Conscious, organized efforts to perpetuate a culture can arise only when a society becomes conscious that there are cultures other than its own and that the existence of its own culture is threatened. Such consciousness, in turn, is a by-product of close and continuous contact with other societies; an acculturation phenomenon under the definition developed by the above-mentioned committee.

The phrase "selected aspects of its culture" also requires elaboration. Nativistic movements concern themselves with particular elements of culture, never with cultures as wholes. This generalization holds true whether we regard cultures as continuums of long duration or follow the usual ethnographic practice of applying the term "a culture" to the content of such a continuum at a particular point in time. The avowed purpose of a nativistic movement may be either to revive the past culture or to perpetuate the current one, but it never really attempts to do either. Any attempt to revive a past phase of culture in its entirety is immediately blocked by the recognition that this phase was, in certain respects, inferior to the present one and by the incompatability of certain past culture patterns with current conditions. Even the current phase of a culture is never satisfactory at all points and also includes a multitude of elements which seem too trivial to deserve deliberate perpetuation. What really happens in all nativistic movements is that certain current or remembered elements of culture are selected for emphasis and given symbolic value. The more distinctive such elements are with respect to other cultures with which the society is in contact, the greater their potential value as symbols of the society's unique character.

The main considerations involved in this selective process seem to be those of distinctiveness and of the practicability of reviving or perpetuating the element under current conditions. Thus the Ghost Dance laid great stress on the revival of such distinctive elements of Indian culture as games and ceremonial observances, elements which could be revived under agency conditions. At the same time it allowed its adherents to continue the use of cloth, guns, kettles, and other objects of European manufacture which were obviously superior to their aboriginal equivalents. In fact, in many cases the converts were assured that when the dead returned and the whites were swept away, the houses, cattle and other valuable property of the whites would remain for the Indians to inherit.

All the phenomena to which the term "nativistic" has been applied have in common these factors of selection of culture elements and deliberate, conscious effort to perpetuate such elements. However, they differ so widely in other respects that they cannot be understood without further analysis. At the outset it is necessary to distinguish between those forms of nativism which involve an attempt to revive extinct or at least moribund elements of culture and those which merely seek to perpetuate current ones. For convenience we will refer to the first of these forms as *revivalistic nativism,* to the second as *perpetuative nativism.* These two forms are not completely exclusive. Thus a revivalistic nativistic movement will be almost certain to include in its selection of elements some of those which are current in the culture although derived from its past. Conversely a perpetuative nativistic movement may include elements which had been consciously revived at an earlier date. However, the emphases of these two forms are distinct. The revivalistic type of nativism can be illustrated by such movements as the Celtic revival in Ireland, with its emphasis on the medieval Irish tradition in literature and its attempt to revive a moribund national language. The perpetuative type of nativism can be illustrated by the conditions existing in some of the Rio Grande Pueblos or in various Indian groups in Guatemala. Such groups are only vaguely conscious of their past culture and make no attempts to revive it, but they have developed elaborate and conscious techniques for the perpetuation of selected aspects of their current culture and are unalterably opposed to assimilation into the alien society which surrounds them.

There is a further necessity for distinguishing between what we may call *magical nativism* and *rational nativism.* It may well be questioned whether any sort of nativistic movement can be regarded as genuinely rational, since all such movements are, to some extent, unrealistic, but at least the movements of the latter order appear rational by contrast with those of the former.

Magical nativistic movements are often spectacular and always troublesome to administrators, facts which explain why they have received so much attention from anthropologists. Such movements are comparable in many respects to the messianic movements which have arisen in many societies in time of stress. They usually originate with some individual who assumes the role of prophet and is accepted by the people because they wish to believe. They always lean heavily on the supernatural and usually embody apocalyptic and millennial aspects. In such movements moribund elements of culture are not revived for their own sake or in anticipation of practical advantages from the elements themselves. Their revival is part of a magical formula designed to modify the society's environment in ways which will be favorable to it. The selection of elements from the past culture as tools for magical manipulation is easily explainable on the basis of their psychological associations. The society's members feel that by behaving as the ancestors did they will, in some usually undefined way, help to recreate the total situation in which the ancestors lived. Perhaps it would be more accurate to say that they are attempting to recreate those aspects of the ancestral situation which appear desirable in retrospect.

Such magical nativistic movements seem to differ from ordinary messianic and millennial movements in only two respects. In the nativistic movements the anticipated millennium is modeled directly on the past, usually with certain additions and modifications, and the symbols which are magically manipulated to bring it about are more or less familiar elements of culture to which new meanings have been attached. In non-nativistic messianic movements, the millennial condition is represented as something new and unique and the symbols manipulated to bring it about tend to be new and unfamiliar. Even in these respects the differences are none too clear. New elements of culture often emerge in connection with magical nativistic movements, as in the case of the distinctive Ghost Dance art. Conversely, messianic movements may lean heavily upon the familiar symbolism of the culture, as in the case of most Christian cults of this type. The basic feature of both messianic cults and magical nativistic movements is that they represent frankly irrational flights from reality. Their differences relate only to the ways in which such flights are implemented and are, from the point of view of their functions, matters of minor importance.

What we have chosen to call rational nativistic movements are a phenomenon of a quite different sort. While such movements resemble the magical ones in their conscious effort to revive or perpetuate selected elements of culture, they have different motivations. What these are can be understood more readily if we reintroduce at this point the distinction previously made between revivalistic and perpetuative nativistic movements. Rational revivalistic nativistic movements are, almost without exception, associated with frustrating situations and are primarily attempts to compensate for the frustrations of the society's members. The elements revived become symbols of a period when the society was free or, in retrospect, happy or great. Their usage is not magical but psychological. By keeping the past in mind, such elements help to re-establish and maintain the self-respect of the group's members in the face of adverse conditions. Rational perpetuative nativistic movements, on the other hand, find their main function in the maintenance of social solidarity. The elements selected for perpetuation become symbols of the society's existence as a unique entity. They provide the society's members with a fund of common knowledge and experience which is exclusively their own and which sets them off from the members of other societies. In both types of rational nativistic movement the culture elements selected for symbolic use are chosen realistically and with regard to the possibility of perpetuating them under current conditions.

It must be emphasized that the four forms of nativistic movement just discussed are not absolutes. Purely revivalistic or perpetuative, magical or rational movements form a very small minority of the observed cases. However, these forms represent the polar positions of series within which all or nearly all given nativistic movements can be placed. Moreover, it will usually be found that a given nativistic movement lies much closer to one end of such a scale than to the other if it is analyzed in terms of the criteria used to establish the polar positions. If we combine the polar positions in the two series, the result is a fourfold typology of nativistic movements, as follows:

1. Revivalistic-magical
2. Revivalistic-rational
3. Perpetuative-magical
4. Perpetuative-rational

Forms 1, 2, and 4 in this typology recur with great frequency, while form 3 is so rare that the writer has been unable to find any clearly recognizable example of it. The reason for this probably lies in the conditions which are usually responsible for magical nativistic movements. The inception of such movements can be traced almost without exception to conditions of extreme hardship or at least extreme dissatisfaction with the *status quo*. Since the current culture is associated with such conditions and has failed to ameliorate them, magical efficacy in modifying these conditions can scarcely be ascribed to any of its elements. Nevertheless, a perpetuative-magical movement might very well arise in the case of a society which currently occupies an advantageous position but sees itself threatened with an imminent loss of that position. It is highly probable that if we could canvass the whole range of nativistic movements examples of this type could be found.

An understanding of the various contact situations in which nativistic movements may arise is quite as necessary for the study of these phenomena as is a typology of such movements. There have been many cases of contact in which they have not arisen at all. The reasons for this seem to be so variable and in many cases so obscure that nothing like a satisfactory analysis is possible. The most that we can say is that nativistic movements are unlikely to arise in situations where both societies are satisfied with their current relationship, or where societies which find themselves at a disadvantage can see that their condition is improving. However, such movements may always be initiated by particular individuals or groups who stand to gain by them and, if the prestige of such initiators is high enough, may achieve considerable followings even when there has been little previous dissatisfaction.

Although the immediate causes of nativistic movements are highly variable, most of them have as a common denominator a situation of inequality between the societies in contact. Such inequalities may derive either from the attitudes of the societies involved or from actual situations of dominance and submission. In order to understand the motives for nativistic movements the distinction between these two sources of inequality must be kept clearly in mind. Inequality based on attitudes of superiority and inferiority may exist in the absence of real dominance, although situations of dominance seem to be uniformly accompanied by the development of such attitudes. As regards attitudes of su-

periority and inferiority, two situations may exist. Each of the groups involved in the contact may consider itself superior or one group may consider itself superior with the other acquiescing in its own inferiority. There seem to be no cases in which each of the groups involved in a contact considers itself inferior. The nearest approach to such a condition is the recognition of mixed inferiority and superiority, i.e., the members of each group regard their own culture as superior in certain respects and inferior in others. Such a condition is especially favorable to the processes of culture exchange and ultimate assimilation of the two groups. It rarely if ever results in the development of nativistic movements.

The type of situation in which each society considers itself superior is well illustrated by the relations between Mexicans and Indians in our own Southwest. In this case factors of practical dominance are ruled out by the presence of a third group, the Anglo-American, which dominates Indian and Mexican alike. Although the two subject groups are in close contact, each of them feels that any assimilation would involve a loss of prestige. The transfer of individuals from one social-cultural continuum to the other is met by equal resistance on both sides and the processes of assimilation never have a chance to get under way. Under such circumstances the life of each of the societies is conscious of its own culture and consciously seeks to perpetuate its distinctive elements. At the same time this consciousness of difference is devoid of envy or frustration and produces no friction. The members of each group pursue their own goals with the aid of their own techniques and, although the situation does not preclude economic rivalries—witness the constant quarrels over water rights—it does preclude social rivalries. It seems that the establishment of such attitudes of mutual social exclusiveness, without hatred or dominance, provides the soundest basis for organizing symbiotic relationships between societies and should be encouraged in all cases where the attitudes of one or both of the groups in contact preclude assimilation.

Contact situations comparable to that just discussed are not infrequent, but they seem to be less common than those in which both groups agree on the superiority of one of the parties. It must be repeated that such attitudes are not neecssarily linked with conditions of actual dominance. Thus the Japanese during the early period of European contact acquiesced in the European's estimate of his own superiority and borrowed European culture elements eagerly and indiscriminately although maintaining national independence. Again, the disunited German states of the eighteenth century acknowledged the superiority of French culture and were eager for French approval even when no political factors were involved.

When two groups stand in such a mutually recognized relationship of superiority and inferiority, but with no factors of actual dominance involved, the contact will rarely if ever give rise to nativistic movements of the magical type. The relationship cannot produce the extreme stresses which drive the members of a society into such flights from reality. On the other hand, the contact may well give rise to rational nativistic movements, but these will rarely if ever appear during the early contact period. At first the superior group is usually so sure of its position that it feels no reluctance toward borrowing convenient elements from the culture of the inferior one. Conversely, the inferior group borrows eagerly from the superior one and looks forward to full equality with it as soon as the cultural differences have been obliterated. During this period impecunious members of the superior group are likely to turn their prestige to practical advantage by marrying rich members of the inferior one and, for a time, genuine assimilation appears to be under way. In such a situation the nativistic trends will normally appear first in the superior group, which is naturally jealous of its prestige. The movements inaugurated will generally be of the perpetuative-rational type, designed to maintain the *status quo,* and will include increasing reluctance to borrow elements of culture from the inferior group and the increase of social discrimination against its members and those of the superior group who consort with them.

When such a nativistic movement gets well under way in the superior group, there will usually be a nativistic response from the inferior one. Finding themselves frustrated in their desire for equality, with or without actual assimilation, the inferiors will develop their own nativistic movements, acting on the well-known sour-grapes principle. However, these movements will be of the revival-istic-rational rather than the perpetuative-rational type. The culture elements selected for emphasis will tend to be drawn from the past rather than the present, since the attitudes of the superior group toward the current culture will have done much to devaluate it. In general, symbolic values will be attached, by preference, to culture elements which were already on the wane at the time of the first contact with the superior group, thus embodying in the movement a denial that the culture of the other group ever was considered superior.

We have already said that attitudes of superiority and inferiority seem to be present in all cases of contact involving actual dominance. Combining these two sets of factors we get the following possible situations for contact groups:

1. Dominant-superior
2. Dominant-inferior
3. Dominated-superior
4. Dominated-inferior

These situations assume agreement on the part of the groups involved not only with respect to dominance, readily demonstrable, but also with respect to attitudes. The frequent lack of such agreement makes it necessary to add a fifth situation, that in which the dominant and dominated group each considers itself superior. The other possible combinations, those involving attitudes of inferiority on the part of both dominant and dominated and those involving attitudes of mixed inferiority and superiority on both sides, may be ruled out from the present discussion. The first of these possible combinations simply does not occur. The second occurs rather frequently, but as in the cases where it occurs without domination, normally results in assimilation rather than the production of nativistic movements.

The idea that nativistic movements may arise in dominant as well as dominated groups appears strange to us, since most of our experience of such movements comes from the contact of Europeans with native peoples. However, we must not forget that Europeans have occupied a singularly favored position in such contacts. Even where the European settles permanently among a native population, he remains a mere outlier of white society and, thanks to modern means of transportation and communication, can keep close touch with the parent body.

This parent body is shielded from contact and assimilation and is thus able to send out to its colonial ruling groups constant increments of individuals who are culturally unmixed. Moreover, the technological superiority of European culture has, until recently, rendered the dominance of colonial groups secure. The nativism of Europeans has, therefore, been largely unconscious and entirely of the perpetuative-rational type. It has manifested itself in such things as the practice of sending children back to Europe to be educated or the Englishman's insistence on dressing for dinner even when alone in a remote outpost of empire. Most dominant groups have been less fortunate. They have found themselves threatened, from the moment of their accession to power, not only by foreign invasion or domestic revolt but also by the insidious processes of assimilation which might, in the long run, destroy their distinctive powers and privileges. This threat was especially menacing when, as in most of the pre-machine age empires, the dominant and dominated groups differed little if at all in physical type. Among such rulers the frustrations which motivate nativistic movements in inferior or dominated groups were replaced by anxieties which produced very much the same results.

Returning to the contact situations previously tabulated, we find that dominant-superior groups tend to initiate perpetuative-rational forms of nativism as soon as they achieve power and to adhere to them with varying intensity as long as they remain in power. Thus the various groups of nomad invaders who conquered China all attempted to maintain much of their distinctive culture and at the height of their power they issued repressive measures directed not only against the Chinese but also against those of their own group who had begun to adopt Chinese culture. It seems probable that revivalist-rational forms of nativism will not arise in a dominant-superior group, at least as regards elements of culture which were moribund at the time of their accession to power, although this form of nativism might develop with respect to culture elements which had fallen into neglect during the period of power. It seems possible also that, under conditions of extreme threat, some form of brief revivalist-magical nativism might arise in such a group, but information

that might verify these conjectures is lacking.

The situation in which a dominant group acknowledges its cultural inferiority to the dominated is one which must arise very infrequently. However, examples of it are provided by such cases as that of the Goths at the time of their conquest of Italy. Such a group immediately finds itself caught on the horns of a dilemma. It can remove its feelings of inferiority only by undergoing cultural if not social assimilation with the conquered society, while such assimilation is almost certain to cost it its dominant position. It seems probable that such a society might develop nativistic movements either when its desire for cultural assimilation with the conquered was frustrated or when it found its dominant position seriously threatened, but again information is lacking.

There is abundant information on nativistic movements among dominated groups and in discussing these we stand on firm ground. A dominated group which considers itself superior will normally develop patterns of rational nativism from the moment that it is brought under domination. These patterns may be either revivalist or perpetuative but are most likely to be a combination of both. One of the commonest rationalizations for loss of a dominant position is that it is due to a society's failure to adhere closely enough to its distinctive culture patterns. Very often such nativism will acquire a semi-magical quality founded on the belief that if the group will only stand firm and maintain its individuality it will once again become dominant. Fully developed magical-revivalist nativism is also very likely to appear in groups of this sort since to the actual deprivations entailed by subjection there are added the frustrations involved by loss of dominance. These frustrations are somewhat mitigated in the cases where the dominant group recognizes the superiority of the dominated group's culture. Such attitudes strengthen the rational nativistic tendencies of the dominated group and diminish the probabilities for magical-revivalist nativism of the more extreme type. Lastly, in cases where the dominant group concurs with the dominated in considering certain aspects of the latter's culture superior but will not grant the superiority of the culture as a whole, this attitude will stimulate the dominated group to focus attention upon such aspects of its culture and endow them with added symbolic value.

A dominated group which considers itself inferior, a condition common among societies of low culture which have recently been brought under European domination, is extremely unlikely to develop any sort of rational nativism during the early period of its subjection. It may, however, develop nativism of the revivalist-magical type if it is subjected to sufficient hardships. The threshold of suffering at which such movements may develop will vary greatly from group to group and will be influenced not only by the degree of hardship but also by the society's patterns of reliance upon the supernatural. A devout society will turn to nativism of this sort long before a skeptical one will. If the hardships arising from subjection are not extreme, the inferior group will usually show great eagerness to assume the culture of the dominant society, this eagerness being accompanied by a devaluation of everything pertaining to its own. Nativistic movements tend to arise only when the members of the subject society find that their assumption of the culture of the dominant group is being effectively opposed by it, or that it is not improving their social position. The movements which originate under these circumstances are practically always rational with a combination of revivalist and perpetuative elements. In this respect they resemble the nativistic movements which originate in inferior groups which are not subject to domination and there can be little doubt that the primary causes are the same in both cases. These movements are a response to frustration rather than hardship and would not arise if the higher group were willing to assimilate the lower one.

Rational nativistic movements can readily be converted into mechanisms for aggression. Since the dominated society has been frustrated in its earlier desires to become acculturated and to achieve social equality, it can frustrate the dominant society in turn by refusing to accept even those elements of culture which the dominant group is eager to share with it. Dominated societies which have acquired these attitudes and developed conscious techniques for preventing further acculturation present one of the most difficult problems for administrators. Passive resistance requires much less energy than any of the techniques needed to break it down, especially if the culture patterns of the dominant group preclude the use of forcible methods.

One final aspect of nativistic movements remains to be considered. The generalizations so far developed have been based upon the hypothesis that societies are homogeneous and react as wholes to contact situations. Very frequently this is not the case, especially in societies which have a well-developed class organization. In such societies nativistic tendencies will be strongest in those classes or individuals who occupy a favored position and who feel this position threatened by culture change. This factor may produce a split in the society, the favored individuals or groups indulging in a rational nativism, either revivalistic or perpetuative, while those in less favored positions are eager for assimilation. This condition can be observed in many immigrant groups in America where individuals who enjoyed high status in the old European society attempt to perpetuate the patterns of that society while those who were of low status do their best to become Americanized.

In a rapidly shrinking world the study of nativistic movements, as of acculturation in general, has ceased to be a matter of purely academic interest. As contacts between societies become more frequent and more general, the need for an understanding of the potentialities of such contact situations becomes more urgent. The troubles which they usually involve can be traced, with few exceptions, to two factors: exploitation and frustration. The first of these is the easier to deal with and may well disappear with the spread of modern science and techniques to all parts of the world. The second is more difficult to deal with, since its removal entails fundamental changes in attitudes of superiority and inferiority. Without these there would be no bar to the assimilation of societies in contact situations or to the final creation of a world society. However, this seems to be one of those millennial visions mentioned elsewhere in this report. Failing assimilation, the happiest situation which can arise out of the contact of two societies seems to be that in which each society is firmly convinced of its own superiority. Rational revivalistic or perpetuative nativistic movements are the best mechanism which has so far been developed for establishing these attitudes in groups whose members suffer from feelings of inferiority. It would appear, therefore, that they should be encouraged rather than discouraged.

BERNARD BARBER

Acculturation and Messianic Movements

Among the many nativistic movements that have been developed in the wake of the impact of white American culture upon the native Indian cultures of the United States, two have been selected for special treatment: the Ghost Dance and the Peyote Cult. The Ghost Dance was a classic example of Linton's magical-revivalistic type of movement and appeared in two waves, both originating among the Northern Paiute Indians in Nevada. The first Ghost Dance started in 1870 and spread mainly to Northern California; the second started in 1890 and spread mainly eastward to the Plains tribes. In this selection Barber develops the thesis that these differential spreads can be accounted for by the relative amounts of deprivation in the two areas.

He then goes on to describe the Peyote Cult as an alternative response to deprivation which, because it was essentially nonviolent and nonthreatening to white American culture and worked in Christian elements and symbols, could spread and survive in areas where the Ghost Dance was forcibly exterminated. We thus seem to have an understandable sequence of acculturation events and native Indian responses—severe deprivation following the extermination of the buffalo herds, and the displacement and resettlement of Indian tribes—setting the cultural stage for acceptance and development of the Ghost Dance, which was to bring back the ancestors driving immense herds of buffalo before them. When the Ghost Dance did not produce the hoped-for results, or was forcibly stamped out by Indian agents and soldiers, the same tribes began to accept the Peyote Cult, which crystallized around passive acceptance and resignation in the face of continuing deprivation.

The outstanding account of the Ghost Dance is found in James Mooney's "The Ghost-Dance Religion" (1896).

Reprinted from *American Sociological Review*, VI (1941), 663–669, by permission of the author and the American Sociological Society.

Robert H. Lowie has recently called our attention again to the problem of messianic movements among the American aborigines. Among the North American Indians one of the fundamental myths was the belief that a culture hero would one day appear and lead them to a terrestrial paradise. Under certain conditions, which this paper will describe and analyze, these myths have become the ideological basis for messianic movements. In the messianic movement, the ushering in of the "golden age" by the messiah is announced for the *immediate* future. Twenty such movements had been recorded in the United States alone prior to 1890.

The messianic doctrine is essentially a statement of hope. Through the intervention of the Great Spirit or of his emissary, the earth will shortly be transformed into a paradise, enjoyed by both the living and the resurrected dead. In anticipation of the happy return to the golden age, believers must immediately return to the aboriginal mode of life. Traits and customs which are symbolic of foreign influence must be put aside. All members of the community—men, women, and children—must participate. Besides reverting to the early folkways, believers must adopt special ritual practices until the millennium arrives. Thus in the

American Ghost Dance movements ceremonial bathing and an elaborate dance were the chief ritual innovations. The doctrine always envisages a restoration of earthly values. These values will be enjoyed, however, in a transcendental setting, for in the age which is foretold there will be no sickness or death; there will be only eternal happiness. The messianic doctrine is peaceful. The exclusion of the whites from the golden age is not so much a reflection of hostility toward them as a symbolization of the fulfillment of the former way of life. The millennium is to be established through divine agency; believers need only watch and pray.

The general sociocultural situation that precipitates a messianic movement has been loosely described as one of "harsh times." Its specific characteristic is the widespread experience of "deprivation"—the despair caused by inability to obtain what the culture has defined as the ordinary satisfactions of life. The fantasy situation pictured in the messianic doctrine attracts adherents chiefly because it includes those things which formerly provided pleasure in life, the loss of which constitutes deprivation. The pervasiveness of the precipitating cultural crisis may be inferred from the broad range of sociocultural items to be restored in the golden age. For example, one of the Sioux participants in the Ghost Dance experienced a vision of an old-fashioned buffalo hunt, genuine in all details. He said that he had beheld the scouts dashing back to proclaim the sighting of a herd. Now, the killing off of the buffalo was probably the greatest blow to the Plains Indians. Another bitter grievance was the expropriation of the Indian lands and the segregation of the tribes on reservations; removal to a new geographical setting had more or less direct repercussions on every phase of the culture. For example, the prophet Smohalla promised, among other things, the restoration of the original tribal lands.

Deprivation may arise from the destruction not only of physical objects but also of sociocultural activities. In the aboriginal Sioux culture, millions of buffalo furnished an unlimited supply of food. Buffaloes and their by-products were perhaps the most important commodity in the Sioux economy, being employed as articles of exchange, as material for tepees, bedding, war shields, and the like. In addition, the buffalo was the focal point of many ritual and social activities of the Sioux. When the buffaloes were destroyed, therefore, the Sioux were deprived not only of food, but also of culturally significant activities. The tribal societies concerned with war and hunting lost their function and atrophied. The arts and techniques surrounding the buffalo hunt, arts and techniques which had once been sources of social status and of pride in "workmanship," were now rendered useless.

The impact of the white culture, besides depriving the Indians of their customary satisfactions, adds to their suffering by introducing the effects of new diseases and intoxicating liquor. In 1889 the Sioux suffered decimating epidemics of measles, grippe, and whooping cough. It is significant that Tenskwatawa prophesied that there would be no smallpox in the golden age. Complaints about the evil influences of firewater were expressed by "Open Door"; by "Handsome Lake," the Iroquois Prophet; by the Delaware Prophet; and by Känakuk, among others.

The messianic movement served to "articulate the spiritual depression" of the Indians. Those groups which faced a cultural impasse were predisposed to accept a doctrine of hope. Correlatively, the tribes that rejected the doctrine were in a state in which the values of their old life still functioned. In a condition of anomie, where there is a disorganization of the "controlling normative structure," most of the members of the group are thrown out of adjustment with significant features of their social environment. The old set of social and cultural norms is undermined by the civilized culture. Expectations are frustrated, there is a "sense of confusion, a loss of orientation," there is no longer a foundation for security. At such a time, messianic prophecies are most likely to be accepted and made the basis of action. Messiahs preach the return to the old order, or rather, to a new order in which the old will be revived. Essentially, their function is to proclaim a *stable order,* one which will define the ends of action. Their doctrines describe men's former life, meaningful and satisfactory.

The stabilizing function of the messianic movement may be illustrated in specific cases. Investigation of the 1870 and 1890 North American Ghost Dance movements shows that they are correlated with widespread deprivation. The two movements, though they originated in the same tribe, the North Paiute of Nevada, spread over different areas, depending upon the presence or absence of a deprivation situation. A comparison of the two movements makes the relationship clear-cut. The Ghost Dance of 1870 spread only through northern California; the tribes in that area had "suffered as great a disintegration by 1870 . . . as the average tribe of the central United States had undergone by 1890." In 1890 the Ghost Dance once again spread from the North Paiute, but this time not to California. By 1875 the movement there had exhausted itself and was abandoned. All the dancing and adherence to the rules of conduct had failed to bring the golden age. Disillusionment supervened upon the discovery that the movement was an inadequate response. The alternative response seems to have been a despondent and relatively amorphous adaptation. The Indians "had long since given up all hope and wish of the old life and adapted themselves as best they might to the new civilization that engulfed them." The 1890 movement did spread to the Plains tribes because by 1890 their old life had virtually disappeared, and the doctrine of the Ghost Dance was eagerly adopted for the hope that it offered. The radical changes among the Plains tribes in the twenty-year period, 1870–90, may best be traced by examining the history of the Teton Sioux. Up to 1868, they were the least affected by white contact of all the tribes of the Plains area. By 1890, however, they were experiencing an intense deprivation situation, the climax of a trend which had begun twenty years before. Especially severe were the years between 1885–90, when crops failed, many cattle died of disease, and a large part of the population was carried off by epidemics.

Further corroboration of the positive correlation of the messianic movement with extended deprivation has been presented by Nash. In 1870 the Ghost Dance doctrine was presented to three tribes which had been brought together on the Klamath reservation six years before, the Klamath, the Modoc, and the Paviotso. Of the three tribes, the Modoc, who had experienced the greatest amount of deprivation, participated most intensely. The Paviotso, who had experienced minimal cultural changes, participated least of all. Moreover, Nash found

that within the tribes the members participated differentially, in rough proportion to the deprivation experienced.

A case study of the Navaho furnishes still further support for our thesis. Until quite recently, the Navaho territory was relatively isolated; few roads crossed it and there were not more than two thousand white inhabitants. The Navaho had managed to maintain the essentials of their own culture; their economic life had remained favorable; and from 1869 to 1931 they increased in numbers from less than 10,000 to 45,000. In 1864, in retaliation for their marauding, the United States Government rounded up the Navaho and banished them to the Bosque Redondo on the Pecos River. This exile was an exception to the fact that in general they had not suffered deprivation. They could not adapt to the agricultural life imposed on them and begged for permission to go home. Many died during epidemics of smallpox, whooping cough, chicken pox, and pneumonia. After four years, they were given sheep, goats, and clothing by the Government and allowed to return to their own country.

The equilibrium of the Navaho culture was quickly restored. The tribe grew rich in herds and silver. The old way of life was resumed in its essentials, despite the greater emphasis on a pastoral economy. The deprivation situation of 1864–68 was left behind; life was integrated around a stable culture pattern. In the winter of 1889–90, when Paiute runners tried to spread the belief in the coming of the Ghost Dance Messiah, their mission was fruitless. "They preached and prophesied for a considerable time, but the Navaho were skeptical, laughed at the prophets, and paid but little attention to their prophecies." There was no social need of a redeemer.

Within the last fifteen years, however, the entire situation of the Navaho tribe has changed. There has been constantly increasing contact with the white culture. Automobiles and railroads have brought tourists. The number of trading stores has increased. The discovery of oil on the reservation has produced rapid changes. Children have been sent to Government schools, far from their homes. Since 1929, the depression has reduced the income from the sale of blankets and silver jewelry. By far the most important difficulty now confronting the Navaho is the problem of overgrazing and soil erosion. To avert disaster, a basic reorganization of the economic activities of the tribe is necessary. Therefore the Government, to meet this *objective* condition, has introduced a soil-erosion and stock-reduction program, but it has been completely unsatisfactory to the Navaho. Stock-reduction not only threatens their economic interests, *as they see them,* but undermines the basis of important sentiments and activities in the Navaho society. To destroy in a wanton fashion the focus of so many of their day-to-day interests cuts the cultural ground from under them.

Thus at present the Navaho are experiencing widespread deprivation. Significantly enough, within the past few years there has been a marked emergence of anti-white sentiment. Revivalistic cults have appeared. There has also been a great increase in recourse to aboriginal ceremonials on all occasions. Long reports of Navaho revivalistic activities were carried recently in *The Farmington Times Hustler,* a weekly published in Farmington, New Mexico. These activities bear a detailed similarity to the Ghost Dance and other American Indian messianic doctrines.

Despite the positive correlation of the messianic movement and deprivation, there is no one-to-one relation between these variables. It is here suggested that the messianic movement is *only one of several alternative responses.* In the other direction, the relationship is more determinate; the messianic movement is comprehensible only as a response to widespread deprivation. The alternative response of armed rebellion and physical violence has already been suggested. The depopulation among the natives of the South Pacific Islands may be viewed as still another response. The moral depression which, it often has been held, is one of the "causes" of the decline of the native races may be construed as a mode of reaction to the loss of an overwhelming number of satisfactions.

The theory of alternative responses may be tentatively checked against another set of data. The Ghost Dance among the Plains tribes lasted little more than a year or two, coming to a sharp end as a result of the

suppression of the so-called "Sioux outbreak" with which it adventitiously had become connected in the minds of the whites. The Government agents on the Indian reservations successfully complied with their instructions to exterminate the movement. However, the deprivation of the tribes remained as acute as ever. It is in this context that the Peyote Cult emerged and spread among the Indians *as an alternative response.* It became the focus of a marked increase of attention and activity after 1890, thus coming in approximate temporal succession to the Ghost Dance. Completely nonviolent and nonthreatening to the white culture, the Peyote Cult has been able to survive in an environment which was radically opposed to the messianic movements.

The general and specific sociocultural matrices of the Peyote Cult are the same as those of the messianic movements. The Indians

fifty years ago, when Peyote first became known to them . . . were experiencing . . . despair and hopelessness over their vanishing culture, over their defeats, over the past grandeur that could not be regained. They were facing a spiritual crisis. . . . Some turned to Peyotism, and as time has but intensified the antagonistic forces, more and more have become converted to the new religion which offers a means of escape . . . [V. Petrullo, *The Diabolic Root*, p. 27].

The Peyote Cult, like the messianic movement, was an "autistic" response, in Lasswell's terms, but the essential element of its doctrine was different. Whereas the Ghost Dance doctrine had graphically described a reversion to the aboriginal state, the Peyote Cult crystallized around passive acceptance and resignation in the face of the existing deprivation. It is an alternative response which seems to be better adapted to the existing phase of acculturation.

Thus we have tested the hypotheses that the primitive messianic movement is correlated with the occurrence of widespread deprivation and that it is only one of several alternative responses. There is a need for further studies, especially in regard to the specific sociocultural conditions which produce responses.

W. W. HILL

The Navaho Indians and the Ghost Dance of 1890

In response to Barber's thesis that the Ghost Dance spread to California tribes in 1870 and to Plains tribes in 1890 because of widespread deprivation, but failed to be accepted by the Navaho Indians because their life was integrated around a stable culture pattern, Hill shows convincingly in his paper that although Barber's general hypothesis may be sound, special cultural patterns in a particular tribe can be crucial in leading a people to reject a movement that is embraced by neighboring tribes. In this case Hill demonstrates that the Navaho fear of the dead and ghosts, which is an underlying and pervasive pattern in Navaho culture, was the critical factor in their rejection of the Ghost Dance. As Hill expresses it, "The Navaho were frightened out of their wits for fear the tenets of the movement were true"—that is, that the ghosts would come back!

Reprinted from *American Anthropologist*, XLVI (1944), 523–527, by permission of the author and the American Anthropological Association.

For years it has been the custom for most anthropologists to revert to economic determinism for an explanation of messianic phenomena. Recently, however, Bernard Barber in his paper "Acculturation and Messianic Movements" called our attention to approaches other than economic, i.e., social, and during the past year Ralph Linton in his article "Nativistic Movements" has outlined a whole new field for researches in the dynamics associated with revivalistic and perpetuative aspects of cultures. Stimulated by these two works I examined my field material on the Ghost Dance of 1890 among the Navaho and, because the data therein varied so from accounts of other tribes, decided to present it for publication.

To those acquainted with Navaho Indians any mention of their association with the Ghost Dance of 1890 must seem anomalous. While strictly speaking no direct participation did occur, this messianic development reached the Navaho and the impact registered profoundly on the minds of the individuals of the period. According to Mooney, news of the movement was conveyed to the Navaho via the Paiute. This was confirmed by some Navaho. However, others assigned it to the Southern Ute, while still others were unable to give any provenience. Most, however, agreed that while it was known throughout the reservation, the focal point for the dissemination of the con-

cepts was in the Shiprock, Nava [Newcomb] Tohatchi region, i.e., northwest New Mexico, a factor which lends weight to their probable diffusion from the Southern Ute.

Most of the familiar traits of the Ghost Dance complex, the resurrection of the dead, the removal of the whites, the reestablishment of the old order of life, and survival through compulsory belief and participation in the movement, were known to the Navaho. The most widespread and significant element was the reported return of the dead. This was variously expressed. Some informants simply state that the dead or ghosts were said to be returning. Elaboration on this theme included the statements that those who had died during the incarceration at Fort Sumner, and those who had been killed by enemies, were coming back, and that the headmen were leading the ghosts back to the reservation.

Other phases of the doctrine were also subject to individual elaboration. The vehicle for white elimination varied in its practical methods, some holding that they were to be exterminated, others that they would leave the Navaho area and return to their former habitat. It was thought that the arrival of the millennium would bring with it the return of the old order, social and religious, plentiful game, ample rainfall, and corn immune from disease. Those who believed in and participated in the movement were to live; those who were skeptical were to die.

It is clear that the Navaho were thoroughly cognizant of all the essential elements of the Ghost Dance of 1890. It has also been established that the movement failed to flourish or find acceptance. We have the testimony of informants alive during this period, the statement of Washington Matthews to Mooney, and Barber's conclusions to this effect. The reasons for this rejection pose some interesting problems in dynamics and configuration.

The question of why the Navaho failed to embrace a doctrine found palatable by so many Indian peoples of North America represents a situation probably unique in the history of messianic movements. Barber has suggested that the rejection was due to a lack of social and spiritual "deprivation." This corresponds to an idea expressed many years ago by Wissler, in connection with the spread of the Ghost Dance in the Plains, and termed by him the occurrence of a cultural vacuum. I should like to present, however, an alternative possibility for the rejection of the 1890 Ghost Dance by the Navaho other than Barber's "life was integrated around a stable culture pattern."

It appears that the lack of acceptance resulted from the functioning of phases of Navaho culture falling into categories described by Kluckhohn as belonging to a covert pattern or configuration. The appended accounts show Navaho attitudes toward the Ghost Dance to have been ones of extreme ambivalence. It is apparent that the acceptance or rejection, per se, on the basis of the benefits which the movement promised was absent from the minds of informants. The question of "life integrated around a stable culture pattern" (if such existed in 1890, it certainly did not in 1870 when according to informants a similar opportunity was rejected) was not a consideration in the decisions. In fact, the idea of rejection or acceptance was of minimum importance; the Navaho interest in the movement was a manifestation of anxiety as to whether or not the reports which reached them were true.

An underlying fear appears even in accounts of the most skeptical informants. It is expressed, according to Navaho pattern, in references to abnormal weather conditions which prevailed during the period, suspicion of witchcraft in connection with the purveyors of the movement, and post-factum rationalizations of dire consequences both to individuals and property. All these were secondary expressions. The real anxiety concern was with the one element which was the core of the movement, i.e., the return of the dead.

Had the "economic" or "social integration" factors been compulsive, a selective element could have been expected to operate; the Navaho might gladly have embraced parts of the complex—the restoration of the old life and the disappearance of the whites—while rejecting the tidings that the dead were to return. However, the compelling element for them was clearly their fear of the dead; so much so that all other tenets were infected by it, hence suspect and to be rejected.

For the Navaho with his almost psychotic fear of death, the dead, and all connected with them, no greater cataclysm than the return of the departed or ghosts could be envisaged. In short, the Navaho were frightened out of their wits for fear the tenets of the movement were true. Thus, a covert pattern or configuration, deep-seated in the unconscious psychology of that people, acted as a barrier to the diffusion of a complex embraced by most of the tribes in western United States.

APPENDIX

The Late Fat One's Son, Tohatchi, N.M.: "The ignorant Navaho like myself were saying at this time, 'Look over toward Nava. [Nava (Newcomb) is north of Tohatchi. The ghosts are thought to reside in the north.] They [ghosts] are there already at Nava and will soon appear on the high ridges between Nava and Cornfields.' Then they would mention the names of the different headmen who had died and who were leading the ghosts back. Among them they mentioned my own father. The majority of the people believed in this. Those who did not believe, would ask, 'What is the purpose of these ghosts coming back?' The believers would say, 'They are just coming back to live with us and to tell us of the things in the other world.' Some of the people were singing to prevent the ghosts from coming back; they were afraid of them. This lasted one whole summer but gradually died out because no ghosts appeared and because the unbelievers ridiculed the believers. They tried to find the source of this rumor but they could not find where it started. They decided that some woman must have started it." The informant said that he does not know how far the Ghost Dance spread but believes that it was known throughout the reservation. The ghosts were to bring with them much rain; there was to be quantities of game in the country again; they were to bring corn which was immune from all diseases; all the old customs were to be reinstated; everything was to be as it was in the beginning because these ghosts knew conditions on both sides [i.e., in life and death] and they were to combine things from both sides and make things perfect. Some of the men even told people that they should be thankful that their relatives were returning. "Old Manuelito, of Fort Sumner time, was the chief unbeliever. He said, 'It is our belief that if ghosts appear it is bad luck. If they do appear we will have to get rid of them.' I was living close to Manuelito so I did not believe in their return, but everyone was talking so strongly about it it was hard not to believe. A woman dreamed that in the future the ghosts would return to the land of the living. That seems to have been the start of it. Manuelito told all the leading men to try and discourage this ghost business. He said, 'We know that ghosts are bad.' He tried to get the people to think of beneficial things, like agriculture and sheep raising. He said, 'Why ask the ghosts to come back; some day you will get a chance to go there.' This ghost dance never caused any harm but this witch business did. Right after [the captivity at] Fort Sumner the Navaho were very poor."

Grey Hair, White Cone, Ariz.: "The people who were saying this were a kind of prophet people. After they had said this thing a number of girls and boys around eighteen years of age died." The informant says that he has heard this prediction of the return of the dead three times during his life. "The first time was when I was about twelve years old [1870]. I heard it again when I was about thirty years old [1890]. The last time I heard it was about fifteen years ago [about 1918]. These prophet men were thinking bad. They must have been thinking that all the Navaho were going to die. A few years after the first time I heard this [1870] there was an epidemic of measles and a great many people died. A few years after the second time [1890] an epidemic of mumps killed a great number of people. Nothing has happened as yet since the last prophecy but I am waiting to see what will."

Slim Curley, Crystal, Ariz.: "I was living at Lukachukai. I was a young man at the time. The days were just hazy and the sun was reddish. Everything looked peculiar. People began to say that the Utes and the Paiutes were talking about the ghosts coming. Many of the people in the country did not believe this. You could tell because they ridiculed the idea. However, there were a number who did believe it. I remember at a gathering for gambling one night there was a man who did not believe it. This man asked another for some money, saying, 'I hear that the ghosts are coming back to this country. No doubt my mother is in the crowd and you can have intercourse with her when she returns.' Those who believed said, 'The Utes are sending word ahead that the ghosts are coming.' In the last month Chi Dodge was giving a group of medicine men a talking to. In the course of the talk he said, 'You must not start all these rumors.' He said, 'Look what happened after Fort Sumner [days]; someone started this rumor that all the white men were to be exterminated and then later this business about the ghosts coming back was started.' One old man wanted to take a party to the west to visit Changing Woman and find out what this return of the ghosts meant."

Mr. Headman, Head Springs, Ariz.: "There were Holy Men among the Navaho who told the old men and women that the dead were coming back. However, the old men and women did not believe it. They said, 'No one is going to come back once they are dead. If they come back it will mean that they will bring back all kinds of sickness. Also, if they come back there will be no rains and no corn.' They told the prophets that they should not say that the dead were coming back. The prophets said, 'When the ghosts come back all the whites . . .'—it hurts an old man like me to say these kind of words [i.e., to talk about ghosts]."

Albert G. Sandoval, Lukachukai, Ariz.: "It was known all over the reservation but most of the people did not believe it. They never danced. The Gods have left the country and have visited the people for the last time. The dead do not come back. In 1920 a preacher on the San Juan predicted a flood. The people were frightened and the majority of them left for the mountains. There was a hell of a mess. Most of the Indians took all their possessions with them. The knowledge [of the Ghost Dance] does not seem to have come from any particular source. Everyone knew of it but it just seems to have been passed along."

Pete Price, Fort Defiance, Ariz.: "The wind and the weather were very unusual at that time. Then word came that the dead were coming back to the earth. However, the majority of the people did not take this very seriously. They used to joke about it."

Mr. Left-Handed, Crown Point, N.M.: "I heard that all the Navaho who had died at Fort Sumner and all those who had been killed by enemies were coming back to life. The Navaho were all to go back where they had been living before and all the whites would have to go back to their own country. This came from around Tohatchi. There was no dance connected with the coming of the ghosts. As a rule it was not believed by the majority. Most of the people thought that this was started by the witches."

The Late Little Smith's Son, Crown Point, N.M.: "When we first heard of it I was living along Tohatchi flat. We heard that the ghosts

were moving in close to where we were. Some of the young scouts told me that my father was coming back and that I had better go over and meet him. They said that all those who did not believe that the ghosts were coming back were going to die; the rest of the poeple would live on. This ghost business started up near Shiprock. A man there started it."

J. S. SLOTKIN

The Peyote Way

Peyote (a name derived from the Nahuatl word *peyotl*) was used in the ceremonies of Indians in central and northern Mexico in pre-Columbian times. The Huichol Indians living in the Sierra Madre mountains of western Mexico still make long pilgrimages on foot to collect peyote for their ceremonies each year. From Mexico the custom of taking peyote spread to the United States Indians and by 1890 it had become an important form of religion among the Plains tribes. Today, as Slotkin points out, Peyote religion is the most widespread contemporary religion among the Indians of the United States. It is organized as the Native American Church and has become a kind of Indian version of Christianity, having adopted white Christian theology, ethics, and eschatology and modified these features to make them more compatible with traditional Indian culture.

The following selection provides a brief but illuminating description of "the Peyote Way" written by an anthropologist who was a member and officer of the Native American Church. In addition to the other technical reports published by Slotkin and mentioned in the selection, there is also a monograph by Weston LaBarre, *The Peyote Cult* (1938), and a recent popular book by Aldous Huxley, *Doors to Perception* (1954), which describes Huxley's experiences in taking mescaline, the same drug that is found in peyote.

Reprinted from *Tomorrow*, IV, No. 3 (1955–1956), 64–70, by permission of the author and Garrett Publications.

Peyote (*Lophophora williamsi*) is a spineless cactus which grows in the northern half of Mexico and for a short distance north of the Texas border. It has attracted attention because it is used as a sacrament in religious rites conducted by Indians in the United States and Canada belonging to the Native American Church. The Peyote Religion or Peyote Way, as it is called by members, is the most widespread contemporary religion among the Indians, and is continually spreading to additional tribes.

From the viewpoint of almost all Peyotists, the religion is an Indian version of Christianity. White Christian theology, ethics, and eschatology have been adopted with modifications which make them more com-

patible with traditional Indian culture. The religion probably originated among the Kiowa and Comanche in Oklahoma about 1885.

The Peyote rite is an all-night ceremony, lasting approximately from sunset to sunrise, characteristically held in a Plains type tipi. Essentially the rite has four major elements: prayer, singing, eating the sacramental Peyote, and contemplation. The ritual is well defined, being divided into four periods: from sunset to midnight, from midnight to three o'clock, from three o'clock to dawn, and from dawn to morning. Four fixed songs sung by the rite leader, analogous to the fixed songs in the Catholic Mass, mark most of these divisions.

The rite within the tipi begins with the Starting Song; the midnight period is marked by the Midnight Water Song; there is no special song at three o'clock; at dawn there is the Morning Water Song, and the rite ends with the Quitting Song. At midnight sacred water is drunk again and a communion meal eaten.

Usually five people officiate at the rite. Four are men: the leader, often referred to as the Roadman because he leads the group along the Peyote Road (that is, the Peyotist way of life) to salvation; the drum chief who accompanies the leader when he sings; the cedar chief who is in charge of the cedar incense; and the fire chief who maintains a ritual fire and acts as sergeant-at-arms. A close female relative of the leader, usually his wife, brings in, and prays over, the morning water.

In clockwise rotation, starting with the leader, each male participant sings a set of four solo songs; he is accompanied on a water drum by the man to his right. The singing continues from the time of the Starting Song to that of the Morning Water Song; the number of rounds of singing therefore depends upon the number of men present. On most occasions there are four rounds, so that each man sings a total of sixteen songs.

During the rite Peyote is taken in one of the following forms: the fresh whole plant except for roots (green Peyote), the dried top of the plant (Peyote button), or an infusion of the Peyote button in water (Peyote tea). Some people have no difficulty taking Peyote. But many find it bitter, inducing indigestion or nausea. A common complaint is, "It's hard to take Peyote."

The amount taken depends upon the individual, and the solemnity of the ritual occasion. There is great tribal variability in amount used, and accurate figures are virtually impossible to obtain. But in general one might say that under ordinary circumstances the bulk of the people take less than a dozen Peyotes. On the most serious occasions, such as rites held for someone mortally sick, those present take as much Peyote as they can; the capacity of most people seems to range from about four to forty Peyote buttons.

Peyotists have been organized into the Native American Church since 1918. These church groups run the gamut of comprehensiveness from the single local group on the one extreme, to the intertribal and international federation known as the Native American Church of North America, on the other extreme.

In a series of other publications I have discussed the early history of Peyotism ("Peyotism, 1521–1891," *American Anthropologist*, LVII [1955], pp. 202–30), presented an historical and generalized account of the religion (in a book to be published in 1956[1]), and given a detailed description of the Peyote Religion in a single tribe ("Menomini Peyotism," *Transactions of the American Philosophical Society*, XLII [1952], Part 4)—all from the viewpoint of a relatively detached anthropologist. The present essay is different. Here I concentrate on the contemporary uses of, and attitudes toward, sacramental Peyote, and write as a member and officer of the Native American Church of North America. Of course the presentation is mine, but I think substantially it represents the consensus of our membership.

Long ago God took pity on the Indian. (Opinions vary as to when this happened: when plants were created at the origin of the world, when Jesus lived, or after the white man had successfully invaded this continent.) So God created Peyote and put some of his power into it for the use of Indians. Therefore the Peyotist takes the sacramental Peyote to absorb God's power contained in it, in the same way that the white Christian takes the sacramental bread and wine.

Power is the English term used by Indians for the supernatural force called *mana* by anthropologists; it is equivalent to the New Testament *pneuma*, translated as Holy Spirit or Holy Ghost. Power is needed to live. As a Crow Indian once remarked to me as we were strolling near a highway, man is like an auto; if the car loses its power it cannot go. Physically, power makes a person healthy, and safe when confronted by danger. Spiritually, power gives a person knowledge of how to behave successfully in everyday life, and what to make of one's life as a whole. The Peyotist obtains power from the sacramental Peyote.

Physically, Peyote is used as a divine healer and amulet.

[1] Ed. Note: *The Peyote Religion: A Study in Indian-White Relations* (Glencoe, Ill.: The Free Press, 1956).

For sick people Peyote is used in various ways. In a mild illness Peyote is taken as a home remedy. Thus when a man has a cold, he drinks hot Peyote tea and goes to bed. In more serious illnesses Peyote is taken during the Peyote rite. Such an illness is due not only to lack of sufficient power, but also to a foreign object within the body. Therefore a seriously sick person who takes Peyote usually vomits, thus expelling the foreign object which is the precipitating cause of the illness; then more Peyote is taken in order to obtain the amount of power needed for health.

In cases of severe illness, the rite itself is held for the purpose of healing the patient; it is often referred to as a doctoring meeting. In addition to having the sick person take Peyote, as in less desperate cases, everyone else present prays to God to give the patient extra power so he or she will recover.

Members may keep a Peyote button at home, or on their person, to protect them from danger. The latter is particularly true of men in the armed forces. The power within the Peyote wards off harm from anything in the area of its influence. In cases of great danger, as when a young man is about to leave for military service, a prayer meeting is held at which everyone present beseeches God to give the man extra power to avoid harm.

Spiritually, Peyote is used to obtain knowledge. This is known as learning from Peyote. Used properly, Peyote is an inexhaustible teacher. A stock statement is, "You can use Peyote all your life, but you'll never get to the end of what there is to be known from Peyote. Peyote is always teaching you something new." Many Peyotists say that the educated white man obtains his knowledge from books—particularly the Bible; while the uneducated Indian has to obtain his knowledge from Peyote. But the Indian's means of achieving knowledge is superior to that of the white man. The latter learns from books merely what other people have to say; the former learns from Peyote by direct experience.

A Comanche once said, "The white man talks *about* Jesus; we talk *to* Jesus." Thus the individual has a vividly direct experience of what he learns, qualitatively different from inference or hearsay. Therefore the Peyotist, epistemologically speaking, is an individualist and empiricist; he believes only what he himself has experienced.

A Peyotist maxim is, "The only way to find out about Peyote is to take it and learn from Peyote yourself." It may be interesting to know what others have to say; but all that really matters is what one has directly experienced—what he has learned himself from Peyote. This conception of salvation by knowledge, to be achieved by revelation (in this case, through Peyote) rather than through verbal or written learning, is a doctrine similar to that of early Middle Eastern Gnosticism.

The mere act of eating Peyote does not itself bring knowledge. The proper ritual behavior has to be observed before one is granted knowledge through Peyote. Physically, one must be clean, having bathed and put on clean clothes. Spiritually, one must put away all evil thought. Psychologically, one must be conscious of his personal inadequacy, humble, sincere in wanting to obtain the benefits of Peyote, and concentrate on it.

Peyote teaches in a variety of ways.

One common way in which Peyote teaches is by heightening the sensibility of the Peyotist, either in reference to himself or to others.

Heightened sensibility to oneself manifests itself as increased powers of introspection. One aspect of introspection is very important in Peyotism. During the rite a good deal of time is spent in self-evaluation. Finally the individual engages in silent or vocal prayer to God, confessing his sins, repenting, and promising to follow the Peyote Road (that is, the Peyotist ethic) more carefully in the future. If he has spiritual evil within him, Peyote makes him vomit, thus purging him of sin.

Heightened sensibility to others manifests itself as what might be called mental telepathy. One either feels that he knows what others are thinking, or feels that he either influences, or is influenced by, the thoughts of others. In this connection a frequent phenomenon is speaking in tongues, which results from the fact that people from different tribes participate in a rite together, each using his own language; Peyote teaches one the meaning of otherwise unknown languages.

For example, during the rite each male participant in succession sings solo four songs at a time. Recently a Winnebago sitting next to me sang a song with what I heard as a Fox text (Fox is an Algonquian language closely related to Menomini, the language I use in the rite), sung so clearly and distinctly I understood every word.

When he was through, I leaned over and asked, "How come you sang that song in Fox rather than Winnebago (a Siouan language unintelligible to me)?"

"I did sing it in Winnebago," he replied. The afternoon following the rite he sat down next to me and asked me to listen while he repeated the song; this time it was completely unintelligible to me because the effects of Peyote had worn off.

A second common way in which Peyote teaches is by means of revelation, called a vision. The vision is obtained because one has eaten enough Peyote under the proper ritual conditions to obtain the power needed to commune with the spirit world. The vision provides a direct experience (visual, auditory, or a combination of both) of God or some intermediary spirit, such as Jesus, Peyote Spirit (the personification of Peyote), or Waterbird.

The nature of the vision depends upon the personality and problems of the individual. The following are typical: He may be comforted by seeing or hearing some previously unexperienced item of Peyotist belief, or departed loved ones now in a happy existence. He may be guided on the one hand by being shown the way to solve some problem in daily life; on the other hand, he may be reproved for evil thoughts or deeds, and warned to repent.

A third way in which Peyote teaches is by means of mystical experience. This is relatively uncommon. It is limited to Peyotists of a certain personality type among the more knowledgeable members of the church; roughly speaking, they have what white people would call a mystical temperament. These Peyotists, in turn, rarely have visions, and tend to look upon them as distractions. The mystical experience may be said to consist in the harmony of all immediate experience with whatever the individual conceives to be the highest good.

Peyote has the remarkable property of helping one to have a mystical experience for an indefinite period of time, as opposed to most forms of mystical discipline under which the mystical experience commonly

lasts for a matter of minutes. Actually I have no idea of how long I could maintain such an experience with Peyote, for after about an hour or so it is invariably interrupted by some ritual detail I am required to perform.

What happens to the Peyotist phenomenologically that makes possible the extraordinary results I have described? It seems to depend on both the physiological and psychological effects of Peyote.

Physiologically, Peyote seems to have curative properties. Many times, after a variety of illnesses brought about by fieldwork conditions, I have left a Peyote meeting permanently well again.

Another physiological effect of Peyote is that it reduces the fatigue to an astonishing extent. For instance, I am not robust, but after taking Peyote I can participate in the rite with virtually no fatigue—a rite which requires me to sit on the ground, cross-legged, with no back rest, and without moving, for 10 to 14 hours at a stretch; all this in the absence of food and water.

Psychologically, Peyote increases one's sensitivity to relevant stimuli. This applies to both external and internal stimuli. Externally, for example, the ritual fire has more intense colors when I am under the influence of Peyote. Internally, I find it easier to introspect upon otherwise vague immediate experiences.

At the same time, Peyote decreases one's sensitivity to irrelevant external and internal stimuli. Very little concentration is needed for me to ignore distracting noises inside or outside the tipi. Similarly, extraneous internal sensations or ideas are easily ignored.

Thus, on one occasion I wrote in my field diary, "I could notice no internal sensations. If I paid very close attention, I could observe a vague and faint feeling that suggested that without Peyote my back would be sore from sitting up in one position all night; the same was true of my crossed legs. Also, my mouth might be dry, but I couldn't be sure."

The combination of such effects as absence of fatigue, heightened sensitivity to relevant stimuli, and lowered sensitivity to irrelevant stimuli, should make it easier to understand how the individual is disposed to learn from Peyote under especially created ritual conditions.

To any reader who becomes intrigued by

Peyote, two warnings should be given. First, I have discussed the effects of Peyote on those who used it as a sacrament under ritual conditions. The described responses of white people to Peyote under experimental conditions are quite different; in fact, they tend to be psychologically traumatic. Second, Peyote is a sacrament in the Native American Church, which refuses to permit the presence of curiosity seekers at its rites, and vigorously opposes the sale or use of Peyote for nonsacramental purposes.

CYRIL S. BELSHAW

The Significance of Modern Cults in Melanesian Development

This selection takes us to a description and analysis of nativistic cults in another part of the world, the Melanesian islands in the South Pacific. Belshaw provides a vivid summary of the main features of the modern nativistic cults that have occurred. He then goes on to show that the movements were widely separated in time and place and that their similarities must be due to similarities in local conditions which produce them. These local conditions are essentially ones in which the Melanesians are halfway between the old and the new way of living. The natives have been in contact with thriving European communities, but none of them have been able to participate in vigorous activity leading to a higher standard of life. Hence they are envious of the Europeans, but without effective means of achieving a European way of life. So like the Ghost Dance, Peyote Cult, and other movements among the North American Indians, these Melanesian cults appear to be triggered by the same kind of conditions among people who find themselves in a transitional state. The people respond by developing cults which explain European success, and attempt to achieve a method of parallel success by adopting and manipulating (in magical fashion) symbols of the European way of life: flags and flagpoles, chairs and rulers, and so on.

Reprinted in abridged form from *The Australian Outlook,* IV (1950), 116–125, by permission of the author and the Australian Institute of International Affairs.

Although we know that in New Caledonia and Fiji the Melanesian people have shown themselves capable of considerable political development, many of us who know the Melanesian in the New Hebrides, British Solomon Islands, and New Guinea are inclined to doubt the possibility, at least in the near future, of Melanesians organizing their own political movements. The "Fuzzy Wuzzy Angels" of the war, emerging from the bush with hardly-come-by garden produce, resisting many forms of agricultural innovation, chewing betel nut, wearing cast-off clothing, speaking seemingly mutilated forms of English, appear to be far removed from any form of modern organization. The British Solomon Island experiments in Native Courts and Councils, though a tremendously promising innovation, have been temporarily arrested by a strange native cult. The suggestion that there might before long be a pan-Melanesian nationalist movement would evoke incredulous smiles from most European Island residents, who point to the impossibility of persuading laborers from different communities to work together in harmony, to the multifarious languages and cultures, and to the absence of anything approaching a centralized organization in traditional life.

It is the purpose of this article to suggest, however, that this is far too simple an interpretation of Melanesian possibilities. An analysis of certain apparently isolated Melanesian cults, which have grown up in European times, will give an indication of some of these possibilities. We may begin by a brief summary of their features.

THE TUKA CULT OF FIJI

About 1885 a prophet arose among the hill tribes of Fiji. He claimed that it had been revealed to him that before long the whole world would be turned upside down, particularly that the whites would serve the natives, the chiefs would serve the common people, and his followers would have eternal life. Jehovah was subordinated to local gods, and through the use of supernatural powers derived from the gods, the prophet was enabled to secure the obedience of a large following. This following drilled in European style to repulse the expected advance of the Administration. The prophet was banished, but the belief in the *tuka* cult continued.

THE BAIGONA CULT OF PAPUA

The *Baigona* Snake Cult of the Northern Division of Papua operated for many years from 1911. The prophet had the secrets of sorcery and prophecy revealed to him by the *Baigona Snake,* and cultivated its good-will by special rites. He sold the secrets of the cult to those who wished to be initiated. The movement was characterized by trances. Its rise coincided with the attempt to bring the area under administrative control. An administrative patrol was endangered and administrative pressure to reduce the trances and abolish the sale of initiation in accordance with antisorcery policy was not completely successful.

THE LONTIS CULT OF BUKA

I have not been able to find details of this cult, which occurred in 1913 during the German administration. Numerous arrests were made.

THE GERMAN WISLIN OF THE TORRES STRAITS

This is the first clear specimen of the genus now known as "Cargo Cult." It occurred in 1913 on the island of Saibai, Torres Straits. The prophet declared that his followers would see the *markai,* the spirits of the dead, who would come to them in a steamer, bringing all kinds of manufactured cargo, and who would kill all the whites. Those who disobeyed the prophet would lose all their money and would be unable to earn any more.

THE TARO CULT AND ITS RELATIVES IN PAPUA

This cult, very much akin to the *Baigona,* but in which the native vegetable taro took the place of the *baigona* snake, was more vigorous in its proselytism and lasted from 1914 into the late twenties. Dreams, ritual, and shaking fits played a prominent part in it. Off-shoots were the *Kava Kava* and *Kekesi* cults in the same area (Northern Division).

THE VAILALA MADNESS OF PAPUA

The *Vailala Madness,* which swept the Gulf Division of Papua from 1919 to 1923, was in the hands of sorcerers who had the power of divination during trances, and who encouraged their followers to take part in orgies of shaking fits. The great bull-roarer ceremonies of the kinship groups were abandoned, and new ceremonies were created to take their place. A steamer was expected, bringing the deceased relatives who were to have white skins. The new ceremonies contained a Christian element, flagpoles were given names and treated as the media through whom messages from the dead were recieved, there was a certain element of military drill, and women were given equality. Public confessionals took place.

THE MURDER OF CLAPCOTT, NEW HEBRIDES

In 1923 the inland people of Espiritu Santo, New Hebrides, were influenced by rumors of death-raising. The prophet concerned claimed that if all the Europeans were killed the dead would arise, with white skins. They would bring European goods with them, and a house was built to receive these. To join the movement, it was necessary to pay a pig, or a fee of 5/- to one pound. During a great feast the prophet's wife died, and a European, Clapcott, was immediately killed. It is stated that the same people killed some Europeans called Greig in 1908, but details do not seem to have been published. These are the only occasions in which Europeans have been assaulted during these movements, though resistance and threats have been offered on several occasions.

THE CARGO CULTS OF BUKA

In 1932 and 1933 a cargo cult arose which appeared to be related to the previously mentioned *Lontis* cult. The prophet claimed that a steamer would arrive, laden with good things, and that all Buka would be ruled from their village. A store was to be built to receive these goods, and the police to be resisted if they interfered. But the ship would not come while food was available, and hence gardens were abandoned for some time. The leaders were imprisoned, but the cult continued.

THE MARKHAM CARGO CULT, NEW GUINEA

In 1933 a prophet arose in this area who claimed that Jehovah was subordinate to Satan. Once again the spirits of the dead were expected to return, bringing goods; gardens lapsed; and séances took place. Villages were destroyed and community houses built, and it was erroneously believed that the Administration would be passive.

THE CHAIR AND RULE MOVEMENT OF THE SOLOMONS

About 1939 a European missionary encouraged the Melanesians of Santa Ysabel, Gela, and Savo to agitate for a seat on the nominated Advisory Council. He emphasized the need for a chairman and rules of procedure. The movement got out of hand and was misinterpreted. The Melanesians elevated a flag, a wooden chair, and a wooden rule into positions of ritual importance. They wrote to friends in San Cristoval and agitated for higher wages. Those involved were punished and the missionary asked to leave the Protectorate. His memory was still revered in 1945 among some people. The Administration was prompted into plans for Native Courts and Councils by this movement.

THE JOHN FRUM MOVEMENT, NEW HEBRIDES

In 1940 a native of the island of Tanna declared himself to be the prophet of John Frum, a spirit which evidently took the place of the ancient spirit of Karaperamun, formerly of great power. John Frum declared that the whole island was shortly to change in nature—its volcanic cone to be replaced by fertile plains, its people to be eternally young and healthy, and to have everything that they could ever desire. In order to achieve this end, it was necessary to hunt

and kill all Europeans, to rid themselves of the taint of European money, to rid themselves of immigrant natives, and to return to the old customs of polygyny, dancing, kava drinking, and so forth, which had been rigidly proscribed by the theocratic Presbyterian Church. Money was taken to the stores and a great spending spree indulged in. The Administration took action; arrests were made.

The movement continued, however, especially in 1942, 1943, and 1947, encouraged by letters from the former leaders, who had been banished to Malekula. A modern touch was added by the construction of an aerodrome for American Liberators. The imprisoned leaders succeeded in converting neighboring villages on Malekula. A similar movement arose on Ambryn, in which a house was built to receive goods from the Messageries Maritimes steamer "Le Polynésien."

THE NAKED CULT, ESPIRITU SANTO

This cult, seen from 1944 to 1948, appears to be connected with the Clapcott murder case mentioned previously. It has, however, rather different features. The followers of the prophet are to go naked and are to cohabit in public. Villages are to be destroyed and replaced by two communal houses, one for the men and one for the women. All animals and property received from the Europeans are to be destroyed. Old customs such as exogamy and marriage payments are to be scrapped. The people are no longer to work for the Europeans, but to wait for the arrival of the Americans, when they will receive all good things. The people are to have immortality.

THE MASINGA RULE MOVEMENT OF THE SOLOMONS

The *Masinga* rule movement first made its appearance at the end of 1945 and in 1946 and is the most political of any of the movements that have yet appeared. In its early stages it appeared to have connections with the earlier Chair and Rule movement, and with disaffection which was rife on Guadalcanal, following the presence of Allied troops. It soon took on its own form, however, with Malaita the center. Buildings were erected to warehouse the expected free gifts from American liberators; monetary contributions were exacted from the adherents of the movement; the leaders were reputed to have boundless wealth in dollars and to pay their followers twelve pounds a month; Melanesians were forbidden to work for Europeans unless a wage of twelve pounds a month was paid; missionary and administrative work was resisted; demonstrations of several thousand natives took place on Government stations demanding education, higher wages, political independence, and the removal of Europeans; "soldiers" were drilled; the central organization on Malaita established connections with Ulawa and San Cristoval and the movement was eventually copied in the Santa Cruz group and the Western Solomons. At first the Administration was prepared to tolerate the movement and wait for it to die out, but as resistance, and particularly drilling, grew in scale, several score of arrests were made. The movement still continues, and so do the arrests.

OTHER CONTEMPORARY MOVEMENTS

At the close of the recent war, Melanesia was left with three described movements, *Masinga* Rule, John Frum, and the Naked Cult. There appears, however, to have been a general revival of similar movements all over Melanesia, with the possible exception of New Caledonia, though we still await published details of them. There is the Apolisi prophet movement of Fiji, a cargo cult in the Loyalty Islands (the first reported) and in New Guinea, and a similar movement in the Purari Delta of Papua. This latter appears to have interesting possibilities, for it is reported that for the first time the Administration, while watching it carefully, is encouraging it and aiding it in its development program—including rebuilding of villages and reorganization of agriculture. (These two objectives were also part of the *Masinga* Rule movement, but neither Melanesian leadership nor Administration pursued them vigorously.)

These then are the principal details of about thirteen movements that have been described over the past fifty years. What is their significance?

The first point to notice is that the movements are widely separated in time and place, from the Torres Straits to Fiji, and that this effectively rules out the possibility that they are copies of each other. Their similarities must be due to similarities in local conditions which produce them.

The movements fall into two main groups, with borderline cases in between. The first of these is seen in its purest form in the *Baigona* and Taro cults in Papua. There is no hint here of conflict with the European until the European Administrator, from the Melanesian point of view, "butts in." In their essentials, the cults are similar to those found everywhere in Melanesia at the time of the arrival of the Europeans. They express the indigenous Melanesian animist interpretation of the world and his centuries-old traditional delight in ceremonial and cult practices. They are novel only in that their origins have been observed and not speculated about, and from this point of view they are of considerable interest to the sociologist.

The other cults are a modern modification of this phenomenon. But before we make this clear, a number of alternative hypotheses may be disposed of.

First, there is the understandable Administrative view that these are dangerous movements, interrupting Melanesian life, threatening good order, and evidencing the unhealthy despotic powers of sorcerers who, by trickery, have bullied the local people, and who make their fortune by the sale of their tricks. Of the political aspects of this view, I will speak later. But as a theory of origins it is most defective. No leader, it must be emphasized, in the absence of mechanical instruments or a police state, can force people to follow him or accept his doctrines. The traditional Melanesian method of avoiding unwanted leaders is simply to move somewhere else, found a new village, grow new gardens, or retaliate by counter-sorcery or murder. It must be accepted that the religious element in these cults is sufficiently near the Melanesian pattern to enable us to believe that their following is by and large popular. As for the sale of the tricks of the trade, that too is common to most forms of Melanesian sorcery, and even the passing on of dance movements and songs. It is, as it were, payment for copyright.

Secondly, there is the view that the cults express a reaction to a particular event or organization. It is superficially possible, for instance, to blame the John Frum movement on to the rather rigid and narrow interpretations of recent Presbyterian proselytizing. Similarly, one could blame the Espiritu Santo movement on to the sale of liquor and to other abuses by the traders. And the *Masinga* Rule movement has been blamed on "Marxist elements" among American troops.

All these views possess an element of truth, but all lack conviction. Why should such diverse historical facts give rise to such unified movements? On the other hand, if we describe the position of these Melanesian communities in the modern world we can see that there is indeed a common element.

None of these communities is untouched by European influence; and none of them has been able to take full advantage of living under that influence. Moving roughly west to east, the Torres Straits have been the happy hunting grounds of pearl fishers and labor recruiters, but at the beginning of the century the island of Saibai was subject to no permanent European influences; the Gulf of Papua is not a favorite area of European exploitation, though there have been European planters there; Buka again is on the fringe of European activity; Gela it is true is very close to the pre-war Solomon Island capital of Tulagi—but here the movement was more definitely political rather than religious and it was stronger in the less developed north than in the more developed south; Malaita is a classic example, for here there was practically no European activity, while the almost overpopulated communities sent their sons to other islands for plantation work; inland Espiritu Santo has hardly been visited by Europeans, though there is a thriving community on the coast; Tanna is a small island well off the beaten track, again exporting a few of its people as seamen; and the Loyalty Islands, unattractive to European settlers, live by exporting produce to Noumea, the New Caledonian capital. Inland Fiji, at the time of the Tuka Cult, was quite primitive.

These people, then, have all been in contact with thriving European communities, but none of them have been able to participate in vigorous activity leading to a higher standard of life. I think it is most significant that the two extremes of Melanesian life do not appear so far to have succumbed to these cults, though they have problems of their own. On the one hand, we have the thriving native settlements in or near such towns as Port Moresby, Rabaul, Vila, and in New Caledonia, and areas of intensive missionary industrial work. Here the people are in the grip of modern life—and have little time or inclination to organize into cults. On the other hand, we have areas such as the interior of New Guinea and Malekula, where cults continue in their native form, unmodified by European intrusion.

If we accept this thesis, it is easy to understand that the similarities in the cults are due to the position of the communities halfway between the old and the new way of living; and that the differences are due almost solely to particular historical circumstances. The universals seem to be these. The "halfway" Melanesian sees other people who possess a way of living that he tends to envy. He has to find some explanation of European power in holding sway over multitudes; of the miraculous arrival of manufactured goods in ships and aeroplanes; of strange European behavior which sends away piles of raw materials; of the peculiar distaste with which Europeans treat him. On the one hand, this gives him an end of activity—he must strive to attain a similar power. On the other hand, it sets him an intellectual problem and gives him an emotional experience. His emotional experience is jealousy, sometimes hatred, of the European, who neither gives him these things as a friend nor initiates him into the mysteries of the process of sale and production—indeed, tries to fob him off with Biblical education. His intellectual problem is, first, to explain European success, and, second, to achieve a method of parallel success.

This problem must be solved in terms of Melanesian experience. There is behind him the great tradition of cults such as the *Baigona,* and animism. It is natural that he should turn to find a superior cult. At first, it was Christianity in many parts, which was conceived as a superior, sometimes as a supplementary, animism. This fails, or is not understood, and is molded on to something new. The new cult endeavors to copy significant European activities. There is the belief in shipping, that is, in the origin of cargoes—for remember, most Melanesians have not seen or experienced the manufacturing process. There is a mystical significance in the revolting white skin of Europeans, and in money, which circulates so strangely; in flags and flagpoles, which the European treats with peculiar reverence; in towns and houses rather than villages; in soldiers and drilling—which *must* be mystical, for what use is there in it? And in later years, of course, there is the myth of American ar-rival, so obviously based upon the big-handedness and freedom of American troops. These things supplied the modern elements in the cargo myth, the myth which explained European successes and indicated the correct road to follow.

YONINA TALMON

Pursuit of the Millennium: The Relation Between Religious and Social Change

Within the last decade many fruitful studies of millenarian movements have been made both in Europe and America, underscoring the importance of such movements historically, psychologically, and sociologically. Dr. Talmon's article reviews the publications of Norman Cohn, Eric J. Hobsbawm, Georges Balandier, Peter Worsley, and Bryan Wilson, and concludes with some statements of her own that are worthy of attention as a careful estimate of what we can say with assurance about millenarian cults and what directions future study should take.

Her characterization of these movements is derived from comparative study in which she finds that these cults view time as a linear process (rather than a cyclic one) leading to a final future, although they do not ignore the past. Salvation is seen as a merger of the spiritual with the terrestrial, combining an other-worldly hope with a new universe and a new social order. Millenarism has a collective rather than an individual orientation, the message being directed toward a group. The part played by the group in bringing about the millennium may range from very passive to very active; the latter is usually predominant. Generally, the more millenarian the movement the more activist it is. Most millenarian movements are messianic; however, a separate charismatic leader may exist alongside the messiah. In terms of organization, the movements are typically ephemeral rather than sect-like. Finally, most of them are highly emotional.

Dr. Talmon anticipates the Aberle article that follows insofar as she feels the conditions giving rise to millenarian movements are those of deprivation, there being a markedly uneven relation between expectations and the means of their satisfaction.

The author does not think that we can make a blanket statement concerning the function of the movements, for each one depends on the situation. She does make the important point, however, that the revolutionary nature of millenarism makes it a powerful agent of change. This does not mean, as has been alleged, that the cult movements tend to be completely absorbed within secular revolutionary movements; in fact, membership in millenarian movements actually competes with militant secular movements.

Hobsbawm and Worsley interject Marxian explanations into their studies of millenarism, a tendency which the author does not always find in accordance with the facts. But she does give serious consideration to the Marxian position that religious and social change must be viewed within a large-scale evolutionary framework.

Reprinted from *Archives Européennes de Sociologie*, III (1962), 125–148, by permission of the author and the *Archives Européennes de Sociologie*.

Millenarian movements have recently attracted the attention of scholars in different fields. Norman Cohn has studied the history of Millenarism in medieval and reformation Europe centering his attention mainly on France and Germany. Eric J. Hobsbawm devoted a considerable part of his analysis in *Primitive Rebels* to millenarian movements in Spain and Italy during the 19th and early 20th centuries. From Georges Balandier's studies we gain insight into several millenarian movements in Africa. Peter Worsley has examined and analysed the history of the millenarian movements which have proliferated in Melanesia during the last century. A more recent addition to this field is Bryan Wilson's book "Sects and Society" in which he deals with an ongoing millenarian movement in Britain. In time the movements studied range from the middle ages to the present day. The geographical spread is as great. Most important of all from a comparative point of view, these studies enable us to examine the millenarian movements in different historical settings and in different types of societies.[1]

Comparative analysis of millenarian movements has a number of distinct axes: (a) *Comparative analysis of different types of millenarian movements*. This is the main task of most of the studies discussed here. (b) *Comparative analysis of millenarian and non-millenarian religious movements.* Hobsbawm engages in such analysis when he compares the millenarian movements to the labour sects. This is the major task of Wilson's book which compares the millenarian Christadelphians to the mildly millenarian Elimites and to the non-millenarian Christian Scientists. He is concerned mainly with comparison of patterns of internal change in different types of religious sects. Comparative analysis between millenarian and non-millenarian religious groups figures to some extent in Balandier's and Worsley's studies as well. (c) *Comparative analysis of*

millenarian movements and non-religious political movements. Elucidation of the relation between millenarism and modern revolutionary movements is a major theme in most of the studies in this field.

The studies of millenarism discussed here present different approaches to the problem. There are considerable disagreements on basic theoretical as well as methodological matters. Yet, when juxtaposed and examined in relation to each other, it emerges that they have a certain continuity and common purpose. The most important underlying common denominator is the concern with the analysis of social change. Most of the scholars engaged in research in this field are not so much interested in millenarism as such but in the light that the study of such radical and potentially explosive religious movements may shed on the relation between religion and social change. Critical analysis of these studies reveals the development of a tentative typology and a cumulative growth of a body of hypotheses on the aetiology of origins and continuance of such movements. It seems worthwhile to elucidate and systematise the main findings and then relate them to the more general theoretical problem of analysis of change.

I

That the task of comparative analysis of such disparate material on millenarian movements that have occurred at different times all over the world is at all possible, is due to the fact that the studies in this field are in one sense or another interdisciplinary. The study of millenarism has brought about a veritable rapprochement between history, sociology and anthropology. The historical studies of Cohn and Hobsbawm are not confined to the description and analysis of unique sequences of events. They aim to detect the recurrent regularities of social events. While recognising that each transient constellation has its own unique irreducible particularity and distinctiveness, they stress recurrent patterns which tend to reappear again and again, revealing as they do similarities which become more and more recognisable. Elements which once produced a certain historical situation reappear in different sequence and different proportion, yet the basic pattern is reproduced. The range of the comparative method employed

[1] N. Cohn, *The Pursuit of the Millennium* (New York, 1957). E. J. Hobsbawm, *Primitive Rebels* (Manchester, 1959). G. BALANDIER, *Sociologie actuelle de l'Afrique Noire* (Paris, 1955). P. Worsley, *The Trumpet Shall Sound* (London, 1957). See also his "Rebellion and Revolution," *Science and Society*, XXV (1961), 26–27. B. R. Wilson, *Sects and Society* (Berkeley and Los Angeles, 1961). Cf. also the special issues of *Archives de Sociologie des religions* on this problem, IV (1957) and V (1958).

differs considerably. While Hobsbawm is wary of the danger of facile generalisation and does not venture much out of his circumscribed period and area, Cohn feels much more free to relate the movements he is dealing with to each other and to equivalent or analogous movements elsewhere. It should be stressed, however, that both of them employ a comparative method—abstracting, selecting, classifying, comparing, and explicitly or implicitly testing general hypotheses.

The rapprochement between history and sociology is brought about in yet another way. Both Cohn's and Hobsbawm's studies are more or less present oriented. Relevance to the main problems of present-day society consciously and intentionally affects their choice of subject matter and modes of analysis. They are interested in the past, more or less primarily, inasmuch as it points or leads to the present. Their conceptions and evaluations of the major trends in modern society differ considerably but both of them constantly and systematically relate past and present, analysing the more distant or more immediate past mainly in order to shed light on patterns of development of contemporary society. There are different degrees of preoccupation with contemporary issues here. Cohn's study is extremely erudite and exhaustive. He over-stresses the analogy with modern totalitarian movements, yet this provides mainly a point of orientation and a general frame of reference and does not affect too much the study of medieval movements which stand in their own right. Exhaustive scholarship is not the object of Hobsbawm's book and, although he is very much on his guard against facile analogies between pre-modern and modern movements, his main concern is the analysis of the transition to modern society. This concern with the major issues of modern society which these historians share with sociologists brings about a certain overlapping of fields and some interchange of techniques.

The recourse to a more sociological, more comparative and more generalising method is in a way imposed by the special nature of the historical material on millenarian movements. Most millenarian movements were subterranean and amorphous popular revolt movements. When dealing with them, historians were compelled to go beyond the official and mainly political accounts of history and

center their attention on the social relations and social processes which underlie political processes. Hence a growing tendency to employ sociological concepts and sociological modes of analysis. The extreme paucity and the questionable nature of most of the available documentary material on these movements exert a similar influence. The people who were the bearers of the millennial ideology were often ignorant and inarticulate and did not leave a satisfactory written account of their movement. Traces of their influence may be discerned in popular traditional lore and popular myths, but many of them have remained largely anonymous. Since most millenarian ideologies contain both heretical and revolutionary elements, these movements were often mercilessly persecuted and suppressed. Much of the scanty documentary evidence concerning them was often destroyed, and in dealing with them the historian has to rely largely on superficial description by outsiders and on tendentious accounts by opponents. The outcome of a long process of collecting and collating, appreciating and reappreciating scraps of evidence culled from different and sometimes very questionable sources is often only a tentative, partial and sketchy account. The historical data are generally speaking too problematical, too poor to use for self-contained and largely independent case studies. The historians dealing with such material are therefore driven to seek external controls and supplementary information by means of a more morphological analysis and more or less systematic comparison with similar movements elsewhere. Even in such a meticulous and rich book as *Pursuit of the Millennium* the analysis of some of the movements is rather thin and uneven. This is no doubt true of most of the historical analysis in *Primitive Rebels*. Comparative analysis supplements and reinforces the analysis of each separate case by introducing a wider perspective. It pulls the different lines of inquiry together by centering the discussion on major recurrent themes and on common problems. Hobsbawm was so much aware of the inadequacy and inappropriateness of ordinary historical methods in the study of such movements that he supplemented his analysis of primary and secondary sources with a certain amount of field work, thus adopting a technique which is typical of sociology and social anthropology.

Examination of anthropological studies in this field reveals a concomitant and complementary change in research methods. The functional-structural school has been for a long time non- and even anti-historical. During the first phases of the development of the discipline, social anthropologists have dealt with comparatively stable and comparatively static societies. Primitive people were illiterate; they had an essentially non-historical time conception and hardly any genuine historical traditions. Historical reconstructions of their past were largely conjectural. The opposition to this type of pseudo-history has resulted in a strong reaction not merely against conjectural constructions but against any historical analysis. The tendency to neglect the time dimension was strengthened by the nature of the socio-anthropological field study which is based on intensive participation in the social life of a community for a certain circumscribed period, usually not exceeding two years. This has inevitably led to a tendency to study fully configurations of social structure at any given time rather than trace development through time. There have been, however, many attempts to overcome this limitation lately. This is largely due to the fact that primitive societies have been drawn into increasingly closer contacts with modern societies and are undergoing deep transformations. The pace of change has quickened and its intensity has increased. This has forced social anthropologists to think about their subject in more developmental terms and adapt their research method accordingly. This was done in many different ways. There have been the attempts to combine diachronic and synchronic analysis by recurrent study in the same community. The recent tendency to introduce detailed case studies traced over a long span of time is another development in the same direction. There is in addition a growing number of more historically oriented anthropological researches which have recorded and analysed all the historical evidence on the societies concerned. This growing emphasis on historical analysis is evident in most anthropological studies on millenarian movements, but Worsley's study is perhaps the most radical example of this reorientation. Most of the book is devoted to an island by island and generation by generation historical account of the millenarian movements in Melanesia during the last 70 years. He has patiently amassed a truly vast amount of evidence which was buried in out-of-the-way journals and in official and unofficial reports by government officials and missionaries. In his task of tracing the developmental cycle of the various movements he used accounts by laymen as well as the work of professional anthropologists. While other attempts to adapt the social anthropological field method to the analysis of change have retained the emphasis on field research study of limited duration and only tried to modify and extend it, Worsley experiments with a predominantly historical research method.

Worsley's study is radically comparative as well, and this is another significant methodological reorientation. As in the case of the historical method, reaction against certain phases of the development of the discipline and the nature of its field techniques worked against the development of a comparative method in social anthropology. Criticism of a comparative method which concentrated on tracing the derivations and affiliations of isolated cultural traits completely torn out of any social and cultural context resulted in a strong and persistent bias against the comparative method. Attempts to reintroduce it into social anthropology have developed in two main directions. One line of development retains the primacy of the monographic study but introduces more continuity between the separate studies by building up a common frame of reference. Each field study is regarded as one in a connected series of case studies and the hypotheses developed by it are retested by subsequent studies in other societies. There is in addition the attempt to draw together in one book a number of monographic case studies in any given field and systematise their results by general discussion and comparative analysis. The second line of development does away with the primacy of the intensive field study. It does not compare only the fortuitously available intensive monographic studies but attempts an exhaustive survey and summary of all the material available in its field of inquiry. Balandier's and Wilson's books are comparative in the first sense, since they are based on intensive case studies. Worsley's book is comparative in the second sense. He aims to arrive at generalisations by means of a theoretical analysis and a systematic comparison of all relevant data in his field. The study of millenarian movements has thus resulted in a certain convergence between the related disciplines. It serves as a common meeting ground and has brought about a reappraisal and exchange of research techniques.

II

Perhaps the most important thing about millenarism is its *attitude towards time*. It views time as a linear process which leads to a final future. There is a fullness of time and end of days which will bring about a decisive consummation of all history. The millennium is not necessarily limited to a thousand years; it symbolises the meta-historical future in which the world will be inhabited by a humanity liberated from all the limitations of human existence, redeemed from pain and transience, from fallibility and sin, thus becoming at once perfectly good and perfectly happy. The world will be utterly, completely and irrevocably changed. Radical millenarian movements regard the millennium as imminent and live in tense expectation and preparation for it.

Coupled with this emphasis on the apocalyptic future is the equally radical rejection of the present as totally evil and abysmally corrupt. The transition from the present into the final future is not a gradual process of progressive approximations to the final goal. It is a sudden and revolutionary leap onto a totally different level of existence. Sometimes this transformation is expected to occur suddenly and miraculously without a preparatory struggle. Yet more often than not we find that the new dispensation is born out of unprecedented cataclysms, disastrous upheavals and bloody calamities. The apocalyptic victory will be won by means of a prodigious and final struggle which will destroy the agents of corruption, purge the sinful world and prepare it for its final redemption. Millenarism is thus basically a merger between an historical and a non-historical conception of time. Historical change leads to a cessation of all change. Divine will is made manifest and realized in the historical process, yet its final consummation will come in a mythical millennium which is the end of all history.

Millenarism is a forward-looking, future-oriented religious ideology. However, while its attitude to the present is outrightly and radically negative, its attitude to the past is more ambivalent. The rejection of the present usually includes the near and often the more distant past as well. Millenarism usually has a strong anti-traditional component and preparation for the millennium has often entailed a ritualised overthrow of traditional norms. Primitive millenarian movements have engaged in a breaking of hallowed taboos and in a desecration of their most valued religious symbols, thus dissociating themselves from their traditional culture. Their main concern was often not the perpetuation or revival of their indigenous tradition but the birth of a new order. Yet this strong anti-past orientation is often mitigated when the millennium is envisaged as a return of a mythical golden age. When the millennium is regarded as a paradise regained, those elements of tradition which are viewed as embedded in it, become also components of the new order. By establishing a connection between the meta-historical past and the meta-historical future, the millenarian movement can be radically change-oriented yet incorporate traditional elements in its view of the final future.

Another important characteristic of millenarian movements is their view of salvation as a *merger to the spiritual with the terrestrial*. The millenarian view of salvation is transcendent and immanent at the same time. The heavenly city is to appear on earth. It is in this world that the saints, the elect, or the chosen people will experience the blessing, not as ethereal saints. Millenarism offers not an otherworldly hope but the fulfilment of divine purpose in a new universe and a new social order. This terrestrial emphasis is more or less evident in all the millenarian movements. In its crudest and more extreme form we encounter it in the Cargo Cults. The core of these cults is a belief that the culture hero, the devil or the spirit of the dead will return in some mechanical means of transportation such as aeroplanes, lorries or ships, loaded with a cargo of imported goods. The cargo has been made in heaven for the use of the natives, but the white men have diverted it from them. The return of the cargo to its rightful owners will bring about an era of universal plenty and happiness. The natives will be liberated from alien domination once and for all and will be completely exempt from all the ills of human existence. Yet even in such a down to earth and materialistic conception of the millennium there is a more or less strong spiritual ingredient. The new order will be also a new moral order based on justice, peace and cooperation.

Closely connected with the former characteristic is the *collective orientation* of millenarism. The aim of millenarian movements is not only the salvation of individual souls but the erection of a heavenly city for a chosen people. The millenarian message is directed to an already existing group or calls for a formation of new groups of elect. It views these groups as divinely appointed bearers of the good tiding and calls on them to prepare for the imminent advent. The group is more or less collectively responsible and will enjoy the wonderful future awaiting it as a group.

What is the *role of the group in bringing about the advent?* There are many variations in this respect. Movements of this type range from the fairly passive and quietist on the one hand, to the extremely activist and aggressive on the other. There are certain elements in the millenarian ideology which work against an outrightly active definition of the role of the follower. The followers of these movements are not makers of the revolution; they expect it to be brought about miraculously from above. Ultimately, initiative and actual power to bring about change rest with divine powers. All millenarian movements share a fundamental vagueness about the actual way in which the new order will be brought about, expecting it to happen somehow by direct divine intervention. In many millenarian movements the part of the people before the change is to gather together, to watch the signs of the inevitable advent, to engage in measures of ritual preparation and purify themselves. Yet there is a strong activist militant ingredient in the millenarian ideology which more often than not outweighs the passive elements in it. Most of the radical millenarian movements define the role of the follower much more actively. In such movements, the believers have the power to hasten and retard salvation. In some cases the advent cannot come to pass without the active help of the elect. Since the vision of redemption is both transcendent and terrestrial, paving the way for it often entails the employment of both ritual and secular measures. Since the onset of the millennium is more often than not viewed as entailing a final struggle, the followers pit themselves against the powers of evil. The hope of a total and imminent salvation which will be brought about by divine powers with the active support and help of the elect throws such movements into spells of hectic and often rebellious activity. The millenarian vision instils in the movement a sense of extreme urgency and a dedication to an all-embracing purpose. Every minute and every deed count and everything must be sacrificed to the cause. The followers are driven to stake everything and spare nothing since their aim is no less than the final solution of all human problems. It would seem that the combination of the historical and the meta-historical in the millennial time conception, the vision of the unification of the transcendent and the terrestrial in a completely transformed and holy social order, the merger between individual and social destinies, coupled with a total rejection of the existing order and a view of an imminent final struggle have a powerful revolutionary potential. No wonder that in most of the movements described in these studies the millenarian ideology has precipitated and instigated active revolt against the established authorities. Comparative analysis seems to indicate that, generally speaking, the more extremely millenarian a movement is the more activist it is. As Worsley has pointed out, there seems to be a correlation between the time conception of each movement and its position in the *passivity-activity continuum.* Movements which view the millennium as imminent and have a total and vivid conception of redemption are, on the whole, much more activist than movements which expect it to happen at some remote date and consequently tend to have a more partial and rather pale conception of the millennium. It would seem that truly great expectations and a sense of immediacy enhance the orientation to active rebellion while postponement of the critical date and lesser expectation breed passivity and quietism.

This generalisation holds more or less true when examined in the material on pre-modern and primitive movements. It has to be modified to some extent with regard to such movements in modern societies. The Christadelphians have a radical millenarian ideology. They live in tense expectation of an imminent and total redemption. They rigorously oppose the social order as totally depraved and view its present difficulties with vindictiveness. Yet their attitudes are not translated into direct action against it. They defied the authorities in the matter of conscription to the army and stuck to their opposition to service in the armed forces. However, they did not oppose the authorities on other matters and did not engage in active rebellion against the established order. They have kept aloof from the world. Tense, impatient and vindictive, they await the divinely appointed time of its downfall. The same seems to be more or less true for other modern millenarian movements such as the Seventh Day Adventist and Jehovah's Witnesses. Wilson hints that modern millenarian movements are less rebellious than their counterparts elsewhere mainly because there are very slender chances for successful rebellion in a modern society. He feels, however, that internal pressures towards militancy are so strong in such a movement that were a revolt at all feasible the Christadelphians would have pitted themselves against the social order and tried to overthrow it.

Most millenarian movements are *messianic*. Redemption is brought about by a messiah who mediates between the divine and the human. Most important, of course, is the figure of Jesus, but there are other figures as well. In many of the medieval movements redemption is brought about by the sleeping monarch who comes to life again and rescues his people. In primitive societies, the messiah is the culture hero or a departed leader who was persecuted and put to death by the authorities. Often it is a multiple messiah seen in the form of the spirits of the dead ancestors. Another important mediator between the divine and the movement is the *leader*. Inspired leaders who claimed to be appointed by divine powers have played an extremely important role in these movements. Sometimes these prophetic figures move from mere prophecy to become messianic incarnations of divine leadership, but more often than not the figure of the messiah and the figure of the leader remain distinct. Leaders act as precursors of the messiah and as his prophets by announcing the good tidings. They develop their special brand of millenarism by emphasising millenarian elements in their traditional culture and by seizing upon millenarian elements in the cultures which impinge on them. They interpret the millennial traditions and vulgarise them,

combining disparate elements and systematising. They supply their followers with secondary exegesis when their hopes fail to materialise. They teach the new ritual and preach the new moral code. They organise their followers and lead them in preparation for the advent.

Inspired and energetic leaders have played such an important role in some of the millenarian movements that when they lost their drive or died, the movements they initiated and organised disintegrated almost immediately. Yet it should be stressed that in many cases leaders function as a symbolic focus of identification rather than as sources of authority and initiative. In some regions, millenarism is an endemic force and when it reaches a flash-point it may seize upon any available figure. The initiative in such case comes primarily from the community which sometimes almost imposes the leadership position on its leader. Some of the leaders are in fact insignificant and their elevation to such a position seems to be accidental—they happened to be there and fulfilled an urgent need for a mediator. That the function of leadership is sometimes primarily symbolic is clearly seen in the cases of movements with absent leaders. In some notable instances the influence of a leader and his integrating power have increased enormously after he left or was removed from his scene of operations. Death, imprisonment or mysterious absence have increased their stature and enhanced their authority. Only when absent did they begin to loom large as powerful prophetic figures.

Often there is also not just one charismatic leader but a multiple leadership. First, we find in a number of instances a division of leadership between the organiser who is concerned with practical matters and the inspired prophet. Secondly, the movements are sometimes based on loyalty to leaders on the local level and do not have an overall leadership. Moreover, the strong fissiparous tendencies which operate in most of these movements work against attempts at unification of leadership. Millenarian movements suffer from frequent cessation and fission partly because they base their recruitment of their leaders on inspiration. A revelatory basis of recruitment facilitates the emergence of numerous leaders and prophets since many may claim divine inspiration. That this is only a partial explanation is suggested by the fact that millenarian movements seem to suffer from fissiparous tendencies more than religious movements with an equally inspirational leadership. It seems that millenarian movements are particularly prone to fissions because they preach rebellion against authority and probably attract rebellious non-conformist and contentious people. The denial of authority seems to be a factor in perpetuating internecine strife. The fissiparous tendence is particularly strong in radical but non-active movements. The attempt to arouse and canalise rebellious feelings but to postpone active rebellion until some future occasion resulted in the case of the Christadelphians in the turning of rebelliousness inwards and in a proliferation of leaders.

Organisationally, millenarian movements vary from the amorphous and ephemeral movement with a cohesive core of leaders and ardent followers and a large ill-defined body of followers, to the fairly stable segregated and exclusive sect-like group. The organisational form of a more or less ephemeral movement is, however, more typical. This is no doubt closely related to the nature of the millenarian message. The promise of an imminent and total redemption awakes enthusiastic hopes and sweeps a large number of followers into the movement. However, its source of strength is also its source of weakness—by promising an imminent delivery and sometimes even fixing a definite date, it brings its own downfall. When the appointed day or period passes without any spectacular happenings or with not the right apocalyptic events, the movement faces a serious crisis which often disrupts and even disperses it completely.

The crisis of non-materialisation of the millennium is a severe one but it need not always lead to disruption. In some notable cases the failures of prophecy did not cause disaffection and immediate disintegration. The commitment to the promise of a millennium was so intense that the shock of temporary disappointment could not shatter it. Paradoxically, non-materialisation was followed in these cases by a burst of vigorous proselytizing activities and drew the believers together. These movements are sometimes able to develop a body of exegesis which accounts for the delay and keeps the hope alive. A frequent solution is the switch from a short-range radical millenarism to a long-range and more or less attenuated version of it. Another solution is refraining from fixing any definite date but still keeping the hope of a speedy delivery in full force. Wilson's study of the Christadelphians proves that such a solution is feasible and can work for a considerable length of time without serious modification of the original doctrine. Hobsbawm shows that radical millenarism has become a permanent though periodically dormant force in Andalusia for more than seventy years, suffering reversal after reversal yet flaring up again and again. The recurrent revival of the movement follows an almost cyclical pattern; the millennial outbursts follow one another after approximately a ten-year interval. Similar though not as cyclical patterns of disruption and revival can be observed in the medieval material as well as in Melanesia and Africa. Sometimes there is a hidden continuity between the different phases of the movement. When the millenarian movement suffers a reverse, it goes under cover. It remains underground until it sees a better chance for its struggle, repeatedly hiding or going out into the open but retaining its radical millenarism. It should be stressed, however, that often there is hardly any direct connection between what may seem to be recurrent phases of the self-same movement. Continuation of similar conditions often breed similar yet independent reactions. In many cases, there is no direct influence or any continuity of either tradition or personnel between the different movements.

Most millenarian movements are *highly emotional.* With the exception of the Christadelphians who discourage emotional release in any form and emphasise exegesis, exhortation and doctrine, almost all the other movements involve wild and very often frenzied emotional display. In many instances we encounter hysterical and paranoid phenomena—mass possession, trances, fantasies. The emotional tension manifests itself in motor phenomena such as twitching, shaking and convulsions which have swiftly spread through wide areas. Closely related to the high emotional tension is a strong antinomian tendency. Millenarian movements deliberately break accepted taboos and overthrow hallowed norms. They engage in many ritualised forms of sin and sacrilege. Sexual aberrations in the form of either extreme asceticism or sexual excess are very common as well. There is often unbridled expression of aggression. Members of such movements have swept over the country, devastating, burning and massacring on their way. Sometimes aggression is turned inwards: the members destroy their own property and even commit mass suicide.

III

What are the *conditions which give rise to* such movements and in which *social groups are they anchored?* The data clearly support the frequently posited relationship between socio-economic conditions and religious expression. Radical millenarism found support in all levels of society at one time or another but essentially it is a religion of the *deprived groups*—oppressed peasants, the poorest of the poor in cities and towns, populations of colonial countries. The millenarian hope usually flares up as a reaction to particularly severe hardships and suffering. Many of the outbursts of millenarism took place against a background of disaster—plagues, devastating fires, recurrent long droughts that were the dire lot of the peasants, slumps that caused widespread unemployment and poverty and calamitous wars. Repeated historical experiences of disaster, living under constant threat of hunger, illness and untimely and cruel death led to rejection not only of actual history but of history as such. The fantastic hope of total redemption was often born out of abysmal despair.

Yet there is much more to it than just that. The analysis clearly shows that the development of millenarism cannot be interpreted only in terms of an extremely severe deprivation. The predisposing factor was often not so much any particular hardship but a markedly *uneven relation between expectations and the means of their satisfaction.* In Cohn's and Hobsbawm's material it is predominantly the inability to satisfy traditional expectations. In medieval Europe millenarism affected mainly people who, because of the pressure of surplus population were cut off from the traditional order and were unable to satisfy wants instilled in them by it. The insidious onslaught of the developing capitalistic order on a backward and isolated peasant economy created the same basic difficulty in Spain and Italy centuries later, although there it affected not only people who were cut off from their

rural base but the rural community as a whole. We encounter the same type of frustration in primitive societies as well but there it increasingly becomes not so much a problem of the lack of means to supply traditional wants but the development of a set of new expectations. The encounter with modern societies engenders enormously inflated expectations without a concomitant and adequate development of institutional means for their supply. This discrepancy creates a void which is often bridged by millenarian hope. That frustration may be much more important than actual hardship becomes evident when we consider the fact that millenarian unrest was caused in certain parts of New Guinea not by any direct contact with the white men. Though there were hardly any changes in the status quo indirect contacts brought about changed expectation and acute frustration. It should be stressed that in many cases millenarian outbursts were caused not by a deterioration of conditions but by a limited amelioration which raised new hopes and new expectations but left them largely unfulfilled.

The incongruity between ends and means is not the only source of frustration. Much of the deep dissatisfaction stems from incongruities and difficulties in the realm of *regulation of ends.* Quick change and encounter with radically different systems of values result in a more or less severe cultural disintegration. When the impinging cultural influences penetrate into the traditional setting and gain a foothold there they often undermine the effectiveness of traditional norms as guides of action. Even the most central traditional values cease to be self-evident and sacred. In many spheres there are contradictory claims and mutually exclusive obligations. Since conflicting claims tend to neutralise and annul each other, the impinging cultural influences often weaken and even destroy the indigenous tradition without substituting a new system of values, thus causing confusion and anomie. When the alien culture is that of a more prestigious upper class or that of a colonial ruling class, it is often willingly or unwillingly, consciously or unconsciously acknowledged as superior. This causes much self-doubt and even self-hatred. Wilson stresses quite rightly that the sense of cultural deprivation and the quest for cultural reorientation are sometimes more important than economic frustration. Millenarism is often born out of the search for a tolerably coherent system of values, a new cultural identity and regained sense of dignity and self-respect.

Another important factor operative in the emergence of millenarism was found to be *social isolation* brought about by the disruption of traditional group ties. Cohn points out that millenarism did not appeal much to people who were firmly embedded in well-integrated kinship groupings and effectively organised and protected in cohesive local communities. The people most exposed to the new pressures and therefore more prone to millenarism were the mal-integrated and isolated who could find no assured and recognised place in cohesive primary groups. The importance of a breakdown of kinship and local groupings is a major theme in the analysis of pre-modern, modern and primitive societies as well.

Yet even the combination of such factors as severe deprivation, severe frustration and extreme isolation does not supply us with a full answer to our question. The most important contribution of Balandier, Worsley and Hobsbawm to this analysis lies in their insistence that millenarism is essentially a *pre-political phenomenon*. In primitive societies it appears mainly in so-called stateless segmentary societies which have rudimentary political institutions or lack any specialised political institutions altogether. When it appears in societies with fairly developed political institutions it appeals to strata which are politically passive and have no experience of political organisation and no access to political power. Instances of such non-political strata in societies with a more or less developed political structure are the peasants in feudal societies, the peasants in isolated and backward areas in modern societies, marginal and politically passive elements in the working class, recent immigrants and mal-integrated and politically inarticulate minority groups. Sometimes millenarism is post-political, appearing after the downfall of a fairly developed political system. The collapse of an entire political system by a crushing defeat and the shattering of tribal or national hopes have sometimes led to widespread millenarism. It is the lack of effective organisation, the absence of regular institutionalised ways of voicing their grievances and pressing their claims that pushes such groups to a millenarian solution.

Not being able to cope with their difficulties by concerted political action, they turn to millenarism. According to this analysis, millenarism is born out of great distress coupled with political helplessness.

That the combination of all the necessary predisposing factors will actually lead to millenarism and not result in the development of other types of religious ideology is ultimately conditioned also by the type of prevalent religious beliefs. Clearly, religions in which history has no meaning whatsoever and religions which have a cyclical repetitive conception of time are not conducive to millenarism. Apocalyptic eschatology is essentially alien to religions of a philosophical and mystical cast which turn the eye of the believer towards eternity where there is no movement and no process. This is certainly the case with some nature and cosmic religions which live in the framework of ever-recurring repetitive cycles of rise and decline. Another important factor operative in this sphere is a "this-worldly" emphasis. Religions with a radical, other-worldly orientation which puts all the emphasis on the hereafter or on a purely spiritual and totally nonterrestrial salvation do not give rise to the vision of the kingdom of God on earth. This explains why there is apparently no apocalyptic tradition in Hinduism and why it has not occupied an important place in Buddhism.

On the whole, millenarism appeared mainly in countries which had direct or indirect contact with the Judeo-Christian messianic traditions. Christianity itself originally derived its initial élan from radical millenarism and, although the millenarian ideology was reinterpreted and relegated to a secondary position, it still played an important part in the history of Europe. The Christian missions were the most important agency for the worldwide spreading of millenarism. Several fundamentalist sects played a particularly important role in this process, but millenarism appeared also in cases where the main contact with it was mediated by less apocalyptic versions of Christianity. The millenarism is reinstated to its central position by a process of selection and reinterpretation.

When millenarism developed in primitive societies it was influenced by pre-existing religious concepts as well. Some primitive mythologies contain eminently suitable beliefs such as the expectation of the future return of the culture hero or the idea of the return of all the dead as a prelude to a messianic era. It should be stressed, however, that these themes appeared in a rather embryonic form and did not occupy a particularly important position in primitive mythology. They were developed, reinterpreted and elaborated into full-fledged millenarian conceptions only under the impact of the new situation and after the contact with Christianity. The pre-existing primitive conceptions affected the development of millenarism in yet another way. The prevalence of millenarism in Melanesia and the importance of expectations of cargo in its view of the millennium are, it would seem, due to the strong and almost exclusive emphasis which the indigenous religion puts on ritual activity oriented to the acquisition of material goods.

IV

What are the *functions of millenarism?* How does it answer the needs of its followers and what does it contribute to the strata and societies where it appears? In this sphere we find different interpretations and different emphases. Cohn's approach to this particular problem is predominantly psychological. He regards millenarism as primarily an outlet for extreme anxiety and as a delusion of despair. He treats it as a collective paranoid fantasy born out of irrational fears and fantastic expectations. He feels that the megalomaniac view of oneself as wholly good, abominably persecuted yet assured of final triumph, the attribution of demonic power to the adversary, the inability to accept the ineluctable limitations of human existence, constitute the unmistakable syndrome of paranoia. The irrational and hysterical emotionality, the destructive and often suicidal activities seem to him clear symptoms of mental illness. Hobsbawm and Worsley reject this psychological interpretation and press for a more sociological approach. Worsley strongly objects to the description of these movements as irrational and tries to prove that if we take into consideration the social conditions and the cultural milieu which gave rise to them they cease to be bizarre and fantastic and become fully understandable and not illogical reactions. The highly emotional and aggressive

behaviour is related to the revolutionary nature of the movement which strives to overthrow the old order and establish a new one. The severing of old ties and the rejection of old norms demand an enormous effort and engender a deep sense of guilt, hence much of the hysteria and the aggression. Many of the antinomian manifestations are a deliberate overthrow of the accepted norms, not in order to throw overboard all morality but in order to create a new brotherhood and a new morality. The paranoid manifestations stem from the contradictions inherent in the situation in which such movements appear and from the difficulties inherent in their revolutionary task and not so much from psychological aberrations of individual followers. Wilson treats the sociological and psychological interpretations as complementary but he too stresses the situational strains rather than the abnormality of the followers. Wilson supplies us here with a careful and balanced analysis of functions versus dysfunctions on three different levels. He distinguishes between the functions and dysfunctions of millenarism for the individual follower, for the movement and for society as a whole. By and large, he feels that millenarism has strong disruptive potentialities. While it supplies the individual followers with strong identification with a cohesive movement and gives him hope for imminent delivery, it creates serious difficulties in the sphere of canalisation of aggression. Such movements always face the crisis of non-materialisation and suffer from the turning of the aggression of its members inwards which manifests itself in numerous fissions. A millenarian movement can counteract more or less successfully the disintegrating tendencies inherent in its religious ideology for a long time but this is achieved at the cost of considerable mal-integration from the point of view of the total society. Christadelphianism institutionalises deviant tendencies without being able to bring about actual change.

A far more positive evaluation of millenarism emerges from the studies of Balandier, Worsley and Hobsbawm. The main hypothesis which underlies these studies is that millenarism is an activating and unifying force in hitherto politically passive and segregated groups and that in recent and contemporary history it has been an important *precursor of political awakening and a fore-*

runner of political organisation. Such functions were performed also by other types of religious movements, but radical millenarism is much more potent in this respect. The main effect of the millenarian movement is to overcome divisions and join previously isolated or even hostile groups together. Though faced by the same common problems and sometimes even sharing the same culture, these groups cannot act as a unified force except on a localised and ad hoc basis. When confronted by crisis and by necessity to take concerted action, they are compelled to create a new unity which transcends kinship and local loyalties. Millenarism helps to draw into activity and organise masses of people on a large scale almost simultaneously. Conversion acts as a sudden overpowering awakening. It brings about a new awareness and a change in men's attitude to life, shaking them out of their apathy. Since millenarism has a strong collective orientation and is also activity-centered, this conversion does not lead them only inwards to repentance and meditation but draws them outwards to involvement and activity in the movement. Millenarism usually evokes exceptionally intense commitment and fervour and, since exaltation eases communication, millenarism expands swiftly almost as if by contagion, cross-cutting and breaking down local barriers. It widens the horizon of identification and participation and creates wider unities.

The revolutionary nature of millenarism makes it a very potent agent of change. It demands a fundamental transformation and not just improvement and reform. The radical versions of millenarism incite the followers to active anticipation of the advent and even to active revolt. It invests their struggle with the aura of a final cosmic drama. It interprets present difficulties as signs of the beginning of the end and views every small success as proof of invincibility and as portents of future triumph. It arouses truly great hopes and therefore can make equally great demands on its followers. By promising complete salvation, it is able to liberate formerly untapped energies and generate a supreme effort without which no major break with the existing order can be achieved.

Millenarism helps to bring about a breakthrough to the future. Yet its special efficacy lies also in its power to bridge future and past. We have already pointed out that inasmuch as the end of days is somehow connected with the mythical beginning, the vision of the apocalyptic future includes certain traditional elements. Even the most anti-traditional version of millenarism is in fact a creative synthesis between the new and old. Even when rejecting and transcending the old, it reinstates important aspects of it. It constantly reinterprets such traditional elements and places them in a new context. It invests the old with new meanings while the new elements may often have traditional connotations. Even when it negates the content of tradition it does not invalidate the principles by which truth is traditionally sought and preserved.

While bridging the gap between future and past, millenarism also connects religion and politics. Operating in societies or in strata completely dominated by religion, millenarism couches its political message in the familiar and powerful language and images of traditional religion employing and revitalising its age old symbols. In such milieus recruitment to new political goals is often possible only when expressed in religious terms. In many cases it is also the only means of establishing cooperation between leaders and followers. Millenarism provides an important mechanism of recruitment of new leaders. It opens up new avenues of ascent and develops a set of new statuses. Although some of the new leaders derive their authority from their central or marginal position in the traditional order, more often than not their authority stems at least in part from their comparatively superior knowledge and greater experience in non-traditional spheres of activity and has no traditional legitimation. Millenarism helps them to establish their authority. Externalisation and sanctification of the source of authority puts the leader above sectional loyalties and helps him to avoid sectional discord. By projecting their authority to the supernatural sphere they objectify and legitimise it. Millenarism helps the leader in this respect in yet another way. It closes the gap which often develops between a more "advanced" and more politically minded leader and the more traditional mass of his followers. In many cases he cannot hope to reach his followers and really communicate with them if he does not express his protest in popular and widely understood religious terms. In some cases, the movement is started by an "advanced" and politically minded leader, but when its political ideology reaches the masses, it is spontaneously interpreted in religious terms. The best example of such a process is the development of Amicalism described by Balandier.

The resort to a religious appeal is sincere and non-manipulative in most cases. During the first stages of reorganisation most of the leaders have got little experience in the political sphere and cannot express their striving except in a religious form. During later phases of development the resort to religion may sometimes become a conscious propagandist and organisational device. The leader clothes his political ideology in religious terms because he realises that this is the only way to mobilise the masses. He often emphasises the religious components of his ideology also for the purpose of hiding his real intentions from the authorities.

Millenarism is thus essentially a *connecting link* between pre-political and political movements. It lubricates the passage from pre-modern religious revolt to a full-fledged revolutionary movement. The process of transition can be actually traced in both primitive and recent pre-modern movements. There are two main distinct avenues of transition. In some cases the movements gradually change their nature, slowly becoming less ritualised and more secular in emphasis. These movements start to pay much more attention to purely political and economic goals. They attach far more importance to strategy and tactics and organise more effectively. Yet they do not sever their ties with their millenarian tradition and continue to derive much of their revolutionary zeal from its promise of final salvation. Another major direction of development entails the complete absorption of the millenarian movement within a secular revolutionary movement. When the millenarian movement fails to achieve its goals and disintegrates, its disappointed followers turn to secular revolutionism, embracing an extreme and militant version of either nationalist or socialist ideology. The millenarian movement serves in such cases as a kind of preparatory school for revolutionaries. When they "graduate" from it they are ready to go over to militant secular movements.

It should be stressed that the hypothesis which posits that millenarism functions as an integrating force and as forerunner of political action is borne out only in material on the contemporary history of Melanesia and Africa on the one hand and in the material on the recent history of Italy on the other. Most of the medieval movements were ephemeral outbursts and only a few of them had strong formative powers and lasting social consequences. Since they had little chance to change the massive structure of medieval society, most of these revolutionary revivals short-circuited and disappeared. Material on the American Indians suggests that radical millenarism has played a limited and largely disruptive role there. Any movement with a revolutionary potential was quickly suppressed, leaving an aftermath of disillusion and disorganisation. The task of rehabilitating and integrating the Indians was performed mainly by reformist cults oriented to peaceful accommodation to the white society. Membership in millenarian movements in modern societies functions more as a competing alternative to membership in militant secular movements rather than as a preparation for it. All these movements reject secular movements and enjoin on their members to keep away from them. It is clear that the actual functions which any millenarian movement performs in any given situation depend on the degree of differentiation between the religious and political sphere in the society in which it operates and on the chances it has to engage in active political action and carry out a successful revolution. Much work needs still to be done before we can arrive at generally valid generalisation in this sphere.

v

All the studies discussed here regard millenarism as in one sense or another a prototype of modern revolutionary movements.

This is demonstrated and justified in four different ways:

(*a*) Secular revolutionary movements differ greatly from other types of secular political movements and have in a certain sense a semi-religious character. Their world view is total and all embracing. It purports to solve basic problems of meaning and trace and interpret the unfolding of world history. The revolutionary ideology is a matter of ultimate concern and utmost seriousness; it demands from the followers unquestioning faith and unconditional loyalty. It is therefore all pervasive and defines every aspect of life. Much like the great religious movements of the past, secular revolutionism has stirred deeply large masses of people evoking intense fervor and dedication to its cause.

(*b*) There is an even more marked affinity between these political movements and millenarism. Secular revolutionism shares with millenarism the apocalyptic element—like millenarism it looks forward to a total and imminent realization of its ideals. Millenarism shares with secular revolutionism its collective and terrestrial emphasis as well as the radical condemnation of the existing social order. Both the religious and secular versions of revolutionism reject gradual and peaceful improvement and prepare for a final decisive struggle. Millenarism has a more passive definition of the role of the follower, but, by and large, we find in both versions of revolutionism a potent merger between inevitability and freedom which assures the revolutionaries of their final triumph, yet endows them with some power to hasten or retard salvation.

(*c*) There is in addition a partial similarity in the conditions which bring about such movements. Like millenarism, secular revolutionism is brought about by a combination of severe deprivation, acute frustration and disintegration of primary groups.

(*d*) Last but not least, there are direct connections and a continuity of tradition between religious and secular revolutionism. Cohn assumes such undercurrent of continuity without proving his contention systematically. Balandier, Worsley and Hobsbawm set about substantiating this thesis by actually tracing direct transitions from one to the other.

To be sure, this type of analysis highlights similarities and glosses over differences which are, in many cases, as great and as important as the affinities. It is certainly a far cry, for instance, to equate communism and Nazism and treat them as one and the same thing for the purpose of comparison with millenarism. Cohn states repeatedly that differences between Nationalist and Socialist revolutionism are largely immaterial in this context. There is little to be gained from pushing such analogies too far. As noted above, the contention of direct continuity between religious and secular revolutionism was borne out only in part of the material. There is no doubt that in many cases religious and secular revolutionism are independent of each other. The affinities stem from the similarity of the predisposing factors and from the dynamics of the common revolutionary position rather than from any direct interchange of ideas or transfer of members from one to the other.

The analogy with modern revolutionism is employed for different purposes. Cohn uses it primarily in order to underline the essentially primitive, mythical and menacing nature of modern revolutionary movements. Worsley and Hobsbawm use it in order to uncover the modern elements in pre-modern movements. Behind this difference of approach there is a fundamentally different evaluation of millenarism. Cohn views millenarism as a dangerous collective madness, as an essentially irrational, destructive and disruptive force. Both Worsley and Hobsbawm stress its underlying realism and its inherent though hidden rationality. They view it as a primarily positive and constructive force.

So far we have summed up and analysed the main conclusions arrived at by recent studies of millenarism. We shall conclude this review by a short critical examination of the theoretical assumptions on which these studies are based and the wider theoretical implications of their findings. There are different degrees of involvement with theoretical problems here. Cohn is not at all concerned with general problems of sociological theory; he just makes a limited use of certain analytical tools supplied to him by sociology. He uses these analytical tools competently and imaginatively, but does not attempt to deal with his problems on a higher level of abstraction. Balandier has a keen interest in the theory of change, but he too is primarily concerned with the application of general theory to his special case rather than with the examination of what his study has contributed to general theory. The other studies dealt with here are more theoretically oriented. The main purpose of Wilson's study is a critical examination of certain general propositions on the dynamics of sect development. He specifies the conditions which facilitate resistance to denominationalising tendencies and analyses the mechanisms which help the established sect to resist external and internal pressures and preserve its initial ideology without serious modifications. Hobsbawm's and Worsley's attempts to deal with problems of change are less systematic but far more ambitious. They examine the relations between religious and social change within a large-scale evolutionary framework concentrating their attention on the transition from pre-modern to modern society.

The analytical tools used by Worsley and Hobsbawm are mainly those forged by Marxian sociology. This is by no means a rigid and simplicist application of Marxian theory. The theoretical analysis is, on the whole, subtle and flexible. It is often enriched and modified by incorporation of modes of analysis and ideas developed by non-Marxian sociologists. If anything, these studies prove that a neo-Marxian theory provides powerful tools for the analysis of change. These studies also make manifest, however, some of its inherent limitations. By and large, religion is treated here as an ideology which just expresses concrete socioeconomic interests rather than moulds and directs them. It is primarily an instrument in the political struggle. Its "pie in the sky" or mystical versions act as opiate to the people and help to preserve the status quo. Its this-worldly, activist and future-oriented versions act as expressions of the drive towards change. On the theoretical level, religion is denied any independent causal significance and there is no adequate analysis of internal, partly independent processes in the religious sphere. Both Hobsbawm and Worsley tend to deal with conditions and consequences of millenarism rather than with development of its doctrine and ritual. This is particularly noticeable in Hobsbawm's book. Hobsbawm is not much concerned and rather bored with the finer details of the theological analysis of millenarism. Sometimes he cannot hide his impatience and distaste for the misplaced ingenuity that goes into building up elaborate universes of symbolism. Worsley devotes a certain amount of attention to the symbols employed by the cargo cults and sometimes manages to supply us with a perceptive analysis of the different levels of meaning of these symbols but his treatment of this matter only occasionally approaches the subtlety of Cohn's analysis. Both Hobsbawm and Worsley recognise the influence of predisposing religious factors on the development of millenarism but tend to minimize their importance. Their analysis of the relation

between hardship and deprivation is not quite balanced. They have a strong tendency to overemphasize the importance of severe hardship and disregard the frustrating effects of partial and discontinued amelioration. Their analysis is sometimes vitiated also by construing religion as an intentionally manipulated propagandist and organisational device. Now and then there is an almost imperceptible shift from imputation of latent functions by the investigator to imputation of semi-conscious distortion and disguise by the actors. Neither of the authors discussed here realises the full implications of the fact that millenarism combines a historical with a mythical time conception. The assumption that a future orientation and a past orientation are mutually exclusive and incompatible vitiates Worsley's just criticism of the characterization of millenarian movements as "nativistic." Millenarian movements are forward looking not backwards looking movements, yet their vision of the future usually contains many reinterpreted elements of native tradition. It is precisely this combination of a radical revolutionary position with traditionalism which accounts for the widespread appeal of these movements. It is because these movements merge a future orientation with either an overt or covert past orientation that they are such potent agents of change.

Both Worsley's and Hobsbawm's studies are based on evolutionary assumptions. A critical reappraisal of evolutionary theory is long due and it is therefore a pity that these assumptions are not clearly defined and are used rather uncritically. In spite of the fact that Hobsbawm's book hinges on the distinction between the archaic and the modern forms of rebellion, he does not define these concepts clearly. Even the basic distinction between the contemporary in a historical sense and the contemporary or modern in a typological sense is left largely implicit. Both Worsley and Hobsbawm view religious movements in modern society as transitional phenomena destined to disappear soon. They feel that the full articulation and spread of processes of institutional differentiation and modernisation will lead to a quick decline and final disappearance not only of millenarism but of all other religious movements as well. This is tacitly assumed without proper discussion or proof.

While their discussion of theoretical problems is at times vigorous and acute, they do

not make full use or even discuss adequately
all the available theoretical formulations in
this field. Worsley's critical review of Max
Weber's theories on the relation between religion and social change is squeezed in and
put out of the way in a short appendix. His
ambiguous and shifting use of the term rationality vitiates much of his otherwise useful criticism of Weber. The aversion to any
type of formal sociology causes an almost
complete disregard of Simmel's theory of
conflict in spite of its relevance to the analysis. K. Mannheim's analysis of utopianism
is overlooked and not mentioned at all.
Mannheim's study has serious shortcomings,
yet it provides many important insights and

should not be totally ignored. Both studies
would have gained much from a widening of
their theoretical base and from a fuller and
more critical examination of their assumptions.

The studies on millenarism have proved
the fruitfulness of a comprehensive comparative and historical approach, yet it would
seem that further progress in this field will
be achieved primarily by means of theoretically oriented yet very detailed case studies.
Further elaboration and specification of the
hypotheses outlined here will be possible
mainly on the basis of additional more
sharply focused and more fully worked out
case studies.

DAVID ABERLE

A Note on Relative Deprivation Theory As Applied to Millenarian and Other Cult Movements

Many scholars have had the impression that cult movements labeled variously as "nativistic," "revitalistic," "messianic," "millenarian," and the like, have a certain unity, and have been dissatisfied with the inability of these terms to single out the common thread running through them all. They are not sufficiently
all-encompassing. To take one instance, the millenarian movements of the Middle Ages in Europe were not nativistic and
certainly had none of the syncretistic, acculturative, or political
overtones found among so many of the cults in question. Another example is provided by the cargo movements of the central New Guinea highlands, where cults have arisen without
the natives ever having seen a white man. David Aberle has
made a genuine contribution toward the solution of the dilemma
by his suggestion that the theme running through these cults
is one of relative deprivation. Thus, although he does not say
so, he has shifted the emphasis from the reaction to the cause
underlying the reaction, thus reaching into the heart of the matter, which after all concerns religion as a force providing hope
and comfort where people perceive their lot as an unhappy one.
He distinguishes three types of reference points for relative
deprivation, as well as four kinds of deprivation, making twelve
categories in all. No cult movement fits neatly into any one com-
partment alone, as becomes obvious if one draws up a table composed of these categories, eliminating, as does Aberle, purely
personal deprivation as opposed to societal ones. Where, for
example would one fit in the Mau Mau of Kenya, or the Black
Muslims of the United States?

Reprinted from "Millenial Dreams in Action," in Sylvia L. Thrupp
(ed.), *Comparative Studies in Society and History,* Supplement II
(The Hague: Mouton & Co., 1962), pp. 209–214, by permission of the
author and the Society for the Comparative Study of Society and History.

I will not attempt to review the history of
theories of deprivation and relative deprivation, especially since they enter, explicitly or

implicitly, into so many explanations of specific religious and political movements and
so many general theories in this area. I will

rather attempt to supply a statement of my own viewpoint, recognizing that many parts of it can be found in the works of others.

Relative deprivation is defined as a negative discrepancy between legitimate expectation and actuality. Where an individual or a group has a particular expectation and furthermore where this expectation is considered to be a proper state of affaris, and where something less than that expectation is fulfilled, we may speak of relative deprivation. It is important to stress that deprivation *is* relative and not absolute. To a hunting and gathering group with an expectation of going hungry one out of four days, failure to find game is not a relative deprivation, although it may produce marked discomfort. It is a truism that for a multi-millionnaire to lose all but his last million in a stock market crash *is* a major deprivation. The deprivation, then, is not a particular objective state of affairs, but a difference between an anticipated state of affairs and a less agreeable actuality. We must furthermore consider the expectations as *standards,* rather than merely as prophecies of what will happen tomorrow.

The discovery of what constitutes serious deprivation for particular groups or individuals is a difficult empirical problem. It requires careful attention to the reference points that people employ to judge their legitimate expectations, as well as to their actual circumstances. Among the obvious reference points that can be, and are used for such judgments are: (1) one's past versus one's present circumstances; (2) one's present versus one's future circumstances; (3) one's own versus someone else's present circumstances.

The first and third types of judgment are easily illustrated. Any one who worked among the Navaho Indians in the 1940's was obliged to notice that for many Navahos the Government livestock reduction of the 1930's had created a situation where they viewed themselves as worse off than they had been, and as worse off than they should have been. And the impression one derives from Margaret Mead's account of the Manus, in *New Lives for Old,* is that these people regard themselves as worse off than they should be, by comparison with full participants in Western material culture.

Perhaps the second type of judgment requires some elucidation. If, let us say, a group of elderly pensioners have a particular standard of living, and have reason to believe that the shrinking dollar value of their pensions will not long permit this, then, with only a little strain they may be regarded as relatively deprived: their *prospective actuality* is worse than their standard of legitimate expectation.

The critical feature of these and subsequent examples is that they involve not only relative deprivation, but a deprivation which stems from *change,* actual or anticipated. It is where conditions decline by comparison with the past, where it is expected that they will decline, in the future by comparison with the present, and where shifts in the relative conditions of two groups occur, that the deprivation experience becomes significant for efforts at remedial action. Indeed it is change itself that creates discrepancies between *legitimate* expectations and actuality, either by worsening the conditions of a group, or by exposing a group to new standards.

The previous examples are very much concerned with material goods. It is not necessary, however, to assume that all deprivation experiences are primarily concerned with such goods. I have attempted a rough classification of types of deprivation. They fall into four groups: possessions, status, behavior, and worth. They may furthermore be classified as *personal* and *group* or *category* experiences. A man whose house is destroyed by fire experiences a personal deprivation of possessions—since this is *not* an experience most of us plan on. An American Indian tribe expropriated from its land, experiences group deprivation of possessions. Allowing for this, we have, in fact, at least three measuring points for deprivation, and at least four areas of deprivation, classified in each case as personal versus group (e.g., tribe) or category (e.g., Negro). This provides a 24-cell table of deprivations, one too large to illustrate in detail.

We can, however, eliminate the purely personal deprivations. If the individual does not find that there are others in like circumstances, their significance for social movements, millenarian or other, political or religious, would appear to be trivial. I will attempt to illustrate the others, using Navaho examples and only one frame of reference for comparison: present (undesirable) versus past (desirable). Navahos who had large herds in the 1920's lost them through livestock reduction in the 1930's. Those with such herds constituted a category, and their loss of stock adversely affected other Navahos who had benefitted from their generosity, so that the Navahos as a group or set of groups experienced deprivation of possessions, with respect to diet, trade goods procured through sale of animal products, etc. In addition, the large owners suffered deprivation of status. The society was reduced to far more egalitarian relationships; the man who had had followers to herd for him, gratitude for generosity, and standing because of his wealth now was almost as badly off as any other Navaho. His comparison here was to his past status in *his* group, not vis-à-vis the outside world. These were among the key deprivations experienced by Navahos during this period.

With the decline in livestock holdings came a necessary decline in certain types of behavior viewed as desirable by Navahos. Kin did not fulfil their obligation to kin, neighbors to neighbors, "rich" to poor, because the wherewithal for reciprocity and generosity was no longer there. There was a pervasive feeling that people did not *behave* as they should, or as they once did, and this I would call a deprivation in the area of behavior. This particular type of deprivation can be equally well illustrated by a shift to a different frame of reference for deprivation. With continued exposure to Americans, under circumstances which make Americans a model, some Navahos have come to feel that they do not behave as they should, by comparison with Americans: they are dirty, or superstitious, or eat "bad" foods (e.g., prairie dogs).

Finally, I come to worth, which is to some degree a residual category. It refers to a person's experience of others' estimation of him on grounds over and above his alterable characteristics—of possessions, status, and behavior. It is best illustrated again by those Navahos who use the outside world as a point of reference. Navahos with most contact have come to realize that to some degree neither wealth, occupational status, nor "proper" behavior can alter the fact that they are Navahos, and that they are therefore regarded as inferior and undesirable. Their total worth, then, is not what they feel it should be, and they experience a sense of deprivation in this regard. Many

Navahos are still sufficiently insulated from the larger world not to have this experience.

Now I conceive of any of these types of deprivation, measured by any of these reference points, to be the possible basis for efforts at remedial action to overcome the discrepancy between actuality and legitimate aspiration. (They can also be the basis for apathy, disorganization, despair, or suicide.) Insofar as the actions are undertaken by individuals and not by groups they are not relevant for present considerations. But the fact of deprivation is clearly an insufficient basis for predicting whether remedial efforts will occur, and, if they occur, whether they will have as aims changing the world, transcending it, or withdrawing from it, whether the remedy will be sought in direct action or ritual, and whether it will be sought with the aid of supernatural powers or without. The Navahos, have, for example, attempted to influence the Indian Service, hide their sheep, form political organizations, and protest to Congress. They have, in isolated instances, had visions of the total destruction of the whites, and in groups, Navaho members of the peyote cult have used the ritual of that cult both to attempt to foresee further Government plans and to seek new wealth through God's help.

I take it that the interest of the conference in millenarian movements was primarily in those movements which seek supernatural help, or which, at any rate, see supernatural intervention in the affairs of men.

A sense of blockage—of the insufficiency of ordinary action—seems to me, as it has seemed to many others, the source of the more supernaturally based millenarian, nativistic, revitalistic, and cargo movements— to use terms applied to various types of movements which we somehow sense as belonging together in some respects. And, difficult as it may be to anticipate whether a group's aspiration will be to return to the past, achieve the standards of the outside world, or transcend earthly standards completely, there is usually no serious difficulty in deciding whether, at a particular time, a particular group faces obstacles which are empirically unsurmountable in short-run terms. No one knew whether the Navahos would become violent over stock reduction, but every one knew that in the 20th century the violence of a few tens of thousands of American Indians could be put down if it became necessary to do so. We then add to our focus on deprivation types, attention to the question whether direct action could be expected to solve the group's problems. If it could not, we expect a correspondingly large increment of religious and magical action, although we cannot outlaw the possibility that this may lead to violence.

If we now turn to types of deprivation, we can have some expectation that the ideology of the movement will be related to the type of deprivation—or at least that emphasis in the ideology will be so related. The Plains Ghost Dance, although it originated elsewhere, spread among the Plains when the buffalo were gone—and anticipated the marvelous removal of the white man and a life of abundant hunting and gathering. It was oriented to deprivation of possessions. The Handsome Lake cult, originating long after the conquest of the Iroquois, focussed vigorously on morality and thus had a strong component of reaction to deprivation in the behavioral area. Peyotism, one of the most viable of American Indian nativistic movements, contains in its beliefs and values: elements of magical aid, including assistance in gaining more wealth; certain compensations for loss of status; a code of morality vigorously opposing drunkenness, adultery, and shiftlessness, three plagues of Reservation life; and hundreds of items designed to restore the self-respect of the Indian as an Indian. It is no accident that peyotism can therefore appeal to the traditional, who have suffered material deprivation, the formerly well-to-do, who have suffered status deprivation, the disorganized sufferers from deprivation in the behavioral area, and the marginal men with their ambivalence about being Indian in a white world. No one peyotist need come to peyotism for all of these, but a variety of sufferers can be accommodated.

This framework seems to me to be a profitable one for the inspection of various cults, including millenarian movements. It is not limited to absolute deprivation, nor to the assumption that the deprived are always those at the bottom of the status hierarchy. By the same token, it has a certain excessive flexibility. It is always possible after the fact to find deprivations. What is important is to be able to predict either the types of deprivations that lead to certain ideological formations, or the degree of deprivation which

crystallizes a cult movement. To date neither of these goals is achieved, although we are closer to the first than to the second. It is more appealing to me, however, to attempt to work within this formula than to assume randomness of social behavior or an indefinite plurality of causes. At a minimum, it is fair to say that millenarian, revitalistic, and cargo cult movements do not arise under circumstances where the members of a group think that the world is so nearly perfect that transformation or translation must be just around the corner. There is sufficient evidence of abundant distress in many instances to make this approach at least valuable for exploration.

Lastly, we come to the millenarian movement itself, rather than to the family of movements of which it is a part. My own experience has been largely with other than millenarian movements, and my exposure to the millenarian materials presented at the conference was a new experience.

The question is, what good is relative deprivation theory for the analysis of such movements? First, I will give to the adherents of the boredom theory of millenarian movements as many specific instances as they choose to claim, provided it is not maintained that *most* millenarian *movements* involving some active participation of believers are inspired by boredom. Second, I grant nothing to the utility of theories which are based on supposedly pan-human experiences, since constants cannot be used to explain variables. Third, the fact that a movement is *millenarian* is a totally insufficient basis for deciding what type of deprivation is important (in cases not involving boredom); both inspection of the ideology and of the condition of the adherents is necessary for this purpose, as Cohn's paper amply demonstrates. There is no reason why only the deprivations of peasants, and why only hunger and landlessness need be considered as bases for deprivation, or why the proof that it wasn't the peasants (or the disoriented new urbanites) that were involved is any reason not to look further for the deprivations of groups that did participate. Fourth —and this is prejudice—I am unwilling to admit that pure existential unease or concern with spiritual discomfort dissociated from the social conditions of participants forms a useful basis for explaining these movements.

This all adds up to the assumption that millenarian movements are susceptible to analysis in terms of deprivation theory, in the same way as cargo cults, the Handsome Lake cult, the peyote cult, and so on. Furthermore, the tense expectation of the millennium is not a sufficient basis for classifying these movements, since the things their ideologies react against are diverse. Hence there is one sense in which they should be parcelled out with their nearest non-millenarian cognates, and this we did not attempt. It is possible that the Tupi-Guarani movements, for example, belong in the family of ideologies of expansion, quite as much as in the family of millenarian movements. This position, however, also leaves something to be desired, since we have an uneasy sense that in one way or another the millenarian movements *do* share something besides tense expectation. I would suggest that many of them have one thing in common. The millenarian ideology often justifies the *removal* of the participants in the movement from the ordinary spheres of life. Indeed, this removal is frequently not only social but spatial, whether it takes the form of withdrawal or of wandering. I would suggest that the deprivations which form the background for the movement not only involve the sense of blockage to which I have referred earlier, which leads to resort to supernaturalism, but also the sense of a social order which cannot be reconstituted to yield the satisfactions desired. The millenarian ideology justifies the removal of the participants from that social order, by reassuring them that the order itself will not long continue, and frees them to indulge in phantasy about the ideal society, or to attempt to build it in isolation or through violent attempts against the existing order. Those who suffer from acute deprivation and cannot withdraw from the world can only constitute sects of the elect, or utilize devices to compensate for deprivation. The millenarian ideology justifies withdrawal, and that is its functional significance.

MELVILLE J. HERSKOVITS

African Gods and Catholic Saints in New World Religious Belief

Another important type of response in culture-contact situations is for a people to achieve a syncretism between their aboriginal religious beliefs and the doctrines and rituals of a Christian church of the Europeans. This syncretism has been especially notable in the case of American Indian contacts with Catholicism in the American Southwest and in Middle America, and, as Herskovits documents in this paper, has also taken place among New World Negroes who live under Catholic influence in Brazil, Cuba, Haiti, and elsewhere.

One of the remaining problems in the study of the dynamics of religion is to discover more systematically the conditions under which a culture-contact situation may lead to a nativistic reaction of some kind, as contrasted to the conditions under which a thoroughgoing syncretism occurs. But in either event both types of response demonstrate that a non-European people do not easily abandon their native religious beliefs and practices when they are confronted by European Christianity; indeed, the weight of the evidence indicates that the basic beliefs and practices of a religious system have a great tenacity—so much so that when they are threatened, the people may react either by engaging in some type of nativistic reaction or by a syncretistic reaction which takes over the outer forms of the European religion but retains for a long time the inner and deeper meanings of the native religious practices and value systems.

Reprinted from *American Anthropologist*, XXXIX (1937), 635–643, by permission of the author and the American Anthropological Association.

The tendency of native peoples who have had long contact with Catholicism to achieve a syncretism between their aboriginal religious beliefs and the doctrines and rituals of the Church has received notice in the case of various folk. Best known in this connection are the Indians of Central America, Mexico, and the southwestern part of the United States, where the phenomenon has been emphasized in the literature. The somewhat more thoroughgoing assimilation of Christian and pagan beliefs which has taken place among New World Negroes has, however, gone in large measure unrecognized. In Mexico and among some Indian tribes of the Southwest, assimilation has generally taken the form of the survival of aboriginal custom in a system of belief and ritual practices the outer forms of which are predominantly Catholic. In the case of the New World Negroes who live under Catholic influence in Brazil, Cuba, and Haiti, however, the exchange has been less one-sided, and the elements ancestral to the present-day organization of worship have been retained in immediately recognizable form.

This phenomenon has been studied with care in Cuba and Brazil, and somewhat less systematically in Haiti. In all three countries it is marked by the following characteristics: the Negroes profess nominal Catholicism while at the same time they belong to "fetish cults" which are under the direction of priests whose functions are essentially African and whose training follows more or less well recognized channels of instruction and initiation; the ceremonialism and ideology of these "fetish cults" exhibit Catholic elements more or less prominently; and everywhere specific identifications are made between African gods and Catholic saints.

It is the last of these characteristics that will be treated in this paper, since here can be most immediately recognized the manner in which these Negroes, in responding to the acculturative process, have succeeded in achieving, at least in their religious life, a synthesis between aboriginal African patterns and the European traditions to which they have been exposed. The emphasis, as far as actual data are concerned, will be placed on information gathered in the course of field work in Haiti; but because of the resemblance between Haitian syncretization of African and Catholic gods and that found in Cuba and Brazil, the material from these countries will also be summarized to permit comparisons.

The historical background of the phenomenon is obvious, since efforts were made everywhere in the New World to convert the slaves to Christianity, and in Haiti, at least, baptism into the Catholic Church was required for all those who were unloaded from the holds of the slave ships. In Cuba and Brazil, as in Haiti, the course of history has enabled Catholicism to continue to play a major role in the life of the people as their official religion. And it is this fact, together with the present-day vestiges of the fear, constantly present in the minds of the Europeans during the time of slavery, that the African cults offered a focus for revolt, that explains the inferior social position held by these "fetish cults" wherever they are found. It is here also that explanation may be sought for the conditions under which African rituals are carried on, since at best they obtain but passive acquiescence on the part of the authorities and, more often, must be conducted under the greatest secrecy.

In the case of these African religious systems, handicapped by social scorn and official disapprobation, the followers are almost inevitably split into local groups, each of which is dominated by the personality of the priest whose individual powers furnish the principal drive toward any outer organization the cult-group under his charge may achieve. This in turn makes it difficult to maintain anything more than a local hierarchy of priests, and is reflected in a resulting confusion of theological concept. Hence in all these countries a general frame of reference concerning the supernatural has been handed down from Africa, and within this a variety of beliefs and modes of worship exist.

In the Haitian *vodun* cult this takes the form of differences of opinion not alone from region to region, but within a given region even between members of the same group, concerning such details of cult belief and practice as the names of deities, modes of ritual procedure, or the genealogies of the gods, to say nothing of concepts regarding the powers and attributes of the African spirits in their relation to one another and to the total pantheon. As a case in point, there may be cited the three separate lists of names of deities which were collected in Haiti from a single valley in the interior, the valley of Mirebalais. When these three lists were compared with each other and with the published roster of names of *vodun* deities given by Dorsainvil, it was seen that while certain designations were found in all lists, there were extreme divergencies as well. Some names were present in all of them, it is true, and these represented the more important deities worshiped over the whole of Haiti, being gods derived from Dahomey and, to a lesser extent, from Nigeria and those other cultures of West Africa which have predominated in determining the form and functions of Haitian *vodun* worship. But the differences between these lists were much greater than the resemblances; and since this had to do only with names of gods, it is not strange that in identifying deities with Catholic saints an even greater divergence of opinion was found.

Two methods were employed in the field to obtain this material. In some cases African deities were equated with Catholic saints in the course of discussions of general theological problems, or, as has been done in Brazil, invocations of songs were recorded which coupled the name of a given saint with that of its corresponding pagan god. The other means used to obtain this information was more direct. As elswhere in the New World, the imagination of the Negroes seems to have been taken by the ordinary chromolithographs found widely distributed in Catholic countries, which depict the saints and are hung in the houses of the faithful. It was possible to present a collection of these *images,* as they are termed in Haiti, to the natives and to obtain information concerning the manner in which the saints are envisaged by the people, and those *loa* or African deities they are believed to represent, by asking the necessary questions.

We may now turn to the correspondences themselves. Legba, the god who in Dahomey guards crossroads and entrances to temples, compounds, and villages, is widely worshiped in Haiti where, as in Dahomey, he must "open the path" for all other supernatural powers and hence is given the first offering in any Haitian *vodun* ceremony. Legba is believed by most persons to be the same as St. Anthony, for the reason that St. Anthony is represented on the *images* as an old man, poorly dressed, carrying a wand which supports him as he walks. Some hold that Legba is St. Peter, on the basis of the eminently logical reason that St. Peter, like Legba, is the keeper of keys and opens the door. By most persons, however, St. Peter is usually believed to be a *loa,* or *vodun* deity, without any African designation, being called the *loa* St. Pierre, though this again is disputed, the *loa* St. Pierre being held by still others to constitute the spirit that validates the neolithic celts which in Haiti as in other parts of the New World and in Africa, are held sacred as "thunderstones."

Damballa, the Dahomean rainbow-serpent deity, is one of the most widely worshiped and important Haitian *vodun* gods. The question of the active existence of the serpent cult in Haiti is one which cannot be considered in this place, but to the extent that it does exist either in actuality or in the sacredness with which serpents are regarded, their worship is undoubtedly associated with this god Damballa, who also retains his aboriginal character of being the rainbow. The saint identified with Damballa is St. Patrick, on whose *image* serpents are depicted. Following this logic further, Moses is held to be the "father of Damballa" because of the miracle he performed before Pharaoh when he threw down his staff on the ground and turned it into a serpent.

The Ogun *loa* include several gods who are generally regarded as brothers. Ogun Ferraille is held to be St. James, while Ogun Balandjo, a deity who gives "remedies" to cure the sick, is identified with St. Joseph because the picture of this saint shows him holding a child, his hand raised in the blessing which heals. Gran' Erzilie is by most persons believed to be Mater Dolorosa, though one informant expressed the belief that this saint is another *loa* named Erzilie Freda Dahomey. The widespread identification of Gran' Erzilie with Mater Dolorosa, however, is based on the attributes accorded the African goddess, since she is believed to be the richest of all the deities, so that the chromolithographic representation of Mater Dolorosa showing her as richly clothed, surrounded by many evidences of great wealth, and wearing many rings and necklaces, is quite in keeping with the wealthiness of Gran' Erzilie. The Dahomean sea god, who has retained his aboriginal function in Haiti, is equated with St. Expeditius. The *marassa,* spirits of twins, are believed to be the twin saints Cosmas and Damien, and St. Nicholas, because of the figures of children on his representations, is regarded as the "protector of the *marassa.*" Simbi, who unlike the deities of predominantly Dahomean origin already mentioned is a Congo god, is believed by some to be St. Andrew, though others state that this saint is Azaka Mede, a *loa* which clearly derives its name from that of the river across which Dahomean belief holds that all dead must pass to reach the next world. One special member of the Simbi group, Simbi en Deux Eaux, is believed to be the equivalent of St. Anthony the Hermit, although this again is disputed by those who hold this saint is rather the *loa* named 'Ti Jean Petro.

The Haitian, however, does not stop merely at identifying saints with African gods, for saints are occasionally themselves conceived as *loa,* or as natural phenomena such as the sun, moon, and stars, which are regarded as saints and occasionally worshiped. Thus St. Louis, the patron of the town of Mirebalais where this field work was carried on, is a *loa* in his own right. Similarly two of the kings who figure in the *image* that depicts the Adoration of the Christ Child, Balthazar and Gaspar, are also held to be *vodun* deities. La Sirène, a character derived from European mythology, is believed to be a water goddess and is identified with Notre Dame de Grâce, while the *loa* Kpanyol, or Spanish *loa,* is equated with Notre Dame d'Alta Gracia.

St. John the Baptist is a powerful nature spirit worshiped as the *loa* St. Jean Baptiste, and is believed to control the thunder and lightning. The chromolithograph depicts this saint as a sweet-faced child holding a lamb, in striking contrast to the great power he is supposed to wield, and the irresponsibility that characterizes his actions. Yet this identification becomes understandable when it is realized that in Dahomean mythology, which has influenced so much of Haitian belief, as in Yoruban concept, the ram is the emblem of the god of thunder; while the basis of the conception of the *loa* St. Jean Baptiste as the thunderer becomes even clearer when it is pointed out that the ram is the sacrificial animal of this *loa* in Haiti. The following myth is told of this deity:

On a given day of the year, God permits each saint to have control over the universe. St. John the Baptist, however, is so irresponsible, and his rage so violent, that God fears for the con-

sequences were he allowed to exert his power on this day. Plying him with drink the day before, he is therefore made so drunk that when he falls asleep he does not awaken until the day after. When he is told his day has already passed, his rage is terrible, and he causes great storms to flay the earth; and it is a commonplace in Mirebalais that this day is marked by tempests of almost hurricane proportions, with great displays of thunder and lightning. Though he can do some damage, his power is now limited, however, to his own sphere.

Concerning the tendency to regard the phenomena of nature as supernatural beings we find St. Soleil (St. Sun), Ste. la Lune (St. Moon), Sts. Étoiles (Sts. Stars) and Ste. la Terre (St. Earth) among those worshiped under this category. Even the conception of a force such as the power that can bring reverses to a man may be anthropomorphized and worshiped, as the belief in the existence of a supernatural being known as St. Bouleversé indicates. An *oraison* to this "saint," well known throughout Haiti, reads as follows:

Saint Bouleversé, vous qui avez le pouvoir de bouleverser la terre, vous êtes un saint et moi, je suis un pêcheur, je vous invoque et vous prends pour mon patron dès aujourd'hui. Je vous envoie chercher un tel; bouleversez sa tête bouleversez sa memoire, bouleversez sa pensée, bouleversez sa maison, bouleversez pour moi mes ennemis visibles et invisibles; faites éclater sur eux la foudre et la tempête.

En l'honneur du Saint Bouleversé dites trois Pater et trois Ave Maria.

Satan, je te renonce, si tu viens de la part du démon, que le démon t'emporte et te jette dans l'abime et dans l'infernal séjour.

Bête méchante, langue de vipère, langue pernicieuse, si tu viens de la part de Dieu pour me tromper, il faut que tu marche de terre en terre, de coin en coin, de village en village, de maison en maison, d'emplois en emplois comme le juif errant, l'insulteur de Jésus Christ.

Seigneur, mon Dieu, viens chercher à perdre un tel, afin qu'il soit disparu devant moi comme la foudre et la tempête.

The data which have been sketched from Haiti will be strikingly familiar to those conversant with the literature on Cuba and Brazil, though the names of the Haitian deities will be unfamiliar to them, and the correspondences, Catholic saint for saint, and African god for god, somewhat different. Thus Legba, the Dahomean trickster held to be St. Anthony or St. Peter in Haiti, ap-

CORRESPONDENCE BETWEEN AFRICAN GODS AND CATHOLIC SAINTS IN BRAZIL, CUBA, AND HAITI[a]

AFRICAN DEITIES AS FOUND IN:	BRAZIL	CUBA	HAITI
Obatala		(O) Virgen de las Mercédes; the Most Sacred Sacrament; Christ on the Cross	
Obatala; Orisala; Orixala (Oxala)	(I) (N) (R) "Nosso Senhor de Bomfim" at Bahía; (N) Saint Anne; (R) "Senhor do Bomfim" at Río (because of the influence of Bahía")		
Grande Mambo Batala Shango	(I) (N) (R) Santa Barbara at Bahía; (R) St. Michael the Archangel at Río; (R) St. Jerome (the husband of Santa Barbara) at Bahía (see Yansan below)	(O) Santa Barbara	(M) Saint Anne
Elegbara, Elegua, Alegua		(O) "Animas benditas del Purgatorio"; "Anima Sola"	
Legba			(M) (H) St. Anthony; (W) (H?) St. Peter
Esu	(I) (N) (R) the Devil		
Ogun	(I) (R) St. George, at Río; (N) St. Jerome; (I) (N) (R) St. Anthony, at Bahía	(O) St. Peter	
Ogun Balandjo			(M) St. James the Elder; (H) St. Joseph
Ogun Ferraille			(H) St. James
Osun	(N) Virgin Mary; N. D. de Candeias	(O) Virgin de la Caridad del Cobre	
Yemanjá	(N) Virgin Mary; (R) N. S. de Rosario (at Bahía); N. D. de Conceiçao (at Río)	(O) Virgin de Regla	
Maîtresse Erzulie; Erzilie; Erzilie Freda Dahomey			(M) (S) the Holy Virgin; especially the Holy Virgin of the Nativity; (P) Santa Barbara (?); (H) Mater Dolorosa
Saponam	(I) the Sacred Sacrament		
Osa-Osé (Oxóssi)	(I) (N) (R) St. George, at Bahía; (R) St. Sebastian, at Río	(O) St. Alberto; (occasionally) St. Hubert	
Ololu; Omolú	(R) St. Bento	(O) St. John the Baptist	
Agomme Tonnere			(M) St. John the Baptist

[a] In this table, the initials before the names of the saints indicate the sources from which the correspondences have been derived:

(H) Herskovits, field data (see also *Life in a Haitian Valley*, Ch. 14).
(I) Ignace.
(M) Price-Mars.
(S) Seabrook.

(W) Wirkus and Taney.
(N) Nina-Rodrigues.
(O) Ortiz.
(P) Parsons.
(R) Ramos.

African deities as found in (Cont.)	Brazil (Cont.)	Cuba (Cont.)	Haiti (Cont.)
Ibeji (Brazil and Cuba); Marassa (Haiti)	(R) Sts. Cosmas and Damien		(H) Sts. Cosmas and Damien
Father of the Marassa			(H) St. Nicholas
Orumbila (Odumbila?)		(O) St. Francisco	
Loco	(R) St. Francisco		
Babayú Ayí		(O) St. Lazarus	
Ifa	(R) The Most Sacred Sacrament		
Yansan (wife of Shango)	(R) Santa Barbara (wife of St. Jerome)		
Damballa			(W) (H) St. Patrick
Father of Damballa			(H) Moses
Pierre d'Ambala			(M) St. Peter
loa St. Pierre			(H) St. Peter
Agwe			(H) St. Expeditius
Roi d'Agoueseau			(M) St. Louis (King of France)
Daguy Bologuay			(M) St. Joseph
la Sirène			(M) the Assumption; (H) N. D. de Grâce
loa Christalline			(H) Ste. Philomena
Adamisil Wedo			(H) Ste. Anne
loa Kpanyol			(H) N. D. de Alta Gracia
Aizan			(H) Christ (?)
Simbi			(H) St. Andrew
Simbi en Deux Eaux			(H) St. Anthony the Hermit
Azaka Mede			(H) St. Andrew (?)
'Ti Jean Petro			(H) St. Anthony the Hermit (?)

pears under his Yoruban name Elegbara, being held in Brazil to be the equivalent of the Devil, and of the Blessed Souls in Purgatory or the Anima Solo in Cuba. Shango, identified with Santa Barbara both in Brazil and Cuba, is not represented in Haiti by his Dahomean counterpart, Xevioso; it is to be remarked, however, that in Dahomey itself, among those natives of the city of Abomey who are members of the Catholic Church, this same identification is made between Xevioso and Santa Barbara. Mawu, the Great God of the Dahomeans, has not been retained in Haiti in the way in which Obatala, her Yoruban counterpart, has lived on in Brazil and Cuba, and though the Nigerian-Dahomean Ogun (designated Gu in Da-

homey) has persisted in all three countries, differences are found in the saints with which he is identified in each. The table that accompanies this discussion shows in concise form the reconciliations that have been effected between gods and saints. It has been abstracted from the available literature on Brazil, Cuba, and Haiti, and in addition is supplemented by data recorded during field work in the latter country.

In a sense, the disparities that exist between the identifications made by the Negroes who live in different countries emphasize the theoretical importance of the materials presented in this paper. Were a given African god everywhere found to be identified with the same Catholic saint, there would be great probability that this had resulted from contacts between slaves subsequent to their arrival in the New World, and thus represented a diffusion from one country to another. As it is, there can be little question that these syncretizations have developed independently in each region where they are found. In the two lands where gods of the same African (Yoruban) tribe predominantly survive—Brazil and Cuba—distance and the absence of historic contacts of any significance make any other explanation untenable. And though Haiti is relatively close to Cuba, the fewness of the contacts between the Negroes of the two countries except in very recent times, added to the fact that in the syntheses that have been achieved in each country the gods of different African tribes figure, make the same point. Considered as a whole, therefore, the data show quite clearly to what an extent the inner logic of the aboriginal African cultures of the Negroes, when brought in contact with foreign traditions, worked out to achieve an end that, despite the handicaps of slavery, has been relatively the same wherever the forces making for change have been comparable.

CLIFFORD GEERTZ

Ritual and Social Change: A Javanese Example

The following article contains a suggested revision of "functional" sociocultural theory, centering the problem around a chronicle of a Javanese burial ceremony and the surrounding events. It also embodies an analysis of the cultural and social phenomena involved in the burial situation from the position of the suggested revision in theory. Actual cultural practice, contained in the ethnographic description, is seen in the diachronic context of changing political and social patterns. The point is made that any "functional" analysis must differentiate between the different systems to which each—cultural practice and social structure—belongs. Culture, Geertz states, exists in a system wherein the parts have consistency and unity on the basis of style, logical implication, meaning, and value. The social structure, on the other hand, is integrated into a "causal web"; each part is integral to the functioning of the whole. It is further suggested that, because of the differing ways in which the two systems are integrated, conflict between them is an inherent potential stemming from the basic independence of each dimension as far as the initiation of change is concerned, yet there is interdependence of each after change has taken place.

In the burial scene the kampong dwellers, adherents of a peasant or folk-like culture, find that the traditional beliefs and practices, integrated through "logico-meaningful" relationships, are in conflict with the "causal-functional" integration of the social structure, derived in part from the urban sphere. The conflict arises from the discontinuity that exists between the two dimensions because of their differing types of integration and their differing points of articulation with the urban sociocultural system.

Many elements found here among the Javanese have been previously cited as occurring in other groups: fear of the dead, concern for the welfare of the living who come into contact with the deceased, a desire to complete the burial as rapidly as possible, and the culturally approved, ritualized expression of emotion generated through the loss of a son, a friend, or a neighbor. The reader might join Geertz and the inhabitants of Modjokuto in pondering the question, "What direction will burial customs take when death next occurs in a Permai family?"

Reprinted in abridged form from *American Anthropologist*, LIX (1957), 32–54, by permission of the author and the American Anthropological Association.

As in so many areas of anthropological concern, functionalism, either of the sociological sort associated with the name of Radcliffe-Brown or of the social-psychological sort associated with Malinowski, has tended to dominate recent theoretical discussions of the role of religion in society. Stemming originally from Durkheim's *The Elementary Forms of the Religious Life* and Robertson Smith's *Lectures on the Religion of the Semites,* the sociological approach (or, as the British anthropologists prefer to call it, the social anthropological approach) emphasizes the manner in which belief and particularly ritual reinforce the traditional social ties between individuals; it stresses the way in which the social structure of a group is strengthened and perpetuated through the ritualistic or mythic symbolization of the underlying social values upon which it rests. The social psychological approach, of which Frazer and Tylor were perhaps the pioneers but which found its clearest statement in Malinowski's classic *Magic, Science and Religion,* emphasizes what religion does for the individual—how it satisfies both his cognitive affective demands for a stable, comprehensible, and coercible world, and how it enables him to maintain an inner security in the face of natural contingency. Together the two approaches have given us an increasingly detailed understanding of the social and psychological "functions" of religion in a wide range of societies.

Where the functional approach has been least impressive, however, is in dealing with social change. As has been noted by several writers, the emphasis on systems in balance, on social homeostasis, and on timeless structural pictures leads to a bias in favor of "well-integrated" societies in a stable equilibrium and to a tendency to emphasize the functional aspects of a people's social usages and customs rather than their dysfunctional implications. In analyses of religion this static, ahistorical approach has led to a somewhat overconservative view of the role of ritual and belief in social life. Despite cautionary comments by Kluckhohn (1944) and others on the "gain and cost" of various religious practices such as witchcraft, the tendency has been consistently to stress the harmonizing, integrating, and psychologically supportive aspects of religious patterns rather than the disruptive, disintegrative, and psychologically disturbing aspects; to demonstrate the manner in which religion preserves social and psychological structure rather than the manner in which it destroys or transforms it. Where change has been treated, as in Redfield's work on Yucatán, it has largely been in terms of progressive disintegration: "The changes in culture that in Yucatán appear to 'go along with' lessening isolation and homogeneity are seen to be chiefly three: disorganization of the culture, secularization, and individualization." Yet even a passing knowledge of our own religious history makes us hesitate to affirm such a simply "positive" role for religion generally.

It is the thesis of this paper that one of the major reasons for the inability of functional theory to cope with change lies in its failure to treat sociological and cultural processes on equal terms; almost inevitably one of the two is either ignored or is sacrificed to become but a simple reflex, a "mirror image," of the other. Either culture is regarded as wholly derivative from the forms of social organization—the approach characteristic of the British structuralists as well as many American sociologists; or the forms of social organization are regarded as behavioral embodiments of cultural patterns—the approach of Malinowski and many American anthropologists. In either case, the lesser term tends to drop out as a dynamic factor and we are left either with an omnibus concept of culture ("that complex whole . . .") or else with a completely comprehensive concept of social structure ("social structure is not an aspect of culture, but the entire culture of a given people handled in a special frame of theory" [Fortes]). In such a situation, the dynamic elements in social change which arise from the failure of cultural patterns to be perfectly congruent with the forms of social organization are largely incapable of formulation. "We functionalists," E. R. Leach has recently remarked, "are not really 'anti-historical' by principle; it is simply that we do not know how to fit historical materials into our framework of concepts."

A revision of the concepts of functional theory so as to make them capable of dealing more effectively with "historical materials" might well begin with an attempt to distinguish analytically between the cultural and social aspects of human life, and to treat them as independently variable yet mutually interdependent factors. Though separable only conceptually, culture and social structure will then be seen to be capable of a wide range of modes of integration with one another, of which the simple isomorphic mode is but a limiting case—a case common only in societies which have been stable over such an extended time as to make possible a close adjustment between social and cultural aspects. In most societies, where change is a characteristic rather than an abnormal occurrence, we shall expect to find more or less radical discontinuities between the two. I would argue that it is in these very discontinuities that we shall find some of the primary driving forces in change.

One of the more useful ways—but far from the only one—of distinguishing between culture and social system is to see the former as an ordered system of meaning and of symbols, in terms of which social interaction takes place; and to see the latter as a pattern of social interaction itself. On the one level there is the framework of beliefs, expressive symbols, and values in terms of which individuals define their world, express their feelings, and make their judgments; on the other level there is the ongoing process of interactive behavior, whose persistent form we call social structure. Culture is the fabric of meaning in terms of which human beings interpret their experience and guide their action; social structure is the form that action takes, the actually existing network of social relations. Culture and social structure are then but different abstractions from the same phenomena. The one considers social action in respect to its meaning for those who carry it out, the other considers it in terms of its contribution to the functioning of some social system.

The nature of the distinction between culture and social system is brought out more clearly when one considers the contrasting sorts of integration characteristic of each of them. This contrast is between what Sorokin has called "logico-meaningful integration" and what he has called "causal-functional integration." By logico-meaningful integration, characteristic of culture, is meant the sort of integration one finds in a Bach fugue, in Catholic dogma, or in the general theory of relativity; it is a unity of style, of logical implication, of meaning and value. By causal-functional integration, characteristic of the social system, is meant the kind of integra-

tion one finds in an organism, where all the parts are united in a single causal web; each part is an element in a reverberating causal ring which "keeps the system going." And because these two types of integration are not identical, because the particular form one of them takes does not directly imply the form the other will take, there is an inherent incongruity and tension between the two and between both of them and a third element, the pattern of motivational integration within the individual which we usually call personality structure.

Thus conceived, a social system is only one of three aspects of the structuring of a completely concrete system of social action. The other two are the personality systems of the individual actors and the cultural system which is built into their action. Each of the three must be considered to be an independent focus of the organization of the elements of the action system in the sense that no one of them is theoretically reducible to terms of one or a combination of the other two. Each is indispensable to the other two in the sense that without personalities and culture there would be no social system and so on around the roster of logical possibilities. But this interdependence and interpenetration is a very different matter from reducibility, which would mean that the important properties and processes of one class of system could be theoretically *derived* from our theoretical knowledge of one or both of the other two. The action frame of reference is common to all three and this fact makes certain "transformations" between them possible. But on the level of theory here attempted they do not constitute a single system, however this might turn out to be on some other theoretical level [Parsons, *The Social System*].

I will attempt to demonstrate the utility of this more dynamic functionalist approach by applying it to a particular case of a ritual which failed to function properly. I shall try to show how an approach which does not distinguish the "logico-meaningful" cultural aspects of the ritual pattern from the "causal-functional" social structural aspects is unable to account adequately for this ritual failure, and how an approach which does so distinguish them is able to analyze more explicitly the cause of the trouble. It will further be argued that such an approach is able to avoid the simplistic view of the functional role of religion in society which sees that role merely as structure-conserving, and to substitute for it a more complex conception of the relations between religious belief and practice and secular social life. Historical materials can be fitted into such a conception, and the functional analysis of religion can therefore be widened to deal more adequately with processes of change.

THE SETTING

The case to be described is that of a funeral held in Modjokuto, a small town in eastern Central Java. A young boy, about ten years of age, who was living with his uncle and aunt, died very suddenly but his death, instead of being followed by the usual hurried, subdued, yet methodically efficient Javanese funeral ceremony and burial routine, brought on an extended period of pronounced social strain and severe psychological tension. The complex of beliefs and rituals which had for generations brought countless Javanese safely through the difficult post-mortem period suddenly failed to work with its accustomed effectiveness. To understand why it failed demands knowledge and understanding of a whole range of social and cultural changes which have taken place in Java since the first decades of this century. This disrupted funeral was in fact but a microcosmic example of the broader conflicts, structural dissolutions, and attempted reintegrations which, in one form or another, are characteristic of contemporary Indonesian society.

The religious tradition of Java, particularly of the peasantry, is a composite of Indian, Islamic, and indigenous Southeast Asian elements. The rise of large, militaristic kingdoms in the inland rice basins in the early centuries of the Christian era was associated with the diffusion of Hinduist and Buddhist culture patterns to the island; the expansion of international maritime trade in the port cities of the northern coast in the fifteenth and sixteenth centuries was associated with the diffusion of Islamic patterns. Working their way into the peasant mass, these two world religions became fused with the underlying animistic traditions characteristic of the whole Malaysian culture area. The result was a balanced syncretism of myth and ritual in which Hindu gods and goddesses, Moslem prophets and saints, and local place spirits and demons all found a proper place.

The central ritual form in this syncretism is a communal feast, called the *slametan*. Slametans, which are given with only slight variations in form and content on almost all occasions of religious significance—at passage points in the life cycle, on calendrical holidays, at certain stages of the crop cycle, on hanging one's residence, etc.—are intended to be both offerings to the spirits and commensal mechanisms of social integration for the living. The meal, which consists of specially prepared dishes, each symbolic of a particular religious concept, is cooked by the female members of one nuclear family household and set out on mats in the middle of the living-room. The male head of the household invites the male heads of the eight or ten contiguous households to attend; no close neighbor is ignored in favor of one further away. After a speech by the host explaining the spiritual purpose of the feast and a short Arabic chant, each man takes a few hurried, almost furtive, gulps of food, wraps the remainder of the meal in a banana-leaf basket, and returns home to share it with his family. It is said that the spirits draw their sustenance from the odor of the food, the incense which is burned, and the Moslem prayer; the human participants draw theirs from the material substance of the food and from their social interaction. The result of this quiet, undramatic little ritual is twofold: the spirits are appeased and neighborhood solidarity is strengthened.

The ordinary canons of functional theory are quite adequate for the analysis of such a pattern. It can rather easily be shown that the slametan is well designed both to "tune up the ultimate value attitudes" necessary to the effective integration of a territorially based social structure, and to fulfill the psychological needs for intellectual coherence and emotional stability characteristic of a peasant population. The Javanese village (once or twice a year, village-wide slametans are held) is essentially a set of geographically contiguous, but rather self-consciously autonomous, nuclear family households whose economic and political interdependence is of roughly the same circumscribed and explicitly defined sort as that demonstrated in the slametan. The demands of the labor-intensive rice and dry-crop agricultural process require the perpetuation of specific modes of technical cooperation and enforce a sense of community on the otherwise rather self-contained families—a sense of community which the slame-tan clearly reinforces. And when we consider the manner in which various conceptual and behavioral elements from Hindu-Buddhism, Islam, and "animism" are rein-terpreted and balanced to form a distinctive and nearly homogeneous religious style, the close functional adjustment between the communal feast pattern and the conditions of Javanese rural life is even more readily apparent.

But the fact is that in all but the more isolated parts of Java, both the simple terri-torial basis of village social integration and the syncretic basis of its cultural homoge-neity have been progressively undermined over the past fifty years. Population growth, urbanization, monetization, occupational dif-ferentiation, and the like have combined to weaken the traditional ties of peasant so-cial structure; and the winds of doctrine which have accompanied the appearance of these structural changes have disturbed the simple uniformity of religious belief and practice characteristic of an earlier period. The rise of nationalism, Marxism, and Is-lamic reform as ideologies, which resulted in part from the increasing complexity of Javanese society, has affected not only the large cities where these creeds first appeared and have always had their greatest strength, but has had a heavy impact on the smaller towns and villages as well. In fact, much of recent Javanese social change is perhaps most aptly characterized as a shift from a situation in which the primary integrative ties between individuals (or between fami-lies) are phrased in terms of geographical proximity to one in which they are phrased in terms of ideological like-mindedness.

In the villages and small towns these ma-jor ideological changes appeared largely in the guise of a widening split between those who emphasized the Islamic aspects of the indigenous religious syncretism and those who emphasized the Hinduist and animistic elements. It is true that some difference be-tween these variant subtraditions has been present since the arrival of Islam; some in-dividuals have always been particularly skilled in Arabic chanting or particularly learned in Moslem law, while others have been adept at more Hinduistic mystical prac-tices or specialists in local curing techniques. But these contrasts were softened by the easy tolerance of the Javanese for a wide range of religious concepts, so long as basic ritual patterns—i.e., slametans—were faith-fully supported; whatever social divisiveness they stimulated was largely obscured by the overriding commonalities of rural and small-town life.

However, the appearance after 1910 of Is-lamic modernism (as well as vigorous con-servative reactions against it) and religious nationalism among the economically and po-litically sophisticated trading classes of the larger cities strengthened the feeling for Islam as an exclusivist, antisyncretic creed among the more orthodox element of the mass of the population. Similarly, secular nationalism and Marxism, appearing among the civil servants and the expanding prole-tariat of these cities, strengthened the pre-Islamic (i.e., Hinduist-animist) elements of the syncretic pattern, which these groups tended to prize as a counterweight to pu-ristic Islam and which some of them adopted as a general religious framework in which to set their more specifically political ideas. On the one hand there arose a more self-con-scious Moslem, basing his religious beliefs and practices more explicitly on the interna-tional and universalistic doctrines of Mo-hammed; on the other hand there arose a more self-conscious "nativist," attempting to evolve a generalized religious system out of the material—muting the more Islamic ele-ments—of his inherited religious tradition. And the contrast between the first kind of man, called a *santri,* and the second, called an *abangan,* grew steadily more acute, until today it forms the major cultural distinction in the whole of the Modjokuto area.

It is especially in the town that this con-trast has come to play a crucial role. The absence of pressures toward interfamilial co-operation exerted by the technical require-ments of wet-rice growing, as well as less-ened effectiveness of the traditional forms of village government in the face of the com-plexities of urban living, severely weaken the social supports of the syncretic village pat-tern. When each man makes his living—as chauffeur, trader, clerk, or laborer—more or less independently of how his neighbors make theirs, his sense of the importance of the neighborhood community naturally di-minishes. A more differentiated class system, more bureaucratic and impersonal forms of government, greater heterogeneity of social background, all tend to lead to the same result: the de-emphasis of strictly geographical ties in favor of diffusely ideological ones. For the townsman, the distinction between santri and abangan becomes even sharper, for it emerges as his primary point of social reference; it becomes a symbol of his social identity, rather than a mere contrast in belief. The sort of friends he will have, the sort of organizations he will join, the sort of political leadership he will follow, the sort of person he or his son will marry, will all be strongly influenced by the side of this ideological bifurcation which he adopts as his own.

There is thus emerging in the town— though not only in the town—a new pattern of social living organized in terms of an altered framework of cultural classification. Among the elite this new pattern has already become rather highly developed, but among the mass of the townspeople it is still in the process of formation. Particularly in the *kampongs,* the off-the-street neighborhoods in which the common Javanese townsmen live crowded together in a helter-skelter profusion of little bamboo houses, one finds a transitional society in which the traditional forms of rural living are being steadily dissolved and new forms steadily reconstructed. In these enclaves of peasants-come-to-town (or of sons and grandsons of peasants-come-to-town), Redfield's folk culture is being constantly converted into his urban culture, though this latter is not accurately characterized by such negative and residual terms as "secular," "individualized," and "culturally disorganized." What is occurring in the kampongs is not so much a destruction of traditional ways of life as a construction of a new one; the sharp social conflict characteristic of these lower-class neighborhoods is not simply indicative of a loss of cultural consensus, but rather indicative of a search, not yet entirely successful, for new, more generalized, and flexible patterns of belief and value.

In Modjokuto, as in most of Indonesia, this search is taking place largely within the social context of the mass political parties, as well as in the women's clubs, youth organizations, labor unions, and other sodalities formally or informally linked with them. There are several of these parties (though the recent general election severely reduced their number), each led by educated urban elites—civil servants, teachers, traders, students, and the like—and each competing with the others for the political allegiance of both the half rural, half urban kampong dwellers and of the mass of the peasantry. And almost without exception, they appeal to one or another side of the santri-abangan split. Of this complex of political parties and sodalities, only two are of immediate concern to us here: Masjumi, a huge, Islam-based political party; and Permai, a vigorously anti-Moslem politico-religious cult.

Masjumi is the more or less direct descendant of the pre-war Islamic reform movement. Led, at least in Modjokuto, by modernist santri intellectuals, it stands for a socially conscious, antischolastic, and somewhat puritanical version of back-to-the-Koran Islam. In company with the other Moslem parties, it also supports the institution of an "Islamic State" in Indonesia in place of the present secular republic. However, the meaning of this ideal is not entirely clear. Masjumi's enemies accuse it of pressing for an intolerant, medievalist theocracy in which abangans and non-Moslems will be persecuted and forced to follow exactly the prescripts of the Moslem law, while Masjumi's leaders claim that Islam is intrinsically tolerant and that they only desire a government explicitly based on the Moslem creed, one whose laws will be in consonance with the teachings of the Koran and Hadith. In any case, Masjumi, the country's largest Moslem party, is one of the major spokesmen on both the national and the local levels for the values and aspirations of the santri community.

Permai is not so impressive on a national scale. Though it is a nation-wide party, it is a fairly small one, having strength only in a few fairly circumscribed regions. In the Modjokuto area, however, it happened to be of some importance, and what it lacked in national scope it made up in local intensity. Essentially, Permai is a fusion of Marxist politics with abangan religious patterns. It combines a fairly explicit anti-Westernism, anti-capitalism, and anti-imperialism with an attempt to formalize and generalize some of the more characteristic diffuse themes of the peasant religious syncretism. Permai meetings follow both the slametan pattern, complete with incense and symbolic food (but without Islamic chants), and modern parliamentary procedure; Permai pamphlets contain calendrical and numerological divinatory systems and mystical teachings as well as analyses of class conflict; and Permai speeches are concerned with elaborating both religious and political concepts. In Modjokuto, Permai is also a curing cult, with its own special medical practices and spells, a secret password, and cabalistic interpretations of passages in the leaders' social and political writings.

But Permai's most notable characteristic is its strong anti-Moslem stand. Charging that Islam is a foreign import, unsuited to the needs and values of the Javanese, the cult urges a return to "pure" and "original" Javanese beliefs, by which they seem to mean to the indigenous syncretism with the more Islamic elements removed. In line with this, the cult-party has initiated a drive, on both national and local levels, for secular (i.e., non-Islamic) marriage and funeral rites. As the situation stands now, all but Christians and Balinese Hindus must have their marriages legitimatized by means of the Moslem ritual. Funeral rites are an individual concern but, because of the long history of syncretism, they are so deeply involved with Islamic customs that a genuinely non-Islamic funeral tends to be a practical impossibility.

Permai's action on the local level in pursuit of non-Islamic marriage and funeral ceremonies took two forms. One was heavy pressure on local government officials to permit such practices, and the other was heavy pressure on its own members to follow, voluntarily, rituals purified of Islamic elements. In the case of marriage, success was more or less precluded because the local officials' hands were tied by Central Government ordinances, and even highly ideologized members of the cult would not dare an openly "illegitimate" marriage. Without a change in the law, Permai had little chance to alter marriage forms, though a few abortive attempts were made to conduct civil ceremonies under the aegis of abangan-minded village chiefs.

The case of funerals was somewhat different, for a matter of custom rather than law was involved. During the year I was in the field, the tension between Permai and Masjumi increased very sharply. This was due in part to the imminence of Indonesia's first general elections, and in part to the effects of the cold war. It was also influenced by various special occurrences—such as a report

that the national head of Permai had publicly called Mohammed a false prophet; a speech in the nearby regional capital by a Masjumi leader in which he accused Permai of intending to raise a generation of bastards in Indonesia; and a bitter village-chief election largely fought out on santri vs. abangan grounds. As a result, the local subdistrict officer, a worried bureaucrat trapped in the middle, called a meeting of all the village religious officials, or *Modins*. Among many other duties, a Modin is traditionally responsible for conducting funerals. He directs the whole ritual, instructs the mourners in the technical details of burial, leads the Koran chanting, and reads a set speech to the deceased at the graveside. The subdistrict officer instructed the Modins—the majority of whom were village Masjumi leaders—that in case of the death of a member of Permai, they were merely to note the name and age of the deceased and return home; they were not to participate in the ritual. He warned that if they did not do as he advised, they would be responsible if trouble started and he would not come to their support.

This was the situation on July 17, 1954, when Paidjan, nephew of Karman, an active and ardent member of Permai, died suddenly in the Modjokuto kampong in which I was living.

THE FUNERAL

The mood of a Javanese funeral is not one of hysterical bereavement, unrestrained sobbing, or even of formalized cries of grief for the deceased's departure. Rather, it is a calm, undemonstrative, almost languid letting go, a brief ritualized relinquishment of a relationship no longer possible. Tears are not approved of and certainly not encouraged; the effort is to get the job done, not to linger over the pleasures of grief. The detailed busy-work of the funeral, the politely formal social intercourse with the neighbors pressing in from all sides, the series of commemorative slametans stretched out at intervals for almost three years—the whole momentum of the Javanese ritual system is supposed to carry one through grief without severe emotional disturbance. For the mourner, the funeral and postfuneral ritual is said to produce a feeling of *iklas,* a kind of willed affectlessness, a detached and static state of "not caring"; for the neighborhood group it is said to produce *rukun,* "communal harmony."

The actual service is in essence simply another version of the slametan, adapted to the special requirements of interment. When the news of a death is broadcast through the area, everyone in the neighborhood must drop what he is doing and go immediately to the home of the survivors. The women bring bowls of rice, which is cooked up into a slametan; the men begin to cut wooden grave markers and to dig a grave. Soon the Modin arrives and begins to direct activities. The corpse is washed in ceremonially prepared water by the relatives (who unflinchingly hold the body on their laps to demonstrate their affection for the deceased as well as their self-control); then it is wrapped in muslin. About a dozen santris, under the leadership of the Modin, chant Arabic prayers over the body for five or ten minutes; after this it is carried, amid various ritual acts, in a ceremonial procession to the graveyard where it is interred in prescribed ways. The Modin reads a graveside speech to the deceased, reminding him of his duties as a believing Moslem; and the funeral is over, usually only two or three hours after death. The funeral proper is followed by commemorative slametans in the home of the survivors at three, seven, forty, and one hundred days after death; on the first and second anniversary of death; and, finally, on the thousandth day, when the corpse is considered to have turned to dust and the gap between the living and the dead to have become absolute.

This was the ritual pattern which was called into play when Paidjan died. As soon as dawn broke (death occurred in the early hours of the morning), Karman, the uncle, dispatched a telegram to the boy's parents in a nearby city, telling them in characteristic Javanese fashion that their son was ill. This evasion was intended to soften the impact of death by allowing them to become aware of it more gradually. Javanese feel that emotional damage results not from the severity of a frustration but from the suddenness with which it comes, the degree to which it "surprises" one unprepared for it. It is "shock," not suffering itself, which is feared. Next, in the expectation that the parents would arrive within a few hours, Karman sent for the Modin to begin the ceremony. This was done on the theory that by the time

the parents had come little would be left to do but inter the body, and they would thus once more be spared unnecessary stress. By ten o'clock at the very latest it should all be over; a saddening incident, but a ritually muted one.

But when the Modin, as he later told me, arrived at Karman's house and saw the poster displaying Permai's political symbol, he told Karman that he could not perform the ritual. After all, Karman belonged to "another religion" and he, the Modin, did not know the correct burial rituals for it; all he knew was Islam. "I don't want to insult your religion," he said piously, "on the contrary, I hold it in the utmost regard, for there is no intolerance in Islam. But I don't know your ritual. The Christians have their own ritual and their own specialist (the local preacher), but what does Permai do? Do they burn the corpse or what?" (This is a sly allusion to Hindu burial practices; evidently the Modin enjoyed himself hugely in this interchange.) Karman was, the Modin told me, rather upset at all this and evidently surprised, for although he was an active member of Permai, he was a fairly unsophisticated one. It had evidently never occurred to him that the anti-Moslem-funeral agitation of the party would ever appear as a concrete problem, or that the Modin would actually refuse to officiate. Karman was actually not a bad fellow, the Modin concluded; he was but a dupe of his leaders.

After leaving the now highly agitated Karman, the Modin went directly to the subdistrict officer to ask if he had acted properly. The officer was morally bound to say that he had, and thus fortified the Modin returned home to find Karman and the village policeman, to whom he had gone in desperation, waiting for him. The policeman, a personal friend of Karman's, told the Modin that according to time-honored custom he was supposed to bury everyone with impartiality, never mind whether he happened to agree with their politics. But the Modin, having now been personally supported by the subdistrict officer, insisted that it was no longer his responsibility. However, he suggested if Karman wished, he could go to the village chief's office and sign a public statement, sealed with the Government stamp and countersigned by the village chief in the presence of two witnesses, declaring that he,

Karman, was a true believing Moslem and that he wished the Modin to bury the boy according to Islamic custom. At this suggestion that he officially abandon his religious beliefs, Karman exploded into a rage and stormed from the house, rather uncharacteristic behavior for a Javanese. By the time he arrived home again, at his wit's end about what to do next, he found to his dismay that the news of the boy's death had been broadcast and the entire neighborhood was already gathering for the ceremony.

Like most of the kampongs in the town of Modjokuto, the one in which I lived consisted both of pious santris and ardent abangans (as well as a number of less intense adherents of either side), mixed together in a more or less random manner. In the town, people are forced to live where they can and take whomever they find for neighbors, in contrast to the rural areas where whole neighborhoods, even whole villages, still tend to be made up almost entirely of either abangans or santris. The majority of the santris in the kampong were members of Masjumi and most of the abangans were followers of Permai, and in daily life, social interaction between the two groups was minimal. The abangans, most of whom were either petty artisans or manual laborers, gathered each late afternoon at Karman's roadside coffee shop for the idle twilight conversations which are typical of small town and village life in Java; the santris—tailors, traders and storekeepers for the most part—usually gathered in one or another of the santri-run shops for the same purpose. But despite this lack of close social ties, the demonstration of territorial unity at a funeral was still felt by both groups to be an unavoidable duty; of all the Javanese rituals, the funeral probably carries the greatest obligation on attendance. Everyone who lives within a certain roughly defined radius of the survivors' home is expected to come to the ceremony; and on this occasion everyone did.

With this as background, it is not surprising that when I arrived at Karman's house about eight o'clock, I found two separate clusters of sullen men squatting disconsolately on either side of the yard, a nervous group of whispering women sitting idly inside the house near the still clothed body, and a general air of doubt and uneasiness in place of the usual quiet busyness of slametan

preparing, body washing, and guest greeting. The abangans were grouped near the house where Karman was crouched, staring blankly off into space, and where Sudjoko and Sastro, the town Chairman and Secretary of Permai (the only nonresidents of the kampong present) sat on chairs, looking vaguely out of place. The santris were crowded together under the narrow shadow of a coconut palm about thirty yards away, chatting quietly to one another about everything but the problem at hand. The almost motionless scene suggested an unlooked-for intermission in a familiar drama, as when a motion picture stops in the mid-action.

After a half hour or so, a few of the abangans began to chip half-heartedly away at pieces of wood to make grave markers and a few women began to construct small flower offerings for want of anything better to do; but it was clear that the ritual was arrested and that no one quite knew what to do next. Tension slowly rose. People nervously watched the sun rise higher and higher in the sky, or glanced at the impassive Karman. Mutterings about the sorry state of affairs began to appear ("everything these days is a political problem," an old, traditionalistic man of about eighty grumbled to me, "you can't even die any more but what it becomes a political problem"). Finally, about 9:30, a young santri tailor named Abu decided to try to do something about the situation before it deteriorated entirely: he stood up and gestured to Karman, the first serious instrumental act which had occurred all morning. And Karman, roused from his meditation, crossed the no-man's-land to talk to him.

As a matter of fact, Abu occupied a rather special position in the kampong. Although he was a pious santri and a loyal Masjumi member, he had more contact with the Permai group because his tailor shop was located directly behind Karman's coffee shop. Though Abu, who stuck to his sewing machine night and day, was not properly a member of this group, he would often exchange comments with them from his work bench about twenty feet away. True, a certain amount of tension existed between him and the Permai people over religious issues. Once, when I was inquiring about their eschatological beliefs, they referred me sarcastically to Abu, saying he was an expert, and they teased him quite openly about what they considered the wholly ridiculous Islamic theories of the afterlife. Nevertheless, he had something of a social bond with them, and it was perhaps reasonable that he should be the one to try to break the deadlock.

"It is already nearly noon," Abu said, "things can't go straight on like this." He suggested that he send Umar, another of the santris, to see if the Modin could now be induced to come; perhaps things were cooler with him now. Meanwhile, he could get the washing and wrapping of the corpse started himself. Karman replied that he would think about it, and returned to the other side of the yard for a discussion with the two Permai leaders. After a few minutes of vigorous gesturing and nodding, Karman returned and said simply, "all right, that way." "I know how you feel," Abu said, "I'll just do what is absolutely necessary and keep the Islam out as much as possible." He gathered the santris together and they entered the house.

The first requisite was stripping the corpse (which was still lying on the floor, because no one could bring himself to move it). But by now the body was rigid, making it necessary to cut the clothes off with a knife, an unusual procedure which deeply disturbed everyone, especially the women clustered around. The santris finally managed to get the body outside and set up the bathing enclosure. Abu asked for volunteers for the washing; he reminded them that God would consider such an act a good work. But the relatives, who normally would be expected to undertake this task, were by now so deeply shaken and confused that they were unable to bring themselves to hold the boy on their laps in the customary fasion. There was another wait while people looked hopelessly at each other. Finally, Pak Sura, a member of Karman's group but no relative, took the boy on his lap, although he was clearly frightened and kept whispering a protective spell. One reason the Javanese give for their custom of rapid burial is that it is dangerous to have the spirit of the deceased hovering around the house.

Before the washing could begin, however, someone raised the question as to whether one person was enough—wasn't it usually three? No one was quite sure, including Abu; some thought three a necessary number. After about ten minutes of anxious discussion, a male cousin of the boy and a carpenter, unrelated to him, managed to work up the courage to join Pak Sura. Abu, attempting to act the Modin's role as best he could, sprinkled a few drops of water on the corpse and then it was washed, rather haphazardly and in unsacralized water. When this was finished, however, the procedure was again stalled, for no one knew exactly how to arrange the small cotton pads which, under Moslem law, should plug the body orifices. Karman's wife, sister of the deceased's mother, could evidently take no more, for she broke into a loud, unrestrained wailing, the only demonstration of this sort I witnessed among the dozen or so Javanese funerals I attended. Everyone was further upset by this development, and most of the kampong women made a frantic but unavailing effort to comfort her. Most of the men remained seated in the yard, outwardly calm and inexpressive, but the embarrassed uneasiness which had been present since the beginning seemed to be turning toward fearful desperation. "It is not nice for her to cry that way," several men said to me, "it isn't proper." At this point, the Modin arrived.

However, he was still adamant. Further, he warned Abu that he was courting eternal damnation by his actions. "You will have to answer to God on Judgment Day," he said, "if you make mistakes in the ritual. It will be your responsibility. For a Moslem, burial is a serious matter and must be carried out according to the Law by someone who knows what the Law is, not according to the will of the individual." He then suggested to Sodjoko and Sastro, the Permai leaders, that they take charge of the funeral, for as party "intellectuals" they must certainly know what kind of funeral customs Permai followed. The two leaders, who had not moved from their chairs, considered this as everyone watched expectantly, but they finally refused, with some chagrin, saying they really did not know how to go about it. The Modin shrugged and turned away. One of the bystanders, a friend of Karman's, then suggested that they just take the body out and bury it and forget about the whole ritual; it was extremely dangerous to leave things as they were much longer. I don't know whether this remarkable suggestion would have been followed, for at this juncture the mother and father of the dead child entered the kampong.

They seemed quite composed. They were not unaware of the death, for the father later told me he had suspected as much when he got the telegram; he and his wife had prepared themselves for the worst and were more or less resigned by the time they arrived. When they approached the kampong and saw the whole neighborhood gathered, they knew that their fears were well founded. When Karman's wife, whose weeping had subsided slightly, saw the dead boy's mother come into the yard, she burst free of those who were comforting her and with a shriek rushed to embrace her sister. In what seemed a split second, both women had dissolved into wild hysterics and the crowd had rushed in and pulled them apart, dragging them to houses at opposite sides of the kampong. Their wailing continued in undiminished volume, and nervous comments arose to the effect that they ought to get on with the burial in one fashion or another, before the boy's spirit possessed someone.

But the mother now insisted on seeing the body of her child before it was wrapped. The father at first forbade it, angrily ordering her to stop crying—didn't she know that such behavior would darken the boy's pathway to the other world? But she persisted and so they brought her, stumbling, to where he lay in Karman's house. The women tried to keep her from drawing too close, but she broke loose and began to kiss the boy about the genitals. She was snatched away almost immediately by her husband and the women, though she screamed that she had not yet finished; and they pulled her into the back room where she subsided into a daze. After awhile—the body was finally being wrapped, the Modin having unbent enough to point out where the cotton pads went—she seemed to lose her bearings entirely and began to move about the yard shaking hands with everyone, all strangers to her, and saying "forgive me my faults, forgive me my faults." Again she was forcibly restrained; people said, "calm yourself, think of your other children—do you want to follow your son to the grave?"

The corpse was now wrapped and new suggestions were made that it be taken off immediately to the graveyard. At this point, Abu approached the father, who, he evidently felt, had now displaced Karman as the man legally responsible for the proceedings. Abu explained that the Modin, being a Government official, did not feel free to approach the father himself, but he would like to know: how did he wish the boy to be buried—the Islamic way or what? The father, somewhat bewildered, said, "Of course, the Islamic way. I don't have much of any religion, but I'm not a Christian, and when it comes to death the burial should be in the Islamic way. Completely Islamic." Abu explained again that the Modin could not approach the father directly, but that he, being "free," could do as he pleased. He said that he had tried to help as best he could but that he had been careful to do nothing Islamic before the father came. It was too bad, he apologized, about all the tension that was in the air, that political differences had to make so much trouble. But after all, everything had to be "clear" and "legal" about the funeral. It was important for the boy's soul. The santris, somewhat gleefully, now chanted their prayers over the corpse, and it was carried to the grave and buried in the usual manner. The Modin gave the usual graveyard speech, as amended for children, and the funeral was finally completed. None of the relatives or the women went to the graveyard; but when we returned to the house—it was now well after noon—the slametan was finally served, and Paidjan's spirit presumably left the kampong to begin its journey to the other world.

Three days later, in the evening, the first of the commemorative slametans was held, but it turned out that not only were no santris present but that it was as much a Permai political and religious cult meeting as a mourning ritual. Karman started off in the traditional fashion by announcing in high Javanese that this was a slametan in remembrance of the death of Paidjan. Sudjoko, the Permai leader, immediately burst in saying, "No, no, that is wrong. At a third-day slametan you just eat and give a long Islamic chant for the dead, and we are certainly not going to do that." Then he launched into a long, rambling speech. Everyone, he said, must know the philosophical-religious basis of the country. "Suppose this American (he pointed to me; he was not at all pleased by my presence) came up and asked you: what is the spiritual basis of the country? and you didn't know—wouldn't you be ashamed?"

He went on in this vein, building up a whole rationale for the present national political structure on the basis of a mystical interpretation of President Sukarno's "Five Points" (Monotheism, Social Justice, Humanitarianism, Democracy, and Nationalism) which are the official ideological foundation of the new republic. Aided by Karman and others, he worked out a micro-macrocosm correspondence theory in which the individual is seen to be but a small replica of the state, and the state but an enlarged image of the individual. If the state is to be ordered, then the individual must also be ordered; each implies the other. As the President's Five Points are at the basis of the state, so the five senses are at the basis of an individual. The processes of harmonizing both are the same, and it is this we must be sure we know. The discussion continued for nearly half an hour, ranging widely through religious, philosophical, and political issues (including, evidently for my benefit, a discussion of the Rosenbergs' execution).

We paused for coffee and as Sudjoko was about to begin again, Paidjan's father, who had been sitting quietly and expressionless began suddenly to talk, softly and with a curiously mechanical tonelessness, almost as if he were reasoning with himself but without much hope of success. "I am sorry for my rough city accent," he said, "but I very much want to say something." He hoped they would forgive him; they could continue their discussion in a moment. "I have been trying to be iklas ("detached," "resigned") about Paidjan's death. I'm convinced that everything that could have been done for him was done and that his death was just an event which simply happened." He said he was still in Modjokuto because he could not yet face the people where he lived, couldn't face having to tell each one of them what had occurred. His wife, he said, was a little more iklas now too. It was hard, though. He kept telling himself it was just the will of God, but it was so hard, for nowadays people didn't agree on things any more; one person tells you one thing and others tell you another. It's hard to know which is right, to know what to believe. He said he appreciated all the Modjokuto people coming to the funeral, and he was sorry it had been all mixed up. "I'm not very religious myself. I'm not Masjumi and I'm not Permai. But I wanted the boy to be buried in the old way. I hope no one's feelings were hurt." He said again he was trying to be iklas, to tell himself it was just the will of God, but it was hard, for things were so confused these days. It was hard to see why the boy should have died.

This sort of public expression of one's feelings is extremely unusual—in my experience unique—among Javanese, and in the formalized traditional slametan pattern there is simply no place for it (nor for philosophical or political discussion). Everyone present was rather shaken by the father's talk, and there was a painful silence. Sudjoko finally began to talk again, but this time he described in detail the boy's death. How Paidjan had first gotten a fever and Karman had called him, Sudjoko, to come and say a Permai spell. But the boy did not respond. They finally took him to a male nurse in the hospital, where he was given an injection. But still he worsened. He vomited blood and went into convulsions, which Sudjoko described rather graphically, and then he died. "I don't know why the Permai spell didn't work," he said, "it has worked before. This time it didn't. I don't know why; that sort of thing can't be explained no matter how much you think about it. Sometimes it just works and sometimes it just doesn't." There was another silence and then, after about ten minutes more of political discussion, we disbanded. The father returned the next day to his home and I was not invited to any of the later slametans. When I left the field about four months later, Karman's wife had still not entirely recovered from the experience, the tension between the santris and the abangans in the kampong had increased, and everyone wondered what would happen the next time a death occurred in a Permai family.

* * *

In sum, the disruption of Paidjan's funeral may be traced to a single source: an incongruity between the cultural framework of meaning and the patterning of social interaction, and incongruity due to the persistence in an urban environment of a religious symbol system adjusted to peasant social structure. Static functionalism, of either the sociological or social-psychological sort, is unable to isolate this kind of incongruity because it fails to discriminate between logico-meaningful integration and causal-functional integration; because it fails to realize that cultural structure and social structure are not mere reflexes of one another but independent, yet interdependent, variables. The driving forces in social change can be clearly formulated only by a more dynamic form of functionalist theory, one which takes into account the fact that man's need to live in a world to which he can attribute some significance, whose essential import he feels he can grasp, often diverges from his concurrent need to maintain a functioning social organism. A diffuse concept of culture as "learned behavior," a static view of social structure as an equilibrated pattern of interaction, and a stated or unstated assumption that the two must somehow (save in "disorganized" situations) be simple mirror images of one another, is rather too primitive a conceptual apparatus with which to attack such problems as those raised by Paidjan's unfortunate but instructive funeral.

CHAPTER 12

NEW METHODS OF ANALYSIS

INTRODUCTION

Perhaps the most challenging problem of all for the student of religious beliefs and patterns of behavior is how to sharpen the methods by which he elicits and analyzes the data. Each field season adds to the corpus of materials that we have on the myths and rituals of diverse cultures of the world, and adds urgency to the need for the development of new and more precise methods of meaningfully analyzing these ethnographic materials.

The current generation of anthropologists has recently shown a great deal of interest and ingenuity in thinking about these methodological problems. We do not refer here to either definitional or basic epistemological problems (although these are also important), but rather to the simple, straightforward question: "Now that you have a collection of myths and/or a series of observations on ritual behavior in one or more cultures, how, precisely, are you going to proceed to analyze them?"

Within the past decade there has been a variety of attempts to cope with this methodological problem, and we can merely provide a small sample of the new methods that are being developed. References to other methods are offered in this introduction and in the introductions to the various articles in the chapter.

The first two selections deal with the structural analysis of myth—first, Lévi-

Strauss's key paper in which he sets forth his methods and copes with the Oedipus myth and the Zuni emergence myth; then Leach's application of Lévi-Strauss's methods to a basic myth in our own society, the story of the Creation as recorded in the Book of Genesis.

The next two selections are drawn from the work of a small group of younger American anthropologists who have been active in developing what has come to be called "ethnoscience." This particular label is somewhat unfortunate, as it carries many different connotations to professionals and laymen. But the important point is that precise methods are employed, with the categories and units for ethnographic description and analysis being elicited (in the native language) from the informants of the culture under investigation, rather than being derived from our own culture. The first selection, from Frake, is a structural description of Subanun religious behavior in the Philippines; the second, by Metzger and Williams, deals with the curer in a Tzeltal community in Mexico.

The selection from Vogt's recent field research in Zinacantan, Mexico, represents an attempt to describe precisely and to analyze how behavioral sequences and concepts, expressed explicitly in the native language, are replicated in various domains of the culture.

The final selections, by Burton and Whiting, and Young, illustrate the cross-cultural method, utilizing data from the Human Relations Area Files on a sample of cultures, in reaching general conclusions about the function of male initiation ceremonies.

Not included in this edition of the *Reader,* but especially deserving of mention, are the recent attempts of Birdwhistell, Hall, and the Barkers to develop more precise methods for the analysis of gestures and behavior

units. Ray Birdwhistell's *Introduction to Kinesics* (1952), Edward T. Hall's recent paper on "A System for the Notation of Proxemic Behavior" (1963), and the Barkers' paper on "Behavior Units for the Comparative Study of Cultures" (1961) all provide stimulating approaches (and additional references) for the student interested in exploring the potentialities of these methods for the analysis of ritual behavior.

CLAUDE LÉVI-STRAUSS

The Structural Study of Myth

The eminent French anthropologist Claude Lévi-Strauss has been providing the anthropological world with a most stimulating and provocative series of articles and books in the past decade, several of them dealing with the analysis of myths, rituals, and native categories of thought. In our judgment, his key paper on myth is "The Structural Study of Myth," which was first published in the *Journal of American Folklore* in 1955 but was revised by the author for his *Anthropologie Structurale* (1958) and then translated into English for *Structural Anthropology* (1963).

In this article Lévi-Strauss makes the suggestion that our sociological and psychological interpretations of mythology have up to this point been far too facile. As he expresses it:

> If a given mythology confers prominence to a certain character, let us say an evil grandmother, it will be claimed that in such a society grandmothers are actually evil and that mythology reflects the social structure and the social relations; but should the actual data be conflicting, it would be readily claimed that the purpose of mythology is to provide an outlet for repressed feelings. Whatever the situation may be, a clever dialectic will always find a way to pretend that a meaning has been unravelled.

He therefore suggests that the basic function of myth is to furnish a culture with a "logical" model by means of which the human mind can evade unwelcome contradictions, and he proceeds to apply this theory to the Oedipus myth and to the Zuni emergence myth.

As the student who attempts to put this provocative theory to a test will soon discover, there are a number of exceedingly difficult operational problems, of which we will mention only a few. Lévi-Strauss suggests that the analysis proceed by dividing the myth into "the shortest possible sentences, and writing each sentence on an index card bearing a number corresponding to the unfolding of the story." The problem here is that if the analyst is operating in the native language (say Zuni), how does he decide on what are "the shortest possible sentences?" Lévi-Strauss then goes on to propose that the cards be arranged into columns, so that ultimately the myth reads like an orchestra score. There is a

Reprinted from *Journal of American Folklore,* LXVII (1955), 428–444, by permission of the author and the American Folklore Society.

question as to whether two or more analysts, working independently, will end up with the same cards in the same columns. Finally, we may ask precisely how an analyst moves from short sentences on index cards to the quite general themes presented in, for example, the four columns devoted to the Oedipus myth.

But having presented these operational difficulties, we are left with the conviction that there is a novel, and we hope ultimately testable, theory in this notion of Lévi-Strauss about mythology. We present his article in order that new students can profit by the insights and proceed to cope with the methodological problems.

1.0. Despite some recent attempts to renew them, it would seem that during the past twenty years anthropology has more and more turned away from studies in the field of religion. At the same time, and precisely because professional anthropologists' interest has withdrawn from primitive religion, all kinds of amateurs who claim to belong to other disciplines have seized this opportunity to move in, thereby turning into their private playground what we had left as a wasteland. Thus, the prospects for the scientific study of religion have been undermined in two ways.

1.1. The explanation for that situation lies to some extent in the fact that the anthropological study of religion was started by men like Tylor, Frazer, ˙nd Durkheim who were psychologically oriented, although not in a position to keep up with the progress of psychological research and theory. Therefore, their interpretations soon became vitiated by the outmoded psychological approach which they used as their backing. Although they were undoubtedly right in giving their attention to intellectual processes, the way they handled them remained so coarse as to discredit them altogether. This is much to be regretted since, as Hocart so profoundly noticed in his introduction to a posthumous book recently published, psychological interpretations were withdrawn from the intellectual field only to be introduced again in the field of affectivity, thus adding to "the inherent defects of the psychological school . . . the mistake of deriving clearcut ideas . . . from vague emotions." Instead of trying to enlarge the framework of our logic to include processes which, whatever their apparent differences, belong to the same kind of intellectual operations, a naive attempt was made to reduce them to inarticulate emotional drives which resulted only in withering our studies.

1.2. Of all the chapters of religious an-thropology probably none has tarried to the same extent as studies in the field of mythology. From a theoretical point of view the situation remains very much the same as it was fifty years ago, namely, a picture of chaos. Myths are still widely interpreted in conflicting ways: collective dreams, the outcome of a kind of esthetic play, the foundation of ritual. . . . Mythological figures are considered as personified abstractions, divinized heroes or decayed gods. Whatever the hypothesis, the choice amounts to reducing mythology either to an idle play or to a coarse kind of speculation.

1.3. In order to understand what a myth really is, are we compelled to choose between platitude and sophism? Some claim that human societies merely express, through their mythology, fundamental feelings common to the whole of mankind, such as love, hate, revenge; or that they try to provide some kind of explanations for phenomena which they cannot understand otherwise: astronomical, meteorological, and the like. But why should these societies do it in such elaborate and devious ways, since all of them are also acquainted with positive explanations? On the other hand, psychoanalysts and many anthropologists have shifted the problems to be explained away from the natural or cosmological towards the sociological and psychological fields. But then the interpretation becomes too easy: if a given mythology confers prominence to a certain character, let us say an evil grandmother, it will be claimed that in such a society grandmothers are actually evil and that mythology reflects the social structure and the social relations; but should the actual data be conflicting, it would be readily claimed that the purpose of mythology is to provide an outlet for repressed feelings. Whatever the situation may be, a clever dialectic will always find a way to pretend that a meaning has been unraveled.

2.0. Mythology confronts the student with a situation which at first sight could be looked upon as contradictory. On the one hand, it would seem that in the course of a myth anything is likely to happen. There is no logic, no continuity. Any characteristic can be attributed to any subject; every conceivable relation can be met. With myth, everything becomes possible. But on the other hand, this apparent arbitrariness is belied by the astounding similarity between myths collected in widely different regions. Therefore the problem: if the content of a myth is contingent, how are we going to explain that throughout the world myths do resemble one another so much?

2.1. It is precisely this awareness of a basic antinomy pertaining to the nature of myth that may lead us towards its solution. For the contradiction which we face is very similar to that which in earlier times brought considerable worry to the first philosophers concerned with linguistic problems; linguistics could only begin to evolve as a science after this contradiction had been overcome. Ancient philosophers were reasoning about language the way we are about mythology. On the one hand, they did notice that in a given language certain sequences of sounds were associated with definite meanings, and they earnestly aimed at discovering a reason for the linkage between those sounds and that meaning. Their attempt, however, was thwarted from the very beginning by the fact that the same sounds were equally present in other languages though the meaning they conveyed was entirely different. The contradiction was surmounted only by the discovery that it is the combination of sounds, not the sounds in themselves, which provides the significant data.

2.2. Now, it is easy to see that some of the more recent interpretations of mythological thought originated from the same kind of misconception under which those early linguists were laboring. Let us consider, for instance, Jung's idea that a given mythological pattern—the so-called archetype—possesses a certain signification. This is comparable to the long supported error that a sound may possess a certain affinity with a meaning: for instance, the "liquid" semivowels with water, the open vowels with things that are big, large, loud, or heavy, etc., a kind of theory which still has its supporters. Whatever emendations the original

formulation may now call for, everybody will agree that the Saussurean principle of the arbitrary character of the linguistic signs was a prerequisite for the acceding of linguistics to the scientific level.

2.3. To invite the mythologist to compare his precarious situation with that of the linguist in the prescientific stage is not enough. As a matter of fact we may thus be led only from one difficulty to another. There is a very good reason why myth cannot simply be treated as language if its specific problems are to be solved; myth *is* language: to be known, myth has to be told; it is a part of human speech. In order to preserve its specificity we should thus put ourselves in a position to show that it is both the same thing as language, and also something different from it. Here, too, the past experience of linguists may help us. For language itself can be analyzed into things which are at the same time similar and different. This is precisely what is expressed in Saussure's distinction between *langue* and *parole,* one being the structural side of language, the other the statistical aspect of it, *langue* belonging to a revertible time, whereas *parole* is non-revertible. If those two levels already exist in language, then a third one can conceivably be isolated.

2.4. We have just distinguished *langue* and *parole* by the different time referents which they use. Keeping this in mind, we may notice that myth uses a third referent which combines the properties of the first two. On the one hand, a myth always refers to events alleged to have taken place in time: before the world was created, or during its first stages—anyway, long ago. But what gives the myth an operative value is that the specific pattern described is everlasting; it explains the present and the past as well as the future. This can be made clear through a comparison between myth and what appears to have largely replaced it in modern societies, namely, politics. When the historian refers to the French Revolution it is always as a sequence of past happenings, a non-revertible series of events the remote consequences of which may still be felt at present. But to the French politician, as well as to his followers, the French Revolution is both a sequence belonging to the past—as to the historian—and an everlasting pattern which can be detected in the present French social structure and which provides a clue for its interpretation, a lead from which to infer the future developments. See, for instance, Michelet who was a politically-minded historian. He describes the French Revolution thus: "This day . . . everything was possible. . . . Future became present . . . that is, no more time, a glimpse of eternity." It is that double structure, altogether historical and anhistorical, which explains that myth, while pertaining to the realm of the *parole* and calling for an explanation as such, as well as to that of the *langue* in which it is expressed, can also be an absolute object on a third level which, though it remains linguistic by nature, is nevertheless distinct from the other two.

2.5. A remark can be introduced at this point which will help to show the singularity of myth among other linguistic phenomena. Myth is the part of language where the formula *traduttore, traditore* reaches its lowest truth-value. From that point of view it should be put in the whole gamut of linguistic expressions at the end opposite to that of poetry, in spite of all the claims which have been made to prove the contrary. Poetry is a kind of speech which cannot be translated except at the cost of serious distortions; whereas the mythical value of the myth remains preserved, even through the worst translation. Whatever our ignorance of the language and the culture of the people where it originated, a myth is still felt as a myth by any reader throughout the world. Its substance does not lie in its style, its original music, or its syntax, but in the *story* which it tells. It is language, functioning on an especially high level where meaning succeeds practically at "taking off" from the linguistic ground on which it keeps on rolling.

2.6. To sum up the discussion at this point, we have so far made the following claims: 1. If there is a meaning to be found in mythology, this cannot reside in the isolated elements which enter into the composition of a myth, but only in the way those elements are combined. 2. Although myth belongs to the same category as language, being, as a matter of fact, only part of it, language in myth unveils specific properties. 3. Those properties are only to be found *above* the ordinary linguistic level; that is, they exhibit more complex features beside those which are to be found in any kind of linguistic expression.

3.0. If the above three points are granted, at least as a working hypothesis, two consequences will follow: 1. Myth, like the rest of language, is made up of constituent units. 2. These constituent units presuppose the constituent units present in language when analyzed on other levels, namely, phonemes, morphemes, and semantemes, but they, nevertheless, differ from the latter in the same way as they themselves differ from morphemes, and these from phonemes; they belong to a higher order, a more complex one. For this reason, we will call them *gross constituent units*.

3.1. How shall we proceed in order to identify and isolate these gross constituent units? We know that they cannot be found among phonemes, morphemes, or semantemes, but only on a higher level; otherwise myth would become confused with any other kind of speech. Therefore, we should look for them on the sentence level. The only method we can suggest at this stage is to proceed tentatively, by trial and error, using as a check the principles which serve as a basis for any kind of structural analysis: economy of explanation; unity of solution; and ability to reconstruct the whole from a fragment, as well as further stages from previous ones.

3.2. The technique which has been applied so far by this writer consists in analyzing each myth individually, breaking down its story into the shortest possible sentences, and writing each such sentence on an index card bearing a number corresponding to the unfolding of the story.

3.3. Practically each card will thus show that a certain function is, at a given time, predicated to a given subject. Or, to put it otherwise, each gross constituent unit will consist in a relation.

3.4. However, the above definition remains highly unsatisfactory for two different reasons. In the first place, it is well known to structural linguists that constituent units on all levels are made up of relations and the true difference between our gross units and the others stays unexplained; moreover, we still find ourselves in the realm of a non-revertible time since the numbers of the cards correspond to the unfolding of the informant's speech. Thus, the specific character of mythological time, which as we have seen is both revertible and non-revertible, synchronic and diachronic, remains unaccounted for. Therefrom comes a new hypothesis which constitutes the very core of our argument : the true constituent units of a myth are not the isolated relations but *bundles of such relations* and it is only as bundles that these relations can be put to use and combined so as to produce a meaning. Relations pertaining to the same bundle may appear diachronically at remote intervals, but when we have succeeded in grouping them together, we have reorganized our myth according to a time referent of a new nature corresponding to the prerequisite of the initial hypothesis, namely, a two-dimensional time referent which is simultaneously diachronic and synchronic and which accordingly integrates the characteristics of the *langue* on one hand, and those of the *parole* on the other. To put it in even more linguistic terms, it is as though a phoneme were always made up of all its variants.

4.0. Two comparisons may help to explain what we have in mind.

4.1. Let us first suppose that archaeologists of the future coming from another planet would one day, when all human life had disappeared from the earth, excavate one of our libraries. Even if they were at first ignorant of our writing, they might succeed in deciphering it—an undertaking which would require, at some early stage, the discovery that the alphabet, as we are in the habit of printing it, should be read from left to right and from top to bottom. However, they would soon find out that a whole category of books did not fit the usual pattern : these would be the orchestra scores on the shelves of the music division. But after trying, without success, to decipher staffs one after the other, from the upper down to the lower, they would probably notice that the same patterns of notes recurred at intervals, either in full or in part, or that some patterns were strongly reminiscent of earlier ones. Hence the hypothesis : what if patterns showing affinity, instead of being considered in succession, were to be treated as one complex pattern and read globally? By getting at what we call *harmony,* they would then find out that an orchestra score, in order to become meaningful, has to be read diachronically along one axis—that is, page after page, and from left to right—and also synchronically along the other axis, all the notes which are written vertically making up one gross constituent unit, i.e. one bundle of relations.

4.2. The other comparison is somewhat different. Let us take an observer ignorant of our playing cards, sitting for a long time with a fortune-teller. He would know something of the visitors : sex, age, look, social situation, etc. in the same way as we know something of the different cultures whose myths we try to study. He would also listen to the séances and keep them recorded so as to be able to go over them and make comparisons—as we do when we listen to myth telling and record it. Mathematicians to whom I have put the problem agree that if the man is bright and if the material available to him is sufficient, he may be able to reconstruct the nature of the deck of cards being used, that is : fifty-two or thirty-two cards according to case, made up of four homologous series consisting of the same units (the individual cards) with only one varying feature, the suit.

4.3. The time has come to give a concrete example of the method we propose. We will use the Oedipus myth which has the advantage of being well-known to everybody and for which no preliminary explanation is therefore needed. By doing so, I am well aware that the Oedipus myth has only reached us under late forms and through literary transfigurations concerned more with esthetic and moral preoccupations than with religious or ritual ones, whatever these may have been. But as will be shown later, this apparently unsatisfactory situation will strengthen our demonstration rather than weaken it.

4.4. The myth will be treated as would be an orchestra score perversely presented as a unilinear series and where our task is to reestablish the correct disposition. As if, for instance, we were confronted with a sequence of the type : 1,2,4,7,8,2,3,4,6,8,1,4,5, 7,8,1,2,5,7,3,4,5,6,8 . . . , the assignment being to put all the 1's together, all the 2's, the 3's, etc. ; the result is a chart :

1	2		4			7	8
	2	3	4		6		8
1			4	5		7	8
1	2			5		7	
		3	4	5			
					6		8

4.5. We will attempt to perform the same kind of operation on the Oedipus myth, trying out several dispositions until we find one which is in harmony with the principles enumerated under 3.1. Let us suppose, for the sake of argument, that the best arrangement is the following (although it might certainly be improved by the help of a specialist in Greek mythology):

being slain. As to the fourth, a word of clarification is needed. The remarkable connotation of the surnames in Oedipus' father-line has often been noticed. However, linguists usually disregard it, since to them the only way to define the meaning of a term is

Kadmos seeks his sister Europa ravished by Zeus			
		Kadmos kills the dragon	
	The Spartoi kill each other		
			Labdacos (Laios' father) = *lame* (?)
	Oedipus kills his father Laios		
			Laios (Oedipus' father) = *left-sided* (?)
		Oedipus kills the Sphinx	
Oedipus marries his mother Jocasta			
	Eteocles kills his brother Polynices		
			Oedipus = *swollen-foot* (?)
Antigone buries her brother Polynices despite prohibition			

4.6. Thus, we find ourselves confronted with four vertical columns each of which include several relations belonging to the same bundle. Were we to *tell* the myth, we would disregard the columns and read the rows from left to right and from top to bottom. But if we want to *understand* the myth, then we will have to disregard one half of the diachronic dimension (top to bottom) and read from left to right, column after column, each one being considered as a unit.

4.7. All the relations belonging to the same column exhibit one common feature which it is our task to unravel. For instance, all the events grouped in the first column on the left have something to do with blood relations which are over-emphasized, i.e. are subject to a more intimate treatment than they should be. Let us say, then, that the first column has as its common feature the *overrating of blood relations*. It is obvious that the second column expresses the same thing, but inverted: *underrating of blood relations*. The third column refers to monsters

to investigate all the contexts in which it appears, and personal names, precisely because they are used as such, are not accompanied by any context. With the method we propose to follow the objection disappears since the myth itself provides its own context. The meaningful fact is no longer to be looked for in the eventual sense of each name, but in the fact that all the names have a common feature: i.e. that they may eventually mean something and that all these hypothetical meanings (which may well remain hypothetical) exhibit a common feature, namely they refer to *difficulties to walk and to behave straight*.

4.8. What is then the relationship between the two columns on the right? Column three refers to monsters. The dragon is a chthonian being which has to be killed in order that mankind be born from the earth; the Sphinx is a monster unwilling to permit men to live. The last unit reproduces the first one which has to do with the *autochthonous origin* of mankind. Since the monsters are overcome by men, we may thus say that the common feature of the third column is *the denial of the autochthonous origin of man.*

4.9. This immediately helps us to understand the meaning of the fourth column. In mythology it is a universal character of men born from the earth that at the moment they emerge from the depth, they either cannot walk or do it clumsily. This is the case of the chthonian beings in the mythology of the Pueblo: Masauwu, who leads the emergence, and the chthonian Shumaikoli are lame ("bleeding-foot," "sore-foot"). The same happens to the Koskimo of the Kwakiutl after they have been swallowed by the chthonian monster, Tsiakish: when they returned to the surface of the earth "they limped forward or tripped sideways." Then the common feature of the fourth column is: *the persistence of the autochthonous origin of man.* It follows that column four is to column three as column one is to column two. The inability to connect two kinds of relationships is overcome (or rather replaced) by the positive statement that contradictory relationships are identical inasmuch as they are both self-contradictory in a similar way. Although this is still a provisional formulation of the structure of mythical thought, it is sufficient at this stage.

4.10. Turning back to the Oedipus myth, we may now see what it means. The myth has to do with the inability, for a culture which holds the belief that mankind is autochthonous (see, for instance, Pausanias, VIII, xxix, 4: vegetals provide a *model* for humans), to find a satisfactory transition between this theory and the knowledge that human beings are actually born from the union of man and woman. Although the problem obviously cannot be solved, the Oedipus myth provides a kind of logical tool which, to phrase it coarsely, replaces the original problem: born from one or born from two? born from different or born from same? By a correlation of this type, the overrating of blood relations is to the underrating of blood relations as the attempt to escape autochthony is to the impossibility to succeed in it. Although experience contradicts theory, social life verifies the cosmology by its similarity of structure. Hence cosmology is true.

4.11.0. Two remarks should be made at this stage.

4.11.1. In order to interpret the myth, we were able to leave aside a point which has until now worried the specialists, namely, that in the earlier (Homeric) versions of the Oedipus myth, some basic elements are lacking, such as Jocasta killing herself and Oedipus piercing his own eyes. These events do not alter the substance of the myth although they can easily be integrated, the first one as a new case of auto-destruction (column three) while the second is another case of crippledness (column four). At the same time there is something significant in these additions since the shift from foot to head is to be correlated with the shift from: autochthonous origin negated to: self-destruction.

4.11.2. Thus, our method eliminates a problem which has been so far one of the main obstacles to the progress of mythological studies, namely, the quest for the *true* version, or the *earlier* one. On the contrary, we define the myth as consisting of all its versions; to put it otherwise: a myth remains the same as long as it is felt as such. A striking example is offered by the fact that our interpretation may take into account, and is certainly applicable to, the Freudian use of the Oedipus myth. Although the Freudian problem has ceased to be that of autochthony *versus* bisexual reproduction, it is still the problem of understanding how *one* can be born from *two:* how is it that we do not have only one procreator, but a mother plus a father? Therefore, not only Sophocles, but Freud himself, should be included among the recorded versions of the Oedipus myth on a par with earlier or seemingly more "authentic" versions.

5.0. An important consequence follows. If a myth is made up of all its variants, structural analysis should take all of them into account. Thus, after analyzing all the known variants of the Theban version, we should treat the others in the same way: first, the tales about Labdacos' collateral line including Agavé, Pentheus, and Jocasta herself; the Theban variant about Lycos with Amphion and Zetos as the city founders; more remote variants concerning Dionysos (Oedipus' matrilateral cousin), and Athenian legends where Cecrops takes the place of Kadmos, etc. For each of them a similar chart should be drawn, and then compared and reorganized according to the findings: Cecrops killing the serpent with the parallel episode of Kadmos; abandonment of Dionysos with abandonment of Oedipus; "Swollen Foot" with Dionysos *loxias,* i.e. walking obliquely; Europa's quest with Antiope's; the foundation of Thebes by the Spartoi or by the brothers Amphion and Zetos; Zeus kidnapping Europa and Antiope and the same with Semele; the Theban Oedipus and the Argian Perseus, etc. We will then have several two-dimensional charts, each dealing with a variant, to be organized in a three-dimensional order so that three different readings become possible: left to right, top to bottom, front to back. All of these charts cannot be expected to be identical; but experience shows that any difference to be observed may be correlated with other differences, so that a logical treatment of the whole will allow simplifications, the final outcome being the structural law of the myth.

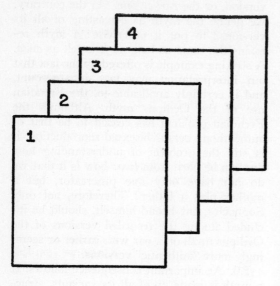

Fig. 1.

5.1. One may object at this point that the task is impossible to perform since we can only work with known versions. Is it not possible that a new version might alter the picture? This is true enough if only one or two versions are available, but the objection becomes theoretical as soon as a reasonably large number has been recorded (a number which experience will progressively tell, at least as an approximation). Let us make this point clear by a comparison. If the furniture of a room and the way it is arranged in the room were known to us only through its reflection in two mirrors placed on opposite

walls, we would theoretically dispose of an almost infinite number of mirror-images which would provide us with a complete knowledge. However, should the two mirrors be obliquely set, the number of mirror-images would become very small; nevertheless, four or five such images would very likely give us, if not complete information, at least a sufficient coverage so that we would feel sure that no large piece of furniture is missing in our description.

5.2. On the other hand, it cannot be too strongly emphasized that all available variants should be taken into account. If Freudian comments on the Oedipus complex are a part of the Oedipus myth, then questions such as whether Cushing's version of the Zuni origin myth should be retained or discarded become irrelevant. There is no one true version of which all the others are but copies or distortions. Every version belongs to the myth.

5.3. Finally it can be understood why works on general mythology have given discouraging results. This comes from two reasons. First, comparative mythologists have picked up preferred versions instead of using them all. Second, we have seen that the structural analysis of *one* variant of *one* myth belonging to *one* tribe (in some cases, even *one* village) already requires two dimensions. When we use several variants of the same myth for the same tribe or village, the frame of reference becomes three-dimensional and as soon as we try to enlarge the comparison, the number of dimensions required increases to such an extent that it appears quite impossible to handle them intuitively. The confusions and platitudes which are the outcome of comparative mythology can be explained by the fact that multi-dimensional frames of reference cannot be ignored, or naively replaced by two- or three-dimensional ones. Indeed, progress in comparative mythology depends largely on the cooperation of mathematicians who would undertake to express in symbols multi-dimensional relations which cannot be handled otherwise.

6.0. In order to check this theory, an attempt was made in 1953–54 towards an exhaustive analysis of all the known versions of the Zuni origin and emergence myth: Cushing, 1883 and 1896; Stevenson, 1904; Parsons, 1923; Bunzel, 1932; Benedict,

1934. Furthermore, a preliminary attempt was made at a comparison of the results with similar myths in other Pueblo tribes, Western and Eastern. Finally, a test was undertaken with Plains mythology. In all cases, it was found that the theory was sound, and light was thrown, not only on North American mythology, but also on a previously unnoticed kind of logical operation, or one known only so far in a wholly different context. The bulk of material which needs to be handled almost at the beginning of the work makes it impossible to enter into details, and we will have to limit ourselves here to a few illustrations.

6.1. An over-simplified chart of the Zuni emergence myth would read as follows:

that belief with the ancient Greeks, and it is not without reason that we chose the Oedipus myth as our first example. But in the American case, the highest form of vegetal life is to be found in agriculture which is periodical in nature, i.e. which consists in an alternation between life and death. If this is disregarded, the contradiction surges at another place: agriculture provides food, therefore life; but hunting provides food and is similar to warfare which means death. Hence there are three different ways of handling the problem. In the Cushing version, the difficulty revolves around an opposition between activities yielding an immediate result (collecting wild food) and activities yielding a delayed result—death has to be-

INCREASE		DEATH	
mechanical growth of vegetals (used as ladders)	emergence led by Beloved Twins	sibling incest	gods kill children
food value of wild plants	migration led by the two Newekwe		magical contest with people of the dew (collecting wild food *versus* cultivation)
		sibling sacrificed (to gain victory)	
food value of cultivated plants		sibling adopted (in exchange for corn)	
periodical character of agricultural work			war against Kyanakwe (gardeners *versus* hunters)
hunting	war led by two war-gods		
			salvation of the tribe (center of the world found)
warfare		sibling sacrificed (to avoid flood)	
DEATH		PERMANENCY	

6.2. As may be seen from a global inspection of the chart, the basic problem consists in discovering a mediation between life and death. For the Pueblo, the problem is especially difficult since they understand the origin of human life on the model of vegetal life (emergence from the earth). They share

come integrated so that agriculture can exist. Parsons' version goes from hunting to agriculture, while Stevenson's version operates the other way around. It can be shown that all the differences between these versions can be rigorously correlated with these basic structures. For instance:

	CUSHING	PARSONS	STEVENSON
Gods ⎫ Kyanakwe ⎭	allied, use fiber strings on their bows (gardeners)	Kyanakwe alone, use fiber string	Gods ⎫ allied, use fiber Men ⎭ string
	VICTORIOUS OVER	VICTORIOUS OVER	VICTORIOUS OVER
Men	alone, use sinew (hunters) (until men shift to fiber)	Gods ⎫ allied, use sinew Men ⎭ string	Kyanakwe alone, use sinew string

Since fiber strings (vegetal) are always superior to sinew strings (animal) and since (to a lesser extent) the gods' alliance is preferable to their antagonism, it follows that in Cushing's version, men begin to be doubly underprivileged (hostile gods, sinew string); in Stevenson, doubly privileged (friendly gods, fiber string); while Parsons' version confronts us with an intermediary situation (friendly gods, but sinew strings since men begin by being hunters). Hence:

	CUSHING	PARSONS	STEVENSON
gods/men	−	−	+
fiber/sinew	−	. +	+

6.3. Bunzel's version is from a structural point of view of the same type as Cushing's.

However, it differs from both Cushing's and Stevenson's inasmuch as the latter two explain the emergence as a result of man's need to evade his pitiful condition, while Bunzel's version makes it the consequence of a call from the higher powers—hence the inverted sequences of the means resorted to for the emergence: in both Cushing and Stevenson, they go from plants to animals; in Bunzel, from mammals to insects and from insects to plants.

6.4. Among the Western Pueblo the logical approach always remains the same; the starting point and the point of arrival are the simplest ones and ambiguity is met with halfway:

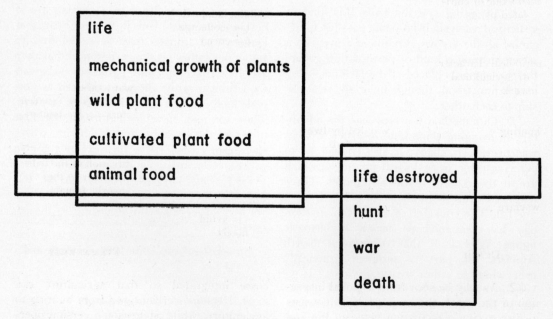

FIG. 2.

The fact that contradiction appears in the middle of the dialectical process has as its result the production of a double series of dioscuric pairs the purpose of which is to operate a mediation between conflicting terms:

1. 2 divine messengers	2 ceremonial clowns		2 war-gods
2. homogeneous pair: dioscurs (2 brothers)	siblings (brother and sister)	couple (husband and wife)	heterogeneous pair: grandmother/ grandchild

which consists in combinatory variants of the same function (hence the war attribute of the clowns which has given rise to so many queries).

6.5. Some Central and Eastern Pueblos proceed the other way around. They begin by stating the identity of hunting and cultivation (first corn obtained by Game-Father sowing deer-dewclaws), and they try to derive both life and death from that central notion. Then, instead of extreme terms being simple and intermediary ones duplicated as among the Western groups, the extreme terms become duplicated (i.e., the two sisters of the Eastern Pueblo) while a simple mediating term comes to the foreground (for instance, the Poshaiyanne of the Zia), but endowed with equivocal attributes. Hence the attributes of this "messiah" can be deduced from the place it occupies in the time sequence: good when at the beginning (Zuni, Cushing), equivocal in the middle (Central Pueblo), bad at the end (Zia), except in Bunzel where the sequence is reversed as has been shown.

6.6. By using systematically this kind of structural analysis it becomes possible to organize all the known variants of a myth as a series forming a kind of permutation group, the two variants placed at the far-ends being in a symmetrical, though inverted, relationship to each other.

7.0. Our method not only has the advantage of bringing some kind of order to what was previously chaos; it also enables us to perceive some basic logical processes which are at the root of mythical thought. Three main processes should be distinguished.

7.1.0. The trickster of American mythology has remained so far a problematic figure. Why is it that throughout North America his part is assigned practically everywhere to either coyote or raven? If we keep in mind that mythical thought always works from the awareness of oppositions towards their progressive mediation, the reason for those choices becomes clearer. We need only to assume that two opposite terms with no intermediary always tend to be replaced by two equivalent terms which allow a third one as a mediator; then one of the polar terms and the mediator become replaced by a new triad and so on. Thus we have:

INITIAL PAIR	FIRST TRIAD	SECOND TRIAD
Life		
	Agriculture	
		Herbivorous animals
		Carrion-eating animals (raven; coyote)
	Hunt	
		Prey animals
	War	
Death		

With the unformulated argument: carrion-eating animals are like prey animals (they eat animal food, but they are also like food-plant producers (they do not kill what they eat). Or, to put it otherwise, Pueblo style: ravens are to gardens as prey animals are to herbivorous ones. But it is also clear that herbivorous animals may be called first to act as mediators on the assumption that they are like collectors and gatherers (vegetal-food eaters) while they can be used as animal food though not themselves hunters. Thus we may have mediators of the first order, of the second order, and so on, where each term gives birth to the next by a double process of opposition and correlation.

7.1.1. This kind of process can be followed in the mythology of the Plains where we may order the data according to the sequence:

Unsuccessful mediator between earth and sky
(Star husband's wife)

Heterogeneous pair of mediators
(grandmother/grandchild)

Semi-homogeneous pair of mediators
(Lodge-Boy and Thrown-away)

While among the Pueblo we have:

Successful mediator between earth and sky
(Poshaiyanki)

Semi-homogeneous pair of mediators
(Uyuyewi and Matsailema)

Homogeneous pair of mediators
(the Ahaiyuta)

7.1.2. On the other hand, correlations may appear on a transversal axis (this is true even on the linguistic level; see the manifold connotation of the root *pose* in Tewa according to Parsons: coyote, mist, scalp, etc.). Coyote is intermediary between herbivorous and carnivorous in the same way as mist between sky and earth; scalp between war and hunt (scalp is war-crop); corn smut between wild plants and cultivated plants; garments between "nature" and "culture"; refuse between village and outside; ashes between roof and hearth (chimney). This string of mediators, if one may call them so, not only throws light on whole pieces of North American mythology—why the Dew-God may be at the same time the Game-Master and the giver of raiments and be personified as an "Ash-Boy"; or why the scalps are mist producing; or why the Game-Mother is associated with corn smut; etc.—but it also probably corresponds to a universal way of organizing daily experience. See, for instance, the French for vegetal smut, *nielle,* from Latin *nebula;* the luck-bringing power attributed to refuse (old shoe) and ashes (kissing chimney-sweepers); and compare the American Ash-Boy cycle with the Indo-European Cinderella: both phallic figures (mediator between male and female); master of the dew and of the game; owners of fine raiments; and social bridges (low class marrying into high class); though impossible to interpret through recent diffusion as has been sometimes contended since Ash-Boy and Cinderella are symmetrical but inverted in every detail (while the borrowed Cinderella tale in America—Zuni Turkey-Girl—is parallel to the prototype):

7.2.0. Thus, the mediating function of the trickster explains that since its position is halfway between two polar terms he must retain something of that duality, namely an ambiguous and equivocal character. But the trickster figure is not the only conceivable form of mediation; some myths seem to devote themselves to the task of exhausting all the possible solutions to the problem of bridging the gap between *two* and *one.* For instance, a comparison between all the variants of the Zuni emergence myth provides us with a series of mediating devices, each of which creates the next one by a process of opposition and correlation:

$$\text{messiah} > \text{dioscurs} > \text{trickster} > \frac{\text{bisexual}}{\text{being}} >$$

$$\frac{\text{sibling}}{\text{pair}} > \frac{\text{married}}{\text{couple}} > \frac{\text{grandmother-}}{\text{grandchild}} >$$

$$\frac{\text{4 terms}}{\text{group}} > \text{triad}$$

In Cushing's version, this dialectic is accompanied by a change from the space dimension (mediating between sky and earth) to the time dimension (mediating between summer and winter, i.e., between birth and death). But while the shift is being made from space to time, the final solution (triad) re-introduces space, since a triad consists in a dioscur pair *plus* a messiah simultaneously present; and while the point of departure was ostensibly formulated in terms of a space referent (sky and earth) this was nevertheless implicitly conceived in terms of a time referent (first the messiah calls; *then* the dioscurs descend). Therefore the logic of myth confronts us with a double, reciprocal exchange of functions to which we shall return shortly (7.3.).

7.2.1. Not only can we account for the ambiguous character of the trickster, but we may also understand another property of mythical figures the world over, namely, that the same god may be endowed with con-

	EUROPE	AMERICA
Sex	female	male
Family Status	double family	no family
Appearance	pretty girl	ugly boy
Sentimental status	nobody likes her	in hopeless love with girl
Transformation	luxuriously clothed with supernatural help	stripped of ugliness with supernatural help

tradictory attributes; for instance, he may be *good* and *bad* at the same time. If we compare the variants of the Hopi myth of the origin of Shalako, we may order them so that the following structure becomes apparent:

(Masauwu: x) $\sim$ (Muyingwu: Masauwu) $\sim$
(Shalako: Muyingwu) $\sim$ (y: Masauwu)

where x and y represent arbitrary values corresponding to the fact that in the two "extreme" variants the god Masauwu, while appearing alone instead of associated with another god, as in variant two, or being absent, as in three, still retains intrinsically a relative value. In variant one, Masauwu (alone) is depicted as helpful to mankind (though not as helpful as he could be), and in version four, harmful to mankind (though not as harmful as he could be); whereas in two, Muyingwu is relatively more helpful than Masauwu, and in three, Shalako more helpful than Muyingwu. We find an identical series when ordering the Keresan variants:

(Poshaiyanki: x) $\sim$ (Lea: Poshaiyanki) $\sim$
(Poshaiyanki: Tiamoni) $\sim$ (y: Poshaiyanki)

7.2.2. This logical framework is particularly interesting since sociologists are already acquainted with it on two other levels: first, with the problem of the pecking order among hens; and second, it also corresponds to what this writer has called *general exchange* in the field of kinship. By recognizing it also on the level of mythical thought, we may find ourselves in a better position to appraise its basic importance in sociological studies and to give it a more inclusive theoretical interpretation.

7.3.0. Finally, when we have succeeded in organizing a whole series of variants in a kind of permutation group, we are in a position to formulate the law of that group. Although it is not possible at the present stage to come closer than an approximate formulation which will certainly need to be made more accurate in the future, it seems that every myth (considered as the collection of all its variants) corresponds to a formula of the following type:

$$f_x(a) : f_y(b) \sim f_x(b) : f_{a-1}(y)$$

where, two terms being given as well as two functions of these terms, it is stated that a

relation of equivalence still exists between two situations when terms and relations are inverted, under two conditions: 1. that one term be replaced by its contrary; 2. that an inversion be made between the *function* and the *term* value of two elements.

7.3.1. This formula becomes highly significant when we recall that Freud considered that *two traumas* (and not one as it is so commonly said) are necessary in order to give birth to this individual myth in which a neurosis consists. By trying to apply the formula to the analysis of those traumatisms (and assuming that they correspond to conditions 1. and 2. respectively) we should not only be able to improve it, but would find ourselves in the much desired position of developing side by side the sociological and the psychological aspects of the theory; we may also take it to the laboratory and subject it to experimental verification.

8.0. At this point it seems unfortunate that, with the limited means at the disposal of French anthropological research, no further advance can be made. It should be emphasized that the task of analyzing mythological literature, which is extremely bulky, and of breaking it down into its constituent units, requires team work and secretarial help. A variant of average length needs several hundred cards to be properly analyzed. To discover a suitable pattern of rows and columns for those cards, special devices are needed, consisting of vertical boards about two meters long and one and one-half meters high, where cards can be pigeon-holed and moved at will; in order to build up three-dimensional models enabling one to compare the variants, several such boards are necessary, and this in turn requires a spacious workshop, a kind of commodity particularly unavailable in Western Europe nowadays. Furthermore, as soon as the frame of reference becomes multi-dimensional (which occurs at an early stage, as has been shown in 5.3.) the board-system has to be replaced by perforated cards which in turn require I.B.M. equipment, etc. Since there is little hope that such facilities will become available in France in the near future, it is much desired that some American group, better equipped than we are here in Paris, will be induced by this paper to start a project of its own in structural mythology.

8.1.0. Three final remarks may serve as conclusion.

8.1.1. First, the question has often been raised why myths, and more generally oral literature, are so much addicted to duplication, triplication or quadruplication of the same sequence. If our hypotheses are accepted, the answer is obvious: repetition has as its function to make the structure of the myth apparent. For we have seen that the synchro-diachronical structure of the myth permits us to organize it into diachronical sequences (the rows in our tables) which should be read synchronically (the columns). Thus, a myth exhibits a "slated" structure which seeps to the surface, if one may say so, through the repetition process.

8.1.2. However, the slates are not absolutely identical to each other. And since the purpose of myth is to provide a logical model capable of overcoming a contradiction (an impossible achievement if, as it happens, the contradiction is real), a theoretically infinite number of slates will be generated, each one slightly different from the others. Thus, myth grows spiral-wise until the intellectual impulse which has originated it is exhausted. Its growth is a continuous process whereas its structure remains discontinuous. If this is the case we should consider that it closely corresponds, in the realm of the spoken word, to the kind of being a crystal is in the realm of physical matter. This analogy may help us understand better the relationship of myth on one hand to both *langue* and *parole* on the other.

8.1.3. Prevalent attempts to explain alleged differences between the so-called "primitive" mind and scientific thought have resorted to qualitative differences between the working processes of the mind in both cases while assuming that the objects to which they were applying themselves remained very much the same. If our interpretation is correct, we are led toward a completely different view, namely, that the kind of logic which is used by mythical thought is as rigorous as that of modern science, and that the difference lies not in the quality of the intellectual process, but in the nature of the things to which it is applied. This is well in agreement with the situation known to prevail in the field of technology: what makes a steel ax superior to a stone one is not that the first one is better made than the second. They are equally well made, but steel is a different thing than stone. In the same way we may be able to show that the same logical processes are put to use in myth as in science, and that man has always been thinking equally well; the improvement lies, not in an alleged progress of man's conscience, but in the discovery of new things to which it may apply its unchangeable abilities.

EDMUND LEACH

Lévi-Strauss in the Garden of Eden: An Examination of Some Recent Developments in the Analysis of Myth

When Edmund Leach served as a Fellow of the Center for Advanced Study in the Behavioral Sciences during 1960–1961, he had the scholarly leisure for the first time to thoroughly examine Lévi-Strauss's theories about myth. As he related to the junior editor (personal communication, January 1961), he began the examination very skeptically, but as he proceeded to read Lévi-Strauss, and, more importantly, to apply the method to one of the basic myths of our own society—the story of the Creation as recorded in the Book of Genesis—he came to have greater respect for the potential in the ideas set forth by Lévi-Strauss. The editors do not think Leach has actually solved the methodological problems they posed in the introduction to the Lévi-Strauss article, but they do think this delightful article helps to understand Lévi-Strauss's basic thesis. They also agree with Leach when he says that "No one will ever again be able to read the early chap-

Reprinted from *Transactions of the New York Academy of Sciences*, Ser. II, Vol. XXIII (1961), 386–396, by permission of the author and the New York Academy of Sciences.

ters of Genesis without taking this pattern [i.e., the structural analysis Leach has undertaken] into account."

Leach has written a subsequent article, "Genesis As Myth" (1962), which he considers to be an improvement on the present one. However, it does not contain the valuable review of the Lévi-Strauss approach that influenced the editors in their selection of the older version. The newer article stresses modern information theory and the light it throws on myth as a form of communication; it maintains that the binary structure of myth is not due to random chance but to oppositions that are intrinsic to the process of human thought. The interested reader is strongly urged to consult the 1962 article for its special orientation and lucidity.

The study of myth has always had a central place in anthropological studies, but the views of anthropologists have varied greatly both on matters of definition and of interpretation. In this respect the celebrities of the past 80 years fall into 2 classes. First, there is a group of writers whom we may call *symbolists*—among whom I would class James G. Frazer, Sigmund Freud, and Ernst Cassirer in his earlier phase—who assume that the elements of myth are to be understood as symbols that are pieced together into a nonrational story much as in a fairy tale or dream. These writers hold that the "purpose" or "meaning" of myth is one of two kinds: (1) myth "explains the inexplicable," for example, the origin of the world, the origin of death, (2) myth is a kind of word magic that purports to alter the harsh facts of reality by manipulating symbolic representations of these facts.

Common to all the symbolist writers is the view that a myth can be understood as "a thing in itself" without any direct reference to the social context in which it is told; the meaning can be discovered from a consideration of the words alone.

The second group of writers are the *functionalists*—among whom I would class Émile Durkheim and his associates, Jane Harrison, B. Malinowski, and Cassirer in his later phase. The key theme here is the assumption of an intimate and direct association between myth and social action; the myth and its associated rite are held to be two aspects of the same unitary whole.

The most explicit formulation of this doctrine was provided by Malinowski in his well known essay *Myth in Primitive Psychology* (Malinowski, 1926). Myth provides a "charter" or justification for facts in the present day social situation. For example, in the Trobriand myth of emergence, it is re-

corded that the brother and sister founder ancestors of each matrilineal subclan emerged from holes in the ground, the position of which is precisely recorded by tradition. Each ancestral hole is located in territory that is today regarded as the hereditary property of the subclan descendants of the original founder ancestors. Thus a tale that, considered in isolation, has all the appearance of fantasy is seen to "make sense" when related to its social context. Within the framework of Trobriand ideas this myth has the force of a legal precedent in a court of law.

As C. Lévi-Strauss puts it: "This theory assumes that myth and rite are homologous . . . the myth and the rite reproduce each other, the one at the level of action the other at the level of ideas." (Lévi-Strauss, 1956, p. 289).

It is a necessary corollary of this functionalist thesis that myth can be studied *only* within its social context. A myth divorced from its associated rite can have no meaning. Myth is never "a thing in itself."

British social anthropologists of my generation were brought up to believe that, on this issue, Malinowski was right. Detailed modifications of his original theory might be possible but the essentials of the argument were unassailable.

One consequence of this acceptance of the functionalist thesis has been that the collections of "literary myths" that exist in ethnographic libraries and in the sacred writings of the more sophisticated religions have come to be neglected by the professional anthropologist. Such myths, in the form in which we now have them, are clearly "divorced from their ritual context," hence, according to the functionalist dogma, they cease to be of interest.

The same line of reasoning eliminates

from the field of serious academic discussion the whole of the works of Frazer and other exponents of the Frazerian "comparative method." Many of the comparisons to which Frazer draws our attention are very striking but, since Frazer consistently ignored the context of his evidence, it is a matter of functionalist dogma that we *must* ignore the apparent implications.

In a number of essays published over the last four years Lévi-Strauss has quite explicitly repudiated the functionalist thesis (the key document is Lévi-Strauss, 1955) in favor of a revised form of "symbolist" analysis that he calls structural. Lévi-Strauss denies the existence of any causal link by which myth overtly justifies the patterning of social action or vice versa. He concedes that myths and rites that occur in the same cultural environment may very well share a common structure. Hence if the elements of a myth or the elements of an associated rite are treated as the elements in a logical statement, the myth and the rite may appear to "say the same thing." Nevertheless, myth and rite are independent and each can be studied in isolation.

According to Lévi-Strauss the best method of ascertaining the "meaning" of a myth is to assemble together all the variant forms in which it has been recorded regardless of their date or source. What we are looking for is the fundamental essence, and this essence, according to Lévi-Strauss, is a matter of logical structure that will persist throughout all the diversities of form by which the myth story has been perpetuated. A comparison of the different versions of a single myth complex will reveal this common structural nexus, and it is this common structure that really gives "meaning" and importance to those who recount the myth.

If we accept this view, then it follows that, despite anything that Malinowski may appear to have demonstrated, the social anthropologist is fully entitled to study myth as "a thing in itself" without regard to detailed consideration of social or ritual context. I do not ask anyone to suspend his critical judgment. Lévi-Strauss' thesis has many weaknesses and some of them seem a good deal more damaging than the alleged weaknesses of functionalism. Nevertheless, he has made out a case. At the very least he has demonstrated that the functionalist thesis, in its more orthodox form, is unnecessarily inhibiting. He has reopened what had begun to look like a closed argument. We need not accept Lévi-Strauss' views in every particular, but it is quite clear that the proper understanding of myth is once again a very open question.

As Lévi-Strauss himself recognizes, his new theory is exceedingly difficult to put to the test. In effect he postulates that the symbolic elements in a myth are analogous to neutral pebbles of diverse colors. One cannot discover what the elements "mean" by any straight forward technique of intuition or verbal interpretation; all that one can do is observe how the pebbles are grouped together into patterns. In principle, this patterning (or structure) of the symbols in relation to each other is a matter of statistics. Lévi-Strauss maintains that a really thorough application of the method would entail the use of punched cards and the services of an electronic computer (Lévi-Strauss, 1955). Since most of us operate under the delusion that some myths appear meaningful in a fairly straightforward way this kind of intellectual sophistication may arouse suspicion; nevertheless I suggest that the matter be given serious consideration.

If we accept Lévi-Strauss' view, the heart of the matter is that myth furnishes a "logical" model by means of which the human mind can evade unwelcome contradictions, such as that human beings cannot enjoy life without suffering death or that rules of incest (which specify that legitimate sex relations can only be between members of opposed kin groups) conflict with a doctrine of unilineal descent. The function of myth is to "mediate" such contradictions, to make them appear less final than they really are and thus more acceptable. This end is not served by isolated myths but by clusters of myths that are similar in some ways but different in others so that, in accumulation, they tend to blur the edges of real (but unwelcome) category distinctions.

Among the examples that Lévi-Strauss has used to illustrate his thesis are the following:

(1) He claims that an analysis of certain Pueblo Indian myths shows that the central problem that the myth cluster seeks to resolve is the opposition between life and death. In the myths we find a threefold category distinction: agriculture, hunting, and war. Agriculture is a means to life for man

but entails the death of animals. It is thus a mediating middle category.

In another version of the same myth cluster a further threefold category distinction emerges: grass-eating animals, ravens, and predatory animals. Grass-eating animals are vegetarians; they need not kill in order to live. Ravens and predators are meat eaters; but ravens need not kill in order to eat. In accumulation, therefore, argues Lévi-Strauss, this succession of symbol patterns

Perhaps you wonder what all this has to do with the Oedipus myth as you know it, and I do not pretend that the Lévi-Strauss example is easy to follow. Figure 1 may help. Lévi-Strauss assumes that the myth has a logical form corresponding to the equation: $a:b :: c:d$ (*op cit.*, pp. 55–56). The theme of incest (the overemphasis of kinship solidarity) is balanced against the themes of patricide and fratricide (the underemphasis of kinship solidarity) and this

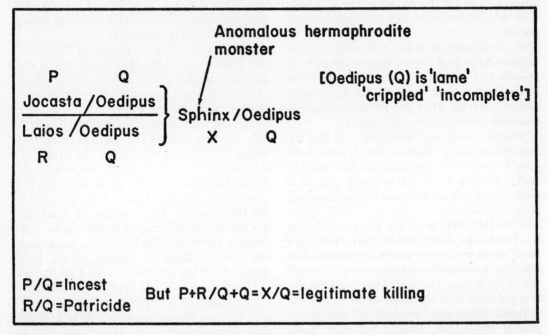

Fig. 1.

creates a logical model that asserts (or seems to assert) that, after all, life and death are *not* just the back and front of the same penny, that death is *not* the necessary consequence of life (Lévi-Strauss, 1955).

(2) Lévi-Strauss furnishes other examples. For instance, he claims, rather surprisingly, that the central problem with which the myth of Oedipus is concerned is that of autochthonous creation. In the beginning man was created; but who precisely was created? A man plus a woman of the same kind? If so, then the perpetuation of mankind must have depended upon incest and we are all born in sin. Or was there a double creation—a man plus a woman of a different kind? In that case what are these two original kinds, and how can we justify a claim to descent from one line of ancestors rather than another?

corresponds to a similar balance between the highly ambivalent sphinx and Oedipus, who, in isolation, is incomplete and crippled. The sphinx is a kind of merging of the two parent figures Jocasta and Laios. Oedipus' legitimate task is to eliminate the sphinx. He accomplishes this end by sinning doubly—incest with Jocasta and patricide against Laios. Oedipus does not actually kill the sphinx. The sphinx, which is primarily female, commits suicide, as does Jocasta. The cause of the suicide is that Oedipus answers the riddle—the answer being, in effect: "the son grows into the father and replaces him" (Lévi-Strauss, 1958, p. 238). On this analysis the myth centers around a problem of patrilineal descent: the requirement that fathers shall be perpetuated in their sons without the intervention of women, which in simple fact is plainly impossible. However, the impossibility is "resolved" in the myth by mediating the antithesis between male and female parents into the ambivalent person of the sphinx. Lévi-Strauss is somewhat free with his editing of the mythology, and I have been decidedly free with my editing of Lévi-Strauss. For further enlightenment I must ask you to read him in the original.

For my part I find the whole analysis extremely interesting. I feel that Lévi-Strauss has a case. We ought to investigate the hypothesis with all the means at our disposal: with or without resort to mathematical computers.

With all this in mind I decided to take another look at the story of the creation as recorded in Genesis. How well do the various theories about myth that I have mentioned stand up when put to the test against this basic myth of our own society?

The first point that struck me was that the different types of theories that I have mentioned throw the emphasis on different aspects of the story, or rather stories for, as is well known, there are two distinct creation stories in Genesis.

The symbolists favor the story concerning the Garden of Eden. Frazer and Freud and most medieval artists are in agreement that the core of the story is the matter of Eve and the serpent and the forbidden fruit. From this point of view the myth seems to provide a rather elementary example of the use of phallic symbolism. Frazer, however, made the further penetrating observation that the Tree of the Knowledge of Good and Evil, from which Eve's apple comes, is unambiguously stated to be the Tree of Death that stands opposed to another special tree, the Tree of Life. Moreover, while Adam and Eve were forbidden to eat of the Tree of Death they were not, in the first instance, forbidden to eat of the Tree of Life. (Genesis 2, v. 17).

A functionalist approach would be quite different. The story of the seven-day creation provides a mythical charter for the seven-day week. Also, in a more round about way, the creation story provides a charter for the Jewish rules of taboo as recorded in Leviticus, chapter 11.

The creation story specifies all living things as belonging to a very limited number of precisely defined categories: fowls of the air, fish, cattle, beasts, and creeping things. Similarly the plants are categorized as grass,

herb-yielding seed (cereals), and fruit trees. It is further specified that the animals are intended to eat the grass while the cereals and the fruit and the meat of the animals themselves are intended for man's exclusive benefit (Genesis 1, vv. 29 and 30). As Mary Douglas has pointed out (Douglas, 1959), the creatures classified as "abominations" in Leviticus 11 are those that break out of these tidy categories: water creatures with no fins, flying creatures with 4 legs, animals and birds that eat meat or fish, and certain animals that are indiscriminate in their eating habits such as dogs and pigs.

This functionalist treatment of the material leads to an orthodox thesis about the close association of ideas concerning taboo, sacredness, and abnormality (Radcliffe-Brown, 1952, chapter VII).

Having said all this one notices that it is only the first part of the creation story that seems to serve as a "charter" in Malinowski's sense. The second part—the Garden of Eden story that appeals so strongly to the symbolists—has no obvious implications for the functionalist. Thus neither the symbolist nor the functionalist approaches can be considered adequate. Each tells us something but neither offers an answer to the total question: What is Genesis 1 to 4 all about?

However, if we now apply a Lévi-Strauss style of analysis everything takes on a completely new shape; moreover it is a shape that recurs in both parts of the story and is repeated again in a third form in the Cain and Abel story that follows. The complex diagram (Figure 2) has been designed to display this structure. At every step we find the assertion of a category opposition followed by the introduction of a "mediating" category. The seven-day creation story (upper section of the diagram) may be analysed as follows:

Genesis 1, vv. 1 to 5 (not on diagram). Light divided from darkness. Initial introduction of concept of category opposition, heaven versus earth.

Genesis 1, vv. 6 to 8 (column 1 of diagram). Fresh water above (fertile rain) opposed to (salt) water below (sea). Mediated by firmament (sky).

Genesis 1, vv. 9 and 10 (column 2 of diagrams). Sea opposed to dry land.

Genesis 1, vv. 11 and 12 (column 3 of diagram). Mediated by grass, herb-yielding

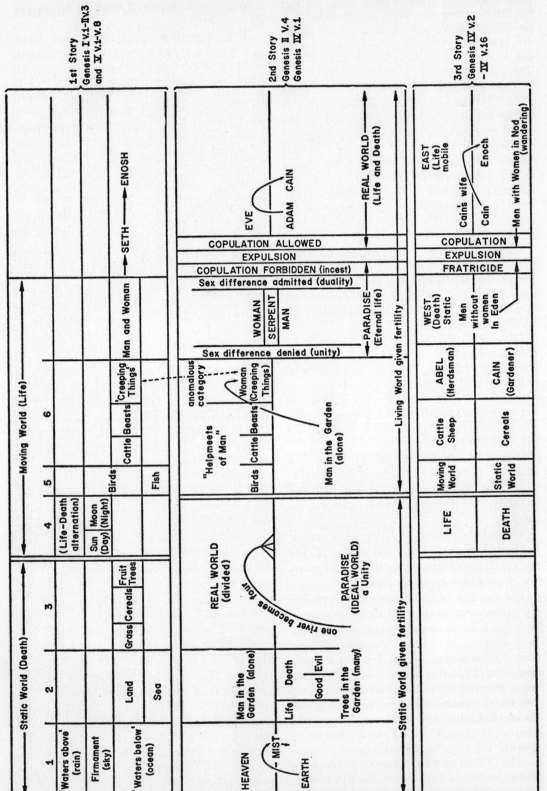

FIG. 2.

seed, and fruit trees. These grow on dry land but need water. Very significantly, they are classed as things "whose seed is in itself" (thereby contrasted with such creatures as animals and birds, which are divided into males and famales).

The creation of the world as a static (that is, dead) entity is now complete, and this whole phase of creation is opposed to the creation of moving (that is, living) things.

Genesis 1, vv. 13 to 18 (column 4 of diagram). The mobile sun and moon are placed in the firmament of column 1. Light and darkness, opposed at the beginning of the story, are now presented as alternations. By implication the life-death opposition is also an alternation.

Genesis 1, vv. 20 to 23 (column 5 of diagram). Fish and birds are living things corresponding to the category opposition of column 2 but they also mediate the oppositions between sky and land and between salt water and fresh water.

Genesis 1, vv. 24 and 25 (column 6 of diagram, left half). Cattle, beasts, and creeping things (that is, domestic animals, wild animals, and anomalous animals) correspond to the static triad of column 3 but are not allocated accordingly. Only grass is allocated to the animals, the rest is reserved for man (vv. 29 and 30).

Genesis 1, vv. 26 and 27 (column 6 of diagram, right half). The final act of creation is the simultaneous creation of man and woman: "Male and female created he them."

The whole system of living creatures is instructed to "be fruitful and multiply," but the problems of life versus death and incest versus procreation are not faced.

The Garden of Eden story that now follows attacks from the start these very problems that have been evaded in the first version. We start again with a category opposition of heaven versus earth, but this is mediated by a fertilizing mist that is drawn up out of the dry infertile earth (Genesis 2, vv. 4 to 6). The same theme recurs throughout the story. Living Adam is formed from "the dust of the ground" (v. 7); so are the living animals (v. 19). The dry lands of the real world are fertilized by a river that comes out of the ground of Eden. In Eden (Paradise) it is a unitary river; in the real world it is divided (vv. 10 to 14). Finally fertile Eve is

formed from the rib of infertile Adam (vv. 22 and 23).

The opposition of Heaven and Earth (column 1) is followed by the opposition of Man and the Garden and, in the Garden, are trees that include a Tree of Life and a Tree of Death (column 2: Genesis 2, vv. 8 and 9). Notice that the Tree of Death is called the "Tree of Knowledge of Good and Evil" which might also be called the "knowledge of sexual difference," or the "knowledge of logical categories." The theme is repeated: isolated unitary categories such as man alone, life alone, one river, occur only in ideal Paradise; in the real world things are multiple and divided; man needs a partner, woman; life has a partner, death.

The other living things are now created because of the loneliness of Man in Eden. The categories are cattle (domestic animals), birds, and beasts (wild animals). These are unsatisfactory as helpmeets of Man, so Eve is drawn from Adam's rib: "they are of one flesh." (columns 5 and 6: Genesis 2, vv. 18 to 24). Comparison of the two stories at this stage shows that Eve in Eden is, from a structural point of view, the same category as "the creeping things" of the first story. Creeping things were anomalous in the category opposition "cattle versus beasts"; Eve is anomalous in the category opposition "man versus animal"; and finally "the serpent" (a creeping thing) is anomalous in the category opposition "man versus woman." The parallels here with the Oedipus-Sphinx story are here extremely close, as may be seen from Figures 1 and 3. The Bible does not specify the serpent's sex. Mediaeval artists made it female, Freud might have argued for a male; the structural argument suggests hermaphrodite qualities.

Adam and Eve eat the apple and become aware of sexual difference, and death becomes inevitable (Genesis 3, vv. 3 to 8)— also of course pregnancy and life becomes possible. Significantly, Eve does not become pregnant until after they have been expelled from Paradise (Genesis 4, v. 1). The curse that is imposed on the serpent deserves especial note (Genesis 3, vv. 14 and 15). There is to be enmity between the serpent and the woman and between "the seed of the serpent" and the "seed of the woman"—the latter being specified as male; *"he* shall bruise thy head; and thou shalt bruise *his* heel."

One is inevitably reminded of Lévi-Strauss' point that autochthonous heroes are very commonly lame (Lévi-Strauss, 1955). Indeed the whole formula parallels that of Oedipus. If "the seed of the serpent" be here read as "the semen of the father," while "the seed of the woman" be read as the son of the father by his impregnated wife, the curse refers to the opposition between man and woman and the hostility between father and incest (compare Genesis 3, vv. 17 to 19 with Genesis 4, v. 11 and 12) he is also declared a sacred person whose life is protected (v. 15). Cain is the ancestor of "wanderers" in general—pastoralists, traveling musicians, traveling metal-workers (Genesis 4, vv. 19 to 24)—groups with special skills but not servile outcastes.

I do not claim that this kind of "structural" analysis is the one and only legitimate

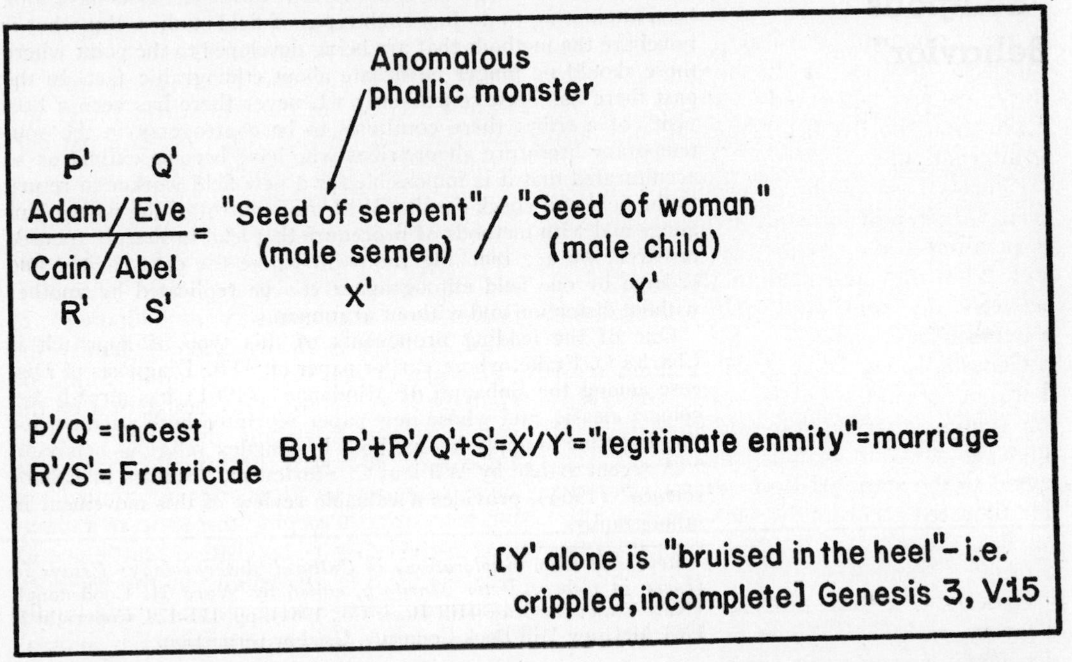

Anomalous phallic monster

$$\frac{\overset{P'}{\text{Adam}} / \overset{Q'}{\text{Eve}}}{\underset{R'}{\text{Cain}} / \underset{S'}{\text{Abel}}} = \frac{\text{"Seed of serpent"}}{\underset{X'}{\text{(male semen)}}} / \frac{\text{"Seed of woman"}}{\underset{Y'}{\text{(male child)}}}$$

P'/Q'= Incest
R'/S'= Fratricide   But P'+R'/Q'+S'=X'/Y'="legitimate enmity"=marriage

[Y' alone is "bruised in the heel"– i.e. crippled, incomplete] Genesis 3, V.15

FIG. 3.

son. It might even be taken as a "charter" for circumcision.

Finally, although very briefly, let us notice that the Cain and Abel story repeats the same story over again. The opposition between Cain the gardener and Abel the herdsman is the same opposition as that between the first three days of the creation and the last three days, the static world versus the living. Cain must eliminate his brother and substitute a wife in order that a sterile homosexual world shall become a fertile heterosexual world (Genesis 4, v. 17). Some extra elements come in here. The dead world of Eden-paradise is said to lie to the west, the living world (significantly called Nod "wandering") lies to the east (Genesis 4, v. 16); moreover, although Cain is cursed for the sin of fratricide in terms nearly identical to those imposed on Adam for the sin of

procedure for the interpretation of myth. It seems to me that whether any particular individual finds this kind of thing interesting or stimulating must depend on personal temperament; some may think it is too like a conjuring trick. For my part, I do find it interesting. All I have done here is to show that the component elements in some very familiar stories are in fact ordered in a pattern of which many have not been previously aware. However, the pattern *is* there; I did not invent it, I have merely demonstrated that it exists. No one will ever again be able to read the early chapters of Genesis without taking this pattern into account. Whether the analysis has any "value" for anthropologists or for anyone else I am not sure, but at least it surely throws new light on the mysterious workings of what Durkheim used to call the "collective conscience."

CHARLES O. FRAKE

A Structural Description of Subanun "Religious Behavior"

The new field of "ethnoscience" has a number of active and creative young anthropologists who promise much in the way of developing more precise methods for eliciting and ordering ethnographic facts in terms of contrasts that are inherent in the data. In the judgment of the editors, the attempt to analyze data in terms of native categories is *not* novel. Anthropologists have long been attempting to do just such types of field studies. But what *is* novel are the methods that are being developed to the point where there should no longer be debate about ethnograhic fact. In the past there has been controversy whenever there has been a "revisit" of a tribe; there continues to be controversy in the contemporary literature about tribes who have become extinct or so acculturated that it is impossible for a new field worker to return to the field and check results. With full control of the native language and with methods of procedure that lead to sharply focused research, we are reaching the point where the data elicited and ordered by one field ethnographer can be replicated by another without distortion and without argument.

One of the leading proponents of this type of approach is Charles O. Frake, whose earlier paper on "The Diagnosis of Disease among the Subanun of Mindanao" (1961) has already become a classic, and whose new paper reprinted here attempts for the first time to apply his methods to complex religious behavior.

A recent article by William C. Sturtevant, "Studies in Ethnoscience" (1964), provides a valuable review of this movement in ethnography.

The purpose of this paper is not to present anything approaching a complete description of Subanun "religion" but rather to raise the question of what kind of statement would constitute an adequate ethnographic description of an aspect of a culture. This is not, I think, a trivial question to ask. A theory of how to describe cultural behavior implies a theory of culture. Ethnography, the science of cultural description, can potentially fill a role as critical to our general theoretical understanding of the nature of culture as has modern descriptive linguistics toward our understanding of the nature of language.

A description of a culture, an *ethnography,* is produced from an *ethnographic record* of the events of a society within a given period of time, the "events of a society" including, of course, informants' responses to the ethnographer, his queries, tests, and apparatus. *Ethnographic technique,* ignored in this paper, is the task of devising means for producing an adequately ample record of events. *Ethnographic methodology* is the task of devising operations for producing an ethnography from an ethnographic record. *Ethnographic theory* is the task of devising criteria for evaluating ethnographies. These three aspects of the ethnographic task are interdependent. The adequacy of the record and the validity of the methodology cannot be determined unless the data are subjected to analysis and the results tested against the criteria of the theory during the course of field investigation. The production of an ethnography should imply a task more challenging than "writing up one's notes."

When an ethnographer first enters a strange society, each encountered event is new, unanticipated, improbable, and, hence, highly informative in the communication-theory sense. As he learns the culture of the society, more and more of what happens becomes familiar and anticipatable. The ethnographer can plan his own activities on the basis of these anticipations. The more he learns of a culture, the more his anticipations match those of his informants. Similarly for a person born in a society, as he learns his culture, the events of his life become more probable, becoming parts of familiar *scenes* which he and his fellows plan for, stage, and play their roles in. To describe a culture, then, is not to recount the events of a society but to specify what one must know to make those events maximally probable. The problem is not to state what someone did but to specify the conditions under which it is culturally appropriate to anticipate that he, or persons occupying his role, will render an equivalent performance. This conception of a cultural description implies that an ethnography should be a theory of cultural behavior in a particular society, the adequacy of which is to be evaluated by the ability of a stranger to the culture (who may be the ethnographer) to use the ethnography's statements as instructions for appropriately anticipating the scenes of the society. I say "appropriately anticipate" rather than "predict" because a failure of an ethnographic statement to predict correctly does not necessarily imply descriptive inadequacy as long as the members of the described society are as surprised by the failure as is the ethnographer. The test of descriptive adequacy must always refer to informants' interpretations of events, not simply to the occurrence of events.

With this criterion of descriptive adequacy in mind the formulation of an ethnographic statement would seem to include at least the following tasks:

1. Discovering the major categories of events or *scenes* of the culture.

2. Defining scenes so that observed interactions, acts, objects, and places can be assigned to their proper scenes as roles, routines, paraphernalia, and settings.

3. Stating the distribution of scenes with respect to one another, that is, providing instructions for anticipating or planning for scenes.

These three methodological problems will be discussed with reference to a portion of the Subanun record, a record which is inadequate at several points because much of this analysis was completed only after I had left the field.

The Subanun are a pagan people practicing swidden agriculture in the mountainous interior of Zamboanga Peninsula on the island of Mindanao in the Philippines. The data of this paper pertain only to the Eastern Subanun of the Gulu Disakan and Lipay regions northeast of Sindangan Bay in the interior of Zamboanga del Norte Province, studied in the field in 1953–1954 and 1957–1958. In terms of segmentation and stratification, Subanun society displays remarkable simplicity. Each nuclear family is the focus of a partially unique and variable network of social ties with kin and neighbors which constitutes, for that family, the "total society." This maximal, nondiscrete sphere of social relationships has no corporate organization and is not segmented into lineages, age-sets, secret societies, territorial districts, political factions, or the like. Despite this simplicity of their social structure, the Subanun carry on constant and elaborate interfamily social activities—litigation, offerings, feasts—all well lubricated with ample quantities of rice wine. Warfare is lacking.

THE IDENTIFICATION OF "RELIGIOUS BEHAVIOR"

One of the most frequent and regularly recurrent events in the Subanun record is eating. Most, *but not all,* Subanun events which we should consider instances of "eating" as a category of activity fall into an easily distinguishable Subanun scene, a 'meal.' To qualify as a 'meal' a scene must include at least one actor, the 'eater,' and a 'cooked starchy-staple food.' A meal characteristically marks a clear interruption of other activity, requiring the performers to squat before a setting of food on the floor or ground; it is scheduled at least once daily; it requires prior planning and preparation; and, although one actor is sufficient, it is generally staged as a social performance.

In the typical recorded meal, those participating in the role "joint eaters" belong to a single nuclear family, the side dish is a nonmeat food, the staple may be a root crop or a cereal, and no 'rice wine' (*gasi*) is served. These are *ordinary meals.* If one of the features of an ordinary meal changes, the others change as well. Meals with multi-family joint eaters, meat side dish, cereal staple, and 'rice wine' are *festive meals* or, simply, *feasts*.

Festive meals occur at irregular intervals and must be occasioned: i.e., there must be a legitimizing event which serves as a reason for the feast. It is always appropriate to ask in Subanun, "What is the reason for this feast?" To ask, "What is the reason for this meal?" would sound somewhat odd in uncontrived contexts. Festive meals substitute for ordinary ones. A meal is scheduled at least once daily. If there is a legitimizing occasion and the necessary components are procurable, a festive meal is staged; otherwise an ordinary meal is staged. A central part of Subanun planning involves anticipating festive occasions so that the necessary components for staging a feast be procurable whenever a legitimizing event occurs. The occurrence of one of the components, as an event, can itself be a reason for a feast, requiring the mustering of the other essential components. If a wild pig (meat-side-dish component) is caught in a trap, its consumption requires a feast. If guests congregate (multifamily-performance component), they must be feasted. The festive meal itself occurs in a context of a wide range of other activities: competitive drinking, displays of verbal art, singing, dancing. All activities occurring from the arrival to the departure of participants in a feast together constitute a *festivity*.

During some festivities occur episodes which themselves seem to be feasts, but of a rather special sort. The festive provisions are set up on distinctive paraphernalia and the 'eaters,' though sometimes audible, are not visible to the ethnographer nor, by report, to the ordinary Subanun. Feasts of this sort whereby 'mortals' feed the various categories of 'nonvisible' or 'supernatural' inhabitants of the Subanun universe, the Subanun call *kanu,* here glossed as 'offerings.' During the course of a festivity, one to several offerings may be performed. A festivity during which offerings occur is a *ceremony*. A ceremony may be *simple* or *complex* depending on whether one or more than one offering is held. This contrast between simple and complex ceremonies is not matched by a lexical distinction in Subanun, but is necessary in order to describe the de-

nota of names for types of offerings and ceremonies. Ceremonies are named for one constituent offering. Thus *beklug* denotes a particular kind of offering or a ceremony in which the *beklug* offering is one of many constituents. If a Subanun offering name is given as "instructions to perform," one must know from context whether the referent is an offering or a ceremony and, if a ceremony, whether it is simple or complex. The term *kanu* may likewise, depending on context, refer to an offering or to a ceremony.

A ceremony, then, is one kind of festivity. Other kinds are 'litigation,' 'labor-recruiting feasts,' 'game-sharing feasts,' 'meat-division feasts,' and 'hospitality feasts.' Several kinds of festivities may be jointly held. If for some reason it is necessary to provide a feast, it is often economic to discharge as many festive functions as possible during its course. Thus a legal case and an offering may occur during a festivity originally staged as a hospitality feast.

To the naïve observer an offering may seem like a minor episode in a festive event. But when one considers how offerings and ceremonies vary in paraphernalia, social participation, routines, planning, and programming, and when one considers the range of events which are relevant to staging ceremonies, it becomes clear that the behavioral complex centering on offerings penetrates deeply into many crucial areas of Subanun life. The programming and staging of ceremonies forms a major segment of Subanun cultural activity comparable in scope and content to the traditional ethnographic category of "religion." This comparability suggests (but does not require) the term *religious behavior* as a label for this activity, and it suggests *Subanun religion* as a label for what is described by an ethnographic statement which accounts for this behavior. But the only criterion of whether a particular act is an instance of *religious behavior* is its relevance to the programming and performing of 'offerings.' The ethnographic (in contrast to the ethnological) issue is not whether instances of *religious behavior* so defined conform to any particular cross-cultural notion of "what religion is," but whether they do in fact comprise a meaningful descriptive category of Subanun cultural activity and, if so, how is this category to be described.

THE PERFORMANCE OF AN 'OFFERING'

The first step in describing Subanun *religious behavior* is to describe the performance of offerings themselves in terms of discovered categories of constituent locales, objects, performers, and acts. Only a brief outline of the constituent structure of offerings as performances can be presented here.

SETTINGS

There are no special buildings, rooms, or outdoor areas reserved for staging offerings. Offerings may be held inside nuclear family residences, in house yards, in fields, in forests, or on stream banks, the specific locale depending on the type of offering as well as on sociological, ecological, and meteorological conditions.

PROVISIONS

A festive meal must be provided for both mortal and supernatural participants. A feast for supernaturals requires special components: the staple must be of rice, eggs are added to the required meat side dish, the proffered wine (or fermented mash) must be of rice and be ritually prepared, the proffered betel quids must be prepared with domesticated betel-pepper leaf and areca palm nuts (mortals often use substitute ingredients). Some categories of supernaturals take their food raw, others in a cooked state. These provisions are first offered to the invited supernaturals on an altar, then removed and consumed, generally as part of a larger feast, by humans. (The supernaturals conveniently consume only the 'intangible essence,' *seŋaw,* of food and drink.) The kind and quantity of provisions within these constituent categories varies with type of offering, with the kind of event occasioning the offering, with the whims of individual supernaturals, and with particular bargains struck beforehand between mortal host and supernatural guest. From an economic standpoint the side dish, requiring sacrifice of valuable livestock, is the most significant feature of an offering. The market value of pigs and chickens slaughtered for the offering and accompanying feast provides a direct index of the occasion's importance.

PARAPHERNALIA

Humans settle for a banana leaf on the floor, but the supernaturals demand elaborate devices from which to partake of their meals. The Subanun construct at least thirty types of altars, varying in number of platforms, method of construction, materials employed, means of support or suspension, decoration, and size. Sometimes the type of altar is determined by the deity being propitiated. Thus the 'raw-food-eating gods' (*kemuŋluq*) always eat from a platformless *seleŋsaŋan,* but a personal 'guardian god' (*tipun*) generally prefers a *bibalay* altar, the defining attributes of which are rectangular shape, no sides, stick floor, and parallel legs. More often the type of altar or altars is specific to a particular kind of offering or ritual occasion, and a variety of supernaturals will in turn eat from it during the ceremony. Some more elaborate offerings require special equipment other than altars: various kinds of barriers to inhibit the movements of malevolent supernaturals, folded cloths to capture lost souls, miniature wooden replicas of weapons, model rafts and canoes, decorative and rustling leaves. With few exceptions all of this equipment is constructed anew (usually in a rather slipshod fashion) for each offering and then discarded. Since human drinking and feasting cannot proceed until the offering is completed, the few Subanun who are prone to spend time lavishing care on the construction of ritual paraphernalia become the butt of criticism from their more secular-minded fellows. Every offering also requires a resonant porcelain bowl (struck rhythmically to announce the occasion to the supernatural guests) and incense (the fumes of which augment the aroma of the offering as a lure).

PARTICIPANTS

The participants in an offering all belong to the category of 'persons' (*getaw*), those 'living things' (*tubuqan*) with whom one can establish communicatory relations. A dichotomous dimension of reported conscious visibility divides 'persons' into two subcategories with fundamentally distinct roles in offerings. 'Persons' reported to be consciously visible to the ordinary Subanun are 'mortals' (*kilawan*). 'Persons' whom the ordinary Subanun are reportedly unable to see consciously are 'supernaturals' (*kanaq kilawan*). Only the exceptional perceptual powers of certain prominent 'mediums' can reportedly record a conscious visual image of the 'supernaturals.' Others may 'see' a supernatural without being aware of it—a possible cause of illness if the unconscious image is particularly terrifying. The nonempirical nature of Subanun 'supernaturals' refers only to the visual sense; these beings are (reportedly) able to make an impression on one's auditory and tactile senses.

The English word 'supernatural' thus serves as a *label* for the Subanun category of 'persons' reportedly not consciously visible to the ordinary Subanun. There are, of course, in the verbally revealed Subanun universe many creatures ('persons' and 'nonpersons') which the ethnographer feels confident he will never see and which many informants admit they have never seen (but only because they have never encountered them, except perhaps in the dark). Some of these "natural" (i.e., visible) but rarely encountered phenomena play an important role in Subanun life, but they do not appear at offerings and hence are not relevant to the present discussion. Only by attending to Subanun criteria can we assign the bow-and-arrow-wound-inflicting *menubuq* pygmies to the category 'supernatural' and the body-dismembering *meɲayaw* marauders to the category 'mortal.' Neither class appears to the ethnographer to have any empirically substantiatable members in the Subanun habitat at the present time, though they both may once have had. Yet to discuss both categories together as aspects of Subanun *religion* because they are both "supernatural" according to the ethnographer's notions would seriously distort the structure of Subanun culture.

At the most general level of terminological contrast the Subanun classify 'supernaturals' as 'souls' (*gimuud*), 'spirits' (*mitubuq*), 'demons' (*getau-telunan*), and 'gods' (*diwata*) (cf. Table 1). Two semantic dimensions suffice to define these four categories in terms of necessary and sufficient contrasts in verbal descriptions:

1. Inherent connection with mortals
   1.1 Inherently connected with a living mortal
   1.2 Once inherently connected with a mortal now dead but still remembered by at least one living mortal
   1.3 Not inherently connected to a living or remembered mortal

2. Habitat connection with mortals
   2.1 Regularly residing with mortals in 'this world' (*glumbaŋ*)
   2.2 Not regularly residing in 'this world'

Using the numbering of the outline above, the four categories are definable as follows:

'Souls'   : 1.1
'Spirits' : 1.2
'Demons'   : 1.3 2.1
'Gods'   : 1.3 2.2

'Souls' play a role in offerings through attempts to use offerings to recapture, for the sake of their owner's health, lost souls lured away by fragrant blossoms, attractive supernaturals, and the offerings of sorcerers. ('Souls,' a kind of 'supernatural,' must be distinguished from *gina* 'life stuff,' associated with consciousness, cognition, and emotion but not a 'person' who attends offerings.)

After death the soul survives to become a 'spirit,' a bodiless soul who wanders about 'this world' until sent on a tour of sacred places and other worlds by a series of offerings performed on his behalf by his survivors. Becoming eventually forgotten in the sky world, he then acquires the necessary attributes of a 'god' (cf. definition above). It is the spirits of the recent dead—close kin whom he remembers personally and toward whom he still has ritual obligations—that concern a Subanun. When he dies, others will remember him, and those he remembered will be forgotten. Ties between spirits and mortals are reformulated in successive generations rather than continuing through time as an ancestor cult—just as the corporate social groups of Subanun society, the nuclear families, do not survive through successive generations as descent groups but are constantly dissolving and reforming.

Remembered spirits are important to the Subanun because they are the closest friends a mortal has among the supernaturals. They willingly attend seances for sentimental reunions with their loved ones (though even they demand an offering of food and drink). At seances they typically act as intermediaries between mortals and less friendly supernaturals, often filling a role not unlike that of a legal authority in arbitrating a dispute between plaintiff (the offended supernatural) and defendant (the mortal offender and victim of the plaintiff's wrath). Spirits respond to emotional appeal "for oldtimes'

TABLE 1. Categories of Participants in Subanun 'Offerings.'

'persons'	getaw:	
^a1.	'supernaturals'	kanaq kilawan
1.1.	'souls'	gimuud
1.2.	'spirits'	mitubuq
1.3.	'demons'	getau-telunan
1.3.1.	'ogres'	menemad
1.3.2.	'goblins'	memenwa
1.3.3.	'pygmies'	menubuq
1.4.	'gods'	diwata
1.4.1.	'sky gods'	getau-laŋit
1.4.2.	'raw-food-eating gods'	kemuŋluq, meŋilaw
1.4.2.1.	'sunset gods'	getau-sindepan
1.4.2.2.	'sea gods'	getau-dagat
1.4.2.3.	'ocean gods'	getau-land
1.4.3.	'sunrise gods'	getau-sebaŋan, tumiag
1.4.4.	'underworld gods'	getau-bayaq
2	'mortals'	kilawan
^a2.1.	'functionaries'	sug mikanu dun
2.1.1.	nonprofessional functionaries	
2.1.2.	'professional functionaries'	belian
2.1.2.1.	'invocators'	bataq belian
2.1.2.2.	'mediums'	gulaŋ belian
2.1.2.2.1.	'shamans'	guleligan
2.1.2.2.2.	'interviewers'	meninduay
2.2.	'assistants'	gimpaŋ
^a2.3.	'beneficiaries'	sug pikanuan dun
2.4.	'audience'	sug suminaup dun

^a Marks categories which must be represented at any offering.

sake" and consequently tend to be less greedy in their demands than other supernaturals. They can be troublesome, however, if their mortal kin shirk their ritual obligations. Also they may become so afflicted with the prevalent Subanun sentiment of 'loneliness' (*bugaq*) that they desire to transform a mortal loved one to spirit status, a transformation few mortals are willing to undergo, no matter how fond they were of the departed. Several informants have voiced a suspicion, founded on their remembrance of the deceased, that the spirit in such cases is not always as sentimental as he pretends; he has merely discovered a neat wedge for extorting food and drink from his survivors.

'Demons,' while not usually so viciously malevolent as the 'raw-food-eating gods,' are dangerous because they live so close at hand. Any chance encounter with them is likely to result in illness, and the disturbance of many of their habitats caused by swidden activities requires regular propitiation.

Of greatest importance among the 'gods' are the various types of 'raw-food eaters' (see Table 1) who periodically ascend the streams of Subanun country to inflict severe illness and epidemics and through their 'pets,' the rats and locusts, cause agricultural disasters. Their annual 'new year's' propitiation at strategic river confluences provides a common ritual interest for all settlements whose drainages converge upon a single convenient blocking place.

Other 'gods,' especially the 'sky gods,' are generally much less malevolent if not actually friendly. Perversely, they do not participate nearly so regularly in human affairs, although some exert important control over rice growth. During the course of an illness-studded life, most adult male Subanun acquire a personal 'guardian supernatural' (*tipun*), frequently a 'sky god,' who must receive annual propitiation at harvest time for the sake of the health of the man's family and rice.

'Gods' and 'demons' come in large numbers of varieties distinguished by habitat specifications, appearance, malevolence, diet, altar preferences, natural phenomena under their provenience, and so on. The verbal expositions of this pantheon vary greatly from informant to informant and from region to region. To present any one of these systems in all of its detail as "the Subanun pantheon" would do violence to cultural reality. The striking feature of Subanun theology is that, at any but the most general levels (see Table 1), it is not a consistent body of cherished lore at the tip of everyone's tongue. Beyond the generalizations given here, Subanun 'supernaturals' are, with some exceptions, diffuse in their functions. Almost any supernatural can cause almost any ailment or interfere in almost any activity. Consequently an elaborate and precise taxonomy of supernaturals correlated with their functional roles need not be shared by all participants in the performance of an offering. Individuals and groups can differ considerably in their theological speculations with little consequence for the practical conduct of *religious behavior*.

Direct observation and Subanun descriptions of role performances both make it clear that a 'mortal' participant in an offering occupies at least one of the following roles: 'funtionary,' 'assistant,' 'beneficiary,' or 'audience' (see Table 1).

The 'functionary' has the task of extending the invitation to the supernatural guests once the offering has been prepared. He invokes the supernaturals by incantation, bowl striking, and incense burning. The functionary, furthermore, assumes the responsibility of supervising all proceedings connected with the offering to ensure their proper performance. Every adult male household head has frequent occasion to serve as functionary for simple household ceremonies. Women rarely assume this role in fact, except during one type of agricultural offering, but are not proscribed from it by custom. A person must always act as his own functionary in offerings to his personal 'guardian god' (*tipun*).

The complexity of Subanun religious techniques, however, demands specialized knowledge of functionaries for all but the simplest offerings. A 'professional functionary' (*belian*) is an acknowledged specialist in religious techniques who regularly acts as a functionary for offerings involving beneficiaries outside his own household. If a 'professional functionary' has one or more supernatural 'familiars' (*bilaq*) and can thereby conduct seances, he is a 'medium' (*gulaŋ belian,* or simply *belian* if context makes the level of contrast clear); otherwise he is an 'invocator' (*bataq belian,* literally, "a little bit of a professional functionary"). There are two kinds of 'mediums': 'shamans' (*guleligan*), who are 'possessed' (*tenaqan*) by their familiars, and 'inter-

viewers' (*meninduay*) who carry on conversations with the supernatural guests as the latter partake of the offering.

Of the special statuses which a Subanun can achieve, that of 'medium' is the most formalized in method of recruitment and in social acknowledgment. It can never, however, replace a Subanun's full-time occupational role of farming. There are two routes, open to any adult man or woman, for becoming a medium: by 'training' (*pigubasan*) and by 'revelation' (*gemaw*). All mediums of my acquaintance selected the former route, involuntarily, when the supernaturals imposed the role upon them as the price of recovery from an illness. In this manner the gods recruit new members to the profession which is so essential to their well-being. A person so selected assists a qualified medium and acts as an 'invocator' until the gods inform him that he is ready to assume a medium's role himself. A medium of the other type (*gemaw*) allegedly receives his training direct from the gods and needs no apprenticeship.

The Subanun expects a good medium to exhibit certain peculiarities of 'habitual behavior' (*kebetaŋ*). His personality should emphasize to a fault the Subanun virtues of a quiet, passive, rather phlegmatic approach to interpersonal relationships with the consequence that he becomes, by Subanun evaluation, somewhat impractical in daily affairs. These traits of the personality type called *melemen* are the polar opposites of the forceful aggressiveness (*gembeluq*) required of a legal authority. Hence the same person cannot easily occupy both the role of mediator with the supernaturals and the role of mediating among human disputants. Furthermore, by Subanun standards, the personality expected of a medium is more commendable, if less entertaining, than that of the extroverted legal authority.

Almost every settlement has someone who can assume the role of 'invocator' for certain ceremonies, but, in the area of my fieldwork, over half of the settlements lacked resident mediums. Mediums must therefore extend their services beyond their own settlements on a community-wide or even a region-wide basis, depending on their reputation. The travel required takes sufficient time from the medium's agricultural and technological tasks at home to counterbalance what material rewards his profession brings

—a problem paralleling that of prominent legal authorities. Probably the most important material reward for mediums is the opportunity they have to attend a large number of feasts and drinking parties without any obligation to reciprocate. In addition, when called upon to perform special ceremonies for the cure of illness, they collect a small fee. They receive no fee for communal ceremonies in which they themselves are beneficiaries.

The other roles assumed by participants at an offering are functions of the particular social context; they are not permanent attributes of a person's status in the society at large. 'Assistants' are any persons who, under the functionary's supervision, prepare and set up the food and material equipment for the offering. They are recruited for the occasion from apprentice mediums, personnel of the beneficiary's household, the beneficiary himself, or simply from people "who like to do that sort of thing." The 'beneficiary' is the person or persons for whose benefit the offering is being given. The beneficiary may be one person, a household, a settlement, or even an entire region, depending on the purpose of the offering. The responsibility of providing a locale for the ceremony, of securing the necessary provisions, and of recruiting assistants falls to the beneficiaries. Any person or family intending to assume the role of beneficiary must make a contribution to the offering.

The 'audience' comprises all persons who are present because of the offering but who have no special role in its actual performance. It may include uninvited people who "happened to drop by" (in unexpressed anticipation of a feast), but it is largely composed of people with a special interest in the beneficiary. Major ceremonies of illness and death provide the only formalized occasions which bring large numbers of a person's dispersed kindred together as participants in a single event. Scheduled agricultural and prophylactic ceremonies, on the other hand, recruit audience and group beneficiaries along lines of local group affiliation. Except during seances, the majority of the audience and even beneficiaries, when these are in large number, generally show very little interest in the proceedings of the offering proper; that is the task of the functionary and his assistants. A Subanun offering is a technique for accomplishing a practical purpose. It is not an obvious source of inspiration or a forceful expression of ultimate values to an awe-stricken congregation. There are, of course, sources of inspiration and forceful expressions of values in Subanun life, but they are more likely to be communicated during secular gatherings around rice-wine jars after the offering is completed. Seances, however, rival legal disputes as foci of lively interest: they provide all persons present with an opportunity to interrogate, beg, cajole, bargain, and debate with the supernaturals themselves.

ROUTINES

To complete a description of the constituent structure of offerings there should be an analysis of the actions or routines followed in the performance. Such a description, however, would require a much more detailed discussion of offerings in all their varieties than is possible here. Consequently I merely list below the categories under which such a description of routines would be organized:

1. Preliminary staging talk
2. Assembly of participants
3. Preparing of provisions and paraphernalia
4. Setting up of offering
5. Invocation
6. Seance, if any
7. Removing provisions
   (Routines 4–7 repeated for each offering of the ceremony)
8. Festivities (routines of festive eating, drinking, singing, etc.)
9. Dispersal of participants
10. Postperformance critique

THE DISTRIBUTION OF 'CEREMONIES'

If we assume that the foregoing description adequately accounts for the identification and performance of offerings within ceremonial contexts, the problem remains of formulating a statement which accounts for the scheduling of ceremonies in relation to other scenes of the culture. A distributional analysis seeks to answer the question: what does the occurrence of a given event imply to the knower of the culture about the occurrences of other possible events in the system? A statement of the distribution of ceremonies will specify what features of a Subanun's experience are relevant to the staging of a religious performance of a given kind at a given time.

Formulating a statement of the distribution of religious scenes requires examination of the ethnographic record for observed and reported events which, by the criteria already formulated, are instances (or "tokens") of this scene. Next we list the other scenes regularly occurring before and after religious scenes. To judge the extent to which the occurrence of one scene implies another, the record of observed sequences must be checked against the record of informant's statements about anticipated sequences and of their interpretations of actual sequences in terms of these anticipations. This list of scenes provides a distributional *frame* for the set of events labeled 'religious scenes' or 'ceremonies.' The diagram A| |B, where A is the set of scenes regularly anticipated before ceremonies and B the set regularly anticipated after ceremonies, represents the frame. Such a distributional frame specifies the necessary conditions for anticipating the occurrence of a ceremony. Note that these conditions depend not only on the actual occurrence of an anticipated event, but also on plans made for producing or coping with future events. The model of distributional structure is a two-sided, before-and-after frame, such as that required in linguistic description, and not a Markov chain in which the probability of an event is a sole function of the outcome of the preceding event. In acting as well as in speaking persons have an image of the pattern to be completed and make plans accordingly.

Description of a frame requires a statement of: (1) the probability of the events that comprise the frame, (2) the alternative scenes, other then ceremonies, that can be anticipated to occur in the same frame, (3) the alternative kinds of ceremonies that can be anticipated to occur given the occurrence of *a* ceremony.

The significance of ceremonies in Subanun life relates strikingly to the probability of events which, in terms of legitimate cultural expectations, imply ceremonies. Among the most probable events of Subanun life are those that make up the scenes of the annual agricultural cycle: swidden slashing, felling, burning, planting, protecting, and harvesting. The annual staging of each of these scenes in this order by each family is an essential feature of the Subanun ecological adaptation. These scenes and their constitu-

ents provide a frame for scheduling about nine annual complex ceremonies, the exact number varying locally. Each of these ceremonies is of a specific named kind with prescribed settings, kinds of provisions, paraphernalia, routines, and social participation. These ceremonies are *scheduled ceremonies*. Their distribution has the following characteristics:

1. The scenes of the distributive frames are highly probable.
2. Each frame calls for a specified kind of ceremony.
3. There are no anticipatable alternatives to any of these ceremonies.

Thus the annual occurrence of a given kind of scheduled ceremony is highly probable, and learning that a given scheduled ceremony has indeed occurred is not very informative (it is not 'news') to the person who knows the culture. The occurrence of a scheduled ceremony is, in effect, a structural marker of the anticipatable sequence of scenes in Subanun culture. It signals that events are unfolding as scheduled. [Compare the linguistic frames marked in the following English utterance: "I want | |go| | Hawaii." The person who knows English can legitimately anticipate only one form, *to,* in the first slot; whereas in the second slot a number of alternatives can be anticipated: *to, through, by, near, away from,* etc. The actual occurrence of a given form in the second slot is less probable and much more informative about the nonlinguistic world than the occurrence of a form in the first slot which can inform us only whether or not the utterance is correctly constructed.]

To the Subanun, the occurrence of a scheduled ceremony not only signals the expected unfolding of events, but it is also necessary if future anticipations of probable events are to be fulfilled. The failure of one of the scenes of the agricultural cycle to occur as anticipated is a sign of a major *crisis* —an unanticipatable occurrence with far-reaching consequences for future anticipations. If harvesting does not follow swidden planting and protecting, then a crisis— drought, locusts, crop disease, human sickness—has occurred. The anticipated structural sequence of scenes has been broken. Correspondingly, to the Subanun, the failure properly to stage the correct ceremony on

schedule can only lead to crisis. Unanticipated crises are caused by the supernaturals
when *their* anticipations of regular feasts are
not met. The explicit rationale for performing scheduled offerings is to prevent the occurrence of crises, to ensure the proper unfolding of events.

The performance of scheduled ceremonies
is necessary to prevent crises, but, as is obvious to any Subanun, it is by no means
sufficient to do so. Serious crises do occur.
The distributive frames of many ceremonies
are composed of unscheduled events that
disrupt the ordinary routine of activities.
Since their scheduling in relation to other
scenes cannot, with great probability, be
planned in advance, ceremonies occupying
such frames are *unscheduled ceremonies.*
Their distribution has the following characteristics:

1. The events which comprise the distributive frame are relatively improbable in
the sense that other events could more legitimately have been expected at that time instead.

2. In a given frame there are often alternative courses of action to staging a religious
scene.

3. Given the staging of a religious scene, a
variety of types of ceremonies can occur in
many of these frames.

Thus, knowing Subanun culture, one cannot predict when the conditions for an unscheduled ceremony will occur, and given
the occurrence of such conditions, one cannot
directly predict if a ceremony or an alternative scene will be staged, and given the staging of a ceremony, one cannot directly predict what kind of ceremony will be held. In a
typical unscheduled situation there are a
number of alternative courses of action—a
range of doubt over what to anticipate.
When a particular course of action is selected from these alternatives, the decision is
highly informative—it is news—even to one
who knows the culture.

The occurrence of illness exemplifies an
unscheduled frame. Oversimplifying somewhat (by ignoring disease stages and states
of 'relapse' and 'recuperation'), the anticipated outcomes of an illness are continued sickness, cure, or death, giving the
frame:

sickness	diagnosis	continued sickness cure death

All English terms comprising the frame are
labels for categories of events as identified
by the Subanun. The alternatives anticipatable are:

1. No formal therapy
2. 'Medication' (one or more of about eight
   hundred alternatives)
3. 'Religious' therapy
   3.1 Consulting the supernaturals
   3.2 'Ritual contract'
   3.3 Performance of a 'contracted offering'
       3.3.1–61 +. (List of alternative types of
       offerings)

The initial choice is made in relation to the
anticipatable outcome, or prognosis, predicated by diagnosis, and subsequent choices
are made in relation to the results of previous choices (Frake, 1961). 'Medication'
(*kebuluŋan*), relying on the special power
inherent in certain, generally botanical, substances, comprises a set of techniques conceptually distinct both from reliance on
'skills' (*kependayan*) and from appeals to
the supernaturals through offerings. These
three contrasting techniques are applicable
to a wide range of endeavors apart from illness: agriculture, technology, social control,
lovemaking, etc.

Because of the greater expense and more
elaborate planning required, religious therapy for illness is resorted to only if medication fails or its failure is immediately obvious from prognosis. If religious therapy
does occur, it is informative of the seriousness of the case. The particular kind of
ceremony required, if any, cannot be determined from diagnosis, but only by consulting
the supernaturals through divination or seance.

Once a patient has learned he must perform a specific kind of ceremony and has
ritually acknowledged his intention to do so,
he has acquired a *binalaq,* a term appropriately glossed as 'ritual debt,' for a Subanun's procrastination and legalistic evasion
with *binalaq* obligations closely parallels his
handling of ordinary 'debts' (*gutaŋ*) with
his fellow mortals. The 'ritual acknowledgment' (*penebiin*) of a *binalaq,* which generally follows considerable haggling with the
supernaturals, can be labeled 'ritual contract.' It is sound policy to contract to pay
one's ritual debt *after* one is cured. In this
way one is assured that the supernaturals

will abide by their side of the agreement. The Subanun knows that even the most generous offering does not always cure his afflictions, and that, if he pays his ritual debts while he is sick, the supernaturals may keep him sick in the hope of extorting more and more from him.

But in this contest between mortal and supernatural, the former shows no more conscientiousness in fulfilling his obligations than the latter. Once he is cured, the Subanun patient becomes very reluctant to expend his resources on the supernaturals. Yet most Subanun have had enough experience with relapses of sickness to be somewhat wary of neglecting their ritual obligations without making an effort to do it legitimately by obtaining an extension of the contract through assiduous divination or through pleading with the supernaturals during a seance. Obtaining an extension often means an increase in the offering as interest, but despite past experience, the Subanun frequently hopes that with enough extensions his supernatural creditors will eventually forget about the debt and not inflict illness on him again in an effort to recover it. These hopes are generally in vain. The supernaturals hound their debtors with the same diligence as mortal creditors. Sooner or later, the Subanun who has neglected a ritual debt becomes ill. Then he remembers his outstanding obligations, which are likely to be numerous, and, if indications from seances and divination are affirmative, he may actually perform the contracted offering. But he may also acquire a new obligation pertinent to his new illness and penalizing him for the long delay in paying the debt for the old. With the new obligation, depending on the course of the illness, he may go through the same delaying tactics until he is once again afflicted. Because of these tactics of debt evasion, in many a crisis ceremony of disease the beneficiary is indeed sick but not with the illness that originally incurred the obligation to perform *that* ceremony. (There are, of course, many complexities and deviations from this simplified description that cannot be dealt with here.)

SUMMARY

In contrasting religious scenes with alternative and complementary kinds of cul-tural activity, it becomes clear that the entire behavior complex of which 'offerings' are the ultimate constituents serves the Subanun essentially as a technique, a way of getting things done. To build a house, to grow crops, to cure disease, or to make love, a Subanun may rely on his own 'skills' (*kepandayan*), resort to the 'medicinal' properties of certain substances (*kebuluŋan*), or call upon the supernaturals for assistance (*kanu*). Religion, generally the most expensive and complex of these techniques, belongs especially to the context of crises or potential crises—unanticipatable events with severe consequences and uncertain outcomes. The regular performance of scheduled ceremonies is designed to prevent crises. Unscheduled ceremonies are staged to cope with crises and put events back on their proper course.

The rationale for *religion* (i.e., 'offering'-focused behavior) as a technique lies in the belief that one can accomplish an end by inducing others to act in his behalf. This principle, valid enough in social relationships, the Subanun extend by peopling the universe with unseen beings who have the power to inflict and thereby cure illness. These beings, the 'supernaturals,' are terminologically a species of 'persons' (*getaw*), and they can be influenced by methods resembling those proved effective in social relationships among mortals: offering food and drink, verbal appeals, attention to paraphernalia. A unique network of relationships, canalized by ritual obligations incurred through illness and the threat of illness, links each Subanun with the supernatural inhabitants of the universe, just as his network of social ties is patterned by secular obligations. The supernaturals sanction their demands with their power over health, whereas one's mortal fellows generally employ subtler sanctions of public opinion. In both cases the sanctions prove effective: social relationships are maintained, the supernaturals are fed, and the Subanun patient, if not cured, is perhaps consoled.

These characterizations of Subanun *religion* are summaries of the distributional properties of a structural segment of Subanun cultural activity with respect to contrasting and complementary activities. They are not, in intention at any rate, simply intuitive impressions of "the meaning of religion in Subanun life" unrelatable to operations performed on ethnographic data. As an adequate ethnographic statement the present

paper is deficient in detail and rigor. It merely suggests some of the methodological features of such a statement.

DUANE METZGER AND GERALD WILLIAMS

Tenejapa Medicine I: The Curer

In the same general tradition as Frake, the ethnographer Metzger and the linguist Williams have collaboratively developed a set of very precise procedures for ethnographic description and analysis, which they have applied to the Highland Chiapas community of Tenejapa in Southern Mexico. Their procedures involve the establishment and employment of specifiable eliciting frames, formulated in the informants' language and in terms that are meaningful to the informants. The use of these eliciting frames enables the ethnographer to produce cultural descriptions which mirror the discriminations made by the informants rather than discriminations that would be made by the observers utilizing categories drawn from our culture.

In their previous (and much longer) article, "A Formal Ethnographic Analysis of Tenejapa Ladino Weddings" (1963), Metzger and Williams provided a fuller exposition of their methods, utilizing data elicited from Spanish-speaking informants in Tenejapa. In the article reprinted here they use the same methods with Tzeltal-speaking informants to describe the role, attributes, and ritual practices of the native curers. They suggest that their techniques are applicable in ethnographic description generally, including other aspects of the religious system.

Reprinted from *Southwestern Journal of Anthropology*, XIX (1963), 216–234, by permission of the authors and the *Southwestern Journal of Anthropology*.

The treatment of serious illness in Tenejapa—a Tzeltal-speaking community in the Chiapas highlands—is primarily the province of the /hpošil/, "curer." We propose to examine the role of the curer, placing particular emphasis on the characteristics and performances which not only define the role but which also, in their internal variation, are the basis for evaluation of curers and selection of one curer rather than another.

The procedures employed in the collection of the data and in the descriptive analysis of it are in part revealed in the body of the paper where eliciting frames and typical responses have been shown. The establishment and employment of specifiable eliciting frames, formulated in the informants' language and in terms "entertainable" by informants, constrains their response in some great degree to a focus or foci which are in turn defined in the informants' terms, rather than by the categories of the investigator. In this sense the description stems from the

material itself. The structure and limits of the description bear a significant relation to structure and limits of the informants' "knowledge."

1. /HPOŠIL/, THE CURER

1.1. THE ROLE OF THE CURER

Working with seven Tenejapa informants from six *parajes,* we were able to compile a list of some three hundred curers known to them. The approximate population of all Tenejapa *parajes* being about 10,000 (1960 Census) and calculating a population of curers of two or three times the size of the list obtained, since our informants' acquaintance did not extend over the whole of the *municipio,* it appears that the ratio of curers to total population is somewhere between one to ten and one to twenty-five. This ratio indicates something of the importance of the performances engaged in by curers and of the situations which call up these performances. It may be observed as well that the variety and frequency of illness are equally of a large order and that, though we have not attempted any sort of statistical confirmation, the subject of illness figures with great frequency in conversation.

Virtually anything that upsets the Tenejapaneco's equanimity is a potential source of illness, while the maintenance of the health of the members of the family is a major drain upon available resources. It is the curer whose role is central to these concerns and who exercises major control over the disposition of these resources. Also, it appears, at least in some instances, it is the curer who decides whether an illness may be treated or not, and thus, at least indirectly, has some power of decision over the life or death of the patient. An illustration of two of these points is the curer's recommendation in instances of apparent imminent death to refrain from great expenditure in a hopeless attempt at a cure. The curer who fails to show such concern for the welfare of the patient's family is accused of avarice and failure to fulfill his obligation to /ya školta te muk' b'ik'it/, "watch over the people." Derogation of this duty leads to punishment in the form of illness.

Being known as a curer confers a status which overrides other status achieved, such as that of great age. It is usual for a respected elder to address even young curers as /tatik pošil/, /tatik/ being the most respectful, reverential term of address available, and, in general, curers are so addressed rather than by name.

1.2. ATTRIBUTES OF CURERS—CRITERIAL AND ENTAILED

Curers may be of any age (including children) or sex (though male curers are more numerous than female). No formal training is provided for those who fill the role.

The primary distinguishing characteristic of curers is their ability to "pulse" (/ya sna?ik lek ?a?y k'ab'al/, "They know well how to 'feel of the hand.' "). /?a?y k'ab'al/ or /pik k'ab'al/ or /¢ahtae k'ab'al/, which refers to the process of pulsing, and thereby sensing, the movement of the blood of the patient, allows the identification of the illness, its etiology, cure, etc. This skill comes to the curer only as a "gift of God," usually discovered in himself by the curer (even while still a child). It is said that by praying to God in the church and burning candles, it is possible to obtain the necessary power to cure for the asking and without danger. Informants, though reporting this to be the case, cannot name any person who has become a curer in this way. More generally, persons attempting to acquire without the gift the knowledge of pulsing that characterizes curers run the danger of being punished by a visitation of illness.

In contrast to pulsing, a second performance characteristic of curers is not limited to them but is shared by non-curers of high status. This is the "true prayer," /b'a¢'il č'ab'/, which is an integral part of the public performances of the civil and religious officials as well as of heads of families, whose perceived function is to /sk'anel kušlehal/, "ask for the life (of the *pueblo* or household)." Public prayer, occurring at conventionally appropriate times, anticipates a potentially great number of dangers to the community and its individual members; within the context of curing, the focus of prayer is upon the life of an individual in relation to a single specific danger to that life.

While any non-curer who is skilled in praying (/ ya sna? lek č'ab'/, "he knows how to pray well") may attempt, and sometimes succeed at, curing, the curer's ability to pulse makes his use of prayer more surely effective. Since there are many varieties of /b'a¢'il č'ab'/, differentiated by the god to whom addressed and specific to the disease, the ability to identify the disease (by pulsing) and the knowledge, which is essentially restricted to curers, of the association between specific diseases and gods is crucial. The would-be curer, like anyone else in the community, can learn these associations by closely observing curers at work when there is illness in his household. However, he must be circumspect in his learning. Attempts at acquiring such knowledge are generally punished by illness/ya stikun tal te hč'ultatik/ ~/te ryos/, "sent by God," because /ya htohb'e ryos tame ya hk'an ya hnop pošile/, "God punishes me if I want to learn to cure."

Like prayer, skill in the use of medicinal plants, which is characteristic of curers, is shared in a general sense by non-curers but becomes unique in the hands of curers because of its association with their other attributes. Medicinal plants are known by all adults in Tenejapa, and association of specific plant remedies with common illnesses is well-known. The curer's use of these plants is special in that, first he alone can surely identify the illness. Then, once the illness is identified, knowledge of the specific herbal remedy for the illness is more or less restricted (as in the case of prayer) to the curer. Finally, /tuhtael/, the preparation and administration of the remedy, involves prayer and spitting into the mixture, both of which invest the medicine with the curer's power.

Other curing skills are exclusive to curers but not common to all of them. Among these are blood-letting, and the curing of various specific types of diseases. Still other curing skills are neither common to all curers nor exclusive to them. These coincide with a set of infirmities which are not /čamel/, "illness(es)": /ti?b'en čan/, "snake bite," /k'asem sb'akel/, "broken bones," /k'ahk'et/, "burns," /b'e¢'em/, "sprains," and /mahel/, "bruises."

Another somewhat peripheral phenomenon sometimes associated with curers is the /sánto/ or /hč'ultatik/, the "talking saint." These generally are in boxes in the house of their owner and may not be seen, though the more reliable are audible, sometimes "speaking" in a high-pitched whining noise, sometimes in recognizable words. The most highly regarded instance reported is that of one which can be heard speaking from inside the house while the listeners remain outside. The primary function of the saint is divinatory and ranges beyond divining the causes of illness and the identification of witches to the finding of lost objects.

The man who owns a saint is the /yahwal hč'ultatik/ or /b'ankilal mučáču yu?un hč'ultatik/, "dueño del santo," and need not be a curer at all. The curer who has a saint, /?ay hč'ultatik ta sna/, "there's a saint in his house," may employ his saint as a substitute for his own pulsing, but more generally uses it to confirm pulsing. The saint, then, is a supplement or substitute for more traditional (and generally more respected) modes of obtaining information; it has no apparent function in other segments of the cure.

1.3. CLASSES OF CURERS

Having established the attributes of /hpošil/ we asked the question /hay ten hpošiletik ?ay ta b'alamilal/, "How many kinds of curers are there in the world?" One reply was /?ay ča?ten/, "There are two kinds," specified as /b'ankilal hpošil/, "(literally, older brother curer) master curer" and /?ih¢'inal hpošil/, "(literally younger sibling curer) junior curer."

1.31. By knowledge. In respect to knowledge, these two classes contrast on several interrelated dimensions. One of these dimensions is the types of knowledge attributed to them. The ability to treat specific illnesses distinguishes all /b'ankilal hpošil/ and some /?ih¢'inal hpošil/ from all others. For example, /spisil b'ankilal hpošiletik ya sna?ik te *hulawe*/, "All master curers know how to let blood (specifically from the head," but /?ay ?olil ?ih¢'inal hpošiletik ma sna?ik te *hulawe*/, "There are some junior curers who do not know how to let blood."

The presentation of the names of other illnesses or modes of treatment elicited further differentiated statements of the same kind in which the following were some of the items substitutable for /hulaw/ in the statements above:

1. /ya sna?ik lek č'ab'/
   "they know how to pray well"
2. /ya sna?ik tuhtawaneh/
   "they know how to prepare and bless medicine"
3. /ya sna?ik čonaw/ *or* /ya sna?ik suhtesel čonel/
   "they know how to send an illness back (to the hostile person who caused it)"
4. /ya sna?ik poštawan yu?un me?tik tatik/
   "they know the cure for /me?tik tatik/"
5. /ya sna?ik špoštael ?ak'b'il čamel/
   "they know the cure for illness caused by witchcraft"

This knowledge, while characteristic of /b'ankilal hpošil/, may be possessed as well by individual /?ih¢'inal hpošil/, but the latter as a class cannot be said to be characterized by the knowledge. It will be noted that at least some abilities are clearly matters of degree (see 1 above), while in other cases the master curer and junior curer are distinguishable by the types of illness they are competent to cure; thus, of a junior curer who pretends to cure a /tulan čamel/, "a strong illness" such as /me?tik tatik/, it is said /ya špoštawan ha?te ma lom s?u¢ub' yu?un te mač'a ya špoštae/, "he cures (treats), but the person treated does not recover well." There are attributed to the

/ʔihȼ'inal hpošil/, who knows the limits of his ability, such statements as /ha ʔin čamel ʔaʔwuʔuni ma šhuʔ kuʔun lek špoštael melel lom tulan čamel ʔaʔtaohi/, "This illness of yours, I cannot cure, because (you have) met with a very strong illness" or /haʔlek leaiktal te mač'a ya snaʔ lek špoštael te tulan čamele/, "Better summon someone who knows well the cures of serious illnesses."

A general statement of the difference may be seen in the following regarding the /ʔihȼ'inal hpošil/: /maʔma spisil ʔak'b'il ta yok ta sk'ab' yuʔun hč'ultatik/, "Not all is given into his hands by God"—while of the /b'ankilal hpošil/ it is said, /spisil ʔak'b'il ta yok ta sk'ab'/, "All is given into his hands."

It will be noted that among the abilities characteristic of /b'ankilal hpošil/ is that of curing /ʔak'b'il čamel/, "given illness," i.e., illness attributed to an act of will of a /hʔak' čamel/, "giver of illness." The classes /hʔak' čamel/ and /hpošil/ intersect in some of the same persons. However, not all /hʔak' čamel/ are /hpošil/, and while all /b'ankilal hpošil/ may be able to cure such illness, not all master curers can induce illness. Those who are so able are said to /čaʔten ya snaʔ/, "he knows two kinds (classes)." A master curer never induces illness in this way in his role as curer, and the cure for /ʔak'b'il čamel/ does not include counter-measures of the same kind.

"Sending the illness back," /suhtesel čonel/, another ability characteristic of the master curer, is concerned not with /ʔak'b'il čamel/, but /čamel yuʔun čonel/, "illness induced through ritual 'sale' (of the victim)." This illness is attributed to a /hčonawal/, who implements his ill will by cutting candles into small pieces and praying over them as they burn. The master curer performs the same ritual as an integral part of the cure for /čamel yuʔun čonel/. Thus, while not all /hčonawal/ are /hpošil/, all /b'ankilal hpošil/ are /hčonawal/; moreover, the latter, unlike the role of /hʔak' čamel/, is entailed in the master curer's role.

One type of specialized knowledge which is characteristic of /b'ankilal hpošil/ is not common to all of them. The ability to handle /čamel yuʔun ʔalahel/, "childbirth," is more or less restricted to women; while there are a few men who share this ability, they are reportedly little used because women are "embarrassed" to be attended by men in childbirth. The knowledge of such curers is not restricted to the problem of childbirth; they are general practitioners as well. The curing skills mentioned earlier as neither exclusive to curers nor shared by all of them—e.g., bone-setting—do not distinguish between /b'ankilal/ and /ʔihȼ'inal/ curers, for many master curers lack some or all of these skills.

1.32. By performance. The knowledge attributed to the master curer which distinguishes him from the junior curer is manifest in his performances in the curing setting. The /b'ankilal/-/ʔihȼ'inal/ contrast, previously defined in general terms of reputation, is carried out on another level in the performances which contribute to—and which at the same time reflect—that reputation.

Within the performances of the curer and others involved in the cure there may be distinguished 1) pulsing: /ʔaʔy k'ab'al/-/ȼahtae k'ab'al/, and 2) prayer saying: /č'ab'atael/.

Previous to performances differentiating curers from other visitors who are not curers, the usual formulae of greeting are exchanged by the visiting curer and the family of the /čamel/, "sick person."

1.32.1. Differentiation of the curer's reception begins with the request of the family that he "pulse" the patient: Head of the family: /maʔyuk šʔob'ol b'ahat šaʔ ȼahtab'en sk'ab'in hčamel kuʔuni/, "Would you not do me the favor of feeling for him his hand?"

Pulsing generally consists indeed of taking the pulse of both wrists for lengths of time ranging from five minutes to a half-hour per wrist. *In extremis,* the pulse at the wrist being too weak to "hear," pulsing may be done inside the elbow joint or inside the upper arm. This stage in the cure and its constituent performances are much more than diagnostic, leading not only to the identification of the illness, but to a variety of other information regarding the illness as well.

Among the information extracted by the master curer from his pulsing are the following:

/ya yal šč'ič'el te hčamel te b'i čamelil ya štiʔwan ya yaʔye/
"The blood of the patient says what illness it is he is suffering"
/te b'i čamelil ya štaot te hčamele/
". . . what illness has seized him, the patient"
/te b'anti ya štaot te hčamele/

". . . where it seized him, the patient"
/te b'a č'ab'atael ya sk'ane/
". . . which prayer is required"
/ta me ˀay čuhkem šč'ulele/
". . . if his soul has been captured"
/ta me ˀay skape/
". . . if there is a combination (of illnesses)"
/ta me ˀay ščohe/
". . . if there is envy (involved)"
/ta me ˀay smeˀ šwiše/
". . . if the soul is not well guarded (by the old woman who is responsible for it)"

Thus, virtually everything concerning a disease, from its provenience, etiology, to specific medicines and locations in which specific prayers must be said, is available to the curer through pulsing. The curer can also point the finger of guilt at the person whose misbehavior has resulted in the illness, even to parents and ancestors:

/ya snaˀb'e lek yaˀyel šč'ič'el te hčamel te b'i smul skolaˀal hahčemtal yuˀun te hmam hmeˀčuntike/
"The blood of the patient knows well what sins of parents (or ancestors)"

During the course of the pulsing, the curer may carry on conversation with the family, the subject of conversation being unlimited, and the occasion not necessarily excluding jokes and laughter. If, during this conversation, the curer makes obvious attempts to elicit from the patient or the attending family the information which is properly forthcoming from pulsing, it is likely to be said that he is /ihȼ'inal/ and not /b'ankilal/.

/te me ya snaˀ yaˀyel k'ab'ale ma ya shohk'o/
"'If he knew how to pulse, he would not ask questions,' he said"

In such a situation, the family may deliberately withhold information:

Curer: /b'it'il ˀaˀ lihk te ščamel te ˀanȼe/
        "How did the illness of the woman begin?" *or*
        /b'anti ˀaˀ sȼakat te čamele/
        "Where did the illness grasp you?"
Family: /hič naš ˀaˀ ȼakot/
        "It just grasped."
Curer: /maˀyuk b'a t'ušah/
        "Couldn't it be she has fallen?"
Family: /maˀyuk/
        "No."

In contrast, the /b'ankilal hpošil/ displays his lack of concern by engaging in small talk, gossip, and jokes. Silence, or any other apparent sign of concern on the part of the

curer (e.g., trembling of the hand while pulsing, /ya šnihk/, "(his hand) trembles") is negatively evaluated.

Duration of the pulsing constitutes another potential point on which differentiation between /b'ankilal/ and /ˀihȼ'inal hpošil/ is based. Thus a short pulsing (followed by a clear, unhesitating explication) is characteristic of the master curer, while a long pulsing (and hesitation in explaining the results) indicates skill of a lesser order.

Family: /b'i yael te sk'ab'e/
         "What says his hand?"
Curer: /ma škil mama ya yal ˀaˀ kaˀy te sk'ab'e/
         "I don't know. His hand does not speak, I feel."

The pulsing completed, the curer is expected to explain what he has learned. The master curer's explication of the circumstances antecedent to the disease generally conforms to what the family and patient know of them, while the junior curer's may not.

An instance of a highly evaluated set of performances by a curer will be seen in this example: The curer, a woman in this case, was called to a "gravely" ill patient. Without asking questions, and after a brief pulsing, she indicated that the patient was suffering illness as a punishment for complaining of the rigors and inconveniences of the *cargo,* "public office," he had recently assumed. The /ryos/ of his cargo was punishing the cargo-holder for remarks which he admitted to having made, the remarks being known as well to the family.

Further, the contrast between master and junior curers extends to the curer's statements with respect to the severity of the disease and the possibility of curing it. Accuracy of such estimation, as evidenced in subsequent developments and in the costs involved in the cure, is characteristic of the master curer. Informants report that /ˀihȼ'inal hpošil/ are prone to underestimate the severity of disease, while the confidence of the /b'ankilal hpošil/ does not deter him from staking his reputation on an extended and expensive cure. The /b'ankilal hpošil/ admits the gravity of the illness and characteristically undertakes the cure with due humility: /sk'an ryos ya šˀuȼub'/, "With the help of God he will recover."

The conclusion of the pulsing is the point of selection between alternative courses in the cure, depending upon the identification of the disease, perceived cause of the disease, etc. The curer may rest while preparations are made for whatever course is to be followed in the subsequent segment, and he will generally be fed.

1.32.2. The succeeding segment of the curing sequence consists of the components directed toward the curing itself. The constituent components depend upon the results of the preceding segment. Among possible components are the preparation and administration of medicine or other physical attempts at curing, the burning of incense and candles, the saying of prayers to appropriate gods (the prayers being said in specific places depending on the illness and its provenience), and possibly a ceremonial meal. Among these potential components, there are relations of mutual exclusion, of sequential order, of co-occurrence, the description of which will constitute a subsequent account of Tenejapa Tzeltal curing practices.

We will confine ourselves here to an outline of the general sequence of performances which constitute this segment.

Encompassing the variability arising from different results of pulsing and the variability arising from apparent changes as the cure proceeds, the three highest order sequential components appear to be as follows: (1) /b'aȼ'il č'ab'/, "prayer," (2) /tuhtael/, "preparation and administration of blessed medicine" and (3) /hulaw/, "bloodletting." The time span of a single sequence (there is always the possibility of

the iteration of the sequence) can be as long as four days. If the pulsing segment indicated that /b'aȼ'il č'ab'/ is appropriate, it will be anterior to other co-occurring components, if any. The /b'aȼ'il č'ab'/ itself is divided into four or six parts (practice appears to vary from one *paraje* to another), the parts being distributed in sequence on succeeding mornings and evenings, the first occurring in the evening. Special routines, however, may be accorded severe illness, or certain specific illnesses such as /me?tik tatik/, and the requisite number of prayers may be said in sequence without interruption. Severity may also dictate simultaneity of several segments, requiring the participation of a person other than the curer. This person, the /hč'ab'owil/, "prayer sayer," is not a curer, but one who can recite the appropriate prayer as determined by the curer. A prayer cycle, once begun, must be carried to its conclusion by the person reciting it without his engaging in any other curing component; thus, in order for other components to be simultaneous with the prayer, the latter must be said by another person (the /hč'ab'owil/) while the other component is carried out by the curer. Prayer, in this sense, is the only component which may be delegated.

Two of the above sequential components, /tuhtael/ and /b'aȼ'il č'ab'/, are both regarded as /č'ab'/, a superordinate category which contrasts directly with /hulaw/, "bloodletting." Within /b'aȼ'il č'ab'/ are a variety of disease-specific prayers, each of which intersects, as shown in Table 1, with

TABLE 1.   The Structure of the Prayer (/č'ab'/)

| In Setting: | tuhtael | | b'aȼ'il čab'ᵃ | | | | | |
	č'ulelal	kušlehal	me?el wišil	skap sk'ab'	me?tik tatik	k'ašim b'ehtael	čonel	šiwel
ta yut na, "in the house"								
1. ta kurus "before the cross"	X	X	X					
2. ta ti?k'al "before the fire"								X
3. ta b'ayuk naš "anywhere"	X			X				
ta ?amak' "before the house"	X				X	X		
ta kurus ta ?anhel "at a (wayside) cross"							X	

ᵃ The names of prayers shown here in Table 1 are renderings, by and large, of homonymous names of diseases to which the prayers are specific. Glossing these names would be at best only vaguely suggestive, and at worst very much misleading. Were this paper part of an already completed description of Tzeltal medicine, these would be cross-referenced to sections in which criterial attributes of /čamel/, "diseases," as a class would be laid out together with the defining dimensions in terms of which members of the class contrast and are differentiated. Only one of these is shown here, i.e., location of the saying of the appropriate prayers, since it relates to one aspect of curers' performances.

settings appropriate to their performance. /tuhtael/ may be applied to the preparation and application of a variety of disease-specific medicines, but the location of their preparation is indifferently before or within the house.

Table 2 shows a simple case (an illness requiring six prayers) in which the curer is performing all components, thus displaying the linear ordering of components most clearly.

The components stand in a transitive relation; at the close of any component, depending upon the state of the patient, the next numbered component may succeed. After the accomplishment of component 2, /tuhtael/,

in the case of the disease of the same name).

If the cure is to be continued, the repetition of the cycle will be limited to /b'aȼ'il č'ab'/, given that the cure is continued by the same curer. Where a different curer is called in, however, the complete cycle may be begun again.

The components of the curing segment proper also show variation in terms of which evaluation of the curer may be made. In prayer, whether the /b'aȼ'il č'ab'/ or that of /tuhtael/, the performance of the /b'ankilal hpošil/ shows variety, that of the /ʔihȼ'inal/ repetitiveness; and the repertory of the /b'ankilal/ allows him to continue longer, with consequent greater effectiveness.

TABLE 2. Cycling of Components of the Cure Proper

Time	Day 1	Day 2	Day 3	Day 4	± Day 5
/sakub'el k'inal/ "becomes light the day"		b'aȼ'il č'ab'	b'aȼ'il č'ab'	b'aȼ'il č'ab'	tuhtael
/č'ul ʔahk'ub'al/ "(holy) night"	b'aȼ'il č'ab'	b'aȼ'il č'ab'	b'aȼ'il č'ab'		± (hulaw + tuhtael)

or 3, /hulaw/, the cycle may be reiterated by returning to component 1, /b'aȼ'il č'ab'/, except that /hulaw/ is invariably succeeded by another instance of /tuhtael/ at the same curing session. The time intervening between the major components may be compressed or it may be expanded such that components succeed each other on succeeding days.

At the beginning of component 2, /tuhtael/, the curer and assembled company may begin drinking, a performance which is mutually exclusive with component 1, /b'aȼ'il č'ab'/. The preparation and administration of medicine generally involves the use of /poš/, "*aguardiente* (in this case, distilled cane alcohol)," together with the saying of prayers (but not /b'aȼ'il č'ab'/) over the medicine.

If /hulaw/, component 3, is to be carried out, a fragment of broken glass is secured with which the necessary wounds will be made. There would seem to be two types of appropriate /hulaw/, one involving small incisions in the skin on the sides of the head and in the scalp, the other, incisions in other parts of the body. In the former case, the blood is collected on leaves and removed from the house, the disease being removed from the body along with or in the blood. In the latter case, in addition to blood, some other substance may be removed by the curer and eaten by him to prevent contagion (/ton č'ič'/, literally "blood stones,"

In the preparation and administration of medicines the /ʔihȼ'inal hpošil/ may always rely on the same medicine; /ma lom snaʔb'e sb'a spisil pošiletike/, "He doesn't know all the kinds of medicines." To the /b'ankilal/ there is attributed, at least, the knowledge of "all classes (of medicine)," /ya snaʔb'e sb'a spisil stukel/.

The physical manipulations of /hulaw/, "blood letting," make clear the curer's confidence or lack thereof, in that the incisions made should be regular and the hand steady, while the trembling hand of the incompetent leads to ragged incisions.

Upon termination of the curing segments, the curer is offered a gift of 10–30 ears of corn. The amount of corn varies neither with his status nor with the success of the cure (although he may decline it if the patient has died), but with the wealth of the patient's family. Daily consumption of corn is estimated at five ears per person per day.

1.32.3. Throughout the curing sequence, then, there are opportunities to evaluate—or to re-evaluate—the curer in terms of the /b'ankilal/-/ʔihȼ'inal/ contrast. (In the course of the cure, a curer who has claimed a master's knowledge and skill may betray his junior status by injudicious eliciting of information, trembling hands, etc.; or, even in the absence of these signs of lesser status, he may incorrectly predict the course of the illness, e.g., the patient may fail to recover or die in contradiction of a favorable prognosis.) An informant's evaluation of a curer is primarily based on the personal observations which he or his close associates have made of that curer. The relative lack of consensus in such evaluations by our informants suggests that these experiences vary greatly and that the classes of /b'ankilal hpošil/ and /ʔihȼ'inal hpošil/ are, in general, not to be regarded as groups with fixed memberships. Where multiple judgments were obtained as to the ability of various curers, there was disagreement between the informants in two-thirds of the cases. However, in the remaining third of the cases, where there was agreement, the overwhelming majority of curers were evaluated as /b'ankilal/, a fact which suggests that there may be a certain amount of consensus at the highly skilled end of the scale. The apparent lack of consensus below this level makes the selection of a curer problematic and involves the trial-and-error employment of /ʔihȼ'inal hpošil/ (labelled after the fact), as well as masters. In any case, there is a floor, as it were, underlying any evaluation, a level below which the definition of a person as a curer will not permit evaluation to go. Thus, an obviously poor curer can still, despite negatively evaluated performances, produce reactions of fear in the family of the patient by a prediction of death. Informants confirm that, in the position of patient, they find themselves vacillating between belief and disbelief of such predictions.

2. THE CURER VIS-A-VIS THE PATIENT-HOUSEHOLD

2.1. CONDITIONS APPROPRIATE TO THE SUMMONING OF THE CURER

The curer is not summoned in every instance in which a person defines himself as /ʔayon ta čamel/ or /čamelon/, "I am sick," or is defined as such by others, /ʔay ta čamel/, "he/she is sick." The criteria which appear to operate in distinguishing between occasions appropriate and inappropriate to calling the curer generally involve the contrast between 1) /muk'ul čamel/, "great illness," /ʔip čamel/, "powerful illness," /tulan čamel/, "hard illness," versus 2) /solel k'ašlel čamel/, "illness which passes," /č'uhč'ul čamel/, "a little illness."

In reply to the question, /b'it'il ya šb'aht taluk te hpošile/, "When do you call the curer?" there emerges the following family of responses:

/haʔ hič ya šb'a yič' tal ʔik'el hpošil/ "One is going to call a curer,"

A. /te me ʔay muk'ul čamele/ "if there is a great illness"

/te me ʔay ʔip čamele/ "if there is a great illness"

/te me ʔay tulan čamele/ "if there is a strong illness"

We take this one level further by asking, /b'inti ʔut'il ʔay te ʔip čamele/, "How is (what is) a powerful illness?" and eliciting the response:

/haʔ ʔip čamel ta me ʔay ma sk'an šhelaw ta ʔora te čamele/ "It is a powerful illness if it does not (wish to) be cured in (normal) course, the illness."

Other conditions for calling the curer include:

B. /ta me ʔay b'ayel k'uš hkok k'ab'tike/ "If there is great pain in our bodies"

/ta me ʔay me šȼ'ihk' stiʔaw te čamel ya kaʔytike/ "If we cannot bear the pain of the illness we feel"

Other conditions require anticipation of illness, as:

C. /haʔ lek ta nail ya šb'aht tal ta ʔik'el te hpošile/ "It is best first to call the curer" *or*

/haʔ lek te ʔalan ya kak' hb'ahtik ta poštaele/ "It is best to send for curing beforehand"

/ta me ʔay b'i šiʔotike/ "if we are *espantado*" *or*

/ya kaʔytik ta me ʔay mač'a ya ščap hk'olaltik ta ʔak'b'il čamele/ "We feel that there is someone trying to give illness (through witchcraft)"

Sometimes the calling of a curer follows the failure of another curer to restore the patient to health. Indeed, the lay diagnosis of "powerful" illness may follow—as the definition in A suggests—from an unsuccessful attempt to cure it; along with the diagnosis goes the after-the-fact evaluation of the curer as /ʔihȼ'inal hpošil/.

2.2. OBTAINING THE SERVICES OF THE CURER

The recognition of the above conditions within the household is up to the head of the house, and the decision to obtain the services of the curer is his. If the head of the house himself is the patient, it may be his wife or one among the children of the household who will make the decision to call the curer, if the head of the house is perceived to be ill but does not act himself. In general, if the patient is perceived as ill, but in such a condition as to refuse or be unable to recognize it, the curer will be called, even against the will of the patient.

Occasionally, if the illness is defined as "powerful" but the patient is not too sick to walk, the patient may go himself to the curer's house with a keg of *chicha* (a fermented sugar cane beverage) to request and participate in the cure. Usually, however, the curer is summoned to the patient's house.

The actual performance of going to request the services falls under the general heading of /ʔabat/, "errand," a performance mutually exclusive with the performances appropriate to the senior members of the household, and particularly to those of the senior male, generally the father in the predominantly nuclear family household. A child or young adult is usually sent, though he (or she) may be reluctant or afraid if he has not done such an errand before. The informants were encouraged to supply hypothetical but appropriate instances of verbal behavior to fit this situation. We constructed the interaction by setting up the question frames used by the person requiring information, in this case the young person who is to run the errand. Thus,

Child: /meʔ b'inti mahtanalil ya kič'b'el yuʔun ¢'in hpošile/
"Mother, what is the gift I should take for the curer?"

Parent: /haʔ ʔič'a b'el htab'uk ʔišimi/
"Take these twenty ears of corn."

The parent's response constitutes a substitution frame for the eliciting of other appropriate gifts:

/haʔ ʔič'a b'el hunuk pulatu čenek'i/
"Take this one bowl of beans." *or*

/haʔ ʔič'a b'el čeb'uk pulatu čenek'i/
"Take those two bowls of beans." *or*

/haʔ ʔič'ab'el hunuk pulatu ʔiči/
"Take this one bowl of *chiles*." *or*

/haʔ ʔič'a b'el čeb'uk pulatu ʔiči/
"Take these two bowls of *chiles*."

Child: /b'inti ya šk'o kalb'e ¢'in hpošile/
"What shall I say (on coming) to the curer?"

Parent: /haʔ ya šk'o walb'e ¢'in te ʔay hčamel kuʔuntike/
"Arriving, tell him that we have a sick person."

Child: /b'inti ya kalb'e ¢'in ta me ʔay ma sk'an štale/
"What shall I say if he does not wish to come?"

Parent: /yaniš ʔaʔwokol k'opta tal ta pórsa ¢'in/
"Ask him please to come under any circumstances." *or*

/te ʔay šʔob'ol b'a štal yilotike melel ʔip hčamel kuʔuntik yaʔwil/
"That he do us the favor of coming to see us, because our sick person is serious(ly ill)."

The errand-boy is quite likely to find the curer is away from home, as curers of good reputation are often employed, and a single cure may require as much as four full days if travelling time to distant patients is included. Moreover, while no curer is busy curing every day, all of them carry on the usual adult occupations as well—the men in the cornfields, the women in their kitchens and courtyards. There are no full-time specialists in curing; the meager fees paid for curer's services are incommensurable with such specialization, and the time that curing subtracts from subsistence activities is so great as to cause curing to be considered a somewhat sacrificial vocation.

The response of the curer to the request and gift may be one of three: (1) he may come as requested, and at once; (2) he may protest a previous obligation, undertaking to come later; or (3) he may refuse the "gift" and thus decline to undertake the cure. The second may be interpreted as a disguised attempt to pursue some work of his own, and the third may indicate some history of conflict between curer and the family of the patient. In both types of situation, the curer places himself in jeopardy of supernatural punishment in that he is refusing what is considered an obligation contingent upon his role as curer.

2.3. THE SELECTION OF A CURER

First and foremost, the curer selected by the patient's household is generally one with whom they have had favorable first-hand experience in previous curing situations; at least initially, curers known only by hearsay are not considered. Proximity is a factor important in the initial stages and often associated with this acquaintance, except that normally the curer does not treat his own children or members of his own household. Proximity may also be crucial in emergency. Given these guiding principles, the selection of a curer takes into account the household's guess diagnosis of the illness and involves an attempt to match the illness and the curer's skills as they have observed them. A "powerful" illness requires a known /b'ankilal hpošil/, while for a "little" illness an /ʔihȼ'inal hpošil/ may be chosen. The guesswork involved both in identifying the illness and in evaluating the curer often means that the first curer called will not be the last. However, the ideal rationalization of the selection of a curer is phrased in firm, positively evaluative terms:

/mač'a hunuk hpošilil ya šb'a kik'tik tal/
"Which curer shall we send for to come?"

/haʔ ya šba kik'tik tal te hʔaluš lopis howil ȼ'iʔe melel haʔ ya snaʔ ščiknatesel spisil te b'i ya štiʔwan ya kaʔytike/
"Let us summon Alonso López 'Mad Dog' because he knows how to explain all the things that we suffer."

3. CONCLUSION

In this paper, some aspects of the role of the Tenejapa Tzeltal curer have been described in terms consistent with discriminations made by the Tenejapa Tzeltal themselves; the discrimination of curers from non-curers, the evaluation of and distinction between curers, the establishment of recognized units within the curing performance (and their relation to the evaluation of the curer), the relation of evaluation to the selection of the curer, etc.

The techniques here employed seem to us to be applicable in ethnographic description generally. Whether through these or other techniques, the arrival at cultural descriptions which mirror the discriminations made by informants is a desirable end for ethnography. The present paper is, of course, only a sample; Tzeltal curers and their activities constitute a focus which if articulated with a number of other such foci will place the Tzeltal curers within a potentially ever-widening description, having as its end a Tzeltal-centered "whole-culture" description of the Tenejapa Tzeltal community.

EVON Z. VOGT

Structural and Conceptual Replication in Zinacantan Culture

Utilizing a combination of systematic sequences of behavior, performed repeatedly in rituals observed over a series of years, and of concepts that are expressed explicitly in the Tzotzil language spoken in the Highland Chiapas community of Zinacantan in Southern Mexico, this article provides methodological suggestions for the description and interpretation of selected elements of a religious system. The rules of behavior for a ritual meal are specified and it is shown how they apply to all structural levels in the society from the small domestic family groups up to the tribal affairs in the ceremonial center. Similarly, the Tzotzil concept of "embracing" is traced through several domains of Zinacanteco life, including socialization within the family, as well as baptismal, wedding, and curing ceremonies, and how it is extended symbolically to the activities of the ancestral gods that are believed to reside inside the mountains. These "replications" of important rules of behavior and key Tzotzil concepts in various domains appear to form an amazingly consistent network of symbols, or "code" of the type that Lévi-Strauss describes in his article on "The Bear and the Barber" (1963).

Reprinted from *American Anthropologist*, LXVII (1965), by permission of the author and the American Anthropological Association.

I. INTRODUCTION

In this essay I propose to examine an organizational principle of Zinacantan culture which I have chosen to call "replication." After seven seasons (1957–1963) of field work in Zinacantan, I believe I am beginning to understand something of the patterns of the culture. One of its patterned aspects that now strikes me forcibly is the systematic manner in which certain ritual behaviors are replicated at various structural levels in the society, and certain concepts, expressed quite explicitly in Tzotzil, are replicated in various domains of the culture. It is as if the Zinacantecos have constructed a model for ritual behavior and for conceptualization of the natural and cultural world which functions like a kind of computer that prints out rules for appropriate behavior at each organizational level of the society and for the appropriate conceptualizing of phenomena in the different domains of the culture.

In my thinking about this principle of "replication" I have been influenced by Evans-Pritchard's description of the concept of *cieng* ("home") among the Nuer, by Kluckhohn's treatment of "patterns" and "configurations," by Lévi-Strauss' ideas about "models" and "codes" for the analysis of social structure and culture, and by Leach's paper on "Rethinking Anthropology," but more especially by what the Zinacantecos have been striving to communicate to me over the past seven years. I have also come to agree strongly with those of my colleagues who propose that a description of cultural behavior is attained by a formulation of what one must know in order to respond in a culturally appropriate manner in a given socio-ecological context. If the ethnographer working in Zinacantan can come to understand the model and the rules that are printed out, then he will have mastered the codes that are necessary to know in order to behave appropriately in the myriad of settings and contexts he confronts in Zinacanteco society. Although I am still some distance from understanding and being able to describe all facets of the model with precision, I offer this description and analysis of the principle of replication as a step in the direction I am following in a monograph now in preparation on Zinacantan.

II. THE MUNICIPIO OF ZINACANTAN

The Highland Maya of Chiapas comprise a nucleus of some 175,000 conservative Indians living in municiple units distributed around the Ladino town of San Cristobal Las Casas. Each municipio speaks a distinct dialect of Tzotzil or Tzeltal, possesses dis-

tinctive styles of dress, and has local customs that differ in varying degrees from neighboring municipios. Zinacantan with a 1960 population of 7600 Indians is located just to the west of San Cristobal Las Casas. I have elsewhere described the settlement pattern as typically Maya with ceremonial center and outlying hamlets, or "parajes" as these are called in Chiapas. About 800 Zinacantecos live in the densely settled valley in which the ceremonial center is located; the other 6800 live in the eleven outlying parajes. The ceremonial center contains the Catholic churches, the "cabildo," and a plaza where markets are held during important fiestas. In and around this ceremonial center are located a series of sacred mountains and waterholes which figure importantly in the religious life.

The most important structural feature of the ceremonial center is a religious hierarchy with 55 cargo positions attached to the cult of the saints and the temples. This hierarchy consists of a ranked series of four levels in a ceremonial ladder. To pass through this ceremonial ladder a man must serve a year at each level, and during the time he holds the cargo he must move into the ceremonial center and engage in a complex annual round of ceremonies. The ceremonies are expensive, costing him as much as 14,000 Mexican pesos for some cargos, and time-consuming. But while he fills the role, he enjoys special prestige and wears special costumes for ritual occasions. At the end of the year he turns the office over to the next incumbent, and moves back to his paraje to become a corn-farmer again. Some year must elapse before he can work himself out of debt and accumulate enough wealth to ask for a cargo position at the next higher level. The process continues until he passes through the ladder and becomes an honored "pasado."

In addition, there are some 100 to 150 *hʔiloletik* in Zinacantan. These *hʔiloletik* are the "curanderos" or shamans in the system. Most of them are men, but some are women, and some are as young as 15 years of age. To become a *hʔilol,* one dreams three times that one's *ch'ulel* ("inner soul") has been called before the council of the ancestral gods inside the most important sacred mountain and taught how to perform ceremonies. The ceremonies performed by the *hʔiloletik* include eight types of curing ceremonies, semi-annual ceremonies (held in May and

October) for waterhole groups and lineage groups in the parajes, new house ceremonies, rain-making ceremonies in the fields, and three annual ceremonies for the "New Year," the "Middle of the Year" and the "End of the Year." A remarkable feature of the *hʔiloletik* is the degree to which they are formally organized. For example, they are all in rank order from one to 100 or 150, the rank order depending upon number of years that have elapsed since the practitioner made his debut as a *hʔilol*.

The subsistence system that supports this complex ceremonial organization is based upon crops of maize, beans, and squash grown in milpas located in the Highlands, but more importantly on lands in Tierra Caliente along the north side of the Rio Grijalva. The diet is supplemented by chickens, eaten especially on ritual occasions, and by beef, especially when cattle are purchased and butchered by cargo-holders for important fiestas in the ceremonial center. Small herds of sheep are owned by Zinacanteco women, with the wool providing materials for many items of clothing woven on the backstrap loom.

III. STRUCTURAL REPLICATION

Just as the settlement pattern of Zinacantan appears to take the form of an aggregate of aggregates ranging from the domestic family house up to the ceremonial center, so also the social structure and ceremonial organization appears to manifest an orderly replication of increasing structural scale.

The social structure of the outlying hamlets is based upon the following residential units: the patrilocal extended family occupying a house compound; the *sna* composed of one or more localized patrilineages; the waterhole groups composed of two or more *snas;* and the paraje.

The house compounds, or "sitios" as they are called in Chiapas, are often enclosed by some type of pole or brush fence and contain one or more dwelling houses, a granary for the storage of maize, a sweat house, and, in the center, a patio cross that serves ritually as the house shrine for the family unit that shares a single corn supply.

The house compounds are grouped into larger units which I call *snas*. The term *sna* means literally "the house of," and it is the term the Zinacantecos themselves use to refer to these residential units that are typically composed of one or more localized patrilineages in which genealogical connections can be traced. The *sna* takes its name from the lineages. In cases where the unit contains only one lineage, there is no problem. The unit is simply called, for example, *sna ʔakovetik,* or the "houses of the wasp nests." In the case of larger *snas* containing two or more lineages, the unit takes its name from the predominant lineage. Thus *sna ʔok'iletik* "the houses of the coyotes," contains the coyote lineage, but also contains two smaller lineages that have settled next to the coyotes and intermarried with them.

The *snas* are in turn grouped into waterhole groups each with distinctive names that are used by the Indians to describe where a person lives within a paraje. The waterholes are highly sacred, and there are myths about each of them describing the circumstances under which the ancestors found the waterhole and how it acquired its distinctive name. Each waterhole group is composed of two to seven *snas,* the size depending basically upon the amount of water available in the waterhole for household water and for watering sheep and other livestock, such as horses and mules.

There is finally the paraje unit which is composed of one or more waterhole groups. Some small parajes, such as *Elamvoʔ,* are composed of a single waterhole group; but all of the large parajes, such as *Pasteʔ, Nachih,* or *Navenchauk,* are subdivided into two or more waterhole groups.

Just as there exists a social order of ascending scale from the patrilocal extended family in its house compound, through the *sna,* the waterhole group, and up to the paraje, so there is also a ceremonial order of ascending scale that exactly parallels and expresses the social order both in terms of ritual paraphernalia and in terms of ceremonies of increasing size and complexity. Each of the social structural units I have described is symbolized by shrines composed of crosses that are conceptualized by the Zinacantecos as "doorways," or in other words, as means of communication with the *totilmeʔiletik* (the ancestral deities living in the mountains) and with *yahval balamil* (the earth god).

Within the context of the patrilocal extended family living in its house compound there are a series of ceremonies that involve basically the members of the family and never require the services of more than one *h'ilol*. Typical examples are curing ceremonies for individual members of the family and new house dedication ceremonies.

For each *sna* there are *k'in krus* ceremonies performed in May and in October that involve the services of all of the *h'iloletik* who live in the *sna* and the participation of all of the families in the *sna*. This ceremony appears to be a symbolic way of expressing the rights of the members of the *sna* in the lands they now occupy which have been inherited from their patrilineal ancestors.

For each waterhole group there are also *k'in krus* ceremonies performed semi-annually, typically preceding by a few days in May and in October the *k'in krus* rituals of the *snas*. Again, all of the *h'iloletik* living in the waterhole group assemble to perform and the participation of all of the families living in the waterhole group is expected. What this ceremony appears to express by its ritual forms are the rights which the members of the waterhole group have to use water from a common waterhole and the obligation they have to care for the waterhole properly.

Finally, the paraje unit is ritually expressed by two annual ceremonies performed by all of the *h'iloletik* living in the paraje. These ceremonies are called *'ach' habil* ("New Year") and *slaheb habil* ("End of Year"), and their function seems to be to symbolize the unity of the paraje and its relationship to the tribal *totilme'iletik* in the ceremonial center.

THE RITUAL MEAL: AN ILLUSTRATION OF
STRUCTURAL REPLICATION

I now focus upon one aspect of ritual behavior which appears to exemplify in its details the printing out of rules from the general model for appropriate behavioral sequences at various levels in the system, and hence to provide a clear illustration of structural replication.

Ordinary meals in Zinacanteco homes are served on the ground in pottery or gourd bowls. The men sit on small chairs and eat the tortillas and beans from the containers; the women eat later sitting on the ground near the fire. But whenever there is a ritual occasion, there is a *ve'el ta mesha* ("meal on a table") which follows carefully pre-scribed etiquette. The important rules are these:

Rule 1: The meal must be served on a wooden rectangular table. Every Zinacanteco house contains one or more of these small wooden tables. Most of them range in size from approximately 30 x 45 cm. to 60 x 90 cm. and are approximately 45 cm. high. Some are constructed by the Zinacantecos; more commonly they are purchased from the neighboring Chamulas who specialize in the making of small wooden tables and chairs which they sell in the market in San Cristobal Las Casas.

Rule 2: The table must always be oriented with the long axis running East-West. The Zinacantecos have no words in their Tzotzil language with which to distinguish North and South by our compass reckoning, but they do express the East to West axis by speaking of *lok'eb k'ak'al* ("rising or coming up sun") and *maleb k'ak'al* ("setting or disappearing sun").

Rule 3: The table must be covered with a pink and white striped cloth, called man-tresh. The women weave this cloth on back-strap looms from cotton thread. The same cloth is used to carry candles from San Cristobal for the ritual.

Rule 4: A bottle of posh ("aguardiente") must be placed in the center of the East end of the table. This action designates the East end of the table as the "head" of the table.

Rule 5: The commensalists must sit in small wooden chairs (also made by Chamulas) at the table in strict rank order. The most common rank order is expressed in [Fig. 1].

Rule 6: The meal consists of posh, maize tortillas, chicken cooked in broth with chile, coffee, and kashlan vah (small round loaves of bread made by Ladinos of wheat flour). Pork or dried fish may be substituted if the family has been unable to afford a chicken, but such substitution is always noted and it is clear that chicken is ideally *the* dish to serve.

Rule 7: The eating of the meal must follow a strictly prescribed sequence which consists of eleven basic steps.

(1) A young man designated as *hp'isvo'* ("drink pourer" or "measurer") serves a round of *posh* using the same shot glass and serving in rank order. The senior man present receives his shot glass of *posh* and engages in appropriate "toasting" and "bowing and releasing" behavior. Briefly, the "toast-

ing" behavior consists of his raising his glass and saying *kichban,* followed by a kin term or name, to each person at the table in rank order and receiving the response of *?icho?*. The "toasting" is accompanied by the "bowing and releasing"—that is, each of the more junior persons bows his head toward this senior man and is released by the senior man touching the back of his right hand to the

stack of tortillas in a gourd container are placed on the table by one of the younger men who receives them from the women cooks. The senior man takes a tortilla, tears off a small piece and dips it into his broth, and eats it. The others follow his lead.

(5) The senior man picks up his bowl and begins to drink the chicken broth. The others follow.

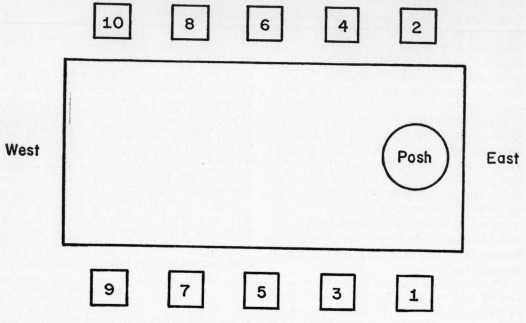

FIG. 1.

forehead of the junior person. The senior man then drinks the shot of *posh* in one gulp, grimaces to show how strong the liquor is, spits a few drops on the floor, and returns the glass of the *hp'isvo?* who proceeds to serve the next man in rank order and the sequence is repeated until the round is complete.

(2) The *mantresh* is either rolled up to the "head" of the table or both sides are rolled to the middle, and a gourd bowl of warm water is placed on the table for washing hands. The senior man washes his hands and is followed by the others in rank order.

(3) A gourd bowl of water is passed for rinsing out the mouth. The senior man rinses his mouth, spits out the water, and is followed by the others in rank order. The *mantresh* is rolled out again to cover the table.

(4) The chicken in the broth is then served in individual pottery bowls and a

(6) The senior man takes a piece of chicken, places it in a tortilla, and eats it. The others follow. All of the commensalists finish eating at approximately the same time, and they must either eat all of the food served them, or wrap the leftover chicken up in a tortilla and take it home with them.

(7) The *hp'isvo?* serves a second round of *posh.* The sequence of behavior is the same as on the first round.

(8) Each commensalist is then served an individual cup of coffee (sweetened with "panela") with a piece of *kashlan vah* on top. The senior man begins to drink the coffee and eat the bread; the others follow.

(9) The *mantresh* is then removed from the table, and the hand rinsing sequence is repeated, initiated by the senior man.

(10) The mouth washing sequence is repeated, initiated by the senior man.

(11) The *hp'isvo?* serves a third round of *posh.* The same sequence of behavior is

followed as on the first and second rounds; and the meal is formally over.

The rules of behavior I have described apply to the *ve?el ta mesha* at all levels in the social system. In the small domestic ceremonies, e.g. at curing or new house dedication ceremonies, a very small table is used and as few as four or five people will eat at the table. The *h?ilol* sits in position 1 and is followed by other men, and then women, in rank order.

In the *k'in krus* ceremonies for the *sna* the table will be larger, and more people will sit at the table. The senior members of the lineage are seated in the most senior position, then followed by the *h?iloletik* in rank order, and finally by the more junior ritual assistants.

For *k'in krus* for a waterhole group, the scale increases. As many as eight to ten *h?iloletik* have to be seated at the table, along with the ritual assistants, and often two or more tables have to be placed together to provide a larger surface for the meal. For the "New Year" and "End of Year" ceremonies for an entire paraje, the scale becomes still larger and as many as fifteen to twenty *h?iloletik* plus assistants are involved.

The maximum scale is reached at the Fiesta of San Sebastian in January when the entire religious hierarchy of 55 cargo-holders plus the *presidente* and his assistants, sit down to eat at an enormous table and are served not just pieces of chicken, but a whole chicken per person!

But whether the *ve?el ta mesha* involves only one family in a small domestic ritual with a handful of people sitting at a ridiculously tiny table, or, at the other end of the scale, involves the entire religious hierarchy seated in full regalia at the enormous table and consuming entire chickens, the rules of behavior are precisely the same. What is done in the small thatched house of individual families is replicated in ever increasing scale for the lineage, for the waterhole group, for the paraje, and for the whole municipio in the ceremonial center.

The same type of analysis can be made for many other aspects of ritual life in Zinacantan. For example, in ritual processions there are also a set of basic rules—the marching order is always junior man in front and senior man in the rear, the movement of the procession from one sacred place to the next is always counterclockwise and the circuit always brings them back to the house where the procession was initiated, etc. Again, these behavioral sequences are followed whether the procession involves three or four people in a small domestic ceremony, or at the other end of the scale, the procession involves the entire religious hierarchy of cargo-holders performing rituals in the ceremonial center.

These ritual patterns have important symbolic connections with the Zinacanteco view of the world and the relation of their social system to it. The most important *totilme?iletik* (ancestral deities) are believed to live in the East, and it is no accident that the principal sacred mountain (see below) lies to the East of the ceremonial center. During a *ve?el ta mesha* these ancestral deities are believed to appear and to partake of the food and *posh* that is served their living descendants. The living descendants are arranged in rank order at the table in such a way that the eldest (and hence ones closest to becoming deceased ancestors) are seated closest to the East end of the table, next to the *totilme?iletik*. The more junior members, with more time still to live, are seated further away. Why the marching order in processions follows the rank order from junior man in front to senior man in the rear is still a mystery to me. Nor can I yet explain why processions move around circuits counterclockwise, except to point out that this appears to be an ancient and quite general Maya pattern.

IV. CONCEPTUAL REPLICATION

I now turn to what I have chosen to call conceptual replication. By this I mean that the world of the Zinacantecos is segmented conceptually in systematic ways that are replicated in different domains of Zinacanteco culture.

"EMBRACING": AN ILLUSTRATION OF CONCEPTUAL REPLICATION

Again, for purposes of explanation, I shall focus upon one Zinacanteco concept which appears to exemplify in its details the printing out of beliefs from the general model for appropriate conceptualizing of phenomena in various domains.

There is a word stem in Tzotzil, *-pet*, which means "to embrace" or "to caress."

Thus, for example *hpetom* means "embracer" or "caresser." The concept of "embracing" occurs in at least the following domains of Zinacanteco life: the socialization process in the family, the baptismal ceremonies, the wedding ceremonies, the curing ceremonies, and the activities of ancestral gods inside the mountains.

Within the Zinacanteco family it is believed that one of the most important duties of the father and the mother called *tot* and *me'*, is to "embrace" a child and care for it well so that it does not lose its *ch'ulel* ("inner soul") composed of 13 parts. For if the child loses one or more parts of its *ch'ulel*, it will become ill, and may die.

At the baptismal ceremony a child always has a godfather and a godmother, called *ch'ultot* and *ch'ulme'*, or literally "divine father" and "divine mother." Their principal duties during the baptismal ceremony are to "embrace" their godchild while this important ritual is taking place. And perhaps the most important function of the ceremony from the Zinacantecos' point of view is to fix more permanently in the body the child's *ch'ulel* so that it will not be lost so easily.

At a wedding ceremony a ritual specialist called *hpetom* ("embracer") is in charge of introducing the bride into her new home— i.e. the groom's father's house in this system of patrilocal residence. In performing these ritual functions he is believed to "embrace" or "caress" the bride and groom, or in other words, to create a new relationship that will last, one in which the bride will come to like and not run home to her parents' house. In performing this duty he goes through a number of ritual sequences, such as taking the bride and groom into the house, removing their wedding clothes, giving the new couple lectures on how they should behave in their new marriage, instructing the bride's mother-in-law on how she should take care of her new daughter-in-law, and then leading the bride's relatives into the house and introducing them to the groom's parents.

During curing ceremonies a patient who is believed to have lost parts of his *ch'ulel* calls the *h'ilol* ("curer") *tot*. The ritual *tot* in this case is believed to "embrace" the patient in the process of helping him recover the lost parts of his *ch'ulel*.

High above Zinacantan center stands an extinct volcano, rising up to 9000 feet, called *bankilal muk'ta wits* ("older brother great mountain"). Inside the mountain, according to the Zinacantecos, are a series of corrals: one full of jaguars, another full of coyotes, another full of ocelots, and still another full of smaller animals such as squirrels, raccoons, and anteaters. These animals are the *chanuletik* of the Zinacantecos, and the total number adds up to 7600, the same as the population, for each Zinacanteco has a *chanul* as an animal spirit companion—a kind of wild animal alter ego, so to speak. The life of a Zinacanteco is intimately bound to his *chanul* in that anything that happens to the *chanul* automatically happens to him.

Ordinarily, the ancestral gods, called *totilme'iletik* (literally "fathers-mothers"), live in their houses inside the mountain and take good care of the *chanuletik*. They have their *mayoletik* ("assistants") feed and water them, and they "embrace" them. In other words, we have here the supernatural father and mother "embracing" the alter ego children, if you will.

However, if a Zinacanteco does something wrong, then the *totilme'iletik* stop "embracing" his *chanul;* in fact, he may be let out of his corral and left to wander loose and uncared for in the forest. In this event, he may be shot at or otherwise injured, and, if so, his human companion will suffer the same fate.

In a very dramatic symbolic way the connection between the real world of people and the supernatural world of *totilme'iletik* and *chanuletik* is made clear in one ritual sequence in the largest and most complex curing ceremony. Toward the end of the ceremony the patient is placed in a platform bed surrounded with pine boughs, just as the corral of his *chanul* inside the mountain is surrounded by pine trees. As the patient passes through the gateway of his decorated platform bed, called a "corral," in this ceremony, he is like a *chanul* being rounded up and herded through the gate into the supernatural corral inside the "older brother great mountain." In this instance, what is done inside the mountain is replicated in the curing ceremony, and in both domains a *tot* is "embracing" and caring for a patient or his alter ego in the spiritual world.

In a word, in the socialization process within the family, in the ritual life of the baptismal, wedding, and curing ceremonies, and in the supernatural world inside the mountain "fathers" and "mothers" are "embracing" their children. What is conceptualized in one of these domains appears to be replicated in the others, and the result is an amazingly consistent network of symbols that forms a "code" of the type that Lévi-Strauss (1963) writes about in his recent article.

The same kind of analysis can be made for many other concepts in Zinacantan culture. I will mention two by way of example. Another important word stem in Tzotzil is *-il*, which means "to see." Thus, for example *hʔilol* means "seer." In the Zinacanteco view of the world, there was an ancient mythological time in the past when all Zinacantecos could "see" into the mountains where the ancestral gods are now living. Now, however, only *hʔiloletik* possess this special ability to "see" the gods and communicate directly with them. It follows that *hʔiloletik* are critically important links between ordinary Zinacantecos and the gods for any important ceremony that requires communication and exchange of goods and services with these ancestral gods. Similarly, it is significant that the large complex curing ceremony (described above) is called *muk'ta ʔilel* ("the big seeing") to describe the process by which a patient goes on a pilgrimage to the sacred mountains and "sees" the gods with the aid of the *hʔilol*.

Another crucial concept in Zinacanteco culture is the contrast between *bankilal* and *ʔits'inal*. Literally, these terms mean "older brother" and "younger brother," and they are expressed in Zinacenteco kinship terminology. But they are replicated in so many domains of Zinacanteco culture that they lead us to conclude that something

much more generic is involved. Indeed, they appear as a way of classifying phenomena in almost any domain in the universe one can mention: there are older and younger brother mountains, crosses, *hʔiloletik*, drums, waterholes, cargo-holders in the religious hierarchy, etc. They are even applied to the Christ figure, for we have discovered that the Nativity scene in the Christmas ceremonies contains Joseph and Mary and then not one, but *two* small Christ children lying in the manger—*bankilal* and *ʔits'inal!*

They certainly appear to serve as symbols expressing some basic contrasts and oppositions in Zinacanteco life (Lévi-Strauss 1963:2), and one hypothesis I am working on is that they give general expression to the contrasts and oppositions found in the principle of age-ranking. If this proves to be correct, *bankilal* and *ʔits'inal* are symbolically expressing both the fact (and probably also the stress) found in not only "older" versus "younger" but also "more powerful" versus "less powerful," "more prestigeful" versus "less prestigeful," etc.

I suggest that these data have implications not only for our understanding of the integration of contemporary Zinacanteco culture, but also for the study of one of the probable processes of Maya cultural development over time. One can imagine how Maya ritual behavior and belief might have developed in complexity by gradual elaboration of the basic elements of domestic ceremonies that were originally performed by small household and hamlet units and were replicated on an increasing scale as the population expanded and the size of the social units increased to encompass the magnificent ceremonial centers with their large sustaining areas containing thousands of households and dozens of small hamlets.

ROGER V. BURTON AND JOHN W. M. WHITING

The Absent Father and Cross-Sex Identity

Quite apart from its intrinsic interest as a study and interpretation of a ritual that has long puzzled anthropologists, this article provides an excellent illustration of the cross-cultural method using data from the Human Relations Area Files and selecting variables that can be coded and analyzed statistically. Burton and Whiting explore the hypothesis that the association between male initiation rites and exclusive mother-child sleeping arrangements (and a long postpartum sex taboo) are related to problems in cross-sex identity. The hypothesis states that in societies with maximum conflict in sex identity, e.g., where a boy initially sleeps exclusively with his mother and where the domestic unit is patrilocal and hence controlled by men, there will be initiation rites at puberty which function to resolve this conflict. The chi-square test of association is found to be significantly beyond chance, since over 87 percent of the 64 societies included in the sample fall in the cells predicted by the hypothesis.

The basic method is further illustrated in the article by Young (1962) challenging the Whiting results, reprinted here to give the student a fuller understanding of the method as well as the nature of the controversy. An even more ambitious effort, using similar methods, in the field of primitive religions can be found in the interesting book by Guy E. Swanson on *The Birth of the Gods* (1960). There has also recently appeared Yehudi Cohen's *Transition from Childhood to Adolescence* (1964), which utilizes the cross-cultural method and presents still another view of the function of initiation rituals.

It is helpful for the reader to know that prior to the appearance of the present article there was one by Whiting, Kluckhohn, and Anthony, "The Function of Male Initiation Ceremonies at Puberty" (1958), wherein it was contended that male initiation ceremonies have developed as institutional mechanisms to separate sons from mothers and to break the sons' psychological dependency upon their mothers in societies in which the infant sons sleep with their mothers and in which there is a postnatal taboo of a year or more on the mothers' sexual relations. It was argued that not only must the psychological dependency be broken, but that the displacement of the sons by the fathers returning to their wives after a year or more of taboo generates deep hostility in the sons. The initiation ceremonies were hypothesized as providing a means by which the adult men could assert authority over the adolescent boys, separate the women, and break the psychological dependency relationship.

Reprinted in abridged form from *Merrill-Palmer Quarterly of Behavior and Development*, VII (1961), 85-95, by permission of the authors and the publishers.

In this paper, we shall present evidence on the effect of the father's position in the family as it relates to the growing child's learning by identification and to the development of his sex identity. This evidence consists first of a cross-cultural study done at the Laboratory of Human Development, Harvard University, and second, a review of recent research in the United States and Europe, relevant to our theory of identification, on the effect of father absence in the household.

THE STATUS ENVY HYPOTHESIS

Before presenting this evidence, however, we would like to state our view on the process of identification and the development of identity. This view we would like to call the *status envy hypothesis*. This hypothesis may be summarily stated as follows: The process of identification consists of the covert practice of the role of an envied status. Identification consists of learning a role by rehearsal in fantasy or in play rather than by actual performance, and this rehearsal is motivated by envy of the incumbent of a privileged status.

Let us consider the mother-infant relationship in which the mother attempts to satisfy all of the infant's needs. According to our theory, if it were possible for the mother to supply everything the infant wanted, he would not identify with her as he already occupies the privileged status. Some learning does, of course, take place in such a complementary relationship. The child learns to give the proper signals when he wants something and to accept and consume it when it is offered. Furthermore, he learns to predict certain sequences of events determined by his mother's behavior. In other words, he has cognizance of his mother's role. Although this cognizance may provide some savings in later learning, if and when he is motivated to perform her role, we would like to distinguish cognizance of a complementary role from identification with its incumbent.

To clarify our view of the motivation leading to identification, we would like to introduce the concept of a resource. A resource is anything, material or nonmaterial, which somebody wants and over which someone else may have control. Resources include food, water, optimum temperature, freedom from pain, and the derived symbolic resources such as love, solace, power, information, and success. Were these resources inexhaustible, and equally and completely available to all, there would be no such thing as status envy and, by our hypothesis, no learning by identification. Such, however, is not the case. As part of the cultural rules of every society, there is a status system which gives privileged access to resources for some positions in the system and, at the same time, disbars other positions from controlling and consuming them.

Returning to our mother-child example: As soon as the mother withholds a resource from her child and, by virtue of her position in the family, either herself consumes it or gives it to someone else, the conditions for status envy obtain. Even during infancy in societies where an infant occupies the most privileged status, complete nurturance is practically impossible. No matter how much a mother might wish to be ever-loving, the exigencies of life are such that there are times when she must withhold some resource that the child wants.

This is particularly true during the process of socialization. By definition this process involves teaching the child to delay gratification and to defer to the rights of others. More specifically, socialization involves teaching the child the privileges and disabilities which characterize the social structure of his society.

We may now restate our major hypothesis: If there is a status that has privileged access to a desired resource, the incumbent or occupant of such a status will be envied by anyone whose status does not permit him the control of, and the right to use, the resource. Status envy is then a motivational component of status disability, and such motivation leads to learning by identification.

This view differs from some other theories of identification in that we hold that a completely satisfying complementary relation between two people will not lead to identification. By this hypothesis, a child maximally identifies with people who consume resources in his presence but do not give him any. He does not identify with the people he loves unless they withhold from him something he wants. Love alone will not produce identification. Thus, the status envy hypothesis advanced here makes identification with the aggressor just a special case, and the Oedipal situation is also simply a special case.

The actual process of learning by identification consists of the covert practice in fantasy or in play of the role of the envied status. So when the child wants to stay up late, for example, and his parents make him go to bed while they themselves stay up, the child says to himself, "I wish I were grown up. Perhaps if I acted as they do I would be grown up," and he goes to sleep rehearsing, in fantasy, grown-up behavior.

ATTRIBUTED, SUBJECTIVE, AND OPTATIVE IDENTITY

We would now like to present our views on another concept which we believe will be useful in distinguishing households with fathers absent from those with fathers present. This is the concept of identity.

In every society, statuses have names or labels. In our society, for example, there are the familiar kinship statuses of mother, father, uncle, aunt, brother, sister; the age-determined statuses of infant, child, adolescent, adult, and aged; the occupational statuses of doctor, lawyer, clerk, workman etc.; and, especially important to our thesis, the sex-determined statuses of male and female.

We would like to define a person's position or positions in the status system of this society as his identity. Furthermore, we would like to distinguish three kinds of identity: attributed, subjective, and optative. *Attributed identity* consists of the statuses assigned to a person by other members of his society. *Subjective identity* consists of the statuses a person sees himself as occupying. And finally, *optative identity* consists of those statuses a person wishes he could occupy but from which he is disbarred. It is this last kind of identity that is most important for this paper.

Obviously, one's optative identity derives from status envy, and nothing much would be added to our theory by introducing this concept if one's optative identity were always objective and realistic. The wish being father to the thought, however, this is frequently not the case, and people often feel "I am what I would like to be." In such a case, the subjective and optative identities merge and become discrepant with the attributed identity.

It is our thesis that the aim of socialization in any society is to produce an adult whose attributed, subjective, and optative identities are isomorphic: "I see myself as others see me, and I am what I want to be." It is further presumed, however, that such isomorphism can only be achieved by passing through a stage in which there is status disbarment, status envy, and thus a discrepancy between one's optative and attributed identities. That is, to become such an adult, a person must have been deprived of the privileged consumption of resources accorded only to adults. This disbarment results in his wanting to be a member of that class. When society then permits him to occupy this privileged status, there is agreement in what he wants to be, in what society says he is, and in what he sees himself to be.

CROSS-CULTURAL EVIDENCE

Having briefly presented our views on learning by identification and on identity, let us now turn to the consideration of some empirical data which may provide a test of these notions. The first such test will be cross-cultural. The independent variables are judgments as to the distribution of resources during infancy and during childhood. Specifically, social structure of a sample of societies was judged for the degree to which the father and adult males in general, or the mother and adult females in general, occupied privileged or equivalent statuses as perceived by the infant and later by the child. Arrangements in infancy lead to *primary identification;* whereas those in childhood lead to *secondary identification.*

It is our assumption, and this has been supported by a previous study, that sleeping arrangements provide the best index of status envy during infancy. The bed seems to be the center of a child's world during the first year or two of his life. This is where the resources of greatest value to him are given or withheld, and those who share this setting with him become the models for his first or primary identification.

In most societies the world over, an infant sleeps during the nursing period either in his mother's bed, or in a crib or cradle right next to it, and within easy reach. Of over 100 societies on which we have data on sleeping arrangements, the American middle class is unique in putting the baby to sleep in a room of his own.

For our purposes, the big difference lies in whether or not the father also sleeps with the mother. In a sample of 64 societies which we would like to report now, 36 of them have the pattern of the father and mother sleeping apart, and the infant thus has the exclusive attention of the mother at night. In the remaining 28 societies, the infant either shares his mother's bed with his father or in a few instances sleeps alone. According to our theory, these two arrangements should be profoundly different in their effect on the infant's first or primary identification.

In the exclusive mother-infant case, the mother should be seen as all-powerful, all-important, and, insofar as she sometimes withholds resources, the person to be envied; and we predict the infant will covertly practice her role, and his optative identity will be female. In societies where the father sleeps with the mother, quite a different picture obtains with respect to valued resources. In this instance, both parents give and withhold important resources. Under these conditions, therefore, we assume the envied status to be that of a parent of either sex. For the infant, the juxtaposition of privilege is seen as between self and adult, rather than between self and female.

Thus the male infant in societies with exclusive mother-child sleeping arrangements should have a primary cross-sex optative identity, whereas the boy reared in societies in which the father sleeps with the mother should have a primary adult optative identity.

After a child is weaned and becomes what Margaret Mead calls a yard child, conditions may change drastically from those of infancy. Privilege may now be defined by marital residence. Three major patterns emerge in our samples of societies: patrilocal, matrilocal, and equilocal.

In societies with patrilocal residence, a man will remain throughout his life in or near the house in which he was born, his wife or wives moving in from another village. In such societies, the domestic unit consists of a group of males closely related by blood, and a group of inmarrying and interloping females. Prestige and power are clearly vested in this group of men, and adult males are the ones to be envied.

Societies with matrilocal residence are a mirror image of the patrilocal case. Here the daughters stay at home and their husbands are the interlopers. In such societies, by contrast with the patrilocal, women occupy the privileged and envied statuses.

Equilocal societies are more familiar to us. Here a young husband and wife set up a household of their own apart from the parents of either, as is generally the case in our own society; or they may choose between, or alternate between, living with the wife's parents and the husband's parents. In this instance, residence does not automatically give advantage to either men or women, and sex identity is thus not an important issue.

Thus residence patterns may provide the conditions for the envy of males or the envy of females; or sex-determined statuses may be relatively unprivileged. This distribution of resources in the domestic unit provides the conditions for what we would like to call secondary identification.

SOME PRIMARY AND SECONDARY OPTATIVE IDENTIFICATION COMBINATIONS

Although the two types of sleeping arrangements and three residence patterns yield six combinations of conditions for primary and secondary identification, we would like here to concentrate on only two of them in contrast to all others. These are, first, the societies which should produce the maximum conflict between primary and secondary optative sex identity: e.g., societies with both exclusive mother-infant sleeping arrangements, which should lead a boy initially to wish he were feminine, and patrilocal residence patterns, which should lead him subsequently and secondarily to want to be masculine. The other societies of interest to us are those which promote feminine identification, both initially and secondarily; that is, societies with both exclusive mother-child sleeping arrangements and matrilocal residence.

Having described our independent variables, let us now turn to the dependent variables which should be predicted by our theory from (*a*) maximum conflict in optative sex identity and (*b*) maximum feminine optative sex identity.

INITIATION HYPOTHESIS

In a previous study, male initiation rites at puberty were shown to be strongly associated with exclusive mother-child sleeping arrangements and a long post-partum sex taboo. Although cross-sex identification was mentioned in a footnote as a possible interpretation of these findings, the authors' major explanation was based on the assumption that these conditions exacerbated the Oedipal conflict, and that initiation rites were the symbolic expression of resolution of this conflict.

We now believe, and would like to present evidence, that the sex identity interpretation is the more valid and fruitful. We would like to present the cross-sex identity and initiation hypothesis explicitly as follows: In societies with maximum conflict in sex identity, e.g., where a boy initially sleeps exclusively with his mother and where the domestic unit is patrilocal and hence controlled by men, there will be initiation rites at puberty which function to resolve this conflict in identity.

This hypothesis suggests that the initiation rites serve psychologically to brainwash the primary feminine identity and to establish firmly the secondary male identity. The hazing, sleeplessness, tests of manhood, and painful genital operation, together with promise of high status—that of being a man if the tests are successfully passed—are indeed similar to the brainwashing techniques employed by the Communists. Indicating how traumatic these rites may be, one ethnographer reports that boys returning home after initiation did not know their village or recognize their parents.

Native theory also supports our interpretation. In most societies with elaborate initiation rites at puberty, there are two terms labeling one's sex identity which are different from the ones with which we are familiar. One term refers to all women and uninitiated boys, whereas the other refers to initiated males only. In these societies, according to native theory, a male is born twice: once into the woman-child status, and then at puberty he symbolically dies and is reborn into the status of manhood.

Let us now turn to our data. In our sample of 64 societies, there were 13 in which there were elaborate initiation ceremonies with genital operations. All 13 of these had the exclusive mother-infant sleeping arrangements which we predicted would cause a primary feminine identification. Furthermore, 12 of these 13 had patrilocal residence which we predicted would produce the maximum conflict in identity and hence the need for an institution to help resolve this conflict. A chi-square test of the association is fantastically beyond chance. Expressed simply, 87½ percent of the 64 societies fall in the cells predicted by our hypothesis.

But what of societies where the female status is seen as privileged both in infancy and in childhood, where the infant sleeps exclusively with his mother and in childhood moves into a world controlled by his mother, his aunts, and his tyrannical maternal grandmother? Here our theory would predict that a man would have a strong optative feminine identity, and the society should provide him some means to act out, symbolically at least, the female role.

From the beginnings of ethnographic reporting, a strange custom has been described for various societies over the world. This custom consists of the husband going to bed and undergoing all the same taboos as his wife during the time she is in labor. This custom is known as the *couvade* and has long been a favorite example for undergraduate texts in anthropology to exemplify the curious customs of primitive peoples. As a test of our hypothesis, however, the couvade is most apt. What event more than childbirth defines that part of a woman's role that is uniquely feminine? It seems to us, at least, that when a man attempts to participate in the birth of his child by closely imitating the behavior of his wife, this should be a good index of his wish to act out the feminine role and thus symbolically to be in part a woman.

Our hypothesis is again strongly confirmed by the data. Of the 12 societies with couvade in our sample, 10 had exclusive mother-child sleeping arrangements and 9 had matrilocal residence. Again, the results are highly significant statistically. In this instance, 90 per cent of the cases fall in the predicted cells.

FRANK W. YOUNG

The Function of Male Initiation Ceremonies: A Cross-Cultural Test of an Alternative Hypothesis

We present this article in complete form, including the "Comment" by Whiting, followed by the "Rejoinder" by Young.

Taking into consideration both of the Whiting *et al.* hypotheses (that based upon the Oedipal conflict and that based upon sex-role conflict), presented in the previous article, Young now presents an alternative theory based upon the need for male solidarity in a social system characterized by polygynous family organization. He argues that the function of the male initiation ceremonies is to dramatize the sex-role characteristics of societies with a high degree of male solidarity; and he proceeds to find a strong association between male initiation ceremonies and family organization.

The student is urged to study the controversy and judge for himself, but the editors would like to add a few thoughts for the future of this type of approach. It is clear that we need more comparative studies, since only by some such type of cross-cultural approach are we going to reach valid conclusions concerning the function of religious beliefs and practices in *Homo sapiens* generally. We predict there will be further refinements in method and theory that will ultimately permit competent anthropologists to come to a consensus. In the meantime, there is likely to be much more controversy since not only are anthropologists, such as Whiting and Young, trying out quite different hypotheses based upon different theoretical assumptions, but too often the basic ethnographic data on which all such studies must be based are simply inadequate for the questions that are being asked.

Hand in hand with further cross-cultural studies, we think there must also be a major thrust in the direction of providing much more adequate and precise ethnographic data and analysis using methods of the types suggested in our sample of papers in this chapter on the analysis of elements of religion in single cultures.

Reprinted from *The American Journal of Sociology*, LXVII (1962), 379–396, by permission of the authors and the University of Chicago.

Many "culture and personality" studies depend on theories which characterize personality as a system of intervening variables or mechanisms by which one aspect of culture—usually child-training practices—influences another aspect such as religious beliefs or particular institutions. Although this view has been criticized and contradictory evidence on some points has been published, it has been difficult to put the theory to a decisive test because so much of its support is in the form of clinical or anthropological evidence that cannot be replicated. There is need for a test which differentiates between a Freudian hypothesis and an alternative, and which, in turn, rejects one but not the other under conditions that are rigidly controlled.

The opportunity for such a test is provided by the appearance of a study by John W. M. Whiting, Richard Kluckhohn, and Albert Anthony in which they test on a sample of fifty-six societies a hypothesis that links certain childhood situations to the presence of male initiation rites. They assert that when the infant sleeps on its mother's bed for a year or more, strong feelings of dependency develop. Similarly, if there is a postnatal taboo of a year or more on the mother's sex relations, when the husband finally returns to his wife the displacement of the dependent boy from his mother's close care generates deep hostility. Both these emotions may become disruptive to society when the boy matures. Adolescence is a particularly dangerous period because at that age the boy is called upon to participate in men's work, independent of his mother's support. At this age he also handles weapons. Since all societies must maintain social control of disruptive behavior, an institutional mechanism of control is functionally necessary. The initiation ceremonies of primitive peoples may be so interpreted as such a mechanism. Hazing and genital operations assert the authority of men over the adolescent boy; the separation of boys from women and submission to tests of fortitude breaks the boys' psychological dependency. A demonstrable association exists between the four initiation customs and the two child-training practices.

It is clear that the foregoing "disruptive emotion" hypothesis follows the classic Freudian framework of impulsive man assailed by a frustrating culture. Although Whiting *et al.* reject a specific Oedipal explanation, their modification is still in the Freudian tradition, and the many general criticisms that have been made of that framework still apply. For instance, it is assumed that the emotions generated in childhood somehow maintain themselves until adolescence, despite the great variety of experience between the two periods. It is further assumed that the two- or three-year-old boy is capable of the complex emotions and preceptions that are postulated by the theory; that is, when the father returns the displaced boy is able to infer that the father is to blame, even though it was the mother who allowed the father to return. Third, it is assumed that initiation ceremonies are primarily inhibitory and that this function is almost completely determined by the peculiar patterning of two small aspects of family organization.

Before introducing an alternative explanation based on symbolic interaction theory, it should be acknowledged that Whiting has already abandoned the disruptive emotion hypothesis (a shift that became known to the author after the termination of the study reported here) and has substituted what may be called a "sex-role conflict" hypothesis. The latter explanation of the empirical association between initiation ceremonies and child care employs some concept of identifi-

cation, namely: "the process of identification consists of the covert practice of the role of an envied status. In learning-theory terms, identification consists (*a*) of learning a role by rehearsal in fantasy or in play rather than by actual performances, and (*b*) such rehearsal is motivated by envy of the incumbent of a privileged status." The initiation ceremony is now interpreted as an institution which resolves a cross-sex identification. The child having a close sleeping relation with his mother (the postnatal taboo is disregarded in the second interpretation) comes to envy her status, which in turn leads to a feminine identification. If he lives in a society where the rule of residence is patrilocal, however, at five or six years of age he perceives that men have the enviable status, which leads him to a male identification. The resulting conflict must be resolved with the help of a social institution.

In view of the second hypothesis, criticism and empirical rejection of the disruptive emotion explanation is more pertinent rather than less so, since the second hypothesis is basically like the first. For example, despite the term identification, the sex-role conflict hypothesis involves the same assumptions regarding childhood emotions and the competence of the child to make complex interpretations. Thus, Whiting argues that when the boy sleeps with the mother he comes to identify with her as a result of his recognition that her status is different from his and that hers is enviable, while if the parents sleep together, the boy identifies with them both to about the same degree. But is not the opposite interpretation equally plausible? If a child thinks at all, is it not more likely that he would be satisfied when he has his mother all to himself and would feel relatively deprived when he must share her with the father? Would he not therefore identify with her when the father is present? Similarly, the interpretation of patrilocal residence is dubious. Even granted that in patrilocal societies men have higher status, it does not follow that such status is any more readily perceived than in matrilocal societies. At any rate, the best study available indicates that males play the instrumental role in all societies, regardless of rule of residence. At least, then, the child must discriminate between the instrumental role of the men and their prestige. Finally, the sex-role conflict hypothesis still assumes that initiation ceremonies are inhibiting—at least Whiting implies this when he uses the term "brainwash" to characterize their function—although now the ceremony also functions to reinforce the boy's male identification, presumably as a result of the hazing and genital operations, which prompt the youth to envy the status of his tormentors.

The present study uses the cross-cultural methodology employed in the Whiting research, and whenever possible uses his coding of items, although this coding, since it is derived from another theoretical framework, tends to work against the test. The same sample is used with the exception of the Khalapur Rajputs and the Druze, inasmuch as these are a caste and a religious group respectively and do not qualify as communities, the basic unit of the present analysis.

AN ALTERNATIVE FORMULATION

According to the symbolic interaction explanation, the function of initiation is to stabilize the boy's sex role at a time when it is particularly problematical, although not in the manner suggested by Whiting. Thus, one's sex role becomes problematical insofar as its definition does not provide sufficient guidance in the diverse social interactions allowed or prescribed by society. Inasmuch as societies have a sexual division of labor and some form of marriage, a well-defined sex role becomes functionally necessary when the boy nears the threshold of participation in such social patterning. However, some societies pose still another socialization problem which is that sex role must conform to more specific requirements imposed by a high degree of male solidarity. Such solidarity may be defined as the co-operation of the men in maintaining a definition of their situation as one which is not only different from that of women, but which involves organized activities requiring the loyalty of all males. Although solidarity is a matter of degree, a crucial threshold develops when the men of a village come to see themselves as a consciously organized group with the power to exclude or discipline its membership. Inasmuch as explanation of the development of male solidarity is outside the scope of this paper, it is sufficient to say that it appears to be an ecological problem in the sense that the physical and social environment determines the degree of cohesion: The environment must permit a simple and stable definition of the situation. Solidarity would not be expected among Eskimo men where the food supply is so meager and diverse that males rarely act in concert. At the other extreme, modern societies have such complex environments that an indifferentiated interpretation is rarely possible. Rather, male solidarity should occur in the "middle-level" societies where the variety of food exploitation patterns is limited and where the resources may be exploited by co-operative groups. Moreover, it is among such societies that intergroup hostilities conducive to male solidarity are possible. In nomadic communities hostility tends to be individualized while in complex societies armies are made up of men from diverse communities. Only in relatively stable, autonomous communities would combat groups include all the males of the village and only those. Of course, as male cohesion develops it is likely that the "approved" interpretation of the environment becomes oversimplified, and if a notion like "all whites are our enemies" develops, then the phenomenal environment may operate to further consolidate the group.

In societies with a high degree of male solidarity, stabilization of sex role is not complete until the boy identifies with the male group, since such identification is a major component of the sex role. Identification is here defined as the process of taking as one's own the cluster of social meanings held by a person or group. Identification requires first that the identifier have sufficient skill in symbolic interaction (usually not acquired until early adolescence) to comprehend the symbolic environment and, second, that he recognize that his society requires him to learn certain specific clusters of social meanings, such as those involved in one's sex role. Strength of identification is determined by the degree to which the identifier co-operates in creating and maintaining the definition of the situation and by the degree of clarity given the social meanings by the group or person generating them.

Given the foregoing assumptions, it might appear that identification with a solidary male group is easy compared to learning the relatively vague attitudes required for participation in work and the family and hence that initiation ceremonies should be unnecessary for the more organized male structure. But the relative clarity of meanings held by the cohesive males is not apparent to the candidate. Typically, the male activities are hidden from the uninitiated. Moreover, once the meanings of the male group are accessible, internalization must be achieved rapidly and precisely. There is no long period of inculcation by way of games, sharing in sex-segregated work, or the differentiated expectations of others. Neither is there the allowable deviation that occurs in most family and work organization. Therefore, the social meaning of male solidarity must be dramatized in a memorable way and the candidate must participate intensely in the presentation. Futhermore, the rest of the community must be alerted to his new status so they can respond appropriately. What could be more impressive to both the youth and the community than to be publicly subincised or to be the center of attention of a group of village men intent upon beating him severely? It is a mistake to interpret initiation ceremonies in terms of culture-bound notions of pain or mutilation. The ethnographic accounts strongly suggest that, given the proper attitude, these are probably accepted with the same equanimity that a woman

The solidarity hypothesis may be empirically tested by cross-tabulation of the child-training items and initiation ceremonies when male solidarity is controlled. Although this hypothesis ultimately requires a recoding of both the child-training items and Whiting's empirical definition of initiation rites, they are adequate for the present test. The only new factor, then, is male solidarity. Empirically it is defined by the presence of an organization in which all adult males are expected to participate and from which women are excluded. The organization must be institutionalized to the point of having its own building or a taboo that protects open meetings from the perception of women or uninitiated boys. The definition includes the cases of the Hopi and Dahomeans where there are a number of male organizations of essentially the same type. It is assumed that such reduplication occurs in larger communities simply as an adaptation to the larger population. When the organizations develop differentiated purposes, they do not qualify.

The cross-tabulation of these three factors is shown in Table 1 and follows the format

TABLE 1. Relation of Male Initiation Ceremonies to Exclusive Mother-Son Sleeping Arrangement and Postnatal Taboo When Presence of Exclusive Male Organization Is Controlled

Exclusive Male Organization	Mother-Son Sleeping	Postnatal Taboo	No. of Societies Having at Least One of Four Initiation Customs[a]	
			Present	Absent
Present	+	+	11	1
	+	−	1	1
	−	+	2	0
	−	−	2	0
			16	2
Absent	+	+	3	4
	+	−	0	2
	−	+	1	4
	−	−	0	22
			4	32

[a] Genital operations, hazing, seclusion from women, and tests of manliness.

submits to beauty care or a man to being tatooed. Similarly, tests of fortitude and social separation (the ethnographic accounts give no basis for Whiting's phrase "separation from women") are another way of dramatizing the boy's new status. Not only does he give a performance to the community, but his separation before or after the performance reminds the community by his absence of his new presence.

of the Whiting *et al.* article. It is clear that when male solidarity is controlled, no relation remains between the typology of child-care items and the presence of initiation ceremonies. The relative efficiency of prediction of the disruptive emotion and solidarity hypothesis is .45 and .70 respectively, as measured by Goodman and Kruskal's lambda and giving Whiting *et al.* the benefit of the doubt on the predictions of the positive-negative combinations of child-care items, even though they made no prediction about these. Essentially the same cross-tabulation applies to the sex-role conflict hypothesis, except that the postnatal taboo is dropped out and the presence of patrilocal residence (as against matrilocal and a general category labeled ambilocal) is substituted. The efficiency of the prediction based on these factors is only .40 compared, as before, to .70 for the more parsimonious solidarity variable. Unfortunately a cross-tabulation of these variables with male solidarity controlled is not feasible due to the paucity of cases.

Among a number of possible objections to these results, one demands immediate analysis: Is the relation between male solidarity and initiation ceremonies tautological? As usual, answers may be given at different levels of abstraction. If the question refers to the concrete level of indicators, then the answer is certainly negative. If the only index of male solidarity was the presence of a specific male organization, one might object that the initiation ceremony is merely an aspect of the organization's activities. But as defined here, male solidarity is more than a specific organization and is indicated in other ways, such as group hunting, organization for local warfare, etc. Moreover, many initiation ceremonies have no apparent relation to the activities of the male organization, and even if they did, it still does not follow that the *degree* of dramatization (the dependent variable) is an integral part of the organization's activities. If, however, the question refers to the conceptual level, there is room for doubt. Of course, there is nothing in either of the two concepts—male definition of the group situation and dramatization of status—that necessarily implies the other, but it might be argued that at a high level of abstraction initiation ceremonies are simply another way of talking about the boundary-maintaining activities of a given, although abstractly conceived, group. Whether this is so or not requires a much deeper theoretical and empirical probing, but the important implication remains unchallenged. If initiation ceremonies and group solidarity are simply different aspects of the same social structure, then it is even more doubtful that an explanation of these in terms of the events of childhood is sufficient. Certainly the basic features of social structure are not determined by events that are consequences of that very structure. Rather, an ecological explanation, such as has been suggested, would appear more plausible.

A RECONCEPTUALIZATION OF INITIATION CEREMONIES

The cross-tabulation in Table 1 shows that when male solidarity is controlled, the association between the child-care items and initiation ceremonies is dissolved. But the indicators of the initial association were based on the rejected hypothesis. It remains now to reconceptualize both of these in terms of the new framework and to show that male solidarity is an even stronger determinant when these variables are recoded.

The solidarity hypothesis would define initiation ceremonies as the more dramatic forms of sex-role recognition. So conceived, initiation ceremonies involve a patterned performance designed to convey a particular impression to an audience. Such dramatization of sex role takes a variety of forms, combining particular customs like tatooing, tooth filing, beatings, fasting, special taboos, social isolation, gifts, dances, participation in raids, circumcision, subincision, etc., in ways that have always attracted the attention of anthropologists. Examples of undramatic sex-role recognition are the informal delineation that results from differentiated subsistence activities among Koryak men and women, the adolescent boy's shift of residence to a youth camp among the Nyakyusa, and the formalized—but undramatic—coeducation in our own society. However, not all customs of the adolescent period are relevant to the social recognition of sex role, and the following rules delineate the limits: (*a*) the custom must occur periodically in the same general form and be supervised at least in part by the adults of the society, (*b*) it must apply to all adolescent males and only to these—ceremonies including females do not qualify, and (*c*) of a series of initiation ceremonies, only the most elaborate, as measured by the scale, is to be coded. Such rules would exclude the tooth filing among children in Alor, the festivities surrounding the young men in wartime Japan who went into the military, the unpatterned hazing of Maori warrior novices, and the marriage-initiation pattern of the Khalapur Rajputs (although they were excluded on other grounds). One major implication of these operational rules is the rejection of the view that initiation marks the attainment of full adult status. There is of course an intimate connection between sex role and responsible adulthood, and in a few societies the recognition of the two statuses merges. But in the large majority, consensual validation of responsible adult status is withheld by prohibitions on marriage, speaking in councils, full participation in warfare, etc., until late adolescence.

These criteria defined a large pool of items, some of which formed a Guttman scale (Table 2). Step 1 of the scale includes

However, at least two relationships between the scale and other data reinforce its interpretation as an undimensional measure. First, essentially the same scale applies to females, and holds for the thirty-four societies of this sample that have dramatic initiation ceremonies for that sex. Second, an elaborate dramatization is most likely to occur when there are a number of initiates, rather than just one, a fact which would also support the present interpretation.

However, a more important consideration is the theoretical plausibility of the scale. The three basic steps appear to reflect an increasing amount of social preparation. The

TABLE 2.   Scale of Degrees of Dramatization of Male Initiation Ceremonies

Step	Item	Per Cent of Societies	Scale Error
1	Customary minimal social recognition (gift, party, change of name, etc.)	100	0
2	Social seclusion (physical and/or social separation such as initiation camp, isolation or taboo on social contact)	75	0
3	Personal dramatization (initiate is ceremonially dressed and/or gives public performance)	55	2
4	Organized social response (group dresses ceremonially and/or performs)	35	1
5	Emotionalized social response (beating or severe hazing)	30	0
	Total cases	(20)	

all the minimal recognition customs, such as gift-giving, a change of name, festive attention, etc., that are periodically maintained with the help of adults. Such public recognition usually lasts less than a day and involves a group no larger than the immediate family. The second and third steps may be taken together to reflect individualized dramatization of the initiate. Social seclusion and decoration and/or performance call attention to the personality of the youth. The last two items also combine to form a general category of "group participation," with the fifth step reflecting an emotionally charged group response. It is significant that items like circumcision, subincision, etc., did not scale, probably because the coding was not sensitive to their precise dramatic context, which is the basis of the scale. Circumcision in itself, as our own society demonstrates, is not necessarily dramatic. Needless to say, none of the scale items occurs in societies with undramatic sex role recognition.

Although the scale has a high coefficient of reproducibility (.97), the small number of cases and the fact that some of the steps contain only one or two societies detracts from its internally demonstrated validity.

easiest thing the adults can do is make a simple gesture, such as a gift. If they wish to call more attention to the boy, but still keep the effort small, they can separate him socially. Further elaboration can be achieved by dramatizing the initiate's person, or by organizing the whole group. Only in the more elaborate forms is there a strong emotional display.

The scale takes on special significance in view of Whiting's interpretation of initiation as "brainwashing." It is difficult to see how these items would support such an interpretation, as indeed, it is difficult to see how the four items chosen by Whiting *et al.* (especially when only *one* of the four need be present) qualify as a social mechanism for resolving a sex-role conflict. It must be admitted, however, that there is an almost total overlap between the presence of initiation ceremonies as coded by Whiting *et al.* and as indicated by the scale. In fact, nineteen of the twenty cases are identical. The scale rejects one society (Chiracahua) which Whiting *et al.* coded as having initiations and adds another (Yap) which they excluded. Such correspondence is reasonable, nonetheless, since all the four items used by Whiting *et al.* are ways of dramatizing sex role. The crucial point is that the four-item index excludes a host of customs that anthropologists and the scale would include.

If the scale of dramatic sex-role recognition is substituted for the four-item index in Table 1, and is used simply to indicate the presence or absence of dramatic customs, there is an increase in the measure of prediction efficiency of the solidarity hypothesis, bringing it to .80 in comparison with .45 for

another side. From the adult point of view an exclusive sleeping arrangement is simply another way of saying that the father is absent. While it is true that the mother need not keep the child on her own mat when the father is away, the two situations are usually the same in practice and it is doubtful whether it would be possible to code the distinction, given present data, even if it existed. Perhaps then, the real question is why the father is absent. The mere fact of polygyny is almost a sufficient explanation.

TABLE 3. Relation of Father's Separation from Nursing Wife to Extent of Polygyny and Presence of Exclusive Male Organization

Extent of Polygyny	Father Typically Separated from Nursing Wife	
	Yes	No
Exclusive male organization present:		
Polygyny, 20 per cent or more	7	1
Limited polygyny, under 20 per cent	3	1
Monogamy	2	4
Total	12	6
Exclusive male organization absent:		
Polygyny, 20 per cent or more	5	8
Limited polygyny, under 20 per cent	1	8
Monogamy	1	13
Total	7	29

the disruptive-emotion hypothesis, where there is no change. The next step is to relate degrees of solidarity to degrees of dramatization, but because of the small number of cases in the present sample, only a trend shows up.

MALE SOLIDARITY AND FAMILY ORGANIZATION

In addition to replacing the interpretation of initiation ceremonies required by the two Freudian hypotheses, the solidarity hypothesis calls for a reinterpretation of the childhood experience items. It has already been shown that the two aspects of what may now be labeled "absent-father family organization" have no empirical relation to initiation ceremonies when male solidarity is controlled. Why, then, was there even a correlation to begin with? It is important, first, to examine the actual data. An "exclusive mother-infant sleeping arrangement" means that the mother keeps the child on her own mat for at least a year and usually until the child is weaned. Often the mother lives in a special hut, a pattern that is frequent when there is polygyny. But these same facts have

Although it is conceivable that a husband might continue to sleep with a wife who is nursing an infant, considerations of sleeping convenience are enough to explain why he stays with other wives. But even in those cases where the husband has no other wives he may not stay with his new family, but go instead to the men's house where life is probably more exciting and at least quieter. And what of the postnatal taboo? It also makes sense in this context as a norm for controlling the frequency of pregnancy, since polygynous wives typically maintain separate households and gardens, and must be free to work. This interpretation is tested in Table 3 by a cross-tabulation of the relation of the father to a nursing wife with the presence of an exclusive male organization and the extent of polygyny. The absent-father family pattern was empirically defined by the combination of both the exclusive mother-son sleeping arrangement and the postnatal taboo, since to rely on only one of these items would admit too many cases where the family type was undeveloped. The distribution of the cases (lambda is .42) indicates that when general polygyny and a male organization are both present, the absent-father family pattern is likely to occur. It is still relatively frequent if only general polygyny exists. In the two cases where a male organization is present but there is no polygyny, we should expect the presence of a men's house where the husband can stay. In fact they (the Yapese and Fijians) do have such houses. Similarly, the society (Ooldea) that does not have the absent-father family pattern despite the presence of a male organization ought not to have a men's house, as indeed is the case. However, this sort of refinement in terms of sleeping quarters may not be carried too far. In some societies, the men sleep apart from their wives despite the lack of men's house while in other societies they do not make use of the clubhouse in this manner. Also, such refinement unduly reduces the already small number of cases.

The foregoing discussion has been extended more than might ordinarily be necessary because it is important to show how faulty operationalization leads to false conclusions. These customs of household organization apply only to adults. Any inference from them to the personality of the child is just that. Admittedly it is difficult to index infant behavior directly, but there are descriptions of boy's play, attitudes, etc., which might serve better. The burden of proof is at least on those who see such a connection. Indeed, it should have been there at the outset. To assume that childhood experiences index personality tendencies is tantamount to defining as true the crucial link in the theory.

The only problem remaining is why polygyny should be associated with male solidarity. Although various hypotheses might be offered, the simplest one is that it takes the work of many women to support the activities of solidary males.

SOME BASIC ISSUES

There are many loose ends to this study, such as the relation of female initiation to female solidarity, the relation of solidarity to the division of social labor and to more particular ecological factors, the prediction of degrees of dramatization, and the relation of other customs, such as the couvade, to types of household organization. Preliminary findings on all of these factors appear to support the solidarity hypothesis and will be published elsewhere. Enough has been said, however, to permit an analysis of some basic issues.

In the image of man and society that stands behind the two Freudian hypotheses, personality is conceptualized as "mediating" between "maintenance systems" and "projective systems." An example given by Whiting illustrates the paradigm: In societies with extended family households, in contrast to mother-child households, mothers tend to indulge infants. Such high indulgence is in turn associated with the belief that human beings can influence the gods. In this example, the organization of the household is part of the maintenance system. The kind of personality found in different household organizations is said to be reflected in the amount of maternal indulgence, and since this indicator is associated with attributes of the gods, it is asserted that personality interacts with the projective system. Initiation ceremonies can be similarly fitted into this paradigm: polygyny is part of the maintenance system and, as Table 3 shows, is associated with an exclusive mother-child sleeping arrangement. The feminine identification alleged to result from this infant experience is a variable of personality which interacts with other variables, particularly male identification. Initiation ceremonies, interpreted as part of the projective system, help to resolve the resultant personality conflict. If childhood training is interpreted as predisposing the child to accept a certain social order, the cases are analogous, although the meaning of "projective" thereby becomes ambiguous. However, the basic point is clear: Whiting's particular hypothesis concerning initiation ceremonies, whether in its first or second form, is to be taken as only one instance of a general paradigm, as a specific derivation from a general theory. Now, if we could be sure that his explanation of initiation ceremonies was a rigorous deduction from this theory, then a negative test of the hypothesis would invalidate the parent structure. But such precision may not be assumed at the present stage of the social sciences, so it is necessary to examine directly, if only theoretically, the basic conceptualization. It may be criticized on several fundamental counts.

In the Whiting model, the direction of causation moves from the subsistence institutions to the personality of the child and thence to the wider social order. Although the possibility is admitted that some sequences by-pass the childhood events, they are exceptions to the rule. Such a framework poses at the outset complex methodological problems. An adequate test of any derived hypothesis should follow the causal sequence from the events in the economy of one generation to the interaction of the next generation with the prevailing ideology. An experiment lasting some twenty years or more is indicated, and it is difficult to believe that adequate controls could be instituted during this period.

But a more substantive question bears on the assumption that social determinants can be generated or transmitted through the mechanisms of childhood personality. For a hundred years or more social scientists have agreed that society exists in and through communication, and it was tacitly assumed that this was adult communication. There were good reasons for this assumption that children do not fully participate in society, that is, in the symbolic environment of a group of people making a living in a particular locality. Since children are not physically able to participate in adult work, they are excluded from full involvement in the symbolic environment. Such participation, there is good reason to believe, is a precondition to adequate comprehension of social meanings. Phrasing this criticism another way, can any modern conception of society disregard the vast accumulation of evidence and theory regarding social control, institutionalization, leadership, and all the other processes that adults appear to maintain? The situation is analogous to that pointed out by Hume in discussing whether we should except the truth of miracles. If such a belief requires the rejection of a larger body of scientific generalization, we are well advised to disbelieve.

But even if the Whiting model granted that "babies don't make culture," as Ellsworth Faris once said, it would still be inadequate. For it appears that the scheme postulates an essentially wordless communication. In both hypotheses, the child assimilates a crucial meaning of his experience quite early in life, certainly before his language skill is fully developed. In the discussion of how the four customs of the initiation ceremony operate, it is implied that the experience of isolation, tests of fortitude, etc., convey particular meanings. Again, in the sex-role conflict hypothesis the boy learns by exposure to genital operations and hazing that identification with males is preferable to identification with females. Phrased generally, the individual is placed in a behavioral situation, and "he gets the message."

Maintaining the position that meaning is conveyed without words is at least awkward. How then does the boy maintain his male identification after his initiation when there is no high-status group to envy? To say that the youth is always inferior to someone invalidates the particular choice of patrilocal residence and the mother-son sleeping arrangement as determinants. Whiting might invoke secondary reinforcement—a wordless variety—but such reinforcement can only account for the narrowest conception of identification. For if male role means anything it means participating in the legal, religious, military, and kinship structures—all of which involve words and consensus—in ways that are different from the activity of females. Sex, dominance, or aggression may or may not be part of the male role, but participation in certain social sectors in prescribed ways always is. At the very least, the empirical association between male solidarity and initiation would appear to imply words and demand an explanation in terms of them.

It appears, then, that Whiting's conception of cultural and personality integration can do without words only if a narrow concept of identification is employed. But it is questionable whether the social sciences can do without a broad, social definition of male identification. How are we to explain the modal shifts in behavior as a person changes roles even when the situation remains the same? How are we to deal with the identical responses made to different stimulus situations? Words seem quite necessary as carriers of the complex and flexible cluster of meanings that appear to be involved in the male role.

However, it is very likely that Whiting would agree that the conventional symbolism of language is necessary for the flexible behavior characteristic of the socialized adult. Secondary reinforcement might be invoked to connect the behavioral situations with the associated words. Perhaps the contrary implication in his empirical research is simply an operational problem, to be remedied by better data. But if this is so, major theoretical problems remain. Concepts like status envy and identification must be broadened to include social meanings and the theory must explain how these meanings are learned. In the present case, initiation ceremonies may not be labeled "brainwashing" and described with no reference to the manipulation and dramatization of ideas that is part of the meaning of that term.

There is another characteristic of Whiting's conception of meaning that may be noted. The model places great emphasis on the isomorphism of the behavioral situation and the meaning that it conveys. Thus, infants that are indulged by their mothers come to believe that the gods will indulge them too. When a boy is displaced from his mother's bed by his father, he believes he is being deprived (rather than favored by both). When, during initiation, a boy is socially isolated, he comprehends that he must give up his dependence on women, and when he is circumcised he is confirmed in his male status through an experience impossible for women. Of course, not all the ascribed meanings reflect this congruency, but there is a strong trend in this direction, reminiscent of early Freudian dream interpretation. However, this implicit assumption is untenable if for no other reason than the lack of enough isomorphisms in the world to account for social behavior. Even if there were, it would require great methodological sophistication to find the connections. For instance, does a digging stick convey the idea of a man or a woman? Admittedly the assumption of isomorphism between situation and meaning is not crucial to the theory, but it does tell us something about Whiting's disinterest in purely conventional symbolism.

A third line of criticism questions whether any theory that explains social facts in terms of parallel individual experiences can adequately account for the uniformities of group behavior. This question, posed long ago by Durkheim, has never been satisfactorily answered by advocates of person-specific theories. In the present case, for instance, it is agreed that all societies that initiate boys do so uniformly. The exceptions are few and clearly deviant. Now, in terms of the sex-role conflict hypothesis each boy sleeps near his mother, comes to identify with her, and later, if he lives in a patrilocal society, comes to envy the status of the men and to identify

with them. But do all boys follow this sequence? It has already been shown that the exclusive mother-child sleeping arrangement is a concomitant of polygyny. But even in polygynous societies not all men have multiple wives and some of the monogamous men very likely sleep at home with their nursing wives. Of what use is initiation to these boys? It does no good to claim that the norm of polygyny exerts a general influence, because the hypothesis requires that each boy experience a close relationship with his mother. Neither is it sufficient to say that some boys have no conflict but go along with initiation anyway, because such a loophole vitiates the hypothesis and undermines the whole task of explanation.

Actually, this criticism of person-specific theories has been implicit in a methodological complaint often lodged against cross-cultural research. It has been argued that a social norm is not an adequate index of individual behavior. There is not assurance that individual behavior is uniform, and the very notion of a norm implies that it will not be. But this stricture had little force as long as investigators obtained correlations between two or more social norms and made a plausible explanation of how individual behavior might operate. On the other hand, the criticism has great force when it is stated, not as an operational problem, but as a fundamental deficiency of a whole class of theory. Regardless of correlations, person-specific theories cannot explain uniformities of behavior like participation in initiation ceremonies.

What then is the alternative conceptual framework? First, it is that symbolic interactionism is still in its early stages of development and requires much more elaboration. But such a conceptual framework would assert that society is a complex of groups within groups—even the smallest primitive community is differentiated—and that each of these subgroups tends to maintain its organization intact in the context of the whole and vis-à-vis the other subgroups. The individual members co-operate to maintain a given definition of the group situation and to communicate it successfully, often by dramatization, to the other groups, which constitute audiences. This interplay always appeals to overriding principles of the social order since few subgroups can afford the destruction of the larger structure. Over and above this organized conversation is the grammar of language itself. This combined structural backbone helps to maintain the contingencies in vocabulary that carry clusters of social meaning.

The relations of the individual to these symbolic structures is one of varying modes and degrees of participation, and the organization of roles acquired in the course of such participation is the basis of personality. Although personality may be said to affect social structure indirectly through individually promulgated social innovation, to say that model personality has an independent effect on the shared system of beliefs makes no sense in these terms. Personality is linked to culture not as a mediator and converter of signals in the manner of a television relay station, but as a special and intense organization of a field of symbols. The degree and mode of each individual's participation in society determine "how much" personality he will have and whether he will reorganize his portion of the symbolic environment in a way that might later affect the whole.

In the picture of society suggested above there is little that is new. The novely lies in the application of this conceptual framework to the phenomena of initiation. Male solidarity has already been defined as the consensus of the men regarding the purpose and activities of the group. Although the present study does not directly index these shared meanings, the ethnographic accounts strongly suggest that definite religious, military, and fraternal attitudes exist and are expressed in the ritual activity, regalia, and mythology. These meanings must be maintained by adults inasmuch as, quite aside from the taboos barring the uninitiated, children cannot comprehend these meanings fully until after early adolescence. Granted that games, observation, and conversation serve as an introduction to adult symbolic structures, the inculcation of these is weak and partial. Certainly this line of thought would reject the unconscious learning asserted by the Freudians to occur during the first several years of life.

Initiation ceremonies are viewed as a mechanism for maintaining the consensus of the males. If the boys did not undergo initiation or if some were allowed to avoid it, the male definition of the situation might be distorted or weakened. It is for this reason that initiation is required of all boys in a community. The ceremony insures conformity by involving the candidate in an intense cooperation with men in the symbolic process. Initiation is the first and perhaps most memorable step in a continued participation in an organized symbolic structure. So long as a man participates in it, the social meanings he has internalized remain strong and he plays his sex role with confidence in diverse situations. The rituals themselves only remind him of what it means to be a man in his society; in themselves they contain no meaning. On this view circumcision is not different in kind from a gift, a new name, a dance, etc. It differs in degree only insofar as its acquisition has a more dramatic and emotional context. Thus, almost anything can figure in the initiation ceremony. The sound of a bull roarer or some test of endurance have an intrinsic dramatic quality. Lacking such, the effect may be heightened by hiring a specialist to direct the ceremony or by encouraging the women to wail.

An initial implication of this conception of initiation ceremonies is that empirical work on ritual must allow for the wide variety of symbolic contents; it may not be limited to particular customs. More generally, it suggests that other rituals might profitably be viewed in terms of a dramaturgical framework. The essence of this approach, it should be noted, is the analysis of the function of rituals for groups, not individuals.

COMMENT

JOHN W. M. WHITING

Frank W. Young is to be commended for giving us a new understanding of the function of male initiation rites at puberty. He has convincingly demonstrated the strong relationship between such rites and the presence of exclusive male organizations in a society. Furthermore, his interpretation that the function of the rites is, in part at least, to dramatize and make explicit the male role in contrast to that of woman's, is quite plausible.

I also commend his attempt to challenge

previous interpretations. It is in this way, in my opinion, that science advances. I do not feel, however, that he has successfully refuted all culture and personality studies that have used events in childhood as indicators of personality.

With specific reference to the Whiting, Kluckhohn, and Anthony study, Mr. Young has quite properly attempted to discover the relative merits of his male solidarity hypothesis and what he has labeled the "disruptive emotions" hypothesis advanced by Whiting, Kluckhohn, and Anthony. He has done this by showing the effect of the predicting variable for each hypothesis with the other held constant. By this procedure he has shown that the relationship of male initiation to male solidarity is stronger than to either exclusive mother-son sleeping arrangements or the *post partum* sex taboo. This is well and good, but I think he has become a little overenthusiastic when he claims that if exclusive male organizations are held constant there is no relationship at all between the childhood factors and male initiation rites. If one looks at his Table 1, this statement is true only when exclusive male organizations are present. Where they are absent there is still a significant relation between the child-rearing variables and initiation rites.

More importantly, however, as far as the more general question of the validity of the culture and personality theory goes, Mr. Young has completely neglected to take into account the functional equivalents to both antecedent and consequent variables presented in the Whiting, Kluckhohn, and Anthony paper. These alternatives are: (1) that change of residence at adolescence is a functional equivalent to male initiation rites, and (2) that the absence of a father's authority over a child, as is the case in certain matrilocal societies, is the functional equivalent of exclusive sleeping arrangements and the *post partum* sex taboo. Since Mr. Young has not published the names of the tribes in his Table 1, it is impossible to conclude as to the relative merits of the "male solidarity" hypothesis or the "disruptive emotions" hypothesis as modified by the above assumptions. However, it seems evident that the most plausible interpretation is that both relationships are strong and valid.

As Mr. Young has indicated in his paper,

Whiting and his associates have abandoned the "disruptive emotions" hypothesis or at least drastically modified it. They now argue that insofar as male initiation rites are designed to curb disruptive emotions it is those emotions arising from a male youth's conflict as to his sex identity and his consequent need to prove himself a man by exhibiting aggressive and antisocial behavior. This interpretation was suggested as an alternative in the Whiting, Kluckhohn, and Anthony article. "If, however, the mother herself is perceived by the child as the one responsible for terminating the early intense relationship, this should lead the boy to both envy her and identify with her. This should produce conflict with respect to his sex role identity, which initiation rites would serve to resolve." The function of male initiation rites are seen as a cultural means of establishing and confirming male identity. The two hypotheses differ in specifying the conditions under which such confirmation is necessary. Mr. Young argues that the rites are necessary in societies which are characterized by a high degree of male solidarity. Mr. Young tentatively suggests that such a need should occur in middle-level societies, but his argument here is neither convincing nor supported by evidence. I would argue that both male solidarity and male initiation rites are a consequence of conflict in sex identity engendered in infancy and early childhood, and evidence in support of this is presented in two of the papers mentioned in Mr. Young's article and more extensively in a forthcoming monograph on cross-sex identity which includes both cross-cultural and cross-individual evidence. If one looks at Mr. Young's Table 1 with the view that both male solidarity and male initiation are consequences of conflict in sex identity, it will be seen that exclusive male organizations are nearly as strongly associated with mother-son sleeping arrangements and the postnatal sex taboo as they are to initiation rites.

Mr. Young has attempted to justify a reverse direction of causation by suggesting that exclusive male organizations cause polygyny which in turn causes the absence of the father and hence exclusive mother-son sleeping arrangements and the *post partum* sex taboo. He has presented data to support this in Table 3. The relation between polygyny and mother-infant relationships shown in the table is partly the consequence of scoring procedures. Societies where the polygynous wives sleep separately and the husband rotates between them have been coded as having exclusive mother-son sleeping arrangements since the father shares the bed no more than half the time and usually not at all if there is a *post partum* sex taboo. The relation between exclusive male organizations and polygyny, however, is not significantly significant; in fact it is virtually non-existent. It can be seen from Mr. Young's Table 3 that only eight of the twenty-one societies with 20 per cent polygyny have exclusive male organizations whereas nearly as many, six of twenty, monogamous societies have male organizations. Thus the reverse direction suggested by Mr. Young is not supported by empirical evidence but rather the culture and personality hypothesis shown in the diagram at the bottom of the page.

Mr. Young cannot accept this causal connection because he rejects the whole Freudian and culture and personality approach. This is, of course, his privilege. But the evidence in favor of this view is to me quite convincing, much more so than the oft-cited critiques of this approach by Sewell and Orlansky, Lindesmith, and Strauss, referred to by Mr. Young. Leaving aside recent clinical and psychological studies which have shown the effect of child-rearing upon personality, the many recent cross-cultural studies that have shown relations between child-rearing and other aspects of culture are too numerous to be convincingly refuted by Mr. Young's study. Many of these studies have been reviewed recently by the present author. They include, in addition to those referred to in Mr. Young's paper, Spiro and D'Andrade, Lambert, Triandis, and Wolf, Barry, Whiting and Child, Stephens, Friendly, Ayres, Whiting, and Whiting *et al.*

The difference in the basic assumptions between these so-called culture and personality studies and the standard sociological or functional anthropological studies has been hinted at by Mr. Young but, I think, should be made clear. What I would like to call somewhat unfairly "old-fashioned functionalism" assumed that culture serves the psychobiological needs of "natural man" and that such needs are universal and a part of human nature. In addition to these psychobiological needs rooted in the individual, there are structural needs or prerequisites which account for variations in other aspects of a culture but do not presume any fundamental psychological difference in the nature of the individual members of the society in question.

The basic assumptions of the culture and personality approach are quite different. Starting with a similar assumption as to the basic psychological needs of man they assume that there are other equally coercive or perhaps even more compelling needs that arise from early life experiences. Such needs may be a strong fear of failure and a need to achieve to compensate for it, an overpowering sense of guilt, a strong distrust of others, or in the present instance a conflict in one's sex identity.

If a reasonable majority of the members of a society are brought up in such a way as to have one or another of these conflicts, it is assumed by the proponents of the culture and personality approach that there will be institutions developed by the society to help its members resolve these conflicts either by protecting them from events which will evoke them or by re-education (initiation ceremonies) or by providing socially approved means of denying them or acting them out.

It is further assumed that these conflicts are usually unconscious, that is to say, that the members of the society are not aware of them and cannot put them into words. Furthermore, it is assumed that parents often have no intention of inducing such conflicts in their children and would avoid it if they knew what they were doing.

Clearly the issue between these two approaches cannot be resolved by a single study but I think that Mr. Young is to be strongly commended for bringing this issue to the fore so that it can be debated.

Polygyny → { Exclusive mother-son sleeping / *Post partum* sex taboo } → Exclusive male organizations / Initiation rites

REJOINDER

FRANK W. YOUNG

Since the central issues of this debate depend on the first and third tables in the article, I shall comment briefly on several important, but less crucial, points. First, I realize that even a successful rejection of this Freudian-derived hypothesis would only raise doubts about the rest of the theory and findings, but I did want to bring the larger framework into the debate in order that the character of these doubts might be examined. Second, I intended that my discussion of middle-level societies and warfare should indicate the direction that research can take. Actually my findings on these "ecological" determinants were not included inasmuch as they would have doubled the length of the paper. Third, I disregarded the functional equivalents that Professor Whiting mentions because most of the variance and his basic theory depend on the child-training items. I felt it was important in a paper of this sort to avoid too many bypaths, although in fact my other results do throw doubt on one of the functional equivalents—the change of residence at adolescence. Finally, I did not publish the coding for the variables because I intend to include the complete code and detailed identifications of the communities in a longer publication.

Whiting, in criticizing the data, feels that I am "a little overenthusiastic" in interpreting Table 1 as showing no relationship between the childhood factors and initiation when male organization is controlled. But Whiting himself admits that the association dissolves when male organization is present, and the lower part of the table should not offer much encouragement. I feel that lambda is a more appropriate statistic for these data than chi square, and in this case lambda is zero for both subtables. However, I confess that I, too, did not find the lower half of Table 1 entirely satisfactory. I was surprised to see even the three cases turn up in favor of Whiting's hypothesis. But now I am happy to report that I have found a way to get rid of even these.

Whiting makes a significant statement when he mentions (in discussing Table 3) that there is a built-in association between polygyny and mother-infant intimacy due to coding separate wives' quarters, a *post partum* taboo and a rotating husband as an exclusive mother-son arrangement. Given the inadequate data in the ethnographies, I can understand this decision, but it leads to difficulties. The fact is that if only direct evidence of exclusive mother-son sleeping arrangements is accepted, the three cases that favor the disruptive emotion hypothesis (lower half of Table 1) melt to one, and there is no significance even by chi square. As will become clear from the discussion below, the effect of coding the combination of rotating husband, separate wives' quarters and a *post partum* taboo as exclusive mother-son sleeping is to build in the male solidarity variable.

Recoding the exclusive mother-son sleeping pattern so as to exclude polygyny also has a marked effect on Table 3, a new version of which is presented in Table 4. Two important facts are evident. First, the absent-father family pattern—as I would prefer to call the combination of the two childhood items—tends to appear only when polygyny and male organization are both present. Second (and rearranging the table accordingly), male organization tends to appear only when both polygyny and the absent-father pattern are present. This enables us to conclude, contrary to the line of argument proposed in Whiting's diagram, that the "childhood factors" are not predictors of male organization, nor does polygyny alone adequately account for their presence. In summary, then, Table 4, together with the revision of Table 1, rejects all the predictions in the theoretical diagram. Rather, these relationships suggest that male solidarity leads to initiation rites, that solidarity combined with polygyny leads to the absent-father family pattern, and that there is no association between such a pattern and initiation ceremonies. Thus:

$$\text{Interaction of}\left\{\begin{array}{l}\text{Male organization}\\\text{Polygyny}\end{array}\right.\begin{array}{l}\longrightarrow\text{Male initiation}\\\\\left.\right\}\text{Absent-father family pattern}\end{array}$$

TABLE 4.[a] Relation of Father's Separation from Nursing Wife to Extent of Polygyny and Presence of Exclusive Male Organization[b]

Extent of Polygyny	Father Typically Separated from Nursing Wife	
	Yes	No
Exclusive male organization present:		
Polygyny, 20 per cent or more	5	2
Limited polygyny, under 20 per cent	3	1
Monogamy	1	5
Total	9	8
Exclusive male organization absent:		
Polygyny, 20 per cent or more	2	8
Limited polygyny, under 20 per cent	2	8
Monogamy	0	14
Total	4	30

[a] Same as Table 3 except that coding of exclusive mother-son sleeping arrangement, which in combination with a *post partum* taboo indexes the separation pattern, excludes the presence of polygyny.
[b] $N = 51$, data lacking on three cases.

These interrelations may be explained as follows: polygyny and male solidarity are mutually functional in that women can compensate with their work for the nonproductive activity of the males and at the same time give each other aid and moral support when the husband is not around. Alternately, only when a man has plural wives can he absent himself to a great extent from the domestic establishment and still maintain it, and only because of the demands of the male group are there reasons to be away or so preoccupied.

There is much more that could be said on these points, but two anthropologists have already taken up too much space in a sociology journal. Let me add only that Whiting and I heartily agree on at least one principle: research should be cumulative. And progress is even easier when one investigator is willing to smooth the path for the second, as Whiting has so generously done for me on more than one occasion.

BIOGRAPHIES OF AUTHORS

David Friend Aberle (1918–   ) was born in Minnesota and obtained his doctor's degree from Columbia University. Currently he is Professor of Anthropology at the University of Oregon. Most of his field work has been done with the Navaho Indians, about whom he has written extensively. His relevant publications include *Navaho and Ute Peyotism* (1957; co-author, Omer C. Stewart).

Erwin Henry Ackerknecht (1906–   ) is director of the Medizinhistorisches Institut of the University of Zurich. He holds a medical degree from the University of Leipzig and a diploma in ethnology from the University of Paris, and has combined this dual background in a long series of articles and books dealing with the medicine and pathology of primitive peoples. From 1947 to 1956 he was Professor of Medical History at the University of Wisconsin. He is the author of *A Short History of Medicine* (1955), *Franz Joseph Gall et sa collection* (with H. Vallois, 1955) and several other works.

Bernard Barber (1918–   ) is Professor and Chairman of the Department of Sociology at Barnard College, Columbia University. He received his education at Harvard, where he was granted his Ph.D. Professor Barber is the author of *Science and the Social Order* (1952) and *Social Stratification* (1957).

Robert Neelly Bellah (1927–   ) was born in Oklahoma and received his doctorate from Harvard, where he has taught since 1958 and currently holds the title of Associate Professor of Sociology and Regional Studies. Interested in the sociology of religion, he is author of *Tokugawa Religion* (1957).

Cyril Shirley Belshaw (1921–   ) was born in New Zealand and educated there at the London School of Economics. He has done administrative work and field research in Melanesia. At present he is Professor of Anthropology at the University of British Columbia. He is the author of *The Great Village* (1957), and *Under the Ivi Tree* (1964).

Bruno Bettelheim (1903–   ) is presently the Stella M. Rowley Professor of Education at the University of Chicago and also Professor in the Departments of Psychology and Psychiatry at the same institution. He was born and educated in Vienna. In his years of association with the Sonia Shankman Orthogenic School at the University of Chicago, he has been a major worker in the field of child psychotherapy and child development. It was at this school that he first developed an interest in initiation rites. His works include *Symbolic Wounds* (1954), *The Informed Heart* (1960), and *Dialogues with Mothers* (1962).

Waldemar Bogoras (Vladimir Germanovich Bogoraz) (1865–1936) was a Russian who was exiled in his youth to Siberia. At the invitation of his friend Waldemar Jochelson he joined the Jesup North Pacific Expedition, working with the Chukchee, Koryak, Yukaghir, and Lamut. For a while he lived in the United States, and then returned to Russia, where he was associated with the Museum of the Academy of Sciences. He wrote novels under the pseudonym "Tan." Among his numerous monographs are *The Chukchee* (1904–1909), *Chukchee Mythology* (1910), and *Koryak Texts* (1917).

Ruth Leah Bunzel (1898–   ) is Lecturer in Anthropology at Columbia, where she was trained under Franz Boas. During the war she was an analyst for the Office of War Information. Her main field research has been done in connection with Zuni ceremonialism, but she has had additional research experience in Middle America and is the author of *Chichicastenango: A Guatemalan Village* (1952). She has also investigated American and Chinese national character.

Roger Vernon Burton (1928–   ) was born in California and holds the doctorate in human development from Harvard. The socialization process, utilizing experimental design in natural settings, now holds his interest. He is Research Psychologist in the Laboratory of Socio-Environmental Studies, National Institute of Mental Health, and Lecturer at George Washington University.

Henry Callaway (1817–1890) was born in England and received his M.D. at King's College, Aberdeen, in 1853. The following year he was ordained a deacon and went to South Africa as a missionary for the Society for the Propagation of the Gospel. In 1855 he was ordained a priest and later became the first bishop of St. John's, Kaffraria. He devoted considerable time to Zulu studies, his first book being *Nursery Tales, Traditions, and Histories of the Zulus* (1868), followed by his great work, *The Religious System of the Amazulu* (1868–1870), which was never completely published.

Walter Bradford Cannon (1871–1945) took his A.B. (1896), A.M. (1897), and M.D. (1900) at Harvard University, and was the holder of numerous honorary degrees from universities throughout the world. He was George Higginson Professor of Physiology at Harvard from 1906 until his retirement in 1942. He was responsible for solving the acute World War I problem of traumatic shock, and he discovered the adrenalin-like hormone "sympathin." Many of his studies dealt with homeostasis, a term which he introduced to the literature. His publications include *Bodily Changes in Pain, Hunger, Fear and Rage* (1915, revised 1929), *Traumatic Shock* (1923), and *The Wisdom of the Body* (1932).

Robert Henry Codrington (1830–1922) was educated at Charterhouse and Wadham College, Oxford. At Oxford, he was a Scholar from 1849 to 1853 and a Fellow in 1855; he was ordained in 1855–1857. His many years of study in Melanesia led to his monograph, *The Melanesians: Studies in Their Anthropology and Folklore* (1891), which remains a standard work on eastern Melanesia. His earlier work, *The Melanesian Languages* (1885), contains 34 grammars of Melanesian languages from the eastern New Hebrides to the central Solomons.

Elizabeth Florence Colson (1917–) was trained in anthropology at Radcliffe, where she received the doctorate. She is Professor of Anthropology at the University of California, Berkeley, having previously been director of the Rhodes-Livingstone Institute and associated with the African Studies Program at Boston University. Her field work was done in California, Washington, and Northern Rhodesia. Among her publications are *Marriage and the Family Among the Plateau Tonga of Northern Rhodesia* (1958), *Social Organization of the Gwembe Tonga* (1960), and *The Plateau Tonga* (1962).

Émile Durkheim (1858–1917), a Frenchman by birth, was descended from a long line of rabbis and at an early age prepared for the rabbinate, but soon decided to become a teacher. He attended the École Normale Supérieur, where he was much influenced by Fustel de Coulanges and Émile Boutroux. For a few years he taught philosophy at various lycées and then turned to sociology. To prepare himself for improving his doctoral dissertation, he spent a year in Paris and Germany. At the University of Bordeaux in 1887 he gave the first course in social science ever offered in France. Six years later he defended his two doctoral theses, one of them being his *De la Division travail social* (1893). He founded the *Année Sociologique* in 1898. He taught sociology for thirty years at Bordeaux and the University of Paris. He was a prolific writer and, in turn, has been the object of scores of expository and critical books and articles.

Adolphus Peter Elkin (1891–) was born and educated in Australia, except for his doctorate, which he received at the University of London. He is Emeritus Professor of Anthropology at the University of Sydney, where he has taught for many years. In 1933 he became editor of *Oceania*, a position which he still holds. His field research has been done in Australia and New Guinea. He is the author of *The Australian Aborigines: How to Understand Them* (1st ed., 1938; 4th ed., 1964). He has also published *Studies in Australian Totemism* (1933) and *Some Rituals of Arnhem Land, North Australia* (1964).

William Ellis (1794–1872) was ordained in the London Missionary Society at the age of 21. In 1817 he was sent to the Pacific, where he remained until 1824. His *Polynesian Researches* (1831) is an able record of his observations of native life in the Society Islands and Hawaii, and is still a valuable source book. During his stay in the Hawaiian Islands he also wrote *A Narrative of a Tour through Hawaii* (1826), and is credited with having established the first printing press in Polynesia. After his return to England, he wrote a two-volume *History of Madagascar* (1838). Later, between 1853 and 1865, he made several trips to the then politically turbulent island of Madagascar.

Edward Evan Evans-Pritchard (1902–) holds the chair in social anthropology at Oxford, where in 1946 he succeeded Radcliffe-Brown. He received his master's degree at Oxford and his doctorate at the University of London. He has taught and done research at the Egyptian University at Cairo, the University of London, and Cambridge. He has carried on field work in the Sudan, the Belgian Congo, Ethiopia, and Kenya. Among his books are *Witchcraft, Oracles and Magic Among the Azande* (1937) and *Nuer Religion* (1956). He has an essay on religion in *The Institutions of Primitive Society* (1954).

Thomas Hornsby Ferril (Childe Herald) (1896–) was born in Denver and graduated from

Colorado College. With his wife he is publisher of *The Rocky Mountain Herald,* Colorado's oldest weekly, founded in 1860. He has won many honors and awards in poetry, and at the same time is active in business and industry. Four books of his poetry have been published and a fifth is on the way.

Raymond William Firth (1901–   ) is Professor of Anthropology in the University of London, at the London School of Economics and Political Science. Born in New Zealand, he first read Economics and later received his graduate training in anthropology under Malinowski in London. His major field research has been carried out on the island of Tikopia and in the Malay State of Kelantan. In 1953–1955 he was President of the Royal Anthropological Institute of Great Britain and Ireland. He is the author of *The Work of the Gods in Tikopia* (1940), *The Fate of the Soul: An Interpretation of Some Primitive Concepts* (1955), and other papers on religion, some of which have been republished in his *Essays on Social Organization and Values* (1964).

Charles O. Frake (1930–   ) was born in Wyoming and did his graduate work in anthropology at Yale. At present he is Assistant Professor of Anthropology at Stanford, having taught previously at Harvard. The southeast Asia area holds his principal regional interest, and he has done field work in the Philippines.

Henri Frankfort (1897–1954) was at the time of his death director of the Warburg Institute and Professor of Pre-Classical Antiquity at London University. Born in Holland, he went to Egypt as a pupil of Flinders Petrie, and did his first archaeological field work at Abydos and Armant with the Egyptian Exploration Society. Soon after, he was induced by James Henry Breasted to supervise seven seasons of excavations in Iraq for the Oriental Institute of the University of Chicago, an institution to which he later repaired for research and writing. Among his numerous publications are *Cylinder Seals* (1939), *Kingship and the Gods* (1948), and *Art and Architecture of the Ancient Orient* (1954).

Henriette Antonia Groenewegen Frankfort (1896–   ) is the widow of Henri Frankfort and collaborated with him on many of his projects. She is author of *Arrest and Movement: An Essay on Space and Time in the Representational Art of the Ancient Near East* (1951).

Sir James George Frazer (1854–1941) was born in Glasgow and educated at Glasgow University and Trinity College, Cambridge. He was called to the bar in 1879, and in 1907 became Professor of Social Anthropology at the University of Liverpool. He was knighted in 1914. Frazer had a strong interest in comparative religion, and it was in this field that he made his chief contributions to anthropological theory. Among his numerous writings the most famous is *The Golden Bough* (1st ed., 1890; 3d ed., 12 vols., 1911–1915). He also wrote *The Belief in Immortality and the Worship of the Dead* (1913-1924), *Folk-Lore in the Old Testament* (1918), *Myths of the Origin of Fire* (1930), and *The Fear of the Dead in Primitive Religion* (1933–1936).

Sigmund Freud (1856–1939), the founder of psychoanalysis, was born in Moravia, then a part of Austria, and at the age of four was brought to Vienna. Although he received a medical degree, he had no real interest in medicine except for its psychiatric aspects. He spent the year 1885 in Paris as a pupil of Charcot, whose use of hypnosis in functional nervous diseases had a profound influence on his thinking. He was even more influenced by certain observations on hysteria made by Dr. Josef Breuer, a highly respected general practitioner, with whom he published an important joint article in 1893. In 1909 Freud went to Clark University and gave five lectures in German, thus marking the formal debut of psychoanalysis in the United States. For many years he taught neurology at the University of Vienna. He moved to London in 1938 to escape the Nazi threat and died there just before the outbreak of the war.

Numa-Denys Fustel de Coulanges (1830–1889) was a French historian who, after he lost his professorship in antiquities at the University of Strasbourg in 1870 when Strasbourg became German, turned to medieval history, where he exerted much influence in the reinterpretation of the history of the Middle Ages. However, his is best remembered for his effort at tracing the influence of early religion on the development of Greek and Roman society, publishing his ideas in his great book, *La Cité antique* (1864). While director of the École Normale Supérieure he attracted the admiration of a young student, Émile Durkheim.

Clifford Geertz (1926–   ) is Professor of Anthropology at the University of Chicago. He was born in San Francisco. After attending Antioch College he went to Harvard and there received his doctorate in social anthropology in 1956. He has carried on field research in Java, Bali, and Morocco. Among his publications is his book, *The Religion of Java* (1960).

John Philip Gillin (1907–   ) is Research Professor of Anthropology at the University of Pittsburgh. During 1959–1962 he was Dean of the Division of Social Sciences at the same institution. He received undergraduate and graduate training in sociology and psychology at Wisconsin but took his doctor's degree in anthropology at Harvard. Although he has done work in North Africa, Europe, and the United States, most of his field research has been in Latin America. He has written a book on general anthropology, *The Ways of Men* (1948).

Alexander A. Goldenweiser (1880–1940) came to the United States from Russia while a young man, and received his training in anthropology at Columbia under Boas. He taught at Columbia, the New School for Social Research, the University of Oregon, Reed College, and the University of Wisconsin. Among his chief writings are *Early Civilization* (1922) and its successor, *Anthropology* (1937), and the well-known article, "Totemism: An Analytical Study" (1910).

Sir George Grey (1799–1883) was a colonial administrator unique for his time, since he deliberately set out to learn the language and the culture of the people he governed. He is especially remembered by ethnologists and folklorists for his classic *Polynesian Mythology and Ancient Traditional History of the New Zealand Race* (1855), which he compiled while governor-general of New Zealand. His direct contact with influential chiefs in the course of his duties made him realize that the myths, proverbs, and poems which they so frequently quoted to him to explain their views had a pragmatic role. Grey, with the help of the Maori, systematically collected and translated as much of the traditional narrative of the people as he could obtain.

Sir Arthur Francis Grimble (1888–1956) was a Britist colonial administrator. He was educated at Cambridge, where he received the master's degree. He entered the colonial service and was District Officer for the Gilbert and Ellice Islands, Administrator and Colonial Secretary for the Windward Islands, and Governor and Commander-in-Chief for the Seychelles. He retired in 1948. He is author of *A Pattern of Islands* (1952), as well as several other works.

Edward Smith Craighill Handy (1892–   ) is a Polynesian specialist trained at Harvard under Roland B. Dixon. He is Research Associate in Ethnology for the Bernice Pauahi Bishop Museum of Honolulu, as well as Research Associate in Ethnology for the Peabody Museum of Salem, Massachusetts. His interests lie essentially in the field of ethnography and historical reconstruction. His Polynesian field researches have been conducted in the Marquesas, Samoa, the Society Islands, and Hawaii. Among his publications is his monograph, *Polynesian Religion* (1927).

Childe Herald. See Thomas Hornsby Ferril.

Melville Jean Herskovits (1895–1963) was born in Ohio and trained in anthropology by Boas at Columbia. In 1927 he began a long association with Northwestern University, where he taught and directed its Program of African Studies. He did field work in Dutch Guiana, Africa, Haiti, Trinidad, and Brazil, his chief interest being in Africo-American ethnology and African culture. He was author of many books, among them being *Dahomey* (1938) and *Man and His Works* (1949).

Willard Williams Hill (1902–   ) is chairman of the Department of Anthropology at the University of New Mexico. He received his doctorate from Yale. Most of his field research has been done among the Navaho, on whom he is one of the outstanding authorities, but he has also worked with the Pueblo, Ute, and Pomo Indians. He is the author of *Navaho Warfare* (1936) and *The Agricultural and Hunting Methods of the Navaho Indians* (1938).

George Caspar Homans (1910–   ) is a sociologist trained at Harvard, where he has taught since 1939 except for a period of military service. He is now Professor of Sociology in the Department of Social Relations. He has served as President of the American Sociological Association (1963–1964). He is the author of *The Human Group* (1950), *Social Behavior* (1961), and *Sentiments and Activities* (1962).

George Lyman Kittredge (1860–1941) was one of the world's foremost authorities on Shakespeare and early English literature. He was educated at Harvard and from 1894 to his retirement in 1936 he was Gurney Professor of English Literature at that institution. Professor Kittredge was the author of many books on Shakespeare, Chaucer, English grammar, Anglo-Saxon literature, and English and Scottish popular ballads and folk songs. His continued interest in the history of Anglo-American witchcraft led to his classic study, *Witchcraft in Old and New England* (1929).

Clyde Kluckhohn (1905–1960) was born in Iowa and did graduate work at the universities of Vienna, Oxford, and Harvard, where he received his doctorate and taught until his death. He served as chairman of the Department of Anthropology at Harvard and was one of the organizers of the Department of Social Relations at that institution, where he also served from 1947 to 1954 as director of the Russian Research Center.He was one of the outstanding authorities on the Navaho Indians, with whom he did extensive field work for a quarter of a century. He was active in the reorganization of the American Anthropological Association, being elected president of that body in 1947; but his dedication to his profession ranged beyond this and he was frequently called upon to serve in various administrative and advisory capacities. Of his numerous publications, those bearing on Navaho religion include *Navaho Classification of Their Song Ceremonials* (1938), *An Introduction to Navaho Chant Practice* (1940), both of which were written with Leland C. Wyman as coauthor, and *Navaho Witchcraft* (1944).

Alfred Louis Kroeber (1876–1960) was born in Hoboken, New Jersey, and trained in anthropology at Columbia by Boas, receiving his doctorate in 1901. From that year until his retirement in 1946 he taught at the University of California at Berkeley and was for many years curator of its museum of anthropology. He was not only one of the most prolific writers in his discipline (over 500 publications) but one of the most active in its various societies, having served as president of the American Folklore Society (1906), the American Anthropological Association (1917–1919), and the Linguistic Society of America (1940). He was also the recipient of several honorary degrees and awards. Most of his field research was done with the Indians of California. Of his publications, some of the most noteworthy were the *Handbook of the Indians of California* (1925), *Configurations of Culture Growth* (1944), and, especially, *Anthropology* (1923; revised 1948), which as a textbook exerted an important influence on generations of students.

Berthold Laufer (1874–1934) was born in Cologne and attended the universities of Berlin and Leipzig. Shortly after receiving his doctorate in 1897 he came to the United States. He made several field trips to China and Tibet, which resulted in original and scholarly research that soon led to his being recognized as one of the world's foremost sinologists. Possessed of an encyclopedic mind, his scholarly publications ranged over an incredible variety of topics. He was associated with the American Museum of Natural History from 1903 to 1906. From 1905 to 1907 he lectured at Columbia University. In 1908 he began his association with the Field Museum of Natural History, where he held curatorships in Asiatic Ethnology (1911) and Anthropology (1915) until his death.

Edmund Ronald Leach (1910–   ) was born in England and educated at the University of Cambridge and the London School of Economics. His field work has been extensive, having been conducted in China, Formosa, Iraq, Burma, Borneo, and elsewhere. He now is on the faculty of Cambridge, where he holds the title of Reader in Social Anthropology. Some of his essays have been collected into a small but influential book, *Rethinking Anthropology* (1961).

William Armand Lessa (1908–   ) is Professor of Anthropology and head of the Pacific Island Program at the University of California, Los Angeles. Born in Newark, he began his work in anthropology with Hooton as an undergraduate at Harvard and later received the doctorate in social anthropology from the University of Chicago. His field work began in Hawaii and has extended to China, Ulithi Atoll, and Samoa. Among his books and monographs the one most relevant to the field of religion is his *Tales from Ulithi Atoll: A Comparative Study in Oceanic Folklore* (1961).

Claude Lévi-Strauss (1908–   ) is Directeur d'Études at the École Pratique des Hautes Études in Paris, and occupies the chair of comparative religion of nonliterate peoples at that institution. He was born in Brussels and educated at the University of Paris. Early in his career he taught at the Université de São Paulo and the New School for Social Research, New York. Later he served as cultural attaché to the French embassy in the United States. His field work was done in South and Central Mato Grosso, Brazil (1935–1936) and North and West Mato Grosso and South Amazonas (1938–1939). He has gained world recognition in anthropology for his pursuit of what has been called the "structural method." Among his writings are *Tristes Tropiques* (1955; trans. 1961), *Le Totémisme aujourd'hui* (1962; trans. 1963), and *Structural Anthropology* (1963).

Ralph Linton (1893–1953) studied anthropology for brief periods at Pennsylvania and Columbia but received his doctorate from Harvard. After serving as assistant curator of the Chicago Natural History Museum, he taught at Wisconsin and Columbia, and was Sterling Professor of Anthropology at Yale at the time of his death. From 1939 to 1945 he was editor of the *American Anthropologist,* and in 1946 was president of the American Anthropological Association. His field researches took him to various parts of the world, including the Marquesas, Madagascar, South Africa, Peru, and Brazil. He is the author of *The Study of Man* (1936), *The Cultural Background of Personality* (1945), and *The Tree of Culture* (1955, posthumous), as well as numerous monographs and articles.

Robert Harry Lowie (1883–1957) at the time of his death was Professor Emeritus of Anthropology at the University of California, Berkeley. He was born in Vienna and educated in the United States, receiving the doctorate in 1908 from Columbia, where he studied under Boas. From 1907 to 1921 he was associated with the American Museum of Nautral History and after that he went to Berkeley. He was editor of the *American Anthropologist* from 1924 to 1933, and president of the American Folklore Society, the American Ethnological Society, and the American Anthropological Association. He wrote numerous books, among them being *Primitive Society* (1920), *Primitive Religion* (1924; revised, 1948), and *The History of Ethnological Theory* (1937).

Bronislaw Malinowski (1884–1942) was born and educated in Poland, where he took his Ph.D. in physics and mathematics. When ill health forced him to leave the University of Cracow in order to recuperate, he accidentally came across a copy of Frazer's *Golden Bough,* which awakened his interest in the study of culture. He went to England in 1910 and studied under C. G. Seligman at the London School of Economics. Beginning in 1914 he spent two-and-a-half years doing research in the Pacific islands, chiefly in the Trobriands, which were made famous by his many books, including *Argonauts of the Western Pacific* (1928) and *Coral Gardens and Their Magic* (1935). In 1927 he was appointed to the first Chair in Anthropology at the University of London, where his weekly seminars became famous. At the time of his death he was a Visiting Professor at Yale University. An article written by S. F. Nadel, "Malinowski on Magic and Religion," appears in *Man and Culture—An Evaluation of the Work of Bronislaw Malinowski,* ed. Raymond Firth (1957).

Duane G. Metzger (1930–   ) is an assistant professor at the University of Illinois, where he holds a joint appointment in the Department of Anthropology and the Institute of Communications Research. He holds a master's and doctor's degree from the University of Chicago, and was a Junior Fellow in the Society of Fellows at Harvard. He has done field work in Chiapas, Mexico.

Horace Mitchell Miner (1912–   ) is Professor of Anthropology and Sociology at the University of Michigan. He was born in St. Paul, Minnesota, and received his doctorate in anthropology from the University of Chicago. His field research includes studies made in Africa, Canada, and Columbia. Among his publications are *St. Denis: A French Canadian Parish* (1939), *The Primitive City of Timbuctoo* (1953), and *Oasis and Casbah* (1960).

Omar Khayyam Moore (1920–   ) is Professor of Psychology at Rutgers. He was born in Utah and received his master's and doctor's degrees in sociology at Washington University, St. Louis. He is currently active in numerous "responsive environments" projects.

Siegfried Frederick Nadel (1903–1956) was born in Vienna and trained there in musical composition and conducting. He received the doctorate in psychology from the University of Vienna. A strong and active interest in comparative musicology drew him toward the study of African languages and ethnology. Consequently, he went to London to study anthropology with Malinowski. His principal field research was done among the Nupe of Nigeria (*A Black Byzantium,* 1942) and the Nuba of Kordofan. He taught at the London School of Economics and the University of Durham, after which he was called to fill the first chair in anthropology at the newly created Australian National University, a post he held at the time of his death. His chief theoretical works are *The Foundations of Social Anthropology* (1951) and *The Theory of Social Structure* (1957).

Morris Edward Opler (1907–   ) is Professor of Anthropology and Asian Studies, and Director of the South Asia Program, at Cornell University. He received his doctorate in anthropology at Chicago. He is best known for his studies of Apache tribes; however, he has also had extensive experience in applied anthropology and is currently interested in the cultures of South Asia. Among his publications are *Myths and Tales of the Jicarilla Apache Indians* (1938), *Myths and Legends of the Lipan Apache Indians* (1940), *Myths and Tales of the Chiricahua Apache Indians* (1942), and *The Character and Derivation of the Jicarilla Holiness Rite* (1943).

George Kerlin Park (1925–   ) was born in Boston and received his doctorate in anthropology from the University of Chicago. After teaching sociology at Ohio State University he went to Makerere College in Uganda as Senior Research Fellow in the East African Institute of Social Research. At present he is Associate Professor of Anthropology, Pitzer College, Claremont, California. His field work has been done in Norway and Tanganyika.

Talcott Parsons (1902–   ) was born in Colorado. After attending the London School of Economics, where he studied with Ginsberg and Malinowski, he went to the University of Heidelberg and there received the doctorate in sociology and economics. He began teaching at Harvard in 1927, at first in economics and later in sociology, and is now Professor of Sociology. He was the first chairman of the Department of Social Relations at that institution (1946–1957), being one of its founders. He has translated and edited some of the works of Max

Weber. Among his own writings are *The Structure of Social Action* (1937), *The Social System* (1951), and *Structure and Process in Modern Societies* (1960).

Raffaele Pettazzoni (1883–1960) was a distinguished exponent of the Religionswissenschaft school of religion. Born near Bologna, he spent most of his academic life teaching at the University of Rome. In 1951 he became president of the International Association for the Study of Religions, and in 1954 was made director of *Numen.* He was author of a large number of books, among them *La confession dei peccati* (1929–1936), a vast study on the question of the confession of sins; *L'essere celeste nelle credenze dei popoli primitive* (1922) : and *L'Onniscienza di Dio* (1955). Several of his works have been translated into English.

Alfred Reginald Radcliffe-Brown (1881–1955) was born and educated in England, where he trained in anthropology under Haddon and Rivers at Cambridge University. His first field trip took him to the Andaman Islands from 1906 to 1908, and his fellowship thesis for Trinity College was a conventional reconstruction of Andamanese culture history. But while teaching at the London School of Economics and at Cambridge he became aware of the French sociologists, especially Durkheim and Mauss, and eventually completely rewrote his Andamanese materials in terms of the meaning and function of their rites, myths, and institutions. From 1910 to 1912 he did field research in Australia. He spent a considerable part of his life abroad, being affiliated with the Pretoria Museum, the University of Cape Town, the University of Sydney, the University of Chicago, Yenching University, the University of São Paulo, Farouk I University, and Grahamstown. He was called to the newly created Chair of Social Anthropology at Oxford in 1937. Radcliffe-Brown is author of *The Andaman Islanders* (1922). Three collections of his essays, addresses, and seminar lectures have been published: *Structure and Function in Primitive Society* (1952), *A Natural Science of Society* (1957), and *Method in Social Anthropology* (1958).

Knud Rasmussen (1879–1933) was born in Greenland, of partially Eskimo parentage. He learned to speak an Eskimo dialect before he was competent in Danish. He had as playmates during his childhood Eskimos who were entirely Christianized, and as a boy he dreamed of exploring and living in the unknown northland. He made the first of nearly a dozen major expeditions to the polar regions in 1902–1904, and this trip resulted in the publication of *The People of the Polar North* (1905), which established him as an authority on the Eskimos. Although particularly interested in folklore, he

contributed greatly to knowledge about Greenland and the polar regions. He wrote on geography, natural history, language, general ethnology, and many other subjects, and in recognition of his research and writings he was awarded a Ph.D. from the University of Copenhagen. He was editor or author of several multivolume works on the Eskimo, of which *The Report of the Fifth Thule Expedition, 1921–24* was one.

Bernardino de Sahagún (1499–1590) has been described as the foremost authority of his time on the ethnology of the Aztec people. Coming from Spain in the year 1529 as a young Franciscan friar, he quickly developed an interest in the history and way of life of his Indian wards. He served as a teacher, missionary, inspector of missions, convent superior, and member of the governing board of the order. His major work, divided into twelve books, is the *Historia de las Cosas de Nueva Espana,* an account of the Aztecs derived from native informants. Written in parallel Spanish and Aztec versions, it has been translated by Anderson and Dibble and published in thirteen parts under the title *Florentine Codex,* after the city of Florence where the manuscript is kept. Fray Bernardino also wrote many lesser items in Spanish, Latin, and Aztec.

Hayyim Schauss (1884–1953) was a historian, lecturer, and teacher born in Lithuania. He taught for over a quarter of a century at the Jewish Teachers Seminary in New York. In Los Angeles he was associated with the College of Jewish Studies and the University of Judaism. He was the author of hundreds of essays and articles, published in the Yiddish press and in various Yiddish journals, on the Jewish religion, Bible, Midrash, history, customs and ceremonies, and folklore. Perhaps his most popular contributions to Jewish scholarship were two companion volumes published in English, *The Jewish Festivals* (1938) and *The Lifetime of a Jew* (1950).

Wilhelm Schmidt (1868–1954) was born in Germany but taught at the University of Vienna and in his later years at Fribourg, Switzerland. Although a member of the Society of the Divine Word for Foreign Missions, he was never assigned an overseas post. He became interested in languages and linguistics after being stimulated by reports and information brought to Vienna by returned missionaries. His work on the comparative linguistics of Australia and southeast Asia brought him many awards and much recognition. He is nonetheless best known in the United States for his contributions to ethnology, particularly theory. As an adherent of the *Kulturkreislehre,* he advanced a historical approach based on the analysis of diffusion, through time and space, of complexes of cultural characteristics (*Handbuch der Methode der kulturhistorischen Ethnologie,* 1937). Father Schmidt trained a long line of excellent fieldworkers and theoreticians, who came to be known as the "Vienna School." In 1926 he founded the distinguished journal, *Anthropos.* Of the hundreds of articles and many books that he wrote, perhaps the best known is his monumental *Der Ursprung der Gottesidee* (1926–1952).

James Sydney Slotkin (1913–1958) at the time of his death was an associate professor in the Department of Social Sciences of the University of Chicago, at which institution he received his training in anthropology. His field research was conducted among the Menomini Indians. Among his pertinent publications are *The Peyote Religion* and *The Menomini Powwow Religion* (1957).

William Robertson Smith (1846–1894) was a theologian and Semitic scholar educated at Aberdeen, Edinburgh, and Bonn. He was Professor of Old Testament Exegesis at Free Church College, Aberdeen, but was discharged in 1881 because of Biblical articles which he wrote for the *Encyclopaedia Britannica,* of which he was coeditor and later editor. In 1883 he became Professor of Arabic at Cambridge, a position he held at the time of his premature death. His best known book is *Lectures on the Religion of the Semites* (1889).

Melford Elliot Spiro (1920–   ) is Professor of Anthropology at the University of Chicago. He received his doctorate in anthropology at Northwestern University. His field work includes studies of the Ojibway, the natives of Ifaluk Atoll, an Israeli kibbutz, and the Burmese. He is the author of *An Atoll Culture: Ethnography of Ifaluk in the Caroline Islands* (with E. G. Burrows, 1953) and *Kibbutz: Venture in Utopia* (1956), and is currently working on a cross-cultural study of religion, and on religion in Burmese society.

William Edward Hanley Stanner (1905–   ) was born in Sydney, Australia, and educated at Sydney University and the University of London, where he received his doctorate. He was Director of the Makerere Institute (Uganda) and served on the South Pacific Commission. Since 1950 he has been Reader in Comparative Social Institutions at the Australian National University, Canberra. In 1961 he was Convener and Chairman of a national conference which led to the formation of the Australian Institute of Aboriginal Studies. He has carried out anthropological research in Australia, Africa and southwest Pacific Islands. His publications include *The South Seas in Transition* (1953) and *On Aboriginal Religion* (1963).

Yonina Talmon (1923–   ) was born in Palestine and is now Senior Lecturer at the Hebrew University in Jerusalem, where she once studied for the doctorate in sociology. She did postdoctoral work at the London School of Economics in 1950–1951 and held a research fellowship at Harvard in 1961–1963. Her current research is on collective settlements. She has published extensively in journals throughout the world.

John Eric Sidney Thompson (1898–   ) was born and educated in England. After several years with the Chicago Natural History Museum, in 1935 he joined the staff of the Carnegie Institution of Washington, where he served as a member of the Department of Anthropology until 1957. He is presently a Fellow of the British Academy. He also holds the Viking Medal from the Wenner-Gren Foundation for Anthropological Research. He is the author of *Mexico before Cortez* (1933), *Maya Hieroglyphic Writing* (1950), and numerous other works.

Mischa Titiev (1901–   ) is Professor of Anthropology at the University of Michigan. He was born in Russia and educated at Harvard, where he received the doctorate in 1935. He is an authority on the Hopi Indians, having written *Notes on Hopi Witchcraft* (1942) and *Old Oraibi: A Study of the Hopi Indians of Third Mesa* (1944). In 1948 and 1963–1964 he did field research with the Araucanian Indians in Chile, and in 1951 with rural Japanese. He is the author of *Introduction to Cultural Anthropology* (1959) and other works.

Harry S. Tschopik, Jr. (1915–1956) received his graduate degrees in anthropology at Harvard. He was Assistant Curator of South American Ethnology at the American Museum of Natural History from 1947 until the time of his death. Most of his field research was with the Indians of Peru, although he aso worked with the Navaho in 1937–1938.

Edward Burnett Tylor (1832–1917) was the foremost anthropologist of his time. Although not a university graduate, having been privately educated, he became Keeper of the University Museum at Oxford and a reader there from 1884 until 1896, when he was given a professorship. He had an unusually wide range of interests. He went to Mexico in 1856 in the company of a prehistorian, and visited some Pueblo villages in 1884, but he was not a fieldworker. However, his critical appraisals and analyses of secondary materials were significant contributions to the nascent fund of anthropological knowledge. He was not strictly an evolutionist, for he insisted on the important part played in the development of culture by diffusion. His best-known works are *Researches in the Early History of Mankind and the Development of Civilization* (1865), *Primitive Culture: Researches into the Development of Mythology, Philosophy, Religion, Language, Art, and Custom* (1871), and *Anthropology: An Introduction to the Study of Man and Civilization* (1881).

Evon Zartman Vogt (1918–   ) was born in Gallup, New Mexico, and educated at the University of Chicago, where he received his doctorate in 1948. Since then he has been teaching at Harvard, where he is now Professor of Social Anthropology and Curator of Middle American Ethnology. He has done extensive field work among the Navaho of New Mexico and the Tzotzil Indians of Chiapas, Mexico. His publications include *Navaho Veterans* (1951), *Modern Homesteaders* (1955), *Water Witching U.S.A.* (with Ray Hyman, 1959), *Desarrollo Cultural de Los Mayas* (with Alberto Ruz, 1964), and *Zinacantan: A Maya Community in the Highlands of Chiapas* (forthcoming).

William Lloyd Warner (1898–   ) is Professor of Social Research at Michigan State University. He received his training at the University of California and Harvard. He has done field research in Australia and supervised extensive community studies in Massachusetts and Illinois as well as work in industrial anthropology. He is the author of *A Black Civilizations: A Social Study of an Australian Tribe* (1937), the "Yankee City" series of books, and *The Family of God: A Symbolic Study of Christian Life in America* (1961).

John Wesley Mayhew Whiting (1908–   ) is Professor of Social Anthropology in the Departments of Social Relations and Anthropology at Harvard. He did his graduate work at Yale and principal field work among the Kwoma of New Guinea. He is author of *Becoming a Kwoma* (1941) and coauthor, with Irvin Child, of *Child Training and Personality* (1953).

Gerald E. Williams (1925–   ) is Associate Professor in the Department of Anthropology, University of Rochester. Born in Ohio, he did his graduate work in anthropology at the University of Chicago, his dissertation being on colloquial Minangkabau. He has done field work in Java, Sumatra, and Mexico.

Edmund Wilson (1895–   ) is a literary critic and writer with an interest in problems of comparative religion. After his graduation from Princeton in 1916 he served as managing editor of *Vanity Fair* from 1920 to 1921, as associate editor of the *New Republic* from 1926 to 1931, and as book review editor of the *New Yorker* from 1944 to 1948. He has published almost a score of books, including *The Scrolls from the Dead Sea* (1955), in connection with which he visited the Dead Sea site where the scrolls were found.

Eric Robert Wolf (1923–   ) was born in Vienna and received his doctorate in anthropology from Columbia. He is Professor of Anthropology at the University of Michigan. He has done field work in Puerto Rico, Mexico, and the Italian Alps. Among his publications is *Sons of the Shaking Earth* (1959).

Frank Wilbur Young (1928–   ) was born in Chicago and received the doctorate in social anthropology from Cornell, where he is now Associate Professor in the Department of Rural Sociology. He has done field work in Nova Scotia and Mexico. Recently published is his *Initiation Ceremonies* (1965).

SELECTED MONOGRAPHS ON
NON-WESTERN RELIGIOUS SYSTEMS

BARTON, R. F. *The Religion of the Ifugaos.* ("Memoirs of the American Anthropological Association," No. 65.) Menasha, Wis., 1946.

This account of "the most extensive and pervasive religion that has yet been reported . . . outside of India" introduces the gods and describes their uses and some occasions on which they are invoked. Interesting features of the work are an attempt at quantification—for example, counting the times a particular benefit is sought in a sample of rites—and an examination of the historical development of the religion based on comparative data from related groups.

BELLAH, ROBERT N. *Tokugawa Religion: The Values of Pre-Industrial Japan.* Glencoe, Ill.: The Free Press, 1957.

The author uses Max Weber's sociological frame of reference to demonstrate the influence of certain religious and political value orientations found in the feudal Tokugawa period which, he proposes, formed the matrix for the prodigious and vigorous later economic and political development of Japan into an industrial nation.

BOGORAS, WALDEMAR. *The Chukchee,* Vol. VII of Franz Boas (ed.), *The Jesup North Pacific Expedition.* ("Memoirs of the American Museum of Natural History," Vol. XI, Parts 2 and 3.) Leyden: E. J. Brill, 1904–1909.

Based on extensive field work among the reindeer-breeding peoples of Siberia, this monograph presents a wealth of detail on Chukchee cosmology and on the ritual means for securing the benefits of good spirits and warding off the effects of evil ones. (The sketches of these spirits by Chukchee are illuminating.) Seasonal sacrifices are associated with the life cycle of the reindeer, while other ritual centers around the hearth, each household having its own sacred objects and signs.

BOWERS, ALFRED W. *Mandan Social and Ceremonial Organization.* Chicago: The University of Chicago Press, 1950.

Although this book is concerned with ritual, describing a variety of ceremonies each built around a specific need (buffalo, eagles, rain), it is valuable also as mythology, since all the rites are dramatizations of myths. Each centers about a bundle of objects which represent the characters and incidents of the myth.

BUNZEL, RUTH. "Introduction to Zuni Ceremonialism," *47th Annual Report of the Bureau of American Ethnology,* pp. 467–545. Washington, D.C., 1932.

In this summary of the rich and varied ceremonialism of Zuni, the author points out that the apparent complexity is one of organization rather than content. She demonstrates this by abstracting a pattern of ritual elements common to all rites and by listing the major cults and their internal organization and interactions. Special emphasis is placed on the aesthetic functions of the ritual in Zuni life.

BUNZEL, RUTH. *Chichicastenango: A Guatemalan Village.* ("Publications of the American Ethnological Society," Vol. XXII.) Locust Valley, N.Y.: J. J. Augustin, 1952.

This study of a Guatemalan community contains a great deal of detail on the organizational aspects of the local religion—the selection and functioning of the rotating officials of the church—and on the *fiesta* round. In addition, consideration is given to the role of the ancestors as supplements to the Catholic saints, the use of the ancient calendar, divination by seeds, and the ideas of sin and penance.

CASO, ALFONSO. *El Pueblo del Sol.* México: Fondo de Cultura Económica, 1953.

Caso sees the worship of the gods (especially the sun) and their maintenance by sacrifices as the central motivating force behind the Aztec nation. He examines the gods—their powers and their demands—and suggests that the requirements of the religion had a profound formative influence on the society. Illustrations in color from the codices contribute to the exposition and make this an attractive book.

EVANS, I. H. N. *The Religion of the Tempasuk*

Dusuns of North Borneo. New York: Cambridge University Press, 1953.

The author gives a detailed account of Dusun religion and custom set in a background of daily life, pointing out the similarities to beliefs and practices found not only in other parts of Borneo but also in the Philippines, Indonesia, and Malaya. Among such similarities he cites the idea of multiple souls, soul wandering and capture, the importance of priestesses or mediums, as well as striking resemblances in ceremonial practice.

EVANS-PRITCHARD E. E. *Witchcraft, Oracles and Magic Among the Azande.* Oxford: Clarendon Press, 1937.

Throughout this skillful account the author explores the dynamics of Zande belief— the balance between faith and skepticism and between empirical and mystical causes. To the Azande, witchcraft is the socially relevant cause of all illness and death; it is a purely psychical act, imputed to others (usually social deviants) and denied in oneself.

EVANS-PRITCHARD E. E. *Nuer Religion.* Oxford: Clarendon Press, 1956.

In this study Evans-Pritchard describes a religion which is distinctive in its markedly monotheistic tendency, its strong sense of dependence on God, and the idea of punishment for sin and the consequent guilt, confession, and expiatory sacrifice. He suggests that Nuer religious thought, in which one spirit has many manifestations, is a reflection of the segmentary structure of the society.

FIRTH, RAYMOND. *The Work of the Gods in Tikopia.* ("London School of Economics and Political Science Monographs on Social Anthropology," Nos. 1 and 2.) London: Percy Lund, Humphries & Co., 1940.

Firth gives a step-by-step, eye-witness account, enriched by his closeness to the people and the vernacular, of the ritual cycle in this small Pacific society. He stresses the unity, perceived by the people themselves, of the series of rites—consecration of canoes and temples, harvest and planting, sacred dances, moral exhortation, and taboos on noise and amusement. Attention is given throughout to the sources of variation, by conscious innovation or error, in the tradition—the dynamics of ritual.

FLETCHER, ALICE, and LA FLESCHE, FRANCIS. "The Omaha Tribe," *27th Annual Report of the Bureau of American Ethnology,* pp. 15– 672. Washington, D.C., 1911.

This study emphasizes ritual, both that of the secret societies and that performed by the clans for the tribe. The camp circle has two ritual divisions—the northern, the clans of which are responsible for rites concerned with creation and the cosmos, and the south-ern, whose clans perform the rites of war, maize, buffalo, and the sacred pole which "holds the tribe together."

FORTUNE, R. F. *Sorcerers of Dobu.* London: George Routledge & Sons, 1932.

The author sees jealousy of possession as a keynote to this culture and traces it in the attitudes toward, and uses of, the incantations which are the means of control over the supernatural. Both garden magic and spells for inflicting disease are privately owned and secret and are employed largely to protect one's property from others. Divination by watergazing is a technique for locating the sorcerer who has caused a particular illness.

FORTUNE, R. F. *Manus Religion.* ("Memoirs, American Philosophical Society," Vol. III.) Philadelphia, 1935.

Dr. Fortune presents an exhaustive account of every facet of Manus religion with a wealth of illustrative case material, native opinions, and so on. Due to his intimacy with the villagers, he describes their personalities and emotional reactions as accurately as the average individual could describe those of his European neighbor.

FOSTER, GEORGE M. *Empire's Children: The People of Tzintzuntzan.* ("Smithsonian Institution, Institute of Social Anthropology, Publications," No. 6.) Washington, D.C., 1948.

In this community, considered by the author as one of the least rural in all rural Mexico, Catholicism of a Mexican variety has replaced the old religion in its entirety. The Church, with its rotating offices, its associations, and its ceremonial calendar, is a social and spiritual focus for the community.

GEERTZ, CLIFFORD. *The Religion of Java.* Glencoe, Ill.: The Free Press, 1960.

Javanese religion is seen as having a Great and a Little tradition, each of which blends an animistic and a Hindu heritage. Their world view and social behavior are contrasted with a third element, *santri,* the more nearly orthodox Islamic tradition. The author links each with residence and occupation, but even more importantly with religious orientation and political alignments. The study emerges as an analysis of the Javanese value system.

GRINNELL, GEORGE B. *The Cheyenne Indians.* 2 vols. New Haven, Conn.: Yale University Press, 1923.

In an account reflecting several decades of acquaintance with the Cheyenne, the author describes in detail two of the four major ceremonies, pointing up the importance of the personal ordeal, private or public, in securing success and averting evil. Healing, also rich in ceremony, receives lengthy consideration.

GUSINDE, MARTIN. *Die Feuerland Indianer.* Band 2. *Die Yamana.* Mödling bei Wien: Verlag der Internationalen Zeitschrift "Anthropos," 1937.

This work contains an account of the religious concepts and practices of the primitive Yahgan of Tierra del Fuego. The author gives particular attention to the myths, which are concerned with the creation of the world and the invention (by a legendary family) of important parts of the social life.

HERSKOVITS, MELVILLE J. *Dahomey.* 2 vols. New York: J. J. Augustin, 1938.

The political complexity of this West African monarchy is here shown to be paralleled by an elaborate theology and a set of specialized religious institutions. In addition to ancestor worship carried on by extended families, there are rites for royal ancestors (at one time including human sacrifice), divination, and rituals performed by the highly trained priests of five separate cults.

JUNOD, HENRI A. *The Life of a South African Tribe.* 2d ed., revised and enlarged. London: Macmillan & Co., Ltd., 1927.

This missionary's work on the Thonga deals rather sympathetically with religious observances and gives explanations for them in native terms. The worship of ancestors is central, and divination with dice is used to determine the occasions for sacrifice; a great variety of the latter are employed for rain making and growth, purification after death, punishment and reconciliation of enemies, and, combined with magic, medicine.

LANTIS, MARGARET. *Alaskan Eskimo Ceremonialism.* ("Publications of the American Ethnological Society," Vol. XI.) New York: J. J. Augustin, 1947.

This survey draws together material on ceremonial from the various Eskimo groups of Alaska, pointing out the distribution and variation of ceremonies at life crises, memorial feasts for the dead, secret societies which impersonate devils to frighten the uninitiated, and hunting ritual (the latter most highly developed). The author attempts a reconstruction of historical relationships on the basis of the distributional data.

LIENHARDT, GODFREY. *Divinity and Experience: The Religion of the Dinka.* Oxford: Oxford University Press, 1961.

This analysis of the religion of the Dinka, a pastoral people of East Africa, is concerned principally with cosmology rather than ritual. The author discusses the Dinka concept of "Divinity" (connoting formlessness or event rather than the more substantive term "God"), the political and religious ascendance of the clans of spear-masters, and the part played by cattle sacrifices in the ceremonials, which he interprets as being social-

symbolic dramas paralleling events, not altering them. Cattle are offered as foils for disaster and as substitutes for men who would otherwise be the victims.

LOWIE, ROBERT H. *The Crow Indians.* New York: Farrar & Rinehart, 1935.

Lowie's insight into Crow culture and his wide knowledge of others give both depth and perspective to this work. He sees the vision quest or guardian-spirit complex as the dominant pattern in Crow relations with the supernatural, and traces this and the idea of "medicine" in a variety of communal ceremonies.

McILWRAITH, T. F. *The Bella Coola.* 2 vols. Toronto: University of Toronto Press, 1948.

This monograph on a vanishing Northwest Coast society presents a view of the world in which all the forces and beings in nature are conceived as persons. Religious belief and practice are consequently multifaceted and ubiquitous. Inheritance of myths and dances through sibs, shamanism, and a series of origin stories involving the ingenious Raven are features of considerable interest.

MALINOWSKI, BRONISLAW. *Coral Gardens and Their Magic.* 2 vols. London: George Allen & Unwin, 1935.

Focusing on agriculture in the Trobriands, Malinowski here enlarges upon his ideas about magic with a coherent and colorful illustration of its nature, its role, and its relationship to technology and practical work. Although there are references to myths which underpin land tenure and the cultivation of gardens, this is primarily a book about practice and not about a system of beliefs.

MEAD, MARGARET. *The Mountain Arapesh,* Vol. II, *Supernaturalism.* ("Anthropological Papers of the American Museum of Natural History," Vol. XXXVII, Part 3, pp. 317–451.) New York, 1940.

In this monograph Mead describes the Arapesh world view, pointing out the absence of cosmology and the recurrence of the basic contrast between the physiological natures of men and women in ideas about human beings, spirits associated with the kin groups, life, and death. She traces this contrast in selected myths and rituals, primarily in rites of passage and harvest ceremonies.

MORLEY, SYLVANUS G. *The Ancient Maya.* 3d ed., revised by George W. Brainerd. Stanford, Calif.: Stanford University Press, 1956.

Morley draws on a lifetime of work in Maya archaeology and ethnology for this description of the Maya gods and the calendrical ritual directed to them. He traces the development of pantheon, priesthood, and ritual as this can be seen in the archaeological record.

MURPHY, ROBERT F. *Mundurucú Religion.*

("University of California Publications in American Archaeology and Ethnology," Vol. XLIX, No. 1.) Berkeley: University of California Press, 1958.

Murphy examines the transformations which the religion of the Mundurucú, an Indian tribe in Brazil, is undergoing today due to profound changes in their culture and social organization. Until very recently the core of their religious beliefs was the relationship between humans and game animals, now declining due to a different economic orientation. He also emphasizes the continued persistence and importance of sorcery.

NADEL, S. F. *Nupe Religion*. London: Routledge & Kegan Paul, 1954.

Nadel's description and discussion of the theology, divination and other rituals, medicine, and witchcraft of this tribe of the Sudan reflects both anthropological sophistication and exhaustive field research. Consideration is given to the borrowing of elements of religion from other tribes and to conversion to Islam, both of which provide insight into the indigenous system.

NIMUENDAJÚ, CURT. *The Eastern Timbira*. Translated by Robert H. Lowie. ("University of California Publications in American Archaeology and Ethnology," Vol. XLI.) Berkeley, Calif., 1946.

The chief emphasis in this study of a Brazilian tribe is on ceremonial and its organization. The annual dry-season rites are the initiation of age classes or dances performed by hereditary men's societies. In the rainy season these societies and ceremonial moieties participate in planting, growth, and harvest ritual.

OPLER, MORRIS E. *An Apache Life-Way*. Chicago: The University of Chicago Press, 1941.

Seeking to convey the Apache's view of life in, as nearly as possible, the Apache's own terms, Opler arranges his material on religious beliefs and practices in the order of their introduction in the individual life cycle. To the same end, he makes extensive use of verbatim reports of his informants on ritual (girls' puberty ceremony, shamanistic ceremonies for curing, love, hunting, and war) and cosmology.

RADCLIFFE-BROWN, A. R. *The Andaman Islanders*. Cambridge: At the University Press, 1922.

After describing the customs and beliefs of the Andamanese, Radcliffe-Brown proceeds to interpret the ceremonies and some of the myths from the point of view of social anthropology. He suggests that both of these serve to maintain and transmit the sentiments on which the social system depends, and shows how certain features of the marriage,

funeral, and puberty rites contribute to this end.

RADIN, PAUL. "The Winnebago Tribe," *37th Annual Report of the Bureau of American Ethnology*, pp. 35–550. Washington, D.C., 1923.

Radin discusses Winnebago religious concepts and describes the four major kinds of ceremony: the clan feast; the rites of four societies of individuals blessed by the same spirit; the Medicine dance, whose membership is voluntary; and the dance following success in war. He provides perspective by a consideration of the introduction of a modern cult, Peyote.

RASMUSSEN, KNUD. *Report of the Fifth Thule Expedition, 1921–24*, Vol. VII, No. 1, *Intellectual Culture of the Iglulik Eskimos*. Copenhagen: Gyldendalske Boghandel, Nordisk Forlag, 1929.

Rasmussen prefaces his work with a group of Eskimo autobiographies which bring out the difficulties of life in the far north. He proceeds, with the aid of myths and first-person statements from articulate informants, to show how the Eskimo views this life. Shamanism, amulets, and magic words as means of reducing the uncertainties of existence are described.

REDFIELD, ROBERT. *Tepoztlan: A Mexican Village*. Chicago: The University of Chicago Press, 1930.

With characteristic and appealing simplicity Redfield describes the fusion of Spanish and Aztec elements which constitutes the religion of these Mexican peasants. He follows the yearly round of *fiestas* and discusses the concepts of *santo* (saint) and *veterano* (military hero) as foci of the sentiments of the community.

REDFIELD, ROBERT, and VILLA ROJAS, ALFONSO. *Chan Kom: A Maya Village*. ("Carnegie Institution of Washington Publications," No. 448.) Washington, D.C., 1934.

In this Maya village the authors find two separate complexes of sacred ritual, each with its own practitioners and general sphere of operations. One uses prayers from the Catholic liturgy recited by professional *cantores;* this complex is usually chosen for baptism, marriage, and death. The other uses Maya priests and prayers to the spirits of the milpa, the village, and the rain, and is used for agriculture and illness.

RIVERS, W. H. R. *The Todas*. London: Macmillan & Co., Ltd., 1906.

The core of the religious life of this people of India's Nilgiri hills is the care of the sacred water buffaloes. This work is done in village dairies, graded by degree of sanctity, by an ordained priesthood; the elaborateness of ritual and the personal requirements of the priests vary accordingly. Religious practices of the common people include rites of passage and the observance of taboos on periodic sacred days.

ROSCOE, JOHN. *The Bakitara.* Cambridge: At the University Press, 1923.

A major focus of this monograph from East Africa is the ritual surrounding the king, described as both "the great high priest of the nation" and "almost a deity himself." Supplementing the king were rain makers, diviners of many kinds, and priests devoted to each of the nineteen gods concerned with cattle raising.

SELIGMAN, C. G., and SELIGMAN, BRENDA Z. *The Veddas.* Cambridge: At the University Press, 1911.

The Seligmans present a detailed account of the culture and religions of the Veddas of Ceylon, who for many years served as a sort of stockpile of a "primitive people." Their religion centers around the ancestral spirits, who enter into the bodies of shamans or other persons in order to communicate with their descendants. Strikingly, belief in magic and sorcery appear to be lacking here.

SHIROKOGOROFF, S. M. *The Psychomental Complex of the Tungus.* London: Kegan Paul, 1935.

This monograph gives systematic treatment to the beliefs of a Siberian people in spirits residing in nature and in the dead and to the methods (most of them individual) of managing these spirits. Particular attention is given to shamanism—the rituals and paraphernalia, the psychological aspects of both performance and belief, the social position of the shaman, and the possible sources of the complex.

SPECK, FRANK G. *Naskapi.* Norman, Okla.: University of Oklahoma Press, 1935.

This work on the religion of the hunting bands of Labrador stresses the individual nature of religious observance and links it with dispersed nomadic settlement; aside from feasts in celebration of hunting success, no religious assembly is known. The author discusses the spiritual guide and the ritual of hunting in which this spirit is invoked by sweat baths, songs, drumming, and divination.

SPENCER, BALDWIN, and GILLEN, F. J. *The Arunta.* 2 vols. London: Macmillan & Co., Ltd., 1927.

A major part of this monograph is concerned with totemism—the relationship between the individual and his totem and the associated *churinga* (sacred object); the traditions, in which totemic ancestors and local topography are linked; and the various rituals whereby the totem animal or plant is increased and the young are initiated into the secrets of the sacred.

STANNER, W. E. H. *On Aboriginal Religion.* ("Oceania Monographs," No. 11.) Sydney, 1963.

This is a masterful and unique effort to examine Australian religion, with the author endeavoring to study it in itself and not as a mirror of something else.

TITIEV, MISCHA. *Old Oraibi.* ("Papers of the Peabody Museum of American Archaeology and Ethnology," Vol. XXI, No. 1.) Cambridge, Mass., 1944.

Titiev describes Hopi ceremonialism in all its complexity and interprets the various rituals in terms of the basic concepts of continuity of life after death and the duality of the year. The colorful Katcina Cult, centering around the impersonation of the dead, displays these concepts as fundamentals, while other rituals, performed by secret societies, share them to some extent.

TSCHOPIK, HARRY, JR. *The Aymara of Chucuito, Peru.* I. Magic ("Anthropological Papers of the American Museum of Natural History," Vol. XLIV, Part 2, pp. 137–308.) New York, 1951.

The aim of this monograph is to suggest a relationship between a highly specialized system of magic (described in detail) and certain salient features of Aymara personality. The author suggests that the specialization of practitioners (six kinds, distinguished by the problems each handles), the proliferation of specific rites, and the private nature of most magic are compatible with the characteristic ways of expressing anxiety and hostility.

UNDERHILL, RUTH. *Papago Indian Religion.* New York: Columbia University Press, 1946.

The author approaches the description of Papago ceremonies from the point of view of the contrast between two coexistent methods of contact with the supernatural—the communal and the individual. Whether of rainmaking ceremony or guardian-spirit quest, the descriptions are well written and enhanced by the inclusion of poetic songs and texts.

VAILLANT, GEORGE C. *Aztecs of Mexico.* Garden City, N.Y.: Doubleday, Doran & Co., 1941.

On the basis of Conquest documents, Vaillant constructs a brief but vivid and discerning picture of Aztec religion. He describes some of the hierarchy of gods who gave their names to the days of the ritual year, and demonstrates with clarity how this ritual calendar set the times for ceremonies—often human sacrifices—performed by the priesthood, itself a hierarchy.

WARNER, W. LLOYD. *A Black Civilization: A Social Study of an Australian Tribe*. Rev. ed. New York: Harper & Bros., 1958.

Totemism among the Murngin of Australia and its elaborate, myth-dramatizing ritual are carefully described and sociologically interpreted in this work. In addition, the role of magicians ("black" ones to cause illness and "white" ones to cure it) is examined, with special reference to arrangements in a northern subgroup which lacks this means of dealing with disease.

GENERAL BIBLIOGRAPHY

ABERLE, DAVID. "A Note on Relative Deprivation Theory As Applied to Millenarian and Other Cult Movements," in Sylvia L. Thrupp (ed.), *Millenial Dreams in Action*. ("Comparative Studies in Society and History," Supplement 2.) The Hague, 1962.

ACKERKNECHT, ERWIN H. "Problems of Primitive Medicine," *Bulletin of the History of Medicine,* XI (1942), 503–521.

BALANDIER, GEORGES. *Sociologie Actuelle de l'Afrique Noire: Dynamique des Changements Sociaux en Afrique Centrale*. Paris: Presses Universitaires de France, 1955.

BARBER, BERNARD. "Acculturation and Messianic Movements," *American Sociological Review,* VI (1941), 663–669.

BARKER, ROGER G. and BARKER, LOUISE SHEDD. "Behavior Units for the Comparative Study of Cultures," in Bert Kaplan (ed.), *Studying Personality Cross-Culturally*. Evanston, Ill.: Row, Peterson and Co., 1961.

BARTON, R. F. *The Religion of the Ifugaos*. ("Memoirs of the American Anthropological Association," No. 65.) Menasha, Wis., 1946.

BASCOM, WILLIAM R. "The Sanctions of Ifa Divination," *Journal of the Royal Anthropological Institute,* LXXI (1941), 43–54.

BASCOM, WILLIAM R. "The Myth-Ritual Theory," *Journal of American Folklore,* LXX (1957), 103–114.

BEAUCLAIR, INEZ DE. "Black Magic on Ifaluk," *American Anthropologist,* LXV (1963), 388–389.

BECKWITH, MARTHA WARREN. *The Kumulipo: A Hawaiian Creation Chant*. Chicago: The University of Chicago Press, 1951.

BELLAH, ROBERT N. *Tokugawa Religion: The Values of Pre-Industrial Japan*. Glencoe, Ill.: The Free Press, 1957.

BELLAH, ROBERT N. "Religious Evolution," *American Sociological Review,* XXIX (1964), 358–374.

BELSHAW, CYRIL S. "The Significance of Modern Cults in Melanesian Development," *The Australian Outlook,* IV (1950), 116–125.

BETTELHEIM, BRUNO. *Symbolic Wounds, Puberty Rites and the Envious Male*. Glencoe, Ill.: The Free Press, 1954.

BIRDWHISTELL, RAY. *Introduction to Kinesics*. Louisville: University of Louisville Press, 1952.

BLACK, JOHN SUTHERLAND, and CHRYSTAL, GEORGE. *The Life of William Robertson Smith*. London: A. and C. Black, 1912.

BLACKFORD, KATHERINE M. H., and NEWCOMB, ARTHUR. *The Job, The Man, The Boss*. New York: Doubleday, Page & Co., 1914.

BOAS, FRANZ. "The Origin of Totemism," *Journal of American Folklore,* XXIII (1910), 392–393.

BOGORAS, WALDEMAR. *The Chukchee*, Vol. VII of Franz Boas (ed.), *The Jesup North Pacific Expedition*. ("Memoirs of the American Museum of Natural History," Vol. XI, Parts 2 and 3.) Leyden: E. J. Brill, 1904–1909.

BOWERS, ALFRED W. *Mandan Social and Ceremonial Organization*. Chicago: The University of Chicago Press, 1950.

BROSSES, CHARLES DE. *Du culte des Dieux Fétiches, ou Parallèle de l'ancienne Religion de l'Égypte avec la Religion actuelle de Nigritie*. Geneve: Cramer, 1760.

BUNZEL, RUTH L. "Introduction to Zuni Ceremonialism," *47th Annual Report of the Bureau of American Ethnology,* pp. 467–545. Washington, D.C., 1932.

BUNZEL, RUTH L. "Zuni Katcinas," *47th Annual Report of the Bureau of American Ethnology,* pp. 837–1086. Washington, D.C., 1932.

BUNZEL, RUTH L. *Chichicastenango: A Guatemalan Village*. ("Publications of the American Ethnological Society," Vol. XXII.) Locust Valley, N.Y.: J. J. Augustin, 1952.

BURCKHARDT, JACOB. *The Civilization of the Period of the Renaissance in Italy*. Translated by S. G. C. Middlemore. London: C. K. Paul & Co., 1878.

BURTON, ROGER V., and WHITING, JOHN W. M. "The Absent Father and Cross-Sex Identity," *Merrill-Palmer Quarterly of Behavior and Development,* VII (1961), 85–95.

CALLAWAY, HENRY. *The Religious System of the Amazulu: Izinyanga Zokubula, or Divination, As Existing among the Amazulu, in Their Own Words*. ("Publications of the Folk-Lore Society," No. 15.) London, 1870.

CANNON, WALTER B. "'Voodoo' Death,"

American Anthropologist, XLIV (1942), 169–181.

CASO, ALFONSO. *El Pueblo del Sol.* México: Fondo de Cultura Económica, 1953.

CAZENEUVE, JEAN. *Les Dieux dansant à Cibola: Le Shalako des Indiens Zunis.* Paris: Gallinard, 1957.

CHAPPLE, ELIOT DISMORE, and COON, CARLETON STEVENS. *Principles of Anthrology.* New York: Henry Holt & Co., 1942.

CODRINGTON, ROBERT H. *The Melanesians: Studies in Their Anthropology and Folklore.* Oxford: Clarendon Press, 1891.

COHEN, YEHUDI. *Transition from Childhood to Adolescence.* Chicago: Aldine Publishing Co., 1964.

COHN, NORMAN. *The Pursuit of the Millennium.* New York: Essential Books, 1957. [Reprinted in revised form in paperback edition, Harper Torchbooks, 1961.]

COLSON, ELIZABETH. "Ancestral Spirits and Social Structure among the Plateau Tonga," *International Archives of Ethnography,* XLVII, Part 1 (1954), 21–68.

COMTE, AUGUSTE. *Cours de philosophie positive.* Paris: Borrani et Droz. 1835–1852.

DOUGLAS, M. "Leviticus XI." Lecture delivered at University College, London, 1959. Unpublished.

DRAPER, GEORGE. *Disease and the Man.* London: Kegan Paul, Trench, Trübner & Co., 1930.

DURKHEIM, ÉMILE. *The Elementary Forms of the Religious Life.* Translated from the French by Joseph Ward Swain. London: George Allen & Unwin, Ltd., 1915.

EGGAN, FRED. "Social Anthropology and the Method of Controlled Comparison," *American Anthropologist,* LVI (1954), 743–763.

ELKIN, A. P. *The Australian Aborigines: How to Understand Them.* 3d ed. Sydney: Angus & Robertson, 1954.

ELLIS, WILLIAM. *Polynesian Researches, during a Residence of Nearly Eight Years in the Society and Sandwich Islands.* 4 vols. 2d ed., enlarged and improved. London: Fisher, Son, & Jackson, 1839–1842.

EVANS, I. H. N. *The Religion of the Tempasuk Dusuns of North Borneo.* New York: Cambridge University Press, 1953.

EVANS-PRITCHARD, E. E. *Witchcraft, Oracles and Magic Among the Azande.* Oxford: Clarendon Press, 1937.

EVANS-PRITCHARD, E. E. *Nuer Religion.* Oxford: Clarendon Press, 1956.

EVANS-PRITCHARD, E. E. "Religion," in E. E. Evans-Pritchard *et al., The Institutions of Primitive Society.* Oxford: Basil Blackwell, 1956.

FERGUSSON, HARVEY. *Modern Man: His Belief and Behavior.* New York: A. A. Knopf & Co., Inc., 1936.

FIRTH, RAYMOND. *The Work of the Gods in Tikopia.* ("London School of Economics and Political Science Monographs on Social Anthropology," Nos. 1 and 2.) London: Percy Lund, Humphries & Co., 1940.

FIRTH, RAYMOND. *Elements of Social Organization.* London: Watts & Co., 1951.

FIRTH, RAYMOND (ed.). *Man and Culture: An Evaluation of the Work of Bronislaw Malinowski.* London: Routledge & Kegan Paul, 1957.

FIRTH, RAYMOND. "Offering and Sacrifice: Problems of Organization," *Journal of the Royal Anthropological Institute,* XCIII (1963), 12–24.

FISCHER, J. L. "The Sociopsychological Analysis of Folktales," *Current Anthropology,* IV (1963), 235–295.

FLETCHER, ALICE, and LA FLESCHE, FRANCIS. "The Omaha Tribe," *27th Annual Report of the Bureau of American Ethnology,* pp. 15–672. Washington, D.C., 1911.

FORTUNE, REO F. *Sorcerers of Dobu.* London: George Routledge & Sons, 1932.

FORTUNE, REO F. *Manus Religion.* ("Memoirs, American Philosophical Society," Vol. III.) Philadelphia, 1935.

FOSTER, GEORGE M. *Empire's Children: The People of Tzintzuntzan.* ("Smithsonian Institution, Institute of Social Anthropology, Publications," No. 6.) Washington, D.C., 1948.

FRAKE, CHARLES O. "The Diagnosis of Disease among the Subanun of Mindanao," *American Anthropologist,* LXIII (1961), 113–132.

FRAKE, CHARLES O. "A Structural Description of Subanun 'Religious Behavior,'" in W. H. Goodenough (ed.), *Explorations in Honor of George Peter Murdock.* New York: McGraw-Hill Book Co., 1964.

FRANKFORT, H., *et al. The Intellectual Adventure of Ancient Man.* Chicago: The University of Chicago Press, 1946.

FRAZER, JAMES G. *Psyche's Task: A Discourse Concerning the Influence of Superstition on the Growth of Institutions.* London: Macmillan & Co., Ltd., 1909.

FRAZER, JAMES G. *The Golden Bough: A Study in Magic and Religion.* 12 vols. 3d ed., revised and enlarged. London: Macmillan & Co., Ltd., 1911–1915.

FRAZER, JAMES G. *Sir Roger de Coverley, and Other Literary Pieces.* London: Macmillan & Co., Ltd., 1920.

FRAZER, JAMES G. *The Fear of the Dead in Primitive Religion.* 3 vols. London: Macmillan & Co., Ltd., 1933–1936.

FREUD, SIGMUND. *Totem and Taboo: Resemblances Between the Psychic Life of Savages and Neurotics.* Authorized English translation, with Introduction, by A. A. Brill. New York: Moffat Yard & Co., 1918.

FREUD, SIGMUND. "Obsessive Acts and Religious Practices,"*Collected Papers,* Vol. II. Translated by Joan Rivière. 5 vols. London: Hogarth Press and the Institute of Psycho-Analysis, 1948–1950.

FROMM, ERICH. *Escape from Freedom.* New York: Rinehart & Co., 1941.

FUNG, YU-LAN. *A History of Chinese Philosophy.* Translated by Derk Bodde. Peiping: H. Vetch, 1937.

FUSTEL DE COULANGES, N. D. *La Cité antique.* Paris: Durand, 1864. [Also published in English translation as *The Ancient City,* various editions, including paperback by Doubleday & Co., 1963.]

GEERTZ, CLIFFORD. "Ritual and Social Change: A Javanese Example," *American Anthropologist,* LIX (1957), 32–54.

GEERTZ, CLIFFORD. *The Religion of Java.* Glencoe, Ill.: The Free Press, 1960.

GEERTZ, CLIFFORD. "Religion as a Cultural System." In press.

GENNEP, ARNOLD L. VAN. *Les Rites de Passage.* Paris: E. Nourry, 1909.

GILL, WILLIAM WYATT. *Myths and Songs from the South Pacific.* London: Henry S. King & Co., 1876.

GILLIN, JOHN. "Magical Fright," *Psychiatry,* XI (1948), 387–400.

GILLMOR, FRANCES. *Windsinger.* New York: Minton, Balch & Co., 1930.

GOLDENWEISER, ALEXANDER A. "Totemism: An Analytical Study," *Journal of American Folklore,* XXIII (1910), 179–293.

GOLDENWEISER, ALEXANDER A. "Religion and Society: A Critique of Émile Durkheim's Theory of the Origin and Nature of Religion," *The Journal of Philosophy, Psychology, and Scientific Methods,* XIV (1917), 113–124.

GOLDENWEISER, ALEXANDER A. "Totemism: An Essay on Religion and Society," in V. F. Calverton (ed.), *The Making of Man: An Outline of Anthropology.* New York: Modern Library, 1931.

GOODE, WILLIAM J. *Religion Among the Primitives.* Glencoe, Ill.: The Free Press, 1951.

GOODWIN, GRENVILLE. *Myths and Tales of the White Mountain Apache.* ("Memoirs of the American Folklore Society," Vol. XXXIII.) New York, 1939.

GOODY, JACK. "Religion and Ritual: The Definitional Problem," *British Journal of Sociology,* XII (1961), 142–164.

GREY, GEORGE. *Polynesian Mythology and Ancient Traditional History of the New Zealand Race.* London: John Murray, 1855.

GRIMBLE, ARTHUR. "Gilbertese Creation Myth," *The Listener,* XLV, No. 1155 (1951), 621–625.

GRIMBLE, ARTHUR. *A Pattern of Islands.* London: John Murray, 1952.

GRINNELL, GEORGE B. *The Cheyenne Indians.* 2 vols. New Haven, Conn.: Yale University Press, 1923.

GUSDORF, GEORGES. *L'Expérience humaine du sacrifice.* Paris: Presses Universitaires de France, 1948.

GUSINDE, MARTIN. *Die Feuerland Indianer.* Band 2. *Die Yamana.* Mödling bei Wien: Verlag der Internationalen Zeitschrift "Anthropos," 1937.

HALL, EDWARD T. "A System for the Notation of Proxemic Behavior," *American Anthropologist,* LXV (1963), 1003–1026.

HALLOWELL, A. IRVING. *Culture and Experience.* Philadelphia: University of Pennsylvania Press, 1955.

HANDY, E. S. CRAIGHILL. *Polynesian Religion.* ("Bernice P. Bishop Museum Bulletins," No. 34.) Honolulu, 1927.

HARRISON, JANE. *Themis: A Study of the Social Origins of Greek Religion.* Cambridge: At the University Press, 1912.

HASTINGS, JAMES (ed.). *Encyclopaedia of Religion and Ethics.* 13 vols. New York: Charles Scribner & Sons, 1921.

HAYDON, A. EUSTACE. "Comparative Religion," in *Encyclopaedia of the Social Sciences,* IV (1931), 131–134.

HERALD, CHILDE [TOM FERRIL]. "Freud and Football," *The Rocky Mountain Herald,* September 10, 1955. Denver, Colorado.

HERSKOVITS, MELVILLE J. "African Gods and Catholic Saints in New World Religious Belief," *American Anthropologist,* XXXIX (1937), 635–643.

HERSKOVITS, MELVILLE J. *Dahomey.* 2 vols. New York: J. J. Augustin, 1938.

HEWETT, E. L. *The Chaco Canyon and Its Monuments.* Albuquerque, N.M.: University of New Mexico Press, 1936.

HILDEBRAND, DIETRICH VON. *In Defense of Purity.* New York: Sheed & Ward, 1935.

HILL, W. W. "The Navaho Indians and the Ghost Dance of 1890," *American Anthropologist,* XLVI (1944), 523–527.

HOAGLAND, HUDSON. "Some Comments on Science and Faith," in "Conference on Science, Philosophy, and Religion." New York, 1941. (Mimeographed.)

HOBSBAWM, E. J. *Primitive Rebels.* New York: The Free Press of Glencoe, 1959.

HOMANS, GEORGE C. "Anxiety and Ritual: The Theories of Malinowski and Radcliffe-Brown," *American Anthropologist,* XLIII (1941), 164–172.

HORTON, ROBIN. "A Definition of Religion, and Its Uses," *Journal of the Royal Anthropological Institute,* XC (1960), 201–226.

HOWELLS, W. W. *The Heathens: Primitive Man and His Religions.* Garden City, N.Y.: Doubleday & Co., 1948.

Hsu, Francis L. K. *Under the Ancestors' Shadow.* New York: Columbia University Press, 1948.

Hubert, Henri, and Mauss, Marcel. "Essai sur la nature et la fonction du sacrifice," *L'Année Sociologique,* II (1897–1898), 29–138.

Hume, David. *Four Dissertations.* I, *The Natural History of Religion.* . . . London: A. Millar, 1757.

Huxley, Aldous. *Doors to Perception.* New York: Harper & Bros., 1954.

Hyman, Stanley Edgar. "The Ritual View of Myth and the Mythic," *Journal of American Folklore,* LXVIII (1955), 462–472.

Jacobs, Melville. *The Content and Style of an Oral Literature: Clackamas Chinook Myths and Tales.* New York: Wenner-Gren Foundation for Anthropological Research, Inc., 1959.

James, E. O. *Comparative Religion: An Introductory and Historical Study.* London: Methuen & Co., 1938.

Jungmann, Joseph A. *The Mass of the Roman Rite: Its Origins and Development.* New ed., revised and abridged; New York: Benziger Brothers, 1961.

Junod, Henri A. *The Life of a South African Tribe.* 2d ed., revised and enlarged. London: Macmillan & Co., Ltd., 1927.

Kitagawa, Joseph. "The Nature and Program of the History of Religions Field," *Divinity School News,* November, 1957, pp. 13–25.

Kittredge, George Lyman. *Witchcraft in Old and New England.* Cambridge, Mass.: Harvard University Press, 1929.

Kluckhohn, Clyde. "Myths and Rituals: A General Theory," *Harvard Theological Review,* XXXV (January, 1942), 45–79.

Kluckhohn, Clyde. *Navaho Witchcraft.* ("Peabody Museum Papers," No. 22.) Cambridge, Mass., 1944.

Kluckhohn, Clyde. "Universal Categories of Culture," in *Anthropology Today: An Encyclopedic Inventory,* prepared under the chairmanship of A. L. Kroeber. Chicago: The University of Chicago Press, 1953.

Kroeber, Alfred L. "Totem and Taboo: An Ethnologic Psychoanalysis," *American Anthropologist,* XXII (1920), 48–55.

Kroeber, Alfred L. "Totem and Taboo in Retrospect," *American Journal of Sociology,* XLV (1939), 446–451.

Kroeber, Alfred L. *Anthropology.* New ed., revised. New York: Harcourt, Brace & Co., 1948.

Kroeber, Alfred L. *The Nature of Culture.* Chicago: The University of Chicago Press, 1952.

La Barre, Weston. *The Peyote Cult.* ("Yale University Publications in Anthropology," No. 13.) New Haven, Conn., 1938.

Lafitau, Joseph François. *Les moeurs des sauvages amériquains comparées aux moeurs des premiers temps.* Paris: Saugrain l'âiné, 1724.

Lang, Andrew. *The Making of Religion.* London: Longmans, Green & Co., 1898.

Langer, Suzanne K. *Feeling and Form: A Theory of Art.* New York: Charles Scribner's Sons, 1953.

Lantis, Margaret. *Alaskan Eskimo Ceremonialism.* ("Publications of the American Ethnological Society," Vol. XI.) New York: J. J. Augustin, 1947.

Laufer, Berthold. "The Development of Ancestral Images in China," *Journal of Religious Psychology,* VI (1913), 111–123.

Leach, E. R. "Lévi-Strauss in the Garden of Eden: An Examination of Some Recent Developments in the Analysis of Myth," *Transactions of the New York Academy of Sciences,* Ser. II, Vol. XXIII (1961), 386–396.

Leach, E. R. "Two Essays on the Symbolic Representation of Time," in *Rethinking Anthropology.* London: Athlone Press, University of London, 1961.

Leach, E. R. "Genesis As Myth," *Discovery,* XXIII (1962), 30–35.

Leighton, Alexander H., and Leighton, Dorothea C. "Elements of Psychotherapy in Navaho Religion," *Psychiatry,* IV (1941), 515–524.

Leighton, Alexander H., and Leighton, Dorothea C. "Some Types of Uneasiness and Fear in a Navaho Indian Community," *American Anthropologist,* XLIV (1942), 194–209.

Lessa, William A. "Somatomancy: Precursor of the Science of Human Constitution," *Scientific Monthly,* LXXV (December, 1952), 355–365.

Lessa, William A. "Oedipus-Type Tales in Oceania," *Journal of American Folklore,* LXIX (1956), 63–73.

Lessa, William A. "Sorcery on Ifaluk," *American Anthropologist,* LXIII (1961), 817–820.

Lessa, William A. *Tales from Ulithi Atoll: A Comparative Study in Oceanic Folklore.* ("University of California Publications: Folklore Studies," No. 13). Berkeley and Los Angeles, 1961.

Lessa, William A. "The Decreasing Power of Myth on Ulithi," *Journal of American Folklore,* LXXV (1962), 153–159.

Lévi-Strauss, Claude. *Les Structures élémentaires de la parenté.* Paris: Les Presses Universitaires, 1949.

Lévi-Strauss, Claude. "Structure et dialectique," in *For Roman Jakobson: Essays on the Occasion of his Sixtieth Birthday,* pp. 289–294. The Hague: Mouton, 1956.

Lévi-Strauss, Claude. *Anthropologie Struc-

turale. Paris: Libraire Plon, 1958.

LÉVI-STRAUSS, CLAUDE. *Tristes tropiques.* Paris: Libraire Plon, 1955. [English edition, *A World on the Wane,* London: Hutchinson & Co., 1961.]

LÉVI-STRAUSS, CLAUDE. "The Bear and the Barber," *Journal of the Royal Anthropological Institute,* XCIII (1963), 1–11.

LÉVI-STRAUSS, CLAUDE. "The Structural Study of Myth," in *Structural Anthropology,* New York: Basic Books, Inc., 1963.

LÉVI-STRAUSS, CLAUDE. *Totemism.* Translated by Rodney Needham. Boston: Beacon Press, 1963. [French edition, *Le Totémisme aujourd'hui,* Paris, 1962.]

LEWIS, OSCAR. "Comparisons in Cultural Anthropology," in *Yearbook of Anthropology, 1955,* ed. William L. Thomas, Jr. New York: Wenner-Gren Foundation for Anthropological Research, Inc., 1955.

LIENHARDT, GODFREY. *Divinity and Experience: The Religion of the Dinka.* Oxford: Clarendon Press, 1961.

LINTON, RALPH. "Totemism and the A.E.F.," *American Anthropologist,* XXVI (1924), 296–300.

LINTON, RALPH. "Nativistic Movements," *American Anthropologist,* XLV (1943), 230–240.

LOWIE, ROBERT H. *Primitive Society.* New York: Liveright Publishing Corp., 1920.

LOWIE, ROBERT H. *The Crow Indians.* New York: Farrar & Rinehart, 1935.

LOWIE, ROBERT H. *Primitive Religion.* Enl. ed. New York: Liveright Publishing Corp., 1948.

LOWIE, ROBERT H. *Indians of the Plains.* ("American Museum of Natural History, Anthropological Handbooks," No. 1.) New York: McGraw-Hill Book Co., Inc., 1954.

LOWIE, ROBERT H. "Religion in Human Life," *American Anthropologist,* LXV (1963), 532–542.

MCILWRAITH, T. F. *The Bella Coola.* 2 vols. Toronto: University of Toronto Press, 1948.

MALINOWSKI, BRONISLAW. *Myth in Primitive Psychology.* New York: W. W. Norton & Co., 1926.

MALINOWSKI, BRONISLAW. *Sex and Repression in Savage Society.* London: Routledge & Kegan Paul, 1927.

MALINOWSKI, BRONISLAW. "Culture," in *Encyclopaedia of the Social Sciences,* IV (1931), 621–646.

MALINOWSKI, BRONISLAW. *Coral Gardens and Their Magic.* 2 vols. London: George Allen & Unwin, Ltd., 1935.

MALINOWSKI, BRONISLAW. *Magic, Science and Religion, and Other Essays.* Boston: Beacon Press, 1948, and Glencoe, Ill.: The Free Press, 1948. (Also printed in paperback edition by Doubleday Anchor Books, 1954.)

MARETT, ROBERT RANULPH. *The Threshold of Religion.* London: Methuen & Co., Ltd., 1909.

MATTHEWS, WASHINGTON. *The Night Chant: A Navaho Ceremony.* ("Memoirs of the American Museum of Natural History," No. 6.) New York: American Museum of Natural History, 1902.

MEAD, MARGARET. *The Mountain Arapesh,* Vol. II, *Supernaturalism.* ("Anthropological Papers of the American Museum of Natural History," Vol. XXXVII, Part 3, pp. 317–451). New York, 1940.

MENDELSOHN, ISAAC (ed.) *Religions of the Near East: Sumero-Akkadian Religious Texts and Ugaritic Epics.* ("The Library of Religion," Vol. IV.) New York: Liberal Arts Press, 1955.

MERTON, ROBERT K. "Social Structure and Anomie," *American Sociological Review,* III (1938), 672–682.

METZGER, DUANE, and WILLIAMS, GERALD. "Tenejapa Medicine I: The Curer," *Southwestern Journal of Anthropology,* XIX (1963), 216–234.

MINER, HORACE. "Body Ritual among the Nacirema," *American Anthropologist,* LVIII (1956)), 503–507.

MITCHELL, J. C. *The Yao Village.* Manchester: Manchester University Press, 1956.

MONEY-KYRLE, R. *The Meaning of Sacrifice.* ("The International Psycho-Analytic Library," No. 16.) London: Hogarth Press, 1930.

MOONEY, JAMES. "The Ghost-Dance Religion and the Sioux Outbreak of 1890," *14th Annual Report of the Bureau of American Ethnology, 1892–93,* Part 2. Washington, D.C.: 1896.

MOONEY, JAMES, and OLBRECHT, FRANS M. *The Swimmer Manuscript.* ("Bureau of American Ethnology Bulletins," No. 99.) Washington, D.C., 1932.

MOORE, OMAR K. "Divination—A New Perspective," *American Anthropologist,* LIX (1957), 69–74.

MORGAN, WILLIAM. "Navaho Dreams." *American Anthropologist,* XXXIV (1932), 390–405.

MORGAN, WILLIAM. *Human Wolves Among the Navaho.* ("Yale University Publications in Anthropology," No. 11.) New Haven, Conn., 1936.

MORLEY, SYLVANUS G. *The Ancient Maya.* 3d ed., revised by George W. Brainerd. Stanford, Calif.: Stanford University Press, 1956.

MÜLLER, F. MAX (trans.). *Rig-Veda-Sanhita: The Sacred Hymns of the Brahmans.* London: Trübner & Co., 1869.

MURDOCK, GEORGE P. *Social Structure.* New York: Macmillan Co., 1949.

MURPHY, ROBERT F. *Mundurucú Religion.* ("University of California Publications in American Archaeology and Ethnology," Vol.

XLIX, No. 1.) Berkeley: University of California Press, 1958.

NADEL, S. F. "A Study of Shamanism in the Nuba Mountains," *Journal of the Royal Anthropological Institute,* LXXVI (1946), 25–37.

NADEL, S. F. *Nupe Religion.* London: Routledge & Kegan Paul, 1954.

NEEDHAM, JAMES (ed.). *Science, Religion and Reality.* New York: Macmillan Co., 1925.

NIMUENDAJÚ, CURT. *The Eastern Timbira.* Translated by Robert H. Lowie. ("University of California Publications in American Archaeology and Ethnology," Vol. XLI.) Berkeley, Calif., 1946.

NORBECK, EDWARD. *Religion in Primitive Society.* New York: Harper & Bros., 1961.

OGDEN, C. K., and RICHARDS, I. A. *The Meaning of Meaning.* New York: Harcourt, Brace & Co., 1923.

OPLER, MORRIS E. "An Interpretation of Ambivalence of Two American Indian Tribes," *Journal of Social Psychology,* VIII, No. 1 (February, 1936), 82–115.

OPLER, MORRIS E. "Further Comparative Anthropological Data Bearing on the Solution of a Psychological Problem," *Journal of Social Psychology,* IX (1938), 477–483.

OPLER, MORRIS E. *An Apache Life-Way.* Chicago: The University of Chicago Press, 1941.

PARK, GEORGE K. "Divination and Its Social Contexts," *Journal of the Royal Anthropological Institute,* XCIII (1963), 195–209.

PARSONS, ELSIE CLEWS. *Pueblo Indian Religion.* 2 vols. Chicago: The University of Chicago Press, 1939.

PARSONS, ELSIE CLEWS. "A Pre-Spanish Record of Hopi Ceremonies," *American Anthropologist,* XLII (1940), 541–542.

PARSONS, TALCOTT. *Essays in Sociological Theory: Pure and Applied.* Glencoe, Ill.: The Free Press, 1949.

PARSONS, TALCOTT. *The Social System.* Glencoe, Ill.: The Free Press, 1951.

PARSONS, TALCOTT. "Religious Perspectives in Sociology and Social Psychology," in Hoxie N. Fairchild (ed.), *Religious Perspectives in College Teaching.* New York: Ronald Press, 1952.

PERRY, RALPH BARTON. *General Theory of Value: Its Meaning and Basic Principles Construed in Terms of Interest.* New York: Longmans, Green & Co., 1926.

PETRULLO, VICENZO. *The Diabolic Root: A Study of Peyotism, the New Indian Religion, among the Delawares.* Philadelphia: University of Pennsylvania Press, 1934.

PETTAZZONI, RAFFAELE. *La confession des péchés.* Translated by R. Monnot. 2 vols. Paris: E. Leroux, 1931–1932.

PETTAZZONI, RAFFAELE. "The Formation of Monotheism," *Essays on the History of Religions.* Translated by H. J. Rose. Leiden: E. J. Brill, 1954.

RADCLIFFE-BROWN, A. R. *The Andaman Islanders.* Cambridge: At the University Press, 1922.

RADCLIFFE-BROWN, A. R. "The Sociological Theory of Totemism," *Proceedings of the Fourth Pacific Science Congress* (Java, 1929). Batavia, 1930.

RADCLIFFE-BROWN, A. R. *Taboo.* ("The Frazer Lecture," 1939.) Cambridge: At the University Press, 1939.

RADCLIFFE-BROWN, A. R. "Religion and Society," *Journal of the Royal Anthropological Institute,* LXXV (1945), 33–43.

RADCLIFFE-BROWN, A. R. "The Comparative Method in Social Anthropology." Huxley Memorial Lecture for 1951. *Journal of the Royal Anthropological Institute,* LXXXI (1951), 15–22. [Republished in *Method in Social Anthropology,* Chicago, 1958.]

RADCLIFFE-BROWN, A. R. *Structure and Function in Primitive Society.* Glencoe, Ill.: The Free Press, 1952.

RADIN, PAUL. "The Winnebago Tribe," *37th Annual Report of the Bureau of American Ethnology,* pp. 35–550. Washington, D.C.: 1923.

RADIN, PAUL. *Primitive Religion: Its Nature and Origin.* New York: The Viking Press, Inc., 1937.

RAGLAN, FITZ ROY RICHARD SOMERSET (LORD). *The Hero: A Study in Tradition, Myth, and Drama.* London: Methuen & Co., Ltd., 1936.

RASMUSSEN, KNUD. *Report of the Fifth Thule Expedition, 1921–24,* Vol. VII, No. 1, *Intellectual Culture of the Iglulik Eskimos.* Copenhagen: Gyldendalske Boghandel, Nordisk Forlag, 1929.

RASSERS, W. H. "On the Javanese Kris," *Bijdragen tot de Taal-, Land- en Volkenkunde van Nederlandsch-Indië,* XCIX (1940), 501–582.

REDFIELD, ROBERT. *Tepoztlan: A Mexican Village.* Chicago: The University of Chicago Press, 1930.

REDFIELD, ROBERT, and VILLA ROJAS, ALFONSO. *Chan Khom: A Maya Village.* ("Carnegie Institution of Washington Publications," No. 448.) Washington, D.C., 1934.

REICHARD, GLADYS A. *Navajo Medicine Man: Sandpaintings and Legends of Miguelito.* New York: J. J. Augustin, 1939.

REINACH, SALOMON. *Orpheus: A History of Religions.* Translated by Florence Simmonds. Enlarged. New York: Liveright Publishing Corp., 1930.

RIVERS, W. H. R. *The Todas.* London: Macmillan & Co., Ltd., 1906.

RODWELL, J. M. (trans.) *The Koran.* London: J. M. Dent & Sons, 1909.

RÓHEIM, GÉZA. "Psycho-analysis of Primitive Culture Types," *International Journal of Psycho-analysis*, XIII (1932), 1–221 (Róheim Australasian Research number).

ROSCOE, JOHN. *The Bakitara*. Cambridge: At the University Press, 1923.

ROUSSEAU, JEAN-JACQUES. *Émile: ou, De l'éducation*. Amsterdam: J. Néaulune, 1762.

SAHAGÚN, BERNARDINO DE. *The Florentine Codex: General History of the Things of New Spain*, Book II, *The Ceremonies*. Translated by A. J. O. Anderson and C. E. Dibble. ("Monographs of the School of American Research," No. 14, Part 3.) Santa Fe, N.M.: Museum of New Mexico, 1951.

SANTAYANA, GEORGE. *Reason in Religion*. New York: Collier Books, 1906.

SCHAUSS, HAYYIM. *The Jewish Festivals*. Cincinnati, Ohio: Union of American Hebrew Congregations, 1938.

SCHLEITER, FREDERICK. *Religion and Culture: A Critical Survey of Methods of Approach to Religious Phenomena*. New York: Columbia University Press, 1919.

SCHMIDT, WILHELM. *The Origin and Growth of Religion: Facts and Theories*. Translated by H. J. Rose. New York: Lincoln Mac-Veagh, 1931.

SCHUTZ, A. *The Problem of Social Reality* (Vol. I of *Collected Papers*). The Hague: Martinus Nijhoff, 1962.

SEBEOK, T. A. (ed.). *Myth: A Symposium*. ("Bibliographical and Special Series," No. 5, American Folklore Society.) Bloomington, 1955.

SELIGMAN, C. G., and SELIGMAN, BRENDA Z. *The Veddas*. Cambridge: At the University Press, 1911.

SELTZER, CARL C. "Constitutional Aspects of Juvenile Delinquency," in *Origin and Evolution of Man*. ("Cold Spring Harbor Symposia on Qualitative Biology," Vol. XV, pp. 361–372.) Cold Spring Harbor, N.Y., 1950.

SHEDON, WILLIAM H., HARTL, EMIL M., and McDERMOTT, M. A. *Varieties of Juvenile Delinquency: An Introduction to Constitutional Psychiatry*. New York: Harper & Bros., 1949.

SHELDON, WILLIAM H., STEVENS, S. S., and TUCKER, W. B. *The Varieties of Human Physique: An Introduction to Constitutional Psychology*. New York: Harper & Bros., 1940.

SHIROKOGOROFF, S. M. *The Psychomental Complex of the Tungus*. London: Kegan Paul, 1935.

SINGER, MILTON. "The Cultural Pattern of Indian Civilization." *Far Eastern Quarterly*, XV (1955), 23–36.

SLOTKIN, J. S. "Menomini Pevotism," *Transactions of the American Philosophical Society*, XLII, Part 4 (1952).

SLOTKIN, J. S. "Peyotism, 1521–1891," *American Anthropologist*, LVII (1955), 202–230

SLOTKIN, J. S. "The Peyote Way," *Tomorrow*, IV, No. 3 (1955–1956), pp. 64–70.

SLOTKIN, J. S. *The Peyote Religion: A Study in Indian-White Relations*. Glencoe, Ill.: The Free Press, 1956.

SLOTKIN, J. S. *The Menomini Powwow Religion*. Milwaukee, Wis.: Milwaukee Public Museum. 1957.

SMITH, SIDNEY. "The Practice of Kingship in Early Semitic Kingdoms," in S. H. Hooke (ed.), *Myth, Ritual, and Kingship*. Oxford: Oxford University Press, 1958.

SMITH, W. ROBERTSON. *Lectures on the Religion of the Semites*. New York: D. Appleton & Co., 1889.

SPECK, FRANK G. *Naskapi*. Norman, Okla.: University of Oklahoma Press, 1935.

SPENCER, BALDWIN, and GILLEN, F. J. *The Arunta*. 2 vols. London: Macmillan & Co., Ltd., 1927.

SPIRO, MELFORD E. "Ghosts, Ifaluk, and Teleological Functionalism," *American Anthropologist*, LIV (1952), 497–503.

SPIRO, MELFORD E. "Sorcery, Evil Spirits, and Functional Analysis: A Rejoinder," *American Anthropologist*, LXIII (1961), 820–824.

STANNER, W. E. H. "The Dreaming," in T. A. G. Hungerford (ed.), *Australian Signpost*. Melbourne: F. W. Chesire, 1956.

STANNER, W. E. H. *On Aboriginal Religion*. ("Oceania Monographs," No. 2.) Sydney, 1963.

STANNER, W. E. H. "Religion, Totemism, and Symbolism," in R. M. and C. H. Berndt (eds.), *Aboriginal Man in Australia*. Sydney: Angus and Robertson, 1965.

STURTEVANT, WILLIAM C. "Studies in Ethnoscience," *American Anthropologist*, LXVI, No. 3, Part 2 (1964), 99–131.

SWANSON, GUY E. *The Birth of the Gods: The Origin of Primitive Beliefs*. Ann Arbor: University of Michigan Press, 1960.

TALMON, YONINA. "Pursuit of the Millennium: The Relation Between Religious and Social Change," *Archives Européennes de Sociologie*, III (1962), 125–148.

THOMPSON, J. ERIC. *The Rise and Fall of Maya Civilization*. ("The Civilization of the American Indian Series," Vol. XXXIX.) Norman, Okla.: University of Oklahoma Press, 1954.

THRUPP, SYLVIA (ed.). *Millenial Dreams in Action: Essays in Comparative Study*. ("Comparative Studies in Society and History," Supplement No. 2.) The Hague: Mouton, 1962.

TITIEV, MISCHA. "A Fresh Approach to the Problem of Magic and Religion." *Southwestern Journal of Anthropology*, XVI (1960), 292–298.

TSCHOPIK, HARRY, JR. "Taboo As a Possible Factor Involved in the Obsolescence of Navaho Pottery and Basketry," *American Anthropologist*, XL (1938), 257–262.

TSCHOPIK, HARRY, JR. *The Aymara of Chucuito, Peru.* I. Magic. ("Anthropological Papers of the American Museum of Natural History," Vol. XLIV, Part 2, pp. 137–308.) New York, 1951.

TYLOR, EDWARD B. *Primitive Culture: Researches into the Development of Mythology, Philosophy, Religion, Language, Art, and Custom.* 2 vols. 2d ed. London: John Murray, 1873.

UNDERHILL, RUTH. *Papago Indian Religion.* New York: Columbia University Press, 1946.

VAILLANT, GEORGE C. *Aztecs of Mexico.* Garden City, N.Y.: Doubleday, Doran & Co., 1941.

VOGT, EVON Z. "Water Witching: An Interpretation of a Ritual Pattern in a Rural American Community," *Scientific Monthly,* LXXV (September, 1952), 175–186.

VOGT, EVON Z. *Modern Homesteaders: The Life of a Twentieth-Century Frontier Community.* Cambridge: Harvard University Press, 1955.

VOGT, EVON Z. "Structural and Conceptual Replication in Zinacantan Culture," *American Anthropologist,* LXVII (1965). (In press.)

VOGT, EVON Z., and HYMAN, RAY. *Water Witching U.S.A.* Chicago: The University of Chicago Press, 1959.

VOLTAIRE, FRANÇOIS MARIE AROUET DE. *Dictionnaire philosophique, portatif.* Nouv. éd., rev. Londres, 1765.

WALLACE, ANTHONY F. C. "Revitalization Movements," *American Anthropologist,* LVIII (1956), 264–281.

WALLIS, WILSON D. *Religion in Primitive Society.* New York: F. S. Crofts & Co., 1939.

WARNER, W. LLOYD. *A Black Civilization: A Social Study of an Australian Tribe.* New York: Harper & Bros., 1937.

WARNER, W. LLOYD. *American Life: Dream and Reality.* Chicago: The University of Chicago Press, 1953.

WARNER, W. LLOYD. *The Living and the Dead: A Study of the Symbolic Life of Americans.* New Haven: Yale University Press, 1959.

WARNER, W. LLOYD. *The Family of God.* New Haven: Yale University Press, 1961.

WAX, MURRAY, and WAX, ROSALIE. "The Notion of Magic," *Current Anthropology,* IV (1963), 495–518.

WAX, ROSALIE, and WAX, MURRAY. "The Magical World View," *Journal for the Scientific Study of Religion,* I (1962), 179–188.

WEBSTER, HUTTON. *Taboo: A Sociological Study.* Stanford, Calif.: Stanford University Press, 1942.

WEBSTER, HUTTON. *Magic: A Sociological Study.* Stanford, Calif.: Stanford University Press, 1948.

WELCKER, FRIEDERICH GOTTLIEB. *Die griechische Götterlehre.* 3 vols. Göttingen, 1857–1863.

WESTERMARCK, EDVARD ALEXANDER. *Origin and Development of Moral Ideas.* 2 vols. London: Macmillan & Co., Ltd., 1906–1908.

WHITEHEAD, ALFRED N. *Symbolism.* New York: G. P. Putnam's Sons, 1927.

WHITING, JOHN W. M. "The Cross-Cultural Method," in Gardner Lindzey (ed.), *Handbook of Social Psychology.* Vol. I, pp. 523–531. Cambridge: Addison-Wesley, 1954.

WHITING, JOHN W. M., KLUCKHOHN, RICHARD, and ANTHONY, ALBERT. "The Function of Male Initiation Ceremonies at Puberty," in Eleanor E. Maccoby, T. M. Newcomb, and E. L. Hartley (eds.), *Readings in Social Psychology.* New York: Henry Holt & Co., 1958.

WILSON, B. R. *Sects and Society.* Berkeley and Los Angeles: University of California Press, 1961.

WILSON, EDMUND. *Red, Black, Blond and Olive.* New York: Oxford University Press, 1956.

WOLF, ERIC. "The Virgin of Guadalupe: A Mexican National Symbol," *Journal of American Folklore,* LXXI (1958), 34–39.

WORSLEY, PETER. *The Trumpet Shall Sound.* London: MacGibbon & Kee, 1957.

WORSLEY, PETER. "Rebellion and Revolution," *Science and Society,* XXV (1961), 26–27.

YOUNG, FRANK W. "The Function of Male Initiation Ceremonies: A Cross-Cultural Test of an Alternative Hypothesis," *The American Journal of Sociology,* LXVII (1962), 379–396.

INDEX OF AUTHORS AND TITLES

655

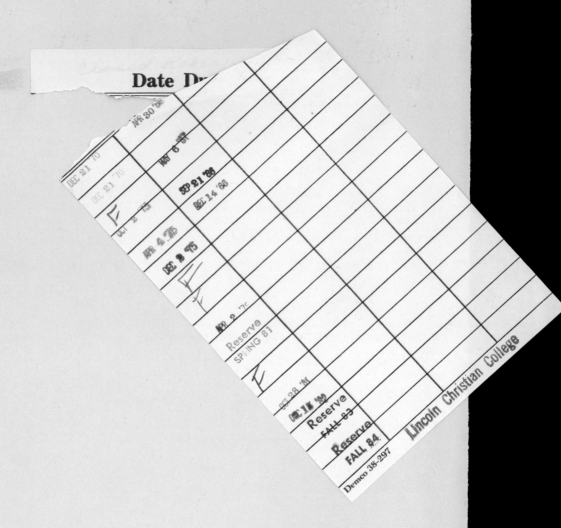